EVIDENCE: TEACHING MATERIALS FOR AN AGE OF SCIENCE AND STATUTES

EVIDENCE: TEACHING MATERIALS FOR AN AGE OF SCIENCE AND STATUTES

Seventh Edition

RONALD L. CARLSON
Fuller E. Callaway Chair of Law Emeritus
University of Georgia Law

EDWARD J. IMWINKELRIED
Edward L. Barrett, Jr. Professor of Law
University of California, Davis

JULIE SEAMAN
Associate Professor of Law
Emory University School of Law

ERICA BEECHER-MONAS
Professor of Law
Wayne State University Law

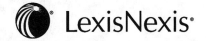

ISBN: 978-0-7698-5288-1
Looseleaf ISBN: 978-0-7698-5304-8
eBook ISBN: 978-0-3271-7821-7

Library of Congress Cataloging-in-Publication Data
Evidence : teaching materials for an age of science and statutes / Ronald L. Carlson ... [et al.]. -- 7th ed.
   p. cm.
Includes index.
ISBN: 978-0-7698-5288-1
1. Evidence (Law)--United States--Cases. I. Carlson, Ronald L., 1934-
   KF8935.E95 2012
   347.73'6--dc23

2012039375

NOTE TO USERS
To ensure that you are using the latest materials available in this area, please be sure to periodically check the LexisNexis Law School web site for downloadable updates and supplements at www.lexisnexis.com/lawschool.

Editorial Offices
121 Chanlon Rd., New Providence, NJ 07974 (908) 464-6800
201 Mission St., San Francisco, CA 94105-1831 (415) 908-3200
www.lexisnexis.com

MATTHEW◊BENDER

PREFACE TO THE SEVENTH EDITION

This edition continues to emphasize the themes of expert testimony, scientific evidence, and statutory construction in the law of evidence. It also retains an interdisciplinary approach, referencing social science and psychology research where relevant to particular evidentiary doctrines. In addition, we hope that students and professors alike will appreciate a more concise, streamlined approach throughout the text.

The new edition comes on the heels of the publication of the critically important NAS Report, STRENGTHENING FORSENSIC SCIENCE IN THE UNITED STATES: A PATH FORWARD (2009), available at www.ncjrs.gov/pdffiles1/nij/grants/228091.pdf. The full impact of this report will not be apparent for some time, but the report raises crucial questions about the use of forensic evidence in criminal prosecutions and the application of *Daubert* in civil as well as criminal cases. The report comes at the same time that the Supreme Court has shown an intense interest in the application of the Sixth Amendment Confrontation Clause to forensic reports. Citing the report and the new Supreme Court decisions, this edition continues the project that it has taken on for many years, namely, examining the intersection of science, law, evidence, and the Constitution. We lay out the issues and consider possible future directions, and raise questions for students to consider. We shall continue to keep a close eye on these issues in future supplements and editions.

This edition also coincides with the 2011 "restyling" of the Federal Rules of Evidence. Given our long emphasis on close reading of the statutory text, this wholesale revision of the language of the Rules must be highlighted. Of course, every new rule is accompanied by an Advisory Committee Note asserting that "[t]here is no intent to change any result in any ruling on evidence admissibility." Yet, given the textualist approach that many judges take to statutory interpretation, the law of unintended consequences may come into play; several commentators have already begun to weigh in on possible substantive effects of the restyling. As in the case of the 2009 NAS Report, it is too soon to tell how the courts will treat the new rules. We have quoted the restyled Rules throughout this text—often contrasting the previous wording of the Rule. Hence, this edition should give students an excellent foundation for understanding the issues posed by the restyling.

Finally, we have continued the project of streamlining and tightening the text, removing extraneous and cumulative material that found its way in over the course of the six prior editions and numerous supplements. There is always a tension between completeness and brevity. However, in an Internet age in which supplementary materials are but a click away, we are committed to making students engagement with the text as smooth and uninterrupted as pedagogically feasible.

This edition comes to press with two new authors and the departure of Edward (Ted) Kionka and Kristine Strachan. We owe Professors Kionka and Strachan a huge debt. Ted was one of the original coauthors, and he was the primary author of the excellent, comprehensive teachers' manual that has accompanied this coursebook since its inception. For several editions, Kristine provided the impetus to shorten and simplify the coursebook. Kristine was the one who forced the rest of us to make the tough coverage

PREFACE TO THE SEVENTH EDITION

choices. We hope that they both will be pleased with this new edition, since in large part it still reflects their major contributions.

RLC

EJI

JS

EBM

PROVENANCE: NOTES FROM EARLIER PREFACES

Sixth Edition:

On the statutory front, this edition comes hot on the heels of the latest amendment to the Federal Rules of Evidence, effective December 1, 2006. Although the ink is barely dry on these amendments, more may be in the offing. We like to think that developments since the publication of our fifth edition in 2002 have again confirmed the wisdom of our earlier decision to stress both statutory construction and expert testimony in this coursebook.

There are also noteworthy developments regarding expert testimony. Recently, more than two-thirds of prosecutors' offices in the United States reported that they routinely resort to DNA evidence either at trial or in plea negotiations. Comment, *Testimonial or Nontestimonial? The Admissibility of Forensic Evidence after* Crawford v. Washington, 94 KY. L.J. 187 (2005/2006). One of the emerging issues is whether the *Crawford* decision bars introduction of crime laboratory reports against the accused. This and a host of other "hot button" issues generated by *Crawford* are examined in this new edition.

Further, the lower courts are struggling with the impact of the Court's post-*Daubert* decision, *Kumho*, on expert testimony. When the Court decided Daubert, we predicted that ultimately the thorniest issue would be development of admissibility standards for non-scientific expertise. That prediction has come to pass. Although *Daubert* listed several factors that trial judges should consider — for the most part those factors were derived from a scientific model. Unfortunately, *Kumho* gave the lower courts little guidance on how to evaluate the reliability of non-scientific expertise; and it has become painfully clear to courts that it is impossible to put round, non-scientific pegs into square, scientific holes. This edition explores the way lower courts are currently struggling to formulate sensible standards for the admissibility of non-scientific expert testimony. Given the fast pace of change on both the statutory and expert testimony fronts, we remain committed to issuing new supplements and editions on a regular basis. We hope that this edition and its supplements will help keep law students abreast of the state of contemporary evidence law.

Fifth Edition:

The role of expert testimony, including scientific evidence, continues to grow — as does the controversy over this subject. The controversy swirls at two levels. At one level, the battle is between the proponents of *Daubert* and the advocates of *Frye*. Like the reports of Samuel Clemens' death, predictions of the demise of *Frye* have turned out to be "greatly exaggerated." Courts in many of the largest and most litigious states, including California, Florida, Illinois, and New York, have decided to adhere to some variation of the traditional general acceptance standard. At another level, in *Daubert* jurisdictions the battle is between the proponents of scientific testimony and the opponents. In some respects, *Daubert* appears to have toughened admissibility standards. In late 2000, the Federal Judicial Center released a study of the admissibility of expert testimony. In 1995, the center asked federal District Judges whether in their most recent trial, they had admitted all the proffered testimony. At that time, 75% of the judges answered in the affirmative. In the most recent study, that figure had fallen to 58%. In 1991, the center asked the judges whether they had ever excluded expert testimony. At that time, 25% of the judges answered yes. In the most recent study, that figure had risen to 41%.

Fourth Edition:

The Devitt casefile has undergone major surgery. In the prior editions, the complainant was an alleged rape victim. In most chapters of the new edition, there is a male victim of a battery. In the chapters discussing the evidentiary rules peculiar to sexual assault prosecutions, the facts are varied to include a rape charge.

The emphasis on scientific problems is evident at two levels. When the Court handed down *Daubert* in 1993, some commentators suggested that the Court had liberalized the standards for admitting purportedly scientific evidence. As the new edition explains, *Daubert* has proven to be a two-edged sword. Although the decision opens a window for admitting testimony about novel scientific theories, in other respects *Daubert* has toughened the standards. The lower courts are enforcing the new empirical validation standard with rigor. Secondly, there is increasing resort to scientific research to critique the underlying assumptions of evidence law. Although *Daubert* has garnered the headlines, perhaps the most significant innovation since the release of our third edition has been the enactment of Federal Rules 413-415. There was certainly a political impetus for that legislation. However, another contributing factor was the reassessment of the empirical research into the validity of character as a predictor of conduct. A number of commentators, including David Bryden, David Crump, Susan Davies, Miguel Mendez, and Roger Park, have contributed to that reassessment. The fourth edition references their contributions.

As in the prior editions, there is a heavy emphasis on statutory construction. If anything, that topic has heated up since the release of the third edition. At that time, the Justices of the Supreme Court seemed largely committed to a textualist approach to the interpretation of the Rules. Since that time, some Justices, notably Justices Breyer and Kennedy, have moved away from that approach. In addition, several scholars have endeavored to construct alternatives to textualism. Randolph Jonakait, Eileen Scallen, Andrew Taslitz, and Glen Weissenberger have been leaders in that endeavor.

Third and Second Editions:

Two key reasons prompt the second and third editions: we wanted to place greater emphasis on developing students' statutory construction skills and we wanted to underscore the potential impact of science on evidence law. Since the release of the second edition, statutory interpretation has become a "hot topic." The conventional wisdom has been that in interpreting statutes, judges should freely consult extrinsic legislative history material such as committee reports to identify the rational purpose inspiring the statute. Conservative jurists, notably Justices Rehnquist and Scalia and Judges Easterbrook and Posner, are now challenging that wisdom. Eskridge, *The New Textualism*, 37 U.C.L.A. L. REV. 621, 624 (1990). Eskridge & Frickey, *Legislation Scholarship and Pedagogy in the Post-Legal Process Era*, 48 U. PITT. L. REV. 691 (1987). Liberal jurists, including Judge Patricia Wald, have rushed to the defense of the conventional practice. The dispute over the proper approach to statutory interpretation has surfaced in evidence decisions. Jonakait, *The Supreme Court, Plain Meaning, and the Changed Rules of Evidence*, 68 TEX. L. REV. 745 (1990). Moreover, the influence of science on evidentiary doctrine is becoming more evident. In some cases, commentators are citing empirical research to support calls for the reform of evidentiary doctrine. *E.g.*, Zacharias, *Rethinking Confidentiality*, 74 IOWA L. REV. 351 (1989). In other cases, the battle over the admissibility of a novel type of evidence such as DNA typing is being fought over the scientific merit of the technique. Thompson & Ford, *DNA Typing: Acceptance and Weight of the New Genetic Identification Tests*, 75 VA. L. REV. 45 (1989). The second edition acknowledged the contribution of Professors Richard Friedman and Dale Nance, whose perceptive criticisms and suggestions made that edition a better teaching tool.

First Edition:

In the preface to the first edition, we explained our reasons for wanting to publish a new evidence coursebook: providing a better analytical approach to the study of evidence; teaching through the problem method based on a civil and criminal case file; emphasis on the procedural context of evidence law; and enhanced focus on logical and legal relevance doctrine. This emphasis reflected our belief that in the courtroom, relevance is by far the most important evidentiary doctrine. Our litigation experience persuaded us that, for better or worse, few trials present really novel or thorny

PROVENANCE: NOTES FROM EARLIER PREFACES

hearsay or privilege problems. However, in every trial, every attorney must deal with the logical relevance doctrine in establishing the materiality of the evidence and the authenticity of any exhibits offered; and problems of legal relevance are most pervasive. Moreover, a sound grasp of logical relevance — the ability to develop an imaginative alternative theory of relevance — is often the key to overcoming an objection based on exclusionary rules such as hearsay or remedial measures. We also noted that the first edition was intended solely as a teaching device rather than a reference work. A relatively small number of cases and case extracts were used, based on our belief that evidence is not a good course in which to use the case method: it is simply too time-consuming. The all-important application of law to facts can best be learned through the use of problems and hypotheticals spun off the problems. Finally, we noted that some of our students commented that they could not understand evidence doctrine because they could not visualize applied use of the doctrine. Thus, we included sample foundations in order to meld concrete application with conceptual theory.

ACKNOWLEDGMENTS

The authors acknowledge their debt to the inspired writings on evidence by the late Mason Ladd, former dean at both the Iowa and Florida State law schools. Professor Carlson was privileged to serve as a casebook co-author with Dean Ladd. Portions of the Ladd and Carlson casebook were helpful in preparing this book, especially with regard to the hearsay rule.

Professor Imwinkelried thanks the University of California, Davis Law School secretaries who helped prepare the sixth edition: Glenda McGlashan and Nina Bell. On earlier editions, he also gratefully acknowledges the help of his research assistants: Theodore Blumoff, Lucy Karl and Thomas Lammert; the Washington University Law School secretaries who prepared the first edition manuscript: Ilse Arndt, Barbara Aumer, Jane Bettlach, Dora Bradley, Susan Hutchings, Mary Ellen Powers, and especially Mary Schelling; and third edition research assistants: Joseph deUlloa and David Kornbluh. Professor Imwinkelried dedicates his work to Cindy, Marie, Ken, and Kindra; his parents, the late Mr. and Mrs. John Imwinkelried; and his parents'in-law, the late Mary Jane Clark and Lyman (Brownie) Clark.

Professor Seaman is grateful for excellent research assistance provided by Jason Antin and Brad Strickland. In addition, she wishes to acknowledge the invaluable contributions of Hawwa Djuned and Daniel Ra in preparing the manuscript and securing permissions. Finally, thanks to all of the many Emory Law School students who participated in the "typo competition" - any remaining typos are entirely the fault of this author.

The authors acknowledge their enormous debt and appreciation to Ms. Theresa Hrenchir of the University of San Diego School of Law for her extraordinary contribution to the preparation of the fourth edition. Successful completion of the project is in large part due to her outstanding legal ability, analytical skill and professionalism in producing the text, overseeing the work of three sets of research assistants, and coordinating the complexity of the communications and work product of the co-authors. Every group of law professors should be blessed with such a dedicated and meticulous editor. The authors are also grateful to their research assistants for their help on the fourth edition: Darren R. Beardsley, University of San Diego School of Law; Ryan Hall and Lynn Loschin, University of California at Davis, School of Law; Chandler Mason, Tripp Self, and Molly Kleiber, University of Georgia School of Law. Professor Carlson also acknowledges Mary Fielding of the University of Georgia staff for her assistance with manuscript preparation.

RLC

EJI

JS

EBM

EXCERPT ACKNOWLEDGMENTS

We gratefully acknowledge the following sources of excerpts:

Belli, Demonstrative Evidence and the Adequate Award, 22 Mississippi Law Journal 284 (1951). Reprinted with permission.

Carlson, A Student's Guide to Elements of Proof 98–100 (2004). Reprinted with the permission of Thomson West.

Carlson, Impeaching Jury Verdicts, 2 Litigation at 31–33 (Fall 1975). Copyright by the American Bar Association. Reprinted with permission.

Comment, The Husband-Wife Privileges of Testimonial Non-Disclosure, 56 Northwestern University Law Review 208, 220–22 (1961). Reprinted with special permission of Northwestern University School of Law, *Northwestern University Law Review.*

Comment, The Identification of Original Real Evidence, 61 Military Law Review 145 (1973).

Cutler, Thigpen, Young & Mueller, The Evidentiary Value of Spectrographic Voice Identification, 63 Journal of Criminal Law and Criminology 343 (1972). Reprinted with special permission of Northwestern University School of Law, *The Journal of Criminal Law and Criminology.*

Easterbrook, Statutes' Domains, 50 University of Chicago Law Review 533, 544–52 (1983). Reprinted with permission.

Garcia, Garbage In, Gospel Out: Criminal Discovery, Computer Reliability, and the Constitution, 38 U.C.L.A. Law Review 1043 (1991). Reprinted with permission.

Hutchins & Slesinger, Some Observations on the Law of Evidence, 28 Columbia Law Review 432, 437–39 (1928).

E. Imwinkelried, P. Giannelli, F. Gilligan & F. Lederer, Courtroom Criminal Evidence, sections 2904–12 (4th ed. 2005). Reprinted with permission.

F. James, G. Hazard & J. Leubsdorf, Civil Procedure, section 7.16 (5th ed. 2001). Reprinted with the permission of Foundation Press.

Kalven, The Jury, the Law, and the Personal Injury Damage Award, 19 Ohio State Law Journal 158, 170–72 (1958). Reprinted with permission.

McCormick, Handbook of the Law of Evidence, section 47 (Cleary ed. 1984). Reprinted with the permission of Thomson West.

McCormick, Evidence, volume 1, section 19, at 110–12 (K. Broun ed., 6th ed. 2006). Reprinted with the permission of Thomson West.

Mendez, California's New Law on Character Evidence: Evidence Code Section 352 and the Impact of Recent Psychological Studies, 31 U.C.L.A. Law Review 1003, 1045–53 (1984). Reprinted with permission.

Risinger, Denbeaux & Saks, Exorcism of Ignorance as a Proxy for Rational Knowledge: The Lessons of Handwriting Identification "Expertise," 137 University of Pennsylvania Law Review 731, 744–47 (1989). Reprinted with permission of *University of Pennsylvania Law Review* and William S. Hein & Company, Inc.

EXCERPT ACKNOWLEDGMENTS

Twining, William, Taking Facts Seriously - Again, 55 J. Legal Ed. (2005)

Walker, Thibaut & Andresli, Order of Presentation at Trial, 82 Yale Law Journal 216–26 (1972). Reprinted with permission.

Waltz & Huston, The Rules of Evidence in Settlement, 5 Litigation at 11 (Fall 1978). Copyright by the American Bar Association. Reprinted with permission.

Waltz & Park, Evidence 82–83 (8th ed. 1995). Reprinted with the permission of Foundation Press.

J. Weinstein & M. Berger, 2 Weinstein's Evidence 410[03]. Reprinted with permission. Matthew Bender & Company, Inc., a member of the LexisNexis Group. All rights reserved.

J. Weinstein & M. Berger, 3 Weinstein's Evidence 601[03]; 607[04]; 607[06]. Reprinted with permission. Matthew Bender & Company, Inc., a member of the LexisNexis Group. All rights reserved.

Zacharias, Rethinking Confidentiality, 74 Iowa Law Review 351, 377–81, 383–86, 394–95, 409–11 (1989). Reprinted with permission.

TABLE OF CONTENTS

TABLE OF CONTENTS

TABLE OF CONTENTS

TABLE OF CONTENTS

TABLE OF CONTENTS

TABLE OF CONTENTS

TABLE OF CONTENTS

TABLE OF CONTENTS

TABLE OF CONTENTS

TABLE OF CONTENTS

TABLE OF CONTENTS

TABLE OF CONTENTS

TABLE OF CONTENTS

TABLE OF CONTENTS

TABLE OF CONTENTS

TABLE OF CONTENTS

TABLE OF CONTENTS

TABLE OF CONTENTS

TABLE OF CONTENTS

TABLE OF CONTENTS

TABLE OF CONTENTS

TABLE OF CONTENTS

TABLE OF CONTENTS

TABLE OF CONTENTS

TABLE OF CONTENTS

Part 1

BACKGROUND, FRAMEWORK AND PROCEDURE

Chapter 1

THE PHILOSOPHY AND HISTORY OF AMERICAN EVIDENCE LAW

A. INTRODUCTION

A trial or hearing in a court or other tribunal is a dispute resolution mechanism. At the hearing, the judge, hearing officer, or jury makes findings of fact necessary to resolve the dispute. Public perception of the effectiveness of the hearing and the soundness of the result is critical. Unless there is a widespread belief that these hearings resolve disputes fairly, accurately, and efficiently, there is a danger that aggrieved parties will attempt to resolve their dispute or seek vindication privately in some socially unacceptable — perhaps violent — manner.

There are three essential functions that must be performed in order to resolve a dispute in a non-arbitrary manner that, ideally, discovers the "truth" at a reasonable cost: (1) defining the issues between the parties (the pleading function), (2) gathering information on the issues (the discovery function), and (3) deciding which information to consider in resolving the issues (the evidentiary function). Those tasks could, of course, be performed with relative informality. Moreover, we could devise a simple evidence code. As Thayer noted in the nineteenth century, there is only one inexorable evidentiary rule: the dictate of logic, which forbids "receiving anything irrelevant, not logically probative." J. THAYER, PRELIMINARY TREATISE ON EVIDENCE 264–66 (1898). We could treat logical relevance as the only evidentiary rule and allow the trier of fact to consider any and all probative information. Even if the stakes are higher in criminal cases, we do not necessarily need more complex rules to determine the admissibility of evidence; we could simply resort to a higher burden of proof to test the cumulative sufficiency of all the evidence admitted.

For reasons that will become apparent, we have chosen not to follow the simple approach. Quite the contrary, we have developed complex procedures and evidentiary rules. Indeed, we have the most complex, restrictive set of evidentiary rules in the world. In this chapter, we shall examine the philosophical and historical reasons for that complexity: our commitment to an adversary system, the use of lay jurors as fact finders, and the use of evidentiary rules to further other social policies. As you analyze each of these aspects of the American legal system and consider the specific procedures and evidentiary rules governing proof at trial, you should attempt to identify the assumptions of the current system and ask yourself whether those assumptions have been empirically validated.

B. THE ADVERSARY SYSTEM

There are two archetypal forms of judicial dispute-resolution systems in the industrialized world: adversarial and inquisitorial. The adversarial system, in which the parties are active in gathering evidence and presenting their dispute to a neutral, umpire-like judge, is the form used in most systems that derive from common-law British roots, including the American system. In inquisitorial systems, in contrast, fact gathering and criminal prosecutions are initiated and controlled by the judiciary, with the parties limited to making arguments about the facts so gathered and the law being implemented. This is the form used in France, Germany, and much of continental Europe as well as in much of Africa, South America, and Asia. Indeed, inquisitorial systems are more common worldwide than adversarial systems. Although the term "inquisitorial" has pejorative connotations in the United States, conjuring images of the Star Chamber, on the European Continent and elsewhere where inquisitorial procedures are common, the term has a very different meaning.

As comparativist Mirjan Damaska has noted, neither adversarial nor inquisitorial systems exist in pure form anywhere. Even in the United States, which has the purest form of the adversary system, well over 90% of criminal cases are disposed of without trial via plea bargaining. In the plea bargaining process, it is the prosecutor who decides what charges will be brought, acts as the adjudicator of facts, assesses their persuasiveness, and determines what sentence should be given in exchange for a plea. Conversely, adversarial traits can be discerned in continental systems, and some countries (such as Russia) use a hybrid of both systems. Recently, New Zealand has decided to move from an adversarial form of adjudication to an inquisitorial form.

The differences between adversarial and inquisitorial legal systems are most clearly reflected in procedure. In the United States, it is the parties' responsibility to gather information about the case. Rather than actively guiding the direction of pretrial discovery, the judge's role is more passive. By and large, the judge merely rules on discovery disputes between the parties. Similarly, at trial, the parties shoulder most of the burden of presenting the case. As we shall see, trial judges have the power to call and question witnesses, yet most judges are reluctant to invoke this power; schooled in the adversary system, they are usually content to let the attorneys "try their own case."

Although the adversary system is firmly entrenched in the United States, it has not gone without criticism. Undoubtedly, the most famous call for reform is Judge Frankel's article, *The Search for Truth: An Umpireal View*, 123 U. PA. L. REV. 1031 (1975). In the article, the judge notes that he has presided at trials at which it was evident that a "wily advocate . . . bested the facts and prevailed." *Id.* at 1034. In Judge Frankel's view, "[O]ur adversary system rates truth too low among the values that institutions of justice are meant to serve." *Id.* at 1032. He stresses that other countries and other disciplines — "history, geography, medicine, whatever — do not emulate our adversary system," *Id.* at 1036, and he urges a relaxation of "our rigid insistence that the parties control the evidence until it is all 'prepared' and packaged for competitive manipulation at [] trial." *Id.* at 1054. For a more recent call to abolish both the adversary and jury systems, see Tidmarsh, *Pound's Century, and Ours*, 81 NOTRE DAME L. REV. 513 (2006).

Others — including most American trial lawyers and judges — vigorously defend the adversary system. The following excerpt is representative of the arguments in favor of the adversary system.

PROFESSIONAL RESPONSIBILITY: REPORT OF THE JOINT CONFERENCE
44 American Bar Association Journal 1159, 1159–61 (1958)

In a very real sense it may be said that the integrity of the adjudicative process itself depends upon the participation of the advocate. This becomes apparent when we contemplate the nature of the task assumed by any arbiter who attempts to decide a dispute without the aid of partisan advocacy.

Such an arbiter must undertake, not only the role of judge, but that of representative for both of the litigants. Each of these roles must be played to the full without being muted by qualifications derived from the others. When he is developing for each side the most effective statement of its case, the arbiter must put aside his neutrality and permit himself to be moved by a sympathetic identification sufficiently intense to draw from his mind all that it is capable of giving — in analysis, patience and creative power. When he resumes his neutral position, he must be able to view with distrust the fruits of this identification and be ready to reject the products of his own best mental efforts. The difficulties of this undertaking are obvious. If it is true that a man in his time must play many parts, it is scarcely given to him to play them all at once.

It is small wonder, then, that failure generally attends the attempt to dispense with the distinct roles traditionally implied in adjudication. What generally occurs in practice is that at some early point a familiar pattern will seem to emerge from the evidence; an accustomed label is waiting for the case and, without awaiting further proofs, this label is promptly assigned to it. It is a mistake to suppose that this premature cataloguing must necessarily result from impatience, prejudice or mental sloth. Often it proceeds from a very understandable desire to bring the hearing into some order and coherence, for without some tentative theory of the case there is no standard of relevance by which testimony may be measured. But what starts as a preliminary diagnosis designed to direct the inquiry tends, quickly and imperceptibly, to become a fixed conclusion, as all that confirms the diagnosis makes a strong imprint on the mind, while all that runs counter to it is received with diverted attention.

An adversary presentation seems the only effective means for combating this natural human tendency to judge too swiftly in terms of the familiar that which is not yet fully known. The arguments of counsel hold the case, as it were, in suspension between two opposing interpretations of it. While the proper classification of the case is thus kept unresolved, there is time to explore all of its peculiarities and nuances.

The true significance of partisan advocacy touch[es] the integrity of the adjudicative process itself. It is only through the advocate's participation that the hearing may remain in fact what it purports to be in theory: a public trial of the facts and issues. Each advocate comes to the hearing prepared to present his proofs and arguments, knowing at the same time that his arguments may fail to persuade and that his proofs may be rejected and inadequate. It is a part of his role to absorb these possible disappointments. The deciding tribunal, on the other hand, comes to the hearing uncommitted.

The matter assumes a very different aspect when the deciding tribunal is compelled to take into its own hands the preparations that must precede the public hearing. In such a case the tribunal cannot truly be said to come to the hearing uncommitted, for it has itself appointed the channels along which the public inquiry is to run. The deciding tribunal is under a strong temptation to keep the hearing moving within the boundaries originally set for it. The result may be that the hearing loses its character as an open trial of the facts and issues, and becomes instead a ritual designed to provide public confirmation for what the tribunal considers it has already established in private. When this occurs adjudication acquires the taint affecting all institutions that become subject to manipulation, presenting one aspect to the public, another to knowing participants.

* * * Viewed in this light, the role of the lawyer as a partisan advocate appears not as a regrettable necessity, but as an indispensable part of a larger ordering of affairs. The institution of advocacy is not a concession to the frailties of human nature, but an expression of human insight in the design of a social framework within which man's capacity for impartial judgment can attain its fullest realization.

NOTES

1.   The "intuitive hypothesis" of the Joint Conference Report has a plausible, common sense appeal. Thibaut, Walker & Lind, *Adversary Presentation and Bias in Legal Decision making*, 86 HARV. L. REV. 386, 397 (1972). However, it can be a grave mistake to confuse the plausible and the proven.

There has been little empirical research into the validity of the Joint Conference's hypothesis; although there is some "empirical support for the general claim that an adversary presentation significantly counteracts decisionmaker bias." *Id.* On the other hand, there are indications that "the adversary system does not provide a generally more vigorous search for facts." Lind, Thibaut & Walker, *Discovery and Presentation of Evidence in Adversary and Nonadversary Proceedings*, 71 MICH. L. REV. 1129, 1143 (1973). Additional empirical investigation is certainly in order.

2.   The debate continues as to the relative merit of the adversary system, as practiced in the United States. *See, e.g.*, Carrie Menkel-Meadow, *The Trouble with the Adversary System in a Postmodern, Multicultural World*, 38 WM. & MARY L. REV. 5 (1996); Norman W. Spaulding, *The Rule of Law in Action: A Defense of Adversary System Values*, 93 CORNELL L. REV. 1377 (2008). For an interesting historical study, see Randolph N. Jonakait, *The Rise of the American Adversary System: American Before England*, 14 WIDENER L. REV. 323 (2009).

The American adversarial model raises significant ethical issues. For a recent discussion of several of these ethical problems that involve evidentiary issues, see the Fordham Law Review Symposium issue: Daniel J. Capra, *Ethics and Evidence*: Introduction, 76 FORDHAM L. REV. 1225 (2007).

C.   THE USE OF LAY JURORS

Continental legal systems differ from ours in another respect: juries are rare. In contrast, in America, juries are used frequently, and the Sixth and Seventh Amendments to the U.S. Constitution guarantee the right to a jury in certain instances. "More than ninety percent of the world's criminal jury trials, and nearly all of its civil jury trials, take place in the United States." Casper & Zeisel, *Lay Judges in the German Criminal Courts*, 1 J. LEGAL STUD. 135 (1972). This extensive use of juries in the United States arises from the commitment to including the voice of the community in the process of legal decision making. For a history of the right to jury trial under the Seventh Amendment, see Charles W. Wolfram, *The Constitutional History of the Seventh Amendment* , 57 MINN. L. REV. 639, 653–71 (1973) (discussing the jury as a feature of separation of powers, providing a popular check on the three branches of government).

The use of lay jurors as decisionmakers has affected both our procedures and the content of our evidentiary rules. Anglo-American jurists have long been skeptical of lay jurors' competence. Thayer remarked that our evidence law is a "product of the jury system . . . where ordinary untrained citizens are acting as judges of fact." J. THAYER, A PRELIMINARY TREATISE ON EVIDENCE AT THE COMMON LAW 509 (1898).

In concluding that the courts developed the modern, restrictive evidentiary rules primarily to control lay jurors, Thayer may have overstated the evidence. Nevertheless, many of the rules that operate to exclude logically relevant evidence appear to reflect doubts about the jurors' capabilities. Rather than risking the jurors' misevaluation of evidence of suspect reliability, the common law sometimes excludes the evidence altogether. The concern that juries will misevaluate evidence was rarely mentioned until the Nineteenth Century; it has not been sufficiently studied, and there is little reason to believe that judges do not suffer from the same cognitive biases as jurors. The pioneering Chicago Jury project gave us the first hard data on the subject. In H. KALVEN & H. ZEISEL, THE AMERICAN JURY, first published in 1966, two University of Chicago law professors reported on their empirical studies of jury behavior:

> We begin our inquiry into what the jury makes of the evidence by establishing two basic propositions. The first is simply that, contrary to an often voiced suspicion, the jury does by and large understand the facts and get the case straight. The second proposition is that the jury's decision by and large moves with the weight and direction of the evidence. . . .
>
> The hypothesis that the jury does *not* understand the case has loomed large in the debate over the jury. It has not infrequently been charged that the modern jury is asked to perform heroic feats of attention and recall well beyond the capacities of ordinary men. A trial, it has been argued, presents to the jury a mass of material which it cannot possibly absorb, and presents it in an artificial sequence which aggravates the jury's intellectual problem. The upshot is said to be that the jury often does not get the case straight

and, therefore, is deciding a case different from the one actually before it.

Id. at 149. The authors go on to refute this hypothesis by comparing the extent to which the judge and jury agreed or disagreed in various trials, classified according to trial length, closeness of the case, and complexity. The authors found overwhelming evidence that jurors by and large do, in fact, understand the evidence as well as the judge, and that their decisions accurately follow the weight and direction of the evidence.

One final caution: Do not assume that every trial is a jury trial. Quite to the contrary, most trials are bench trials: the judge sits without a jury and serves as trier of fact as well as presiding judge. Furthermore, if we include administrative hearings as well as judicial trials, it is clear that jury trials represent only a small percentage of the total number of hearings conducted each year in the United States.

NOTES

1.   Does it make sense to apply the same set of evidentiary rules — even those created in part because of jury concerns — in bench trials as well as in jury trials? Would it be feasible to apply different sets of evidentiary rules in jury and bench trials? Does it make any difference whether the rules are decisional (judge-created) or statutory? Note that, on their face, the Federal Rules of Evidence do not recognize any exceptions for bench trials.

2.   The Federal Rules have recently been revised, although the stated intent of the revisions has been to clarify rather than change the rules. At the state level, there are several jury reform projects either recently completed or underway. *See* www.crcf.org/americanjury/reform.html. The American Bar Association's *Principles Relating to Juries and Jury Trials* (2005) recommended, among other ways to improve the jury process, permitting jurors to take notes, ask questions and discuss evidence. § 13 (A), (C), (F).

3.   Are jurors rational decisionmakers? Are our rules of evidence optimized for the process by which jurors find facts? The debate goes on. *See, e.g.*, Craig R. Callen, *Symposium, Visions of Rationality in Evidence Law*, 2003 MICH. ST. L. REV. 847–1364; R. JONAKAIT, THE AMERICAN JURY SYSTEM (2003). And the work of the ABA Commission on the American Jury Project continues. *See* www.abanet.org/jury/home.html. For a recent comprehensive treatment, see NEIL VIDMAR & VALERIE HANS, AMERICAN JURIES: THE VERDICT (2007).

D.   EVIDENTIARY RULES BASED ON EXTERNAL SOCIAL POLICIES

As a bare minimum, any rational system of evidence should exclude irrelevant evidence. And, if the potential for drawing unwarranted inferences is high (or, as Fed. R. Evid. 403 provides, if the unduly prejudicial effect outweighs the probative value) exclusion may similarly serve rationality goals. It may also be defensible to exclude evidence which, although relevant, is of suspect trustworthiness, such as some forms of hearsay. However, it is quite another matter to exclude evidence not for reasons of logic, but based on extrinsic social policies. Rather than enhancing the accuracy of fact-finding, the exclusion of evidence for that purpose may distort the ultimate decision. When we deprive the trier of fact of relevant, reliable evidence, we increase the risk of a miscarriage of justice.

Yet, to a greater extent than any other legal system, the American legal system frequently excludes relevant, reliable evidence on the theory that the exclusion serves a social policy separate from the truth-finding function of the trial. Many of these exclusions are based on the Constitution. For example, the Fourth Amendment's judicially created exclusionary rule and the Fifth Amendment's privilege against self-incrimination have substantial evidentiary consequences.

We also exclude evidence to promote non-constitutional social policies, most notably in the privileges excluding communications between persons in confidential relationships (*e.g.*, husband and wife, attorney and client, psychotherapist and patient). We exclude privileged communications in the hope that the exclusion will facilitate a freer flow of information between the parties to the relationship. But here the trade-off is even more debatable: we exclude relevant evidence and increase the risk of miscarriage of justice to protect policies that are not of constitutional dimension.

E.   OTHER REASONS FOR EVIDENTIARY RULES

In addition to the factors discussed in the preceding sections — the adversary system, the use of lay jurors, and external social policies — there are other considerations that underlie various rules of evidence. Rules of evidence (and related rules of trial procedure) may also rest on considerations of fairness to victims, witnesses or other participants in the process as well as minimizing expense and delay. *See* FED. R. EVID. 102, 403.

As we examine each rule of evidence, try to determine its underlying policy bases, its purposes, and the assumptions upon which it is premised.

F.   A RESEARCH AGENDA FOR THE FUTURE

Most evidentiary doctrines rest on assumptions about human behavior — the conduct of judges, jurors, witnesses on the stand, and actors outside the courtroom. Many of these assumptions are potentially testable by empirical techniques. In a landmark study of American jury behavior, R. HASTIE, S. PENROD & N. PENNINGTON, INSIDE THE JURY (1983), the authors assert that given the availability of social science and statistical methods, it is no longer tolerable for legal policymakers to rely "on the vagaries of intuition and personal experience." In the following excerpt, the authors discuss possible methodologies of jury research and evaluate their respective strengths and weaknesses.

R. HASTIE, S. PENROD & N. PENNINGTON INSIDE THE JURY
at 37–41 (1983) (citations omitted)

The experimental simulation paradigm was used in the present jury study. Over one thousand citizens called for jury duty in state trial courts were asked to view a three-hour filmed reenactment of a murder trial. After viewing the trial twelve jurors retired to a jury room to deliberate to a verdict on the case as if they were actual impaneled jurors. This method is called a jury simulation or a mock jury experiment. . . .

Two major methodological concerns face a researcher when designing a study, namely internal validity and external validity. Internal validity refers to the degree to which changes in the measured dependent variables can be attributed to the manipulated independent variables. External validity refers to the degree to which the findings or results of research in one setting, such as a laboratory experiment, can be generalized to another setting, such as an actual courtroom. . . .

There is a tension between the concerns of internal and external validity. The more control one has over an experimental environment, the more one can ensure that all variables other than the dependent variable are held constant, thereby decreasing or eliminating the possibility that these extraneous or con-founding variables have a causal role in producing the observed effects. This means increased confidence in the internal validity of experimental findings. However, experimental control usually comes at the cost of increased artificiality of the research environment. This means decreased external validity or generalizability of any observed cause-and-effect relationships. In the other direction, the closer an experimental environment is to a real world setting, the more likely that any experimental result will be valid in the real world situation. But by drawing the complexities of the real world into an experiment, one usually sacrifices the control and simplicity of design that increase internal validity. For example, one field study identified a correlational relationship between the race of a defendant and the severity of sentence for interracial crimes. However, it would be difficult to conclude with any confidence that the race of the defendant alone caused the differences in sentencing. Any one of a number of other factors that may not have been measured and which certainly were not controlled could have contributed to the observed difference in sentencing. Indeed, subsequent research showed that the observed differences may have been attributable to the prior criminal history of the defendants rather than to racial factors. . . .

The main advantages of studying mock juries as opposed to real juries derive from the high internal validity of the controlled experiment. One of the most serious threats to internal validity is the possibility that the apparent cause in a cause-and-effect relationship is not the true cause. . . . To be confident that a particular cause is actually producing an observed effect, it is desirable to hold all conditions besides the independent or causal variable constant. Thus, for example, to study the effect of the defendant's race on sentencing would require making sure that all variables other than race were the same in each group of cases. This is not possible in a natural setting, where each trial is different, each defendant is different, and a large set of variables besides race may differentiate two groups of cases which have been divided into categories by race. In a simulation, these potentially confounding variables may be controlled.

Extraneous differences in a real trial, such as the facts of the case or the characteristics of the defendant, are not the only possible sources of confounding of a relationship. Differences in the personal characteristics of members of a real jury can also confound a relationship. Here the advantage of a jury simulation is that the same stimulus trial may be shown to many sets of experimental juries. The performance of multiple replications removes the potentially confounding effect of individual differences, such as social class or gender. The method also permits study of a distribution of juror behavior, making it statistically possible to assess the replicability of observed differences.

The experimental control in a jury simulation which allows for increased confidence in observed effects also allows for systematic evaluation of an independent variable far beyond what could be done in a natural setting. One can ask mock jurors questions that the legal system would not usually ask real jurors. Mock jurors may be asked demographic questions, attitude questions, and questions concerning their feelings toward jury deliberation and verdicts or their assessments of other jurors. In addition to flexibility in the choice of measures, the jury simulation allows for observation of the mock jury's reactions to the trial and juror behavior during deliberations.

While methodological and practical reasons thus compel use of the simulation method for extensive jury research, the jury simulation entails drawbacks in the area of external validity. The seriousness of these drawbacks depends on the questions to be answered by the simulation and the way it is carried out. One problem has to do with the subject population. The vast majority of jury simulations have used students as mock jurors; only 12.5 percent have used subjects from an actual jury pool. . . . But the use of student subjects is questionable . . . Because students differ as a group from actual jurors in terms of age, education, income, and ideology, students' behavior differs systematically from the behavior of real jurors. . . . In general, evidence suggests that differences between students and real jurors pose a threat to the external validity of many conclusions from jury simulations that use only student subjects.

Still another important issue for jury simulations is the difference between the consequences of real jury and mock jury decisions. A real jury decides the fate of an actual defendant; a mock jury usually knows that its decision will have no such impact. Comparison of the verdicts of "alternate" jurors (subjects from the jury pool who observed as a group in the gallery of a courtroom) with real jurors in ten cases, revealed a greater tendency toward conviction among the alternate juries. . . . In contrast, comparison of two groups of student jurors, half of whom were told they were actually deciding a student discipline case and half of whom were told they were mock jurors, found the mock juries more lenient. . . . A similar study found no verdict differences between mock juries and real juries.

———

NOTE

Throughout this text, we shall refer to empirical studies questioning the underlying assumptions of evidentiary doctrines. However, just as we urge the reader to have a critical attitude toward evidentiary doctrine, we recommend that the reader review the cited studies with a healthy skepticism. As you read the various studies included in the text, keep these questions in mind:

- Does the author of the study provide enough background information about the study to enable us to independently assess its internal and external validity?

- Did the researchers control all the variables that might explain their findings? Did the researchers rely on an incomplete model of human behavior?

- Can we confidently transfer the research findings to the real world? Was the data set sufficiently large and representative? Was the study conducted under conditions that approximate real world situations? As Hastie et al. warn, mock jurors usually realize that their decisions carry no real consequences. Knowing that their decisions are not legally binding, they may put less effort into their decision-making than actual jurors do. Similarly, many legal psychology studies use college-age subject populations. The issue is whether the findings in those studies can be generalized across other age groups.

- Are the conclusions in the study about causal relations consistent with ordinary human experience? Is the relationship practically as well as statistically significant? For example, it has been reported that there is "a strong positive correlation between teachers' salary increases and sales of liquor." W. CURTIS, STATISTICAL CONCEPTS FOR ATTORNEYS 158 (1983).

G.   THE HISTORY OF AMERICAN EVIDENCE LAW

1.   Introduction

American jurisprudence has common law origins, but statutes have become the dominant source of modern American law. Most major areas of American law are undergoing "statutization." Evidence law is no exception.

The Federal Rules of Evidence took effect in 1975. Until then, the law of evidence in both state and federal courts derived mostly from judicial decisions. Few states had evidence codes, and few statutes or court rules concerned evidence.

2.   Prior to the Federal Rules

Among the earliest codification efforts was the Field Code of Civil Procedure. Few lawyers are aware that Field's code also contained rules of evidence. Although not adopted in Field's home state of New York, Oregon (1862) adopted all and California (1872) adopted substantially all of these evidence rules. In 1860, Georgia undertook to codify the common law, including its law of evidence. However, except for these few states, statutory codification and reform of the law of evidence were limited to occasional enactments covering isolated rules until well into the twentieth century.

In 1904, the massive body of American evidence case law that had developed to that time was synthesized in the first edition of Northwestern law professor John Henry Wigmore's monumental treatise. Wigmore's influence cannot be overstated; his work has remained the dominant authority in the field to this day. Perhaps this treatise was in part responsible for the fact that codification did not begin to take hold until the 1970's.

California opted for its own code of evidence, effective January 1, 1967. The California rules are more detailed and comprehensive than other codifications and contain a number of well-drafted provisions that have been influential in other jurisdictions.

3.   The Federal Rules of Evidence

By far the most important event in the history of American evidence law was the enactment of the Federal Rules of Evidence. The Federal Rules mark the beginning of a new era, the dawn of the Age of Statutes in evidence law. They are the central focus of our study of the law of evidence.

In 1961, Chief Justice Earl Warren appointed a Special Committee on Evidence, charged with determining whether uniform rules of evidence for the federal courts were advisable and feasible. Nine months later, the committee reported in the affirmative. One of the questions addressed was whether the Supreme Court's rulemaking power extended to the promulgation of rules of evidence. The committee concluded that it did, and that the *Erie* doctrine was not a significant obstacle. In short, the assumption was that almost all rules of evidence were "procedural" in the sense of *Erie*, and hence were matters on which federal law would control, even in a diversity case.

In March 1965, Chief Justice Warren appointed an advisory committee to draft the proposed rules, with renowned attorney Albert E. Jenner, Jr., of Chicago as its chairperson and Professor Edward W. Cleary as reporter. That draft — known as the Revised Draft — was approved by the Judicial Conference in October 1970, and forwarded to the Supreme Court.

The Court elected not to promulgate the Rules immediately, but instead returned the Revised Draft to the Judicial Conference to be published again to the profession. This time, organized opposition surfaced, notably from the United States Department of Justice. A third version of the Rules was sent to the Court, which included many of the Justice Department's suggested changes. After making a few further changes agreed to by the committee, the Supreme Court approved the Rules on November 20, 1972, and authorized the Chief Justice to transmit them to Congress in accordance with the Rules Enabling Act procedures.

If Congress had done nothing, the Rules would have become effective in ninety days. But the Rules reached Congress in the aftermath of Watergate — a time when many of its members sought to reclaim powers believed to have been lost by that branch to the executive and judiciary.

On March 30, 1973, Congress passed a law providing that the Rules would not go into effect until the adjournment of the Ninety-third Congress's first session, unless expressly approved by the Congress before that time. Meanwhile, hearings on the Rules began in the House Judiciary Committee's Special Subcommittee on Reform of Federal Criminal Laws, the so-called "Hungate Subcommittee." After a number of significant revisions, the Rules (in the form of H.R. 5463) were reported out on November 15. On February 6, 1974, after debate and a few amendments, the House passed the bill.

In June 1974, the Senate Judiciary Committee (chaired by Senator Sam Ervin) held hearings on the House bill. Many amendments later, the bill was reported out on October 18. The Senate debated and passed the bill on November 21–22. The Senate's version differed substantially from the House-passed bill; it was closer to the Rules originally promulgated by the Court. A conference committee resolved the differences in short order, usually in favor of the House version. The Conference Report passed both houses in December, and the Federal Rules of Evidence became law when President Ford signed the bill on January 2, 1975. The Rules took effect on July 1, 1975.

To insure that it would continue to have effective supervisory power over the Rules, Congress added explicit limitations on the Supreme Court's rulemaking power:

(a) The Supreme Court of the United States shall have the power to prescribe amendments to the Federal Rules of Evidence. Such amendments shall not take effect until they have been reported to Congress by the Chief Justice at or after the beginning of a regular session of Congress . . . .

(b) Any such rule creating, abolishing, or modifying an evidentiary privilege shall have no force or effect unless approved by Congress.

28 U.S.C. § 2074 (section (a) no longer reads this way).

One of the arguments used by the proponents of the Federal Rules was that their adoption would have a "domino" effect; that is, the states would tend to adopt evidence codes modeled after them. This prediction has proved to be correct. After they became effective, the Federal Rules triggered the establishment of study committees in many states, most of which eventually adopted an evidence code or rules closely approximating a version of the Federal Rules of Evidence. In most of these states, the rules eventually became law, either as rules of that jurisdiction's highest court or by legislative enactment.

The Federal Rules of Evidence are becoming the American law of evidence. Most states have largely "borrowed" their evidence law from the Federal Rules. Not only is the wording of the codes strikingly similar to that of the Federal Rules; in construing their own state codes, courts in the "borrowing" jurisdictions tend to adopt the gloss placed on the Federal Rules by the federal courts.

NOTES

1.   On April 11, 2011, the Supreme Court transmitted to Congress a set of comprehensive amendments, which took effect on December 1, 2011. These so-called "stylistic" amendments are intended to clarify, but not change, the meaning of the rules. According to one member of the drafting committee, "[t]he goal has been to make the rules clearer, more consistent, and more readable — all without changing their meaning."[1]

2.   Though most American jurisdictions have now codified their evidence law, either by statute or court rules, the debate over the wisdom of specific provisions nonetheless continues, as does the debate over whether it is even desirable to codify evidence law. This debate is but one example of the pervasive tensions in the law between specific and general rules of decision, and between (1) judge-made law with its greater flexibility and relative ease of modification and (2) codified law, with its greater certainty, predictability, and ease of determination.

Note that formal rules are not necessarily codified rules. For example, even at common law, the hearsay rule was a simple, formal rule subject to a large number of judicially created formal exceptions. Conversely, a codified rule can be non-formal, such as the rule that allows a judge to exclude evidence if he or she determines that its probative value is outweighed by its tendency toward unfair prejudice (Fed. R. Evid. 403).

3.   Instead of a formal, strict hearsay rule with a number of specific exceptions, we might adopt a general, flexible rule such as that proposed by Dean McCormick: "Hearsay is inadmissible except where the judge in his discretion finds it needed and trustworthy." McCormick, *The Borderland of Hearsay*, 39 Yale L.J. 489, 504 (1930). However, in this context, most lawyers would reject such a rule because, in their view, it vests too much discretion in the judge, the result is too unpredictable, and it would be subject to very limited review on appeal. After we have studied the hearsay rule, see if you agree.

4.   As we will see, Congress refused to adopt the specific privilege rules that the Advisory Committee drafted for Article V of the Federal Rules of Evidence. Instead, Congress delegated responsibility for developing privilege law to the courts. Does this mean that some areas of evidence law are more resistant to codification and therefore are good candidates for non-formal, judge-made rules?

---

[1] Joseph Kimble, *A Drafting Example from the Proposed New Federal Rules of Evidence*, 88 Mich. B.J. 52 (Aug. 2009).

Chapter 2

EVIDENCE: TYPES, SOURCES AND SUBSTITUTES

A. THE TYPES OF INFORMATION TO WHICH THE EVIDENTIARY RULES ARE APPLIED

At its most basic, evidence is information, and the law of evidence concerns information that is used in the context of litigation. This is quite a broad concept: As Twining explains, "a single 'bit' of information that counts as admissible or inadmissible 'evidence' at the adjudicative stage may perform similar, but not identical, functions in respect of other decisions at other stages in the same process." WILLIAM TWINING, RETHINKING EVIDENCE 248 (2d ed. 2006). For example, "a 'confession' may be the start of a process of cooperation with authority, the forerunner to a guilty plea (with or without bargaining) or, after retraction, may be admissible or inadmissible as evidence or its reception may provide a ground for appeal." *Id.* Thayer defined evidence more narrowly as "any matter of fact which is furnished to a legal tribunal, otherwise than by reasoning or a reference to what is noticed without proof, as the basis of inference for ascertaining some other matter of fact." James B. Thayer, *Presumptions in the Law of Evidence*, 3 HARV. L. REV. 141 (1889). But how does this information come into court?

California Evidence Code § 140 defines evidence as: "testimony, writings, material objects, or other things presented to the senses that are offered to prove the existence or nonexistence of a fact."

This rule first tells us that evidence includes **testimony**. A witness may give oral testimony about his own perceptions or opinions. As we shall study later in greater detail, an ordinary lay witness may testify on the basis of personal knowledge — that is, what he has seen, smelled, heard, tasted, or felt firsthand. Such testimony might include a police officer testifying about drugs she saw in the defendant's apartment, the odor of marijuana she smelled before breaking in the door, and the defendant's statements to her immediately after the arrest. In addition, witnesses with specialized knowledge are often permitted to testify to opinions based on that knowledge: A drug enforcement agent, for example, might be permitted to express an opinion about the street value of the drugs in question. *United States v. Hernandez*, 218 F.3d 58, 70 (1st Cir. 2000) (holding testimony about street value admissible).

The California rule next states that evidence includes "writings [and] material objects." Documents are very commonly admitted as evidence. However, they are only one illustration of the broader category of "material objects" known as **physical evidence**. That category might include such varied items as a pistol, a knife, a muffler, or a photograph. The category is not even limited to objects historically connected with the case (so-called "real" or "original" physical evidence); for purposes of trial, the attorneys can prepare drawings, models and charts, known as "demonstrative" evidence. The introduction of physical evidence usually requires a witness to testify in order to "lay a foundation" for the object or document: The witness "sponsors" the exhibit by testifying to its authenticity. However, physical evidence differs from oral testimony in an important respect: The jurors themselves can observe the object and use their own firsthand sense impressions to assess the witness's testimony about the object.

Indeed, in some cases the jurors are not even limited to situations in which a witness introduces them to the physical evidence. In a "jury view," a court official takes the jurors to a location outside the courtroom where the jurors make their own observations without the intermediation of a sponsoring witness. In the *O. J. Simpson* case, for example, the trial judge allowed the jurors to visit the location where Nicole Brown Simpson and Ronald Goldman were murdered.

NOTES

1. Note the reference at the end of California Evidence Code § 140 to "other things presented to the senses." While a witness is on the stand, she presents her demeanor to the senses of the trier of fact. Should demeanor be considered a form of evidence? The cases are divided over this question. *See* Imwinkelried, *Demeanor Impeachment: Law and Tactics*, 9 AM. J. TRIAL ADVOC. 183, 189–92 (1985).

On the one hand, the trial court record cannot adequately reflect a witness's demeanor. To the extent that a finding of fact at the trial rests on demeanor, the appellate court will be unable to judge the rationality of a resulting decision or ruling.

On the other hand, it seems unrealistic to deny evidentiary status to demeanor. Communications experts commonly assert that when one person speaks to another, the speaker's nonverbal conduct accounts for more than 50% of the information communicated. J. KESTLER, QUESTIONING TECHNIQUES AND TACTICS § 2.49 (3d ed. 1999). If the speaker's statement is laden with emotion, more than 90% of the message can be communicated nonverbally. K. TAYLOR, R. BUCHANAN & D. STRAWN, COMMUNICATION STRATEGIES FOR TRIAL ATTORNEYS 49 (1984). Moreover, when the listener perceives a conflict between the speaker's statement and the accompanying nonverbal cues, the listener ordinarily disbelieves the statement, since "we trust actions more than . . . words." Peskin, *Non-Verbal Communications in the Courtroom*, TRIAL DIPL. J., Winter 1980, at 8. In the Cleveland Jury Project conducted in the mid-1980s, the researchers found that when witnesses disagreed, jurors often decided the case by focusing on the witnesses' demeanor. Austin, *Why Jurors Don't Heed the Trial*, NAT'L L.J., Aug. 12, 1985, at 18. Though much of this research is preliminary, almost all of the studies to date support the intuition that fact-finders rely on demeanor when judging a person's credibility.

2. How reliable is demeanor evidence? Research suggests that it may be relatively unreliable, especially in cross-racial situations. *See* Rand, *The Demeanor Gap: Race, Lie Detection, and the Jury*, 33 CONN. L. REV. 1 (2000). In one study, subjects who read the transcript of a witness's testimony more accurately assessed

credibility than those who saw the witness testify in person. And a survey of professional fact-finders — administrative law judges — found that they tend to give little weight to demeanor evidence. Ogden, *The Role of Demeanor Evidence in Determining Credibility of Witnesses in Fact Finding: The Views of ALJs*, 20 J. NAALJ 1 (2000).

B.   THE SOURCES OF EVIDENCE LAW

1.   Constitutional Considerations

Especially in criminal practice, the U.S. Constitution limits the information that may be available at trial. The key provisions that tend to impact the admissibility of evidence are the Fourth Amendment's prohibition against unreasonable searches and seizures (along with its judicially derived Exclusionary Rule), the Fifth Amendment's privilege against self-incrimination, and the Sixth Amendment's Confrontation Clause and right to counsel guarantee. If the government obtains evidence by violating one of these provisions, Supreme Court doctrine generally requires that the evidence be excluded. *See, e.g., Mapp v. Ohio*, 367 U.S. 643 (1961) (holding evidence obtained by unconstitutional search inadmissible).

The exclusionary rules based on the Fourth, Fifth, and Sixth Amendments are also enforceable against the states. The Fourteenth Amendment's Due Process clause explicitly applies to the states, and the Supreme Court has held that it incorporates many of the Bill of Rights guarantees, including the Fourth, Fifth, and Sixth Amendment exclusionary rules. *See, e.g., Griffin v. California*, 380 U.S. 609 (1965) (holding that judicial and prosecutorial comments on the defendant's failure to testify violated the Fifth Amendment); *Malloy v. Hogan*, 378 U.S. 1 (1964) (holding that the Fifth Amendment prohibition against compulsory self-incrimination is protected by the Fourteenth Amendment against abridgement by the states). Indeed, many of the leading criminal procedure precedents are cases that originated in state court. *See Mapp v. Ohio, supra* (Fourth Amendment exclusionary rule); *Miranda v. Arizona*, 384 U.S. 436 (1966) (Fifth Amendment requirement for warnings during custodial interrogation); *Gilbert v. California*, 388 U.S. 263 (1967) (Sixth Amendment right to counsel at lineups).

2.   Court Rules

In the process of creating the Federal Rules of Evidence, a dispute arose as to whether the Supreme Court had the authority to promulgate the Rules. In an order dated November 20, 1972, the Court purported to exercise that authority. In a dissenting opinion, Justice Douglas cautioned that "[t]here are those who think that fashioning of rules of evidence is a task for the legislature, not for the judiciary." RULES OF EVIDENCE — COMMUNICATION FROM CHIEF JUSTICE OF THE UNITED STATES vi (1973). Congress intervened, blocked the Rules from taking effect, and made significant modifications. Congress ultimately enacted the Rules as an Act of Congress — the Federal Rules of Evidence are a federal statute.

Furthermore, Congress has retained a role for itself in the evidence rulemaking process. Amendments to the rules enabling statutes, 28 U.S.C. §§ 2072–2074, extended their scope to include rules of evidence. New rules must be transmitted to Congress and Congress can prevent any proposed rule from taking effect.

A similar battle was fought in many of the states that considered adopting the Federal Rules. In some jurisdictions, the legislatures prevailed and adopted a statutory code of evidence; in other states, the highest court succeeded in adopting an evidence code as rules of court. *See* Giannelli, *The Proposed Ohio Rules of Evidence: The General Assembly, Evidence, and Rulemaking*, 29 CASE W. RES. L. REV. 16 (1978).

NOTES

1. Which branch is better suited to draft an evidentiary code? At first blush, the judiciary seems the more likely candidate, since courts work with the evidentiary rules on a daily basis and can see how the rules interface with other bodies of law such as civil and criminal procedure. What are the arguments on the other side? If additional empirical investigation of the assumptions underlying the rules is critically needed (as we suggest), which branch is better equipped to conduct that investigation?

2. If a code of evidence is adopted by court rule, what happens if there is a conflict between a particular court-adopted rule and a statutory rule of evidence adopted by the legislature? *See* Gamble & Fowlkes, *Comprehensive Principles Governing the Interaction Between the Alabama Rules of Evidence and Alabama Statutory Rules of Evidence: The Need for Judicial Initiative and Legislative Deference When Both Branches of Government Hold Constitutional Power to Adopt Rules of Evidence*, 56 ALA. L. REV. 937 (2005).

3. Statutes and Statutory Interpretation

Arguably the most important source of evidence law in the United States is statutory law. As noted in the prior section, Congress has enacted the Federal Rules of Evidence as a statute, and some 41 states (and other jurisdictions) have adopted evidence codes patterned after the Federal Rules. Since several states, notably California and New York, had adopted their own evidence codes before the promulgation of the Federal Rules, the vast majority of states now have a largely statutory body of evidence law. In these jurisdictions, in the final analysis, determining evidence law is largely an exercise in statutory interpretation. Whether the evidence code in a particular jurisdiction was adopted by the legislature (statute) or by the judiciary (court rule), similar issues of interpretation arise.

Statutory interpretation is, as you probably know by now, highly contentious. The following excerpt summarizes the main positions and proposes a "practical reasoning" solution:

William N. Eskridge, Jr.
Philip P. Frickey
Statutory Interpretation As Practical Reasoning
42 Stan. L. Rev. 321 (1990) (citations omitted)

In the last decade, statutory interpretation has reemerged as an important topic of academic theory and discussion. This development is welcome, since few topics are more relevant to legal craft and education than the interpretation of statutes, now our primary source of law. The recent theoretical views, however, contrast with practicing lawyers' strategies of statutory interpretation. When practitioners give advice to clients about what a statute means, their approach is usually eclectic: They look at the text of the relevant statutory provisions, any legislative history that is available, the context in which the legislation was enacted, the overall legal landscape, and the lessons of common sense and good policy. But when law professors talk about statutory interpretation, they tend to posit a more abstract, "grand" theory that privileges one or another of these approaches as "foundational." The commentators' grand theories contrast with the more ad hoc, fact-based reasoning of the practicing lawyer.

How do judges interpret statutes? How should they? Many commentators argue that judicial interpretation is, or at least ought to be, inspired by grand theory. We think these commentators are wrong, both descriptively and normatively: Judges' approaches to statutory interpretation are generally eclectic, not inspired by any grand theory, and this is a good methodology. Stated another way, we argue that foundationalism is a flawed strategy for theorizing about statutory interpretation and that a more modest approach, grounded upon "practical reason," is both more natural and more useful.

*   *   *

The philosophical inspiration for our model is Aristotle's theory of practical reasoning (*phronesis*). Aristotle's practical philosophy starts with the proposition that one can determine what is right in specific cases, even without a universal theory of what is right. * * * Both the hermeneutical and pragmatic traditions emphasize themes of Aristotelian practical reasoning — the concrete situatedness of the interpretive enterprise, which militates against overarching theories; the complexity of interpretation and argument, which recognizes that different values will pull the interpreter in different directions; and the importance of workable resolutions to complex questions. * * *[T]hese traditions and our model of practical reasoning offer methods and criteria for criticizing the Court's approach. In some cases, we claim, the Court distorts some of the interpretive factors or appears to ignore or minimize relevant evolutive factors, in an attempt to make the cases easier than in fact they are. In these moments, the Court seems to be gripped by a form of "counter-majoritarian anxiety": As unelected judges, applying statutes enacted by our elected legislators, they feel some pressure to tie their results rigorously to the expectations that legislators had when they enacted the statute. Any result not related to majoritarian expectations may seem illegitimate in a democracy.

*   *   *

I. THE FAILURE OF FOUNDATIONALIST THEORIES OF STATUTORY INTERPRETATION

Traditional theories have always considered a variety of factors relevant for statutory interpretation. In the post-World War II era, however, legal scholars have preferred theories that offer a unitary foundation for statutory interpretation. Much of the theoretical debate has been over which of the competing foundations is the best one. The three main theories today emphasize (1) the actual or presumed intent of the legislature enacting the statute ("intentionalism"); (2) the actual or presumed purpose of the statute ("purposivism" or "modified intentionalism"); and (3) the literal commands of the statutory text ("textualism"). We call these theories "foundationalist," because each seeks an objective ground ("foundation") that will reliably guide the interpretation of all statutes in all situations.

Each of the three grand theories seeks to reconcile statutory interpretation by unelected judges with the assumptions of majoritarian political theory. Toward this end, each seeks an objective standard that will constrain the discretion of judicial interpreters. And each theory fails. In light of both modern scholarship on interpretation and concrete experience in statutory cases, all three theories suffer from flawed assumptions, indeterminacy, and nonexclusivity. To begin with, each theory posits an anchoring value — legislative "intent" or "purpose," or statutory "plain meaning" — that rests upon certain questionable assumptions. When we examine these assumptions, each anchoring idea loses its close link to majoritarian legitimacy. Moreover, upon close scrutiny the essential indeterminacy of the anchoring ideas becomes clear. Thus, legislative intent and purpose prove to be distressingly malleable, and even such "hard" evidence as statutory text turns out to be quite flexible. A grand theory loses much of its *raison d'être*, we argue, if it cannot reliably assure determinate results. Finally, even if its results were fully consistent with democratic principles and determinate, if rigorously applied each theory would yield anomalous results that most legal interpreters could not stomach. The anomalies arise in part because none of the three anchors (intent, purpose, text) can altogether exclude the other two. Nor does any of them adequately accommodate evolutive factors — current values and policies, as well as the dynamics of the statutory policies as implemented over time. * * *

A. *Intentionalism*

The most popular grand theory is probably intentionalism. Under this view, the Court acts as the enacting legislature's faithful servant, discovering and applying the legislature's original intent. Traditional treatises on statutory interpretation generally acknowledge the primacy of legislative intent, qualifying the canons of construction with the caveat, "unless the legislature otherwise intends." Although traditional intentionalism was subjected to withering attack in the 1930s and 1940s, recent scholarship has revived academic interest in the theory and posited some form of intentionalism as the anchor for a grand theory of interpretation.

Intentionalism makes a strong claim to be the only legitimate foundation for statutory interpretation in a representative democracy. If the legislature is the primary lawmaker and courts are its agents, then requiring the courts to follow the legislature's intentions disciplines judges by inhibiting judicial lawmaking, and in so doing seems to further democracy by affirming the will of elected representatives. Not surprisingly, then, a number of Supreme Court opinions state that original legislative intent is the touchstone for statutory interpretation.* * *

B. *Purposivism*

The legal realists* * * raised some of the objections to intentionalism noted above and proposed as an alternative theory a flexible "mischief" approach to statutory interpretation. Professors Henry Hart and Albert Sacks in the 1950s expanded the realists' approach into a "purposivist" theory of interpretation that seemed as faithful to the principle of legislative supremacy as intentionalism, but without the rigidity and definitional problems of intentionalism. According to the Hart and Sacks legal process materials, "every statute must be conclusively presumed to be a purposive act. The idea of a statute without an intelligible purpose is foreign to the idea of law and inadmissible." Because "every statute and every doctrine of unwritten law developed by the decisional process has some kind of purpose or objective," identifying that purpose and deducing the interpretation with which it is most consistent resolves interpretive ambiguities.

First, purposivism's apparent majoritarian justifications rest upon questionable assumptions about the legislative process. Hart and Sacks assumed that the legislature is filled with reasonable people who will reach reasonable, purposive results by following established procedures. Whether Hart and Sacks thought this assumption reflected the realities of the legislative process is unclear. But it was a plausible working assumption for the legal community in the 1950s, given the state of political science. And since Hart and Sacks expressed no caveat along these lines, much less attempted any elaborate normative justification for these assumptions if they were deemed unrealistic, it appears that at least some of the legitimacy of their approach depends upon the empirical accuracy of these assumptions.

These optimistic legal process assumptions have received a considerable amount of theoretical and empirical testing since the 1950s and must now be considered naive. Public choice theory, the application of economic analysis to public decision making, posits that "rational" legislators responding to rational interest groups will not, in fact, produce purposive statutes. Economic game theory suggests that, frequently, nothing more than who controls the legislature's agenda determines legislative results. Interest group theory suggests that much legislation simply distributes benefits to well-organized groups, typically at the expense of the general public. To speak of a statute's "purpose" is incoherent, unless one means the deal between rent-seeking groups and reelection-minded legislators. To be sure, public choice is a controversial approach to legislation, but the insights presented here — the potential arbitrariness and unfairness of many legislative decisions — are supported by more traditional institutional political theory as well. Leading scholars of legislative institutions stress the ability of committees and power figures to manipulate legislative procedure, and the importance of "subgovernments" of bureaucrats, lobbyists, and subcommittee leaders who push the legislative agenda toward distributing favors to organized groups.

Modern political theory, especially public choice theory, renders the political theory assumptions of purposivist statutory interpretation highly controversial. It seems clear not only that reasonable people in the legislature do not always produce reasonable results, but that in some cases that is the last thing they want to do. Some statutes are little else but backroom deals. Judicial attempts to fancy up those deals with public-regarding rhetoric either are naive or simply substitute the judge's conception of public policy for that of the legislature. And when a court uses purposivist analysis to elaborate a statute, it may actually undo a deliberate and precisely calibrated deal worked out in the legislative process. Such judicial lawmaking can often be justified, we think, but the point is that this is judicial lawmaking and not, as some legal process thinkers might suggest, merely carrying out the original statutory purposes.

Second, purposivism is indeterminate, for some of the reasons just developed. The complex compromises endemic in the political process suggest that legislation is frequently a congeries of different and sometimes conflicting purposes. To be enacted, a statute must be acceptable to a range of interest groups, each of which will have their own reasons for supporting, or at least not opposing, the statute. Some commentators argue that these various purposes cannot be aggregated into a *public* purpose. Moreover, even if such an aggregation were theoretically possible, supporters of legislation will usually appeal to more than one public purpose in order to maximize political support.

Third, although purposivism often permits statutes to develop over time, [it] cannot be accepted as a general theory because it neglects other values we consider critically important. Representative democracy places some value on faithfulness to original legislative intentions. It also is committed to following determinate texts: Because text is the only thing actually enacted into law, it is formally the most legitimate expression of legislative intent or purpose. Moreover, it is argued, citizens ought to be able to rely on clear statutory text to determine their rights and duties.

C. *Textualism*

The legal realists and legal process thinkers discredited intentionalism as a grand strategy for statutory interpretation; in its place they suggested purposivism. That theory has in turn been extensively criticized, especially by scholars influenced by the law and economics movement. As argued above, the recent trend is to view the legislature as not necessarily purposive; "attributing" purposes to ad hoc statutory deals is nothing if not judicial lawmaking. Accordingly, several judges of the law and economics school have responded to the critique of purposivism by urging as a grand theory the return to some version of the old "plain meaning rule": The beginning, and usually the end, of statutory interpretation should be the apparent meaning of the statutory language.

The arguments for textualism are strong ones. As suggested above, textualism appeals to the rule-of-law value that citizens ought to be able to read the statute books and know their rights and duties. By emphasizing the statutory words chosen by the legislature, rather than (what seem to be) more abstract and judicially malleable interpretive sources, textualism also appeals to the values of legislative supremacy and judicial restraint.

There are at least two varieties of textualism. The stricter version posits the statutory text as (at least ordinarily) the sole legitimate interpretive source. A characteristically pithy Holmesianism says it well: "We do not inquire what the legislature meant; we ask only what the statute means." The second, and less ambitious, variety of textualism uses statutory language not in place of, but rather as the best guide to, legislative intent or purpose. "There is, of course, no more persuasive evidence of the purpose of a statute than the words by which the legislature undertook to give expression to its wishes." Similarly, "when words are free from doubt they must be taken as the final expression of the legislative intent." As a grand theory, both versions of textualism suffer from similar defects: They oversimplify the meaning of statutory texts, are not so determinate as they sound, and ignore other values our polity considers important. * * *

Textualism can control statutory interpretation only if the text itself offers a complete and reasonably determinate source of meaning. This proposition has long been contested, and it is more controversial than ever today. Whether or not language itself is intrinsically indeterminate, one would have to concede that general, politicized terms such as "discrimination" are susceptible of different interpretations. * * * "Discrimination" has acquired nuances that are hard to capture. For example, in common usage we do not say we "discriminate" against peaches because we prefer pears (although this would arguably be a correct use of the word). Is it any more natural to say we are "discriminating" when we establish a program to try to rectify past misdeeds by hiring or training more people who have suffered invidious "discrimination" at our hands in the past?

An additional problem with any strict textualist theory is its failure to consider that the meaning of text is strongly influenced by context. If we were to write you a note, "Go fetch us some meat," you could not interpret that note without knowing and understanding its context. This same sort of analysis is readily applicable to legal texts. When Congress told us in 1964 that we should not "discriminate" on the basis of race in employment decisions, did we not know from ten years of experience with *Brown*, from the horrific pictures of Bull Connor's firehoses pummeling black youths marching against racism, from the March on Washington, and from Dr. Martin Luther King's eloquent speeches and letters, that the point of the statute was to seek justice for a group that had systematically been treated unjustly in our society? * * *

A final problem undercuts textualism: the importance of the interpreter's own context, including current values. Philosophy and literary theory suggest to us that interpretation cannot aspire to universal objectivity, since the interpreter's perspective will always interact with the text and historical context. * * * The more general point, of course, is that current values cannot easily be excluded from statutory interpretation. Where current values and historical context strongly support an interpretation, a determinate text will not stand in the way.

*   *   *

Easterbrook, *Statutes' Domains*
50 U. Chi. L. Rev. 533, 544–52 (1983)

Unless the statute plainly hands courts the power to create and revise a form of common law, the domain of the statute should be restricted to cases anticipated by its framers and expressly resolved in the legislative process. Unless the party relying on the statute could establish either express resolution or creation of the common law power of revision, the court would hold the matter in question outside the statute's domain. The statute would become irrelevant, the parties (and court) remitted to whatever other sources of law might be applicable. Because legislatures comprise many members, they do not have "intents" or "designs," hidden yet discoverable. Each member may or may not have a design. The body as a whole, however, has only outcomes. This follows from the discoveries of public choice theory. Although legislators have individual lists of desires, priorities, and preferences, it turns out to be difficult, sometimes impossible, to aggregate these lists into a coherent collective choice. Every system of voting has flaws. The one used by legislatures is particularly dependent on the order in which decisions are made. Legislatures customarily consider proposals one at a time and then vote them up or down. This method disregards third or fourth options and the intensity with which legislators prefer one option over another. Additional options can be considered only in sequence, and this makes the order of decision vital. It is fairly easy to show that someone with control of the agenda can manipulate the choice so that the legislature adopts proposals that only a minority support. The existence of agenda control makes it impossible for a court — even one that knows each legislator's complete table of preferences — to say what the whole body would have done with a proposal it did not consider in fact. Few of the best-intentioned, most humble, and most restrained among us have the skills necessary to learn the temper of times before our births, to assume the identity of people we have never met, and to know how 535 disparate characters from regions of great political and economic diversity would have answered questions that never occurred to them.

A principle that statutes are inapplicable unless they either plainly supply a rule of decision or delegate the power to create such a rule is consistent with the liberal principles underlying our political order. Those who wrote and approved the Constitution thought that most social relations would be governed by private agreements, customs, and understandings, not resolved in the halls of government. There is still at least a presumption that people's arrangements prevail unless expressly displaced by legal doctrine. All things are permitted unless there is some contrary rule. It is easier for an agency to justify the revocation of rules (or simple nonregulation) than the creation of new rules. A rule declaring statutes inapplicable unless they plainly resolve or delegate the solution of the matter respects this position.

———

In Judge Easterbrook's view, the unreliability of extrinsic legislative history material is a potent reason for placing greater stress on the text of the statute. After all, the text is "all that Congress enacts into 'law'. . . ." Eskridge, *The New Textualism*, 37 U.C.L.A. L. Rev. 621, 648 (1990). Only the text has the force of law. *Id.* at 671. In Seventh Circuit Judge Richard Posner's words, Congress "does not legislate by issuing committee reports." *American Hosp. Ass'n v. N.L.R.B.*, 899 F.2d 651, 657 (7th Cir. 1990). The textualists have resurrected Holmes' approach to statutory interpretation: "We do not inquire what the legislature meant; we ask only what the statute means." Holmes, *The Theory of Legal Interpretation*, 12 HARV. L. REV. 417, 419 (1899).

While Judge Easterbrook has concentrated his criticism on routine reliance on extrinsic legislative history material, Judge Posner has attempted to redefine the question judges should ask while they search through legislative history. In the past, due in part to the writings of Professors Hart and Sacks, we tended to assume that the legislature is comprised of reasonable persons pursuing the public interest in good faith. *See* W. ESKRIDGE, JR., P. FRICKEY, & E. GARRETT, LEGISLATION: STATUTES AND THE CREATION OF PUBLIC POLICY (3d ed. 2001). On that assumption, each piece of legislation has a rational, organizing purpose; the judge's task in reviewing the legislative history material is to identify that purpose. However, law-and-economics theorists such as Judge Posner claim that this theory of legislation is unrealistic. They assert that a statute should be viewed as a rational deal between the legislature and interest groups. *See* Eskridge & Frickey, *Legislation Scholarship and Pedagogy in the Post-Legal Process Era*, 48 U. PITT. L. REV. 691, 710, 718 (1987) ("statutory law, and its concomitant political compromises [should] be treated with more deference"). Statutes "are the eventual product of strong competing political currents . . ." *Woodland Joint U. School Dist. v. Comm'n*, 2 Cal. App. 4th 1429, 4 Cal. Rptr. 2d 227, 241 (1992). Under this view, the judge's task is to ascertain the nature of the compromise underlying the legislation and to implement that compromise.

The dispute over statutory interpretation has, of course, surfaced in cases arising under the Federal Rules of Evidence. *See* Jonakait, *The Supreme Court, Plain Meaning, and the Changed Rules of Evidence*, 68 TEX. L. REV. 745, 749 (1990) (arguing that the Supreme Court's application of the plain meaning standard to the Rules of Evidence may produce "uncontemplated outcomes"). Professor Edward Cleary, the reporter for the advisory committee that drafted the Federal Rules of Evidence, believed that because of the nature of the audience for the Federal Rules of Evidence (lawyers and judges) and the history of evidence law in the United States (built on a large body of case law precedent), the meaning of the rules cannot be divorced from their historical background and legislative history.

Cleary, *Preliminary Notes on Reading the Rules of Evidence*
57 NEB. L. REV. 908 (1978) (citations omitted)

* * *

If the Congress can speak only as specified in the Constitution, that is, by passing bills . . . , then a plausible argument can be made that as a matter of constitutional theory nothing said by the Congress in any other way has any force as law and ought to be disregarded. On policy grounds, the use of legislative history is criticized as inviting easy answers and drawing attention away from conveyed meaning, purpose, and general scheme. The British practice has been against referring to legislative history at all. But in the United States legislative history has proved irresistibly tempting, and it must be admitted that, in exploring nuances of meaning, the reasoning and thought processes of those involved may be helpful as a source of explication and illumination, without necessarily attributing to them the authority of law.

The principal considerations in the use of legislative history are its authoritativeness and its availability. Authoritativeness concerns the extent to which given materials reflect the thinking that actually went into the legislation. Availability is important for very practical reasons. In the public interest, how far should the profession and its menial diggers be expected, or even permitted, to excavate and sift for minute shards of legislative history? . . . [T]he components of legislative history [for the Federal Rules of Evidence are] listed in a roughly descending order of importance as measured in terms of authoritativeness and availability.

1. *The Rules prescribed by the Supreme Court.* The Rules prescribed by the Court constituted the official document transmitted to the Congress. . . . Moreover, they were the basis of the bills introduced in the Congress.

2. *The Advisory Committee's Notes.* The notes of the Advisory Committee served the purposes of both supporting and explaining the Rules. They accompanied the Rules through the successive stages of consideration by the Committee on Rules of Practice and Procedure, the Judicial Conference of the United States, and the Supreme Court. The Chief Justice transmitted them to the Congress with the Rules. They were carefully scrutinized by the involved congressional committees and subcommittees, and, except in those instances where superseding changes were made in the Rules by the Congress, must be taken to represent the thinking of that body as the equivalent of a committee report effectively serving as the basis of legislation . . . .

3. *Congressional materials.* The materials emanating from the Congress are of varying degrees of authority. Committee reports include those of the Subcommittee on Criminal Justice of the House Judiciary Committee, the House Committee on the Judiciary, the Senate Committee on the Judiciary, and the Conference Report. All are helpful and highly authoritative. Some materials in the Congressional Record are of authority equivalent to a committee report, e.g., statements by the committee chairman, sponsor of the bill, or sponsor of an amendment. . . .

In principle, under the Federal Rules no common law of evidence remains. "All relevant evidence is admissible, except as otherwise provided." [FED. R. EVID. 402.] In reality, of course, the body of common law knowledge continues to exist, though in the somewhat altered form of a source of guidance in the exercise of delegated powers. . . .

NOTES

1.   State constitutions may also serve as a source of evidentiary rules. What is the relationship between a ruling based on a state constitution and one based on the federal Constitution?

2.   Justice Frankfurter explained his approach to statutory construction: "If the

purpose of construction is the ascertainment of meaning, nothing that is logically relevant should be excluded." Frankfurter, *Some Reflections on the Reading of Statutes*, 47 COLUM. L. REV. 527, 541 (1947). Judge Easterbrook, on the other hand, has argued for a strict textualist construction. Judge Posner attempts to strike a more accommodating middle way. Which of these positions do you find the most persuasive?

3. In the following chapters, we shall encounter numerous questions of interpretation posed by the wording of the Federal Rules of Evidence. As you work through these questions, ask yourself whether it would make a difference if the judge construing the statute was a textualist, interpretivist, or purposivist.

4. Should the techniques for interpreting statutes be identical to those for construing a constitution?

4. The Common Law

Absent a controlling statute or court rule, the judge deciding an evidentiary issue can fall back on a vast body of common law. The staggering size of the common law of evidence led to the publication of some of the most influential American treatises, including James Bradley Thayer's A PRELIMINARY TREATISE ON EVIDENCE AT COMMON LAW (1898) and the various editions of Wigmore's monumental work, A TREATISE ON THE ANGLO-AMERICAN SYSTEM OF EVIDENCE IN TRIALS AT COMMON LAW.

Although the volume of decisional evidence law dwarfs the statutory and constitutional law on evidence, constitutional and statutory law have higher places in the hierarchy of evidence law. Thus, if a statute conflicts with a constitutional provision, the latter prevails. *A fortiori*, when a decisional rule is at odds with a statute, the statute invalidates the case law rule. For example, before the adoption of the Federal Rules of Evidence, many jurisdictions held that expert witnesses could base their opinions only on independently admissible data; if an evidentiary rule such as the hearsay doctrine barred the admission of the evidence as substantive proof, the expert could not rely upon the data as part of the basis of her opinion. *See e.g. Pritchett v. Steinker Trucking Co.*, 247 N.E.2d 923 (Ill. App. Ct. 1969). However, Federal Rule of Evidence 703 overturned that holding by allowing the expert to base an opinion on any data reasonably employed in the actual practice of his specialty even if "the facts or data [are] . . . not . . . [independently] admissible in evidence." FED. R. EVID. 703. The statute compels the courts to follow its lead and abandon the prior common-law view.

NOTES

1. When the California Evidence Code was enacted in the mid-1960s, the California Law Revision Commission manifested an intent to "wipe out all court-created exclusionary rules of evidence not based on a statutory or constitutional provision." 1 B. JEFFERSON, CALIFORNIA EVIDENCE BENCHBOOK § 21.1 (3d ed. 2006). Like Federal Rule of Evidence 402, California Evidence Code § 351 proclaims that "[e]xcept as otherwise provided by statute, all relevant evidence is admissible." In *People v. Starr*, 11 Cal. App. 3d 574, 583, 89 Cal. Rptr. 906, 912

(1970), the court grappled with the question of whether the corroboration requirements for accomplice testimony survived the adoption of the California Evidence
Code. Although the requirements were of common-law origin, the court refused to
hold that the Code impliedly abolished them; the court announced that more explicit
language was needed to repeal "such a firmly established and fundamental rule." Do
you agree?

2. What approach should the court take to the construction of a purportedly
comprehensive evidence code such as the Federal Rules? On the one hand, it is well
settled that remedial statutes are to be liberally construed. 3 N. SINGER, SUTHER-
LAND STATUTES AND STATUTORY CONSTRUCTION § 60:1 (6th ed. 2001). But there is an
equally strong tradition of strict construction of statutes in derogation of the
common law. *Id.* at §§ 61:1–61:5.

3. Consider Federal Rule of Evidence 402. What light does it shed on the
proper approach to interpreting the Federal Rules? *See* Imwinkelried, *A Brief
Defense of the Supreme Court's Approach to the Interpretation of the Federal Rules
of Evidence*, 27 IND. L. REV. 267 (1993).

4. In a 1984 decision, the U.S. Supreme Court approvingly quoted a passage
from Professor Cleary's article: "In principle, under the Federal Rules no common
law of evidence remains." *United States v. Abel*, 469 U.S. 45, 46–49 (1984). The Court
did so again in *Daubert v. Merrell Dow Pharmaceuticals*, 509 U.S. 579 (1993). Some
commentators, however, believe that uncodified, common law evidentiary rules have
survived the enactment of the Federal Rules, or that the Federal Rules do not
preclude additional common law rules. Weissenberger, *Are the Federal Rules of
Evidence a Statute?*, 55 OHIO ST. L.J. 393 (1994). Which side is right? Is it possible
that both are?

C. SUBSTITUTES FOR EVIDENCE: OTHER METHODS OF ESTABLISHING FACTS

In addition to proving facts through the admission of evidence at trial, there are
several other ways in which facts can be established. These include (1) judicial
notice, (2) stipulation, (3) judicial admission, and (4) preclusion.

1. Judicial Notice

Read Federal Rule of Evidence 201.

A commonly invoked technique of establishing a fact is judicial notice. The judge
notes the existence of a fact and instructs the jury that the fact exists. Judicial
notice expedites the trial by dispensing with formal proof of the fact.

The courts can use judicial notice to feed more empirical information into the
decision-making process. Professor Kenneth Culp Davis has long called upon the
courts to employ a more "full-bodied factual technique" to investigate the
assumptions underlying rules of law. *See* K. DAVIS & R. PIERCE, ADMINISTRATIVE LAW
TREATISE § 10.5 (4th ed. 2002). The Advisory Committee liberally cites Professor
Davis in the Note accompanying Rule 201.

a. Judicial Notice of Facts

In the following excerpt, Professor Davis articulated the critical distinction between adjudicative and legislative facts. By its terms, Federal Rule of Evidence 201, governing judicial notice, is limited to judicial notice of "adjudicative" data. FED. R. EVID. 201(a). The distinction is important because subsections (d) through (g) contain detailed procedures for judicial notice which are expressly inapplicable to the input of legislative facts.

Davis, *Judicial Notice*
55 COLUM. L. REV. 945, 952–53 (1955) (citations omitted)

Legislative and Adjudicative Facts

*   *   *

When a court or an agency finds facts concerning the immediate parties — who did what, where, when, how, and with what motive or intent — the court or agency is performing an adjudicative function, and the facts so determined are conveniently called adjudicative facts. When a court or an agency develops law or policy, it is acting legislatively; the courts have created the common law through judicial legislation, and the facts which inform the tribunal's legislative judgment are called legislative facts.

Stated in other terms, the adjudicative facts are those to which the law is applied in the process of adjudication. They are the facts that normally go to the jury in a jury case. They relate to the parties, their activities, their properties, their businesses. Legislative facts are those which help the tribunal to determine the content of law and policy and to exercise its judgment or discretion in determining what course of action to take. Legislative facts are ordinarily general and do not concern the immediate parties. In the great mass of cases decided by courts and by agencies, the legislative element is either absent, unimportant, or interstitial, because in most cases the applicable law and policy have been previously established. But whenever a tribunal is engaged in the creation of law or of policy, it may need to resort to legislative facts, whether or not those facts have been developed on the record.

The formulation of law and policy, both in the judicial process and in the administrative process, obviously gains strength to the extent that information replaces guesswork or ignorance or intuition or general impressions. Questions of law and policy often yield to comprehensive factual study, as the magnificent leadership of Justice Brandeis in that direction so eloquently testifies. But the present development of the social sciences unfortunately brings us no more than to the threshold of ability to solve our basic problems of law and policy through a full-bodied factual technique. The result is an uneven mixture of *a priori* conjectures and partially informed guesses, with occasional factual investigations of varying depth.

The Advisory Committee addressed the same distinction between adjudicative and legislative facts in its Note to Rule 201(a).

NOTES

1. The new revision to Fed. R. Evid. 201 make explicit the limited scope of the rule by specifying that only adjudicative facts are covered. To appreciate the difference between adjudicative and legislative facts, recall that Davis refers to adjudicative facts as those "which relate to the parties," or more fully:

> When a court or an agency finds facts concerning the immediate parties — who did what, where, when, how, and with what motive or intent — the court or agency is performing an adjudicative function, and the facts are conveniently called adjudicative facts. . . .

> Stated in other terms, the adjudicative facts are those to which the law is applied in the process of adjudication. They are the facts that normally go to the jury in a jury case. They relate to the parties, their activities, their properties, their businesses. . . .

2. Then compare, Davis' reference in his article to Justice Brandeis. As a counsel before the Supreme Court, Brandeis developed the type of brief now named after him — a Brandeis brief, including economic, political, and sociological data. J. MAGUIRE, COMMON SENSE AND COMMON LAW 172–74 (1947). Perhaps the best example of such a brief is the brief filed by thirty-five social scientists in *Brown v. Board of Educ.*, 347 U.S. 483 (1954). The brief contained legislative data on the psychological effects of segregation on black children. Much of that data surfaced in footnote 11 of Chief Justice Warren's opinion. Legislative data plays a pivotal role in modern appellate advocacy; a good brief is a social impact statement, showing the court how a current or proposed rule of law affects society.

3. Can a court take judicial notice of the contents of a business's web site? *Compare Victaulic Co. v. Tieman*, 499 F.3d 227, 236 (3d Cir. 2007); *O'Toole v. Northrop Grumman Corp.*, 499 F.3d 1218, 1224–25 (10th Cir. 2007); *Enterprise Rent-A-Car Co. v. U-Haul Int'l*, 327 F. Supp. 2d 1032, 1042 (E.D. Mo. 2004). What about minutes of a city council meeting posted on the city's web site? *Freedom From Religion Foundation v. City of Green Bay*, 581 F. Supp. 2d 1019, 1024 (E.D. Wis. 2008). *See Seifert v. Winter*, 555 F. Supp. 2d 3, 11 n.5 (D.D.C. 2008) (discussing judicial notice of information posted on government web sites). How about a study from an internet web site on identity theft and a list of data breach incidents reported in California during a two-year period? *Ruiz v. Gap, Inc.*, 540 F. Supp. 2d 1121, 1124 (N.D. Cal. 2008). A Wikipedia article? *See Palisades Collection, L.L.C. v. Graubard*, 2009 N.J. Super. Unpub. LEXIS 1025 (Apr. 17, 2009).

4. Judicial notice is applied more broadly in administrative proceedings. *See Singh v. Ashcroft*, 393 F.3d 903, 905–06 (9th Cir. 2004).

5. **Despite the influence of** Professor Davis' writings over the Advisory Committee, it would be an understatement to say that Professor Davis is displeased with the final draft of Rule 201. He faults the Committee for being too narrow: "the effect of Rule 201 is almost the equivalent of zero, because the vast majority of cases of judicial notice involve legislative facts, to which Rule 201 does not apply." 3 K.

DAVIS & R. PIERCE, ADMINISTRATIVE LAW TREATISE ß 10.6 (4th ed. 2002). He faults the courts for compounding the problem by misconstruing Rule 201, charging that almost all facts noticed under Rule 201 are legislative facts, not adjudicative facts. For example, in *EEOC v. Delta Air Lines*, 485 F. Supp. 1004, 1009 (N.D. Ga. 1980), the court referred to Rule 201 as a basis for noticing the proposition that "only females become pregnant." "The fact is obviously not adjudicative, and Rule 201 by its terms did not apply." K. DAVIS & R. PIERCE, *supra*.

6. If the procedures of Rule 201 are only applicable to taking judicial notice of adjudicative facts, what is the procedure for noticing legislative facts? Should the parties at least be given the opportunity to challenge extra-record legislative fact prior to the court's decision to take judicial notice? *Cf.* FED. R. EVID. 201(e). *See* Keeton, *Legislative Facts And Similar Things: Deciding Disputed Premise Facts*, 73 MINN. L. REV. 1 (1987).

7. Rule 201 typically does not apply to facts considered by a court when ruling on the admissibility of evidence. *Invest Almaz v. Temple-Inland Forest Products Corp.*, 243 F.3d 57, 69 (1st Cir. 2001) (taking judicial notice of a period of economic depression).

Defining "adjudicative fact" is only half the problem. The question remains: Which types of adjudicative facts should be judicially noticed? When should we dispense with formal evidence? The courts and commentators are in agreement on two categories of data — and in disagreement over a third.

Matters of common knowledge. At early common law, the only type of noticeable fact was a matter of common knowledge. Federal Rule of Evidence 201(b)(1) codifies the doctrine by permitting notice of facts "generally known within the territorial jurisdiction of the trial court. . . ." Conrad gives a particularly colorful rationale for the doctrine: "Courts . . . cannot be presumed to be ignorant. Courts should at least know what everybody else knows." 2 E. CONRAD, MODERN TRIAL EVIDENCE § 983 (1956). If a fact is generally known in the vicinity, it is foolish to waste court time by requiring formal evidence to prove the fact. If a reasonable person of average knowledge and intelligence would be familiar with the fact, the judge may dispense with formal evidence. *See, e.g.*, *Solomon v. Miami Woman's Club*, 359 F. Supp. 41 (S.D. Fla. 1973) (town population), *Donie State Bank v. Knight*, 620 S.W.2d 698 (Tex. App. 1981) (county boundaries), *Johnson v. Penrod Drilling Co.*, 510 F.2d 234 (5th Cir. 1975) (inflation); the *Allen v. Allen*, 518 F. Supp. 1234 (E.D. Pa. 1981) (date of Father's Day in a particular year). The judge may even take notice of well-known international events such as domestic turmoil in Iran, (*Itek Corp. v. First Nat'l Bank*, 511 F. Supp. 1341 (D. Mass. 1981)) and civil war in El Salvador. *Orantes-Hernandez v. Smith*, 541 F. Supp. 351 (C.D. Cal. 1982).

PROBLEMS

1. **Problem 2-1.** A Morena statute provides that the speed limit in the business district of any incorporated town is twenty-five miles an hour. At trial, Ms. Hill requests judicial notice that (a) El Dorado is an incorporated town; and (b) the corner where the collision occurred is in El Dorado's business district. As trial

judge, would you grant the request? *See Varcoe v. Lee*, 180 Cal. 338, 342–47, 181 P. 223, 224–27 (1919).

2. **Problem 2-2.** In the *Devitt* case, the prosecutor seeks to rebut evidence that the day before the occurrence, Mr. Paterson had been drinking in a bar. A Morena statute provides that no alcoholic beverages may be sold on Sunday. May the court judicially notice that March 14, 20YR, was a Sunday? *See Pack v. Proffitt*, 463 F. Supp. 761, 761 (E.D. Tenn. 1976).

Verifiable certainty. Although common knowledge is the more familiar basis for judicial notice, the growth principle for the doctrine has been the alternative basis, verifiable certainty. As the 2011 revision to Rule 201 explains, only "facts not subject to reasonable dispute" should be judicially noticed. Even if an adjudicative fact is not a matter of common knowledge, the judge may notice it if it is "capable of accurate and ready determination by resort to sources whose accuracy cannot reasonably be questioned." FED. R. EVID. 201(b)(2). *See In re Marquam Invest. Corp.*, 942 F.2d 1462 (9th Cir. 1991) ("unquestionable" sources); *Assembly of State of California v. United States Dept. of Commerce*, 797 F. Supp. 1554 (E.D. Cal. 1992) ("authoritative" sources).

Federal courts may judicially notice matters of public record, such as prior court and administrative proceedings, within and without the federal court system. However, such notice is limited to the existence, facial content, and authenticity of the document. Judicial notice ordinarily cannot be used to prove the truth of the factual content of the document, nor does it extend to another court's findings of fact. *See United States v. Southern Calif. Edison Co.*, 300 F. Supp. 2d 964, 973–76 (E.D. Cal. 2004) (granting judicial notice of agency order but denying it for documents whose authenticity and completeness was disputed).

NOTES AND PROBLEM

1. We commonly refer to this basis for judicial notice as "verifiable certainty." What does "certainty" mean in this context? How high must the likelihood be? As the director for the Center for Modern Technologies has pointed out, "with monotonous regularity, apparently competent men have laid down the law about what is technically possible and impossible — and have been proved utterly wrong, sometimes while the ink was scarcely dry from their pens." A. CLARKE, PROFILES OF THE FUTURE: AN INQUIRY INTO THE LIMITS OF THE POSSIBLE (1984). In 1878, while Edison neared the perfection of his invention of the electric light bulb, a special British Parliamentary committee announced that the concept was "unworthy of the attention of practical and scientific men." A year before the Soviet Union launched *Sputnik I*, the Astronomer Royal, Dr. Richard van der Riet Woolley, stated that proposals for space travel were "utter bilge." Even if a proposition qualifies as a verifiable scientific "certainty" today, the proposition may be discredited in a decade. In *Daubert v. Merrell Dow Pharmaceuticals*, 509 U.S. 579 (1993), Justice Blackman observed that "arguably, there are no certainties in science."

2. In the context of copyright litigation, courts frequently take judicial notice of the content of copyrighted and allegedly infringing materials. *See, e.g., Wild v. NBC*

Universal, Inc., 788 F. Supp. 2d 1083 (C.D. Cal. 2011) (granting motion to dismiss, after taking judicial notice of contents of Season 4 of Heroes and a 3-book series, Carnival of Souls and finding lack of substantial similarity); *Davis v. American Broadcasting Companies, Inc.*, 2010 U.S. Dist. LEXIS 76145 (W.D. Mich. 2010) (granting motion to dismiss after taking judicial notice of the "generic elements of creative works"); *Campbell v. Walt Disney Co.*, 718 F. Supp.2d 1108 (N.D. Cal. 2010) (taking judicial notice of written screenplay and allegedly infringing motion picture in granting motion to dismiss for lack of substantial similarity). Does this practice comply with the rule's requirement that judicially noticed facts be undisputed?

3. The Advisory Committee Note to Rule 201 states: "These . . . rules [Rule 44.1 of the Federal Rules of Civil Procedure and Rule 26.1 of the Federal Rules of Criminal Procedure] are founded upon the assumption that the manner in which law is fed into the judicial process is never a proper concern of the rules of evidence but rather of the rules of procedure. The Advisory Committee on Evidence, believing that this assumption is entirely correct, proposes no evidence rule with respect to judicial notice of law, and suggests that those matters of law which, in addition to foreign-country law, have traditionally been treated as requiring pleading and proof and more recently as the subject of judicial notice be left to the Rules of Civil and Criminal Procedure." Nevertheless, courts sometimes do take judicial notice of law under Rule 201. *United States v. Feldman*, 324 F. Supp. 2d 1112, 1118 (C.D. Cal. 2004) (treaty with Spain).

On this issue, *see Getty Petroleum Marketing, Inc. v. Capital Terminal Co.*, 391 F.3d 312, 320–30 (1st Cir. 2004) (comprehensive discussion in dissent). Rule 44.1 provides, in part: "In determining foreign law, the court may consider any relevant material or source, including testimony, whether or not submitted by a party or admissible under the Federal Rules of Evidence. The court's determination must be treated as a ruling on a question of law."

Problem 2-3. In *Hill*, the plaintiff wants to prove that Mr. Worker had the time to notice the imminent danger, brake, and avoid the collision. Her attorney hands the judge a document entitled, "Table of Stopping Distances — Morena Highway Patrol." The attorney then says, "Your Honor, we'd like you to notice these correlations. For example, that at thirty miles an hour, the total stopping distance is eighty-eight feet." As trial judge, how would you rule? *See Recent Case*, 38 Mo. L. REV. 678 (1973). Would it make a difference if Ms. Hill's attorney had said, "For example, that at thirty miles an hour under normal conditions, the average stopping distance is eighty-eight feet." Why?

Highly probable facts. Almost all courts limit the substantive scope of the judicial notice doctrine to matters of common knowledge and verifiable certainties. If the fact falls within either category, it is virtually indisputable. Requiring formal evidence to prove such a fact would be a waste of time. However, some commentators have urged the extension of the doctrine beyond these parameters to highly probable facts. In *Judicial Notice — Excerpts Relating to the Morgan-Wigmore Controversy*, 14 VAND. L. REV. 779 (1961), Professor McNaughton succinctly described the controversy:

Professor Morgan and Dean Wigmore do not differ with respect to the application of the doctrine to "law." Their difference relates to judicial notice of "facts." Here Wigmore, following Thayer, insists that judicial notice is solely to save time where dispute is unlikely and that a matter judicially noticed is therefore only "prima facie," or rebuttable, if the opponent elects to dispute it. It is express in Thayer and implicit in Wigmore that (perhaps because the matter is rebuttable) judicial notice may be applied not only to indisputable matters but also to matters of lesser certainty. Morgan on the other hand defines judicial notice more narrowly, and his consequences follow from his definition. He limits judicial notice of fact to matters patently indisputable. And his position is that matters judicially noticed are not rebuttable. He asserts that it is wasteful to permit patently indisputable matters to be litigated by way of formal proof and furthermore that it would be absurd to permit a party to woo a jury to an obviously erroneous finding contrary to the noticed fact. Also, he objects to the Wigmorean conception on the ground that it is really a "presumption" of sorts attempting to pass under a misleading name. It is, according to Morgan, a presumption with no recognized rules as to how the presumption works — what activates it and who has the burden of doing how much to rebut it.

Wigmore and Thayer argue that the orthodox categories, common knowledge and verifiable certainty, do not exhaust the potential of the judicial notice doctrine. If the doctrine is designed to expedite trials and secondarily to regulate the rationality of verdicts, why not permit the judge to notice disputable facts that nevertheless have a high degree of likelihood? Or is the indisputability standard a more appropriate dividing line between judicial notice and formal evidence? Once we allow the opponent to attack the judicially noticed fact, judicial notice seems to become a sort of "glorified presumption." E. MORGAN, BASIC PROBLEMS IN EVIDENCE 10 (1963).

b. Judicial Notice of Law

The courts traditionally invoked judicial notice as the vehicle for feeding legal authorities into the decision making process. E. MORGAN, BASIC PROBLEMS IN EVIDENCE 1 (1963). In state court, the trial judge may notice "the common law and public statutes in force in the state. . . ." *Id.* The expression "public statutes" includes "the public Acts of Congress and the provisions of the Constitution of the United States and of the state. . . ." *Id.* In federal district court, the judge may notice "the common and statutory laws of every state in the Union." *Id.* 44 U.S.C. ß 307 states that "the contents of the Federal Register shall be judicially noticed," and it is arguable that this federal statute requires state courts to notice the federal laws published in the Register.

At common law, the courts were reluctant to extend the judicial notice doctrine beyond these types of authorities. *See Campbell v. Mincey*, 413 F. Supp. 16 (N.D. Miss. 1975) (finding state agency regulations beyond the scope of judicial notice).

NOTES

1. Does it make sense to apply the same input technique to legal and factual data? Does the input of legal authorities even belong within the domain of evidence? Federal Rule of Civil Procedure 44.1 and Rule of Criminal Procedure 26.1 both govern the determination of foreign law. The last sentence of each rule reads: "The court's determination shall be treated as a ruling on a question of law." What is the significance of the statement that a particular determination "shall be treated as a ruling on a question of law"?

2. Do the Federal Rules treat the determination of law as an aspect of judicial notice? *See* FED. R. EVID. 201(a).

3. Courts not only judicially notice law embedded in constitutional provisions, statutes, and cases, but also notice legal events, such as the entry of judgments and orders. If we are going to use judicial notice as a theory for the input of legal authorities, should we limit the theory to judicial decisions and legislative enactments? Why not extend the doctrine to ordinances and regulations? At one time, the limitation could be defended on the ground that there was less ready access to written materials setting forth the ordinances and regulations. Does that ground have merit today?

2. Other Methods of Establishing Facts

There are other substitutes for evidence — alternative methods by which facts can be established in litigation. Typically, these other methods are more appropriate to courses in civil and criminal procedure, but they will be mentioned briefly here because they are alternatives to formal proof of facts.

Stipulation. It is not uncommon for parties to stipulate to a fact. Although it can be done by a formal document, more often a stipulation is oral, made during trial or a pre-trial hearing or conference. A stipulation is simply an agreement between the parties or a commitment by one party not to contest the existence of a particular fact. For example, counsel may state, on the record, "Your Honor, we will stipulate that the traffic light was red when the truck entered the intersection." Such a stipulation, if otherwise agreeable or "accepted" by the other parties and the court (or required to be accepted by the court) is binding, and obviates the need for proof of that fact. *See* 22 C. WRIGHT & K. GRAHAM, FEDERAL PRACTICE AND PROCEDURE: EVIDENCE § 5194 (1978).

Judicial admission. There are two types of formal judicial admissions that can preclude proof of a fact. First, before trial in a civil case, a party can formally request that another party admit a fact. The procedure for doing so is spelled out in the Federal Rule of Civil Procedure 36; every state has a comparable rule. Rule 36 (a) provides that the request can be to admit the truth of "any matters within the scope of Rule 26 (b) (1) set forth in the request that relate to statements or opinions of fact or of the application of law to fact, including the genuineness of any documents described in the request." Each matter so described is deemed admitted unless, within 30 days, the party to whom the request was made serves a written answer or objection. The answer may admit or deny the fact, or may state that the party cannot truthfully admit or deny the fact, and why. The answer may be qualified or admitted in part and denied in part. Lack of information or knowledge may not be given as a reason for denial unless the party has made a reasonable effort to obtain the information or knowledge. Rule 36 (b) provides that "[a]ny matter admitted under this rule is conclusively established unless the court on motion permits withdrawal or amendment of the admission." Properly used, this device can obviate proof of undisputed or indisputable facts. For example, it is often used to eliminate the need to lay a foundation for the authentication of documents.

Another type of judicial admission occurs when a party, on the record, unequivocally alleges a fact under circumstances where the court will treat this allegation as binding on that party. For example a party may plead that he is a citizen of Morena. As a general rule, the court will treat that allegation as binding and incontrovertible, obviating the need for proof of that fact, and in some cases that party will be precluded from later disclaiming or withdrawing that factual allegation. In addition, a failure to deny a fact in the appropriate pleading constitutes an admission, obviating the need for proof of the fact alleged. *See* 5 C. WRIGHT & A. MILLER, FEDERAL PRACTICE AND PROCEDURE: CIVIL 2D § 1279 (1990).

Binding judicial admissions must be distinguished from "mere" evidentiary admissions. As a general rule, any relevant statement a party has ever made can be admitted if offered against that party by another party. *See* FED. R. EVID. 801(d)(2). Although admissible, such "admissions" are not conclusive against the party making them and may be controverted.

Preclusive prior fact determinations. Sometimes a fact issue will be deemed to have been conclusively decided in another proceeding, and therefore must be taken as decided and cannot be relitigated. No doubt you encountered this doctrine in the course in civil procedure, under the topic referred to as "issue preclusion" or "collateral estoppel." *See* 18 C. WRIGHT, A. MILLER & E. COOPER, FEDERAL PRACTICE AND PROCEDURE: JURISDICTION §§ 4416–4426 (1981). To the extent that this doctrine applies, it can also preclude the need for proof of facts.

Chapter 3

THE CHRONOLOGY OF A TRIAL

A. INTRODUCTION

This chapter gives the reader a brief, simplified overview of the way in which a trial is typically organized. In addition to reviewing this material, any student would be well advised to visit a local courthouse and spend a day or so observing a jury trial — something many law students have never done. Or you might watch a jury trial on one of the television channels that broadcasts complete trials live. Observing a trial, in combination with this background reading, will give you a much better understanding of the context in which the rules of evidence are applied. As you will see, evidence law affects every stage of the process.

B. THE ORGANIZATION OF THE TRIAL AS A WHOLE

1. Jury Selection and Voir Dire

Before a jury trial can begin, the jurors must be selected. The judge begins the selection process by first introducing the attorneys and parties to the panelists (the prospective jurors) and describing in general terms the nature of the case. Then comes the *voir dire* examination of the panelists. The judge (and, in many jurisdictions, the attorneys) questions the prospective jurors to determine who is qualified to sit.

In all jurisdictions that permit attorneys to question prospective jurors during *voir dire*, the attorney may ask questions logically relevant to grounds for challenge for cause. A number of jurisdictions also allow the attorneys to ask questions designed to facilitate "intelligent" exercise peremptory challenges. However, it is no secret that *voir dire* examination is often used for two other important purposes.

The first is factual indoctrination: the trial attorney exposes the jury to key items of evidence that will be introduced during trial. Surprisingly, conventional wisdom has it that the most effective strategy is for the attorney to expose the jury to the most damaging items of evidence. For example, suppose that in the *Devitt* case the defense attorney knows that Devitt has several prior convictions. The defense attorney is certain that, when Devitt takes the witness stand, the prosecutor will attempt to impeach Devitt with these prior convictions. To preempt the prosecutor, the defense attorney might state during *voir dire* examination: "Now, Mr. Grant, the evidence will show that my client, Mr. Devitt, has two prior criminal convictions. If he takes the stand and testifies, will you reject his testimony simply because of those convictions?" The reasoning underlying the "expose your weaknesses" strategy is simple: The impact of the evidence will be less damaging to your case if you mention the evidence first. If you let the opponent be the first to mention the evidence to the jury, the evidence may sound more damning, and some jurors might suspect that you were attempting to conceal the truth from them.

In addition to *factual* indoctrination, the attorneys often use the *voir dire* examination for the purpose of *legal* education or indoctrination: The attorney teaches the jury about the legal doctrines most helpful to the attorney's case; these are often evidentiary rules. For example, in the *Devitt* case, the defense attorney might devote some *voir dire* questioning to the prosecution's burden of proof and the presumption of innocence:

Q: Ms. Martinez, if you had to vote in this case right now, before hearing any evidence, what would your verdict be?

A: I guess "not guilty."

Q: So you understand that the defendant is presumed innocent?

A: Yes.

Q: You realize, don't you, that the prosecution has the burden of proving Mr. Devitt's guilt beyond any reasonable doubt?

A: Yes.

2. Opening Statements

After the jury has been selected and impaneled, the attorneys present their opening statements. The plaintiff or prosecutor goes first. In most jurisdictions, the defense attorney may present an opening immediately, or may reserve opening until the beginning of the defense's case-in-chief. (Except in certain criminal cases, it is usually not a good idea to reserve opening statement.)

The function of the opening statement is to preview the admissible evidence for the jury. The attorney customarily tells the jury, "The evidence will show. . . ." Unless the attorney has carefully analyzed the evidentiary problems likely to arise during the trial, she can easily commit error during the opening statement. The error may not only result in a mistrial, it could also lead to disciplinary sanctions. Rule 3.4(e) of the American Bar Association's Model Rules of Professional Conduct states that a lawyer shall not "allude to any matter that the lawyer does not reasonably believe is relevant or that will not be supported by admissible evidence."

The most common objection to the content of an opening statement is that an attorney is being "argumentative." As Professor Jeans explains, to avoid this objection the attorney must understand evidence law, especially the norms limiting the admission of opinion testimony: "Opening statements should not be an argument — a tool of persuasion yes — but not an argument. It is objectionable, for instance, for your opponent to state that 'the evidence will show that the defendant negligently drove at an excessive rate of speed' or 'the poor plaintiff has suffered a most grievous injury that will severely affect her for the rest of her life.' How best to recognize an objectionable argument? As you listen to your opponent's opening statement ask yourself, 'Will a witness testify in such fashion?' Relating to the examples, who will testify that 'the defendant was negligent and drove at an excessive rate of speed?' These are conclusions and as such inadmissible. . . . Or who will testify that 'plaintiff suffered grievous injuries?' This too is conclusionary, thus inadmissible as evidence, and consequently improper in opening statement." J. JEANS, TRIAL ADVOCACY § 10.15 (2d ed. 1993). Hence, in *Devitt*, it would be objectionable if the prosecutor stated during opening, "Now, I'm going to give you three solid reasons why you should believe Mr. Paterson's testimony rather than the defendant's." Or, in the *Hill* case, the plaintiff could not state, "This is the common sense reason why you should conclude that . . . ." The opinion rules (which we will explore further in Chapter 23) would prohibit a witness from making those statements, and consequently the attorney cannot make them during opening statements.

3. The Plaintiff's or Prosecutor's Case-in-Chief

It is a fundamental principle of the adversary system that the parties generally control the presentation of evidence. S. LANDSMAN, READINGS ON ADVERSARIAL JUSTICE: THE AMERICAN APPROACH TO ADJUDICATION 2 (1988). Evidence law recognizes several methods of establishing the existence of a fact at trial. These include: (1) formal introduction of evidence by a party; (2) stipulation between the parties; and (3) judicial notice. Although the latter two methods are often used, the vast majority of the evidence in most cases is presented by the first method.

The Anglo-American norm is that evidence is presented one witness at a time, and that one party presents its evidence fully before the other party offers contrary proof. The rationale for this structure is that it is more orderly, increases juror comprehension, and gives each party an opportunity to present his or her version of the facts in a relatively uninterrupted fashion.

The plaintiff (in a civil case) or prosecutor (in a criminal case) has the first opportunity to present evidence to the jury. This portion of the trial is usually called the "plaintiff's (or government's) case-in-chief." The plaintiff or prosecutor has the initial chance to present evidence to the jury because that party has the ultimate burden of proof on most of the factual issues in the case. During the case-in-chief, the party may present any evidence logically relevant to any factual issue on which that party has the burden of proof, so long as admission of the evidence does not otherwise violate the rules of evidence. Indeed, in many jurisdictions, the scope is even broader; the party may present any admissible evidence logically relevant to *any* factual issue in the case. In such jurisdictions, the plaintiff or prosecutor in its case-in-chief is permitted to anticipate defenses and to offer evidence rebutting those defenses.

The plaintiff or prosecutor has discretion as to which witnesses will be called during the case-in-chief. They may even call adverse parties. For example, in the *Hill* case, the plaintiff Ms. Hill could call Polecat Motors' president as a witness during the her case-in-chief. It is common practice in medical malpractice actions to call the defendant doctor during the plaintiff's case. Of course in a criminal case, the Fifth Amendment's privilege against self-incrimination precludes the prosecutor from calling the defendant as a witness during the government's case-in-chief.

4.   Defense Motion for Nonsuit or Directed Verdict

At the close of the plaintiff's or prosecutor's case-in-chief, the plaintiff or prosecution will announce that it "rests." Suppose that the defense counsel at that point believes that the evidence is legally insufficient to sustain the plaintiff's or prosecutor's burden of production — even if the jury believes all the evidence, the defense argues that the evidence is insufficient to permit the trier of fact to find all the facts on which the plaintiff or prosecutor has the burden of proof. The defense counsel accordingly moves for dismissal of the case (variously called a motion for a nonsuit, judgment of acquittal, finding of not guilty, directed verdict, or judgment as a matter of law). Whatever its title, the motion challenges the legal sufficiency of the evidence.

In ruling on this motion, the judge decides whether the plaintiff or prosecutor has sustained the initial burden of going forward (or "production"). We shall analyze the burdens of proof in depth in Chapter 30. If the judge agrees with the defense counsel, the judge grants the motion and terminates the trial. If the judge disagrees, the trial proceeds to the defendant's evidence.

As we shall see in Chapter 30, just as there are different ultimate burdens of proof in civil and criminal cases (preponderance of the evidence vs. beyond a reasonable doubt), the judge will use a different standard in civil and criminal cases in determining whether to direct a verdict.

5.   The Defense's Case-in-Chief

The next major component of the trial is the defense's case-in-chief. The rules governing the defense case are similar to the rules governing the opening case. The scope of the defense case includes evidence logically relevant to any fact at issue in the case. As with the plaintiff's or prosecutor's case, the defendant may call adverse witnesses. Hence, in our torts case, defendant Polecat Motors could call Ms. Hill during the defense case-in-chief.

Several empirical studies have investigated the question whether this ordering of plaintiff's or prosecutor's evidence followed by defense's evidence makes sense. Consider the following excerpts from a study by the Human Behavior and Legal Process Project, funded by the National Science Foundation.

Walker, Thibaut & Andresli, *Order of Presentation at Trial*
82 YALE L. J. 216, 216–26 (1972)

The order of evidence in an adversary proceeding has an important effect upon the final determination of guilt or innocence. This effect is complicated by the fact that the adversary process is ordered in two distinct ways: a "gross order" of presentation by each party; and, within this gross order, an "internal order" for the presentation of each party's case.

Gross order is determined by statute and judicial decision for the three parts of the traditional adversary process: opening statements, presentations of evidence, and closing arguments. The prosecution or plaintiff usually has the right to make the first opening statement, present evidence first, and make both the first and the final closing arguments. The usual justification for this ordering is that the party with the burden of proof should have the advantage of making the first and last presentation.

The results of this experiment suggest that in a legal setting the impact of the final bits of evidence, in both gross order and internal order, is pervasive: In gross order, the side going second is strongly advantaged; internal order favors strong evidence occurring toward the end of the presentation except when the defense presents first.

In seeking to account for the gross order results, it is important to examine why facts presented first have less impact in a legal setting than elsewhere. First impressions normally have strong impact when individuals receive information about relatively stable characteristics of others, such as attitudinal and personality dispositions and abilities. However, the determination of whether another person has performed an unlawful act entails judgments not on permanent characteristics but rather on specific events. Thus the legal inquiry may reduce the natural impact of this type of early information. Another circumstance thought to strengthen early impressions is a finding of an inconsistency between earlier and later information. Once an early impression is formed, later inconsistent information is often "discounted" because the recipient of the information has relied on the first impression. However, the recipient of the information presented by each party in an adversary process knows that such information has been screened by the advocate and is thus plainly incomplete. Luchins has shown that by forewarning subjects of the imminence of additional information, the impact of early information is suppressed. Thus, when fact-finders know that early information is imperfect and that contrary information will follow, first impressions are not so strong that later information will be discounted. Similarly, early information presented in a legal setting is not likely to produce the strong bias that may in other settings lead to the "assimilation" of subsequent information. Moreover, even if fact-finders enter the case with a strong bias toward the side presenting first, the adversary system is designed to counter such biases.

Indeed, it appears that in legal settings it is the material presented first which is discounted. Sears has demonstrated that fact-finders exposed only to one side of a case (as compared with those exposed to both sides) made less extreme judgments on the relative merits of the presentation. This suggests that after having heard only the first presentation, decision-makers in a legal setting will reserve judgment until they have heard the remaining evidence. Moreover, Sears found that, where subjects who had heard both sides of the case were approximately equally interested in hearing additional information favoring one or the other party, those who had heard only one side were not as interested in receiving further information supporting that side but rather preferred to hear information favoring the opposition. It is this posture of legal fact-finders, with their suspension of commitment and heightened receptivity to the subsequent presentation, that may favor the party going second. Such effects are further promoted, of course, by a sharpened recall of the more recently presented evidence.

The results of this experiment suggest: (1) it makes a difference whether one goes first or second in the adversary presentation of legal materials, and the second position is the more advantageous; (2) the ordering of weak and strong elements within presentations also produces a difference in results, and the weak to strong (climactic) order is the more effective. But this second finding is true regardless of gross order only for the plaintiff or prosecution; the climactic order is advantageous for the defense only within second presentations and there only to a relatively minor degree.

Assuming that the ideal order for adversary fact-finding is a sequence of evidence which eliminates any advantage gained solely because of order, these two findings suggest an optimal sequence for an adversary system: The advocate asserting guilt or fault should go first and present his case in a climactic order; the advocate defending should follow and also present his case in a climactic order. Both advocates are thus given effective resources: This sequence gives a gross order advantage to the defense, offset by the climactic order advantage given to the preceding prosecution or plaintiff presentation. One of the groups in the experiment heard the hypothetical case in this sequence, and a high degree of balance was achieved. This result suggests the value of the traditional adversary system in generating balanced judgments by affording both parties fair access to their most effective resources.

The system, with its traditional gross order for opening statements and the presentation of evidence (prosecution or plaintiff first), provides the ideal order as long as both advocates follow their self-interest and present their evidence in a climactic order. The traditional adversary trial thus appears remarkably well arranged to neutralize the effects of order and thus maintain the fact-finding process relatively free of this powerful yet legally irrelevant influence.

6. The Plaintiff's or Prosecutor's Rebuttal

After the defense's case-in-chief, the plaintiff or prosecutor can present rebuttal evidence. As the label "rebuttal" suggests, this part of the trial has a limited scope. The judge generally restricts the plaintiff or prosecutor to testimony that "is precisely directed to rebutting new matter or new theories presented by the defendant's case-in-chief." *Bowman v. General Motors Corp.*, 427 F. Supp. 234, 240 (E.D. Pa. 1977). *Accord Peals v. Terre Haute Police Dept.*, 535 F.3d 621, 629–30 (7th Cir. 2008). However, the judge has wide discretion to broaden the scope and to permit the plaintiff or prosecutor to introduce evidence mistakenly omitted during the case-in-chief; an appellate court will reverse the trial judge's ruling on this issue only when there has been a clear abuse of discretion.

7. The Defense Surrebuttal or Rejoinder

The norms applicable to the surrebuttal are similar to those for rebuttal. The defendant has a right to surrebuttal only when new ground has been covered during the rebuttal. Here too, the trial judge has broad discretion and appellate courts ordinarily uphold a judge's decision to preclude surrebuttal. It is rare that a trial actually proceeds to the surrebuttal stage. However, in an extreme case, a denial of surrebuttal can constitute error.

8.   Witnesses Called by the Trial Judge

The trial judge need not be content with the witnesses the parties choose to call. The judge may decide that the interests of justice require that additional witnesses be called to testify. Under Federal Rule of Evidence 614(a), "[t]he court may call a witness on its own or at a party's request. Each party is entitled to cross-examine the witness."

The following problem frequently arises in practice: A witness possesses highly relevant knowledge but has such an unsavory background and is so easily impeached that neither party wants to call him or her as a witness. Both sides may fear that if the jury associates them with that witness, the jury's suspicions about the witness will spill over and impair the credibility of their other witnesses. In such cases, one of the parties may ask the judge to call the witness.

In addition, occasionally the trial court itself may want to call a witness in the interests of justice. Although this power is more often exercised in a bench trial, it is available and is used (albeit infrequently) in jury trials as well. In a criminal case, there is authority that the trial court cannot call a witness where the government's case would be insufficient as a matter of law without the court's witness. *See United States v. Karnes*, 531 F.2d 214 (4th Cir. 1976). In addition, the trial court should instruct the jury that a witness is not entitled to any greater credibility because he or she was called by the court. *Id.* In general, the power of the judge to call witnesses is used sparingly. Excessive intervention by the judge runs counter to the adversary tradition and may undermine the role of the judge as an impartial arbiter and result in prejudice to a party. *See generally* 4 WEINSTEIN'S FEDERAL EVIDENCE §§ 614.03–.05 (rev. 2009).

9.   Closing Argument or Summation

As we have seen, the attorneys may not mention inferences during the opening statement, and evidence law also limits their ability to elicit opinions from witnesses, especially witnesses who do not qualify as experts. However, after all of the evidence has been presented, the counsel are permitted to argue inferences during closing argument or summation. The plaintiff or prosecutor ordinarily argues first, the defense attorney then presents his or her closing argument, and then plaintiff or prosecutor is permitted a reply argument. As the party with the burden of proof, the plaintiff or prosecutor usually has the privilege of both opening and closing this stage of the trial.

There are several types of inferences the attorneys may properly argue during closing. First, the attorneys may argue regarding the credibility of witnesses. Suppose for example that in *Devitt*, during cross-examination, the defendant had admitted that he had a previous conviction for perjury. The prosecutor could argue during summation: "Now, ladies and gentlemen, I'm going to tell you why you should disbelieve the defendant and reject his testimony. During his testimony, you heard him admit that he has previously been convicted of perjury. This man, Devitt, is a convicted perjurer, ladies and gentlemen. He took the stand in another courtroom. He took the oath in another courtroom. And he lied — just as he's lying today."

The attorneys may also argue inferences from the circumstantial evidence. Assume that in *Hill* there was a dispute over the point of impact between Ms. Hill and Mr. Roe's cars. Roe's attorney might argue in his or her closing: "It's true that Ms. Hill says that Mr. Worker struck the rear of her car while her car was still in the intersection. But, ladies and gentlemen, look at the physical evidence in this case. The policeman, Patrolman Officer, gave us a very detailed description of the accident scene. Most of the debris, including the broken glass, was found 100 feet from the intersection. And our expert testified that glass matched Mr. Worker's headlight glass. When you consider all the circumstances, ladies and gentlemen, it's clear that the only reasonable inference is that the point of impact was not in the intersection, as the plaintiff claimed, but rather well down the street, as Mr. Worker testified."

Although the attorneys may argue inferences and conclusions during summation, such inferences must be conclusions from the evidence formally introduced at the trial. Under Rule 3.4(e) of the ABA's Model Rules of Professional Conduct, a lawyer may not "allude to any matter that the lawyer does not reasonably believe is relevant or that will not be supported by admissible evidence, assert personal knowledge of facts in issue except when testifying as a witness, or state a personal opinion as to the justness of a cause, the credibility of a witness, the culpability of a civil litigant or the guilt or innocence of an accused."

10.   The Judge's Instruction (or "Charge") to the Jury

In some jurisdictions, the attorneys argue after the judge gives the jurors their final instructions, but the prevailing practice is that the judge instructs the jury after closing arguments. In the final jury charge, the judge explains the substantive law, describes any pertinent evidentiary rules, and mentions the voting procedures the jury must use. The final charge may include up to six different types of evidentiary instructions.

Admissibility: In most cases, the judge decides whether an individual item of evidence is admissible, and the jurors' only task is to decide how much weight to ascribe to the item. However, in certain limited instances the jurors must decide the admissibility of evidence. In some jurisdictions, for instance, the jury determines the admissibility of dying declarations and of confessions challenged on voluntariness grounds. Moreover, as we shall see in Chapter 5, under Federal Rule of Evidence 104(b) the jurors make the final decision on issues of conditional relevancy. After instructing the jury on the test to be used to determine the admissibility of the evidence, the judge instructs the jurors to consider the evidence during their deliberations only if they decide that the evidence is admissible; if they decide that the evidence is inadmissible, they must disregard it and give it no weight at all during their deliberations.

Corroboration: In some civil law countries, there are special corroboration requirements. In those systems, to make out a submissible case the proponent may have to present the testimony of two eyewitnesses or the testimony of one eyewitness plus documentary corroboration. Corroboration requirements are rare in common-law countries such as the United States. In the United States, the admissible testimony of one witness to a fact is usually sufficient evidence to support a jury finding of that fact.

However, even in the United States, an attorney occasionally encounters special corroboration requirements. As a case in point, many states require corroboration for an accomplice's testimony. Since an accomplice may be prosecuted and has an incentive to curry favor with the prosecution, the courts are wary of the testimony of accomplices called by the prosecution. In these jurisdictions, the final jury charge instructs the jury that it cannot convict the defendant on the accomplice's testimony standing alone but rather must be satisfied that there is other credible evidence to connect the defendant with the commission of the offense. The United States Constitution contains a corroboration requirement in Article III, § 3, which provides that "[n]o person shall be convicted of treason unless on the testimony of two witnesses to the same overt act, or on confession in open court."

Cautionary: This type of instruction directs the jury to be wary in evaluating the weight of particular evidence. In addition to — or instead of — the corroboration requirements described above, many jurisdictions use a cautionary instruction about the testimony of accomplices who appear as prosecution witnesses. Because the accomplice frequently has an interest in currying favor with the prosecution, the judge instructs the jury to be skeptical in evaluating the accomplice's testimony. Other jurisdictions employ cautionary instructions for eyewitness testimony, instructing the jury that in stressful situations even an honest witness can make a mistaken identification. Still other jurisdictions have developed cautionary instructions about testimony by drug addicts.

In most cases, the need for a cautionary instruction is premised on the type of witness who is the source of the testimony: An accomplice, an eyewitness, or a drug addict. However, in some cases, the need arises because of weaknesses in the inferences underlying the theory of logical relevance for the testimony. For example, in *Miller v. United States*, 320 F.2d 767 (D.C. Cir. 1963), immediately after a robbery the defendant fled the scene. At trial, there was no direct evidence — no one saw the defendant pick the victim's pocket. The government's case rested heavily on the inference of guilt it claimed arose from the defendant's flight. On appeal, the court ruled that the jury should have been given a cautionary instruction to the effect that flight does not necessarily imply guilt.

The appellate court identified two factual assumptions underlying the claimed relationship between flight and guilt: (1) one who flees shortly after a criminal act is committed or when he is accused of committing it does so because he feels some guilt concerning that act; and (2) one who feels some guilt concerning an act has committed that act. The court criticized the first assumption on the ground that common experience does not support it, noting that those "who are entirely innocent do sometimes fly from the scene of a crime through fear of being apprehended as the guilty parties, or from an unwillingness to appear as witnesses." (quoting)

The court also challenged the second assumption by quoting none other than Sigmund Freud: "You may be led astray . . . by a neurotic who reacts as though he were guilty even though he is innocent — because a lurking sense of guilt already in him assimilates the accusation made against him on this particular occasion."[1]

The *Miller* case illustrates the possible need for an instruction to counteract a common misconception. The case also illustrates the role which science — in this instance psychiatry — can play. On the other hand, flight evidence is only one example of circumstantial proof. As we shall see, by definition circumstantial evidence may involve a chain of inferences, including intermediate inferences that must be drawn before reaching the final inference. In most cases there are possible explanations and inferences other than the intermediate inferences the proponent wants to draw. Are you persuaded that the inferences involved in flight evidence are uniquely (a) weak, or (b) likely to be misunderstood by jurors?

Limiting: The admissibility of an item of evidence often turns on the purpose for which it is offered. If an item of evidence is admissible for one purpose but inadmissible for another, ordinarily that item is admissible so long as it is offered for the proper purpose. The same is true if the item of evidence is admissible against one party but not against another. F.R.E. 105 codifies the common-law rule: "If the court admits evidence that is admissible against a party or for a purpose — but not against another party or for another purpose — the court, on timely request, must restrict the evidence to its proper scope and instruct the jury accordingly." In other words, the opponent's remedy is a limiting instruction to the jury, telling the jury the purpose for which the evidence was admitted and instructing it to confine the evidence to that purpose. If the risk is too great that the jury will be unable to follow that instruction or will use the evidence for the improper purpose, the judge has discretion to exclude the evidence or take other steps to minimize that risk.

As an example, assume that in the *Devitt* case the trial judge admitted proof of the defendant's prior convictions solely to impeach the defendant. The judge might give the jury this limiting instruction: "Ladies and gentlemen, during this trial you heard evidence that the defendant has a previous conviction in state court. You are not to consider that as evidence that the defendant is a bad man, and for that reason probably committed the assault he is charged with. You may consider that evidence for only one purpose, namely, determining his credibility. You may consider the fact of the conviction in deciding whether the defendant is an honest, trustworthy person and worthy of belief."

Curative: A curative instruction directs the jurors to disregard something they have already heard. Assume, for instance, that a police officer is testifying in the *Devitt* case and unexpectedly blurts out the fact that Devitt has been arrested on 12 prior occasions. The evidence of the arrests are inadmissible, but the jury has already heard the testimony. To cure the error, the trial judge would instruct the jury: "Now, ladies and gentlemen, you just heard Officer Monroe refer to some previous arrests of the defendant. I instruct you to disregard that statement. You should not consider that statement at all in your deliberations on the defendant's

---

[1] Freud, *Psychoanalysis and the Ascertaining of Truth in Courts of Law* (1906), in Collected Papers (1959), Vol. 2, p. 13. Freud subsequently observed that a "sense of guilt" may derive from "criminal intentions" rather than from an actual past misdeed, and in so-called "normal" as well as neurotic individuals. *See, e.g.*, Freud, *Criminality From a Sense of Guilt* (1915), in Collected Papers (1959), Vol. 4, p. 342; Freud, *The Ego and the Id* (1923), in Complete Psychological Works (1961), Vol. 19, p. 48 ff.

guilt or innocence. You must strike that statement from your minds." Keep in mind that if the statement is highly prejudicial and the judge concludes that the jury will be unable to disregard it, he or she will grant a mistrial.

Although at one time courts routinely assumed that the jury was capable of following such limiting or curative instructions, empirical research in the 1960s by the celebrated Chicago Jury Project resulted in a more realistic assessment of the jury's capabilities. *See* H. KALVEN & H. ZEISEL, THE AMERICAN JURY (1966). The Supreme Court has indicated that there are limits to its belief in the jury's capacity. *See Bruton v. United States*, 391 U.S. 123, 129 (1968) ("The naive assumption that prejudicial effects can be overcome by instructions to the jury . . . all practicing lawyers know to be unmitigated fiction").

Several empirical studies raise substantial doubts about the jury's ability to follow curative instructions. *E.g.*, Marcotte, *"The Jury Will Disregard . . . ,"* 73 A.B.A. J. 34 (Nov. 1, 1987) (an American Bar Foundation study); Priolo, *Can a Curative Instruction Effectively Remedy Impermissible References to a Defendant's Past Criminal Behavior?*, 30 SUFFOLK U. L. REV. 583 (1995). In one study, M.I.T. psychologist John Carroll discovered that curative instructions sometimes "make matters worse. [T]he jurors tend to think, 'The evidence may be even more important if they have to tell me to ignore it.' " Cole, *Can Jurors Ignore Inadmissible Evidence*, 24 TRIAL 80, 81 (Sept. 1988).

Sufficiency: While the judge passes on the *legal* sufficiency of the evidence, the jurors determine its *factual* sufficiency. They decide whether to believe particular witnesses and, ultimately, whether the historical facts of the case have been proven. To guide the jury's decision, the judge provides instructions on the ultimate burden of persuasion on the facts.

The judge's instruction deals with both the *allocation* of the burden — on which party it rests — and the level of the burden — to what degree must the facts be proven. If the jurors cannot decide whether a fact exists, the party that bears the burden of persuasion must lose. In the *Hill* case, the trial judge would undoubtedly assign the plaintiff the burden on the question whether Worker was driving negligently. Similarly, in the *Devitt* prosecution, the government will bear the burden of establishing that there was an assault.

Regarding the level or measure of the burden of persuasion, on the negligence issue in *Hill*, the plaintiff's burden will likely be a preponderance of the evidence. Under this standard, the evidence must make it more probable than not that Worker drove carelessly. However, Count Five of the *Hill* complaint alleges misrepresentation. If the count alleged knowing misrepresentation — fraud — many jurisdictions require the plaintiff to establish the fraud by a higher standard, namely, clear and convincing evidence. Of course, in criminal cases the prosecution must prove its case by the familiar standard of beyond a reasonable doubt.

In some jurisdictions, the judge is not limited to instructions on the law governing the allocation and measure of the burden; the judge may also comment on the sufficiency of particular items of evidence to satisfy the burden. In doing so, the judge must make it clear to the jurors that his or her comments do not bind them. In other jurisdictions, the judge may sum up the relevant evidence but may not expressly comment on its sufficiency. In still other states, the judge may neither sum up nor comment; the judge may instruct only on the pertinent law.

Chapter 4

THE EXAMINATION OF A WITNESS

Read Federal Rules of Evidence 106, 611, 614 and 615.

A. THE ORDER OF THE EXAMINATION OF A WITNESS

1. Sequestration or Exclusion of Witnesses

When a judge "sequesters" a prospective witness, the judge orders the witness excluded from the courtroom. The judge may sequester witnesses before the trial begins. In some jurisdictions, judges automatically sequester most witnesses; in others, judges must do so on the motion of either party; and in still others, judges have discretion whether or not to sequester. The governing Federal Rule of Evidence is Rule 615:

At a party's request, the court must order witnesses excluded so that they cannot hear other witnesses' testimony. Or the court may do so on its own. But this rule does not authorize excluding:

(a)   a party who is a natural person;

(b)   an officer or employee of a party that is not a natural person, after being designated as the party's representative by its attorney;

(c)   a person whose presence a party shows to be essential to presenting the party's claim or defense; or

(d)   a person authorized by statute to be present.

The judge may order prospective witnesses to leave the courtroom or may place them in the custody of an officer of the court. In addition to excluding the witness from the courtroom when they are not testifying, the judge customarily places sequestered witnesses "under the rule" by ordering them not to discuss their testimony with other witnesses in the case. As the court remarked in *United States v. Sepulveda*, 15 F.3d 1161, 1176 (1st Cir. 1993), "such non-discussion orders are generally thought to be a standard concomitant of basic sequestration fare." Although the Rule does not expressly authorize such additional orders, the vast majority of courts have concluded that trial judges have inherent authority to issue them.

If a prospective witness violates a sequestration order, in some jurisdictions the judge may penalize the violation by ruling the person incompetent to testify. Even in those jurisdictions, though, the prospective witness's disqualification is not automatic and the judge has discretion to decide whether disqualification is the most appropriate sanction. *United States v. English*, 92 F.3d 909, 913 (9th Cir. 1996). In exercising that discretion, judges consider such factors as whether the witness's violation was inadvertent or willful; whether the party or counsel colluded in the violation; and how important the prospective witness's testimony is. If the judge decides against disqualifying the prospective witness, he or she can take other remedial action. For example, in the final charge to the jury, the judge might comment on the witness's violation of the sequestration order and give the jury a cautionary instruction about that witness's testimony. The judge also has the options of declaring a mistrial and holding the witness in contempt. Or the judge might simply strike the part of the witness's testimony that directly related to the violation. *Zeigler v. Fisher-Price, Inc.*, 302 F. Supp. 2d 999 (N.D. Iowa 2004). Courts generally view complete disqualification as a last resort, reserved for the most blatant violations of the rule.

NOTES AND PROBLEMS

1. What purpose is served by sequestering a prospective witness? How does sequestration contribute to the reliability of the witness's testimony at trial? What are the risks if the judge permits a witness to remain in the courtroom while other witnesses testify? In considering these questions, first assume bad faith on the part of the witnesses. Then assume good faith.

2. Problem 4-1. In *Devitt*, at the very beginning of the trial Devitt is disruptive and boisterous. The judge warns Devitt once, but within a few minutes Devitt interrupts again. The prosecutor requests that the trial judge sequester Devitt. What result under Federal Rule 615(a)? Also consider *Illinois v. Allen*, 397 U.S. 337, 343 (1970).

3. Problem 4-2. To assist her during the trial, the prosecutor wants the detective in charge of the investigation at the counsel table. Under Rule 615, could the judge exempt the detective from the sequestration order? For that matter, does the prosecutor have an absolute right to have the detective exempted from the order? Is this problem governed by Rule 615(b) or Rule 615(c)? Does a person designated under 615(b) have to be a current employee of the entity? *United States ex rel. Bahrani v. Conagra, Inc.*, 624 F.3d 1275, 1296–97 (10th Cir. 2010) (although Gustafson did not work for the named party, he was an employee of the real party in interest).

4. Problem 4-3. In *Hill*, the defense intends to present the testimony of an accident reconstruction expert. During the defense case-in-chief, the defense plans to ask the expert a hypothetical question based on earlier witnesses' testimony about the damage to the vehicles, the location of the debris, and other physical facts. Should the accident reconstruction expert be exempted from any sequestration order under Rule 615? Suppose, alternatively, that the plaintiff will also present an accident reconstruction expert's testimony. Now the defense wants its expert present in the courtroom to help the defense attorney follow and understand the plaintiff's expert testimony. Does the defense have a right to an "at the elbow expert" to help the attorney prepare for cross-examination? *Compare Malek v. Federal Ins. Co.*, 994 F.2d 49, 53–54 (2d Cir. 1993) (error to sequester plaintiff's expert), *with Opus 3 Ltd. v. Heritage Park, Inc.*, 91 F.3d 625 (4th Cir. 1996) (not error to sequester defendant's expert who was also a fact witness; there is no *per se* rule allowing "elbow" experts).

2. Direct, Cross, Redirect, and Recross Examinations

When an attorney wants to present a prospective witness's testimony, the attorney calls that person as a witness. In our adversary system, the attorneys representing the opposing parties largely control the questioning of the witnesses. S. LANDSMAN, READINGS ON ADVERSARIAL JUSTICE: THE AMERICAN APPROACH TO ADJUDICATION 3–4 (1988). A court official such as the reporter or bailiff administers the oath to the witness or, if the witness has conscientious scruples against an oath, permits the witness to affirm under penalty of perjury. The witness takes the stand, and the questioning attorneys progress through the direct, cross, redirect, and recross stages of examination, which the California Evidence Code describes in this fashion:

§ 772. Phases of examination.

    (a)   The examination of a witness shall proceed in the following phases: direct examination, cross-examination, redirect examination, and recross-examination, and continuing thereafter by redirect and recross-examination.

    (b)   Unless for good cause the court otherwise directs, each phase of the examination of a witness must be concluded before the succeeding phase begins.

    (c)   Subject to subdivision (d), a party may, in the discretion of the court, interrupt his cross-examination, redirect examination, or recross-examination of a witness, in order to examine the witness upon a matter not within the scope of a previous examination of the witness.

    (d)   If the witness is the defendant in a criminal action, the witness may not, without his consent, be examined under direct examination by another party.

§ 760. Direct examination.

"Direct examination" is the first examination of a witness upon a matter that is not within the scope of a previous examination of the witness.

§ 761. Cross-examination.

"Cross-examination" is the examination of a witness by a party other than the direct examiner upon a matter that is within the scope of the direct examination of the witness.

§ 762. Redirect examination.

"Redirect examination" is an examination of a witness by the direct examiner subsequent to the cross-examination of the witness.

§ 763. Recross-examination.

"Recross-examination" is an examination of a witness by a crossexaminer subsequent to a redirect examination of the witness.

3. Questions by the Trial Judge

Even in an adversary system, the trial judge is not required to be a mere umpire or passive moderator at the trial. *United States v. Montas*, 41 F.3d 775 (1st Cir. 1994), *cert. denied sub nom. Felix-Montas v. United States*, 514 U.S. 1121 (1995). Not only is the trial judge permitted to call witnesses on his or her own motion, the judge can also question witnesses called by the parties. Federal Rule of Evidence 614 provides:

(a)   Calling. The court may call a witness on its own or at a party's request. Each party is entitled to cross-examine the witness,

(b)   Examining. The court may examine a witness regardless of who calls the witness.

(c)   Objections. A party may object to the court's calling or examining a witness either at that time or at the next opportunity when the jury is not present.

The judge may question actively to clarify the testimony elicited by the attorneys. Nonetheless, the philosophy underlying our adversary litigation system places some restrictions on the judge's right to call and question witnesses. Ordinarily, there must be an extremely high level of interference by the judge before judicial intervention crosses the line. The following case is illustrative.

UNITED STATES v. HICKMAN
592 F.2d 931 (6th Cir. 1979)

KEITH, CIRCUIT JUDGE.

[At a joint trial, Hickman and Head were convicted of being felons in possession of firearms. In addition, Head was found guilty of marijuana possession. The jury was unable to agree on charges against both men of possession of marijuana with intent to distribute. Pursuant to a search warrant, police found four pounds of marijuana when they searched the defendant's apartment.]

Although this case is routine, the conduct of the trial judge was not. Appellants charge that the district court's conduct of the trial rendered a fair verdict impossible. Appellant Head, in his brief, asserts that the district court voluntarily interjected itself in the proceedings over 250 times. Our examination of the entire record of the case bears out the truth of this allegation. Although this bare figure, by itself, is not dispositive, it serves to emphasize the serious problems we have concerning the way this trial was handled.

The law in this area is as easy to state as it is difficult to apply. The proper role of a federal trial judge was best summarized by the Supreme Court in the following oft-quoted words:

In a trial by jury in a federal court, the judge is not a mere moderator, but is the governor of the trial for the purpose of assuring its proper conduct and of determining questions of law. *Quercia v. United States*, 289 U.S. 466, 469 (1933). Thus, the mere asking of questions is not at all improper:

> The trial judge in the federal court is more than a mere arbitrator to rule upon objections and to instruct the jury. It is his function to conduct the trial in an orderly way with a view to eliciting the truth and to attaining justice between the parties. It is his duty to see that the issues are not obscured and that the testimony is not misunderstood. He has the right to interrogate witnesses for this purpose.

United States v. Carabbia, 381 F.2d 133, 139 (6th Cir. 1967).

The problem is that potential prejudice lurks behind every intrusion into a trial made by a presiding judge. The reason for this is that a trial judge's position before a jury is "overpowering." *United States v. Hoker*, 483 F.2d 359, 368 (5th Cir. 1973). His position makes "his slightest action of great weight with the jury." *United States v. Lanham*, 416 F.2d 1140, 1144 (5th Cir. 1969). For this reason, this Circuit has disapproved of extensive questioning of witnesses by a trial judge. *United States v. Ball*, 428 F.2d 26, 30 (6th Cir. 1970) ("It is not 'desirable practice' for him to interrupt the proceedings by questioning the witness.").

As is apparent, determining when a trial judge oversteps is difficult. Numerous factors need be considered. First, the nature of the issues at trial. In a lengthy, complex trial, intervention by the judge is often needed to clarify what is going on. *See United States v. Smith*, 561 F.2d 8, 13–14 (6th Cir.), *cert. denied*, 434 U.S. 958 (1977).

Second, the conduct of counsel. If the attorneys in a case are unprepared or obstreperous, judicial intervention is often called for. If the facts are becoming muddled and neither side is succeeding at attempts to clear them up, the judge performs an important duty by interposing clarificatory comments or questions. *See United States v. Frazier*, [584 F.2d] at 793.

Third, the conduct of witnesses. It is often impossible for counsel to deal with a difficult witness without judicial intervention. Similarly, a witness'testimony may be unbelievable and counsel may fail to adequately probe. *See United States v. Liddy*, 509 F.2d 428, 437–42 (1974), *cert. denied*, 420 U.S. 911 (1975). More commonly, judicial intervention will operate to clear up inadvertent witness confusion. *See United States v. McColgin*, 535 F.2d 471, 474–75 (8th Cir. 1976), *cert. denied*, 429 U.S. 853 (1976).

The nature and scope of the district judge's questions present problems. The destructive effects of the judge's intrusions are apparent from his handling of the defense's cross-examination of expert witness Stokes, the government chemist. The chemist testified that he performed three different tests for marijuana upon the substance that he was given to analyze. After defense counsel elicited the admission that the first test, the microscopic test, was not conclusive for marijuana, the judge interrupted and stated "He says it's not conclusive. That's why he made three tests." After defense counsel continued cross-examination as to the reliability of the second test performed by the chemist, the court interrupted once again:

By the Court:	Well, I'll save time. Have you got any chemist that's going to show that this is not marijuana?
Mr. Kagin:	No.
By the Court:	You're just relying on your ability to satisfy the jury that this man doesn't know what he's talking about?
Mr. Kagin:	That's right.
By the Court:	Proceed. You haven't tested 'it?
Mr. Kagin:	No, your Honor.
By the Court:	You haven't tested.
Mr. Kagin:	I want to see if he has —
By the Court:	(Interrupting) Well, he says he has and there's no evidence to the contrary.

Counsel was then permitted to continue and amply cross-examine the witness further. Unfortunately, immediately after counsel had finished, the district judge stepped in at once and rehabilitated the witness' testimony. The entire sequence deserves reproduction:

Q.	Is the thin layer chromatography test in and of itself conclusive for the presence of marijuana?
A.	No, sir. It could have been hashish, it could have been Cannabin [sic], which is an active ingredient of marijuana.
Q.	And it could have been something else that you've gotten here that's totally unrelated to marijuana and something that's not under control?
A.	Well, if I hadn't done the microscopic test —
Q.	(Interrupting) All right. Let's take that and say if you hadn't.
A.	All right.
By the Court:	Well, now, you're arguing with the gentleman. You remember he's the one that made the tests. You're not going to testify yourself. I'm not going to let you.
Q.	Are you telling me that this test is not of itself conclusive, is that correct?
A.	That is correct.
Q.	So we have Test No. 1 that is not conclusive, Test No. 2 that is not conclusive, and Test No. 3 that's not conclusive. And from that you conclude it's marijuana, is that correct, sir?
A.	That's correct.
Q.	No further questions.

By the Court: Well, let's get this finished, and you can step down. Did you use the standard testing procedure that all United States chemists use in testing a substance to determine whether it is marijuana?

The Witness: I used three, the three.

By the Court: The standard ones that they use?

The Witness: Well, some people use two of them, but I used these three.

By the Court: I understand you used all three of them.

The Witness: That's correct.

By the Court: And in your professional opinion, the substance in each of the three samples is marijuana?

A.   That's correct.

By the Court: Step down.

The district judge's brilliant redirect examination would have been entirely proper had it been done by the prosecutor. It was improper for the judge to have assumed the prosecutor's role under the circumstances. . . .

Our conclusion is reinforced because the judge's actions were so unnecessary. This was a one-day trial. The principal issue for the jury was whether it would impute possession of the contraband in the apartment to one or another defendant. Counsel for both sides were able, and at all times, conducted themselves properly. The testimony was relatively clear and any difficulties could easily have been handled by counsel had the judge restrained himself. There was no need for judicial intervention to assist the jury by clarifying the facts.

Given what occurred here we are persuaded that the district court's instructions to the jury could not offset the effects of his conduct. Nor do we hold the failure to object against defense counsel. We think that the following statement of the Seventh Circuit in *United States v. Hill*, 332 F.2d 105, 106–07 (7th Cir. 1964) is fully applicable here:

> Counsel for defendant in a criminal case is indeed in a difficult and hazardous predicament in finding it necessary to make frequent objections in the presence of a jury to questions propounded by the trial judge.

[T]he trial court's conduct amounted to plain error.

NOTES

1. Empirical research by psychologist Robert Rosenthal bears out Judge Keith's observation that the judge's "slightest action" can be "of great weight with the jury." Blanck, Rosenthal & Cordell, Note, *The Appearance of Justice: Judges' Verbal and Nonverbal Behavior in Criminal Jury Trials*, 38 STAN. L. REV. 89 (1985). The Note describes a research project funded by the National Science Foundation. The researchers attempted to determine: (1) whether a judge's knowledge of the defendant's criminal record affects the judge's attitude toward the defendant during a jury trial, and (2) if so, whether the judge's attitude is communicated nonverbally

to the jury and influences the jury verdict. The researchers found that, to some extent, a judge's belief in the defendant's guilt can be transmitted to the jury "through judges' subtle verbal and nonverbal behaviors," such as the way in which the judge reads the jury instructions. *Id.* at 92. These behaviors "leak" the judge's attitude to the jury and, at least in some cases, influence the jury's verdict. *Id.* at 150–51.

2. For another example of improper judicial intervention, see *Nationwide Mut. Fire Ins. Co. v. Ford Motor Co.*, 174 F.3d 801 (6th Cir. 1999). There the same court that decided *Hickman* reversed a judgment due to judicial misconduct. The trial judge repeatedly interrupted plaintiff's opening statement, at one point telling counsel that two witnesses should not be called in his case-in-chief, repeatedly engaged in one-sided questioning of witnesses, and invited objections by defense counsel. The court held that although the standard of review is abuse of discretion, "the harmless error doctrine is inapplicable in cases where judicial bias and/or hostility is found to have been exhibited at any stage of a judicial proceeding." 174 F.3d at 808. Whether the judge was in fact biased against plaintiff was "irrelevant: His interruptions were so numerous and his questions so one sided, they must inevitably have left the jury with the impression that the judge believed Nationwide's actions were egregious and improper." *Id.*

4. Questions by the Jurors

Some commentators have long urged that trial jurors be encouraged to ask questions. Harms, Comment, *The Questioning of Witnesses by Jurors*, 27 AM. U. L. REV. 127 (1977). At first, such suggestions fell on deaf judicial ears. Most trial judges did not tell the jurors that they could suggest questions for a witness, and many appellate courts made it clear that they did not want the jurors encouraged to ask questions. *E.g., United States v. Bush*, 47 F.3d 511, 515 (2d Cir. 1995). Some courts even went so far as absolutely forbidding questions by jurors. *State v. Zima*, 237 Neb. 952, 468 N.W.2d 377 (1991); *Morrison v. State*, 845 S.W.2d 882 (Tex. Crim. App. 1992).

More recently, there is a growing chorus of voices in favor of permitting questions by jurors during the trial, provided the procedure is strictly regulated. The literature is extensive. *See, e.g.*, Diamond, Rose & Murphy, *Jurors' Unanswered Questions*, 41 CT.REV. 1 (Spring 2004); Heuer, *Increasing Jurors' Participation in Trials: A Field Experiment with Jury Note taking and Question Asking*, 12 LAW & HUM. BEHAV. 231–56 (1988). In Diamond, *Juror Questions at Trial*, 78 N.Y. ST. B.J. 23 (2006), the author describes one experiment:

> While the practice remains controversial, experience with pilot programs permitting jurors to submit questions during trial is producing "converts" among judges and attorneys who participate in these trials. One . . . convert is Judge James Holderman, co-chair of the Seventh Circuit Bar Association's American Jury Project, which tested seven ABA Principles between October 2005 and May 2006. Judge Holderman's initial skepticism about juror questions disappeared after he found through experience that the procedure worked smoothly, the questions were generally relevant and provided beneficial insights to the attorneys, and, the jurors appreciated

the opportunity to submit questions. Other Seventh Circuit judges and attorneys reached the same conclusions.

The American Bar Association has published PRINCIPLES FOR JURIES AND JURY TRIALS. Principle 13 states, in part:

C. In civil cases, jurors should, ordinarily, be permitted to submit written questions for witnesses. In deciding whether to permit jurors to submit written questions in criminal cases, the court should take into consideration the historic reasons why courts in a number of jurisdictions have discouraged juror questions and the experience in those jurisdictions that have allowed it.

1.   Jurors should be instructed at the beginning of the trial concerning their ability to submit written questions for witnesses.

2.   Upon receipt of a written question, the court should make it part of the court record and disclose it to the parties outside the hearing of the jury. The parties should be given the opportunity, outside the hearing of the jury, to interpose objections and suggest modifications to the question.

3.   After ruling that a question is appropriate, the court may pose the question to the witness, or permit a party to do so, at that time or later; in so deciding, the court should consider whether the parties prefer to ask, or to have the court ask, the question. The court should modify the question to eliminate any objectionable material.

4.   After the question is answered, the parties should be given an opportunity to ask follow-up questions.

NOTES

1.   What are the risks of permitting jurors to ask questions? Are those risks adequately addressed by the procedures outlined in the A.B.A. PRINCIPLES?

2.   Are there special reasons why juror questions should not be permitted in jury trials of criminal cases?

3.   Is a juror likely to attach inordinate weight to an answer to a question which she posed to a witness? Judge Lay has observed that there are "no empirical studies [of] the effect of juror questions on [juror] neutrality." *United States v. Johnson*, 892 F.2d 707, 713 n.3 (8th Cir. 1989).

5.   Excusing the Witness

When the questioning is completed, the witness is excused. Typically, the witness is permanently excused. If nothing is said when the witness leaves the stand, the witness is considered permanently excused. If the witness is permanently excused and an attorney later desires to elicit additional testimony from him, the attorney must seek leave of the court. In some cases, though, the witness is excused subject to recall. In that case, the attorney has the right to recall him and elicit additional testimony. The difference between permanent excuse and excuse subject to recall can sometimes be critical — as we shall see later when we discuss prior inconsistent statement impeachment in Chapter 16.

B. THE SCOPE OF THE EXAMINATION OF A WITNESS

1. Direct Examination

It is frequently said that the scope of direct examination includes any evidence logically relevant to any material fact of consequence in the case. That statement is somewhat imprecise. More accurately, the scope of direct examination depends upon the segment of the case in which the direct examination occurs. For example, the scope of the plaintiff's case-in-chief is broader than the scope of the plaintiff's rebuttal. Hence, the scope of direct examination during the case-in-chief exceeds the scope of direct examination during rebuttal.

2. Cross-Examination

a. The Split of Authority over the Proper Scope of Cross-Examination

It is a commonplace observation that there is a wide split of authority over the proper scope of cross-examination, and there is an element of truth in that observation. However, to avoid overstatement, we should first specify the many points of agreement among courts on the scope of cross-examination. All courts concur that it includes a witness's credibility. Consequently, during cross-examination, the questioner may always attempt to impeach the witness. Further, most courts agree that the judge has discretion to broaden or narrow the normal scope of cross-examination on the historical merits of the case. The main point of disagreement is the proper norm for cross-examination on the historical merits. There are three views.

Federal Rule 611(b) opts for the majority (restrictive) view:

> (b) Scope of cross-examination. Cross-examination should not go beyond the subject matter of the direct examination and matters affecting the witness's credibility. The court may allow inquiry into additional matters as if on direct examination.

Under this view, the proper scope of cross is limited to the scope of direct. Thus, the direct examiner may preclude the cross-examiner from probing an issue during cross by not raising the issue on direct. This view gives the direct examiner some control over the latitude of cross.

A second, minority view is that the scope of cross-examination is wide open — this is often called the "English Rule." Almost one-third of the states have adopted this position. *See, e.g.*, MICHIGAN RULES OF EVIDENCE RULE 611(b); MISSISSIPPI RULES OF EVIDENCE RULE 611(b); TENNESSEE RULES OF EVIDENCE RULE 611(b); MASSACHUSETTS EVIDENTIARY STANDARD 611(b). The draft version of Rule 611(b) that the Supreme Court first transmitted to Congress would have adopted this view:

(b) A witness may be cross-examined on any matter relevant to any issue in the case, including credibility. In the interests of justice, the judge may limit cross-examination with respect to matters not testified to on direct examination.

Under the English Rule, the scope of the direct examination does not limit the cross-examination. Depending on the segment of the case in which the cross-examination occurs, the cross-examiner may attempt to elicit any evidence logically relevant to any material fact of consequence in the case. Congress, however, was more conservative than the Court and opted for the restrictive rule in the final version of Rule 611(b).

A few states (for example, Pennsylvania, Vermont, and West Virginia) have adopted a third approach. In this small number of jurisdictions, the restrictive rule applies to any witness except a party in a civil case, as to whom the wide-open rule applies.

NOTES AND PROBLEMS

1.   Which of the above views do you think is the soundest? Most academic commentators support the wide-open view, arguing that it promotes more expeditious examination; judicial economy favors eliciting all the witness's testimony at one time rather than recalling the witness later to give additional testimony. Litigators, in contrast, tend to prefer the restrictive view, contending that it makes for a more orderly presentation of testimony to the jury. *See* Carlson, *Cross-Examination of the Accused*, 52 CORNELL L.Q. 705, 706–07 (1967). The restrictive approach also happens to give litigators the greatest control over the content of their cases-in-chief. Which view promotes more accurate testimony? Do the contrasting views reflect different estimates of the jury's capacity to comprehend testimony?

2.   Like most formulations of the American view, Rule 611 presents an obvious problem: how to define "the subject matter of the direct examination"? Should we equate "the matters covered on direct examination" with the historical transactions mentioned on direct? Suppose that on direct Devitt testified only about the circumstances surrounding his arrest 10 hours after the alleged assault? Could the prosecutor then cross-examine Devitt about the offense itself? Or should we equate "the matters covered on direct" with the essential legal elements of the cause of action or crime mentioned on direct? Another possibility is to permit the cross-examiner to ask any questions that tend to rebut either express statements on direct or implications from the express statements made during direct. Which definition is most conducive to an orderly presentation of the evidence to the jury? Which definition would be the most manageable and predictable in application?

3.   **Problem 4-4.** In the *Devitt* case, on direct examination Devitt merely denied hitting Paterson. Could the prosecutor cross-examine Devitt about whether Paterson consented to a fight with Devitt? There are occasional statements to the effect that consent is a defense to a battery charge at least when the battery results only in minor bodily injuries. LAFAVE, CRIMINAL LAW § 7 16.2(e) (5th ed. 2010).

4. Problem 4-5. Suppose that after the alleged battery, Paterson wrote a note to a close personal friend. The note's wording suggests that Paterson consented to a fight with Devitt due to an argument over how much Paterson owed Devitt for installing shelving in the kitchen. At trial, on direct examination Paterson denies consent. On cross-examination, the defense attorney would like to question him about the note and also to introduce the note into evidence. When the defense attorney attempts to do so, the prosecutor objects, "[b]eyond the proper scope of cross. The defense can't introduce exhibits during the cross-examination of a prosecution witness." Analyze this problem under Federal Rule 611(b). *Compare* A. TANFORD, THE TRIAL PROCESS: LAW, TACTICS AND ETHICS 292 (4th ed. 2009)(permissible) *with* R. HUNTER, FEDERAL TRIAL HANDBOOK § 22.3 (3d ed. 1993)(impermissible).

b. The Consequences of Undue Restriction of the Scope of Cross-Examination

Even when the evidence in question relates to a witness's credibility, "a trial judge can opt to exclude evidence that is marginally relevant and highly prejudicial." *United States v. Davis*, 490 F.3d 541 (6th Cir. 2007). Therefore, trial judges have some discretion to limit the extent to which the cross-examiner questions about a topic, even though that topic is within the proper scope.

It is a wholly different matter, though, if the trial judge unreasonably limits or completely forecloses cross-examination on a vital topic. The Sixth Amendment right to confrontation guarantees a criminal defendant an opportunity for adequate cross-examination. *Davis v. Alaska*, 415 U.S. 308 (1974); *Smith v. Illinois*, 390 U.S. 129 (1968). The cross-examination guarantee is a right of first magnitude, and appellate courts carefully scrutinize any restriction on its scope.1 McCORMICK, EVIDENCE § 19, at 113 (6th ed. 2006). In the words of one court,

> An accused's constitutional right of confrontation is violated when either (1) he or she is absolutely prohibited from engaging in the otherwise appropriate cross-examination designed to show a prototypical form of bias on the part of a witness, or (2) a reasonable jury would have received a significantly different impression of the witness's credibility had counsel been permitted to pursue his or her proposed line of cross-examination.

State v. Banks, 771 N.W.2d 75 (Neb. 2009).

If the witness testifies on direct examination but either the witness or the judge restricts the scope of the cross-examination, the question arises whether all or part of the direct examination should be stricken. In the decision whether to strike, two factors are crucial: (1) the cause of the restriction; and (2) the importance of the subject on which cross-examination was foreclosed. The following is the best short treatment of the first factor.

1 McCORMICK, EVIDENCE § 19, at 110–112 (6th ed. 2006)

What are the consequences of a denial or failure of the right? There are several common, recurring situations. First, a party testifying on his own behalf might unjustifiably refuse to answer questions necessary to a complete cross-examination. In this fact situation, the consensus is that the adversary is entitled to have the direct testimony stricken, a result that seems warranted.

Second, a non-party witness might similarly refuse to be cross-examined, or to answer proper cross-examination questions. Here the proper result is less clear, but many judges and writers seem to approve of the same remedy of excluding the direct. This remedy minimizes the party's temptation to procure the witness'srefusal, a collusion which is often hard to prove; the remedy forcefully protects the right of cross-examination. However, there is also some authority for the view that the matter should be left to the judge's discretion. In particular, there is support for the notion that if the privilege against self-incrimination is invoked as to cross-examination questions which are collateral, that is, logically relevant only to the witness's credibility, the direct testimony should not be stricken; or at the least the judge ought to have a measure of discretion in ruling on that matter.

Third, the witness may become, or purport to become, sick or otherwise physically or mentally incapacitated, before cross-examination is begun or completed. The facts in many of these cases arouse suspicion of simulation, particularly when the witness is a party. Consequently, the party's direct examination is often stricken. In the case of the non-party witness, the same result usually obtains. However, at least in civil cases, this result should arguably be qualified: The judge should exclude the direct unless he is clearly convinced that the incapacity is genuine. In that event he ought to let the direct testimony stand. He should then give the jury a cautionary instruction to explain the weakness of uncross-examined evidence. (Temporary incapacity may change this result, as indicated below.)

The fourth situation is that of the witness's death before the conclusion of the cross-examination. Here again it is usually said that the party denied cross-examination is entitled to have the direct testimony stricken, unless, presumably, the death occurred during a postponement of the cross-examination consented to or procured by that party. Indeed, its exclusion may very well be constitutionally compelled if the person was a state's witness in a criminal case. Yet, at least in the case of death, there is no adequate reason for striking the direct testimony. It has been suggested that striking the direct ought to be discretionary. That suggestion has merit. No matter how valuable cross-examination may be, common sense tells us that the half-loaf of direct testimony is better than no bread at all. It seems excessive to deny the jury all the testimony from that potential source of valuable information. To let the direct testimony stand was the accepted practice in equity. It is submitted that except for the testimony of prosecution's witnesses, the judge should let the direct testimony stand but on request instruct the jury to consider the lack of opportunity to cross-examine in weighing the direct testimony.

The above results may be modified in certain situations. For instance, it has been held that where the incapacity is temporary, the cross-examiner may not insist upon immediate exclusion of the direct testimony. Rather, he must be content with the offer of a later opportunity to cross-examine even when this makes it necessary for him to submit to a mistrial.

[The foregoing assumes a substantial failure to cross-examine. If there has been partial but incomplete cross-examination, the trial judge should have discretion either to strike only the uncross-examined part of the direct, or, where appropriate, to treat the partial cross-examination as adequate.]

PROBLEM

Problem 4-6. In *Devitt*, Paterson, has just completed his direct examination. On cross-examination, he refuses to answer a question.

- In one variation of this problem, the question he refuses to answer is, "Isn't it true that two years ago you filed a false claim for welfare benefits?"

- In another variation of this problem, the question is, "Isn't it true that a year ago you filed a false assault charge against another man, a Mr. Johnson?"

- In a final variation of this problem, the question he refuses to answer is, "Isn't it true that the day after you reported this so-called battery to the police, you told your daughter that you had freely agreed to fight Mr. Devitt because of an argument over the price of his carpentry work?"

Assume that in all three scenarios, the question itself is unobjectionable and proper. In addition to considering the cause of the restriction of the scope of cross, the judge weighs the importance of the topic on which cross was foreclosed. In which variation of the problem does the defense have the strongest case for striking the direct? In which the weakest case? Why? The leading case, *United States v. Cardillo*, 316 F.2d 606, 612–13 (2d Cir. 1963), draws a distinction between purely "collateral" cross-examination that "would [develop] the general unsavory character of the witness" and "untruthfulness with respect to specific events of the crime charged." *Id.* at 613. *Cf. United States v. Marzook*, 435 F. Supp.2d 708, 749–50 (N.D. Ill. 2006).

c. Expansion of the Scope of Cross-Examination

Suppose that the judge goes to the opposite extreme: Rather than unduly restricting the scope of cross, the judge permits the cross-examiner to range well the normal scope. Assume, for example, that in our torts case the jurisdiction normally limits cross-examination to the historical events mentioned on direct. As one of her witnesses, Ms. Hill calls her husband, Arthur Hill, who accompanied her to Jefferson Motor Car Co. when she bought the automobile. On direct examination, Arthur testifies only about the oral representations the salesperson made to Ms. Hill. On cross-examination, the defense attorney begins questioning Arthur about his observation of the extent of the plaintiff's personal injuries suffered in the accident. The plaintiff objects that the question is beyond the scope of the direct. The judge responds, "You're right, of course. But I think I'll exercise my discretion to allow this line of inquiry." The cross-examiner has thus exceeded the normal scope of cross with the judge's permission. In this situation, the traditional view is that the cross-examiner "adopts" the witness with respect to the matter beyond the scope of the direct.

The question is: what are the procedural consequences of such an adoption?

NOTE

As we shall see later in this chapter, leading questions are generally not permitted on direct examination. Conversely, leading questions are usually allowable on cross. When the cross-examiner exceeds the normal scope of cross, should he or she forfeit the right to lead the witness with respect to the new matter?

3. Redirect Examination

The common-law rule is that, as of right, the proponent of the witness may conduct redirect about topics the opponent broached for the first time during cross-examination. *United States v. Moran*, 493 F.3d 1002, 1003 (9th Cir. 2007), is illustrative. There, the defendant was charged with tax violations. On cross-examination, the prosecutor questioned the defendant about her receipt of an expert's letter questioning the legality of her business practices. The Ninth Circuit held that trial judge erred by precluding redirect examination about contrary legal opinions the defendant had received from other experts.

Just as the trial judge has some discretion to constrict the scope of redirect, there is also leeway in the other direction. The judge has discretion to permit the proponent of the witness to exceed this scope and cover topics that could have been mentioned on direct.

PROBLEM

Problem 4-7. In our torts case, Ms. Hill's husband, Arthur, is on the stand. On direct examination, he testifies only about the signing of the written contract with Jefferson Motor Car Co. On cross-examination, the defense interrogates Arthur about what the salesperson said at the time the parties signed the written contract. On redirect, Ms. Hill's attorney would like to elicit Arthur's testimony that Arthur and the plaintiff made it clear to the salesperson that they were relying on his judgment in picking out a safe, suitable automobile. Does Ms. Hill have the right to elicit that testimony on redirect?

4. Recross Examination

The guidelines for recross parallel those for redirect. As of right, the cross-examiner may question about topics mentioned for the first time on redirect, but ordinarily may not examine otherwise. *Hale v. United States*, 435 F.2d 737, 751 (5th Cir. 1970). Here too the judge has broad discretion as to whether to broaden the normal scope of the examination.

5. The Rule of Completeness

The so-called "rule of completeness" decrees that if one party introduces part of an item of evidence — such as a deposition — during one stage of a witness's examination, the opponent has the right to introduce other parts relevant to the same subject matter during the next stage. So conceived, the rule is a doctrine of scope: it provides that if one party introduces a half-truth during an examination of the witness, the opposing party has the right to show the whole truth during the next examination. Consider two codifications of the rule.

Federal Evidence Rule 106 provides:

> If a party introduces all or part of a writing or recorded statement, an adverse party may require the introduction, at that time, of any other part — or any other writing or recorded statement — that in fairness ought to be considered at the same time.

When invoking Rule 106, the opponent must both specify the portion that he or she wants the proponent to read and explain why that portion is necessary context for the portion the proponent contemplates reading. *McCoy v. Augusta Fiberglass Coatings, Inc.*, 593 F.3d 737 (8th Cir. 2010).

Now consider California Evidence Code § 356:

> Where part of an act, declaration, conversation, or writing is given in evidence by one party, the whole on the same subject may be inquired into by an adverse party; when a letter is read, the answer may be given; and when a detached act, declaration, conversation, or writing is given in evidence, any other act, declaration, conversation, or writing which is necessary to make it understood may also be given in evidence.

NOTES AND PROBLEM

1.   How do the two rules differ? To trigger FRE 106, is it sufficient to show that the other pages of the deposition transcript relate to the same topic? If not, what is the test? Does the California Evidence Code employ the same test?

Under the federal rule, is the second attorney's only right to introduce the pertinent parts of the item of evidence during his or her next examination of the witness? Does the attorney have the same rights under the California statute?

On its face, the federal statute is inapplicable to oral statements. *United States v. Collicott*, 92 F.3d 973, 983 (9th Cir. 1996); *United States v. Castro*, 813 F.2d 571, 576 (2d Cir. 1987) ("in practice verbal precision cannot be expected when the source of evidence as to an utterance is the memory of a witness"). However, some courts have held that it is appropriate to effectively expand the scope of Rule 106 by invoking the judge's authority under Rule 611(a). *Compare United States v. Castro*, 813 F.2d 571, 576 (2d Cir.) (the rule applies only to written documents; "verbal precision cannot be expected when the source of evidence as to an utterance is the memory of a witness"), *cert.denied*, 484 U.S. 844 (1987), *with United States v. Li*, 55 F.3d 325, 329 (7th Cir. 1995) (judge may invoke the rule of inclusion for oral statements). Which is the sounder rule?

2.   Statutory construction and the rule of completeness: While the California statute basically codifies the common-law rule of completeness, Rule 106 deviates from the common law. Does Rule 106 mean that parties to federal trials may not invoke the common-law rule? Read Rule 106 in conjunction with Rules 402 and 611(a). The McCormick treatise asserts that the common-law rule of completeness is not abrogated by Federal Rule of Evidence 106. 1 McCORMICK, EVIDENCE § 56, at 284 (6th ed. 2006). The Advisory Committee Note to Rule 106 states that "[t]he rule

does not in any way circumscribe the right of the adversary to develop the matter on cross-examination or as part of his own case."

As we shall see later in Chapter 12, in *Daubert v. Merrell Dow Pharmaceuticals*, 509 U.S. 579 (1993) the Supreme Court held that Federal Rule 402 impliedly supersedes uncodified exclusionary rules of evidence. Does Rule 402 sweep away uncodified procedural rules in the same way? Less than a handful of provisions in the Federal Rules deal with purely procedural issues. Moreover, the Federal Rules of Civil and Criminal Procedure regulate procedural issues in detail. In *Beech Aircraft Corp. v. Rainey*, 488 U.S. 153 (1988), the Supreme Court asserted that Rule 106 "partially codified" the common-law doctrine of completeness — indicating that the uncodified aspect of the doctrine is still in effect in federal practice.

3. Problem 4-8. In our torts case, Ms. Hill's husband is unavailable at the time of trial. Rather than calling her husband to the witness stand, Ms. Hill's attorney introduces pages 17–22 of his deposition relating to the signing of the written contract. The defendant would now like to introduce pages 23–30. Those pages also relate to the signing of the contract, but the plaintiff has a sound hearsay objection to the material on page 28. Does the rule of completeness override the hearsay objection? 1 McCormick, Evidence § 56, at 286–88 (6th ed. 2006) (a split of authority).

C. THE FORM OF THE EXAMINATION OF A WITNESS

1. In General

There are restraints on the form of a witness's examination as well as the examination's sequence and scope. The trial judge has discretionary control over the form of the examination. Although the judge has wide discretion at common law, in some areas the rulings have become so standardized that norms have emerged. Although most of these norms are common sense propositions, it is critical that the trial attorney master them, since most of the objections voiced at trial relate to problems of form rather than the substantive evidentiary doctrines. Consider these notes and problems.

NOTES AND PROBLEMS

1. Federal Rule of Evidence 611(a) gives the trial judge general, discretionary control over the form of questions at trial:

(a) Control by the court; Purposes. The court should exercise reasonable control over the mode and order of examining witnesses and presenting evidence so as to:

    (1) Make those procedures effective for determining the truth;

    (2) Avoid wasting time; and

    (3) Protect witnesses from harassment or undue embarrassment.

Some commentators assert that the common-law form rules survived the adoption of the Federal Rules. Langum, *Uncodified Federal Evidence Rules Applicable to Civil Trials*, 19 WILLAMETTE L. REV. 513, 516 (1983). However, other commentators argue that, under statutory provisions such as Rule 611(a), the common-law rules are now nonexistent. Graham, *California's "Restatement" of Evidence: Some Reflections on Appellate Repair of the Codification Fiasco*, 4 LOY. L.A. L. REV. 279, 281 (1971). Which view is sounder? *See* ADVISORY COMMITTEE'S NOTE to Rule 611(a), paragraph 1. If you are inclined toward the latter view, can you distinguish these form rules from the common-law completeness rule which arguably survived the adoption of Federal Rule 106?

2. **Problem 4-9.** In the *Devitt* case, during his case-in-chief, the prosecutor conducts the direct examination of Mr. Paterson. The prosecutor asks:

Q.   When you first spoke with the police, did you say that there had been a battery, and did you then identify the defendant as the attacker?

What objection would you as defense counsel raise? What is the danger of this form of question? As trial judge, would you sustain the objection?

3. **Problem 4-10.** On redirect of Mr. Paterson, for purposes of emphasis, the prosecutor wants to re-ask questions he had posed on direct examination. Can defense counsel object? What is the relevance of California Evidence Code § 774 "('A witness once examined cannot be reexamined as to the same matter without leave of the court....')."

4. **Problem 4-11.** During the defense's case-in-chief, your client, Mr. Devitt, takes the stand. The prosecutor conducts the cross-examination. Your client has a prior conviction that under the local law the prosecutor may use to impeach Devitt's credibility. He has also been arrested several times, but the arrests themselves are inadmissible for impeachment. On cross, the prosecutor asks:

Q.   What kind of trouble with the law have you had?

Can you object? On what ground? Do you evaluate the clarity of the question from the witness's perspective or the attorney's perspective? If the judge sustains your objection, what should the prosecutor do? Should the prosecutor completely abandon this line of inquiry?

5. **Problem 4-12.** During the same cross-examination of your client, the prosecutor asks:

Q.   And isn't it a fact that you were in the victim's apartment that day?

Devitt responds: Yes, but it wasn't a battery. As I've said all along, we got into an argument over how much I was going to charge him, and he threw the first punch.

What can the prosecutor do at this point to rein in a runaway witness? What procedural device should the prosecutor use? If the prosecutor calls the judge's attention to the problem but the judge concludes that the defendant's answer is otherwise admissible, must the trial judge grant the prosecutor the requested relief? Suppose that the defense attorney did not want the defendant to add that statement. Could the defense attorney request the same relief? If the only vice is that party of the answer exceeds the scope of the prosecutor's question, who is the aggrieved party? Suppose that the trial judge concludes that the nonresponsive part of the answer is so prejudicial that realistically, the jurors may be unable to follow a curative instruction to disregard it. On that assumption, what relief could the judge grant?

2.   Leading Questions

The above kinds of form problems arise with some frequency during the trial. The three most important form problems are (1) leading questions, (2) narrative questions, and (3) argumentative questions.

The definition of a "leading" question. California Evidence Code § 764 sets out one of the simplest — and best — definitions of a "leading" question:

> A "leading question" is a question that suggests to the witness the answer that the examining party desires.

Judges listen carefully to the way in which the attorney's question begins. If the question begins with words such as "who," "what," "which," "when," "where," "how," and "why," the judge usually assumes that the question is nonleading. These are natural interrogatory words, the way a layperson usually begins a question when he or she does not know what answer to expect. In contrast, questions that begin with words such as "is," "are," "were," "do," and "did," tend to be mildly leading. There are two ways of making a question strongly leading. The prosecutor could ask:

Q.   Isn't it a fact (Isn't it true) (Isn't it correct) (Won't you admit) (Won't you concede) that you were in his apartment that day?

Or, shifting to the very end of the question, the prosecutor could ask:

Q.   You were in his apartment that day. Isn't that true (Isn't that a fact) (Isn't that correct) (Won't you admit that) (Won't you concede that)?

The second query includes two sentences. The first sentence is a declarative assertion of a fact. The second sentence is a short question, sometimes referred to as a "tag." If after a few answers it is clear to the questioner that the witness is compliant, the questioner sometimes drops the "tag." The attorney simply makes assertions and signifies that the assertion is a question by raising his or her voice at the end of the sentence. This is sometimes called "conversational" cross-examination. Ruthberg, *Conversational Cross-Examination*, 29 Am.J.Trial Advoc. 353, 365–66 (2005).

NOTES AND PROBLEM

1.   Is a question automatically leading if it can be answered categorically, yes or no? If not, phrase a question for the defense counsel to ask Devitt on direct that can be answered categorically but is not leading. Be prepared to explain why the question is not leading.

2.   **Problem 4-13.** During the direct examination of Mr. Paterson, the prosecutor asks:

Q. At the lineup, did you pick out the man on the extreme right or the defendant who was standing roughly in the middle and wearing a blue jacket and brown slacks?

Though this question cannot be answered categorically, it is arguably still a leading question. Can you think of other ways to phrase a noncategorical question to make it leading? These types of subtly leading questions are the most difficult for the opponent to detect in the heat of battle at trial. The opponent must develop an "ear" for leading questions. A trial attorney has to be a good, intense listener.

Leading questions on direct examination. Psychological studies have found that testimony elicited by specific, leading questions is more complete — but less accurate — than testimony elicited by questions calling for narrative responses. Gardner, *The Perception and Memory of Witnesses*, 18 CORNELL L.Q. 391, 404 (1933); Marston, *Studies in Testimony*, 15 J. CRIM. L. & CRIMINOLOGY 1 (1924). That finding lends support to the rule restricting leading questions on direct in Federal Evidence Rule 611(c)(2):

> Leading questions. Leading questions should not be used on the direct examination of a witness except as may be necessary to develop the witness's testimony. Ordinarily, the court should allow leading questions: . . . when a party calls a hostile witness, an adverse witness, or a witness identified with an adverse party.

The fear is that through leading questions, the attorney can furnish the witness with "a false memory." *United States v. Hansen*, 434F.3d 92, 104–05 (1st Cir. 2006). Courts assume that the normal relationship between the direct examiner and the witness will be friendly and that a friendly, cooperative witness is likely to respond to a suggestive question by the attorney.

Contemporary courts and legislatures, however, have relaxed the rigor of the prohibition against leading questions on direct:

> We find no reported case in the last 50 years in which a reversal resulted solely from failure to control leading in the questioning process, and only one in which it was a major factor in the decision to reverse.

Denbeaux&Risinger, *Questioning Questions: Objections to Form in the Interrogation of Witnesses*, 33 ARK. L. REV. 439, 465 (1979). Rule 611(c)'s statutory language, "necessary to develop the witness's testimony," gives the trial judge wide discretion. *McCabe v. Parker*, 608 F.3d 1068, 1076–77 (8th Cir. 2010). As a practical matter, there are several more or less settled exceptions to the norm. The following notes illustrate some of the more important exceptions.

NOTES

1. The direct examiner may use leading questions on "preliminary" matters. For example, when the examiner is questioning the witness about the witness's personal background, leading questions are usually permitted. What is the justification for that exception? How broadly should "preliminary" facts be defined?

2. The direct examiner may use leading questions to interrogate a hostile witness. At common law, the witness became "hostile" only after there was some reflection of hostility on the record such as a refusal to answer or evasion. Contrast the approach of 611(c)(2). How does the rule differ from the common-law approach? When attorneys call adverse witnesses in jurisdictions with statutes such as Rule 611(c), they often announce, "Your Honor, I now call the defendant's wife as an adverse witness pursuant to Rule 611(c)."

3. The direct examiner may use leading questions to refresh the witness's memory when the witness's memory is "exhausted." How do you show on the record that the witness's memory is "exhausted"? Why does that justify deviating from the norm against leading questions on direct? If the direct examiner invokes this exception to the norm, should the judge require that the examiner first employ mildly leading questions before resorting to the "Isn't it true?" variety of leading questions?

4. The direct examiner may use leading questions to interrogate witnesses such as children, retarded persons, and persons who are not fluent in English. What characteristic do all these types of witnesses share? Do you see a connection between this exception and the last exception discussed in Note 3?

5. Many courts "liberally allow" specific, leading questions during the direct examination of an expert witness. 1 McCormick. Evidence § 6, at 27 (6th ed. 2006). What is the rationale for this exception to the norm? *See Dunn v. Owens-Corning Fiberglass*, 774 F. Supp. 929, 943 (D.V.I. 1991) ("complicated testimony"), *aff'd in part, vacated in part*, 1 F.3d 1362, 1371 (3d Cir. 1993).

Leading questions on cross-examination. In contrast to the norm for direct examination, the second sentence of Rule 611(c) assumes that the normal relationship between the witness and the cross-examiner is hostile. For that reason, the witness is much less likely to follow the lead of a suggestive question. Of course, that danger can arise in the rare case in which the relationship between the witness and the cross-examiner is a friendly one. Consider the Advisory Committee's Note to Rule 611(c):

> The rule . . . conforms to tradition in making the use of leading questions on cross-examination a matter of right. The purpose of the qualification "ordinarily" is to furnish a basis for denying the use of leading questions when the cross-examination is cross-examination in form only and not in fact, as for example the "cross-examination" of a party by his own counsel after being called by the opponent (savoring more of re-direct) or of an insured defendant who proves to be friendly to the plaintiff.

3. Questions Calling for a Narrative Response

If the attorney is convinced that the person is a good witness — a person who will project honesty and intelligence to the jury — the attorney usually prefers to elicit the witness's testimony by questions calling for a narrative. Because leading questions tend to elicit yes or no answers, leading such a witness will not present such a witness in her most persuasive light. If the witness gives a narrative, the witness is "displayed" to the maximum possible advantage; the jurors will have a substantial opportunity to observe and be impressed by the witness's sincerity and perception. To elicit a narrative response, the attorney makes the simple request, "In your own words, tell us what happened."

Even at common law in many jurisdictions, there is no absolute rule against narrative testimony. 1 McCormick, Evidence § 5, at 19 (6th ed. 2006). The trial judge has considerable discretion in deciding whether to permit such an examination, and a powerful case can be made for narrative testimony. Recall the psychological studies indicating that testimony elicited in this fashion is more trustworthy than testimony elicited in response to specific questions. Furthermore, as the preceding paragraph suggests, it is often tactically advantageous to elicit testimony in narrative form. Researchers at Duke University have studied the effect of different questioning styles on jurors. Conley, *Language in the Courtroom*, 15 Trial, Sept. 1979, at 32. They discovered that some jurors are acute enough to realize that a witness is being led rather than being asked to give a narrative response. Some of those jurors then infer that the questioning attorney lacks faith in the witness and consequently adopt the same attitude toward the witness — they discount the witness's credibility. *Id.* at 35.

NOTE

Given these advantages, what can explain the fact that trial judges are often reluctant to permit testimony in narrative form? What practical problems arise when the witness testifies in narrative form? Do all lay witnesses have a good sense of chronological organization? If a lay witness testifies without the benefit of chronological guidance in the form of leading questions, what problem will arise? Moreover, lay witnesses know little about the technical evidentiary rules. What problem might that present? Can the attorney calling the witness prevent these problems from materializing at trial by properly coaching the witness before trial?

4. Argumentative Questions

Leading and narrative questions are the form problems most frequently encountered on direct examination. On cross-examination, the most important form objection is that the question is "argumentative." We have already seen that opening statements may not be "argumentative." As is often the case in the law, though, we must beware the "one word-one meaning" trap: we must not assume that "argumentative" means the same thing here that it meant in the opening statement context. In fact, in this context, "argumentative" has another meaning.

"An argumentative question is a speech to the jury masquerading as a question." *People v. Higgins*, 191 Cal.App.4th 1075, 119 Cal.Rptr.3d 856, 873 (2011). Perhaps the best explanation of the concept is an article by a California trial judge: Goff, *Argumentative Questions: Counsel, Protect Your Witness!*, 49 Cal. St.B.J. 140 (1974). In the article, Judge Goff synthesizes the case law and advances the thesis that argumentative questions have two characteristics. Negatively, they are not designed to elicit new substantive testimony from the witness. Rather, affirmatively, they are calculated to challenge the witness with respect to an inference from testimony already in the record. The author gives numerous examples of objectionable argumentative questions, for example: "Do you mean that seriously? Well, now, can you reconcile the two statements? And you are telling us, are you, that when . . . [the sheriff] asked those questions and you gave those answers, you were telling the truth; is that right?" The author cautions, though, that in deciding whether a question is argumentative, the judge should consider not only the wording of the question but also the questioner's "voice, inflection, emphasis, and gestures accompanying the words." Obviously, since the trial transcript usually does not reflect those matters, the trial judge is in a much better position to regulate those matters than the appellate court.

NOTES AND PROBLEMS

1. Problem 4-14. Paterson is testifying in the *Devitt* case. The first part of this problem is an excerpt from his direct testimony. The second part is a section of his cross-examination. Identify all the possible objections to these questions.

The prosecutor has already elicited Paterson's testimony about the assault. Now the prosecutor turns to the identification of Devitt as the attacker:

Q1.	Mr. Paterson, you've just testified about the assault. Was the room where the attack occurred dark, or was it well lit with four 100-watt globes?
A.	It was welllit. I think there were four or five 100-watt globes in the room.
Q2.	Then there was nothing obstructing your view?
A.	No.
Q3.	Did you recognize the man who attacked you?
A.	Yes.
Q4.	And wasn't that man the defendant at the defense table right there?
A.	Yes.
Q5.	Had you ever had any difficulty with him before the day of the attack?
A.	No.
Q6.	Did you give him any provocation on that day or any other prior day?
A.	No.
Q7.	So he attacked you without any good reason. Isn't that true?
A.	Yes.
Q.	Thank you, Mr. Paterson. (Turning to the defense attorney.)Your witness.
Q8.	Mr. Paterson, I have a few questions I'd like to ask on cross-examination. Isn't it true that you told your daughter that you freely consented to have a fight with Mr. Devitt?
A.	Maybe I did, but later I said positively that I didn't.

Q9.   Please don't try to evade the question. I asked you about what you told your daughter. Isn't that what you told her?

A.   I guess so.

Q10.   All right. You told your daughter one thing. Now you tell us something different. Which story do you expect us to believe?

A.   The one I'm telling now because it's the truth.

Q11.   Sure. Let's shift to another topic to see if you can answer these questions. What was the lighting in the room where the alleged attack occurred?

A.   I already told you.

Q12.   I'm so interested that I'd love to hear it again.

A.   I told you that it was well lit.

Q13.   Let's be specific. Were all the light bulbs working? How good is your eyesight?

A.   Just fine.

2. **Problem 4-15.** Assume that the defense attorney is relatively unsuccessful in eliciting favorable responses from Paterson, becomes desperate, and decides to re-ask a number of the questions posed on direct in the faint hope that Paterson will change his story and make a prior inconsistent statement. Defense counsel begins asking questions such as, "So you say that Devitt attacked you. Correct?" The prosecutor objects, "Asked and answered." As trial judge, how would you rule on the objection? *See United States v. Caudle*, 606 F.2d 451, 456–58 (4th Cir. 1979) (objection overruled). Is California Evidence Code § 774 pertinent? As previously stated, that section provides that, '[a] witness once examined cannot be reexamined as to the same matter without leave of the court....' Would the defense attorney's repetition of a question posed by the prosecutor constitute a forbidden reexamination?

3. **Problem 4-16.** Assume that in answer to one question, Paterson does change his story. The defense counsel then asks, "Let's go over that again." Is this fact situation distinguishable from Problem 4-15?

4. The *form-of-the-question* objections that we have explored in this chapter do not exhaust all of the possibilities. Other common objections include:

•   The question is misleading and assumes [a fact] [facts] not in evidence.

•   Counsel is misquoting [the witness] [a prior witness].

•   The question is [ambiguous] [vague] [unintelligible].

•   Counsel is making a statement, not asking a question.

    Although the attorney can usually anticipate the substantive evidentiary issues such as hearsay that will arise at trial, form problems arise on the spur of the moment. The importance of identifying form problems on the spot is one of the reasons why a litigator's most important skill is listening.

Chapter 5

THE ROLES OF JUDGE, JURY AND ATTORNEYS

Read Federal Rules of Evidence 103 and 104.

A. THE ROLE OF THE ATTORNEYS IN THE ADMISSION AND EXCLUSION OF EVIDENCE

1. Pretrial Motions to Admit or Exclude Evidence

In our adversary system, the attorneys representing the parties are the primary movers in the process of determining the admissibility of evidence. A motion *in limine* may be made by either party. The proponent of an item of evidence can make a motion *in limine* (literally "at the threshold," or before the trial begins) to obtain an advance ruling admitting evidence; similarly, the opponent can make a motion *in limine* to exclude evidence. These motions are usually made in the judge's chambers before trial.

A pretrial motion to admit can have advantages for both the proponent and the trial judge. It may enhance the possibility of settling the case before trial, since settlement is more likely when the parties' predictions of the outcome of the case reach a certain congruity. A pretrial evidentiary ruling, which reduces uncertainty, can bring the parties' predictions closer together.

In addition, an advance ruling to admit an item of evidence may influence the proponent's trial strategy, for example, by affecting the party's opening statement. If there is uncertainty about whether certain evidence will be admitted, it is quite risky to mention that evidence in the opening statement. If the evidence ultimately is excluded, a mistrial may result. In any event, the party is likely to lose credibility in the eyes of the jury if the promised evidence is not forthcoming.

If certain evidence, particularly opinion testimony, will require a lengthy foundation, offering the evidence for the first time at trial can be quite risky. If after two hours of foundational testimony the judge rules the opinion inadmissible, the ruling may embarrass the proponent. Or the judge may conclude that the foundational testimony was so prejudicial that a curative instruction to disregard will be ineffective. When the judge reaches that conclusion but the jury has already heard the evidence, the judge may declare a mistrial.

Pretrial motions to exclude evidence come in two forms: Motions to *suppress* assert constitutional grounds for excluding evidence. *Mapp v. Ohio*, 367 U.S. 643 (1961). The defendant must ordinarily assert constitutional grounds for exclusion before trial under pain of waiver. Nonconstitutional grounds for excluding the evidence call for a motion *in limine*. R. CARLSON, SUCCESSFUL TECHNIQUES FOR CIVIL TRIALS Ch.1 (2ded. 1992).

One example of a pretrial *in limine* motion to exclude arises in civil automobile accident cases in certain jurisdictions in which evidence that one of the drivers has consumed alcohol is not, by itself, admissible; there must also be evidence to show that the drinking resulted in intoxication. *E.g., McGrew v. Pearlman*, 710 N.E.2d 125, 130 (Ill. App. Ct. 1999). If the defendant's attorney suspects (or expects) that the plaintiff's attorney might attempt to insinuate that the defendant had been drinking shortly before the accident, but there was insufficient evidence of intoxication, the defense attorney could move *in limine* to bar any reference to the drinking.

In a criminal case, many jurisdictions permit the judge to exclude evidence of prior convictions that are similar to the crime for which the defendant is on trial. If the prosecutor is allowed to introduce evidence of those convictions for the stated purpose of impeaching the defendant's credibility, there is a grave risk that the jurors will misuse the evidence. Rather than limiting their consideration of the evidence to the evaluation of credibility, the jurors might decide to convict simply to protect society even if they are not convinced beyond a reasonable doubt that he is guilty of the crime charged. In this situation, the defense attorney might move *in limine* to prohibit any mention of the prior convictions at trial. We will discuss this issue in detail in Chapter 14 when we consider the subject of character evidence.

The trial judge generally has discretion whether to entertain a motion *in limine*, though there are situations in which a judge arguably has a duty to decide a pretrial motion to admit or exclude. A few jurisdictions require the trial judge to rule on a criminal defendant's *in limine* motion challenging the use of his or her prior convictions for impeachment, as described above. *E.g., People v. Patrick*, 233 Ill.2d 62, 330 Ill. Dec. 149, 908 N.E.2d 1 (2009). However, many evidentiary issues cannot be decided pretrial; the admissibility of the item of evidence often depends on the posture of the rest of the record that is created during the trial. Courts often caution that a trial judge should grant an *in limine* motion to exclude evidence "only when the evidence is clearly inadmissible on all potential grounds." *In re Methyl Tertiary Butyl Ether Litigation*, 643 F. Supp. 2d 461, 463 (S.D.N.Y. 2009).

Suppose that the judge entertains the motion to exclude on the merits but denies the motion before trial. Must the defense attorney make renew the objection at trial to preserve the issue for appeal? Until 2000, the answer was uncertain and the case law was in conflict. The issue was resolved by a 2000 amendment to Rule 103(a)(2). The substance of the amendment is now set out in restyled Rule 103(b): "Once the court rules definitively on the record — either before or at trial — a party need not renew an objection or offer of proof to preserve a claim of error for appeal." *E.g., Abraham v. BP America Production Co.*, 685 F.3d 1196 (10th Cir. 2012)(a definitive ruling).

According to the Advisory Committee Note accompanying the 2000 amendment:

The amendment imposes the obligation on counsel to clarify whether the *in limine* . . . ruling is definitive when there is doubt on that point. *See, e.g., Walden v. Georgia-Pacific Corp.*, 126 F.3d 506, 520 (3d Cir. 1997) (although "the district court told plaintiffs' counsel not to reargue every ruling, it did not countermand its clear opening statement that all of its rulings were tentative, and counsel never requested clarification"). Even where the court's ruling is definitive, nothing in the amendment prohibits the court from revisiting its decision when the evidence is offered. If the court changes its initial ruling, or if the opposing party violates the terms of the initial ruling, objection must be made when the evidence is offered to preserve the claim of error for appeal. The error, if any, in such a situation occurs only when the evidence is offered and admitted.

2.   Offering Evidence at Trial

Suppose that the plaintiff's attorney in a civil tort case wants to introduce a letter written by an employee of the defendant company because the letter contains language that could be construed as an express warranty. The *sponsoring witness* for the letter is a casual acquaintance of the employee; the witness is somewhat familiar with the person's handwriting style.

Following is an illustration of a typical exchange that might occur in such a case:

Q1:	(To the judge) I request that this be marked plaintiff's exhibit number one for identification.
J:	It will be so marked.
Q2:	(To the judge) Please let the record reflect that I am showing the exhibit to the opposing counsel.
J:	It will so reflect.
Q3:	(To the judge) I request permission to approach the witness. J.Granted.
Q4:	(To the witness) I now hand you plaintiff's exhibit number one for identification. What is it?
A:	A letter from the defendant's sales manager.
Q5:	How do you recognize it?
A:	I know his handwriting style.
Q6:	How did you become familiar with his handwriting style? A. We're close friends and associates.
A:	We're close friends and associates.
Q7:	How long have you known him?
A:	At least five years.
Q8:	How often have you seen him sign his name?
A:	Probably tens of times.
Q9:	(To the judge) Your Honor, I now offer [or move the admission of] plaintiff's exhibit number one for identification into evidence as plaintiff's exhibit one.

[Opposing counsel would object at this point if an objection is appropriate.]

J: [Overruled.] The exhibit will be received.

Q10:   (To the judge) Your Honor, I request permission to publish the exhibit to the jurors and allow them to inspect the exhibit at this time.

J: Permission granted.

We shall now dissect this line of questioning.

Marking the exhibit and showing it to the opponent and witness. (Questions 1 through 4). Note that the proponent described the letter only as "plaintiff's exhibit number one for identification." Some jurisdictions permit the proponent to go a bit farther and say, "the letter marked as plaintiff's exhibit number one for identification."

However, the proponent attorney may not reveal the contents of the document prior to its admission. For example, the proponent may not refer to the document as "a letter signed by the defendant." If he or she did so, in effect, this would amount to testifying though the attorney is not under oath. The record will also be much clearer if the proponent uses the accepted expression "plaintiff's exhibit number one for identification."

The foundation or predicate. (Questions 5 through 8). The expressions "foundation" and "predicate" refer to the testimony the proponent must introduce before offering any item of evidence, including the letter in this example. The substantive evidentiary doctrines discussed in the remainder of this book dictate the content of the foundation for the various types of evidence that may be offered. In our hypothetical, the only foundation the proponent must lay is authentication. As we shall see in Chapter 9, the rules of evidence require that documents such as letters be authenticated as a condition precedent to admission. The proponent, to satisfy the authentication requirement, must prove that the article is what it is purported to be; if the plaintiff claims that the article is a letter written by the defendant, the plaintiff can lay the foundation by presenting the testimony of one of the defendant's acquaintances that the letter is written in the defendant's hand-writing style.

Although the judge commonly requires that the proponent lay the foundation before offering the exhibit, the judge has discretion to admit the exhibit condition-ally on the proponent's assurance that the necessary foundational testimony will be introduced later. In such a case, if the proponent fails to complete the foundation prior to resting, the opponent should move to strike the exhibit. Although the judge may permit the proponent to reopen his or her case to complete the foundation, intervening events may have made it difficult for the proponent to supply the missing foundational testimony. And without a key exhibit, the opponent may be in a position to move successfully for judgment as a matter of law (in some jurisdictions called a "directed verdict").

The formal tender or motion for admission. (Question 9). When the proponent believes that the foundation is complete, the proponent formally tenders the exhibit into evidence. In some jurisdictions, the proponent "move[s] the admission of plaintiff's exhibit number one for identification into evidence as plaintiff's exhibit one." In other jurisdictions, the proponent "offers" the exhibit into evidence. The formal tender is the opponent's signal to make any objections such as hearsay or lack of authentication; the tender is the trigger for those objections.

The publication of the exhibit to the jury. (Question 10). If the court admits the exhibit, the attorney may want to get the exhibit into the jurors' hands immediately. Reading the exhibit may be essential to the jurors' understanding of the balance of the witness's testimony. In other cases, the attorney may want to defer publishing the exhibit until the end of the witness's testimony in order to avoid distracting the jury during the testimony.

If the court decides not to admit the exhibit, the next step can be critical.

The offer of proof. Federal Evidence Rule 103 states: "(a) Preserving a Claim of Error. A party may claim error in a ruling to. . . exclude evidence only if the error affects a substantial right of the party and (2) If the ruling excludes evidence, a party informs the court of its substance by an offer of proof, unless the substance was apparent from the context."

This is the so-called "offer of proof" or "avowal" procedure. If the judge sustains an objection to the tender of evidence, the proponent generally must make an offer proof in order to preserve the issue for appeal. If the proponent fails to make such an offer, any error is ordinarily waived. The proponent can lose the right to challenge the most important adverse ruling during the trial simply because the proponent neglected to comply with Rule 103(a)(2). In addition to this formal function, offers of proof may serve the practical functions of educating the trial judge as to the relevance of the evidence as well as creating a clear record for the appellate court of what the evidence would have shown had it been admitted.

As an example of an offer of proof, suppose that, in the *Hill* case, the defendant Polecat Motors wishes to present evidence of a telephone conversation between the witness, Jenkins, and Ms. Hill. The foundation would be proof that Jenkins is familiar with Ms. Hill's voice. The tender is the question, "And what did Ms. Hill say during that telephone conversation?" If the plaintiff's counsel thought that the foundation was inadequate, the plaintiff would object. If the judge agreed and sustained an authentication objection, the proponent might use this procedure:

Q: Your Honor, may I approach the bench?

J: Yes.

Q: Your Honor, I would like to make an offer of proof for the record.

J: Very well. Proceed.

Q: If you had permitted the witness to answer the question, the witness would have testified that in this conversation, Ms. Hill stated that she had made a full recovery from her injuries. I would like to offer this evidence as an admission that her testimony in this case concerning her injuries is exaggerated. The witness is sufficiently familiar with Ms. Hill's voice to identify it; the witness has already testified that he's spoken face to face with Ms. Hill "on numerous occasions."

The last "Q" is the offer of proof.

3. Objections to Evidence at Trial

If the opponent waits until trial to object to admission of evidence, three questions arise.

1. What procedural device may be used to assert the ground for excluding the evidence? The most common device is an objection. The opponent uses such phrasing as:

"Objection, Your Honor. The question."

"Your Honor, I object to the question on the ground that."

An objection is a challenge to the question itself; it can raise either the contention that the question's *form* is improper or the argument that the question calls for *substantively* inadmissible evidence.

A motion to strike, by comparison, challenges the witness's answer rather than the proponent's question. For example, if a witness unexpectedly refers to inadmissible hearsay, the opponent might use this language:

"Your Honor, I move to strike the last sentence on the ground that it contains a reference to incompetent hearsay."

The opponent may also resort to a motion in situations where the witness has already given some testimony and it later becomes apparent that the testimony was inadmissible, or where the witness begins the answer so quickly that the opponent does not have a fair opportunity to object to an improper question. In the latter situation, the opponent moves to strike the answer "for the purpose of interposing an objection to the question."

2. When should the ground be asserted? The objection or motion must be "timely." If the asserted ground challenges the question, the opponent should voice the objection before the witness begins the answer. If the ground relates to the answer, the opponent should ordinarily make the motion before the examiner poses the next question.

Just as an objection is not timely if it is voiced too late, it can also violate the timeliness requirement if it is premature. When the ground for the objection is the violation of a form rule (such as "leading"), the opposing attorney may state the objection as soon as the improper question is posed. However, when the ground is substantive (such as a violation of the hearsay doctrine), the opposing attorney must ordinarily wait until the proponent of the item of evidence seeks to actually introduce the inadmissible item of evidence. For example, the opposing attorney should not object when the proponent asks the witness: "Did the driver say anything?" The objection is proper when the proponent asks the question actually calling for the inadmissible hearsay: "What did he say?"

3. *How should the objection or motion be phrased?* In addition to being "timely," an objection or motion must be "specific." The case law requires that the objection be specific in several respects.

First, the objection must specify <u>the part of the question or answer</u> the opponent is challenging. It is best to identify the very word, phrase, or sentence the opponent believes is improper. The requirement for specificity explains why it is so critical that the trial attorney be a good listener.

Second, the objection should specify <u>the party on whose behalf</u> the objection is being asserted. Suppose that Devitt were being tried with an alleged conspirator, who had confessed; the confession would be admissible against the conspirator but might be inadmissible hearsay as against Devitt. If you represent both Devitt and his alleged conspirator and the prosecutor has just asked the question calling for the conspirator's confession, you should state that you are objecting "on behalf of the defendant Devitt" or that the confession is inadmissible "as against the defendant Devitt."

Finally, the objection must specify <u>the ground(s) on which it is based,</u> namely, the evidentiary rule(s) being violated. FRE 103(a)(1)(B) provides: "Preserving a claim of error. A party may claim error in a ruling to admit . . . evidence only if the error submits a substantial right of the party and: (1) If the ruling admits evidence, a party, on the record: (B) states the specific ground, unless it was apparent from the context.

In most jurisdictions, a general objection such as "incompetent and inadmissible" does not preserve an error for appeal. However, the traditional view is that it is sufficient to name the generic evidentiary rule being violated:

"Your Honor, I object to the introduction of that letter for lack of authentication."

"Your Honor, I object to the introduction of that copy on the ground that it is not the best evidence."

"Your Honor, I object to that question on the ground that it calls for inadmissible hearsay."

The titles of the articles in the Federal Rules provide the appropriate wording for the objection. For example, the title of Article VII refers to "opinion," Article VIII to "hearsay," and Article IX to "authentication." Most judges would accept phrasing mentioning "improper opinion," "inadmissible hearsay," or "inadequate authentication."

In some situations, though, it is safer to be more specific. There is a risk that an appellate court may demand greater specificity than the traditional view. For example, in *United States v. Fendley*, 522 F.2d 181 (5th Cir. 1975), the defendant was convicted of tax offenses. On appeal, he claimed that the trial judge had improperly admitted a computer printout, on the ground that the government had not complied with the business records hearsay exception. The court noted that business records are admissible under this exception if three conditions are met: (1) The records must be kept pursuant to a routine procedure designed to assure their accuracy; (2) they must be created for motives that would tend to assure accuracy (preparation for litigation is not such a motive); and (3) they must not be mere accumulations of hearsay or uninformed opinion. Defendant's objection at trial was worded as follows:

"Then, Your Honor, we will renew our objection to Government's exhibit 9-108-B [sic] on the basis that there is no showing that the instrument is accurate as to the figures it reflects;

"And that the preparer was someone other than the witness here; that we cannot determine the accuracy of it, and therefore, it shouldn't be admitted;

"Because it would be hearsay and, again I cannot cross-examine the paper, obviously, without having the party assigned to compiling the figures on it before us.

"We object on that basis."

The appellate court held that this was an insufficient, vague hearsay objection (*id.* at 185, 186–87):

[T]his loosely formulated and imprecise objection at most comes to this: (1) the document was hearsay; (2) the witness laying the foundation for its introduction was someone other than the preparer; and (3) the witness laying the foundation was unable to personally attest to the accuracy of the figures contained in the document. . . . The grounds asserted in the defendant's objection are clearly insubstantial. While obviously the document was hearsay, this in itself fails to state an objection.

However, *Fendley* is a distinct minority view. Most courts believe that it is unfair to demand that the opponent be that specific – and in effect educate the proponent about the relevant Evidence law.

B.   THE ROLE OF THE TRIAL JUDGE

It is a commonplace observation that during the trial the judge resolves "questions of law" while the petit jurors decide "questions of fact." However, the distinction between law and fact is sometimes quite unclear; furthermore, certain preliminary factual questions are reserved for the judge. Some commentators have therefore suggested that we entirely abandon the law-fact dichotomy and speak rather in terms of jury questions and judge questions. H. HART & A. SACKS, THE LEGAL PROCESS: BASIC PROBLEMS IN THE MAKING AND APPLICATION OF LAW 344–60 (Eskridge & Frickey eds., 1994).

1.   Questions of Law

The trial judge always decides pure questions of law. Depending on the jurisdiction and the type of case, sometimes the judge also resolves questions of law that have a fact component, often referred to as "mixed questions of law and fact." Under Rule 403, for instance, the judge has discretion to exclude evidence where the dangers of prejudice, confusion, or undue time consumption outweigh the probative value of the evidence. Since the judge must assess the probative value of the evidence in order to make this balancing decision, it is not a pure question of law. However, it also is not a pure issue of fact in the same sense as jury decisions such as how fast Worker's vehicle was going when it struck Ms. Hill's car.

2.   Preliminary Facts Conditioning the Admissibility of Evidence

The statement that jurors decide questions of fact is an over simplification. The jurors do resolve questions of historical fact on the merits of dispute, but often the judge must also rule on questions of fact. Because the judge must determine the admissibility of proffered items of evidence, which often requires a factual determination, judges frequently decide so-called "preliminary" issues of fact. Rule 104 addresses this subject:

(a)   In General. The court must decide any preliminary question about whether a witness is qualified, a privilege exists, or evidence is admissible. In so deciding, the court is not bound by evidence rules, except those on privilege.

(b)   Relevance That Depends on a Fact. When the relevance of evidence depends on whether a fact exists, proof must be introduced sufficient to support a finding that the fact does exist. The court may admit the proposed evidence on the condition that the proof be introduced later.

Rule 104 indicates that there are two types of preliminary facts. The first type, governed by subsection (a), is decided by the judge. The second, controlled by subsection (b), is decided by the jurors; the trial judge makes only the limited determination that the proponent has introduced "evidence sufficient to support a [rational] finding" of the existence of the fact.

What is the basis of the distinction between these two types of preliminary facts? The preliminary fact of a document's authenticity is an example of a Rule 104(b) conditional relevance question. Jurors are not only capable of deciding such a straightforward factual question; even more to the point, we can also be confident that if the jurors decide the document is a forgery, common sense will lead them to disregard it as irrelevant. These preliminary facts "condition" the logical relevance of the evidence in a fundamental sense that is evident even to lay jurors. Contrast the fact of a third party's presence at an attorney-client conversation, a fact that falls under Rule 104(a). If the third party was present to the knowledge of the attorney and client, that presence ordinarily negates the privacy needed for the attorney-client privilege to attach. On the one hand, jurors are certainly competent to decide the factual question whether a third party was physically present at the conversation. On the other hand, assume that the conversation contains a damaging admission by the client. Even if the jurors decide that no third party was present and that the conversation was consequently privileged, can we have the same confidence that the jurors will be able to disregard the damaging admission during deliberation?

This distinction between 104(a) facts for the judge, and 104(b) facts for the jury is among the most difficult topics in evidence law. Probably the most detailed and explicit treatment of the topic appears in the text and Assembly Committee Notes for California Evidence Code §§ 403 and 405. Section 403 roughly corresponds to Federal Rule 104(b), while § 405 corresponds to Federal Rule 104(a):

§ 403. Determination of foundational and other preliminary facts where relevancy, personal knowledge, or authenticity is disputed.

(a) The proponent of the proffered evidence has the burden of producing evidence as to the existence of the preliminary fact, and the proffered evidence is inadmissible unless the court finds that there is evidence sufficient to sustain a finding of the existence of the preliminary fact, when:

   (1) The relevance of the proffered evidence depends on the existence of the preliminary fact;

   (2) The preliminary fact is the personal knowledge of a witness concerning the subject matter of his testimony;

   (3) The preliminary fact is the authenticity of a writing; or

   (4) The proffered evidence is of a statement or other conduct of a particular person and the preliminary fact is whether that person made the statement or so conducted himself.

(b) Subject to Section 402, the court may admit conditionally the proffered evidence under this section, subject to evidence of the preliminary fact being supplied later in the course of the trial.

(c) If the court admits the proffered evidence under this section, the court:

   (1) May, and on request shall, instruct the jury to determine whether the preliminary fact exists and to disregard the proffered evidence unless the jury finds that the preliminary fact does exist.

   (2) Shall instruct the jury to disregard the proffered evidence if the court subsequently determines that a jury could not reasonably find that the preliminary fact exists.

§ 405. Determination of foundational and other preliminary facts in other cases

With respect to preliminary fact determinations not governed by Section 403 . . . :

(a) When the existence of a preliminary fact is disputed, the court shall indicate which party has the burden of producing evidence and the burden of proof on the issue as implied by the rule of law under which the question arises. The court shall determine the existence or nonexistence of the preliminary fact and shall admit or exclude the proffered evidence as required by the rule of law under which the question arises.

(b) If a preliminary fact is also a fact in issue in the action:

   (1) The jury shall not be informed of the court's determination as to the existence or nonexistence of the preliminary fact.

(2)   If the proffered evidence is admitted, the jury shall not be instructed to disregard the evidence if its determination of the fact differs from the court's determination of the preliminary fact.

Comment — Assembly Committee on Judiciary

* * *

Illustrative of the preliminary fact questions that should be decided under Section 405 are the following:

Section 701 — Disqualification of a witness for lack of mental capacity. Under existing law, as under this code, the party objecting to a proffered witness has the burden of proving the witness' lack of capacity. . . .

Section 720 — Qualifications of an expert witness. Under Section 720, as under existing law, the proponent must persuade the judge that his expert is qualified, and it is error for the judge to submit the qualifications of the expert to the jury. . . .

Sections 900-1070 — Privileges. Under this code, as under existing law, the party claiming a privilege has the burden of proof on the preliminary facts. . . . The proponent of the proffered evidence, however, has the burden of proof upon any preliminary fact necessary to show that an exception to the privilege is applicable. . . .

Sections 1200-1341 — Hearsay evidence. When hearsay evidence is offered, two preliminary fact questions may be raised. The first question relates to the authenticity of the proffered declaration — was the statement actually made by the person alleged to have made it? The second question relates to the existence of those circumstances that make the hearsay sufficiently trustworthy to be received in evidence — e.g., was the declaration spontaneous, the confession voluntary, the business record trustworthy? Under this code, questions relating to the authenticity of the proffered declaration are decided under Section 403. But other preliminary fact questions are decided under Section 405. For example, the court must decide whether a statement offered as a dying declaration was made under a sense of impending death, and the proponent of the evidence has the burden of proof on this issue. . . .

Sections 1500-1510 — Best evidence rule. Under Section 405, as under existing law, the trial judge is required to determine the preliminary fact necessary to warrant reception of secondary evidence of a writing, and the burden of proof on the issue is on the proponent of the secondary evidence. . . .

NOTES AND PROBLEMS

1.   Some writers have criticized the manner in which the California Evidence Code applies the distinction to various preliminary facts. California recognizes the hearsay exceptions for statements made by agents and coconspirators. CAL. EVID. CODE §§ 1222–23. In its comment to Evidence Code § 403, the Assembly Committee states: "[A]uthorized admissions [by an agent of a party] . . . are admitted upon the introduction of evidence sufficient to sustain a finding of the foundational fact. The

admission of a co-conspirator is another form of an authorized admission. Hence, the proffered evidence is admissible upon the introduction of evidence sufficient to sustain a finding of the conspiracy." Many jurisdictions, including the federal courts, treat these preliminary issues instead as facts conditioning the admissibility of evidence (104(a)) rather than its logical relevance (104(b)). *See Bourjaily v. United States*, 483 U.S. 171 (1987). Which position is sounder?

2.   There has also been criticism of the line drawn by the Supreme Court in *Huddleston v. United States*, 485 U.S. 681 (1988). In that case, under Federal Rule of Evidence 404(b), the prosecution intended to offer evidence of other crimes allegedly committed by the defendant. The question was whether the judge or the jury should decide the factual issue of the defendant's identity as the perpetrator of the other crimes. Prior to *Huddleston*, most jurisdictions assumed that the judge should resolve that question under 104(a). However, in *Huddleston*, the Court declared that the issue falls under Rule 104(b). Justice Rehnquist reasoned that if the jurors decided that the defendant did not commit the alleged prior act, common sense would naturally lead them to disregard any testimony about it.

Several states have refused to follow *Huddleston*. Minnesota amended its version of Rule 404(b) to reject *Huddleston* in criminal cases. *See also People v. Garner*, 806 P.2d 366 (Colo. 1991) (the judge should use the preponderance standard); *Phillips v. State*, 591 So. 2d 987 (Fla. Dist. Ct. App. 1991) (clear and convincing evidence).

3.   At this juncture, it is expected that you will find the Federal Rule 104(a)–(b) material difficult. You cannot master these materials until you understand the individual evidentiary doctrines conditioned by these preliminary facts. However, we shall use two problems to illustrate the procedures.

4.   **Problem 5-1.** In *Devitt*, assume that the defendant wants to introduce evidence that Paterson, the victim, was grossly intoxicated at the relevant time. The hospital that treated Paterson tested a blood sample, and the defendant wants to introduce the hospital laboratory report stating that a lab technician named Peters tested the blood sample and found a blood alcohol content of 0.19 percent. To lay the foundation, the defense attorney calls Ms. Imbau, the chief of the hospital lab. Ms. Imbau testifies that she is familiar with Peters' handwriting style and that the signature on the report "generally looks like Peters' writing." The defendant then offers the document in evidence, but the prosecutor objects on authentication grounds.

Is the preliminary question whether the document is genuine a question for the judge under FRE 104(a) or for the jury under FRE 104(b)? Why?

Is Ms. Imbau's testimony sufficient to satisfy Rule 104(b)? In other words, does the testimony have sufficient probative value to permit a rational juror to find that the document is genuine?

If it does, must the judge listen to controverting evidence from the government before admitting the document? If not, when does the prosecutor present evidence attacking the document's authenticity, such as testimony of a questioned document examiner that the report is forged?

Does the judge finally decide whether the document is genuine? Does the jury? If the jury makes the final decision, what should the judge tell the jury during the instructions about the authenticity of the exhibit?

5.   **Problem 5-2.** Assume next that the prosecutor also objects that the report is hearsay (a statement prepared out of court by a person who is not on the witness stand now). The defendant attempts to qualify the report as a business record (which would make it admissible hearsay under one of the many exceptions to the rule against hearsay). One of the requirements of the business records exception is that the report have been prepared in the regular course of business "at or near the time" of the fact recorded. The witness, Ms. Imbau, testified to that effect; but the prosecutor has evidence from another witness that the lab technician who wrote the report was very sloppy and did not prepare the report until several months after the test.

Does the preliminary factual question whether the document was timely prepared in the regular course of business fall under Rule 104(a) or 104(b)?

Under 104(a), would the judge consider only the defendant's evidence before deciding whether the document was timely prepared? Assume that the witness who claims that the report was actually prepared months after the test is present and prepared to testify. Should the judge hear the testimony before ruling whether the exhibit qualifies as a business record?

When the opponent believes that he or she has the right to present contrary evidence before the judge rules on a tender of evidence, counsel asks permission to "take the witness on *voir dire* examination." We have already encountered the *voir dire* of prospective jurors. This is a second meaning of the expression "*voir dire.*" If opposing counsel takes the witness on *voir dire*, the opponent conducts a cross-examination in the middle of the proponent's direct examination of the witness.

Does the judge rule finally on this preliminary fact?

6.   **Problem 5-3.** It is conceivable that a preliminary fact will coincide with a fact on the historical merits of the case. For instance, assume that a criminal defendant is charged with rape. Defendant claims that he was married to the complaining witness at the time of the alleged attack and, hence, under the law of his jurisdiction (Morena) he cannot be guilty of rape. Assume that under Morena's substantive criminal law, a husband cannot be convicted of raping his wife. Although the prosecutor has learned that defendant and the complaining witness went through a marriage ceremony, the prosecutor also discovered that defendant was previously married. The prosecutor believes that defendant's marriage to the complaining witness was bigamous and void. At trial, the prosecutor calls the complainant, wife number two. Defendant objects that as his wife, she is incompetent to testify against him. (Assume Morena does not recognize the injured spouse exception to the marital disqualification in this type of case.) The judge must rule on the admissibility of evidence, including the competency of witnesses. His decision turns on resolving the question of whether defendant is lawfully married to the second wife. Yet, is not that one of the very issues the jury is supposed to decide? It may be helpful to consider Federal Evidence Rule 104(c). That rule gives the judge the opportunity of ruling on the admissibility of evidence out of the jury's hearing. If the

judge decided that defendant was not lawfully married to the second wife and, on that theory, permitted her to testify, should the judge inform the jury of the judge's finding of fact? Note the guidance in CAL. EVID. CODE § 405(b).

C. THE ROLE OF THE PETIT JURORS

1. Questions of Law

At early American law in many jurisdictions, jurors had power to decide questions of law. John Jay, the first Chief Justice of the United States, recognized the widespread practice of trial judges informing jurors that they had the power to ignore the judicial instructions on the law. However, since the Supreme Court's 1895 decision in *Sparf v. United States*, 156 U.S. 51 (1895), the marked trend has been toward restricting the jury's authority to decide issues of law. While contemporary jurors thus have no formal power to determine questions of law, in the secrecy of their deliberations they may decide to disregard the law. For example, if jurors believe that an applicable rule of law as charged by the judge is unjust, they can "nullify" that rule — perhaps by acquitting a technically guilty defendant or by compensating a comparatively negligent plaintiff. In some jurisdictions, nullification is considered jury misconduct and is grounds for a new trial; but as we shall see in Chapter 7 a shroud of secrecy surrounds jury deliberations and makes it very difficult to know whether and when nullification has occurred. Most trial judges forbid an attorney — sometimes under threat of contempt — from inviting the jury to nullify the controlling substantive law.

2. Questions of Fact on the Historical Merits

The term "fact" typically refers to the historical data relevant to adjudicating the merits of the dispute: what happened, where, when, why, and to whom? The primary role of the jury is to decide these disputed questions of historical fact, although, often, juries also decide mixed questions of law and fact (e.g., whether the defendant acted "negligently").

To provide an accurate picture, we must point out that most adjudicative hearings in the United States are bench trials without a jury. In a bench hearing, the trial judge, magistrate, or administrative law judge also serves as the trier of fact.

Furthermore, juries resolve only *disputed* questions of fact. In some cases, the evidence on one side is so overwhelming that any rational juror would accept that evidence and enter a verdict accordingly. In these extreme cases, the facts are so clear and so one-sided that the judge may decide "as a matter of law." When he or she does so, the judge takes the case (or a factual issue in the case) away from the jury and announces the party's victory on the case in whole or part. Note, however, that the judge is forbidden to find such facts in favor of the prosecution in criminal cases because of the constitutional right of criminal defendants to trial by jury.

3. Preliminary Questions of Fact Conditioning Admissibility

While the jury's power over questions of law has waned, its power over preliminary questions of fact has increased. Under the early English view, the trial judge had the exclusive authority to decide preliminary facts; today, the jury shares some of that power. As described in section B, this jury power to resolve questions of foundational or preliminary fact turns on whether the factual issue falls under Rule 104(a) or Rule 104(b).

In most jurisdictions, the only preliminary issues of fact that are reserved for the jury are so-called "conditional relevancy" issues. With respect to those facts, which are reserved to the jury by Federal Rule 104(b), the judge plays a limited, screening role: the judge decides only whether the proponent's evidence is sufficient to support a finding by a reasonable jury that the fact exists. In making that decision, the judge accepts the testimony at face value and does not consider its credibility. If the foundational testimony is facially sufficient, the judge admits the evidence and the jury exercises ultimate fact-finding power to decide whether, for example, a letter was genuine. The letter is conditionally relevant because it is logically relevant only on the condition that it is genuine. Once the proponent fulfills the condition by presenting sufficient evidence of the letter's genuineness, the letter is admissible; the jury can then make a final decision on the letter's authenticity.

NOTES AND PROBLEM

1. As we have seen, under Rule 104(b) the jurors finally decide preliminary facts conditioning pure logical relevance. However, the judge must decide the preliminary facts conditioning almost all other evidentiary doctrines — for example, the opinion rule, best evidence, hearsay, and privilege. If these issues are preliminary "facts," why allocate this authority to the judge? We earlier suggested that the allocation is a reflection of the system's skeptical view of the jury's capacity to properly weigh certain types of evidence. Consider also the related administrative problems. If the jury were to decide these preliminary questions, how would that affect the conduct of the trial? If the jurors reserved all their determinations of preliminary facts until the jury deliberations, how would that affect the complexity of the final jury deliberations? What "mental gymnastics" would the jurors have to engage in?

2. **Problem 5-4.** In *Devitt*, the prosecutor has a confession signed by the defendant. In his confession, Devitt admits that he attacked Paterson. Morena procedure permits Devitt to delay any objection to the admissibility of the confession until trial, and Devitt does so. When the prosecutor attempts to introduce the confession, Devitt objects on voluntariness grounds. To support his objection, Devitt testifies as follows: that just before the interrogation he had experienced sharp abdominal pains; he had taken some sedatives to ease the pain; he was groggy when the questioning began; during the questioning, the police refused to let him go to the bathroom; and he finally gave the police the admissions they wanted after they threatened him with violence. The interrogating officer denies Devitt's charges.

The voluntariness of the confession is a preliminary fact that determines the admissibility of the confession. Who should decide this preliminary fact — judge or jury? In addition to analyzing this question under the evidence rules, consider the potential constitutional dimensions of the problem. *See Jackson v. Denno*, 378 U.S. 368 (1964).

D. PROOF OF FOUNDATIONAL FACTS

There is one final, notable provision in Rule 104(a). The last sentence reads: "In so deciding, the court is not bound by evidence rules, except those on privilege." *See also* Rule 1101(d)(1). At first blush, it seems heretical and self-contradictory for an evidence code to dispense with compliance with evidentiary rules. What is the meaning of that sentence? The Supreme Court explored that question in the following case.

BOURJAILY v. UNITED STATES
483 U.S. 171 (1987)

CHIEF JUSTICE REHNQUIST delivered the opinion of the Court.

Federal Rule of Evidence 801(d)(2)(E) provides, "A statement is not hearsay if . . . [t]he statement is offered against a party and is . . . a statement by a coconspirator of a party during the course and in furtherance of the conspiracy." We granted certiorari to answer [two] questions regarding the admission of statements under Rule 801(d)(2)(E): (1) whether the court must determine by independent evidence that the conspiracy existed and that the defendant and the declarant were members of this conspiracy; [and] (2) the quantum of proof on which such determinations must be based.

[In 1984 Greathouse, an FBI informant, arranged a sale of cocaine to Lonardo. Lonardo agreed that he would find individuals to distribute the drug. In a conversation before the sale, Lonardo stated that he had a "gentleman friend" who had some questions about cocaine. In a subsequent telephone call, Greathouse spoke to the "friend" about the drug's price and quality. Greathouse then spoke again with Lonardo. They agreed that the sale would take place in a designated parking lot, and Lonardo would transfer the drug from Greathouse's car to the "friend" waiting in the parking lot in his own car. Greathouse proceeded with the transaction. FBI agents arrested Lonardo and petitioner immediately after Lonardo placed the drugs in petitioner's car in the parking lot. The agents found over $20,000 in the car. At petitioner's trial, the Government introduced Lonardo's statements to Greathouse about the participation of the "friend" in the transaction. The District Court found that, considering the events in the parking lot and Lonardo's statements, the Government had established by a preponderance of the evidence that a conspiracy involving Lonardo and petitioner existed, and that Lonardo's statements had been made in the course of and in furtherance of the conspiracy.]

Before admitting a co-conspirator's statement over an objection . . . under Rule 801(d)(2)(E), a court must be satisfied that the statement actually falls within the definition of the rule. There must be evidence that there was a conspiracy involving the declarant and the nonoffering party, and that the statement was made "in the course and in furtherance of the conspiracy." Federal Rule of Evidence 104(a) provides: "Preliminary questions concerning . . . the admissibility of evidence shall be determined by the court." Petitioner and respondent agree that the existence of a conspiracy and petitioner's involvement in it are preliminary questions of fact that, under Rule 104, must be resolved by the court. The Federal Rules, however, nowhere define the standard of proof the court must observe in resolving these questions.

We are . . . guided by our prior decisions regarding admissibility determinations that hinge on preliminary factual questions. We have traditionally required that these matters be established by a preponderance of proof. Evidence is placed before the jury when it satisfies the technical requirements of the evidentiary Rules, which embody certain legal and policy determinations. The inquiry . . . is not whether the proponent of the evidence wins or loses his case on the merits, but whether the evidentiary Rules have been satisfied. Thus, the evidentiary standard is unrelated to the burden of proof on the substantive issues, be it a criminal case, *see In re Winship*, 397 U.S. 358 (1970), or a civil case. The preponderance standard ensures that before admitting evidence, the court will have found it more likely than not that the technical issues and policy concerns addressed by the Federal Rules of Evidence have been afforded due consideration. . . . Therefore, we hold that when the preliminary facts relevant to Rule 801(d)(2)(E) are disputed, the offering party must prove them by a preponderance of the evidence.

Even though . . . the courts below applied the proper standard of proof with regard to the preliminary facts relevant to Rule 801(d)(2)(E), [petitioner] challenges the admission of Lonardo's statements. Petitioner argues that in determining whether a conspiracy exists and whether the defendant was a member of it, the court must look only to independent evidence — that is, evidence other than the statements sought to be admitted. Petitioner relies on *Glasser v. United States*, 315 U.S. 60 (1942), in which this Court first mentioned the so-called "bootstrapping rule." The . . . issue in *Glasser* was whether Glasser's counsel, who also represented another defendant, faced such a conflict of interest that Glasser received ineffective assistance. Glasser contended that conflicting loyalties led his lawyer not to object to statements . . . by one of Glasser's co-conspirators. The Government argued that any objection would have been fruitless because the statements were admissible. The Court rejected this proposition:

> "[S]uch declarations are admissible over the objection of an alleged coconspirator, who was not present when they were made, only if there is proof *aliunde* that he is connected with the conspiracy. . . . Otherwise, hearsay would lift itself by its own bootstraps to the level of competent evidence." *Id.*, at 74–75.

The Court revisited the bootstrapping rule in *United States v. Nixon*, 418 U.S. 683 (1974), where . . . the Court stated, "Declarations by one defendant may also be admissible against other defendants upon a sufficient showing, *by independent evidence*, of a conspiracy among one or more other defendants and the declarant and if the declarations at issue were in furtherance of that conspiracy." *Id.*, at 701, and n.14. . . .

Both *Glasser* and *Nixon*, however, were decided before Congress enacted the Federal Rules of Evidence in 1975. Rule 104(a) provides: "Preliminary questions concerning . . . the admissibility of evidence shall be determined by the court. . . . In making its determination it is not bound by the rules of evidence except those with respect to privileges." The question . . . is whether any aspect of *Glasser's* bootstrapping rule remains viable after the enactment of the Federal Rules of Evidence.

Petitioner concedes that Rule 104, on its face, appears to allow the court to make the preliminary factual determinations relevant to Rule 801(d)(2)(E) by considering any evidence it wishes, unhindered by considerations of admissibility. [However,] petitioner claims that Congress evidenced no intent to disturb the bootstrapping rule . . . , and we should not find that Congress altered the rule without affirmative evidence so indicating. It would be extraordinary to require legislative history to confirm the plain meaning of Rule 104. The Rule on its face allows the trial judge to consider any evidence whatsoever, bound only by the rules of privilege. [T]he Rule is sufficiently clear that to the extent that it is inconsistent with petitioner's interpretation of *Glasser* and *Nixon*, the Rule prevails.[2]

[T]here is little doubt that a co-conspirator's statements could themselves be probative of the existence of a conspiracy and the participation of both the defendant and the declarant in the conspiracy. Petitioner's case presents a paradigm. The out-of-court statements of Lonardo indicated that Lonardo was involved in a conspiracy with a "friend." The statements indicated that the friend had agreed with Lonardo to buy a kilogram of cocaine and to distribute it.

The statements also revealed that the friend would be at the hotel parking lot, in his car, and would accept the cocaine from Greathouse's car . . . . Each one of Lonardo's statements may itself be unreliable, but taken as a whole, the entire conversation between Lonardo and Greathouse was corroborated by independent evidence. The friend, who turned out to be petitioner, showed up at the prearranged spot at the prearranged time. He picked up the cocaine, and a significant sum of money was found in his car. On these facts, the trial court concluded, in our view correctly, that the Government had established the existence of a conspiracy and petitioner's participation in it.

We need not decide in this case whether the courts below could have relied solely

---

[2] The Advisory Committee Notes show that the Rule was not adopted in a fit of absent-mindedness. The Note to Rule 104 specifically addresses the process by which a federal court should make the factual determinations requisite to a finding of admissibility:

"If the question is factual in nature, the judge will of necessity receive evidence pro and con on the issue. The rule provides that the rules of evidence in general do not apply to this process."

The Advisory Committee further noted: "An item, offered and objected to, *may itself be considered in ruling on admissibility*, though not yet admitted in evidence." (emphasis added). We think this language makes plain the drafters' intent to abolish any kind of bootstrapping rule. Silence is at best ambiguous, and we decline the invitation to rely on speculation to import ambiguity into what is otherwise a clear rule.

upon Lonardo's hearsay statements to determine that a conspiracy had been established by a preponderance of the evidence. To the extent that *Glasser* meant that courts could not look to the hearsay statements themselves for any purpose, it has clearly been superseded by Rule 104(a). It is sufficient for today to hold that a court, in making a preliminary factual determination under Rule 801(d)(2)(E), may examine the hearsay statements sought to be admitted.

JUSTICE STEVENS filed a concurring opinion [omitted].

JUSTICE BLACKMUN, with whom JUSTICE BRENNAN and JUSTICE MARSHALL join, dissenting.

. . . Rule 801(d)(2)(E) . . . was a codification of the common-law exemption of co-conspirator statements from the hearsay definition, an exemption that included the independent evidence requirement. An examination of the legislative history of Rule 801(d)(2)(E) reveals that neither the drafters nor Congress intended to transform this requirement in any way. [A] more complete analysis casts significant . . . doubt on the Court's "plain meaning" easy solution.

. . . [U]nlike many common-law hearsay exceptions, the co-conspirator exemption from hearsay with its agency rationale was not based primarily upon any particular guarantees of reliability or trustworthiness . . . intended to ensure the truthfulness of the admitted statement and to compensate for the fact that a party would not have the opportunity to test its veracity by cross examining the declarant. Although, under common law, the reliability of the co-conspirator's statement was never the primary ground justifying its admissibility, there was some recognition that this exemption from the hearsay rule had certain guarantees of trustworthiness, albeit limited ones. This justification for the exemption has been explained:

> "Active conspirators are likely to know who the members of the conspiracy are and what they have done. When speaking to advance the conspiracy, they are unlikely to describe non-members as conspirators, and they usually will have no incentive to misdescribe the actions of their fellow members." R. LEMPERT & S. SALTZBURG, A MODERN APPROACH TO EVIDENCE 395 (2d ed. 1982).

. . . . [T]he components of the exemption were understood to contribute to this reliability. In particular, the requirement that a conspiracy be established by independent evidence . . . is seen to contribute to the reliability . . . .

The Federal Rules of Evidence did not alter in any way this common-law exemption to hearsay. [B]y explicitly retaining the agency rationale . . . , the Advisory Committee expressed its intention that the exemption would remain identical to the common-law rule and that it would not be expanded in any way. The . . . Committee . . . thought that the traditional exemption appropriately balanced the prosecution's need for a co-conspirator's statements and the defendant's need for the protections against unreliable statements, protections provided by the components of the common-law exemption. *See* 4 WEINSTEIN & BERGER, ¶ 801(d)(2)(E)[01], p. 801-235. The . . . Committee . . . expressed its doubts about the agency rationale and, on the basis of these doubts, plainly stated that the exemption should not be changed or extended: "the agency theory of conspiracy is at best a fiction and ought not to serve as a basis for admissibility beyond that already established." Advisory Committee's Notes on Fed. Rule Evid. 801 . . . . In light of this intention *not* to alter the common-law exemption, the Advisory Committee's Notes thus make very clear that Rule 801(d)(2)(E) was to include *all* the components of this exemption, including the independent-evidence requirement.

NOTES

1. The last sentence of Rule 104(a) applies only to Rule 104(a) determinations by the court. In ruling on preliminary determinations under Rule 104(b), the court is limited to considering only admissible evidence. Do you see why this must be so? Remember Thayer's classic remark that the exclusionary rules are the "child of the jury" system, born of doubts about lay jurors' capacity. J. THAYER, A PRELIMINARY TREATISE ON EVIDENCE AT COMMON LAW 47 (1898). Is there any need to apply those rules when the decision-maker is the judge.

2. Almost all states have adopted the same or a similar version of Rule 104(a), and presumably will follow the U.S. Supreme Court's interpretation of Rule 104(a) that permits otherwise inadmissible hearsay to be considered by the trial court in ruling on foundations. Only a few jurisdictions continue to follow the contrary view that the technical exclusionary rules of evidence apply to foundational testimony. *See, e.g., Romani v. State,* 542 So.2d 984, 985–86 (Fla. 1989). The California legislature rejected the California Law Commission's recommendation that the rules of evidence not apply to determinations made by the trial court under CAL. EVID. CODE § 405. Mendez, *The Role of Judge and Jury: Conforming the Evidence Code to the Federal Rules,* 37 U.S.F. L. REV. 1003 (2003). One jurisdiction gives the trial judge discretion. MD. RULE 5-104(a) reads: "In making its determination, the court may, in the interest of justice, decline to require strict application of the rules of evidence, except those relating to privilege and competency of witnesses."

Chapter 6

OVERVIEW: A CONCEPTUAL FRAMEWORK

Evidence law is a vast subject, and it is easy to become lost in its mass of detail. For that reason, before beginning our study of specific evidentiary doctrines, we pause to consider the conceptual framework of evidence law. If you can develop a broader overview of evidence law, the individual doctrines will make more sense.

Despite the size of the domain of American evidence law, it is reducible to a simple analytic framework. There are two key questions. First, is this individual item of evidence **admissible?** Second, considered cumulatively, are all the party's items of evidence **sufficient** to prove the fact in issue?

A. ADMISSIBILITY

Admissibility is the threshold question. To qualify, an item of evidence must clear several hurdles. Initially, the evidence must originate from a **competent witness.** Even if the prospective witness's proposed testimony is otherwise unobjectionable, the judge may exclude it if the person is incompetent to be a witness. As we will see in chapter X, though the common law disqualified several classes of persons on grounds of interest, bias, or lack of credibility, under current evidence law nearly every person is presumed competent to be a witness.

Once the judge concludes that a prospective witness is competent, the next step is to establish the **logical relevance** of the evidence. Here we shift from the witness's personal qualifications to the content of the witness's proposed testimony. To be relevant, testimony must have probative value in two senses. First, on its face, the item of evidence must have some logical connection with the facts in dispute in the case. The item of evidence must have a tendency, in reason and experience, to increase or decrease the probability that one of the disputed facts exists.

Second, the proponent of the evidence must make a threshold showing that the evidence is what it is claimed to be. Anglo-American evidentiary doctrine is imbued with a spirit of skepticism; thus, if the plaintiff claims that an exhibit is a letter written by the defendant, the plaintiff must ordinarily present some testimony that shows that the document was written by the defendant. Likewise, if a defendant calls a witness to testify to the circumstances of a traffic accident, the defendant must submit some testimony establishing that the witness observed the accident. These are the requirements of authentication (Rule 901) and personal knowledge (Rule 602), which we will cover later chapters.

Even if the evidence has logical relevance, the judge may exercise discretion to exclude the evidence on the ground that it is unfairly prejudicial, misleading, or confusing to the jury (Rule 403). This rule, along with other exclusionary rules that prevent admission of specific types of evidence for particular purposes, represent an attempt to shield the trier of fact from evidence that may cause the trier to commit an inferential error in evaluating the testimony.

In essence, the legal irrelevance doctrine rests on institutional policies — assumptions about the way jurors should behave. Ideally, we want jurors to: (a) treat testimony as evidence only of the facts the judge admits the evidence to prove; (b) attach appropriate weight to the testimony; and (c) avoid being distracted from the central issues in the case. The trial judge plays amateur psychologist and inquires whether the admission of an item of evidence is likely to cause the jurors to deviate from those ideals.

Another hurdle to admissibility is a set of **competence doctrines based on the supposed unreliability or untestability of certain types of evidence.** The evidentiary doctrine many laypersons are most familiar with is the hearsay rule. The rule sometimes excludes in-court testimony about out-of-court statements; the rule may prevent the witness on the stand from testifying about a statement that the witness or someone else made outside the courtroom. The rationale for the rule is our preference that the person giving evidence be subjected to the test of cross-examination. This set of doctrines, most notably, the best evidence rule, the hearsay rule, and the opinion rules, restrict a witness's ability to paraphrase documents, relate statements made outside the courtroom, and express conclusions. Ideally, witnesses should give live testimony, produce writings they intend to quote, and confine their testimony to recitations of fact. The common law prefers those types of evidence; but as we shall see, those preferences can yield in cases of necessity.

Extrinsic social policy can also lead to the exclusion of evidence. In contrast to the rules discussed above, which are focused on the value of the evidence in the service of arriving at the "truth," these extrinsic policies restrict the admissibility of evidence to further social policies separate from — and sometimes in tension with — the truth finding function of the trial. Such policies have led, for example, to the development of the rules of privilege. Privileged communications may be highly relevant and reliable. When a judge excludes evidence on grounds of privilege, the judge does so to promote the social policy of protecting the privacy of certain relationships such as attorney and client. The exclusion of the relevant evidence is part of the social cost of the policy of protecting the relationship. In short, even if evidence passes muster under both the logical and legal relevance requirements, extrinsic social policy can render the evidence inadmissible.

B. SUFFICIENCY

Assume that the individual item of evidence comes from a competent witness; is logically as well as legally relevant; and does not run afoul of rules such as privilege or hearsay. If the proponent conquers all these hurdles, the procedural consequence is that the judge will admit the individual item of evidence. However, the case still may not go to the jury; the judge may grant a "directed verdict" or, as it is now called in federal civil procedure, judgment as a matter of law (FED. R. CIV. P. 50). (In criminal cases, the corresponding terminology is a motion for a judgment of acquittal. FED. R. CRIM. P. 29). Why? Because although the judge admits a party's individual items of evidence, the judge may conclude that even when considered together, that party's items of evidence have insufficient probative value to support a rational judgment in that party's favor.

When the judge passes on the **legal sufficiency** of the proponent's evidence, the judge applies the initial burden of production or going forward. If the judge finds that the proponent's case is legally sufficient, the judge submits the case to the jury. In deciding whether to return a verdict for the party, the jury also evaluates the evidence; the jury passes on the **factual sufficiency** of the evidence. The jury applies the ultimate burden of proof; and in deciding whether the proponent has satisfied that burden, the jury considers the credibility of the testimony.

The presentation of evidence to the judge and jury is not the only way of establishing facts at trial. As Chapter 3 noted, alternatively, the judge can judicially notice some very well-settled facts, and parties sometimes stipulate that certain facts exist. However, in most instances, the party must prove the fact with evidence, and that evidence must satisfy the **sufficiency** rules as well as the **admissibility** standards.

The following outline is a more detailed review of the conceptual framework described above and detailed in the remainder of this book.

A CONCEPTUAL FRAMEWORK FOR THE COURSE BOOK

OVERVIEW: **Background, Framework and Procedure**		
	Chapter 1.	The Philosophy and History of American Evidence Law
	Chapter 2.	Evidence: Types, Sources and Substitutes
	Chapter 3.	The Chronology of a Trial
	Chapter 4.	The Examination of a Witness
	Chapter 5.	The Roles of Judge, Jury and Attorneys
	Chapter 6.	Overview: A Conceptual Framework
CASE FILES		
	Civil:	***Hill v. Roe & Polecat Motors***
	Criminal:	***State v. Devitt***
ADMISSIBILITY: **Competence, Relevance and Social Policy**		
	Chapter 7.	Witness Competency
	Chapter 8.	Logical Relevance: Probative Value
	Chs. 9–12.	Specialized Aspects of Logical Relevance
	Chapter 13.	Legal Irrelevance: The Court's Discretion to Exclude
	Chapter 14.	Specialized Aspects of Legal Irrelevance
	Chs. 15–17.	Credibility Evidence
	Chs. 18–22.	Hearsay
	Chapter 23.	Opinion Evidence
	Chapter 24.	The Best Evidence Rule
	Chs. 25-26.	Privileges
	Chapter 27.	Compromise
	Chapter 28.	Remedial Measures
	Chapter 29.	Liability Insurance

Part 2

CASE FILES

CIVIL CASE FILE — *HILL v. ROE & POLECAT MOTORS*

CRIMINAL CASE FILE — *STATE v. DEVITT*

Civil Case File

CIVIL CASE FILE — *HILL v. ROE & POLECAT MOTORS*

POLICE — TRAFFIC ACCIDENT REPORT

POLICE ACCIDENT NO. A 38771
INCIDENT NUMBER

710375

Sheet ____ of ____ Sheets

I.D.O.T. USE ONLY

COUNTY El Dorado
TOWNSHIP OR CITY El Dorado

ON: Number or Name of Highway or Street
ILLINOIS — MISSOURI ST.

At Intersection With
(Circle One) N E S W of
(Number or Name of Intersecting Highway or Street)

If Not At Intersection ____ Feet or ____ Miles ____
(Nearest Highway, Street, Bridge or Other Landmark)

DATE OF ACCIDENT
MO 5 / DAY 15 / YR
TIME OF ACCIDENT 4:00 AM/PM

DAY OF THE WEEK M T W T F S S

TOTAL UNITS INVOLVED 2

TYPE OF REPORT
1 Conventional
2 Dead
3 Animal
4 Private Property
5 Hit and Run
6 Supplementary

CIRCLE ONE OR MORE
1 Fatal
2 Injury
3 Property Damage
4 Arrest
5 Interstate/Expressway

DRIVER'S NAME HILL, DEBRA (Last, First, M.I.)
TAKEN TO County Hosp.
TAKEN BY Ambulance
SAF. EQPT.
INJ. CODE A

1. MALE 2. FEMALE

DRIVER'S ADDRESS 123 Meadow Ln.
CITY/STATE/ZIP/PHONE Jefferson, Morena
DATE OF BIRTH MO 1 / DAY 20 / YR

DRIVER'S LICENSE NO. K 521-2404-9039
STATE Mor.
CLASSIFICATION OP.
RESTRICTIONS

VEHICLE TYPE 4 Door Sedan
MAKE Polecat
MODEL
COLOR L. Blue
YEAR 19YR
VEH. REGIST. K1001
STATE Mor.
TAG NO. APRIL
TAG YEAR 12YR

Total Occ. Including Driver 2

VEHICLE OWNER Arthur / Debra Hill
VEHICLE IDENTIFICATION NO.
1. DRIVEN AWAY 2. TOWED AWAY

OWNER'S ADDRESS 123 Meadow Ln.
CITY/STATE/ZIP/PHONE Jefferson

VEHICLE REMOVED BY Acme Towing
VEHICLE REMOVED TO

CIRCLE POINT OF CONTACT
APPROX. COST TO REPAIR OR REPLACE
UNDER $250 OVER $250 / TOTAL

IF WITNESS, PLACE IN UNIT NO. BOX

PASSENGERS AND/OR WITNESSES

NAME		ADDRESS	CITY	AGE	SEAT POS.	SAF. EQPT.	TAKEN TO	TAKEN BY	INJ. CODE	M.I.
7. HILL, CINDY	123 Meadow Ln.	Jefferson	Mor.	8	3		County Hosp.	Ambulance	K	1.M 2.F

UNIT NO. 1

NAME SMITH, ROBERT
ADDRESS 200 So. Illinois
CITY Jefferson
STATE Mor.
AGE
SEAT POS.
SAF. EQPT.
TAKEN TO
TAKEN BY
INJ. CODE
1.M 2.F

DRIVER'S NAME WORKER, RALPH (Last, First, M.I.)
☒ PEDESTRIAN

1. MALE 2. FEMALE

DRIVER'S ADDRESS 456 State St.
CITY/STATE/ZIP/PHONE Jefferson, Morena
DATE OF BIRTH MO 3 / DAY 3 / YR

DRIVER'S LICENSE NO. W 581-2606-4432
STATE Mor.
CLASSIFICATION CH
RESTRICTIONS

VEHICLE TYPE Pickup
MAKE Ford
MODEL Workhorse
COLOR Red
YEAR 19YR
VEH. REGIST. B 2003
STATE Mor.
TAG NO. June
TAG YEAR 12YR

Total Occ. Unit 2 Including Driver ONE

VEHICLE OWNER JACK, ROE
VEHICLE IDENTIFICATION NO.
1. DRIVEN AWAY 2. TOWED AWAY

OWNER'S ADDRESS 789 Capitol Ave.
CITY/STATE/ZIP/PHONE El Dorado, Morena
OWNER

VEHICLE REMOVED BY Acme Towing
VEHICLE REMOVED TO

CIRCLE POINT OF CONTACT
APPROX. COST TO REPAIR OR REPLACE
UNDER $250 OVER $250

DAMAGE TO PROPERTY OTHER THAN VEHICLE
ADDRESS OF OWNER

NAME OF OWNER OF PROPERTY
NATURE OF DAMAGE
APPROX. COST TO REPAIR OR REPLACE $

CODE FOR INJURY
Use only code that describes one in each space for injury.
K — Dead before report made.
A — Severe (bleeding wounds, distorted member, or had to be carried from scene.)
B — Other visible injury, i.e. bruises, swelling, limping, etc.
C — No visible injury, but complaint of pain.

	AGE	SEAT POS.	SAF. EQPT.	TAKEN TO	TAKEN BY	STATE	INJ. CODE	M.I.
NAME								1.M 2.F

SEATING IN VEHICLE
1 2 3
4 5 6
STATION WAGON
7 8 9

SAFETY EQUIPMENT USE
0 — UNKNOWN, NOT STATED
1 — SAFETY BELTS USED
2 — SAFETY BELTS NOT USED
3 — HELMET USED
4 — HELMET NOT USED
5 — CHILD RESTRAINT PRESENT-NOT USED
6 — CHILD RESTRAINT USED-NOT BELTED
7 — CHILD RESTRAINT PRESENT-NOT USED
8 — AIR BAG ACTIVATED

TIME NOTIFIED OF ACCIDENT 4:05 AM/PM
ARRIVED AT SCENE 4:08 AM/PM
DATE NOTIFIED OF ACCIDENT MONTH 5 / DAY 15 / YEAR
DATE REPORT COMPLETED MONTH 5 / DAY 17 / YEAR

FIRST (NAME)
THIRD (NAME) — Cole Offutt
ID NUMBER
BEAT/ZONE
SECTION NUMBER
TICKET NUMBER
COURT DATE / /
REVIEWING OFFICER
TICKET NUMBER

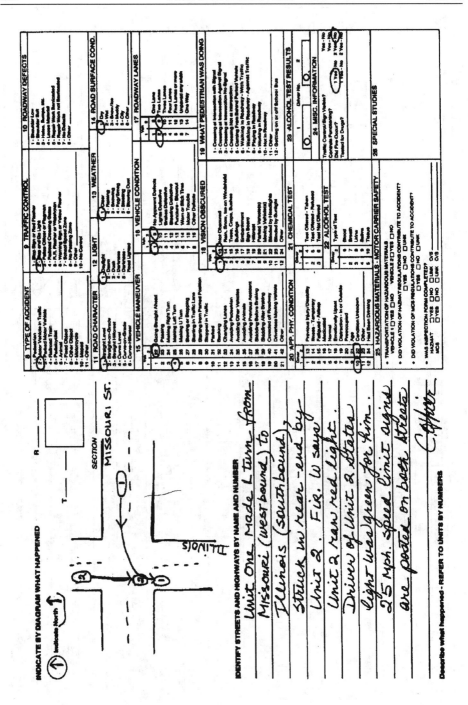

IN THE CIRCUIT COURT FIRST JUDICIAL CIRCUIT EL DORADO COUNTY, MORENA

DEBRA HILL, Individually
and as Administrator of the
Estate of Cindy Hill,
Deceased,

Plaintiff,

-vs-

JACK ROE and POLECAT
MOTORS,
INC., a Corporation,

Defendants.

Civil No. 12345

COMPLAINT

COUNT ONE

[Hill v. Roe]
[Negligence — Personal Injury]

DEBRA HILL, complaining of JACK ROE, alleges:

1. On May 15, 20YR, at approximately 4:00 p.m., Debra Hill was operating a 20YR Polecat automobile in a westerly direction on Missouri Street in the city of El Dorado, state of Morena.

2. Cindy Hill, then eight years of age and the daughter of Debra Hill, was a passenger in the automobile.

3. The Hill automobile entered the intersection of Missouri Street and Illinois Avenue and made a left turn from Missouri Street to the southbound lanes of Illinois Avenue.

4. At that same time and place, Ralph Worker was operating a truck in a southerly direction on Illinois Avenue.

5. At that time and place, Ralph Worker was an agent, servant, and employee of Jack Roe, d/b/a Roe Construction Company, and Ralph Worker was then and there acting in the course and scope of his employment.

6. At that time and place, and immediately prior thereto, Ralph Worker was negligent in one or more of the following ways:

    a.   He was operating his vehicle at a speed in excess of the posted speed limit and too fast for existing conditions, in violation of Morena Rev. Stat. c. 100, § 11-601;

    b.   He failed to obey a traffic control device, *i.e.*, a red traffic light, in violation of Morena Rev. Stat. c. 100, § 11-305;

c. He failed to keep a proper lookout as he approached and entered the intersection.

7. As a direct and proximate result of one or more of the foregoing negligent acts, the truck being operated by Ralph Worker collided with great force with the Hill automobile immediately after the Hill automobile had completed its turn onto Illinois Avenue.

8. As a direct and proximate result of this collision, Debra Hill and Cindy Hill were thrown about the inside of the Hill automobile; and the fuel tank of the Hill automobile became distorted, disconnected, and ruptured; and gasoline and gasoline vapor entered the interior of the automobile and ignited.

9. As a direct and proximate result of the foregoing, Debra Hill was injured in the following ways:

a. She suffered a broken right arm;

b. She sustained numerous cuts, abrasions, and contusions;

c. She was severely burned over a large part of her body;

d. She has experienced severe physical and mental pain and suffering, and she will continue to experience severe physical and mental pain and suffering in the future;

e. She has been required to expend large sums for medical, doctor, and hospital bills and she will incur such expenses in the future;

f. She has lost earnings and will lose earnings in the future;

g. She has become disfigured and will remain disfigured;

h. She has been hospitalized for extended periods of time and has had to undergo surgery on several occasions;

i. She has been deprived of the ability to engage in the various activities of life, either entirely or to the extent she was able prior to her injuries.

WHEREFORE, DEBRA HILL prays judgment against JACK ROE in a sum which will fairly, adequately, and justly compensate her for her injuries, plus costs of this suit, and demands trial by a jury of twelve persons.

COUNT TWO

[Debra Hill, Admr. of Estate of Cindy Hill v. Roe]
[Negligence — Wrongful Death]

DEBRA HILL, as Administrator of the Estate of Cindy Hill, Deceased, complaining of JACK ROE, alleges:

1. Plaintiff realleges paragraphs 1 through 8, inclusive, of Count One as similarly numbered paragraphs of this Count Two.

9. As a direct and proximate result of the foregoing, Cindy Hill was injured in the following ways:

a. She sustained numerous cuts, abrasions, and contusions;

b. She was severely burned over a large part of her body;

c. She experienced severe physical and mental pain and suffering;

d.   She incurred medical, doctor, and hospital bills.

10. As a direct and proximate result of the foregoing, Cindy Hill died approximately 36 hours after the occurrence described.

11. Cindy Hill left surviving her mother, Debra Hill, and her father, Arthur Hill, as her next of kin.

12. As a direct and proximate result of the death of Cindy Hill, her next of kin:

a.   Have been deprived of the support and services which Cindy Hill would have provided them but for her death;

b.   Have been deprived of the society, companionship, love, and affection which Cindy Hill would have provided them but for her death;

c.   Have incurred expense for the funeral and burial of the deceased.

WHEREFORE, DEBRA HILL, as Administrator of the Estate of Cindy Hill, Deceased, prays judgment against JACK ROE in a sum which will fairly, adequately, and justly compensate her estate and next of kin for the injuries and damages alleged, plus costs of this suit, and demands trial by a jury of twelve persons.

COUNT THREE

[Hill v. Polecat Motors, Inc.]
[Strict Product Liability — Personal Injury]

DEBRA HILL, complaining of POLECAT MOTORS, INC., alleges:

1. On and for a long time prior to January 16, 20YR, Polecat Motors, Inc. was engaged in the business of designing, assembling, manufacturing, and marketing automobiles.

2. Some time prior to January 16, 20YR, Polecat Motors, Inc. designed, assembled, manufactured, and marketed a certain 20YR Polecat automobile, Vehicle No. 98765432, and placed that automobile into the stream of commerce by offering it for sale and selling it to its dealer, Jefferson Motor Car Co. of El Dorado, Morena.

3. On January 16, 20YR, Arthur and Debra Hill purchased the above described 20YR Polecat automobile from Jefferson Motor Car Co.

4. On May 15, 20YR, the above-described 20YR Polecat automobile was in the same design condition as when it left the possession and control of Polecat Motors, Inc.

5. At the time the above-described 20YR Polecat automobile left the possession and control of Polecat Motors, Inc., and continuously thereafter until the occurrence described, that automobile was in a defective condition unreasonably dangerous to the user or consumer by reason of one or more of the following conditions:

a.   its fuel tank was located so as to be unnecessarily vulnerable to damage and leakage in the event of a rear-end collision;

b.   Its fuel tank was designed and constructed of materials, and configured, so as to be vulnerable to damage and leakage in the event of a rear-end collision;

c.   The filler pipe of its fuel tank was designed, constructed and located so that in the event of a rear-end collision, it would too readily become separated from the fuel tank and allow gasoline and gasoline vapor to escape into the interior of the automobile;

d.   Its fuel tank did not have a collapsible plastic bladder;

e.   There was no fire shield between the fuel tank and the interior of the automobile;

f.   It did not come equipped with adequate warnings to the user or consumer of the foregoing design conditions and of the resulting fire danger.

6. On May 15, 20YR, at approximately 4:00 p.m., Debra Hill was operating the above-described 20YR Polecat automobile in the vicinity of the intersection of Missouri Street and Illinois Avenue in the city of El Dorado, state of Morena, when it was struck in the rear end by a truck being operated by Ralph Worker.

7. As a direct and proximate result of one or more of the conditions described in paragraph 5, the fuel tank of the above-described 20YR Polecat automobile became distorted, disconnected, and ruptured and gasoline and gasoline vapor entered the interior of the automobile and ignited.

8. Plaintiff realleges paragraph 9 of Count One as paragraph 8 of this Count Three.

WHEREFORE, DEBRA HILL prays judgment against POLECAT MOTORS, INC., in a sum which will fairly, adequately, and justly compensate her for her injuries, plus costs of this suit, and demands trial by a jury of twelve persons.

COUNT FOUR

[Debra Hill, Admr. of Estate of Cindy Hill v. Polecat Motors, Inc.]
[Strict Product Liability — Wrongful Death]

DEBRA HILL, as Administrator of the Estate of Cindy Hill, Deceased, complaining of POLECAT MOTORS, INC., alleges:

1. Plaintiff realleges paragraphs 1 through 7, inclusive, of Count Three as similarly numbered paragraphs of this Count Four.

8. Cindy Hill, then eight years of age and the daughter of Debra Hill, was a passenger in the automobile.

9. Plaintiff realleges paragraphs 9 through 12, inclusive, of Count Two as similarly numbered paragraphs of this Count Four.

WHEREFORE, DEBRA HILL, as Administrator of the Estate of Cindy Hill, Deceased, prays judgment against defendant POLECAT MOTORS, INC., in a sum which will fairly, adequately, and justly compensate her estate and next of kin for the injuries and damages alleged, plus costs of this suit, and demands trial by a jury of twelve.

COUNT FIVE

[Hill v. Polecat Motors, Inc.]
[Misrepresentation — Rest. of Torts § 402B — Personal Injury]

DEBRA HILL, complaining of POLECAT MOTORS, INC., alleges:

1. Plaintiff realleges paragraphs 1, 2, and 3 of Count Three as similarly numbered paragraphs of this Count Five.

4. On and prior to January 16, 20YR, Jefferson Motor Car Co., acting as the agent of POLECAT MOTORS, INC., made certain representations of material facts concerning the above-described automobile to Arthur Hill, including one or more of the following:

   a. The fuel tank and appurtenant structures were reasonably safe, and were not vulnerable to fire in the event of low-speed rear-end collisions.

   b. The automobile, and especially the fuel system, was crashworthy.

   c. The fuel tank would not rupture in the event of a rear-end collision at impact speeds lower than 45 miles per hour.

5. On January 16, 20YR, Arthur Hill purchased the above-described automobile in reliance upon these representations.

6. At the time the above-described 20YR Polecat automobile left the possession and control of Polecat Motors, Inc., and continuously thereafter until the occurrence described, those representations were false, in that:

   a. Its fuel tank was located so as to be vulnerable to damage and leakage in the event of a rear-end collision;

   b. Its fuel tank was designed and constructed of materials, and configured, so as to be vulnerable to damage and leakage in the event of a rear-end collision;

   c. The filler pipe of its fuel tank was designed, constructed, and located so that in the event of a rear-end collision, it would readily become separated from the fuel tank and allow gasoline and gasoline vapor to escape into the interior of the automobile;

   d. Its fuel tank did not have a collapsible plastic bladder;

   e. There was no fire shield between the fuel tank and the interior of the automobile.

7. On May 15, 20YR, at approximately 4:00 p.m., Debra Hill was operating the above-described 20YR Polecat automobile in the vicinity of the intersection of Missouri Street and Illinois Avenue in the city of El Dorado, state of Morena, when it was struck in the rear end by a truck being operated by Ralph Worker at an impact speed of 25 miles per hour or less.

8. As a direct and proximate result of this collision, the fuel tank of the above-mentioned 20YR Polecat automobile became distorted, disconnected, and ruptured and gasoline and gasoline vapor entered the interior of the automobile and ignited.

9. Plaintiff realleges paragraph 9 of Count One as paragraph 9 of this Count Five.

WHEREFORE, DEBRA HILL prays judgment against POLECAT MOTORS, INC., in a sum which will fairly and adequately compensate her for her injuries, plus costs of this suit, and demands trial by a jury of twelve persons.

COUNT SIX

[Debra Hill, Admr. of Estate of Cindy Hill v. Polecat Motors, Inc.]
[Misrepresentation — Rest. of Torts § 402B — Personal Injury]

DEBRA HILL, as Administrator of the Estate of Cindy Hill, Deceased, complaining of Polecat Motors, Inc., alleges:

1. Plaintiff realleges paragraphs 1, 2, and 3 of Count Three as similarly numbered paragraphs of this Count Six.

4. Plaintiff realleges paragraphs 4, 5, 6, 7, and 8 of Count Five as similarly numbered paragraphs of this Count Six.

9. Plaintiff realleges paragraphs 9, 10, 11, and 12 of Count Two as similarly numbered paragraphs of this Count Six.

WHEREFORE, DEBRA HILL, as Administrator of the Estate of Cindy Hill, Deceased, prays judgment against POLECAT MOTORS, INC., in a sum which will fairly and adequately compensate her estate and next of kin for the injuries and demands alleged, plus costs of this suit, and demands trial by a jury of twelve persons

[This complaint is an abbreviated version of one that might actually be filed in a lawsuit based on these facts. Pleading requirements vary among jurisdictions; the foregoing cannot be taken as a model for use in all courts. In addition, in a real case plaintiff would probably also sue the retailer and Worker, and might make additional allegations of negligence and perhaps reckless conduct against the auto manufacturer. Also, the wrongful death and survival claims would probably be pleaded in separate counts. A complaint with this much specificity would most likely be filed in a fact pleading state, as opposed to a notice pleading jurisdiction (such as federal court) where less detail is necessary. However, in an abundance of caution, many lawyers file detailed complaints, even in notice pleading jurisdictions.]

Criminal Case File

CRIMINAL CASE FILE — *STATE v. DEVITT*

Criminal case files vary from one jurisdiction to the next, so we will not attempt to reproduce sample documents here. Assume the following facts.

Accused:	Daniel R. Devitt, age 31
Victim:	Patrick Paterson, age 49
Victim's Daughter:	Lynn Paterson, age 19
Location:	Aurora Apartments, El Dorado,
Investigating Officers:	MorenaKarl Katz and George Hernandez

The police arrest record includes the following crime report, which was prepared by one of the investigating police officers, Officer Hernandez:

Crime Report

Victim, Paterson, is 49, a car salesman. He resides with his daughter, 19, a student at Smith Business College. They live in the Aurora Apartments in north El Dorado. The father hired suspect, Devitt, to do some carpentry at the apartment — building some shelves and doing some repair work in the kitchen. On morning of March 15, victim admitted suspect to apartment before leaving before work. He returned from work at approximately 1600 hours same day. Suspect was still in apartment. Victim noticed beer cans and a bottle, apparently of liquor. The victim noticed the suspect was going through drawers in a dresser in victim's bedroom. When victim told suspect to get out of the bedroom, suspect pulled knife and said, "Get out of my God damn way." Suspect then attempted to run by the victim toward the front door. When the victim endeavored to block the suspect's exit, the suspect first stabbed the victim and then hit him with his right fist. The victim then pretended to be unconscious. He thinks suspect remained another hour. When he was sure suspect had left, he ran to apartment of witness, Matilda Larson, 75-year-old widow living in same apartment complex. Witness tells this officer that victim came to door in disarray and bleeding slightly. Victim at first was incoherent. Witness gave him tea and calmed him. When victim told Larson what had happened, witness phoned north El Dorado police station. Call came in approximately 1830. This officer and officer Katz immediately responded to scene.

[The case file also contains the following statement, signed by the accused:]

Statement of Arrested Person

I am a handyman carpenter. That's how I've made my living since getting out of the Marines. Last week this guy by the name of Paterson phones me and tells me that he wants some work done at his apartment. He tells me that he wants me to do some work like putting up shelves in the kitchen. I said that I could do it for

$150. We agreed, and he told me to show up early Monday, March 15th. That's just what I did. When I got there, Paterson was gone; but his daughter let me in. She left for school, and I got right to work. I worked straight through the morning and almost finished. I took a lunch break and got some beer from the local 7-11. I had finished off a couple of beers and wrapped up the job when the old guy came home. By that time, it was late in the afternoon and real hot. He asked me if I wanted to share a beer, and I said sure. He must have had some booze already because he was acting pretty weird. We get to talking, and for no reason he starts cursing me. I tried to ignore him and get back to work. He wouldn't let me be. While I was trying to slice some tile with my linoleum knife, he walked up behind me and grabbed my arm real hard. He was saying something like, "Don't ignore me when I'm talking to you." I instinctively pulled my arm back, and the knife accidentally cut him. He goes ballistic and starts screaming and punching. I had enough of him. I just shoved him out of my way and left.

I left and went home. That same night, I was just sitting home when these two cops butt in. They didn't shove me around or nothing like that, but they tell me that Paterson had accused me of trying to steal from him and beating him up. I told the cop that the whole thing was with the old guy's fault, but they wouldn't listen. So here I am sitting in jail on a frame-up.

/s/ Daniel R. Devitt

Assume that Devitt has been formally charged by an appropriate procedure — indictment or information — with (1) simple battery, (2) aggravated battery, and (3) attempted theft.

Morena statutes define the following crimes:

Battery (Morena Stat. 5/12–3).

(a)   A person commits battery if he intentionally or knowingly without legal justification and by any means,

    (1)   causes bodily harm to an individual or

    (2)   makes physical contact of an insulting or provoking nature with an individual.

(b)   Sentence. Battery is a Class A misdemeanor.

Aggravated Battery (Morena Stat. 5/12–4).

(a)   A person who, in committing a battery, intentionally or knowingly causes great bodily harm, or permanent disability or disfigurement commits aggravated battery.

(b)   In committing a battery, a person commits aggravated battery if he or she:

    (1)   Uses a deadly weapon other than by the discharge of a firearm;

(e)   Sentence. Aggravated battery is a Class 3 felony.

Theft (Morena Stat. 5/16–1).

(a)   A person commits theft when he knowingly:

    (1)   Obtains or exerts unauthorized control over property of the owner; or

    (2)   Obtains by deception control over property of the owner; or

(3) Obtains by threat control over property of the owner;

. . . .

(b) Sentence.

(1) Theft of property, other than a firearm, not from the person and not exceeding $300 in value is a Class A misdemeanor.

Attempt (Morena Stat. 5/8–4).

(a) Elements of the offense. A person commits an attempt when, with intent to commit a specific offense, he does any act which constitutes a substantial step toward the commission of that offense.

. . . .

(c) Sentence. A person convicted of an attempt may be fined or imprisoned or both not to exceed the maximum provided for the offense attempted but

. . .

(5) the sentence for attempt to commit any felony other than those specified in Subsections (1), (2), (3) and (4) hereof is the sentence for a Class A misdemeanor.

Part 3

ADMISSIBILITY OF EVIDENCE

Chapter 7

WITNESS COMPETENCY

Read Federal Rules of Evidence 601, 605 and 606.

A. INTRODUCTION

The term "competent," as used throughout this text, refers to the issue of whether a person called as a witness is eligible to testify. For the most part, the prospective witness's eligibility depends upon the person's *status* rather than the *content* of the person's proposed testimony. These rules can have the dramatic procedural effect of keeping a person off the witness stand. Therefore, whether the witness is competent is the threshold issue in analyzing the admissibility of evidence presented through that witness. Before we consider the content of any proposed testimony, we must ensure that the testimony comes from a proper source, a competent witness.

At one time in the history of the common law, there were several categories of persons who were not permitted to be witnesses, including parties to the action and others interested in its outcome, spouses of parties, and persons convicted of certain crimes. The common law was virtually obsessed with the prevention of perjury, and it was thought that these categories of witnesses had too much incentive for false testimony. As we will see in this chapter, virtually all of the common law grounds of incompetency have been converted into grounds for impeachment of the witness. Under the federal rules, there are few remaining automatic disqualifications for witnesses.

B. THE EARLY COMMON LAW COMPETENCY DOCTRINE

In a modern trial, almost all of the evidence consists of witnesses' testimony or tangible things for which a witness's testimony has laid the foundation. But it was not always so.

> Historically, the modern witness does not appear as a main source of evidence to the jury until the 1600s. The jurors, originally, being taken from the neighborhood, were supposed to know something of the case; and they were free to make inquiry for themselves out of court. Moreover, the oath of a witness, in those earlier days, was an impressive, almost a decisive act; when sworn, it might impress the jury decisively; and its only proper place was in the other mode of trial, "wager of law," where the party's oath was decisive. Furthermore, the fear of being charged with "maintenance," that

is, of influencing the jurors by persuasion in favor of one of the parties, kept possible witnesses away; and until Queen Elizabeth's period (say 1562) there was no regular compulsory process for them. Thus, when the jury developed and were no longer supposed or allowed to have knowledge of their own, and the ordinary witness became common and took oath, he was admitted only under strict limitations. He must be well qualified. Hence, [there are] many rules which lasted until modern time — for example, the rules excluding all parties in the case and other interested persons.

But with the development of the art of cross-examination in the 1700s and the spread of rationalism in the community, these traditional rules of limitation were gradually seen to be unwise and unpractical. By the middle of the 1800s a strong movement to abolish them took effect; and most of them are now gone. What remains has mostly some practical foundation.

J. Wigmore, A Student's Textbook of the Law of Evidence § 92 (1935).

C. THE PREVAILING MODERN DOCTRINE

Today, the traditional blanket disqualifications have almost entirely disappeared. Nearly all jurisdictions have a statute similar to the federal provision:

Federal Rule of Evidence 601. General Rule of Competency.

Every person is competent to be a witness except as otherwise provided in these rules. However, in civil actions and proceedings, with respect to an element of a claim or defense as to which State law supplies the rule of decision, the competency of a witness shall be determined in accordance with State law.

However, as we shall see, some vestiges of the former incompetencies persist.

1. General Competency Requirements

Competency is predicated upon the witness possessing four distinct capacities: (a) sincerity; (b) observation; (c) memory; and (d) narrative ability. On an appropriate objection, the trial judge must rule on the preliminary issue of whether the prospective witness possesses these four capacities.

a. Capacity for Sincerity: The Oath

When the law ultimately accepted the oath as a predicate for a witness's testimony (rather than as the testimony itself), it became a corollary that the witness was incompetent unless she believed in a Supreme Being who punished false testimony. A witness was incompetent unless she recognized a religious obligation to speak the truth.

That moral obligation has been replaced by a legal obligation to tell the truth, and the law's punishment for perjury has replaced a Supreme Being's retribution as the sanction that induces truthful testimony. The opponent may no longer challenge a witness's competency on the ground that the witness does not believe in a Supreme Being or divine punishment for perjury. In fact, Rule 610 makes a witness's beliefs or opinions on religious matters specifically inadmissible on the issue of credibility.

Although the prospective witness need not recognize a religious duty to testify truthfully, a witness cannot testify unless and until he takes an oath or affirms that he will tell the truth. *See* FED. R. EVID. 603. In a sense, this is a vestige of a competency rule. However, today it has become a rule of trial administration designed to subject the witness to penalties for perjury and to signal to the witness the great importance of truthful testimony. If the witness (for whatever reason) refuses to take an oath, she may "affirm" that her testimony will be the truth; in fact, "affirming" is not even necessary if the witness's proposed statement is the functional equivalent. Rule 603 provides that the oath or affirmation be "administered in a form calculated to awaken his conscience and impress his mind with his duty to" testify truthfully. To require more is usually error. In *United States v. Ward*, 989 F.2d 1015 (9th Cir. 1992), the court ruled that the First Amendment free exercise clause entitled the accused to take an oath that he would speak with "fully integrated honesty."

The proposed witness must have sufficient mental capacity to understand the oath's significance and his duty to tell the truth. For instance, California Evidence Code § 701(a)(2) reads: "A person is disqualified to be a witness if he is . . . [i]ncapable of understanding the duty of a witness to tell the truth." Thus, what began as a religious test has become essentially a cognitive standard.

The age at which a child becomes competent to testify as a witness revolves around this cognitive standard. As early as 1895, the Supreme Court observed that "there is no precise age which determines the question of competency" and noted that "[it] depends on the capacity and intelligence of the child, his appreciation of the difference between truth and falsehood, as well as of his duty to tell the former."[1] Some jurisdictions employ rebuttable presumptions regarding competency of young children. But even where such presumptions are employed, they can be rebutted by showing that the child possesses the requisite understanding.

Thomas D. Lyon, et al., *Young Children's Competency to Take the Oath: Effects of Task, Maltreatment and Age*
34 LAW & HUM. BEHAV. 141 (2010)

Under the law in most jurisdictions, children demonstrate oath-taking capacity if they understand that "truth" refers to factual statements and that one ought to tell the truth. Research has suggested that this basic understanding first appears during the pre-school years. Children as young as 4 years exhibit above-chance performance on tasks requiring them to understand that "truth refers to factual statements and "lies" to counter-factual statements, as well as tasks requiring them to recognize that "truth" is more virtuous than "lies."

* * *

Still younger children may have an inarticulable understanding of true and false

---

[1] Wheeler v. U.S., 16 S. Ct. 93 (1895).

statements. They may understand a concept of truth and falsity, and adhere to the belief that one ought to make true statements, but not be capable of labeling true and false statements as such. . . . [C]hildren as young as 2.5 years who failed to accurately label true and false statements as "good" or "bad" and "truth" or "lie," nevertheless reliably rejected false statements and accepted true statements. This is consistent with research concerning children's ability to reject counterfactual statements, a skill demonstrated in children as young as 20 months. Not everyone agrees that the ability to tell truth from lies is the right question. For an article contending that the real question is the ability of the child witness to tell reality from fantasy, see Laurie Shanks, *Evaluating Children's Capacity to Testify, Developing a Rational Method to Assess a Young Child's Capacity to Offer Reliable Testimony in Cases of Child Sexual Abuse*, 58 Cleve. St. L. Rev. 575, 602 (2010) (contending that the "competency hearing should be restructured to determine the child's level of developmental maturity, her ability to accurately relate a series of events, and her capacity to distinguish reality from fantasy"). There is some research showing that children are able to differentiate fact from fantasy. "By age three, children are quite good at making an explicit distinction between pretense and reality. . . . Experimental and observational studies of pretense play have demonstrated that by age four, children not only can readily shift back and forth between the real and pretend world, but they can also reason quite consistently within each of these two worlds." MYERS, § 2.13 (quoting research). Thus, the fact that the child believes in Santa Claus or other imaginative fantasies does not disqualify the child as a witness. *Id.*

---

b. Mental Capacity to Observe

In addition to the oath requirement, the common law allowed the judge to determine whether the prospective witness had the ability to observe. The term "observe" ordinarily connotes the sense of sight. However, in this context, the term has a broader meaning: a person can "observe" a fact or event through any sense organ. A blind or deaf person can be a competent observer.

At what time must the prospective witness possess this capacity? In the *Devitt* case, suppose that at the time of the alleged attack, Paterson could see but he becomes blind before trial. At trial, may he testify to the assailant's facial features he saw during the attack? Or, in *Hill*, assume that a witness heard Ms. Hill make an admission but the witness becomes deaf before trial. Can the witness still testify about the statement?

c. Mental Capacity to Remember

In addition to having the mental capacity to observe the relevant fact or event, the prospective witness must be able to accurately recall the data at the time of trial. When it comes to children, a large body of research has accumulated concerning their cognitive ability, memory, and other testimonial considerations. For an excellent summary, see J.E.B. MYERS, 1 MYERS ON EVIDENCE IN CHILD, DOMESTIC & ELDER ABUSE CASES, Chapters 1 and 2 (2005) (hereafter "MYERS"). Of course, a child's perception and memory — just like an adult's — can be affected by various factors. Memory decays with time, a factor which may be greater with young children. MYERS, § 1.02[C]. Stress may or may not inhibit memory. MYERS, § 1.04. A child's sense of time develops slowly, and does not fully mature until early adolescence, but even young children can order events in a sequence. MYERS, § 1.22. This can have implications for a child's testimony. MYERS, § 1.23.

There is related debate, with strong advocates on both sides, about the nature and extent of children's suggestibility. MYERS, §§ 1.07–1.11. Although research suggests that young children may be more suggestible than older children or adults (*id.*), there are techniques that can be used to lower suggestibility and to determine whether the child was subjected to an improper interview procedure. MYERS, §§ 1.11, 1.15–1.17. Some courts have approved pre-testimony "taint hearings" to determine whether the way in which the child was interviewed affected or "tainted" the child's memory. MYERS, § 1.14.

Suppose that, before trial, the witness has difficulty remembering relevant facts. Assume further that, under hypnosis, the witness purports to recall seemingly forgotten facts. Is the witness competent to testify to those facts at trial? What possible effects might so-called "hypnotic induction of memories" have on a person's ability to accurately recall events? The following opinion addresses these questions. In this case, the prosecution presented hypnotically enhanced testimony by "M.A.," the victim of a sexual assault. Note the opinion's reliance on scientific research and the central role which empirical research may play in the evolution of evidentiary doctrine.

STATE v. MOORE
188 N.J. 182, 902 A.2d 1212 (2006)

CHIEF JUSTICE PORITZ delivered the opinion of the Court.

[M.A. was asleep in her bedroom when she was awakened and sexually assaulted by an attacker. He repeatedly told her not to look at him, but at one point she briefly opened her eyes. She was able to give police a description of her attacker, but because of the poor lighting in the room and the fact that she saw him only once, she was unable to provide enough information to develop a composite sketch. During the investigation, she was hypnotized by a licensed clinical psychologist, Dr. Samuel Babcock. Before bringing her out of the hypnosis, he told her she "will remember the face [of her assailant], crystal clear, very clearly." A few days later, M.A. chose defendant Moore from a photo array, and later, from two more arrays, one of which was a photo of a lineup. At trial, on the witness stand, M.A. made an in-court identification of defendant Moore as the person who assaulted her. Dr. Babcock testified for the state, and the audiotapes of his session with M.A. were played to the jury, which was also given transcripts of the tapes. M.A. admitted that during the attack she caught only a "glimpse" of her attacker's face in what could have been but a "split second." M.A. maintained, however, that the glimpse was "enough to remember" and that Moore's face "was the same face." She further stated that there was "no question" but that the person she identified in the photo arrays was her assailant, recounting that when she picked Moore's photo she "recognize[d] that face, everything about it." Although she had described a person with a light beard during the police investigation (Moore actually had a mustache at the time of the assault), when she first identified Moore's photograph, M.A. testified, she "wasn't concerned with a beard or a mustache or any kind of facial hair[;] [she] was just looking at the whole face." In respect of the lighting conditions in her bedroom, M.A. testified that there was enough light to see facial features and to "remember someone." She testified that she was not wearing her contact lenses during the assault, but that she was able to see without them and, in fact, had driven without her lenses. When confronted with her prior statements regarding her inability to see objects more than a few feet away without her contacts, M.A. responded that "before I was hypnotized that was accurate."

M.A. acknowledged that her recollection of her assailant had been altered by her hypnotic experience. She explained that hypnosis made her assailant's face "much clearer" with "the features . . . more detailed," that "[i]t was much easier to describe [his face] in more detail afterwards," and that her vision of his face and clothing appeared "brighter." Asked whether she would have recognized her assailant prior to being hypnotized, M.A. replied, "I think so, but I couldn't have been positive." She conveyed in her testimony a clear and strong conviction that Moore was the person who assaulted her.

On remand, the trial court heard testimony from three experts. The court concluded that hypnotically refreshed testimony should be precluded; that "at the very least," the *Hurd* guidelines should be supplemented; and that, regardless of the decision on those two issues, M.A.'s testimony should be barred because Dr. Babcock did not comply with the *Hurd* guidelines. The case then went back up to the New Jersey Supreme Court.]

*   *   *

Twenty-five years ago, in *State v. Hurd*, this Court was presented for the first time with the question "whether the testimony of a witness who has undergone hypnosis to refresh her recollection is admissible in a criminal trial and, if so, in what circumstances." . . . After reviewing the expert testimony presented to the trial court, including the scientific literature available at the time, we held that a witness who has been hypnotized in an attempt to improve his or her recollection may testify at trial "subject to strict safeguards to ensure the reliability of the hypnotic procedure." . . .

[T]he *Hurd* Court traced the evolution of hypnosis as a "memory recall" procedure. . . . The Court observed that most courts considering the question had ruled that hypnotically induced testimony "should be treated like any other present recollection refreshed." . . . At that time, only a few courts had held such testimony per se inadmissible in a criminal trial based on a finding that hypnosis was not generally accepted by experts in the field. . . . The *Hurd* Court agreed that "hypnotically refreshed testimony must satisfy the standard of acceptability for scientific evidence before it is admissible in a criminal trial, but found that it met the standard." . . . More specifically, the Court held that the procedure used to stimulate hypnotic recall must be capable of producing reliable results, and that the worth of the evidence must outweigh the disadvantages of confusion and consumption of resources that would occur every time expert testimony is needed to evaluate the reliability of hypnotic procedures. . . .

The Court reasoned that hypnosis need not be "generally accepted as a means of reviving truthful or historically accurate recall," . . . ; rather, the procedure would be considered "reasonably reliable if [in a particular case] it is able to yield recollections as accurate as those of an ordinary witness, which likewise are often historically inaccurate." . . . Most important in respect of the question before us today, the *Hurd* Court reviewed the substantial extant authority discussing problems associated with post-hypnotic memory, noting that "while hypnosis often can produce remarkably accurate recall, it is also prone to yield sheer fantasy, willful lies, or a mixture of fact with gaps filled in by fantasy." . . . Citing Dr. Orne, the Court recognized three troubling concerns: that a person undergoing hypnosis is extremely vulnerable to suggestion, which even an expert observer may not be able to identify; that such a person loses critical judgment, and consequently will speculate and respond with greater confidence than other persons; and that memories evoked under hypnosis are often confounded with prior recall. . . . Despite those concerns, the Court concluded that "a rule of per se inadmissibility is unnecessarily broad and will result in the exclusion of evidence that is as trustworthy as other eyewitness testimony." . . .

Because the Court found that hypnotically refreshed testimony, in appropriate circumstances, could be as reliable as ordinary recall, it held that such testimony would be "admissible in a criminal trial if the trial court finds that the use of hypnosis in the particular case was reasonably likely to result in recall comparable in accuracy to normal human memory." . . . To aid in that determination, the Court adopted the procedural safeguards suggested by Dr. Orne and directed trial courts to "evaluate both the kind of memory loss that hypnosis was used to restore and the specific technique employed." . . . Under the safeguards, "a psychiatrist or psychologist experienced in the use of hypnosis must conduct the session"; that person "should be independent of and not regularly employed by the prosecutor, investigator or defense"; "any information given to the hypnotist by law enforcement personnel or the defense prior to the hypnotic session must be recorded, either in writing or another suitable form"; the hypnotist must elicit a detailed description of the facts from the subject before hypnosis; "all contacts between the hypnotist and the subject must be recorded"; and "only the hypnotist and the subject should be present during any phase of the hypnotic session." . . . The burden of proof, by clear and convincing evidence, was assigned to the party offering the hypnotically refreshed testimony. . . .

* * *

. . . [I]n 1982 the California Supreme Court issued a seminal decision in . . . [*People v. Shirley*, 31 Cal.3d 18, 723 P.2d 1354 (1982) — eds.]. . . .

Most important in the context of our inquiry in this case, the California court relied on "major voices in the scientific community [that] oppose[d] the use of hypnosis to restore the memory of potential witnesses, with or without procedural safeguards, on the ground of its intrinsic unreliability." *Id.* Those voices spoke of problems associated with hypnosis: of suggestiveness that may be unintended, or even unperceived, by the hypnotist; of confabulation that receives unwarranted credence; of the inability of expert witnesses and lay observers to distinguish between true memories and pseudomemories; and of increased confidence in recall that is unwarranted and renders cross-examination largely ineffective. . . . The court determined that "the testimony of a witness who has undergone hypnosis for the purpose of restoring his memory of the events in issue is inadmissible as to all matters relating to those events, from the time of the hypnotic session forward." *Id.*

* * *

Finally, we note one other trend in respect of this issue. Nine states have adopted an alternative to the three approaches previously discussed (per se admissibility, procedural safeguards, and per se inadmissibility) known as the ad hoc approach. *See, e.g., State v. Iwakiri*, [Idaho 1984]; *State v. Armstrong*, [Wis. 1983]. Those jurisdictions place "the burden on the state in each case to satisfy the trial court that the testimony of witnesses previously subjected to hypnotism is reliable." *State v. Seager*, [Iowa 1983]. Sometimes referred to as the "totality of the circumstances" test, . . . this approach considers, among other things, whether the purpose of the hypnosis was therapeutic or investigative, whether corroborating evidence exists, and whether the post-hypnotic recollection was substantially similar to the pre-hypnotic recollection. The Supreme Court of Colorado, for example, has held that in determining admissibility, trial courts must consider the level of training and independence of the hypnotist, whether all contacts between the witness and the hypnotist were recorded, the circumstances under which the hypnosis occurred, and the appropriateness of hypnosis for the kind of memory loss involved. *People v. Romero*, [Colo. 1987] . . . .

Today, as the debate continues, four states consider hypnotically refreshed testimony per se admissible, with the trier of fact determining its weight . . . ; six allow such testimony when certain procedural safeguards are met . . . ; twenty-six have adopted variations on the per se inadmissible rule . . . ; and nine have adopted some type of "totality of the circumstances" test . . . .

The defense presented two experts, Dr. Steven J. Lynn and Dr. Scott Lilienfeld. Dr. Lynn testified that hypnotically induced testimony is not reliable and that hypnosis, in fact, has an adverse effect on accuracy. He echoed historically expressed concerns about false confidence and confabulation, and indicated that the more hypnotizable people are, the more likely they are to report false memories. In his own research, he found that cross-examination of a hypnotized individual could prove difficult or impossible "if [the] witness confidently believes that a false memory mirrors reality and has problems distinguishing pre- and post-hypnotic memories." Dr. Lynn concluded that the *Hurd* guidelines do not reduce the effects of hypnosis in respect of false confidence, confabulation, uncued errors, recall problems, and response to pseudomemory. He opined that the guidelines simply do not obviate problems [such as] the fact that the hypnotized subject enters with expectations that the procedure will be very helpful, expectations that the memories elicited will be accurate, and . . . any problems in memory that may be present prior even to the implementation of hypnosis and the *Hurd* guidelines.

Defendant's other expert, Dr. Lilienfeld, also challenged the sufficiency of the *Hurd* guidelines in reducing the risk of false or inaccurate memories. He stated that the guidelines incorrectly "assume that by obtaining a full recording of the interactions between the hypnotist and the subject and [then] comparing system-atically the pre-versus [the] post-hypnotic report, [it is possible to determine] whether or not any of the information provided by the hypnotist was leading or misleading." He opined that there should be a per se ban on hypnotically enhanced testimony because such testimony was likely to produce invalid memories. In that regard, he referred to research "suggest[ing] that hypnosis by itself can incur an increased risk of pseudo memories or false memories" and that hypnosis appears "to have an incremental or additional effect above and beyond leading questions" or other confounding influences on memory. Finally, Dr. Lilienfeld rejected the notion that because leading questions and other similar techniques permitted in the courtroom distort ordinary recall, hypnosis should be similarly permitted. He would not "lower the bar even more" simply because there are already problems with certain forms of suggestive influence.[9]

Based on the expert testimony and scientific research submitted by the parties, the trial court decided that hypnotically refreshed testimony should be per se inadmissible. In so concluding, the court used a cost-benefit analysis, identifying as benefits an increase in recall, an opportunity for the witness to focus and attempt to reconstruct his or her memory, and an opportunity "to revisit a traumatic event in a relatively non-harmful and non-threatening context." Conversely, the court identified the costs as a potential adverse effect on accuracy, an increased state of suggestibility, the risk of confabulation, and a tendency toward concreting (or the "honest liar" syndrome).[10]

The trial court also noted that "[h]ypnosis is likely to be used where identification is at issue and there [i]s not a lot of other evidence on the identification issue." The court opined that determining the credibility of a witness when the witness believes what he or she is saying is difficult, and that hypnosis "does have a significant adverse effect on the ability of an advocate to effectively cross-examine" . . . Even [a post-*Hurd* jury instruction] was found by the court to be inadequate because problems such as increased confidence, the aura of scientific objectivity presented by hypnosis, and concreting, are not addressed in the charge.

. . . [W]e would not abandon the template established in *Hurd* unless we had become convinced that the scientific evidence presented below, and relied on by other courts, counsels another course. The difference between the testimony of the experts at the time *Hurd* was decided, and the experts who testified on remand in this case, is largely a difference in degree, not substance. Yet, that difference is telling. Although the scientific community has not reached a definitive consensus on the issue, more recent studies reaffirm and strengthen earlier understandings about how hypnosis affects both memory and attitude. We now conclude on the basis of this data that hypnotically refreshed testimony cannot meet the general acceptance standard of admissibility.

Moreover, there has been a shift in expert opinion suggesting that the problems

---

[9] Those who view memory as "reconstructive" understand it to be influenced by many factors, including information conveyed by third parties and the individual's knowledge, beliefs, and understanding in respect of a remembered event.

[10] Concreting is a phenomenon in which hypnotized individuals become convinced that their memories are correct because they remembered them in hypnosis. Giuliana, Note, *Between a Rock and a* Hurd *Place: Protecting the Criminal Defendant's Right to Testify After Her Testimony Has Been Hypnotically Refreshed*, 65 FORDHAM L. REV. 2151, 2169 (1997).

associated with the use of hypnotically refreshed testimony are less amenable to correction through controls on the hypnotic process. Dr. Orne himself has concluded that the procedural safeguards he advocated in *Hurd* are inadequate to their purpose. [Orne, *et. al., Hypnotically Induced Testimony*, in EYEWITNESS TESTIMONY: PSYCHOLOGICAL PERSPECTIVES 171, 210 (Wells & Loftus eds., 1984 — eds.] We are unable to determine whether hypnotically refreshed testimony is as reliable as ordinary recall (a point important to the *Hurd* Court) or even to implement a process to ensure that such testimony can meet that criterion.

In sum, the experts that testified on remand agreed that hypnosis does not produce more accurate recall, but rather, instills a false confidence in the hypnotized individual thereby producing an aura of truthfulness that subverts effective cross-examination, a cornerstone of the adversarial system. Moreover, the cumulative import of the testimony below, the scientific literature, and the case law from other states is that there is at this point no way to gauge the reliability of hypnotically induced testimony. There is a consensus among scientists and clinical practitioners, including the experts below, that memory is reconstructive and that recall generally is a complicated process in which the individual draws material from many sources. In relation to hypnotically refreshed memory, specifically, because numerous factors "influence how events are perceived, [there are] psychologists and psychiatrists [who] believe hypnosis itself can affect recall." Daniel R. Webert, Note, *Are the Courts in a Trance? Approaches to the Admissibility of Hypnotically Enhanced Witness Testimony in Light of Empirical Evidence*, 40 AM. CRIM L. REV. 1301, 1304 (2003).

Most important here, the testifying experts and the scientific literature are consistent in their description of the effects of hypnosis — suggestibility, confabulation or "gap filling," pseudomemory or "false memory," memory hardening or "false confidence" in one's recollections, source amnesia, and loss of critical judgment. Antonia F. Giuliana, Note, *Between a Rock and a* Hurd *Place: Protecting the Criminal Defendant's Right to Testify After Her Testimony Has Been Hypnotically Refreshed*, 65 FORDHAM L. REV. 2151, 2166–69 (1997); Webert, 40 AM. CRIM. L. REV. at 1320–23; *see* Martin T. Orne, *et al., Hypnotically Refreshed Testimony: Enhanced Memory or Tampering with Evidence?, Issues and Practices in Criminal Justice*, Jan. 1985, at 5–27. In contrast, there is a lack of empirical evidence supporting the popular notion that hypnosis improves recall. Webert, 40 AM. CRIM. L. REV. at 1318–20; Nancy Mehrkens Steblay and Robert K. Bothwell, *Evidence for Hypnotically Refreshed Testimony: The View from the Laboratory*, 18 Law & Hum. Behav. 635, 648 (1994) ("[t]he hypothesized increase in recall accuracy for hypnotized subjects has not been substantiated by research to date."). In this vein, we add only that the general public believes that "hypnosis [is] a powerful tool to recover accurate memories." Webert, 40 AM. CRIM. LAW. REV. at 1320–23. Eighty-eight percent of respondents in a 1999 survey agreed at some level that "hypnosis enables people to accurately remember things they could not otherwise remember." *Ibid.* (*citing* Myles E. Johnson & Coleen Hauk, *Beliefs and Opinions About Hypnosis Held by the General Public: A Systematic Evaluation*, 42 AM. J. CLINICAL HYPNOSIS 10, 17 (1999)). That confidence in the power of hypnosis to produce accurate recall affects individuals undergoing hypnosis who are convinced — wrongly — that they will remember precisely what happened to them after they are hypnotized, and affects jurors, who are likely to reach a favorable verdict when a witness has been hypnotized. *Id.* at 1324 (*citing* Barbara L. Coleman et al., *What Makes Recovered-Memory Testimony Compelling to Jurors?*, 25 LAW & HUM. BEHAV. 317, 324–25 (2001)).

. . . The theory that hypnosis is a reliable means of improving recall is not generally accepted in the scientific community. . . . Because we are no longer confident that procedural safeguards can guard effectively against the risks associated with hypnotically refreshed testimony, we reject the *Hurd* approach and hold that M.A.'s testimony is inadmissible . . . .

NOTES AND PROBLEMS

1.   "Incompetent" is one of those ambiguous terms that must be used with care. It is occasionally employed to refer to the inadmissibility of a particular item of evidence by reason of one of the exclusionary rules. For example, in the *Devitt* case, the El Dorado Police Crime Report may be "incompetent" as evidence because it is inadmissible hearsay. This is the sense of the term in the inartful Perry Mason-type objection, "Your Honor, I object: that evidence is incompetent, irrelevant, and immaterial."

2.   Similarly, it is sometimes said that a person is "incompetent" as a witness concerning a matter unless he or she has personal, "first hand" knowledge of that matter. If a person has no personal knowledge, his testimony is either based on hearsay or a fabrication. We do not use "competent" in this sense either in this chapter. The personal knowledge requirement is a logical relevancy concept that we shall cover later.

3.   The *Moore* case is notable for a number of reasons, particularly its reliance on scientific evidence and its willingness to overturn a rule of law based on the results of ongoing research in forensic psychology. Note the court's reference to the *Frye* rule as one of the standards for the authentication of scientific expert testimony. In an omitted part of the opinion, the court also discusses the more recently adopted *Daubert* rule. These issues will be developed in Chapters 12 and 23. In fact, some courts have treated the issue of hypnotically refreshed testimony as primarily a scientific evidence question. *E.g., People v. Shirley*, 31 Cal. 3d 18, 723 P.2d 1354 (1982) (holding hypnotically refreshed testimony inadmissible); *People v. Gonzales*, 415 Mich. 615, 329 N.W.2d 743 (1982) (post-hypnotic recollections inadmissible because not generally accepted in the scientific community). In these jurisdictions, the issue is not one of competency but admissibility under the rules governing scientific evidence.

4.   In *Rock v. Arkansas*, 483 U.S. 44 (1987), the U.S. Supreme Court held that a criminal defendant could not be denied her constitutional right to testify because of a state rule that excluded post-hypnotic testimony. The Court determined that the "[w]holesale inadmissibility of a defendant's testimony is an arbitrary restriction on the right to testify in the absence of clear evidence by the State repudiating the validity of all post hypnosis recollections." *Id.* at 61. Writing for the majority, Justice Blackmun conceded that "scientific understanding of the phenomenon and

of the means to control the effects of hypnosis is still in its infancy." *Id.* However, he concluded that the available research has "not shown that hypnotically enhanced testimony is always . . . untrustworthy and . . . immune to the traditional means of evaluating credibility . . . ." *Id.* This means that any state court rule that bars hypnotically enhanced testimony in all cases is invalid as applied to a criminal defendant's testimony. However, *Rock's* rationale does not necessarily apply to witnesses other than the accused. *Burral v. State,* 352 Md. 707, 724 A.2d 65, 79 (1999) (holding that defendant's compulsory process right did not include the right to the hypnotically refreshed witness testimony).

In *Moore,* Justice Rivera-Soto concurred in part and dissented in part. He agreed that M.A.'s post-hypnotic statements were inadmissible because they violated the *Hurd* guidelines. However, he would have created an exception for a victim's hypnotically refreshed testimony mirroring the *Rock* exception for the accused's hypnotically refreshed testimony, based on the New Jersey Constitution's Crime Victim's Bill of Rights. 902 A.2d at 1212–14.

Some courts have held that the *Rock* ruling does not prohibit a state from imposing guidelines to improve the reliability of the accused's post-hypnotic testimony. *Morgan v. Florida,* 537 So. 2d 973, 976 (Fla. 1989) (holding that medical diagnosis based on hypnotically refreshed information from defendant was admissible). *Cf. United States v. Scheffer,* 523 U.S. 303, 308 (1998) (an accused's right to present evidence is not unlimited, but rather is subject to reasonable restrictions; state and federal rule makers have broad latitude under the Constitution to establish rules excluding evidence from criminal trials so long as are not arbitrary or disproportionate to the purposes they are designed to serve).

5. No federal decision in this area has ever used Rule 601 as a basis for decision. So far, the federal courts have treated hypnotically refreshed testimony as a credibility issue, not a competency issue, and as such, governed by federal law and determined on a case-by-case basis.

All federal courts agree that the use of hypnotically refreshed testimony against an accused in a state court trial under state law is not a per se federal constitutional violation entitling the accused to habeas corpus relief. *See, e.g., Mancuso v. Olivarez,* 292 F.3d 939, 955 (9th Cir. 2002) ("The admission of post-hypnotic testimony does not violate the Sixth Amendment right to confrontation"). However, its application in a particular case could raise due process issues.

6. Refer back to our discussion of preliminary facts conditioning the admissibility of evidence. Should the judge finally determine witness competency (Rule 104(a)), or does the judge make only a preliminary determination that there is evidence sufficient to support a finding of competency by the jury (Rule 104 (b))? Why?

7. **Problem 7-1.** In the *Hill* case, one of Ms. Hill's witnesses is Mr. Phipps, who claims to have seen the collision. Observing the collision was such a traumatic experience for Phipps that immediately after the accident, he began consulting a psychiatrist, Dr. McCoy. McCoy is convinced that Phipps is suffering from partial amnesia, that the amnesia includes the date of the collision, and, hence that Phipps is lying when he claims to remember details of the collision. Polecat Motors

challenges Phipps's competency. As trial judge, would you listen to McCoy's testimony before ruling on the competency objection? How does this problem relate to the preceding question? Weihofen, *Testimonial Competence and Credibility*, 34 GEO. WASH. L. REV. 53, 55 (1965).

d.   Mental Capacity to Narrate

The last required capacity is the witness's ability to narrate — to relate what she remembers about the perceived event. California Evidence Code § 701 provides:

> (a)   A person is disqualified to be a witness if he or she is: (1) incapable of expressing himself or herself concerning the matter so as to be understood, either directly or through interpretation by one who can understand him;
>   . . .

The rule restates the common law. Bear in mind that a witness is not incompetent simply because of an inability to communicate in English; a witness may testify through a qualified interpreter.

NOTES AND PROBLEMS

1.   Problem 7-2. Is the critical time for determining competency the time of the event or the time of trial? Suppose that in *Hill*, a young child observed the collision. At that time, the child was only three, but by the time of the trial the child is eight. Polecat Motors objects to the child's competency as a witness. Does it matter whether Polecat is challenging the child's perceptual ability rather than the child's capacity to remember or relate? If so, why? Stafford, *The Child as a Witness*, 37 WASH. L. REV. 303, 306–07 (1962).

2.   Remember that the substantive law of contracts and crimes recognized limitations on the competency of minors. To what extent should the law of Evidence also recognize limitations? Should those limitations be fixed or flexible? Can we find answers in the teachings of child psychology?

3.   Problem 7-3. Assume that you are the trial judge in *Devitt*. The prosecutor calls Mr. Paterson as a witness. It is apparent from his answers to the first few questions that he is deeply mentally disturbed and not very coherent. You call counsel to the bench, and the prosecutor informs you that Paterson is suffering from a severe psychosis brought on by the attack upon him. Defendant moves for a psychiatric examination. How would you proceed? *Compare Nobrega v. Commonwealth*, 628 S.E.2d 922 (Va. 2006) (trial court has no authority to order independent psychiatric or psychological examination of complaining child witness in rape case) *with Commonwealth v. Aitahmedlamara*, 823 N.E.2d 408, 411 (Mass. App. Ct. 2005) (trial court has discretion whether to order psychiatric examination of mentally retarded witness to determine competency) *and People v. Anderson*, 25 Cal. 4th 543, 22 P.3d 347, 369 (2001) (same). Federal courts have no power to order a non-party witness to be examined by a psychiatrist. The most the court can do is condition a witness's testimony on a prior examination, and that power should be exercised sparingly. *United States v. Zizzo*, 120 F.3d 1338, 1347 (7th Cir. 1997) (observing that "even the most dastardly scoundrels, cheats, and liars are generally competent to testify").

4. **Problem 7-4.** Assume that in the last problem, you ordered a psychiatric examination. Following the examination, the psychiatrist concluded that although Paterson is generally well adjusted, he suffers from insane delusions about violent attacks and often fantasizes such attacks. Do such delusions render him incompetent as a witness? Is it relevant how often he has fantasies?

5. **Problem 7-5.** Assume that in the last problem, the psychiatrist instead concluded that Paterson is psychotic and suffers from a schizophrenic reaction. As trial judge, would you rule that he is incompetent to testify? Suppose that the psychiatrist added that Paterson's mental illness "might affect" the content of his testimony? Or that the psychiatrist testified that Paterson "is in poor contact with reality"? Would you sustain the objection now?

D. THE FEDERAL RULES

Rule 601 purports to abolish all non-statutory grounds for rendering prospective witnesses incompetent. The Advisory Committee's Note makes the intent explicit: "No mental or moral qualifications for testifying as a witness are specified. Standards of mental capacity have proved elusive in actual application. The question is one particularly suited to the jury as one of weight and credibility. . . ."

If we are to interpret Rule 601 and the accompanying Note literally, the Rule works a revolution. Rather than merely reforming the old moral and mental capacity requirements, the Rule overthrows and abandons them. The only remnant of the moral capacity requirement of sincerity seems to be Rule 603 (the oath requirement); the only vestige of the mental capacity doctrine is Rule 602 (personal knowledge); and the only ability-to-communicate requirement is Rule 604 (interpreters).

Although the legislative history of Rule 601 and its state counterparts almost conclusively demonstrates that this literal interpretation of the statute is correct, many courts continue to assume that the judge retains the common law power to bar a prospective witness by finding as a matter of fact that the witness lacks one of the capacities required at common law. *E.g., United States v. Whittington,* 26 F.3d 456, 466 n.9. (4th Cir. 1994) (holding that "except where a witness is shown to lack personal knowledge of the matters about which he or she intends to testify, does not have the capacity to recall, or does not understand the duty to testify truthfully, a witness is presumed to be qualified"). Judges, schooled in the common law and comfortable with their ability to exercise discretion wisely, sometimes find it difficult to recognize the meaning of statutes intended to revolutionize the common law.

NOTES

1. If the trial judge under Rule 601 has no discretion to refuse to permit a witness to testify on grounds of mental incapacity or immaturity, is there any other basis on which the trial judge can properly exclude the testimony? Read Rules 402, 403, and 611(a).

2. Judge Weinstein's well-known evidence treatise concludes that under the Federal Rules, the trial judge may bar a witness's testimony if "no one could reasonably believe the witness could have observed, remembered, communicated or told the truth with respect to the event in question." 3 WEINSTEIN'S FEDERAL EVIDENCE ¶ 601.03[1][a], at 601–10 (J. McLaughlin ed., 2d ed. 2007). Assume that that is the correct scope of the judge's remaining discretionary power to rule on "competency" issues. How does that power compare with the scope of the judge's power before the adoption of the Federal Rules? Think back to the discussion of preliminary fact-finding procedures under Rule 104(a). Before the adoption of the Federal Rules, did the judge rule on competency as a matter of fact or of law?

3. In 1994, Congress enacted 18 U.S.C. § 3509(c) as part of a comprehensive crime bill designed in part to strengthen the national campaign against child abuse. Section 3509(c), applicable in federal criminal cases, reads:

(c)   Competency examinations.

  (1)   Effect on Federal Rules of Evidence. Nothing in this subsection shall be construed to abrogate rule 601 of the Federal Rules of Evidence.

  (2)   Presumption. A child is presumed to be competent.

  (3)   Requirement of written motion. A competency examination regarding a child witness may be conducted by the court only upon written motion and offer of proof of incompetency by a party.

  (4)   Requirement of compelling reasons. A competency examination regarding a child may be conducted only if the court determines, on the record, that compelling reasons exist. A child's age alone is not a compelling reason.

  (5)   Persons permitted to be present. The only persons who may be permitted to be present at a competency examination are —

    (A)   the judge;

    (B)   the attorney for the Government;

    (C)   the attorney for the defendant;

    (D)   a court reporter; and

    (E)   persons whose presence, in the opinion of the court, is necessary to the welfare and well-being of the child, including the child's attorney, guardian ad litem, or adult attendant.

  (6)   Not before jury. A competency examination regarding a child witness shall be conducted out of the sight and hearing of a jury.

  (7)   Direct examination of child. Examination of a child related to competency shall normally be conducted by the court on the basis of questions submitted by the attorney for the Government and the attorney for the defendant including a party acting as an attorney pro se. The court may permit an attorney but not a party acting as an attorney pro se to examine a child directly on competency if the

court is satisfied that the child will not suffer emotional trauma as a result of the examination.

(8)   Appropriate questions. The questions asked at the competency examination of a child shall be appropriate to the age and developmental level of the child, shall not be related to the issues at trial, and shall focus on determining the child's ability to understand and answer simple questions.

(9)   Psychological and psychiatric examinations. Psychological and psychiatric examinations to assess the competency of a child witness shall not be ordered without a showing of compelling need.

What light, if any, does § 3509(c) shed on the proper interpretation of Rule 601? Note the disclaimer in § 3509(c)(1). Yet does § 3509(c)(2) make sense if Rule 601 sweeps away all competency requirements? Bear in mind the Supreme Court's oft-repeated caveat that "the views of a subsequent Congress form a hazardous basis for inferring the intent of an earlier one." *Consumer Product Safety Comm'n v. GTE Sylvania, Inc.*, 447 U.S. 102, 117–19 (1980).

E.   SPECIALIZED ASPECTS OF COMPETENCY

1.   Disqualification for Interest: Dead Man's Acts

Rule 601's revolution has left a few corners of evidence law untouched, among them various state Dead Man's Acts. Although the old common law disqualification for interest (based on the theory that certain classes of persons were so likely to testify falsely that total exclusion from the witness stand was needed as a safeguard) is now virtually obsolete in all jurisdictions there is one major exception:

> Known generally as Dead Man's Acts, these statutory exceptions vary widely in their terms. Generally, they prohibit the party-witness and other interested persons from testifying to conversations, transactions, or other dealings with a decedent or incompetent when the decedent's estate or the incompetent's representative is an adverse party.

3 WEINSTEIN'S FEDERAL EVIDENCE ¶ 601.05[1][a], at 601–26 (J. McLaughlin ed., 2d ed. 2006).

At one time, Dead Man's Acts were in force in about two thirds of U.S. jurisdictions and were enforced in the federal courts by virtue of Federal Rule of Civil Procedure 43(a). Ray, *Dead Man's Statutes*, 24 OHIO ST. L.J. 89 (1963). Despite vigorous attack by legal writers and judges, the statutes have proved remarkably difficult to overturn.

Although Dead Man's Acts vary greatly in wording and coverage (and can seem complex), the problem they seek to address is uncorroborated (interested) testimony, and their goal is to preclude fraudulent claims against decedents' estates.

By way of example, here is a statute from New York:

N.Y. Civ. Prac. Law § 4519. Personal transaction or communication between witness and decedent or mentally ill person.

Upon the trial of an action or the hearing upon the merits of a special proceeding, a party or a person interested in the event, or a person from, through or under whom such a party or interested person derives his interest or title by assignment or otherwise, shall not be examined as a witness in his own behalf or interest, or in behalf of the party succeeding to his title or interest against the executor, administrator or survivor of a deceased person or the committee of a mentally ill person, or a person deriving his title or interest from, through or under a deceased person or mentally ill person, by assignment or otherwise, concerning a personal transaction or communication between the witness and the deceased person or mentally ill person, except where the executor, administrator, survivor, committee or person so deriving title or interest is examined in his own behalf, or the testimony of the mentally ill person or deceased person is given in evidence, concerning the same transaction or communication. A person shall not be deemed interested for the purposes of this section by reason of being a stockholder or officer of any banking corporation which is a party to the action or proceeding, or interested in the event thereof. No party or person interested in the event, who is otherwise competent to testify, shall be disqualified from testifying by the possible imposition of costs against him or the award of costs to him. A party or person interested in the event or a person from, through or under whom such a party or interested person derives his interest or title by assignment or otherwise, shall not be qualified for the purposes of this section, to testify in his own behalf or interest, or in behalf of the party succeeding to his title or interest, to personal transactions or communications with the donee of a power of appointment in an action or proceeding for the probate of a will, which exercises or attempts to exercise a power of appointment granted by the will of a donor of such power, or in an action or proceeding involving the construction of the will of the donee after its admission to probate.

Nothing contained in this section, however, shall render a person incompetent to testify as to the facts of an accident or the results there from where the proceeding, hearing, defense or cause of action involves a claim of negligence or contributory negligence in an action wherein one or more parties is the representative of a deceased or incompetent person based upon, or by reason of, the operation or ownership of a motor vehicle being operated upon the highways of the state, or the operation or ownership of aircraft being operated in the air space over the state, or the operation or ownership of a vessel on any of the lakes, rivers, streams, canals or other waters of this state, but this provision shall not be construed as permitting testimony as to conversations with the deceased.

———————

a. Statutory Interpretation and Analysis

1) Types of Actions

The wording of the various statutes differs. Statutes differ in identifying the protected party who may object and claim the benefit of the statute. Some statutes apply only to civil actions in which a decedent's or incompetent's personal representative (e.g., executor or guardian) is a party; other statutes apply more broadly to any civil action in which a person claiming through the decedent or incompetent (heir, devisee, or successor in interest) is joined as a party. Furthermore, some statutes protect this party only when he or she is sued; other statutes more liberally allow the party to invoke the statute whether the party is suing or being sued.

2) Disqualified Witnesses

Whose testimony does the statute bar? The variations are (a) all parties who claim adversely to the protected party; or (b) all parties and other interested persons whose interests are adverse to the protected party. This is the more common form.

The definition of an "interested person" has produced much litigation. The expression has been held to include a party's partners, shareholders, and even his attorneys, spouse, and employees. Ordinarily a pecuniary interest is required. In most jurisdictions, one cannot remove his disqualification by assigning the interest to another. We shall refer to the person whose testimony is barred as the disqualified person.

3) Scope of the Incompetence

The variations are numerous. The most common statute prohibits the disqualified person from testifying to certain facts. A few statutes bar testimony by the disqualified person about all matters occurring before the death or incompetency.

The statute prohibits only testimony against the protected party. The statute does not prohibit the protected party from calling a disqualified person as a witness. Thus, the statutes operate more like privileges than full-fledged competency rules.

4) Subject Matter of the Incompetence

In most states the testimonial incompetence is not blanket; the statutes preclude only testimony that falls within one of these categories:

(a) A "transaction with or statement by" the decedent or incompetent person;

(b) A "personal transaction or communication" between the disqualified person and the decedent or incompetent;

(c) A "verbal statement of or transaction with" the decedent;

(d) A "conversation with or event which took place in the presence of the deceased or incompetent person; and

(e) Oral communications between the decedent and the disqualified person.

Much litigation has centered on the question whether the events giving rise to a personal injury action, especially automobile accidents, are "transactions" with the decedent so as to bar a plaintiff's testimony about the accident when the alleged tortfeasor dies. The cases split, but many courts preclude such testimony. When we hear the expression "transaction," it usually connotes a consensual dealing such as a contract. A traffic accident is not a transaction in that sense. However, although the courts are generally hostile to these statutes, many have said that the expression "transaction" must be construed purposively. The purpose of the statute is to protect the estate from the injustice created by the unavailability of the decedent's testimony based on personal knowledge. Given that purpose, "transaction" should arguably be interpreted as including any fact or event which the decedent could have testified about on the basis of personal knowledge.

Some jurisdictions permit the disqualified person to testify for the limited purpose of authenticating business records. Although the party may not testify directly to the transactions, these courts permit the party to authenticate records that evidence the transactions.

5) Exceptions

Since Dead Man's Acts frequently defeat meritorious claims, there has been great hostility to the acts. Numerous exceptions to their operation have been recognized. Some are statutory; others are judicially created by artful statutory "construction." Most exceptions exempt parties standing in specified relationships from the act's operation. The relationships commonly exempted are employer-employee and partner-partner. These are important business relations. The fear is that if the act applied and precluded one party from testifying to normal business transactions, the interference with the relationship would be intolerable.

6) Waiver

If the Dead Man's Act is otherwise applicable and there is no exception, the party opposing the admission of the evidence should explicitly object. The party should use the following language: "[T]he witness is incompetent to answer the question asked because it calls for testimony of a personal transaction [or communication] with a person since deceased . . . , in violation of Section ___ of the State Code." M. LADD & R. CARLSON, CASES AND MATERIALS ON EVIDENCE 295 (1972). Whenever the party opposing the evidence neglects to make such an express and specific objection, he or she runs the risk that the court will find that the party waived the objection. Just as the skepticism about the acts' wisdom has led to several exceptions to the acts' scope, the hostility to the acts has made the courts receptive to waiver arguments. The courts have found — or strained to find — a waiver in a wide range of fact situations.

If the protected party calls a disqualified person as a witness, the incompetency is waived generally or at least as to the subjects on which the protected party examines the witness. All states recognize this exception.

There is similarly a waiver when the protected party introduces evidence of the deceased or incompetent person's statement. This will be in the form of a deposition or by virtue of a hearsay exception. The disqualified person may then testify about the same subject matter. This exception is also universal. There is a split, however, over whether the mere taking of the deposition effects a waiver, if the protected party does not offer it in evidence.

b.   The Future of Dead Man's Acts

The prevailing modern sentiment is that the risk that one party's death may create an evidentiary problem does not justify compounding the problem by depriving the finder of fact of other relevant evidence. The objections to these acts — and the countervailing objections to reform — are well summarized in the commentary of Prof. Vincent C. Alexander to the New York statute (CPLR 4519 *Practice Commentaries*):

> CPLR 4519, the so-called "Dead Man's Statute," is a vestige of the common law rule that parties and other interested persons were incompetent to testify in their own behalf. Such testimony was deemed unreliable as a matter of law. Although CPLR 4512 and its predecessor statutes have abolished incompetency based on interest, in general, CPLR 4519 and its predecessor statutes have preserved the rule of incompetency with respect to the testimony of an interested person concerning a transaction or communication with a decedent or mentally ill person. Such testimony is considered to be rife with the potential for perjury because it can be given without fear of contradiction by the other party to the transaction. Thus, when death or mental illness seals the lips of one of the parties to a transaction, the Dead Man's Statute seeks to achieve adversarial balance in civil trials by sealing the lips of the surviving party. Transactions or communications between the interested witness and the decedent or mentally ill person must therefore be proven through documentary evidence and the testimony of disinterested witnesses.

> One of the problems with the statute, aside from its questionable presumption about human nature, is that application of its hypertechnical language sometimes produces results that are at odds with its rationale. There is also an abiding belief by some that the statute produces injustice, especially in cases in which the only available evidence against an estate is the testimony of an interested party. Some critics are willing to accept the protectionist policy of the statute when claims are made against an estate, but feel that the statute should be inapplicable when the estate seeks affirmative relief. One court aptly observed that the complexity of the rule, together with an inclination toward "leniency or distinction in application" in cases of perceived injustice, "has led to innumerable contradictory decisions both at the trial and appellate court levels." . . .

> Advocates of the statute's abolition have argued that modern juries are sophisticated enough to give the testimony of an interested witness its proper weight. Proponents of reform would permit an interested witness to

testify, subject to one or another various procedural limitations that would help even the odds between the estate and its adversaries. These alternatives to the statute include permitting the admission of hearsay declarations of the decedent even if they do not fall within existing hearsay exceptions, requiring corroboration of the testimony of interested witnesses or imposing an increased burden of proof on the estate's adversary.

A substantial number of New York estate practitioners and Surrogate's Court personnel, however, are convinced that the statute does more good than harm and effectively prevents perjured claims against estates. . . . The Legislature rejected a 1958 proposal by the Advisory Committee on Practice and Procedure for abolition, and recent efforts to eliminate the rule from the Law Revision Commission's Proposed Code of Evidence for New York have been abandoned. *See* N.Y. Law Rev'n. Comm'n., Proposed N.Y. Code of Evidence § 602(e) (1991). A recent attempt to invalidate the statute on due process grounds as applied to a party defending against an estate's claim for affirmative relief was also rejected. For better or worse, the Dead Man's Statute "remains a part of the law of this State." . . .

NOTES AND PROBLEM

1. Should a Dead Man's Act apply to a will contest among the decedent's relatives? Can you distinguish a will contest from a lawsuit in which a stranger files a contract claim against the decedent's estate? Realistically, are the relatives claiming against the decedent? "Probate judges . . . seem to favor such statutes to prevent unscrupulous raids on estates." 3 WEINSTEIN'S FEDERAL EVIDENCE ¶ 601.05[1][a], at 601–26 (J. McLaughlin ed., 2d ed. 2006).

2. Problem 7-6. In the *Hill* case, Worker's deposition was taken and filed. Shortly before trial, Worker died from causes unrelated to the accident, and his administrator was substituted as party defendant. What evidentiary problems would you anticipate in introducing the following items of evidence under the Dead Man's Act of New York; or the Dead Man's Act of your state, if any?

(a)   Debra Hill's testimony about the accident;

(b)   Debra Hill's testimony that Worker visited her at the hospital and what he told her during that visit;

(c)   Testimony of Debra's husband, Arthur, about what he saw when he arrived at the accident scene; or

(d)   Worker's deposition.

3. Several jurisdictions have developed an innovative solution. Instead of barring the survivor's testimony, they repealed or modified their Dead Man's Act so that declarations made by the decedent before her death (which otherwise would have been inadmissible hearsay) can be admitted into evidence. Thus, both the survivor's testimony and the decedent's statements are placed before the trier of fact. *See e.g.*, CAL. EVID. CODE §§ 1260–61; CONN. GEN. STAT. § 52-172; D.C. STAT. 1981

§ 14-302(b); Mich. Comp. Laws § 600.2166; Mo. Ann. Stat. § 491.010; S.D.C.L. § 19-16-34; Utah Rules of Evid. 601; Va. Code Ann. § 8.01-397; Wyo. Stat. Ann. § 1-12-102.

2. Judges, Jurors and Attorneys

a. Judges

A judge is a competent witness in a trial so long as the judge is not presiding over that trial. For instance, when a state prisoner files a federal habeas corpus action, the state judge can testify about the trial that resulted in the prisoner's conviction. But what prevents the judge from testifying during a trial at which the judge is presiding? Perhaps it seems self-evident that the presiding judge should not take the witness stand and testify on behalf of a party. It would be extremely difficult for the jurors to resist the temptation to attach extraordinary weight to the judge's testimony. Moreover, the opposing attorney would find it awkward (to say the least) to cross-examine the judge.

Almost all jurisdictions now disqualify the judge as a witness in the trial in which she is sitting. Federal Rule of Evidence 605 provides: "The judge presiding at the trial may not testify in that trial as a witness. No objection need be made in order to preserve the point." The Advisory Committee Note further explains:

> The solution here presented is a broad rule of incompetency, rather than such alternatives as incompetency only as to material matters, leaving the matter to the discretion of the judge, or recognizing no incompetency. The choice is the result of the inability to evolve satisfactory answers to questions which arise when the judge abandons the bench for the witness stand. Who rules on objections? Who compels him to answer? Can he rule impartially on the weight and admissibility of his own testimony? Can he be impeached or cross-examined effectively? Can he, in a jury trial, avoid conferring his seal of approval on one side in the eyes of the jury? Can he, in a bench trial, avoid an involvement destructive of impartiality?

> The rule provides an "automatic" objection. To require an actual objection would confront an opponent with a choice between not objecting, with the result of allowing the testimony, and objecting, with the probable result of excluding the testimony but at the price of continuing the trial before a judge likely to feel that his integrity has been attacked by the objector.

PROBLEM

Problem 7-7. You represent defendant Devitt. The case is being tried without a jury. At the conclusion of the evidence, the judge announces her verdict — guilty. In giving the reasons for so finding, she states: "Now, I did not believe defendant's testimony. I visited the scene myself, and based on what I saw, I find that the events in question simply could not have unfolded the way he testified." On appeal, could you invoke Rule 605 to argue that the judge was a witness in violation of the rule? *See United States v. Nickl*, 427 F.3d 1286, 1292–93 (10th Cir. 2005).

b. Jurors

It may seem equally obvious that a juror should not step out of the jury box and onto the witness stand. The other jurors might be tempted to ascribe special significance to their fellow juror's testimony. Normally, this problem should never arise. If the prospective jurors are properly questioned during voir dire examination, their personal knowledge of the case should be ascertained and should disqualify them as jurors. However, at early common law, when the problem did arise, courts permitted the juror to testify. Federal Rule of Evidence 606(a) is clear on the modern rule:

(a) *At the trial.* — A member of the jury may not testify as a witness before that jury in the trial of the case in which the juror is sitting. If the juror is called so to testify, the opposing party shall be afforded an opportunity to object out of the presence of the jury.

The more difficult issue is the extent to which a juror, after verdict, may testify about juror misconduct to impeach the verdict in support of the losing party's motion for a new trial. Consider Federal Rule 606(b):

(b) *Inquiry into validity of verdict or indictment.* — Upon an inquiry into the validity of a verdict or indictment, a juror may not testify as to any matter or statement occurring during the course of the jury's deliberations or to the effect of anything upon that or any other juror's mind or emotions as influencing the juror to assent to or dissent from the verdict or indictment or concerning the juror's mental processes in connection therewith. But a juror may testify about (1) whether extraneous prejudicial information was improperly brought to the jury's attention, (2) whether any outside influence was improperly brought to bear upon any juror, or (3) whether there was a mistake in entering the verdict onto the verdict form. A juror's affidavit or evidence of any statement by the juror may not be received on a matter about which the juror would be precluded from testifying.

The Advisory Committee Note explains:

Subdivision (b). Whether testimony, affidavits, or statements of jurors should be received for the purpose of invalidating or supporting a verdict or indictment, and if so, under what circumstances, has given rise to substantial differences of opinion. The familiar rubric that a juror may not impeach his own verdict, dating from Lord Mansfield's time, is a gross oversimplification. The values sought to be promoted by excluding the evidence include freedom of deliberation, stability and finality of verdicts, and protection of jurors from annoyance and embarrassment. . . . On the other hand, simply putting verdicts beyond effective reach can only promote irregularity and injustice. The rule offers an accommodation between these competing considerations.

The mental operations and emotional reactions of jurors in arriving at a given result would, if allowed as a subject of inquiry, place every verdict at the mercy of jurors and invite tampering and harassment . . . As to matters other than mental operations and emotional reactions of jurors, substantial authority refuses to allow a juror to disclose irregularities which occur in the jury room, but allows his testimony as to irregularities occurring outside and allows outsiders to testify as to occurrences both inside and out. However, the door to the jury room is not necessarily a satisfactory dividing point . . . .

Under the federal decisions the central focus has been upon insulation of the manner in which the jury reached its verdict, and this protection extends to each of the components of deliberation, including arguments, discussions, mental and emotional reactions, votes, and any other feature of the process. Thus testimony or affidavits of jurors have been held incompetent to show a [compromise verdict, quotient verdict, speculation as to insurance coverage, misinterpretation of instructions, mistake in returning verdict, and interpretation of guilty plea by one defendant as implicating others.] The policy does not, however, foreclose testimony of jurors as to prejudicial extraneous information or influences injected into or brought to bear upon the deliberative process. Thus a juror is recognized as competent to testify to statements by the bailiff or the introduction of a prejudicial newspaper account into the jury room . . . .

This rule does not purport to specify the substantive grounds for setting aside verdicts for irregularity; it deals only with the competency of jurors to testify concerning those grounds.

Section (b)(3) of Rule 606 was added by amendment effective December 1, 2006. The Advisory Committee describes the reason for the amendment:

Rule 606(b) has been amended to provide that juror testimony may be used to prove that the verdict reported was the result of a mistake in entering the verdict on the verdict form. The amendment responds to a divergence between the text of the Rule and the case law that has established an exception for proof of clerical errors . . . . In adopting the exception for proof of mistakes in entering the verdict on the verdict form, the amendment specifically rejects the broader exception, adopted by some courts, permitting the use of juror testimony to prove that the jurors were operating under a misunderstanding about the consequences of the result that they agreed upon. . . . Thus, the exception established by the amendment is limited to cases such as "where the jury foreperson wrote down, in response to an interrogatory, a number different from that agreed upon by the jury, or mistakenly stated that the defendant was 'guilty' when the jury had actually agreed that the defendant was not guilty."

Carlson, *Impeaching Jury Verdicts*, 2 LITIG., Fall 1975, at 31–33, discusses this issue. Professor Carlson first poses a hypothetical in which a juror brings into the jury room an erroneous newspaper account of certain trial testimony that then serves as the basis for the verdict:

That the verdict was based upon an extraneous account which was inaccurate is clear. Now what? Can the party who lost get the verdict overturned? What if, in the course of a jury's deliberations, events take a slightly different turn? Instead of the jurors taking unsworn evidence from a newspaper, suppose they adopt an improper method of reaching a decision, such as drawing lots or using a quotient verdict to determine damages?

Newspaper clipping and quotient verdict problems seem to be more prevalent than other reported examples of jury "free enterprise." However, reported misconduct has ranged from unauthorized visits to a crime or accident scene by some jurors on their own, to the following situation: A defendant was being tried for illegal sale of alcoholic beverages. Exhibits in the case included three such bottles, all full, and these went with the jurors to the jury room when they retired to deliberate. Later, the bailiff was notified by the jurors that they had reached a verdict. The bailiff opened the door of the jury room and discovered that all three bottles had been opened and emptied. On review, the state supreme court ruled that "both parties have a right to the cool, dispassionate and unbiased judgment of each juror, and the rule seems to be well established that prejudice will be presumed if liquor is drunk after the jury has retired to consider the case." Whether jury misconduct is of the bizarre type as in the last example, or the more regularly encountered problem of the jury deciding the case on non-record information, the question remains — what may counsel do to remedy the situation?

State law is divided into the two competing positions. A strong minority view permits jurors to testify to objective misconduct — overt acts which can either be corroborated or disproved by the testimony of other jurors. Unauthorized trips by jurors to view the scene of a crime fall within this category, as do improper methods for arriving at a verdict. Under this view, deliberations do not lose all secrecy. Several items remain private. For example, a juror would be incompetent as a witness to report matters thought to "inhere in the verdict." Misconduct in this category is not objective misconduct and is not properly the subject of post-verdict attack. Examples include a juror's testimony that he misunderstood the judge's instructions, or one juror impugning another's reasoning in arriving at a verdict.

Rule 606(b) of the Federal Rules of Evidence permits juror testimony attacking a verdict only when "extraneous prejudicial information was improperly brought to the jury's attention" or when "outside influence was improperly brought to bear upon any juror." Thus, the jury's use of newspaper clippings may be exposed in a post-trial attack on the verdict because the clippings would constitute extraneous information which was improperly brought before the jury within the meaning of the federal rule. Similarly, when a juror is approached by a party or any other person during a trial, the second provision of Rule 606(b) may be invoked to show that improper influence was brought to bear on a juror.

However, the rule insulates from attack a favorite ground for post-verdict complaint by defense lawyers in personal injury cases — the quotient verdict. Rule 606 provides that statements made during a jury's deliberations are not later reportable, except to show extraneous prejudicial information or improper outside influence.

PROBLEM

Problem 7-8. In *Hill*, which of the following could be shown by a juror's testimony under Rule 606(b):

(a)   Most jurors misunderstood key instructions;

(b)   Everyone ignored the judge's admonition not to be influenced by the fact that defendant could afford to pay a large judgment;

(c)   A juror slept through the deliberations;

(d)   The jurors agreed in advance that each would write a verdict amount on a slip of paper, they would add the amounts on the twelve slips, and they would be bound by the quotient of the sum divided by twelve;

(e)   During the trial, a juror went to the public library and got some books on automobile design. She read excerpts aloud during the jury's deliberations;

(f)   Several jurors read newspaper accounts of the trial;

(g)   The jurors agreed to deliberate for a maximum of four hours;

(h)   During deliberations, a juror related a similar personal experience with his automobile and that story influenced the verdict;

(i)   During deliberations, several jurors made remarks clearly evidencing racial bias. (Ms. Hill is African-American.) *Shillcutt v. Gagnon*, 827 F.2d 1155 (7th Cir. 1987); *Dobbs v. Zant*, 720 F. Supp. 1566, 1571–79 (N.D. Ga. 1989), *aff'd*, 963 F.2d 1403 (11th Cir. 1991), *rev'd on other grounds*, 506 U.S. 357, 113 S. Ct. 835 (1993); *Powell v. Allstate Ins. Co.*, 652 So. 2d 354 (Fla. 1995).

(j)   Throughout the trial several jurors consumed alcohol and drugs at lunch and tended to be sleepy in the afternoon sessions of the trial. *Tanner v. United States*, 483 U.S. 107 (1987);

(k)   At the beginning of the deliberations, the foreperson announced that she "strongly favored" a defense verdict and used "strong arm tactics" during deliberations to coerce other jurors to vote in favor of the defense. *United States v. Casamayor*, 837 F.2d 1509, 1515 (11th Cir. 1988).

c.   Attorneys

In light of the wording of Rule 601, does a federal judge have the authority to exclude an attorney's testimony? Although Rules 605 and 606 regulate the admissibility of testimony by judges and jurors, a provision on attorney's testimony is conspicuously absent from Article VI.

The American Bar Association's Model Rules of Professional Conduct, Rule 3.7(a) generally proscribes a lawyer's testimony in a case in which the lawyer is serving as an advocate unless (1) the testimony relates to an uncontested issue, (2) the testimony relates to the nature and value of legal services rendered in the case, or (3) disqualification of the lawyer would work a substantial hardship on the client. Most jurisdictions have a comparable rule. The former ABA Model Code of Professional Responsibility (DR 5-101(B)) contained a similar proscription. The Model Code, Ethical Consideration 5-9 articulates the rationale for the rule:

> If a lawyer is both counsel and witness, he becomes more easily impeachable for interest and thus may be a less effective witness. Conversely, the opposing counsel may be handicapped in challenging the credibility of the lawyer when the lawyer also appears as an advocate in the case. An advocate who becomes a witness is in the unseemly and ineffective position of arguing his own credibility. The roles of an advocate and of a witness are inconsistent; the function of an advocate is to advance or argue the cause of another, while that of a witness is to state facts objectively.

As a matter of policy, should the courts convert these ethical norms into competency rules and exclude testimony in violation of the professional responsibility rules?

Chapter 8

LOGICAL RELEVANCE: PROBATIVE VALUE

Read Federal Rules of Evidence 401, 402, 602 and 901.

A. INTRODUCTION

In the preceding chapter we discussed the threshold admissibility question of whether a person is competent to serve as a witness. If a person does not qualify as a competent witness, that person cannot give any testimony at the trial. Assuming the competency hurdle can be overcome, there are several other hurdles that must be cleared to guarantee the testimony's admission. The next hurdle presented is the requirement of logical relevance.

The competency doctrine focuses on the prospective witness; we test the prospective witness' personal qualifications such as the ability to perceive and remember. However, the logical relevance doctrine shifts our focus to the substantive content of the witness's proposed testimony and how it relates to issues in the trial. Even if the person is qualified to give some testimony in the case, that conclusion does not guarantee the admissibility of everything to which the witness proposes to testify.

At the very least, to be admissible, evidence must have probative value. Federal Evidence Rule 402 states the principle succinctly: "Irrelevant evidence is not admissible." That leaves open the question of what exactly relevance is. The 2011 Amendments to the Rules seek to clarify the concept of relevance by dividing it into two sub-parts: "Evidence is relevant if a) it has any tendency to make a fact more or less probable than it would be without the evidence; and b) the fact is of consequence in determining the action." It is the first subsection that we are referring to as "logical evidence." Sub-part (b) is what we refer to as "materiality."

The evidentiary concept of logical relevance has several subtle aspects. To grasp the concept, the student must master three basic distinctions covered in this chapter: (1) the distinction between logical relevance and materiality; (2) the distinction between direct and circumstantial logical relevance; and (3) the distinction between facial and underlying logical relevance. As we study this area, it will become increasingly clear that the Federal Rules of Evidence display a strong bias in favor of admitting logically relevant evidence.

B. THE DISTINCTION BETWEEN LOGICAL RELEVANCE AND MATERIALITY

1. Logical Relevance

Logical relevance of a piece of evidence — a fact — depends on whether there is a rational connection between the fact and what is sought to be proved or disproved. Those rational connections have typically been described as deductive (as used in mathematical proofs), inductive (observations about items applied to similar items), and abductive (plausible explanation) logic. As Professor Brewer explains:

"In a valid deductive argument, the truth of the premises guarantees the truth of the conclusion. In an inductive argument, the truth of the premises cannot guarantee the truth of the conclusion, but when they are well chosen their truth can warrant the conclusion's probable truth. In abductive argument the plausibility of a proposed hypothesis that would explain some event that is believed to have occurred . . . suggests, though it cannot come close to guaranteeing, the truth of the hypothesis itself."

Scott Brewer, *Exemplary Reasoning: Semantics, Pragmatics, and the Rational Force of Reasoning by Analogy*, 109 Harv. L. Rev. 925, 942 (1996).

The form the logic takes, however, is not of paramount concern to legal actors, because legal relevance consists of *any* tendency to make an issue more or less probable than it would be without the evidence. All that is required is a rational connection. But whether there is a rational connection between a fact and an issue is not entirely a matter of logic; it depends on basic assumptions about the world. *See, e.g.*, Susan Haack, *Proving Causation: The Holism of Warrant and the Atomism of Daubert*, 4 J. Health & Biomedical L. 253, 286 (2008) (noting that "whether and to what degree p is relevant to q, that is, is not a matter of pure logic, but depends on facts about the world").

The key question in determining the relevance of a particular fact is, relevant to what? As the Advisory Committee Notes explain: "Relevancy is not an inherent characteristic of any item of evidence but exists only as a relation between an item of evidence and a matter properly provable in the case." (2011 Amendments) In order to determine whether a particular fact is relevant to a given issue, it is necessary to have a theory about how the fact and issue fit together. As Professor Twining explains the centrality of these questions about facts:

William Twining *Taking Facts Seriously — Again*
55 J. Legal Educ. 360 (2005)

* * *

When Jerome Frank argued that over 90 percent of adjudication and pretrial work is more concerned with doubts and uncertainties about facts than with disputed questions of law, he partly understated the case because he was only concerned with litigation and his main focus was on the contested jury trial. But the general message is basically correct — that inferential reasoning and other aspects of information processing are important in most contexts of legal practice and have been relatively neglected in legal education and training. The emphasis on the Federal Rules in American bar examinations and on the rules of evidence in police training to the neglect of inferential reasoning are prime examples.

*   *   *

I suggest that "The Rationalist Tradition of Evidence Scholarship" model provides the most coherent view of the principles of proof. This can be encapsulated in the Benthamite proposition that the direct end of legal procedure is the pursuit of justice under the law through achieving rectitude of decision by rational means. One does not have to subscribe to all of the elements in this ideal type to use it as an organizing device; indeed, my particular formulation of the Rationalist model was specifically designed to signal potential significant points at which skeptics might challenge it. Rather, the model is robust for two reasons: first, because it represents a stable set of assumptions that have largely been shared by leading writers on the law of evidence in the common law tradition for over two centuries. These assumptions also underpin important attempts to rationalize the law of evidence, including the American Federal Rules. Second, the ideal type sets the study of evidence at the outset in its ideological context, that is to say the underlying values involved in the design and operation of legal procedures. Since the main values involved — truth, reason, justice, and the public interest — are regularly, perhaps essentially, contested, far from being a naïve, dogmatic, functionalist model, it provides a context for considering controversial issues.

Historically, most of the controversies in Anglo-American evidence scholarship can be accommodated *within* the Rationalist model because they relate to priorities between truth and other values or represent different views of rationality (for example, Baconians versus Pascalians), or different epistemological theories (for example, correspondence versus coherence theories of truth), or between political priorities (for example, process values/due process versus social control). These can be seen as debates within the Rationalist Tradition. However, the model identifies a range of potential points of departure from one or more of the assumptions of that tradition, for example challenges from strong philosophical skeptics, cultural relativists, post-modernists, or those who doubt the desirability, or the feasibility, or the sense in expecting litigation to be centrally concerned with truth, justice, or reason.

*   *   *

Can the law of evidence be given a coherent framework so that it is not seen just as a rather fragmented confusing collection of loosely related topics? . . . There are, no doubt, several ways to present the rules of evidence within a coherent framework. My view, which is quite orthodox, is that our law of evidence is based on the Thayerite theory that the rules of evidence are a series of disparate exceptions to a principle of free proof, where free proof means ordinary principles of practical inferential reasoning. One needs to understand the principle before studying the exceptions. That means understanding the logic of proof. Thayer may have exaggerated the importance of the jury in the historical development of the law of evidence; he may have taken an unnecessarily narrow view of the law of evidence by equating it with exclusionary rules in disputed trials (but he did write about presumptions, burdens of proof, and judicial notice); but he was surely right in maintaining that the rules of evidence need to be conceived within a framework of *argumentation.*

From the point of view of pedagogy, the topic of relevance is the obvious bridge between the logic of proof and the rules of evidence. Understanding relevance involves understanding the logic of proof within a framework that treats both the principles of proof and the rules of evidence as belonging to a single, coherent subject. . . . [U]nderstanding the logic of proof involves skills as well as knowledge. Studying that topic directly for a substantial period at the start of a course and reinforcing the concepts and skills throughout is a more economical and effective way of understanding evidence. Further it develops some valuable general intellectual skills.

Logical relevance is a matter of logic and experience, not a matter of law or policy. That is, whether evidence is relevant depends on some basic assumptions we make about the way the world works. When we ask whether an item has "logical relevance," we are testing to see whether as a matter of logic and our experience, the item tends to support a particular inference; we try to determine whether there is a rational nexus or connection between the item of evidence and the inference the item is offered to prove. To visualize the test, think of this diagram:

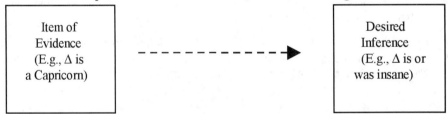

To draw the arrow, we must conclude that the item of evidence has some effect upon the balance of probabilities regarding the truth of the desired inference — either increasing or decreasing its probability. Note that if, and only if, astrology is true does the defendant's astral sign have any bearing at all on whether defendant was insane. *See* Susan Haack, *Of Truth in Science and in Law*, 73 Brook. L. Rev. 985, 996 (2008) (explaining that whether evidence is relevant depends on facts about the world, facts about which we may be mistaken). Even if astrology were part of your worldview, for defendant's astral sign to be relevant, you must have a theory as to how it affects the desired inference of insanity, and be able to demonstrate the logic of the link. For example, as the Supreme Court noted, information about the phases of the moon may be relevant to whether the night was dark, if that is an issue in the case; but evidence that the moon was full will not affect the balance of probabilities regarding whether an individual behaved irrationally on that night unless there are "creditable grounds" to support such a logical link. *See Daubert v. Merrell Dow Pharms., Inc.*, 509 U.S. 579, 591 (1993) (explaining relevance).

If the item increases or decreases the probability — no matter how slightly — the item has logical relevance. Do not be concerned with how greatly the item increases or decreases the probability; we shall turn to the matter of the quantum of probative value when we consider legal irrelevance (or balancing probative value against prejudicial effect). At this point we are interested only in whether the evidence being offered has any effect at all on the balance of probabilities.

PROBLEMS

Problem 8-1. In the *Devitt* case, the defense is attempting to prove that Devitt was insane at the time of the alleged battery. Which of the following items of evidence would be logically relevant? Why?

- Proof that there was a full moon the night of the alleged battery.

- Proof that Devitt is a Capricorn.

- Proof that Devitt was under psychiatric care 20 years ago.

- Testimony by a lay witness that she observed Devitt two hours before the alleged battery and that in her opinion, he was "acting a bit peculiar."

- Testimony of a licensed psychiatrist that Devitt is psychotic.

In answering these questions, pretend that you had never attended law school. Answer each question from the perspective of a logical and reasonably knowledgeable, adult layperson. Would such a layperson find a difference between proof of the full moon and evidence of Devitt's psychiatric treatment 20 years ago? If so, why?

Problem 8-2. In *Devitt*, the defense would like to offer evidence that the defendant took and passed a polygraph test. During the test, Devitt denied attacking Paterson. At trial, the defense calls Dr. Abrahams, the polygraphist who administered the test to Devitt. On the one hand, Dr. Abrahams testifies that the polygraph test is generally accurate 70–85% of the time. On the other hand, he concedes that as a scientist, he uses the rule of thumb that a scientific technique's validity is not proven until it attains an accuracy level of 90% or better. The prosecutor objects that Dr. Abraham's testimony is "absolutely irrelevant" given Abraham's admissions about the fallibility of the polygraph. Who should prevail?

Problem 8-3. In our torts case, after the accident Ms. Hill files a claim for personal injury and property damage with her insurer, Midwest Mutual. Midwest Mutual denies the claim, and Ms. Hill later sues Midwest Mutual. She sues not only to recover the policy proceeds covering her losses but also for attorney's fees. The law of this jurisdiction allows an insured to recover attorney's fees in a suit against the insurer if the insurer denied the claim in bad faith. At the trial of her suit against Midwest Mutual, Ms. Hill offers evidence that she offered to submit a polygraph test administered by any examiner of Midwest Mutual's choosing. Midwest's attorney objects that the evidence is irrelevant. (Assume that polygraph evidence is generally inadmissible in this jurisdiction.) *See Criss v. Springfield Township*, 564 N.E.2d 440 (Ohio 1990); *Murphy v. Cincinnati Ins. Co.*, 772 F.2d 273, 277 (6th Cir. 1985); DeFranco, *Using Polygraph Results To Decide "Good Faith Denial Of Coverage" Cases*, 91 ILL. B.J. 32 (2003).

Problem 8-4. In her lawsuit against Roe and Polecat, Ms. Hill offers evidence that before trial, Worker refused to submit to a polygraph test about the accident. The defense attorneys object that the evidence is irrelevant and polygraph evidence is inadmissible per se. *See* D. FAIGMAN, ET AL., MODERN SCIENTIFIC EVIDENCE: THE LAW & SCIENCE OF EXPERT TESTIMONY § 40:3 (2006). Suppose that Ms. Hill asked the judge to consider the following testimony from Dr. Miriam Laurens before ruling on the relevance objection: She operates a polygraph firm in town; Worker was formerly one of her employees; and she often heard Worker say that he considered the polygraph to be "highly reliable." (Once again, assume that polygraph evidence is ordinarily inadmissible in this jurisdiction.) Should the judge do so?

Problem 8-5. One month after the accident in the *Hill* case, Polecat redesigned the gas tank of the model of car involved in the accident. Polecat began marketing automobiles with the redesigned gas tank one year after the accident. At the trial, Ms. Hill's attorney offers evidence of the redesign. Polecat's attorney objects that "what we did later isn't at all relevant to whether we were at fault at the time of the accident. The only question is what happened then — not what might have occurred a whole year later." Is that correct?

Problem 8-6. In the *Hill* case, to show the defective nature of the gas tank Ms. Hill's attorney offers evidence of two accidents that occurred six years before the accident in *Hill.* In both of the prior accidents, the vehicles had gas tanks similar to the tank in Ms. Hill's car; the gas tanks exploded in the manner in which Ms. Hill's did; and the drivers suffered injuries similar to Ms. Hill's. However, neither injured party sued Polecat; and in this jurisdiction, there is a five-year statute of limitations on such claims. When Ms. Hill's attorney offers evidence of the prior accidents, Polecat's attorney objects that "those accidents can't be used against us now; since the period of limitations has passed, they're no longer actionable and, hence, irrelevant." *See Arrow Intern., Inc. v. Sparks*, 81 Ark. App. 42, 98 S.W.3d 48 (2003). How should the judge rule?

Problem 8-7. In the *Devitt* case file, the pivotal question is whether Devitt attacked Paterson without provocation. Assume alternatively a prosecution in which the central issue is the assailant's identity. The victim, Paterson, testifies that during the fight, the assailant accidentally cut himself on his own knife so badly that the assailant bled on Paterson's shirt. The prosecutor lays a proper chain of custody for the shirt from the crime scene to Dr. Margolin at the crime laboratory. Dr. Margolin is prepared to testify that: She is an expert in blood identification; she analyzed the stain on the shirt and a sample of blood she drew from the defendant; both samples were type A blood; and approximately 42% of the world's population has type A blood. *See* A. MOENSSENS, J. STARRS, C. HENDERSON & F. INBAU, SCIENTIFIC EVIDENCE IN CIVIL AND CRIMINAL CASES § 13.10, at 778 (4th ed. 1995). The defense attorney objects that "so many persons have type A blood that this evidence has absolutely no probative value." Do you agree?

Problem 8-8. In the *Devitt* case, suppose the victim testifies that the assailant kidnapped him and forced him to go to a nearby apartment. He testifies that the apartment in question had a moose head on one wall, a triangle-shaped mirror on another wall and a picture of the Empire State Building on a third wall. The prosecutor then calls the defendant's landlord to testify that the victim's description corresponds to objects on the walls in the defendant's apartment. The defense objects that "the testimony has nothing to do with this case." *See Bridges v. State*, 247 Wis. 350, 19 N.W.2d 529, 534–36 (1945). What should the judge rule? Suppose alternatively that the victim testifies only that the apartment contained a bed and a television. Once again the landlord is willing to testify that the defendant's apartment contains the items the victim described. Relevant?

2. Materiality

a. Introduction

Materiality involves the question of whether an item of evidence has any bearing on an issue properly before the court. This is determined primarily by the pleadings. In defining relevance, the Federal Rules ditched the word "materiality" by insisting that proof be "of consequence" to the determination of the case. Fed. R. Evid. 401. In other words, not only must the evidence have a logical connection to facts in issue, but the evidence must also bear on important issues in the case. *See, e.g., Strickland v. Washington*, 466 U.S. 668, 694 (1984) (in the context of a criminal defense, "material to the defense" means a reasonable probability that the result would be different if the information were disclosed to the defense).

Suppose that in Morena, insanity is an affirmative defense in criminal cases. Further, Morena procedure requires that the defendant plead the defense at the time of arraignment. Devitt's attorney failed to do so. Nevertheless, Devitt's attorney offers the items of testimony in Problem 8-1 above at trial. In this situation, at common law, the prosecutor would have to object that the testimony was "immaterial" rather than "irrelevant": The testimony has logical relevance to prove insanity, but insanity is not properly at issue in the case. In other words, if Devitt's attorney had properly pleaded insanity, some of the items in Problem 8-1 would be both logically relevant and material. However, because of the pleading error, such evidence is objectionable as immaterial. It still has pure logical relevance (*i.e.*, it is probative of insanity), but it lacks materiality (*i.e.*, insanity is not an issue in the case).

NOTES AND PROBLEMS

1. What factors do you consider in determining whether a proposition is material? Do you look only to the substantive law governing the case? How do the pleadings figure into your determination? Focus particularly on the defense's responsive pleading such as the answer. Can that pleading enlarge or contract the scope of "material fact"?

2. **Problem 8-9.** Now review the indictment in the *Devitt* case file. Be prepared to list all the ultimate facts in issue under the indictment.

3. **Problem 8-10.** In the *Devitt* case, the prosecutor offers evidence that the alleged battery occurred within the limits of the city and county of El Dorado. Is that evidence material? To what?

4. **Problem 8-11.** In our torts case, Ms. Hill prays for punitive damages and that prayer is still in the complaint when the case goes to trial. Could she introduce evidence of Polecat Motors' wealth? Would that be material? Why? *See Rose v. Brown & Williamson Tobacco Corp.*, 10 Misc. 3d 680, 709–11, 809 N.Y.S.2d 784, 805–07 (Sup. Ct. 2005).

5. **Problem 8-12.** In the *Devitt* case, the state charges the defendant with both battery and first-degree assault. Under Morena law, first-degree assault is a specific *mens rea* crime. Could Devitt introduce evidence that he had been drinking heavily three hours before the alleged incident? To what would that evidence be material? What if the state charged Devitt with third-degree assault, a general *mens rea* crime?

b. Curative Admissibility

We have already identified two factors we consider in deciding what is material: the substantive law and the pleadings. There is a third factor, namely, the evidence that has been introduced to date in the trial. Strictly speaking, the doctrine of curative admissibility comes into play only when an adverse party introduces immaterial evidence — that is, you could object on the ground that the evidence is irrelevant, but instead you make no objection. Can you, having failed to object, now respond in kind and introduce otherwise immaterial evidence on the same subject in order to "cure" the prejudice caused by the inadmissible evidence? In other words, should we treat the issue as "material" now that a party has seen fit to inject it into the case?

Neither the Federal Rules of Evidence nor other evidence codifications contain a rule on curative admissibility, but most jurisdictions recognize the doctrine. It can be justified as a kind of estoppel or forfeiture, a product of the adversary system, and as such it can be applied even in the absence of a specific enabling rule. Having introduced incompetent evidence, the first attorney has forfeited the protection of evidence law and consequently is in "no position to complain" when the opponent proffers technically inadmissible, responsive testimony. The opponent is entitled to "fight fire with fire." Estoppel, waiver, and forfeiture are not evidentiary rules; they are broader concepts which are sometimes applied in an evidentiary context.

For example, in *Blake v. Clein*, 903 So. 2d 710, 726–27 (Miss. 2005), a medical malpractice case, the issue arose in the following context:

> Prior to the surgery, and during the subsequent course of Clein's treatment, there are entries in his medical records which were introduced into evidence by agreement. Clein stated that he believed his dead mother, who practiced witchcraft, had placed a curse on him, which resulted in his amputation and condition. At trial, the judge ruled that the use of the words "curse" or "witchcraft" could not be used or referred to because of the alleged prejudicial effect the words might have upon the jury.

> The plaintiff "opened the door" to this inquiry by offering into evidence his medical records, without redacting the records. There are numerous references to Clein's belief in a curse within the medical records. Evidence, even if otherwise inadmissible, can be properly presented where a party has "opened the door." . . . In this case, a significant component of plaintiff's claims are related to emotional distress and mental anguish, i.e. psychological or psychic injuries. As such the defense was denied an opportunity to legitimately explore the plaintiff's own statements regarding the origin and/or source, cause, and extent of his psychological injury, agitation, and disturbance.

The doctrine is applied in federal as well as state courts. *See, e.g., Nguyen v. Southwest Leasing & Rental Inc.*, 282 F.3d 1061, 1067–68 (9th Cir. 2002) (holding that admission of expert's curative testimony was not abuse of discretion). There is a three-way split of authority over the doctrine. A few courts do not recognize the doctrine at all; unless the evidence is relevant to the substantive law and pleadings, the evidence is inadmissible. These courts reason that "the admission of incompetent evidence without objection never justifies a rebuttal in kind." Two wrongs do not make a right. In effect, these courts give the opponent only one option: objecting to exclude the inadmissible evidence.

Other courts have developed a more sophisticated version of the majority view. Under this approach, the opponent may introduce irrelevant, responsive testimony only when it is needed to remove unfair prejudice caused by the proponent's evidence. The linchpin of this view is a fairness rationale; the evidentiary rules yield when it would be unfair to permit the opponent to meet the proponent's evidence. However, when there is little or no resultant prejudice, the rules should remain in force.

Most jurisdictions, however, permit rebuttal evidence more or less without restriction. Even in these jurisdictions, the trial judge has discretion as to whether to invoke the doctrine and permit the opponent to introduce responsive, otherwise inadmissible evidence. *See* Gilligan & Imwinkelried, *Bringing the "Opening the Door" Theory to a Close: The Tendency to Overlook the Specific Contradiction Doctrine in Evidence Law*, 41 SANTA CLARA L. REV. 807 (2001) (noting the "dangers posed by mounting confession" about the differences between specific contradiction and curative admissibility). Although the proponent has violated the evidentiary rules, the opponent does not have a full-fledged right to introduce the inadmissible evidence. Moreover, the courts always retain the right to exclude evidence under Rule 403 or its common-law counterpart. We will examine that Rule in a later chapter.

NOTE AND PROBLEM

1. Which view is soundest? The majority rule has the support of the weight of the authority, but does it really rest on legitimate evidentiary considerations? Or are we simply penalizing the other party for having violated the evidentiary rules? Is that a proper consideration in the formulation of relevance doctrine? If the evidence improperly admitted was otherwise irrelevant and we permit the party to meet that evidence, are we not running the risk that the jury will be diverted from the real issues in the case?

2. Problem 8-13. In the *Devitt* case, the prosecutor has inadmissible evidence that four years before the alleged battery, Devitt had made an unprovoked attack on a supervisor at work. The evidence would normally be inadmissible because of the character evidence rules that we shall discuss. However, add a fact: on direct examination by his own attorney, Devitt volunteers the statement that "I've never committed a battery or attacked anybody or done anything bad like that in my life." Would that statement "open the door" to rebuttal by otherwise inadmissible evidence?

3. Modern Statutory Treatment of Logical Relevance and Materiality

As we previously indicated, the early common law separated the doctrines of logical relevance and materiality. If the proponent's evidence did not prove what he or she offered it to prove, the opponent had to voice the objection that the evidence was "irrelevant." In contrast, if the desired inference was not within the range of dispute in the case, the opponent had to make the "immaterial" objection. The trial judge could overrule the objection if the opponent confused the two concepts.

Federal Evidence Rule 401 is typical of the modern statutory treatment of the two concepts:

> Evidence is relevant if: (a) it has any tendency to make a fact more or less probable than it would be without the evidence; and (b) the fact is of consequence in determining the action.

This statute merges the two concepts. Given this definition of "relevant evidence," the opponent no longer has to differentiate between the "immaterial" objection and the "irrelevant" objection. To raise either contention, the opponent need only object that the evidence is "irrelevant."

Under this definition, determining the logical relevance of evidence is a two-step process. First, the proponent must identify all the material facts of consequence in the case. These facts can include preliminary facts such as venue, the historical facts on the merits such as an essential element of a crime, and collateral facts such as the credibility of all the witnesses who have already testified in the case. (In this respect, relevance as an evidentiary concept is narrower than relevance in the context of pretrial discovery. An item is discoverable before trial so long as it is logically relevant to a claim or defense of any party, and, for good cause, the court may order discovery of any matter relevant to the subject matter involved in the action. Relevant information need not be admissible at the trial if the discovery appears reasonably calculated to lead to the discovery of admissible evidence. Federal Rule of Civil Procedure 26(b)(1). In contrast, apart from the operation of the curative admissibility doctrine, for evidentiary purposes at trial the item must relate to an issue which has actually been pleaded.)

Second, the proponent must convince the judge that the item of evidence is logically relevant to one of the material facts. Notice the standard announced in Rule 401: "more or less probable than it would be without the evidence." As one court has remarked:

> [I]n determining whether evidence is relevant, the . . . court must not consider the weight or sufficiency of the evidence. Even if a . . . court believes the evidence is insufficient to prove the ultimate fact for which it is offered, it may not exclude the evidence [under Rule 401] if it has even the slightest probative worth.

Douglass v. Eaton Corp., 956 F.2d 1339, 1344 (6th Cir. 1992).

NOTES

1. Notice what Rule 401 does *not* say.

2. California Evidence Code § 210 defines "relevant evidence" as:

> "Relevant evidence" means evidence, including evidence relevant to the credibility of a witness or hearsay declarant, having any tendency in reason to prove or disprove any disputed fact that is of consequence to the determination of the action.

How does that language differ from the wording of Federal Evidence Rule 401? Suppose that, in its answer in our torts case, Polecat Motors admits that it manufactured the instrumentality or that Polecat later formally tenders a stipulation to that effect. Given the admission or stipulation, must Ms. Hill offer proof of manufacture to make out a submissible case? Even if Ms. Hill need not do so, may she do so under Rule 401? Under California Evidence Code § 210? The Advisory Committee Note to Rule 401 indicates that the drafters deliberately rejected Evidence Code § 210 as a possible model, and in the same paragraph the Note adds that "[t]he fact to which the evidence is directed need not be in dispute." Rule 401 commits the federal courts to the most liberal trial relevance standard in effect anywhere in the United States.

3. Why do both the Federal Rules and the California Evidence Code use the term "of consequence" instead of "material"? Can an item of evidence be "of consequence to the determination of the action" but not material to an element of a party's claim or defense? *See, e.g., United States v. Westbrook,* 125 F.3d 996, 1007 (7th Cir. 1997) (evidence is relevant if its exclusion would leave a "chronological and conceptual void" in the story); *United States v. Aguwa,* 123 F.3d 418, 421 (6th Cir. 1997) (provide "background information"); *cf. Old Chief v. United States,* 519 U.S. 172, 179 (1997) (name of prior offense admissible even though not strictly material).

C. THE DISTINCTION BETWEEN DIRECT AND CIRCUMSTANTIAL LOGICAL RELEVANCE

1. Directly Relevant Evidence

Even lay people have heard of the distinction between direct and circumstantial evidence. They have seen movies in which the criminal defense attorney attempted to persuade the jury by disparaging the prosecution's evidence as "circumstantial." There is an intuitive reaction that somehow direct evidence is more reliable than circumstantial proof. However, in truth, there is only one clear difference between the two types of evidence: the manner in which they are logically relevant to the material facts.

Evidence is directly "relevant" (as defined in Rule 401) if the immediate inference from the evidence is the existence or nonexistence of a material fact. Direct evidence is "[e]vidence, which if believed, proves [the] existence of [the] fact in issue without inference or presumption." *E.E.O.C. v. MCI Intern., Inc.,* 829 F. Supp. 1438, 1447 (D.N.J. 1993) (holding that neither direct nor indirect evidence established age discrimination). One of the material facts in dispute in our torts case is whether Ms. Hill was in pain immediately after her collision with Worker; the pain is one of Ms. Hill's elements of damage. It would be direct evidence if Ms. Hill testifies that she was conscious after the collision and can distinctly recall suffering excruciating pain.

To visualize the definition, the evidence and the logical relevance are direct if we can draw an arrow in a straight, uninterrupted line from the item of evidence to the item in the box:

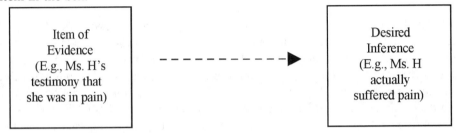

The only remaining question for the jurors is the witness's credibility, that is, whether the witness is believable. Other than that, the jury does not have to draw any intermediate inference between the testimony and the desired inference.

2. Circumstantially Relevant Evidence

Assume now that the proffered item of evidence does not create an immediate inference that a material fact exists. The evidence can still be logically "relevant" as defined in Rule 401 — but it would be circumstantially relevant.

Again we must resort to logic and experience: Our experience tells us that the item of evidence can serve as a step in a process of logical reasoning toward the existence or nonexistence of a material fact. The jury must draw an intermediate inference, but the item can serve as a link in a chain of reasoning steps leading to the ultimate, desired inference. Visualize circumstantial evidence in this fashion:

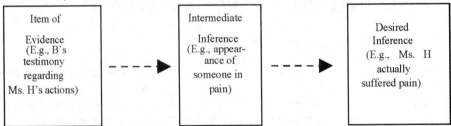

For example, in the *Hill* case, a bystander's testimony that he observed Ms. Hill bent over and holding her head would be circumstantial evidence that she was in pain. Even if the jurors decide that the bystander's testimony is credible, they must also decide to infer Ms. Hill's pain from the circumstances to which the bystander testified. The jury may decide to make the additional inference or decline to do so, drawing the contrary inference that Ms. Hill was merely slightly disoriented after the accident. Testimony by Ms. Hill that she was in pain would be direct evidence;

the only step needed to get from Ms. Hill's testimony to the desired inference is whether the jury believes her testimony.

PROBLEMS

Are the following items of evidence direct or circumstantial? If they are circumstantial, lay out the entire line of reasoning leading from the item of evidence to the ultimate, desired inference:

Problem 8-14. As in Problem 8-7, the prosecutor offers testimony of a physician that the defendant's blood type is A. Assume that the following evidence has already been admitted: The victim Paterson testifies that during the fight the assailant accidentally cut himself on his own knife; Paterson thinks that the assailant bled a bit during the fight; the investigating police officer testified that he found red stains at the alleged crime scene and took them to the police laboratory. A laboratory serologist testifies that the stains were blood of type A. Remember that roughly forty-two percent of the population has type A blood. *See People v. Vernon*, 89 Cal. App. 3d 853, 869, 152 Cal. Rptr. 765, 775 (1979).

Problem 8-15. In the battery prosecution, Paterson testifies that the assailant attacked him from behind and that consequently, he cannot recognize his face. However, he adds that the attacker did speak during the scuffle and that he can recognize the attacker's voice. He testifies that he heard the defendant testify at an earlier hearing in the case and that he can identify the defendant's voice as the assailant's voice. Assume a worst-case scenario from the prosecution's perspective: an extreme case in which Paterson admits that to the best of his knowledge, before the alleged attack he had never met or spoken with the defendant. *See Patterson v. State*, 598 S.W.2d 265, 270 (Tex. Crim. App. 1980).

3. The Significance of the Distinction Between Direct and Circumstantial Evidence

In most respects, there is no distinction between the two types of relevant evidence. Some commentators have even charged that the distinction is of purely academic significance — still another thin distinction with which to torture law students. However, the distinction has some formal and practical significance.

In some jurisdictions, when a party is relying primarily or exclusively upon circumstantial evidence, the trial judge must give the jury a special cautionary instruction. In Georgia, for example, the trial judge often gives the jury an instruction tracking the language of GA. CODE ANN. § 24-4-6: "To warrant a conviction on circumstantial evidence, the proved facts shall not only be consistent with the hypothesis of guilt, but shall exclude every other reasonable hypothesis save that of the guilt of the accused." In Florida, "A motion for judgment of acquittal should be granted in a circumstantial evidence case if the State fails to present evidence from which the jury can exclude every reasonable hypothesis except that of guilty." *Hawkins v. State*, 933 So. 2d 1186, 1189 (Fla. Dist. Ct. App. 2006) (reversing a third-degree murder conviction based on the improper admission of evidence).

The view that circumstantial evidence is somehow less worthy is increasingly disfavored. In some of the jurisdictions that still permit the instruction, it will not be given if there is any direct evidence in support of the state's case. *See, e.g.,People v. McCoy*, 30 A.D.3d 441, 443, 817 N.Y.S.2d 337 (2006) (declining to give a circumstantial evidence charge where the government had direct evidence to support its case). There has been a trend toward abandoning the special, circumstantial evidence instruction altogether. In *Holland v. United States*, 348 U.S. 121, 139–40 (1954), for example, the United States Supreme Court found no error in the refusal to give such an instruction:

> The petitioners assail the refusal of the trial judge to instruct that where the Government's evidence is circumstantial it must be such as to exclude every reasonable hypothesis other than that of guilt. There is some support for this type of instruction in the lower court decisions [citations], but the better rule is that where the jury is properly instructed on the standards for reasonable doubt, such an additional instruction on circumstantial evidence is confusing and incorrect. . . .
>
> Circumstantial evidence in this respect is intrinsically no different from testimonial evidence. Admittedly, circumstantial evidence may in some cases point to a wholly incorrect result. Yet this is equally true of testimonial evidence. In both instances, a jury is asked to weigh the chances that the evidence correctly points to guilt against the possibility of inaccuracy or ambiguous inference. In both, the jury must use its experience with people and events in weighing the probabilities. If the jury is convinced beyond a reasonable doubt, we can require no more.

Aside from these formal distinctions between direct and circumstantial evidence, the fundamental question arises whether direct evidence is more trustworthy than circumstantial evidence. Eyewitness testimony is "direct" evidence; the only question the jury must answer is whether to believe the witness when he says that with his own eyes he saw the defendant commit the crime. Lay jurors are quite willing to rely on eyewitness testimony. Studies have shown that lay jurors are more willing to convict on the basis of eyewitness testimony than on the basis of high quality scientific proof such as fingerprints or questioned document analysis. *See* Heller, *The Cognitive Psychology of Circumstantial Evidence*, 105 MICH. L. REV. 241 (2006) (contending that jurors routinely undervalue circumstantial evidence and overvalue direct evidence).

Yet witness psychology has given us some disturbing insights into the reliability of purported eyewitness identifications, and the weakness of eyewitness identifications has been known for some time. *See, e.g.*, Levine & Tapp, *The Psychology of Criminal Identification: The Gap from* Wade *to* Kirby, 121 U. PA. L. REV. 1079 (1973) (discussing the constitutionality of police practices and procedures in obtaining eyewitness identifications). *United States v. Wade*, 388 U.S. 218, 228–29 (1967) is the landmark decision in which the Court recognized the defendant's right to counsel at post-indictment lineups. Writing for the Court in *Wade*, Justice Brennan stated:

> The vagaries of eyewitness identification are well-known; the annals of criminal law are rife with instances of mistaken identification. Mr. Justice Frankfurter once said: "What is the worth of identification testimony even when uncontradicted? The identification of strangers is proverbially un-

trustworthy. The hazards of such testimony are established by a formidable number of instances in the records of English and American trials. These instances are recent — not due to the brutalities of ancient criminal procedure." The Case of Sacco and Vanzetti 30 (1927). A major factor contributing to the high incidence of miscarriage of justice from mistaken identification has been the degree of suggestion inherent in the manner in which the prosecution presents the suspect to witnesses for pretrial identification. A commentator has observed that "[t]he influence of improper suggestion upon identifying witnesses probably accounts for more miscarriages of justice than any other single factor — perhaps it is responsible for more such errors than all other factors combined." Wall, Eye-Witness Identification in Criminal Cases 26. Suggestion can be created intentionally or unintentionally in many subtle ways. And the dangers for the suspect are particularly grave when the witness' opportunity for observation was insubstantial, and thus his susceptibility to suggestion the greatest.

Moreover, "[i]t is a matter of common experience that, once a witness has picked out the accused at the line-up, he is not likely to go back on his word later on, so that in practice the issue of identity may (in the absence of other relevant evidence) for all practical purposes be determined there and then, before the trial."

In 1999, the U.S. Department of Justice published guidelines for the collection and preservation of eyewitness evidence. *See* D. Faigman, et al., Modern Scientific Evidence: The Law & Science of Expert Testimony § 20:1 (2006). *See also id.* §§ 20:13–20:45 (2006), for a comprehensive review of the science by Prof. Gary Wells, Professor of Psychology at Iowa State University.

Contrast direct eyewitness testimony with scientific evidence. In most cases, scientific evidence will be circumstantial. Suppose, for instance, that Devitt denied ever entering Paterson's bedroom but a fingerprint expert testifies that latent fingerprints found on a plastic comb in the bedroom belong to the defendant. That evidence is only circumstantial proof of guilt; but given Devitt's denial, the fingerprint evidence has great probative value.

Perhaps the most intelligent position is the stance the Supreme Court took in *Holland v. United States*, 348 U.S. 121, 140 (1954): "Circumstantial evidence . . . is intrinsically no different from testimonial [direct] evidence." Most courts are persuaded of the wisdom of that position. That position leads us back to our starting point and explains why, in most respects, courts treat circumstantial evidence in the same fashion as direct evidence.

D. THE DISTINCTION BETWEEN FACIAL AND UNDERLYING LOGICAL RELEVANCE

1. Facial Logical Relevance

To understand the concept of relevance under Rule 401, it is helpful to distinguish between "facial" and "underlying" logical relevance. In deciding the question of facial relevance, the question is whether the item of evidence — "on its face" — appears to be logically relevant to the material facts. The basic questions are: What does the proponent claim that the item is? If it is what it is claimed to be, is it "relevant" to the material facts (*i.e.*, will the item of evidence increase or decrease the probability of the existence of any material fact)? Initially, the judge ascertains what the proponent *claims* that the item is; and under Rule 401, the judge inquires whether the item affects the balance of probabilities of the existence of a material fact *if* the item is what it is claimed to be. For example, in a murder trial, a love letter from defendant to the victim, on its face, tends to suggest that defendant had a love affair with the victim. The true relevancy of this depends upon whether defendant actually wrote (or somehow adopted) the love letter.

2. Underlying Logical Relevance

To understand the concept of underlying logical relevance, one must understand that the common law was imbued with a spirit of skepticism. In everyday life, if we receive a letter purportedly signed by "Grant Hanson," we routinely assume that Grant Hanson wrote the letter. The common law obstinately refused to make that assumption.

More specifically, the common law refused to accept evidence at face value. The proponent must not only persuade the judge that the item is relevant under Rule 401 *if* the item is what it is claimed to be (facial relevance); the proponent must also prove that the item of evidence *is* what the proponent claims it to be (underlying relevance). This requirement for a showing of underlying relevance takes two forms.

Personal knowledge. First, before a witness can testify to a fact or event the witness purportedly observed, there must be foundational proof of the witness's personal knowledge of the event. Federal Evidence Rule 602 states:

> A witness may testify to a matter only if evidence is introduced sufficient to support a finding that the witness has personal knowledge of the matter. Evidence to prove personal knowledge may consist of the witness's own testimony. This rule does not apply to a witness's expert testimony under Rule 703.

Even though the witness's testimony on its face would be logically relevant to the material facts in the case, the common law will not permit the witness to testify until there is proof that the witness will be testifying from firsthand knowledge — to the common-law way of thinking, a necessary guarantee of the testimony's underlying probative value. Thus, the common law will not permit a witness to describe the way Ms. Hill and Mr. Worker's cars collided unless the witness was in a position to have observed the collision. The description is unquestionably relevant under Rule 401, but inadmissible until the proponent also complies with Rule 402.

Authentication. Second, in most cases, before the proponent formally introduces a physical exhibit such as a knife or letter, the proponent must introduce a sponsoring witness's testimony that the item is what it purports to be. The generic term for the presentation of such testimony is "authentication." Rule 901 explains that the authentication of physical evidence is "a condition precedent to admissibility." Again, although on its face the content of a letter was highly relevant to the material facts in the case, the common law will not allow the letter's introduction until there is an added guarantee that the letter is what it appears to be. Suppose that Polecat Motors had a letter, purportedly written by Ms. Hill, in which the writer acknowledged "full responsibility" for the collision. Again, *on its face* the letter is certainly relevant to the material facts of consequence in the case: the contents of the letter satisfy Rule 401. However, the defendant may not introduce the letter until the defendant satisfies Rule 901 with proof that Ms. Hill actually wrote the letter. The defendant claims that the exhibit is a letter written by Ms. Hill, and Rule 901 requires that the defendant establish the letter's genuineness and *underlying* relevance by proving that she did write it.

NOTES

1. The imposition of the personal knowledge and authentication requirements is an added guarantee of the reliability of the judicial fact-finding process.

But is that incremental increase in reliability worth the trouble and expense the proponent must go through? Why not allocate the burden to the opponent to show lack of authenticity? After all, in the normal social and business intercourse, when we receive a letter in the mail we generally assume that it is genuine.

2. What is the pertinence of discovery procedures, especially the procedure for requests for admission? As discovery becomes more liberal, does the authentication requirement become more or less defensible? Why not assume that people are testifying from personal knowledge or that exhibits are genuine and force the opponent to prove the contrary — at least when the pretrial discovery rules would have permitted the opponent to depose the witness or inspect the exhibit?

Local rules of federal district courts and pretrial orders frequently provide that all exhibits be identified in advance of trial, and the authenticity of all exhibits will be deemed established unless written objection is filed (either in a pretrial memorandum or by motion) within a certain time before trial. In addition, Federal Rule of Civil Procedure 26(a)(3)(C) requires mandatory disclosure (even absent a request by the opposing party) of a list of "each document or other exhibit . . . which the party expects to offer" at trial. The concluding language of 26(a)(3)(C) reads:

> Unless otherwise directed by the court, these disclosures shall be made at least 30 days before trial. Within 14 days thereafter, unless a different time is specified by the court, a party may serve and file a list disclosing . . . any objection, including the grounds therefor, that may be made to the admissibility of materials identified under subparagraph (C). Objections

not disclosed, other than objections under Rules 402 and 403 of the Federal Rules of Evidence, shall be deemed waived unless excused by the court for good cause shown.

a.   Underlying Logical Relevance — Personal Knowledge

To ensure the underlying probative value of their oral testimony, lay witnesses must ordinarily base their testimony on personal observation. Proof of personal knowledge is thus part of the foundation for their testimony. As we have seen, the Federal Evidence Rules revolutionized the law of the competency of witnesses. In particular, Rule 601 junked most of the traditional mental qualifications for prospective witnesses. However, the Rules retained the personal knowledge requirement. Under Rule 602, as at common law, the courts generally apply the requirement to both in-court witnesses and out-of-court hearsay declarants. *See United States v. Owens-El*, 889 F.2d 913 (9th Cir. 1989) (holding that evidence of the assault victim's personal knowledge for out of court identification, was sufficient to be submitted to the jury). The following case illustrates the personal knowledge doctrine.

ELIZARRARAS v. BANK OF EL PASO
631 F.2d 366 (5th Cir. 1980)

KRAVITCH, CIRCUIT JUDGE.

In a jury trial appellee Elizarraras was awarded damages of $89,800 due to appellant bank's failure to honor appellee's check. . . . [W]e reverse the judgment and remand for a new trial solely on the issue of damages.

On April 2, appellee, a citizen and resident of Mexico, issued a check for $12,000 to Joe Rey as partial payment for a tractor. The check was written on appellee's account at the Bank of El Paso, appellant herein. On April 5, Rey, also a depositor at the Bank of El Paso, presented the check for payment. The bank applied $1,115.07 to one note owed to the bank by Rey and $7,539.04 to another note which it marked "paid" and delivered to Rey. The balance, $3,345.89, was deposited by the bank in Rey's account. On the same day, the appellee delivered to the bank a stop payment order, on a form provided by appellant, which included an agreement by appellee to indemnify appellant for all expenses and costs resulting from appellant's honoring the stop payment order. On either April 5 or April 6, appellant reversed the entries it had made with respect to Rey. On April 6, appellee issued a check for $64,000, which he believed to be the amount he had on deposit in the Bank of El Paso, payable to Financiera Del Norte, S.A., a Mexican bank. On April 15, Rey filed suit against appellee and appellant, alleging that appellee wrongfully stopped payment on the check and that appellant wrongfully reversed the entries it had made. On April 26, Pedro Jurado, vice president of the Bank of El Paso "acting as commercial loan and regular installment loan officer," notified appellee that there was a shortage of $756.68. Appellee testified that he emphasized to Jurado that it was important that the $64,000 check not be returned for insufficient funds, since such a return would have serious repercussions in Mexico, including a penalty and loss of credit. According to appellee, Jurado assured him that there would be no problem covering the $64,000 check. On April 30, without giving notice to appellee, appellant returned the $64,000 check to the Mexican bank for insufficient funds and deposited $12,000 from appellee's account into the federal court in which Rey's suit was pending, interpleading Rey and appellee. When Rey's suit was subsequently dismissed for lack of subject matter jurisdiction and Rey sued in state court, the appellant interpled the money into state court.

Appellee subsequently filed suit in federal district court alleging that the wrongful dishonor of the $64,000 has damaged him in Mexico. Appellee prevailed in a jury trial. The jury awarded damages in the amount of $89,800: $75,000 for loss of credit and damage to reputation, $12,800 for the penalty the Mexican bank charged appellee, and $2,000 for interest on the $64,000 still owed to the Mexican bank.

The appellant contends that the trial court erred in several respects. Appellant contends that essential evidence to support the award of $12,800 penalty and $2,000 interest to the Mexican bank was wrongfully admitted.

At trial appellant objected to the following statement made by appellee: "I paid the $64,000; then $12,800 and twenty-three and something else." Under Fed. R. Evid. 602, a "witness may not testify to a matter unless evidence is introduced sufficient to support a finding that he has personal knowledge of the matter." The Advisory Committee on the Federal Rules, in its notes on Rule 602, points out that "[t]his rule would prevent [a witness] from testifying to the subject matter of [a] hearsay statement, as he has no personal knowledge of it." The problem in the instant case is that the appellee did not carry the burden Rule 602 puts on him of showing personal knowledge of the matter testified to (although appellant objected on hearsay grounds, not personal knowledge, we will not draw such a fine line). In context, it is clear that as to the penalty and interest appellee was not testifying to any act of payment he committed, but rather to the fact his account was charged $12,800 and $2,800; thus, this is not an instance where one can infer personal knowledge from the testimony itself.[21] The only basis appellee appeared to have for his testimony concerning the payment of the penalty and interest was the Mexican bank officers' oral assertions[22] and the Mexican bank notice appellant received; yet this evidence had been excluded as inadmissible hearsay.[23] Neither the conversation nor notice is in the record on appeal. Therefore, we do not rule on the admissibility of this evidence.

Nor can we agree that admission of the appellee's testimony was harmless error. The testimony was introduced to show that the appellee paid the Mexican bank a penalty of $12,800 and interest of $2,000 due to the return of the check. The only other evidence introduced with regard to these facts was expert testimony on whether Mexican law would have required a 20% penalty on the return of the check and authorized the interest charge, and appellee's testimony that the bank asserted

---

[21] An example would be "I saw X in the room."

[22] On *voir dire*, appellee began to testify that the Mexican bank officials told him about the $12,800 penalty and the $2,000 interest (in context this seemed to be what he was about to say), but an objection to this as hearsay was sustained.

[23] If this testimony had been based on admissible hearsay, this would presumably satisfy Rule 602, though we do not decide the question.

that he owed it interest due to the return of the check. Although to reach its verdict the jury had to find that under Mexican law the Mexican bank was entitled to a penalty of $12,800 and interest of $2,000 from the appellee, and that the Mexican bank asserted there was an interest charge, the jury might very well have not found these facts alone without proof of payment sufficient to establish the disputed damages. *See Liner v. J.B. Talley & Co., Inc.*, 618 F.2d 327 (5th Cir.1980) (articulating harmless error standard). We therefore reverse the judgment insofar as it awards the appellee $12,800 and $2,000 and remand for a new trial on those issues.

NOTES AND PROBLEMS

1. How does the personal knowledge requirement differ from the former competency requirements? Is proof of the possession of the basic capacity to observe part of competency or personal knowledge? What about proof of the opportunity to observe? What about proof of actual observation?

2. In *Elizarraras*, the court alludes to both the personal knowledge and hearsay doctrines and mentions the "fine line" between the doctrines. What is the relation between the two doctrines? It is tempting to say that the distinction is this: The personal knowledge objection is available when it negatively appears that the testimony does not rest on personal knowledge while the hearsay objection is available when it affirmatively appears that the testimony rests on a third party's out-of-court statements.

3. Problem 8-16. In the *Devitt* case, the prosecutor calls Mr. Garrett, one of Paterson's neighbors, as a witness. Garrett is prepared to testify that soon after the time of the alleged battery, he saw Devitt fling open Paterson's apartment door, run out the door, leap into a car, and speed away. Before he begins this testimony, Devitt's attorney interrupts:

D: Your Honor, I object on the grounds that this witness has no personal knowledge.

P: Your Honor, the witness has indicated that he saw all this happen.

D: Your Honor, may we approach the bench?

J: Yes.

D: (At sidebar) Your Honor, we have a witness, Mr. Michelson, who is prepared to swear that at this point in time, he and Garrett were drinking at a bar twenty miles from the apartment complex. I'd like you to listen to Mr. Michelson's testimony before you rule on my objection.

As trial judge, must you consider Michelson's testimony before ruling? Does this preliminary fact fall under Federal Rule 104(a) or 104(b)? Does the fact of personal knowledge condition the competence or the logical relevance of Garrett's testimony? *See M.B.A.F.B. Federal Credit Union v. Cumis Ins. Soc'y*, 681 F.2d 930, 932–33 (4th Cir. 1982). Consider the first two sentences of Rule 602. How would you rule on the objection assuming that the only proof of Garrett's firsthand knowledge is Garrett's own testimony?

4.   Problem 8-17. Under Rule 602, is the judge limited to inquiring whether the witness has some personal knowledge of the facts he or she is testifying to, or may the judge also assess the adequacy of the personal knowledge? *McCrary-El v. Shaw*, 992 F.2d 809, 810–11 (8th Cir. 1993). Pay special attention to the "unless" clause in the first sentence of Rule 602. In *Elizarraras*, the court stated that the issue was whether it could "infer" personal knowledge. Suppose that in the last problem, Garrett admits that he did not have a frontal view of the person who fled from Paterson's apartment. Instead he saw part of the profile as the fugitive ran past some bushes; Garrett concedes that his identification of Devitt as the fugitive rests primarily on "the peculiar shape of the guy's nose that I happened to notice." Does Garrett's testimony satisfy Rule 602? (This problem draws on the fact situation in *United States v. Sears*, 332 F.2d 199 (7th Cir. 1964).)

5.   Problem 8-18. In the *Hill* case, the plaintiff calls a mechanic who worked on Roe's truck before the accident. The mechanic inspected the truck's brakes a few days before the accident. The mechanic testifies that he handed Roe a sheet of paper stating that the mechanic had found a number of specific deficiencies in the brakes. When the plaintiff attempts to elicit the mechanic's further testimony that he, the mechanic, "could tell" that after reading the sheet of paper, Roe "understood that the brakes were bad," the defense objects. Roe's attorney argues that the mechanic "can't have any personal knowledge of what's going on in another person's mind"? What ruling? *United States v. Kupau*, 781 F.2d 740, 745 (9th Cir. 1986) (citing Federal Rule of Evidence 602).

In Problem 8-18, when objecting, many defense attorneys would also have objected that the plaintiff's attorney's question called for "improper speculation." We shall revisit this issue, *infra*, when we cover the materials on lay opinion testimony. Should the mechanic at least be permitted to testify that Roe "appeared" or "seemed" to understand that the brakes were bad?

6.   Commonly, courts do not capitalize on the available scientific method of investigation. Assume, for example, that the question is whether, under the circumstances at the time of the relevant event, the witness could actually have seen or heard what he or she claims. A witness may testify that although she was 70 feet away and there was only a crescent moon, she made out the letters and numbers on the license plate of a car that sped away from the crime scene. Witness psychologists point out that it is possible to conduct a visibility test — duplicating the conditions, including the witness's vision — to determine scientifically whether the witness could actually have observed those details. *See generally* A. TRANKELL, RELIABILITY OF EVIDENCE (1972); Levine & Tapp, *The Psychology of Criminal Identification: The Gap from* Wade *to* Kirby, 121 U. PA. L. REV. 1079 (1973). In testing claims of personal knowledge, the law has not fully exploited the available scientific techniques. To be sure, it would be unduly time-consuming to test every witness's personal knowledge claim in this fashion. However, when there is substantial doubt about the ability of an important witness to have perceived a pivotal fact in the case, it would seem worthwhile to resort to scientific testing. Note that in certain circumstances, Fed. R. Civ. P. 35 empowers the courts to order physical or mental examinations.

b. Underlying Logical Relevance — Authentication

As in the case of the personal knowledge requirement, the authentication requirement is satisfied by proof sufficient to support a rational jury finding that the document is authentic. If the proponent presents that quantum of foundational proof, the judge admits the exhibit; and during deliberations, the lay jurors finally resolve the question of the document's authenticity. In this respect Federal Rule of Evidence 901(a) prescribes the same fact-finding procedure as Rule 104(b). Can we trust lay jurors to resolve questions of personal knowledge and authenticity? Suppose that after considering the foundational testimony, the jurors decide that a particular exhibit is a forgery. Is the jurors' exposure to the exhibit likely to distort their deliberations?

With some types of evidence, fairly hard and fast norms on the manner of authentication of evidence have emerged. Some fact patterns have recurred so frequently and the courts have ruled so consistently that one can predictably conclude that an item of evidence can be authenticated in a particular fashion. We shall address most of the well-settled norms, *infra*, as we cover various specialized applications of the authentication doctrine. However, one must never lose sight of the fact that under Rule 901(a) the fundamental test is *not* whether the proponent has complied with a well-settled norm, but rather whether the proponent has marshaled sufficient surrounding circumstances to create a rational, permissive inference that the item of evidence is authentic. The only limits on the authentication doctrine itself are the rules of logic and the attorney's creativity, as illustrated by the following case.

UNITED STATES v. WILSON
532 F.2d 641 (8th Cir. 1976)

LAY, CIRCUIT JUDGE.

Defendants Gray (a/k/a Punkin), Wilson (a/k/a Big Man), and Brenda Brown appeal from their convictions for conspiracy to distribute heroin in violation of 21 U.S.C. § 846. The issue presented on appeal is whether the trial court erred in admitting two notebooks and their contents which a government witness read to the jury. We find no error and affirm the convictions.

The sufficiency of the evidence supporting the conspiracy conviction of each defendant is not challenged. However, a review of the facts is essential to the ruling on the controversial notebooks. . . .

McCoy, the informant, testified that on various occasions he purchased heroin from each of the defendants and had sold heroin for them as well. McCoy described the defendants' operations, stating that he received heroin from each of the three defendants which he would sell at "a rate." He testified that the defendants ran their operation from various houses in St. Louis.[1] These houses were on Elliott and St.

---

[1] McCoy described in detail how a "house" was operated:

> Q. Now, in the actual running of a house what would be the jobs of the individuals that were running the house?

Louis, Evans and Sarah, and Grand and Herbert in St. Louis. The money and heroin would be passed through a hole in the door and then, according to McCoy, the transactions were usually recorded in code in a book by either "Pauncho" (an unindicted co-conspirator) or Brenda. He stated heroin was sold either in "spoons" or in capsule form called "buttons." The "house" at Grand and Herbert was an apartment run by someone known to the informant as "Jimmy."

Detective Klier of the St. Louis Police Department went to the "house" at Grand and Herbert on April 30, 1975, on information that drugs were being sold there. Detective Klier found James Shelton in the apartment. The door had a two-inch hole in it and the apartment was practically vacant except for certain small items. Klier testified that he found numerous empty red capsules in one room and syringes and two notebooks in the bedroom.

Over defendants' objections, the government introduced the notebooks *and* their contents. The trial court overruled defendants' objections. Detective Klier was allowed to read all the contents of the notebooks to the jury. The notations specifically identified "Brenda" and "Punkin" (Gray's nickname) as taking drugs and money. Defendant Wilson was not mentioned in the notebook.[3]

A. Well, the first thing the job is you got to have a protection in a house so somebody would have to have something there to protect what you got in that house because, let's face it, people, you know, stick you up, highjack you, take your stuff. So once you get your protection set up in the house then it's a simple matter of dealing once people know where you're dealing from and if the stuff is there such where, you know, where when junkies will buy. Well, then it's easy to run a house. You just go to the house; they know you; you stick your money through the hole; they stick the stuff back out; and that's that.

Q. Did you ever open the door or was that a normal procedure?

A. Well, it's not a normal procedure unless you know a person real good, exceptionally good.

Q. But normally it would be sent through a hole, is that correct?

A. Right.

Q. How big would the hole be?

A. Just a small hole big enough to put a spoon through.

Q. What would be the purpose of putting a spoon through?

A. Well, you see, you stick your money through the hole and if you're getting say — let's say you're getting two or three things; well, you can put that on a spoon and stick it right back through the hole.

Q. And that way the door would never have to be opened?

A. No, it wouldn't have to be opened.

Q. Did you ever run any of these houses?

A. Well, no I wouldn't say run a house but I have been up in one of the houses. Transcript at 96–97.

[3] Government Exhibit No. 3 contained the following entries: On page one:

4-26-75

$112.00 cash and 21 in the bottle 24, and 60 in the plastic bags. So you started with 105, buttons.

S/J.R.

On page two:

Left Nut

I started with 78 buttons. He brought 80, but gave me two for myself. Brenda picked up $133 Dollars for 19 buttons Brenda picked up $210 Dollars for 30 buttons, She has picked up the last

The defendants presented no evidence, relying on their motions for acquittal at the end of the government's evidence. The jury returned verdicts of guilty. The defendants argue that no proper foundation has been laid for the notebooks, since the identity of the writer or writers was not shown. We find sufficient evidence to show *prima facie* authenticity or genuineness of the notebooks.

The entries in the notebooks are hand printed by one or more persons. The government represents that it does not know the identity of the author.

Rule 901 of the Federal Rules of Evidence provides:

(a)   General provision. The requirement of authentication or identification as a condition precedent to admissibility is satisfied by evidence sufficient to support a finding that the matter in question is what its proponent claims.

(b)   Illustrations. By way of illustration only, and not by way of limitation, the following are examples of authentication or identification conforming with the requirements of this rule:

. . . .

(4)   Distinctive characteristics and the like. Appearance, contents, substance, internal patterns, or other distinctive characteristics, taken in conjunction with circumstances.

Under this rule, the contents of a writing may be used to aid in determining the identity of the declarant. The primary concern in relying on the contents of an instrument to prove its authenticity is the danger of forgery or substitution of a fraudulent document. However, as has been authoritatively explained:

> For this principle to operate the [writing] must deal with a matter sufficiently obscure or particularly within the knowledge of the persons corresponding so that the contents of the [writing] were not a matter of common knowledge.
>
> The evidential hypothesis in the authentication step is this: only those who knew the details in the [writing] could have written it; if the purported writer can be shown to have probably known the details and if no other person is likely to have known them when the [writing] was written, it is likely that he wrote it. The force of the inference decreases as the number of people who know the details and may have written the [writing] increases. Moreover, if there is a serious question of forgery, the inference is subject to being rebutted by the possibility that the details were added by someone to give an air of verity to the document rather than by the purported author who obtained the information in the usual way.

5 J. Weinstein & M. Berger, Weinstein's Evidence ¶ 901(b)(4)[01], at 46.

It is well settled that the genuineness of a writing can be established by

---

$203 Dollars for 29 buttons. All total she has picked up $546 Dollars for 78 buttons.

Brenda brought 74 buttons, gave Lesa two and Punkin 4 that 6 buttons counted for All total Punkin took 8 buttons.

I'm leaving 54 buttons, and $84 Dollars. [other pages to same effect — eds]

circumstantial proof without resort to the handwriting or typewriting. Where the writings are such that only those persons acquainted with the particular transactions involved could have written them, the authenticity of the evidence is considered more reliable.

Under these principles, we find the contents of these notebooks refer to activities (in this case, drug trafficking) and are characterized by a code of which only someone connected with the transactions would have known. The writer uses nicknames of individuals and the code term "buttons" which the informant had testified were heroin capsules. The writer was obviously familiar with the procedures used by the defendants in their drug operations. Although the precise identity of the declarant is unknown, we think there was at least a *prima facie* showing that the declarant was a member of the drug conspiracy charged in the indictment.

Moreover, there is other evidence which corroborates the authenticity of the notebooks. The books were found in an apartment which the informant said both "Punkin" and Brenda frequented, and in which drugs were sold. The apartment had an unusual hole in its door fitting the informant's description and a known co-conspirator was found there at the time of the raid. The informant further testified that the defendants' drug transactions were recorded in notebooks. This evidence in our view provides a *prima facie* showing of authenticity of the notebooks. This showing could have been, but was not, countered by any evidence from defendants that the documents were forged or otherwise not what the government claimed. . . .

Judgments are affirmed.

NOTES AND PROBLEMS

1. Federal Evidence Rule 901 contains a lengthy list of the accepted authentication techniques. Is that list exclusive, or as at common law may the proponent rely on any circumstantial inference of authenticity? Notice the initial clause of Rule 901(b).

2. Early chapters argued the generalized proposition that the Federal Rules of Evidence swept away uncodified, common law evidentiary doctrine. Rule 901 (b) requires that we refine that generalization. To an extent, Rule 901(b) preserves common law process; judges may find adequate authentication of an item of evidence even if the proponent's foundational testimony does not satisfy one of the specific authentication techniques codified in Rules 901(b)(1)-(10). In effect, Rule 901(b) opens a window to the common law.

3. Do you agree with the result in *Wilson*? The evidence certainly supports the court's conclusion that the notebooks were connected with a drug-trafficking conspiracy. But is that what the prosecution claimed that the notebooks were? If you had been the prosecutor, would you have laid a more complete foundation? What additional facts would you have established? As a practical matter, how do you prove that the information contained in a document is so "obscure or particularly within the knowledge" of the person claimed to be the author? You are essentially being asked to prove a negative.

4. **Problem 8-19.** In our torts case, Ms. Hill is testifying to authenticate the original contract of purchase. The unsigned contract was left in a room on a table; there was also a pen on the table. She saw her husband, Arthur, enter the only door to the room. A few moments later she saw Arthur emerge from the room; at the time, she noticed ink stains on his shirt. She walked into the room and saw the contract, still on the table. The contract bore Arthur's purported signature; the signature was in ink, and the ink was obviously still wet and fresh — the ink smudged a bit when she picked up the contract. On this foundation, the plaintiff's attorney offers the exhibit into evidence. The defense counsel objects:

O.   Your Honor, I must object. There's insufficient authentication for this exhibit. She's so much as admitted that she didn't see him sign, and there's no evidence yet that she's sufficiently familiar with his handwriting style.

As trial judge, how would you rule on the objection? *See* 7 J. WIGMORE, EVIDENCE § 2131, at 712–13 (Chadbourn rev. 1978) (authentication by "sundry circumstances"). *See also United States v. Natale*, 526 F.2d 1160, 1173 (2d Cir. 1975).

5. **Problem 8-20.** At trial Ms. Hill's attorney wants to use a model of the intersection to illustrate the witnesses' testimony about the collision. Does the authentication doctrine apply to the model in the same fashion that it applies to the contract in Problem 8-19? Does the doctrine apply at all? Go back to fundamentals; authentication consists in proving that an item is what you claim it to be. What does Ms. Hill's attorney claim that the model is? Does a model necessarily have to be "substantially similar" to the intersection to be helpful to the jury? Must the model at least be "similar"? *See* 2 MCCORMICK ON EVIDENCE § 214 (6th ed. 2006); Dombroff, *Innovative Developments in Demonstrative Evidence Techniques and Associated Problems of Admissibility*, 45 J. AIR L. & COM. 139, 145–50 (1979).

E. CONCLUSION: LOGICAL RELEVANCE

We have seen that the proponent of evidence must demonstrate the logical relevance of the item of evidence in several respects. Rule 401 requires that the proponent persuade the judge that the item has "facial" logical relevance: that the item either increases or decreases the probability that one of the material facts of consequence exists. The relevance can be either direct or circumstantial. We also studied underlying relevance. Simply stated, the common law will not accept an item of evidence at face value. The proponent must prove that the item *is* what he or she claims it to be. Federal Evidence Rules 602 and 901 impose this requirement on the proponent. For example, if the proponent claims that a witness is testifying from personal knowledge, Rule 602 provides that the proponent must show the witness's personal knowledge. If the proponent claims that an item is the defendant's letter or pistol, Rule 901 mandates that the proponent authenticate the item as such.

In the material ahead, we will analyze the most common, specialized applications of the authentication doctrine: authentication of writings by identifying their author; identification of physical evidence; authentication of tape recordings by identifying the speaker; verification of the accuracy of photographs; and validation of scientific evidence.

Chapter 9

SPECIALIZED ASPECTS OF LOGICAL RELEVANCE: AUTHENTICATION OF WRITINGS

Read Federal Rules of Evidence 901 and 902.

A. INTRODUCTION

As we have seen, part of the "foundation" for an item of documentary evidence is the requirement of authentication. In response to a relevancy objection to a particular item of evidence, the proponent must respond by making a claim about how the evidence relates to an issue in the case, which includes — either implicitly or explicitly — a claim about what the item of evidence *is*. Imagine, for example, that the plaintiff in a commercial lawsuit offers a writing and the defense objects that the writing is not relevant under FRE 401. To show that the writing is relevant, the plaintiff might respond that it is the plaintiff's contract with the defendant, which forms the basis of the lawsuit. That response would satisfy Federal Rule 401; *if* the document is what the plaintiff claims is to be, its contents will certainly affect the probability of the existence of a fact of consequence in the case. However, a showing of relevance under Rule 401 is not enough to support the admission of the evidence. Under Rules 901 and 902, the proponent must also "authenticate" the item, which entails proof that the item *is* what he or she *claims it to be*. The application of the authentication requirement to writings usually — though not always — involves identifying the author of the document.

Before we turn to some specific examples of how a proponent can properly authenticate a document, we should briefly review the context and the procedures for offering an item of evidence such as a letter, check, or invoice. The proponent first marks the exhibit for identification. After showing the exhibit to the opponent, the proponent hands it to the sponsoring witness. It is at this point that the proponent elicits the foundation for the exhibit's introduction, which usually includes proof of the document's authenticity. If the opponent makes a timely objection on grounds of insufficient authentication, the judge will apply the doctrines described in this chapter.

B. PRIVATE WRITINGS

1. Introduction

Modern technology and business practices account for the emergence of so-called "documents cases," complex commercial or antitrust litigation in which attorneys spend years in pretrial discovery to sort through thousands or even millions of relevant documents. For example, in one case, the Washington Public Power Supply System Securities (*WPPSS*) litigation, the parties exchanged more than 200 million pages of documents before settling. Sugarman, *Coordinating Complex Discovery*, 15 LITIG., Fall 1988, at 41. But even in less complex cases, attorneys frequently use documentary evidence; such evidence tends to be persuasive to juries, which often seem to find it more credible than testimony of potentially biased witnesses. For that reason, the common law developed several doctrines for authenticating private writings, which have been incorporated into the Federal Rules of Evidence.

As Chapter 5 pointed out, the authenticity of an object is a preliminary factual question that is within the province of the jury under Federal Rule of Evidence 104(b). The general test under 104(b) is minimal. The proponent need "only [provide] a rational basis for th[e] party's claim that the document is what it is asserted to be." *Jones v. National American University*, 608 F.3d 1039, 1045 (8th Cir. 2010); *Ciampi v. City of Palo Alto*, 790 F. Supp. 2d 1077 (N.D. Cal. 2011). Over the years, the courts have recognized many types of direct and circumstantial evidence as adequate authentication. The California Evidence Code contains an excellent codification of many of the recognized doctrines, some examples of which are set out below:

§ 1413. Witness to the execution of a writing.

A writing may be authenticated by anyone who saw the writing made or executed, including a subscribing witness.

§ 1414. Admission of authenticity; acting upon writing as authentic.

A writing may be authenticated by evidence that:

(a) The party against whom it is offered has at any time admitted its authenticity; or

(b) The writing has been acted upon as authentic by the party against whom it is offered.

§ 1415. Authentication by handwriting evidence.

A writing may be authenticated by evidence of the genuineness of the handwriting of the maker.

§ 1416. Proof of handwriting by person familiar therewith.

A witness who is not otherwise qualified to testify as an expert may state his opinion whether a writing is in the handwriting of a supposed writer if the court finds that he has personal knowledge of the handwriting of the supposed writer. Such personal knowledge may be acquired from:

(a) Having seen the supposed writer write;

(b) Having seen a writing purporting to be in the handwriting of the supposed writer and upon which the supposed writer has acted or been charged;

(c)   Having received letters in the due course of mail purporting to be from the supposed writer in response to letters duly addressed and mailed by him to the supposed writer; or

(d)   Any other means of obtaining personal knowledge of the handwriting of the supposed writer.

§ 1420. Authentication by evidence of reply.

A writing may be authenticated by evidence that the writing was received in response to a communication sent to the person who is claimed by the proponent of the evidence to be the author of the writing.

§ 1421. Authentication by content.

A writing may be authenticated by evidence that the writing refers to or states matters that are unlikely to be known to anyone other than the person who is claimed by the proponent of the evidence to be the author of the writing.

For its part, Federal Rule of Evidence 901 provides both a standard for authentication and a list of ten examples of adequate authentication techniques. The rule makes it clear that this list is not exhaustive, but only illustrative. For example, if a litigant requests a certain document during pretrial discovery and the opponent produces a writing in response to the request, the very act of production is sufficient authentication of the writing, even though that authentication technique is not explicitly laid out in Rule 901. *See, e.g., Vulcan Golf, LLC v. Google, Inc.*, 726 F.Supp.2d 911, 914–15 (N.D. Ill. 2010). In this chapter, we will examine a few of the most common techniques for authenticating a writing, but keep in mind that the proponent is not restricted to demonstrating authenticity through these precise avenues.

2.   Comparison by the Trier of Fact

Federal Rule 901(b)(3) authorizes authentication of a handwritten document by comparison by the trier of fact. Under this authentication procedure, the jury (or judge in a bench trial) compares one or more "exemplars" (samples shown or claimed to be authentic samples of the handwriting of the person in question) with the disputed document. Although many writers and judges have questioned the ability of untrained lay persons to make reliable handwriting comparisons, Rule 901(b)(3) is in accord with a long-standing common-law tradition approving this technique.

The issue of the exemplars' authenticity presents a thorny issue because at first glance, it would seem to be a preliminary fact conditioning the logical relevance of the exemplars. 5 J. WEINSTEIN & M. BERGER, WEINSTEIN'S FEDERAL EVIDENCE ¶ 901.02[4], at 901–18 (rev. 2009). As such the final decision on the exemplars' genuineness should be a question of preliminary fact for the jury. However, some jurisdictions assign this determination to the judge because reserving it for the jury can give rise to administrative difficulties. *E.g.*, CAL. EVID. CODE § 1417. Nevertheless, Rule 901(b)(3) treats the issue of the authenticity of the exemplar as a Rule 104(b) issue for the jury. *See* Advisory Committee Note to Rule 901, subdivision (b).

3. Non-Expert Opinion

Another time-honored technique for authenticating a handwritten document is to elicit an opinion from a non-expert witness who is familiar with the handwriting style of the person claimed to be (or not to be) the author of the questioned writing. Like the common law, both California Evidence Code § 1416 and Federal Rule 901(b)(2) authorize the receipt of such testimony for purposes of authentication; the rules are liberal as to what counts as sufficient familiarity with the person's handwriting. "[F]amiliarity with the handwriting of another person may be acquired by seeing him write, by exchanging correspondence, or by other means. . . ." Advisory Committee Note to Rule 901(b)(2).

Studies suggest that such lay testimony can be highly unreliable. Inbau, *Lay Witness Identification of Handwriting*, 34 U. ILL. L. REV. 433 (1939). The late Professor Inbau, the Wigmore Professor Emeritus at Northwestern University School of Law, conducted an informal handwriting identification experiment using his law faculty colleagues as subjects. He asked them to determine whether other colleagues had authored certain specimen writings — persons whose handwriting styles the subjects were familiar with. Their accuracy scores were so low that Inbau concluded that "[l]ay witness identifications . . . are too unreliable to be considered acceptable as legal evidence." *Id.* at 440. Nevertheless, the evidence statutes and rules continue to permit this mode of authentication.

4. Expert Opinion Testimony

Lay jurors may not find non-expert opinion testimony as impressive as testimony by an expert witness. In major cases such as felony prosecutions and civil actions involving substantial sums of money, the attorneys will often employ professional "questioned document examiners" to study the writings in question and offer their expert opinions as to the authorship of the writings. Federal Rule 901(b)(3) and California Evidence Code § 1418 each codify the common-law rule authorizing this method.

The examiner's opinion is based on a comparison of the questioned document with exemplars, which may be of a "request" or "nonrequest" type. A request exemplar is a sample provided by the suspected author to the examiner. The typical nonrequest exemplar is a pre-existing document that the suspected author created for a purpose wholly unrelated to the litigation, such as a signature on an earlier check or letter. The examiner then compares the questioned document with the exemplars to look for certain characteristics claimed to be unique to the suspected author. Examiners typically use tools such as microscopes, digitally enhanced photographs, and computer-assisted analysis. To make their testimony more impressive, they often use blow-ups and other visual aids to show the trier of fact the bases for their opinions.

Such handwriting specialists have been permitted to testify as expert witnesses since the nineteenth century. *See* Mnookin, *Scripting Expertise: The History of*

Handwriting Identification Evidence and the Judicial Construction of Reliability, 87 VA. L. REV. 1723 (2001). From the beginning, however, the field has been controversial; many scholars outside the field have argued that the opinions of questioned document experts are too unreliable to be accepted as evidence. In a 1989 article, Risinger, Denbeaux & Saks, *Exorcism of Ignorance as a Proxy for Rational Knowledge: The Lessons of Handwriting Identification "Expertise,"* 137 U. PA. L. REV. 731, 739–51 (1989), the authors reviewed several Forensic Sciences Foundation studies. In one test, three handwritten letters containing bomb threats were said to have been received by the news media and followed by bombings by a terrorist organization:

> Forty-one participating laboratories employing document examiners were sent the three letters plus twelve pages of known handwriting samples (two pages for each of six suspects). Examiners were asked to determine whether the same person wrote all of the questioned letters, and whether any of the questioned letters were written by any of the authors of the known writings. Two of the letters were written by one person, whose writing was not submitted, and the third letter was written by one of the suspects whose exemplar was in his normal hand but who in writing the questioned letter attempted to simulate the writing in the other two letters. Only twenty-three of the forty-one laboratories submitted reports: 17 (74%) caught the different authorship of the third letter; 6 (26%) said erroneously that all the letters were written by the same person; 23 (100%) failed to recognize the author of one of the questioned letters among the known exemplars. Thus they were all correct concerning letters 1 and 2 and all wrong concerning letter 3. Every examiner failed to recognize the author of one of the questioned letters among the exemplars.

> [In another test,] [t]welve checks all bearing a signature in the same name were sent to forty-two participating laboratories. They were asked to determine which if any of the signatures were made by the same person. . . . . Only thirty-two of the forty-two laboratories returned the 1985 test. Of those, 13 (41%) gave correct results; 2(6%) of the responses were incorrect in attributing one of the forgeries to the real repeat signatory; 10 (31%) said they were unable to reach conclusions; 7(22%)were substantially wrong.

> Because of complaints from document examiners that [these] tests were too difficult, the Proficiency Advisory Committee decided to make [another] test easy. According to the report, "[t]his test was designed to be a relatively easy and straightforward test . . . . All the writings in this test were natural and free of disguise." This test involved a single questioned extortion note written by one suspect. Both request and non-request known exemplars from four suspects were provided to the participants. After comparing the questioned and the known, examiners were to offer an opinion concerning which, if any, of the known exemplars was written by the same person who wrote the questioned note. Of fifty-five laboratories requesting materials, thirty-three returned reports: 17 (52%) gave correct answers; 1(3%) incorrectly eliminated the correct suspect; 15 (45%) were unable to reach a conclusion.

The publication of the Risinger article prompted further empirical studies on the accuracy of questioned document examination and, in particular, on whether experienced QD examiners can perform identification tasks more successfully than laypersons such as jurors. In 1994, Kam, Wetstein & Conn found that professional questioned document examiners were far more successful than laypersons in making authorship determinations:

> The hypothesis that professionals and nonprofessionals are equally proficient in performing writer identification was found to have the probability of less than 0.001. These findings give indication that handwriting identification expertise indeed exists. . . .

Proficiency of Professional Document Examiners in Writer Identification, 39 JOURNAL OF FORENSIC SCIENCES 5 (1994). Dr. Kan and his associates have now completed several studies, all reaching essentially the same conclusion. In its 2009 report, the National Research Council of the National Academies of Sciences had faint praise for the research:

> "Recent studies have increased our understanding of the individuality and consistency of handwriting . . . and suggest that there may be a scientific basis for handwriting comparison, at least in the absence of intentional obfuscation or forgery. Although there has been only limited research to quantify the reliability and replicability of the practices used by trained document examiners . . . , there may be some value in handwriting analysis." Nat'l Research Council, Strengthening Forensic Science in the United States: A Path Forward 166–67 (2009).

Chapter 12 explores the Supreme Court's 1993 decision in *Daubert v. Merrell Dow Pharmaceuticals, Inc.*, 509 U.S. 579 (1993), which announced a new test for the admissibility of scientific evidence. In *Daubert*, the Court stated that to decide whether proffered testimony qualifies, the judge should consider many factors, including the error rate for the scientific technique. Citing the Risinger article and *Daubert*, some commentators have argued that the courts should reconsider the longstanding admissibility of testimony by questioned document examiners. *E.g.*, Jonakait, *Real Science and Forensic Science*, 1 SHEPARD'S EXP. & SCI. EVID. Q. 435, 447 (1994). To date, most courts continue to admit questioned document examiners' opinions, but the trend has been to reclassify the discipline as non-scientific expertise. *United States v. Prime*, 431 F.3d 1147, 1154 (9th Cir. 2005) ("all six circuits that have addressed the admissibility of handwriting expert testimony"); *United States v. Demjanjuk*, 367 F.3d 623, 635 n.2 (6th Cir. 2004) ("more practical in character rather than scientific").

NOTES AND PROBLEMS

1. **Problem 9-1.** Imagine that Polecat Motors denies that Jefferson's sales manager signed one of the letters which purports to describe a warranty by Polecat. To attack the signature's authenticity, the defense intends to call a questioned document examiner. The defense wants the expert to compare the exhibit with several samples of the sales manager's handwriting style. The sales manager prepared the samples a few days before trial. Should the trial judge permit the

witness to use those samples in making a comparison on the witness stand? Is it significant that the sales manager prepared the exemplars so close in point of time to the trial? *See United States v. Lam Muk Chiu*, 522 F.2d 330, 331–32 (2d Cir. 1975) (applying the common-law *post litem motam* limitation).

In *Lam Muk Chiu*, which antedates the Federal Rules of Evidence, the court cites common-law authorities for the proposition that *post litem motam* exemplars — those that are prepared after litigation has arisen — are "inherently suspect." Did that common-law restriction survive the adoption of the Federal Rules? May the judge factor the credibility of an item of evidence into a Rule 403 analysis? The overwhelming majority of courts have answered that question in the negative. Imwinkelried, *The Meaning of Probative Value and Prejudice in Federal Rule of Evidence 403: Can Rule 403 Be Used to Resurrect the Common Law of Evidence?*, 41 VAND. L. REV. 879, 886 (1988). If the courts construed the expression "probative value" in Rule 403 as subsuming the credibility of the source of the evidence, how would that construction affect Rule 104(b)? *Id.* at 887–88. Just as we ought to attempt to harmonize Rules 402 and 403, we must endeavor to reconcile Rules 104(b) and 403.

2.   **Problem 9-2.** In the *Devitt* case, Paterson testifies that a few days after the attack, he received an unsigned, handwritten letter. The letter related minute details about the attack — details that had not been mentioned in any of the newspaper articles about the attack. The letter's final sentence was, "I got you once, and if you don't stop blabbing to the police I'll be back to get you again." There is no witness prepared to testify that they saw Devitt write the letter. You are the prosecutor and you want to introduce the letter against Devitt. What authentication techniques would you attempt to use? Can you at least authenticate it as a letter sent by the perpetrator? *See United States v. Beecroft*, 608 F.2d 753, 760–61 (9th Cir. 1979) (the contents of a writing may be sufficient to authenticate it).

3.   How should these doctrines apply to social media postings, emails, texts, or other electronic communications? *See* Joseph, *Internet and Email Evidence (Part I)*, 58 THE PRACTICAL LAWYER 19 (2012). Of course there is no question in these cases of "handwriting" identification, but some "forensic linguists" claim to be able to identify a person's writings based on features apart from their "handwriting" as such — for example diction, grammar, spelling, punctuation, and word choice. The technique was most famously used in the Unabomber case here in the U.S. In the U.K., it resulted in a notorious murder conviction where the prosecution was able to prove that the defendant sent certain text messages from the victim's cell phone. *See* Elizabeth Mitchell, The Case for Forensic Linguistics, BBC News, *available at* http://news.bbc.co.uk/2/hi/science/nature/7600769.stm.

Suppose that the prosecutor in *Devitt* wishes to offer a printout of a page from Devitt's Facebook profile and wall posts. In such a case, the proponent typically must establish two propositions: The exhibit is an authentic printout from a social media profile page; and the posting is attributable to a certain person. What kinds of lay and expert testimony can the proponent use to establish these propositions? Although this is a relatively new problem, it is already well settled that the proponent need not call a representative of the social media company to authenticate the evidence. *E.g., Dockery v. Dockery*, 2009 Tenn. App. LEXIS 717 (Oct. 29, 2009).

Suppose that the prosecutor shows that:

— Devitt had adopted the user name shown on the profile page;

— Devitt had not shared his password with anyone else (*People v. Calderon*, 2010 Cal. App. Unpub. LEXIS 7172 (App. Sept. 9, 2010));

— a photograph on the profile page was a picture of Devitt;

— information posted on the profile page such as the person's birthday, occupation, or nickname matched the Devitt's background; and

— a computer expert recovered copies of the postings from the hard drive of Devitt's computer (*People v. Clevenstine*, 68 A.D.3d 1448 (N.Y. 2009) ("an investigator from the computer crime unit of the State Police")).

You are the trial judge applying Rule 104(b). At what point, would you rule that the foundation was adequate?

4. *Rodriguez v. State*, 273 P.3d 845 (Nev. 2012) is one of the leading cases on authentication of text messages. The court held that there was inadequate authentication of 10 of 12 text messages. The court ruled that "a person cannot be identified solely on evidence that the message was sent from a cellular phone bearing the telephone number assigned to that person." The court demanded corroboration "such as where the messages 'contain factual information or references unique to the parties involved.'"

C. BUSINESS WRITINGS

In criminal cases, the documentary evidence often takes the form of private writings. However, both in white collar crime prosecutions and civil actions, the documents are more often business writings. We begin with the assumption that any technique available to authenticate a private writing is equally available to authenticate a business writing. This section explains several additional, special techniques for authenticating business documents.

1. Custody

When we refer to "custody," we mean the place where the document is found. There is a large body of authority that the proponent may authenticate a business writing simply by proving that the document came from the proper custody. The proponent elicits the sponsoring witness's testimony that the witness has personal knowledge of the filing system of the business in question; the witness went to the right file cabinet, drawer, and file; the witness removed the document from that file; and the witness recognizes the exhibit as the document he or she removed from the file.

NOTES

1. Why should proof of proper custody suffice to authenticate a business writing? What assumption is the court making about the procedures and routines of the typical business? Suppose that in a particular case the opponent had evidence that the business in question was very sloppy in its records filing. Would the opponent's evidence preclude the admission of a record from that company on the basis of insufficient authentication, or should the evidence be admitted only to attack the weight of the business record?

2. In most instances, the sponsoring witness will be an agent of the institution or business that generated the record. Must the sponsoring witness be an employee of the business? Suppose that witness were the bookkeeper of the parent corporation or of a company that had extensive dealings with the business. Should that status automatically qualify the witness to authenticate the record? If not, what additional foundational testimony would the proponent have to elicit? *See United States v. Blake*, 488 F.2d 101, 104–06 (5th Cir. 1973).

2. Computer Records

One of the major technological advances in data storage has been the emergence of the computer. Many businesses transfer data from documents to computer storage, and a growing number feed data directly into the computer without generating an intermediate document. Thus, the computer-generated printout of the electronic record has become a vital type of business document.

Just as in the case of paper records, there can be doubts about the reliability of computer-generated documents. In Garcia, *"Garbage In, Gospel Out": Criminal Discovery, Computer Reliability, and the Constitution*, 38 U.C.L.A. L. Rev. 1043 (1991), the author identifies several reliability concerns about computerized data, including the quality and source of the underlying information, biases or errors inherent in the software programs, and inadequate security. Furthermore, it is often very difficult — and, even if possible, very expensive — to ascertain whether an electronic record has been altered.

Before the adoption of the Federal Rules of Evidence, some jurisdictions required detailed, comprehensive foundations for the admission of computerized records. Peritz, *Computer Data and Reliability: A Call for Authentication of Business Records Under the Federal Rules of Evidence*, 80 Nw. U. L. Rev. 956, 958 (1986). Since the adoption of the Rules, most courts have been more receptive to the admission of computerized data, generally admitting the evidence so long as the proponent shows that the business in question has relied on the particular computer system for a substantial period of time. *Id.* at 961. Some have argued that the courts should return to their earlier, more skeptical attitude toward computerized data. "Because program changes or data manipulations can be accomplished without leaving any trace and without affecting the day-to-day operation of a computer system, both unintentional error and intentional fraud are difficult to discover behind a perfect-looking document." *Id.* at 960. As a general proposition, the courts disagree; they continue to apply the minimal Rule 104(b) standard. *See Hardison v. Balboa Ins. Co.*, 2001 U.S. App. LEXIS 2409 (10th Cir.

Feb. 16, 2001); *United States v. Moore*, 923 F.2d 910, 915 (1st Cir. 1991) ("it is not required that computers be tested for programming errors before computer records can be admitted. . . ."); *United States v. Briscoe*, 896 F.2d 1476, 1494 (7th Cir. 1990) (the proponent of computerized records need not show that the computer has been tested for internal programming errors).

No subsection of Federal Rule of Evidence 901 specifically covers authentication of computer-generated documents, but "Rule 901(b) provides flexibility in applying the requisite standard of sufficiency set forth in Rule 901(a)." McCORMICK, EVIDENCE § 227, at 74–76 (6th ed. 2006). The contents of the required foundation vary with the nature of the document:

> [H]ow much information will be required about data input and processing to authenticate the output will depend on the nature and completeness of the data, the complexity of the manipulation, and the routineness of the operation. If the records are pre-existing and are simply stored in a computer, . . . the information about their retrieval may be minimal. Basic computer operations relied on in the ordinary course of business are admitted without an elaborate showing of accuracy. The accuracy of the individual computer will not be scrutinized unless specifically challenged, and even perceived errors in the output are said to go to the weight of the evidence, not its admissibility. A more elaborate foundation may be required to satisfy Rule 901(b)(9) if the computer is performing more complex manipulations. Testimony about the computer equipment, the hardware and software, the competency of the operators, the procedures for inputting data and retrieving the outputs may be necessary, particularly if these elements are challenged. *Id.*

The following decision of the Ninth Circuit Bankruptcy Appellate Panel, involving American Express records, is illustrative.

IN RE VEE VINHNEE
336 B.R. 437 (9th Cir. 2005)

KLEIN, BANKRUPTCY JUDGE:

The paperless electronic record involves a difference in the format of the record that presents more complicated variations on the authentication problem than for paper records. Ultimately, however, it all boils down to the same question of assurance that the record is what it purports to be.

The logical questions extend beyond the identification of the particular computer equipment and programs used. The entity's policies and procedures for the use of the equipment, database, and programs are important. How access to the pertinent database is controlled and, separately, how access to the specific program is controlled are important questions. How changes in the database are logged or recorded, as well as the structure and implementation of backup systems and audit procedures for assuring the continuing integrity of the database, are pertinent to the question of whether records have been changed since their creation.

This ever-expanding complexity of the cyberworld has prompted the authors of the current version of the Manual for Complex Litigation to note that a judge should "consider the accuracy and reliability of computerized evidence" and that a "proponent of computerized evidence has the burden of laying a proper foundation by establishing its accuracy." MANUAL FOR COMPLEX LITIGATION (Fourth) § 11.446 (2004). . . . In effect, it is becoming recognized that early versions of computer foundations were too cursory. . . .

Rule 901(b)(9) . . . describes the appropriate authentication for results of a process or system and contemplates evidence describing the process or system used to achieve a result and demonstration that the result is accurate. . . . The advisory committee note makes plain that Rule 901(b)(9) was designed to encompass computer-generated evidence and also that it did not preclude taking judicial notice in appropriate circumstances.

Indeed, judicial notice is commonly taken of the validity of the theory underlying computers and of their general reliability. IMWINKELRIED, EVIDENTIARY FOUNDTIONS § 4.03 [2] (5th ed. 2002). Theory and general reliability, however, represent only part of the foundation. Professor Imwinkelried perceives electronic records as a form of scientific evidence and discerns [a multi]-step foundation for computer records:

1. The business uses a computer.

2. The computer is reliable.

3. The business has developed a procedure for inserting data into the computer. The procedure has built-in safeguards to ensure accuracy and identify errors.

4. The business keeps the computer in a good state of repair.

5. The witness had the computer readout certain data.

6. The witness used the proper procedures to obtain the readout.

7. The computer was in working order at the time the witness obtained the readout.

8. The witness recognizes the exhibit as the readout.

9. The witness explains how he or she recognizes the readout.

10. If the readout contains strange symbols or terms, the witness explains the meaning of the symbols or terms for the trier of fact.

Although this is a generally serviceable modern foundation, the third step warrants amplification, as it is more complex than first appears. The "built-in safeguards to ensure accuracy and identify errors" in the third step subsume details regarding computer policy and system control procedures, including control of access to the database, control of access to the program, recording and logging of changes, backup practices, and audit procedures to assure the continuing integrity of the records . . . .

Here, the declarant merely asserted that he is employed by American Express and is personally familiar with the hardware and software and computer recordkeeping systems in use in the credit card industry. He did not indicate his job title or anything about his training and experience that would import an aura of verisimilitude to his assertions.

The trial court ruled that this was not adequate qualification of the witness because the "declaration contains no information at all about [declarant's] background and training or whether and to what extent he is knowledgeable about the American Express computers, or how he obtained such information." [T]he trial court did not know whether the declarant was a seasoned professional manager of computer records or a janitor . . . .

The declaration merely identified the makes and models of the equipment, named the software, noted that some of the software was customized, and asserted that the hardware and software are standard for the industry, regarded as reliable, and periodically updated. There is no information regarding American Express' computer policy and system control procedures, including control of access to the pertinent databases, control of access to the pertinent programs, recording and logging of changes to the data, backup practices, and audit procedures utilized to assure the continuing integrity of the records. In view of the cursory nature of the declaration and the lack of basic information that would provide assurance that the record reproduced from the electronic media is identical to the record that was originally stored, we perceive no error . . . .

NOTES AND PROBLEMS

1. As noted in the next section, Rule 902(11) provides an alternative, simplified method for authenticating business records, in tandem with Rule 803(6), which provides a simplified method for satisfying the business records exception to the hearsay rule. Does Rule 104(a) apply to authentication under Rule 902?

2. The records in the *Vee Vinhnee* case were private business documents. If the electronic or computer-generated document comes from a government computer or database and is properly certified, it will usually be treated as self-authenticating and very little foundation will be required. *See* Federal Rule of Evidence 902(4).

3. Problem 9-3. In our torts case, the defense contends that Ms. Hill cannot sue on the contract because Mr. and Mrs. Hill defaulted in their installment payments before the accident in which she was injured. The defense wants to offer a printout from Jefferson Motor Cars' computer; the printout shows that the day before the accident, the plaintiff was two installments delinquent in her payments. The sponsoring witness is the head of Jefferson's accounting department. She helped design the computer system when it was installed eight years ago. Prepare the part of her direct examination in which she will authenticate the computer printout. Do not be content to satisfy the minimal evidentiary requirements; attempt to make the line of testimony as persuasive as possible.

4. Problem 9-4. When you offer the computer printout into evidence, the plaintiff objects on a different ground:

> Your Honor, that printout was prepared specifically for purposes of this trial. The witness admitted only a few moments ago that she made this

printout at the defense attorney's request only two days ago. I cite *Lam Muk Chiu*, 522 F.2d 330, 331–32 (2d Cir. 1975) as authority for my position.

Assume for the moment that the *post litem motam* restriction survived the adoption of the Federal Rules of Evidence. Can you distinguish the exemplars in the *Lam* case from the printout in this problem? When is the computer "record" created?

5. Of course, computers represent only one of the modern technologies to which the authentication doctrine must adapt. The technology has marched from FAX to web-site postings and on to e-mail and text messages.

Suppose that in the *Hill* case, the plaintiffs want to introduce a posting at Polecat's website, describing safety features of the fuel tank. It is certainly sensible to impute that posting to the defendant. *Jones v. National American University*, 608 F.3d 1039, 1044–46 (8th Cir. 2010) (the section of a university's website devoted to job postings). However, suppose that another portion of the website permits purchasers to post comments about their Polecat cars. How should a court treat that type of posting? If the plaintiffs wanted to introduce a posting from that section of the site, what authentication foundation should the judge demand?

Now consider emails. The sender might have resorted to sophisticated encryption techniques to protect the privacy of his or her message. Froomkin, *The Essential Role of Trusted Third Parties in Electronic Commerce*, 75 Or. L. Rev. 49 (1996). In such cases, technology allows a relatively strong showing of whether the email originated from such a sender. However, most persons do not use such advanced security measures; even if they do, courts generally do not require such a showing to authenticate the message. Rather, courts permit the proponent to employ other, simpler authentication techniques. Falling back on Rule 104(b), they accept any foundational showing adequate to support a reasonably inference that that person was the sender. Which provision(s) of Rule 901(b) might support authentication of an email?

3. Simplified Procedures for Introducing Business Records

In the Comprehensive Crime Control Act of 1984, Congress authorized the use of an attestation to authenticate some categories of foreign business records. 18 U.S.C. § 3505. Federal prosecutors frequently use the attestation procedure in drug smuggling prosecutions.

In 2000, the Federal Rules of Evidence were amended to go beyond 18 U.S.C. § 3505. Subdivisions (11) and (12) were added to Rule 902. Rule 902(11) generally permits the authentication of domestic business records by certification while Rule 902(12) similarly allows the authentication of foreign business records by certificate. A notice requirement is included to provide the opponent an opportunity to conduct a pretrial investigation and, if appropriate, contest foundational adequacy at trial.

PROBLEM

Problem 9-5. In our torts case, Ms. Hill moved for the production of Polecat Motors' safety test records for the two years preceding her accident. Could Polecat Motors respond by submitting copies and a certificate complying with Federal Rule 902(11)? What exactly must the certificate state to satisfy Rule 902(11)?

D. OFFICIAL WRITINGS

Like businesses, government has become a more and more important source of documentary evidence. As government regulation becomes more and more pervasive, government file cabinets and databases have grown to include more and more information and attorneys frequently have occasion to use official records as evidence. Any technique for authenticating a private or business writing can be used to authenticate an official writing. Moreover, special rules such as Federal Evidence Rule 902 are designed to facilitate the use of official records.

Rule 902 governs the admission of official records in federal trials. In addition, under the full faith and credit clause of the Constitution, Congress has the power to dictate the circumstances under which the courts of one state must accept official records from another state and it has exercised that power in enacting the following two provisions of Title 28, United States Code:

§ 1738. State and Territorial statutes and judicial proceedings; full faith and credit

The Acts of the legislature of any State, Territory, or Possession of the United States, or copies thereof, shall be authenticated by affixing the seal of such State, Territory or Possession thereto.

The records and judicial proceedings of any court of any such State, Territory or Possession, or copies thereof, shall be proved or admitted in other courts within the United States and its Territories and Possessions by the attestation of the clerk and seal of the court annexed, if a seal exists, together with a certificate of a judge of the court that the said attestation is in proper form.

Such Acts, records and judicial proceedings or copies thereof, so authenticated, shall have the same full faith and credit in every court within the United States and its Territories and Possessions as they have by law or usage in the courts of such State, Territory or Possession from which they are taken.

§ 1739. State and Territorial nonjudicial records; full faith and credit

All nonjudicial records or books kept in any public office of any State, Territory, or Possession of the United States, or copies thereof, shall be proved or admitted in any court or office in any other State, Territory, or Possession by the attestation of the custodian of such records or books, and the seal of his office annexed, if there be a seal, together with a certificate of a judge of a court of record of the county, parish, or district in which such office may be kept, or of the Governor, or secretary of state, the chancellor or keeper of the great seal, of the State, Territory, or Possession that the said attestation is in due form and by the proper officers.

If the certificate is given by a judge, it shall be further authenticated by the clerk or prothonotary of the court, who shall certify, under his hand and the seal of his office, that such judge is duly commissioned and qualified; or, if given by such Governor, secretary, chancellor, or keeper of the great seal, it shall be under the great seal of the State, Territory, or Possession in which it is made.

Such records or books, or copies thereof, so authenticated, shall have the same full faith and credit in every court and office within the United States and its Territories and Possessions as they have by law or usage in the courts or offices of the State, Territory, or Possession from which they are taken.

The effect of these rules is to make official documents "self-authenticating," meaning that the proponent need not present live, sponsoring testimony. *Starski v. Kirzhnev*, 682 F.2d 51 (1st Cir. 2012). Instead, the proponent marks the exhibit for identification, shows the judge the exhibit, and then tenders the exhibit into evidence. The exhibit is admissible so long as there is an attached certificate or chain of certificates that complies with the controlling Rule or statute. Below is an example of the type of certificate that might be attached to a copy of an official record to make the copy self-authenticating:

No._____   Dept._____

SUPERIOR COURT
STATE OF CALIFORNIA
COUNTY OF SAN DIEGO

AUTHENTICATED COPY OF

In above entitled matter.

STATE OF CALIFORNIA, }

                               ss.

COUNTY OF SAN DIEGO, }

    I, JESSE OSUNA, Clerk of the County of San Diego and ex-officio Clerk of the Superior Court of the State of California for the County of San Diego, which is a court of record having a seal, do hereby certify that by law I have custody of the seal and all the records, books and documents of or pertaining to said court.

    I further certify that the document or documents described below and annexed hereto contain a full, true and correct copy of the original document or documents of or pertaining to the Superior Court which is/are on file in my office.

               WITNESS my hand and the seal of the court this __day of _____, 19__

               JESSE OSUNA, County Clerk and ex-officio Clerk of the Superior Court of the State of California for the County of San Diego

    I, _____, Judge of the Superior Court of the State of California, for the County of San Diego, do hereby certify that JESSE OSUNA, whose signature is affixed to the above certificate, is the Clerk of the County of San Diego and ex-officio Clerk of the Superior Court of the State of California for said County. As such clerk, he is the proper certifying officer of the court, and by law has custody of the seal and all the records, books and documents of or pertaining to the court, and his certificate is in due form as used in this state.

               IN WITNESS WHEREOF I have hereunto set my hand this __ day of _____, 19__

               Judge of the Superior Court of the State of California, for the County of San Diego

STATE OF CALIFORNIA, }

                               ss.

COUNTY OF SAN DIEGO, }

    I, JESSE OSUNA, Clerk of the County of San Diego, State of California, and ex-officio Clerk of the Superior Court thereof, which is a court of record having a seal, do hereby certify that the Honorable _____ whose name is subscribed to the above certificate of qualification, was at the date thereof a Judge of the Superior Court of the State of California, for the County of San Diego, duly appointed or elected and qualified and acting; that he is authorized to make such certificates; that full faith and credit are due to his official acts as such judge. I further certify that the signature subscribed on the certificate is genuine and that the certificate is executed according to the laws of the State of California.

               WITNESS my hand and the seal of the Superior Court this __day of _____, 19__

               JESSE OSUNA, County Clerk and ex-officio Clerk of the Superior Court of the State of California, for the County of San Diego

NOTES AND PROBLEMS

1. Why single out official documents and treat them differently than private and business writings? Does it reflect an underlying judgment about the reliability of official documents? What problems would arise if courts demanded live, sponsoring testimony to authenticate public records or if attorneys were entrusted with *original* official documents for use in the courtroom?

2. Under these special procedures, the key is ensuring that the copy of the official record bears a proper attesting or authenticating certificate. *An attesting certificate* usually states that the signatory is the custodian of the original official document and that the attached document is a true and accurate copy of the original. The court judicially notices or presumes the signature's authenticity. That step triggers a chain reaction. If the signature on the certificate is presumed genuine, what effect does that have on the certificate? In turn, if the certificate is then presumed authentic, what effect does that have on the attached copy of the official record?

3. Most jurisdictions limit the presumption to the signature of relatively high-ranking officials. If the custodian is a low-ranking official, the proponent must resort to *an authenticating certificate*, which states that the signatory holds a particular government office (high enough to trigger the presumption and set off the chain reaction); the signatory is familiar with the lower ranking official; and the signature on the attesting certificate is the genuine signature of that low-ranking official.

4. Problem 9-6. In *Devitt*, the prosecutor wants to impeach the defendant with evidence of a prior conviction for perjury. What type of supporting documentation would the prosecutor have to offer in court if: (a) The judgment of conviction had been entered in Kansas and the copy of the judgment of conviction from Abilene itself bore a seal; (b) the conviction had been entered in New York; when the copy of the judgment arrived in the mail, the prosecutor noticed that there was no seal on the copy; or (c) the conviction had been entered in France?

5. Problem 9-7. The prosecutor wants to impeach Devitt with evidence of a Cambodian conviction. However, Cambodian officials inexplicably refused to cooperate with the local American consul. Consequently, the prosecutor could not obtain the necessary certification of the copy of the judgment of conviction. In some situations, lack of local cooperation is not unusual. May the prosecutor nevertheless introduce the conviction? Consider Evidence Rule 902(3). *See United States v. Leal,* 509 F.2d 122, 126 (9th Cir. 1975) (the government had done all it could to comply with the final certification procedure; there was good cause for dispensing with the final certification).

6. Unless the proponent can invoke *Leal*, to satisfy Rule 902 the proponent must produce a final certification from an American official. However in 1991, Federal Rule of Civil Procedure 44(a)(2) was amended to provide:

> If reasonable opportunity has been given to all parties to investigate the authenticity and accuracy of the documents, the court may, for good cause shown, (i) admit an attested copy without final certification or (ii) permit the foreign official record to be evidenced by an attested summary with or

without a final certification. The final certification is unnecessary if the record and the attestation are certified as provided in a treaty or convention to which the United States and the foreign country in which the official record is located are parties.

The 1961 Hague Convention Abolishing the Requirement of Legalization for Foreign Public Documents came into force for the United States on October 15, 1981. T.I.A.S. 10072, U.N.T.S. 189; 67 A.B.A. J. 1705 (1981). Under the convention, the foreign official attaches a special certificate called an apostille and maintains a register showing the serial number of the apostille. An American court can then check the foreign register to verify the authenticity of the apostille. *See generally* Comment, *The United States and the Hague Convention Abolishing the Requirement of Legalization for Foreign Public Documents*, 11 HARV. INT'L L.J. 476, 482, 488 (1970).

Chapter 10

SPECIALIZED ASPECTS OF LOGICAL RELEVANCE: IDENTIFICATION OF PHYSICAL EVIDENCE

Read Federal Rules of Evidence 104(a)–(b) and 901(b)(1) and (4).

A. INTRODUCTION

Thus far we have looked at the authentication of one type of physical object, namely, a document. But trial attorneys have occasion to introduce as evidence a variety of physical objects other than writings. An experienced litigator knows that visual aids can make a case much more persuasive to a jury. Psychological research indicates that we gather as much as eighty-five percent of our data about the external world through the sense of sight and only ten percent exclusively through the sense of hearing. Perlman, *Preparation and Presentation of Medical Proof*, 2 TRIAL DIPL. J. 18 (Spring 1979). Moreover, according to other empirical studies, the respective long-term retention rates are twenty percent of what we hear, thirty percent of what we see, and fifty percent of what we both hear and see.

Because of the widespread use of DNA evidence at trial, authentication of this type of physical evidence has taken on greater importance. In 2001, more than two thirds of prosecutors' offices in the United States used DNA evidence either in plea negotiations or at trial. John M. Spires, Comment, *Testimonial or Nontestimonial: The Admissibility of Forensic Evidence After* Crawford v. Washington, 94 KY. L.J. 187, 187 (2005/2006). DNA typing has also become the dominant testing methodology in civil parentage cases. There are already hundreds of published opinions dealing with DNA evidence. As part of the required foundation for DNA evidence, the proponent must authenticate the samples tested, demonstrating that they are specimens originating from the crime scene, accused, or putative father. The proponent ordinarily authenticates the samples by proving a chain of custody, discussed in Section B.2 of this chapter.

Physical exhibits can also be important for reasons other than their intrinsic evidentiary value. The psychological phenomenon of associational logic enhances the importance of exhibits: the presence of the exhibits in the jury room helps jurors remember the testimony of the witnesses who laid the foundation for the particular exhibits. As of right or in the judge's discretion, the exhibits often accompany jurors into the jury room. Many experienced attorneys make it a practice to admit at least one exhibit during each key witness's testimony, to strongly associate the witness with that exhibit in closing argument, and request that the exhibit be sent to the jury. The lesson is clear: if a trial attorney wants the jury to understand the evidence in the short term and remember it in the long term, the attorney should integrate physical evidence into the presentation. The display of the physical object will help the jurors visualize the proponent's theory of the case. When that second sense comes into play, the proponent's theory becomes much more plausible and believable.

The process of authenticating physical evidence such as a DNA sample is usually termed the "identification of the evidence." Federal Evidence Rule 901(b) expressly uses the term "identification."

When the proponent is ready to use the evidence, the proponent typically takes the following steps. The proponent first has the court reporter mark the exhibit for identification, shows it to the opposing counsel, and then hands the exhibit to the sponsoring witness. The witness next lays the foundation for identification, as described further in this chapter. After laying the appropriate foundation, the proponent formally offers the exhibit into evidence. If the judge admits the evidence, to heighten the impact on the jurors, the proponent usually requests permission to hand the exhibit to the jurors for their personal examination and inspection.

The following diagram depicts these procedures. In effect the proponent walks a triangle. The proponent starts the first leg of the triangle by presenting the exhibit to the court reporter [CR] to be marked "for identification." The proponent then turns and walks the first leg of the triangle. At the end of that leg of the triangle, the proponent shows the exhibit to the opposing counsel [OC]. Then the proponent walks the second leg of the triangle and approaches the witness [W]. At the end of the second leg, the proponent hands the exhibit to the witness and elicits the foundational testimony. Finally, the proponent turns and walks the third, short leg toward the judge [J], where the proponent formally tenders the exhibit into evidence. If the judge agrees that the foundation is complete, the court reporter strikes "for identification" from the title of the exhibit. The item is now formally in evidence.

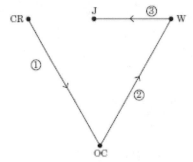

B.   REAL OR ORIGINAL PHYSICAL EVIDENCE

Real or original physical evidence has a historical connection to the facts of the case. For example, in our torts case, Ms. Hill's attorney might want to show the jurors the gas tank of Ms. Hill's car. The gas tank would be real, original evidence. Or in the *Devitt* prosecution, a shirt with bloodstains on it would be original physical evidence if the prosecutor alleged that the exhibit was the shirt Mr. Paterson was wearing when he struggled with his attacker. To authenticate an item, the proponent must prove that it is what he or she claims that it is. Here, since the proponent claims that the object has a historical connection to the case, the authentication doctrine requires that the proponent establish that historical nexus. There are several techniques the proponent may use to prove that nexus.

1. Ready Identifiability

At first, the authentication of an item of physical evidence might seem to be difficult and time consuming. In truth, the foundation can be laid with surprising brevity. Suppose that in a prosecution for assault and battery, the police officer who responded to the scene is testifying. The prosecutor marks a pistol for identification and hands it to the witness:

Q: I now hand you state's exhibit one for identification. What is it?

A: It's the pistol I found at the crime scene.

Q: How can you recognize it?

A: I remember the serial number.

Q: What was that number?

A: 15273956.

Q: When did you first notice the serial number?

A: I carefully noted it when I first picked up the weapon at the scene of the alleged attack.

Q: How can you recognize that number now?

A: I've always had a great memory for numbers. There's no question in my mind. This is the pistol I picked up that afternoon.

Q: Your Honor, I now offer state's exhibit one for identification into evidence as state's exhibit one.

Wigmore described the theory underlying the ready identifiability doctrine. He points out that the authentication process is sometimes aided by a combination of features or marks on an exhibit:

> It is by adding circumstance to circumstance that we obtain a composite feature or mark which as a whole cannot be supposed to be associated with more than a single object. The process of constructing an inference of Identity thus consists usually in adding together a number of circumstances, each of which by itself might be a feature of many objects, but all of which together make it more probable that they coexist in a single object only. A mark common to two supposed objects is receivable to show them to be identical whenever the mark does not in human experience occur with so many objects that the chances of the two supposed objects are too small to be appreciable. But it must be understood that this test applies to the total combination of circumstances offered as a mark, and not to any one circumstance going with others to make it up.

2 WIGMORE ON EVIDENCE §§ 411–412 (3d ed. 1940).

The courts have been quite liberal in treating objects as readily identifiable. When the witness is prepared to say that he or she recognized the exhibit as a particular object seen on an earlier, relevant occasion, on that basis, the courts have admitted such objects as a machine gun, *United States v. Carlos Cruz*, 352 F.3d 499, 506 (1st Cir. 2003); wire cutters, *State v. Houston*, 439 N.W.2d 173, 179 (Iowa 1989); screwdriver, *Lopez v. State*, 490 S.W.2d 565 (Tex. Crim. App. 1973); a pair of scissors, *Westwood v. State*, 693 P.2d 763 (Wyo. 1985); a money bag, *Overton v. State*, 490 S.W.2d 556 (Tex. Crim. App. 1973); a bottle, *State v. Paladine*, 2 Conn. Cir. Ct. 457, 201 A.2d 667 (1964); a leather key case, *Raullerson v. People*, 157 Colo. 462, 404 P.2d 149 (1965); a piece of rope, *Burris v. American Chicle Co.*, 120 F.2d 218 (2d Cir. 1941); and a tire, *United States v. Pagerie*, 15 C.M.R. 864 (A.F.B.R. 1954).

NOTE AND PROBLEM

1.   Do the Federal Rules codify the ready identifiability doctrine? Be prepared to identify the controlling language in the statutory text of Rule 901. What is the test for determining whether an item should be treated as a readily identifiable article? *See Transclean Corp. v. Bridgewood Services, Inc.*, 77 F. Supp. 2d 1045, 1074 (D. Minn. 1999) (the test is whether the proponent has made "a prima facie showing"). *See United States v. Kandiel*, 865 F.2d 967, 974 (8th Cir. 1979) ("[a]ny question concerning the credibility of the identifying witness simply goes to the weight the jury accords this evidence, not to its admissibility"); *United States v. Reilly*, 33 F.3d 1396, 1409 (3d Cir. 1994) ("contradictory evidence goes to the weight to be assigned by the trier of fact and not to admissibility"). In formulating the test, consider Federal Evidence Rules 901(b)(1) and (b)(4) as well as Rules 104(a)–(b). The judge must decide whether to characterize an object as readily identifiable. The question of whether a tire has a particular mark on it is obviously a preliminary "fact" within the meaning of that expression in Rule 104. However, that determination is not enough. To invoke the ready identifiability doctrine, the judge must further find that the mark makes the item one-of-a-kind.

2.   **Problem 10-1.** In *Devitt*, Paterson claims that Devitt threatened him with a knife before fleeing from the apartment. When the police arrived at the scene, they found a knife laying by the bed. The knife had no distinctive natural markings; but following standard operating procedure in most police departments, the seizing officer scratched her initials and the date on the knife blade. Do those marks convert the object into a readily identifiable article? *See United States v. Madril*, 445 F.2d 827, 828 (9th Cir.) (officers identified their markings on the grip of a pistol; pistol properly admitted into evidence); *vacated on other grounds*, 404 U.S. 1010 (1972).

2.   Chain of Custody

It is commonly assumed that once an object like a gun or knife has been seized, particularly in a criminal case, it will be kept in an uninterrupted way in "official" custody until the time of trial. And often that is the case. *See United States v. Carlos Cruz*, 352 F.3d 499, 506 (1st Cir. 2003) (concluding machine guns properly authenticated where agent testified that weapons were seized immediately after arrest, taken to police headquarters, and thereafter remained in custody of Bureau of Alcohol, Tobacco, and Firearms agent). However, things are not always that simple. Many times an objection is asserted claiming that a seized item was out of official custody for a time, breaking the chain of custody, and defeating admission of the exhibit. The response of the courts is to look closely at whether the break in chain was substantial. If only minimal, the break will be excused. See *United States v. Mejia*, 597 F.3d 1329, 1335 (D.C. Cir. 2010) (noting that original acquisition and subsequent custody are what make objects admissible in evidence, and a short ten-minute gap in custody between the arrest by unidentified members of the Salvadoran police and the turning over of the evidence to the FBI was not enough to defeat admissibility; it was "implausible" that a list of DEA agents' names was planted by police in the defendant's wallet).

The chain of custody technique for identifying and gaining admission of physical objects is a well-settled avenue for authenticating exhibits. It operates in the case of solid objects as well as results of laboratory analysis of fluids and drugs. The next article presents a straightforward overview of the issues raised by the chain of custody technique:

E J Imwinkelried, Comment, *The Identification of Original, Real Evidence*
61 MIL. L. REV. 145 (1973)[1]

When must the proponent prove a chain of custody?

There are three situations in which the proponent ordinarily resorts to proof of a chain of custody.

The first situation is where the item is not readily identifiable. As previously stated, the courts are exceedingly liberal in deciding to treat articles as readily identifiable items. However, there are some items which even the most liberal court would not label readily identifiable. If the issue is the identity of a specimen of blood, urine, or drugs, the court will not admit the specimen solely on the basis of the witness' purported identification of the substance. To identify a fungible item, the proponent ordinarily must prove a chain of the item's custody.

The second situation is where by its nature the item is readily identifiable but the witness neglected to note the characteristics which make the item readily identifiable. For example, suppose that the item is a serially numbered pistol but the witness failed to note the serial number. If he had noted the number, the court would treat the item as readily identifiable; as long as the witness testified that he remembered the number, the pistol's identification would be complete. However, if the witness failed to note the number, the proponent could still identify the pistol by proving the chain of its custody. Where the witness fails to note the special

---

[1] The opinions and conclusions presented herein are those of the author and do not necessarily represent the views of the Department of Defense, the Department of the Army, The Judge Advocate General's School, or any other governmental agency.

identifying characteristics of a readily identifiable item, proof of the chain of its custody is "a more than adequate substitute."

The third situation is where the item is a delicate article and its condition at the time of seizure is a pivotal issue in the case. The chain of custody is a method of establishing both the item's identity and its condition at the time of seizure. McCormick takes the position that if the item is "susceptible to alteration by tampering or contamination, sound exercise of the trial court's discretion may require" proof of a chain of custody. He gives the example of chemical specimens. Another illustration would be a delicate part of the engine of a crashed aircraft. Suppose the instrument is serially numbered. Assume further that the setting of the instrument at the time of crash would determine the ultimate liability for the accident. . . . [P]laintiff's counsel attempts to offer the instrument in evidence. He calls as a witness a Federal Aviation Administration investigator. The investigator testifies that he found the instrument at the crash site. The plaintiff's counsel hands the instrument to the witness and asks him to identify it. The witness identifies it on the basis of the serial number. The plaintiff's attorney then offers the item in evidence. Would the trial judge be justified in requiring proof of a chain of the instrument's custody? The answer is probably yes. The witness' testimony proves the item's identity, but the critical question is whether the instrument was at the same setting at the time of crash as it is when offered in evidence. Since the item is a delicate instrument, the judge would be justified in exercising discretion to require proof of a chain of custody. If the item has been subject to careless or rough handling in the interim between seizure and trial, the handling might have jarred the instrument into a different setting. Even though the item is readily identifiable, the posture of the case warrants the requirement for proof of the chain of custody.

What is the length of the chain of custody? What period of time must the proponent account for?

To answer this question, counsel should distinguish between two fact situations.

The first situation is where the item's logical relevance depends upon a witness' in-court identification of the item. The trial counsel wants to authenticate the knife by proving a chain of custody. In this situation, the chain must run from the time of seizure to the time the knife is offered in evidence. The proponent must prove an identity between the item seized and the item offered, and he must assume the burden of proving a chain running from the time of seizure to the time of offer.

The second situation is where the proponent is relying upon the real evidence as the basis for expert testimony of the evidence's chemical analysis . . . . [T]he overwhelming, majority view is that the chain must run only from the time of seizure to the time of analysis or test. In *United States v. Singer*,[67] the court stated that the evidence of the analysis is admissible even if the sample analyzed is lost or destroyed after the test. In fact, it is "nowise customary to produce in court a specimen or part upon which an analysis has been made." The majority view is the better-reasoned rule. If the proponent is offering only the results of the analysis, he must prove identity between the substance seized and the substance analyzed.

---

[67] 43 F. Supp. 863 (E.D.N.Y. 1942).

There is no rule of evidence or logic which compels him to offer the substance in evidence. In some jurisdictions, the party opponent is entitled to inspect the substance and subject it to an independent test; but it is specious to suggest that the proponent's duty to formally offer the substance into evidence is a necessary correlative of the opponent's right to discover and examine the substance.

Which persons comprise the links in the chain of custody?

. . . It is well-settled that persons who merely had access to the item do not constitute links in the chain and that the proponent need not make any affirmative showing of their conduct with respect to the item. Such persons have an opportunity to come in contact with the item; but unless there is some indication that they in fact came into contact with the item, they do not constitute links in the chain of proof.

There is some authority that the proponent need not make any affirmative showing of the conduct of a person who handled the article but who (1) held the item for a very short time and (2) performed only mechanical functions with the item. In *Commonwealth v. Thomas*,[73] the court held that the proponent did not have to make any showing of the conduct of the laboratory technician who merely placed the brushings in question under a microscope . . . . [The court's] reasoning probably ran along these lines: Proof of a chain of custody is a method of negativing any probability that substitution or tampering occurred; a person should be held to be a link, whom the proponent must account for, only if the person had a substantial opportunity to substitute for or tamper with the item; and, finally, persons who handle the item momentarily to perform purely mechanical functions do not have a substantial opportunity for substitution or tampering. There is a strong counter-argument that in the case of fungible, malleable goods, even a person who possesses the article only momentarily has a substantial opportunity for substitution or tampering. To date, the counter-argument has prevailed and the *Thomas* doctrine remains a distinct minority view . . . .

The most significant concession the courts have made is their rule that the proponent need not make any affirmative showing of postal employees' handling of mailed items. Here the courts apply presumptions that postal employees properly discharge their duties and that articles "regularly mailed are delivered in substantially the same condition in which they were sent." It is indisputable that the postal employees who handle a mailed article are custodians of the article. However, if the sender uses the mail, it is virtually impossible to identify all the postal employees who handled the article; and the courts are understandably reluctant to adopt a rule of evidence which, in practical effect, would prevent evidence custodians from using the mail to transmit articles.

What showing must the proponent make to prove the chain of custody?

The courts have expressed the proponent's burden in various ways. Some have said that he must prove the chain by a "clear preponderance" of the evidence. Others have said that he must establish a "reasonable certainty." Others say that he

---

[73] 448 Pa. 42, 292 A.2d 352 (1972).

must prove the chain "unequivocally." Still others say that he must create a "clear assurance." The most definite and often used expression is that the proponent must prove a "reasonable probability."

What is the nature of the probability the proponent must establish? In the leading federal case, *United States v. S.B. Penick & Co.*,[82] the Court of Appeals attempted to define the content of the showing the proponent must make. Affirmatively, he must show it is probable that the item offered in evidence is the same item originally acquired in substantially the same condition it was in at the time of acquisition. Negatively, he must show that it is improbable that either substitution or tampering occurred. In making this determination, the judge must weigh three factors: the nature of the article, the circumstances surrounding its preservation and custody, and the likelihood of any tampering by intermeddlers.

With respect to each link in the chain, the proponent must demonstrate: (1) his receipt of the item; (2) his ultimate disposition of the item, i.e., transfer, destruction, or retention; and (3) his safeguarding and handling of the item between receipt and ultimate disposition. The third element poses the most difficult problem of proof for the proponent.

The courts have held that proof that the article was kept in a sealed container in the interim is an adequate showing of safekeeping and handling. The very "nature of a sealed container" makes substitution or tampering unlikely. It is now the standing operating procedure of law enforcement agencies to place seized fungibles in locked, sealed envelopes . . . . A recent case, *State v. Simmons*[89] demonstrates the probative value of sealed containers even more dramatically. In Simmons, a tissue sample taken from a girl's body was placed in the hospital's tissue laboratory refrigerator. The tissue sample was in a sealed bag. The evidence next indicated that a policeman picked the bag up at the hospital desk. There was no evidence of the bag's safekeeping in the interim between its deposit in the refrigerator and the time when the officer picked up the bag at the desk. There was no evidence identifying the person who transported the bag from the refrigerator to the desk. Nevertheless, the court held that the proof of the chain of custody was sufficient. The court emphasized that although there was a gap in the chain of proof . . . . [t]here was, however, testimony that each of the specimens had been sealed in a bag and that the seals were intact at all times and did not reveal evidence of tampering.

The courts have also held that proof that the article was kept in a secure area in the interim is an adequate showing of safekeeping. The courts have held that articles kept in the following areas were adequately safeguarded: a secured closet, a locked automobile, an evidence locker, a police safe, a police lock box, a locked evidence cabinet, a locked evidence file, a police department evidence room, and a locked narcotics cabinet.

Finally, even in the absence of other proof of safekeeping, the courts have upheld showings of chain of custody where (1) the proponent at least accounted for the

---

[82] 136 F.2d 413 (2d Cir. 1943).

[89] 203 N.W.2d 887 (Wis. 1973).

article's whereabouts and (2) the whereabouts were places where it was unlikely that intermeddling would occur.

As a practical matter, the standard of proof in chain-of-custody cases is rather slight. The proponent need not negate every possibility of substitution or tampering . . . . The courts have even gone so far as to sustain chains when there were glaring discrepancies in the proponent's evidence. In one case, the court sustained the chain even though the name written on the narcotics container was a name other than that of the government special employee who allegedly obtained the narcotics. In another case, the envelope containing the drug stated an analysis date which conflicted with the government chemist's testimony. Again the chain was sustained. In still another case, the police lost the knife before trial. The police found the knife after trial began. A government witness testified that he could identify the knife because of the brown envelope in which it was placed. Again the chain was upheld.

[However, t]here are two types of cases in which the courts tend to impose a strict standard of proof.

The first type of case is one in which there is a strong possibility that the article has been confused with other, similar articles. In *Nichols v. McCoy*,[123] the item in question was a blood sample. The sample had been extracted from a body at the coroner's mortuary. The evidence indicated that bodies were customarily kept at the mortuary and that samples were ordinarily extracted there. The proponent did not make any affirmative showing that the body or blood sample had been segregated from the other bodies and blood samples at the mortuary. The evidence raised a serious question concerning the blood sample's identity, and the court held that the proof of the chain was insufficient.

The second type of case is one in which the article is delicate and malleable. The trial judge has discretion to determine the amount of evidence necessary to lay a proper foundation; and he can vary the standard of proof, depending upon the ease or difficulty with which the item can be altered. If, in a particular case, the judge has "more than a captious doubt about the authenticity of the exhibits," he may require "a very substantial foundation . . .". Some courts frankly admit that they impose a higher standard of proof when the object is "easily alterable" or "easily susceptible to undetected alteration." In contrast, they apply a lower standard of proof if the article is a solid object.

Blood samples are malleable articles. One commentator remarked that blood samples are:

> . . . easily susceptible to accidental alteration through carelessness in taking, storing, or testing, and to willful tampering by intermeddling litigants. In addition, the mechanics of calculating alcoholic content will greatly magnify even a slight change in the condition of the specimen, whatever its cause.

For this reason, the courts tend to impose a stricter standard of proof for the chain of a blood sample's custody.

---

[123] 106 Cal. App. 2d (Adv. 661), 235 P.2d 412 (1951).

NOTES AND PROBLEMS

1. What are the limits of the *Thomas* doctrine mentioned in the excerpted article? Suppose that the laboratory technician had held the article for an hour. Three hours? Overnight? At what point does the technician become such an important custodian that the proponent must make an affirmative showing of his or her safekeeping?

2. Problem 10-2. In the *Devitt* case, Paterson told the police that he was certain that before leaving, the attacker rested his hand on a plastic jewelry box in the bedroom. The officer scratched her initials on the box and took it to the police laboratory. At the laboratory, she handed the box to a technician. In turn, the technician delivered the box to the head of the fingerprint division. The head of the division developed latent fingerprints on the box and is prepared to compare photographs of those prints with the defendant's fingerprints. Do the markings make the box readily identifiable? Do we need a chain of custody? If so, why? If the prosecutor wants to offer the fingerprint testimony, what issue arises when the analyst attempts to testify to the results of a test of the box? *See Whaley v. Commonwealth*, 214 Va. 353, 355–58, 200 S.E.2d 556, 558–59 (1973) (undershorts admissible which were seized from defendant, because shorts were placed with police custodian immediately after seizure; however, any effort to admit a chemical analysis of red smear on shorts in this rape case would require chain of custody showing).

3. Problem 10-3. In the last problem, the prosecutor calls three witnesses: the officer, the technician, and the head of the fingerprint division. At what point should the prosecutor first have the box marked for identification? When should the prosecutor formally offer the box into evidence? After the first link's testimony? After the second link's testimony? After the third link's testimony?

4. Problem 10-4. On cross-examination, the technician admits the following: The officer delivered the box to him just before the close of business on March 12th; for that reason, he did not analyze the box on the 12th; he left the box on his workbench overnight; only police and janitorial employees have keys to the work area; and when he came to work the morning of the 13th, his work area appeared undisturbed. The defense counsel now moves to strike the technician's testimony and exclude the box. As judge, would you grant the motion? *See Wright v. State*, 420 S.W.2d 411, 413 (Tex. Crim. App. 1967) (although marijuana cigarettes were lying on laboratory chemist's desk, chemist swore they were always in his possession; no proof of tampering, so evidence was admitted); *Thomas v. Astrue*, 674 F. Supp. 2d 507, 512 (S.D.N.Y. 2009) (noting that if there is a reasonable assurance of correctly identified and unaltered evidence, as there was in this case where the only gap in the chain was the transfer between the state police and the state toxicology lab and no foul play by the plaintiff was suggested, any defect in the chain of custody affects only the weight of evidence and not admissibility); *Samaniego v. State*, 2002 Tex. App. LEXIS 5408, at *10 (July 26, 2002) (stating that chain of custody was satisfied where "appellant has shown the possibility which existed for someone to tamper with the evidence, but nothing more. Appellant's objection goes to the weight, and not the admissibility of the evidence"). Evidence of tampering, of course, could change the analysis.

5.   The paradox is that at the same time the courts appear to be toughening the standards for proving chain of custody, some legislatures are intervening to relax the standards. Until recently, appellate courts rarely ruled that the proof of a chain of custody was inadequate. However, the advent of DNA evidence seems to have sensitized the courts to this issue. In the year of 2000, for example, there were a number of appellate decisions sustaining attacks on chain of custody. *E.g., United States v. Edwards*, 235 F.3d 1173, 1178 (9th Cir. 2000); *United States v. Ellis*, 15 F. Supp. 2d 1025, 1032 (D. Colo. 1998); *State v. Scott*, 33 S.W.3d 746, 761 (Tenn. 2000).

This reflects a concern about a risk of contamination of DNA samples. Cross-contamination can be particularly serious. In any DNA laboratory "the contamination controls must be heightened." *State v. Scott*, 33 S.W.3d 746, 757 (Tenn. 2000).

6.   More broadly, with all physical objects and laboratory evidence, courts are vigilant to insure that evidentiary items have not been altered, corrupted or contaminated. *State v. Shepard*, 768 N.W.2d 162 (S.D. 2009) (party offering evidence must establish by reasonable probability that the real evidence offered is that object which was involved in the transaction, and that the object is in a substantially unchanged condition). In criminal prosecutions testimony by police, detectives or government agents will usually be required to comply with this feature of chain of custody rules; *United States v. Turner*, 591 F.3d 928, 935 (7th Cir. 2010) (affirming the district court's admission of cocaine into evidence because not every person who handled an exhibit is required to be called as a witness to establish the chain of custody, the substance was in official custody at all times, and the detective testified at trial that the drugs appeared to be in substantially the same condition as when he received them from the undercover officer); *State v. Houston*, 439 N.W.2d 173, 179 (Iowa 1989) emphasizes that introduction of proof is aided "where the possibility of alteration of an exhibit is slight."

7.   Sometimes there is a failure by the offering party to tie the exhibit to the facts of the litigated transaction. It must be shown that the physical exhibit, like a gun or knife, was connected to the criminal incident on trial. The same rule applies to laboratory evidence. *See State v. Cannon*, 254 S.W.3d 287, 298 (Tenn. 2008) (holding that "the trial court erred by admitting into evidence the DNA analysis of semen found on the pantyhose because the pantyhose were not sufficiently identified as belonging to the victim by a witness with knowledge").

8.   Ready identifiability and chain of custody are long-accepted techniques of authenticating physical evidence. However, as we have repeatedly stressed, in the field of logical relevance the proponent is not limited to the well-settled doctrines. At common law, the proponent can be creative so long as the proponent can marshal sufficient circumstances to support a permissive inference of genuineness. Federal Rule 901 preserves that latitude for creative lawyering. In some cases, authentication is satisfied by circumstantial evidence. *United States v. Jackson*, 345 F.3d 59, 65 (2d Cir. 2003) (finding government established sufficient chain of custody with videotape showing defendant giving a substance to informant, agent's testimony of government surveillance of informant before, during, and after transaction, agent's testimony regarding field testing and storage of drugs, and testimony of chemist who tested substance).

C. DEMONSTRATIVE PHYSICAL EVIDENCE

In addition to real or original evidence, there is another type of evidence — demonstrative evidence. There is no logical necessity for limiting the attorneys to objects historically connected with the case. A mannequin, model, replica, or chart can be very helpful to the jury. Even if the aid is prepared specially for purposes of trial, the object can assist the jurors in visualizing and understanding the testimony. *State v. Holmes*, 609 S.W.2d 132 (Mo. 1980). In addition, a visual aid can be a powerful tool of advocacy. For years, the late Melvin Belli was one of the most innovative masters of demonstrative evidence. Mr. Belli's anecdote in the following classic article confirms the finding of psychological researchers that physical evidence can have a major impact on the outcome of a trial.

Belli, *Demonstrative Evidence and the Adequate Award*
22 Miss. L.J. 284 (1951)

The Jeffers Case

To illustrate demonstrative evidence, I refer you to a case I tried against our Municipal Railway: Catherine Jeffers had suffered the traumatic amputation of her right limb below the knee as she was getting off a streetcar on Market Street at its regular stopping point in San Francisco.

At the first trial, the verdict was $65,000. At the first trial I employed all of my ability as a trial man, all of my attributes of sincerity and humility. I failed to use one thing. I didn't use *demonstrative evidence*. Perhaps I should say I did not use imagination. Imagination to me in the courtroom is merely another way of saying I did not think the case through clearly enough so that I could portray to others in the most dramatic fashion what was so obvious to me. I failed to realize that I was trained in the courtroom, I went to law school and had become a specialist, that jurors are chosen because they know nothing of law, know nothing of the procedure of the courtroom, nothing of medicines, and they are mystified as much as they are frightened at the thought of "going to law."

On motion for new trial, excessiveness of verdict, the trial judge set the verdict of $65,000 for a lost limb aside.

I reset the case for trial before another judge and another jury. On the next trial, the verdict was $100,000, and there was another motion for excessive damages. This time the verdict of $100,000 was sustained.

Why the difference? . . .

The first trial judge in my *Jeffers* case had never seen an artificial limb. When I came into court on the second trial it occurred to me, "I am asking this jury to give my client something. I must show them, if possible, just exactly what it is. I can't show them an intangible commodity: pain and suffering and tears."

As if to emphasize my thoughts, defendant's counsel had commented to me that he was going to prove that science has now progressed to the point that an amputee can be fitted with a prosthesis which is just as good as the amputated limb the Lord had given him. . . . I drive cars, play bridge, dance, swim, eat, tie neckties, and do practically everything . . . a normal limb can do. . . . This is exactly the argument that the City Attorney made. I saw the jury impressed by this argument.

On the first day of trial, at the time of the opening argument, I had brought into court a large object wrapped in yellow butcher paper. I placed this down on the counsel table and left it there during the entire trial. Of course, the jury, the judge and opposing counsel were curious. I moved it from the side of the table to the back of the table to the front of the table, close to the jury . . . .

When it came time for me to argue the case, I took the object in the paper before the jury box. It took me about five minutes to unwrap it. When I did, I said, "This is what this young girl is going to have to wear for the rest of her life — this artificial limb, this marvelous scientific invention. You have seen the metal and the harness and the strapping and the brutality of an artificial limb no matter how adeptly made."

I took the artificial limb and I asked Number One Juror to handle it and then to pass it among the other jurors. I asked them to "feel the fine texture of the flesh, to feel the warm blood coursing through the veins, to move the noiseless joints, to compare them with the articulating parts of their own knees." I told them here was this great piece of scientific achievement my friend had spoken of and which anyone would gladly substitute for their own limb.

The jury passed the limb from juror to juror. All this time my plaintiff sat in the courtroom in plain view with only one natural leg! It took about a half an hour for them to pass it about. I could see the verdict sealed in the looks on their faces as this limb was being passed around. The jury was convinced; the trial judge was convinced. The jury was out thirty minutes!

NOTES

1. As defense attorney in *Jeffers*, would you have objected to the manner in which Mr. Belli used the artificial limb during summation? If so, on what ground? Remember the Prosecution Function Standard cited in the introduction to this chapter. What if it were applied to civil actions?

2. It is easy to see how the authentication doctrine applies to real or original physical evidence. Does the doctrine apply as well to demonstrative evidence? Rule 401 mandates that the proponent make a claim about an item of proffered evidence that renders the item logically relevant to a fact of consequence in issue, and the essence of authentication under Rule 901(a) is that the proponent must prove up that claim. What does the proponent claim that an item of demonstrative evidence is? What did Mr. Belli impliedly claim that the artificial limb was?

3. Judges ordinarily admit models only when the sponsoring witness testifies that the object is "substantially similar" to the object historically involved in the case. The trial judge has wide discretion in deciding whether the proponent has made a sufficient showing of similarity. Is the requirement of substantial similarity solely a corollary of authentication? Under Rule 105, when a judge admits an exhibit on the theory that it is demonstrative rather than original evidence, what sort of limiting instruction should the judge give the jury? Suppose that the police could not locate the very knife which Devitt allegedly used to threaten Paterson but that the judge allowed the prosecutor to use a similar knife during Paterson's direct examination to illustrate Paterson's testimony about the battery. In the instruction, what should the judge tell the jury about the knife displayed during Paterson's testimony? How would that instruction limit what the prosecutor could say about the knife during closing argument?

4.   Demonstrative evidence is handled differently by courts:

> Some courts treat demonstrative exhibits exactly as they do substantive exhibits, that is, by formally admitting them into evidence and allowing the jury to view the exhibits during deliberations. Other courts admit demonstrative exhibits into a twilight zone reserved for "demonstrative purposes only," apparently indicating that such exhibits can be identified for the record but must be precluded from use by the jury during deliberations. Still other courts admit demonstrative exhibits "for limited purposes," but nevertheless permit the jury to view the exhibits during deliberations. Finally, some courts explicitly refuse to "admit" demonstrative exhibits into evidence at all, but allow witnesses to refer to them during testimony. . . .
> — some permitting the jury to view this unadmitted evidence during deliberations, while others do not.

Brain & Broderick, *The Derivative Relevance of Demonstrative Evidence: Charting Its Proper Evidentiary Status*, 25 U.C. DAVIS L. REV. 957, 965–66 (1992). *See also* ME. R. EVID. 616 ("illustrative aids" "shall not accompany the jury during deliberations unless by consent of all parties or order of court on good cause shown"); *United States v. Wood*, 943 F.2d 1048, 1053 (9th Cir. 1991) ("such pedagogical devices should be used only as a testimonial aid and should not be admitted into evidence or otherwise be used by the jury during deliberations").

In any event, if the judge admits the evidence for this purpose, at least on request under Federal Rule 105 the judge should give the jury a limiting instruction, specifying the evidentiary status of the exhibit. How would you word the instruction?

The foregoing text notes suggest that if an object like a knife described by a stabbing victim cannot be found, the prosecutor may use one at trial, so long as it looks highly similar to the victim's description. A bottle was employed in this manner in the following case.

STATE v. FREEMAN
269 S.W.2d 422 (Mo. 2008)

RUSSELL, JUDGE

Defendant and the female victim were regular patrons at the Poplar Bluff VFW club. On the night of the murder, they had been there for four to five hours. At some point in the evening, they argued over whose turn it was to use a pool table.

Witnesses noted their raised voices and Defendant's slight agitation. Later, he attempted to flirt with her, briefly sitting down next to her and offering to buy her a drink, which she rebuffed. Defendant remembered having no direct physical contact with the victim or, at most, it was limited to his tapping her on the shoulder.

At last call, Defendant left the bar with an empty bottle of Galliano liqueur, which the waitress had given to him as a souvenir. Fifteen minutes later, the victim left the bar heading home, which was approximately a quarter-mile away. Her upstairs neighbor heard her arrive shortly thereafter and, going to his window, saw her exit her car and struggle to open her apartment's door. At this point a man approached from behind her, and they entered her apartment together. The neighbor did not see the man drive up, and there were no other cars in sight. The next day, the neighbor was only able to give a very general description of the man and apparently had not suspected foul play.

[The victim's body was found in her apartment the next afternoon by her mother. She was naked except for one knee-high stocking remaining on her leg. The other stocking was tied tightly around her neck, and her cause of death was found to be asphyxia. The autopsy also revealed a hemorrhage behind her ear, which was perhaps caused by some type of blow to the head before her death by an instrument with a smooth surface. There was evidence of sexual penetration by a foreign object. The jury returned a guilty verdict for first degree murder. The Missouri Supreme Court agreed with the jury, and disposed of the defendant's complaints that the prosecution improperly used Galliano liqueur bottles as demonstrative evidence. Defendant argued the evidence was not relevant, and inflamed the jury with the image of a sexual assault performed with a bottle.]

The fact that Defendant left the VFW club that night with a Galliano bottle was connected to the State's theory of the case. As such, the bottles were logically relevant. In addition, the bottles were legally relevant because they did not have a tendency to mislead the jury and did not unduly prejudice Defendant. Two waitresses testified that the bottles presented were of the type seen in his possession. Since a Galliano bottle has a very unique shape that is not commonly known, the presentation of the bottles likely served to clarify rather than mislead. And, notably, the State made it clear that the bottles were being presented for demonstrative purposes only. Indeed, the prosecutor's clear statement that the bottles were mere demonstrative evidence, taken with the initial timing of their presentation during testimony about the activities at the VFW club, negates any potential to mislead the jury.

* * *

For all these reasons, it was not a clear abuse of discretion that the trial court allowed these bottles as demonstrative evidence.

NOTE

Other cases align with *Freeman* in permitting a weapon at trial which looks like the actual instrumentality. In one sexual assault case the defendant attacked the victim with a pair of nunchakus, a martial arts weapon. The use of a similar set of nunchakus for demonstrative purposes was proper. A prosecution witness, an expert in martial arts, was allowed to demonstrate the use of the instrument by breaking boards with it. *Toledo v. State*, 651 S.W.2d 382, 384 (Tex. Ct. App. 1983).

Chapter 11

SPECIALIZED ASPECTS OF LOGICAL RELEVANCE: IDENTIFICATION OF SPEAKERS AND VERIFICATION OF PHOTOGRAPHS AND CHARTS

Read Federal Rules of Evidence 901(a) and (b)(5)–(6).

A. THE IDENTIFICATION OF A SPEAKER

In the authentication of writings, the essential task is identifying the author. In the authentication of oral statements, the task is identifying the speaker. The techniques for authenticating statements and conversations largely parallel the techniques for authenticating documents. As with documents, the proponent can rely on direct evidence: For example, a witness might identify the speaker of a statement made in the witness's presence. Where authentication takes the form of circumstantial evidence, there are a number of different methods that might be used. A brief review of several of these techniques for circumstantially identifying the speaker will further demonstrate the parallels to the authentication of written documents that we examined in Chapter 9.

1. The Telephone Directory Doctrine

Rule 901(b)(6) codifies the common law "telephone directory doctrine," as follows:

Rule 901. Authenticating or Identifying Evidence

(b) Examples. The following are examples only — not a complete list — of evidence that satisfies the requirement:

* * *

(6) Evidence About a Telephone Conversation. For a telephone conversation evidence that a call was made to the number assigned at the time to:

(A) a particular person, if circumstances, including self-identification, show that the person answering was the one called; or

(B) a particular business, if the call was made to a business and the call related to business reasonably transacted over the telephone.

This doctrine rests on the quite reasonable assumption that the telephone directory is reliable. That is certainly an assumption we readily make in our daily lives. This is one instance in which the law of evidence has been willing to accept an everyday assumption. Given that assumption, the doctrine tells us that the pattern of circumstances identified in Rule 901(b)(6) is sufficient to allow a jury to make a reasonable inference of the speaker's identity.

2. Identification Based on the Content of an Oral Statement

Alternatively, a spoken statement can be authenticated by proof that only a particular person is likely to know the data disclosed in the statement. We examined a similar method of authenticating writings in Chapter 9. If the proponent can establish that certain facts were disclosed in the oral statement and that only a particular person was likely to know those facts, we may conclude that the speaker was that person.

3. Lay Observer Testimony

One of the most common techniques for authenticating oral statements is testimony of a witness who is familiar with the person's voice, sometimes referred to as "skilled lay observer testimony." Federal Evidence Rule 901(b)(5) codifies the technique:

> An opinion identifying a person's voice — whether heard firsthand or through mechanical or electronic transmission or recording — based on hearing the voice at any time under circumstances that connect it with the alleged speaker.

This technique parallels authentication based on familiarity with a person's handwriting as permitted by Rule 901(b)(2). The foundation requires proof that the witness is sufficiently familiar with the person's voice. Annot., 79 A.L.R.3d 79 (1977). Some of the older decisions suggest that it suffices if the witness heard the alleged speaker talk on even a single prior occasion, but many modern opinions require that the witness have had more significant exposure to the alleged speaker's voice. In *United States v. Albergo*, 539 F.2d 860 (2d Cir.), *cert. denied*, 429 U.S. 1000 (1976), the witness testified that "he had heard appellant's voice on tape some 500 different times and that he had on one occasion visited . . . [a] [b]ar and listened to appellant talking with a group of men at the [b]ar." 539 F.2d at 862. Thus, *Albergo* is an easy case to resolve even under the modern standard. However, the following problems are a bit more challenging.

NOTES AND PROBLEMS

1. **Problem 11-1.** In *Devitt*, the day before the incident, Paterson received an angry telephone call. At the time, he did not recognize the voice. Assume Devitt was not asked to speak at the lineup, and he elected not to testify at the preliminary hearing. Hence, while testifying during the prosecution case-in-chief, Paterson cannot and does not testify that he recognized Devitt's voice on the telephone. However, after testifying, he remains in the courtroom and is present to hear Devitt testify in his own defense. During the prosecution rebuttal, the prosecutor recalls Paterson as a witness. He is prepared to identify Devitt's voice on the basis of

hearing him testify in court. The defense attorney objects that "the courtroom environment is too artificial a setting for any voice identification to be reliable." What ruling? *United States v. Duran*, 4 F.3d 800 (9th Cir. 1993). (bank tellers heard robber speak during robbery, then at trial; held, identification made at court proceeding was proper); *United States v. Neighbors*, 590 F.3d 485, 492–94 (7th Cir. 2009) (detective had conversation with defendant on day of arrest, then heard him speak during court proceedings).

2. Suppose Devitt never took the stand at trial. Courtroom voice identification can be aided in such situations by compelling the accused to provide a voice exemplar in the presence of the jury. Does this process violate the Fifth Amendment privilege against self-incrimination? In *Burnett v. Collins*, 982 F.2d 922 (5th Cir. 1993), the defendant was required to repeat the exact words of the armed robber, even though he chose not to testify during trial. According to the court, "[a] voice exemplar does not violate one's Fifth Amendment privilege against self-incrimination because the exemplar is merely a source of physical evidence."

3. Problem 11-2. The police have a tape recording of a threatening call to Paterson, made after the incident. To identify the speaker as Devitt, the prosecutor calls John Roselle. Roselle has never met Devitt face to face, but he transacts business with him over the telephone several times a week. On the basis of those telephone conversations, he is prepared to say that he can identify Devitt's voice. Specifically, he is prepared to testify that the voice on the recording is Devitt's. Is Roselle's lack of personal contact with Devitt fatal to the admissibility of his testimony? *See United States v. Green*, 40 F.3d 1167 (11th Cir. 1994) (tapes and transcripts of intercepted telephone conversations properly admitted; monitoring government agents became familiar with defendants' voices after the conversations were intercepted); *United States v. Williams*, 2008 U.S. App. LEXIS 765, at *18–*21 (11th Cir. Jan. 10, 2008) (finding that in order "[t]o prove a defendant's involvement in a particular offense, the government may rely on a witness's identification of the defendant's voice on an incriminating tape recording so long as [the] witness was familiar with the defendant's voice").

4. Sometimes a witness testifies that she received a telephone call from an unidentified caller. Occasionally a lawyer asks such a witness the question "was it a White voice?" Or perhaps "was it a Black voice?" Are such questions proper? Recent cases and scholarship have addressed the issue. *See Kohler, Racial Voice Identification: Judicial Condoning the Bogus Science of "Hearing Color,"* 77 Temp. L. Rev. 757 (2004); Son, *In-court Racial Voice Identifications: They Don't All Sound the Same*, 37 Loy. L.A. L. Rev. 1317 (2004). *See also Clifford v. Chandler*, 333 F.3d 724 (6th Cir. 2003) (witness testified that a voice he heard in an apartment belonged to a black male; held, vast majority of courts that have addressed the issue have concluded that racial identification testimony is admissible).

Most courts have adopted a liberal approach to voice identification, even though some psychologists claim that lay opinions identifying voices are unreliable. McGehee, *The Reliability of the Identification of the Human Voice*, 17 J. Gen. Psychol. 249 (1937). In the McGehee study, there were 49 "reader" (31 male and 18 female) and 740 "auditors." In most of the experiments, five readers spoke behind a screen. The auditor had heard only one of the readers' voices before, and the auditor was asked to identify that reader. In some of these experiments, there was only a one day lapse between initially hearing the reader's voice and the screen test. The researchers retested the auditors at a longer period up to five months since the initial hearing. In the study, after five months, only 13% of the auditors correctly identified the reader they initially heard. The researchers concluded that the reliability of lay opinions routinely admitted in court is "relatively low." However, like Professor Inbau's study of lay opinions on handwriting and the proficiency studies of questioned document examiners, these studies of voice identification have not persuaded courts to preclude or restrict the admissibility of lay opinion testimony on this topic.

4.   Expert Testimony Based on Sound Spectrography

Many forms of criminal and civil evidence lend themselves to specialized analysis by forensic experts. Sound recordings are no exception. A recorded telephone call to a victim's family asking for ransom money provides but one example of the sort of voice identification challenge facing a voiceprint examiner. *United States v. Angleton*, 269 F. Supp. 2d 892 (S.D. Tex. 2003) provides an introduction to the technique of voiceprint evidence:

> First, the investigator [expert] must check the recording of the unknown speaker to determine whether it has a sufficient amount of speech for analysis. The investigator then obtains a recording of an exemplar of the known speaker's speech, in which the subject repeats the recorded statements of the unknown speaker. The investigator listens for such factors as accent and dialect, inflection, syllable grouping and breath patterns, and the presence of speech pathologies or other unusual speech habits. In the spectrographic comparison, the examiner visually compares a spectrogram of recordings of the known and unknown speakers. A spectrogram is "a graphic display of the recorded signal on the basis of time and frequency with a general indication of amplitude." The investigator looks for both similarities and differences in various psychoacoustical features of speech, such as bandwidth, mean frequencies, distribution of format energy, and nasal resonances.

Just as an expert document examiner can authenticate a writing, an expert in sound spectrography may be willing to testify that the same voice produced two spectrograms. The following article describes the spectrography technique and some of the research conducted to determine the technique's efficacy.

Cutler, Thigpen, Young, & Mueller, *The Evidentiary Value of Spectrographic Voice Identification*
63 J. Crim. L., Criminology, and Police Science 343 (1972)

The Technique

Speaker recognition by spectrographic voice analysis is a seemingly simple, but fundamentally complex, method of personal identification. In making an identification by this method, the first step is to tape-record an exemplar of an individual's voice. The sound spectrum of his speech sample is then scanned electronically by a high-speed sound spectrograph which produces a spectrogram, a visible amplitude-frequency-time display of the speech sounds recorded. This visible portrayal of the frequency variations in an individual's voice can then be subjectively compared with spectrograms of phonetically identical sounds produced by "unknown" individuals. The sound patterns represented on the spectrogram are the product of the energy expelled during speech and are shaped and determined by the dynamic interplay between the individual's vocal mechanism and the coupling and placement of his articulators. The validity of the technique as a means of personal identification rests on the premise that the sound patterns produced in speech are unique to the individual and that the spectrogram accurately and sufficiently displays this uniqueness.

Kersta: Theory, Experiments, and Replication

Lawrence Kersta, an electrical engineer and physicist, has been the fore-most advocate of the validity of personal identification by spectrographic voice analysis. His claim that the technique is accurate and reliable is founded on two propositions.

The theory of invariant speech is the cornerstone of his hypothesis that individuals can be identified by the spectral characteristics of their voices. The theory posits that the characteristic spectral patterns of phonetically identical utterances vary more between two individuals (interspeaker variability) than between two such utterances spoken by the same individual (intraspeaker variability). Although so far the theory has not been proven directly, Kersta has buttressed the theory by applying his own hybrid form of statistical probability to the acoustic theory of speech production. He argues that since both the dimensions of the vocal cavities and the coupling of the articulators, which define the spectrum for a given sound, are affected by heredity, sex, age, and socio-environmental factors, it is extremely unlikely that two individuals would develop spectrographically identical speech patterns. While a superficially attractive rationale for voice uniqueness, a proper application of probability theory demands substantially more precision than this.

[Kersta's initial experiments with spectrographic voice analysis demonstrated extremely low error rates. Kersta concluded that spectrograms of an individual's speech patterns for particular words are as unique in their identifying characteristics as fingerprints, thus rendering the technique a reliable method of personal identification when performed by a trained examiner. In addition, Kersta claimed that neither passage of time nor conscious efforts at mimicry could frustrate a system of identification based on spectrographic voice analysis. He further maintained that the relatively higher pitch of the female voice would not affect the accuracy of such an identification technique.

Other experimenters, all reputable scientists in speech, phonetics, or associated fields, were unable to duplicate Kersta's high accuracy rates. However a study completed in 1970 under the direction of Oscar Tosi at Michigan State University replicated Kersta's original experiments and confirmed his high accuracy rates.]

The Tosi Study: Format and Results

Since in the matching-to-sample tests conducted by Kersta and others a match for the "unknown" spectrogram always existed, the trial became merely a process of elimination. This type of trial has no relation to a forensic application of the technique, and the results obtained through such trials cannot be extrapolated to validate the technique as a means of identification. The format of the Tosi study, however, was designed to test varying conditions which could be expected to have a major impact on the reliability of the technique in a forensic setting.

[First, both open and closed trials were conducted. Second, the effect of a reduction in cue material on identification accuracy rates was tested. A third very important feature of the Tosi study was its use of both contemporary and non-contemporary matching spectrograms in testing speaker identification. A fourth variable tested was the effect of the context of the cue material and its mode of recording on the reliability of the technique.]

In selecting a speaker population of two hundred fifty males, drawn from a population of twenty-five thousand at the university, Tosi attempted to meet one of the requirements for validation of the technique: homogeneity of the speaker group. The speakers selected had no speech defects and utilized a standard American English dialect.

Each of the twenty-nine examiners used in the experiment was given one month of training in basic acoustic speech principles and in the interpretation of speech spectrograms. Moreover, the examiners were given several objective points of similarity to look for when making comparisons between spectrograms. This training was far more extensive than that given examiners in previous speaker recognition experiments utilizing spectrograms.

In each of the nearly thirty-five thousand random trials, aural comparison of the speech samples was prohibited. The examiner was forced to come to a positive conclusion, either rejecting or accepting one of the "known" spectrograms as identical with the "unknown", and an average time of only fifteen minutes was devoted to study of the spectrograms before a conclusion was demanded. These inhibiting factors, while necessary as a control in the experiment, would not be present in forensic application of the technique.

The statistical results of the open set trials, which tested the reliability of the technique in various forensic applications, indicate that overall accuracy levels of 82–85% are possible under the conditions tested. Although these figures indicate an error range of 15–18%, this gross error rate includes two types of error: *false elimination* (a match was present but the examiner failed to perceive it) and *false identification* (a match was not present but the examiner mistakenly thought there was one, or a match was present but the examiner chose the wrong one). Only the latter error, false identification, is particularly troublesome from a legal standpoint. Moreover, a breakdown of the gross error rate to reflect the differentiation between types of error reveals that the risk of false identification is only 5–6% while that of false identification is only 10–12%.

NOTES

Perhaps the primary lesson to be learned from the debate over the admissibility of sound spectrography is that the courts must not accept at face value an expert's assertion that "numerous experiments" have validated the hypothesis of the accuracy of a technique such as sound spectrography. In testing the assertion, courts should ask questions which check the internal and external validity of a process.

- What was the composition of the group of subjects in the experiment? The early sound spectrography experiments involved almost exclusively white male subjects. Suppose that the expert relied on sound spectrography as the basis for identifying a black female speaker. E. IMWINKELRIED, THE METHODS OF ATTACKING SCIENTIFIC EVIDENCE § 10-6(B), at 297 (3d ed. 1997).

- What were the test conditions? In the early sound spectrography experiments, the speakers made no attempt to disguise their voice. National Academy of Sciences, ON THE THEORY AND PRACTICE OF VOICE IDENTIFICATION 24 (1979). Assume that in a given case, the expert relied on the sound spectrography technique to attempt to identify the person who made a threatening call. It is obvious from the audiotape of the call that the speaker was attempting to disguise his voice. *People v. Law*, 40 Cal. App. 3d 69, 114 Cal. Rptr. 708 (1974).

(procedure has not been demonstrated to be reliable, especially "with respect to disguised and mimicked voices").

––––––––––

There is currently a sharp split of authority over the admissibility of sound spectrography evidence. Many states exclude voiceprint evidence. *E.g., Hyppolite v. State*, 774 N.E.2d 584, 601 (Ind. Ct. App. 2002); *State v. Gortarez*, 141 Ariz. 254, 686 P.2d 1224 (1984); *People v. Kelly*, 17 Cal. 3d 24, 130 Cal. Rptr. 144, 549 P.2d 1240 (1976); *Cornett v. State*, 450 N.E.2d 498 (Ind. 1983). One point of objection to this form of evidence in such courts involves the difficulty which spectrography proof has experienced in achieving general scientific acceptance. A Committee on Evaluation of Sound Spectrograms of the National Academy of Sciences has announced its position that the experimental verification of some of sound spectrography's underlying premises is inadequate. National Academy of Sciences, ON THE THEORY AND PRACTICE OF VOICE IDENTIFICATION (1979).

However, federal courts as well as some other states have been much more receptive to voiceprint evidence. *United States v. Smith*, 869 F.2d 348 (7th Cir. 1989); *United States v. Williams*, 583 F.2d 1194 (2d Cir. 1978); *United States v. Maivia*, 728 F. Supp. 1471 (D. Haw. 1990); *State v. Williams*, 4 Ohio St. 3d 53, 446 N.E.2d 444 (1983); *State v. Williams*, 388 A.2d 500 (Me. 1978). The decision in *Maivia* illustrates the reasoning of courts taking this view. An important piece of government evidence was a threatening tape recorded message of some 65 words left on the alleged victim's telephone answering machine. An expert in spectrographic voice identification was proffered by the defense. The court relied upon the Tosi study, *supra*, in deciding to allow the defense expert to give his opinion of the identity of the speaker on the tape. In this case, the court felt that the testimony of both the defense and government voice experts would be of "appreciable help" to the jury. The message on the phone machine was the primary evidence against the accused. The court observed: "[w]hile the federal courts heavily favor admissibility, state courts are more evenly split on the issue. . . ."

Current jurisprudence continues to display the ambivalence of courts on the question. *United States v. Angleton*, 269 F. Supp. 2d 892 (S.D. Tex. 2003) observed that since the time of *Daubert*, "no federal appellate court has approved the admission of voice spectrographic expert testimony into evidence." The court cited studies which are critical of the reliability of voiceprint evidence:

> The studies, by different researchers, performed over decades, show that the voice spectrographic technique has been tested and found wanting in aspects critical for admission under Rule 702. The studies emphasize the subjective nature of the voice spectrographic analysis, even when combined with an aural analysis component, which is subjective. Several variables, difficult to detect or control, affect the analysis. Although aspects of the voice spectrographic method have been subject to review in published studies, many of the studies conclude that voice spectrographic analysis is of questionable scientific validity as a method of identifying an unknown speaker.

It is not surprising that this court, in view of the foregoing comments, granted the government's motion to exclude defense testimony of a voice analyst. Also rejecting voiceprint proof, see *United States v. Bahena*, 223 F.3d 797, 810 (8th Cir. 2000); *State v. Morrison*, 867 So. 2d 740 (La. Ct. App. 2003) (citing uncertainty regarding the reliability and admissibility of expert voice identification evidence).

On the other hand, some modern court decisions have embraced voiceprint technology. In a 1999 decision citing *Daubert*, the Alaska Supreme Court ruled sound spectrography testimony admissible. *State v. Coon*, 974 P.2d 386 (Alaska 1999). The court did so even though the court acknowledged that the "scientific literature cited by the [defendant] permits a conclusion that there is significant disagreement among experts in the field of voice spectrographic analysis regarding the reliability of the technique." *Id.* at 402. You will need to revisit this when you review the next chapter and consider the impact of the *Daubert* case.

5. Tape Recordings

Although many celebrated cases have focused public attention on the evidentiary importance of audiotapes, the traditional attitude of the courts toward sound recordings has been one of skepticism. The courts' fear of possible tampering with audiotapes led them to insist on a thorough foundation. The courts ordinarily demand a more complete foundation for the admission of a tape recording than they do in the case of a photograph. A recent decision illustrates the foundational steps, and the hazards of not complying with them.

McALINNEY v. MARION MERRELL DOW, INC.
992 F.2d 839 (8th Cir. 1993)

WOLLMAN, CIRCUIT JUDGE.

[A former employee brought suit against an employer. The employee alleged employment discrimination on the basis of national origin. McAlinney was born in Northern Ireland, where he attended medical school. Later, he was hired in the Kansas City area, and served as defendant's Associate Medical Director. When he concluded he was not receiving fair annual reviews as a result of ethnic discrimination based on his Irish ethnicity, he began recording numerous conversations with particular employees. He employed a microcassette recorder hidden in one of his socks.]

McAlinney makes four arguments attacking the propriety of the district court's evidentiary rulings at trial. We note initially that "[w]e give substantial deference to the district court's rulings on the admissibility of evidence, and we will not find error in the absence of a clear showing of abuse of discretion." *Freidus v. First National Bank*, 928 F.2d 793, 794 (8th Cir. 1991).

McAlinney first argues that the district court erred in refusing to permit him to offer tape recordings of conversations between McAlinney and various Marion management-level employees, particularly Dr. Flicker, during his case-in-chief.

As noted earlier, McAlinney had compiled numerous microcassette tapes of surreptitiously recorded conversations, mostly between himself and Dr. Flicker, recorded at work and from his home telephone. McAlinney re-recorded selected portions of these microcassette tapes onto eight cassette tapes. McAlinney then submitted these eight cassette tapes, containing approximately nine hours of conversations, to the district court prior to trial. Marion subsequently filed a motion in limine to exclude the tapes from evidence. After listening to all of the tapes, the district court observed that many of the cassettes were inaudible and that some of the cassettes were fairly audible, but that the conversations on them were difficult to track. The district court determined that although some of the tapes were potentially relevant, they had foundational problems and might confuse or mislead the jury. Accordingly, it excluded the tapes from McAlinney's case-in-chief.

We set forth the requirements for introducing tape recordings into evidence in *United States v. McMillan*, 508 F.2d 101, 104 (8th Cir. 1974), *cert. denied*, 421 U.S. 916, 95 S. Ct. 1577, 43 L. Ed. 2d 782 (1975). In order to be admissible, the proponent must establish that (1) the recording device was capable of taking the conversation offered into evidence; (2) the operator of the device was competent to operate the device; (3) the recording is authentic and correct; (4) changes, additions, or deletions have not been made; (5) the recording has been preserved in a manner that is shown to the court; (6) the speakers are identified; and (7) the conversation elicited was made voluntarily and in good faith, without any kind of inducement. *Id.* We have also held that "[r]elevant evidence may nevertheless be excluded if its probative value is substantially outweighed by a danger of confusion of the issues or of undue delay." *Hogan v. American Telephone & Telegraph Co.*, 812 F.2d 409, 411 (8th Cir. 1987); *see* Fed. R. Evid. 403.

A careful review of all nine hours of the tapes has confirmed the wisdom of the district court's decision to exclude them from McAlinney's case-in-chief. With the exception of three telephone conversations, only one of which is with Dr. Flicker, McAlinney recorded the balance of the conversations on a tiny microcassette recorder hidden in his sock. The resulting tapes are mostly garbled, often unintelligible, and suffer from an excess of background noise. Moreover, the tapes exhibit serious problems of continuity because, either through editing or recorder malfunction, there are numerous blank spots on each tape. Last, certain conversations appear twice on the tapes. Consequently, serious issues arise concerning whether changes, additions, or deletions have been made. *See McMillan*, 508 F.2d at 104. Indeed, McAlinney concedes that he edited the tapes. Moreover, McAlinney testified at great length concerning the statements allegedly made on the tapes. Accordingly, we find no error in the district court's refusal to permit McAlinney to use the tapes in his case-in-chief.

The *McAlinney* case involved a pretrial investigation wherein the district court painstakingly listened to all nine hours of the tapes. Sometimes the issue does not reach the judge until trial. At that point, a classic article in the field describes the process:

> The wire or tape recording should be marked and offered in evidence. Upon receiving such offer of proof, the wire or tape recording should be played before the judge, in the absence of the jury. Upon consideration of objections to the recording as a whole or parts thereof, the court should permit the recording or competent portions thereof to be played to the jury. While the tapes are being played, the court reporter should take down such recorded statements.

Conrad, *Magnetic Recordings in the Courts*, 40 VA. L. REV. 23, 35–36 (1954).

Some courts list the elements of the foundation in mechanical, checklist fashion. *E.g., United States v. Stone*, 960 F.2d 426, 436 (5th Cir. 1992); *United States v. Branch*, 970 F.2d 1368, 1372 (4th Cir. 1992). The checklist ensures that the proponent lays the usual, strict foundation outlined in the McAlinney case. For sound recordings, see *State v. Cusmano*, 274 N.J. Super. 496, 644 A.2d 672 (App. Div. 1994); Comment, 48 RUTGERS L. REV. 263 (1995).

NOTES

1.   Recently, there has been a trend in some courts to relax the strict foundation requirements for tape recordings. *United States v. Buchanan*, 70 F.3d 818 (5th Cir. 1995) (established steps are important and the preferred method of proceeding, but the absence of compliance with one or more of the steps is not fatal; trial court may admit recording in absence of compliance with requirements if the recording accurately reproduces the auditory experience); *United States v. Norman*, 415 F.3d 466, 472–73 (5th Cir. 2005) (no abuse of discretion where district court admitted recording as evidence and concluded that "inaudible portions of the tape were insufficient to make the tape as a whole inadmissible" and those portions would affect the weight of the evidence rather than its admissibility).

However, there remains a need to show an absence of changes or deletions. In *McCormick v. Brevig*, 322 Mont. 112 (2004), failure to show an absence of changes in the recording was fatal to authentication. "In this case, the District Court found that the tape recording had been intentionally altered and the original version of the recording was no longer available." The tape recording was therefore properly rejected by the trial court. Other courts continue to require a heightened showing of non-alteration. *See Penguin Books U.S.A. Inc. v. New Christian Church of Full Endeavor, Ltd.*, 262 F. Supp. 2d 251, 263 (S.D.N.Y. 2003) ("Because tape recordings are likely to have a strong effect on the jury and are susceptible to alteration, the Second Circuit requires their authenticity to be established by clear and convincing evidence") (citing *United States v. Morrison*, 153 F.3d 34, 56 (2d Cir. 1998)).

2.   In a criminal case where the government proffers a tape recording of a drug transaction or an interrogation of a suspect, the government has the burden of demonstrating that the recording is an accurate reproduction of relevant sounds. In several cases, police or other officers who had verbal contact with a defendant were allowed to make positive identification of a voice on a tape recording as belonging to the defendant. *United States v. Norman*, 415 F.3d 466, 473–73 (5th Cir. 2005) (hour long conversation between DEA agent and defendant sufficient to connect defendant's voice to defendant, thus DEA agent's testimony identifying voice from recording admissible); *United States v. Degaglia*, 913 F.2d 372 (7th Cir. 1990).

3.   When tape recordings are used, the attorneys often prepare transcripts for the jurors to follow while the tape is being played. In *United States v. Stone*, 960 F.2d 426 (5th Cir. 1992), a DEA agent's conversation with a drug conspirator was recorded on audiotape. The agent testified he had worn a hidden transmitter, that the tape of the conversation had been kept in a secure place from the time it was made, and that no alterations had been made. A heavy thunderstorm during the conversation interfered with the recording and made portions of the tape hard to understand. As the tape was played, the jury listened and at the same time reviewed a typed transcript, and the defendant objected to the use of transcript. The court instructed the jury: "It [the transcript] is not evidence in this case. The tape is the evidence." On review, the court of appeals concluded the district court's handling of the situation was within its discretion.

4.   The preferred practice is for the court not to submit transcripts of tape recordings to the jury unless the parties stipulate to their accuracy. If the parties cannot agree, the second method is for the court to determine the accuracy of the transcript by reading the transcript against the tapes. This review is accomplished *in camera*. *United States v. Scarborough*, 43 F.3d 1021 (6th Cir. 1994). Care must be exercised in performing this function, because when tapes are difficult to hear, a transcript intended as an aid to the jury inevitably becomes, in the minds of the jury, the evidence itself. *United States v. Segines*, 17 F.3d 847 (6th Cir. 1994).

5.   Sometimes the jurors are allowed to take the transcripts into the jury room as they deliberate on the case. *United States v. Nixon*, 918 F.2d 895 (11th Cir. 1990). Judges who allow this practice seem to view the transcripts as evidence. Contrary to the jury charge in *United States v. Stone, supra*, the decision in *United States v. Valencia*, 957 F.2d 1189 (5th Cir. 1992), adopts the view that "transcripts may be used as substantive evidence to aid the jury in determining the real issue presented,

the content and the meaning of the tape recordings. It is therefore incorrect to think of the transcripts as simply an 'aid' — as better lighting fixtures in the courtroom would be an 'aid' to the jury's vision of witnesses — and not as evidence of any kind. They are evidence and, like other evidence, may be admitted for a limited purpose only." Even in these cases, however, the tape recording controls if there is an inconsistency between tape and transcript: "When both a tape and a transcript are admitted, or a transcript is used by the jury as an aid when listening to the tape, the jury is generally given a limiting instruction that if it encounters a discrepancy between the tape and the transcript, the tape controls."

6. In addition to providing transcripts, sometimes juror understanding of drug tapes is aided by an expert on the vocabulary of the drug trade interpreting terms for the jury. *See United States v. Dukagjini*, 326 F.3d 45 (2d Cir. 2003) (testimony admitted in drug conspiracy trial to explain taped conversations was not objectionable on ground that conversations were readily understandable; alleged conspirators used jargon extensively and were deliberately ambiguous, and defendants' arguments at trial, which included efforts to establish different interpretations of conversations, belied idea that language used was self-explanatory and easily understood).

7. It seems clear that the transcript must be a verbatim rendition of the words and sounds on the tape, and not a summary. The point is made in C. Fishman, *Recordings, Transcripts, and Translations as Evidence*, 81 Wash. L. Rev. 473, 494 (2006) (reviews seven foundational elements for admission of tape recording; technician testified he listened to conversations as he correctly recorded them).

If the transcript is received as evidence of what the recording contains, the transcript is governed by the "mirror the tape" rule. Common sense dictates that, other than the identity of the conversant, the transcript should contain only what can actually be heard on the recording. Although a *witness* may "narrate" the recording while testifying, explaining what physical actions accompanied each passage or sound on the tape, the transcript that is distributed to the jury "should . . . mirror the tape and should not be an amalgam of the recording and the hearsay testimony of persons present at the conversation."

B. PHOTOGRAPHS

The widespread realization of the persuasive value of visual aids accounts for the frequent use of photographic evidence. Some students of photographic evidence estimate that photographs are used in roughly half the cases in the United States.

Before examining the various techniques for authenticating photographs, we must pause to analyze the basic theory of admissibility. The proponent ordinarily introduces the photograph during the testimony of a sponsoring witness. The witness testifies about the object or scene and then adds that the photograph is a "true," "accurate," "fair," or "correct" depiction of the object or scene. On that foundation, the judge admits the photograph. The question is this: Once the photograph is admitted, to what evidentiary status is the photograph entitled?

BERGNER v. STATE
397 N.E.2d 1012 (Ind. Ct. App. 1979)

CHAPMAN, JUDGE.

Indiana courts traditionally have stressed three requirements for the admission of photographic evidence. First, an adequate foundation must be laid. Our courts have consistently held this requires the testimony of a witness who can state the photograph is "a true and accurate representation of the things it is intended to depict." *Wilson v. State,* (1978) Ind., 374 N.E.2d 45. Relevancy is the second requirement for the admission of photographic evidence in Indiana. Like all evidence, a photograph must meet the usual relevancy standard, *i.e.*, it must tend to prove or disprove a material fact. Finally, some Indiana cases require the photographs aid juror's understanding of other evidence. *See Whitfield v. State* (1977) 266 Ind. 629, 366 N.E.2d 173.

Although all three requirements for the admission of photographic evidence are important, in this case we are singularly concerned with the foundation requirement. Indiana's approach to the admission of photographs, as guided by the current foundation requirement, falls within what has been characterized as the "pictorial testimony theory" of photographic evidence. 3 J. WIGMORE, EVIDENCE § 790 (Chadbourn rev. 1970). This theory categorizes photographs with maps, models and diagrams, and thus treats photographs purely as demonstrative evidence. As such, a photograph is not evidence in itself, but is used merely as a nonverbal method of expressing a witness' testimony and is admissible only when a witness can testify it is a true and accurate representation of a scene personally viewed by that witness.

The "silent witness theory" for the admission of photographic evidence permits the use of photographs at trial as substantive evidence, as opposed to merely demonstrative evidence. Thus, under the silent witness theory there is no need for a witness to testify a photograph accurately represents what he or she observed; the photograph "speaks for itself." 3 J.WIGMORE, EVIDENCE § 790 (Chadbourn rev. 1980).

One of the most frequent, and often unintentional, utilizations of the silent witness theory occurs when X-rays are admitted into evidence. Obviously, no witness can testify he or she saw what an X-ray depicts, thus rendering the pictorial testimony theory logically inapplicable. 3 C. SCOTT, PHOTOGRAPHIC EVIDENCE § 1262 (1969). Nevertheless, every jurisdiction admits X-ray photographs as substantive evidence upon a sufficient showing of authentication.

In other words, these courts have not blindly followed the formal, traditional requirement of admitting photographs solely as demonstrative evidence. Instead, these jurisdictions have analyzed the theory behind the traditional requirements, and have recognized the probative potential of photographic evidence. As a result, these courts view photographic evidence in a modern, realistic light and admit photographs where their authenticity can be sufficiently established in view of the context in which the photographs are sought to be admitted. We think this creative analysis and refusal to follow traditional standards merely because such standards exist is laudable as the highest form of a progressive judiciary [*sic*]. We hereby accept the State's invitation and adopt the silent witness theory for the admission of photographic evidence as the law in Indiana. In so doing, we cannot help but note the good company in which we find ourselves. *See e.g. U.S. v. Gray*, 531 F.2d 933 (CA 8 1976); *People v. Bowley*, 59 Cal. 2d 855, 31 Cal. Rptr. 471, 382 P.2d 591 (1963); *People v. Byrnes*, 33 N.Y.2d 343, 352 N.Y.S.2d 913, 308 N.E.2d 435 (1974); *Franklin v. State*, 69 Ga. 36 (1882).

We recognize our adoption of the silent witness theory permits the admission of photographs as substantive or demonstrative evidence. We stress we are not changing existing Indiana law; we are adding a second basis for the admissibility of photographic evidence. Thus, our holding in no way affects the use of photographs as demonstrative evidence; the traditional requirements for admissibility as laid down in numerous Indiana cases remain wholly effective.

The foundation requirements for the admission of photographs as substantive evidence under the silent witness theory are obviously vastly different from the foundation required for demonstrative evidence. However, we feel it would be wrong to lay down extensive, absolute foundation requirements. Every photograph, the context in which it was taken, and its use at trial will be different in some respect. We therefore hold only that a strong showing of the photograph's competency and authenticity must be established. Whether a sufficiently strong foundation has been laid is left to the sound discretion of the trial court, reviewable only for abuse.

Photography is not an exact science. The image a camera produces on film can be affected by a variety of things that may lead to distortion and misrepresentation. However, assuming any misleading qualities of a photograph are not so egregious as to result in an inadequate foundation, complaints concerning a photograph's distortion go on to the weight to which a photograph is entitled, not admissibility.

NOTES AND PROBLEMS

1. Which view do you prefer — the "pictorial testimony" theory or the "silent witness" theory? Which view better guarantees the underlying probative value of photographs admitted at trial? Given the impressive scientific evidence of the reliability of the photographic process, doesn't it seem logical that a photograph should qualify as substantive evidence? Most commentators support the "silent witness" theory. In Gardner, *The Camera Goes to Court*, 24 N.C. L. REV. 233, 245 (1946), the author lambasts the "pictorial testimony" theory for its "baffling, Alice-in-Wonderland quality far removed from the realistic directness of the man-on-the-street." The author adds that only the "tortured" logic of the law, "wrought from centuries of philosophic inbreeding," could account for such a result. *Id.* Cases make the point that under the silent witness theory, still photos are treated as substantive evidence. *McHenry v. State*, 820 N.E.2d 124 (Ind. 2005). This view has been extended to videotapes. *Stevens v. Provitt*, 2003 Ohio App. LEXIS 6517 (2003) (the "silent witness" theory is applicable when the evidence speaks for itself and is substantive evidence of what it portrays); McIntosh v. State, 2003 Ark. App. LEXIS 517 (2003) (contrasting "pictorial testimony" theory, under which photo is merely illustrative of witness's testimony, with "silent witness" theory); *Mays v. State*, 907 N.E.2d 128 (Ind. Ct. App. 2009) (reiterating the standard under the silent witness theory that "videotapes may be admitted as substantive evidence, but 'there must be a strong showing of [the videotape's] authenticity and competency" ') (quoting *McHenry v. State, supra*)).

2. Problem 11-3. In *Devitt*, one of Paterson's neighbors saw a green Mustang parked outside his apartment at the time of the alleged battery. Another prosecution witness, one of Devitt's neighbors, verifies a photograph of Devitt's green Mustang. Devitt's neighbor testifies that the photograph is a "true and accurate" depiction of Devitt's car. The photograph is in color and shows Devitt's car to be green; but the witness does not specifically describe Devitt's car as "green." During closing argument, could the prosecutor say, "One of Mr. Paterson's neighbors, Mrs. Nelson, said she saw a green Mustang parked right outside Mr. Paterson's apartment at that time. And we know that the defendant owns and drives a green Mustang." Does the propriety of making the remark depend on whether the court subscribes to the "pictorial testimony" or "silent witness" theory?

3. Like the trend among the commentators referenced in Note 1, cases also are moving in the direction of the silent witness theory. *State v. Berky*, 447 S.E.2d 147, 148 (Ga. Ct. App. 1994) (citing federal and state cases); *People v. Vaden*, 336 Ill. App. 3d 893, 784 N.E.2d 410 (2003). *See* Graham, *Real and Demonstrative Evidence, Experiments and Views*, 46 CRIM. L. BULL. 792, 807–08 (July–Aug. 2010).

1. Still Photographs

Photography is a complex, technical field. For that reason, the courts could in theory require a very detailed foundation as the predicate for admitting a photograph. For example, since the lens can have a profound impact on the quality of the end-product photograph, courts could demand a showing of the type of lens used. However, the courts have opted not to impose those foundational requirements. *United States v. Stearns*, 550 F.2d 1167 (9th Cir. 1977). It is not that the technical information is irrelevant; quite to the contrary, on cross-examination the opponent may attack the photograph's accuracy by questioning about the camera setting, film type, and development process. *Id.* However, those matters are not part of the foundation for admitting the photograph.

Many courts have imposed very lax foundational requirements for admitting photographs. The witness ordinarily testifies that he or she is familiar with the object or scene depicted; explains how this familiarity was acquired; and lastly opines that the photograph is a "fair" depiction of the object or scene. *Banghart v. Origoverken*, 49 F.3d 1302 (8th Cir. 1995). *See American Wrecking Corp. v. Secretary of Labor*, 351 F.3d 1254, 1262 (D.C. Cir. 2003) (where demolition supervisor with knowledge testified photograph was accurate depiction of accident scene, reliance on photograph was appropriate where photo reflected fair representation of site prior to accident).

Notwithstanding the low threshold required for authentication of photographic proof, sometimes the proponent of a picture fails to satisfy even this low bar. In *Schmidt v. City of Bella Villa*, the plaintiff in a civil rights action complained about police photographing her hip tattoo at headquarters and offered her own posed photo, which was made by her some time after her arrest. The court rejected the evidence as lacking in foundation because it failed to duplicate the plaintiff's clothing on the night of the arrest. "In order to be admissible, a photograph must be shown to be an accurate representation of the thing depicted *as it appeared at the relevant time.*" *Schmidt v. City of Bella Villa*, 557 F.3d 564 (8th Cir. 2009) (emphasis added).

NOTES AND PROBLEM

1. **Problem 11-4.** In our torts case, Ms. Hill wants to introduce a photograph of the intersection where the collision occurred. Must the sponsoring witness be the photographer? Does Federal Rule 104(b) or 901(a) require that the photographer testify? Does the familiarity requirement necessitate testimony by the photographer? *See United States v. Holmquist*, 36 F.3d 154 (1st Cir. 1994) (witness qualifying a photograph need not be the photographer nor see the picture taken so long as he testifies the photo fairly and correctly represents the objects which are pictures); *Wegman-Fakunle v. State*, 626 S.E.2d 170 (Ga. Ct. App. 2006) (not necessary that witness on stand have taken the photograph himself or was even present when the photo was taken as long as he is familiar with the scene depicted in the photo).

2. Objections which are frequently heard when a party offers a photograph include "inadequate foundation" as well as "prejudicial." As to foundation, it is important to ask the sponsoring witness whether the picture is a fair representation of what it purports to portray. *Zerega Ave. Realty v. Hombeck Offshore Transp.*, 571 F.3d 206 (2d Cir. 2009) (when counsel failed to ask the customary question as to whether a photo "fairly and accurately portrayed the area shown," objection based upon lack of proper foundation was correctly sustained). Counsel must also be prepared to defend against the objection that the photo is unduly prejudicial; this issue is decided pursuant to Rule 403, which is explored more fully in Chapter 13. In some cases, the Rule 403 balancing will lead to exclusion of the photographs. In one case, for example, the defendant moved to exclude a photo of an injured leg, which looked like "hamburger." Under Evidence Rule 403, the photos were deemed more prejudicial than probative. The photos depicted "blood and gore which is highly prejudicial to the defendant in this case," held the North Dakota Supreme Court. *Hamilton v. Oppen*, 2002 ND 185, 653 N.W.2d 678 (2002). In many other cases, however, the objection is overruled. *E.g.*, *Maxwell v. State*, 250 Ga. App. 628, 552 S.E.2d 870 (2001) (photos of severely injured victim of assault, however gruesome, are not objectionable merely because there is other evidence of severity of victim's injuries).

2. X-Rays

The use of x-rays is critical in many cases, including of course personal injury litigation. Proof of damages can often be the more important part of the battle, and x-rays can be the most persuasive evidence of injury. Since the "pictorial testimony" theory of verifying photographs cannot be applied to x-rays, courts long ago fashioned an adaptation to the authentication doctrine for proof of the accuracy of an x-ray.

Scott, *X-Ray Pictures As Evidence*
44 Mich. L. Rev. 773 (1946)

Before an X-ray can be admitted in evidence, someone who has knowledge of the fact must take the stand and verify the accuracy of the picture, for X-ray photographs are not admissible in evidence without preliminary proof of their accuracy. But this proof need only relate to the particular X-ray picture in question, for today the science of X-ray photography is too well founded and generally recognized to render it any longer necessary for a witness to testify to the reliability and trustworthiness of the X-ray process itself before X-ray pictures are admitted in evidence.

Since an X-ray picture purports to show only shadows of objects not otherwise visible to the eye, it is evident that a witness' verification of an X-ray photograph ordinarily must be based on the scientific fact that the properly taken X-ray photograph accurately pictures the shadows of internal objects as does the ordinary photograph picture an object's external surface. Therefore, in verifying an X-ray picture ordinarily the following requirements should be met, although it is not uncommon for X-rays to be admitted in evidence without one or more of them being satisfied.

1. The X-ray film should be identified as a picture of the person whose condition is in question. Since X-ray pictures usually are taken by technicians who make hundreds of pictures a week, usually the only practical way to identify a film as being a picture of the person in question is by the use of identification marks verified by some competent witness.

2. There should be proof that the physical condition of the subject at the time of being X-rayed was the same as at the time in issue. This requirement is usually satisfied by testimony of the injured party that after the time in question and before the X-ray pictures were taken he suffered no additional injury to the part of the body under consideration.

3. It should be shown that the X-ray apparatus used was dependable and in good working condition.

4. There should be testimony that the person who took the picture was qualified by training and experience to take accurate X-ray pictures of the human body.

5. The manner of taking the X-ray picture should be completely described, especially in such particulars as the distance from the X-ray tube to the subject, the distance between subject and film, the angle from which the X-rays were directed through the body onto the film, and the length of exposure.

Whenever possible the authentication of an X-ray picture should be made by the physician, dentist or X-ray technician who took the picture. But it has been held that even though the X-ray photographer is not called as a witness, an X-ray film may be sufficiently identified by a physician, dentist or X-ray technician who was present when the picture was made and knows the conditions under which it was made, even though he did not take the picture himself. Authentication by a witness who did not see the picture taken is unsatisfactory and does not render the picture admissible according to the better reasoned cases, but there are decisions to the contrary.

Some recent x-ray cases have demonstrated a loosening of these traditional foundation requirements. *In the Interest of J.P.B.*, 2005 Tex. App. LEXIS 1159 (2005) allowed a doctor to authenticate x-rays which had the patient's name on them and the date of the images. Based on the doctor's testimony about the procedure used in taking a patient from the emergency room to radiology to obtain an x-ray, the x-ray was admitted, even though the doctor was not present when the images were taken. *See also Jones v. State*, 111 S.W.3d 600 (Tex. App. 2003).

Once in evidence, interpretation of x-rays is normally done by a physician. *Gunderson v. United States Dep't of Labor*, 601 F.3d 1013, 1056–57 (10th Cir. 2010) (greater weight awarded to x-ray readings presented by physicians who possess superior radiological qualifications). In a typical personal injury case, for example, a plaintiff's attorney might use the courtroom's document camera, projecting an enlarged image of an x-ray of the plaintiff's pelvic area on the screen while the plaintiff's treating physician is on the witness stand. Using a laser pointer, she will call the attention of the jurors to breaks and fractures created by an auto accident.

NOTES AND PROBLEMS

1. **Problem 11-5.** Doctor Walton is called to the witness stand by Ms. Hill. She testifies that she treated Hill for reversal of normal cervical curve, a whiplash injury. In part, the diagnosis relied upon x-rays of Hill's neck. When asked if she saw the x-rays, Dr. Walton replies: "No. But I carefully reviewed the report of the radiologist who performed the x-ray procedure." Polecat objects to further testimony about whiplash, as follows: "Inadequate foundation, this doctor never looked at the x-rays." Should the court permit the testimony? See *Crowe v. Marchand*, 506 F.3d 13, 16 (1st Cir. 2007) (in doctor malpractice case, the court honored the discretion of the trial court in allowing an expert's testimony to stand regardless of the fact that he had not examined the particular x-rays first hand).

2. Digital x-rays are a new form of x-ray technology, and are commonly used in litigation to explain injuries. Digital x-rays are digital images of the original x-rays which are scanned into a computer and frequently are used in the courtroom in a PowerPoint presentation. *Renzi v. Paredes*, 452 Mass. 38, 50, 890 N.E.2d 806, 816 (2008). The final technological frontier in this area seems to be digital motion x-rays, referred to as DMX. The DMX machine takes thirty x-ray frames per second for ninety seconds while the patient moves. The images are then viewed on a computer. DMX has been approved, but has received a mixed reaction in some appellate courts. *See Graftenreed v. Seabaugh*, 100 Ark. App. 364, 367, 268 S.W.3d 905, 911 (2007); *Johnson v. Burkey-Kelly*, 859 N.Y.S.2d 895 (2007) (use of DMX in personal injury case). *Compare Fowler v. Schweitzer*, 876 N.E.2d 386 (Ind. Ct. App. 2007) (DMX technology is too experimental for courtroom use).

3. Automated Photographic Systems

Automated photographic systems are becoming increasingly common. For example, many retail stores use cameras to detect shoplifting. Banks also make extensive use of automated systems, particularly surveillance cameras. Convenience stores film transactions for security purposes.

Authentication is a simple matter when there are eyewitnesses who recall the event. Thus, if a surveillance camera takes a series of still photographs of a bank robbery, an eyewitness in the bank at the time can verify the film. *United States v. Neal*, 527 F.2d 63 (8th Cir. 1975), *cert. denied*, 429 U.S. 845 (1976). However, sometimes there are no eyewitnesses (as when a break-in occurs after hours) or the eyewitnesses were unobservant. Authenticating the surveillance photographs in this situation is a much more challenging task.

The following case wherein a bank teller was convicted of forgery illustrates how this is sometimes accomplished. The accused was charged with an unauthorized withdrawal of $6,500 from the account of a bank customer.

McHENRY v. STATE
820 N.E.2d 124 (Ind. 2005)

DICKSON, JUSTICE.

The defendant also contends that the trial court committed reversible error in admitting the bank's surveillance video. The video shows that no person was at the defendant's teller window at the time she entered the questioned transaction. The defendant's objection at trial was that the videotape was not a business record and that there was an inadequate foundation, the particulars of which were not specified. On appeal, the defendant does not present argument as to the business record issue but rather argues generally that because the state did not present information to support the reliability of the surveillance tape other than the affidavit of a records custodian, it failed to lay a proper foundation for the admission of the video.

The parties agree that under a "silent witness" theory, videotapes may be admitted as substantive evidence, but "there must be a strong showing of authenticity and competency" and that when automatic cameras are involved, "there should be evidence as to how and when the camera was loaded, how frequently the camera was activated, when the photographs were taken, and the processing and changing of custody of the film after its removal from the camera."

The State argues that witness testimony established the videotape's authenticity. The bank manager removed the videotape, and a police detective checked it to assure that it was the tape covering the date in question. The detective then watched the tape to match the transactions and customers' account numbers with the representations on the videotape. In addition, the bank's custodian of records verified by affidavit that the tape was a regularly conducted activity of the bank and that she had examined the records to verify its trustworthiness.

Rulings on the admission of evidence are subject to appellate review for abuse of discretion. We are not persuaded that the trial court abused its discretion in admitting the videotape.

NOTES AND PROBLEMS

1.   **Problem 11-6.** In *Devitt*, suppose that the defense is alibi. Devitt wants to prove that he was shopping in another town at the time of the alleged assault. The defense attorney contacts the store, May Shoes, where Devitt says he was shopping. The store manager tells the defense attorney that their records show that Devitt purchased a pair of shoes and cashed a check in the store at the time the assault was allegedly occurring forty miles away. Better still, the store maintains an observation camera near the shoe department, and the film shows Devitt at that location. Unfortunately, no store employee remembers Devitt. How can the defense attorney verify the photography? Should the attorney call the May Shoes employee who maintains the camera? *See United States v. Whittingham*, 2009 U.S. App. LEXIS 20910, at *1–*4 (2d Cir. Sept. 22, 2009) (the still images were printed from a surveillance video; a bank employee testified how the videos had been recorded, collected, and time-stamped). Surveillance videotape was held properly admitted to convict of theft by shoplifting in *Ross v. State*, 262 Ga. App. 323, 585 S.E.2d 666 (2003) (citing OCGA 24-4-48). A video recording from a restaurant's surveillance camera was helpful to resolving issues in an action against police, with the plaintiff charging excessive force. The DVD showed several uses of a taser against the party, as well as punching him. *Kies v. City of Lima, Ohio*, 612 F. Supp. 2d 888 (N.D. Ohio 2009).

2.   A body of law is developing which authorizes bank personnel familiar with the operation of automatic teller machine (ATM) cameras to authenticate ATM photographs. *United States v. Fadayini*, 28 F.3d 1236 (D.C. Cir. 1994); *United States v. Rembert*, 863 F.2d 1023 (D.C. Cir. 1988) (silent witness theory). *See also Brooks v. Commonwealth*, 15 Va. App. 407, 424 S.E.2d 566 (1992).

4.   Motion Pictures, Videotapes and Electronic Imagery

"Day-in-the-Life" Films

Motion pictures can have an even more dramatic impact than still photographs. They depict action and, for that reason, can easily capture the jurors' attention. Some attorneys have even filmed reenactments of accidents, acted by Hollywood stunt doubles. TRIAL, Mar. 1982, at 14. In personal injury cases, the civil plaintiff often presents a "day-in-the-life" film. Margolis, *Motion Pictures-An Effective Tool in the Presentation of the Personal Injury Claim*, TRIAL DIPL. J. 32 (Spring 1980). In his article, Margolis outlines the content of a typical "day-in-the-life" film:

(1) *Exterior Day.* Establishing shot of where Client lives, to set stage for later shots of transportation difficulties in leaving home. Open on *close-up* of sign, "Handicapped Resident." Camera *zooms out* to show apartment building, and then *zooms in* to bedroom window of her upper story apartment.

(2) Interior. Low angle *medium shot* of client in bed, framed by bed rails in foreground. Bedside drainage bag will be visible here (although other more

detailed shots of toilet activities should probably be omitted in the interests of good taste). Bed rails are lowered by Client's husband.

(3) *Medium shot* as Client's husband begins to sponge bathe her in bed.

(4) *Wide shot* as Client's husband begins to dress his wife in her bed. Some closer shots here will also be useful in showing need for assistance in getting hands in sleeves, handling buttons and other simple elements of getting dressed that we tend to take for granted.

*   *   *

(6) Series of *medium close-ups* show the nature of the net that will hold and lift her, and show Husband's activities as he attaches hooks, makes adjustments, sees to her comfort and begins to operate the lift.

(7) *Wide shot.* Client being moved from bed to wheel chair, as Husband operates lift. When transfer is complete, he sees to her comfort, disconnects lift (*close-ups*) and removes it. At this point, if her wheel chair has been made operational, she will move herself to her accustomed location in front of the television set. Otherwise, Husband returns and moves chair to that position.

(8) Another series of *close-ups* as he sees to her comfort. These shots will particularly emphasize the hand wrappings that keep her wrists stiff, the difficulty she has in sliding her hands to positions of comfort, and the adjustments that must be made to the chin brace holding her head upright.

(9) *Medium shot. Low angle.* Husband turns on television set, as an indication of the only kind of passive entertainment and activity she has available to her.

(10) *Wide shot* as Husband moves feeder device into place behind wheel chair.

*   *   *

(13) *Low angle medium shot* as she works at feeding herself. This may also include *close-ups* of hands as she tries to grip utensils and of Husband's hands as he assists her. We need only show the beginning of this eating process, keeping with it long enough to indicate the types of difficulties she has.

(14) *Fade in on wide shot* as visiting therapist enters.

(15) Series of *medium close-ups* indicate some of the activities and exercises she goes through with the therapist. Sequence ends with *fade to black* . . . .

*   *   *

(20) *Wide shot* as Husband and fire department representative enter and prepare to carry her for trip to hospital.

(21) *Close-ups* of preparation, including readying of two-man carry and movement to Client from wheel chair.

(22) *Wide shot* from hallway outside apartment, as they maneuver her through apartment and doorway.

(23) *Low angle and wide shot* looking up stairs from bottom, as they carry her down.

(24) *Exterior wide shot* as she is brought out of building, positioned on stretcher, and maneuvered into ambulance. Doors are closed, and vehicle drives away. *Fade out* to black.

Day-in-the-life films are vigorously resisted by defense lawyers, who frequently object on grounds of prejudice or that the evidence will mislead the jury. For court opinions overriding objections, see *Colon v. Rinaldi*, 2006 U.S. Dist. LEXIS 86418(D. Puerto Rico 2006) ("the court determines that the probative value outweighs any prejudice that the film might have under Fed. R. Evid. 403"); *Eckman v. Moore*, 876 So.2d 975 (Miss. 2004) (day-in-the-life video consists of fifteen to twenty minutes of edited tape which portrays an injured party's daily activities). The *Eckman* court observed that demonstrative evidence has evolved from still photographs to films, color slides, videotapes, and computer-generated demonstrations. "However, the standard is the same," announced the court, applying similar probative worth versus prejudicial impact guidelines to all forms of graphic proof. In *Eckman*, the first trial resulted in a $5 million verdict for the plaintiff. Subject to edits suggested by the court, the video showing the injured party being washed, clothed and fed by staff, and being visited by his wife and son were proper scenes in a day-in-the-life video. "[T]he proper purpose of the day-in-the-life video is to show an actual day in the life of the victim." 876 So.2d at 985. Approving such video in a burn case is *Colon v. Bic USA, Inc.*, 199 F.Supp.2d 53 (S.D.N.Y. 2001).

The emotional impact of a "day-in-the-life" film should be obvious. Nor has the persuasive power of videotapes and motion pictures been lost on civil defendants. Like civil plaintiffs, they frequently resort to motion pictures. For instance, a defendant auto manufacturer such as Polecat Motors may use a film depicting safety tests of the model involved in the case; a film showing the model withstanding the very type of impact involved in the case can be impressive evidence of the car's crash worthiness. On the other hand, a film can be especially potent evidence if the opponent prepared the film but the proponent obtained the film during pretrial discovery:

> In products liability cases, plaintiffs sometimes seek to secure and use test . . . films made by the manufacturer. In the California case of *Richard Grimshaw v. Ford Motor Company*, the jury voted a verdict of several million dollars in damages against the defendant. Grimshaw was burned when the 1972 Pinto he was riding in was struck in the rear, and the gas tank ruptured and exploded. The trial proof featured a showing of Ford's own test film of a Pinto backed into a wall at 20 m.p.h. The gas tank ruptured. One juror commented: "In my mind, that film beat the Ford Motor Co."

R. Carlson, Successful Techniques for Civil Trials § 3:34, at 234 (2d ed. 1992).

In the past twenty years, there has been an explosion of interest in courtroom use and adaptation of videotape technology. The use of videotape technology to film out-of-court events is commonplace. For example, police can videotape an undercover drug transaction. *United States v. Roach*, 28 F.3d 729 (8th Cir. 1994). A defendant's confession can be videotaped as graphic proof that the police administered the proper warnings and that the defendant was not coerced. *United States v. Benitez*, 34 F.3d 1489 (9th Cir. 1994); *Battle v. Delo*, 19 F.3d 1547 (8th Cir. 1994). With prior court authorization, a videotape machine can even be installed surreptitiously in a defendant dentist's office to record unlawful sexual assaults on unconscious or semiconscious patients. *People v. Teicher*, 90 Misc. 2d 638, 395 N.Y.S.2d 587 (Sup. Ct. 1977).

Of course, before this evidence can be shown to the jury, it must be authenticated. Since the film has both sound and action, the bodies of law on authenticating sound recordings and films interface here. *Roy v. State*, 608 S.W.2d 645 (Tex. Crim. App. 1980) discusses the interface. *Roy* involved videotapes of transactions in which police posed as "fences" for stolen property. The court addressed the admissibility issue:

> Appellant contends that the trial court erred in permitting the video-tapes to be shown to the jury. Videotapes are a simultaneous audio and visual recording of events. As such, a predicate is required to establish their accuracy and reliability. This Court has unswervingly upheld the seven-pronged predicate for the admission of sound recordings that was first set forth in *Edwards v. State*, 551 S.W.2d 731, 733 (Tex. Crim. App. 1977), as follows:
>
> (1) a showing that the recording device was capable of taking testimony, (2) a showing that the operator of the device was competent, (3) establishment of the authenticity and correctness of the recording, (4) a showing that changes, additions, or deletions have not been made, (5) a showing of the manner of the preservation of the recording, (6) identification of the speakers and (7) a showing that the testimony elicited was voluntarily made without any kind of inducement. . . . [W]e also find that at least some of the requirements can be inferred from the testimony and need not be shown with the same particularity required for admissions of other mechanically acquired evidence . . . .

Other courts have used the bodies of law on motion pictures as well as sound recordings to establish admissibility requirements for videotapes. "A sufficient foundation is laid for a motion picture when a witness with personal knowledge of the filmed object testifies that the film is an accurate portrayal of what it purports to show. . . . A sufficient foundation is laid for a sound recording when a party to the conversation testifies to the accuracy of the recording and the defendant makes no claim of any changes or deletions in the recordings." *People v. Smith*, 749 N.E.2d 986 (Ill. App. Ct. 2001). The court found the foundation for admitting the audio portion of the videotape was flawed in this case.

In addition to authority drawn from motion picture and sound recording cases, courts also find videotapes to be governed by many of the same rules of evidence as still photographs. *Straughn v. State*, 876 So. 2d 492 (Ala. Crim. App. 2003). Again, as with still photographs, objection will be lodged on the ground of "undue prejudice" where the video carries dramatic impact. *See Tinen v. Lederer*, 2010 N.J. Super. Unpub. LEXIS 1141 (N.J. Super A.D. 2010) (indicating that a video *reconstruction* of an accident or occurrence may be admitted into evidence if the probative value outweighs the possible undue prejudice; undue prejudice "occurs when the jury places excessive weight on the video due to its dramatic effect . . .").

Reenactments and computer animations

In a separate, but also frequently used, category are reenactments or simulations of historical events. In an airplane crash case, a litigator might use synchronized videotape simulations-one depicting the activity in the cockpit and the other a view of the plane's exterior, showing the plane's descent and maneuvers. Marcotte, *Putting Jury in Your Shoes*, 73 A.B.A. J. 20 (July 1, 1987). Videotaped animations or recreations have a dramatic impact. In *Robinson v. Missouri Pacific R. Co.*, 16 F.3d 1083 (10th Cir. 1994), an expert witness created a video by first making a scale model of the accident scene. He simulated an accident by using models of a passenger car and a train which resulted in a dramatic two-minute silent color video. The video depicted the plaintiff's theory of a railroad crossing collision. The Tenth Circuit's decision approved the decision of the district court, which permitted the animation to be shown at trial. The opinion added:

> Having determined that the district court did not abuse its discretion, we add some additional comment. Video animation adds a new and powerful evidentiary tool to the trial scene. McCormick's work on evidence observes that with respect to one party's staged reproduction of facts "not only is the danger that the jury may confuse art with reality particularly great, but the impressions generated by the evidence may prove particularly difficult to limit. . . ." 2 McCORMICK ON EVIDENCE 19 (4th ed. 1992) (footnote omitted). Because of its dramatic power, trial judges should carefully and meticulously examine proposed animation evidence for proper foundation, relevancy and the potential for undue prejudice. Normally, the trial judge should review the video outside of the jury's hearing. . . . Courts in appropriate circumstances may permit demonstrative use of audio or visual presentations which may assist the jury. . . .

Reenactments can also emanate from a computer. Juries in modern trials have witnessed computer imaging technology recreating auto accidents, sewer explosions, airplane crashes, or other litigated incidents. Computer graphics evidence is analyzed in M. BRIGHT, R. CARLSON & E. IMWINKELRIED, OBJECTIONS AT TRIAL 51 (5th ed. 2008). *See Commercial Union Ins. Co. v. Boston Edison Co.*, 412 Mass. 545, 591 N.E.2d 165 (1992) (computer simulation evidence admissible). When the objection is made that a graphic recreation of an accident will mislead the jury, the trial judge must assess the reliability of the depiction. *See Dugle v. Norfolk Southern Ry. Co.*, 2010 U.S. Dist. LEXIS 72523 (E.D. Ky. 2010) (when animation which recreates collision carries danger of confusing or misleading the jury, exclusion is proper). Compare *Harris v. Ward*, 2003 WL 22995021 (W.D. Okla. 2003) (reenactment of a shooting in a simulation and a computer animation; court relied on fact that there was evidentiary support for the depictions, including expert opinion, in upholding videotapes).

The line between reenactment of known historical fact and animation of forensic theory can be a blurry one, especially to the jury. One case approving computer-generated animation is *Datskow v. Teledyne Continental Motors Aircraft Prods.*, 826 F. Supp. 677 (W.D.N.Y. 1993). The district court held that a computer-generated animation illustrating an expert's theory of where a fire began inside an airplane engine and how it spread was admissible in a products liability action against the engine manufacturer. The trial judge rejected the defendant's argument that the jury might view the animation as a recreation of the airplane crash and give the video undue weight. It concluded that most jurors are fairly sophisticated and that it had given a cautionary instruction that the animation was not a re-creation of the accident but a series of computer pictures to help the jury understand the expert's testimony.

Computer-generated animation (CGA) is now in vogue. Verizon Directories Corp. v. Yellow Book USA, Inc., 331 F.Supp.2d 136 (E.D.N.Y. 2004) (images are effective in clarifying sometimes dense expert testimony; held, computer-generated peda-gogical devices are admissible in evidence). If the proponent is content to proffer the animation merely for demonstrative purposes, the requisite foundation is minimal. In that event, it suffices if the witness testifies that he or she has viewed the animation and that the animation fairly and accurately depicts the witness' version of the event. *People v. McHugh*, 124 Misc.2d 559, 476 N.Y.S.2d 721 (1984). However, a more elaborate foundation is necessary when the proponent wants to introduce the demonstrative evidence for substantive purposes. The foundation then must include testimony about the computer hardware and software as well as the information input that generated the animation. *Comm. Union Ins. Co. v. Boston Edison Co.*, 412 Mass. 545, 591 N.E.2d 165 (1992).

Jury instructions play a role when a graphic animation is used during the trial to illustrate a witness's (usually an expert's) sworn testimony. When a computer animation is admitted, the trial court gives a cautionary instruction that the video represents only a re-creation of one party's version of events, and may call attention to any assumptions upon which the re-creation is based. *Webb v. CSX Transp., Inc.*, 615 S.E.2d 440 (S.C. 2005); Commonwealth of Penn. v. Serge, 586 Pa. 671, 896 A.2d 1170 (2006) (court must deliver a limiting instruction explaining the illustrative nature of a CJA).

For an overview of electronic imaging technology, see Morande, A Class of Their Own: Model Procedural Rules and Evidentiary Evaluations of Computer-Generated "Animations," 61 U. Miami L. Rev. 1069 (2007); Aronson and McMurtrie, The Use and Misuse of High-Tech Evidence by Prosecutors: Ethical and Eviden-tiary Issues, 70 Fordham L. Rev. 1453 (2007) (computer animations, simulations, PowerPoint presentations, DNA technology).

Digital Technology

Digital technology has raised challenges to insuring accuracy of exhibits. In the following selection, the author reviews traditional foundation requirements for photos, documentary records and audiotapes and then argues that these are inadequate for problems created by modern document technology. Paul, *The "Authenticity Crisis" in Real Evidence*, 15 THE PRACTICAL LITIGATOR 45, 47–48 (Nov. 2004):

The requirement to admit a photograph into evidence is a mere conclusion by a witness that it "accurately represents the scene depicted." The photographer is not called to the stand. Nor is anyone who handled the image. Nor is there evidence required of the first image in the chain — the one created by the information existing at the time of the historical event. . . . All that is necessary is for someone — not necessarily someone present when the photograph was taken — to declare that a photograph is accurate. *See U.S. v. Mojica*, 746 F.2d 242, 244–245 (5th Cir. 1984). Most often this happens *years* after the event.

[The author then describes the manner in which images as well as records can be manipulated]. In short, because of digital technology's ability to chop up records into tiny information fragments, manipulate such information at will, and then reassemble everything, society possesses a power not really contemplated when the authentication rules were adopted in the 1970s.

The author makes an earnest plea for stringent authentication tests to guard against image alteration and manipulated information. He concludes: "The digitalization of information marks a societal sea change." *Id.* at 52.

In accord is Professor Imwinkelried in his article, *Can This Photo Be Trusted?* TRIAL 48 (Oct. 2005) (As impressive as it appears, digital technology has limitations and, in some respects, is inferior to traditional, film photography). *See* Witkowski, *Can Juries Really Believe What They See? New Foundational Requirements for the Authentication of Digital Images*, 10 WASH. U. J. L. & POL'Y 267, 271 (2002) (noting that digital technology makes videos highly susceptible to manipulation and alteration). *But see United States v. Seifert*, 351 F. Supp. 2d 926 (D. Minn. 2005) (digitally enhanced video admitted).

Victim Videotapes

Creating videos is relatively easy with today's computer and video technology, as anyone who has used YouTube can attest. Videos offered in evidence can range from low budget homemade portrayals to extensive productions. In death penalty sentencing hearings, some victim impact videos have extended 20 minutes in length and have featured photos and film clips of the murder victim's life, often accompanied by background music and sometimes narrated by the victim's family members. The Supreme Court denied review in 2008 of two California Supreme Court decisions allowing such a victim impact video to be played for the jury, which then sentenced the defendants to death. *People v. Kelly*, 42 Cal. 4th 763 (2007), cert. denied, 129 S. Ct. 564 (2008). Justice Stevens, dissenting from the denial of review, wrote:

Victim impact evidence is powerful in any form. . . . Equally troubling is the form in which the evidence was presented [here]. As these cases demonstrate, when victim impact evidence is enhanced with music, photographs, or video footage, the risk of unfair prejudice quickly becomes overwhelming. While the video tributes at issue in these cases contained moving portrayals of the lives of the victims, their primary, if not sole, effect was to rouse jurors' sympathy for the victims and increase jurors' antipathy for the capital defendants. The videos added nothing relevant to the jury's deliberations and invited a verdict based on sentiment, rather than reasoned judgment.

PROBLEMS

1. Problem 11-7. In *Hill*, Polecat Motors films a safety test of its product. The defendant's vice president in charge of industrial operations was present when the test was filmed. The defense attorney expected to use the photographer to verify the film, but unexpectedly the photographer becomes seriously ill on the trial day on which the attorney wants to use the film. Unlike the photographer, the vice president knows nothing about the type of equipment or film used or even custody of the film since the day of the test. Does that preclude the vice president from authenticating the film? Does it help Polecat if the film is used solely for demonstrative purposes?

2. Problem 11-8. In the previous problem, does your analysis or answer change if it is a videotape rather than a film? If it is a computer imaging technique, such as an electronic photograph? Some of these scan conventional film, some eliminate the need for film because of magnetic computer disks, and some do not involve the reproduction of any extant image. Image synthesis technology creates photographically realistic images through mathematics.

5. Enhanced Photographs

STATE v. HAYDEN
90 Wash. App. 100, 950 P.2d 1024 (1998)

KENNEDY, Acting Chief Judge.

Eric H. Hayden appeals his conviction of felony murder in the first degree, contending that the trial court erred in admitting enhanced-fingerprint evidence after conducting a *Frye* hearing. Finding no error, we affirm.

*　*　*

[Hayden was accused of the rape and murder of Dawn Fehring, who was found nude near the foot of her bed with her top bed sheet and T-shirt wrapped around her head and neck. Blood stains were found on the carpet near her body and bloody hand prints were visible on the fitted bed sheet covering the mattress.]

During the ensuing investigation, police interviewed occupants of the other apartments in the building, one of whom was appellant Eric Hayden. Hayden became a suspect when he was unable to account for his whereabouts on the night of the murder and seemed nervous during a police interview. He told police that he had been drinking with friends on Friday evening but was unable to identify the friends. He told his girlfriend that he was too drunk that evening to remember where he had been.

The Kirkland Police Department took the fitted bed sheet to Daniel Holshue, a

King County latent print examiner. Holshue cut out the five areas of the bed sheet that contained the most blood prints. He then treated the pieces of sheet with a dye stain called amido black that reacted with the protein in the blood, turning the sheet navy blue. Next, he rinsed the pieces of sheet in pure methanol to lighten the background, leaving only the protein stains dark blue. Finally, he dipped the pieces in distilled water to set the prints. Still, after these chemical processes were completed, the contrast between the latent prints and the pieces of bed sheet was too subtle for Holshue to identify the minimum of eight points of comparison required to make a positive identification.

Holshue took the pieces of sheet to Erik Berg, an expert in enhanced digital imaging at the Tacoma Police Department, for computer enhancement. Berg took computer photographs, or digital images, of the pieces of sheet and then utilized computer software to filter out background patterns and colors to enhance the images so that the prints could be viewed without the background patterns and colors. Using the enhanced photographs of the latent prints, Holshue found twelve points of comparison on one of the fingerprints and more than forty on one of the palm prints. Thus, he concluded that the prints on the bed sheet belonged to Eric Hayden.

On June 5, 1995, the State charged Hayden by information with one count of felony murder in the first degree. Specifically, it alleged that Hayden committed the crime of rape against Fehring, causing her death in the course of, in furtherance, and in immediate flight from that crime. After an 8-day trial, a jury found Hayden guilty. Hayden appeals.

*   *   *

[T]he trial court held a *Frye* hearing to determine the admissibility of the prints identified by use of the enhanced digital imaging process. The State presented testimony from two experts, Holshue and Berg, who explained the steps they took to ultimately identify Hayden's palm and fingerprint from the fitted bed sheet. The State also provided the trial court with forensic literature regarding digital image enhancement. Hayden did not present any witnesses at the *Frye* hearing and presented no controverting literature. Based upon the testimony, the trial court found that the amido black chemical dipping process is generally accepted by forensic scientists and that the enhanced digital imaging process is not novel scientific evidence to which the *Frye* test applies. Nonetheless, the court also concluded that the enhanced digital imaging process passed the *Frye* test.

Hayden . . . argues that the enhanced digital imaging process has not obtained general acceptance in the relevant scientific community because its use for this purpose is recent and because the computer programs used to enhance the images were not designed for forensic science. He maintains that the procedure used to produce the enhanced prints did not satisfy the *Frye* standard and, therefore, that the trial court erred in admitting the evidence . . . .

A. Novel Scientific Evidence

In 1994, the enhanced digital imaging process was described by Berg, the State's digital imaging expert, as "a totally new process based upon research and development done in the late 1960's and early 1970's for the space program." E. Berg, Latent Image Processing-A Changing Technology, The Pacific Northwest International Association for Identification Examiner, Second Quarter 1994. This and other literature presented reflects that the technology used to enhance photographs of latent prints evolved from jet propulsion laboratories in the NASA space program to isolate galaxies and receive signals from satellites. The Tacoma Police Department began using digital imaging technology in forensics in January of 1995.

The State contends that because the underlying scientific theory behind enhanced digital imaging is not new, its application to forensic science does not constitute a novel process; it suggests that it was merely the high cost of the process that prevented law enforcement organizations from using it earlier. Yet, a 1987 article from the FBI Academy's International Symposium on Latent Prints observed:

> Latent print examiners across the country react differently when image enhancement of latent prints is discussed. Often, the initial reaction is one of disapproval. The concern is that nonexistent detail is added to the latent print. Image enhancement techniques are not designed to create detail but to improve images for human interpretation.

A.L. McRoberts, Digital Image Processing as a Means of Enhancing Latent Fingerprints, Proceedings of the International Forensic Symposium on Latent Prints, FBI, July 7–10, 1987, at 166. Although this article may not be reflective of the current latent print examiner community because it was written 10 years ago, it indicates that skepticism, in addition to high costs, may have contributed to the delay in the use of digital image enhancement in forensic science.

In support of its argument that the process is not novel, the State relies further upon *State v. Noltie*, 57 Wash. App. 21, 786 P.2d 332 (1990), *aff'd*, 116 Wash. 2d 831, 809 P.2d 190 (1991). At issue in *Noltie* was the admissibility of enlarged views of a child abuse victim's sex organs obtained using a colposcope, a microscope developed and used to diagnose cancer. *Id.* at 28–29, 786 P.2d 332. This court concluded: "We find no basis for Noltie's contention that colposcopy constitutes a 'novel' field or scientific technique, even though its use in child abuse cases may be relatively recent." *Id.* at 29, 786 P.2d 332. It called the colposcope "a magnifying glass with a fancy name" and concluded that it was not subject to the *Frye* test. *Id.* at 29-30, 786 P.2d 332.

*   *   *

Certainly digital photography is not a novel process. Neither is the use of computer software to enhance images. It is only the forensic use of these tools that is relatively new. Although we find the State's argument that the process is not novel to be persuasive, because this is a question of first impression we analyze the admissibility of the evidence under the *Frye* standard.

B. The *Frye* Test

*   *   *

At trial and in his articles, Berg explained the process of enhanced digital imaging in detail. *See also* B.E. Dalrymple & T. Menzies, Computer Enhancement of Evidence Through Background Noise Suppression, 39 J. Forensic Sciences, Mar. 1994. The advantage of digital photographs, rather than analogue film photographs, is that digital photography can capture approximately 16 million different colors and can differentiate between 256 shades of gray. Digital photographs work with light sensitivity, just like film photographs, except the computer uses a chip and a hard drive in place of the camera's film. At trial, Berg testified that there is no subjectivity in this process.

The digital photographs are enhanced using software that improves sharpness and image contrast. In addition, pattern and color isolation filters remove interfering colors and background patterns. This is a subtractive process in which elements are removed or reduced; nothing is added. At trial, Berg testified that the software he used prevented him from adding to, changing, or destroying the original image. In contrast with "image restoration," a process in which things that are not there are added based on preconceived ideas about what the end result should look like, "image enhancement" merely makes what is there more usable. *See* William J. Watling, Using the FFT in Forensic Digital Image Enhancement, 43 J. Forensic Ident. 574 (1993).

On cross examination at trial, Berg admitted this was the first time he had ever taken a latent print off of a fabric. Still, nothing in the literature presented to the trial court and for this appeal indicates that the validity of the process depends upon the nature of the material upon which the print is found. We have examined the fabric and the digitally enhanced photographs in the course of our review. It is clear even to the untrained eye that the fabric contains a hand print and that nothing appears in the digitally enhanced photograph that was not present on the fabric. Rather, the image of the hand print is merely enhanced by removing background detail unrelated to the points of identification by which the hand print was identified as Hayden's. The evidence in the record supports the trial court's unchallenged findings that the technique utilized by Berg has a reliability factor of 100 percent and a zero percent margin of error and that the results are visually verifiable and could be easily duplicated by another expert using his or her own digital camera and appropriate computer software.

The literature presented by the State indicates that digital image processing has been used as a means of enhancing latent fingerprints by the Los Angeles County Sheriff's Department since at least 1987. *See* A.L. McRoberts, Digital Image Processing as a Means of Enhancing Latent Fingerprints, Proceedings of the International Forensic Symposium on Latent Prints, July 7–10, 1987 at 165–66. Because there does not appear to be a significant dispute among qualified experts as to the validity of enhanced digital imaging performed by qualified experts using appropriate software, we conclude that the process is generally accepted in the relevant scientific community. Accordingly, we reject Hayden's contention that the trial court erred by admitting the challenged evidence and affirm his conviction.

NOTES AND QUESTIONS

1. To produce an enhanced image, researchers study the degradation produced when certain types of photographic equipment are used to produce images of particular types of objects. G. Joseph, Modern Visual Evidence § 8.04[2] (1999). The process of image enhancement reverses the degradation. The technique has been used in many contexts "including medicine, physics, meteorology, resource exploration, factory automation and robotics control." *Id.* at 8-22. Before using the computer software which reverses the degradation, the expert converts the normal, analogue photograph into a digital image: "Digital images are composed of millions of tiny dots, referred to as 'pixels.' " Dolan v. State, 743 So. 2d 544, 545 (Fla. Dist. Ct. App. 1999). The software manipulates the pixels to brighten certain areas and thereby improve the contrast with the details in the other areas of the photograph.

2. Distinguish an enhanced photograph from both enlarged and restored photographs. Enlargement is a multiplication process. That process has been in use for so long and is so widely accepted that its validity is judicially noticeable. The *Hayden* court mentions a third technology, image restoration. How does an enhanced image differ from a restored image?

3. What foundation would an enhanced photograph require in a *Frye* jurisdiction? What foundation is necessary in a *Daubert* jurisdiction?

C. CHARTS, INCLUDING MAPS

The category of demonstrative evidence includes many varieties of evidence, for example, maps and charts. The technique for authenticating a map or chart is strikingly similar to the method of authenticating a photograph. A witness familiar with the object or area depicted vouches that the chart is an "accurate," "fair," or "true" representation.

Although some of the techniques discussed in this chapter, such as sound spectrography and videotapes, are expensive advanced technology, rudimentary charts can be both effective and inexpensive. In traffic accidents such as that at issue in *Hill*, one of the most difficult tasks for the jury is to visualize the respective positions of the automobiles at successive points in time: How were the cars situated with respect to each other 15 seconds before impact? Ten seconds before impact? It is virtually impossible for an attorney to clearly describe a traffic accident without using a chart. Better still, the attorney can use a series of simple charts:

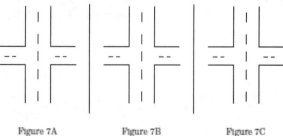

Figure 7A   Figure 7B   Figure 7C

Assume, for instance, that in a traffic accident case, the plaintiff's attorney has the chart on the extreme left marked Plaintiff's Exhibit 7A, the middle chart 7B, and the final chart 7C. During the plaintiff's direct examination, the attorney might ask the plaintiff to depict the position of the two cars 30 seconds before impact. The attorney could then invite the witness to mark the positions of the cars 10 seconds before the impact on 7B and just before impact on 7C. The use of multiple charts — sequential graphics — helps the jury visualize how the accident unfolded.

Charts are not only helpful for presenting an attorney's version of the case; they are equally useful in attacking the opposition's theory. At Ms. Hill's deposition, Polecat's attorney might ask her to draw a diagram or series of diagrams indicating how she remembers the accident developing. At trial, the defense attorneys can use the diagrams as prior inconsistent statements. In one respect, the diagrams are more effective impeachment than oral inconsistent statements. In an oral statement, Ms. Hill might have used an ambiguous word that allows her to explain away the inconsistency at trial. It may be more difficult for her to find an ambiguity in a diagram, especially if the diagram was drawn to scale. Charts can also be used to set up contradictions between witnesses for the same side. Assume that in the *Hill* case, in addition to testifying herself, Ms. Hill calls an eyewitness, Mr. Coronado. Suppose further that at Polecat's request, Mr. Coronado was sequestered and excluded from the courtroom during Ms. Hill's testimony. During her cross-examination, the defense attorney forces Ms. Hill to draw a diagram of her version of the accident. Similarly, during the cross-examination of Mr. Coronado, the defense attorney directs him to prepare a chart. There is a high probability that there will be significant differences between the two depictions of the accident. During summation, the defense can hold up the charts, point to the differences, and argue "the plaintiff's witnesses don't even agree among themselves."

NOTES

1.   Must a chart be drawn to scale to be admissible? In any event, will the "to scale" feature of a chart aid admissibility? What type of instruction should the judge give the jury when the chart is introduced? Consider FED. R. EVID. 105. *See* S. GOLDBERG, THE FIRST TRIAL: WHERE DO I SIT? WHAT DO I SAY? 152–53 (1982).

2.   Courts have allowed maps, charts and diagrams under their broad discretion to admit demonstrative evidence to illustrate a witness's testimony. *People v. Mills*, 106 Cal. Rptr.3d 153 (2010). *See Safety Nat. Cas. Corp. v. United States Dept. of Homeland Sec.*, 2007 U.S. Dist. LEXIS 99225 (S.D. Texas 2007) (where summary and organizational charts are *not* offered into evidence, but are merely used to clarify or illustrate the relevance of admitted documents, the trial court will have discretion to allow the use of those charts).

Chapter 12

SPECIALIZED ASPECTS OF LOGICAL RELEVANCE: ASSESSING THE VALIDITY OF SCIENTIFIC EVIDENCE

Read Federal Rules of Evidence 104(a) and 702.

A. INTRODUCTION

Specialized knowledge — knowledge that is "beyond the ken" of ordinary people — presents judges with the perplexing task of how to evaluate its relevance in court. Is the testimony really based on valid knowledge that is pertinent to this case? How to resolve this question has been an ongoing debate. Since at least the Seventeenth Century, experts have been called upon to enlighten common-law courts about some aspect of the case beyond common knowledge. *See* Tal Golan, *Revisiting the History of Scientific Expert Testimony*, 73 BROOK. L. REV. 879, 898 (2008) (chronicling the debate about scientific testimony in the courts from the earliest days of "proto-science"). What counts as specialized knowledge has been controversial for just as long. Judges, lawyers and the public have been skeptical about the ability of courts to resolve issues on which even experts disagree. Nonetheless, expert testimony has become an increasingly pervasive aspect of modern trials. In this chapter, we will examine the bases for admissibility for such specialized testimony.

B. ADMISSIBILITY STANDARDS

1. General Acceptance

Initially, common-law courts permitted experts to testify where the issue under consideration was "beyond the ken" of an ordinary person to understand, as long as a court found that the expert's testimony would be helpful to the jury, and the expert had training and experience in the subject. These remained the standards for admissibility until 1923. In 1923, *Frye v. United States*, 293 F. 1013 (D.C. Cir. 1923) added another important qualification: the expert must be testifying to generally accepted scientific principles. *Frye* was a murder trial in which the defendant, James Frye, pled not guilty and offered to prove his truthfulness through expert lie detector testimony. The judge excluded the expert testimony and Frye appealed. In addition to the traditional criteria of logical relevance, helpfulness to the factfinder, and witness qualifications (none of which was contested), the appellate court devised an unprecedented new test. The expert testimony had to be grounded in scientific principles that were "sufficiently established to have gained general acceptance in the field in which it belongs." *Id.*

at 1014. Finding that "the systolic blood pressure deception test has not yet gained such standing," the court affirmed the trial court's decision to exclude the testimony.

NOTES AND PROBLEMS

1.   One consequence of the *Frye* test is that it may well promote a degree of uniformity of decision. Individual judges, whose particular conclusions may differ regarding the reliability of particular scientific evidence, may nonetheless discover substantial consensus within the scientific community. Is this kind of uniformity a good thing?

2.   Critics of *Frye* have charged that the *Frye* test rests on unsubstantiated, elitist assumptions about the inability of lay jurors to evaluate scientific testimony. In *People v. Kelly*, 17 Cal. 3d 24, 130 Cal. Rptr. 144, 549 P.2d 1240 (1976), for example, the California Supreme Court made several unflattering assertions about the capacity of laypersons to weigh scientific evidence. What do you think? *See* H. Kalven & H. Zeisel, The American Jury 137 (1966) (finding that jurors were capable of understanding the evidence, even where many of the cases involved scientific testimony). Several studies of polygraph evidence, including both surveys of courtroom use and controlled experimental simulations, indicate that jurors are not overwhelmed by that species of scientific evidence. Imwinkelried, *The Standard for Admitting Scientific Evidence: A Critique from the Perspective of Juror Psychology*, 28 Vill. L. Rev. 554, 567–68 (1983) (collecting the studies). In 1998, Professor Neil Vidmar and many of the leading American legal psychologists filed an amicus curiae brief in the *Kumho* case then pending before the United States Supreme Court. In their brief, the amici presented a comprehensive review of the empirical investigations into this question. They noted the common assertions that "juries fail to critically evaluate expert testimony [and] that they are overawed by experts." However, their analysis of available studies led them to conclude that "[t]he heavy preponderance of data from more than a quarter century of empirical jury research points to just the opposite view of jury behavior." Brief Amici Curiae of Neil Vidmar *et al.* in Support of Respondents, *Kumho Tire Company, Ltd. v. Carmichael*, No. 97-1709, at 25 (Oct. 19, 1998).

3.   As the Georgia Supreme Court observed in its opinion rejecting *Frye*, under *Frye* the admissibility of scientific testimony turns on "counting heads." *Harper v. State*, 249 Ga. 519, 292 S.E.2d 389 (1982). Attorneys with a liberal arts background may feel more comfortable litigating the general acceptance or popularity of a purported scientific proposition; but to put the matter bluntly, the general acceptance test is a crude, indirect and uncertain measure of the validity of the scientific theory or technique. Isn't a more meaningful question whether the theory rests on solid empirical research? *See State v. York*, 564 A.2d 389, 390–91 (Me. 1989).

4.   Assume that *Frye* still governs in Morena. Should *Frye* apply only to scientific evidence that involves use of technology such as a polygraph machine, or should it also extend to such fields as psychiatry? *Compare People v. Shirley*, 31 Cal. 3d 18, 52–53, 181 Cal. Rptr. 243, 263-64, 723 P.2d 1354, 1374–75 (1982) *with People v. McDonald*, 37 Cal. 3d 351, 373–74, 208 Cal. Rptr. 236, 250-51, 690 P.2d 709, 723–24 (1984). One of the rationales underlying *Frye* is the fear that scientific evidence will overawe the jury. Suppose that in the *Hill* case, as an element of damages, Ms. Hill claims that the accident caused her to suffer post-traumatic stress disorder (PTSD) and seeks to present expert testimony of a psychologist or psychiatrist on that point. Does PTSD evidence pose the danger of "overawing" the jury to the same extent as instrumental evidence?

Problem 12-1. In the battery prosecution, Devitt denies fighting with Paterson. The prosecutor wants to prove that there were fibers from Paterson's clothing on the defendant's clothing. The police removed certain fiber strands from the defendant's clothing and submitted them, together with a sample of Paterson's clothing, to the police laboratory. The laboratory conducted a scanning electron microscope (SEM) examination of the two samples; the microscopist is prepared to testify that under the SEM, the two samples were "indistinguishable — a match." SEM is a relatively new advancement in microscopy; it permits magnifications much more powerful than a conventional optical microscope. At trial, the analyst testifies that SEM is "an established, well-known technique" in microscopy. On the other hand, he admits that he knows of no court cases admitting SEM evidence. Is that admission fatal under the *Frye* test? *See People v. Palmer*, 80 Cal. App. 3d 239, 253–56, 145 Cal. Rptr. 466, 472–74 (1978).

Suppose that the microscopist wants to go further and testify that the "match indicates that the strands came from Mr. Paterson's clothing." Is a showing that SEM is generally accepted as a technique for visualizing minute objects an adequate foundation for such testimony? Although many scientific techniques employ impressively exact instruments, it is a mistake to equate "the precision of the measurements in the earlier analytic stages" with "the validity of the ultimate inference drawn in the later, evaluative stage." Imwinkelried & Tobin, *Comparative Bullet Lead Analysis (CBLA) Evidence: Valid Inference or Ipse Dixit?*, 28 Okla. City U. L. Rev. 43, 72 (2003). For example, in 2004, the National Research Council of the National Academy of Science published a report on CBLA evidence. The report concluded that whereas CBLA analysts had used very imprecise instrumentation to determine the elemental composition of bullets, in many cases the testifying expert had overstated the inference that could reliably be drawn from the available empirical data.

The primary advantage of the *Frye* test lies in its essentially conservative nature. For a variety of reasons, later courts used the *Frye* standard to interpose a substantial obstacle to the unrestrained admission of evidence based upon new scientific principles. "There has always existed a considerable lag between advances and discoveries in scientific fields and their acceptance as evidence in a court proceeding." *People v. Spigno*, 156 Cal. App. 2d 279, 289, 319 P.2d 458, 464 (1957) (upholding court's exclusion of psychological testimony of intent). Several reasons have been given to support a posture of judicial caution in this area. Courts have assumed that lay jurors tend to give considerable weight to "scientific" evidence when presented by "experts" with impressive credentials and therefore worry about the existence of a " misleading aura of certainty which often envelops a new scientific process, obscuring its currently experimental nature." *Huntingdon v. Crowley*, 64 Cal. 2d 647, 656, 414 P.2d 382, 390 (1966).

2. The Threshold of Helpfulness to the Jury

Federal Rule of Evidence 702 makes helpfulness to the jury the threshold requirement for expert testimony. The rule provides: "A witness who is qualified as an expert by knowledge, skill, experience, training, or education may testify in the form of an opinion or otherwise if: **(a)** the expert's scientific, technical, or other specialized knowledge will help the trier of fact to understand the evidence or to determine a fact in issue."

How does the expert "assist the trier of fact"? When the underlying data can be described — for example, the physician can list all the symptoms he or she observed — the expert's unique ability is drawing conclusions from the data. In our example, the doctor's training and expertise allows her to come to a diagnosis based on those symptoms, which lay witnesses presumably could not do. The traditional rule was that expert opinion testimony was admissible only when it was strictly necessary; when the subject-matter was within the jury's comprehension, courts often held that expert opinion was superfluous. *Bartak v. Bell-Galyardt & Wells, Inc.*, 629 F.2d 523 (8th Cir. 1980) (finding that while expert testimony was necessary to establish negligence based on highly technical architectural requirements, expert testimony was not necessary for issues of negligence that did not require knowledge of special skills).

Under Rule 702, however, courts have been quite liberal in finding that a topic is proper subject-matter for expert opinion testimony. As the court noted in *Dunn v. Hovic*, 1 F.3d 1362 (3d Cir. 1993) (admitting plaintiff's expert testimony that defendant manufacturer knew about the dangers of asbestos exposure), "even when jurors are well equipped to make judgments on the basis of their common knowledge and experience, experts may have specialized knowledge to bring to bear on the same issue which would be helpful." In personal injury actions, for example, the courts increasingly allow testimony by human factors engineers who may testify, e.g., that yellow paint on a curb would make a defect in the curb inconspicuous to the average person. *See Scott v. Sears, Roebuck & Co.*, 789 F.2d 1052, 1054–56 (4th Cir. 1986) (permitting expert testimony on the effect of color on human perception). In medical and legal malpractice cases, expert opinion testimony regarding the pertinent standard of care is not only permitted but, in most cases, it is required in order for the plaintiff to make out a submissible case. In criminal cases involving drug activity, expert testimony regarding methods used by confederates in street-level drug sales has been admitted as helpful to the jury. *See State v. Nesbitt*, 888 A.2d 472 (N.J. 2006). These cases illustrate the courts' liberality. However, there remain limits to the courts' receptivity to expert opinion testimony, as illustrated in the following case.

UNITED STATES v. AMARAL
488 F.2d 1148 (9th Cir. 1973)

TURRENTINE, DISTRICT JUDGE, sitting by designation.

On May 14, 1973, a two count indictment was filed against appellantAmaral and co-defendant Nordfelt. Count one charged Nordfelt with the January 23, 1973, robbery of a national bank in violation of 18 U.S.C. § 2113(a). Count two charged appellant Amaral with the February 12, 1973, robbery of a national bank, and Nordfelt with aiding and abetting in violation of 18 U.S.C. § 2. A motion to sever was granted. On April 6, 1973, Nordfelt was tried by a jury and convicted on both counts. Defendant Amaral pleaded not guilty. The case was tried by a jury on April 4-6, 1973 and the defendant was found guilty.

Defendant Amaral appeals his conviction. Appellant maintains that the trial court abused its discretion in refusing to allow the defense to present testimony by an alleged expert witness regarding the reliability of eye-witness testimony. We find that these contentions are without merit, and we accordingly affirm the conviction.

The basic purpose of any proffered evidence is to facilitate the acquisition of knowledge by the triers of fact, thus enabling them to reach a final determination. As often stated, our system of evidence rests on two axioms: only facts having rational probative value are admissible and all facts having rational probative value are admissible unless some specific policy forbids. 1 Wigmore, Evidence §§ 9, 10 (3d ed., 1940). Evidence which has any tendency in reason to prove any material fact has rational probative value.

The general test regarding the admissibility of expert testimony is whether the jury can receive "appreciable help" from such testimony. 7 Wigmore, Evidence § 1923 (3d ed., 1940). The balancing of the probative value of the tendered expert testimony evidence against its prejudicial effect is committed to the "broad discretion" of the trial judge and his action will not be disturbed unless manifestly erroneous. *Salem v. United States Lines Co.*, 370 U.S. 31 (1962).

The countervailing considerations most often noted to exclude what is relevant and material evidence are the risk that admission will 1) require undue consumption of time, 2) create a substantial danger of undue prejudice or of confusing the issues or of misleading the jury, 3) or unfairly and harmfully surprise a party who has not had a reasonable opportunity to anticipate the evidence submitted. Scientific or expert testimony particularly courts the second danger because of its aura of special reliability and trustworthiness.

Because of the peculiar risks of expert testimony, courts have imposed an additional test, *i.e.* that the testimony be in accordance with a generally accepted explanatory theory. *Frye v. United States*, 293 F. 1013 (1923). "The theory upon which expert testimony is excepted from the opinion evidence rule is that such testimony serves to inform the court [and jury] about affairs not within the full understanding of the average man." *Farris v. Interstate Circuit*, 116 F.2d 409, 412 (5th Cir. 1941). Therefore, expert testimony must also be in regards to a proper subject. Finally, expert testimony is admissible only when the witness is in fact an expert and is accepted as such by the trial court.

[Because the defense had a full opportunity to cross-examine eyewitnesses, the court held that any deficiencies in the witness' perceptions could be spotted by jurors who did not require expert assistance to evaluate the testimony.]

NOTES AND PROBLEMS

1. *Amaral* is the leading case on the subject of the admissibility of expert testimony on the unreliability of eyewitness identification. A few courts have admitted such testimony, but most of the reported appellate opinions are cases affirming a trial judge's exclusion of the evidence. *E.g., People v. Campbell*, 785 P.2d 153 (Colo. Ct. App. 1989); *State v. Bell*, 788 P.2d 1109 (Wash. Ct. App. 1990). Do you agree with this result? It is true that lay jurors realize that eyewitnesses can be mistaken, but does that dictate the conclusion that an expert would not be helpful to the lay jurors?

There are good arguments that the lay jurors do not fully appreciate the extent or causes of the unreliability. *See generally* Levine & Tapp, *The Psychology of Criminal Identification: The Gap from* Wade *to* Kirby, 121 U. Pa. L. Rev. 1079 (1973). Some experimental data indicates that lay jurors are more willing to convict on the basis of fallible eyewitness testimony than on the basis of technical evidence such as fingerprints. *See* N.Y. Times, Mar. 17, 1981, at Y16.

2. The experimental data mentioned above was gathered by Dr. Elizabeth Loftus of the University of Washington. Dr. Loftus not only favors admitting psychological testimony to apprise the jurors of the weaknesses of eyewitness testimony; she has testified as an expert in such cases. *See* Loftus, *Silence Is Not Golden*, 38 Am. Psychologist 564 (1983). However, other witness psychologists oppose the admission of such testimony. *See* Egeth & McCloskey, *Eyewitness Identification — What Can a Psychologist Tell a Jury?*, 38 Am. Psychologist 550 (1983). One writer observes: "In the recent Duke University lacrosse scandal, three white team members were indicted on rape charges based largely on photographic lineups. The African-American accuser admitted that all the team members looked the same . . . Unfortunately, erroneous eyewitness identifications, including cross-racial misidentifications, are rarely this obvious. Eyewitness identifications are often reliable and persuasive evidence. Yet 30 years of social science research and the contributions of the Innocence Project, a national organization dedicated to exonerating wrongfully convicted persons through DNA testing, have shown that erroneous eyewitness identifications are the single greatest cause of wrongful convictions nationwide." D. Aaronson, *Cross-Racial Identification of Defendants in Criminal Cases: A Proposed Model Jury Instruction*, 23 Crim. Just. 4 (Spring 2008).

3. In most of the appellate opinions affirming the exclusion of expert testimony on the unreliability of eyewitness identification, courts stop short of announcing a categorical rule that such testimony is inadmissible; rather, they often hold only that the trial judge did not abuse his or her discretion in excluding the evidence. If the standard is abuse of discretion, when, if ever, will the appellate courts find the exclusion to be error? Suppose that Paterson had never seen Devitt before the alleged assault and that he first identified him in a photographic lineup more than a year after the crime. Would expert evidence on behalf of *Devitt* be admissible then? Assume further that there were significant differences between Devitt's facial features and the initial description that Paterson gave the police of the attacker's face. *See State v. Chapple*, 660 P.2d 1208, 1217–24 (Ariz. 1983).

4. The debate over the admissibility of eyewitness experts continues. *See* Michael R. Barnett, Note, *The Admissibility Determination of Expert Testimony on Eyewitness Identification*, 70 U. CIN. L. REV. 751 (2002). *See also United States v. Smithers*, 212 F.3d 306 (6th Cir. 2000) (expert testimony on eyewitness identification is not per se inadmissible; decision to admit is left to sound discretion of trial judge). New York and several federal courts have joined "a handful of other states in enabling judges to allow testimony by expert witnesses about why eyewitnesses can be unreliable." Rovella, *Eyewitness Testimony Faces Increasing Criticism*, NAT'L L.J. (May 21, 2001).

A more liberal and receptive view toward eyewitness experts post-*Smith* is illustrated by *United States v. Brownlee*, 454 F.3d 131 (3d Cir. 2006). This decision held that expert testimony regarding the accuracy of eyewitness identifications, identifications which were the primary basis upon which the accused was convicted, would have been helpful to the trier of fact. Exclusion by the trial judge was error.

However, the path to open admissibility of such experts is often one or two steps forward, then one step back. With *Brownlee, supra*, compare the opinion in *United States v. Rodriguez-Felix*, 450 F.3d 1117 (10th Cir. 2006). This latter decision observed that while the majority of federal circuits reject a per se rule of exclusion, expert psychological testimony in the instant case was unlikely to assist the jury.

Psychological and social science research has explored the accuracy of eyewitnesses. *See* Rutledge, *They All Look Alike: The Inaccuracy of Cross-Racial Identifications*, 28 AM. J. CRIM. L. 207 (2001); Natarajan, Note, *Racialized Memory and Reliability: Due Process Applied to Cross-Racial Eyewitness Identifications*, 78 N.Y.U. L. REV. 1821 (2003); Brimacombe, *Perceptions of Older Adult Eyewitnesses: Will You Believe Me When I'm 64?*, 27 LAW & HUM. BEHAV. 507 (2003).

3.   Validity and Reliability as Relevance Concerns

When the Federal Rules of Evidence were codified in 1975, they did not mention *Frye*, nor did they discuss its general consensus standard for admitting novel scientific evidence.

Although the majority of states adopted the Federal Rules of Evidence, most courts continued to analyze expert admissibility under the *Frye* criteria. *Frye*'s general acceptance test remained the dominant standard for determining expert admissibility until 1993, when the Supreme Court decided *Daubert v. Merrill Dow Pharmaceuticals, Inc.*, 509 U.S. 579 (1993).

DAUBERT v. MERRELL DOW PHARMACEUTICALS, INC.
509 U.S. 579 (1993)

JUSTICE BLACKMUN delivered the opinion of the Court.

In this case we are called upon to determine the standard for admitting expert testimony in a federal trial.

I

Petitioners Jason Daubert and Eric Schuller are minor children born with serious birth defects. They and their parents sued respondent in California state courts, alleging that the birth defects had been caused by the mothers' ingestion of Bendectin, a prescription anti-nausea drug marketed by respondent. Respondent removed the suits to federal court on diversity grounds.

After extensive discovery, respondent moved for summary judgment, contending that Bendectin does not cause birth defects in humans and that petitioners would be unable to come forward with any admissible evidence that it does. In support of its motion, respondent submitted an affidavit of Steven H. Lamm, physician and epidemiologist, who is a well-credentialed expert on the risks from exposure to various chemical substances. Doctor Lamm stated that he had reviewed all the literature on Bendectin and human birth defects — more than 30 published studies involving over 130,000 patients. No study had found Bendectin to be a human teratogen (i.e., a substance capable of causing malformations in fetuses). On the basis of this review, Doctor Lamm concluded that maternal use of Bendectin during the first trimester of pregnancy has not been shown to be a risk factor for human birth defects.

Petitioners did not (and do not) contest this characterization of the published record regarding Bendectin. Instead, they responded to respondent's motion with the testimony of eight experts of their own, each of whom . . . possessed impressive credentials. These experts had concluded that Bendectin can cause birth defects. Their conclusions were based upon "in vitro" (test tube) and "in vivo" (live) animal studies that found a link between Bendectin and malformations; pharmacological studies of the chemical structure of Bendectin that purported to show similarities between the structure of the drug and that of other substances known to cause birth defects; and the "reanalysis" of previously published epidemiological (human statistical) studies.

The District Court granted respondent's motion for summary judgment. The court stated that scientific evidence is admissible only if the principle upon which it is based is "sufficiently established to have general acceptance in the field to which it belongs." The court concluded that petitioners' evidence did not meet this standard. Given the vast body of epidemiological data concerning Bendectin, the court held, expert opinion which is not based on epidemiological evidence is not admissible to prove causation. Thus, the animal-cell studies, live-animal studies, and chemical-structure analyses on which petitioners had relied could not raise by themselves a reasonably disputable jury issue regarding causation. Petitioners' epidemiological analyses, based as they were on recalculations of data in previously published studies that had found no causal link between the drug and birth defects, were ruled to be inadmissible because they had not been published or subjected to peer review.

The United States Court of Appeals for the Ninth Circuit affirmed. Citing *Frye* . . . , the court stated that expert opinion based on a scientific technique is inadmissible unless the technique is "generally accepted" as reliable in the relevant scientific community. The court declared that expert opinion based on a methodology that diverges "significantly from the procedures accepted by recognized authorities in the field . . . cannot be shown to be 'generally accepted' as a reliable technique." Contending that reanalysis is generally accepted by the scientific community only when it is subjected to verification and scrutiny by others in the field, the Court of Appeals rejected petitioners' reanalyses as "unpublished, not subjected to the normal peer review process and generated solely for use in litigation." The court concluded that petitioners' evidence provided an insufficient foundation to allow admission of expert testimony that Bendectin caused their injuries and, accordingly, that petitioners could not satisfy their burden of proving causation at trial.

We granted certiorari, in light of sharp divisions among the courts regarding the proper standard for the admission of expert testimony.

II

A.

In the 70 years since its formulation in the *Frye* case, the "general acceptance" test has been the dominant standard for determining the admissibility of novel scientific evidence at trial. Although under increasing attack of late, the rule continues to be followed by a majority of courts. . . .

The *Frye* test has its origin in a short and citation-free 1923 decision concerning the admissibility of evidence derived from a systolic blood pressure test, a crude precursor to the polygraph machine. In what has become a famous . . . passage, the then Court of Appeals for the District of Columbia . . . declared: "Just when a scientific principle or discovery crosses the line between the experimental and demonstrable stages is difficult to define. Somewhere in the twilight zone the evidential force of the principle must be recognized, and while courts will go a long way in admitting expert testimony deduced from a well-recognized scientific principle or discovery, the thing from which the deduction is made must be sufficiently established to have gained general acceptance in the particular field in which it belongs." Because the deception test had "not yet gained such standing and scientific recognition among physiological and psychological authorities . . . ," evidence of its results was ruled inadmissible.

The merits of the *Frye* test have been much debated. . . . Petitioners' primary attack, however, is not on the content but on the continuing authority of the rule. They contend that the *Frye* test was superseded by the adoption of the Federal rules of Evidence. We agree.

We interpret the legislatively-enacted Federal Rules of Evidence as we would any statute. *Beech Aircraft Corp. v. Rainey*, 488 U.S. 153, 163 (1988). Rule 402 provides the baseline: "All relevant evidence is admissible, except as otherwise provided by the Constitution of the United States, by Act of Congress, by these rules, or by other rules prescribed by the Supreme Court pursuant to statutory authority. Evidence which is not relevant is not admissible." "Relevant evidence" is defined as that which has "any tendency to make the existence of any fact that is of consequence to the determination of the action more probable or less probable than it would be without the evidence." Rule 401. The Rule's basic standard thus is a liberal one.

Frye, of course, predated the Rules by half a century. In *United States v. Abel*, 469 U.S. 45 (1984), we considered the pertinence of background common law in interpreting the Rules of Evidence. We noted that the Rules occupy the field but, quoting Professor Cleary, the Reporter, explained that the common law neverthe-less could serve as an aid to their application: "In principle, under the Federal rules no common law of evidence remains. 'All relevant evidence is admissible except as otherwise provided. . . .' In reality, of course, the body ofcommon law knowledge continues to exist, though in the somewhat altered form of a source of guidance in the exercise of delegated powers." We found the common-law precept at issue in the *Abel* case entirely consistent with Rule 402's general requirement of admissibility and considered it unlikely that the drafters had intended to change the rule. In *Bourjaily v. United States*, 483 U.S. 171 (1987), on the other hand, the Court was unable to find a particular common-law doctrine in the Rules, and so held it superseded.

Here there is a specific Rule that speaks to the contested issue. Rule 702, governing expert testimony, provides: "If scientific, technical, or other specialized knowledge will assist the trier of fact to understand the evidence or to determine a fact in issue, a witness qualified as an expert by knowledge, skill, experience, training, or education, may testify thereto in the form of an opinion or otherwise." Nothing in the text of this Rule establishes "general acceptance" as an absolute prerequisite to admissibility. The drafting history makes no mention of *Frye*, and a rigid "general acceptance" requirement would be at odds with the "liberal thrust" of the Federal Rules and their "general approach of relaxing the traditional barriers to 'opinion' testimony." *Beech Aircraft Corp. v. Rainey*, 488 U.S. at 169. Given the Rules' permissive backdrop and their inclusion of a specific rule on expert testimony that does not mention "general acceptance," the assertion that the Rules somehow assimilated *Frye* is unconvincing. *Frye* made "general acceptance" the exclusive test for admitting scientific testimony. That austere standard, absent from and incompatible with the Federal Rules of Evidence, should not be applied in federal trials.

B

That the *Frye* test was displaced by the Rules of Evidence does not mean, however, that the Rules themselves place no limits on the admissibility of purportedly scientific evidence. Nor is the trial judge disabled from screening such evidence. To the contrary, under the Rules the trial judge must ensure that any and all scientific testimony or evidence admitted is not only relevant, but reliable.

The primary locus of this obligation is Rule 702, which clearly contemplates some degree of regulation of the subjects and theories about which an expert may testify. "If scientific, technical, or other specialized knowledge will assist the trier of fact to understand the evidence or to determine a fact in issue" an expert "may testify thereto." The subject of an expert's testimony must be "scientific . . . knowledge."[7] The adjective "scientific" implies a grounding in the methods and procedures of science. Similarly, the word "knowledge" connotes more than subjective belief or unsupported speculation. The term "applies to any body of known facts or to any body of ideas inferred from such facts or accepted as truths on good grounds." Webster's Third New International Dictionary 1252 (1986). Of course, it would be unreasonable to conclude that the subject of scientific testimony must be "known" to a certainty; arguably, there are no certainties in science. *See, e.g.,* Brief for Nicolaas Bloembergen et al. as Amici Curiae 9 ("Indeed, scientists do not assert that they know what is immutably 'true'. . . ."); Brief for American Association for the Advancement of Science and the National Academy of Sciences as Amici Curiae 7-8 ("Science is not an encyclopedic body of knowledge about the universe. Instead, it represents a process for proposing and refining theoretical explanations about the world that are subject to further testing and refinement"). But, in order to qualify as "scientific knowledge," an inference or assertion must be derived by the scientific method. Proposed testimony must be supported by appropriate validation. . . . In short, the requirement that an expert's testimony pertain to "scientific knowledge" establishes a standard of evidentiary reliability.[8]

Rule 702 further requires that the evidence or testimony "assist the trier of fact to understand the evidence or to determine a fact in issue." This condition goes primarily to relevance. "Expert testimony which does not relate to any issue in the case is not relevant and, ergo, non-helpful." 3 Weinstein & Berger 702[02], p. 702-18. *See also United States v. Downing,* 753 F.2d 1224, 1241(CA3 1985) ("An additional consideration under Rule 702 — and another aspect of relevancy — is whether expert testimony proffered in the case is sufficiently tied to the facts of the case that it will aid the jury in resolving a factual dispute"). The consideration has been aptly described by Judge Becker as one of "fit." *Ibid.* "Fit" is not always obvious, and scientific validity for one purpose is not necessarily scientific validity for other, unrelated purposes. The study of the phases of the moon, for example, may provide valid scientific "knowledge" about whether a certain night was dark, and if darkness is a fact in dispute, the knowledge will assist the trier of fact. However . . . , evidence that the moon was full on a certain night will not assist the trier of fact in determining whether an individual was unusually likely to have behaved irrationally on that night. Rule 702's "helpfulness" standard requires a valid scientific connection to the pertinent inquiry as a precondition to admissibility.

C

Faced with a proffer of expert scientific testimony, the trial judge must determine at the outset, pursuant to Rule 104(a), whether the expert is proposing to testify to (1) scientific knowledge that (2) will assist the trier of fact to understand

---

[7] Rule 702 also applies to "technical, or other specialized knowledge." Our discussion is limited to the scientific context because that is the nature of the expertise offered here.

[8] We note that scientists typically distinguish between "validity" (does the principle support what it purports to show?) and "reliability" (does application of the principle produce consistent results?). [O]ur reference here is to evidentiary reliability that is, its trustworthiness. In a case involving scientific evidence, evidentiary reliability will be based upon scientific validity.

or determine a fact in issue.[11] This entails a preliminary assessment of whether the reasoning or methodology underlying the testimony is scientifically valid and of whether that reasoning or methodology properly can be applied to the facts in issue. We are confident that federal judges possess the capacity to undertake this review. Many factors will bear on the inquiry, and we do not presume to set out a definitive checklist or test. But some general observations are appropriate.

Ordinarily, a key question to be answered in determining whether a theory or technique is scientific knowledge that will assist the trier of fact will be whether it can be (and has been) tested. "Scientific methodology . . . is based on generating hypotheses and testing them to see if they can be falsified; indeed, this methodology is what distinguishes science from other fields of human inquiry." *See also* C. Hempel, Philosophy of Natural Science 49 (1966) ("[T]he statements constituting a scientific explanation must be capable of empirical test"); K. Popper, Conjectures and Refutations: The Growth of Scientific Knowledge 37 (5th ed. 1989) ("[T]he criterion of the scientific status of a theory is its falsifiability, or refutability, or testability").

Another pertinent consideration is whether the theory or technique has been subjected to peer review and publication. Publication (which is but one element of peer review) is not a *sine qua non* of admissibility; it does not necessarily correlate with reliability . . . , and in some instances well-grounded but innovative theories will not have been published . . . Some propositions, moreover, are too particular, too new, or of too limited interest to be published. But submission to the scrutiny of the scientific community is a component of "good science," in part because it increases the likelihood that substantive flaws in methodology will be detected. The fact of publication (or lack thereof) in a peerreviewed journal thus will be a relevant, though not dispositive, consideration in assessing the scientific validity of a particular technique or methodology. . . .

Additionally, in the case of a particular scientific technique, the court ordinarily should consider the known or potential rate of error, *see, e.g., United States v. Smith*, 869 F.2d 348, 353–54 (CA7 1989) (surveying studies of the error rate of spectrographic voice identification technique), and the existence and maintenance of standards controlling the technique's operation.

Finally, "general acceptance" can yet have a bearing on the inquiry. A "reliability assessment does not require, although it does permit, explicit identification of a relevant scientific community and an express determination of a particular degree of acceptance within that community." *United States v. Downing*, 753 F.2d at 1238. Widespread acceptance can be an important factor in ruling particular evidence admissible, and "a known technique that has been able to attract only minimal support within the community," *Downing*, at 1238, may properly be viewed with skepticism.

---

[11] Although the Frye decision itself focused exclusively on "novel" scientific techniques, we do not read the requirements of Rule 702 to apply specially or exclusively to unconventional evidence. Of course, well-established propositions are less likely to be challenged than those that are novel, and they are more handily defended. Indeed, theories that are so firmly established as to have attained the status of scientific law, such as the laws of thermodynamics, properly are subject to judicial notice under Fed. Rule Evid. 201.

The inquiry envisioned by Rule 702 is, we emphasize, a flexible one. Its overarching subject is the scientific validity — and thus the evidentiary relevance and reliability — of the principles that underlie a proposed submission. The focus, of course, must be solely on principles and methodology, not on the conclusions they generate.

Throughout, a judge assessing a proffer of expert scientific testimony under Rule 702 should also be mindful of other applicable rules. Rule 403 permits the exclusion of relevant evidence "if its probative value is substantially outweighed by the danger of unfair prejudice, confusion of the issues, or misleading the jury. . . ." Judge Weinstein has explained: "Expert evidence can be both powerful and quite misleading because of the difficulty in evaluating it. Because of this risk, the judge in weighing possible prejudice against probative force under Rule 403 . . . exercises more control over experts than over lay witnesses." 138 F.R.D., 631, 632 (1991).

We conclude by briefly addressing what appear to be [some] underlying concerns. . . . Respondent expresses apprehension that abandonment of "general acceptance" as the exclusive requirement for admission will result in a "free-for-all" in which befuddled juries are confounded by absurd and irrational pseudoscientific assertions. In this regard respondent seems to be overly pessimistic about the capabilities of the jury, and of the adversary system generally. Vigorous cross-examination, presentation of contrary evidence, and careful instruction on the burden of proof are the traditional and appropriate means of attacking shaky but admissible evidence. Additionally, in the event the trial judge concludes that the scintilla of evidence presented supporting a position is insufficient to allow a reasonable juror to conclude that the position more likely than not is true, the court remains free to direct a judgment, Fed. Rule Civ. P. 50 (a), and likewise to grant summary judgment, Fed. Rule Civ. P. 56. These conventional devices, rather than wholesale exclusion under an uncompromising "general acceptance" test, are the appropriate safeguards where the basis of scientific testimony meets the standards of Rule 702.

IV

To summarize: "general acceptance" is not a necessary precondition to the admissibility of scientific evidence under the Federal Rules of Evidence, but the Rules of Evidence — especially Rule 702 — do assign to the trial judge the task of ensuring that an expert's testimony both rests on a reliable foundation and is relevant to the task at hand. Pertinent evidence based on scientifically valid principles will satisfy those demands.

The inquiries of the District Court and the Court of Appeals focused almost exclusively on "general acceptance". . . . Accordingly, the judgment of the Court of Appeals is vacated and the case is remanded for further proceedings consistent with this opinion.

NOTES

1.   On remand, the Ninth Circuit applied the new test but again concluded that the plaintiffs' evidence was inadmissible. *Daubert v. Merrell Dow Pharmaceuticals*, 43 F.3d 1311 (9th Cir. 1995). Writing for the panel, Judge Alex Kozinski (who *also* had written the earlier *Daubert* opinion) explained:

> One very significant fact to be considered is whether the experts are proposing to testify about matters growing naturally and directly out of research they have conducted independent of the litigation, or whether they have developed their opinions expressly for purposes of testifying.

> That an expert testifies for money does not necessarily cast doubt on the reliability of his testimony, as few experts appear in court as an eleemosynary gesture. But in determining whether proposed expert testimony amounts to good science, we may not ignore the fact that a scientist's normal workplace is the lab or the field, not the courtroom or the lawyer's office. While plaintiffs' scientists are all experts in their respective fields, none claims to have studied the effect of Bendectin on limb reduction defects before being hired to testify in this or related cases. If the proffered expert testimony is not based on independent research, the party proffering it must come forward with other objective, verifiable evidence that the testimony is based on "scientifically valid principles."

Id. at 1317–18. Judge Kozinski added that he could not find any "other objective, verifiable" evidence supporting the plaintiffs' experts' opinions in the record. The Advisory Committee's Note accompanying the December 1, 2000 amendment to Rule 702 approvingly cites Judge Kozinski's opinion.

2.   In *Kumho Tire Co. v. Carmichael*, 526 U.S. 137 (1999), the general *Daubert* validity test was extended to all expert testimony.

Writing for the majority, Justice Breyer ruled that like scientific expert testimony, non-scientific expertise must also satisfy a reliability standard. Emphasizing that the trial judge need not accept the *ipse dixit* of the practitioners of an assertedly expert discipline, he cautioned that "the discipline itself [might] lack reliability, as, for example, do theories grounded in any so-called generally accepted principles of astrology and necromancy."

3.   The reach of *Daubert* and *Kumho* has extended to far-flung fields like experts who study financial statements and testify as to lost profits in breach of contract, antitrust and commercial cases. *See generally* Lloyd, *Proving Lost Profits After* Daubert: *Five Questions Every Court Should Ask Before Admitting Expert Testimony*, 41 U. RICH. L. REV. 379 (2007). Does *Kumho* provide a workable approach for the trial judge? In light of *Kumho*, as a trial judge how would you approach the task of evaluating the reliability of the testimony of a musician in a copyright infringement action or of an economist in an antitrust case? *See* Imwinkelried, *Evaluating the Reliability of Nonscientific Expert Testimony: A Partial Answer to the Questions Left Unresolved by* Kumho Tire Co. v. Carmichael, 52 ME. L. REV. 19 (2000). The author suggests that in the following situations, a trial judge could find non-scientific expertise sufficiently reliable:

- A well-designed empirical study demonstrates that the practitioners of the discipline can generally arrive at more accurate opinions than laypersons. For example, there is some research indicating that professional questioned document examiners can perform certain identification tasks more accurately than laypersons.

- In the real world, there is substantial reliance on the opinions of the members of the discipline. For example, for decades, motorists have turned to auto mechanics when their cars malfunction. Motorists generally accept their opinions and find their services useful. Is there a sufficiently strong inference of the reliability of the non-scientific expertise in those situations? What other circumstances would give rise to an adequate inference of the reliability of the expertise?

4. Although the *Kumho* opinion gave trial judges little guidance in exercising their new discretion, lower courts have developed varying approaches to assessing the reliability of non-scientific testimony. Imwinkelried, *The Meaning of "Appropriate Validation" in* Daubert v. Merrell Dow Pharmaceuticals, Inc., *Interpreted in Light of the Broader Rationalist Tradition, Not the Narrow Scientific Tradition*, 30 Fla. St. U. L. Rev. 735 (2003). For example, the court might inquire what type of claim the proponent is making about the theory or technique. There are various types of possible claims, but the two most common are descriptive and inferential claims. At bottom, in a descriptive claim, the expert is merely summarizing his or her prior experience. For example, when a lawyer or doctor testifies about the standard of care in her field, the expert is simply describing her experience in similar cases. In contrast, the expert could make an inferential claim. A dog handler might opine that when her dog "alerted," the alert indicated that there were drugs in the luggage the dog was sniffing.

In a descriptive claim, the expert testifies to the existence of a custom or norm; in an inferential claim, the expert goes further and attempts to draw an inference from the custom or norm. In descriptive claims, the foundation consists of proof of the expert's involvement in numerous, similar transactions. In inferential claims, by comparison, the foundation is more extensive. The proponent must demonstrate that the results of prior use of the technique or theory show that the expert can accurately draw the inference. For example, in the case of the dog handler, the proponent might be required to present testimony about the track record of the dog and handler: in what percentage of cases in which the handler interpreted the dog's conduct as an "alert" did a subsequent search lead to the discovery of drugs?

5. When Rule 702 was amended in 2000 in response to *Daubert* and *Kumho Tire*, the Advisory Committee's Note listed other factors courts have found relevant in assessing reliability:

- Whether experts are "proposing to testify about matters growing naturally and directly out of research they have conducted independent of the litigation or whether they have developed their opinions expressly for purposes of testifying." *Daubert v. Merrell Dow Pharmaceuticals, Inc.*, 43 F.3d 1311, 1317 (9th Cir. 1995).

- Whether the expert has unjustifiably extrapolated from an accepted premise to an unfounded conclusion. *See General Elec. Co. v. Joiner*, 522 U.S. 136, 146 (1997) (noting that in some cases a trial court "may conclude that there is simply too great an analytical gap between data and the opinion proffered").

- Whether the expert has adequately accounted for obvious alternative explanations. *See Claar v. Burlington N.R.R.*, 29 F.3d 499 (9th Cir. 1994) (testimony excluded where the expert failed to consider other obvious causes for the plaintiff's condition). *Compare Ambrosini v. Labarraque*, 101 F.3d 129 (D.C. Cir. 1996) (the possibility of some uneliminated causes presents a question of weight, so long as the most obvious causes have been considered and reasonably ruled out by the expert).

6.   The Advisory Committee's Note to revised Rule 702 attempted to clarify the procedural burden attached to the court's gatekeeping function regarding the reliability of expert testimony. Noting that the applicable standard in applying the 2000 amendment is Rule 104(a), the committee cautioned that "[a ruling] that an expert's testimony is reliable, does not necessarily mean that contradictory expert testimony is unreliable." The Note elaborated:

> As the court stated in *In re Paoli R.R. Yard PCB Litigation*, 35 F.3d 717, 744 (3d Cir. 1994), proponents "do not have to demonstrate to the judge by a preponderance of the evidence that the assessments of their experts are correct, they only have to demonstrate by a preponderance of evidence that their opinions are reliable. . . . The evidentiary requirement of reliability is lower than the merits standard of correctness." *Seealso Daubert v. Merrell Dow Pharmaceuticals, Inc.*, 43 F. 3d 1311, 1318 (9th Cir. 1995) (scientific experts might be permitted to testify if theycould show that the methods they used were also employed by a "recognized minority of scientists in their field."); *Ruiz-Troche v. Pepsi Cola*, 161 F.3d 77, 85 (1st Cir. 1988) ("*Daubert* neither requires nor empowers trial courts to determine which of several competing scientific theories has the best provenance.").

7.   There are literally thousands of articles on legal standards for scientific evidence. For a variety of viewpoints, *see, e.g.*, Nance, *Reliability and the Admissibility of Experts*, 34 SETON HALL L. REV. 191 (2003); Giannelli, *The Supreme Court's "Criminal" Daubert Cases*, 33 SETON HALL L. REV. 1071 (2003); Caudill & LaRue, *Why Judges Applying the* Daubert *Trilogy Need to Know About the Social, Institutional, and Rhetorical — and Not Just the Methodological — Aspects of Science*, 45 B.C. L. REV. 1 (2003); Imwinkelried, *The Meaning of "Appropriate Validation" in* Daubert v. Merrell Dow Pharmaceuticals, Inc., *Interpreted in Light of the Broader Rationalist Tradition, Not the Narrow Scientific Tradition*, 30 FLA. ST. U. L. REV. 735 (2003).

8.   In federal court, judges must adhere to *Daubert* trilogy and to amended Rule 702. State courts, not bound by Supreme Court interpretations of the federal rules, vary in their approaches to admissibility of scientific and other expert evidence. Most state courts have formally adopted the *Daubert* standard, and some states have also adopted the amended version of Rule 702. A significant minority, however, have retained the *Frye* standard: *Frye* jurisdictions include California, Florida,

Illinois, New York, Pennsylvania, and the District of Columbia. North Carolina and Wisconsin maintain a traditional relevance standard. And a few states follow their own formulations. But whatever formulation they follow, judges' awareness of the problem of unreliable expert testimony appears to have changed significantly after *Daubert.* Most commentators now agree that *Daubert* has in practice resulted in more frequent exclusion of expert testimony. On the other hand, although the emphasis of the two admissibility tests is strikingly different — *Daubert* jurisdictions require judges to evaluate the empirical basis of the testimony before them, while *Frye* jurisdictions require only that the judges evaluate the consensus of scientific opinion — in practice, the tests often result in similar admissibility outcomes. *See, e.g., Parker v. Mobil Oil Corp.,* 7 N.Y.3d 434, 448&n.4 (2006) (requiring, in a *Frye* jurisdiction, a threshold inquiry into "whether there is an appropriate foundation for the experts' opinions" in order to provide "a reliable causation opinion" linking gasoline exposure to leukemia and recognizing that cases employing a *Daubert* analysis are instructive in this regard).

C.   THE INCREASING IMPORTANCE OF EXPERT TESTIMONY

Expert testimony has become increasingly prevalent in civil and criminal trials. In a Rand Corporation study of 529 civil trials in California, researchers found that 86% involved expert testimony and that on average there were 3.3 experts per trial. *See* Gross, *Expert Evidence,* 1991 Wis. L. Rev. 1113, 1119. At the same time that more and more expert testimony is being offered in the courtroom, the validity of several types of commonly admitted expert evidence is becoming increasingly contested. In the mid-1970s the Law Enforcement Assistance Administration conducted the Laboratory Proficiency Testing Program to evaluate the accuracy of crime laboratories throughout the United States. That program documented a very real possibility of error in the analysis conducted by forensic laboratories in the United States. Peter Huber of the Manhattan Institute also asserted that American courts were frequently permitting the introduction of "junk science" in civil actions. P. Huber, Galileo's Revenge: Junk Science in the Courtroom (1991). In 1996, the National Institute of Justice released the study: Convicted by Juries, Exonerated by Science: Case Studies in the Use of DNA Evidence to Establish Innocence After Trial (1996), which presented 28 case studies of defendants who had been wrongfully convicted but were later exonerated by DNA evidence. In a later study of the DNA exoneration cases handled by the Innocence Project at Cardozo School of Law, the most common contributing cause was mistaken eyewitness testimony. However, "erroneous forensic science expert testimony [was] the second most common contributing factor to wrongful convictions, found in 63% of those cases." Saks & Koehler, *The Coming Paradigm Shift in Forensic Identification Science,* 309 Science 892, 893 (2005).

Although these revelations of error are unsettling, it is even more disturbing to realize that until very recently few attorneys — or judges — took a close, critical look at forensic evidence offered at trial against criminal defendants. The judicial treatment of sound spectrography (voiceprint) is a case in point. At first, the courts seemed eager to admit voice identifications based on this technique. *See, e.g., United*

States v. Wright, 17 C.M.A. 183, 37 C.M.R. 447 (1967). Later, after the courts realized the lack of experimental verification of some of the technique's premises, the trend turned markedly toward inadmissibility. *People v. Kelly*, 17 Cal. 3d 24, 130 Cal. Rptr. 144, 549 P.2d 1240 (1976). The explanation for the early cases admitting voiceprint was simple; as the court pointed out in *Hodo v. Superior Court*, 30 Cal. App. 3d 778, 106 Cal. Rptr. 547 (1973), in approximately eighty percent of the cases in which such expert opinion testimony was admitted, there was no opposing expert testimony on the issue of reliability and general acceptability by the scientific community. When a National Academy of Sciences committee studied the voiceprint issue, the committee found that "the very large proportion (of cases) in which the only experts testifying were those called by the state" was "striking." Committee on Evaluation of Sound Spectrograms, NATIONAL ACADEMY OF SCIENCES, ON THE THEORY AND PRACTICE OF VOICE IDENTIFICATION 49 (1979). In part because they were unfamiliar with the relevant scientific learning, most trial attorneys did not probe and challenge such evidence.

The same pattern was repeated with DNA evidence. As in the early voiceprint cases, opposing counsel in the early DNA cases essentially accepted the experts' scientific claims at face value. *See* Lewin, *DNA Typing on the Witness Stand*, 244 SCIENCE, June 2, 1989, at 1033. The tide turned only when opposing counsel took a more critical look at the manner in which the tests were conducted and began calling their own experts to critique DNA evidence. *See People v. Castro*, 144 Misc. 2d 956, 545 N.Y.S.2d 985 (Sup. Ct. 1989) (excluding DNA lab results as unreliable). Of course, today DNA evidence is viewed as the "gold standard" against which many of the other forensic techniques are measured. Yet there remains the problem that defense attorneys are ill-equipped to challenge problems with the labs and the statistical claims of prosecutors who offer such evidence.

1. A Framework for Presenting Expert Testimony

It is, of course, understandable that many attorneys — who often have a liberal arts background — are reluctant to probe and challenge such evidence. Mounting an effective challenge may require mastering a formidable amount of scientific knowledge. It seems all too easy to become lost in a maze of atomic absorption, DNA, electrophoresis, scanning electron microscopes, and trace metal detection technique. To overcome this reluctance, the student must realize that the appearance is deceiving. Although many scientific techniques appear mystifying, laying the foundation for scientific evidence usually involves some simple, fundamental elements. Even in the most complex cases involving sophisticated instrumentation, the scientific testimony ordinarily follows a fairly predictable pattern.

First, the expert will need to be qualified. How the expert is qualified will depend to a great extent on what it is that the expert intends to testify about. Once qualified (and sometimes in order to be qualified), the expert will need to explain the theory on which the opinion rests, and how that theory can help resolve an issue before the jury — how it can "assist the jury." For example, in a toxic tort case, the expert will need to establish the theory of general causation; how the particular chemical at issue is thought to cause the disease that the plaintiff suffered. One way to look at this "theory expert" is as the **educational expert**, whose function is to educate the judge (in a *Daubert* hearing) and the jury (at trial) about the theoretical basis for the expert's ultimate opinion. An expert must also explain the empirical foundation — the methodology — used to reach the conclusion (in our toxic tort example, that a particular chemical causes the particular disease suffered will no doubt rest on a number of different studies, each forming a link in the causal chain). Here, the expert can be thought of as a **reporting expert**, who will also need to explain the data achieved using the methodology employed, and how that helps to resolve the issue (in our example of general causation, how each of the studies leads to the expert's conclusion). A third aspect of the expert testimony is interpretive testimony. The purpose of this **interpretive expert** testimony is to evaluate the test results and illuminate the significance of these results. Whether only one or more than one expert is required to complete these three tasks, this process of explaining the theory, methodology, data and results is crucial to the process. Although few cases actually end up using three separate experts, we think it is helpful to separate the expert testimony into the three functions of educating, reporting and interpreting, as we will describe in more detail in Chapter 23. If more than one expert is presented, each of the experts will need to be qualified before testifying, and what is required for their qualification will depend to some extent on the expert's function.

2.   Qualification of the Witness

Whatever aspect of expert testimony the proponent seeks to admit, Fed. R. Evid. 702 requires that to qualify as an expert, the witness must possess relevant "knowledge, skill, experience, training, or education." The trial judge has wide discretion in deciding whether a person qualifies as a witness.

Perhaps the most important point to bear in mind, though, is that the level of requisite expertise is relative to the subtlety and complexity of the subject-matter of the proposed testimony. After all, the judge's gatekeeping duties under *Daubert* include ensuring that an expert's proffered testimony "both rests on a reliable foundation and is relevant to the task at hand." *Daubert*, 509 U.S. at 597. In order to determine the expert's qualifications, the judge must determine not whether the expert is qualified in some abstract general way, but whether the expert's qualifications provide a foundation for the witness to answer a specific question. *See Berry v. City of Detroit*, 25 F.3d 1342, 1351 (6th Cir. 1994) (upholding exclusion of police officer's testimony that failure to discipline officers was proximate cause of shooting). Qualifications and reliability of the opinion are intimately related. *See, e.g., In re Heparin Prods. Litig.*, 803 F. Supp. 2d 712 (N.D. Ohio 2011) (finding pharmacologist qualified to testify about the effects of contaminated heparin in humans despite most of her research having been animal and chemical studies).

The teaching witness, for example, testifies at a relatively high plane of abstraction about the validity of an underlying scientific theory and the reliability of an instrument implementing the theory. Consequently, this witness usually needs impressive academic credentials. In the words of Federal Rule 702, the witness has "knowledge" gained through "education." In 1994, the Federal Judicial Center released the first edition of its Reference Manual on Scientific Evidence.

In this edition, Professor Margaret Berger called on judges to ensure that "the actual qualifications" of the expert will enable him or her to assist the trier of fact on the precise issue before the court. BERGER, *Evidentiary Framework*, in REFERENCE MANUAL ON SCIENTIFIC EVIDENCE 37, 58–64 (1994). Recall that in *Daubert* the Supreme Court stressed that the expert must be qualified to perform the specific "task at hand."

There are signs that the lower courts have begun to respond to Professor Berger's call to toughen qualification standards. In a growing number of cases, trial judges are exercising their discretion to conclude that the proffered witness lacked the specialized expertise necessary to answer the precise question posed in the case. For instance, although the old bromide is that a witness need not be a specialist to qualify as an expert (*Wheeler v. John Deere Co.*, 935 F.2d 1090 (10th Cir. 1991) (finding that psychiatrist need not be a specialist in cognitive psychology to testify about cognitive considerations in product design)), in *Alexander v. Smith & Nephew, P.L.C.*, 90 F. Supp. 2d 1225 (N.D. Okla. 2000) (excluding medical causation testimony in products liability suit), the court ruled that a proffered witness was not an expert in part because the witness was not board certified in the relevant medical specialty.

NOTES

1. How does a *Daubert* foundation compare with a *Frye* foundation? Which foundation is likely to be more elaborate? In both *Daubert* and the Court's later decision, *Kumho Tire Co. v. Carmichael*, 526 U.S. 137 (1999), the Court stressed that the expert's theory or technique must enable the expert to accurately perform the specific "task at hand." A leading commentator has persuasively argued that in that light, the proponent cannot be content to establish the "global" validity of the expert's discipline; rather, the proponent's foundation must detail research demonstrating the validity of the specific theory or technique that the expert contemplates relying on. *See* Risinger, *Defining the "Task at Hand": Non-Science Forensic Science After* Kumho Tire Co. v. Carmichael, 57 WASH. & LEE L. REV. 767 (2000). Thus, even if one accepts the general reliability of the field of questioned document examination, that assumption would not necessarily dictate the admissibility of testimony identifying the author of hand printed Japanese characters. *See United States v. Fujii*, 152 F. Supp. 2d 939 (N.D. Ill. 2000) (declining to extend handwriting expertise to hand printing).

2. Before *Kumho Tire*, many *Frye* jurisdictions exempted what they called "soft" scientific evidence such as psychological and social science testimony from the general acceptance standard. Is this a valid distinction? Is there such an exemption under *Daubert*?

3. *Daubert* has emboldened the criminal defense bar to attack a wide range of forensic techniques, including hair comparisons, firearms identification, bite mark comparisons, and social science evidence. *See* Giannelli & Imwinkelried, *Scientific Evidence: The Fallout from Supreme Court's Decision in* Kumho Tires, 14 CRIM. JUST. 12 (Winter 2000). In early 2002, relying on *Daubert*, a distinguished Federal District Court judge took the dramatic step of barring fingerprint evidence. *United States v. Llera Plaza*, 179 F. Supp. 2d 492 (E.D. Pa. 2002). In his original opinion, the judge ruled that although experts could testify as to points of similarity or dissimilarity between the latent and known prints, they could not testify on the ultimate issue of whether the latent print could be attributed to the defendant.

Although the judge later did an about-face and accepted the testimony, he admitted the evidence only as "non-scientific" expertise. *United States v. Llera Plaza*, 188 F. Supp. 2d 549 (E.D. Pa. 2002). In 2003, critics focused on the comparative bullet lead analysis (CBLA) evidence which forensic experts use to link bullets in a defendant's possession to bullets used in a crime. *See* Imwinkelried & Tobin, *Comparative Bullet Lead Analysis (CBLA) Evidence: Valid Inference or Ipse Dixit?*, 28 Okla. City U. L. Rev. 43 (2003). In 2004, the National Research Council released its report, Forensic Analysis: Weighing Bullet Lead Evidence (2004), which concluded that in the past, some CBLA experts had given testimony exceeding the permissible inferences from the available research data. The courts are now seriously questioning CBLA evidence. *State v. Behn*, 375 N.J. Super. 409, 868 A.2d 329 (App. Div. 2005) (granting new trial based on studies casting doubt on CBLA analysis). The FBI has since discontinued the use of CBLA. And CBLA is far from the only problematic technique. The National Research Council's February 2009 report on forensic science will undoubtedly add fuel to the controversy. As the National Academy of Sciences noted, "Among existing **forensic** methods, only nuclear DNA analysis has been rigorously shown to have the capacity to consistently, and with a high degree of certainty, demonstrate a connection between an evidentiary sample and a specific individual or source." The National Academy of Science Report castigated the lack of systematic research to validate forensic techniques common in criminal cases, finding that most of the time-honored criminal identification techniques such as fingerprints, ballistics, hair analysis, bite marks, and handwriting analysis had "little rigorous systematic research to validate the discipline's basic premises and techniques [although] [t]here is no evident reason why such research cannot be conducted." Nat'l Research Council, Nat'l Acad. of Scis., Strengthening Forensic Science in the United States: A Path Forward 39 (2009). It remains to be seen whether — and how — the findings in the report will affect admissibility of these types of forensic evidence going forward.

4. How much subjectivity can the law of evidence tolerate in interpretive testimony? At what point do the standards used become so subjective that the opinion based on the standards is of no use to lay jurors? *See* Simon A. Cole, *Who Speaks for Science? A Response to the National Academy of Sciences Report on Forensic Science*, 9 Law, Probability & Risk 25 (2010) (discussing the problem of subjectivity in fingerprint analysis). Note the reference to "assist" in Federal Rule of Evidence 702 — a reference which the *Daubert* court went to pains to emphasize.

5. This element of the foundation raises the question of the specificity of the interpretive standard as well as its subjectivity. In a tort suit, a toxicologist might be called to testify only about general causation: Exposure to this chemical can cause a particular illness. However, the foundation for that testimony would not necessarily suffice to permit the expert to take the next step and testify as to specific causation (that the particular chemical caused the plaintiff's illness). Before permitting the expert to do so, the trial judge might demand additional testimony that: (a) an exposed individual will probably develop the illness once he or she has received a certain dose of the chemical; (b) this plaintiff was exposed to that dose of the chemical; and (c) using the methodology of differential etiology, that this chemical rather than some other factor, caused the disease.

6. In most instances, the proponent offers expert testimony to prove a factual proposition. This century has witnessed a dramatic liberalization of the rules governing the admissibility of expert testimony on factual issues. However, notwithstanding that liberalization "it remains black-letter law that expert legal testimony is not permissible." Note, *Expert Legal Testimony*, 97 HARV. L. REV. 797 (1984). The rationale for the black-letter rule harks back to the traditional view that expert testimony is admissible only when it is necessary. One commentator has condemned expert testimony when it is given in open court on the state of the law of the forum jurisdiction in which the court is sitting, or the state of federal law. *See* Baker, *The Impropriety of Expert Witness Testimony on the Law*, 40 U. KAN. L. REV. 325 (1992). *See United States v. Weitzenhoff*, 1 F.3d 1523 (9th Cir. 1993) (court's admission of expert testimony on contested issues of law in lieu of instructing the jury was manifestly erroneous, but error held harmless). An exception to this rule is the "complex legal regime exception." *See U.S. v. Offill*, 666 F.3d 168, 173 (4th Cir. 2011) (admitting expert testimony on securities law based on the complex legal regime exception). Even so, courts attempt to preclude legal conclusion testimony. *See U.S. v. Bilzerian*, 926 F.2d 1285 (2d Cir. 1991) (permitting law professor to testify about Schedule 13D filing requirements in securities law case because he was not testifying to legal conclusions).

7. Does Federal Rule of Evidence 702 bar the admission of expert legal testimony? What is the significance of the expression, "to determine a fact in issue," in Rule 702? For example, is proximate causation a "fact in issue"? *See Peckham v. Cont'l Cas. Ins. Co.*, 895 F.2d 830, 837 (1st Cir. 1990) (admitting expert testimony on the meaning of proximate causation in insurance law).

8. **Problem 12-2.** During the investigation in the *Devitt* case, the police seized some incriminating physical evidence from Devitt's apartment the day after the arrest. Devitt files a pre-trial motion to suppress the evidence on the ground that the police lacked probable cause to believe that any relevant objects would be found in his apartment. Assume that in Morena, the evidentiary rules apply at the hearing on the motion to suppress. At the hearing, the prosecutor calls an attorney from the Morena Attorney General's Appellate Department. She is prepared to testify that she is the Deputy Attorney General with primary responsibility for litigating Fourth Amendment issues and that in her expert opinion, there was probable cause for the search. The defense attorney objects that "this would amount to grossly improper opinion on a question of law." As the judge presiding at the hearing, how would you rule? *See Di Bella v. County of Suffolk*, 574 F. Supp. 151, 152–54 (E.D.N.Y. 1983).

9. **Problem 12-3.** At trial in the *Hill* case, Ms. Hill calls Professor Bertram Oakley, who teaches Contemporary Ethics in the University of Morena Philosophy Department. He is prepared to testify that he has studied contemporary American social ethics and that in his opinion, marketing a product as dangerous as the Polecat model Mr. Hill purchased is "the sort of socially irresponsible act that almost all Americans would regard as misconduct richly deserving punishment and censure." Ms. Hill offers to accept a limiting instruction that the jurors may

consider Professor Oakley's testimony only on the punitive damages issue. Polecat's attorney objects that "like opinion testimony on the law, opinions about morality have no place in the courtroom." As trial judge, how would you rule? *See* Delgado & McAllen, *The Moralist as Expert Witness*, 62 B.U. L. Rev. 869, 881–85, 923–24 (1982).

10. What other topics lend themselves to expert opinion? Do words and terms used in contracts merit expert explanation? What about the question of whether particular remarks are libelous? Urging expert assistance in these situations, *see* Solan, *Can the Legal System Use Experts on Meaning?*, 66 Tenn. L. Rev. 1167 (1999) (lawyers have been consulting with linguists and language experts in a diverse array of legal cases).

11. Since the advent of *Daubert* with its reliability requirements, and the prevalence of pre-trial hearings on the admissibility of expert testimony under Rule 702, the theoretical basis as well as facts and data underlying an expert opinion will most likely be thoroughly vetted in a pre-trial challenge to the admissibility of the expert's testimony. Moreover, Federal Rule of Civil Procedure 26 and Federal Rule of Criminal Procedure 16 both contain expert disclosure provisions, so pre-trial disclosure of expert reports including the expert's theoretical basis, facts and data underlying the expert opinion are now the norm. Failure to meet these disclosure requirements may result in exclusion of the expert. *See U.S. v. Jones*, 664 F.3d 966, 975 (5th Cir. 2011) (failure to disclose expert's reliance on GAO Reports in violation of Federal Rule of Criminal Procedure 16 precluded expert testimony based on the reports); *Clifford v. Crop Production Services, Inc.*, 627 F.3d 268 (7th Cir. 2010) (upholding trial court's exclusion of plaintiff's expert for failure to disclose the basis of the expert's opinion under Federal Rule of Civil Procedure 26).

D. STATISTICAL TESTIMONY AND ITS EMPIRICAL BASIS

The following pre-*Daubert* case involves testimony about statistical probability. Does the judge hold that all expert opinions based on statistical probability are inadmissible? If so, how to account for the wide admissibility of statistical probability assessments in cases involving DNA testimony? If not, how is the judge to evaluate the testimony?

PEOPLE v. COLLINS
68 Cal. 2d 319, 66 Cal. Rptr. 497, 438 P.2d 33 (1968)

Sullivan, Justice.

We deal here with the novel question whether evidence of mathematical probability has been properly introduced and used by the prosecution in a criminal case. While we discern no inherent incompatibility between the disciplines of law and mathematics and intend no general disapproval or disparagement of the latter as an auxiliary in the fact-finding processes of the former, we cannot uphold the technique employed in the instant case. [T]he testimony as to mathematical probability infected the case with fatal error and distorted the jury's traditional role of determining guilt or innocence according to long-settled rules. Mathematics, a veritable sorcerer in our computerized society, while assisting the trier of fact in the search for truth, must not cast a spell over him. We conclude that on the record before us defendant should not have had his guilt determined by the odds and that he is entitled to a new trial. We reverse the judgment.

A jury found defendant Malcolm Collins and his wife defendant Janet Collins guilty of second degree robbery (Pen. Code, §§ 211, 211a, 1157). Malcolm appeals from the conviction.

On June 18, 1964, about 11:30 a.m. Mrs. Juanita Brooks, who had been shopping, was walking home along an alley in Los Angeles. She was pulling behind her a wicker basket carryall containing groceries and had her purse on top of the packages. She was using a cane. As she stooped down to pick up an empty carton, she was suddenly pushed to the ground by a person whom she neither saw nor heard approach. She was stunned by the fall. She managed to look up and saw a young woman running from the scene. According to Mrs. Brooks, the latter appeared to weigh about 145 pounds, was wearing "something dark," and had hair "between a dark blond and a light blond," but lighter than the color of defendant Janet Collins' hair as it appeared at trial. Immediately after the incident, Mrs. Brooks discovered that her purse, containing between $35 and $40, was missing.

About the same time as the robbery, John Bass, who lived on the street at the end of the alley, was in front of his house watering his lawn. His attention was attracted by "a lot of crying and screaming" coming from the alley. As he looked in that direction, he saw a woman run out of the alley and enter a yellow automobile parked across the street from him. He was unable to give the make of the car. The car started off immediately and pulled wide around another parked vehicle so that in the narrow street it passed within six feet of Bass. The latter then saw that it was being driven by a male Negro, wearing a mustache and beard. At the trial Bass identified defendant as the driver of the yellow automobile. However, an attempt was made to impeach his identification by his admission that at the preliminary hearing he testified to an uncertain identification at the police lineup shortly after the attack on Mrs. Brooks, when defendant was beardless.

In his testimony Bass described the woman who ran from the alley as a Caucasian, slightly over five feet tall, of ordinary build, with her hair in a dark blonde ponytail, and wearing dark clothing. He further testified that her ponytail was "just like" one which Janet had in a police photograph taken on June 22, 1964.

On the day of the robbery, Janet was employed as a housemaid in San Pedro. Her employer testified that she had arrived for work at 8:50 a.m. and that defendant had picked her up in a light yellow car about 11:30 a.m. On that day, according to the witness, Janet was wearing her hair in a blonde ponytail but lighter in color than it appeared at trial. There was evidence from which it could be inferred that defendants had ample time to drive from Janet's place of employment and participate in the robbery. Defendants testified, however, that they went directly from her employer's house to the home of friends, where they remained for several hours.

In the morning of June 22, Los Angeles Police Officer Kinsey, who was investigating the robbery, went to defendants' home. He saw a yellow Lincoln automobile with an off-white top in front of the house. He talked with defendants. Janet, whose hair appeared to be a dark blonde, was wearing it in a ponytail. Malcolm did not have a beard. The officer explained to them that he was investigating a robbery specifying the time and place; that the victim had been knocked down and her purse snatched; and that the person responsible was a female Caucasian with blonde hair in a ponytail who had left the scene in a yellow car driven by a male Negro. He requested that the defendants accompany him to the police station and they did so.

At the trial the prosecution experienced some difficulty in establishing the identities of the perpetrators of the crime. The victim could not identify Janet and had never seen the defendant. The identification by the witness Bass, who observed the girl run out of the alley and get into the automobile, was incomplete as to Janet and may have been weakened as to defendant. There was also evidence that Janet had worn light-colored clothing on the day in question, but both the victim and Bass testified that the girl they observed had worn dark clothing.

In an attempt to bolster the identifications, the prosecutor called an instructor of mathematics at a state college. Through this witness he sought to establish that, assuming the robbery was committed by a Caucasian woman with a blond ponytail who left the scene accompanied by a Negro with a beard and mustache, there was an overwhelming probability that the crime was committed by any couple answering such distinctive characteristics. The witness testified, in substance, to the "product rule," which states that the probability of the joint occurrence of a number of *mutually independent* events is equal to the product of the individual probabilities that each of the events will occur.[8] *Without presenting any statistical evidence whatsoever in support of the probabilities for the factors selected*, the prosecutor then proceeded to have the witness *assume* probability factors for the various characteristics which he deemed to be shared by the guilty couple and all other couples answering to such distinctive characteristics.[10]

---

[8] In the example employed for illustrative purposes at the trial, the probability of rolling one die and coming up with a "2" is 1/6, that is, any one of the six faces of a die has one chance in six of landing face up on any particular roll. The probability of rolling "2's" in succession is 1/6 x 1/6, or 1/36, that is, on only one occasion out of 36 double rolls (or the roll of two dice), will the selected number land face up on each roll or die.

[10] Although the prosecutor insisted that the factors he used were only for illustrative purposes to demonstrate how the probability of the occurrence of mutually independent factors affected the probability that they would occur together — he nevertheless attempted to use factors which he personally related to the distinctive characteristics of defendants. In his argument to the jury he invited the jurors to apply their own factors, and asked defense counsel to suggest what the latter would deem as reasonable. The prosecutor himself proposed the individual probabilities set out in the table below. Although the transcript of the examination of the mathematics instructor and the information volunteered by the prosecutor at that time create some uncertainty as to precisely which of the characteristics the prosecutor assigned to the individual probabilities, he restated in his argument to the jury that they should be as follows:

Characteristic	*Individual Probability*
A. Partly yellow automobile	1/10
B. Man with mustache	1/4
C. Girl with ponytail	1/10

Applying the product rule to his own factors the prosecutor arrived at a probability that there was but one chance in 12 million that any couple possessed the distinctive characteristics of the defendants. Accordingly, under this theory, it was to be inferred that there could be but one chance in 12 million that defendants were innocent and that another equally distinctive couple actually committed the robbery. Expanding on what he had thus purported to suggest as a hypothesis, the prosecutor offered the completely unfounded and improper testimonial assertion that, in his opinion, the factors he had assigned were "conservative estimates" and that, in reality "the chances of anyone else besides these defendants being there, . . . having every similarity, . . . is somewhat like one in a billion."

Objections were timely made to the mathematician's testimony on the grounds that it was immaterial, that it invaded the province of the jury, and that it was based on unfounded assumptions. The objections were "temporarily overruled" and the evidence admitted subject to a motion to strike. When that motion was made at the conclusion of the direct examination, the court denied it, stating that the testimony had been received only for the "purpose of illustrating the mathematical probabilities of various matters, the possibilities for them occurring or reoccurring."

Defendant (contends) that the introduction of evidence pertaining to the mathematical theory of probability and the use of the same by the prosecution during the trial was error prejudicial to defendant.

As we shall explain, the prosecution's introduction and use of mathematical probability statistics injected two fundamental prejudicial errors into the case:

(1) The testimony itself lacked an adequate foundation both in evidence and in statistical theory; and (2) the testimony and the manner in which the prosecution used it distracted the jury from its proper and requisite function of weighing the evidence on the issue of guilt, encouraged the jurors to rely upon an engaging but logically irrelevant expert demonstration, foreclosed the possibility of an effective defense by an attorney apparently unschooled in mathematicalrefinements, and placed the jurors and defense counsel at a disadvantage in sifting relevant fact from inapplicable theory.

We initially consider the defects in the testimony itself. As we have indicated, the specific technique presented through the mathematician's testimony and advanced by the prosecutor to measure the probabilities in question suffered from two basic and pervasive defects — an inadequate evidentiary foundation and an inadequate proof of statistical independence. First, as to the foundation requirement, we find the record devoid of any evidence relating to any of the six individual probability factors used by the prosecutor And ascribed by him to the six characteristics as we have set them out in footnote 10, *ante*. To put it another way, the prosecution produced no evidence whatsoever showing, or from which it could be in any way inferred, that only one out of every ten cars which might have been at the scene of

Characteristic	*Individual Probability*
D. Girl with blond hair	1/3
E. Negro man with beard	1/10
F. Interracial couple in car	1/1000

the robbery was partly yellow, that only one out of every four men who might have been there wore a mustache, that only one out of every ten girls who might have been there wore a ponytail, or that any of the other individual probability factors listed were even roughly accurate.[12]

The bare, inescapable fact is that the prosecution made no attempt to offer any such evidence. Instead, through leading questions having perfunctorily elicited from the witness the response that the latter could not assign a probability factor for the characteristics involved,[13] the prosecutor himself suggested what the various probabilities should be and these became the basis of the witness' testimony (*see* fn. 10, *ante*). It is a curious circumstance of this adventure in proof that the prosecutor not only made his own assertions of these factors in the hope that they were "conservative" but also in later argument to the jury invited the jurors to substitute their "estimates" should they wish to do so. We can hardly conceive of a more fatal gap in the prosecution's scheme of proof. A foundation for the admissibility of the witness' testimony was never even attempted to be laid, let alone established. His testimony was neither made to rest on his own testimonial knowledge nor presented by proper hypothetical questions based upon valid data in the record. (*See generally:* 2 WIGMORE ON EVIDENCE (3d ed. 1940) §§ 478, 650–652, 657, 659, 672–684; *State v. Sneed*, (1966) 76 N.M. 349, 414 P.2d 858.) In the *Sneed* case, the court reversed a conviction based on probabilistic evidence, stating: "We hold that mathematical odds are not admissible as evidence to identify a defendant in a criminal proceeding *so long as the odds are based on estimates, the validity of which have* [sic] *not been demonstrated.*" (Italics added.) (414 P.2d at p. 862.)

But, as we have indicated, there was another glaring defect in the prosecution's technique, namely an inadequate proof of the statistical independence of the six factors. No proof was presented that the characteristics selected were mutually independent, even though the witness himself acknowledged that such condition was essential to the proper application of the "product rule" or "multiplication rule." (*See* Note, DUKE L.J. 665, 669–670, fn. 25.)[14] To the extent that the traits or characteristics were not mutually independent (e.g. Negroes with beards and men with mustaches obviously represent overlapping categories),[15] the "product rule"

---

[12] We seriously doubt that such evidence could ever be compiled since no statistician could possibly determine after the fact which cars, or which individuals, "might" have been present at the scene of the robbery; certainly there is no reason to suppose that the human and automotive populations of (Los Angeles), include all potential culprits — or, conversely, that all members of these populations are proper candidates for inclusion. Thus the sample from which the relevant probabilities would have to be derived is itself undeterminable. (*See generally,* YAMAN, STATISTICS, AN INTRODUCTORY ANALYSIS (1964), ch I.)

[13] The prosecutor asked the mathematics instructor: "Now, let me see if you can be of some help to us with some independent factors, and you have some paper you may use. Your specialty does not equip you, I suppose, to give us some probability of such things as a yellow car as contrasted with any other kind of car, does it? I appreciate that you can't assign a probability for a car being yellow as contrasted to some other car, can you? A. No, I couldn't."

[14] It is there stated that "A trait is said to be independent of a second trait when the occurrence or non-occurrence of one does not affect the probability of the occurrence of the other trait. The multiplication rule cannot be used without some degree of error where the traits are not independent."

[15] Assuming *arguendo* that factors B and E (*see* fn. 10, *ante*), were correctly estimated, nevertheless it is still arguable that most Negro men with beards *also* have mustaches (exhibit 3 herein, for instance, shows defendant with both a mustache and a beard, indeed in a hirsute continuum); if so, there is no basis

would inevitably yield a wholly erroneous and exaggerated result even if all of the individual components had been determined with precision. (Siegel, Nonparametric Statistics for the Behavioral Sciences (1956) 19.)

In the instant case, therefore, because of the aforementioned two defects — the inadequate evidentiary foundation and the inadequate proof of statistical independence — the technique employed by the prosecutor could only lead to wild conjecture without demonstrated relevancy to the issues presented. It acquired no redeeming quality from the prosecutor's statement that it was being used only "for illustrative purposes" since, as we shall point out, the prosecutor's subsequent utilization of the mathematical testimony was not confined within such limits.

We now turn to the second fundamental error caused by the probability testimony. Quite apart from our foregoing objections to the specific technique employed by the prosecution to estimate the probability in question, we think that the entire enterprise upon which the prosecution embarked, and which was directed to the objective of measuring the likelihood of a random couple possessing the characteristics allegedly distinguishing the robbers, was gravely misguided. At best, it might yield an estimate as to how infrequently bearded Negroes drive yellow cars in the company of blonde females with ponytails.

The prosecution's approach, however, could furnish the jury with absolutely no guidance on the crucial issue: *Of the admittedly few such couples, which one, if any, was guilty of committing this robbery?* Probability theory necessarily remains silent on that question, since no mathematical equation can prove beyond a reasonable doubt (1) that the guilty couple *in fact* possessed the characteristics described by the People's witnesses, or even (2) that only *one* couple possessing those distinctive characteristics could be found in the entire Los Angeles area.

As to the first inherent failing, we observe that the prosecution's theory of probability rested on the assumption that the witnesses called by the People had conclusively established that the guilty couple possessed the precise characteristics relied upon by the prosecution. But no mathematical formula could ever establish beyond a reasonable doubt that the prosecution's witnesses correctly observed and accurately described the distinctive features which were employed to link defendants to the crime. (*See* 2 WIGMORE ON EVIDENCE (3d ed. 1940) § 478.) Conceivably, for example, the guilty couple might have included a light-skinned Negress with bleached hair rather than a Caucasian blonde; or the driver of the car might have been wearing a false beard as a disguise; or the prosecution's witnesses might simply have been unreliable.[16]

The foregoing risks of error permeate the prosecution's circumstantial case.

---

for multiplying 1/4 by 1/10 to estimate the proportion of Negroes who wear beards *and* mustaches. Again, the prosecution's technique could never be meaningfully applied, since its accurate use would call for information as to the degree of interdependence among the six individual factors. Such information cannot be compiled, however, since the relevant sample necessarily remains unknown. (*See* fn. 10, *ante.*)

[16] In the instant case, for instance, the victim could not state whether the girl had a ponytail, although the victim observed the girl as she ran away. The witness Bass, on the other hand, was sure that the girl whom he saw had a ponytail. The demonstration engaged in by the prosecutor also leaves no room for the possibility, although perhaps a small one, that the girl whom the victim and the witness observed was, in fact, the same girl.

Traditionally, the jury weighs such risks in evaluating the credibility and probative value of trial testimony, but the likelihood of human error or of falsification obviously cannot be quantified; that likelihood must therefore be excluded from any effort to assign a *number* to the probability of guilt or innocence. Confronted with an equation which purports to yield a numerical index of probable guilt, few juries could resist the temptation to accord disproportionate weight to that index; only an exceptional juror, and indeed only a defense attorney schooled in mathematics, could successfully keep in mind the fact that the probability computed by the prosecution can represent, at best, the likelihood that a random couple would share the characteristics testified to by the People's witnesses — *not necessarily the characteristics of the actually guilty couple.*

As to the second inherent failing in the prosecution's approach, even assuming that the first failing could be discounted, the most a mathematical computation could *ever* yield would be a measure of the probability that a random couple would possess the distinctive features in question. In the present case, for example, the prosecution attempted to compute the probability that a random couple would include a bearded Negro, a blonde girl with a ponytail, and a partly yellow car; the prosecution urged that this probability was no more than one in 12 million. Even accepting this conclusion as arithmetically accurate, however, one still could not conclude that the Collinses were probably *the* guilty couple. On the contrary, as we explain in the Appendix, the prosecution's figures actually imply a likelihood of over 40 percent that the Collinses could be "duplicated" by at least *one other couple who might equally have committed the robbery.* Urging that the Collinses be convicted on the basis of evidence which logically establishes no more than this seems as indefensible as arguing for the conviction of X on the ground that a witness saw either X or X's twin commit the crime.

Again, few defense attorneys and certainly few jurors could be expected to comprehend this basic flaw in the prosecution's analysis. Conceivably even the prosecutor erroneously believed that his equation established a high probability that *no* other bearded Negro in the Los Angeles area drove a yellow car accompanied by a ponytailed blonde. In any event, although his technique could demonstrate no such thing, he solemnly told the jury that he had supplied mathematical proof of guilt.

Sensing the novelty of that notion, the prosecutor told the jurors that the traditional idea of proof beyond a reasonable doubt represented "the most hackneyed, stereotyped, trite, misunderstood concept in criminal law." He sought to reconcile the jury to the risk that, under his "new math" approach to criminal jurisprudence, "on some rare occasion . . . an innocent person may be convicted." "Without taking that risk," the prosecution continued, "life would be intolerable . . . because . . . there would be immunity for the Collinses, for people who chose not to be employed, to go down and push old ladies down and take their money, and be immune because how could we ever be sure they are the ones who did it?"

In essence this argument of the prosecutor was calculated to persuade the jury to convict defendants whether or not they were convinced of their guilt to a moral certainty and beyond a reasonable doubt. Undoubtedly the jurors were unduly impressed by the mystique of the mathematical demonstration but were unable to assess its relevancy or value. Although we make no appraisal of the proper application of mathematical techniques in the proof of facts (Finkelstein, *The Application of Statistical Decision Theory to the Jury Discrimination Cases* (1966), 80 HARV. L. REV. 338, 338–340)), we have strong feelings that such applications, particularly in a criminal case, must be critically examined in view of the substantial unfairness to a defendant which may result from ill conceived techniques with which the trier of fact is not technically equipped to cope. We feel that the technique employed in the case before us falls into the latter category.

We conclude that the court erred in admitting over defendant's objection the evidence pertaining to the mathematical theory of probability and in denying defendant's motion to strike such evidence.

The judgment is reversed.

NOTES AND PROBLEMS

1. Perhaps the most frequently quoted sentence in *Collins* is the court's assertion that "[m]athematics, a veritable sorcerer in our computerized society, while assisting the trier of fact in the search for truth, must not cast a spell over him." The *Collins* court assumes that scientific evidence — in this case, statistical testimony — will overawe the jury. What do you think? There have been few studies of the effect of statistical testimony on laypersons. However, some of the leading research studies have found that the lay subjects in those studies tended to underutilize the statistical testimony; the subjects gave far less weight to the testimony than one might suppose. *See* Kaye & Koehler, *Can Jurors Understand Probabilistic Evidence?*, 154 J. ROYAL STAT. SOC'Y 74, 79–80 (1991) ("[t]he clearest and most consistent finding" in the studies conducted to date); Faigman & Baglioni, *Bayes' Theorem in the Trial Process: Instructing Jurors on the Value of Statistical Evidence*, 12 LAW & HUM. BEHAV. 1, 13–16 (1988); Thompson & Schumann, *Interpretation of Statistical Evidence in Criminal Trials: The Prosecutor's Fallacy and the Defense Attorney's Fallacy*, 11 LAW & HUM. BEHAV. 167, 183 (1987) ("[F]inal judgments of guilt . . . tended to be significantly lower than a [statistical] analysis suggests they should have been.").

2. In the years since the *Collins* decision, many courts have admitted statistical evidence. Statistical evidence is very common in discrimination cases; plaintiffs rely on statistics as evidence to support the inference of discriminatory intent. *See* Montlack, *Using Statistical Evidence to Enforce the Laws Against Discrimination*, 22 CLEV. ST. L. REV. 259 (1973). DNA cases rely heavily on statistics, as do many causation arguments in toxic torts.

3. At several points in its opinion, the *Collins* court stressed that the defense attorney was unschooled in mathematics. The court suggested that it was unfair to expect the defense counsel to detect the flaws in the prosecution's statistical evidence. Is that suggestion sound? Isn't it the defense counsel's responsibility to learn enough about the proposed statistical evidence to effectively attack the evidence? How do a judge's gatekeeping responsibilities factor into this analysis?

4. The *Collins* court found several flaws in the prosecutor's use of statistical evidence. List separately each flaw that the court identified. Which flaws were the most important in the court's mind? What flaws do you observe in the expert testimony?

5. Problem 12-4. In *Devitt*, the defendant denies ever being at the scene of the battery. Paterson testifies that during the struggle, the attacker accidentally cut himself on his own knife and bled. The police laboratory technicians find blood stains at the apartment, and conventional red cell tests (ABO, MN, and Rh) exclude Paterson as the source of the stains. At trial, the prosecutor calls Dr. Paul Merton of the University of El Dorado Medical School. Dr. Merton is prepared to testify that his laboratory uses both ABO and white cell tests, so-called HLA (human leukocyte antigen) tests; he conducted comparative ABO and HLA tests of the bloodstains at the crime scene and a sample of Devitt's blood; the ABO test revealed that both samples belonged to a grouping including only 2% of the American population; the HLA test showed that both samples belonged to a grouping including a mere 0.5% of the population; and the two blood grouping systems are independent. Given these findings, what opinion is Dr. Merton permitted to testify to? How close does *Collins* come to announcing a categorical rule against phrasing the expert's opinion in mathematical terms? Under *Collins*, when, if ever, may the witness do so?

6. Problem 12-5. In the last problem, Dr. Merton asserts that the ABO blood grouping includes only 2% of the American population and that the HLA population frequency was only 0.5% of the population. Certainly, in light of *Collins*, proof of these individual probabilities is a key to gaining the admission of the statistical evidence. As prosecutor, would you rely solely on Dr. Merton's assertion? If the defense challenged Dr. Merton's assertion, how would you prove the individual probabilities? Be prepared to list the types of evidence you would offer to corroborate Dr. Merton's assertion. Consider Federal Evidence Rules 104, 201, 703, and 803(18). How do these Rules interrelate?

7. In 1992, the National Research Council released its initial report on DNA: DNA TECHNOLOGY IN FORENSIC SCIENCE. The report discussed the use of the multiplication or product rule in DNA cases. DNA testimony presents some of the same problems as the statistical evidence in *Collins*.

To ensure the independence of the genetic markers, the report recommended the use of single-locus probes targeting sites on different chromosomes. Previously, many laboratories had used multi-locus probes. Multi-locus probes can target sites which are close together on the same chromosome. There is a risk that genetic markers proximate on the same chromosome will be transmitted together — the problem of linkage disequilibrium. If so, the markers are not independent; and the use of the product rule would therefore be inappropriate.

Moreover, there were concerns about the reliability of the population frequencies which are multiplied. The 1992 report acknowledged that although many of the laboratories employing the rule rely on population frequencies for broad categories (Caucasian, Hispanic, and Afro-American), there was a distinct possibility of substructuring within these groups. For instance, the frequencies of Hispanics of Cuban ancestry in Miami may differ from those of Hispanics of Mexican ancestry in Los Angeles. When there is an extraordinary degree of intermarriage within the subpopulation, the frequencies may no longer be in Hardy-Weinberg equilibrium.

In the long term, to compensate for the problem of substructuring, the report urged the laboratories to use a so-called "ceiling" principle. The report stated: "To determine ceiling frequencies, the committee strongly recommends the following approach: (1) Draw random samples of 100 persons from each of 15-20 populations that represent groups relatively homogeneous genetically. (2) Take as the ceiling frequency the largest frequency of any of these populations or 5%, which is larger." Thus, even if the accused were Irish but the largest frequency for a particular marker occurred for Native Americans, the computation for the accused would use the frequency for Native Americans.

In the short term, before the new random samples are compiled, the report recommended that the laboratories apply a modified version of the ceiling principle to the existing data bases. The draft stated: "In applying the multiplication rule, the 95% upper confidence limit of the frequency of each allele should be calculated for separate U.S. 'racial groups' and the highest of these values or 10% (whichever is higher) should be used. Data on at least three major races (*e.g.* Caucasians, blacks, Hispanics, Asians, and Native Americans) should be analyzed."

8.   Initially, several courts cited the 1992 NRC report as a basis for excluding testimony about random match probabilities in DNA cases. *See* 2 P. GIANNELLI & E. IMWINKELRIED, SCIENTIFIC EVIDENCE § 18-5(c) (3d ed. 1999). Particularly when the issue arose in *Frye* jurisdictions, the courts excluded testimony about computations that did not comply with the NRC guidelines. The courts reasoned that in light of the NRC report, it could not be said that the computational techniques used in the past are generally accepted.

Next, the courts began to admit computations made in the more conservative fashion recommended by the NRC. *Id.* They argued that such computations are generally accepted as, if anything, understatements of the improbability of a random match in DNA markers.

In mid-1996, the National Research Council released a new report, THE EVALUATION OF FORENSIC DNA EVIDENCE. That report noted the empirical studies indicating that substructuring is a less serious risk than the 1992 report assumed. At several points in its new report, the NRC explicitly stated that the new research rendered it unnecessary to employ the ceiling or modified ceiling principle. In the report's words, "abundant data" now indicate that random match probabilities computed by the traditional product rule are appropriately conservative. Random match probabilities, computed in the traditional fashion, are now almost universally accepted. *See* 1 FAIGMAN, KAYE, SAKS & SANDERS, MODERN SCIENTIFIC EVIDENCE § 15-4.0 (2002); 2 P. GIANNELLI & E. IMWINKELRIED, SCIENTIFIC EVIDENCE § 18-5(c) (3d ed. 1999).

It would be an overstatement, though, to assert that there is now complete consensus over the use of random match probabilities in DNA cases. In the past, the testimony was admitted in cases involving "confirmation" matches: Non-DNA evidence pointed to a suspect, the police obtained a DNA sample from that suspect, and that sample matched the crime scene sample. However, as DNA databases grow, experts are increasingly testifying to "database" matches: The crime scene evidence did not point to a particular suspect, the police collected DNA evidence at the scene, the local authorities compared that sample to the samples in a DNA database, and that comparison led to the charges against the defendant. *See* Kaye, *Rounding Up the Usual Suspects: A Legal and Logical Analysis of DNA Trawling Cases*, 87 N.C. L. Rev. 425 (2009). This development has triggered a controversy over the appropriate method of computing the match probability in such cases. Some commentators and courts believe that a rarity statistic, computed in the normal fashion, is admissible in database cases as well as confirmation cases. *See People v. Nelson*, 43 Cal. 4th 1242, 78 Cal. Rptr. 3d 69, 185 P.3d 49, *cert. denied*, 129 S. Ct. 357, 172 L. Ed. 2d 219 (2008). Others argue that the use of the database renders the normal statistic inappropriate because such use increases the probability of a coincidental match. They suggest, for example, that the random match probability should be multiplied by the number of persons in the database. Still other commentators support the Balding-Donnelly position that the probative value of the match is even greater in database cases because the database search has eliminated other potential suspects. Most jurisdictions have yet to reach this question.

Chapter 13

THE DISCRETION OF THE COURT TO EXCLUDE LOGICALLY RELEVANT EVIDENCE

Read Federal Rule of Evidence 403

A. INTRODUCTION

The logical relevance of an item of evidence is a necessary, but not sufficient, condition for its admissibility. Ideally, we want the jury to employ an item of evidence only to prove the facts that the item may legitimately be used to establish, ascribe the correct weight to the item of evidence, and concentrate on the key issues in dispute in the case. As a matter of intrinsic trial policy, these behaviors maximize the likelihood of an accurate decision. Dolan, *Rule 403: The Prejudice Rule in Evidence*, 49 S. CAL. L. REV. 220, 284 (1976). Realistically, the admission of technically relevant evidence sometimes creates a risk that the jury will deviate from this model. Drawing on his or her assumptions about jury psychology, the judge may fear that the jury will misuse a particular item of evidence as proof of another proposition, overvalue its weight, or be distracted by it from the pivotal issues in the case. The common-law "legal irrelevance doctrine" gives the judge discretion to exclude logically relevant evidence that realistically triggers these dangers; this doctrine is now embodied in Rule 403, though the term "legal irrelevance" is not used in the Federal Rules and has generally fallen into disuse. MCCORMICK, EVIDENCE § 185, at 741 n.71 (6th ed. 2006).

B. EXCLUSION OF EVIDENCE UNDER FRE 403: THE MODERN DOCTRINE

Numerous pre-Rules precedents, including Supreme Court decisions, recognized the common-law version of the legal irrelevance doctrine. *Eichel v. New York Cent. R. Co.*, 375 U.S. 253 (1963); *Tipton v. Socony Mobil Oil Co.*, 375 U.S. 34 (1963). Rule 403 is the starting point for any analysis of the modern doctrine. Not only is Rule 403 significant in itself, but it also forms part of the context of virtually every provision in the Federal Rules. With the exception of convictions admissible under Rule 609(a)(2), every item of evidence is subject to discretionary exclusion under Rule 403 (or, some instances, one of a limited number of alternative balancing tests codified by another evidence rule such as Rule 609; we will look more closely at those special balancing tests in other chapters). Rule 403 reflects a bias favoring the admission of logically relevant evidence, based on the assumption that the trial judge can reliably forecast the impact of an item of evidence on lay jurors.

Under Rule 403, the court assesses probative value and then balances that value against the countervailing concerns of unfair prejudice, likelihood of confusion, and waste of time. If any of those dangers substantially outweighs the probative value of the evidence, the judge will exclude the evidence under Rule 403.

C.   APPLYING RULE 403

Of course, in order to balance the probative value of an item of evidence against the potential for unfair prejudice or one of the other countervailing dangers, it is necessary to assess the probative value and to gauge the extent of the countervailing danger. In this section, the balancing process is broken down into its component steps and described in further detail.

1.   Step One: Determining the Probative Value of the Item of Evidence

Federal Rules of Evidence 401 and 402 use the adjective "relevant." In contrast, Rule 403 employs the language "probative value." The expression is admittedly ambiguous, but the drafters' use of a different expression in Rule 403 suggests that they had in mind a concept broader than bare logical relevance. Dolan, *supra*, at 234. When a drafter uses different expressions in two similar statutory provisions, we ordinarily presume that the choice was purposeful and that the drafter meant different things. *Soliman v. Gonzales*, 419 F.3d 276 (4th Cir. 2005).

Courts and commentators agree that the concept of probative value allows the trial judge to consider at least four elements in analyzing the "plus side" of the balancing test under Rule 403. *See generally* Imwinkelried, Article, *The Meaning of Probative Value and Prejudice in Federal Rule of Evidence 403: Can Rule 403 Be Used to Resurrect the Common Law of Evidence?*, 41 V AND. L. REV. 879 (1988). First, the judge may consider patent flaws such as facial vagueness or uncertainty in the proposed testimony. When the weakness of the testimony is evident on its face, a judge certainly should be permitted to consider that flaw.

Next, the judge may consider the number of intermediate propositions between the item of evidence and the ultimate consequential fact that the item is offered to prove. In general, the larger the number of intermediate inferences the jury must draw, the weaker the probative value of the evidence. This is because, as we saw when we discussed circumstantial evidence in Chapter 8, such evidence is only as strong as its weakest inferential link, and each link in the circumstantial chain from the evidence to the fact in issue poses the chance of inferential error.

Third, and related to the prior point, the judge may consider the logical strength of the inference from the item to the consequential fact that it is offered to prove. Suppose that to prove Devitt's motive to attack Paterson, the prosecutor attempts to introduce a letter which Devitt wrote several years before the alleged attack; the letter indicates that at that time, Devitt took offense at something he thought Paterson had done. The remoteness in time lowers the probative value of the evidence. Remoteness in place can have the same effect. Whenever the item of evidence is removed in space or time from the events alleged in the pleadings, such geographic or temporal distance creates the possibility of intervening events such as Devitt's discovery that a third party — rather than Paterson — did the act which offended Devitt. Under such circumstances, the probative value of the evidence to prove Devitt's motive is obviously weaker.

Finally, the Advisory Committee Notes to Rule 403 state that "[t]he availability of other means of proof may be an appropriate factor." In our hypothetical, assume that the prosecutor has no evidence of Devitt's motive other than the somewhat dated letter. The unavailability of alternative evidence increases the prosecutor's need to resort to the letter as proof of Devitt's motive. On the other hand, if the prosecutor has other evidence, such as an admission by Devitt that he was angry at Paterson, this would factor into the judge's assessment of the probative value of the letter.

This final factor figured prominently in the Supreme Court's 1997 decision in *Old Chief v. United States*, 519 U.S. 172 (1997). There, the defendant was charged with both assault and being a felon in possession of a firearm. At trial, the prosecution proffered a copy of the defendant's prior conviction for assault to prove his status as a felon. The document stated that in 1988, the defendant "did knowingly and unlawfully assault Rory Dean Fenner, said assault resulting in serious bodily injury. . . ." In support of his objection, the defendant offered to stipulate to the prior conviction element of the charged offense. He argued that in light of his offer, the judge should bar the prosecution from informing the jury of the name and nature of his prior offense because it was highly prejudicial. The judge refused to require the prosecution to accept the stipulation, but the Supreme Court disagreed. Justice Souter, writing for a 5-4 majority, declared:

> [W]hat counts as to the Rule 403 "probative value" of evidence . . . may be calculated by comparing evidentiary alternatives. The Committee Notes to Rule 401 explicitly say that a party's concession is pertinent to the court's discretion to exclude evidence on the point conceded. Such a concession, according to the Notes, will sometimes "call for the exclusion of evidence offered to prove [the] point conceded by the opponent . . . ." The Notes to Rule 403 . . . state that when a court considers "whether to exclude on grounds of unfair prejudice," the "availability of other means of proof may be an appropriate factor." The point gets a reprise in the Notes to Rule 404(b), dealing with admissibility when a given evidentiary item has the dual nature of legitimate evidence of an element and illegitimate evidence of character:
>
> > "No mechanical solution is offered. The determination must be made whether the danger of unfair prejudice outweighs the probative value of the evidence in view of the availability of other means of proof. . . ."

According to Justice Souter, the defendant's stipulation would have given the prosecution "seemingly conclusive evidence of the element." Although the Court acknowledged that the prosecution ordinarily has the right to present a natural, coherent narrative, that consideration "has . . . virtually no application when the point at issue is a defendant's legal status, dependent on some judgment . . . wholly independent . . . of the concrete events of later criminal behavior charged against him." The majority concluded that the stipulation possessed substantially the same probative value as the judgment proffered by the prosecution and that Rule 403 therefore compelled the acceptance of the tendered stipulation.

It would be a mistake to read too much into *Old Chief*. The decision has not resulted in a large number of defense victories in the lower courts. The lower courts have found numerous bases for distinguishing and limiting *Old Chief*. *E.g., United States v. Dorsey*, 523 F.3d 878, 880–81 (8th Cir. 2008) (noting "*Old* Chief's narrow holding"); E. Imwinkelried & D. Schlueter, Federal Evidence Tactics § 4.03[5][b][ii], at 4-34.2–34.9 (rev. 2010) (listing nine bases courts have relied on to distinguish *Old Chief* on this point). For instance, in *Old Chief* Justice Souter noted that the conviction was relevant "solely to prove the element of prior conviction" in the § 922 (b)(1) charge. In footnote 2, the Court indicated that the facts would have presented a different case if the conviction had also been relevant for impeachment under Rule 609. Furthermore, in *Old Chief* the defense tendered a full, unconditional stipulation to the fact which the evidence was offered to prove. If the stipulation had been incomplete or conditional, the prosecution might not have been required to accept the stipulation. Saltzburg, *Stipulations by the Defense to Remove Other Act Evidence*, 9 Crim. Just. 35, 39 (Winter 1995).

NOTES

1.   The common denominator shared by the four factors is that the judge can evaluate them by considering the face of the evidence; the judge need not impinge on the jury's role by considering the credibility of the source of the evidence.

2.   There is a split of authority over a fifth factor, namely, the question of whether the judge may consider credibility in assessing probative value under Rule 403. The minority view is that the judge may do so. For example, one commentator contends that a judge may consider whether the source of the evidence has been impeached. Sharpe, *Two-Step Balancing and the Admissibility of Other Crimes Evidence*, 59 Notre Dame L. Rev. 556, 589 (1984). In the same vein, one court has indicated that the judge may consider whether the item of evidence has been corroborated. *United States v. Murzyn*, 631 F.2d 525, 529 (7th Cir. 1980), *cert. denied*, 450 U.S. 923 (1981). However, the prevailing view is to the contrary.

3.   Consider the issue as a problem of statutory interpretation. In the American trial system, the jury traditionally evaluates credibility. The Sixth and Seventh Amendments secure a constitutional right to jury trial. Would empowering the judge to pass on credibility raise any doubts about the constitutionality of Rule 403? 22 C. Wright & K. Graham Federal Practice and Procedure: Evidence § 5214, at 266 (1978) (arguing that it would). As you are no doubt aware, an important canon of statutory interpretation states that a court should prefer an interpretation of a statute that moots any substantial questions about its constitutionality. 3 N. Singer, & J. Singer, Statutes and Statutory Construction § 57.24 (7th ed. 2007).

Furthermore, consideration of the broader statutory scheme of the Federal Rules suggests that Rule 403 did not contemplate courts would pass judgment on credibility. Specifically, Rules 104(b), 602, and 901(a) all suggest that when the court assesses the admissibility of an item of evidence, it should accept the item at face value. As parts of the same statutory scheme, those Rules and Rule 403 should be harmonized.

2.   Step Two: Identifying the Countervailing Probative Dangers

After assigning a probative value to the item of evidence, the judge turns to the "minus side" of the equation: The probative dangers cutting against the admission of the evidence. These dangers represent the risks that, in one respect or another, the jury will deviate from the ideal model of jury behavior. We can visualize the model, as depicted in the diagram below:

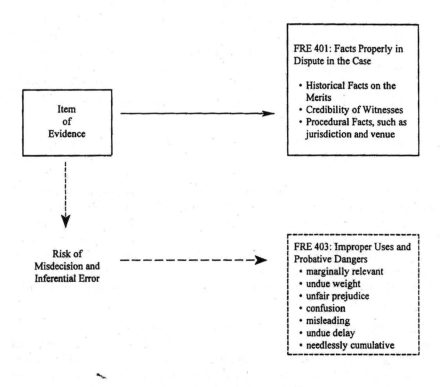

Again, we ideally want the jury to use the item of evidence only as proof of the fact or facts the judge admits the item to prove. The solid arrow from the item of evidence should run directly to one of the facts in the Rule 401 box; there should be a straight line from the item to the fact. The jurors should concentrate on their principal task, which is to decide whether the historical events alleged in the pleadings occurred — and not become distracted by the irrelevant or influenced by the prejudicial.

Misdecision

The inferential process is imperiled when a judge admits an item of evidence that is likely to tempt the jury to decide the case on an improper basis, as suggested by the dotted line. The British philosopher Jeremy Bentham called this problem the risk of "misdecision." 6 J. BENTHAM, THE WORKS OF JEREMY BENTHAM 105–09 (J. Bowring ed. 1962). The Advisory Committee Note to Rule 403 states that the term "[u]nfair prejudice" means "an undue tendency to suggest decision on an improper basis, commonly, though not necessarily, an emotional one." *Laymon v. Bombardier Transp. (Holdings) USA*, 656 F. Supp. 2d 540, 548 (W.D. Pa. 2009).

Suppose, for example, that the trial judge in the *Devitt* case admits testimony about another, extremely violent assault committed by Devitt. On the one hand, this testimony may be relevant for a permissible purpose (for example, one justified under Rule 404(b)). For instance, Devitt may have committed the prior attack with a *modus operandi* strikingly similar to the manner in which Paterson was attacked, which would make the attack arguably relevant to establish Devitt's identity as Paterson's assailant. On the other hand, the testimony about the assault also gives rise to an inference that Devitt has a bad character and a propensity for committing violent acts — an improper basis on which the jury may not rely. Even if the judge gives the jury a limiting instruction that forbids consideration of the testimony about the earlier battery as bad character evidence, it may still have an improper subconscious effect.

In criminal cases, more often than not it is prosecution evidence which poses a risk of misdecision. However, defense evidence can also create this type of risk, and what Rule 403 does is not limited to any particular type of case or any party. Suppose, for instance, that the judge thought that some defense testimony that impeached Paterson was so scurrilous that having heard the testimony, the jurors would detest Paterson and nullify the substantive law criminalizing an assault on him. At least at a subconscious level, the jurors might be tempted to reason, "Paterson deserved it." "While jury nullification is a 'fact' of judicial life, the United States Supreme Court has explicitly recognized that modernly, juries have no right to nullify. *See Standefer v. United States*, 447 U.S. 10, 22 . . . (1980)." *United States v. Rosenthal*, 266 F. Supp. 2d 1068, 1075 (N.D. Cal. 2003).

The same problem can arise in civil cases. Thus, unless punitive damages are in issue, courts often exclude evidence of a defendant's wealth. The jury should not reason that "the defendant should respond in damages because he is rich and the Plaintiff is poor . . . ." *United States ex rel. Miller v. Bill Harbert International Construction, Inc.*, 608 F.3d 871, 897 (D.C. Cir. 2010).

Overvaluation

The jury might commit another type of inferential error, namely, ascribing more weight to the item of evidence than it deserves or concentrating too much of their attention on a minor or marginally important issue. The judge may fear that the jury will draw a stronger inference than is warranted by the evidence. As Chapter 12 notes, many courts assume that lay jurors overestimate the objectivity and certainty of scientific testimony. Suppose, by way of example, that the prosecutor in *Devitt* attempts to introduce expert testimony about a new genetic marker, autoantibodies. The expert, who has just won the Nobel Prize, is prepared to testify that Devitt has the same autoantibody type as the bloodstains found at the crime scene. However, because the autoantibody marker system is so new, the expert cannot quantify the percentage of the population having that autoantibody type. The judge might exclude the expert testimony on the ground that the jury would overvalue the testimony about the match in autoantibody types.

Before excluding evidence under Rule 403, though, the judge must do more than conclude that the jury will probably attach a great deal of value to the testimony; rather, the judge must conclude that the jury will *over* value the testimony. In *Old Chief*, the dissenters stressed that the judge may not exclude relevant evidence simply because the evidence will "hurt" or "damage" the opposition. In an adversary system, the proponent has the right to do precisely that.

Suppose that a movie star testifies as a witness on a marginally important issue for only 10 minutes, but because of the witness's celebrity status, the opposing lawyer fears the jury will accept the testimony as absolute truth. Consequently, the lawyer wants to spend two hours devoted to impeaching the witness's credibility. Admitting that much testimony on credibility might divert the jurors' attention from their most important task, which is deciding the historical merits of the case. The Federal Rules place significant restrictions on the admissibility of evidence logically relevant only to a witness's credibility; the rationale is to reduce the probative danger of distracting the jury's attention.

QUESTIONS AND NOTES

1. The Advisory Committee Notes indicate that evidence is "unfairly" prejudicial when it tempts the jury to decide the case on an emotional basis. Especially in personal injury litigation, the plaintiff's evidence will naturally tend to create sympathy for the injured plaintiff. Madeira, *Lashing Reason to the Mast: Understanding Judicial Constraints on Emotion in Personal Injury Litigation*, 40 U.C. DAVIS L. REV. 137, 147 (2006). Can the judge differentiate between legitimate and "undesirable" emotions? *Id.* at 150, 173. Is it merely a question of degree? *Id.* at 149.

2. Suppose that in *Hill*, Polecat's attorney offers an expert report that the plaintiff's attorney has not had an opportunity to inspect during discovery. Assuming that withholding the report did not violate any pretrial discovery rule in the jurisdiction, may Ms. Hill's attorney object under Rule 403? At common law, it was unclear whether surprise was a valid ground for exclusion under the legal irrelevance doctrine. Is it a ground under Rule 403? Consider this language from the Advisory Committee's Note:

> The rule does not enumerate surprise as a ground for exclusion, in this respect following Wigmore's view of the common law. 6 Wigmore § 1849. *Cf.* McCormick § 152, p. 320, n. 29, listing unfair surprise as a ground for exclusion but stating that it is usually "coupled with the danger of prejudice and confusion of issues." While it can scarcely be doubted that claims of unfair surprise may still be justified despite procedural requirements of notice and instrumentalities of discovery, the granting of a continuance is a more appropriate remedy than exclusion of the evidence.

3. Suppose that the proponent offers a very expensive computer-generated animation (CGA) in a civil case such as *Hill.* Assume further that the opponent objects under Rule 403 and asserts that the judge should consider the fact that the opponent lacks the financial resources to either hire an expert to thoroughly critique the CGA or prepare a CGA for the opponent. Is that argument cognizable under Rule 403?

In a survey of 15 Federal District Court judges, "[e]ight . . . stated that a disparity in resources would not be considered at all." Savikas & Silverman, *Making the Poverty Objection*, NAT'L L.J., July 26, 1999, at C6. The other seven judges indicated that they thought that it was proper to weigh a disparity in economic resources. "Virtually all [of those] judges stated that they would make 'appropriate' remarks to the jury if only one side was using the technology." *Id.* What remarks would be "appropriate" in those circumstances? *Commonwealth v. Serge*, 896 A.2d 1170 (Pa.), *cert. denied*, 549 U.S. 920 (2006) suggested that a trial judge may exclude otherwise admissible expert testimony when the opponent lacks the financial means to afford rebuttal testimony. Do you agree? Neither the text of Rule 403, nor its legislative history, indicates that the trial judge may act as an equalizer and exercise 403 power to level the playing field at trial. In many — if not most — cases, there are feasible alternatives to exclusion, including liberal application of the learned treatise hearsay exception, judicial notice, and cautionary instructions. Imwinkelried, *Impoverishing the Trier of Fact: Excluding the Proponent's Expert Testimony Due to the Opponent's Inability to Afford Rebuttal Evidence*, 40 CONN. L. REV. 317 (2007).

3.   Step Three: Striking the Balance Between Probative Value and Probative Dangers

The last step in the process Rule 403 balancing is the trial judge's determination whether the probative dangers substantially outweigh the probative value of the evidence. In effect, the judge must conduct a "cost/benefit" analysis. It is important to pay careful attention to Rule 403's standard for making this determination. Evidence may not be excluded "unless its probative value *is substantially outweighed*" by the countervailing concerns (emphasis added). *Lee v. Small*, 829 F.Supp.2d 728 (N.D.Iowa 2011). The passive voice of the sentence suggests that the opponent has the burden of demonstrating that the probative dangers substantially outweigh the probative value of the evidence; the word "substantially" indicates that the opponent's burden is a heavy one.

There is legislative history to support this interpretation. In the early hearings on the then proposed Federal Rules of Evidence before the House of Representatives, Albert Jenner, the chair of the Judicial Conference Advisory Committee on Federal Rules of Evidence, asserted that "the overall philosophy and thrust of the Rules" is to "place the burden upon he who seeks the exclusion of relevant evidence." *Quoted in* RULES OF EVIDENCE, HEARINGS BEFORE SPECIAL SUBCOMM. ON REFORM OF FEDERAL CRIMINAL LAWS OF THE HOUSE COMM. ON THE JUDICIARY, 93d Cong., 1st Sess. 77, 78. Moreover, a 1990 Advisory Committee Note to a Rule 609(a) amendment comments that generally under Rule 403, the party opposing the admission of relevant evidence must be able to point to a real danger of prejudice that substantially outweighs the probative value of the evidence. Such language has persuaded many lower courts that Rule 403 allocates the risk of non-persuasion to the party opposing the introduction of logically relevant evidence.

NOTES AND PROBLEMS

1.   In striking the balance, the trial judge is said to have "discretion." What does that mean? Some commentators argue that there are two types of discretion: primary discretion to render a decision and secondary discretion, namely, a high degree of insulation from appellate scrutiny. Waltz, *Judicial Discretion in the Admission of Evidence Under the Federal Rules of Evidence*, 79 Nw. U. L. Rev. 1097, 1102 (1985). Does Rule 403 give the trial judge the power to formulate substantive evidentiary doctrine, or is the discretion simply a procedural by-product of the appellate court's limited supervisory powers? *See* Leonard, *Power and Responsibility in Evidence Law*, 63 S. Cal. L. Rev. 937, 977, 980 (1990) ("when trial courts apply evidentiary rules that call for the balancing of factors based on the circumstances of each case, they are exercising that weak form of discretion that simply connotes the use of judgment;" the judge does not exercise "strong" discretion "in the sense" that she is "not bound by standards established by a higher authority").

2.   Does Rule 403 apply in bench trials? *Compare Gulf States Utils. Co. v. Ecodyne Corp.*, 635 F.2d 517, 519 (5th Cir. 1981) (no) *with* Dolan, *Rule 403: The Prejudice Rule in Evidence*, 49 S. Cal. L. Rev. 220, 280–83 (1976) (yes). On the one hand, considerations of "undue delay, waste of time, [and] needless presentation of cumulative evidence" can certainly arise in a bench trial, and the rule on its face is not limited to jury trials. On the other hand, when the trier of fact is a trained judge, there arguably is a lesser risk of misuse of the evidence by the trier. *Schultz v. Butcher*, 24 F.3d 626 (4th Cir. 1994).

3.   **Problem 13-1.** In the *Hill* case, be prepared to argue both against, and in favor of the admission of a "day-in-the-life" film depicting Ms. Hill's painful personal injuries. *See Bolstridge v. Central Me. Power Co.*, 621 F. Supp. 1202, 1203–04 (D. Me. 1985) (excluding such a film); Alexander, *Day-in-the-Life Video Admissibility*, Cal. Lawyer, Nov. 2011, at 58.

4.   **Problem 13-2.** In *Devitt*, the defendant proposes to call 10 character witnesses to testify to their opinion of Devitt's good moral character. (Note that the defendant may introduce such evidence under Federal Rule of Evidence 404(a), as we shall see in Chapter 14.) The prosecutor objects and requests that the trial judge limit the defense to two witnesses. Under Rule 403, should the judge impose that limitation?

5.   Do not assume that the application of Rule 403 is an "all or nothing" proposition. Rather than invoking Rule 403 as a cleaver and requesting that the judge exclude all the proffered evidence, it is often advisable for the opponent to use the rule as a scalpel and ask the judge to excise a marginally relevant but highly prejudicial detail. *Gerber v. Computer Associates Intern., Inc.*, 303 F.3d 126 (2d Cir. 2002); *Scott v. City of Chicago*, 724 F. Supp. 2d 917 (N.D. Ill. 2010) (admitting the video but not the audio portion of a suspect's videotaped confession).

D. RECURRING ISSUES UNDER RULE 403

Most of the provisions in Articles IV and VI of the Federal Rules of Evidence are, in whole or in part, specific, standardized applications of the general principles of Rule 403, and we shall study those specific rules in later chapters. But there are several recurring fact situations for which, although the doctrine remains discretionary, there is a large body of precedent giving trial judges guidance as to how to exercise his or her discretion.

1. Tangible Objects, Photographs, and Other Visual Evidence

The most frequent objections are to tangible objects and photographs that may shock or "inflame" the jury. For example, in *United States v. Marino*, 658 F.2d 1120 (6th Cir. 1981), the defendant objected to the admission of several weapons found in a briefcase he was carrying at the time of arrest. The defendant was charged with conspiracy to import a large quantity of cocaine. Invoking Rule 403, the defendant claimed that the evidence was prejudicial because it tempted the jury to convict him on the ground that he had a bad, violent character. However, the court found the weapons to be highly probative, commenting that dealers in large quantities of drugs need guns to protect their "assets." Like weapons, gruesome photographs such as those at issue in the following case are a common Rule 403 problem.

STATE v. ROWE
210 Neb. 419, 315 N.W.2d 250 (1982)

PER CURIAM.

[Rowe was convicted of murder and arson. On the morning of May 1, 1980, passersby noted the Rowe residence was burning and called the fire department. Firefighters discovered the badly mutilated body of Layne Rowe, the defendant's wife, wrapped in a blanket and laying on a bed in one of the second floor bedrooms. One of her breasts had been cut off; and an incision had been made in her torso from just below the sternum through the vaginal and rectal areas, exposing several internal organs. An autopsy disclosed that she had also suffered a skull fracture.

A pathologist testified to the following opinions: The skull fracture was consistent with a blow with a clawhammer found on a landing at the head of the stairs near the entrance to the bedroom; it was improbable that the fracture was caused by the head striking a flat object such as a floor; the skull fracture would have ultimately resulted in death; the skull fracture occurred before the mutilation, since there were no signs of resistance; and the immediate cause of death was bleeding, a consequence of the mutilations.

The defendant admitted he had cut his wife's body. However, the defense argued that the skull fracture occurred when she fell down a stairway. The defendant admitted that he had cut his wife's body, but argued that when he did so he was suffering from a "brief reactive psychosis," a consequence of his grief over his belief his wife was dead. The defendant testified that he found Layne, unconscious and bleeding, at the bottom of the steps and unsuccessfully attempted to revive her. According to defense psychiatrists, his belief that she was dead triggered the psychosis, during which he unsuccessfully attempted to shoot himself and then cut her body to remove a baby he thought she was carrying.]

The defendant argues it was error for the court to receive in evidence over his objection four photographs, exhibits 30, 31, 32 and 33. The photographs were, respectively: (1) One picture of Layne Rowe's body in the condition it was delivered to the hospital for the autopsy, partially covered with a burned quilt. (2) One picture of the torso showing the mutilations. (3) Two photographs of the victim's skull taken during the autopsy. The objections to these exhibits are: (1) They are irrelevant because the defendant had stipulated he did the cutting. (2) The risk of unfair prejudice outweighs the marginal relevance the photographs might have. (3) Sufficient foundation was not established because it is not clear from the evidence when the skull photos were taken.

In objecting to these exhibits, the defendant relies upon the principles stated in Neb. Rev. Stat. § 27-403 . . . as follows: "Although relevant, evidence may be excluded if its probative value is substantially outweighed by the danger of unfair prejudice, confusion of the issues, or misleading the jury, or by considerations of undue delay, waste of time, or needless presentation of cumulative evidence."

The objection on the grounds of relevance is founded upon the defendant's stipulation that the defendant did the cutting and the pathologist described adequately his observations, what he did during the autopsy, and his conclusions. The objection on the basis of unfair prejudice is founded upon the proposition that the photographs are "grisly" and "gruesome." It must be conceded they are. The third objection is based upon the claim that the jury might have believed the photos of the skull showed injuries made by the defendant rather than wounds from the autopsy.

In *State v. Williams*, 205 Neb. 56, 67, 287 N.W.2d 18, 25 (1979), we said: "The admission of photographs of a gruesome nature rests largely within the sound discretion of the trial court, which must determine their relevancy and weigh their probative value against their possible prejudicial effect. Although it is true that the probative value of gruesome photographs should be weighed against the possible prejudicial effect before they are admitted, if a photograph illustrates or makes clear some controverted issue in a homicide case, a proper foundation having been laid, it may be received, even if it is gruesome. In a homicide case, photographs of the victim, upon proper foundation, may be received in evidence for purposes of identification, to show the condition of the body, the nature and extent of wounds or injuries, and to establish malice or intent."

The defendant's judicial admission covered only the fact that he mutilated his wife's body. He did not admit he caused the skull fracture. It is clear from the testimony that exhibits 32 and 33 were made during the autopsy; one photo being taken after the scalp had been laid back and the other after the skull had been opened. The testimony showed that the head wound which occurred when the skull was fractured was not evident from casual external examination, and there was no external bleeding from the wound. These two photographs show quite clearly the depth and, to some extent, the configuration of the fracture in a way that words cannot express. These photographs would assist the jury in determining the validity of the pathologist's testimony that the fracture occurred in the way he stated it did. One photograph in particular illustrates the severity of the impact which caused the fracture. These photographs would tend to lead a layman to the conclusion that such a fracture could not be caused by a fall on wooden steps. The court would have erred if it had refused the admission of these photographs, even though the State would have no recourse had they not been received.

The picture of the torso and the blanket-wrapped body fall into the category which we believe lies within a proper judicial discretion. The picture of the torso shows the nature of the major incision and would tend to cast doubt on the defendant's statement to the psychiatrists that a purpose of the cutting was to remove a baby, which defendant believed Layne might be carrying. This photo also tended to show either the defendant's insanity or, on the other hand, the extent of his rage. The photo of the blanket-covered body was marginally relevant, but would tend to support the contention that the purpose of the fire was to conceal the crime by burning, thus casting some doubt upon the defendant's claim that the fire was set to purge the house of the evil spirit he believed was present. The admission of these last two photographs on retrial will be at the discretion of the district judge.

NOTES AND PROBLEMS

1.   What stipulation, if any, by Rowe would have blocked the admission of all four exhibits? How does a stipulation affect the analysis under Rule 403? Remember the *Old Chief* case discussed above in section C.1.

2.   The courts have been notoriously liberal — some would say cavalier — in the admission of shocking photographs. In *United States v. Bowers*, 660 F.2d 527, 529–30 (5th Cir. 1981), the court sustained the admission of a color photograph of a two-year-old child's lacerated heart. Bowers had stipulated to the cause of death, and the court acknowledged that the photograph "had the potential to inflame the jury." On occasion, in justifying the admission of gruesome photographs, courts have remarked that "[m]urder is seldom pretty" (*People v. Long*, 38 Cal. App. 3d 680, 113 Cal. Rptr. 530 (1974)) or that murder "cannot be explained in a lily-white manner." *State v. Adams*, 458 P.2d 558 (Wash. 1969), *rev'd on other grounds*, 403 U.S. 947 (1971).

3.   **Problem 13-3.** In *Hill*, the plaintiff offers into evidence photographs of burn victims in 12 other crashes involving the same make and model of Polecat automobiles struck in the rear by another vehicle, similar to the occurrence here. Argue for and against admission.

4.   **Problem 13-4.** In *Hill*, the plaintiff suffered burns over 70% of her body. In her prayer for relief, she asks for both medical expenses and damages for pain and suffering. During a two-year period, she underwent 10 complex operations, and her attorney had photographs taken of the various stages of the plaintiff's treatment. At trial, the plaintiff's primary-treating physician testifies about the operations and describes the pain which the plaintiff endured at each stage of her treatment. At the end of his direct examination, the plaintiff's attorney attempts to introduce 78

photographs depicting the various stages of the plaintiff's treatment and rehabilitation. The defense objects that the photographs are unduly gruesome and prejudicial. What result? *Washburn v. Beatt Equipment Co.*, 120 Wash. 2d 246, 840 P.2d 860 (1992) (ruling the photos admissible).

2. Experiments and Tests

Oral testimony about out-of-court experiments is often challenged under Rule 403. As we saw in the last subsection, gruesome physical evidence is normally challenged on the ground of unfair prejudice. Objections to testimony about experiments, in contrast, are usually based on a different probative danger: That of misleading the jury. To guard against that danger, most courts require that the proponent of an out-of-court experiment prove that the test conditions were substantially similar to those obtaining at the time of the relevant event. *E.g., Burchfield v. CSX Transp. Inc.*, 636 F.3d 1330, 1334–38 (11th Cir. 2011). However, courts are ordinarily lax in enforcing the substantial similarity requirement; a court is likely to admit such testimony so long as the witness can identify the differences and explain the significance of each difference to the jury.

However, there are limits to this tolerance. In *Jackson v. Fletcher*, 647 F.2d 1020 (10th Cir. 1981), the Court of Appeals held that the trial judge erred in admitting an accident reconstruction expert's testimony about a test of a tractor's stopping distance. The appellate court found "vast" differences between the circumstances at the time of the test and those at the time of the collision and stressed that those differences "cause[d] concern that the jury could have been misled. . . ." *Id.* Simiilarly, *French v. City of Springfield*, 357 N.E.2d 438, 442 (Ill. 1976) held that a "posed" movie showing the view out of the windshield of an automobile being driven past the accident scene was improperly admitted:

> This movie was taken 4 years after the incident. It was filmed in daylight, while the accident occurred at night. [O]ne of the wooden barricades involved in the accident was painted white and would reflect the headlights of an approaching vehicle. This effect was not shown in the film. The City also contends that flare pots, illuminated at night, would tend to make the barricades more visible than shown in the daylight.

NOTE

Assume that before Morena adopted the Federal Rules of Evidence, it was a well-settled common-law rule in the jurisdiction that the proponent of testimony about an out-of-court experiment was required to establish that the circumstances at the time of the experiment were "substantially similar" to those obtaining at the time of the relevant event. After the passage of the Federal Rules, may the trial judge insist on this showing as a categorical requirement? Consider the interplay between Rules 402 and 403. Hoffman, *If the Glove Don't Fit, Update the Glove: The Unplanned Obsolescence of the Substantial Similarity Standard for Experimental Evidence*, 86 NEB. L. REV. 633, 668–70 (2008) (arguing that the enactment of Rule 403 overturned the rigid substantial similarity standard enforced at common law in many jurisdictions).

3. Exhibitions

a. Jury Views

With the judge's permission, a party may exhibit objects to the jury. Some objects, however, cannot practicably be brought to the courtroom. Suppose that one of Ms. Hill's experts is going to testify about a large machine used in the manufacture of Polecat automobiles and you think it is important for the jury to be able to see the machine in order to fully understand the testimony. You are convinced that a purely oral description would be confusing if not incomprehensible, a photograph would not be much better, and a model would not impress the jury with the intimidating scale and awkwardness of the machinery. Another option is a "jury view" — taking the jury to visit the scene outside the courtroom. The rationale of the jury view doctrine is that if an object or scene cannot be brought into the courtroom, the jury can be brought to the object or scene.

A jury view implicates Rule 403 concerns because it poses severe administrative problems for a judicial system geared to the receipt of evidence in court. These problems are usually more substantial than those incident to a simple in-court exhibition. The unanticipated might occur, as in the well-known "Twilight Zone" manslaughter trial:

> [P]roducer John Landis found himself defending allegedly dangerous conditions in an outdoor Vietnam battle set where Vic Morrow and two child actors were killed in a crashing helicopter. The jurors were taken to view the actual scene of the accident. In the middle of the proceeding, a large helicopter made an unexpected fly-by. The defense moved for a mistrial, claiming that the unanticipated presence of the helicopter had a powerful emotional effect on the jurors.

Lipson, *"Real" Real Evidence*, 19 LITIG., Fall 1992, at 29, 32.

In deciding whether to grant a jury view, the judge weighs the complexity of the proposed testimony: The more complex the testimony, the greater is the likelihood that the judge will authorize a view. The judge also considers the time lapse between the incident in question and the time of the request. The longer the time lapse, the greater the likelihood is that the object or scene has changed, and the less the likely the judge will grant a view.

In *Snyder v. Massachusetts*, 291 U.S. 97 (1934), the Supreme Court held that even in a criminal case the defendant does not have a right to be present at a jury view. Presently, however, either by statute, decision, or custom in almost every jurisdiction the parties are entitled to accompany the jurors to the scene. *People v. Garcia*, 36 Cal. 4th 777, 31 Cal. Rptr. 3d 541, 115 P.3d 1191 (2005). The judge ordinarily designates a court official (such as a marshal or sheriff) to serve as the "shower." At the scene, the shower makes brief, factual, descriptive statements about the object or scene viewed. The jurors may not make their own measurements or inspection during the view. Nor may they converse at the scene with each other or with third parties. Hauck, *Jury View of Site — Help or Hindrance?*, 48 J. MO. B. 362, 367 (July–Aug. 1992) ("Comments, discussions, or arguments by jurors . . . are improper. Jurors viewing the scene should be dissuaded from making notes, taking measurements, or drawing maps or diagrams"). The traditional practice precluded receipt of testimony at the scene of the jury view, but more and more jurisdictions now permit it. Under the usual practice, the judge, court reporter, witness, and counsel accompany the parties and jury to the scene. California Code of Civil Procedure § 651(b) provides that "[t]he court shall be in session throughout the view. The proceedings at the view shall be recorded to the same extent as the proceedings in the courtroom."

NOTES

1. What is the evidentiary status of a view? Suppose that in an eminent domain case, the government's expert witness testifies that the parcel is worth $100,000 and the condemnee's expert testifies to a market value of $125,000. After viewing the parcel, the jury returns an award of $150,000. The traditional view is that the sense impressions the jurors gain at the jury view are not "evidence," at least absent a stipulation by the parties. *Noble v. Kertz & Sons Feed & Fuel Co.*, 72 Cal. App. 2d 153, 164 P.2d 257 (1945). On that premise, is the jury's verdict sustainable? Do the Federal Rules speak to this question?

2. Is it realistic to show the jury an object or scene during a view and then instruct the jury that the data gathered during the view is "not evidence"? What arguments can be made in favor of the traditional view? In a jurisdiction abandoning the traditional view, how could the appellate judges exercise control over the rationality of the jury's findings? *See Gonzalez-Perez v. Gomez-Aguila*, 296 F Supp. 2d 117, 119–20 (D. Puerto Rico 2003) (although the traditional view "is still the majority [view], . . . the momentum appears to be headed in an opposite direction. . . . It is unlikely . . . that 'jurors, confronted with testimonial evidence at odds with what they have seen, will apply the metaphysical distinction suggested and ignore the evidence of their own senses' ").

b. Displays of a Person or Parts of the Body

Exhibitions are not limited to inanimate objects. The judge may also permit the passive display of a person or a part of a person's body. Indeed, courts have gone very far in permitting displays. One of the masters of the use of physical evidence was the late Melvin Belli. *See* M. BELLI, MODERN TRIALS §§ 60.1, 60.9–13 (2d ed. 1982). As Belli noted, a "Victorian sense of modesty and indecency" formerly made trial judges reluctant to permit displays of bodily parts. Today, however, judges take "a far more practical approach" to such displays, especially when relevant to "the determination of the injuries" in a case. In *Burnett v. Caho*, 7 Ill. App. 3d 266, 285 N.E.2d 619 (1972), the plaintiff removed his artificial eye while on the witness stand. In *Sullivan v. Minneapolis, St. Paul & S.S.M. Railroad*, 55 N.D. 353, 213 N.W. 841 (1927), the plaintiff displayed an injury to a genital organ. Belli asserted that there is ample authority for the proposition that "[i]t will usually be permissible to expose the bare stump of an amputated limb to the jury in any case involving an amputation."

An exhibition may also consist of a simple display of a person to the jury. Suppose that in a paternity case at the time of trial, the child is seven months old. In the plaintiff's mind, the child bears a striking resemblance to the putative father. Should the judge permit the plaintiff to display the baby to the jury as evidence of the defendant's paternity? Courts are badly divided on this issue. Some routinely permit the display; others just as routinely forbid it. Many will permit the display if the child is old enough to have "settled" facial features. Suppose that, in the defense attorney's opinion, there are obvious racial differences between the child and the putative father. In this situation, the courts generally agree that a display is allowable. Do you think that the widespread use of DNA evidence will ultimately eliminate exhibitions in paternity cases?

4. Demonstrations

In an exhibition, the attorney passively displays the object to the jurors. In a demonstration, in contrast, the attorney shows the jury some process in action. For instance, in our torts case, Ms. Hill's attorney might conclude that it would be helpful if the jury understood how a gas injection system functions. Whereas an oral description of a complex object may be marginally adequate, a purely oral description of a complex, multistep *process* is almost always confusing to jurors. Hence, there may be an even greater need for a demonstration in these situations than there is for an exhibition. In one medical malpractice case, using latex models of the colon, cecum, appendix, and peritoneum, the defendant doctor reenacted an appendectomy on a small platform before the jurors. O'Reilly, *Defending a Doctor Against All Odds*, 72 A.B.A. J. 44, 45 (1986).

As with a request for an exhibition, a request for a demonstration is committed to the judge's discretion and the usual Rule 403 considerations apply. The judge will typically insist that the proponent demonstrate that the conditions for the in-court demonstration are substantially similar to those that prevailed at the time of the relevant event. The typical demonstration entails more difficulties than a mere display of a person or object but fewer problems than a jury view. The following problems highlight some factors that the judge normally should consider in addition to the purely logistical difficulties.

PROBLEM AND QUESTION

1.   Problem 13-5. In our torts case, Ms. Hill claims that as a result of the accident, she no longer has a full range of motion in her left arm. What would be the best way to show that injury to the jury? What objection should the defense attorney raise? How can the opponent effectively cross-examine to attack the demonstration? What other methods of attack are available to Polecats' attorney?

2.   Problem 13-6. In *Hill*, suppose that the plaintiff contends that as a result of the collision her hand has hardened and become immovable. Her attorney requests permission to have each juror grasp the plaintiff's hand. As trial judge, would you grant the request? *See* Madeira, *Lashing Reason to the Mast: Understanding Judicial Constraints on Emotion in Personal Injury Litigation*, 40 U.C. Davis L. Rev. 137, 148 (2006) (some courts fear that this kind of evidence "brings the trier of fact too close to the experience of an injury"; these courts attempt to maintain a "distance" between the plaintiff's injured body and the trier of fact). *But see Curry* *v. American Enka, Inc.*, 452 F. Supp. 178, 180–82 (E.D. Tenn. 1977) (permissible in the judge's discretion).

Chapter 14

EVIDENCE OF CHARACTER, HABIT, AND OTHER ACTS AND TRANSACTIONS

Read Federal Rules of Evidence 404–406, 412–415.

In the previous chapter, we looked at the general framework used to analyze the admissibility of otherwise logically relevant evidence whose probative value is arguably outweighed by one of the countervailing concerns of unfair prejudice, misleading the jury, confusion of issues, or waste of time. As noted in that discussion, several other rules of evidence — and in particular those that follow Rule 403 in Article IV of the Federal Rules of Evidence — are actually specific applications of that framework in which the balancing has, in effect, already been done. Thus, the Rules have determined that particular kinds of evidence, when used for certain purposes, are unfairly prejudicial in light of their probative value. In this chapter, we turn to perhaps the most important set of rules concerned with the danger of unfair prejudice: The rules dealing with evidence of character, habit, and other acts or transactions.

A. CHARACTER EVIDENCE

Though it is often said that evidence of character is inadmissible, there are many instances in which character evidence — or evidence that looks a lot like character evidence — will be admitted. For example, judges typically permit the proponent of a witness to elicit briefly the witness's description of his or her personal background. In the words of one court, "reasonable background information about a witness is always admissible, precisely because it allows the jury to make better informed judgments about the credibility of a witness. . . ." *U.S. v. McVeigh*, 153 F.3d 1166, 1202 (10th Cir. 1998), *cert. denied*, 526 U.S. 1007 (1999). Most judges thus permit witnesses to testify to neutral facts about employment and education. On the other hand, evidence law does impose real limits on both the proponent's ability to introduce evidence of a person's good character and the opponent's right to present bad character evidence.

1. Character as Direct Evidence

This section discusses two fundamental questions that must be answered in order to assess the admissibility of evidence that raises a character inference: (1) Whether character is in issue; and (2) whether the proponent has used an appropriate method of proof.

a. When Is Character Itself in Issue?

Chapter 8 discussed the difference between direct and circumstantial evidence. An item of evidence is directly relevant when the immediate inference from the evidence is the existence or nonexistence of a material fact. In certain rare cases, the character of a party to a lawsuit will be one of those material facts under Rule 401. In such cases, proof of character is an end in itself and character is said to be "directly in issue." If you were to visualize a box containing all the facts of consequence under Rule 401, the character trait itself would be inside the box.

Consider these examples: A newspaper publishes an editorial charging that a politician is "an habitual liar and thief." The politician sues the newspaper for libel, and the newspaper raises the affirmative defense of truth. When the newspaper files its answer setting out that affirmative defense, the truth of the charge (the politician's character for honesty, that is, whether she is "an habitual liar and thief") is added to the range of issues in dispute in the case under Rule 401. Or assume that a truck strikes a pedestrian and the injured pedestrian sues both the employee driver and the employer. The complaint alleges that the employer is vicariously liable on a *respondeat superior* theory (permitting the recovery of compensatory damages) and that the employer was guilty of negligent entrustment (supporting a recovery of punitive damages). On the second count, the complaint alleges that the employee "is a careless driver," that the employer should have realized the employee was a careless driver, and that the employer was negligent in entrusting such a dangerous instrumentality as a large truck to a careless driver. The second count's allegation that the employee "*is* a careless driver" makes the employee's character trait as a careless driver a material fact that is directly "in issue" in the case.

NOTES

1. Suppose Mr. and Mrs. Hill were going through a divorce and fighting over custody of their children. Section 33 of the Morena Family Law Statutes provides that in custody disputes, the judge must consider "the interests of the child" and award custody to "the party more fit to be a parent." Would Ms. Hill's character be an ultimate issue in the custody dispute?

2. Some of the "offenses" in juvenile court are "status" offenses such as the status of being a delinquent or a person in need of supervision (PINS). *In re Dennis J.*, 72 Cal. App. 3d 755, 761, 140 Cal. Rptr. 463, 466 (1977). When a juvenile is alleged to be a PINS, is the juvenile's character in issue? (In subsection 2, we shall soon see why true "status" offenses are peculiar to juvenile court.)

b. If So, What Methods of Proof Are Admissible?

If proof of character is permissible, how would a party go about proving a person's character trait? There are usually said to be three possible ways to prove character: Reputation; opinion, and specific instances of conduct. Think about what you would do if you were considering doing business with someone and were interested in her character for honesty, or if you were contemplating dating someone and were interested in his character for faithfulness. You would probably rely on the person's reputation within some relevant community as to the particular trait. You might also ask the opinion of people who know the person. And you would be interested in hearing about prior occasions when the person did something that seemed to demonstrate that character trait. All three types of evidence are relevant to prove a person's character, but all three are not necessarily admissible in court for that purpose. Federal Rule of Evidence 405 governs the question and provides that when character itself is in issue, all three methods of proof are permitted: reputation, opinion, and specific instances of conduct. The Advisory Committee's Note adds that this view is the "conventional contemporary common law doctrine."

In contrast, when character is used circumstantially, there are severe restrictions on the available methods of proof. When you have reviewed the next section of this chapter, ask yourself whether the difference between direct and circumstantial use of character justifies the disparity in methods of proof.

2. Character as Circumstantial Evidence of the Conduct of a Party

In the overwhelming majority of cases, character evidence is offered as circumstantial proof of the person's conduct. Proof of character is not an end in itself; rather, the end objective is proving conduct on a particular occasion relevant in the case, and character is merely employed as a means to that end. The only fact within the Rule 401 box is the conduct. In the words of Federal Rule of Evidence 404(a), the proponent proves character and then invites the jury to infer that on the occasion in question, the person "acted in accordance with the character or trait."

In the leading Supreme Court precedent, *Michelson v. United States*, 335 U.S. 469 (1948), Justice Jackson explained this theory of circumstantial relevance: "[T]he defendant may introduce affirmative testimony that the general estimate of his character is so favorable that the jury may infer that he would not be likely to commit the offense charged." The proponent argues that the party is not the *type* of person who is likely to perform that *type* of act. In closing argument, the defense counsel might tell the jury: "Consider all the testimony showing what a peaceful person Mr. Devitt is. Ladies and gentlemen, he's simply not the type of person who would commit the brutal, violent crime that he's charged with."

Although *Michelson* sanctions the use of character evidence, common-law courts were notably reluctant to admit this type of evidence. Federal Rule of Evidence 404(a) reflects the traditional hostility toward character evidence. A powerful case can be made for the hostility.

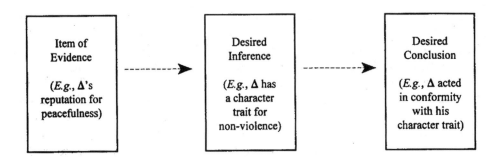

Consider the above diagram. When the proponent of character evidence uses the theory of logical relevance depicted in the diagram, he or she invites the jury to draw this ultimate inference: This particular character trait makes it more probable that the defendant acted "in character" — consistently with the trait — on the occasion in question. There are obvious risks in inviting the jury to engage in this reasoning process.

The first inferential step presents a classic example of Bentham's risk of "misdecision," discussed in Chapter 13. Initially the jury must consciously focus on the type of person the defendant is. When the defendant has a long criminal record or violent past, there is a grave risk that at least at the subconscious level the jurors will be tempted to penalize him for his antisocial past. In short, they may punish the defendant for his or her past or status rather than because they are convinced beyond a reasonable doubt that the defendant committed the charged act. Punishing the defendant for his or her status would violate the Eighth Amendment. *See Robinson v. California*, 370 U.S. 660 (1962) (in adult prosecutions, the prohibition of cruel and unusual punishment precludes status offenses).

After deciding the type of person the defendant is, the jury must decide whether to treat the defendant's character as proof of his or her conduct on a specific occasion. At this step, there is the danger that the trier of fact will overestimate the probative value of character evidence. The following article defends the traditional hostility to character evidence by examining psychological studies that show that people indeed tend to overvalue such evidence. In the past, many psychologists subscribed to the theory that a person's general traits are highly influential in determining his or her conduct. However, more recent situationist research has undercut that theory.

Mendez, *California's New Law on Character Evidence: Having Code Section 352 and the Impact of Recent Psychological Studies*
31 Ucla L. Rev. 1003, 1045–53 (1984)

. . . Psychologists have found that people give greater weight to unfavorable, unpleasant or socially derogatory information about a person than to information of equal intensity but of a positive dimension.[227] . . . Thus, although both sides may

---

[227] *See, e.g.*, Hamilton & Huffman, *Generality of Impression — Formation Processes for Evaluative*

introduce character evidence, the jury is likely to place more weight on the prosecution's evidence of bad conduct or untrustworthiness than on the accused's countervailing evidence. A prior conviction, for example, will be likely to impress the jury in a way that the accused cannot counteract by evidence of a pardon or of having led a blameless life since the conviction.

Perhaps the factor that most induces jurors to overestimate the probative value of character evidence is what psychologists term the "halo effect."[233] In the present context it might be more aptly called the "devil's horns effect." The term refers to the propensity of people to judge others on the basis of one outstanding "good" or "bad" quality. This propensity may stem from a tendency to overestimate the unity of personality to see others as consistent, simple beings whose behavior in a given situation is readily predictable.[235] Gustav Ichheiserhas described the effects of this need to oversimplify

> [The mental processes] function so as to transcend in many ways and many directions the pure raw material and to construct out of this material a more or less well-organized and integrated image of the given personality.

This oversimplification, says Ichheiser, magnifies the impact of character evidence, even when the evidence is barely probative, if at all:

> A man is under suspicion of murder. During the investigation certain definite abnormalities of his sexual behavior come to light, even though there is no evidence that they are related in any way to the committed murder. Again, the frequent reaction in many people, if verbalized, would read something like this: "This man whose sexual life deviates so strangely from the norm can also be expected to deviate from other social norms in any other respect."

Early psychological theories supported the intuition that character evidence was predictive of behavior. Gordon Allport . . . helped formulate the theory that "traits" are "the fundamental dispositions of personality." "Trait theory" essentially holds that the behavior of a given individual is governed by personality traits that exert sufficient influence to produce generally consistent behavior in widely divergent situations.[264] Subsequent empirical research, however, has not only failed to validate trait theory but has generally rejected it.[265]

Instead, the research shows that behavior is largely shaped by specific situational determinants that do not lend themselves easily to predictions about individual behavior. Mischel, a leading exponent of the new theory of specificity, explains:

---

and Nonevaluative Judgments, 20 J. PERSONALITY & SOC. PSYCHOLOGY 200, 201, 204 (1971); . . . .

[233] *See* G. ALLPORT, PERSONALITY — A PSYCHOLOGICAL INTERPRETATION 5521 (1937).

[235] Ichheiser, *Misunderstandings in Human Relations — A Study in False Social Perception*, 55 AM. J. SOC. 27–28 (Supp. 1949).

[264] *See id.* at 289; H. EYSENCK, THE STRUCTURE OF HUMAN PERSONALITY 3 (1970); W. MISCHEL, PERSONALITY AND ASSESSMENT 6 (1968).

[265] Burton, *Generality of Honesty Reconsidered*, 70 PSYCHOLOGY REV. 481, 482 (1963).

First, behavior depends on stimulus situations and is specific to the situation: response patterns even in highly similar situations often fail to be strongly related. Individuals show far less cross-situational consistency in their behavior than has been assumed by trait-state theories. The more dissimilar the evoking situations, the less likely they are to lead to similar or consistent responses from the *same* individual. *Even seemingly trivial situational differences may reduce correlations to zero.* [268]

These findings threaten the basic assumptions about the probative value of character evidence. If even seeming trivial situational differences can render behavioral predictions totally invalid, then character evidence may possess little or no probative value. From this psychological perspective, evidence that a witness has been convicted of a felony involving dishonesty or has cheated on his taxes . . . may not tell us anything about whether he was truthful on the stand.[269] Likewise, evidence that the accused was engaged in an altercation after a New Year's Eve party may tell us nothing about his behavior during a peace demonstration. As Mischel emphasizes, "The assessor who tries to predict the future without detailed information about the exact environmental conditions influencing the individual's criterion behavior may be more engaged in the process of hoping than of predicting."[270] Indeed, the work of Mischel and other psychologists, including Allport who acknowledged the weaknesses of his original theory,[271] has moved one legal commentator to conclude that "the theory of behavior that was so compatible with the [lay] notions about character [has] ceased to have *any* scientific recognition."[272]

---

[268] Mischel, *supra* n. 264, at 177 (emphasis added).

[269] *See, e.g.*, the studies of Hugh Hartshorne and Mark May examining the propensity of school children to deceive. Although they concluded their research over fifty years ago, their findings were remarkably similar to Mischel's:

> What we actually observed is that the honesty or dishonesty of a child in one situation is related to his honesty or dishonesty in another situation mainly to the degree that the situations have factors in common. For example, a child may cheat on his arithmetic test and ten minutes later, in the same room, under the same examiner, under the same general conditions, be perfectly honest in a spelling test. In like manner, he may be dishonest in all classroom situations but be perfectly honest in his dealing with his fellow pupils in the playground or at party games. Indeed, the most striking thing about the conduct of children is the amount of *inconsistency* exhibited. If we call perfect consistency one hundred and perfect inconsistency zero, the average consistency score . . . is only twenty, and there are a great many more scores between twenty and zero, than there are between twenty and one hundred.

H. HARTSHORNE, CHARACTER IN HUMAN RELATIONS 209 (1932) (emphasis added). Not surprisingly, they concluded by rejecting the validity of trait theory in these situations: "The results of these studies show that neither deceit nor its opposite, 'honesty,' are [sic] unified character traits, but rather specific functions of life situations. . . . Lying, cheating, and stealing as measured by the test situations used in these studies are only *very loosely* related." H. HARTSHORNE & M. MAY, STUDIES IN THE NATURE OF CHARACTER — STUDIES IN DECEIT 411 (1928) (emphasis added). These studies, of course, involved children in school situations, not adults in the formalized surroundings of the courtroom, but the doubts raised are at least disturbing.

[270] W. MISCHEL, *supra* note 264, at 140.

[271] Allport, *Traits Revisited*, 21 AM. PSYCHOLOGIST 1, 9 (1966).

[272] Lawson, *Credibility and Character: A Different Look at an Interminable Problem*, 50 NOTRE DAME L. REV. 758, 783 (1975) (emphasis in original).

NOTES

1.   Some commentators contend that even when the inference is a propensity on the defendant's part, it is not necessarily the type of propensity that should trigger the character evidence prohibition. Leonard, *The Use of Uncharged Misconduct Evidence to Prove Knowledge*, 81 NEB. L. REV. 115, 123, 126, 151, 167 (2002). It might not be a propensity to engage in criminal or discreditable conduct. Palmer, *The Scope of the Similar Fact Rule*, 16 ADELAIDE L. REV. 161, 163 (1994). Though any propensity inference poses the danger of reasoning prejudice — the risk that the jury will overestimate the propensity as proof of conduct on the occasion in question — however in these cases, there is little or no risk of *moral* prejudice, that is, the jury's revulsion at the prior conduct. *Id.* at 171–72. That moral prejudice has been described as "the chief reason" for the character evidence prohibition. *Id.* at 177. In practice, proponents usually overlook the possibility of making this alternative argument. When the argument has been advanced, the courts have split. *Id.* at 178–80. Whatever the policy merits of the alternative argument, does the wording of Rule 404 allow the proponent to rely on the argument? Does "character" have a moral connotation?

2.   While Professor Mendez defends the conventional character rule, other commentators have criticized the orthodox view. Laypersons routinely rely on character reasoning in everyday decision-making. Uviller, *Evidence of Character to Prove Conduct: Illusion, Illogic, and Injustice in the Courtroom*, 130 U. PA. L. REV. 845, 883, 890 (1982). Moreover, other commentators argue that the psychological literature lends itself to more nuanced readings. In Leonard, *The Use of Character to Prove Conduct: Rationality and Catharsis in the Law of Evidence*, 58 U. COLO. L. REV. 1 (1986–87), Professor Leonard generally supports Professor Mendez' position but notes that the modern understanding is that, for some persons, character is an excellent predictor of conduct in specific situations. In Crump, *How Should We Treat Character Evidence Offered to Prove Conduct*, 58 U. COLO. L. REV. 279, 283 (1987), Professor Crump sharply disputes Professor Mendez' position, arguing that "social science is by no means monolithic in condemning trait theory. Modern textbooks for college courses teach Allport's view without categorically rejecting it, and they suggest that a modern trait theory might have considerable validity. Although the addition of situational factors may enhance the validity, the literature suggests an ambivalence toward both trait and situation theory." Likewise, Davies, *Evidence of Character to Prove Conduct: A Reassessment of Relevancy*, 27 CRIM. L. BULL. 504 (Nov.–Dec. 1991) challenges Professor Mendez' position. She points out that just as situationism supplanted trait theory, interactionism is now replacing situationism. Interactionists are of the view that, given a large sample of a person's prior conduct in very similar situations, a reliable prediction of the person's behavior in an analogous setting is possible. Since the publication of Ms. Davies' article, support for interactionism has grown in the field of psychology.

Although Rule 404(a) codifies the traditional prohibition against character evidence, the Rule sets out several exceptions to the prohibition. The following subsections address these exceptions.

a.   Circumstantial Character Evidence in Criminal Cases

The Traditional Approach — At the Defendant's Election

Under Federal Rule of Evidence 404(a)(2)(C), the defendant can elect to introduce evidence of his good character, which then "opens the door" to contrary evidence by the prosecutor. The choice is the defendant's. *United States v. Gilliland*, 586 F.2d 1384 (10th Cir. 1978). Furthermore, as we shall see later in this chapter, by virtue of a 2000 amendment to Rule 404(a)(2)(c), the defendant also opens the door to prosecution evidence of character by introducing evidence of the same character trait of the alleged victim of the charged offense.

Customarily, the defendant "opens" the issue by calling a witness to give reputation or opinion testimony regarding the defendant's good character. The defendant could testify to his or her own good reputation in the community, but the defendant is such an obviously biased source for the testimony that the testimony is virtually self-impeaching. Hence, the accused usually calls third parties as defense witnesses to give the character testimony. The defendant may even trigger the 404(a)(2)(C) exception by attempting to elicit favorable evidence during the cross-examination of prosecution witnesses. *Franklin v. State*, 303 S.E.2d 22 (Ga. 1983).

Under Rule 404(a)(2)(A), a witness may testify only to a *"pertinent trait"* of the defendant's character. (emphasis added). This language seems to limit the defendant to testimony about specific character traits. Some jurisdictions, such as California, explicitly permit the defendant to introduce evidence of specific relevant character traits or general, moral, law-abiding character.

NOTES AND PROBLEMS

1.   If character evidence has as little probative value as Professor Mendez contends, why permit even the defense to introduce character evidence? Consider whether the probative dangers implicated by character evidence are more likely to disadvantage the prosecution or the defense. If the defendant is the more likely victim of those risks, perhaps it makes sense to permit the defendant to waive the character evidence ban. The Advisory Committee's Note to Rule 404(a) states that the rule "is so deeply embedded in our jurisprudence as to assume almost constitutional proportions and to override doubts of the basic relevancy of the evidence."

2.   The Rule states that the defendant may present evidence of a "pertinent" character trait. In this context, what does "pertinent" mean? What traits are pertinent in a battery prosecution such as the *Devitt* case? A larceny prosecution? What if the defendant raises an entrapment defense? A prosecution for obstructing an official proceeding? *United States v. Yarbrough*, 527 F.3d 1092, 1100–01 (10th Cir. 2008) (relevant to introduce character evidence of the defendant's integrity and status as a law-abiding police officer). A perjury prosecution?

3.   **Problem 14-1.** In *Devitt*, at the outset of his direct examination the defendant testifies to the following facts: He has always lived in El Dorado; he went

to grammar and high school in El Dorado; immediately after graduating from high school, he went to work for Ganesh Fixit and Carpentry; he has worked there for seven years and now holds the title of assistant manager; he is married; and he and his wife have three children. While each of these facts standing alone appears to be neutral background information, cumulatively the facts create the impression that Devitt is a stable, responsible family person — the type of person who would be unlikely to commit an unprovoked battery. After this testimony, may the prosecutor attack Devitt's character? *See Wilson v. Vermont Castings*, 977 F. Supp. 691, 699 (M.D. Pa. 1997) ("Information about a party or a witness' background, job and education is certainly appropriate and admissible in every action. Juries cannot make assessment of credibility in a vacuum. Such information gives background on the witness and a point of reference in assessing that individual's credibility"), *aff'd*, 170 F.3d 391 (3d Cir. 1999).

4.   Problem 14-2. In *Devitt*, on direct examination the defendant goes on at length about his battlefield decorations from Afghanistan and his position with the local Episcopal church. (As we shall see, even when the defendant places his or her character in issue, the defendant ordinarily may not introduce specific instances of good conduct. Hence, the prosecutor could have objected to this testimony.) After the defendant's testimony, may the prosecutor attack the defendant's character? Think back to the concept of curative admissibility discussed in Chapter 8. Is this problem distinguishable from Problem 14-1?

The FRE Approach: Rules 413-14 — The Abolition of the Defendant's Veto

Under the traditional view, in effect the defendant has the power to veto the use of his or her character as circumstantial evidence of conduct at trial. Federal Rules 413 and 414 are recent statutory innovations that depart from the traditional approach. (Rule 415 further extends the practice to civil cases.) Under these Rules, the prosecution may offer evidence of a defendant's similar sexual assaults or child molestations to prove "any matter to which it is relevant." Under Rule 401, such acts are logically "relevant" as circumstantial proof to establish the defendant's commission of the charged *actus reus*. Unlike Rule 404(a), this type of evidence can be admitted during the prosecution case-in-chief; there is no requirement that the defendant "open the door" to consideration of his character for this purpose. The rules provide:

Federal Rule of Evidence 413. Similar Crimes in Sexual Assault Cases.

(a)   Permitted Uses. In a criminal case in which the defendant is accused of a sexual assault, the court may admit evidence that the defendant committed any other sexual assault. The evidence may be considered on any matter to which it is relevant.

Federal Rule of Evidence 414. Similar Crimes in Child Molestation Cases.

(a)   Permitted Uses. In a criminal case in which the defendant is accused of child molestation, the court may admit evidence that the defendant committed any other child molestation. The evidence may be considered on any matter to which it is relevant.

Note the operative phrase in each subdivision: "may admit." The wording raises the question of whether the judge can exercise Rule 403 discretion to exclude evidence that is otherwise admissible under Rule 413 or 414. In Rule 609(a)(2), when the drafters wanted to make it clear that certain types of convictions were automatically admissible for impeachment, they used the verb "shall." Under a strict textualist approach, these rules may be ambiguous enough to permit the court to resort to extrinsic legislative history material. When the Justice Department initially submitted the rules, they were accompanied by a statement which explicitly noted that judges could continue to exercise their Rule 403 discretion under the proposed rules. All the lower federal courts have ruled that trial judges retain their Rule 403 discretion to exclude evidence otherwise admissible under Rules 413–15. *E.g., United States v. Meacham*, 115 F.3d 1488, 1492 (10th Cir. 1997).

NOTES

1.   Rules 413 and 414 single out prosecutions for sexual assault and child molestation. Is it defensible to divest defendants accused of those crimes of the protection of the traditional rules excluding character evidence? In a 1984 Bureau of Justice Statistics study, the respondents rated rape and child abuse as the second and third most serious — and potentially most repulsive — crimes. THE SEVERITY OF CRIME, BUREAU OF JUST. STATISTICS BULL. (Jan. 1984). In a 1989 study conducted by the Bureau of Justice Statistics, the recidivism rate for rape was the second lowest. Bryden & Park, *"Other Crimes" Evidence in Sex Offense Cases*, 78 MINN. L. REV. 529, 572 (1994). In short, the crimes singled out by these rules appear to present the probative dangers inspiring the character evidence rules to a greater degree than crimes still subject to the character evidence prohibition. Both the United States Judicial Conference and the A.B.A. House of Delegates went on record as opposing the promulgation of Rules 413–14. Congress thought otherwise.

2.   On the other hand, it may be that the adoption of Rules 413 and 414 were not as radical a break from historical practice as they might at first appear. Prior to the adoption of the Federal Rules, many states recognized a "lustful disposition" exception to the character evidence prohibition which allowed evidence of prior sex crimes in sexual assault prosecutions. Reed, *Reading Gaol Revisited: Admission of Uncharged Misconduct Evidence in Sex Offender Cases*, 21 AM. J. CRIM. L. 127 (1993). Indeed, the legislative history of Rules 413 and 414 suggests that the drafters were concerned that states adopting the Federal Rules of Evidence might otherwise abolish their lustful disposition exceptions. In addition, so-called "date- or acquaintance-rape" cases often boil down to "He said, she said." In that context, there is an argument that the evidence has special relevance:

> If two other women . . . accuse [the defendant] of date rape, he may be able to raise . . . doubts about each of their individual accounts. . . . If one considers all three accusations together, however, and no reason exists to suspect collaboration among the accusers, each of the charges will corroborate the others' to a much greater degree than in cases involving eyewitness identifications derived from "mugshot books" of rapists. Although it

remains conceivable that the defendant is innocent of the crime charged, the danger of an erroneous conviction appears to be less in this sort of case than in many ordinary criminal trials.

Bryden & Park, *supra*, at 577.

3.   A group of states, including Arizona, California, Illinois, Indiana, and Missouri, have followed the lead of the federal drafters and carved out exceptions to the character evidence prohibition in child molestation cases. *See, e.g.*, CAL. EVID. CODE §§ 1108–09; IND. STAT. ANN. § 35-37-4-15; MO. REV. STAT. § 566.025. Two state courts have invalidated such statutes under their respective state constitutions. *State v. Cox*, 781 N.W.2d 757 (Iowa 2010); *State v. Burns*, 978 S.W.2d 759 (Mo. 1998). However, apart from those two instances, state courts have uniformly upheld the constitutionality of these statutes. *United States v. Mound*, 149 F.3d 799 (8th Cir. 1998), *cert. denied*, 525 U.S. 1089 (1999).

1)   What Methods of Proof Are Permissible?

Defense Evidence

As we have seen, the defendant normally has the choice whether to open up the issue of his or her character. If the defendant chooses to do so, what kind of evidence may he introduce to prove his character? Consider the example of evidence presented during the inquest following the famous shootout at the O.K. Corral, Wyatt Earp filed an affidavit signed by several leading citizens of Dodge City. In part, it read:

> We, the undersigned citizens of Dodge City, . . . Kansas, . . . certify that we are personally acquainted with Wyatt Earp, late of this city; that he came here in 1876; that during the years of 1877, 1878, and 1879, he was Marshal of our city; that he left our place in the fall of 1879; that during his whole stay here he . . . was regarded and looked upon as a high-minded, honorable citizen; and while kind and courteous to all, he was brave, unflinching, and on all occasions proved himself the right man in the right place. Hearing that he is now under arrest, charged with . . . the killing of those men termed "Cow Boys," from our knowledge of him we do not believe that he would wantonly take the life of his fellow men, and that if he was implicated, he only took life in the discharge of his sacred trust to the people. . . .

Notice that the affidavit contains a mix of reputation and opinion. The affiants state that they "are personally acquainted with" the defendant and that from their "knowledge of him" they do not believe the charged act is in keeping with his character. This is opinion evidence. They also state that Earp "was regarded and looked upon" as having a high character, which is evidence in the form of reputation.

The classic article analyzing the permissible methods for using character as circumstantial evidence of conduct under the common law was written by Dean Mason Ladd, Professor Carlson's late co-author. Ladd, *Techniques and Theory of Character Testimony*, 24 IOWA L. REV. 498 (1939). Dean Ladd noted that the common law did not authorize the proponent to introduce specific acts to prove character.

The rationale was the fear that if "the law were to permit proof of the bad acts [and then] allow those be countered by showing the good deeds . . . , all trials would become burdened with confusion and be endlessly prolonged." That fear, of course, is a consideration cognizable under both the common-law legal irrelevance doctrine and Federal Rule of Evidence 403.

Dean Ladd then pointed out that the traditional common-law view also excluded evidence of opinion as to the person's character thus permitting proof of character only by evidence of reputation. Ladd joined Wigmore in criticizing the exclusion of opinion evidence. He argued that while it could be highly probative of character, opinion testimony presented less risk of undue time consumption than evidence of specific acts. He applauded an incipient trend toward explicitly permitting the admission of opinion testimony about character.

Finally, Dean Ladd described reputation as "the general concurrence of a great number of people reflecting the sentiment" about a person. In his judgment, as aggregate hearsay, reputation was less trustworthy than opinion testimony. Dean Ladd approved, though, of the expansion of the concept of "community" beyond just the local residential neighborhood to include churches, lodges, police departments, and businesses.

Dean Ladd's article was influential in the drafting Federal Rules of Evidence 404 and 405 governing character evidence. Cleary, *Mason Ladd*, 66 Iowa L. Rev. 701, 702–08 (1981). Rule 405 specifies the permissible methods of proof where character evidence is admissible. The Rule retains the traditional common-law ban on specific instances of conduct where character is not directly in issue. Not only is a character witness forbidden from testifying directly to specific acts; a character witness testifying to an opinion may not even cite specific instances of conduct on direct examination for the limited purpose of showing the basis of the opinion. However, the restrictions on reputation and opinion were relaxed, and both are permitted under Rule 405(a). In addition the courts have continued to expand the meaning of "community," for purposes of reputation testimony, gradually broadening the meaning of the term to include any substantial social group in which the person is likely to have a settled reputation. *United States v. Mandel*, 591 F.2d 1347 (4th Cir. 1979) (a particular law office); *O'Bryan v. State*, 591 S.W.2d 464 (Tex. Crim. App. 1979) (a business circle); *Freeman v. State*, 132 Ga. App. 742, 209 S.E.2d 127, 130–31 (1974) (church congregation).

NOTES AND PROBLEMS

1   **Problem 14-3.** In *Devitt*, the defendant is a student at a university and offers evidence of his campus reputation. Would that be admissible? *United States v. Oliver*, 492 F.2d 943, 945–47 (8th Cir. 1974) (yes), *cert. denied*, 424 U.S. 973 (1976). What additional facts would you like to know? Would it be relevant that Devitt was a senior rather than a freshman? Would it be helpful to know the size of the student body?

2   **Problem 14-4.** If you had a witness prepared to testify to Devitt's reputation for peacefulness in El Dorado, what foundational questions would you have to ask?

3 Problem 14-5. If you were going to present favorable opinion testimony about Devitt, what foundation would you have to lay? How does the reputation foundation differ from the opinion foundation? Does a reputation witness have to personally know the defendant? Must an opinion witness?

4 Should expert testimony regarding a person's character be admissible? *See People v. Stoll*, 49 Cal. 3d 1136, 265 Cal. Rptr. 111, 783 P.2d 698 (1989) (yes); *contra United States v. Webb*, 625 F.2d 709, 710–11 (5th Cir. 1980). The Advisory Committee Note to Rule 405 alludes to "the opinion of [a] psychiatrist based upon examination and testing." However, the Congressional hearings and committee reports do not reflect any realization that the adoption of Rule 405 would open the door to expert opinions or any appreciation of the special problems posed by expert opinions. 22 C. WRIGHT & K. GRAHAM. FEDERAL PRACTICE AND PROCEDURE: EVIDENCE § 5265, at 588–95 (1978). Is the statutory text broad enough to permit the receipt of expert as well as lay testimony?

5 Problem 14-6. At his trial, Devitt chooses to testify. On direct examination, the defense attorney attempts to elicit Devitt's testimony that he, Devitt, has never before been charged with or even arrested for a crime. The prosecutor objects that this "is an improper method of proving character." What ruling? *Compare Government of the Virgin Islands v. Grant*, 775 F.2d 508, 511–13 (3d Cir. 1985) (inadmissible), *with United States v. Blackwell*, 853 F.2d 86, 87–88 (2d Cir. 1988) (admissible though of "relatively low probative value"). Is Devitt attempting to smuggle in evidence of specific good acts? *Grant* appears to be the prevailing view.

Prosecution evidence.

Once the defendant has opened the door by offering evidence of his own good character, the prosecutor may rebut the defense evidence. During the rebuttal, the prosecutor can respond in kind with rebuttal testimony by adverse reputation and opinion witnesses. The courts generally apply the same rules to character evidence introduced during the prosecution's rebuttal that they do to evidence admitted during the defense case-in-chief; reputation and opinion testimony must satisfy the same foundational requirements as defense evidence, and prosecution witnesses may not testify on direct examination to specific instances of conduct.

The slippery problem, though, is prosecution cross-examination of *defense* character witnesses. In addition to calling bad character witnesses during its rebuttal, the prosecution may cross-examine the defense's good character witnesses. In doing so, the prosecution is permitted to ask the witness about relevant specific acts. If the witness is aware of acts of the defendant that are contrary to the character to which the witness has testified, this undermines the credibility of the witness's testimony.

NOTES

1. Think about the scenario just described, in which the prosecutor cross-examines the defendant's character witness by asking whether he or she is aware of specific acts that are inconsistent with the good character trait. What is its impeachment value if the witness answers yes? How does that answer reflect on the

soundness of the witness's standard for assessing good reputation or in forming his or her opinion? What is its impeachment value if the witness answers no? How does that answer reflect on the extent of the witness's knowledge of the defendant's reputation or the basis for his or her opinion? What sort of limiting instruction should the judge give the jury? Consider who is being impeached — is it the defendant or the defense character witness?

As trial judge, would you permit the prosecutor to make the following closing argument if the character witness denied hearing the report?

> On cross-examination I asked Mr. Stacey, the defendant's character witness, whether he'd heard that three years ago the defendant was convicted of a battery. Mr. Stacey answered that he'd never heard such a report. Think about that answer. Mr. Stacey expects you to believe that he knows the defendant's reputation for peacefulness well, but he's never heard a report about a battery conviction three years ago. A battery is a violent crime. A battery is just plain inconsistent with the defendant's supposedly peaceful reputation. Yet Stacey claims that he never heard of the report. That answer tells you that Stacey really doesn't know the defendant's reputation. If he knew the defendant's reputation as well as he claims, he certainly would have heard that report.

Would you allow the following closing argument if the character witness admitted hearing the report?

> Think about that answer. On the one hand, Stacey testifies that the defendant has a good reputation for peacefulness, and he expects you to believe that he — Stacey — is a good judge of character. On the other hand, he admits that he's heard that the defendant was convicted of battery a mere three years ago. Ladies and gentlemen, Mr. Stacey must have a pretty strange standard for deciding whether someone has a good reputation for peacefulness. When a person is reported to have been convicted of a battery, most reasonable people would say that that person has a terrible reputation for peacefulness. But not Mr. Stacey. Either he has a weird standard for judging character, or he's a biased witness. In either case, you just can't trust Stacey's testimony.

2.   At early common law, just as the courts uniformly permitted the "Have you heard . . .?" form of cross-examination, they almost unanimously condemned the "Do you know . . .?" form. At first blush, this might seem to be a nonsensical distinction. However, remember that these courts began with a premise that the only proper form of direct examination was reputation testimony and not opinion testimony. Is the "Have you heard?" form in some sense a corollary of the reputation form of direct examination? As the courts began to accept opinion testimony on direct examination, they also increasingly sanctioned the "Do you know?" form of cross-examination.

3.   What position do the Federal Rules take on the proper form of the prosecutor's questions on cross-examination? Consider both the last sentence in Rule 405(a) and this paragraph in the Advisory Committee's Note:

According to the great majority of cases, on cross-examination inquiry is allowable as to whether the reputation witness has heard of particular instances of conduct pertinent to the trait in question. *Michelson v. United States*, 335 U.S. 469 (1948); Annot., 47 A.L.R.2d 1258. The theory is that, since the reputation witness relates what he has heard, the inquiry tends to shed light on the accuracy of his hearing and reporting. Accordingly, the opinion witness would be asked whether he knew, as well as whether he had heard. The fact is, of course, that these distinctions are of slight if any practical significance, and the second sentence of subdivision (a) eliminates them as a factor in formulating questions.

4. This line of inquiry can be so prejudicial that in addition to the above form limitations, there are procedural restrictions on this type of cross-examination. The prosecutor must have a good faith basis in fact for asking the question. *Michelson, supra*; State v. *Johnson*, 389 So. 2d 372, 376 (La. 1980). For instance, the prosecution might have a police report or eyewitness statement describing the act. The information constituting the basis for believing that the defendant committed the act need not be independently admissible under the technical rules of evidence such as hearsay. However, if the defense objects to the line of inquiry, at sidebar the prosecutor should be prepared to both describe the information and insert any pertinent documents into the record.

The FRE Approach: Rules 413–14 — Specific Acts

As previously stated, in sexual assault and child molestation cases, Rules 413–14 no longer accord the defendant the right to decide whether his or her character may be used as circumstantial proof of conduct. The rules depart from tradition in another respect. The preceding paragraphs point out that under the general rule contained in FREs 404 and 405, both defense and prosecution are restricted to reputation and opinion testimony in proving character on direct examination and may ask about relevant specific acts only on cross-examination. Rules 413–14, in contrast, expressly permit the admission of direct testimony about specific acts.

Do Rules 413–14 also permit the admission of testimony about reputation and opinion?

b. Circumstantial Character Evidence in Civil Cases

1) The General Rule

Most courts traditionally have prohibited the circumstantial use of character evidence in civil cases and thus have held that the exceptions for criminal defendants to elect to open the door with evidence of their good character do not apply in civil cases. Prior to 2006, though, a minority of courts did allow defendants to offer such evidence in civil cases with criminal overtones, such as assault actions. *Bolton v. Tesoro Petr. Corp.*, 871 F.2d 1266, 1277–78 (5th Cir.) (in a civil securities fraud action, a party offered character testimony by former President Gerald Ford; "[s]uch evidence can be admissible in a civil trial raising quasi-criminal allegations against a defendant"), *cert. denied*, 493 U.S. 823 (1989). A 2006 amendment to Rule 404(a) settled this dispute. The Advisory Committee Note reads:

> The Rule has been amended to clarify that in a civil case evidence of a person's character is never admissible to prove that the person acted in conformity with the character trait. . . .

The accompanying report of the Committee on Rules of Practice and Procedure explains:

> The risks of character evidence historically have been considered worth the costs where a criminal defendant seeks to show his good character or the pertinent bad character of the victim. This so-called "rule of mercy" is thought necessary to provide a counterweight to the resources of the government, and is a recognition of the possibility that the accused, whose liberty is at stake, may have little to defend with other than his good name. But none of those considerations is operative in civil litigation.

Does the probative value of the evidence mysteriously disappear simply because it is offered in a civil case? Why give the criminal defendant "a special dispensation"?

2) Remaining Areas of Use of Circumstantial Character Evidence in Civil Cases

The 2006 amendment to Rule 404(a) was not intended to affect the admission of uncharged misconduct in civil cases under Rule 404(b), which we shall look at in later in this chapter. In addition, evidence of the "sexual predisposition" of the victim in a civil sexual misconduct case may be admissible under Rule 412(b)(2) — which we will study in the next section. Finally, look carefully at Rule 415(a):

> Federal Rule of Evidence 415. Similar Acts in Civil Cases Involving Sexual Assault or Child Molestation.
>
> (a) Permitted Uses. In a civil case involving a claim for relief based on a party's alleged sexual assault or child molestation, the court may admit evidence that the party committed any other sexual assault or child molestation. The evidence may be considered as provided in Rules 413 and 414.

Congress approved Rule 415 in the same bill which promulgated Federal Rules 413–14. How does Rule 415 change the state of the law? Under this Rule, does either party have the power to "veto" the use of character reasoning? When the Rule comes into play, are the parties restricted to reputation and opinion evidence? Would reputation or opinion even be admissible under Rule 415?

3. Character as Circumstantial Evidence of the Conduct of a Non-Party

Rule 404(a) refers to the character of "the alleged victim" as well as that of a criminal "defendant." Although mentioned in the indictment or information, the victim is not a formal party in a prosecution. In most instances, the common law prohibits the introduction of evidence regarding the character of non-parties. The only two notable exceptions are the victims of violent offenses and sex crimes.

a. The Victims of Violent Crime

Sometimes the defense can rationalize the introduction of evidence of the alleged victim's violent character without arguing that the evidence is circumstantial proof that the alleged victim in fact began the fight, that is, was the aggressor. Suppose that the defendant claims self-defense. The subjective element of self-defense is the defendant's reasonable belief that he or she is about to be attacked. Assume that before a fight with the alleged victim, the defendant heard a report that the alleged victim had a violent temper. The defendant need not offer evidence of the alleged victim's character trait of violence as circumstantial character evidence, that is, to increase the likelihood that the alleged victim threw the first punch. Rather, there is an entirely alternative theory of logical relevance. Can you figure out what it is? *See Martinez v. Wainwright*, 621 F.2d 184, 188 (5th Cir. 1980). However, if the defendant had not heard any report of the acts before the encounter with the alleged victim, the defendant would be forced to resort to a character theory. As before, the two recurring questions are: When is it legitimate to use character evidence, and how may the character, if admissible, be proven?

1)   When Is Proof of the Victim's Violent Character Admissible as Circumstantial Evidence of the Victim's Conduct?

Sometimes the only tenable theory of logical relevance for evidence of the victim's character is that it is circumstantial evidence of conduct. Under these circumstances, we must reach the question of whether the character evidence is admissible for this purpose. The rules are roughly parallel to the rules for the introduction of evidence of the defendant's own character. In both settings, the defendant may open the door on the issue. Thus, Federal Rule of Evidence 404(a)(2)(B) permits the defendant to attack "an alleged victim's pertinent trait" such as violence. Once the defendant has done so, the prosecution can rejoin with evidence of the victim's peaceful character. Moreover, by virtue of a 2000 amendment to Rule 404(a)(2)(B)(ii), once the defendant has done so, the prosecution may also introduce "evidence of the defendant's same trait." The accompanying Advisory Committee Note states that "[t]he amendment makes clear that the accused cannot attack the alleged victim's character and yet remain unshielded from the disclosure of equally relevant evidence concerning the same character trait of the accused."

Furthermore, under Rule 404(a)(2)(C), in a homicide case the prosecution need not wait until the defense formally attacks the victim's character. Under that rule, the defendant opens the door by offering any type of "evidence that the [alleged] victim was the first aggressor." It suffices that the defendant or any defense witness testifies that the alleged victim threw the first punch. Many states have taken a contrary view and admit prosecution character evidence only if the defense attacks the alleged victim's character.

2)   What Methods of Proof Are Available?

If evidence of the victim's character is admissible, what form may it take? Here the courts are badly divided. Again, there are three conceivable methods of proving character: reputation, opinion, and specific instances of conduct. Some courts permit the use of the same methods usable to prove the defendant's character. The Federal Rules of Evidence take this approach and thus forbid the use of specific instances of the victim's conduct on direct examination. In contrast, some jurisdictions go to the extreme of allowing proof of specific instances of the victim's violent character. Still other courts will admit proof of specific prior violent acts only if they were directed at the defendant. *State v. Black*, 587 S.W.2d 865 (Mo. Ct. App. 1979). In the view of these courts, acts directed at the defendant have far greater probative value than acts committed against third parties.

NOTES

1.   Why does this sort of evidence pose a Rule 403 problem? How great is the risk that the jury will decide the case on an improper basis? If the jurors hear enough evidence of the alleged victim's violent character, might they not subconsciously nullify the law, thinking that the victim was such a vile person that "he deserved what he got"?

2.   Which position do you prefer: (1) the traditional view that the prosecutor may prove up the alleged victim's peaceful character only after the defendant makes a frontal assault on the victim's character, or (2) Rule 404(a)(2)'s provision allowing the prosecutor to introduce evidence of the victim's good character whenever in a homicide case the defense contends that the alleged victim began the affray? Why is the Rule limited to homicide cases? Is there a special need for the evidence in those cases?

b.   Victims of Sex Crimes

When we study credibility evidence in Chapter 15, we will see that a few jurisdictions still admit evidence of a complainant's promiscuous conduct on the tenuous theory that such conduct impeaches the complainant's credibility. Our focus here is very different: The defendant wants to introduce evidence of the victim's past consensual intercourse with others to support the inference that she consented to intercourse with the defendant on the occasion in question. The defendant thus is attempting to use the victim's character as circumstantial proof of her conduct on a particular occasion.

Until recently, many courts routinely permitted the defendant to introduce evidence of the complainant's reputation for "unchastity" as well as specific sexual acts. Suppose, in the *Devitt* case, that it was Mr. Paterson's daughter — rather than Paterson himself — who walked in on Devitt burglarizing the apartment. Ms. Paterson claims that after she confronted Devitt, he attacked and raped her. In a rape prosecution against Devitt, courts in the past might well have admitted a psychiatrist's testimony stating that Ms. Paterson is a "nymphomaniac" who constantly fantasizes about sexual attacks. As originally written, Federal Rule 404(a)(2) seemed generally to sanction the continuation of the practice of liberal admission of evidence of unchastity. Indeed, the Advisory Committee Note to the original version of FRE 404(a)(1) used this example to illustrate a pertinent character trait of a victim that the defendant might choose to attack.

However, with the advance of the feminist movement and the growing awareness of the gravity of the problem of rape in the United States, more and more jurisdictions abandoned the old view. In some cases, the courts by decisional rule adopted restrictions on evidence of the alleged victim's specific sexual acts, e.g., *State v. Mastropetre*, 400 A.2d 276 (Conn. 1978), or reputation, e.g., *McLean v. United States*, 377 A.2d 74 (D.C. 1977). In other jurisdictions, legislatures enacted so-called "rape shield" laws. The same reform movement led to the adoption of Federal Rule of Evidence 412:

> Rule 412. Sex Offense Cases; The Victim's Sexual Behavior or Predisposition.
>
>   (a)   Prohibited Uses. The following evidence is not admissible in a civil or criminal proceeding involving alleged sexual misconduct:
>
>   (1)   Evidence offered to prove that a victim engaged in other sexual behavior; or
>
>   (2)   Evidence offered to prove a victim's sexual predisposition.
>
>   (b)   Exceptions
>
>   (1)   Criminal Cases. The court may admit the following evidence in a criminal case:
>
>   (A)   Evidence of specific instances of a victim's sexual behavior, if offered to prove that someone other than the defendant was the source of semen, injury, or other physical evidence;
>
>   (B)   Evidence of specific instances of a victim's sexual behavior with respect to the person accused of the sexual misconduct, if offered by the defendant to prove consent or if offered by the prosecutor; and
>
>   (C)   Evidence whose exclusion would violate the defendant's constitutional rights.
>
>   (2)   Civil Cases. In a civil case, the court may admit evidence offered to prove a victim's sexual behavior or sexual predisposition if its probative value substantially outweighs the danger of harm to any victim and of unfair prejudice to any party. The court may admit evidence of a victim's reputation only if the victim has placed it in controversy.

NOTES AND PROBLEMS

1. Are the evidence rules that govern admissibility of sexual conduct and reputation — Rules 412 through 415 — the product of extrinsic social policy concerns, intrinsic truth-finding concerns, or both? In late 1994, Congress approved

an updated version of Rule 412 in the same package of legislation that included new Rules 413–15. The amendment extended Rule 412 to civil actions and to more types of prosecutions. The approval of Rules 413–15 was driven in part by Congress' belief that the new rules would contribute to the national campaign against rape, and the inclusion of the expanded version of Rule 412 in the same bill signals that the rape shield law is justified by related policy concerns.

2. **Problem 14-7.** In *Devitt*, the defense wants to offer evidence that, three months before the alleged rape, the defendant and Ms. Paterson met at a disco in downtown Morena. The defendant is prepared to testify that they went to his apartment that night and had consensual intercourse. Is that evidence admissible under Federal Rule of Evidence 412? Which provision controls?

3. **Problem 14-8.** Devitt offers the testimony of Bruce Langley, who is prepared to testify that he met Ms. Paterson at a party the night before the alleged rape. At the time, she told him that she was depressed because she had just broken up with her boyfriend; they went to his apartment and had consensual intercourse there. Again, which provision in Rule 412 governs?

4. Why is this kind of evidence potentially problematic? Suppose that we liberally admit evidence of Ms. Paterson's nonmarital intercourse. As in the case of evidence of the violent character of alleged victims of forcible offenses, there is a danger that the jury may acquit a rapist on an improper basis. In addition, federal and state rape shield rules were partly a response to the widespread perception that victims were being re-victimized on the witness stand by having their sexual histories paraded before juries; many victims were reluctant to come forward because of this common practice and thus many rapes were going unprosecuted.

5. Rule 412(b)(2) prescribes a balancing test. How does that test compare to the test under Rule 403? *See Rodriguez-Hernandez v. Miranda-Velez*, 132 F.3d 848, 856 (1st Cir. 1998) ("Rule 412 . . . reverses the usual approach of the Federal Rules of Evidence on admissibility by requiring that the evidence's probative value 'substantially outweigh' its prejudicial effect").

6. Rape shield rules vary by jurisdiction, with some states offering broader protection to victims than others. In a few jurisdictions, rape shield laws apply only in criminal cases. Hines, Note, *Bracing the Armor: Extending Rape Shield Protection to Civil Proceedings*, 86 NOTRE DAME L. REV. 879 (2011). The federal rule, however, is broader. A 1994 amendment to Rule 412 explicitly extended it to civil cases. In addition, federal courts have generally read "sexual behavior" broadly and have construed the rule as applying to "all activities that involve actual physical conduct, such as sexual intercourse or contact; those activities that imply sexual intercourse or sexual contact, such as evidence of use of contraceptives; and even activities of the mind, such as fantasies or dreams and viewing pornography." Nicolas, *"They Say He's Gay": The Admissibility of Evidence of Sexual Orientation*, 37 GA. L. REV. 793, 803 (2003); Note, *The Next Generation of Sexual Conduct: Expanding the Protective Reach of Rape Shield Laws to Include Evidence Found on MySpace*, 13 SUFF. J. TRIAL & APP. ADV. 211, 229 (2008).

7. However, there are limits. For instance, despite the rule many courts permit the defendant to impeach an adult complainant by proof of prior false accusations

of sexual conduct. Colquitt, *Evidence and Ethics: Litigating in the Shadows of the Rules*, 76 Fordham L. Rev. 1641, 1650 (2007). Most demand persuasive proof that the prior accusation was false, *Morgan v. State*, 54 P.3d 332 (Alaska Ct. App. 2002), but given such proof these courts reason that a prior accusation about sexual conduct is not "sexual behavior" within the meaning of that expression in the statute.

In addition, some courts admit the complainant's prior sexual conduct on the question of whether the complainant invited or welcomed the allegedly offensive conduct in a sexual harassment action. *Wilson v. City of Des Moines*, 442 F.3d 637, 643 (8th Cir. 2006). Further, when the alleged victim is a young child, there is extensive authority that the defendant may introduce evidence of the child's prior sexual experiences that might explain the child's familiarity with sexual matters. *People v. Morse*, 231 Mich. App. 424, 586 N.W.2d 555 (1998); Buttrey, *Michigan's Rape-Shield Statute and the Admissibility of Evidence That a Child Complainant Has Been Previously Molested*, 15 T.M. Cooley L. Rev. 391 (1998). Without the benefit of that evidence, jurors might assume that a young child would otherwise be ignorant of sexual matters and, therefore, regard the child's very knowledge as corroboration of the child's accusation.

B.   HABIT OR ROUTINE PRACTICE

Proof of a person's habit can be used as direct or circumstantial evidence of the person's conduct. In occasional cases a person's habit can become a material fact of consequence in the case under Rule 401. Evidence of the habit is then directly relevant. However, as in the case of character evidence, in most instances the proponent uses proof of a person's habit as circumstantial proof of the person's conduct on a particular occasion.

1.   The Difference Between Character and Habit Evidence

There are major conceptual differences between the concept of a habit and that of character, which in turn account for differences in the evidentiary rules governing habit and character. Character is a generalized concept: we are referring to character when we say that a person is "a good, moral, law-abiding individual," and even the description of the person as "a good driver" is a statement of a character trait. Habit is a different "beastie." Perhaps the most insightful exposition of the two concepts appears in the Advisory Committee's Note to Federal Rule of Evidence 406:

> An oft-quoted paragraph, McCormick § 162, p. 340, describes habit in terms effectively contrasting it with character:
>
> "Character and habit are close akin. Character is a generalized description of one's disposition, or of one's disposition in respect to a general trait, such as honesty, temperance, or peacefulness. 'Habit,' in modern usage, both lay and psychological, is more specific. It describes one's regular response to a repeated specific situation. If we speak of character for care, we think of the person's tendency to act prudently in all the varying situations of life, in business, in family life, in handling automobiles and in walking across the

street. A habit, on the other hand, is the person's regular practice of meeting a particular kind of situation with a specific type of conduct, such as the habit of going down a particular stairway two stairs at a time, or of giving the hand-signal for a left turn, or of alighting from railway cars while they are moving. The doing of the habitual acts may become semi-automatic."

Equivalent behavior on the part of a group is designated "routine practice of an organization" in the rule. Agreement is general that habit evidence is highly persuasive as proof of conduct on a particular occasion. Again quoting McCormick § 152, p. 341:

"Character may be thought of as the sum of one's habits though doubtless it is more than this. But unquestionably the uniformity of one's response to habit is far greater than the consistency with which one's conduct conforms to character or disposition. Even though character comes in only exceptionally as evidence of an act, surely any sensible man in investigating whether X did a particular act would be greatly helped in this inquiry by evidence as to whether he was in the habit of doing it."

In short, proffered testimony describes a habit only when the testimony relates to a specific, repeated behavioral pattern — for instance, if the witness were to testify that on numerous occasions the witness saw the person execute a right-hand turn in a particular fashion and the issue is whether the person, the defendant, executed a right-hand turn in that particular, careful fashion at the time in question. There must be a high reaction-to-situation ratio: On all or substantially all the occasions on which the person finds herself in the same situation, she follows the same, particularized behavioral pattern. *Mobil Exploration v. Cajun Const. Services*, 45 F.3d 96, 99–100 (5th Cir. 1995). Given the specificity and repetition of the behavioral pattern, habit has more probative value than character. On that assumption, the limitations on habit evidence should be laxer than the restrictions on character evidence.

This definition of "habit," requiring proof of a repetitive, specific behavioral pattern, is sometimes termed the "probability theory." Mengler, *The Theory of Discretion in the Federal Rules of Evidence*, 74 Iowa L. Rev. 413, 417 (1989). The above quotation from the Committee Note to Rule 406 lends support to that theory.

However, there is a competing definition — the so-called "psychological theory." *Id.* Like the probability theory, this theory requires that the proponent of alleged habit evidence prove that the evidence relates to a frequently repeated, specific behavioral pattern. However, the psychological theory imposes the further restriction that the conduct in question is "unconsciously mechanical — Pavlovian." *Id.* Dean Mengler explains:

[O]n this psychological theory, the routine practice of reading a novel before going to bed, while customary, could not be habitual because it is volitional. In contrast, the regular practice of turning the pages of the novel with one's left hand could be habitual because of its mechanical or automatic nature.

Id. This theory also finds support in the Advisory Committee Note to Rule 406, which cites *Levin v. United States*, 338 F.2d 265 (D.C. Cir. 1964), *cert. denied*, 379 U.S. 999 (1965). That case excluded testimony offered as habit for the stated reason that "the very volitional basis of the activity raises serious questions as to its invariable nature." *Id.* at 272. Many courts seem to subscribe to this theory. *Becker v. ARCO Chemical Co.*, 207 F.3d 176, 204 (3d Cir. 2000) (semi-automatic, situation-specific); *Gamerdinger v. Schaefer*, 603 N.W.2d 590 (Iowa 1999) (invariable); *Washington St. Physicians Ins. v. Fisons Corp.*, 122 Wash. 2d 299, 858 P.2d 1054 (1993) ("semi-automatic, almost involuntary and invariabl[y] specific responses to fairly specific stimuli").

NOTES

1. How can we explain the presence of passages supporting two, inconsistent definitions of "habit" in the Advisory Committee Note? Mengler suggests that the Committee disagreed over the definition of "habit," set out its disagreement in its Note, and invited the courts to resolve the issue. Could the courts resolve the issue by applying the psychological theory to evidence of a person's habit but the probability theory to evidence of an entity's routine practice?

2. The next question is which courts may legitimately resolve this ambiguity — the trial courts or the appellate courts? In a common-law system, the answer would be the appellate courts. They would settle the definition as a question of law and then announce that rule as binding on the trial bench. However, Mengler argues forcefully that in the statutory scheme of the Federal Rules, the decision should be left to the trial courts on a case-by-case basis. Several factors support his argument. The habit provision rests largely on Rule 403 policy concerns. As we have seen, the trial judiciary exercises Rule 403 discretion on an ad hoc basis. Furthermore, "a principal cause for the codification movement" was "skepticism about appellate decision-making." *Id.* at 423–24. Thus, like 403, Rule 406 may effect a subtle shift in the balance of power between the trial and appellate courts.

2. When is Habit Evidence Admissible?

Federal Rule of Evidence 406 governs the admission of evidence of a person's habit (or an organization's routine practice). On its face, the Rule makes evidence of habit freely admissible and makes no distinction between criminal and civil cases. The prosecutor thus need not wait until the defendant places his or her habit in issue. Hence, there is a marked contrast between the habit norms announced in Rule 406 and the character norms in Rules 404 and 405. Rule 406 authorizes any litigant to use habit or routine practice as circumstantial proof of conduct.

At common law, many jurisdictions admitting habit evidence imposed one of the following limitations on its admissibility. Some courts admitted habit evidence only when there was some corroborating evidence that the person acted consistently with the habit on the occasion in question. *State v. Wadsworth*, 210 So. 2d 4 (Fla. 1968). A second common restriction was to allow habit evidence only when there was an exceptional need for circumstantial evidence of conduct, namely, when there were no eyewitnesses. Snell, *Eyeing the Iowa No Eyewitness Rule*, 43 Iowa L. Rev.

57 (1957). These limitations remain alive and well in some jurisdictions today. *Gann v. Oltesvig*, 491 F. Supp. 2d 771, 779 (N.D. Ill. 2007) (the Illinois Pattern Instruction); Schroeder, *Evidence of Habit and Routine Practice*, 29 Loy. U. Chi. L.J. 385 (1998) (discussing Illinois law). Does Rule 406 preserve those limitations?

3. What Methods of Proof are Admissible?

There are two recognized methods of proving the existence of a person's habit or an organization's custom: specific instances and opinion. The original draft of Federal Rule 406 set forth both methods: "(b) Habit or routine practice may be proved by testimony in the form of an opinion or by specific instances of conduct sufficient in number to warrant a finding that the habit existed or that the practice was routine." Congress ultimately deleted section (b), leaving it to the courts to deal with on a case-by-case basis.

NOTES AND PROBLEMS

1. **Problem 14-9.** In *Hill*, one count in the plaintiff's complaint alleges that Polecat Motors was guilty of negligent manufacture. Polecat wants to show that its quality control procedures would have caught the defect if it existed in the product at the time of manufacture. The head of quality control is prepared to testify that the safety checks include a check for leaks in the gas tank, one of the defects that allegedly caused the injury in this case; she trains all the defendant's quality control inspectors to conduct that test before the product leaves the assembly line; and she has personally seen the inspectors conduct that test "thousands of times." The courts tend to admit evidence of business customs more liberally than testimony about personal habits. "This may be because there is no confusion between character traits and business practices, as there is between character and [personal] habit, or it may reflect the belief that the need for regularity in business and the organizational sanctions which may exist when employees deviate from the established procedures give extra guarantees that the questioned activity followed the usual custom." 1 McCormick, Evidence § 195, at 785–86 (6th ed. 2006).

2. **Problem 14-10.** Devitt wants to defend on an alibi theory. He would testify that "for the past year or so, on Monday at 3:30 in the afternoon, I almost always stop by Ernie's Bar and Grill and hang around for about two hours." The assault on Paterson occurred on a Monday during that time frame. Is the evidence of Devitt's customary visit to the bar admissible? *See Levin v. United States*, 338 F.2d 265, 272 (D.C. Cir. 1964) (not sufficiently automatic or regular to qualify as habit evidence), *cert. denied*, 379 U.S. 999 (1965).

C. OTHER ACTS AND TRANSACTIONS

1. Introduction

We might summarize the character evidence rules described thus far as follows: (1) In the narrow class of cases in which a person's character is directly in issue, evidence of the relevant character trait is admissible, and the character trait may be proven by reputation, opinion, or specific acts; (2) Otherwise, the general rule is that character evidence is not admissible to prove that the person acted in conformity with that character trait on a particular occasion at issue in the case; (3) However, there are exceptions to the general ban on character evidence used circumstantially to prove conduct — these exceptions apply in criminal cases and allow the defendant to elect to "open the door" to the use of such evidence (or the prosecution in the case of sex crimes under 413–415). When Rules 413-15 apply, the parties are limited to specific acts. However, if character is provable under one of the other exceptions, it may be shown only by reputation or opinion evidence but not by evidence of specific acts; yet on cross-examination, character witnesses may be asked about relevant specific instances for the limited purpose of testing the character witness's credibility. Finally, (4) if the proponent can persuade the court that the evidence shows a habit rather than character, evidence of the habit, in the form of opinion or specific instances of conduct, is permitted.

But what if a party wishes to introduce evidence of a party's specific acts of conduct not to prove the person's character (or to prove a habit), but to prove something else? In that case, the general bar on character evidence would not apply, because the evidence would not be offered to prove character. On the other hand, the evidence of the specific act(s) would still tend to raise a character inference, which presents the same dangers of unfair prejudice and misdecision that underlie the character evidence doctrine. Under these circumstances we say that the item of evidence has "dual relevance," and that it is inadmissible to prove character but may be admissible to prove some other fact that is logically relevant in the case, subject to Rule 403.

To put this problem into more concrete terms, suppose that the prosecutor in a criminal trial wishes to prove an act by the defendant separate from the specific act for which the defendant is on trial. Assume that the act is relevant for a non-propensity purpose. Further suppose that the other act the prosecutor wants to prove is another crime by the defendant. The introduction of proof of that other act may convince some of the jurors that the defendant is a habitual criminal who deserves to be imprisoned, whether or not the defendant is guilty of the charged crime, or that it is likely the defendant committed the charged crime because he has done other crimes in the past. Moreover, there is a risk of distracting and confusing the jurors — another probative danger recognized in Rule 403.

A large body of doctrine has grown up around this issue; the applicable rule has been codified by FRE 404(b):

404(b). Crimes, Wrongs, or Other Acts.

(1) *Prohibited Uses* . Evidence of a crime, wrong, or other act is not admissible to prove a person's character in order to show that on a particular occasion the person acted in accordance with the character.

(2) *Permitted Uses; Notice in a Criminal Case.* This evidence may be admissible for another purpose, such as proving motive, opportunity, intent, preparation, plan, knowledge, identity, absence of mistake, or lack of accident. On request by a defendant in a criminal case, the prosecutor must [provide reasonable notice of the nature of the evidence].

There are several important things to notice about this rule. First, unless Rule 413, 414, or 415 applies, other acts evidence must be offered on an entirely different theory of logical relevance than character evidence. While character evidence may sometimes be offered as circumstantial proof of the conduct of a person (*i.e.*, that the person acted in conformity with the character trait, disposition, or propensity), "other acts" evidence may *never* be offered on that theory of relevance (unless the facts trigger Rule 413, 414, or 415). Other acts evidence must have "special" or "independent" logical relevance — other than a character theory. Federal Rule of Evidence 404(b) codifies the common law requirement for a showing of such *noncharacter* relevance.

Second, the method of proving other acts evidence differs from the method of proof for character evidence. When the proponent of character evidence offers it as circumstantial proof of a party's conduct, the proponent is usually restricted to reputation or opinion. The proponent cannot introduce evidence of specific acts. The rules for other acts evidence are the mirror image. Affirmatively, the proponent of other acts evidence may and must prove a specific act, namely, the other act. Negatively, unless Rule 413, 414, or 415 applies, the proponent may not resort to reputation or opinion.

2. Other Acts Evidence in Criminal Cases

While Rule 404(b) by its terms is not restricted to criminal cases (except for the notice requirements set out in 404(b)(2)), in practice the issue often arises in criminal cases. Initially, students should be aware that many of the terms used by courts and commentators in this area of evidence law are potentially misleading. For example, commentators often refer to 404(b) evidence as "uncharged misconduct," but this means only that the other acts are not the subject of the charge *in the current case.* Furthermore, while many of the cases and commentaries refer to this species of proof as "similar crimes" evidence, that title is also inaccurate. The crime need not be similar to the crime charged to have independent logical relevance and be admissible under 404(b). For instance, many courts admit proof of a defendant's narcotics addiction to prove the defendant's financial motive to commit a charged robbery. *United States v. Parker*, 549 F.2d 1217 (9th Cir.), *cert. denied*, 430 U.S. 971 (1977); *United States v. Lee*, 509 F.2d 400 (D.C. Cir. 1974), *cert. denied*, 420 U.S. 1006 (1975).

For that matter, there is no necessity that the other act be a crime at all — notice that the rule is labeled "Crimes, Wrongs, or Other Acts." Consider this hypothetical. The defendant is charged with murdering his mistress's husband. The prosecution may offer evidence of the defendant's intercourse with the decedent's wife because the evidence is indisputably relevant to prove the defendant's motive to commit the murder. The evidence would be admissible whether or not adultery was a crime in the jurisdiction. The act is not admissible because it is a crime; the act is admissible because of its independent logical relevance and in spite of the fact that it is prejudicial evidence of a crime (but subject, of course, to Rule 403). *United States v. Beechum*, 555 F.2d 487 (5th Cir. 1977), *cert. denied*, 440 U.S. 920 (1979).

This topic is of enormous practical importance. In many jurisdictions, alleged errors in the admission of other acts evidence are the most frequent ground for appealing criminal cases. 22 C. WRIGHT & K. GRAHAM, FEDERAL PRACTICE AND PROCEDURE: EVIDENCE § 5239 (1978). Moreover, in some jurisdictions errors in the admission of such evidence are the most common ground for reversal. In the federal courts, Rule 404(b) has generated more reported cases than any other subsection of the rules. 1 E. IMWINKELRIED, UNCHARGED MISCONDUCT EVIDENCE § 1:04 (rev. ed. 1999). "It has been cited in 5,603 federal . . . decisions since [its] adoption" in 1975. Reed, *Admitting the Accused's Criminal History: The Trouble with Rule 404(b)*, 78 TEMP. L. REV. 201, 211 (2005). There are so many reported cases because prosecutors offer uncharged misconduct evidence so frequently, and they do so because they appreciate how potent the evidence is.

a. The Independent Logical Relevance Requirement

Unless Rules 413–415 apply, the key task facing the proponent of other acts evidence under Rule 404(b) is articulating a noncharacter theory of logical relevance. The early American view was that uncharged misconduct evidence was admissible in criminal cases so long as it was logically relevant to some fact of consequence other than the defendant's bad character. Stone, *The Rule of Exclusion of Similar Fact Evidence: America*, 51 HARV. L. REV. 988 (1938). However, in the 1840s the courts began developing the so-called "exclusionary doctrine," under which such evidence was admissible only if it was logically relevant on certain specific, well-recognized theories such as motive, identity, or intent. Under this exclusionary approach, some courts announced a rigid rule excluding uncharged misconduct evidence and treated such theories as motive and identity as pigeonhole "exceptions" to the norm. Note, *Developments in Evidence of Other Crimes*, 7. U. MICH J.L. REFORM 535, 536 (1974). Some courts reduced the doctrine to a mnemonic: MIMIC: M=motive, I=intent, M=mistake, I=identity, C=common plan or scheme. Comment, 9 U. BALT. L. REV. 245, 266 (1980).

However, this exclusionary approach in criminal cases was subject to withering criticism. Professor Anthony Amsterdam wrote:

> It is often stated as a general rule of evidence that proof of a defendant's prior record and unrelated crimes is inadmissible; then a number of "exceptions" to the rule — use of other offenses to show identity, motive, common scheme, and so forth — are defined. This may be well and good if the trial judge believes it, but there is no such general rule. Prior record and unrelated crimes are inadmissible, like other facts, unless they are relevant. If relevant, they are admissible, and the socalled exceptions simply state several grounds of relevancy. The actual evidentiary principle . . . involved here [is that t]here is one specific purpose for which prior crime evidence may not be used; that is, to show that the defendant is an evil or a vicious person, as a basis for the further inference that s/he therefore is guilty of the present charge.

3 A. AMSTERDAM, TRIAL MANUAL FOR THE DEFENSE OF CRIMINAL CASES § 368, at 123 (5th ed. 1988). Professor Amsterdam in this passage is articulating the "inclusionary approach," which is now the clear majority view in both state and federal courts.

The language of Rule 404(b) adopts this approach.

Under the inclusionary approach, the prosecutor may offer evidence of a defendant's other crimes, wrongs, or acts for any logically relevant purpose other than the purpose explicitly forbidden by the first sentence of Rule 404(b): "to prove a person's character in order to show that on a particular occasion the person acted in accordance with the character." Hence, if the facts support a theory of logical relevance other than the "verboten" one, the prosecutor may use the uncharged misconduct evidence — for example, to show the defendant's identity as the perpetrator of the charged crime or to prove the defendant's possession of the requisite *mens rea*.

As you can see, Rule 404(b) goes on to list several of the most common noncharacter uses of other acts evidence, including the following:

> ***Modus operandi to prove identity.*** One identity technique is to establish that the defendant committed another crime and that both that crime and the charged crime share a very distinctive *modus operandi*. The similarities between the crimes must be so great that they support an inference that the charged crime was the defendant's handiwork. *United States v. Phaknikone*, 605 F.3d 1099, 1108 (11th Cir. 2010). Further, the *modus operandi* must be sufficiently unique or unusual that it serves as the defendant's "signature." *United States v. Curtin*, 443 F.3d 1084, 1092 (9th Cir. 2006).

> If the prosecution relies on this theory, the trial judge might give the jury the following limiting instruction: "Evidence has been introduced for the purpose of showing that the defendant committed a crime other than the offense for which he is on trial. Even if you believe this evidence, you may not treat it as proof that the defendant is a person of bad character or that he has a disposition to commit crimes. You may consider the evidence only for the limited purpose of determining if it tends to show the identity of the person who committed the crime of which the defendant is accused."

> If the judge gives the above limiting instruction, during closing argument the prosecutor would initially marshal the testimony indicating that the defendant perpetrated the uncharged crime. The prosecutor could then highlight all the points of similarity between the charged and uncharged offenses. Next, the prosecutor would tell the jury that the *modus operandi* of the two offenses was so distinctive that "common sense tells you that the same man committed both crimes." At this point the prosecutor would probably quote the judge's limiting instruction. The prosecutor could conclude by stating: "Ladies and gentlemen, the same man committed the other robbery. Therefore, according to her Honor's instruction, you're entitled to conclude that the same man — this defendant — perpetrated the charged offense."

> ***Consciousness of guilt.*** The defendant's post-arrest attempt to escape or to bribe a prosecution witness is relevant to show a consciousness of guilt on the defendant's part. *United States v. Myers*, 550 F.2d 1036 (5th Cir. 1977).

Identity. Modus operandi is not the only permissible theory for proving the defendant's identity as the perpetrator. The prosecution may prove another act of misconduct putting the defendant in possession of an instrument linked to the crime for which the defendant is now being tried. For instance, it would be relevant to show that the defendant stole the getaway car used in the charged bank robbery. *United States v. Waldron*, 568 F.2d 185 (10th Cir. 1977), *cert. denied*, 434 U.S. 1080 (1978). Note that this evidence would also tend to prove *Preparation*, which is a separate noncharacter purpose.

Mens rea such as knowledge. The prosecutor may offer uncharged misconduct evidence on noncharacter theories of logical relevance to establish the *mens rea* element required for the charged offense. Assume, for example, that the defendant is charged with the knowing receipt of stolen goods. The court may allow the prosecutor to introduce evidence of the defendant's earlier receipt of other stolen property from the same transferor under suspicious circumstances to strengthen the inference of guilty knowledge. *Lanier v. State*, 172 Tex. Crim. 238, 356 S.W.2d 671 (1962). A prior transaction with the same transferor under such circumstances can put the defendant on notice that the transferor is a "fence," and that notice might lead the defendant to suspect that the other goods the same transferor later gave the defendant were stolen.

Motive. Proof of the defendant's involvement in the Watergate break-in of a psychiatrist's office supplied the motive for his participation in the Watergate conspiracy to cover up the break-in. *United States v. Haldeman*, 559 F.2d 31 (D.C. Cir. 1976). Similarly, as previously stated, evidence of a defendant's addiction to expensive narcotics can supply the motive for the commission of a property offense such as robbery or burglary. *United States v. Lee*, 509 F.2d 400 (D.C. Cir. 1974).

Plan. If the charged crime and other crimes appear to be part of a common plan, proof of the plan is admissible at the trial for the charged crime. Suppose, for instance, that the defendant, one of the heirs to Greenacre, decides to gain title to Greenacre by murdering all the other heirs. The overall objective, gaining Greenacre, necessitates the commission of a number of crimes, all inspired by the same objective. Proof of the overall plan tends to establish the defendant's guilt of the killing of any one of the other heirs. This hypothetical illustrates what is often called a "chain" plan.

The courts also agree that there is legitimate noncharacter relevance in the case of "sequential" plans: The defendant first burglarizes the bank president's residence to steal the key to the bank entrance and then uses the key to burglarize the bank. Imwinkelried, *Using a Contextual Construction to Resolve the Dispute over the Meaning of the Term "Plan" in Federal Rule of Evidence 404(b)* , 43 U. KAN. L. REV. 1005 (1995).

In addition, there is arguably genuine independent relevance in "template" cases — fact situations in which there is evidence that the defendant thought about the method of committing the crimes before perpetrating the initial offense in a series of crimes, all displaying the same methodology. However, what if the prosecution's only evidence is that the defendant committed recent, similar crimes? Is that enough to prove the existence of a "plan"? How would you distinguish that situation from proving character to show propensity?

In the following pre-Rules case, the court grapples with the question whether the prosecutor may employ uncharged misconduct evidence to establish that there was an *actus reus*. In *Woods*, the defendant was charged with infanticide. The defendant's foster son, Paul, died as a result of cyanosis, a condition caused by lack of oxygen. The defendant claimed that the death was an accident. The prosecution offered evidence that nine children in the defendant's custody had suffered a minimum of 20 cases of cyanosis. The prosecution offered the evidence to prove that the death was due to an *actus reus* rather than natural accident. The trial judge admitted the evidence, but on appeal the defendant noted that the Fourth Circuit had not previously approved of that use of uncharged misconduct evidence.

UNITED STATES v. WOODS
484 F.2d 127 (4th Cir. 1973), *cert. denied*, 415 U.S. 979 (1974)

WINTER, CIRCUIT JUDGE.

The evidence of what happened to the other children was not, strictly speaking, evidence of other crimes. There was no evidence that defendant was an accused with respect to the deaths or respiratory difficulties of the other children, except for Judy. Simultaneously with her trial for crimes alleged against Paul, defendant was being tried for crimes alleged against Judy, but there was no direct proof of defendant's guilt and the district court ruled that the circumstantial evidence was insufficient for the government to have proved its case. Thus, with regard to no single child was there any legally sufficient proof that defendant had done any act which the law forbids. Only when all of the evidence concerning the nine other children and Paul is considered collectively is the conclusion impelled that the probability that some or all of the other deaths, cyanotic seizures, and respiratory deficiencies were accidental or attributable to natural causes was so remote, the truth must be that Paul and some or all of the other children died at the hands of the defendant. We think also that when the crime is one of infanticide or child abuse, evidence of repeated incidents is especially relevant because it may be the only evidence to prove the crime. A child of the age of Paul and of the others about whom evidence was received is a helpless, defenseless unit of human life. Such a child is too young, if he survives, to relate the facts concerning the attempt on his life, and too young, if he does not survive, to have exerted enough resistance that the marks of his cause of death will survive him. Absent the fortuitous presence of an eyewitness, infanticide or child abuse by suffocation would largely go unpunished. *See Minnesota v. Loss*, 295 Minn. 271, 204 N.W.2d 404 (1973).

The government and the defendant agree that evidence of other crimes is not admissible to prove that an accused is a bad person and therefore likely to have committed the crime in question. Indeed, the rule is beyond dispute: *Michelson v. United States*, 335 U.S. 469, 475–476 (1948). Defendant argues that while there are certain recognized exceptions to this rule, the instant case cannot be fitted into any of them, emphasizing that corpus delicti is not an exception. The government, in meeting this approach, contends that the evidence was admissible on the theory that ittended to prove (a) the existence of a continuing plan,[7] (b) the handiwork or signature exception,[8] (c) that the acts alleged in the indictment were not inadvertent, accidental, or unintentional, and (d) the defendant's identity as the perpetrator of the crime. We are inclined to agree with the defendant that the evidence was not admissible under the scheme or continuing plan exception because there was no evidence that defendant engaged in any scheme or plan, or, if so, the objective or motive. The evidence may have been admissible under the lack of accident exception, although ordinarily that exception is invoked only where an accused admits that he did the acts charged but denies the intent necessary to constitute a crime, or contends that he did the acts accidentally. McCormick, [Evidence] p. 450. However, in *State v. Lapage*, 57 N.H. 245, 294 (1876), there was dictum that under certain circumstances where several children of the same mother had died, evidence of the previous deaths ought to be admissible because of the unlikelihood of such deaths being accidental.

McCormick, in listing the instances in which evidence of other crimes may be admissible, cautions "that the list is not complete, for the range of relevancy outside the ban is almost infinite. . . ." *Id.* 448. And then, McCormick states:

> [S]ome of the wiser opinions (especially recent ones) recognize that the problem is not merely one of pigeonholing, but one of balancing, on the one side, the actual need for the other crimes evidence in the light of the issues and the other evidence available to the prosecution, the convincingness of the evidence that the other crimes were committed and that the accused was the actor, and the strength or weakness of the other crimes evidence in supporting the issue, and on the other, the degree to which the jury will probably be roused by the evidence to overmastering hostility.

Id. p. 453. This approach is one which finds support in *Dirring v. United States*, 328 F.2d 512 (1st Cir. 1964), *cert. denied*, 377 U.S. 1003 (1964); and *United States v. Hines*, 470 F.2d 225 (3d Cir. 1972), *cert. denied*, 410 U.S. 968 (1973). These cases stand for the proposition that evidence of other offenses may be received, if relevant, for any purpose other than to show a mere propensity or disposition on the part of the defendant to commit the crime, provided that the trial judge may exclude the evidence if its probative value is outweighed by the risk that its admission will create a substantial danger of undue prejudice to the accused.

We think that the evidence would prove that a crime had been committed because of the remoteness of the possibility that so many infants in the care and custody of defendant would suffer cyanotic episodes and respiratory difficulties if they were

---

[7] *Makin v. Attorney General of New South Wales*, [1894] A.C. 57 (P.C. 1893) (N.S. Wales) and *Regina v. Roden*, 12 Cox Cr. 630 (1874) support this view. Makin was a prosecution for infanticide by a professional foster parent. Evidence that the bodies of twelve other infants, who had been entrusted to him with inadequate payment for their support, was held admissible. In *Roden*, a prosecution for infanticide by suffocation, evidence that three of defendant's other children died in her lap, was held admissible.

[8] *Rex v. George Joseph Smith*, [1914–15] All E.R. Rep. 262 ("Brides of Bath" case) and *People v. Peete*, 26 Cal. 2d 306, 169 P. 2d 924 (1946) permitted proof of unique methods of previous homicides to establish guilt of the accused.

not induced by the defendant's wrongdoing, and at the same time, would prove the identity of defendant as the wrongdoer. Indeed, the evidence is so persuasive and so necessary in case of infanticide or other child abuse by suffocation if the wrongdoer is to be apprehended, that we think that its relevance clearly outweighs its prejudicial effect on the jury.[10] We reject defendant's argument that the proof was not so clear and convincing that its admissibility should not be sustained. If the evidence with regard to each child is considered separately, it is true that some of the incidents are less conclusive than others; but we think the incidents must be considered collectively, and when they are, an unmistakable pattern emerges. That pattern overwhelmingly establishes defendant's guilt.[13]

NOTES AND PROBLEMS

1.   Some critics have attacked the independent logical relevance doctrine on the ground that the distinction between character and noncharacter theories is illusory. Note, *The Character of Discrimination Law: The Incompatibility of Rule 404 and Employment Discrimination Suits*, 114 YALE L.J. 1063 (2005). These critics contend that even the accepted theories of "independent" relevance involve propensity inferences. Kuhns, *The Propensity to Misunderstand the Character of Specific Acts Evidence*, 66 IOWA L. REV. 777 (1981). For example, Professor Kuhns critiques the case law admitting evidence of the defendant's commission of an uncharged crime with the same distinctive *modus operandi* as the charged offense. Professor Kuhns argues that admitting this evidence to establish the defendant's identity:

> necessarily requires a generalized propensity inference. The only factor that makes commission of the other crime relevant to identify the perpetrator of the charged crime is the assumption that some individual has a propensity to commit both crimes, and this assumption is dependent upon the inference that people generally have a propensity not to perpetrate a crime in the same unusual manner in which another person has perpetrated a crime. *Id.* at 787.

The theory of logical relevance sanctioned by *Woods* relies on the so-called doctrine of objective chances. 1 E. IMWINKELRIED, UNCHARGED MISCONDUCT EVIDENCE § 4:03 (rev. 2008) The theory is that if the defendant suffered a particular type of loss — the death of a spouse or child as in *Woods* — more frequently than the average, innocent citizen would sustain such losses, the defendant's claim of accident is objectively implausible. That theory can be depicted in this fashion:

---

[10] Although the average juror, when confronted with such evidence, could have little doubt of defendant's guilt, it is not unlikely that, in view of the abundant evidence of defendant's emotional distress at the loss or illness of each child, he would recognize that there was a pitiable absence of some factor in defendant's personality which would permit her to engage in such repeated conduct.

[13] *State v. Schleigh*, 210 Or. 155, 310 P.2d 341, 348 (1957) (repeated fires by spontaneous combustion unlikely; eight fires along one country road immediately after defendant, his father and other drove by show "a deliberate plan to set them") . . . .

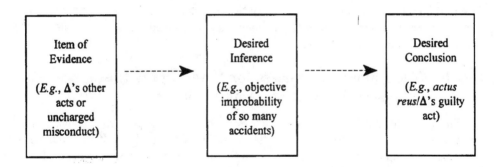

Formally, the theory does not require any assumption about the defendant's personal, subjective bad character. Nevertheless, it does seem to pose a real risk that the jury will be tempted to punish the defendant for past crimes. Is the theory merely propensity evidence under the guise of pop statistics? The Supreme Court appeared to endorse the doctrine of objective chances in *Estelle v. McGuire*, 502 U.S. 62 (1991).

2. In *Woods*, the prosecution used the theory to prove the occurrence of an actus reus. Can the doctrine be utilized to prove mens rea? Suppose that the defendant is charged with knowing possession of drugs. Although drugs were found in the trunk of a car the defendant was driving, he adamantly denies knowing of the presence of the drugs. On two prior occasions when the defendant was similarly stopped, the police found drugs in vehicles he was driving. It is true that innocent people sometimes find themselves enmeshed in suspicious circumstances. However, how likely is that the defendant would innocently become involved in three such situations?

3. Distinguish the *admissibility* of doctrine of chances evidence from its *sufficiency* to sustain a conviction. In *Woods*, the prosecution presented a forensic pathologist's testimony that, given Paul's case history, there was a 75% probability that his death was a homicide. Without more, the doctrine of chances establishes only that one or some of the incidents were not accidents. There is nothing in the internal logic of the doctrine that singles out the charged incident as a crime.

4. **Problem 14-11.** In *Devitt*, the defendant denies the battery and claims that Paterson was mistaken in identifying him. Another man, Anderson, was beaten a week before the alleged battery in this case. Anderson is prepared to identify Devitt as his attacker. Is his testimony admissible under Rule 404(b)? Suppose that Anderson adds that his attack also occurred on Monday, the day of the week Paterson was attacked. His attack occurred at 4:00 in the afternoon, the same time Paterson was beaten. What if, as in the instant case, the assailant wore brown pants and a yellow shirt? What if, as in the instant case, the assailant threatened the victim with a thin, silvery knife? At what point, if any, would you as judge be persuaded to admit the evidence?

5. **Problem 14-12.** Suppose that Anderson's beating occurred a week after — rather than a week before — the attack on Paterson. The courts sometimes refer to uncharged misconduct as "prior crimes." Should the doctrine be limited to acts occurring before acts alleged in the pleading? See *United States v. Hearst*, 563 F.2d

1331, 1336 (9th Cir. 1977) (evidence of publishing heiress Patty Hearst's participation in a crime a month after the robbery she was tried for). Does Rule 404(b) include a timing requirement?

b. The Balancing Process for Determining the Admissibility of Other Acts Evidence

Finding that uncharged misconduct evidence has independent, noncharacter relevance does not end the analysis. That finding satisfies Rule 404(b); but since this evidence is potentially so damaging to the defense, the evidence must still pass muster under the Rule 403 balancing test. Under Rule 403, the judge must balance the prosecution's need for the evidence against its prejudicial character.

1)   The Prosecution's Need for the Evidence

The prosecution's need for the evidence depends on four factors: (a) the strength of the evidence that the defendant committed the other act; (b) the extent to which the other act is probative of the fact of consequence the prosecutor offers it to establish; (c) the availability of other, less prejudicial evidence to prove the fact of consequence; and (d) the degree to which that fact of consequence is disputed.

Factor (a). It is not enough that the uncharged misconduct evidence has bare logical relevance; the cases often proclaim that to overcome its prejudicial character, the evidence must possess "substantial" relevance. The identification of the defendant as the perpetrator of the uncharged crime should be relatively positive and unequivocal. It was formerly the majority rule that the prosecution must present clear and convincing evidence that the defendant was the perpetrator before evidence of the other act could be presented to the jury. *United States v. Kinney,* 598 F. Supp. 883, 887 (D. Me. 1984). However, in *Huddleston v. United States,* 485 U.S. 681 (1988), the Supreme Court held that the majority view was not adopted by the Federal Rules and that the preliminary factual questions whether the prior act occurred and whether the defendant was the actor are to be decided by the jury under Rule 104(b). Thus, according to the Court, the evidence of these preliminary facts need only be sufficient to support a rational, permissive inference that the facts are true. The *Huddleston* Court made it clear that the court's role in this situation is to screen the evidence under Rule 403, not Rule 104(a). Assume that the identifying evidence in such a case is rather vague or indefinite; the witness to the uncharged crime might be prepared to say only that "the defendant looks an awful lot like the guy who I saw commit" that crime. Under *Huddleston,* this testimony would probably satisfy Rule 104(b), but given the facial uncertainty of the testimony, the judge might exclude the evidence under Rule 403.

Factor (b). Ideally, there should be only a short time lapse between the two acts. The more remote the uncharged act is in time or place from the charged crime, the less probative it is. However, unlike Rule 609(b), 404(b) does not contain any general guidelines for evaluating remoteness in time.

Factor (c). The prosecution's need for the uncharged misconduct evidence is certainly bona fide when the prosecution has no other evidence to prove the fact of consequence or the other evidence is "weak and inadequate." *State v. Billstrom,* 276

Minn. 174, 149 N.W.2d 281 (1967). Recall the discussion of *Old Chief* in Chapter 13: The court must evaluate the need for the evidence in light of the availability of alternative, less prejudicial evidence. *United States v. DiZenzo*, 500 F.2d 263 (4th Cir. 1974). If the prosecution has a strong case without the uncharged misconduct evidence, the judge should exclude the evidence. *United States v. Cochran*, 546 F.2d 27 (5th Cir. 1977). The prosecution may not overkill with cumulative testimony; the prosecution should not prove its case to the hilt with uncharged misconduct evidence. *People v. Perez*, 42 Cal. App. 3d 760, 117 Cal. Rptr. 195 (1974).

Factor (d). Lastly, the court should factor in the extent to which the fact of consequence is genuinely disputed. In many jurisdictions, if the defendant pleads not guilty, the courts routinely find that every element of the charged offense is sufficiently disputed to warrant the introduction of uncharged misconduct. *United States v. Roberts*, 619 F.2d 379 (5th Cir. 1980). In these jurisdictions, the defendant must give the prosecution some "enforceable pretrial assurance" that he or she does not intend to dispute an issue to negate the prosecution need for the evidence. *United States v. Webb*, 625 F.2d 709 (5th Cir. 1980). There is a pertinent passage in the Advisory Committee Note to Rule 401:

> The fact to which the evidence is directed need not be disputed. While situations will arise which call for the exclusion of evidence offered to prove a point conceded by the opponent, the ruling should be made on the basis of such considerations as waste of time and undue prejudice (see Rule 403)
> . . . .

PROBLEMS

1. **Problem 14-13.** Suppose that, in *Devitt*, the prosecution offers uncharged misconduct for the stated purpose of proving Devitt's identity as the assailant. Before trial, Devitt offers to stipulate to his identity and defend only on the ground of self-defense. Should the judge in effect force the prosecutor to accept the stipulation, or should the judge nevertheless admit the evidence? *United States v. Coades*, 549 F.2d 1303, 1306 (9th Cir. 1977) ("a deplorable example of prosecutorial overzealousness"); *People v. Perez, supra*, at 765–68, 117 Cal. Rptr. at 197–99 ("the usual stipulation to the testimony of the police chemist as to the fact that the substance acquired from the defendant was a narcotic was not forthcoming . . . ."); *cf. Old Chief v. United States*, 519 U.S. 172 (1997).

2. **Problem 14-14.** On direct examination, Devitt frankly admits that he had fought with Paterson but claims self-defense. Does that bar uncharged misconduct on the identity issue? If the issue must be genuinely disputed, what will constitute a sufficient dispute? Is it enough that at a pretrial hearing, the defendant indicates that he will dispute that issue? *United States v. Kirk*, 528 F.2d 1057, 1061 n.3 (5th Cir. 1976) (yes). What if defense counsel suggests the defense in the opening statement? What if defense counsel vigorously cross-examines the prosecution witnesses who testify to Devitt's identify as the assailant? Should we require that the prosecutor always reserve uncharged misconduct evidence to the rebuttal stage after the defense case-in-chief?

2)   The Prejudicial Character of the Evidence

The four factors discussed above determine the probative worth of the other acts evidence, but under Rule 403 the judge must balance probative value against the countervailing probative dangers. While almost all uncharged misconduct evidence will be harmful to the defense, there are of course varying degrees of prejudice. It is one thing to admit as uncharged misconduct proof of a petty theft by the defendant; the degree of prejudice is much greater if we permit the prosecutor to introduce evidence of an uncharged act of child molestation by the defendant — a crime that most jurors would find highly repulsive. *United States v. Cook*, 538 F.2d 1000 (3d Cir. 1976). In the early 1980s, the Department of Justice released the findings of its National Survey of Crime Severity. The bureau wanted to determine the public perceptions of the seriousness of various crimes. Sixty thousand adults participated and were asked to rate the gravity of several offenses. The survey resulted in the following ratings, *inter alia*:

72.1   A person plants a bomb in a public building. The bomb explodes, and 20 people are killed.

52.8   A man forcibly rapes a woman. As a result of physical injuries, she dies.

47.8   A parent beats his young child with his fists. As a result, the child dies.

33.8   A person runs a narcotics ring.

32.7   An armed person skyjacks an airplane and holds the crew and passengers hostage until a ransom is paid.

21.2   A person kidnaps a victim.

20.1   A man forcibly rapes a woman. Her physical injuries require treatment by a doctor but not hospitalization.

19.5   A person kills a victim by recklessly driving an automobile.

16.9   A legislator takes a bribe of $10,000 from a company to vote for a law favoring the company.

12.2   A person pays a witness to give false testimony in a criminal trial.

11.4   A person knowingly lies under oath during a trial. 10.8 A person steals a locked car and sells it.

10.4   A person intentionally hits a victim with a lead pipe. The victim requires hospitalization.

6.5   A person uses heroin.

5.4   A person has some heroin for his own use.

4.5   A person cheats on his federal income tax return. 1.6 A person is a customer in a house of prostitution.

1.4   A person smokes marijuana.

1.1   A person disturbs the neighborhood with loud, noisy behavior.

Trial judges are accustomed to hearing counsel "cry wolf" and make bald assertions about the prejudicial character of the proponent's evidence. Judges are much more impressed when the opponent marshals empirical data such as the BJS study.

NOTES

1.   At common law, most courts assigned the prosecutor the burden of showing that the probative value of uncharged misconduct evidence outweighs any attendant probative dangers. The courts often declared that the prosecutor's burden was "heavy." *Smith v. State*, 646 S.W.2d 452, 458 (Tex. Crim. App. 1983). Do the Federal Rules continue the common-law norm? Rule 404(b) does not mention the balancing process, however, the Advisory Committee Note refers the reader to Rule 403. On its face, Rule 403 seems to turn the common-law norm upside down; the passive voice of the sentence suggests that the opponent has the burden, and the adverb "substantially" indicates that the opponent's burden is now a heavy one. Would it be possible to construe Rule 404(b) as incorporating the factors listed in Rule 403 without adopting the allocation and measure of the burden suggested by Rule 403? *See* Kuhns, *The Propensity to Misunderstand the Character of Specific Acts Evidence*, 66 Iowa L. Rev. 777, 797 n.74 (1981).

2.   It is sometimes assumed that only the prosecutor can employ the uncharged misconduct doctrine. Is that assumption correct? Does the text of Rule 404(b) contain that restriction? Suppose that Devitt's attorney uncovered evidence that a third party had committed other batteries and used exactly the same *modus operandi* as employed in the Paterson attack. Would Rule 404(b) forbid Devitt from offering that evidence to exculpate himself? Should Rule 403 apply to exculpatory Rule 404(b) evidence proffered by the defense in the same way in which it applies to inculpatory Rule 404(b) evidence offered by the prosecution? In *State v. Garfole*, 76 N.J. 445, 388 A.2d 587 (1978), the court stated that the standard for admitting a third party's misdeeds to exculpate the defendant should be less stringent than the test for admitting testimony about the defendant's uncharged misconduct.

3.   Other Acts Evidence in Civil Actions

Uncharged misconduct evidence is of growing importance in civil cases. In civil rights cases, it is often introduced to prove the defendant's discriminatory animus. Marshall, Note, *The Character of Discrimination Law: The Incompatibility of Rule 404 and Employment Discrimination Suits*, 114 Yale L.J. 1063 (2005). On damages, it is frequently used to establish malice as a predicate for recovering punitive damages. Gash, *Punitive Damages, Other Acts Evidence, and the Constitution*, 2004 Utah L. Rev. 1191. In civil cases, the proponent of other acts evidence cannot offer the evidence simply to (1) increase the probability that the party committed the act alleged in the pleading or (2) support a generalized inference of the party's fault. On those theories of logical relevance, the evidence has minimal probative value — probative value insufficient to overcome the danger of distracting the jury from the central issues in the case. The proponent must offer the evidence for "more sharply refined" noncharacter purposes. *Britton v. Rogers*, 631 F.2d 572 (8th Cir. 1980). Depending on the purpose, the court might admit evidence of another contract entered into by a party, another lawsuit filed by that party, or another tort committed by that party.

a.   Other Contracts

Suppose that in a contract action, the plaintiff attempts to offer evidence of another contract. The classic discussion of this topic appears in Slough, *Relevancy Unraveled*, 6 U. KAN. L. REV. 38 (1957). Slough noted that when the evidence related to another contract between the same two persons currently litigating a contract dispute, the marked tendency in the cases was to admit the evidence if it shed light on the meaning of the contract *so long as* the two agreements were "substantially similar." In contrast, the courts were reluctant to admit evidence of another contract between a party to the current suit and a stranger to the litigation. Today, there is no absolute ban on evidence of contracts with third parties. For example, in *Firlotte v. Jessee*, 76 Cal. App. 2d 207, 172 P.2d 710 (1946) the question was whether Jessee reserved the right to graze cattle on land he had sold to Firlotte. Firlotte offered testimony by a third party that "Jessee had approached him with an offer to sell . . . the same land and that Jessee had said nothing about reserving the right to pasture his own cattle. . . ." Although the testimony related to Jessee's bargaining with a third party, the evidence was admissible because of its considerable probative worth: "[t]he circumstance of the defendant's offering the identical land to another without reservation afforded a strong probability that the course followed in one instance would be followed in another." The purpose of the evidence — not the identity of the contracting parties — should be determinative.

PROBLEMS

1.   **Problem 14-15.** In our torts case, Ms. Hill alleges that at the time the parties signed the written contract Jefferson's representative made an express oral warranty that the car was "top flight" and "virtually malfunction proof." In its answer, Polecat Motors denies that the warranty was ever made. At trial, could Ms. Hill call as witnesses other customers of Jefferson Motor Co. to elicit their testimony that Jefferson's salespeople made similar representations to them? Does the evidence have "independent" relevance if Ms. Hill offers the evidence to prove that the representation was made as a basis for creating a warranty? Is Ms. Hill simply arguing, "They did it once, therefore they did it again"?

2.   **Problem 14-16.** Would your analysis in the last problem change if Ms. Hill wanted to avoid the contract on the ground of fraud? Ms. Hill has evidence that, two months before her husband's purchase, the same Jefferson salesperson made identical representations to another customer, Mr. Felice. purchased the identical model of Polecat which Mr. Hill bought. One month later, Mr. Felice's car developed severe mechanical problems. Felice brought the car back to the dealership and called the problems to the salesperson's attention. How does the logical relevance of this evidence differ from that of the evidence proffered in Problem 14-15, *supra*? Would this evidence run afoul of the prohibition of using other acts to support a general inference of fault, or does this evidence have "independent" or "special" noncharacter logical relevance?

b. Tort Actions

1)   Other Claims by the Plaintiff

Consider the notorious case of *San Antonio Traction Co. v. Cox*, 184 S.W. 722 (Tex. Civ. App. 1916):

[Cox sued the Traction Company for personal injuries, which he claimed he received in alighting from a street car. He alleged that while he was getting off the car at a crossing, the car was started suddenly without notice, causing the plaintiff to fall from the car. Defendant alleged that Cox and several members of his family have continuously "worked together, conspired, assisted, and abetted each other in propounding false and fraudulent claims against this defendant," and "that this suit and the claim propounded herein is a part and parcel of said co-operation, conspiracy, and abetting of the above-mentioned parties for the purpose of obtaining money from this defendant." The plaintiff prevailed at trial.]

Appellant complains of the exclusion of certain testimony. . . . The testimony excluded shows a remarkable condition of affairs. About 17 claims were propounded by Cox and his relatives, all of which, except 2, were for injuries alleged to have been sustained in alighting from cars. To get off of a street car is a simple thing, and it is inconceivable that all of these people could have been caused to fall by reason of negligence of the operatives of the cars. Surely the company had no desire to willfully inflict injuries upon the members of this family, and surely these people were not all suffering from infirmities such as to prevent them from getting off of a street car without assistance. In spite, however, of the warnings furnished by similar accidents to members of the family, they appear not to have learned caution, but continued taking the risk, a terrible one as to them, of getting off of street cars, with the result that every now and then one of them would be injured just like the others were. We think it so highly improbable that all of these claims could be honest ones, that a jury would be justified in inferring that fraud had been practiced with regard to some of them. The testimony indicates a bad state of affairs, but we do not think, had it been admitted, it would, with the other testimony, have justified a charge on conspiracy. The evidence fails to connect plaintiff with the other claims, except in one instance in which he was with a cousin when he had his fall, and also witnessed the release executed by him to the company. . . .

The issue in this case was whether plaintiff was injured by reason of the negligence of the company as alleged by him, or whether, as is contended by defendant, no such incident as testified to by plaintiff occurred, or if it did, that it was willfully brought about by him, and not caused by negligence of the company. Proof of a conspiracy and of his connection therewith would undoubtedly tend strongly to corroborate the testimony of the employees of defendant that no such incident occurred, or might lead the jury to believe that he willfully permitted himself to be thrown from the steps. But as above pointed out the evidence admitted fails to show any conspiracy between any of the members of the family who propounded claims, and the evidence excluded, considered alone or with that admitted, would not justify a charge on conspiracy, for it merely shows transactions of a similar nature, not connected with each other. . . .

NOTES AND PROBLEMS

1. Notice the court's use of such expressions as "conspiracy," "willfully," and "ulterior object." Those passages suggest the court's conception of what would constitute independent relevance. What showing would the court have found satisfactory?

2. Did the traction company's attorney commit a tactical mistake in alleging that Cox and his family members had entered into a conspiracy to defraud the traction company? The court acknowledges that "it is inconceivable that all of these people could have been caused to fall by reason of negligence of the operatives of the cars." Given that logical relevance, the incidents' striking similarity, and the alleged victims' close family relationships, perhaps the traction company's attorney could have succeeded without alleging a conspiracy. The traction company might argue that, in light of these circumstances, it was objectively unlikely that all these incidents were bona fide accidents. Would this argument require the jury to draw any inference about the plaintiff's subjective, personal character? Remember the *Woods* case excerpted earlier in this chapter.

3. **Problem 14-17.** How can a defendant prove that the plaintiff is a "claim-minded" individual who files frivolous suits? Suppose that in our torts case there is evidence Ms. Hill filed three unsuccessful products liability cases against other manufacturers in the past five years. Would that evidence have sufficient independent noncharacter logical relevance to be admissible? Suppose that the prayer in one of the earlier suits asked for damages for injuries to the plaintiff's back, just as the prayer in the instant case seeks damages for personal injuries to the back. What theory of logical relevance suggests itself now? Would that qualify as "independent" logical relevance?

2) Other Torts by the Defendant

Evidence of another misdeed by a civil defendant can have a dramatic impact on the outcome of the case. In one empirical study, researchers found that if a civil jury learns that the defendant has a criminal record, the plaintiff can expect a verdict 9% higher than normal. D. Herbert & R. Barrett, Attorney's Master Guide to Courtroom Psychology 321 (1980). More commonly, the plaintiff offers evidence of another tort committed by the defendant. Especially when the defendant is a mass manufacturer as in our torts case, the plaintiff will often be able to find evidence of similar torts committed by the defendant. However, the plaintiff may not offer evidence of the other torts merely to prove that the event alleged in the complaint occurred. Nor may the plaintiff offer the evidence to support a general inference that, as in the prior cases, the defendant was at fault. These theories of admissibility fall short of "independent" relevance.

Nowhere in civil actions is the stress on independent logical relevance greater than in product liability cases. Connolly, *Evidentiary Products in Products Cases*, in PRODUCTS LIABILITY: LAW, PRACTICE, AND SCIENCE 11:46–48 (1967), is illustrative. Connolly lists some of the theories of logical relevance the courts have found acceptable. The theories include, *inter alia*:

- The other accident tended to show the existence of the condition which resulted in the plaintiff's injury. If a third party slipped and fell on the same step the day before the plaintiff's accident, the short time lapse makes it likely that the condition still existed when the plaintiff attempted to use the same stairway.

- The other accident evidenced the instrumentality's potential to cause injury which rendered the instrumentality or condition unsafe. For this purpose, the plaintiff could introduce both prior and subsequent accidents.

- The other accident put the defendant on notice that the instrumentality or condition was unsafe. On this theory of logical relevance, the plaintiff is restricted to prior accidents.

- The other accident involving the defendant's instrumentality or conditions shows that the instrumentality or condition caused the plaintiff's injury.

Connolly notes that when the courts invoke one of these theories, they often generalize that only "substantially similar" accidents are admissible. However, he adds that as a practical matter, the courts relax the similarity standard when the plaintiff relies on the notice theory. Under that theory, the other incident need merely "attract the defendant's attention to the dangerous situation." The incident could have a wide "warning radius."

NOTES AND PROBLEMS

1. Connolly refers to "the warning radius of the [prior] happening." What does that mean? Suppose that the prior accident involved a slip and fall on the fourth step on a stairway. The following day the plaintiff is injured in a slip and fall on the fifth step.

2. **Problem 14-18.** At trial, Polecat Motors calls Dr. Eckert. Eckert is an expert in the design of automobiles and did his Ph.D. work on the design hazards of gas tanks. Eckert testifies that it would have been physically impossible for Ms. Hill's gas tank to explode as she described merely because Worker's car struck her moving car at the speed Ms. Hill testified to. Eckert adds that the only possible explanation is that Ms. Hill panicked, stepped on the brake rather than the gas, came to an abrupt stop before Worker's car struck hers, and thereby increased the force of the collision. During her rebuttal, Ms. Hill would now like to introduce evidence of four other accidents in which the gas tanks of moving Polecat cars exploded when they were rear-ended. Is the evidence of the other accidents admissible? *Auzene v. Gulf Pub. Serv. Co.*, 188 So. 512, 515 (La. Ct. App. 1939).

3. **Problem 14-19.** Suppose that Ms. Hill had offered the same evidence during her case-in-chief rather than waiting until her rebuttal. How does that fact change the legal irrelevance analysis?

4. **Problem 14-20.** In her suit, Ms. Hill alleges a strict products liability cause of action based on a claimed design defect in the Polecat's gas tank. Suppose instead that she had alleged that Polecat negligently manufactured the particular gas tank in her car. How does the inclusion of a design defect allegation in the pleading affect the admissibility of the evidence of the other accidents involving similarly designed products? Does the design defect allegation make it easier to tie the pleaded incident to the uncharged incidents?

5. **Problem 14-21.** Polecat Motors has evidence of the "safety history" of the model of car that Ms. Hill was driving at the time of the accident. The complaint department's records show that during the three years that Polecat marketed and sold over 300,000 cars of that model, only fifteen complaints were made by customers and none related to the gas tank. Is that evidence admissible in Ms. Hill's products liability suit? *Stark v. Allis Chalmers & Northwest Rds. Inc.*, 2 Wash. App. 399, 467 P.2d 854, 858 (1970) ("The trial court may allow . . . testimony of lack of accidents where circumstances are similar . . . .").

6. **Problem 14-22.** Suppose again that instead of invoking a products liability theory, Ms. Hill alleged negligent manufacture. How would that affect the "safety history" evidence? In what sense is a products liability allegation a two-edged sword from the plaintiff's perspective? *See* Morris, *Proof of Safety History in Negligence Cases*, 61 Harv. L. Rev. 205 (1948) (the judge has more latitude to admit defense evidence of lack of accidents in product liability cases).

7. Uncharged misconduct also plays an important role in civil rights cases. Just as prosecutors often use it to prove criminal intent, plaintiffs frequently resort to it to prove discriminatory animus. An age discrimination case, *Sprint/United Mgmt. Co. v. Mendelson*, 552 U.S. 379 (2007), is illustrative. *Mendelson* involves "me too" testimony — that is, evidence by similarly situated employees claiming that they were subjected to the same type of discrimination as the plaintiff. The Tenth Circuit read the District Court opinion as adopting a categorical rule that another employee is similarly situated only if the employee has the same supervisor as the plaintiff. The Tenth Circuit rejected this categorical approach, applied Rule 403, and found that the evidence of the age discrimination against other employees was sufficiently probative to be admissible. The Supreme Court reversed, finding that the district court opinion was susceptible to the interpretation that it simply found the evidence insufficiently probative under Rule 403. The Supreme Court added that even if the district court erred by adopting a per se rule, the Tenth Circuit should have remanded to permit the trial judge to engage in the balancing in the first instance. The Court emphasized that trial judges are in a superior position to conduct "fact-intensive, context-specific" balancing. Starr & Wilson, *Employment Law: "Me Too" Evidence*, Nat'l L.J., Jan. 21, 2008, at 12.

8. Do not limit your imagination to theories relevant to the merits of liability. As previously stated, plaintiffs attorneys often rely on evidence of a defendant's uncharged misconduct as a predicate for recovering punitive damages. However, uncharged misconduct can be a two-edged sword on damages. Defense attorneys have developed a number of creative damages theories for introducing evidence of a *plaintiff's* uncharged misconduct. For example, suppose that the plaintiff seeks lost wages as an element of damages. Some courts have admitted evidence of the

plaintiff's criminal record on the theory that the plaintiff's record would make it more difficult for the plaintiff to obtain highly remunerative employment. *Toombs v. Manning*, 640 F. Supp. 938 (E.D. Pa. 1986), *aff'd in part, vacated in part*, 835 F.2d 453 (3d Cir. 1987). Or suppose that the amount of the plaintiff's damages depends in part on the plaintiff's life expectancy. In such situations, a number of courts have allowed the defense to introduce evidence of the plaintiff's drug abuse. *Harvey by and through Harvey v. General Motors Corp.*, 873 F.2d 1343 (10th Cir. 1989); *Smith v. Southland Corp.*, 738 F. Supp. 923 (E.D. Pa. 1990). The evidence is relevant at least if the defense also offers expert testimony that the type of substance abuse reduces a person's life expectancy.

4. A Comparison of the Admissibility of Other Acts Evidence in Civil and Criminal Cases

As a practical matter, in many jurisdictions the standards for admitting evidence of other acts in civil actions are stricter than those applied to the admissibility of evidence of other crimes in criminal prosecutions. "[I]n [some] jurisdictions, evidence of a criminal defendant's other homicides is more readily admissible than proof of a civil defendant's other tire failures." Article, *Uncharged Misconduct Evidence: Getting It Out Into the Light*, TRIAL, Nov. 1984, at 60. Contrast the trend in criminal cases toward an *inclusionary* approach to uncharged misconduct with the generally *exclusionary* approach taken in the majority of jurisdictions toward the admissibility of evidence of other acts in civil cases. Moreover, even if the evidence of another accident falls within a recognized exception, the courts often demand near identity of circumstances with the pleaded tort. In contrast, the academic commentators have generally been critical of the lax manner in which the courts apply the similarity requirement in prosecutions.

NOTES

1. Consider these divergent approaches as a matter of policy. Should Rule 403 and the doctrine of legal irrelevance be applied differently in criminal than in civil cases? The stakes are arguably higher in criminal cases. Which species of evidence is more likely to be prejudicial: proof of another tort or evidence of another crime? Consider the ratings in the Bureau of Justice Statistics' National Survey of Crime Severity set forth above.

2. Now analyze the problem as one of statutory construction. For civil cases, the doctrine of other acts is largely a creature of common or decisional law. Some commentators assert that the Federal Rules of Evidence leave these rules uncodified and that the courts may continue to enforce them under the general aegis of Rule 403. Langum, *Uncodified Federal Evidence Rules Applicable to Civil Trials*, 19 WILLAMETTE L. REV. 513, 519 (1983). Do you agree? Consider the wording of the first sentence of Rule 404(b). What significance do the words, "wrongs . . . or acts," have if the Rule applies only to evidence of other crimes? *See* 2A N. SINGER & J. SINGER, STATUTES AND STATUTORY CONSTRUCTION § 46.06 (7th ed. 2007). If we assume *arguendo* that the words, "wrongs . . . or acts," are expansive enough to include evidence of other contracts, torts, accidents, and lawsuits, is admissibility governed by the general statute Rule 403 or the more specific provisions of Rule

404(b)? *Busic v. United States*, 446 U.S. 398, 406 (1980) ("a more specific statute will be given precedence over a more general one . . .").

3.   The number of citations to Rule 404(b) in civil cases is growing exponentially. In the past two decades, civil practitioners have come to realize that uncharged misconduct evidence can be highly useful for such purposes as proving discriminatory intent, Marshall, Note, *The Character of Discrimination Law: The Incompatibility of Rule 404 and Employment Discrimination Suits*, 114 YALE L.J. 1063 (2005), and establishing the malice necessary to permit a recovery of punitive damages. Gash, *Punitive Damages, Other Acts Evidence, and the Constitution*, 2004 UTAH L. REV. 1191. In numerous states, there is an enhanced burden of proof when the plaintiff seeks punitive damages. Many jurisdictions require clear and convincing evidence, *Photias v. Graham*, 14 F. Supp. 2d 126 (D. Me. 1998) (Maine law); *McDermott v. Party City Corp.*, 11 F. Supp. 2d 612 (E.D. Pa. 1998) (Pennsylvania law), and one state prescribes proof beyond a reasonable doubt as the standard. *Karnes v. SCI Colorado Funeral Services, Inc.*, 162 F.3d 1077, 1082 (10th Cir. 1998). Evidence of the defendant's other similar intentional misconduct can help the plaintiff meet that heavy burden.

Chapter 15

CREDIBILITY EVIDENCE: BOLSTERING AND IMPEACHING

Read Federal Rules of Evidence 607, 608(a), 801(d)(1)(C) and 806.

A. INTRODUCTION

Although credibility evidence is indisputably material and relevant, that does not guarantee its admission. Credibility evidence can be extremely prejudicial, distracting or likely to pose other probative dangers. A complex body of law has evolved in response to these dangers. To understand this body of law, it is important to realize that there are three types of credibility evidence. The first is **bolstering** evidence. A party bolsters her own witness's credibility when she presents evidence designed to increase the witness's credibility in the jurors' eyes even before the opposing party has attacked that credibility. Second is attacking — **impeachment** — evidence. Impeachment is the general term for an attack on a witness's credibility. Such attacks are designed to convince the jury that a witness is unworthy of belief. Finally, there is **rehabilitating** evidence. Rehabilitation is the general term for evidence designed to rebuild or restore a witness's credibility after it has been attacked.

B. THE EVIDENTIARY STATUS OF CREDIBILITY EVIDENCE

For the most part, evidence offered on a credibility theory is admissible only for that purpose and will not be admitted "substantively," that is, to prove or disprove a historical fact or substantive issue in the case. The reason for its substantive inadmissibility may be simply that it is irrelevant. Suppose that Jones saw Devitt outside Mr. Paterson's apartment about the time an anonymous, threatening note was slipped under Mr. Paterson's door. The note warned Patterson not to testify against Devitt. Patterson does testify and includes telling about the timing and contents of the note he received. Jones then testifies about when he saw Devitt near the Patterson apartment. After his direct examination, Jones is cross-examined about a prior felony conviction for perjury. The fact that Jones was once convicted of perjury usually has no bearing on the substantive issues in the case. In other words, it neither increases nor decreases the probability that Paterson was assaulted or that Devitt was the person who left the note.

Even if credibility evidence is relevant to a substantive issue in the case, it may be inadmissible for that purpose because it violates some other rule of evidence. Thus, a prior inconsistent statement might violate the rule against hearsay. Suppose that on cross-examination, Devitt impeaches Jones by showing that Jones told his neighbor that he, Jones, did not think it was Devitt he saw near Paterson's apartment. Devitt may certainly use this prior inconsistent statement to impeach Jones. The fact that Jones made a prior inconsistent statement reduces his credibility, and the judge will admit the statement as credibility evidence. However, if Devitt attempted to use Jones' statement as substantive proof that Devitt was not near Paterson's apartment, an objection on hearsay grounds would be sustained.

PROBLEM

Problem 15-1. In *Devitt*, after the defense impeaches Jones with the prior inconsistent statement, the prosecutor asks for a "limiting" instruction under Rule 105. You are the trial judge. Should you give such an instruction? If so, how should the instruction be worded? *See United States v. De La Torre*, 599 F.3d 1198 (10th Cir. 2010) (finding that the district court did not abuse its discretion where the court delivered an appropriate limiting instruction; defendant's statements concerning his prior methamphetamine use were admitted for the sole purpose of allowing the jury to consider the witness's credibility; statements were introduced in order to impeach the witness, but were not allowed as substantive evidence on the issue of guilt); *Newsome v. Penske Truck Leasing Corp.*, 437 F. Supp. 2d 431 (D. Md. 2006) (prior inconsistent statements are admissible only as impeachment evidence).

C. BOLSTERING BEFORE IMPEACHMENT

As soon as Jones testifies for the prosecution in *Devitt*, his credibility becomes one of the material facts in the case. Consequently, it would be logically relevant for the prosecution to bolster Jones' believability even before any attack is made upon it. However, the common law generally forbade bolstering. The common law rule is followed in modern cases. *State v. Kackley*, 92 P.3d 1128 (Kan. Ct. App. 2004); *United States v. Perez*, 30 F.3d 1407 (11th Cir. 1994); *Berman v. State*, 632 S.E.2d 757 (Ga. Ct. App. 2006).

There is a straightforward rationale for this rule. At the point at which the prosecutor attempts bolstering, before Devitt's cross-examination of Jones, we do not know whether or how Devitt may attack Jones' believability. Devitt may decide, for various reasons, not to cross-examine Jones. In that event, any time devoted to the bolstering evidence would essentially have been wasted; the prosecutor would have spent time building up the credibility of a witness who was never attacked. Most jurisdictions therefore force the witness's proponent, the party calling the witness, to wait until redirect to offer evidence designed to enhance the witness's credibility. If the opposing party does not attack, we have saved precious court time; if the opposing party attacks, the proponent can then offer the evidence as rehabilitation. In the words of Rule 403, until the opposing party sharpens the issue of the witness's credibility by impeachment, devoting hearing bolstering evidence would be a "waste of time."

Cases underline the point. The court examined the prosecutor's approach in *United States v. Porges*, 2003 U.S. App. LEXIS 22730 (2d Cir. Nov. 4, 2003), where the prosecution bolstered witnesses by bringing out, on direct, special agreements to tell the truth contained in "cooperation agreements" which the witnesses had entered into with the government. The defendant successfully argued on appeal that this evidence improperly bolstered the witnesses' testimony because evidence of the cooperation agreements was introduced prior to any attack on the credibility of those witnesses. "[A]lthough the prosecutor may inquire into impeaching aspects of cooperation agreements on direct, *bolstering* aspects such as promises to testify truthfully or penalties for failure to do so may only be developed to rehabilitate the witness *after a defense attack on credibility.*"

The Federal Rules codify the prohibition. Rule 608(a) provides:

> (a) Reputation or Opinion Evidence. A witness's credibility may be attacked or supported by testimony about the witness's reputation for having a character of untruthfulness, or by testimony in the form of an opinion about that character. But evidence of truthful character is admissible only after the witness's character for truthfulness has been attacked.

> Notwithstanding the general rule against bolstering, courts do occasionally permit the practice. Many jurisdictions, for example, recognize the "fresh complaint" doctrine. 4 J. WIGMORE, EVIDENCE §§ 1134-40 (Chadbourn rev. 1972); 6 J. WIGMORE, EVIDENCE §§ 1160, 1171 (3d ed. 1940). Hence, during a rape victim's direct examination, the victim could testify that she phoned in a report to the police an hour after the alleged attack. *See State v. Kackley*, 92 P.3d 1128, 1135 (Kan. Ct. App. 2004) (a recognized exception to the rule against bolstering exists in rape cases). Similarly, some jurisdictions admit evidence of a witness's pretrial identification to bolster the witness's in-court identification. *State v. Draughn*, 121 N.J. Super. 64, 296 A.2d 79 (1972); *People v. Nival*, 33 N.Y.2d 391, 353 N.Y.S.2d 409, 308 N.E.2d 883 (1974). Suppose that during his direct examination, Paterson pointed to Devitt and identified him as his assailant. Under this exception to the bolstering prohibition, before concluding his direct, Paterson could add that he also singled Devitt out at a lineup the day after the alleged battery.

> There are settled reasons for these two exceptions. Historically, juries often found sexual assault prosecutions hard to decide, especially where the trial became a swearing contest between the complainant and the defendant. There was a special need in these situations for additional credibility evidence. Courts also assumed that lay jurors would be troubled by the absence of a fresh complaint to the authorities. Accordingly, this exception to the bolstering rules was formulated. If evidence of a fresh complaint existed, most courts considered it admissible. The pretrial identification exception proceeded on different reasoning. A pretrial identification of the suspect by the victim is always closer in time to the actual events in the case than an identification made at trial. Usually, it comes a few days or perhaps even hours after the crime. It has generally been assumed that proximity in time to the litigated events decreases concerns about the quality of the victim's memory, and thus courts have found

it particularly relevant to admit evidence of the earlier identification.

Finally, although it is not an "exception" to the general ban, it is important to distinguish corroboration from bolstering. If witness #1 testifies to fact *A*, it is *improper bolstering* to call witness #2 to testify that witness #1 is a truthful person, unless witness #1 is attacked on cross-examination. In contrast, it is *proper corroboration* to call witness #2 to give additional testimony about fact *A*.

NOTES AND PROBLEMS

1. **Problem 15-2.** In *Devitt*, the prosecutor calls Jones as the first government witness. Jones testifies that he saw Devitt "hanging around near Mr. Paterson's apartment." Suppose Devitt waives any cross-examination of Jones, and Jones is excused from the stand. The prosecutor next calls Paterson and seeks to have him testify that he had known Jones "for years" and that in his opinion, he is "an honest, truthful individual." The defense counsel objects on bolstering grounds. What ruling?

2. **Problem 15-3.** Suppose that in the last problem Ms. Garfield is called as a witness for the prosecution. She is a neighbor of Jones. Ms. Garfield attempts to testify that a couple of days after the assault Jones told her that "I am sure it was Devitt who was casing the Paterson apartment." The defense objects. What ruling? *See Woodard v. State*, 269 Ga. 317, 496 S.E.2d 896 (1998) ("Unless a witness' veracity has affirmatively been placed in issue, the witness' prior consistent statement is pure hearsay evidence, which cannot be admitted merely to corroborate the witness, or to *bolster the witness' credibility in the eyes of the jury.*") (*emphasis added*).

3. **Problem 15-4.** In *Devitt*, the defense counsel knows that the prosecutor intends to call Jones. During his opening statement, defense counsel states, "During this trial, you'll hear evidence that only a few short months ago, this witness Jones was convicted of perjury — perjury, ladies and gentlemen." The prosecutor calls Jones as her first witness. On direct examination of Jones, the prosecutor elicits the fact that Jones pleaded guilty to the perjury charge pursuant to a plea bargain. The prosecutor next attempts to elicit the fact that, in the bargain, Jones agreed to testify truthfully in *Devitt.* At that point, the defense counsel objects that the prosecutor is "improperly bolstering Jones' credibility." The prosecutor responds that she is "merely rehabilitating the witness from the attack the defense has already mounted." What ruling? *See United States v. Maniego*, 710 F.2d 24, 27 (2d Cir. 1983). Note the court's construction of the expression, "or otherwise," in Rule 608(a). Is the defense counsel's assertion during opening statement a sufficient attack to allow bolstering of the witness? The judge typically instructs the jury that an attorney's assertions during opening are not evidence in the case.

4. In *United States v. Santiago*, 46 F.3d 885 (9th Cir. 1995), the government showed by direct examination questions that witnesses had little incentive to lie. The court held that the attempt to bolster the witnesses was permissible because the defense had attacked their credibility in opening statement. "[T]his court has held that 'vouching' for witnesses by the prosecution is permissible if the defense

has attacked the credibility of those witnesses in its opening statement." Here, the defense counsel's opening called the government witnesses people who "are perfectly happy to lie." In another case, when a federal trial judge improperly excluded evidence of a party's good character for truthfulness, the error was not harmless. The opponent had urged in opening remarks that the party was corrupt, would lie, and had filed false charges against a person. *Renda v. King*, 347 F.3d 550 (3d Cir. 2003) (new trial ordered).

5. Violations of the prohibition on bolstering can occur in a number of ways. First, the proponent of witness #1 can attempt to bolster that witness by having witness #2 swear that in a conversation prior to trial, witness #1 described the litigated incident in exactly the same fashion that witness #1 testified on direct. This is the way the bolstering issue was raised in Problem 15-3, *supra*. However, that is not the only manner in which the rule against bolstering may be undercut. Sometimes it comes from the mouth of witness #1 herself. Suppose that in the *Hill* case, Debra Hill describes the accident fully on direct. At this point the plaintiff's attorney asks her if she also described the accident to the police, right after the collision and she answers "yes." Her lawyer then invites her to repeat her description as she gave it to the police. This is bolstering, just as much as getting duplicating information from a third person, as in Problem 15-3. Witness self-quotation has arisen in a number of cases, and a bolstering objection has not always been honored to block the improper material. *See Atwell v. State*, 293 Ga. App. 586, 667 S.E.2d 442 (2008) (introduction of a witness's prior statements does not constitute improper bolstering; a witness's testimony about what he previously said is not bolstering, because improper bolstering refers to character evidence to show the witness is truthful). This represents a narrow view of what constitutes bolstering. In these circumstances, what other objection should counsel have ready if the court overrules a bolstering objection? In addition to bolstering, is witness self-quotation also hearsay? *See* Chapter 18(B)(4), *infra* (if she was not testifying in this case at the time she made the earlier statement, the statement is hearsay; the declarant's assertion is hearsay if it was an "out-of-*this*-court statement").

D. IMPEACHMENT

1. Overview

While most jurisdictions are hostile to bolstering evidence, they liberally receive impeaching evidence. There are numerous methods of attacking credibility, but basically they all boil down to a charge that the witness is mistaken or lying. California Evidence Code Section 780 lists some of the many recognized factors relevant to credibility:

> Except as otherwise provided by statute, the court or jury may consider in determining the credibility of a witness any matter that has any tendency in reason to . . . disprove the truthfulness of his testimony at the hearing, including but not limited to any of the following:
>
> (a)   His demeanor while testifying and the manner in which he testifies.
>
> (b)   The character of his testimony.

(c)   The extent of his capacity to perceive, to recollect, or to communicate any matter about which he testifies.

(d)   The extent of his opportunity to perceive any matter about which he testifies.

(e)   His character for honesty or veracity or their opposites. (f) The existence of a bias, interest, or other motive.

(h)   A statement made by him that is inconsistent with any part of his testimony at the hearing.

(i)   The nonexistence of any fact testified to by him.

(j)   His attitude toward the action in which he testifies or toward the giving of testimony.

(k)   His admission of untruthfulness.

Some impeachment techniques focus on the witness's testimony in the present case:

Prior inconsistent statements. On some prior occasion, the witness made a statement which is inconsistent with the testimony he has just given in court.

Interest, bias, prejudice, or motive to fabricate. The witness has (a) a personal stake in the outcome of this lawsuit, (b) a bias in favor of one of the parties, (c) a prejudice against one of the parties, or (d) a motive to fabricate (*e.g.*, his testimony has been purchased).

Prior convictions and former dishonest acts. The past record of the witness in committing crimes or promulgating falsehoods is deemed a factor which impacts his credibility as a witness.

Some impeachment techniques have a much broader focus. Consider subsections of the California Evidence Code § 780 which authorize wide-ranging *ad hominem* attacks:

Character impeachment. The witness's character is defective in a way that affects the believability of his or her testimony. Evidence of character usually consists of proof that the witness (a) has been convicted of a certain type of crime, (b) has engaged in conduct that evidences dishonesty, or (c) is known or reputed to be a dishonest person.

Perception, memory, or narration. The witness did not have sufficient capacity or opportunity to perceive that about which he or she is now testifying; the witness cannot adequately remember; or the witness cannot articulate his or her testimony in an understandable form.

In sum, impeachment can take a narrow focus suggesting that the witness's testimony is unreliable for case-specified reasons (*e.g.*, a stake in the outcome of this lawsuit) or can be a broadside attack on the witness' general believability. In some forms, the attack can be inoffensive. Devitt could impeach Jones' testimony by calling Dr. Shultz, Jones' optometrist, to testify about Jones' poor eyesight. At the other end of the spectrum, the attack can be insulting in the extreme. Devitt might call Ms. Fulton, one of Jones' acquaintances, to testify that in her opinion Jones "is a liar — the truth is not in the man."

NOTES

1. Earlier, we noted the split of authority over whether a witness's demeanor qualifies as evidence. Evidence Code § 780(a) lists witness demeanor as the very first type of credibility evidence. Empirical research indicates that, when persons communicate, they attach a good deal of significance to the nonverbal conduct accompanying each other's verbal statements. In particular, the results of the Cleveland Jury Project suggest that in "swearing contests" — trials in which witnesses give diametrically opposed testimony-many jurors decide the case by focusing on the witnesses' demeanor. Judge Frank, one of the leading Legal Realist jurists, shared that assessment of the practical importance of demeanor:

> The liar's story may seem uncontradicted by one who merely reads it, yet it may be "contradicted" in the trial court by his manner, his intonation, his grimaces, his gestures, and the like — all matters which "cold print could not preserve" . . . the witness' demeanor, not apparent in the record, may alone have "impeached" him. *Broadcast Music, Inc. v. Havana Madrid Restaurant Corp.*, 175 F.2d 77, 80 (2d Cir. 1949).

2. Does Judge Frank's assessment of the importance of demeanor help explain why appellate courts ordinarily refuse to redetermine the credibility of the witnesses who testify in the trial court? Are there methods for overcoming the practical difficulties in transmitting demeanor evidence to appellate judges?

3. As noted in Chapter 4, there is a right to cross-examine, and to impeach. *See United States v. Owens*, 484 U.S. 554 (1988). While prior inconsistent statement cross-examination can occur with a party's own witness — see the last section of this chapter — the vast majority of such cross-examinations will be conducted upon adversary witnesses called by one's opponent. In criminal cases, the right to cross-examine is so pervasive that even *Miranda*-tainted statements can be used by prosecutors to impeach. *See Harris v. New York*, 401 U.S. 222, 91 S. Ct. 643, 28 L. Ed. 2d 1 (1971). In *Harris*, the United States Supreme Court ruled that incriminating statements made to the police without the benefit of *Miranda* warnings, although inadmissible in the state's case-in-chief, were admissible for impeachment purposes. In *Oregon v. Haas*, 420 U.S. 714, 95 S. Ct. 1215, 43 L. Ed. 2d 570 (1975), the United States Supreme Court expanded the holding in *Harris* to include statements made in violation of a defendant's Fifth Amendment right to counsel. The thrust of these rulings was confirmed in 2009 in *Kansas v. Ventris*, 129 S. Ct. 1841 (2009) (using voluntary statement obtained without waiver of Sixth Amendment right to counsel is proper for impeachment; *Harris* was cited approvingly).

2. Who Can Be Impeached

By now, we should have a sense of the *how* of impeachment: the methods of attacking a witness's credibility. The next question is whom: *whom* may we impeach?

The most obviously permissible object of impeachment is a witness who has been called by the opposing party. While there can be various aims of cross-examination-one is to impeach. Indeed, the right to impeach has constitutional dimensions, as further discussed in Chapter 32. *Davis v. Alaska*, 415 U.S. 308 (1974); *Smith v. Illinois*, 390 U.S. 129 (1968). Every jurisdiction would agree that after Jones testifies for the prosecution, Devitt has a right to cross-examine Jones to impeach his credibility. Suppose alternatively that Jones was unavailable at trial but the trial judge allowed another witness, Garner, to testify to Jones' statement placing Devitt near the crime scene. In this variation of the hypothetical, Devitt has two proper targets for impeachment: Garner and Jones, the hearsay declarant. Federal Rule of Evidence 806 declares that like an in-court witness, the credibility of a hearsay declarant is also subject to impeachment. In *United States v. Lawson*, 608 F.2d 1129 (6th Cir. 1979), the court held that the defendant placed his credibility in issue although he never testified; the defense attorney cross-examined a prosecution witness to elicit the fact that the defendant had denied involvement in the crime. That cross-examination allowed the prosecution to attack the defendant's credibility.

The law is less well-settled when you attempt to impeach your own witness rather than a witness called by the other side in the case. Suppose that the prosecutor called Jones but, to the prosecutor's surprise, Jones testified that he was fairly certain that the man standing outside Paterson's apartment was not Devitt. Could the prosecutor attack Jones' credibility?

At early common law, the answer was an emphatic "No." 3 D. LOUISELL & C. MUELLER, FEDERAL EVIDENCE § 297 (1979). The courts assumed that by calling the witness, the prosecutor "vouched" for the witness's credibility. If the party chose to call the person as a witness and offer the witness's testimony, the courts inferred that the party impliedly warranted the person's believability. Working from that inference, they forbade the party from attacking the credibility of his own witnesses. There were various inroads and exceptions to this so-called "voucher rule," the primary one being that a party could impeach her own witness if, to the party's surprise, the witness gave testimony affirmatively damaging to the party's case. *St. Clair v. United States*, 154 U.S. 134, 150 (1894). But before qualifying for this exception, the party had to satisfy two requirements: surprise and harm. It was not enough that the testimony was merely disappointing to the party.

Even the inroads made by the surprise doctrine, however, did not satisfy the critics of the voucher rule. Their basic complaint was that the historic assumption underlying the rule (namely, that since parties are free to select their own witnesses, they are therefore somehow accountable for them) has "no application in a modern adversary system: Seldom does a party have a choice among witnesses. . . ." 3 D. LOUISELL & C. MUELLER, FEDERAL EVIDENCE § 297 (1979). Ms. Hill, for example, had little role in selecting the eye-witnesses to her accident, and similarly the prosecutor could not determine who happened to witness Devitt's entry to and exit from Paterson's apartment. In light of that reality, critics viewed the voucher rule as a silly anachronism. That view has led to the adoption of statutory reforms such as Federal Rule of Evidence 607: "The credibility of a witness may be attacked by any party, including the party calling him." Even in the remaining jurisdictions without the Federal Rules of Evidence, the voucher rule has fallen into disuse.

Chambers v. Mississippi, 410 U.S. 284 (1973), which we shall discuss in greater detail in Chapter 32, gave constitutional impetus to the movement to reform the voucher rule. In *Chambers*, the defendant was charged with murdering a police officer named Liberty. The defendant's theory of the case was that the real murderer was one Gable McDonald. McDonald had confessed to several persons that he was the culprit. However, before trial, McDonald repudiated his confession. Both before and during trial, Chambers requested permission to call McDonald and treat him as an adverse witness. In essence, Chambers wanted to cross-examine and impeach McDonald. The trial judge denied the defendant permission to lead or impeach. The Supreme Court held that in doing so, the judge committed constitutional error. Writing for the Court, Justice Powell observed that under primitive English trial practice "oath-takers" or "compurgators" were called to stand behind a particular party's position in any controversy. "Their assertions were strictly partisan and, quite unlike witnesses in criminal trials today, their role bore little relation to the impartial ascertainment of the facts." He ruled that the "voucher" doctrine was out of date:.

> It might have been logical for the early common law to require a party to vouch for the credibility of witnesses he brought before the jury to affirm his veracity. Having selected them especially for that purpose, the party might reasonably be expected to stand firmly behind their testimony. But in modern criminal trials, defendants are rarely able to select their witnesses: they must take them where they find them. Moreover, as applied in this case, the "voucher" rule's impact was doubly harmful to Chambers' efforts to develop his defense. Not only was he precluded from cross-examining McDonald, but, as the State conceded at oral argument, he was also restricted in the scope of his direct examination by the rule's corollary requirement that the party calling the witness is bound by anything he might say. He was, therefore, effectively prevented from exploring the circumstances of McDonald's three prior oral confessions and from challenging the renunciation of the written confession.

Today, impeachment of one's own witness is an established technique. *See United States v. Ray*, 2009 U.S. App. LEXIS 5232 (4th Cir. Mar. 13, 2009), finding that the defendant was not deprived of a fair trial where the prosecution successfully impeached its own witness. In this case the Government's impeachment of its own witness came after it was surprised by adverse testimony, and inquiry was made into the possible bias of the witness and his motivation for deviating from expected testimony.

NOTES AND PROBLEMS

1.   Courts no longer require the impeaching lawyer to be surprised. Although surprise need not be shown by the impeaching party, a strong showing of inconsistency is frequently required. In other words, the examiner is not entitled to read a prior written statement to a witness under the guise of impeachment unless it is clear that the trial testimony of the witness is contradicted by the writing. *See Evans v. Verdini*, 466 F.3d 141, 147 (1st Cir. 2006) (noting that it was the witness's statement that he had not seen the defendant with a gun that opened the door for the prosecution to impeach their own witness's testimony with a prior statement which stated that the witness had seen the defendant shoot the victim).

2.   **Problem 15-5.** Assume the prosecutor in *Devitt* calls witness Jones to say that Jones saw Devitt run from Patterson's apartment building. Observers were shocked when Jones testified: "You know, I have decided it was not Danny Devitt who was running away. It was somebody else." Under the federal rule, could the prosecutor interrogate Jones about his pretrial statement wherein he swore it was Devitt who ran away? Does the inconsistency entitle the witness's proponent to use any type of impeachment to attack the witness? Is there a distinction between allowing the proponent to impeach with prior inconsistent statements *versus* a character trait for untruthfulness or commission of a crime? If the content of the witness's testimony surprises the proponent, should the proponent be restricted to impeachment techniques attacking the specific testimony in the case? Should a showing of surprise or inconsistency be a prerequisite to impeaching by other methods? *See Jones v. State*, 270 Ga. 25, 505 S.E.2d 749 (1998) (law requires that the witness's trial testimony be shown to be inconsistent with his prior statements, and absent this fact, no impeachment may be made by prior conviction or other means). Even if the proponent is surprised at trial, before trial the proponent had an opportunity to investigate the witness's background. Should that opportunity preclude the proponent from attacking by the technique of character trait or crime?

3.   The Advisory Committee Note to Rule 607 states that "[t]he traditional rule against impeaching one's own witness is abandoned as based on false premises. A party does not hold out his witnesses as worthy of belief, since he rarely has a free choice in selecting them."

4.   **Problem 15-6.** It is often good trial advocacy to anticipate the impeachment of your own witness and preempt it. Suppose, for example, that the prosecutor intends to call Jones but knows that Jones told his friend Waterford that he, Jones, "has real doubts whether the guy by Paterson's door was Devitt." The prosecutor could disregard the prior inconsistent statement and allow the defense counsel to mention the statement for the first time on cross-examination. However, the jurors may infer that the prosecutor was trying to hide something; furthermore, the statement may be elicited in a less damning way or with milder effect if the prosecutor beats defense counsel to the punch and elicits the statement during Jones' direct examination. *United States v. Mobile Materials, Inc.*, 881 F.2d 866 (10th Cir. 1989) (entirely proper for government to disclose immunity agreements with witnesses in opening statements for the purpose of minimizing damage to the witness's credibility). *See Delozier v. Sirmons*, 531 F.3d 1306, 1323 (10th Cir. 2008) ("reduce the sting"), *cert denied*, 129 S. Ct. 2058, 173 L.Ed.2d 1138 (2009); *United*

States v. Stapleton, 2008 U.S. App. LEXIS 21782, at *13–*16 (6th Cir. Oct. 15, 2008) ("remove the sting").

Consider this tactic again when studying impeachment by prior conviction. Does the proponent of the witness need to resort to Rule 607 in order to take the "sting" out of expected prior conviction impeachment of a witness? Is this really an impeachment? Or rather an effort to enhance the credibility of the witness, or at least to preserve it?

5.   **Problem 15-7.** In *Hill*, the plaintiff produced testimony from a police officer that a bystander had been hit by flying debris and was seriously injured. Before being taken to the hospital, the bystander related that he saw the accident and told the officer "the truck blew the red light." The bystander later died, but the officer's oral report of this exchange was admitted against Roe under a hearsay exception. Now Roe wants to impeach the bystander by proof that the man was convicted of perjury three years ago. What result? *See* Rule 806.

6.   A foundation must be established when impeaching one's own witness. The witness may be directly confronted with his own alleged statement, and afforded an opportunity to explain or deny the allegations made therein. *United States v. Buffalo*, 358 F.3d 519 (8th Cir. 2004).

Since most courts allow impeachment of one's own witness, it is helpful to see how the process works. In some trials, this methodology will be critical to salvaging the case.

R. CARLSON, A STUDENT'S GUIDE TO ELEMENTS OF PROOF
81–82 (2011)

Direct Examination

In the hallway outside the courtroom the witness assures the plaintiff's attorney that he will come through for the plaintiff in a car wreck case. "Look," he tells plaintiff's counsel, "I saw the whole thing and your guy — the driver of the silver Honda — had the green light." The witness is now called to the stand.

Q: Will you please state your name?

A: Willis X. Fortson.

Q: Where do you live?

A: 920 Madison Avenue in this city.

Q: What is your business or occupation?

A: Plumber. I have worked for Reliable Plumbing for 12 years.

Q: Going back to last June 12, do you remember something unusual that day?

A: Big accident. I was outside a job near the corner of Broad and High Streets, taking a break and having a smoke. I saw the whole thing.

Q: Could you please tell us what happened?

A: Sure. The silver Honda came from the east on Broad Street, approached the intersection at a high rate of speed, and ran the red light. Then the big crash with the black Cadillac.

Q: Mr. Fortson, I believe you may be mistaken as to the car which ran the red light. Wasn't it the black Cadillac?

A: No way. It was the silver Honda that blew the red light.

Q: Mr. Fortson, I now hand you a signed statement which has been marked Plaintiff's Exhibit 3. Will you please look at it?

A: Sure. (witness does so)

Q: Does that jog your memory about who ran the red light?

A: Well, it says at the top "Statement of Willis Fortson," and that is my signature at the bottom, but no, I say it was the Honda that was in the wrong.

Q: You do recognize this statement as the one you signed in my office just one month after the wreck?

A: Yes.

Q: And you freely signed it, after describing the accident in your own words to my investigator?

A: Yes.

Q: Do you remember saying this, and for the record, I am reading from the second paragraph of the witness' prior statement: "The silver Honda waited for the green light, then went into the intersection real slow."

A: Let me see my writing. (witness looks at Plaintiff's Exhibit 3 for identification) Yes, I guess I did say exactly that.

Q: What statement was given closer to the time of the accident, your testimony today or the one you just read?

A: The one I just read, of course.

Plaintiff's Attorney: That's all.

Chapter 16

CREDIBILITY: IMPEACHMENT TECHNIQUES

Read Federal Rules of Evidence 608, 609, 610 and 613.

A. ATTACKS ON COMPETENCY

1. Introduction

Earlier we studied the elements of witness competency: (1) moral capacity, or the capacity to swear or to affirm to testify truthfully; (2) capacity to observe; (3) capacity to remember; and (4) capacity to relate, or narrate. We saw that as a general proposition, these former grounds for disqualification have evolved into grounds for impeachment.

2. The Testimonial Quality of Sincerity

Atheism was once grounds for disqualification. Courts allowed the cross-examiner to inquire whether the witness believed in a God who punishes perjury. Swancara, *Impeachment of Non-Religious Witnesses*, 13 ROCKY MTN. L. REV. 336 (1941). Theism was considered an important incentive for truthful testimony.

Over the years, judicial attitude toward this type of impeachment changed radically. The prevailing modern view is that religious belief is no longer required to be a competent witness, nor is the witness's religious belief admissible on the issue of the witness's credibility. In almost all jurisdictions and under Federal Rule of Evidence 610, evidence of a witness's religious opinions is inadmissible to enhance or detract from his character for truthfulness. The Note to Rule 610 explains:

> While the rule forecloses inquiry into the religious beliefs or opinions of a witness for the purpose of showing that his character for truthfulness is affected by their nature, an inquiry for the purpose of showing interest or bias because of them is not within the prohibition. Thus disclosure of affiliation with a church which is a party to the litigation would be allowable under the rule.

Rule 610 implements the values embodied in the First Amendment, which protects the free exercise of religion; the Supreme Court has been vigilant in protecting freedom of conscience. *Wallace v. Jaffree*, 472 U.S. 38 (1985). In *United States v. Sampol*, 636 F.2d 621, 666 (D.C. Cir. 1980), the court noted that "[t]he purpose of [Rule 610] is to guard against the prejudice which may result from disclosure of a witness's faith. The scope of the prohibition includes unconventional or unusual religions." In *Government of the Virgin Islands v. Petersen*, 553 F.2d 324 (3d Cir. 1977), the court invoked Rule 610 to bar evidence that a witness was a member of the Rastafarian sect. Questions which amounted to an attack on the tenets of the Jehovah's Witnesses were deemed improper in *Redman v. Watch Tower Bible and Tract Society*, 630 N.E.2d 676 (Ohio 1994). Where, over repeated objections, the trial court permitted counsel to ask the plaintiff's accountant about whether he had other Hasidic clients and whether his teaching position was part of the Yeshiva University system, the appellate court found error. *Malek v. Federal Ins. Co.*, 994 F.2d 49 (2d Cir. 1993).

In *People v. Wood*, 66 N.Y.2d 374, 497 N.Y.S.2d 340, 488 N.E.2d 86 (1985), the witness affirmed rather than swore to testify truthfully. The court held that it was error to question the witness about his refusal to swear an oath. Courts are alert to this problem when a witness affirms, rather than taking an oath. In *State v. Rodriguez-Garcia*, 23 Kan. App. 2d 847, 937 P.2d 446 (1997), a state statute provided that "[e]very person has a privilege to refuse to disclose his or her theological opinion or religious belief." When the prosecutor quizzed a witness about affirming and later argued that in her trial testimony "she didn't swear to God, she affirmed," this was error.

NOTES AND PROBLEMS

1. While Rule 610 is a general rule of exclusion, exceptions exist. A person's affiliation with a religious group is properly admissible where probative of an issue in a criminal prosecution. The government inquired into religious practices and beliefs in *United States v. Beasley*, 72 F.3d 1518 (11th Cir. 1996), and the court of appeals approved the inquiries against a Rule 403 challenge. Similarly, in *McQueen v. Napel*, 2010 U.S. Dist. LEXIS 143706 (E.D. Mich. Apr. 27, 2010), the petitioner's beliefs could not be admitted to establish the lack of credibility of a witness or to establish guilt, but were allowed where the affiliation with a religious group itself was probative on an issue in the criminal prosecution. Here, the petitioner's spiritual affiliation was admitted to establish his views on his wife's biblical duties, which were based on his interpretation of the Bible. The prosecutor's questions had nothing to do expressly with religion, but the information was used to establish "the existence of [defendant's] sexual expectations that were not being fulfilled, which the prosecutor argued compelled him to assault his stepdaughter." There can be other, limited reasons for exploring religion. In most cases, however, reliance upon religion either to enhance or to attack credibility is barred. *See United States v. Cooper*, 286 F. Supp. 2d 1283 (D.C. Kan. 2003) (Government's motion to exclude evidence of defendant's religious beliefs was granted pursuant to Fed. R. Evid. 610 to extent the evidence might be offered to enhance defendant's credibility).

2. **Problem 16-1.** In *Hill*, Polecat calls an accident reconstructionist, Wentworth. On direct examination, Wentworth testifies favorably to Polecat. On cross-examination, Ms. Hill would like to elicit that Wentworth is a member of the New Church of the Holy Deity and that the church owns $10,000 of stock in Polecat. Does Rule 610 preclude the cross-examination? *See Firemen's Fund Ins. Co. v. Thien*, 63 F.3d 754, 761 (8th Cir. 1995) (evidence that two witnesses were members of the same religious group as one of the parties was properly admitted to show bias).

3. The examination by the direct examiner sometimes authorizes cross-examination in the otherwise forbidden area of religious beliefs. In a rape case, for example, if the prosecution introduces evidence of the victim's religious beliefs pertaining to sexual intercourse outside of marriage, the defendant may be permitted to confront and impeach the victim on this issue. In *Postell v. State*, 407 S.E.2d 412 (Ga. Ct. App. 1991), the defendant claimed consent. The state argued that because of the victim's religious beliefs, she would not have had consensual intercourse with him. "[O]n cross-examination by the defense, the victim testified that on an occasion prior to the rape, she willingly performed oral sex at the defendant's request, and admitted that this was contrary to the teachings of her church."

To what extent should scientific evidence relating to sincerity — most notably, polygraph examinations and statements made under the influence of "truth sera" — be admissible? Here, the fundamental issue is the test's scientific validity. However, there is an additional, often unstated, consideration — our reluctance to admit expert evidence that directly infringes on the lay jury's traditional role of independently evaluating sincerity. The courts often balk at allowing scientific evidence to interfere with that role.

A leading illustration of this problem is the controversy over polygraph or "lie detector" evidence. The courts are split. Some allow it, but with various limitations and conditions. Other courts give the trial judge discretion to evaluate the proponent's foundation discretion ordinarily exercised to exclude the evidence. A clear majority of courts, however, have announced a categorical rule that polygraph evidence is inadmissible. The following case is illustrative of the majority view.

PEOPLE v. GARD
158 Ill. 2d 191, 632 N.E.2d 1026 (1994)

Harrison, Justice.

[A jury found the defendant guilty of two counts of arson. The intermediate appellate court affirmed, but the Illinois Supreme Court reversed because of the introduction of evidence regarding polygraph examinations. Two witnesses for the State, Diana King and John Clutter, testified about taking polygraph tests. During King's testimony, she referenced the "lie detector test." Clutter's testimony was that after he was advised he flunked the polygraph, he began telling the truth. The court first considered the impact of polygraph proof when a party (such as a criminal defendant) has taken the test. It then analyzes the ramifications when nonparty witnesses (like the two witnesses in this case) have been tested.]

This court has consistently held evidence pertaining to polygraph examination of a defendant generally inadmissible, declaring unequivocally in *People v. Baynes*, 88 Ill. 2d 225, 244, 58 Ill. Dec. 819, 430 N.E.2d 1070 (1981), that such evidence is inadmissible in Illinois because it is insufficiently reliable. Moreover, the court observed, "[n]o other form of evidence is as likely to be considered as completely determinative of guilt or innocence as a polygraph examination." (*Baynes*, 88 Ill. 2d at 244, 58 Ill. Dec. 819, 430 N.E.2d 1070). Because the results of polygraph examinations appear to be quasi-scientific, jurors are likely to give such results undue weight. *People v. Taylor*, 101 Ill. 2d 377, 391–92, 78 Ill. Dec. 359, 462 N.E.2d 478 (1984). As a consequence, the prejudicial effects of polygraph evidence substantially outweigh its probative value.

Shortly after its decision in *Baynes*, this court found the guidance provided there controlling in *People v. Yarbrough*, 93 Ill. 2d 421, 426, 67 Ill. Dec. 257, 444 N.E.2d 493 (1982). In *Baynes* the court had held polygraph evidence inadmissible in a criminal trial despite the defendant's stipulation prior to the polygraph examination that the results of the test would be admissible: stipulation cannot and does not render unreliable evidence reliable.

*   *   *

As the quotations from the record reveal, polygraph evidence was very much a part of this defendant's trial. It would serve no useful purpose to catalogue all of the references to polygraph testing that abound in this record. Suffice it to say that at defendant's trial such references were casual and commonplace, virtually ubiquitous. Testimony concerning the polygraph examinations of both Diana King and John Clutter permeates the transcript of proceedings at trial. Indeed, during the course of defendant's trial the polygraph examination of John Clutter became the lodestar by which the jury was invited to measure truth: that which Clutter spoke until and during his polygraph examination was false; that which he spoke once advised by police that he had failed the polygraph examination was true. Clutter's testimony at trial was consistent with the latter; ergo, by implication, Clutter's testimony at trial was true. By further implication, other witnesses' testimony consistent with that of Clutter was necessarily true.

For the same reasons that this court has held evidence of polygraph examination of defendant inadmissible at trial, we hold evidence of polygraph examination of a witness inadmissible at trial. Evidence of polygraph testing is rendered no more reliable, and jurors deem it no less worthy of belief, because the person tested was a witness rather than a defendant. Whether the examination is of defendant or witness, evidence of polygraph testing is equally unreliable and likely to be accorded undue weight with the result that its prejudicial effect far exceeds its probative value. As this record amply demonstrates, the use of polygraph evidence at a defendant's trial is no less repugnant and no less an affront to the integrity of the judicial process when the examination has been given to a witness at the defendant's trial than it is when the examination has been given to the defendant himself.

It is a familiar rule that an objection to the introduction of evidence not made at the time of admission and an error not raised in a post-trial motion will be deemed waived for review. (*Baynes, supra* at 230). However, this court may notice error rising to the level of plain error in spite of the defendant's failure to record objections and to preserve properly the record for review. (*Baynes, supra* at 230). If the admission of evidence constitutes plain error that causes a miscarriage of justice upon a defendant or a tainting of the integrity and reputation of the judicial process, the error is considered although it was not brought to the attention of the trial court. (*Baynes, supra* at 231). While one purpose of the plain error rule is to afford certain protections to the accused, the other is to protect and to preserve the integrity and the reputation of the judicial process. (*Baynes, supra* at 230–31). As it was in *Baynes*, the latter purpose is the focus of our concern here. Like the evidence in *Baynes*, the evidence here is not so closely balanced that the defendant may be said to have been prejudiced by the introduction of the polygraph evidence and thereby prevented from receiving a fair trial. Like the defendant in *Baynes* this defendant himself caused, in part, the admission of polygraph evidence. Nevertheless, in *Baynes* this court determined that the stipulated admission of polygraph evidence rose to the level of plain error because it was error impinging upon the integrity of our judicial system. So, too, do we today rule that the admission of evidence of polygraph testing of witnesses at defendant's trial constituted plain error because it was error compromising the integrity and tarnishing the reputation of the judicial process itself.

Judgments reversed; cause remanded.

NOTES

1. There are several scenarios in which parties attempt to offer polygraph evidence at trial. Polygraph results are sometimes offered to support the credibility of a witness who passed the test. *Gard* supplies a twist on this formula, with the testimony of Clutter, providing evidence of a failed test. As a consequence of that result, it was urged, Clutter began telling the truth. Occasionally, a prosecutor attempts to elicit evidence that the defendant was offered a test but refused to take it.

All of the foregoing scenarios are generally met with the same response from the courts: No mention of polygraph tests or results will be permitted at trial.

2. Note that the actual basis of the decision in *Gard* was that polygraph evidence is unreliable. In general, courts approach the admissibility of polygraph as a question of scientific reliability under *Daubert* or the applicable state rule. Furthermore, *Gard* is typical of such decisions in its fear that polygraph evidence will overwhelm the jury. That fear is an often unstated premise in many cases excluding polygraph evidence. However, the courts' bias against polygraphy is arguably overblown:

> Several scholars have observed that the judicial reaction against credibility expertise, and lie detection evidence in particular, has been wholly out of proportion to its purported lack of scientific reliability . . . In the wake of the Supreme Court's decision in *Daubert v. Merrell Dow Pharmaceuticals*, which rejected the *Frye* "general acceptance" test under the Federal Rules of Evidence, several scholars predicted that courts would reevaluate their longstanding per se rejection of polygraph evidence. Yet after some initial signs of a trend in that direction, most courts have continued to exclude polygraph evidence. In doing so, they frequently cite the danger that such evidence will usurp the province of the jury to determine witness credibility.

Seaman, *Black Boxes*, 58 EMORY L.J. 427, 460–61 (2008) (footnotes omitted).

Some of the debate over the admissibility of polygraph in federal courts has been stilled by the following Supreme Court decision.

UNITED STATES v. SCHEFFER
523 U.S. 303 (1998)

JUSTICE THOMAS announced the judgment of the Court.

[The Air Force accused an airman of using an illegal drug. He submitted to a polygraph test given by the Air Force and passed. At trial, admission was denied the polygraph results, and the Supreme Court approved exclusion of the evidence. The Court found no consensus that polygraph results are reliable, and also held that the jury is the lie detector.]

Respondent sought to introduce the polygraph evidence in support of his testimony that he did not knowingly use drugs. The military judge denied the motion, relying on Military Rule of Evidence 707, which provides in relevant part

(a)   Notwithstanding any other provision of law, the results of a polygraph examination, the opinion of a polygraph examiner, or any reference to an offer to take, failure to take, or taking of a polygraph examination shall not be admitted into evidence.

The military judge determined that Rule 707 was constitutional because "the President may, through the Rules of Evidence, determine that credibility is not an area in which a fact finder needs help, and the polygraph is not a process that has sufficient scientific acceptability to be relevant." He further reasoned that the factfinder might give undue weight to the polygraph examiner's testimony, and that collateral arguments about such evidence could consume "an inordinate amount of time and expense."

* * *

By a 3-to-2 vote, the United States Court of Appeals for the Armed Forces reversed. . . .

Rule 707 serves several legitimate interests in the criminal trial process. These interests include ensuring that only reliable evidence is introduced at trial, preserving the jury's role in determining credibility, and avoiding litigation that is collateral to the primary purpose of the trial. The rule is neither arbitrary nor disproportionate in promoting these ends. Nor does it implicate a sufficiently weighty interest of the defendant to raise a constitutional concern under our precedents.

State and federal governments unquestionably have a legitimate interest in ensuring that reliable evidence is presented to the trier of fact in a criminal trial. Indeed, the exclusion of unreliable evidence is a principal objective of many evidentiary rules.

The contentions of respondent and the dissent notwithstanding, there is simply no consensus that polygraphic evidence is reliable. To this day, the scientific community remains extremely polarized about the reliability of polygraph techniques. 1 D. FAIGMAN, D. KAYE, M. SAKS, & J. SANDERS, MODERN SCIENTIFIC EVIDENCE 565 §§ 14-2.0-3.0 (1997); *see also* 1 P. GIANNELLI & E. IMWINKELRIED, SCIENTIFIC EVIDENCE § 8-2(C), pp. 225-227 (2d ed. 1993); 1 J. STRONG, MCCORMICK ON EVIDENCE § 206, p. 909 (4th ed. 1992). Some studies have concluded that polygraph tests overall are accurate and reliable. *See e.g.* S. Abrams, THE COMPLETE POLYGRAPH HANDBOOK 190-191 (1968) (reporting the overall accuracy rate from laboratory studies involving the common "control question technique" polygraph to be "in the range of 87 percent"). Others have found that polygraph tests assess truthfulness significantly less accurately — that scientific field studies suggest the accuracy rate of the "control question technique" polygraph is "little better than could be obtained by the toss of a coin," that is, 50 percent. *See* Iacono & Lykken, *The Scientific Status of Research on Polygraph Techniques: The Case Against Polygraph Tests*, in 1 MODERN SCIENTIFIC EVIDENCE, *above*, § 14-5.3, p. 629 (hereinafter Iacono & Lykken).

This lack of scientific consensus is reflected in the disagreement among state and federal courts concerning both the admissibility and the reliability of polygraphic evidence. Although some Federal Courts of Appeal have abandoned the *per se* rule excluding polygraph evidence, leaving its admission or exclusion to the discretion of district courts under *Daubert, see e.g., United States v. Posado*, 57 F.3d 428, 434 (C.A.5 1995); *United States v. Cordoba*, 104 F.3d 225, 228 (C.A.9 1997), at least one Federal Circuit has recently reaffirmed its *per se* ban, see *United States v. Sanchez*, 118 F.3d 192, 197 (C.A.4 1997), and another recently noted that it has "not decided whether polygraphy has reached a sufficient state of reliability to be admissible." *United States v. Messian*, 131 F.3d 36, 42 (C.A.2 1997). Most states maintain *per se* rules excluding polygraph evidence. New Mexico is unique in making polygraph evidence generally admissible without the prior stipulation of the parties and without significant restriction. *See* N.M. Rule Evid. § 11-707. Whatever their approach, state and federal courts continue to express doubt about whether such evidence is reliable.

The approach taken by the President in adopting Rule 707 — excluding polygraph evidence in all military trials — is a rational and proportional means of advancing the legitimate interest in barring unreliable evidence. Although the degree of reliability of polygraph evidence may depend upon a variety of identifiable factors, there is simply no way to know in a particular case whether a polygraph examiner's conclusion is accurate, because certain doubts and uncertainties plague even the best polygraph exams. Individual jurisdictions therefore may reasonably reach differing conclusions as to whether polygraph evidence should be admitted. We cannot say, then, that presented with such widespread uncertainty, the President acted arbitrarily or disproportionately in promulgating a *per se* rule excluding all polygraph evidence. . . .

For the foregoing reasons, Military Rule of Evidence 707 does not unconstitutionally abridge the right to present a defense. The judgment of the Court of Appeals is reversed.

[Opinion of JUSTICE KENNEDY, with whom JUSTICES O'CONNOR, GINSBURG and BREYER joined, concurring in part and concurring in the judgment, omitted — eds.]

NOTES

1.   Look carefully at the *Scheffer* decision: Does it hold that polygraph evidence is always inadmissible? Does it hold that polygraph cannot satisfy the *Daubert* standard? How would you state the precise holding of *Scheffer*? As we shall see in Chapter 32, the threshold for triggering the constitutional right to present evidence is higher than the standard for laying an adequate *Daubert* foundation. Note, however, that subsequent cases for the most part continue to flatly reject polygraph evidence in the absence of stipulation. For example, Polygraph examination results were rejected in *United States v. Campos*, 217 F.3d 707 (9th Cir. 2000). Prior to her trial for transporting marijuana, Campos underwent a polygraph test. During the examination, Campos was asked whether she knew there were drugs in the van she drove into the United States from Mexico. When she answered no, the polygraph examiner concluded Campos was answering truthfully. Campos sought admission at her trial of this polygraph evidence, but the district court precluded its admission and the Court of Appeals affirmed. Applying the rule that experts may not state an opinion that the defendant lacked the mental state to commit the crime, the court held that the examiner's proposed testimony improperly attempted to relate the defendant's mental state. See also *United States v. Gardiner*, 463 F.3d 445 (6th Cir. 2006) (evidence that co-conspirator failed polygraph test inadmissible); *Cook v. State*, 928 So. 2d 589 (La. Ct. App. 2006) (polygraph evidence inadmissible in civil trials).

2.   Occasionally an evidentiary doctrine such as curative admissibility or the rule of completeness will provide an exception to the "no polygraph" rule. *See State ex rel. Kemper v. Vincent*, 191 S.W.3d 45 (Mo. 2006) (polygraph test admissible under rule of completeness). So can a stipulation in some jurisdictions. *Horne v. State*, 614 S.E.2d 243 (Ga. Ct. App. 2005) (polygraph testimony not usually admissible, but parties may stipulate to its admissibility).

3.   The Testimonial Qualities of Perception, Memory, and Narration

We shall see later that according to the best available empirical evidence, the most common cause of erroneous testimony is misperception or misrecollection rather than deliberate perjury. Moreover, a claim that a witness is mistaken is certainly less insulting to the witness than a claim that she is lying. Both factors-the relative frequency of the different causes of erroneous testimony and the more offensive nature of sincerity attacks-cut in favor of the more liberal admissibility of evidence attacking the other testimonial qualities.

Many kinds of information are relevant to the witness's ability to observe, remember, and narrate. These include her education, intelligence, and interests. This information may be brought out as part of routine cross-examination.

However, the trial judge has considerable discretion to protect the witness from harassment.

The cross-examiner may test sight, hearing, or memory by asking questions about the events in question or even unrelated events. The examiner may also conduct an in-court demonstration to test the witness's ability to observe, remember, or relate. Courtroom demonstrations are dangerous; they can backfire if the witness performs well. A demonstration should not be undertaken without careful planning and preparation. If the examiner resorts to the "hop, skip, and jump" technique of cross-examination — questioning the witness about events out of chronological sequence and rapidly shifting from one event to another the cross-examiner may succeed in confusing the witness. However, the likelihood is that the jurors will also be confused and dismiss the witness's mistake as an innocent, excusable misrecollection.

Memory and perception can be affected by drugs or alcohol. The attacking party may show that the witness was intoxicated or under the influence of drugs at the time of the events to which she testifies. *United States v. Leonard*, 494 F.2d 955, 971 (D.C. Cir. 1974). Similarly, it may be shown that the witness is under the influence at the time of testifying. *United States v. Banks*, 520 F.2d 627, 631 (7th Cir. 1975). Courts sometimes instruct the jury that the testimony of such a witness should be considered with caution and great care. *United States v. Yarbough*, 55 F.3d 280 (7th Cir. 1995).

Proof that the witness is a chronic alcoholic is another matter. Most courts exclude evidence of chronic drunkenness unless the evidence shows that the witness was intoxicated at the time of the relevant event. *Springer v. Reimers*, 4 Cal. App. 3d 325, 84 Cal. Rptr. 486 (1970). In *United States v. DiPaolo*, 804 F.2d 225 (2d Cir. 1986), the court held that it is within the proper scope of cross-examination to determine whether a witness was under the influence of alcohol or narcotics either at the time of observation of events in dispute or at the time of testifying. The court further noted: "As Wigmore points out, however, 'a general habit of intemperance tells us nothing of the witness's testimonial incapacity [unless it involves] actual intoxication at the time of the event observed or at the time of testifying.'"

There is some variation on this theme where drug addiction is the issue rather than alcoholism. Although the view is not universal, some courts admit proof of a witness's drug use to show the witness's more general lack of credibility. *See Furlong v. Circle Line Statue of Liberty Ferry, Inc.*, 902 F. Supp. 65 (S.D.N.Y. 1995) (if it is shown that a witness was a drug user at the time of a litigated event, the drug use may be relevant to credibility since it can affect perception).

The issue of drug use might be broached on cross-examination. Or, a cross-examiner, suspecting drug use, might demand that a witness roll up his sleeve, in order for the fact-finder to detect possible needle marks. Assuming a good faith basis for the request, should the judge allow the demonstration? Occasionally a physical exhibition is necessary to make the cross-examination effective, and the trial court has discretion to allow it. In *People v. Lewis*, 25 Ill. 2d 396, 185 N.E.2d 168 (1962), a witness for the state in a criminal prosecution testified that he had not taken narcotics for over six months. On cross-examination defense counsel asked the witness to take off his coat and exhibit his arm for the presence or absence of fresh needle marks. The trial court disallowed this request, but was reversed on appeal.

NOTES AND PROBLEMS

1. Is the differential treatment of chronic alcoholism and drug addiction justified? Dean McCormick contended that at least in part the discrimination reflects the "social odium . . . attached" to drug abuse. C. McCormick, Handbook of the Law of Evidence § 44, at 163 (4th ed. 1992). Is that the only basis? Suppose that the drug in question is contraband. Is illegal drug use logically relevant to credibility on more than one theory?

2. Problem 16-2. In *Hill*, during her case-in-chief the plaintiff calls Mr. Menlow, who claims to have witnessed the collision. During its case-in-chief, Polecat calls Mr. Jensen. Jensen is prepared to testify that he was with Menlow shortly before the collision and saw Menlow swallow two white capsules. Ms. Hill objects, arguing that "the witness can't identify the contents of the capsule." What ruling? What if Jensen were also prepared to testify that soon after swallowing the pills, Menlow's speech became slurred and he had "a sort of dazed appearance"?

As we have seen, most jurisdictions liberally admit evidence of deficiencies in the witness's perceptual, retentive, and narrative capacities. Some commentators urge courts to go further and to authorize widespread psychological evaluation of trial witnesses; however, this raises significant issues. Can the party attacking the witness's credibility ask that the witness be tested or observed in the courtroom by a psychiatrist or psychologist, and then have that expert testify about the witness's ability to perceive, remember, or relate? What about psychological testimony evaluating the motives of a witness?

J. WEINSTEIN & M. BERGER, 3 WEINSTEIN'S EVIDENCE ¶ 607[04]

At first glance, the promise of such expert aid is appealing. Juries, after all, though the final arbiters of fact, have always been allowed the help of experts in evaluating facts whose significance laymen could not be expected to understand. Certainly psychiatrists or psychologists are more cognizant of the complexities of the human mind than the average juror or judge. Accordingly, there are those who argue that the expert — particularly the psychiatrist — should be used in evaluating the credibility of a witness as "the policy of admitting any relevant material demands that he be heard." To such advocates, rejection of psychiatric testimony is an example of rigid adherence to outmoded ideas and a refusal to acknowledge that psychiatry is a science.

But the writings of other commentators and judges suggest that psychiatric testimony often confuses rather than enlightens. Experts often disagree with each other, are unclear and contradictory in their terminology, and do not relate their diagnosis of the witness to his ability to give credible testimony since they are not geared to answering the questions in which a court is interested.

The consequence is that although there is undoubtedly a national tendency toward admitting psychiatric testimony, the federal courts have been hesitant about moving in this direction. In accordance with most other jurisdictions, they have refused to admit the results of lie detector tests and truth-serum interviews where they have not generally recognized the trustworthiness and reliability of such tests as being sufficiently well-established to accord the results the status of competent evidence. The federal courts have also been reluctant to order psychiatric examinations of witnesses. At least one judge has concluded that courts lack inherent power to order such an examination of a witness in a criminal case.

The current hesitation of the federal judiciary is particularly striking because federal courts pioneered the use of a psychiatrist to evaluate the testimony of a witness. In *United States v. Hiss*, 88 F. Supp. 559 (D.C.N.Y. 1950), a prosecution for perjury, the defendant attempted to impeach the cardinal government witness, Whittaker Chambers, with psychiatric testimony that Chambers was a psychopathic personality disposed to making false accusations. Defendant's psychiatrist witness was permitted to state his diagnosis on the basis of a twenty-three page hypothetical question embodying facts testified to in court by Chambers, his in-court observations of Chambers, and his study of Chambers' writings. But although all discussions of the use of psychiatric testimony dwell at length on the Hiss trial, and the case has been hailed as the dawn of a new era, in the twenty years that have elapsed, *United States v. Hiss* has been cited more frequently in the federal courts in distinguishing the case at hand than as a precedent.

Perhaps one reason for the lack of enduring impact of the *Hiss* opinion is the complete, destructive cross-examination inflicted on the psychiatrist by prosecutor Thomas F. Murphy. As noted, the psychiatrist testified that Chambers fit the profile of a pathological liar, based in large measure upon the doctor's observation of Chambers as a witness. In lieu of examining Chambers, the psychiatrist substituted his observations of Chambers during the latter's court testimony. Because Chambers regularly looked up at the ceiling, the defense expert seized upon this as a signal that the witness had an emotional disorder. What happened next is summarized in Gorman, *Spies, Lies and a Witness to Analyze: The Direct and Cross Examination of Dr. Carl Binger in* United States v. Hiss II, 30 LITIGATION 53, 67 (Summer 2004):

> Binger had drawn diagnostic significance from Chamber's gazing at the ceiling from time to time, apparently unable or unwilling, in Binger's view, to connect with the examiner. Murphy worked the point in this [cross-examination] exchange:

Q: Now Doctor, we made a count this morning of the number of times that you looked at the ceiling, and during the first ten minutes you looked at the ceiling 19 times; the next 15 minutes 20 times; and the next 15 minutes ten times; and the following ten minutes ten times, making a total in 50 minutes of 59 times, and I was wondering,

Doctor, whether that had any symptoms of a psychopathetic personality?

A: Not alone.

In the end, Binger's testimony collapsed on its subjective and vague underpinnings.

While the expert was allowed to explain his belief in *Hiss*, that Chambers suffered from a psychological disorder, the case underlines the importance of the expert generating a proper clinical foundation for his or her conclusions.

NOTES

1. In McCord, *Syndromes, Profiles, and Other Mental Exotica: A New Approach to the Admissibility of Nontraditional Psychological Evidence in Criminal Cases*, 66 OR. L. REV. 19, 47 (1987), the author observes that "[w]hile several cases suggest support for . . . *Hiss*, only one court seems to follow it." There is a plausible argument that a psychiatric opinion based on a pretrial examination would be far more probative than the Hiss testimony based on in-court observations.

2. Do you think that the real reason for the courts' reluctance to admit expert testimony on credibility is a doubt about the validity of the scientific techniques? Or is it an intuitive belief that the jurors are generally capable of assessing witnesses' credibility without expert testimony?

Occasionally a witness or a party is challenged on cross-examination to comment upon whether his accusers are lying. Courts are regularly called upon to adjudicate the issue of whether a proper cross-examination may embrace such questions. *See* Problem 23-9, *infra*. The point is illustrated in the following case.

PEOPLE v. ZAMBRANO
124 Cal. App. 4th 228, 21 Cal. Rptr. 3d 160 (2004)

KING, J.

[Defendant was convicted of a drug offense. He contended that the trial court prejudicially erred by allowing the prosecutor to ask him, on cross-examination, whether two police officers were lying about his involvement in an alleged drug transaction, and that the prosecutor committed misconduct by asking such questions. He argues that the prosecutor's "were they lying" questions were improper cross-examination because they called for his inadmissible lay opinion on the officers' veracity, invaded the province of the jury to determine the credibility of witnesses, and were irrelevant.]

The prosecutor did not ask defendant one or two "were they lying" questions to clarify his testimony. Instead, she repeatedly and improperly asked defendant to opine whether the officers were lying about each aspect of their testimony that differed from defendant's. She used the "were they lying" questions to berate defendant and to inflame the passions of jury. [The court quoted some of the cross-examination questions which the prosecutor addressed to the accused on the witness stand.]

Q.   So in your version of events today, what you're telling this jury is
        that the only thing Corporal Escarpe testified to truthfully was the
        fact that you were arrested that night?

A.   Yes ma'am.

Q.   So Corporal Escarpe is lying about everything he testified to except
        for the fact that you were arrested that night?

A.   Yes.

Q.   And Officer Dorsey is lying about everything that took place that
        night except for the fact that you were arrested October 10th, 2001,
        correct?

A.   Yes, ma'am.

Q.   So what you want this jury to believe is that Officer Dorsey and
        Corporal Escarpe are going to risk their jobs and come in here and
        lie to them?

Defense Counsel: Objection, relevance. Speculation.

The Court: Overruled. You can answer it, sir.

A.   I don't know if they are going to lose their jobs or not. I — what I
        am telling you is that I had no drugs nor do I use drugs.

Q.   So everybody is lying except for you?

A.   Like I tell you, ma'am, I never had drugs and I never received
        money from no one, nor did I see money either.

Q.   Well, you didn't answer my question, though, Mr. Zambrano, did
        you? I asked you, everybody is lying but you today?

A.   Yes, ma'am.

Cross-examination — described by Wigmore as "the greatest legal engine ever
invented for the discovery of truth" — has two purposes. Its chief purpose is to test
the credibility, knowledge and recollection of the witness.

The other purpose is to elicit additional evidence. *Fost v. Superior Court* (2000)
80 Cal. App. 4th 724, 733, 95 Cal. Rptr. 2d 620. But proper attack on a witness'
credibility does not consist solely of berating the witness; it requires presenting or
eliciting additional evidence which bears on the witness' credibility. "Unless
precluded by statute, any *evidence* is admissible to attack the credibility of a witness
if it will establish a *fact* that has a tendency in reason to disprove the truthfulness
of the witness' testimony. . . . If a defendant takes the stand and generally denies
the crime with which he is charged, the permissible scope of cross-examination is
'very wide.' When a defendant voluntarily testifies, the prosecutor 'may fully amplify
his testimony by inquiring into the *facts and circumstances* surrounding his
assertions, or by introducing evidence through cross-examination which explains or
refutes his statements or the inferences which may necessarily be drawn from
them." *People v. Humiston* (1993) 20 Cal. App. 4th 460, 479, 24 Cal. Rptr. 2d 515
(italics added).

Here, the prosecutor's "were they lying" questions were inadmissible, because they were irrelevant to any issue in this case. The questions did not clarify defendant's prior testimony, because he had already testified that his recollection of the alleged drug transaction differed from the officers' in every material respect. Nor did the questions inquire into any *facts or circumstances* surrounding defendant's testimony, or develop independent evidence which ran contrary to his testimony. The questions served no purpose other than to elicit defendant's inadmissible lay opinion concerning the officers' veracity. The questions merely forced defendant to opine, without foundation, that the officers were liars.

*   *   *

[T]he first line of cases cited and discussed in *People v. Foster* (2003) 111 Cal. App. 4th 379, 385, 3 Cal. Rptr. 3d 535, holds that asking "were they lying" questions *always* constitutes misconduct, in part because it is the jury's function to determine credibility questions. [Although misconduct, the court held the prosecutor's questions in *Zambrano* which forced the defendant to call the officers liars did not create reversible error. The prosecutor's methods were deemed "reprehensible." "Nevertheless, it is not reasonably probable that the jury would have reached a result more favorable to defendant had the misconduct not occurred."]

NOTES

1.   The foregoing case raises the issue of witness A commenting upon the perception, memory, and narration of witness B. By and large, a lay witness is not permitted to engage in this sort of speculation, nor may he be required to do so. *Athridge v. Iglesias*, 167 F. Supp. 2d 389 (D.D.C. 2001) (one witness may not express the opinion that another witness is not telling the truth); *Berman v. State*, 632 S.E.2d 757 (Ga. Ct. App. 2006) (under no circumstances can the credibility of a witness be bolstered by the opinion of another, even an expert, as to whether the witness is telling the truth). This topic is revisited when we study lay opinion in Chapter 23.

What about an expert assessing whether one party told the truth, or that a witness lied when he gave his testimony. In today's legal world, a psychiatrist can be used to describe a mental condition that affects credibility, and can ascribe the affliction to a specific witness. However, the expert cannot take it a step further by telling a jury that the witness lied while on the stand in this particular case. Nor can the witness state that the person told the truth. Criticizing this limitation on credibility proof, see Simmons, *Conquering the Province of the Jury: Expert Testimony and the Professionalization of Fact-Finding*, 74 U. Cin. L. Rev. 1013 (2006). Consider the relationship of this rule to the treatment of polygraph, discussed above.

2.   Applying the general rule, see *United States v. Harris*, 471 F.3d 507, 511 (3d Cir. 2006) (asking one witness whether another is lying is improper because "[S]uch questions invade the province of the jury and force a witness to testify as to something he cannot know"); *Hunter v. State*, 919 A.2d 63 (Md. 2007) (error to allow prosecutor to ask five were-they-lying questions); *Liggett v. People*, 135 P.3d 725

(Colo. 2006) (range of views on the issue, with majority rejecting "were they lying" questions).

3. Rare exceptions have been developed depending upon the identity of the witness. In one jurisdiction, while witnesses generally cannot be pitted against each other, the criminal defendant can be cross-examined by asking him: "Was Officer Smith lying when he said you stole the vehicle?" *Hawkins v. State*, 281 Ga. App. 852, 637 S.E.2d 422 (2006). Another exception is sometimes applied. There is a distinction between asking witness B if witness A was mistaken versus asking him if witness A was lying. *United States v. Wallace*, 461 F.3d 15 (1st Cir. 2006). In *Wallace*, the prosecutor cross-examined the defendant about whether testimony of other witnesses was "wrong" or "mistaken." However, prosecutor questions here were deemed to be proper because Wallace was not required to brand another witness as a purveyor of falsehoods. As noted in R. CLARK, G. DEKLE & W. BAILEY, CROSS-EXAMINATION HANDBOOK 163 (2011): Some courts "draw a distinction between asking a witness whether someone else is lying and asking a witness whether she disagrees with another witness. Although this distinction may at first blush seem disingenuous, many courts have found it proper if the questioner avoids the word 'lying.' "

B. PRIOR INCONSISTENT STATEMENTS AND SPECIFIC CONTRADICTION

1. Prior Inconsistent Statements and Acts

The logical relevance of prior inconsistent statement impeachment is obvious. If on a prior occasion the witness made a statement inconsistent with his testimony at trial, the inconsistency *at least* calls into question the quality of the witness's memory — and maybe more. This mode of impeachment is quite common in civil cases because of the availability of deposition transcripts. The transcript is an ideal source for inconsistent statements. The following text explains and illustrates the effective impeaching use of a deposition transcript.

A. MORRILL, TRIAL DIPLOMACY § 4.29
(2d ed. 1972)

A definite style and technique should be adopted by every trial lawyer in using a deposition to impeach a witness. The following is one of the techniques used to impeach a witness:

Q: You testified in court today that when you first saw Mr. White's automobile, it was traveling about 40 M.P.H.

A: That's correct.

Q: Now, Mr. Smith, do you recall giving your deposition about six months ago?

A: Yes.

Q: That deposition was taken in your lawyer's office, was it not?

A: Yes.

Q: And your lawyer was present the entire time I was asking you those questions?

A: Yes.

Q: There was a court stenographer present at that time, just as there is one here in court today?

A: Yes.

Q: And that court stenographer was taking down all of the questions I asked of you and all of the answers that you gave?

A: Yes.

Q: Before you testified, were you sworn to tell the truth?

A: Yes.

Q: Before I proceeded to ask you any questions, I asked you to listen carefully to my questions and told you I would be happy to repeat any questions you did not understand; is that correct?

A: That is correct.

Q: Do you remember this question being asked of you and this answer being given by you?

[At this juncture, the examining attorney turns to opposing counsel and gives the page reference in the deposition from which he is about to read.]

Q: "Can you estimate the speed of Mr. White's automobile when you first saw it?"

A: "Yes. It was traveling about 25 M.P.H."

Q: Do you recall that question being asked of you and that answer being given by you while you were under oath?

A: Yes.

[At this point, the witness has been impeached. There are several possible questions to ask next in following up the impeachment in order to highlight the inconsistencies. Some of the more commonly used are as follows:]

Q: Were you lying then or are you lying now?

Q: At the time you gave your deposition, less time had gone by and you undoubtedly remembered the facts more clearly at that time, is that not so?

Q: Mr. Smith, would you like to change your testimony at this time?

I feel it is usually preferable to say nothing at all. If the point has been properly made by the cross-examiner, it is not necessary to give the witness a slap in the face. I do not feel such a slap adds any emphasis to the point already made, and it is always possible that the jurors may sympathize with the witness and dislike the examiner for what they may feel is an unnecessary affront.

NOTES AND PROBLEMS

1. Problem 16-3. In *Hill*, Polecat cross-examines Mr. Menlow, who witnessed the collision. Polecat produces a pretrial statement from Menlow wherein he says he really did not see the whole thing, and attempts to impeach him by referring to the statement. There is an objection: "Beyond the scope. We said nothing about any pretrial statement during our direct, your honor." What ruling? *See* Rule 611(b). Remember the provision for matters of credibility contained in the federal rule and mentioned earlier in the material on scope of cross-examination.

2. After review of the foregoing passage, it is apparent why Wigmore characterized cross-examination as "the 'greatest legal engine ever invented for the discovery of truth.'" *California v. Green*, 399 U.S. 149, 158, 90 S. Ct. 1930, 1935, 26 L. Ed. 2d 489, 497 (1970) (quoting 5 Wigmore on Evidence § 1367, at 32 (Chadbourn rev. 1974)). In *State v. Silva*, 621 A.2d 17 (N.J. 1993), the court listed modes of impeachment, and the prominent place of contradiction by prior statement is noteworthy: "[T]he law recognizes five acceptable modes of attack upon the credibility of a witness: (1) prior inconsistent statements, (2) partiality, (3) defect of character, (4) defect of capacity of the witness to observe, remember, or recount matters, and (5) proof by others that material facts are otherwise than as testified to by the witness under attack. Wigmore (Chadbourn rev. 1974), § 33, at 111–12."

3. In addition to depositions, prior inconsistent statements emanate from a number of other sources. One of these sources is the opponent's own documents. If an opposing witness refreshes his recollection on the witness stand from a writing, the cross-examiner can demand to see the document and impeach the witness from it. *See* Fed. R. Evid. 612. The proponent of the witness frequently attempts to block impeachment by objecting to disclosure on privilege grounds, but many cases sweep aside the objection and allow the impeachment to proceed. Floyd, *A "Delicate and Difficult Task": Balancing the Competing Interests of Federal Rule of Evidence 612, the Work Product Doctrine, and the Attorney-Client Privilege*, 44 Buff. L. Rev. 101 (1996).

4. As noted, sometimes prior inconsistent statements which are used to impeach come from the opponent's own documents, such as business files in *Travelers Ins. Co. v. Smith*, 991 S.W.2d 591 (Ark. 1999), an insurance company was sued over the conduct of one of its claim adjusters. At trial, a company supervisor swore that the adjuster did not have a history of misconduct. The plaintiff then put in evidence an investigative report drawn from another case wherein a claims department manager for the defendant insurance company concluded that the adjuster who was sued in the *Smith* case had misrepresented facts. The supervisor's trial testimony denying that the company had ever previously thought that the adjuster misrepresented his actions opened the door to this form of impeachment under Rule 613.

5. Prior inconsistent statements can also be found in declarations made by one's opponent during mediation. If a party testifies at trial, a statement made earlier by that party during unsuccessful mediation proceedings may be brought up by the opponent. But will the opponent be able to impeach with such statements? A 2006 amendment to Federal Evidence Rule 408 prohibits the use of compromise statements for later impeachment of the party who made the statement.

a. Cross-Examination about a Prior Inconsistent Statement or Act

In most cases, the inconsistent statement is an assertion about factual data. Here is an easy example. In *Hill*, assume that Mr. Worker testifies on direct examination that Roe ordered him to deliver a package across town but told him to "take your time cause there's no rush." At his deposition, Worker stated that Roe instructed him "to hustle — it's a rush order."

What if the inconsistency stems from opinion rather than factual data? Suppose on direct, Worker merely described his conduct in terms suggesting that he was driving carefully. Could Ms. Hill impeach Worker with a pretrial statement to a friend that he, Worker, was "at fault" in the accident? At common law, the answer was no; the inconsistency had to be a factual statement rather than an opinion. G. LILLY, AN INTRODUCTION TO THE LAW OF EVIDENCE § 83 (1978). Both Wigmore and McCormick attacked the limitation. Responding to the argument, most courts now permit impeachment by prior statements in opinion form.

More fundamentally, does the evidence even have to take the form of a statement? Can a nonverbal act qualify? Common sense suggests an affirmative answer. On impeachment by inconsistent acts, see *Brandt v. Vulcan, Inc.*, 30 F.3d 752 (7th Cir. 1994). In some contexts, courts have accepted scientific testimony about the inconsistencies of conduct. For example, suppose that, in a child sexual abuse prosecution, the defendant is the father of the alleged victim. On cross-examination of the alleged victim, the defense counsel attempts to elicit the fact that she delayed reporting the alleged offense to anyone, including her mother. This is inconsistency by conduct. The prosecutor objects and proffers that he can submit testimony by a child psychologist that in cases of intra-family child abuse, it is "common and quite normal" for the victim to be too afraid to report the abuse. Should the judge preclude the cross-examination? Or should the judge permit the cross-examination but allow the prosecutor to introduce the expert's testimony later in the trial? Most jurisdictions have opted for the latter solution, allowing the "inconsistent act" impeachment to proceed. 2 G. JOSEPH & S. SALTZBURG, EVIDENCE IN AMERICA: THE FEDERAL RULES IN THE STATES § 51.3, at 94–97 (Supp. 1992).

Sometimes a witness makes an extensive explanation of a point at trial, even though he was silent on the point earlier when he gave a pretrial statement. Can the impeaching attorney confront the witness with his prior omission or silence as an inconsistent statement or an inconsistent act? The following excerpt addresses that question:

J. WEINSTEIN & M. BERGER, 3 WEINSTEIN'S EVIDENCE ¶ 607[06]
(some citations omitted)

[A] perplexing point is whether a failure to assert a fact it would have been natural to affirm amounts to an assertion of the nonexistence of the fact which can be used to impeach testimony in which the witness admitted the fact's existence.

According to Wigmore such a failure to make an assertion should be admitted as a prior inconsistent statement, and the federal cases are in accord.

The Supreme Court in *Jenkins v. Anderson*[29] cited Wigmore with approval in holding that a defendant's failure to tell police authorities that he had killed in self-defense could be used to impeach him after he testified that he had acted solely in self-defense. Distinguishing its decision in *Doyle v. Ohio*[30] on the ground that defendant's silence in that case had been induced by the government through *Miranda* warnings informing the defendant of his right to silence, the majority of the court held that impeachment by use of prearrest silence does not violate the Fourteenth Amendment."

This is not to say that prearrest silence will be usable in every instance: it "cannot be used for impeachment where silence is not probative of a defendant's credibility and where prejudice to the defendant might result." Except for silence induced by governmental action, the Supreme Court's decision in *Jenkins* leaves impeachment by silence an evidential rather than a constitutional matter. . . .

Jenkins's distinction between pre-and post-*Miranda* silence seems unsound. *Miranda* was designed to equalize the position of the uninformed defendant with the person who knows his rights. *Jenkins* puts at a disadvantage the defendant who knew enough to remain silent without a warning. On its facts, however, *Jenkins* is not particularly objectionable. After allegedly killing in self-defense, the defendant disappeared for two weeks. Arguably, a reasonable person would have remained to tell the police of the presence of the cadaver. "Hit- and-run" tactics are arguably evidence of a guilty mind, although defendant, then apparently on probation, might well have run out of fear of an unfair and unfavorable impression on his probation officer and other law enforcement officials even if he were guiltless. Had defendant remained on the scene and said to the police before *Miranda* warnings, "I know my rights and I am going to remain silent," use of this refusal to talk would have been shocking on both reasonable inference and constitutional grounds. On Rule 403 grounds the technique used by the prosecutor seems particularly unfortunate since it brought clearly to the jury's attention the defendant's prior criminal history. *Jenkins* puts an added burden on trial courts to weigh carefully Rule 403 implications of this form of impeachment. Prohibiting cross-examination based on silence in *Jenkins*, had the proper objection been made, would have been desirable.

The most unsettled aspect of determining what amounts to an inconsistency is presented when a witness denies all recollection of a matter about which he had formerly made a statement. Can this former statement be regarded as inconsistent? The common law practice — still probably followed in most jurisdictions — would not consider such statements inconsistent and would not, therefore, permit their use even for impeachment purposes. Wigmore objected to a rule of blanket exclusion noting that:

> the unwilling witness often takes refuge in a failure to remember, and the astute liar is sometimes impregnable unless this flank can be exposed to an

---

[29] 447 U.S. 231, 100 S. Ct. 2124, 65 L. Ed.2d 86 (1986).

[30] 426 U.S. 610, 96 S. Ct. 2240, 40 L. Ed.2d 91 (1976).

attack of this sort. An absolute rule of prohibition would do more harm than good, and the trial Court should have discretion.

NOTES AND PROBLEMS

1.   The foregoing passage suggests two separate scenarios. It is important to keep the competing patterns in mind. In the first, the witness testifies fully at trial about facts he did not mention when he was initially interviewed or deposed. The second situation is one where the witness gave a full pretrial statement, but then claims at trial he cannot remember the events at issue. The latter situation raises some special questions. Counsel may not need to rely exclusively upon an impeachment theory where the trial witness claims he cannot remember. The details of the earlier statement may be elicited under a "refreshing recollection" theory. Dean Ladd's article in the next subsection suggests the technique.

2.   **Problem 16-4.** This problem relates to the first scenario referenced in Note 1. Devitt's friend Wickersham lives next door to Devitt in Devitt's apartment building. He visited Devitt shortly after the Paterson attack, but before the police arrived. During their conversation Wickersham said: "They just had on the news that the old guy you were working for got attacked. They said it was an unprovoked attack by somebody with a knife. Danny boy, that looks like your work to me." Devitt did not respond. He simply smiled. Wickersham is now cooperating with police. At trial, Devitt testified in accord with his pretrial statement that Paterson was the aggressor triggering the confrontation, and the stabbing was an accident. The prosecutor asked Devitt why he never told Wickersham that story. This is impeachment by prior silence. Proper impeachment?

3.   The second situation which is referenced in Note 1 relates to a claim of failed recollection by the witness during the time he is on the witness stand. He cannot remember the litigated incident, he says, nor can he recall ever making a statement about it.

Recent years have witnessed considerable erosion of the bar against impeaching a witness who presently denies all recollection of an event. When the same person made an earlier statement about that event, he can be attacked by it. Courts continue to fall back from the common law practice noted near the end of the Weinstein and Berger passage. See *State v. Martin*, 614 N.W.2d 214 (Minn. 2000), holding that in order to impeach a witness with prior inconsistent statements, a foundation is supplied when the declarant fails to recollect the prior statement. Failure of a witness to recall his prior statement is sufficient foundation to impeach the witness using extrinsic evidence.

4.   While a witness may claim lack of recollection when she is on the witness stand, the attorney more frequently encounters the situation of direct contradictions between a deposition or pretrial statement and the testimony ultimately given at trial.

How directly must a prior statement conflict with the witness's trial testimony in order to impeach with it? One standard for the requirement of inconsistency in prior statements used for impeachment allows the cross-examiner to impeach when there is "any material variance" between the testimony of the witness and the witness's previous statement. *State v Johanesen*, 873 P.2d 1065, 1069 n.6 (Or. 1994). "The prior statement 'need only bend in a different direction' " than the trial testimony. J. McNaught & H. Flannery, Massachusetts Evidence: A Courtroom Reference 13-5 (1988). Who decides whether an "inconsistency" exists? Is it governed by Rule 104 (a) or (b)? *See United States v. Bonnett*, 877 F.2d 1450, 1463 (10th Cir. 1989) ("the determination as to whether the prior testimony is truly inconsistent is a matter within the discretion of the trial judge").

5. Rule 613(a) expressly states that, when cross-examining a witness about a prior inconsistent statement, "the statement need not be shown nor its contents disclosed to the witness at that time. . . ." As we shall see in the excerpt from Dean Ladd's article in the next subsection, at common law when the prior inconsistent statement was in writing, "the writing [had to] be shown to the witness before . . . interrogation upon its content. . . ." Rule 613(a) seems to abolish that requirement. However, Judge Posner has ruled that the trial judge has discretion to require the cross-examination to follow the common law practice. *United States v. Marks*, 816 F.2d 1207, 1211 (7th Cir. 1987) ("If defense counsel had been reading from a transcript of a previous trial or deposition, there would have been no justification for the district judge's procedure. But since a statement appearing in an interview report could easily be garbled, yet seem authoritative when read from a paper that the jury would infer was an official FBI document, the judge was reasonable in insisting that the witness be allowed to examine his purported statement before being impeached by it").

6. The subject of prearrest silence comes up again in the tacit admissions section of the Admissions chapter, *infra*. On that topic, see Hunter, *The Man on The Stairs Who Wasn't There: What Does a Defendant's Pre-Arrest Silence Have to Do with* Miranda, *The Fifth Amendment or Due Process?*, 28 Hamline L. Rev. 227 (2005). When allowing silence to impeach, some courts focus on pre-arrest conduct or silence which collides with a testifying defendant's account at trial. *State v. Brown*, 190 N.J. 144, 919 A.2d 107 (2007) (where defendant asserted self-defense at trial, prosecutor was permitted to impeach him with fact he did not come forward and assert this explanation in the weeks prior to his arrest). The general rule seems to allow pre-arrest silence to impeach. There is less consensus on whether the silence stands as affirmative evidence of guilt. Courts are divided on the question of whether the privilege against self-incrimination forbids use of pre-arrest silence substantively. *Weitzel v. State*, 863 A.2d 999, 1004 (Md. 2004) (holding that pre-arrest silence in police presence is not admissible as substantive evidence of guilt under Maryland evidence law). The Supreme Court of Michigan observed that the Fifth Amendment does not prohibit impeaching a defendant with pre-arrest silence. However, the prosecutor overstepped when the state used post-*Miranda* silence substantively and for impeachment. The prosecution violated defendant's due process rights, in a prosecution for two counts of second-degree criminal sexual conduct, by repeatedly using defendant's post-arrest, post-*Miranda* silence as evidence of defendant's guilt in its case-in-chief and to impeach the defendant's testimony that he was innocent.

b.   Extrinsic Evidence of a Prior Inconsistent Statement or Act

The witness you cross-examined has recently left the stand. You want to impeach him further. The party which originally called the witness has now rested its case. May you call a witness during your part of the case to testify about prior inconsistent statements or acts by the earlier witness? Cross-examining witness #1 about his or her own statement is sometimes referred to as intrinsic impeachment while calling witness #2 to establish witness #1's statement is styled extrinsic impeachment. In the case of prior inconsistent statements, you may present the extrinsic evidence if you satisfy three conditions.

First, at common law, you must lay a foundation during the initial witness's cross-examination. Dean Ladd analyzes the foundational requirement. The Rule of The Queen's Case, mentioned in Dean Ladd's article, is the rule announced in 1820 in the English decision *Queen Caroline's Case*: "If it be intended to bring the credit of a witness into question by proof of anything he may have said or declared touching the case, the witness is first asked, upon cross-examination, whether or not he has said or declared that which is intended to be proved." In the case of written prior inconsistent statements, many trial judges construed the rule to mean that the cross-examiner had to show the writing to the witness before questioning the witness about the inconsistent statement in writing.

Though the Rule of Queen Caroline's case is not codified in the Federal Rules of Evidence and is arguably rejected by FRE 613, some courts continue to enforce the foundation requirement. *United States v. Schnapp*, 322 F.3d 564, 571–72 (8th Cir. 2003) (holding exclusion of defendant's impeachment testimony regarding alleged prior inconsistent statements of government witness was warranted where defense counsel failed to ask witness to explain or deny alleged prior statements while witness was on stand during government's case-in-chief).

Ladd, *Some Observations on Credibility: Impeachment of Witnesses*
52 CORNELL L. Q. 239, 245 (1967)

The Rule of The Queen's Case required that the writing be shown to the witness before permitting interrogation upon its content, thus eliminating what may be an effective part of the impeachment. Likewise, in reference to an oral statement made out of court, counsel on cross-examination may prefer, for the purpose of impeachment, first to ask the witness what he had said, if anything, rather than confront him initially with the statement. In the situation either of a writing or of an oral statement, if the witness were asked what he said before being confronted with the statement, he might give a different story, thus disclosing his desire to evade the effect of what he had said previously. . . . [The issue is the timing of when a contradictory declaration should be made known to the declarant. In most jurisdictions the modern rule is that, before extrinsic proof is made of the statement or the writing,] the statement must be made known or the writing shown to the declarant so that he will have the opportunity to identify and explain or deny it. . . .

A common practice is to proceed as though attempting to refresh the recollection of the witness, making the content of the statement known to him; then, if he denies making the statement, proof by extrinsic evidence may be offered. The detailed steps for impeachment by proof of prior statements of a witness contradictory to the testimony given in court fit into a simple formula. A foundation should be laid, identifying the time, place, occasion, and the person to whom it is claimed the declaration in question was made. The witness should then be informed of the statement and asked if he made it. Only if he denies making the statement may those to whom the statement was made be called to present the impeaching testimony. They, too, will be examined in a similar manner to establish the making of the statement. If the alleged statement was in writing, it would be shown to the declarant with opportunity to admit or deny it as his. In event of denial, the writing should be authenticated and offered in evidence. Some courts permit only the reading of the statement to the jury.

A significant exception applies when the witness is a party and has made an out-of-court declaration inconsistent with his testimony. The statement would be used by the adverse party only if deserving to the declarant and, therefore, is admissible as an admission. It is substantive evidence requiring no foundation other than proof of the fact that the statement was made by the party against whom it is offered.

Federal Rule of Evidence 613(b), borrowing heavily from California Evidence Code §§ 768 and 770, provides:

> (b) Extrinsic Evidence of a Prior Inconsistent Statement. Extrinsic evidence of a witness's prior inconsistent statement is admissible only if the witness is given an opportunity to explain or deny the statement and an adverse party is given an opportunity to examine the witness about it, or if justice so requires. This subdivision (b) does not apply to an opposing party's statement under Rule 801(d)(2).

PROBLEM

Problem 16-5. In *Devitt*, the defense learns that Paterson told a friend, Ms. Garret, that "I made the whole thing up, and those stupid cops are buying it hook, line, and sinker." At trial, Paterson becomes faint and claims shortness of breath at the end of the direct examination, and the defense counsel is reluctant to confront him directly with his statements to Ms. Garret. Moreover, the defense counsel believes that the later in the trial Ms. Garret testifies, the more surprising and dramatic her testimony will be. As Paterson begins to leave the witness stand, the defense counsel requests that he "be excused subject to recall." The judge grants the request. During the defense case-in-chief, the defense calls Ms. Garret. When it becomes clear to the prosecutor that Ms. Garret is going to testify about Mr. Paterson's statement, the prosecutor objects:

O.   Your Honor, I must object. This is obviously extrinsic evidence to impeach the victim, and there was absolutely no foundation during cross.

What ruling? Morena has adopted Federal Rule of Evidence 613(b). *See In the Matter of Nautilus Motor Tanker Co., Ltd.*, 862 F. Supp. 1251 (D.N.J. 1994) (while witness must be afforded opportunity to address statement, no particular sequence or timing is necessary). However, at some point a foundation must be laid by confronting the witness with his prior statement. *See United States v. Schnapp*, 322 F.3d 564, 571 (8th Cir. 2003) (holding exclusion of defendant's impeachment testimony regarding alleged prior inconsistent statements of government witness was warranted where defense counsel failed to ask witness to explain or deny prior statements while witness was on stand during government's case-in-chief). *Compare United States v. Pridgen*, 518 F.3d 87, 91 (1st Cir. 2008) (holding proper foundation was laid to impeach witness, including opportunity for witness to explain or deny her inconsistent statements).

If the court insists upon a foundation during cross-examination, the second condition for introducing extrinsic evidence is that the witness' answer must ordinarily be a denial or evasion. If the witness fully admits the inconsistent statement, there is no need to present cumulative, extrinsic evidence of the statement. Rule 403 would dictate the exclusion of the extrinsic evidence as a "waste of time." In contrast, the witness' flat denial of the statement creates the most compelling need for the extrinsic evidence. Modernly, most courts are lax in enforcing this condition and admit evidence of the prior statement even if the witness's answer falls short of a flat denial. C. McCormick, Handbook of the Law of Evidence § 37, at 20 (4th ed. 1992). The third condition is the collateral fact rule, below.

NOTE AND PROBLEMS

1. **Problem 16-6.** Assume a variation of the facts in Problem 16-5. When Paterson is on the stand he is asked about his statement to Ms. Garret. He answers: "I don't remember saying that to her," or is evasive, "I could have, but I doubt it." Defense counsel argues that Paterson's evasions and claims of memory lapse amount to implied denials of the facts he earlier admitted to Ms. Garret. What ruling? *See United States v. Insana*, 423 F.2d 1165 (2d Cir.), *cert. denied*, 400 U.S. 841 (1970).

2. **Problem 16-7.** Assume that when confronted by the defense counsel, Paterson fully admits the statement to Ms. Garret, and simply adds, "I don't know why I said that to her, it was wrong to do so." Now the defense counsel seeks to call Ms. Garret "to further prove Paterson's improper statement." The prosecution objects on the ground that since Paterson admitted the prior statement, further evidence is not needed. What ruling?

3. Some variation in approach may be encountered with respect to the last problem, depending upon the court. Lax enforcement of Rule 403 prompts some judges to permit extrinsic evidence. However, in federal practice a strict approach is often encountered. *See Bank Atlantic v. Paine Webber, Inc.*, 955 F.2d 1467 (11th Cir. 1992) ("[w]hen a witness admits making a prior inconsistent statement, extrinsic proof of the statement is excludable"); *United States v. Soundingsides*, 820

F.2d 1232 (10th Cir. 1987) (when witness admits prior statement, witness is adequately impeached and further evidence is not needed). *Compare United States v. Lashmett*, 965 F.2d 179 (7th Cir. 1992). State courts sometimes allow introduction of the statement itself, even in the face of an acknowledgment of it by the declarant. *See, e.g., Duckworth v. State*, 268 Ga. 566, 492 S.E.2d 201 (1997) (cross-examiner does not have to offer prior written statement into evidence before impeaching witness; however, whether witness admits or denies making statement, written statement may be admissible).

4. Courts continue to be receptive to delivering a limiting instruction as to the nature of the evidence when requested by the lawyer whose client is impeached. This was remarked upon earlier in the text. *See* Problem 15-1. The approach applies to inconsistent statement impeachment. *See United States v. Watkins*, 591 F.3d 780 (5th Cir. 2009), where a rental application was properly admitted during cross-examination to contradict defendant's prior testimony denying that an alleged member of a conspiracy was his landlord. The application was admitted under a limiting instruction that contradicting information was only allowed to show that the defendant had made a prior inconsistent statement. Courts are alert to improper use of impeaching evidence by a party, even where a limiting instruction is given. Despite such an instruction, the Government urged the jury in closing to make substantive use of contradicting statements in *United States v. Wood*, 2007 U.S. App. LEXIS 24114 (10th Cir. Oct. 12, 2007). The court ruled that upon admission of prior inconsistent statements, "it is well settled that contradictory statements introduced for the purpose of impeachment are not admissible as substantive evidence." Failure of Government counsel to abide by an instruction to that effect was fatal to the prosecution's effort. The conviction of the defendant was reversed.

2. Specific Contradiction

This impeachment technique is closely related to, and often confused with impeachment by prior inconsistent statement. To illustrate the difference, suppose that in *Hill*, witness A testified for the plaintiff that, "[W]orker was going at least fifty miles an hour just before impact." If Polecat's attorney employed prior inconsistent statement impeachment, the attorney could call witness B to testify that witness A told her that, "the car was really going only abut 35-tops." However, Polecat's attorney might specifically contradict witness A by presenting witness B's testimony that she also observed the accident and that in her opinion, "The car was really going only about 35 — tops."

The impeaching effect of specific contradiction is indirect. The second witness does not charge that the first witness is a liar or even describe an inconsistent statement by the first witness. The second witness merely gives a contrary version of the facts on the merits of the case. However, inferentially, the specific contradiction is logically relevant to the first witness's credibility; if the second witness is correct, the first witness must be lying or mistaken. In short, specific contradiction evidence has dual logical relevance; on its face, it purports to relate to the historical merits, but it also indirectly attacks the credibility of the opposing witnesses.

Like the prior inconsistent statement technique, this technique raises legal irrelevance problems. We want the jury to concentrate on the historical merits of the case. Cross-examining a witness about his or her credibility may distract a jury somewhat from the merits, but calling a second witness for the purpose of impeaching another witness's credibility arguably poses the danger of distraction to an even greater degree. For that reason, the common law placed restrictions on the use of extrinsic evidence such as calling a secondary witness: Impeachment by prior inconsistent statement and specific contradiction are both subject to the Collateral Fact Rule. Accordingly, that is our next subject.

NOTE

It is clear from the decided cases that, under the Federal Rules, courts continue to permit impeaching attorneys to use the specific contradiction technique. *E.g.*, *United States v. Tarantino*, 846 F.2d 1384, 1409 (D.C. Cir.), *cert. denied*, 488 U.S. 840 (1988). In *United States v. Castillo*, 181 F.3d 1129 (9th Cir. 1999), after a defendant in a drug transporting case took the stand and described himself as an anti-drug crusader who never used drugs, the prosecution was allowed to call a rebuttal witness to tell about the defendant's 1997 arrest for possession of cocaine. This specific contradiction impeachment was approved on appeal.

Other cases have confirmed the place of impeachment by contradiction. *See United States v. Gilmore*, 553 F.3d 266 (3d Cir. 2009) (impeachment by contradiction is a permissible means of impeachment under the Federal Rules; moreover, it is not subject to the limitations prescribed by Rule 609); *Wegener v. Johnson*, 527 F.3d 687 (8th Cir. 2008) (attacking witness by evidence that facts asserted by witness are wrong is to impeach by contradiction).

3.   The Collateral Fact Rule

The collateral fact rule can be stated simply: The attorney may not use extrinsic evidence to impeach a witness on a collateral matter. The rule's phrasing poses two obvious definitional problems: What is "extrinsic evidence"? What is a "collateral" matter?

There is a general agreement on the first definition. All courts concur that evidence is extrinsic if it is presented after the judge has excused the witness to be impeached. For example, after the judge excuses Paterson from the witness stand in *Devitt*, the defense counsel might attempt to (1) introduce a certified copy of the grand jury transcript of Paterson's testimony, reflecting prior inconsistent statements or (2) call another witness, Garret, to whom Paterson made an inconsistent statement. Both items of evidence would be "extrinsic" to the testimony of Paterson, the witness the defense is attempting to impeach.

The only remaining dispute over the meaning of "extrinsic" is the extent to which the attorney may introduce impeaching documentary evidence during Paterson's cross-examination. The trend in the decided cases is to hold that the attorney may do so as long as the witness willingly authenticates the document. *See e.g., Carter v. Hewitt*, 617 F.2d 961, 970–71 (3d Cir. 1980). Introducing the documentary evidence during the cross-examination may slightly prolong the examination and, to that extent, raise the probative danger of time consumption. However, in the words of the *Carter* court:

> When . . . the extrinsic evidence is obtained from and through examination of the very witness whose credibility is under attack, . . . we must recognize that the rule's core concerns are not implicated.

Id. at 970. Thus, for all practical purposes, you must worry about the collateral fact rule only when you are presenting extrinsic evidence after the excuse of the witness you are attacking.

Even then the rule may be inapplicable. At common law, the rule is not a general limitation on all impeachment techniques. Quite to the contrary, the rule applies to less than a handful of the recognized impeachment techniques. For example, it is well-established that the rule is inapplicable to impeachment for bias. The witness's bias is "always independently provable" by extrinsic evidence. *United States v. Harvey*, 547 F.2d 720 (2d Cir. 1976). The admissibility of extrinsic bias evidence reflects the courts' judgment that bias is so probative of credibility that it is always worth the court's time to hear extrinsic evidence on that issue. In other cases, the rule is inapplicable because the very nature of the impeachment technique necessitates extrinsic proof. For example, under Federal Rule of Evidence 608(b)(2), the attorney may call witness B to testify that witness A has a character trait of untruthfulness. The character witness's testimony will always be extrinsic to the testimony of the witness to be impeached. Once we have made the policy decision to recognize the 608(b)(2) method of impeachment, we must permit extrinsic evidence; and the collateral fact rule cannot be applied.

In truth, the rule applies to only three impeachment techniques: prior inconsistent statement and specific contradiction as well as specific instances of misconduct under Rule 608(b). When the attorney employs one of these techniques, the second definitional problem immediately rears its ugly head: Is the fact "collateral," barring extrinsic evidence?

It is easy to answer the question in the context of Rule 608(b). The statute specifically provides that the attorney may cross-examine the witness about specific instances of conduct "if probative of . . . untruthfulness . . ." FED. R. EVID. 608(b). Thus, if Paterson had attempted to file a fraudulent welfare application, Devitt's attorney could question about it. A fraudulent grant or employment application is logically relevant to show untruthfulness. However, the statute adds that the act "may not be proved by extrinsic evidence." *Id.* In that sense, the cross-examiner must "take the answer." That expression is a colorful way of saying that the act is a "collateral" fact. The misdeed is relevant only to the witness's credibility and has no bearing on the case's historical merits. Given its minimal probative value, the courts allow inquiry on cross-examination, but cut off the questioning at that point.

It is more difficult to define "collateral" in the context of specific contradiction or prior inconsistent statement impeachment. The problem is that sometimes the inconsistent statements and contradictory testimony relate to collateral facts and sometimes they relate to noncollateral facts. Fortunately, there is an excellent, succinct statement of the definition of "collateral" fact.

C. McCORMICK, HANDBOOK OF THE LAW OF EVIDENCE
§ 47
(Cleary ed. 1984)

[There are several types of facts that are not collateral and hence allow the introduction of extrinsic evidence.]

The first kind are facts that are relevant to the substantive issues in the case. It may seem strained to label this proof of relevant facts with the terms "contradiction" or "impeachment." But it does have the dual aspect of relevant proof and of reflecting on the credibility of contrary witnesses. Here the "contradiction" theory has at least one practical consequence, namely, it permits contradicting proof, which without the contradiction would be confined to the case in chief, to be brought out in rebuttal.

[Another] kind of fact must be considered. Suppose a witness has told a story of a transaction crucial to the controversy. To prove him wrong in some trivial detail of time, place or circumstance is "collateral." But to prove untrue some fact recited by the witness that if he were really there and saw what he claims to have seen, he could not have been mistaken about, is a convincing kind of impeachment that the courts must make place for, although the contradiction evidence is otherwise inadmissible because it is collateral under the tests mentioned above. To disprove such a fact is to pull out the linchpin of the story. so we may recognize this type of allowable contradiction, namely, the contradiction of any part of the witness' account of the background and circumstances of a material transaction, which as a matter of human experience he would not have been mistaken about if his story were true. This test is of necessity a vague one because it must meet an indefinite variety of situations, and consequently in its application a reasonable latitude of discretionary judgment must be accorded to the trial judge.

The expression "facts relevant to the substantive issues in the case" means evidence "logically relevant to the historical issues in the case." If evidence falls into this category, it is not only relevant to credibility, it has dual relevance, and the quantum of probative value justifies the additional expenditure of time necessary to introduce the extrinsic evidence.

A similar analysis obtains in the second category mentioned. If the fact is so fundamental that "he could not have been mistaken about [it] if he were really there and saw what he claims to have seen," the fact is not just relevant to credibility. Disproving the fact also creates the inference that the witness' testimony about the historical merits is necessarily untruthful or mistaken.

The characterization of the test as "a vague one" is certainly accurate. In *United States v. Higa*, 55 F.3d 448 (9th Cir. 1995), the court remarked that the test "is easy to state and difficult to apply." To get a feel for the test, consider the following notes and problems.

NOTES AND PROBLEMS

1.   Problem 16-8. In *Devitt*, Paterson is testifying. The defense attorney begins cross-examination. During the cross-examination, she asks Paterson whether he ever filed a false unemployment compensation claim. Paterson denies doing so. The examination continues:

D: Mr. Paterson, let me remind you of the penalties for perjury in this state.

P: Your Honor, I object. This is collateral impeachment, and the defense counsel knows that she must take the witness's answer.

D: Your Honor, I have the right to press for an answer.

What ruling? *See* J. WEINSTEIN & M. BERGER, WEINSTEIN'S EVIDENCE ¶ 608[05] (1996) (opportunity for cross-examiner to press for an answer is authorized by federal rule).

2.   Problem 16-9. The next prosecution witness is Mr. Store, one of Paterson's neighbors. He testified at the grand jury hearing that he saw the defendant exit the Paterson apartment shortly after the time of the alleged battery. He testified, "I was standing in front of a store across the street and talking with three of my friends when I see this guy run out the door to Paterson's apartment." At trial, on direct examination Mr. Store testified that he was talking with two friends. On cross-examination, Store insisted that the correct number was two. After Store leaves the witness stand, may the defense counsel introduce a certified copy of the grand jury transcript containing Store's statement about three friends? *See People v. Dice*, 120 Cal. 189, 201, 52 P. 477, 482 (1898) (witness to shooting who could not remember how many cows he was milking at the time could not be impeached by his preliminary hearing testimony that he was milking nine cows).

3.   Problem 16-10. Defense continues to cross-examine Store, and asks his age. Store responds: "I am 59." The defense attorney challenges the testimony: "I submit you are 60, and I will call to the stand two of your friends who were at your 60th birthday party last month to prove it." Can the friends be called?

That courts continue to apply the collateral fact rule is evident in modern cases. *United States v. Higa*, 55 F.3d 448 (9th Cir. 1995) (extrinsic evidence to impeach rejected; collateral contradiction is one not related to matters at issue); *United States v. Cowling*, 648 F.3d 690 (8th Cir. 2011) (holding that, while defendant has the right to an opportunity to impeach a witness, that right will not extend to immaterial matters as proposed by the defendant here; evidence was not pertinent to the substantive issues of the trial); *People v. Steele*, 769 N.W.2d 256 (Mich. Ct. App. 2009) (supporting the modern use of the collateral fact rule).

C. BIAS

1. Introduction

At early common law, the parties and their spouses were incompetent to testify; these persons had a motive for perjury, and the common law's response was to disqualify these potential witnesses as a means of preventing perjury. Modernly, the former grounds for disqualification serve as grounds for impeachment. Hence, a party may now testify in his own behalf, but the judge may instruct the jury that "[i]n weighing his testimony, . . . you may consider the fact that the [party] has a vital interest in the outcome of this trial." *United States v. Hill*, 470 F.2d 361 (D.C. Cir. 1972).

Bias is not only one of the routine bases for impeachment; in the minds of many courts, it is the most probative impeachment technique. Schmertz & Czapanskiy, *Bias Impeachment and the Proposed Federal Rules of Evidence*, 61 Geo. L.J. 257, 264 (1972).

2. Bias Impeachment in General

The late John Kaplan of Stanford Law School thought that the case for bias impeachment should be rested squarely on the psychological research, documenting the potentially distorting effect of a witness's bias. To prove his point, he often gave friends a copy of the following study. On November 23, 1951, the Dartmouth and Princeton football teams played in the last game of the season for both teams. The game was highly publicized even before kickoff. The game proved to be a rough one; there were serious injuries and numerous penalties against both teams. After the game, the two student newspapers ran strongly worded editorials, each accusing the other team of dirty play. The researchers obtained a film of the game. They showed the same film to a group of Dartmouth undergraduates and another group of Princeton undergraduates. After the undergraduates viewed the film, the researchers questioned them about their perceptions of the film.

Hastorf & Cantril, *They Saw a Game: A Case Study*
49 J. Abnormal and Soc. Psychol. 129 (1954)

Nearly all Princeton students judged the game as "rough and dirty" — not one of them thought it "clean and fair." And almost nine-tenths of them thought the other side started the rough play.

When Princeton students looked at the movie of the game, they saw the Dartmouth team make over twice as many infractions as their own team made. And they saw the Dartmouth team make over twice as many infractions as were seen by Dartmouth students. When Princeton students judged these infractions as "flagrant" or "mild," the ratio was about two "flagrant" to one "mild" on the Dartmouth team, and about one "flagrant" to three "mild" on the Princeton team.

As for the Dartmouth students, while the plurality of answers fell in the "rough and dirty" category, over one-tenth thought the same was "clean and fair" and over a third introduced their own category of "rough and fair" to describe the action.

Although a third of the Dartmouth students felt that Dartmouth was to blame for starting the rough play, the majority of Dartmouth students thought both sides were to blame.

When Dartmouth students looked at the movie of the game they saw both teams make about the same number of infractions. And they saw their own team make only half the number of infractions the Princeton students saw them make. The ratio of "flagrant" to "mild" infractions was about one to one when Dartmouth students judged the Dartmouth team, and about one "flagrant" to two "mild" when Dartmouth students judged infractions made by the Princeton team.

Interpretation: The Nature of a Social Event

It seems clear that the "game" actually was many different games and that each version of the events that transpired was just as "real" to a particular person as other versions were to other people. A consideration of the experiential phenomena that constitute a "football game" for the spectator may help us both to account for the results obtained and illustrate something of the nature of any social event.

Of crucial importance is the fact that an "occurrence" on the football field or in any other social situation does not become an experiential "event" unless and until some significance is given to it: an "occurrence" becomes an "event" only when the happening has significance. And a happening generally has significance only if it reactivates learned significances already registered in what we have called a person's assumptive form-world.

Hence the particular occurrences that different people experienced in the football game were a limited series of events from the total matrix of events potentially available to them. People experienced those occurrences that reactivated significances they brought to the occasion; they failed to experience those occurrences which did not reactivate past significances.

NOTES AND PROBLEMS

1. It is a matter of common knowledge that a person's bias can affect her testimony. However, do laypersons fully appreciate the extent of the potential impact of bias? Should courts admit expert testimony on the causes and extent of bias?

2. Problem 16-11. In *Devitt*, the defense calls Mr. Anzalone as a witness. On direct examination, Anzalone testifies that one week after the alleged assault, he was standing at the bar in a local saloon. He adds that Mr. Paterson was standing a few feet away. He testifies that he overheard Paterson say that he had "framed" Devitt. On cross-examination, the prosecutor asks:

Q: Mr. Anzalone, isn't it true that until a few months ago, you were a
            member of a gang called the Survivors?

A: Yes.

Q: And Mr. Devitt was a member of the same gang? Wasn't he?

A: Yes.

Q: To join the gang, you take an oath. Right?

A: Yes.

Q: An oath you promise you'll keep for your entire life?

A: Yes.

Q: Doesn't that oath include a promise to lie for other gang members?

A: Yes.

The defense objects to the entire line of questioning. The defense attorney adds: "Even if this has some minimal probative value on bias, it's inadmissible. This jurisdiction has adopted the Federal Rules of Evidence, and those rules make no mention of bias impeachment." Before ruling on the defense's objection, consider the Supreme Court's decision in the following case.

UNITED STATES v. ABEL
469 U.S. 45 (1984)

JUSTICE REHNQUIST delivered the opinion of the Court.

[T]he Federal Rules of Evidence . . . do not by their terms deal with impeachment for "bias," although they do expressly treat impeachment by character evidence and conduct, Rule 608, by evidence of conviction of a crime, Rule 609, and by showing of religious beliefs or opinion, Rule 610. Neither party has suggested what significance we should attribute to this fact. Although we are nominally the promulgators of the Rules, and should in theory need only to consult our collective memories to analyze the situation properly, we are in truth merely a conduit when we deal with an undertaking as substantial as the preparation of the Federal Rules of Evidence. In the case of these Rules, too, it must be remembered that Congress extensively reviewed our submission, and considerably revised it. *See* 28 U.S.C. § 2076; 4 J. Bailey III & O. Trelles II, Federal Rules of Evidence: Legislative Histories and Related Documents (1980).

Before the present Rules were promulgated, the admissibility of evidence in the federal courts was governed in part by statutes or Rules, and in part by case law. *See*, e.g., Fed. Rule Civ. Proc. 43(a) (prior to 1975 amendment); Fed. Rule Crim. Proc. 26 (prior to 1975 amendment); *Palmer v. Hoffman*, 318 U.S. 109 (1943); *Funk v. United States*, 290 U.S. 371 (1933); *Shepard v. United States*, 290 U.S. 96 (1933). This Court had held in *Alford v. United States*, 282 U.S. 687 (1931), that a trial court must allow some cross-examination of a witness to show bias. This holding was in accord with the overwhelming weight of authority in the state courts as reflected in Wigmore's classic treatise on the law of evidence. *See Id.*, at 691, citing 3 J. Wigmore, Evidence § 1368 (2d ed. 1923).

With this state of unanimity confronting the drafters of the Federal Rules of Evidence, we think it unlikely that they intended to scuttle entirely the evidentiary availability of cross-examination for bias. One commentator, recognizing the omission of any express treatment of impeachment for bias, prejudice, or corruption, observes that the Rules "clearly contemplate the use of the above-mentioned grounds of impeachment." E. Cleary, McCORMICK ON EVIDENCE § 40, p. 85 (3d 1984). Other commentators, without mentioning the omission, treat bias as a permissible and established basis of impeachment under the Rules. 3 D. LOUISELL & C. MUELLER, FEDERAL EVIDENCE § 341, p. 470 (1979); 3 J. WEINSTEIN & M. BERGER, WEINSTEIN'S EVIDENCE ¶ 607[03] (1981).

We think this conclusion is obviously correct. Rule 401 defines as "relevant evidence" evidence having any tendency to make the existence of any fact that is of consequence to the determination of the action more probable or less probable than it would be without the evidence. Rule 402 provides that all relevant evidence is admissible, except as otherwise provided by the United States Constitution, by Act of Congress, or by applicable rule. A successful showing of bias on the part of a witness would have a tendency to make the facts to which he testified less probable in the eyes of the jury than it would be without such testimony.

The correctness of the conclusion that the Rules contemplate impeachment by showing of bias is confined by the references to bias in the Advisory Committee Notes to Rules 608 and 610, and by the provisions allowing any party to attack credibility in Rule 607, and allowing cross-examination on "matters affecting the credibility of the witness" in Rule 611(b). The Court of Appeals have upheld use of extrinsic evidence to show bias both before and after the adoption of the Federal Rules of Evidence.

We think the lesson to be drawn from all of this is that it is permissible to impeach a witness by showing his bias under the Federal Rules of Evidence just as it was permissible to do so before their adoption.

NOTES

1.　The Court asserts that the Federal Rules "do not by their terms deal with impeachment" for bias. Is that true? Read Rule 411. Can Rule 411 be considered part of the context of Article VI?

2.　The *Abel* decision is undeniably important because it clarifies the status of bias impeachment under the Federal Rules and reveals at least part of the Court's conception of the statutory scheme of the Federal Rules. How does Rule 402 figure into that scheme, according to *Abel*?

3.　Think back to specific contradiction impeachment, *supra*. Just as Article VI is silent on bias impeachment, it makes no mention of specific contradiction. Given that common denominator, does *Abel* help explain why the courts continue to permit specific contradiction impeachment?

3.　The Two Stages of Bias Impeachment

A party attempting to show a witness's bias may do so in two ways. One way is to cross-examine the witness himself or herself to expose the bias. The other possibility is calling a second witness to establish the first witness's bias. The courts usually employ the expression "extrinsic evidence" to describe the testimony of the second witness.

a.   Cross-Examination to Prove Bias

1)   Relevance of Bias Impeachment

An attorney may cross-examine a witness to show the witness's bias against the attorney's side of the case or in favor of the opposing side. The scope of cross-examination about bias is quite broad. The courts allow the attorney to inquire about such diverse matters as family ties, *Adams v. State*, 280 Ala. 678, 198 So. 2d 255 (1967); romantic involvement, *People v. Jones*, 7 Cal. App. 3d 48, 86 Cal. Rptr. 717 (1970); and financial ties, *United States v. Kerr*, 464 F.2d 1367 (6th Cir. 1972). The courts tolerate a wide-ranging inquiry about bias. For example, the defense can cross-examine a prosecution witness to elicit the witness's admission that he has been granted immunity, *United States v. Musgrave*, 483 F.2d 327, 328 (5th Cir. 1973); is bargaining for a reduced sentence, *Gordon v. United States*, 344 U.S. 414 (1953); *United States v. Lopez-Medina*, 596 F.3d 716 (10th Cir. 2010) (witnesses may be cross examined about cooperating with government for reduced sentence in order to show interest or bias); or is a paid informant, *Wheeler v. United States*, 351 F.2d 946 (1st Cir. 1965). Efforts of the witness to avoid the consequences of his own crimes, and the incentive for him to slant his testimony may be shown. *United States v. Cooks*, 52 F.3d 101 (5th Cir. 1995) (jury should have been informed of all pertinent facts surrounding witness's motivation).

Further, the courts even allow attorneys to invoke bias impeachment theories to circumvent other evidentiary rules. Two or three illustrations will suffice. Federal Rule of Evidence 404(b) limits the admissibility of the defendant's other acts of misconduct. The statute specifically provides that the prosecutor may not introduce evidence of the other acts "to prove the character of [the defendant] to show that he acted in conformity therewith." However, suppose that the defendant calls a witness who has been involved in other crimes with the defendant. There is respectable case authority that the prosecutor may cross-examine the defense witness about other crimes the defendant and witness perpetrated together; the witness's prior criminal association with the defendant is evidence of bias in the defendant's favor. *United States v. Robinson*, 530 F.2d 1076 (D.C. Cir. 1976). *See also Gilbert v. United States*, 366 F.2d 923 (9th Cir. 1966), *cert. denied*, 388 U.S. 922 (1967). In a cocaine prosecution the trial court excluded all cross-examination about internal DEA incentives for agents to obtain convictions of drug traffickers. "This testimony would have revealed the specific benefits that would accrue to the agents should [defendant] be convicted." By excluding the DEA agent's motives favoring the prosecution, the trial judge violated the defendant's Confrontation Clause rights. *Vega v. Colorado*, 893 P.2d 107 (Colo. 1995) (error, but not reversible deprivation of rights; harmless error rule).

Mere arrests are usually excluded, unless reduced to a criminal conviction. However, where bias proof is involved, the rule against arrests, as well as the rule against impeachment by ordinary misdemeanor, is sometimes circumvented. *See United States v. Harper*, 527 F.3d 396 (5th Cir. 2008) (evidence of confidential informant's conviction for misdemeanor offense admissible to show his bias in prosecution for drug offenses; since charges were pending at the time informant agreed to work for government, pendency of criminal case and his conviction demonstrated motive to curry favor with government).

The courts are so impressed with the probative value of bias evidence that they have even allowed attorneys to override evidentiary rules that seemingly block the introduction of bias evidence. In *Davis v. Alaska*, 415 U.S. 308 (1974), which we shall discuss at length in the materials on the Confrontation Clause, the accused was charged with a burglary. The star prosecution witness was Richard Green. Earlier, Green had been adjudged a juvenile delinquent for burglarizing two cabins. Green was on probation for those offenses at the time of the accused's trial. An Alaska statute and court rule generally cloaked juvenile court proceedings with confidentiality. Based on the statute and court rule, the prosecutor obtained an *in limine* order forbidding the defense counsel from questioning Green about the prior juvenile offense. Writing for the majority, Chief Justice Burger concluded that the order violated the accused's confrontation rights. In the course of his opinion, the Chief Justice explained the logical relevance of the excluded evidence.

> [P]etitioner's counsel made it clear that he would not introduce Green's juvenile adjudication as a general impeachment of Green's character as a truthful person but, rather, to show specifically that at the same time, Green was assisting the police in identifying petitioner, he was on probation for burglary. From this petitioner would seek to show that Green acted out of fear or concern of possible jeopardy to his probation. Not only might Green have made a hasty and faulty identification of petitioner to shift suspicion away from himself as one who robbed the Polar Bar, but Green might have been subject to undue pressure from the police and made his identifications under fear of possible probation revocation. Green's record would be revealed only as necessary to probe Green for his bias and prejudice and not generally to call Green's good character into question.

More recently, the Supreme Court confirmed the approach of *Davis*. In *Olden v. Kentucky*, 488 U.S. 227 (1988), the defendant claimed that the trial court's refusal to allow him to impeach the complaining witness's testimony by introducing evidence supporting a motive to lie deprived him of his Sixth Amendment right to confront witnesses against him. When the complainant claimed rape, the defendant attempted to cross-examine her as to whether she "concocted the rape story to protect her relationship with [another man]." The Supreme Court ruled, pursuant to *Davis* and *Delaware v. Van Arsdall*, 475 U.S. 673 (1986), that there is a constitutionally protected right to impeach a witness for bias. *See also Daniels v. State*, 767 P.2d 1163 (Alaska Ct. App. 1989); *State v. Finley*, 300 S.C. 196, 387 S.E.2d 88 (1989).

Courts continue to follow this approach. *United States v. Manske*, 186 F.3d 770 (7th Cir. 1999) (conviction reversed where accused was denied opportunity to question government witnesses about their bias in favor of an accomplice who had already pleaded guilty; the Court of Appeals felt this was a "quintessentially appropriate topic for cross-examination" and should have been allowed because the bias of a witness is always probative).

PROBLEMS

1. **Problem 16-12.** A defendant is charged with rape. Police pulled into a parking building late at night and a woman leaped from the defendant's car when the police came into view. She claimed defendant was attacking her, while the defendant claims she had taken $100 for sexual intercourse, which the police interrupted. At trial, the defendant offers evidence that on two prior occasions the complaining witness had been arrested in the same parking building for acts of prostitution. The jurisdiction has a rape shield law like Federal Evidence Rule 412. When the defendant attempts to cross-examine the complainant about whether she was attempting to avoid arrest this time and fabricated the claim of rape, the prosecutor objects, relying upon Rule 412. The defendant responds: "Bias, your honor." What ruling? Is there an analogy to *Davis v. Alaska*? *See Commonwealth v. Joyce*, 415 N.E.2d 181, 186–87 (Mass. 1981); (defendant's right to show bias outweighed the rape shield law; complainant ran naked from her parked car to a police car and made the accusation); *Jackson v. Norris*, 734 F. Supp. 2d 606 (E.D. Ark. 2010) (recognizing the state statutes operating to restrict evidence in order to protect the privacy rights of individuals, including rape-shield laws, must have adequate balance so as to not unduly interfere with a defendant's ability to defend himself against criminal charges); *State v. Jalo*, 27 Or. App. 845, 557 P.2d 1359, 1362 (1976); (motive for complainant to fabricate accusation against defendant could be exposed); *Commonwealth v. Black*, 487 A.2d 396, 401 (Pa. Super. Ct. 1985) (Pennsylvania's Rape Shield Law may not be used to exclude relevant evidence showing a witness's bias).

2. **Problem 16-13.** In *Devitt*, the prosecution calls Mr. Larson as a witness. On direct examination, Larson testifies that he sometimes works with Devitt. Larson adds that the day before the alleged assault, he had a conversation with Devitt. Larson states that during the conversation, Devitt said that: He, Devitt, had seen "some fine stuff in that apartment that would look great on me." On cross-examination, the defense counsel attempts to elicit Larson's admission that one month before his alleged conversation with Devitt, he was arrested for selling marijuana. The prosecutor objects that "Mr. Larson's arrests are absolutely irrelevant." *See Commonwealth v. Schand*, 420 Mass. 783, 653 N.E.2d 566 (1995) (defendant has constitutional right to cross-examine witness to inquire whether witness expects more favorable treatment from the government on pending charges in exchange for his testimony in defendant's prosecution). On the propriety of prosecutor's granting favorable deals in exchange for testimony, see Finklea, Note, *Leniency in Exchange for Testimony: Bribery or Effective Prosecution?* 33 IND. L. REV. 957 (2000).

3. **Problem 16-14.** Larson is asked by Devitt's lawyer on cross-examination whether he would like to see Devitt out of the way because "you are both competing for the same girl." When the prosecutor objected and demanded to know the factual basis for the question, the defense attorney responded that "this is bias impeachment, and I do not have to reveal a good faith basis for my questions." What result? *Newman v. United States*, 705 A.2d 246 (D.C. 1997) (must be basis to support a genuine belief that the witness is biased).

4. Problem 16-15. Later during the cross-examination of Larson, the defense counsel asks whether Larson refused to talk to her (the defense counsel) before trial. On cross-examination, defense counsel asks Larson:

Q.   Mr. Larson, didn't you refuse to speak with me before this trial?

A.   Yes, I didn't want to talk to you.

Q.   But you did cooperate with the prosecutor?

A.   (belligerently) So what!

At this point the prosecutor objected: "Objection, the witness has no legal obligation to talk to the defense. Witnesses are free to talk, or refuse to talk, to whomever they please. His refusal to speak has nothing to do with this case, and is irrelevant." What ruling? *United States v. Crouch*, 478 F. Supp. 867, 871 (E.D. Cal. 1979) ("a witness' refusal to talk to counsel may be brought out in trial in that it may be evidence which relates to the witness' possible bias").

2)   Balancing Probative Value and Prejudice

Although the courts ascribe great probative value to bias impeachment, Rule 403 balancing often accounts for the exclusion of evidence logically relevant to prove bias.

In *Hafner v. Brown*, 983 F.2d 570, 576 (4th Cir. 1992), the defendants in a civil rights action were police officers. The court ruled that the trial judge "acted well within his discretion" in precluding cross-examination of a plaintiff's witness about the witness's past arrests; the defendants unsuccessfully argued that the arrests were relevant to show the witness's "bias against the police." However, in *United States v. Spencer*, 25 F.3d 1105 (D.C. Cir. 1994), a contrary result occurred. The court found a prior charge admissible as a possible source of a witness's hostility to law enforcement.

Even if such balancing does not completely foreclose a topic, it may restrict the extent of inquiry. *Thornton v. Vonallmon*, 456 S.W.2d 795 (Mo. Ct. App. 1970), exemplifies the restrictive effect. In *Thornton*, the defendant attempted to impeach a plaintiff's witness by showing that the witness had a sexual relationship with the plaintiff. On the one hand, the court held that the trial judge erred by precluding all inquiry about the witness's sexual relations with the plaintiff. However, the court added that "specific occasions or particular acts may not be inquired into." The court attempted to strike a balance by permitting a limited inquiry about the biasing relationship. The lurid details of the relationship may shed little additional light on the magnitude of the bias, and the details may be highly distracting to the jurors.

Rule 403 balancing again excluded proof of bias in *United States v. Davis*, 490 F.3d 541 (6th Cir. 2007). Cross-examination of a witness about her extramarital relationship with a doctor was excluded. "While bias is always relevant with regard to a witness's credibility, it remains the case that a trial court can opt to exclude evidence that is marginally relevant and highly prejudicial."

NOTES AND PROBLEMS

1. Is it material that the bias is directed against a class of persons (the police) rather than a particular individual? How does that affect the probative value of the bias evidence? Schmertz & Czapanskiy, *Bias Impeachment and the Proposed Federal Rules of Evidence*, 61 GEO. L.J. 257, 262 (1972).

Proof of personal bias is routinely allowed. If a witness strongly dislikes one of the parties to the case, it is clear that such fact is showable to demonstrate the witness's bias. What if the witness does not personally know any of the parties, but instead hates the racial or ethnic group to which the plaintiff or defendant belongs? Are the witness's prior expressions of bias against an ethnic group or class admissible? *State v. Loyd*, 459 So. 2d 498, 508 (La. 1984) (personal bias vs. general bias). *Compare Simmons v. Collins*, 655 So. 2d 330 (La. 1995). What if, in an employment discrimination case, a supervisor is sought to be cross-examined about whether he harbors "a bad attitude against women"?

Regarding impeachment based upon group bias consisting of a witness's prejudice against the legal system and legal process, see *Tobin v. Leland*, 804 So. 2d 390, 394 (Fla. Dist. Ct. App. 2001).

2. Problem 16-16. In *Hill*, Polecat calls Professor Sjostrom as an expert witness. On direct examination, Professor Sjostrom testifies that the placement of the gas tank was "in full compliance with modern safety standards." On cross-examination, Ms. Hill would like to force Sjostrom to admit that:

- During the past five years, he has testified on 20 occasions for automobile manufacturers in suits against the manufacturers.

- During that time, he earned a total of $83,000 as compensation for appearing as a witness for automobile manufacturers.

- The $83,000 represents thirty-six percent of his total income for the period.

- He has testified at the request of Polecat's defense attorney on two other occasions, and collected $4,000 and $5,000 respectively for those two court appearances.

Is this evidence logically relevant? Is it legally relevant? Why? *See* Graham, *Impeaching the Professional Expert by a Showing of Financial Interest*, 53 IND. L.J. 35, 50 (1977). *See also Collins v. Wayne Corp.*, 621 F.2d 777 (5th Cir. 1980); (a showing of a pattern of compensation in past cases raised inference that witness slanted testimony in those cases to be hired in future cases); *United States v. Edwardo-Franco*, 885 F.2d 1002, 1009–10 (2d Cir. 1989) (cross-examination of government's handwriting expert as to whether expert received several thousand dollars each time he testified for government was relevant to show potential bias). Under the usual rule, witnesses may be cross-examined about compensation for testifying. *Crowe v. Bolduc*, 334 F.3d 124 (1st Cir. 2003) (admissible on issue of bias).

3. Can inquiry about expert fees be overdone? In *State v. Negron*, 810 A.2d 1152 (N.J. Super. App. Div. 2002), the court initially acknowledged the propriety of an attorney cross-examining about and commenting upon payments made by an opponent to an expert witness. Such inquiry can serve as a basis for presenting the jury with an argument of bias on the part of the witness. However, counsel should not abuse the license to make reasonable inquiries about fees. In *Negron*, "[t]he prosecutor's conduct in this case crossed the line." Several cross-examination questions were subjects for concern on the part of the court. When one defense expert, a neurosurgeon with extensive practice and research experience in brain injuries, testified for the defense, this doctor stated his bill would be $2,900. The prosecutor observed:

Q: You had to stumble on that. It probably hurts you have to charge so low, correct?

A: You're making me nervous. That's why I'm stumbling. I came here —

Q: Sixty, 50, you've testified however many times as an expert, correct?

A: That's right.

Q: This is not the first time you're on the stand, correct?

A: Well, I have —

Q: Correct? That calls for a yes or no.

The Court: He says he can't answer it with a yes or no answer. That's his answer.

[The Prosecutor]: I'll withdraw the question. We'll move on.

Q: What makes you nervous, doctor, is that you are distorting the facts in this case to come up with your silly opinion, isn't that what makes you nervous?

A: No.

Another defense expert was paid a higher fee, and the cross-examination of this doctor also concentrated upon the amount of his compensation. The prosecutor's summation thereafter remarked: "[One defense witness] is a consultant which means he can't get a real job. Okay? That means he's got to pick up work in the courts as an expert." The prosecutor referenced both defense experts with another remark: "If they were good at what they did they wouldn't be here. For [one expert's] testimony, $10,000. What did he say that made any sense?" The prosecutor concluded: "$10,000 to fabricate evidence, to beat a murder charge. Great country, America, it really is, when you can pay a witness to come up with fraud like this."

The court castigated the prosecutor's unsupported assertions that the experts had sold their integrity, and reversed the defendant's conviction: "The foregoing cross-examination and summation excerpts speak for themselves. They clearly disclose a pattern of prosecutorial excesses that had every capacity to deny defendant the fair and impartial jury review to which he was entitled."

4. Problem 16-17. On further cross-examination of Professor Sjostrom, Ms. Hill attempts to elicit his admission that earlier this year he sent an advertisement of his services as an expert witness to every member of a national organization of defense attorneys, including Polecat's firm. *Weatherly v. Miskle*, 655 S.W.2d 842, 844 (Mo. Ct. App. 1983) (admitted a letter sent to over 2,000 lawyers by expert, advertising his services).

See Johnson v. Family Health Plan, 473 N.W.2d 609 (Wis. Ct. App. 1991) (doctor advertising is subject to exposure).

b.   Extrinsic Evidence to Prove Bias

The attorney attempting to impeach the witness may not be content with cross-examination. The attorney may press the attack even after that witness has left the stand. To continue the attack, the attorney will have to resort to extrinsic evidence. What are the evidentiary restrictions on the use of such evidence to prove bias?

The most important point to make is that the collateral fact rule is not a restriction. The inapplicability of the rule further reflects the courts' belief that bias is highly probative on the issue of credibility. *United States v. Dunson*, 142 F.3d 1213 (10th Cir. 1998) (bias is never classified as a collateral matter which lies beyond the scope of inquiry).

However, do not leap to the conclusion that extrinsic evidence is always admissible to prove bias. Although the collateral fact rule is inapplicable, in many jurisdictions there is a foundational requirement. The attorney must lay a proper foundation on cross-examination as a condition precedent to introducing the extrinsic proof. C. McCORMICK, HANDBOOK OF THE LAW OF EVIDENCE § 39, at 134–35 (4th ed. 1992). *See also United States v. Weiss*, 930 F.2d 185 (2d Cir. 1991), noting that extrinsic evidence of bias is allowed "although a foundation in the form of a preliminary question is often required."

D.   PROOF OF A CHARACTER TRAIT OF UNTRUTHFULNESS AND SPECIFIC UNTRUTHFUL ACTS

1.   Introduction

There are several conceivable ways of proving that a witness is a liar. The opposing attorney could prove that the witness has the reputation of being a liar. Next, the attorney could introduce the testimony of an acquaintance of the witness that in the acquaintance's opinion, the witness is a liar. Finally, we could allow the attorney to prove specific acts of untruthfulness by the witness. In some jurisdictions, only reputation evidence is permissible; in other jurisdictions, reputation and specific acts; and in still other states, all three types of proof are acceptable.

All three types of evidence are undeniably logically relevant on the issue of the witness's credibility. The question is the legal irrelevance of the evidence. Evidence of a witness's untruthful character poses thorny problems. You can understand part of the difficulty if you imagine that your reputation were on public trial. It is a hard issue to try and fraught with potential for abuse and prejudice. As we progress through this chapter, balance the probative value of each type of evidence (reputation, opinion, and specific acts) against the attendant probative dangers.

2.   The General Permissibility of Introducing Evidence of the Character Trait of a Witness for Untruthfulness

Unfortunately, the expression "character evidence" is often used ambiguously. It is critical to differentiate among the different uses of "character evidence." There are a number of ways in which character evidence can be logically relevant:

a.   Character in Issue

Although it is rare, a person's character trait can be an element of the substantive claim or defense. For example, in the *Hill* case one of the charges of negligence might be that Roe negligently entrusted the motor vehicle to Worker. To plead a negligent entrustment cause of action, Ms. Hill would have to allege that Worker is a careless driver, Roe knew or should have known that Worker is a careless driver, and Roe nevertheless entrusted the motor vehicle to Worker. Under these pleadings, Worker's character trait would be logically relevant to the historical merits of the case. Indeed, Worker's character is one of the ultimate issues.

b.   Character as Circumstantial Evidence of Historical Facts of the Merits

If the issue is whether a person performed a particular act, would it be helpful to the trier of fact to know something about that person's character trait? If you answer yes, you probably believe that people have a general propensity to act consistently with their character. Therefore, if you know the person's pertinent character trait, you will infer that he is more or less likely to have done the act in question. For example, in the *Devitt* case, if you know the defendant is or is not a peaceful, law-abiding person, his character makes it less or more likely that he attacked Paterson. The following diagram depicts this use of character as circumstantial evidence of the historical facts of the merits:

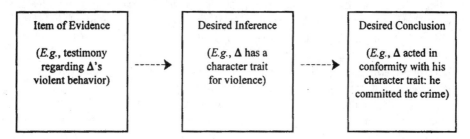

c.   Character as Circumstantial Evidence of Credibility

By parity of reasoning, a person's character with respect to truthfulness or mendacity is relevant to his credibility when he testifies as a witness. If the person is a habitual liar, that character trait increases the likelihood that his testimony is perjurious. This diagram depicts the underlying theory of logical relevance:

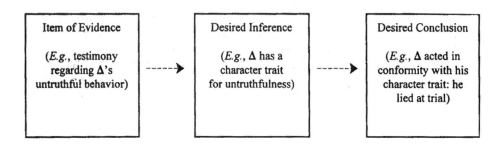

There is a striking similarity between the two diagrams. Under both theories of logical relevance, the proponent of the evidence employs the character evidence as circumstantial proof of a person's conduct on a specific occasion. In one instance, the prosecutor argues that Devitt's character trait for violence increases the likelihood that he committed the crime. In the other instance, the proponent argues that the untruthful witness acted "in character" while testifying and consequently perjured himself. In both cases, the proponent of the evidence invites the jury to draw an inference of specific conduct from the person's character trait.

Despite the essential similarity between the two uses of character evidence, the common law and the Federal Rules treat the two uses very differently. As we shall see in this chapter, both at common law and under the Federal Rules, character evidence is routinely admissible on a credibility theory. In sharp contrast, as we have already seen, the common law and the Federal Rules severely restrict the use of character evidence as circumstantial proof of the historical merits. However, as we saw, the adoption of Federal Rules of Evidence 413-15 eliminated some of the asymmetry between the two bodies of law.

What light does the available empirical research shed on the probative value of character evidence? Professor Mendez' survey of the psychological literature on the predictive value of character, based largely on Mischel's research, concludes that the general construct of character is a poor predictor of conduct in specific situations. Other commentators agree. *See* Lawson, *Credibility and Character: A Different Look at an Interminable Problem*, 50 NOTRE DAME L. REV. 758, 779–85 (1975) (one leading study of the degree of consistence between a character trait of truthfulness and conduct on specific occasions reported that "the most striking thing . . . is the amount of inconsistency exhibited"); Munday, *Stepping Beyond the Bounds of Credibility: The Application of Section I(f)(ii) of the Criminal Evidence Act 1898*, 1986 CRIM. L. REV. 511, 513–14; Spector, *Rule 609: A Last Plea for Its Withdrawal*, 32 OKLA. L. REV. 334, 351–53 (1979) ("For example, a prior conviction for perjury will generally say nothing about the willingness of a person to lie on this occasion"). In short, there appears to be little scientific basis for the differential treatment of the two circumstantial uses of character.

Might the difference be justified in terms of the doctrine of legal irrelevance?

3. Specific Methods of Proving the Character Trait of a Witness for Untruthfulness

There are four types of evidence which the impeaching attorney may offer, to prove a witness's character trait for untruthfulness: the witness's reputation for untruthfulness, another person's opinion that the witness is untruthful, an untruthful act by the witness (which has not yet resulted in a conviction), or a conviction for such an act. The last type of evidence poses special problems and will be covered in detail at the end of this chapter.

a. Reputation and Opinion Testimony

If the impeaching attorney decides to offer reputation or opinion evidence of a witness's untruthfulness, the evidence usually takes the form of testimony by a second, character witness. The witness to be impeached has already left the stand, and a later witness is now prepared to testify that the earlier witness is reputed to be untruthful or that, in her opinion, the earlier witness is untruthful. There are restrictions on the direct and cross-examination of such character witnesses.

1) Direct Examination

It is generally agreed that the character witness may testify only to the principal witness's specific character trait for truthfulness or veracity. The principal witness's general immoral character may not be shown (on the credibility issue). Prior to the Federal Rules of Evidence, some courts permitted a slightly broader scope: the character trait of "honesty." However, Rule 608(a)(1) expressly confines the scope of the testimony to the "character for truthfulness or untruthfulness."

At common law most jurisdictions limited the form of this proof to testimony by the character witness regarding the reputation of the principal witness for truthfulness. The courts excluded the character witness's personal opinion about the principal witness's veracity. Nor could the character witness bolster her testimony with specific illustrations of the principal witness's truthful conduct.

It might seem anomalous that we not only allow but require proof in the form of reputation-gossip. The stated rationale is that reputation is the most reliable form of evidence because it is based upon collective knowledge acquired over a period of time by those who would know best. Opinion, it was thought, would be too much influenced by the character witness's friendship with the principal witness. Thus, the traditional form of the questions and answers would be as follows. After establishing the extent of the character witness's experience with the relevant community, the questioner asks:

Q: Does X have a general reputation in El Dorado regarding her truthfulness?

A: Yes, she does.

Q: Do you know what that reputation is?

A: Yes, I do.

Q: Please tell the jury what the reputation is.

A: It is bad.

Under Federal Rule 608(a), testimony in the form of reputation or opinion is permissible.

NOTES AND PROBLEMS

1. As previously stated, most jurisdictions now exclude evidence of the principal witness's general, moral, law-abiding character when it is offered to prove the witness's credibility. Is that evidence logically irrelevant? Or should the evidence be barred under the legal irrelevance doctrine?

2. **Problem 16-18.** In *Hill*, Mr. Worker testifies for Mr. Roe for three hours. Ms. Hill hired Doctor Schultz, a physician, to attend the trial and observe Worker's testimony. Schultz observed all of Worker's testimony. During her rebuttal, Ms. Hill calls Schultz as a witness. After stating his qualifications and a definition of "pathological liar," Schultz' direct examination continues:

Q: Where were you earlier today, Doctor?

A: Right here in this courtroom.

Q: What were you doing?

A: At your request, I was observing and studying Mr. Worker's behavior and demeanor on the witness stand.

Q: What sort of conduct did you observe?

A: I noted that he repeatedly refused to meet the gaze of the questioner, frequently placed his hand over his mouth while answering, and often changed his position in his chair before beginning an answer.

Q: Doctor, do you have an opinion whether Mr. Worker is a pathological liar, as you previously defined the term.

O: Objection, Your Honor. This question calls for clearly improper matter.

You are the trial judge. What ruling? Does Rule 608(a) bar this testimony? On its face, does Rule 608(a) limit the impeaching attorney to lay opinions?

3. Assume that Rule 608(a) sanctions the introduction of otherwise admissible expert opinions. Is there nevertheless a ground for objecting to Dr. Schultz' testimony? There is a general rule against any witness stating that another lied when he gave his sworn trial testimony. But is that what Schultz is doing? Rather, is he describing a general psychological condition? Would it make a difference if Schultz had examined Worker for five hours at Schultz' clinic before trial? *See United States v. Hiss*, 88 F. Supp. 559, 559–60 (D.C.N.Y. 1950). In a more recent case, a forensic psychiatrist concluded that plaintiff's record indicated that he had lied about himself and fabricated psychiatric symptoms. The expert opinion was excluded as unfairly prejudicial. *Hodges v. Keane*, 886 F. Supp. 352 (S.D.N.Y. 1995).

4. Problem 16-19. After Dr. Schultz leaves the stand, *Hill* calls Mr. Bartosic. Bartosic testifies that, in addition to working for Mr. Roe, Worker is employed part-time at his company. Bartosic testifies that he is familiar with Worker's reputation for truthfulness at his company. *Hill* then asks, "What is that reputation?" As soon as the question is asked, Roe's attorney objects and requests permission to take the witness on *voir dire* before the judge rules on the objection. Does the opposing attorney have a right to *voir dire*? Does this issue fall under Federal Rule 104(a) or Rule 104(b)? Suppose that Roe's attorney conducts a *voir dire* and forces Bartosic to admit that there are only four employees at his company and that he has known Worker for only six months. What ruling? *See Wisinski v. State*, 508 So. 2d 504, 505–06 (Fla. Dist. Ct. App. 1987) (judge refused to admit testimony because small number of people provided only a limited cross section, and because witness had only known party for short period).

For a case excluding reputation drawn from a few people at a skating rink, see *People v. Erickson*, 883 P.2d 511 (Colo. Ct. App. 1994).

5. Defendants testified on their own behalf in a federal drug trial. A government informant was from Mexico. That fact alone did not give the defendants, also from Mexico, the right to testify to the informant's bad reputation for truthfulness. *United States v. Ruiz-Castro*, 92 F.3d 1519 (10th Cir. 1996). In order to establish a foundation for reputation testimony, a witness should show acquaintance with the person under attack, "the community in which he has lived and the circles in which he has moved" in order to speak with authority about the manner in which the attacked person is regarded.

2)　Cross-Examination

Federal Evidence Rule 608(b) permits a character witness to be cross-examined about specific instances of the principal witness's conduct which are inconsistent with the reputation or opinion to which the character witness testified. The rule specifies that individual incidents of conduct, if probative of truthfulness or untruthfulness, may be inquired into on cross-examination.

Suppose, for instance, that during rebuttal, the prosecutor called a witness who attacked Devitt's character trait of truthfulness. During surrebuttal Devitt called his cousin, Mr. Frontiero, to vouch for his truthfulness. On cross-examination of Frontiero, the prosecutor may ask whether Frontiero has heard that two years ago Devitt testified falsely in a drunk-driving prosecution. The ostensible purpose of this question is to show that Frontiero's testimony is not credible. If Frontiero has not heard of the incident, his knowledge of Devitt's reputation is suspect. If Frontiero knows of the incident but still believes that Devitt is a truthful person, the jury may question Frontiero's standard for assessing credibility. (Of course, an illegitimate purpose may also be present — to get otherwise inadmissible evidence of Devitt's alleged perjury and drunk driving before the jury.)

Since we are now getting pretty far afield, this evidence is treated as collateral; the question may be asked, but the cross-examiner must "take the witness's answer." If the witness disputes the specific instance or denies knowledge of the instance inquired about, that is the end of the matter. The cross-examiner cannot later introduce extrinsic evidence of the specific instance to disprove the denial.

In 2003, Federal Evidence Rule 608(b) was amended "to clarify that the absolute prohibition on extrinsic evidence applies only when the sole reason for proffering that evidence is to attack or support the witness' character for truthfulness. . . . By limiting the application of the Rule to proof of a witness' character for truthfulness, the amendment leaves the admissibility of extrinsic evidence offered for other grounds of impeachment (such as contradiction, prior inconsistent statement, bias and mental capacity) to Rules 402 and 403." 2003 Adv. Comm. Note, FED. R. EVID. 608.

The first sentence of Rule 608(b) now reads:

"Except for a criminal conviction under Rule 609, extrinsic evidence is not admissible to prove specific instances of a witness's conduct in order to attack or support the witness's character for truthfulness."

NOTES AND PROBLEMS

1.   The usual manner of raising a specific incident on cross-examination is with a "have you heard" question. *See United States v. Parker*, 553 F.3d 1309 (10th Cir. 2009) (prosecution may ask a character witness questions of the "have you heard" variety when a witness testifies about personal opinion of the defendant's character; district court did not abuse discretion in allowing the questioning by the government on cross-examination of defendant's character witnesses where none of the questions assumed defendant's guilt). When a character witness is cross-examined, the cross-examiner is not limited to confronting the character witness with a defendant's prior felony convictions. Other forms of misconduct are appropriate for use during cross-examination. *See United States v. Bah*, 574 F.3d 106 (2d Cir. 2009) (in prosecution for operating an unlicensed money-transmitting business, district court did not abuse discretion in permitting government to question defendant's character witness about a former customer's complaint accusing defendant of fraud).

2.   **Problem 16-20.** In *Devitt*, after the defendant testifies, the prosecutor calls Mr. Lang as a rebuttal witness. Lang testifies that Devitt has "a bad reputation in El Dorado for lying all the time." In surrebuttal, Devitt calls Ms. Wilson, another El Dorado resident, who contradicts Lang. A week before trial, a police officer told the prosecutor that "there's a rumor floating round that Devitt cheated on his last year's income tax." During his cross-examination of Ms. Wilson, the prosecutor asks: Ms. Wilson, have you heard a report that the defendant cheated on his taxes last year?

D: Your Honor, may we approach the bench?

J: Yes.

D: I'd like to know the basis for that question. In fact, I demand to know it.

J: Ms. Prosecutor, what is the basis?

Is a police officer's report a satisfactory basis? What if Devitt had been arrested for tax evasion? What if the local federal grand jury had already indicted Devitt for tax evasion? If a final conviction is unnecessary, at what point should we draw the line? *See* Graham, *Evidence and Trial Advocacy Workshop*, 21 CRIM. L. BULL. 495,

510–11 (1985) (cross-examiner must have a good faith basis for inquiry about specific instances of misconduct; knowledge of conduct which led to arrest or indictment supplied basis; rumor alone does not suffice).

3. Courts require a good faith basis before permitting a party to cross-examine about prior bad acts. Earlier, we touched upon this requirement in connection with bias impeachment. This general requirement of an evidentiary basis for cross-examination underlies other impeachment techniques as well, such as prior conviction impeachment.

b. Specific Untruthful Acts (Which Have Not Resulted in a Conviction)

As we will study next, one method of establishing a mendacious character is proving that the witness has been convicted of certain crimes. Another technique permits proof of specific instances of the witness's untruthful conduct even if that conduct has not led to a judgment of conviction. The issue of the admissibility of this type of evidence has badly divided the courts. Younger, *Three Essays on Character and Credibility Under the Federal Rules of Evidence*, 5 HOFSTRA L. REV. 7, 12–13 (1976). The courts have split into three schools of thought.

One group of courts excludes this evidence altogether. In essence, this school deems the evidence worth the court's time only if there is highly reliable proof of the act's commission, namely, a conviction.

At the other extreme, many courts purport to allow the cross-examiner to inquire beyond acts of untruthfulness — into any bad, illegal, or immoral act by the witness. These courts might permit the prosecutor to cross-examine a rape defendant about another alleged rape for the purpose of impeaching defendant's credibility. *State v. Caruthers*, 676 S.W.2d 935 (Tenn. 1984). In sex offense prosecutions some of these jurisdictions even go to the length of allowing the cross-examiner to question the victim about her prior sexual misconduct on a credibility theory. Annot., 97 A.L.R.3d 967 (1980); Annot., 94 A.L.R.3d 257 (1979); Ordover, *Admissibility of Patterns of Similar Sexual Misconduct: The Unlamented Death of Character for Chastity*, 63 CORNELL L. REV. 90, 120 (1977). As we have seen, under Federal Rule 412 and in many states, the trend is toward limiting the admission of sexual misconduct whether it is offered to prove the complainant's consent or to attack her credibility. *Stephens v. Miller*, 13 F.3d 998 (7th Cir. 1994); *Slater v. State*, 310 Ark. 73, 832 S.W.2d 846 (1992). One of the reasons for this trend is that we have come to question the connection between sexual morality and credibility. Ordover, *supra*, at 120–26. This same, questioning attitude accounts for the emergence of the third, majority view on the admissibility of specific acts of misconduct.

The majority of jurisdictions permit cross-examination concerning specific acts of misconduct, but only if the acts relate directly to veracity. Rule 608(b) requires that they be "probative of untruthfulness." Deceitful acts, including forgery, bribery, tax fraud, bankruptcy fraud, false statements, false swearing, cheating, embezzlement, swindling, false advertising, issuing bad checks, unlawful use of credit cards, criminal impersonation, and unlawfully concealing a will ordinarily qualify. *United States v. Amahia*, 825 F.2d 177 (8th Cir. 1987) (perjury, subornation of perjury, false statement, and false pretenses); *Bonilla v. Jaronczyk*, 2009 U.S. App. LEXIS 26167 (2d Cir. Dec. 2, 2009) (prisoner's use of false papers to reenter United States illegally was admissible and went to the prisoner's character for truthfulness or untruthfulness). Introduction of false income tax returns was approved under the majority view as Rule 608(b) evidence in *Gaillard v. Jim's Water Service, Inc.*, 535 F.3d 771, 773 (8th Cir. 2008) (inflated returns used to attack credibility of plaintiff in accident injury case).

Borderline cases such as smuggling are left to the trial judge's discretion. Acts primarily involving force or intimidation are excluded. The definite trend is toward this majority view, limiting the cross-examiner to acts "probative of . . . untruthfulness." Note the parallel between the evolution of this body of law and character evidence, discussed in section B of this chapter. In that section, we observed a trend toward limiting the opposing attorney to the character trait of untruthfulness rather than general moral character. The law governing specific acts impeachment is moving in the same direction.

One commentator, Professor Friedman, has proposed still another, compromise view. Friedman, *Character Impeachment Evidence: Psycho-Bayesian [!?] Analysis and a Proposal Overhaul*, 38 UCLA L. REV. 637 (1991). On the one hand, he would absolutely preclude the use of this technique to impeach a criminal accused. On the other hand, subject to the trial judge's discretionary balancing, he would permit the use of the technique to impeach any other type of witness. *See* Friedman, *Character Impeachment Evidence: The Asymmetrical Interaction Between Personality and Situation*, 43 DUKE L.J. 816 (1994).

The limitations on extrinsic evidence of the act are even more severe than the restrictions on cross-examination. Evidence of specific acts of misconduct is deemed collateral. If the witness denies the misconduct, the cross-examiner must "take the answer" and cannot introduce extrinsic evidence to disprove the denial. *Shipman v. State*, 604 S.W.2d 182 (Tex. Crim. App. 1980). Federal Rule of Evidence 608(b) codifies this rule. *Nicholas v. Pennsylvania State Univ.*, 227 F.3d 133 (3d Cir. 2000); *Becker v. ARCO Chemical Co.*, 207 F.3d 176 (3d Cir. 2000); Note, 4 NEW ENG. L. REV. 133, 139 (1981). Under Rule 608(b), the courts have excluded conviction records, arrest records, Internal Revenue Service reports, and other documents when offered as "extrinsic evidence" of the untruthful act. Annot., 36 A.L.R. Fed. 564, 578–81 (1978). Thus, the collateral fact rule applies to this mode of impeachment. Yet, some courts allow extrinsic evidence when the witness admits the misconduct. *United States v. Zandi*, 769 F.2d 229, 236–37 (4th Cir. 1985); *United States v. Jackson*, 876 F. Supp. 1188, 1197–98 (D. Kan. 1994). Many commentators, though, take the position that properly construed, Rule 608(b) bars the introduction of extrinsic evidence whether the witness admits or denies the misconduct. R. CARLSON, 3 CRIMINAL LAW ADVOCACY: TRIAL PROOF & 12.29 (1994).

NOTES AND PROBLEMS

1. How broadly should Rule 608(b) be construed? The crucial language in the rule is "probative of truthfulness or untruthfulness. . . ." Compare that language with the wording of Rule 609(a)(2), "dishonest act or false statement." When a legislature uses different words, the courts typically presume that the legislature meant different things. *Kuhs v. Superior Court*, 201 Cal. App. 3d 966, 974, 247 Cal. Rptr. 544, 549 (1988) (as a general rule of statutory construction, where the legislature uses different terms, different meanings are intended).

See Robinson v. Shell Oil Co., 70 F.3d 325 (4th Cir. 1995) (in explaining statutory language, words are given their common usage, and courts should apply statute as written).

Which language is broader?

In *United States v. Cudlitz*, 72 F.3d 992 (1st Cir. 1996), the prosecutor cross-examined Cudlitz about whether he had solicited a man to burn down a building. The defendant denied doing so. The court held that Cudlitz might have been questioned under Rule 608(b) as to prior instances of forgery or perjury; but soliciting arson is not "probative of untruthfulness."

Similarly, a physician witness for the plaintiff in *Unmack v. Deaconess Medical Center*, 967 P.2d 783 (Mont. 1998) was cross-examined about the fact that at a prior time he had been disciplined by a professional association for misconduct. Using the disciplinary action against him during cross-examination was improper, said the Montana Supreme Court. The disciplinary action was not probative of untruthfulness; and it also carried with it the baggage of extreme prejudice under Evidence Rule 403.

Nor was it proper to bring up a prior incident against a professor who had sued a university. The cross-examiner made the claim that she allegedly invited students to her house for a hot tub party. *Speers v. University of Akron*, 196 F. Supp. 2d 551 (N.D. Ohio 2002) (actions do not reflect on plaintiff's truthfulness; court also holds prior shoplifting charge against her followed by conviction is plainly inadmissible because this is not a crime involving dishonesty).

2. Problem 16-21. In *Devitt*, two months before trial, the defendant was playing poker with an acquaintance, Mr. Belville. Devitt drank to excess and leaped to the conclusion that Belville was cheating him. Devitt struck Belville, grabbed all the money on the card table, and fled. Under Morena law, Devitt's conduct amounted to the statutory offense of theft by violence. If Devitt testifies, may the prosecutor cross-examine him about the theft?

3. Problem 16-22. Before trial, Devitt's attorney learns that Mr. Paterson's employer recently fired him because he misstated facts on his original job application. One part of the job application asked applicants to list all prior convictions. Although Paterson had a prior conviction for marijuana possession, he omitted any mention of the conviction. When the defense attorney begins questioning him about the job application, the following conversation occurs at sidebar:

P: Your Honor, I have reason to believe that the defense counsel is trying to elicit the fact that on his job application, Mr. Paterson lied about a prior for marijuana possession.

J: Is that true?

D: Yes.

J: What's your theory of admissibility?

D: Rule 608(b), Your Honor.

P: If that's the case, Your Honor, it's clearly inadmissible. Rule 608(b)
                      is limited to acts relevant to "truthfulness or untruthfulness," and
                      marijuana possession had nothing to do with that.

D: That misses the point, Your Honor. It's the lie I'm going after.

What ruling? *See United States v. Owens*, 21 M.J. 117, 123 (C.M.A. 1985) (false
statements were made by defendant on his application for promotion to Warrant
Officer; proper to impeach him with that falsity when he testified in trial for
shooting his wife).

See also Browne v. Signal Mountain Nursery, L.P., 286 F. Supp. 2d 904 (E.D.
Tenn. 2003) (evidence of inaccurate information on plaintiff's employment applications was relevant to her credibility and was properly admitted).

4.   A frequently repeated generalization is that mere arrests cannot be asked
about on cross-examination. While that may be literally true in many instances,
what about the conduct which led to the arrest? In *United States v. Robertson*, 39
M.J. 211 (C.M.A. 1994), the court held that an arrest alone is not probative of
credibility; but where the underlying facts which gave rise to the arrest relate to
untruthfulness, they may form the basis for questions under Rule 608 (b).

5.   The law of impeachment by prior conviction, the next topic in the text, bars
use of convictions which are remote in time, *i.e.*, stale convictions. Does the same bar
apply under Rule 608(b)? Not always. Some decisions have favored admission of old
incidents which occurred a long time prior to current trial. *See Hampton v. Dillard
Dept. Stores, Inc.*, 18 F. Supp. 2d 1256 (D. Kan. 1998) (evidence of incidents of
untruthfulness, one of which was over 20 years old, was admissible to impeach
credibility).

E.   CONVICTION OF A CRIME

1.   An Overview of Impeachment By Proof of a Conviction

a.   Logical Relevance

The logical relevance of a witness's criminal conviction is undeniable. The fact of
the conviction is some evidence of the witness's willingness to disregard social
norms. The theory of logical relevance of the prior conviction is that it increases the
probability that at the time of trial, the witness will violate another social norm and
testify untruthfully. The conviction is circumstantial proof of the perjurious nature
of the witness's trial testimony. As the Advisory Committee explained, a "demonstrated instance of willingness to engage in conduct in disregard of accepted
patterns is translated into willingness to give false testimony." 45 F.R.D. 161, 297

However, there are grave doubts about the reliability of that translation. Unlike
Rule 608(b), conviction impeachment is not limited to conviction for offenses which
are directly germane to credibility. By way of example, under Rule 609(a)(1), the
impeaching attorney can prove that the witness suffered a prior conviction for

voluntary manslaughter or felony drunk driving. Dean Ladd was particularly critical of the probative value of the courts' willingness to admit evidence of convictions for "crimes-at-large." Ladd, *Credibility Tests — Current Trends*, 89 U. PA. L. REV. 166, 177–78 (1940). The courts' willingness to stretch the impeachment that far compounds the doubts raised by the psychological studies. *Id.* In this light, is it sensible to treat conviction impeachment more liberally than Rule 608(b) impeachment?

There is, though, a counter-argument that the bare fact of the conviction raises the probative value of this type of impeachment evidence. The conviction is seemingly trustworthy proof that the witness in fact committed the underlying act. Some courts have asserted that the conviction is "the strongest proof" that the witness committed the act. Note, *Evidence of Other Crimes in Montana*, 30 MONT. L. REV. 235, 238 (1969). When there has been no conviction, it can be highly debatable whether the witness committed the untruthful act. The conviction thus heightens the probative worth of the impeaching evidence.

PROBLEMS

1.   **Problem 16-23.** In *Devitt*, on direct examination the defendant testifies that "I've never been in trouble with the law before." The prosecutor has a certified copy of a judgment of a conviction of Devitt in 20YR. Does the prosecutor have to resort to Rule 609 to justify the admission of the conviction?

2.   **Problem 16-24.** The prosecutor calls Mr. Melrose as a witness against Devitt. Melrose testifies on direct examination that he "happened to be near" Paterson's apartment at the time of the alleged battery and that he saw Devitt running from the apartment. The defense counsel has evidence that in 20YR, Melrose was convicted of sexual assault in Morena and that he is still on probation for the assault. Does the defense counsel have to resort to Rule 609 to justify the admission of the conviction? *See Davis v. Alaska*, 415 U.S. 308, 316–18 (1974) (proof of past misconduct followed by parole or probation raises inference of bias on the part of a witness who is on probation; he may be trying to curry favor with the state during his testimony).

b.   Prejudice

Evidence of a conviction raises a number of Rule 403 concerns. The evidence carries with it a substantial risk of unfair prejudice. The fact that the witness is a "criminal" or an "ex-con" may induce an emotional reaction by the trier of fact against the witness. Even if he is merely a witness, the judge or jury may discredit his testimony solely because they dislike him. If he is a party, a close case may go against him because of the jury's dislike.

The prejudice becomes acute when the witness is the criminal defendant. When in doubt, the jury may decide to resolve the doubts against him; the jury may be more willing to convict a "criminal." This danger reaches its zenith when the crime for which he was convicted is the same as or similar to the crime now charged. In H. KALVEN & H. ZEISEL, THE AMERICAN JURY 160 (1966), the researchers found that when the strength of the evidence was constant, sixty-five percent of the defendants without a record were acquitted but only thirty-eight percent of the defendants whom the jury knew or suspected had a criminal record. If the jury learns of the defendant's criminal record, they may use a "different. . . calculus of probabilities" in deciding whether to convict. *Id.* at 179.

The advocates of this method of impeachment argue that the opponent is entitled to a limiting instruction and the instruction protects the opponent against misuse of the evidence. Others counter that limiting instructions are notoriously ineffective. Note the comments of one trial judge:

> The defendant is a dead duck once he is on trial before a jury and you present a record that he was convicted . . . twenty-five years ago. . . . If it's any way close, the jury is going to hang him on that record, not on the evidence.

People v. Montgomery, 47 Ill. 2d 510, 514, 268 N.E.2d 695, 697 (1971). On appeal, the court referred to these remarks in discussing the effectiveness of a limiting instruction:

> The remarks of the trial judge reflect his disbelief in the effectiveness of that safeguard. That same disbelief was expressed in more scholarly terms by Dean Griswold: "We accept much self-deception on this. We say that the evidence of the prior conviction is admissible only to impeach the defendant's testimony, and not as evidence of the prior crimes themselves. Juries are solemnly instructed to this effect. Is there anyone who doubts what the effect of this evidence in fact is on the jury? If we know so clearly what we are actually doing, why do we pretend that we are not doing what we clearly are doing?" Griswold, *The Long View* (1965), 51 A.B.A. J. 1017, 1021. *Id.*

Note, 4 Colum. J.L. & Soc. Probs. 3, 218 (1968), reports the results of a survey of judges' and attorneys' attitudes toward limiting instructions. Ninety-eight percent of the attorneys surveyed and forty-three percent of the judges surveyed believe that juries are unable to follow such limiting instructions.

More recent empirical research supports this widespread belief. In a Boston College study, 160 randomly chosen subjects received written descriptions of the evidence in a criminal case, a prosecution for either murder or auto theft. Wissler & Saks, *On the Inefficacy of Limiting Instructions — When Jurors Use Prior Conviction Evidence to Decide Guilt*, 9 Law & Hum. Behav. 37 (1985). The only variation in each case was the impeachment evidence; some jurors were told the defendant had a prior conviction for murder, others auto theft, and still others perjury. All jurors were instructed to limit their consideration of the conviction to the defendant's credibility. Sixty percent of the jurors voted to convict when the impeaching conviction was perjury. However, seventy-five percent voted to convict when the charged crime and the impeaching conviction were identical. In short, the jurors were inclined to use the impeaching conviction as character evidence on the merits rather than confining it to credibility. In addition, "[a]s part of the University of Chicago Jury Project, Dale Broeder interviewed jurors after they had . . . rendered verdicts in criminal trials. Broeder asserted that the 'jurors almost universally used defendant's record to conclude that he was a bad man and hence was more likely than not guilty of the crime for which he was then standing trial.' "

Beaver & Marques, *A Proposal to Modify the Rule on Criminal Conviction Impeachment*, 58 TEMP. L.Q. 585, 602 (1985).

Other commentators agree with the prejudice analysis. In Dodson, *What Went Wrong With Federal Rule of Evidence 609: A Look at How Jurors Really Misuse Prior Conviction Evidence*, 48 DRAKE L. REV. 1, 45 (1999), this observation appears:

> The current version of Rule 609 sacrifices individual rights and turns traditional notions of American criminal law on its head. The goal has been to increase convictions and get criminals off the street, but what has been forgotten are the underlying social goals and policies behind American criminal law. It has long been recognized that a person should not suffer criminal sanctions because he is a bad person or has done bad things in the past. Criminal justice in this country is premised on the assumption that we should only punish specific acts which the state can prove beyond a reasonable doubt.

NOTE

Courts continue to place great confidence in limiting instructions. *United States v. Buchanan*, 70 F.3d 818 (5th Cir. 1995): "Although the danger of prejudice associated with prior conviction evidence is often great, the district court in this case substantially reduced the possibility of prejudice to *Bonner* by carefully instructing the jury on how they could consider the evidence." The holding in *United States v. Lopez*, 979 F.2d 1024 (5th Cir. 1992), is in accord. In view of the foregoing survey results, is this confidence justified?

2.   Cross-Examination of a Witness About a Prior Conviction

First consider the restrictions on cross-examining a witness about a prior conviction. There are several points of agreement among the courts. When the attorney is relying on Rule 609 rather than Rule 608(b), the evidence must take the form of a conviction. Even before sentencing and formal entry of judgment, the verdict is persuasive evidence of guilt. In *United States v. Mitchell*, 886 F.2d 667 (4th Cir. 1989), although the defendant had been convicted but not yet sentenced, the court's acceptance of the jury's verdict was a sufficient predicate for the use of the verdict for impeachment in a subsequent trial. A related problem is the effect of a pending new trial motion or appeal on the admissibility of the conviction. Almost all courts agree that the judgment is nevertheless admissible. *McGee v. State*, 206 Tenn. 230, 332 S.W.2d 507 (1960). For example, Rule 609(e) provides that "[t]he pendency of an appeal . . . does not render evidence of a conviction inadmissible." FED. R. EVID. 609(e).

There is also a consensus that the conviction must be valid. The Supreme Court has announced that the conviction is inadmissible if it was obtained in violation of a criminal defendant's Sixth Amendment counsel right. *Loper v. Beto*, 405 U.S. 473 (1972). The prosecution may not use a conviction resulting from a trial at which the right to counsel attached but the defendant neither waived nor was afforded counsel.

There is also general agreement that there are only certain details which the cross-examiner may inquire about — typically, nature of the crime, the date of the offense and the disposition. *Gibson v. Moskowitz*, 523 F.3d 657 (6th Cir. 2008) (exclusion of evidence regarding circumstances of prior conviction); *Gora v. Costa*, 971 F.2d 1325 (7th Cir. 1992); *Hodges v. State*, 229 Ga. App. 475, 494 S.E.2d 223 (1997); *State v. Higgins*, 422 N.W.2d 277 (Minn. Ct. App. 1988).

See United States v. Street, 548 F.3d 618 (8th Cir. 2008). In *Street*, the court found that while a witness may be questioned regarding certain essentials surrounding a prior conviction in order to establish that a witness was convicted following a jury trial, to inquire further may be improper. For example, to contest the truthfulness of the witness's individual past statements in the earlier trial which led to his conviction would be, in effect, relitigating his prior conviction. This type of "confusing, collateral issue" is to be avoided. Matters like the date and nature of the prior crime, the basic details, are ordinarily reflected on the face of any copy of the judgment of conviction. As previously stated, one of the rationales for the liberal treatment of conviction impeachment is that the availability of the documentary evidence of the judgment reduces the likelihood that the evidence will distract the jury; it is improbable that the jurors will have to devote an inordinate amount of time to the question of whether the witness committed the act. To some extent that time saving would be lost if the cross-examiner could inquire about aggravating details which are not stated on the face of the document. That inquiry might trigger the very type of lengthy dispute which the availability of the document supposedly precludes. *See Cummings v. Malone*, 995 F.2d 817, 826 (8th Cir. 1993).

The consensus over conviction impeachment ends abruptly at this point. The two questions that have divided the courts relate to the fundamental logical and legal relevance concerns that we mentioned in the previous section. Must the underlying crime involve fraud or dishonesty? And even if the conviction satisfies the normal foundational requirements, should the trial judge have a residual power to balance the conviction's probative value against incidental probative dangers?

a. The Types of Crimes

Before the Federal Rules of Evidence, support could be found in federal cases "for each of the following propositions: a witness may be impeached by inquiry about any conviction of crime, whether felony or misdemeanor; felonies may be shown but misdemeanors may not; only crimes involving moral turpitude may be shown; any felony may be shown but misdemeanors only if they involve moral turpitude; felonies and misdemeanors amounting to *crimen falsi*; or that only crimes resting on dishonest conduct may be shown." 2 C. WRIGHT, FEDERAL PRACTICE AND PROCEDURE: CRIMINAL § 416 (1969). The state cases were also in disarray. California Evidence Code § 788 allowed all felonies to be shown. A respectable number followed the Model Code (Rule 106(b)) and the 1954 Uniform Rules (Rules 20–22) and admitted only crimes involving dishonesty or false statement. However, the majority of courts seemed to allow the proponent to use any felony "without regard to the nature of the particular offense" and *crimen falsi* offenses "without regard to the grade of the offense." Adv. Comm. Note, FED. R. EVID. 609.

If the Advisory Committee's description of the majority view is accurate, Rule 609(a) should be characterized as a relatively conservative provision; the Rule reflects that view. Rule 609(a) presents several statutory construction issues, and you should read its text carefully. The Conference Report gives us some aid in interpreting the text. The Report explains that the expression, "dishonesty and false statement," includes crimes "such as perjury, subornation of perjury, false statement, criminal fraud, embezzlement, or false pretense, or any other offense in the nature of *crimen falsi*, the commission of which involves some element of deceit, untruthfulness, or falsification . . ." *Quoted in* 3 J. WEINSTEIN & M. BERGER, WEINSTEIN'S EVIDENCE ¶ 609–81 (1985).

NOTES AND PROBLEMS

1. Concentrate on a comparison between the scope of Rules 609(a)(1) and (a)(2). Are the two provisions mutually exclusive, or is there a possibility of overlap? If so, be prepared to give an example of a crime falling in the area of overlap.

2. **Problem 16-25.** In *Devitt*, the prosecution calls Mr. Melrose. In 2011, Melrose was convicted of shoplifting. The maximum imposable punishment was six months' imprisonment. Morena has adopted Federal Rule 609(a). Can the defense rely on Rule 609(a)(2) as the basis for cross-examining Melrose about the conviction? The defense argues that any theft "inherently involves an element of dishonesty." What ruling? *See* J. WEINSTEIN & M. BERGER, 3 WEINSTEIN'S EVIDENCE ¶ 609-72-73 (1985). Remember Professor Cleary's comment on this problem in his article quoted in Chapter 2. Professor Cleary marshalls the legislative history indicating that Congress intended to confine Rule 609(a)(2) to crimes involving an element of false statement. He argues that, in the collision "between legislative history and the seemingly unmistakable meaning" of the text of Rule 609(a)(2), the legislative history should prevail. Cleary, *Preliminary Notes on Reading the Rules of Evidence*, 57 NEB. L. REV. 908, 917 (1978). Do you agree with Cleary's argument? Under the traditional doctrine of *ut res magis valeat quam pereat*, courts presume that every provision in a statute is intended to have independent effect. *DeSisto College, Inc. v. Town of Howey-in-the-Hills*, 706 F. Supp. 1479, 1485 (M.D. Fla.), *aff'd*, 888 F.2d 766 (11th Cir. 1989). Courts prefer to avoid constructions which render even part of a statute surplusage. *People v. Wesley*, 198 Cal. App. 3d 519, 523, 243 Cal. Rptr. 785, 786 (1988). What effect does Professor Cleary's position have on the meaning of "dishonesty or" in Rule 609(a)(2)? Would Judge Easterbrook favor Professor Cleary's position? Is this one of those instances in which the court's philosophy of statutory construction is outcome-determinative?

3. Misdemeanors which lack dishonesty or false statement characteristics are frequently excluded. *See Daniels v. Loizzo*, 986 F. Supp. 245 (S.D.N.Y. 1997), excluding misdemeanor convictions for unauthorized use of a vehicle, resisting arrest and disorderly conduct. The case also illustrates the use of a motion *in limine* to exclude proof of prior offenses. Other cases employ a similar approach. In *Harris v. Wal-Mart Store, Inc.*, 630 F. Supp. 2d 954 (C.D. Ill. 2009) the court excluded a prior conviction of theft under $300 as improper impeachment evidence. The prior crime lacked the requisite elements of dishonesty or false statement.

Substantial dispute attends the issue of whether a particular crime falls within Rule 609 (a)(2). Perjury, false statement offenses, criminal fraud, embezzlement and false pretenses all come under the rule. *F.D.I.C. v. Jeff Miller Stables*, 573 F.3d 289 (6th Cir. 2009) (holding that embezzlement is a crime of dishonesty that is *always* admissible in order to attack the character of a witness); *S.E.C. v. Sargent*, 229 F.3d 68 (1st Cir. 2000). So does criminal impersonation. *Brundidge v. City of Buffalo*, 79 F. Supp. 2d 219 (W.D.N.Y. 1999). Whether shoplifting fits the formula has been the subject of debate. One point of view is expressed in *United States v. Dunson*, 142 F.3d 1213 (10th Cir. 1998) (no). In accord with *Dunson*, see *United States v. Galati*, 230 F.3d 254 (7th Cir. 2000) (but shoplifting items of "significant value" can change rule). See also the *Speers* decision cited in Note 1 to the text section on Specific Untruthful Acts (Which Have Not Resulted in a Conviction), *supra*. A contrary holding on shoplifting is noted in *State v. Al-Amin*, 578 S.E.2d 32 (S.C. Ct. App. 2003) (shoplifting is a crime of dishonesty). On the question of whether armed robbery is a dishonesty offense, this case says yes. The court cites supportive decisions from Florida, Mississippi, New Mexico, Oregon, Pennsylvania, and others. Further, the court approves admission without a probative value/prejudicial effect analysis, an approach which is appropriate under Rule 609(a)(2), once the decision is made that the crime involves dishonesty.

4. Some jurisdictions limit impeaching convictions to those involving "moral turpitude." Questions of interpretation frequently involve the issue of whether a past offense involved this element. Should a judge receive extrinsic evidence respecting the circumstances of the crime in order to determine whether moral depravity was involved? While some courts may proceed in this manner, a competing approach bars the court from taking evidence and going behind the conviction. The latter courts restrict the trial judge to an inspection of the statutory definition of the crime. *People v. Bautista*, 217 Cal. App. 3d 1, 265 Cal. Rptr. 661 (1990). An amendment, effective December 1, 2006, to Rule 609(a)(2) clarified the point that dishonesty crimes are automatically admissible. The rule provided:

> (2) [admission into evidence is provided] for any crime regardless of the punishment . . . if the court can readily determine that establishing the elements of the crime required proving — or the witness's admitting — a dishonest act or false statement.

The Advisory Committee Note also gives examples of "ready proof" of a dishonest act or false statement: "where the deceitful nature of the crime is not apparent from the statute and the face of the judgment . . . a proponent may offer information such as an indictment, a statement of admitted facts, or jury instructions to show that the factfinder had to find, or the defendant had to admit, an act of dishonesty or false statement in order for the witness to have been convicted."

5. Problem 16-26. In *Hill*, the plaintiff calls Mr. Garfield as a witness to the accident. Three years ago, in Wyoming, Garfield was convicted for the third time of drunken driving. Under Wyoming law, as a recidivist, Garfield faced a potential maximum punishment of two years' imprisonment. In fact, he was sentenced to only three months' confinement in the county jail. Under Morena law, even for a third offense, Garfield would have faced a maximum prison term of six months. Morena has adopted Federal Rule 609(a)(1). Is the conviction admissible against Garfield?

6. *Preserving the issue for appeal: The* Luce *ruling.* Suppose that the defendant moves, in limine, to exclude impeachment by evidence of her prior convictions under FRE 609 and the judge denies the motion. The defendant might rationally then decide not to testify for fear that the prior convictions will prejudice the jury against her. If she does not testify and is convicted, may she challenge the judge's in limine ruling on appeal? In *Luce v. United States*, 469 U.S. 38 (1984), the United States Supreme Court held that in some situations he or she must. Luce was convicted of drug offenses. At trial, he moved *in limine* to bar his impeachment with a prior state conviction. The trial judge denied the motion. Defendant made neither a commitment to testify if the motion were granted nor an offer of proof as to what his testimony would be. In denying the motion, the trial judge noted that the nature and scope of defendant's trial testimony could affect the court's evidentiary rulings; for example, the court was prepared to exclude the prior conviction if defendant limited his testimony to explaining his attempt to flee from the arresting officers. However, if defendant took the stand and denied any prior involvement with drugs, he could then be impeached by the earlier conviction. Defendant did not testify and was found guilty.

The United States Supreme Court affirmed:

> [H]ad petitioner testified and been impeached by evidence of a prior conviction, the District Court's decision to admit the impeachment evidence would have been reviewable on appeal. . . . . The Court of Appeals would then have had a complete record detailing the nature of petitioner's testimony, the scope of the cross-examination, and the possible impact of the impeachment on the jury's verdict.

> A reviewing court is handicapped in any effort to rule on subtle evidentiary questions outside a factual context.[4] This is particularly true under Rule 609(a)(1), which directs the court to weigh the probative value of a prior conviction against the prejudicial effect to the defendant. To perform this balancing, the court must know the precise nature of the defendant's testimony, which is unknowable when, as here, the defendant does not testify.[5]

> Any possible harm flowing from a district court's *in limine* ruling permitting impeachment by a prior conviction is wholly speculative. The ruling is subject to change when the case unfolds, particularly if the actual testimony differs from what was contained in the defendant's proffer. Indeed even if nothing unexpected happens at trial, the district judge is free, in the exercise of sound judicial discretion, to alter a previous *in limine* ruling. On a record such as here, it would be a matter of conjecture whether the District Court would have allowed the Government to attack petitioner's credibility at trial by means of the prior conviction.

---

[4] Although the Federal Rules of Evidence do not explicitly authorize *in limine* rulings, the practice has developed pursuant to the district court's inherent authority to manage the course of trials. *See generally* FED. RULE EVID. 103(c); *cf.* FED. RULE CRIM. P. 12(e).

[5] Requiring a defendant to make a proffer of testimony is no answer; his trial testimony could, for any number of reasons, differ from the proffer.

When the defendant does not testify, the reviewing court also has no way of knowing whether the Government would have sought to impeach with the prior conviction. If, for example, the Government's case is strong, and the defendant is subject to impeachment by other means, a prosecutor might elect not to use an arguably inadmissible prior conviction.

Because an accused's decision whether to testify "seldom turns on the resolution of one factor," *New Jersey v. Portash*, 440 U.S. 450, 467 (1979) (Blackmun, J., dissenting), a reviewing court cannot assume that the adverse ruling motivated a defendant's decision not to testify. In support of his motion a defendant might make a commitment to testify if his motion is granted; but such a commitment is virtually risk free because of the difficulty of enforcing it.

Even if these difficulties could be surmounted, the reviewing court would still face the question of harmless error. *See generally United States v. Hasting*, 461 U.S. 499 (1983). Were *in limine* rulings under Rule 609(a) reviewable on appeal, almost any error would result in the windfall of automatic reversal; the appellate court could not logically term "harmless" an error that presumptively kept the defendant from testifying. Requiring that a defendant testify in order to preserve Rule 609(a) claims, will enable the reviewing court to determine the impact any erroneous impeachment may have had in light of the record as a whole; it will also tend to discourage making such motions solely to "plant" reversible error in the event of conviction. . . .

[T]o raise and preserve for review the claim of improper impeachment with a prior conviction, a defendant must testify.

7.   Although most states have opted to follow *Luce*, there is a split of authority over the question. *Commonwealth v. Little*, 906 N.E.2d 286, 292 (Mass. 2009) (rejecting *Luce*); Annot., 80 A.L.R.4th 1028 (1990). When the draft of the 2000 amendment to Rule 103(a) (discussed above) was circulated for public comment, it contained language that would have codified *Luce* and extended it to civil cases. However, this language was eliminated in the final draft, and the *Luce* discussion was relegated to the Advisory Committee's Note: "Nothing in the amendment is intended to affect the rule set forth in *Luce* . . . and its progeny."

The *Luce* decision itself concerns only impeachment of an accused under Rule 609. However, as the Advisory Committee notes, "The *Luce* principle has been extended by many lower courts to other situations. *See United States v. Goldman*, 41 F.3d 785, 788 (1st Cir. 1994) ('Although *Luce* involved impeachment by conviction under Rule 609, the reasons given by the Supreme Court for requiring the defendant to testify apply with full force to the kind of Rule 403 and 404 objections that are advanced by Goldman in this case.'); *United States v. Ortiz*, 857 F.2d 900 (2d Cir. 1988) (where uncharged misconduct is ruled admissible if the defendant pursues a certain defense, the defendant must actually pursue that defense at trial in order to preserve a claim of error on appeal)."

Suppose that the trial court rules that the prosecutor may use the defendant's prior conviction for impeachment, and the defendant decides to testify. What are the

Rule 103 consequences if defense counsel decides to blunt the impact of the impeachment by admitting the conviction on direct examination? In *Ohler v. United States*, 529 U.S. 753 (2000), a 5-4 decision, the Supreme Court held that by introducing her conviction on direct examination, defendant had waived any error in the ruling on the motion *in limine*. The Court's syllabus states:

> A defendant who preemptively introduces evidence of a prior conviction on direct examination may not challenge the admission of such evidence on appeal. Ohler attempts to avoid the well-established commonsense principle that a party introducing evidence cannot complain on appeal that the evidence was erroneously admitted by invoking the Federal Rules of Evidence 103 and 609. She . . . argues that applying such a waiver rule in this situation would compel a defendant to forgo the tactical advantage of preemptively introducing the conviction in order to appeal the *in limine* ruling. But both the Government and the defendant in a criminal trial must make choices as the trial progresses. Ohler's submission would deny to the Government its usual right to choose, after she testifies, whether or not to use her prior conviction against her. She seeks to short-circuit that decisional process by offering the conviction herself (and thereby removing the sting) and still preserve its admission as a claim of error on appeal. But here she runs into the position taken by the Court in *Luce v. United States*, 469 U.S. 38, 41 . . . that any possible harm flowing from a district court's *in limine* ruling permitting impeachment by a prior conviction is wholly speculative. Only when the Government exercises its option to elicit the testimony is an appellate court confronted with a case where, under normal trial rules, the defendant can claim the denial of a substantial right if in fact the district court's *in limine* ruling proved to be erroneous.

Do you agree with this result? As in the case of *Luce*, there is a split of authority. Perrin, *Pricking Boils, Preserving Error: On The Horns of a Dilemma After* Ohler v. United States, 34 U.C. Davis L. Rev. 615 (2001). Several state courts have refused to follow *Ohler. State v. Swanson*, 707 N.W.2d 645, 654 (Minn. 2006); *Zola v. Kelley*, 826 A.2d 589, 591–92 (N.H. 2003). Are there any better ways to protect the interests of both the government and the accused in this situation?

b.   The Judge's Discretion to Exclude an Otherwise Admissible Conviction

Since conviction evidence poses severe probative dangers, it would have been only natural if the appellate courts had early given the trial judge discretion to balance the conviction's probative value against any dangers the evidence might generate. Surprisingly, that was not the case. The traditional attitude was that if the evidence satisfied all the routine foundational requirements (*i.e.*, the evidence was a valid final conviction for the right type of crime), the conviction was automatically admissible.

This state of the law was dramatically unsettled when the Court of Appeals for the District of Columbia decided *Luck v. United States*, 348 F.2d 763 (D.C. Cir. 1965). In *Luck*, Judge McGowan proclaimed that the trial judge should have discretion to exclude a conviction if she concluded that "the prejudicial effect of impeachment far outweighs the probative relevance of the prior conviction on the issue of credibility." *Id.* at 768. The *Luck* rule authorized the trial judge to engage in the sort of balancing analysis that is the core of the legal irrelevance doctrine. The case law following *Luck* elaborated the kinds of factors the judge should consider. Among them were:

- the nature of the conduct underlying the conviction

- the similarity or dissimilarity between that conduct and the conduct charged

- the importance of the testimony given by the witness whose credibility is sought to be impeached by the conviction

For example, suppose that the charged offense is murder, the witness is the accused, and the prior conviction is for murder. Suppose the witness is not the accused, but is nevertheless the "star" witness for the defense. In both these examples, the probative danger of allowing impeachment by the conviction would probably be considered high.

The *Luck* approach generated a lot of criticism — which surfaced again during the congressional debate over Federal Rule 609. The 1975 version of that Rule originally specified that the judge must balance the prejudicial effect of the evidence "to the defendant." However, the ambiguity of the Rule generated even further controversy. The Supreme Court attempted to clarify some of the uncertainty in *Green v. Bock Laundry Mach. Co.*, 490 U.S. 504 (1989). The plaintiff in *Green* was a prisoner on work release who was severely injured on the job. He filed a products liability action against the manufacturer of the machine that caused his injury. At trial, the defense was permitted over objection to impeach the plaintiff with his prior convictions for burglary and conspiracy to commit burglary. On appeal, the Supreme Court examined whether or not the trial judge had discretion to exclude otherwise admissible convictions in civil actions:

> We next must decide whether Rule 609(a)(1) governs all prior felonies impeachment, so that no discretion may be exercised to benefit civil parties, or whether Rule 609(a)(1)'s specific reference to the criminal defendant leaves Rule 403 balancing available in the civil context.
>
> Several courts, often with scant analysis of the interrelation between Rule 403 and Rule 609(a)(1), have turned to Rule 403 to weigh prejudice and probativeness of impeaching testimony in civil cases. Prodigious scholarship highlighting the irrationality and unfairness of impeaching credibility with evidence of felonies unrelated to veracity indicates that judicial exercise of discretion is in order. If Congress intended otherwise, however, judges must adhere to its decision.
>
> A general statutory rule usually does not govern unless there is no more specific rule. *See D. Ginsburg & Sons, Inc. v. Popkin*, 285 U.S. 204, 208 (1932). Rule 403, the more general provision, thus comes into play only if Rule 609, though specific regarding criminal defendants, does not pertain to civil witnesses. *See* Advisory Committee's Note to Proposed Rule 403, 56 F.R.D., at 218. The legislative history evinces some confusion about Rule 403's applicability to a version of Rule 609 that included no balancing

language. That confusion is not an obstacle because the structure of the Rules as enacted resolves the question.

Rule 609(a) states that impeaching convictions evidence "shall be admitted." With regard to subpart (2), which governs impeachment by *crimen falsi* convictions, it is widely agreed that this imperative, coupled with the absence of any balancing language, bars exercise of judicial discretion pursuant to Rule 403. Subpart (1), concerning felonies, is subject to the same mandatory language; accordingly, Rule 403 balancing should not pertain to this subsection either.

In summary, we hold that Federal Rule of Evidence 609(a)(1) requires a judge to permit impeachment of a civil witness with evidence of prior felony convictions regardless of ensuant unfair prejudice to the witness or the party offering the testimony. Thus, no error occurred when the jury in this product liability suit learned through impeaching cross-examination that plaintiff Green was a convicted felon. The judgment of the Court of Appeals is *Affirmed.* (footnotes omitted)

NOTES

1. What does *Green* tell us about the Court's view of Rule 403? Professor Rothstein suggested that Rule 403 "apparently cuts across the entire body of the [Federal] Rules." Rothstein, *Some Themes in the Proposed Federal Rules of Evidence*, 33 FED. B.J. 21, 29 (1974). In light of *Green*, is that generalization universally true? Why does the majority attach so much significance to Congress' use of the verb "shall" in Rule 609(a)?

After *Green*, the Supreme Court proposed amendment of Rule 609(a)(1) — which is now the present version:

(1) [When attacking a witness by means of a prior conviction] for a crime that, in the convicting jurisdiction, was punishable by death or by imprisonment for more than one year, the evidence:

    (A) must be admitted, subject to Rule 403, in a civil case in which the witness is not a defendant; and

    (B) must be admitted in a criminal case in which the witness is a defendant, if the probative value of the evidence outweighs its prejudicial effect to that defendant.

2. It might seem anomalous that the same Supreme Court which decided *Green*, proposed the amendment to overrule *Green*. A significant disadvantage of codifying a body of law is that codification makes it more difficult to correct an erroneous policy choice. If *Green* had been a common law case, the Court could have reevaluated the policy considerations, overruled contrary prior precedents, and simply announced a new decisional rule. However, since the Federal Rules governed, the Court's function was limited to construing the statute. Under Federal Rule 1102, when the Court wants to amend a provision of the Rules, the Court must comply with 28 U.S.C. § 2074, which reads:

(a)   The Supreme Court shall transmit to the Congress not later than May 1 of the year in which a rule prescribed under section 2072 is to become effective a copy of the proposed rule. Such rule shall take effect no earlier than December 1 of the year in which such rule is so transmitted unless otherwise provided by law. The Supreme Court may fix the extent such rule shall apply to proceedings then pending, except that the Supreme Court shall not require the application of such rule to further proceedings then pending to the extent that, in the opinion of the court in which such proceedings are pending, the application of such rule in such proceedings would not be feasible or would work injustice, in which event the former rule applies.

(b)   Any such rule creating, abolishing, or modifying an evidentiary privilege shall have no force or effect unless approved by Congress.

3.   Opponents of codification have argued that once Congress reduced the Rules to statutory form, evidence law would tend to stagnate. Jonakait, *The Supreme Court, Plain Meaning, and the Changed Rules of Evidence*, 68 TEX. L. REV. 745, 784–85 (1990). In large part, the validity of this criticism turns on the difficulty of invoking this amendment procedure. How onerous is this procedure? In most instances, before taking effect, does an amendment require the express approval of Congress?

––––––––––

The certainty which the Court sought to infuse into prior conviction impeachment law by the amendment of Rule 609 seems to have been effective. Cases decided after the amendment, uniformly apply the balancing test to the use of prior convictions in civil cases. *Wilson v. Groaning*, 25 F.3d 581 (7th Cir. 1994) ("It is well settled that evidence of prior convictions is admissible in a civil case to impeach the credibility of the plaintiff-subject to the constraints of Rule 403"); *Wilson v. Union P.R.R. Co.*, 56 F.3d 1226, 1231 (10th Cir. 1995) (excluding evidence of a drug conviction against a party in a civil case because "such evidence can be highly prejudicial and arouse jury sentiment against a party-witness").

Some federal circuits employ a five-part test for determining when the probative value of a prior conviction outweighs its prejudicial effect:

1.   The impeachment value of the prior crime.

2.   The point in time of the conviction and the witness's subsequent history.

3.   The similarity between the past crime and the charged crime.

4.   The importance of the defendant's testimony.

5.   The centrality of the credibility issue.

United States v. Nururdin, 8 F.3d 1187, 1191 (7th Cir. 1993) (court found impeachment evidence proper, and prejudicial impact was lessened by jury instruction to consider prior felony convictions only to impeach defendant's testimony, and not to demonstrate a propensity to crime); *United States v. Alexander*, 48 F.3d 1477, 1488 (9th Cir. 1995) (defendant urged that similarity of prior offense to the charged crime weighed against admitting it; however, impeachment of defendant with prior robbery conviction approved in current armed robbery trial). Convictions for the same crime are sometimes seen as unduly prejudicial because of a jury tendency to conclude "if he did it before, he likely did it this time."

In addition to weighing the probative value of the individual conviction, courts sometimes invoke a quantitative factor. In *Wilson v. Groaning*, 25 F.3d 581 (7th Cir. 1994) the defense sought to use prior convictions to impeach a plaintiff. The court balanced the prejudice of admitting the plaintiff's six convictions against the defendant's right to impeach. The judge decided that allowing admission of three convictions did not pose a danger of unfair prejudice. The court of appeals approved, holding that this was not a case where the defendants were permitted to "harp on the plaintiff's crime, parade it lovingly before the jury in all its gruesome details, and thereby shift the focus of attention from the events at issue to the plaintiff's conviction in the prior case." *Id.* at 586.

Lawyers deal with the prejudicial impact of a client's prior convictions in different ways. Some opt to bring it up themselves, if they are certain the prior record is going to be exposed. Others ask the trial judge who has ruled the conviction admissible to withhold from the jury the exact name of the crime. What about the court admitting the fact that a prior conviction occurred and the sentence, without naming the prior crime because of its prejudicial nature? *See Perryman v. H&R Trucking, Inc.*, 2005 U.S. App. LEXIS 12052 (3d Cir. June 22, 2005) (trial court did not abuse its discretion in allowing impeachment of defendant in motor vehicle accident case with fact of his conviction of crime without allowing disclosure of nature of offense, on basis that prejudicial nature of disclosure that offense was sexual assault would have outweighed its probative value).

NOTES AND PROBLEMS

1. In *Wilson v. Groaning*, the plaintiff's counsel opted to soften the impact of the prior conviction evidence by eliciting Wilson's convictions during his direct examination. Is this a good tactic? What psychological effect is taken away from the opponent when the direct examiner employs this technique? *United States v. DeLoach*, 34 F.3d 1001, 1004 (11th Cir. 1994) (to blunt expected attacks on credibility, defense may elicit evidence of defendant's conviction). Moreover, there is authority that when a direct examiner fully brings out his witness's prior convictions, cross-examination on the same point is disallowed. *Nicholas v. State*, 49 Wis. 2d 683, 183 N.W.2d 11 (1971) ("[t]his tactic is permissible; and the matter may not be pursued on cross-examination — provided the answers on direct are truthful and accurate"). The cross-examiner can elicit specific information if not elicited on direct; *for example*, the date and place of the conviction, and the length of the sentence imposed,-but that is about all.

2. While softening the impact of the conviction by bringing it out on direct is often a favorable strategy, there are dangers. If defense counsel goes beyond the name, date, location, and punishment for the crime and explores factual nuances, the cross-examiner can also go into details. In addition, the decision in *Ohler v. United States*, 529 U.S. 753 (2000), poses a hazard for criminal case defendants who testify and bring out their prior offenses on direct. The decision holds that

defendants who preemptively introduce evidence of prior convictions during direct testimony may not claim on appeal that admission of such evidence was error. This case should be considered in connection with *Luce v. United States*, 469 U.S. 38 (1984), discussed earlier in this text.

3. Confirming the current vitality of *Ohler*, see *Clarett v. Roberts*, 657 F.3d 664 (7th Cir. 2011). Citing *Ohler*, the court held that "criminal defendants who introduce evidence of their own prior convictions in an effort to remove the 'sting' forego the right to appeal the trial court's decision to admit those convictions into evidence."

Further discussion of *Ohler* and *Luce* appears in Perrin, *Pricking Boils, Preserving Error: On the Horns of a Dilemma After* Ohler v. United States, 34 U.C. DAVIS L. REV. 615, 671–72 (2001). Professor Perrin observes that parties cannot complain about evidence they introduce. "That principle is nothing more than a straightforward application of waiver. A party waives any error created by the admission of evidence which that party chooses to introduce into evidence." The difficulties for defense attorneys posed by Supreme Court law in this area are summarized: "*Ohler* places lawyers on the horns of a dilemma. A lawyer can preemptively disclose a weakness and thus waive any error, or he or she can withhold disclosure of the weakness and preserve the error. Neither option is attractive, in that, neither gives the party everything that it wants and needs. The former choice forecloses appeal in the event of conviction, the latter increases the likelihood of conviction." Commentary on how trial lawyers are impacted by the Court's jurisprudence concludes the Perrin article: "The decision imposes on lawyers a high cost for making the imminently reasonable and common sense decision to prick the boils in their cases. Perhaps trial lawyers can find some solace in the fact that *Ohler* applies only to federal trials and that not all state courts follow the approach adopted by the Supreme Court. Yet, for those trial lawyers who find themselves trying cases in federal courtrooms across the United States, there will be little solace. Instead, there will be continuing frustration as they try to practice effective trial advocacy while navigating the thicket of procedural barriers designed to make it difficult for them to do so."

4. Suppose the prior convictions are not brought out on direct. Can a cross-examiner inquire by dropping a long sheet of computer paper on the floor, suggesting it to be a printout of the witness's prior convictions, when the fact is that the witness has been convicted only once or twice? How does such a display impact the rule that there must be a good faith basis for cross-examination questions? Will misimpressions created by examiners sometimes rise to the level of reversible error? *See Sanders-El v. Wencewicz*, 987 F.2d 483 (8th Cir. 1993) ("computer printout fiasco").

5. We are reminded of the good-faith requirement on cross-examination, which applies when inquiring about prior convictions or other forms of alleged misconduct. Improper cross-examination created reversible error in *Walker v. State*, 373 Md. 360, 818 A.2d 1078 (2003) (prosecutor's assertions of personal knowledge of facts not in evidence during cross-examination of the witness entitled the defendant to a mistrial). On the general rule that a cross-examiner must have a good-faith basis for her questions, see *Medlock v. State*, 263 Ga. 246, 430 S.E.2d 754 (1993). There has been specific application of this rule to prior conviction impeachment. In *United*

States v. Ruiz-Castro, 92 F.3d 1519 (10th Cir. 1996), the defense wanted to cross-examine a government witness about alleged prior convictions in Mexico for drug offenses. However, the court found the defendants failed to present any evidence supporting the alleged convictions, and barred cross-examination on the point. The appellate court observed that the basis for impeachment "cannot be speculation and innuendo with no evidentiary foundation".

6. Problem 16-27. In *Devitt*, the defense introduces the signed statement of Walter Clarkston. He is a friend of Devitt, and in the statement says that Devitt could not have attacked Paterson because Clarkston and Devitt were out on the town looking for prostitutes at the time of the assault. The trial judge found the statement sufficiently "self-denigrating" to permit its admission into evidence. Clarkston has disappeared and cannot be found for the trial. The prosecutor seeks to impeach Clarkston's testimony by showing he was convicted of lying to a federal agent two years ago. The defense objects. What result? Rule 806 allows hearsay declarants to be attacked by a number of forms of impeachment. *United States v. Saada*, 212 F.3d 210 (3d Cir. 2000) (the credibility of a hearsay declarant may be impeached, among other means, by evidence of criminal convictions under Rule 609).

7. An additional procedural point involves the respective burdens of proof when a criminal defendant is impeached by prior convictions as opposed to impeachment of other witnesses. Rule 609(a) establishes its own balancing provision for criminal defendants, and mandates Rule 403 for other witnesses. While Rule 403 is in the passive voice — suggesting that the opponent of the evidence has the burden of persuasion — the criminal defendant provision in Rule 609(a)(1) is in the active voice. In construing it, courts have made clear that the burden is with the government to prove that the probative value of the prior conviction for impeachment purposes outweighs its prejudicial effect to the criminal accused. *United States v. Jackson*, 863 F. Supp. 1462, 1467 (D. Kan. 1994).

3. Extrinsic Evidence of a Prior Conviction

The attorney attacking the witness's credibility is not limited to cross-examining the witness about a conviction. The collateral fact rule is inapplicable to this impeachment technique, and the attorney may resort to extrinsic evidence of the conviction. *Montgomery v. State*, 277 Ark. 95, 100–01, 640 S.W.2d 108, 112 (1982). The Illinois statute is illustrative. ILL. COMP. STAT. ANN. CH. 735 § 5/8-101 (1993) provides:

8-101. Interested witness

(A) conviction may be shown for the purpose of affecting the credibility of [a] witness; and the fact of [a] conviction may be proven like any fact not of record, either by the witness himself or herself (who shall be compelled to testify thereto) . . . or by any other competent evidence.

This does not mean that extrinsic evidence of the conviction is always admissible. Suppose that during direct or cross-examination, the witness admits the prior conviction. In a similar situation, when a witness fully admits a prior inconsistent statement, most courts exclude cumulative extrinsic evidence as a waste of time. By parity of reasoning, the judge can exclude extrinsic evidence of any conviction to which the witness admits. However, if the witness equivocates or denies the conviction, she may be deemed to have invited the presentation of extrinsic evidence, such as a certified copy of the conviction.

NOTES AND PROBLEMS

1. It is not invariably required that the cross-examiner proceed, at least initially, with a certified copy of the prior conviction. A report that the conviction occurred, secured by the examiner from an official agency, will supply the examiner with a good-faith basis to simply ask the witness about the conviction during cross-examination. It is only when the witness denies the occurrence of the conviction that things get complicated. One authority observes that the usual manner of impeachment with a prior conviction is to ask the witness about it; if denied, the cross-examiner then produces a certified copy of the conviction. K. Blackburn, *The Expansion of Allowable Impeachment: Admission of Juvenile Priors, Misdemeanor Convictions, and Good Faith Cross-Examination by Prosecutors*, 1 CHAP. J. Crim. JUST. 213, 218 (2009).

2. The factor of remoteness in time has generated much litigation. Federal Rule 609(b) attempts to clarify the state of the law governing stale convictions. Under the final version of Rule 609(b), a prior conviction ordinarily will not be usable if more than 10 years have expired since the witness was convicted and "served his time." *United States v. Orlando-Figueroa*, 229 F.3d 33 (1st Cir. 2000) (exclusion by trial court of more-than-ten-year old conviction of government witness for mail fraud). *See Boomsma v. Star Transp., Inc.*, 202 F. Supp. 2d 869 (E.D. Wis. 2002) (exclusion of conviction because more than 14 years had passed since truck driver's release from prison). In any case, in order to offer proof of a conviction more than 10 years old, the proponent must give advance written notice.

3. **Problem 16-28.** In the *Devitt* case, the trial takes place on September 15, 20YR. Devitt has four prior convictions:

Crime	Date of Conviction	Maximum Sentence	Disposition
Computer theft	5 yrs. ago May 5	Supervision* for 1 year	Supervision* completed successfully
Contributing to the delinquency of a child	13 yrs. ago June 6	3 years	Suspended sentence, probation
Unlawful firearms possession	12 yrs. ago April 1	4 years	Served 2 years; 2 years parole

---

* In this jurisdiction, "supervision" does not involve incarceration.

Crime	Date of Conviction	Maximum Sentence	Disposition
Attempted Murder	8 yrs. ago Sept. 9	5 years	Served 6 months, conviction set aside on habeas corpus for violation of right to counsel; guilty plea to assault, sentenced to time served

For the prosecution, argue for the admission of these convictions. For the defendant, argue against their admission.

4. Courts continue to police the age of old convictions. *See Schmude v. Tricam Industries, Inc.*, 556 F.3d 624 (7th Cir. 2009) (worker's action against ladder manufacturer; exclusion of plaintiff's prior felony); *Simpson v. Thomas*, 528 F.3d 685 (9th Cir. 2008) (prior convictions over 10 years old likely prejudiced the jury; reversed and remanded); *United States v. Yielding*, 2009 U.S. Dist. LEXIS 38579 (E.D. Ark. 2009) (finding that the government was not entitled to cross examine a defendant regarding state court conviction where it was entered many years earlier, making it too remote in time so that its prejudicial effect outweighed its probative value).

Chapter 17

CREDIBILITY: REHABILITATION

Read Federal Rule of Evidence 801(d)(1)(B).

A. INTRODUCTION

There are three stages of credibility analysis. Previous chapters covered the first two stages: bolstering the witness's credibility before attempted impeachment and impeachment This chapter covers the last stage of credibility analysis: rehabilitating the witness's credibility after the witness has been impeached.

We shall examine five methods of rehabilitation: (1) the use of redirect examination to deny or explain the impeaching fact; (2) prior consistent statements by the witness; (3) corroboration of the witness's testimony by other witnesses; (4) proof of the witness's character trait of truthfulness; and (5) expert testimony used to demonstrate the credibility of the witness.

B. THE USE OF REDIRECT EXAMINATION FOR REHABILITATION

We have observed that as the examination proceeds through its various stages of direct and cross, the scope narrows. By the time we reach redirect examination, the only questions the examiner may ask as of right are questions aimed at issues raised for the first time during cross-examination. In most cases, the new issues raised on cross are the impeaching facts that the cross-examiner elicits to attack the witness's credibility. These will be addressed upon redirect, and the examiner frequently uses this opportunity to cover ground which is highly favorable to the examiner. The most challenging part of conducting a good redirect is finding an effective way to deny or explain the impeaching facts that the cross-examiner elicited. T. MAUET, TRIAL TECHNIQUES § 5.14 (6th ed. 2002). The redirect should concentrate on a few significant points that definitely can be developed, including explanations or clarifications. S. LUBET, MODERN TRIAL ADVOCACY 154 (3d ed. 2010).

Suppose, for example, that in *Hill*, during Mr. Roe's direct examination, he testified that he considered Worker a careful driver and had no hesitation entrusting the car to Worker. On cross-examination, Ms. Hill's attorney asks:

Q: Isn't it true that a month before the accident in this case, you told your secretary that you knew that Worker had been involved in a serious traffic accident in 2010?

A: Yes.

On redirect, the defense attorney can invite Roe to explain away the seemingly impeaching fact elicited on cross:

Q: What else did you tell your secretary in that conversation?

A: I told her that I had spoken with the police officer who investigated the 2010 accident.

Q: What did you tell her about the accident?

A: I mentioned that the police officer assured me that the accident was entirely the fault of the other driver.

NOTES AND PROBLEMS

1.   **Problem 17-1.** In *Devitt*, the prosecution calls Mr. Thompson as a witness. On direct, Thompson testifies that he saw Devitt emerge from Paterson's apartment at the time of the alleged assault. On cross-examination, Thompson admits that a week later, he told the police that the man he saw was definitely not Devitt. On redirect, may the prosecutor elicit Thompson's testimony that he made the inconsistent statement because Devitt had confronted and physically assaulted Thompson prior to his subsequent inconsistent statement to the police? May the prosecutor introduce extrinsic evidence of the assault and Thompson's fear of future reprisal from Devitt, in order to rehabilitate Thompson? *See People v. Hawkins*, 10 Cal. 4th 920, 42 Cal. Rptr. 2d 636, 897 P.2d 574 (1995), *cert. denied*, 116 S. Ct. 1685 (1996) (when a witness is impeached by a prior inconsistent statement, evidence is clearly admissible on redirect to rehabilitate the witness's credibility; discrepancy in testimony was explained because witness changed his account out of fear, and was afraid of defendant who stabbed him).

2.   **Problem 17-2.** During the cross-examination of Mr. Paterson, he admits that he did not report the assault for several hours. On redirect examination, may the prosecutor elicit his testimony that he knew that Devitt had previously been convicted of a violent crime and that Paterson initially feared his reprisal? *State v. Parris*, 592 A.2d 943, 947 (Conn. 1991) (delay of nine months in reporting incident; victim was frightened of defendant, and court held the delay was not a sufficient ground to exclude the testimony).

3.   **Problem 17-3.** Suppose Devitt is cross-examined with a prior conviction. On redirect, may he be rehabilitated by his own explanation of the prior conviction? *See United States v. Boyer*, 150 F.2d 595 (D.C. Cir. 1945) (witness should be able to proceed with any reasonably brief protestations on his own behalf which he may wish to make). However, consider all of the consequences. Some courts apply the rule that a witness who has rehabilitated himself by explaining the circumstances of a previous conviction can be cross-examined concerning the facts surrounding the conviction. *Vincent v. State*, 264 Ga. 234, 442 S.E.2d 748 (1994). Presumably this might come during recross, in the case of witness who has used redirect examination to provide favorable details which mitigate a former conviction.

4.   While the scope of redirect and recross-examination are within the discretion of the trial judge, several norms have evolved. The purpose of redirect is to clarify or rebut problems raised by opposing counsel on cross, and the redirect examiner

will be given latitude to do so. Even otherwise inadmissible evidence may be unearthed on redirect to accomplish this purpose. *United States v. Noe*, 411 F.3d 878, 886 (8th Cir. 2005). The scope of redirect is limited to subjects explored on cross-examination. *Fluellen v. State*, 264 Ga. App. 19, 22 (2003). Recross-examination is properly limited to matters raised on redirect. *United States v. Payne*, 437 F.3d 540, 550 (6th Cir. 2006). If nothing new is raised, recross may even be denied. *United States v. Perez-Ruiz*, 353 F.3d 1 (1st Cir. 2003). However, in a criminal case when new matters are brought out by a prosecutor's redirect, the Confrontation Clause of the Sixth Amendment mandates that the opposing party be given the right to recross-examination on those new matters. *Payne, supra.*

C.   PRIOR CONSISTENT STATEMENTS

Another use of redirect examination is to prove the witness' prior consistent statements. Just as a prior inconsistent statement detracts from the witness's credibility, a previous consistent statement may enhance the credibility. Common experience tells us that a consistent story indicates stability in memory and narration. In general, it is meaningful to us whether the witness has said the same thing before. D. Blinka, *Why Modern Evidence Law Lacks Credibility*, 58 BUFF. L. REV. 357 (2010). The author points out that the timing, place, and circumstances of making a prior statement are critical. These factors coalesce to provide an intricate set of rules which control admissibility. In fact, the body of law governing the admissibility of prior consistent statements is rather complex. To master that body of law, we must grapple with two questions: What must occur on cross-examination to trigger the admissibility of prior consistent statements? Are there any special timing requirements for the statement elicited on redirect?

1.   What Triggers Admissibility of Prior Consistent Statements

Not every form of impeachment enables the proponent to rehabilitate the witness by use of the witness's prior consistent statements. California Evidence Code § 791 typifies the approach of many jurisdictions to prior consistent statements:

> § 791. Prior consistent statement of witness.
>
> Evidence of a statement previously made by a witness that is consistent with his testimony at the hearing is inadmissible to support his credibility unless it is offered after:
>
> (a)   Evidence of a statement made by him that is inconsistent with any part of his testimony at the hearing has been admitted for the purpose of attacking his credibility, and the statement was made before the alleged inconsistent statement; or
>
> (b)   An express or implied charge has been made that his testimony at the hearing is recently fabricated or is influenced by bias or other improper motive, and the statement was made before the bias,

motive for fabrication, or other improper motive is alleged to have arisen.

Other courts embrace the concept contained in (b) above. However, several jurisdictions do not follow the approach contained in (a). This latter deviation from the California pattern constitutes a variation which is applied in numerous courts. These courts disallow witness support if the only form of impeachment consists of contradiction by inconsistent statements.

The only mention of prior consistent statements in the text of the Federal Rules of Evidence appears in Rule 801(d)(1)(B):

A statement is not hearsay if . . .

the declarant testifies and the prior statement is consistent with the declarant's testimony and is offered to rebut an express or implied charge that the declarant recently fabricated it or acted from a recent improper influence or motive in so testifying.

Professor Graham explains the admission of prior consistent statements in *Prior Consistent Statements: Rule 801(d)(1)(B) of the Federal Rules of Evidence, Critique and Proposal*, 30 Hastings L.J. 575, 584 (1979):

Rule 801(d)(1)(B), in conformity with the common law, recognizes that when during cross-examination an express or implied charge is made that the witness' in-court testimony is false as a result of an improper influence or motive, a consistent statement made prior to the alleged existence of the improper influence or motive is admissible to rebut the charge. Unfortunately, neither term, "improper influence" or "motive," as incorporated into Rule 801(d)(1)(B) is specifically defined in the rule nor clearly defined in the authorities. Under generally accepted definitions of these terms, motive may be said to be an emotional state of an individual, such as racial prejudice, greed, love, or revenge, that may have prompted the individual to falsify his testimony. An influence, on the other hand, may be defined as an outside force such as a bribe that induces an individual to testify in a particular manner.

If the foregoing definitions are employed, an influence may be said to produce a motive to falsify. Thus "motive" is the thrust of our concern. An "improper" motive is any motive that tends to induce the witness to do anything but tell the whole truth.

Wigmore categorizes the kinds of emotions to which Rule 801(d)(1)(B) refers as "untrustworthy partiality." Such partiality has the following components:

Bias, in common acceptance, covers all varieties of hostility or prejudice against the opponent *personally* or of favor to the proponent personally.

Interest signifies the specific inclination which is apt to be produced by the relation between the witness and the *cause at issue* in the litigation.

Corruption is here to be understood as the *conscious false intent* which is inferrible [sic] from giving or taking a bribe or from expressions of a general unscrupulousness for the case in hand.

In order to complete the definition of partiality this author suggests the inclusion of [another] category: *Coercion*, intended to include any form of mental, emotional, or physical duress or compulsion that overcomes a witness' duty to tell the truth . . . .

To illustrate the distinction between an express and an implied charge of partiality, assume that, on cross-examination of the witness, counsel inquires, "You are the mother of the defendant, aren't you?" Counsel has made an implied charge of partiality. Although the question is a direct inquiry as to a fact, it does not inquire as to the natural inference the cross-examiner hopes the trier of fact will draw. Now assume that counsel continues on cross-examination, "You would do anything you could to help your son, wouldn't you?" This is an express charge because the inference previously left to be inferred is now asserted.[39]

NOTES AND PROBLEMS

1. The United States Supreme Court, in *Tome v. United States*, 115 S. Ct. 696 (1995) (excerpted below), pointed out that prior consistent statements may not be admitted to counter all forms of impeachment or to bolster the witness merely because she has been discredited. Admissibility is confined to statements which rebut charges of fabrication or improper influence. When the attack on the witness is impeachment of her character, proof of bad reputation, prior convictions, or past dishonest acts, the Court endorsed the view that "there is no color for sustaining [the witness] by consistent statements." See also *Woodard v. State*, 269 Ga. 317, 496 S.E.2d 896 (1998), following the view that veracity is placed in issue so as to permit the introduction of prior consistent statements only when there has been a charge of recent fabrication, improper influence, or improper motive. In accord with this approach is *United States v. Belfast*, 611 F.3d 783 (11th Cir. 2010), holding that prior consistent statements are treated as admissible non-hearsay only where they are used to rebut a *specific* allegation of recent fabrication. The prior consistent statements will not be admitted to simply rehabilitate a witness's credibility that has only been generally called into question.

Accordingly, when there is an effort to support a witness with a prior consistent

---

[39] Note that should the examiner go a step further and question, "Isn't it true that you made up this story to protect your son?," the question would probably be objectionable as argumentative. Heafey states that "a question is argumentative and therefore objectionable if it: (1) Is asked for the purpose of persuading the trier of fact, rather than to elicit information or; (2) Calls for an argument in answer to an argument contained in the question or; (3) Calls for no new facts, but merely asks the witness to assent to inferences drawn by the examiner from proved or assumed facts." Heafey, California Trial Objections § 14.1, at 67 (1967). In asking the witness whether he has made up his testimony, the cross-examiner is not attempting to elicit information; the real purpose of the question is to persuade the trier of fact. The question merely asks the witness to assent to the inference that counsel has drawn from the witness's testimony. Thus, the cross-examiner's question is subject to the objection that it is argumentative.

statement, it is important that the trial judge make sure that fabrication has been charged. A claim that a crime victim "made up her story from the start" is the sort of allegation that satisfies the rule. When prior consistent statements are introduced to support a witness who has been subjected only to lesser forms of impeachment, the support is improper. Appellate courts will sometimes reverse for violation of the rule. *United States v. Kenyon*, 397 F.3d 1071 (8th Cir. 2005), illustrates the point. Testimony of a physician's assistant concerning prior statements made by a child relating to alleged sexual abuse corroborated the victim. However, the child had not been charged with fabricating the testimony which the physician assistant's testimony supported. The Court of Appeals overturned the defendant's conviction because of introduction of the hearsay.

    2. Problem 17-4. In the *Hill* case, the following occurred during the cross-examination of Mr. Worker:

Q: Mr. Worker, you testified on direct examination that you lost control of your vehicle because another car suddenly cut in front of you. Didn't you?

A: Yes.

Q: You did speak with a police officer right after the collision. Isn't that true?

A: Yes.

Q: But you didn't mention the other car to the police officer.

A: That's right.

Q: Is that because it was never there, and you just "remembered" it for this trial?

A: You have me confused.

    On redirect, would the defense attorney be allowed to elicit Worker's prior consistent statements? *See United States v. Castillo*, 14 F.3d 802, 806 (2d Cir. 1994) (prior consistent statements admissible to clarify the apparent contradiction brought out during cross-examination). *See United States v. Frazier*, 469 F.3d 85, 89 (3d Cir. 2006) (attack on witness by cross-examiner suggested witness fabricated a story, after which direct examiner was properly permitted to bolster the credibility of the witness).

    3. Problem 17-5. In the previous problem, the following occurred:

Q: But you didn't mention the other car to the police officer.

A: No.

Q: Doesn't that fact tell us that the story you told us today is fishy?

A: Well, —

Q: Your Honor, I'm sorry. I'd like to withdraw that question.

J: Very well.

    Would the defense attorney still be able to elicit prior consistent statements on redirect? *See People v. Williams*, 274 Ill. App. 3d 598, 653 N.E.2d 899, 907 (1995) (former statements authored by witness were received on redirect to rehabilitate witness who had been impeached on cross).

For a discussion of withdrawn questions, see *United States v. Coleman*, 631 F.2d 908, 914 (D.C. Cir. 1980) (although the question was withdrawn, the inference that the witness had changed his testimony was left lingering; consequently, the prior consistent statement was proper to demonstrate that the pretrial statement and the account by the witness at trial were consistent and unchanged).

4.　Ordinarily it takes a slashing attack on cross-examination containing allegations of fabrication to justify consistent statement rehabilitation. What if the cross-examination in *Devitt* asks Mr. Thompson:

Q:　　　　　　Weren't you arrested for assault just two months ago, and the prosecutor threatened you with prosecution unless you 'came through' against Devitt?

Can consistent statements by Thompson now be offered on redirect? *See People v. Kennedy*, 115 P.3d 472 (Cal. 2005) (rehabilitation allowed; prior consistent statements are admissible on redirect where the cross-examiner charges the witness gave false testimony due to bias or other improper motive).

5.　Prior consistent statements used to rehabilitate a witness constitute substantive evidence, not simply credibility support. The Advisory Committee Note to Rule 801 concluded that prior consistent statements "are substantive evidence." But the weight to be attached to Advisory Committee Notes remained uncertain until *Tome v. United States, supra.* The Supreme Court relied upon the Notes to decide the case, calling them a "useful guide in ascertaining the meaning of the Rules." Their sometimes compelling import derived from the fact that the "Notes are also a respected source of scholarly commentary." Thus, the Supreme Court held that the Advisory Committee Notes were both persuasive commentary as well as a guide to legislative intent. Taslitz, *Interpretive Method and the Federal Rules of Evidence: A Call for a Politically Realistic Hermeneutics*, 32 Harv. J. on Legis. 329 (1995).

2.　Timing Requirements for Prior Consistent Statements

Once the opposing counsel initiates one of the three types of impeachment on cross-examination, either charges of fabrication, improper influence, or in some courts inconsistent statement, rehabilitation by consistent statement may follow. A few jurisdictions allow the witness's proponent on redirect to elicit any prior consistent statements by the witness, whenever the statement was made. *Kizziar v. State*, 628 S.W.2d 243 (Tex. Ct. App. 1982). However, under California Evidence Code § 791(a), if the impeachment takes the form of a prior inconsistent statement, the consistent statement must have been "made before the alleged inconsistent statement." Similarly, under subsection (b), when the cross-examiner alleges recent fabrication or improper motive, the consistent statement must have been "made before the bias, motive for fabrication, or other improper motive is alleged to have arisen." This restrictive view is the prevailing rule in the United States. *Tome v. United States*, 115 S. Ct. 696 (1995); C. McCormick, Evidence § 47 (6th ed. 2006).

Even the jurisdictions subscribing to the majority view sometimes differ over the rationale. In some cases, they declare that the consistent statement is logically irrelevant unless the statement is prior: "Only then [is] the . . . consistent statement 'relevant' on the issue of credibility." *United States v. Quinto*, 582 F.2d 224, 232–33 (2d Cir. 1978). These courts argue that if the charge is improper motive, the consistent statement rebuts the charge only when the statement antedates the improper motive. Otherwise, the consistent statement is subject to the same charge as the trial testimony. *Patterson v. State*, 907 P.2d 984, 988 (Nev. 1995). However, other courts rationalize the prevailing view on Rule 403 grounds. They would probably concede relevance under Federal Rule of Evidence 401, but they contend that a subsequent statement "does not have significant force." *United States v. Payne*, 944 F.2d 1458 (9th Cir. 1991). A subsequent statement may also be subject to a charge of improper motive, but the motive reduces the weight of the statement without destroying its materiality. These courts exclude subsequent statements because they demand a greater quantum of probative value on redirect than on cross-examination.

The United States Supreme Court entered the fray in 1995 when it decided the following case:

TOME v. UNITED STATES
115 S. Ct. 696 (1995)

JUSTICE KENNEDY.

[The first witness for the Government in a sexual assault case was cross-examined for two days. The cross-examiner implicitly charged that the witness had a motive to falsify. Thereafter seven pretrial statements of the witness were produced which fortified the direct. On appeal the Court of Appeals affirmed defendant's conviction, holding the out-of-court statements to be admissible even though they had been made after the witness' alleged motive to fabricate arose. The Court of Appeals refused to follow the rule which required the statements to predate the time of fabrication, rejecting the so-called pre-motive requirement. The Supreme Court reversed, aligning its view with the common law and the Federal Rules Advisory Committee.]

The prevailing common-law rule for more than a century before adoption of the Federal Rules of Evidence was that a prior consistent statement introduced to rebut a charge of recent fabrication or improper influence or motive was admissible if the statement had been made before the alleged fabrication, influence, or motive came into being, but it was inadmissible if made afterwards.

As Justice Story explained: "[W]here the testimony is assailed as a fabrication of a recent date . . . in order to repel such imputation, proof of the antecedent declaration of the party may be admitted." *Ellicott v. Pearl*, 35 U.S. (10 Pet.) 412, 439, 9 L. Ed. 475 (1836). *See also People v. Singer*, 300 N.Y. 120, 124–125, 89 N.E.2d 710, 712 (1949).

The underlying theory of the Government's position is that an out-of-court consistent statement, whenever it was made, tends to bolster the testimony and so tends also to rebut an express or implied charge that the testimony has been the product of an improper influence. Congress could have adopted that rule with ease, providing, for instance, that "a witness' prior consistent statements are admissible whenever relevant to assess the witness' truthfulness or accuracy." The theory would be that, in a broad sense, any prior statement by a witness concerning the disputed issues at trial would have some relevance in assessing the accuracy or truthfulness of the witness' in-court testimony on the same subject. The narrow Rule enacted by Congress, however, cannot be understood to incorporate the Government's theory.

Our analysis is strengthened by the observation that the somewhat peculiar language of the Rule bears close similarity to the language used in many of the common law cases that describe the premotive requirement. "Rule 801(d)(1)(B) employs the precise language — 'rebut[ting] . . . charge[s] . . . of recent fabrication or improper influence or motive' — consistently used in the panoply of pre-1975 decisions." E.O. Ohlbaum, *The Hobgoblin of the Federal Rules of Evidence: An Analysis of Rule 801(d)(1)(B), Prior Consistent Statements and a New Proposal*, 1987 B.Y.U. L. Rev. 231, 245. *See, e.g., Ellicott v. Pearl*, 35 U.S. (10 Pet.) 412, 439, 9 L. Ed. 475 (1836); *Hanger v. United States*, 398 F.2d 91, 104 (CA8 1968); *People v. Singer*, 300 N.Y. 120, 89 N.E.2d 710 (1949).

The language of the Rule, in its concentration on rebutting charges of recent fabrication, improper influence and motive to the exclusion of other forms of impeachment, as well as in its use of wording which follows the language of the common-law cases, suggests that it was intended to carry over the common-law pre-motive rule.

NOTES AND PROBLEMS

1.   *Tome* accepts statements made prior to a biasing event but rejects subsequent statements. Which view do you prefer: the minority view or the majority doctrine embraced by *Tome*? Why? Subsequent cases have emphasized the point that a prior consistent statement is admissible only if it was made before the onset of the alleged influence or the date of the biasing event. *United States v. Drury*, 396 F.3d 1303 (11th Cir. 2005) (excluding a statement made after the motive to fabricate arose; prior statement admissible only if made prior to the onset of motive to falsify); *McInnis v. Fairfield Communities, Inc.*, 458 F.3d 1129 (10th Cir. 2006) (employment discrimination suit; premotive requirement for prior consistent statements not met because supportive emails were written by company official after conflict developed between him and employee). *See United States v. Snell*, 2009 U.S. Dist. LEXIS 18851 (E.D. Pa. 2009), where the court held that defendant's statements did not predate his motive to lie. Defendant was a police officer. His motive to lie "arose upon his apprehension by police following his flight from the scene of a home invasion." Any statements made after that apprehension could not be used as a prior consistent statement. Statements made after his apprehension were too obviously at risk of being altered by the defendant, who had an interest in not only avoiding imprisonment, but in saving his career as a police officer.

2.   **Problem 17-6.** In *Hill*, before trial, Worker has a conversation with the police officer who investigated the accident scene. Early in the interview Worker states, "I feel sorta guilty about the whole thing. I can't help thinking that there was something that I could have done to have avoided the accident." Five minutes later

during the same conversation, Worker said, "But I guess when I look at it objectively, there really wasn't anything I could have done. I honestly don't think I was at fault." During Worker's cross-examination, Ms. Hill's attorney forces Worker to admit the statement he made early in his interview with the police officer. On redirect, Roe's attorney elicits the statement Worker made later in the conversation. Worker testifies to the statement and then adds that although he was in an uncertain mood when he made the earlier statement, he had "real conviction in my voice" when he made the later statement. As his next witness, Roe calls the police officer to whom Worker made the statement. The officer is prepared to testify that Worker "seemed much more positive" when he made the second statement. As soon as Roe's attorney begins questioning the officer about his conversation with Worker, Ms. Hill's attorney objects "to all this extrinsic evidence about Worker's credibility. Besides, prior consistent statements cannot be proved through the testimony of third parties, like this officer." Should extrinsic evidence of prior consistent statements be admissible? *See United States v. Montague*, 958 F.2d 1094, 1099 (D.C. Cir. 1992) (prior statement can be proved through the testimony of a third party).

3. Trial transcript testimony in *Tome*, including that of the first witness as well as corroborative statements reported by other witnesses, is reported in Burns, *Bright Lines and Hard Edges: Anatomy of a Criminal Evidence Decision*, 85 J. Crim L. & Criminology 843 (1995).

D. CORROBORATION

By definition, corroborating testimony is extrinsic evidence-extrinsic to the testimony of the first witness who is being corroborated. Under the corroboration doctrine, the court is not admitting prior consistent statements by the witness; rather, the court is admitting consistent testimony by another witness. This is a key distinction. The corroborating witness testifies to a relevant event, for example, and the description of it may coincide with that supplied by the main witness. However, when the corroborating witness seeks to testify about the main witness's out-of-court statements, special rules operate. The *Tome* case makes this clear.

The prior consistent statement rules apply limitations and restrictions when, after witness #1 testifies to fact *A*, witness #2 attempts to testify about another, similar statement by witness #1 about fact *A*. Corroboration proof proceeds with far fewer obstacles. It is corroboration if witness #2 gives his or her own testimony about fact *A*.

Corroboration is the converse of specific contradiction. Courts freely and routinely admit corroborating evidence at numerous places in the trial — not merely on redirect. How does corroboration support the main witness? Does the mere coincidence between the two witnesses' testimony give the supported witness's testimony superior credibility?

E. PROOF OF THE CHARACTER TRAIT OF A WITNESS FOR TRUTHFULNESS

Another type of extrinsic rehabilitating evidence is evidence of the witness's character trait of truthfulness. Like evidence of a witness's prior consistent statement, proof of the witness's truthfulness raises two questions: What types of impeachment trigger the proponent's right to prove the witness's truthfulness? What form must the proof of truthfulness take?

The second question can be answered readily. If a court allows the unfavorable character witness to testify to reputation within a business circle rather than a residential community, the court will accept favorable reputation testimony drawn from the same circle. Further, if the jurisdiction accepts unfavorable opinion testimony as well as unfavorable reputation evidence, the witness's proponent may resort to favorable opinion or reputation.

The first question, however, is more troublesome. What impeachment techniques amount to attacks on the witness's character?

Throughout this chapter, we have seen that the courts' rule of thumb on rehabilitation is response in kind. To minimize the danger of distracting the jury, the courts require the rehabilitation to be a response in kind to the impeachment. On that assumption, the courts should certainly admit favorable character evidence when the opposing counsel called a character witness to testify directly to the prior witness's character trait of untruthfulness. Federal Rule of Evidence 608(a) so provides:

> (a) Reputation or Opinion Evidence. A witness's credibility may be attacked or supported by testimony about the witness's reputation for having a character for truthfulness or untruthfulness, or by testimony in the form of an opinion about that character. But evidence of truthful character is admissible only after the witness's character for truthfulness has been attacked.

When will the attack come? Usually this happens during cross-examination, but sometimes it occurs earlier. *See Renda v. King*, 347 F.3d 550, 554–56 (3d Cir. 2003) (holding that arrestee's opening statement suggesting corruption by officer went beyond alleging bias and was indirect attack on witness's character for truthfulness, opening door for evidence of witness's good character for truthfulness). The approach of the *King* case was followed in another trial. *See United States v. Johnson*, 437 F.3d 665 (7th Cir. 2006) (prosecution did not improperly bolster a government witness's credibility where defense counsel indicated during voir dire and opening statement that the defense theory would be to attack the witness's credibility).

Sometimes the attack is deemed to fall short. That is, the attack on credibility is not sufficiently intense or severe. It does not authorize the proponent of the witness to shore him up. *See United States v. Drury*, 396 F.3d 1303 (11th Cir. 2005) (evidence of witnesses' truthful character is admissible only after his character for truthfulness has been attacked; conduct of counsel in pointing out inconsistencies in witness's testimony and in arguing that testimony was not credible did not constitute an attack on witness's reputation for truthfulness).

Note the similarity in approach used by the courts in connection with two rehabilitation techniques. The approach appears when a party wishes to support a witness who has been attacked. For either character support or support by showing prior consistent statements of the witness (treated earlier in this chapter), the attack must be of a particularly penetrating kind. As noted, generally this sort of attack comes during cross-examination of the witness, although it can be carried out during opening statement.

In previous materials cataloguing the various impeachment techniques, we distinguished between *ad hominem* attacks versus attacks on the content of the witness's testimony. Common sense suggests that the courts should treat the *ad hominem* attacks as assaults on the witness's character. Impeachment evidence of a witness's conviction or untruthful act "open the door to character support." C. McCORMICK, EVIDENCE 84 (6th ed. 2006). Lesser attacks do not. *People v. Miller*, 890 P.2d 84, 96 (Colo. 1995), held that merely questioning a witness's credibility on cross-examination does not necessarily constitute an attack which opens the door. Even if we apply the *ejusdem generis* maxim of statutory interpretation to the language, the *ad hominem* attacks should fall within Rule 608(a).

Once we decide that a slashing cross-examination which accuses the witness of lying opens the door to evidence supporting the witness, issues nonetheless remain.

The point of disagreement among the courts is whether the opponent's use of any of the other impeachment techniques should permit the proponent to introduce favorable character evidence. Some courts have been reluctant to admit favorable character evidence in response, for example, to prior inconsistent statement impeachment. *People v. Wheatley*, 805 P.2d 1148 (Colo. Ct. App. 1990). A decisive statement appears in *Renda v. King*, 347 F.3d 550, 554 (3d Cir. 2003): "[E]vidence of bias or prior inconsistent statements generally does not open the door for evidence of good character for truthfulness." *Compare State v. Hall*, 390 S.E.2d 169, 173 (N.C. Ct. App. 1990). As trial judge, how would you rule in the following problems?

PROBLEMS

1. **Problem 17-7.** In *Hill*, the plaintiff calls Professor Monsky, an expert on accident reconstruction. During cross-examination, Roe's attorney questions Monsky about his fee in the *Hill* case and the percentage of income he earns every year by testifying in court. *Syken v. Elkins*, 644 So. 2d 539 (Fla. Dist. Ct. App. 1994). As her next witness, Ms. Hill calls Professor Lawrence. Professor Lawrence is prepared to testify to Monsky's good reputation for truthfulness among the faculty members at El Dorado State University. Roe's attorney objects under Rule 608(a). While many federal courts do not allow bias impeachment to open the door to character support, some states take a contrary view.

See People v. Ah Fat, 48 Cal. 61, 64 (1874) (financial interest in testifying was alleged during cross; responsive proof that witness possessed good character was proper).

2.   Problem 17-8. In *Devitt*, the defendant testifies that he never had any difficulty with Mr. Paterson. On cross-examination, the prosecutor asked: "Isn't it true that a week after this incident you told your friend Dave Clark that you had clobbered Mr. Paterson?" As his next witness, Devitt calls Father Benedetti, a local priest. Father Benedetti is prepared to testify that in El Dorado, Devitt has a reputation as a truthful person. The prosecution objects, citing Rule 608(a).

See State v. Hall, 390 S.E.2d 169, 173 (N.C. Ct. App. 1990) (sometimes a cross-examiner's reliance on a prior statement relating to important matters constitutes the sort of attack on credibility that justifies a response; evidence of the reputation for truthfulness of the witness allowed).

Would the result be the same if Devitt's inconsistent statement related to the color of the shirt he saw Paterson wearing the day of the alleged assault? Is it significant that Devitt might easily be mistaken about the color of the shirt?

F.   EXPERT TESTIMONY

As we saw in the last chapter, *United States v. Hiss*, 88 F. Supp. 559 (D.C.N.Y. 1950), supported the use of expert psychiatric testimony for the purpose of impeachment. More recently, attorneys have begun using scientific evidence as rehabilitation. In rape or child sexual abuse cases, for example, expert psychiatric testimony has been used to explain why a victim sometimes recants her account of the crime, or delays reporting it. *People v. Taylor*, 75 N.Y.2d 277, 552 N.Y.S.2d 883, 552 N.E.2d 131, 138 (1990) ("the reaction of a rape victim in the hours following her attack is not something within the common understanding of the average lay juror"; rape trauma syndrome evidence can assist jurors in reaching a verdict). In *State v. Hall*, 330 N.C. 808, 412 S.E.2d 883 (1992), evidence that a victim's symptoms are consistent with those of sexual or physical abuse victims was held to be admissible, but only to aid the jury in assessing the complainant's credibility.

A good summary of the posture of the law appears in Risinger, *Navigating Expert Reliability: Are Criminal Standards of Certainty Being Left on the Dock?*, 64 ALB. L. REV. 99, 116–17 (2000). Professor Risinger reports that a minority of jurisdictions allow prosecutors to use syndrome evidence openly, but an expert would generally not be allowed to say explicitly that the victim was truthful. *See Taylor v. Director*, 2011 U.S. Dist. LEXIS 56953 (E.D. Tex. May 26, 2011) (court affirmatively stated that an attempt to offer an expert witness to the truthfulness of any particular witness will be inadmissible; as well as holding that an expert is not allowed to offer a direct opinion on the truthfulness of a child complainant's allegations).

On the other hand, in many courts the expert could educate the jury regarding features of the syndrome, affirm that the characteristics of the victim were consistent with the syndrome, and could explain why there might be a delay in reporting the crime.

In addition, experts on battered women's syndrome have been used to rehabilitate victims in assault cases. However, while a psychiatrist may be permitted to testify that recantation is consistent with the conduct of many women subjected to battering, numerous courts draw the line when the expert is asked if he believed the victim in this case. *State v. Borrelli*, 227 Conn. 153, 629 A.2d 1105 (1993). In *Borrelli* the expert, a sociologist, provided a possible explanation for this assault victim's recantation of her account of her husband's abuse, threats, and assaults. The court carefully pointed out that the expert did not testify that this victim was in fact battered; rather, the expert supported the state's position that the victim's recantation was a pattern of typical behavior consistent with battered women's syndrome. A similar distinction has been drawn in cases admitting an expert witness's testimony on the general behavioral characteristics of child abuse victims.

On battered women's syndrome, see Michelson, *The Admissibility of Expert Testimony on Battering and Its Effects After Kumho Tire*, 79 Wash. U. L.Q. 367 (2001); Schuller, *Expert Evidence and Its Impact on Jurors' Decisions in Homicide Trials Involving Battered Women*, 10 Duke J. Gender L. & Pol'y 225 (2003).

These considerations lead us back to the concept of scientific validation. When a scientist states that a theory or technique has been "validated," he or she means that it has been experimentally verified that the technique can accurately perform a certain task. In *State v. Saldana*, 324 N.W.2d 227, 229–31 (Minn. 1982), the court surveyed some of the scientific literature on rape trauma syndrome, including the heralded study by Burgess and Holmstrom. The court concluded that the syndrome had been validated "not [as] a fact-finding tool, but [only as] a therapeutic tool useful in counseling." *Id.* at 230. In *People v. Shirley*, 31 Cal. 3d 18, 181 Cal. Rptr. 243, 723 P.2d 1354, *cert. denied*, 459 U.S. 860 (1982), the hypnotic enhancement case excerpted earlier, the California Supreme Court drew a parallel distinction. The court acknowledged that hypnosis has been validated as a therapeutic tool for treating mental patients troubled by repressed memories. However, the court concluded that hypnosis has not been validated as a technique for helping witnesses retrieve accurate memories of prior events. *Id.* at 66, 723 P.2d at, 1381 Cal. Rptr. at 243

Other courts, of course, take a contrary view. In *Roark v. Commonwealth*, 90 S.W.3d 24 (Ky. 2002), the Kentucky Supreme Court approved hypnosis to aid a sexual abuse victim to identify her assailant. Hypnosis is discussed in Webert, Note, *Are the Courts in a Trance? Approaches to the Admissibility of Hypnotically Enhanced Witness Testimony in Light of Empirical Evidence*, 40 Am. Crim. L. Rev. 1301 (2003).

NOTE

How would you design an experiment to validate the hypothesis that hypnosis is an effective therapeutic tool for patients troubled by repressed memories of child abuse? In contrast, how would you plan an experiment to validate the hypothesis that the memories a patient purports to retrieve through hypnosis are accurate recollections of actual events? A scientific experiment does not validate all possible applications of a theory or technique; it verifies only a particular hypothesis about a particular application. *See* Duncan, Note, *"Lies, Damned Lies, and Statistics"? Psychological Syndrome Evidence in the Courtroom After* Daubert, 71 Ind. L.J. 753 (1996), pointing out some of the flaws in the Burgess and Holmstrom research.

Chapter 18

THE RULE AGAINST HEARSAY: THE ADMISSIBILITY OF OUT-OF-COURT STATEMENTS

Read Federal Rules of Evidence 201, 401, 702, 801 and 802.

A. THE REASONS FOR THE HEARSAY RULE

As Chapter 6 pointed out, the common law developed a number of "preferential" rules designed to ensure the reliability of trial testimony. Nance, *The Best Evidence Principle*, 73 Iowa L.Rev. 227 (1988). The common law prefers that:

- Witnesses limit their testimony to recitations of observed fact and allow the trier of fact to decide which inferences to draw from the facts;

- Witnesses produce the document when they propose referring to a document's contents; and

- Persons who are the real source of testimony subject themselves to cross-examination in the trier's presence.

The first preference accounts for the opinion rule (Chapter 23), the second underpins the best evidence rule (Chapter 24), and the third leads to the emergence of the rule against hearsay (Chapters 18–22).

Though we will look more closely at the precise definition of hearsay in the next section of this chapter, for now you can think of hearsay simply as a statement made out of court and offered in court to prove what it says. There are four main reasons typically cited as underlying this basic aversion to use of out-of-court statements for their truth. First, hearsay evidence is usually unsworn, whereas the common law and modern evidence statutes require that, before testifying, a prospective witness acknowledge by oath or affirmation their obligation to testify truthfully. FED. R. EVID. 603. One purpose of requiring this acknowledgment is to awaken the witness's conscience before testifying; the oath will hopefully make it more probable that the witness testifies sincerely. Many statements that fall within the definition of hearsay are unsworn; the lack of an oath or affirmation heightens doubts about the reliability of the statement. 5 J. WIGMORE, EVIDENCE §§ 1362, 1373–77 (3d ed. 1940). Note, however, the mere fact that a statement is sworn does not necessarily make it admissible under the hearsay rules. *Id.* §§ 1362, 1364. Thus, this factor is not the primary rationale for the hearsay rule.

The second reason underlying the rule against hearsay is the possibility of error in the oral transmission of information. 2 McCORMICK, EVIDENCE § 245 (6th ed. 2006). The person relaying information orally may misspeak, and the person receiving the information and repeating it to the factfinder (the witness now on the stand) may err in hearing, remembering, or relating. The longer the chain of transmission, the greater is the chance of error. However, the reduction of a statement to writing does not necessarily make it admissible. *Id.*

Third is the jury's inability to observe the contemporaneous demeanor of the person who made the out-of-court statement. In *Barber v. Page*, 390 U.S. 719, 725 (1968), the Supreme Court underscored the importance of affording "the jury [the occasion] to weigh the demeanor of the witness." We commonly assume that nonverbal behavior is an important clue to a person's credibility. If a witness fidgets on the stand, perspires, and refuses to look the attorney in the eye, we sometimes suspect the witness is being untruthful.

Finally, we come to what is widely regarded as the primary rationale for the rule against hearsay: The admission of a declarant's hearsay statement denies the opposing party an opportunity to cross-examine the declarant about the statement. We exclude hearsay to ensure that, as a general rule, the opposing party has an opportunity to challenge the statement by cross-examination.

It is important to realize that the hearsay rule crystallized during a rather romantic era in trial advocacy. One Victorian writer on trial technique declared that "[t]here is never a cause contested, the result of which is not mainly dependent upon the skill with which the advocate conducts his cross-examination." Cox, *The Advocate* 434, *in* REED, CONDUCT OF LAWSUITS 277 (2d ed. 1912). Many of the paeans written to the hearsay rule assume that it is all in a day's work for a brilliantly intuitive cross-examiner to unmask even the cleverest perjurer. Wigmore characterized cross-examination as the "greatest legal engine ever invented for the discovery of truth." 5 J. WIGMORE, EVIDENCE § 1367 (3d ed. 1940).

The modern view of the value of cross-examination is somewhat more realistic. Most cases are won by methodically prepared direct examination rather than by divinely inspired cross-examination. In fact, overly aggressive cross-examination can actually be counterproductive — to put it bluntly, you sometimes slit your own throat when you go for the witness's jugular. The best use of cross-examination is usually to elicit a few favorable admissions from the witness rather than to attempt to browbeat the witness into tears or confession. *Id.* at 338. In the contemporary view, cross-examination has more limited effectiveness than the Victorians assumed; we consequently have been willing to recognize more hearsay exceptions.

Nevertheless, cross-examination is still regarded as a valuable right; indeed, in our criminal jurisprudence, the right has constitutional status. *Davis v. Washington*, 547 U.S. 813 (2006); *Crawford v. Washington*, 541 U.S. 36 (2004); *Davis v. Alaska*, 415 U.S. 308 (1974); *Alford v. United States*, 282 U.S. 687 (1931). If you recall from our discussion of the general elements of competency, to qualify as a witness a person must have moral capacity and the mental capacities to observe, remember, and relate. These correspond to the testimonial qualities of sincerity, perception, memory, and narration. Cross-examination enables the opposing attorney to test these qualities. As we have seen, modern evidence law takes an extremely liberal view of competency and courts as a matter of course allow persons with questionable sincerity or mental capacity to testify. The more liberal the competency standards, the more compelling is the need to subject the testimony of these persons to the safeguard of cross-examination.

B. THE DEFINITION OF HEARSAY

As important as the hearsay rule is, one might expect a crystal clear definition of hearsay. It would be ideal if hearsay were easily recognizable. Unfortunately, this is not the case. M. LADD & R. CARLSON, CASES AND MATERIALS ON EVIDENCE 802 (1972); McCormick, *The Borderland of Hearsay*, 39 YALE L.J. 489 (1930). The rule is beset with numerous complexities and splits of authority; some of the most important disagreements relate to the definition of hearsay.

Most laypersons think that the hearsay rule forbids any in-court testimony about out-of-court statements. Quite to the contrary, the rule's scope is actually quite narrow. We can tentatively define hearsay as *an **assertion** by an out-of-court human **declarant**, offered to **prove the truth** of the assertion. Cf.* FED. R. EVID. 801(a)–(C). To fully understand the definition, we must examine three main definitional aspects of the rule: (1) "Assertion" — the types of statements that fall within the rule; (2) "prove the truth" — the purpose for which the statement is offered; and (3) "an out-of-court human declarant" — the proper understanding of who (or what) counts as a hearsay declarant for purposes of the rule. As will become clear when we tackle these issues, every element of the definition is ultimately explicable in terms of cross-examination policy.

1. "An Assertion" — The Types of Statements Testable By Cross-Examination

In some cases, it is initially difficult to determine whether the witness is referring to hearsay. The witness may artfully use such expressions as he or she "ascertained," "discovered," or "learned" in order to slip hearsay into the record without drawing an objection. However, as Chapter 5 noted, when the potential objection relates to the hearsay doctrine, under Federal Rule 104(a) the opponent may both object and conduct voir dire in support of the objection. If it is unclear whether the witness is implicitly relying on inadmissible hearsay, you may conduct a voir dire to clarify whether the witness is referring to an inadmissible hearsay statement.

Assertive Statements

In most jurisdictions, the hearsay rule applies to only assertions. Federal Rule of Evidence 801(c) limits the scope of the rule to "statement[s]," and subsection 801(a) then defines "statement" as "a person's oral assertion, written assertion, or nonverbal conduct, if the person intended it as an assertion." If the utterance or conduct is assertive, it satisfies this element of the hearsay definition whether it is made in a private, oral conversation, an email (*Whitesell Corp. v. Whirlpool Corp.*, 666 F. Supp. 2d 765 (W.D.Mich. 2009)), during a television program (*Kallstrom v. City of Columbus*, 165 F. Supp. 2d 686 (S.D. Ohio 2001)), a law review article (*Bartholomew v. Unum Life Ins. Co. of America*, 588 F.Supp.2d 1262, 1267–68 (W.D. Wash. 2008)), a Mapquest printout (*Jianniney v. State*, 962 A.2d 229, 231–32 (Del. 2008)), or a newspaper article. *Torres v. White*, 685 F. Supp. 2d 1283, 1286 (N.D. Okla. 2010), or any number of other imaginable contexts.

The rule's limitation to assertions is a corollary of the primary rationale for the rule, which is to guarantee the opposing party an opportunity to cross-examine to expose latent weaknesses in sincerity, perception, memory, or narration. Certain types of utterances are essentially immune to such weaknesses. For example, if on observing the collision in *Hill* a bystander utters the exclamation "My God!" there is little reason to be concerned about latent weaknesses in testimonial qualities. Realistically, this type of statement is not testable by cross-examination; there is ordinarily no serious concern about the person's perception or memory when the testimony takes the form of an exclamatory, imperative, or interrogatory sentence. *E.g., Katzenmeier v. Blackpowder Products, Inc.*, 628 F.3d 948, 951 (8th Cir. 2010) (instructions); *Biegas v. Quickway Carriers, Inc.*, 573 F.3d 365, 378–79 (6th Cir. 2009) (an exclamation); *S.E.C. v. Nacchio*, 704 F. Supp. 2d 1099, 1115 (D. Colo. 2010) (a question or request). The conventional wisdom is that the need for cross-examination to unmask weaknesses arises only in connection with assertive statements — sentences that make assertions about facts and events. The sentence must declare or assert a fact susceptible of being true or false. *Craig v. State*, 630 N.E.2d 207 (Ind. 1994).

Given this reasoning, courts will all agree that the definition of "assertion" includes statements that are in the form of declarative sentences. While there is little need for cross-examination if the bystander to the collision in *Hill* shouts "My God!," if the same person adds, "That car (Worker's car) was going at least 40 miles an hour," there is an obvious need to cross-examine the bystander to gauge her testimonial qualities before admitting the sentence as proof of the car's speed. Did she correctly estimate the speed? Does she accurately remember the incident?

It is sometimes necessary to look beyond the sentence's form and inquire whether — functionally — the proponent is using it as a declarative assertion. Suppose that before the accident in *Hill* Polecat's president, Mr. Famiglietti, had a conversation with the chief of safety engineering in the presence of a witness, Mr. Wright. During the conversation, Wright heard Famiglietti tell the safety engineer, "I'm not asking you; I'm flat out ordering you to figure out some way to move that gas tank out of the dangerous position we've got it in now." On its face, this sentence is imperative rather than declarative. However, if Hill's attorney offers Wright's testimony to prove that the gas tank is dangerous, that part of Famiglietti's statement is being used as an assertion that the gas tank was in a dangerous position. In effect, there is an assertion embedded in the imperative sentence. Most judges would therefore treat the sentence as hearsay. *See KW Plastics v. U.S. Can Co.*, 130 F. Supp. 2d 1297, 1299 (M.D. Ala. 2000) ("One cannot avoid the hearsay rule by tacking a question mark at the end of an essentially factual statement. My law clerk said that would be the end of the hearsay rule?").

Assertive Acts

There is also broad agreement that assertive conduct falls within the hearsay definition. Assume that Mr. Paterson attends a lineup of battery suspects, including Devitt. After he has viewed the lineup, an officer asks Paterson, "Do you see the assailant up there?" Paterson points at Devitt. The declarant, Mr. Paterson, has not uttered a word; but his act of pointing at Devitt is the functional equivalent of saying, "That man there is the attacker." Paterson clearly intended his act to be a substitute for speech, and Devitt has the same need to cross-examine Paterson's as he would if Paterson had spoken rather than pointed. Suppose alternatively that, as a result of the injuries he sustained in the attack, Paterson has been rendered mute and partially paralyzed; he can neither speak nor use his hands. However, he is conscious and evidently in possession of his mental faculties. A police officer tells him to blink twice if the assailant was the man in the middle of the lineup (which is Devitt). He does so. Again, Devitt would need to cross-examine him, just as surely as if Paterson had said that the man in the middle was the assailant. *United States v. Katsougrakis*, 715 F.2d 769 (2d Cir. 1983) (a nod in response to a question is an assertive statement). That need dictates the conclusion reached by Federal Rule 801(a): the definition of hearsay includes "nonverbal conduct, if the person intended it as an assertion." (Note that the trial judge resolves the question of the declarant's intent under Federal Rule 104(a)).

Implied Assertions or "Morgan Hearsay"

In all the above cases — explicitly declarative sentences, sentences used as declarations, and assertive conduct — the need for cross-examination is evident. In each case, the opposing party may have justifiable doubts about the declarant's testimonial qualities. The need is less clear in the case of the last and most controversial category, nonassertive conduct or "Morgan hearsay." The leading authority for extending the hearsay definition to include this last category is a famous English precedent.

WRIGHT v. DOE D. TATHAM
7 Ad. & El. 313, 112 Eng. Rep. 488 (Ex. 1837)

[The heirs of John Marsden sued to eject the devisee under a will of Marsden from property that Marsden owned at the time of his death. The issue was the sanity of Marsden when the will was executed. To prove that Marsden was mentally competent the defendant offered in evidence several letters written to Marsden by acquaintances who were deceased at the time of the trial. One letter involved a business dispute in which Marsden was asked to direct his attorney to submit settlement terms. The other letters were friendly and of a type that would not be written to a person regarded to be insane. The trial judge excluded the letters.]

PARKE, B. The question for us to decide is, whether all or any of the three rejected letters were admissible evidence, on the issue raised in this case, for the purpose of showing that Mr. Marsden was, from his majority in 1779 to and at the time of the making of the alleged will and codicil in 1822 and 1825, a person of sane mind and memory, and capable of making a will?

Each of the three letters, no doubt, indicates that in the opinion of the writer the testator was a rational person. He is spoken of in respectful terms in all. Dr. Ellershaw described him as possessing hospitality and benevolent politeness; and Mr. Marton addresses him as competent to do business to the limited extent to which his letter calls upon him to act; and there is no question but that, if any one of those writers had been living, his evidence, founded on personal observation, that the testator possessed the qualities which justified the opinion expressed or implied in his letters, would be admissible on this issue. But the point to be determined is, whether these letters are admissible as proof that he did possess these qualities?

I am of opinion that . . . the letters are all inadmissible for such a purpose. The question is, whether the contents of these letters are evidence of the fact to be proved upon this issue — that is, the actual existence of the qualities which the testator is, in those letters, by implication, stated to possess: and those letters may be considered in this respect to be on the same footing as if they had contained a direct and positive statement that he was competent. For this purpose they are mere hearsay evidence, statements of the writers, not an oath, of the truth of the matter in question, with this addition, that they have acted upon the statements on the faith of their being true, by their sending the letters to the testator. That the so acting cannot give a sufficient sanction for the truth of the statement is perfectly plain; for it is clear that, if the same statements had been made by parole or in writing to a third person, that would have been insufficient. Yet in both cases there has been an acting on the belief of the truth, by making the statement, or writing and sending a letter to a third person; and what difference can it possibly make that this is an acting of the same nature by writing and sending the letter to the testator? It is admitted that you have no right to use in evidence the fact of writing and sending a letter to a third person containing a statement of competence, on the ground that it affords an inference that such an act would not have been done unless the statement was true, or believed to be true, although such an inference no doubt would be raised in the conduct of the ordinary affairs of life, if the statement were made by a man of veracity. But it cannot be raised in a judicial inquiry; and, if such an argument were admissible, it would lead to the indiscriminate admission of hearsay evidence of all manner of facts.

Further, it is clear that an acting to a much greater extent and degree upon such statements to a third person would not make the statements admissible. For example, if a wager to a large amount had been made as to the matter in issue by two third persons, the payment of that wager, however large the sum, would not be admissible to prove the truth of the matter in issue. You would not have had any right to present it to the jury as raising an inference of the truth of the fact, on the ground that otherwise the bet would not have been paid. It is, after all, nothing but the mere statement of that fact, with strong evidence of the belief of it by the party making it. Could it make any difference that the wager was between the third person and one of the parties to the suit? Certainly not. The payment by other underwriters on the same policy to the plaintiff could not be given in evidence to prove that the subject insured had been lost. Yet there is an act done, a payment strongly attesting the truth of the statement, which it implies, that there had been a loss. To illustrate this point still further, let us suppose a third person had betted a wager with Mr. Marsden that he could not solve some mathematical problem, the solution of which required a high degree of capacity; would payment of that wager to Mr. Marsden's banker be admissible evidence that he possessed that capacity? The answer is certain; it would not. It would be evidence of the fact of competence given by a third party not upon oath.

Let us suppose the parties who wrote these letters to have stated the matter therein contained, that is, their knowledge of his personal qualities and capacity for business, on oath before a magistrate, or in some judicial proceedings to which the plaintiff and defendant were not parties. No one could contend that such statement would be admissible on this issue; and yet there would have been an act done on the faith of the statement being true, and a very solemn one, which would raise in the ordinary conduct of affairs a strong belief in the truth of the statement, if the writers were faith worthy. The acting in this case is of much less importance, and certainly is not equal to the sanction of an extra judicial oath.

The conclusion at which I have arrived is, that proof of a particular fact, which is not of itself a matter in issue, but which is relevant only as implying a statement or opinion of a third person on the matter in issue, is inadmissible in all cases where such a statement or opinion not on oath would be of itself inadmissible; and, therefore, in this case the letters which are offered only to prove the competence of the testator, that is the truth of the implied statements therein contained, were properly rejected, as the mere statement or opinion of the writer would certainly have been inadmissible.

NOTES AND PROBLEMS

1. In 1992, the English House of Lords affirmed the continuing precedential value of *Wright. Regina v. Kearley*, 2 App. Cas. 228 (1992). *See* Callen, *Symposium on Hearsay and Implied Assertions: How Would (or Should) the Supreme Court Decide the* Kearley *Case?*, 16 Miss. C. L. Rev. 1 (1995). However, in 2010 in *Regina v. Chrysostomou*, [2010] EWCA Crim 1403, the Lords construed the 2003 Criminal Justice Act as abolishing the previous common-law rule.

2. The Federal Rules Advisory Committee noted that with almost all nonassertive conduct, the declarant is willing to act on his or her belief. The declarant's willingness to do so is certainly some evidence of sincerity. But is the declarant's presumable sincerity sufficient to remove the evidence from the hearsay definition? Professor Morgan argued that the opposing party still has a legitimate need to test the declarant's other testimonial qualities of perception, memory, and narration. Morgan, *Hearsay Dangers and the Application of the Hearsay Concept*, 62 Harv. L. Rev. 177, 214, 217 (1948).

Most witness psychologists believe that errors in perception and memory cause far more erroneous testimony than insincerity. Stewart, *Perception, Memory, and Hearsay: A Criticism of Present Law and the Proposed Federal Rules of Evidence*, 1970 Utah L. Rev. 1, 9–10. Psychologists generally agree that the emphasis on deliberate perjury in evidence law is excessive. Stewart, *supra*, at 8–9. Shifting the emphasis to errors in perception and memory would cut in favor of Professor Morgan's position. However, the Federal Rules of Evidence clearly take the contrary view and focus on the testimonial infirmity of sincerity in defining hearsay.

3. **Problem 18-1.** Ms. Hill would like to prove that a week after she filed suit against Roe, Roe began transferring title to all his assets to his brother. Is this evidence logically relevant? Is it hearsay? *See Chaufty v. De Vries*, 41 R.I. 1, 102 A. 612, 616–17 (1918) (admissible evidence of consciousness of liability).

4. **Problem 18-2.** At trial, Polecat Motors calls Mr. Schultz. Schultz testifies that he has been the head of Polecat's Customer Complaint Department for the past 15 years. May Schultz testify over a hearsay objection that during that time there have been no other customer complaints about the gas tank on the Polecat model

that Ms. Hill was driving at the time of the accident? Can silence be considered a statement? *See Howe v. Hull*, 873 F. Supp. 70, 72 (N.D. Ohio 1994) ("While silence can be assertive in limited situations, the failure to say something is simply not a statement for purposes of Rule 801.").

5. **Problem 18-3.** In *Devitt*, the prosecutor believes that the defendant may claim that someone else attacked Mr. Paterson. The prosecutor attempts to elicit Police Officer Gravelle's testimony that he interviewed all the occupants of the apartment complex the day of the incident; he asked them whether they had seen any prowlers around the complex that day; and he "ascertained that there were no other strange men around the apartment building that day." Devitt objects on hearsay grounds. Be on the alert when the opposing witness says that she "ascertained," "learned," "determined," or "discovered" something.

6. **Problem 18-4.** At trial, Devitt claims that the attack was committed by someone else. The defense counsel's theory is that the assailant was a man named Gene Fulbright. Devitt calls Robert Montgomery, who testifies that: He was Fulbright's roommate; the day after the alleged attack he saw Fulbright reading the newspaper article about the incident; as soon as he finished reading the article, Fulbright became "nervous"; and that night, Fulbright "got out of town without telling me where he was goin' or even taking any of his stuff with him." The prosecutor objects to Montgomery's testimony on hearsay grounds.

2. "Offered to Prove the Truth of the Assertion"

Determining that the statement has an assertive character establishes only that the statement can potentially be tested by cross-examination in a meaningful fashion. That alone is not enough to make it hearsay. There must also be a need for cross-examination. A genuine need for cross-examination arises only when the proponent of the evidence offers it for "a hearsay purpose," that is, to prove the substance of the assertion. In that circumstance, the opposing attorney should generally be allowed to test the out-of-court declarant's testimonial qualities, since the probative value of the evidence depends upon the declarant's sincerity, perception, memory, and narration. When the testimony is offered for a hearsay purpose, the out-of-court declarant is the real witness — the real source of the substantive evidence. McElhaney, *The Heart of the Matter*, 89 A.B.A. J. 50, 52 (May 2003).

In contrast, if the proponent offers the statement to prove something other than the truth of what the declarant asserted, the need for cross-examination decreases. When the evidence is offered for a nonhearsay purpose, the primary need is to cross-examine the witness on the stand rather than the out-of-court declarant because the *fact of the statements having been said* is logically relevant even if the *facts asserted by the statement* are false. There are three common nonhearsay purposes.

a. Verbal Act or Legally Operative Language

One common nonhearsay use of evidence is to prove a verbal act or operative fact. Here, the fact that the words were said, rather than their underlying "truth," has either legal or factual significance in the case: The significance of the statement lies in the fact that the statement was made. *Transportes Aereos Pegaso v. Bell Helicopters*, 623 F. Supp. 2d 518, 529–30 (D. Del. 2009). Suppose that the issue was whether a person was even capable of speaking. The witness is prepared to testify that she heard the person say something. The person's statement is a verbal act – the act of speaking. Tribe, *Triangulating Hearsay*, 87 Harv.L.Rev. 957, 958-61 (1974).

Or suppose that in the *Hill* case, Mr. Hill attempted to testify about oral warranties by the salesman of the car. The warranties, describing the car's condition, might be declarative sentences. The salesman was out of court when he made the statement, and he might be unavailable at the time of trial. However, Ms. Hill is not offering the salesman's assertions to prove their truth. Quite to the contrary, she will want to prove that the assertions were untrue, thereby establishing a breach of warranty cause of action. If she establishes that the assertions are true, she proves herself out of court. Under warranty law, it is relevant that the salesman made the statements; the statements have direct legal consequences because they *are* the warranties. For this purpose, we are primarily interested in *Mr. Hill's* (rather than the salesman's) testimonial qualities: Is Mr. Hill lying about the salesman's representations? Did he hear the salesman correctly? Does he remember the statements accurately? Polecat's opportunity to cross-examine Mr. Hill satisfies the policy concerns underlying the hearsay rule.

There are numerous examples of verbal acts. Although the *Hill* hypothetical focuses on a specific type of statement constituting part of a contract, a warranty representation, more broadly under the objective theory of mutual assent all the statements forming a contract are verbal acts. *Kepner-Tregoe, Inc. v. Leadership Software, Inc.*, 12 F.3d 527 (5th Cir.), *cert. denied*, 513 U.S. 820 (1994). Thus, an offer or an acceptance is a verbal act. *Cloverland-Green Spring v. Pennsylvania Milk*, 298 F.3d 201, 218 (3d Cir. 2002). The statements affect the legal rights of the parties because legal consequences flow directly from the fact that the words were uttered. *Echo Acceptance Corp. v. Household Retail Serv.*, 267 F.3d 1068, 1087 (10th Cir. 2001). When one party utters an offer, that party confers a power to accept on the offeree; and when the offeree utters an acceptance, the offeree has created a contract.

Likewise, in a defamation case, the allegedly libelous statement is admissible as a verbal act. "The making of the defamatory statement is itself of legal significance." *Hickey v. Settlemier*, 318 Or. 196, 864 P.2d 372, 376–77 (1993). When the plaintiff offers evidence of the defendant's allegedly defamatory statement, the farthest thing from plaintiff's mind is offering that statement for its truth. In all these cases, the statement is "performative" — "a change in legal rights, duties, powers, privileges, or disabilities" is "wrought by the utterance itself." Park, *The Definition of Hearsay: To Each Its Own*, 16 Miss. C. L. Rev. 125, 133 (1995).

The "trace" theory is a variation on the theme of verbal act. Professor Graham has provided a lucid explanation of the theory:

Hearsay questions arise only when the relevancy of the circumstantial evidence, such as a tag or sign, derives solely from the truth of the mechanical trace. Take . . . the situation of a tag on a briefcase containing a weapon bearing the name "Bill Snow" found . . . in a public locker. Since the relevancy of the evidence to identify the defendant whose name is Bill Snow derives from the truth of the assertion made on the tag, i.e. the briefcase belongs to Bill Snow, the tag is hearsay . . . .

To be distinguished is the situation where the relevancy of the mechanical trace . . . does not derive from the truth of the statement itself. Consider a book of matches bearing the name Red Fox Inn found on the defendant accused of a murder committed at the Red Fox Inn. If authenticated solely as having been taken off the person of the defendant, the matchbook is hearsay since its relevancy depends on the acceptance of the assertive statement on the matchbook that its origin is the Red Fox Inn. Now assume that the owner of the Red Fox Inn testifies that the matchbook found on the defendant is identical to the matchbooks he places on the tables for use by customers. [T]he relevancy of the matchbooks is no longer dependent on the truth of the matter asserted but is based upon personal knowledge and the process of comparison.

Graham, *Employing Hearsay Statements Improperly to Establish Authenticity of Identification and Commercial Documents Connected or Affiliated with Accused Under Fed. R. Evid. 901(b)(4)*, 44 CRIM. L. BULL. 789, 800–02 (Sep. — Oct. 2008).

b. Effect on the State of Mind of the Hearer or Reader

Another accepted nonhearsay use of evidence is showing the effect of the statement on the hearer's or reader's state of mind — sometimes referred to as a "mental input" theory of logical relevance. *Fred Harvey Corp. v. Mateas*, 170 F.2d 612 (9th Cir. 1948). Suppose that Ms. Hill seeks punitive damages on the theory that Polecat knew that the placement of the gas tank was hazardous but nevertheless recklessly failed to make corrective repairs. Ms. Hill calls Mr. Miles as a witness. Miles was present at a conversation one year prior to the accident between Famiglietti, the president of Polecat, and Mr. Winslow, a consultant from a safety engineering firm. During the conversation, Miles heard Winslow tell Famiglietti that "the way you've placed the tank on that model creates a horrendous risk of explosion and fire on impact." The consultant's statement puts the president on notice of the hazardous condition. When offered for this purpose, the statement is not hearsay. Our primary focus is cross-examining the witness Miles: Is he lying? Was he close enough to hear exactly what Winslow said? Has he confused this conversation with another conversation he overheard? Ms. Hill's attorney will have to present other, independent evidence that the placement of the tank was an unreasonably dangerous design defect, but she can put Miles' testimony to a nonhearsay use. Suppose that as trial judge, you agreed to admit Miles'testimony for the nonhearsay purpose of establishing Famiglietti's notice of the hazardous condition. As trial judge, how would you word the limiting instruction identifying the proper and improper uses of the testimony? Also, in closing argument, the attorney may not treat the statement as proof of the asserted facts; she must walk the tightrope and use the statement only for the nonhearsay purpose for which it was admitted.

Or suppose that in a wrongful discharge case, the question is whether the employer acted in good faith in firing the employee. For that purpose, complaints about the employee by customers (*Blanks v. Waste Management of Arkansas, Inc.*, 31 F. Supp. 2d 673 (E.D. Ark. 1998)) and co-workers (*Vallabhapurapu v. First Nat'l Bank of Chicago*, 998 F. Supp. 906 (N.D. Ill. 1998)) are admissible as nonhearsay. Even if the complaints are in error, their receipt could give the employer reason to form a bona fide belief that the employee should be terminated. The testimony "show[s] the information relied upon or considered in making [the] decision." *Fenje v. Feld*, 301 F. Supp. 2d 781, 811 (N.D. Ill. 2003).

c.   State of Mind of the Declarant

One other nonhearsay use of evidence deserves mention: circumstantial proof of state of mind of the speaker or writer sometimes referred to as a mental output theory of logical relevance. Hence, if the issue is whether a person knew a fact, the person's statement disclosing that knowledge is nonhearsay. *In re National Century Financial Enterprises, Inc.*, 846 F.Supp.2d 828, 876 (S.D.Ohio 2012). Assume that in a trademark infringement case, the issue is whether the defendant's trade name is so similar to that of the plaintiff that consumers are confused over the source of the goods they are purchasing. In that case, testimony about emails or public opinion polls evidencing confusion would be admissible over a hearsay objection. *Suarez Corp. Industries v. Earthwise Technologies*, 636 F.Supp.2d 1139 (W.D.Wash. 2008). The moving party is not attempting to prove that the customers were correct in asserting that a particular good was manufactured by a certain company. Rather, the movant is endeavoring to prove that those assertions are false; the best evidence of confusion is proof that the customers' assertions were incorrect. Although early on the hearsay status of public opinion polls troubled the courts, under the modern view the responses are admissible. If the plaintiff claims that the defendant's trademark is confusingly similar to the plaintiff's, responses evidencing confusion are admissible as nonhearsay. *Medic Alert Foundation U.S., Inc. v. Corel Corp.*, 43 F. Supp. 2d 933 (N.D. Ill. 1999).

Or imagine that when the police question Devitt about the crime, he says, "At the time of the crime I was in North Dakota visiting my sick mother." When the police contact Devitt's mother, she says that she has not seen him in four years. At trial, the prosecution could present both the mother's testimony and the police testimony about Devitt's statement. The last thing the prosecutor wants to do is prove the truth of Devitt's statement; if the prosecutor "succeeded" in proving that, the prosecutor would establish an alibi for Devitt! Rather, the proof of Devitt's false exculpatory statement is logically relevant to show Devitt's consciousness of guilt.

Prior inconsistent statements used for impeachment purposes are also admitted under a version of this nonhearsay theory. Suppose that before trial, a witness in the *Devitt* case tells the police that he saw Devitt lurking around Paterson's apartment at 4:00 P.M. the day of the alleged battery. At trial, he testifies that he recalls seeing Devitt near his apartment at 10:00 A.M. that day. Both statements might be false; the truth of the matter might be that Devitt was standing outside the apartment at

1:00 P.M. However, irrespective of the statement's truth, the fact that the witness made the prior statement is logically relevant. The fact *of* the inconsistent statement is relevant even if the fact asserted *in* the statement is false. The fact that the witness made a pretrial statement inconsistent with his trial testimony is circumstantial proof that the witness is at least uncertain. Thus, the evidence gives the trier of fact an insight into the witness's state of mind.

NOTES AND PROBLEMS

1. This section highlights the interface between the relevance and hearsay doctrines. Before analyzing the hearsay aspect of any item of evidence, you should identify all the theories on which the item is relevant under Federal Rule of Evidence 401. Test the theories one by one, and ask: Does the theory require that the statement be offered for its substantive truth? As in so many other areas of evidence law, the premium is on the imaginative development of alternative theories of logical relevance. For a helpful and concise summary of nonhearsay theories, see Garland, *An Overview of Relevance and Hearsay: A Nine Step Analytical Guide*, 22 Sw. U. L. Rev. 1039, 1051–62 (1993).

2. Problem 18-5. Assume that Devitt's defense is insanity. At trial, Devittcalls Ms. Solomon as a witness. Ms. Solomon is prepared to testify that she saw Devitt two hours after the incident and that at the time Devitt told her that a Martian invasion was imminent. The prosecutor objects that the testimony is "nothing more than self-serving hearsay." Is the statement "an assertion"? Even if it is, is it offered for a hearsay purpose?

3. Problem 18-6. In the *Hill* case, the plaintiff calls Dr. Gartner to testify about the extent of her injuries. Dr. Gartner was a member of a team of three treating physicians. The plaintiff wants to elicit Gartner's final opinion that many of Ms. Hill's injuries will be permanent. Before eliciting the ultimate opinion, Ms. Hill asks Gartner to relate the two other physicians' opinions of the severity and probable duration of her injuries. Polecat objects on hearsay grounds. Consider the relevance of Federal Rule of Evidence 703.

4. Problem 18-7. Polecat contends that the real cause of the accident was that the brakes on Worker's car were in disrepair. Polecat alleges that Roe took the car in to an auto brake shop three days before the accident, obtained an estimate of the cost of repairs, and then decided against the repairs when he learned that the repair bill would be over $1,100. At trial, Polecat calls Jake Beroni, a repairman at the brake shop. Polecat has Beroni authenticate the repair estimate given to Roe and offers the estimate into evidence. Roe objects on hearsay grounds.

5. Problem 18-8. Devitt moves to suppress a statement he gave the police on the ground that the statement is the product of an illegal arrest. *Wong Sun v. United States*, 371 U.S. 471 (1963). He contends that the police lacked probable cause to arrest him. At the hearing on the motion, the prosecutor calls Police Officer Gravelle. Gravelle attempts to testify that two occupants of the apartment complex saw Devitt running from Mr. Paterson's apartment shortly after the alleged battery. Devitt's attorney objects on hearsay grounds. Are the occupants' statements hearsay when offered to establish probable cause? *See Draper v. United States*, 358 U.S. 307, 311–14 (1959) (no).

6. **Problem 18-9.** Assume that the evidence of the occupants' statements should be admitted at the suppression hearing. The judge denies the motion, and the case goes to trial. Would the police officer's testimony about the statements be equally admissible at the trial on the merits? *See* McElhaney, *It's Not for Its Truth*, 77 A.B.A. J. 80, 82 (Oct. 1991) ("Judge, if this evidence is no good for its truth, then what is it good for?").

Suppose that at the trial on the merits, the prosecutor argued that the officer was going to testify that she arrested Devitt and that she was offering the statements for the limited purpose of explaining the officer's conduct. Does that change the analysis? *Swanigan v. Trotter*, 645 F. Supp. 2d 656, 666–67 (N.D. Ill. 2009) (why the officer decided to conduct a stop). However, on this theory it is a discredited "Old Wives' Tale" that the jury needs to hear all the details of the information reported to the officer. *Zemo v. State*, 646 A.2d 1050 (Md. Ct. Spec. App. 1994).

7. **Problem 18-10.** The prosecutor wants to prove that immediately after his arrest, Devitt gave the police a false alibi. Devitt claimed that at the time of the battery he was with his uncle, Josh Devitt, at a nearby lake. Devitt's uncle denies that he was with Devitt at that time. The prosecutor calls Officer Franklin, the police officer who initially interrogated Devitt. Franklin attempts to testify that Devitt said he was with his uncle. Is Franklin's testimony hearsay? (Disregard any argument that the testimony qualifies as the admission of a party-opponent.)

3. "By a Human Declarant" — Hearsay Issues Versus Scientific Validity Problems

In some cases, the source of the out-of-court statement is not considered a hearsay declarant. Federal Rule 801(b) defines "declarant" as "the person who made the statement." Consider the printout "0.15" from an intoxilyzer machine. "0.15" is elliptical, representing the statement, "The breath alcohol concentration of the person who just blew into this machine is 0.15%." That statement is assertive; and if a prosecutor wants to use the statement to prove that the person was intoxicated, the statement is unquestionably offered for the truth of the assertion. The issue, though, is whether the intoxilyzer should be considered a hearsay declarant.

On the one hand, printouts of computer-stored information are deemed hearsay. A human being — "a person" — generates the initial report of the sale, and that report finds its way into the company's database. On the other hand, in the case of the intoxilyzer, the printout is computer generated rather than computer stored; no human being previously found that the concentration was 0.15 and then fed that data into the instrument. It is true that human beings programmed the software, but the software consists of a series of commands or orders, that is, non-assertive imperatives. To validate the printout, the proponent will have to establish the validity of the scientific principles embedded in the software. As we saw in Chapter 12, in some cases the principles will be judicially noticeable under Federal Rule 201(b)(2) while in other cases the proponent will have to lay a foundation satisfying

Daubert v. Merrell Dow Pharmaceuticals, Inc., 509 U.S. 579 (1993) and Federal Rule 702. However, in the case of computer-generated data, the instrument is not a hearsay declarant under Rule 801(b). *United States v. Lamons*, 532 F.3d 1251 (11th Cir.) (machine-generated CD of data collected from telephone calls), *cert. denied*, 555 U.S. 1009 (2008); *United States v. Hamilton*, 413 F.3d 1138, 1142–43 (10th Cir. 2005) (computer-generated "header" information accompanying pornographic images); *United States v. Crockett*, 586 F. Supp. 2d 877 (E.D. Mich. 2008) (printouts of readings from laboratory instruments such as a mass spectrometer and a gas chromatograph); *Smith v. State*, 866 S.W.2d 731 (Tex. Ct. App. 1993) (an intoxilyzer printout slip); *Tatum v. Commonwealth*, 17 Va. App. 585, 440 S.E.2d 133 (1994) (the display of a telephone number on a caller identification device).

4. "By an Out-Of-Court Declarant" — Satisfying the Need for Cross-Examination

Suppose that the original source of the information was unquestionably a hearsay declarant. Assume further, though, that that declarant becomes a witness at trial. The declarant's appearance at trial enables the opponent to cross-examine about both the declarant's trial testimony and the declarant's prior out-of-court statements. In this situation, does the person cease to be an out-of-court declarant, removing her prior statements from the scope of the hearsay definition? Now Rule 801(d)(2) comes into play. We have seen that if the statement is assertive and its proponent offers it as proof of the assertion, the opposing party has a need for cross-examination. The remaining question is whether this need for cross-examination has been satisfied where the declarant is also the witness at trial.

The Traditional View

The traditional view is that the only way to meet the need is to subject the statement to cross-examination when it is made. Simply stated, the traditional view is that "once an out-of-court declarant, always an out-of-court declarant." Under this view, the person remains an out-of-court declarant even when she subsequently becomes a witness at trial; if she was not testifying in this case at the time she made the statement, the statement is hearsay. *Comer v. State*, 222 Ark. 156, 257 S.W.2d 564 (1953). Under this view, the statement is not admissible for its truth even if it is admissible for a nonhearsay purpose. For example, suppose that in *Hill*, an eyewitness to the accident gave the police a statement shortly after the collision. At trial the eyewitness testifies inconsistently with her statement to the police. Her prior statement to the police would qualify as a prior inconsistent statement, and the judge would admit it on a mental output theory for the limited purpose of impeaching her credibility. However, even though the eyewitness is now available for cross-examination and the statement is indisputably admissible on a credibility theory, the traditional view would bar the use of the statement as substantive evidence.

The traditional view reflects the great value that the early courts attached to the opportunity for contemporaneous cross-examination. Perhaps the most emphatic statement of this reasoning appears in the California Supreme Court's opinion in

People v. Johnson, 68 Cal. 2d 646, 68 Cal. Rptr. 599, 441 P.2d 111 (1968), *cert. denied*, 393 U.S. 1051 (1969). The court addressed the argument that the present opportunity to cross-examine the witness about prior statements is sufficient:

> We cannot share the optimism of this reasoning. As Maguire has candidly admitted, "many trial lawyers will have none of this. They say it is a professorial pipe-dream. They have in mind considerations of practical policy. . . ." (Maguire, Evidence: Common Sense and Common Law (1947) p. 59) Perhaps the foremost practical objection to the academic approach is that it grossly underestimates the value of one of the characteristics which make cross-examination "the greatest legal engine ever invented for the discovery of truth." (5 Wigmore, op. cit. *supra*, at p. 29.) To assert that the dangers of hearsay are "largely nonexistent" when the declarants can be cross-examined at some later date, or to urge that such a cross-examination puts the later trier of fact in "as good a position" to judge the truth of the out-of-court statement as it is to judge contemporary trial testimony, is to disregard the critical importance of *timely* cross-examination . . . .
>
> . . . In the leading case of *State v. Saporen* (1939) 205 Minn. 358, 285 N.W. 898, 900–901, . . . after observing that the witness' oath does not solemnize his prior extrajudicial statement, the opinion turns to the alleged adequacy of the belated cross-examination of the witness: "The chief merit of cross-examination is not that at some *future* time it gives the party opponent the right to dissect adverse testimony. Its principal virtue is in its *immediate* application of the testing process. Its strokes fall while the iron is hot. False testimony is apt to harden and become unyielding to the blows of truth in proportion as the witness has opportunity for reconsideration and influence by the suggestion of others, whose interest may be, and often is, to maintain falsehood rather than truth."

The Polar Extreme Position

Although *Johnson* represents the traditional view at common law, there are competing views. The most extreme view is that the person ceases to be an out-of-court declarant as soon as he or she becomes a witness at trial; the person's availability for questioning at trial satisfies the need for cross-examination and automatically removes his or her prior statements from the definition of hearsay. To date, Kansas is the only jurisdiction clearly committed to this view, KAN. CIV. PROC. CODE. § 60-460(a), though a few Georgia cases also support it. R. CARLSON, HANDBOOK FOR GEORGIA LAWYERS § 25.3 (3d ed. 2003). One passage in the Advisory Committee Note to Rule 801 evinces sympathy with this approach:

> Considerable controversy has attended the question of whether a prior out-of-court statement by a person now available for cross-examination concerning it, under oath and in the presence of the trier of fact, should be classified as hearsay. If the witness admits on the stand that he made the statement and that it was true, he adopts the statement and there is no hearsay problem.

An occasional federal case seizes on this passage as support for ruling that the hearsay objection disappears when the declarant makes the prior statement "part of his oath-supported, court-given testimony subject to cross-examination." *Amarin Plastics, Inc. v. Maryland Cup Corp.*, 946 F.2d 147, 153 (1st Cir. 1991).

Like the traditional position, this view rests on assumptions about the value of cross-examination. Revising his earlier view, Wigmore argued that when the witness was available for cross-examination, "[t]he whole purpose of the hearsay rule has been . . . satisfied" even with respect to the witness's prior statements. 3A J. WIGMORE, EVIDENCE § 1018, p. 996 (Chadbourn rev.). Judge Learned Hand amplified on Wigmore's reasoning. In *Di Carlo v. United States*, 6 F.2d 364 (2d Cir. 1925), Judge Hand explained that when the witness is available at trial, the jury may use the witness's present demeanor to evaluate the credibility of even prior statements: "If from all that the jury sees of the witness, they conclude that what he says now is not the truth, but what he said before, they are none the less deciding from what they see and hear of that person and in court." *Id.* at 368.

The Compromise View

As you might have guessed, there is also compromise view. Federal Rule 801 is illustrative. Rule 801(d)(1) removes certain prior statements of a witness from the hearsay definition:

(d) Statements that are not hearsay. A statement that meets the following conditions is not hearsay:

(1) A Declarant-Witness's Prior Statement. The declarant testifies and is subject to cross-examination about a prior statement, and the statement:

(A) is inconsistent with the declarant's testimony and was given under penalty of perjury at a trial, hearing, or other proceeding or in a deposition; (B) is consistent with the declarant's testimony and is offered to rebut an express or implied charge that the declarant recently fabricated it or acted from a recent improper influence or motive in so testifying; or (C) identifies a person as someone the declarant perceived earlier.

To an extent, Rule 801(d)(1) adopts Hand's reasoning whenever the prior statement would be otherwise admissible for a nonhearsay purpose. If the statement is admissible as a prior identification to bolster credibility (801(d)(1)(C)), a prior inconsistent statement to impeach credibility (801(d)(1)(A)), or a prior consistent statement to rehabilitate credibility (801(d)(1)(B)), the Rule allows the statement's admission as substantive evidence. But the Rule embraces Hand's reasoning somewhat grudgingly. If the prior statement would be admitted in any event, the jury will be forced to evaluate the statement's credibility and weight in part on the basis of the witness's present demeanor. The drafters reasoned that in this situation, they might as well admit the statement as both substantive proof and credibility evidence. Unfortunately, as we shall now see, the drafters left the courts with several, difficult issues of statutory construction to resolve.

NOTES AND PROBLEMS

1. The traditional doctrine and Hand's view embody opposing assumptions about the need for cross-examination. Which view is sounder? Does *Johnson* overestimate the need for cross-examination? Or does Hand underestimate the danger that the witness will retreat behind the claim, "I know that the statement was correct when I said it, but I'm a little hazy now about the accident itself."? When the witness retreats in that fashion, how effectively can the opponent cross-examine the witness? It is arguable that the answers themselves impeach the witness. During closing argument, the cross-examiner can point to the "hazy" nature of the answers and invite the jury to disbelieve the witness on that basis.

2. In many jurisdictions following the compromise view, the analysis proceeds in two steps. You initially decide whether the prior statement is admissible for a nonhearsay purpose such as a credibility theory of impeaching or rehabilitating. If the statement is admissible for such a purpose, the proponent then invokes Hand's reasoning and urges its admission as substantive proof.

3. The application of the federal version of the compromise view is a bit more complex. Under the federal version, it is not enough that a prior inconsistent statement satisfies Rule 613; Federal Rule 801(d)(1)(A) allows the admission of prior inconsistent statements only when the statement is given "under penalty of perjury at a trial, hearing, or other proceeding or in a deposition." There is no such requirement under (B) or (C). Nineteen states admit prior inconsistent statements as substantive evidence even when the statement was not made under oath. Goldman, *Guilt by Intuition: The Insufficiency of Prior Inconsistent Statements to Convict*, 65 N.C. L. Rev. 1, 46 (1986).

4. Problem 18-11. In *Devitt*, Paterson picked the defendant out in a pretrial lineup. The prosecutor wants to elicit Officer Gravelle's testimony that he stood next to Mr. Paterson during the lineup and that Paterson identified Devitt as the assailant. Over Devitt's hearsay objection, may the prosecutor elicit this testimony even before calling Paterson as a witness?

5. Problem 18-12. The prosecutor has Officer Gravelle authenticate a photograph of Devitt's car, including the license plate number. As her next witness, the prosecutor calls Mr. Riley. Riley lives in the same apartment complex as Paterson. Riley identifies the car in the photo as a car that he saw parked near Paterson's apartment the day of the incident. Over Devitt's hearsay objection, may Riley testify that he also identified Devitt's car at the police parking lot the day after the incident? *See Harley v. United States*, 471 A.2d 1013, 1015–16 (D.C. 1984) (yes). Rule 801(d)(1)(C) refers only to an "identification of a person." Can that statutory language reasonably bear the meaning ascribed to it by *Harley*?

6. The courts have a somewhat ambivalent attitude toward 801(d)(1)(C). In some respects, they construe the provision liberally. Thus, the courts have held that testimony about a witness's prior identification is admissible even if the witness cannot confirm the identification at trial. *United States v. Salameh*, 152 F.3d 88, 125 (2d Cir. 1998), *cert. denied sub nom. Abouhalima v. United States*, 525 U.S. 1112 (1999). In other respects, though, the courts have cabined the provision cautiously. For example, the prevailing view is that the provision does not authorize the receipt of a witness's pretrial accusation, "The defendant did it"; most courts apply the provision only to identification statements made at or after a lineup, showup, photo array, or preliminary hearing. *United States v. Kaquatosh*, 242 F. Supp. 2d 562, 563–67 (E.D. Wis. 2003).

7.   As we saw in Chapter 17, discussing rehabilitation after impeachment, under the prevailing common-law view a consistent statement may be used to rehabilitate the witness's credibility only if the statement predates the impeaching event or influence. We saw further that in *Tome v. United States* the Supreme Court held that Rule 801(d)(1)(B) codified this so-called "premotive" requirement. Under the majority reasoning in *Tome*, a prior inconsistent statement that fails to satisfy the premotive requirement is not relevant for any purpose, including any nonhearsay purpose. Thus, unlike the use of prior inconsistent statements that might not satisfy Rule 801(2)(1)(A) but might still be admissible for the nonhearsay impeachment purpose of showing that the witness "blows hot and cold," there is no analogous permissible nonhearsay purpose for prior consistent statements that do not fall under Rule 801(d)(1)(B). This interpretation of *Tome* has been adopted by the clear majority of lower courts that have considered the question.

NOTE

Under the majority opinion, what precisely must the statement antedate? Suppose that in the *Hill* case, a passenger in Ms. Hill's car settled with Polecat prior to trial and appeared as a defense witness at trial. Under the terms of the settlement agreement, Polecat paid the witness $20,000. During cross-examination, to impeach the witness for bias, the plaintiff's attorney forces the witness to admit that he has entered into a settlement agreement with Polecat. When would "the improper influence or motive" arise: when the possibility of a settlement between the witness and Polecat was first broached, when they signed the settlement contract, or when Polecat made the first settlement payment to the witness?

C.   CONCLUSION

The analysis outlined in this chapter yields five basic methods of defeating a hearsay objection. The proponent may argue: (1) The statement is not assertive; (2) the statement, albeit assertive, is being offered for a nonhearsay purpose; (3) the statement was generated by an instrument, not a human declarant; (4) the declarant is a witness at trial and her prior statements fall under Rule 801(d); or (5) the statement falls within the scope of some hearsay exemption or exception. Differing procedural consequences flow from these theories:

- If the theory for defeating the objection is that the statement is nonassertive, the judge will admit the statement only for the purpose of showing that the statement was made. Rule 801(a).

- If the theory is that the statement is offered for a nonhearsay purpose, again the statement will not be admitted as substantive evidence. The trial judge will admit the statement for a specified, nonhearsay purpose but give a limiting instruction identifying that purpose and forbidding the jurors from using the statement for a hearsay purpose. Rules 105, 801(c).

- If the theory is that the statement was generated by an instrument, the statement will be admitted as substantive evidence so long as the proponent validates the instrument by judicial notice or a foundation satisfying *Daubert.* Rule 801(b)

- If the theory is that the speaker is currently a witness at the trial or hearing, the statement is admitted as substantive proof without a limiting instruction. Rule 801(d)(1).

- Similarly, if the theory is that the statement is admissible because it falls within an exception or the exemption for admissions, the statement will qualify as substantive evidence; and the judge will not give a limiting instruction. Rules 801(d)(2), 803–04, 807.

D.   HEARSAY DRILL

In part, the ability to recognize hearsay in the courtroom is an experiential skill. To give the student more realistic practice with the hearsay definition, we have included the following drill, raising the various aspects of the hearsay definition.

1. Problem 18-13. The following evidence is offered in the *Devitt* prosecution. Is the evidence hearsay? (At this stage, please disregard the question of whether the evidence might be admissible within a hearsay exemption or exception.)

Pretrial

(a) The prosecution charged Greg Martin with being an accessory before the fact to the battery. Martin confessed. Devitt also gave the police a confession. However, before trial, Devitt moves to suppress his confession on the ground that the confession is involuntary. Specifically, Devitt contends that the police coerced him into making a confession imitating Martin's. At the suppression hearing, the prosecution calls Officer Gomez as a witness. Gomez took the confessions from both Martin and Devitt. The prosecution attempts to elicit Gomez' testimony about the two confessions to show that Devitt's confession does not imitate Martin's; the prosecution points to the differences between the two confessions. The defense counsel objects that Gomez' testimony is hearsay. (Assume that the evidentiary rules, including the hearsay rules, apply at the suppression hearing.) *See Tennessee v. Street,* 471 U.S. 409 (1985) (nonhearsay).

Trial — Prosecution Case-in-Chief

(b) At trial, the prosecution calls Mr. Paterson as a witness. He testifies that before trial, he met with a police artist. Using an Identikit, the artist helped him prepare a sketch of the assailant's face. At that point, the prosecution marks a sketch as Prosecution Exhibit #1 for identification. Paterson identifies the sketch as the one he prepared with the police artist's help. When the prosecutor offers the exhibit into evidence, the defense counsel objects on hearsay grounds. *See State v. Motta,* 659 P.2d 745, 749–50 (Haw. 1983) (discussing the split of authority).

(c) Assume that a victim has been kidnapped and taken to the kidnapper's apartment. On direct examination, victim seeks to testify that shortly after the alleged incident, he gave the police a description of the kidnapper's apartment; he seeks to testify that he told the police that the apartment had a moosehead on one wall, a triangle-shaped mirror on another wall, and a picture of the Empire State Building on a third wall. The defense counsel objects that such testimony would be hearsay. The prosecutor is prepared to call the victim's landlord to describe the defendant's apartment. *See Bridges v. State*, 247 Wis. 350, 19 N.W.2d 529, 534–36 (1945) (the evidence was admissible for the nonhearsay purpose of showing her state of mind, that is, her knowledge of the features in the apartment).

(d) On cross-examination by the defense counsel, Paterson admits that when he was initially interviewed by the police, he said, "At first, I thought the assailant was that guy Devitt I hired to do the carpentry work, but the more I thought about it the more uncertain I became." The prosecutor requests a limiting instruction that the jury may consider the statement only insofar as it reflects on Paterson's credibility. The defense counsel objects and argues that since Paterson is on the witness stand, the statement "can come in as substantive evidence." What result under Federal Rule of Evidence 801(d)(1)(A)? *See United States v. Livingston*, 661 F.2d 239, 242–43 (D.C. Cir. 1981) (the lack of an oath).

(e) In (d), suppose that Mr. Paterson made an inconsistent statement in a sworn battery complaint against Devitt rather than in his interview with the police. *See State v. Smith*, 651 P.2d 207, 209–10 (Wash. 1982) (the court notes the split of authority but observes that "[a]t least one other state court . . . would admit an affidavit signed by a witness any time it is taken under oath before an official who is authorized to hear evidence and administer oaths").

(f) As its next witness, the prosecution calls Officer Gomez. He testifies that shortly after Paterson's battery report, he conducted a photographic display to help him identify the assailant. He testifies that he included a photograph of the defendant in the photo spread. When he attempts to testify that Paterson selected the defendant's photograph from the stack of photographs, the defense counsel objects on hearsay grounds. *See Jones v. State*, 300 A.2d 424, 425–26 (Md. Ct. Spec. App. 1973) (assertive conduct).

(g) Assume that the trial judge overrules the hearsay objection in (f). Suppose further that the prosecutor next attempts to offer the photograph Paterson selected into evidence. He marks the photograph as Prosecution Exhibit #2 for identification. When he shows it to the opposing counsel, the defense attorney notes that the back of the photograph bears the notation, "Chosen by victim Paterson. Officer Gomez." The prosecutor then offers the exhibit into evidence. The defense counsel objects to "the hearsay writing on the photo." The prosecutor responds, "Hearsay! Your Honor, the so-called statement isn't even a complete sentence. How can it be hearsay?" *See State v. Walker*, 654 S.W.2d 129, 131 (Mo. Ct. App. 1983) (double hearsay).

(h) Officer Gomez next attempts to testify that Paterson told him that Devitt was the assailant. The defense counsel objects that "the officer's testimony about Paterson's statements is inadmissible hearsay." Assume that: In Morena, the bolstering rules permit proof of a victim's pretrial identification even before attempted impeachment; when the identification is offered as bolstering evidence, only the victim may testify to the identification; and Morena has enacted Federal Rule of Evidence 801(d)(1)(C). *See People v. Gardner*, 265 N.W.2d 1, 12–16 (Mich. 1978) (the third-party testimony is inadmissible as substantive evidence).

(i) Later, on direct examination, Gomez adds that as part of his investigation, he collected physical evidence to send to the crime laboratory for scientific analysis. He testifies that when he asked Paterson for the clothing he wore during the incident, Paterson handed him a shirt and jeans. The defense attorney objects that the testimony about Paterson's conduct amounts to hearsay. *See Stevenson v. Commonwealth*, 237 S.E.2d 779, 781 (Va. 1977) (assertive conduct). Or suppose that after Gomez asked for the clothing, and without saying a word, Paterson walked over to a dresser and pulled open a drawer containing a shirt and jeans. In Paterson's presence, Gomez reached into the drawer, removed the clothing, and took the clothing with him. Does this conduct amount to hearsay? *See State v. Satterfield*, 316 N.C. 55, 340 S.E.2d 52, 53–54 (1986) (assertive conduct).

(j) Gomez then testifies that after interviewing Paterson, he went to Devitt's apartment to arrest him. During a lawful search incident to the arrest, Gomez found a slip of paper bearing Paterson's name and address. The prosecutor argues that the notations show that Paterson "was on the defendant's mind." (It is stipulated that the notations are in Devitt's handwriting.) The defense counsel objects that the notations are hearsay. *See United States v. Anello*, 765 F.2d 253, 261 (1st Cir. 1985) (the writing was admissible for the nonhearsay purpose of showing the author's knowledge of the subject).

(k) In (j) assume that there was no stipulation or evidence that the notations were in Devitt's handwriting. However, there are stipulations that the slip of paper was found in Devitt's apartment and that Devitt was the sole tenant of the apartment.

(l) On continued cross-examination of Officer Gomez, the defense counsel asked, "Isn't it true, Officer, that you put my client's photo in that stack of photographs because you and several of the other officers at the station have a grudge against my client?" On redirect examination, the prosecutor attempts to elicit Gomez' testimony that shortly after the alleged battery, he received an anonymous telephone tip that Devitt was the assailant. The defense counsel objects that the testimony would "be the worst sort of hearsay." *See State v. Perez*, 638 P.2d 335, 336–37 (Haw. 1981) (admissible for the nonhearsay purpose of showing that the officer's focus on the defendant was legitimate and not the result of a grudge).

(m) On cross-examination of Officer Gomez, the defense counsel asked, "In fact, isn't it true that you wanted to get Mr. Devitt so badly that after arresting him, you didn't bother to investigate any other men who might have been around the apartment that day?" On redirect examination, the prosecutor attempts to elicit Gomez' testimony that after Devitt's arrest, Paterson viewed Devitt in a lineup, pointed out Devitt, and said he was "absolutely, 100% positive" that Devitt was the assailant. Again the defense counsel objects on hearsay grounds. *See State v. Giannini*, 606 S.W.2d 780, 781 (Mo. Ct. App. 1980) ("to explain the officer's conduct in not investigating whether anyone had signed in and out of the halfway house that morning").

(n) As its next witness, the prosecution calls Greg Martin. Martin initially testifies that at one time, he was charged with being an accessory before the fact to Devitt's battery of Paterson. When the prosecutor asks, "How did you plead to that charge?," the defense counsel makes a hearsay objection. (Martin entered a guilty plea.) *See United States v. Melton*, 739 F.2d 576, 578–79 (11th Cir. 1984) (the evidence was properly admitted for the limited purpose of blunting the defendant's anticipated impeachment and to minimize the impression that the government was trying to conceal the witness's guilty plea).

(o) Later in Martin's direct examination, the prosecutor attempts to elicit Martin's admission that after the battery but before his plea, he made an attempt on Paterson's life "to eliminate the key witness." The defense counsel objects that the testimony about Martin's conduct "would constitute implied hearsay."

Trial — Defense Case-in-Chief

(p) During the defense case-in-chief, the defense calls Mr. Andrew Peltier a witness. Peltier testifies that he is a bartender at a saloon near Paterson's apartment. Peltier testifies that earlier the day of the alleged attack, Paterson visited the bar and had a few drinks. He attempts to testify that before leaving the bar, Paterson requested that the bartender arrange a buy of illegal drugs, including marijuana, for him. The prosecutor objects that "this man's testimony about Paterson's statements is plainly hearsay." *See Harrison v. State*, 686 S.W.2d 220, 222 (Tex. Ct. App. 1984) ("merely a question").

(q) During his own direct testimony, Devitt states that after the alleged battery and before his arrest, he had a conversation with Mr. Bart Lawson, a neighbor who happens to be a police officer. Devitt attempts to testify that during the conversation, he told Lawson that he had been at Paterson's apartment. The prosecutor objects that "any testimony about the conversation with Lawson is self-serving hearsay." The defense counsel responds that the testimony is critical to the defense case: "Since my client knew that Lawson was a policeman, he would never have made the statement to Lawson if he had believed that he was guilty of any crime." *See United States v. Webster*, 750 F.2d 307, 330–31 (5th Cir. 1984) ("Dickson's testimony was offered as circumstantial evidence of the declarant's ignorance of some fact").

(r) On cross-examination by the prosecutor, the prosecutor initially attempts to elicit Devitt's admission that when the police tried to arrest him, he gave the name Michael Dunning. The defense counsel objects that "my client was out of court at the time, and so his statements would be hearsay." *See United States v. Bankston*, 603 F.2d 528, 531 n.1 (5th Cir. 1979) (to prove consciousness of guilt, the prosecution wants to show that the statement was false, not true).

(s) Later on cross-examination, Devitt admits that he has a cousin named Andrea Gertz. The prosecutor next asks, "Later the same day (the day of the alleged battery), didn't you phone her and order her to give false alibi testimony that she was with you at the time of the attack?" The defense counsel objects that "whatever my client said to Ms. Gertz is blatant hearsay." *See United States v. Coven*, 662 F.2d 162, 174 (2d Cir. 1981) ("direct evidence of Coven's act of obstruction of justice").

(t) As the next defense witness, the defense counsel calls Ms. Gertz. On the one hand, she admits the telephone call mentioned in (s). On the other hand, when the defense counsel asks what occurred during the call, Ms. Gertz says, "As I've said all along, we just talked about family matters. Dan didn't say anything about an attack or an alibi or anything like that." The prosecutor moves to strike the reference, "As I've said all along" on the ground that it amounts to a description of the content of earlier out-of-court statements and is therefore hearsay. *See United States v. McLennan*, 563 F.2d 943, 952–53 (9th Cir. 1977). Pay special attention to n.5 on page 953 of the opinion. In his concurrence, Judge Choy states that he would "do away with [the] rule that makes declarant-witness self-quoting hearsay."

Trial — Prosecution Rebuttal

(u) During the prosecution rebuttal, the prosecutor calls Officer Welsh. Welsh testifies that he is the custodian of records for the El Dorado Police Department. He attempts to testify that he learned from the department's computer that Ms. Gertz has a prior conviction for false statement. The defense counsel objects that the testimony is hearsay. *United States v. Escobar*, 674 F.2d 469, 473–74 (5th Cir. 1982) ("what he learned from the computer" was "beyond doubt, inadmissible under the hearsay rule").

(v) Later during direct examination, Officer Welsh testifies that he interviewed Ms. Gertz a week after the alleged battery. Welsh testifies without objection that at that time, Ms. Gertz initially said that she was with Devitt at the time of the alleged battery. Over defense hearsay objections, Welsh testifies that: He next told Gertz that the police had already found eyewitnesses to disprove the alibi; he then told Gertz that she could be sentenced to 25 years in jail for perjury; and Gertz responded by saying, "Oh, my God! How can I throw away 25 years of my life?"

(w) Assume that, during her direct examination, Ms. Gertz had testified to an alibi for Devitt; she testified that they spent the entire day of March 15, 20YR together at a music festival in a nearby town. As its next rebuttal witness, the prosecution calls Nicole Stewart. Ms. Stewart testifies that she is a good friend of Ms. Gertz. She adds that, in March of 20YR, she received a postcard from Ms. Gertz. She states that she kept the postcard, because the face of the postcard is a particularly beautiful view of an Hawaiian sunset.

She identifies the handwriting on the postcard as Ms. Gertz'. The prosecutor then offers the postcard into evidence. The postcard bears a purported postmark reading: "Honolulu, Hawaii 15 Mar 20YR." The defense objects that the postmark is hearsay. The prosecutor replies, "How can it be hearsay? A machine made that mark! You can't cross-examine a machine; a machine can't be a hearsay declarant." What ruling? *United States v. Cowley*, 720 F.2d 1037, 1044–45 (9th Cir. 1983), *cert. denied*, 465 U.S. 1029 (1984) ("the postmark is hearsay"). Do you see a distinction between records stored in a machine such as a computer and records generated by a machine such as the digital output of an intoxilyzer machine? *Ly v. State*, 908 S.W.2d 598, 600 (Tex. Ct. App. 1995) (electronic monitoring system); Schlueter, *Hearsay — When Machines Talk*, 53 Tex. B.J. 1135 (Oct. 1990).

Chapter 19

HEARSAY: THE EXEMPTION FOR A PARTY'S OWN STATEMENTS OFFERED AGAINST THE PARTY

Read Federal Rule of Evidence 801(d)(2).

A. INTRODUCTION

In the last chapter, we studied the general rule excluding hearsay evidence. This chapter begins our discussion of the exemptions from and exceptions to that rule. Most of these exemptions and exceptions rest on considerations of reliability and necessity.

This chapter is devoted to the subject of statements of a party that are offered against him at trial, often referred to — somewhat confusingly — as the "admissions doctrine." Though courts and commentators use the term "admissions," the statements admissible under this doctrine need not "admit" anything in the colloquial sense of the term. Rather, the doctrine potentially covers any statement that a party has made that is offered against him at a later trial. The restyled Rules use the broad terminology, "an opposing party's statement."

We have given this category of statements singular treatment for several reasons. One is that trial attorneys probably use this doctrine more frequently than any other hearsay exemption or exception. That is particularly true in civil actions in which litigants routinely conduct pretrial depositions of prospective witnesses. Moreover, the admissions exemption stands alone because it has a peculiar rationale. Though courts ordinarily do not permit the introduction of hearsay unless the circumstances create a strong inference of the statement's trustworthiness, an opponent's own out-of-court statements may be introduced against him even if they are not based on personal knowledge and, worse still, were self-serving when made. McCormick suggests that "the most satisfactory justification of the admissibility of admissions is that they are the product of the adversary system." 2 McCormick, Evidence § 254, at 179 (6th ed. 2006). Professor Morgan concurs but adds that the doctrine squares with the cross-examination rationale for the hearsay rule: "A party can hardly object that he had no opportunity to cross-examine himself." E. Morgan, Basic Problems of Evidence 266 (1962).

The unique rationale for the admissibility of admissions led some early commentators to urge that admissions be classified as nonhearsay in the Federal Rules of Evidence. These commentators, including Professor Morgan, reasoned that the hearsay definition should not include admissions, since the cross-examination policy underlying the hearsay definition does not extend to admissions. This reasoning appealed to the drafters of the Federal Rules and influenced the language of Rule 801(d)(2):

> (d) Statements That Are Not Hearsay. A statement that meets the following conditions is not hearsay:

> (2) An Opposing Party's Statement. The statement is offered against an opposing party and:

> (A) was made by the party in an individual or representative capacity;

> (B) is one the party manifested that it adopted or believed to be true;

> (C) was made by a person whom the party authorized to make a statement on the subject;

> (D) was made by a party's agent or employee on a matter within the scope of that relationship and while it existed; or

> (E) was made by the party's coconspirator during and in furtherance of the conspiracy.

Consequently, in federal parlance, the admissions doctrine constitutes an "exemption" rather than an "exception." Despite the change in terminology, however, in federal practice admissions "function as exceptions to the hearsay rule for most purposes." *Macuba v. DeBoer*, 193 F.3d 1316, 1324 n.14 (11th Cir. 1999).

B. PERSONAL ADMISSIONS

The common law has long assumed that a person must accept the consequences of her own voluntary acts. That assumption is reflected in hearsay doctrine as well as in criminal and tort law. Federal Rule of Evidence 801(d)(2)(A) recognizes the admissibility of a person's own statement made "in an individual or representative capacity." The evidence must be a statement or assertive act of the party-opponent. However, the other requirements for a personal admission are minimal.

The statement can take myriad forms. At one extreme, the statement could be a casual, offhand remark made to a neighbor over a backyard fence. At the other extreme, the statement could be a formal pleading or stipulation filed in another lawsuit. Even pleadings in prior suits and pleadings which were later amended in the previous suit are usable as evidentiary admissions in subsequent litigation. 2 MCCORMICK, EVIDENCE § 257 (6th ed. 2006). A minority of courts balk at this, reasoning that treating ancillary or amended pleadings as admissions interferes with the policies underlying the liberal pleading and amendment provisions of the Federal Rules of Civil Procedure. *Computer Associates Intern. v. American Fundware*, 831 F. Supp. 1516, 1529 (D. Colo. 1993). For other policy reasons, *nolo contendere* pleas are inadmissible in subsequent civil actions. FED. R. EVID. 410(2); *Quigley v. Travelers Property Cas. Ins. Co.*, 630 F. Supp. 2d 1204 (E.D. Cal. 2009).

Admissions can be spoken or written. A written admission can take any number of forms, including a letter, *United States v. Pickard*, 278 F. Supp. 2d 1217, 1234 (D. Kan. 2003), or a press release. *Zeigler v. Fisher-Price, Inc.*, 302 F. Supp. 2d 999 (N.D. Iowa 2004).

The admission can even take the form of conduct, if that conduct is intended as an assertion. If a police officer confronted a crowd and asked, "Who did this?", the defendant's act of raising his or her hand would be both hearsay (an assertive act) and an admission. Many courts refer to acts such as a defendant's escape from custody as "an admission of guilt by conduct." *See* Annot., 3 A.L.R.4th 1085 (1981). Is that terminology precise? Is this hearsay to begin with? Is this assertive conduct or "Morgan hearsay"?

Whatever form the statement takes, it must be relevant to the issues in the case. Some authorities go farther and declare that the statement must be inconsistent with the position the party-opponent takes at trial. As a practical matter, unless the statement is in some respect unfavorable or disserving to the party-opponent's position at trial, the adversary will not offer the evidence. In federal practice, it is more useful to conceive of the test affirmatively: Is this item of evidence logically relevant under Federal Rule 401 to prove some fact that the proponent has a right to prove under the pleadings and substantive law? If the test is phrased in this fashion, there is no "need of inquiry as to the disserving aspect of . . . [the] statement." M. LADD & R. CARLSON, CASES AND MATERIALS ON EVIDENCE 859 (1972). The crux is relevance, not whether the statement is unfavorable to the party.

NOTES AND PROBLEMS

1. Compare Rule 613(b) on prior inconsistent statements with admissions under Rule 801(d)(2)(A). Is a foundation needed to introduce extrinsic evidence of an admission?

2. At common law, a statement is admissible as an admission even when the speaker lacked personal knowledge of the statement's subject-matter. *Ohlendorf v. Feinstein*, 636 S.W.2d 687 (Mo. Ct. App. 1982). Thus, in *Hill*, if Roe told Ms. Hill in the hospital that "it seems that the person who was driving my truck was speeding," Roe's statement would be admissible as a statement of a party-opponent even though Roe was not with Worker, who was driving at the time of the collision. Does Federal Rule 801(d)(2) constitute an implied exception to Rule 602? Does Rule 602 apply to hearsay declarants? The Advisory Committee Note to Rule 801 refers to "[t]he freedom which admissions have [traditionally] enjoyed from . . . the rule requiring firsthand knowledge."

3. Problem 19-1. Under Morena law, Worker is liable to indemnify Roe for the damage to Roe's vehicle if Worker's negligence caused the collision with Ms. Hill. A month after the collision, a customer, Mr. Quartz, heard Worker and Roe arguing in an office at Roe's plant. During the argument, Roe told Worker, "You know that you were at fault in that accident. And your carelessness cost me almost $1400 in repairs to the damn vehicle." In Ms. Hill's suit against him, Roe files an answer denying Worker's negligence. At trial, Ms. Hill calls Quartz as a witness and attempts to elicit his testimony about Roe's statement to Worker. Roe's attorney objects that the question "calls for unreliable hearsay. It was clearly self-serving when made." What ruling? *Compare* Federal Rule of Evidence 801(d)(2) *with* Rule 804(b)(3). *State v. Walls*, 637 S.W.2d 812, 813 (Mo. Ct. App. 1982) ("[a]dmissions, unlike declarations against interest, need not be against the declarant's interest when made"). *See Jewell v. CSX Transp., Inc.*, 135 F.3d 361, 365 (6th Cir. 1998) ("[t]rustworthiness is not a separate requirement for admission under Rule 801(d)(2)(A)").

4.   **Problem 19-2.** Suppose that, in Problem 19-1, Roe's attorney moved to strike the answer on the ground that "at fault" is obviously an inadmissible opinion. What ruling now? *Compare United States v. Bakshinian*, 65 F. Supp. 2d 1104, 1109 (C.D. Cal. 1999) (opinions are freely admissible when made by a party-opponent) with *Eagleston v. Guido*, 41 F.3d 865, 874 (2d Cir. 1994) ("[i]n any event, his views on that subject would be inadmissible because they are legal conclusions concerning an ultimate issue in the case"). In its Note to Rule 801(d)(2), the Advisory Committee states that admissions are liberally admitted and that they enjoy freedom "from the restrictive influences of the opinion rule."

C.   ADOPTIVE ADMISSIONS

Adoptive admissions differ radically from personal admissions. In the case of personal admissions, we have the best possible justification for imputing a statement to the party-opponent: The party-opponent himself or herself made the statement constituting the admission. Not so in the case of adoptive admissions. In this setting, some third party — perhaps even a complete stranger — makes the statement; but in the words of Federal Rule of Evidence 801(d)(2)(B), the party-opponent "manifested that it adopted or believed [the statement] to be true." The pivotal question is whether the surrounding circumstances support an inference of assent to the contents of the statement.

1.   Affirmative Adoption

Suppose that in *Hill* the plaintiff sued to collect for a knee injury that she claims was caused by her collision with Worker. Two years earlier, when applying for a job with Acme Corporation, Ms. Hill was required to submit a medical report. Ms. Hill visited a Dr. Ferguson, obtained a report from him, and submitted the report to Acme's Personnel Office. Polecat and Roe could use the report against Ms. Hill at trial as evidence that her knee injury was preexisting. By voluntarily tendering the report to Acme, Ms. Hill affirmatively manifested assent to its contents. *Russo v. Metropolitan Life Ins. Co.*, 125 Conn. 132, 3 A.2d 844 (1939). A party can affirmatively adopt another's words by agreeing with the speaker. *E.g., United States v. Jinadu*, 98 F.3d 239, 245 (6th Cir. 1996) (accused answered an accusation with "yes"). In some circumstances, even laughter can constitute an adoption. *People v. Pappadiakis*, 705 P.2d 983 (Colo. Ct. App. 1985), *aff'd*, 728 P.2d 1271 (Colo. 1986). The adoption can be made by an entity as well as a natural person. If someone submits a report containing recommendations to a corporation, there is an adequate inference of adoption when the entity acts on and implements the recommendations. *Wright-Simmons v. City of Oklahoma City*, 155 F.3d 1264, 1268–69 (10th Cir. 1998).

Who decides whether there is a sufficiently strong inference of assent? Think back to our discussion of preliminary fact-finding procedures. In their comments to California Evidence Code § 403 (the California counterpart of Federal Rule 104(b)), the Assembly Committee stated:

Under existing law, both authorized admissions (by an agent of the party) and adoptive admissions are admitted upon the introduction of evidence sufficient to sustain a finding of the foundational fact.

Thus, the question for the court under Rule 104(a) is whether the jury could rationally infer under the circumstances that the party-opponent manifested assent to the third party's statement by her words or actions. The jury makes the final decision whether to draw the inference.

PROBLEMS

1.   **Problem 19-3.** Suppose that Acme Corporation had Dr. Ferguson on retainer and required that Ms. Hill go to Ferguson for her pre-employment physical examination. Would Ferguson's report still be admissible against Hill as an adoptive admission? Is Ferguson's report less reliable now? Is the reliability of Ferguson's report even relevant on an adoptive admission theory?

2.   **Problem 19-4.** In *Hill*, the trial judge decided to sever Ms. Hill's suit against Roe from her suit against Polecat. Ms. Hill's suit against Roe goes to trial first. At the trial, Ms. Hill calls Mr. Laroby, an eyewitness to the accident. Laroby's testimony is generally favorable to Ms. Hill, but he does say that he detected a slight odor of alcohol on her breath immediately after the collision. Later Ms. Hill's suit against Polecat comes to trial. May Polecat offer Laroby's testimony about the alcoholic breath against Ms. Hill?

3.   **Problem 19-5.** Assume instead that in Problem 19-4 Ms. Hill had deposed Laroby before the first trial and offered Laroby's deposition transcript at the trial because of Laroby's unavailability. Does that fact strengthen or weaken Polecat's argument?

2.   Negative Adoption — Tacit Admissions

In some cases, it may be rational to infer a person's assent to a statement from the person's silence in the face of the statement. Since the person's silence is the key to creating the inference, this type of adoption is sometimes called a "tacit admission." In most cases in which the courts find tacit admissions, the following facts are present:

- A third party made a statement.

- The third party made the statement in the party-opponent's hearing and presence.

- The party-opponent understood the statement.

- The party-opponent was physically and mentally capable of replying to the statement.

- The party-opponent made no reply or made an evasive response.

- The statement accused the party-opponent of some misconduct.

- In similar circumstances, a reasonable innocent person would have immediately disputed the statement.

Note, *Tacit Criminal Admissions*, 112 U. PA. L. REV. 210 (1963). In these circumstances, there is a common sense inference that the party-opponent agreed with the substantive content of the third party's statement if the party-opponent did not "demur." *People v. Rodrigues*, 8 Cal. 4th 1060, 36 Cal. Rptr. 2d 235, 276, 885 P.2d 1 (1994), *modified*, 9 Cal. 4th 579a, *cert denied*, 516 U.S. 851(1995).

Focus for a moment on the third party's statement. Suppose that in *Hill*, immediately after the accident Mr. Laroby walked up to Ms. Hill and said, "There's alcohol on your breath. You've obviously been drinking." If a reasonable person in Ms. Hill's position would respond in some way to that statement unless it were true, then the statement is admissible for its truth against Ms. Hill as an adopted admission.

Commentators such as Professor Gamble have sharply questioned the psychological validity of the underlying assumption that, in these circumstances, the most reasonable explanation for the person's silence is the person's realization of the truth of the accusation. Gamble, *The Tacit Admission Rule: Unreliable and Unconstitutional — A Doctrine Ripe for Abandonment*, 14 GA. L. REV. 27 (1979). One commentator charges that the assumption is "no more than a[n unproven] scientific hypothesis." *Id.* at 32. Former Chief Justice Burger himself noted that "there is not a scintilla of empirical data to support" the assumption. *United States v. Hale*, 422 U.S. 171, 181 (1975). In the *Miller* case cited in Chapter 3, Judge Bazelon pointed out that a person's neurosis may prompt the person to "react . . . as though he were guilty even though he is innocent." *Miller v. United States*, 320 F.2d 767, 772 (D.C. Cir. 1963) (citing 2 S. FREUD, COLLECTED PAPERS 13 (1959)). The continued recognition of the tacit admission doctrine may be another instance of the courts' reliance on "common sense psychology" — at odds with the psychological reality. Gamble, *supra*, at 34.

NOTES

1.   The commentators' criticisms of the tacit admission doctrine are slowly winning converts among the courts. In 1989, the Alabama Supreme Court severely limited the use of the doctrine in criminal cases. *Ex parte Marek*, 556 So. 2d 375 (Ala. 1989). The court rejected the "underlying premise . . . that an innocent person always objects when confronted with a baseless accusation." *Id.* at 381. The court specifically cited the Gamble article. *Id.* at 381 n.1.

2.   Courts apply the tacit admission doctrine in criminal as well as civil cases. The criminal context poses special problems. *Griffin v. California*, 380 U.S. 609 (1965), forbids a prosecutor from commenting on the defendant's invocation of the privilege against self-incrimination, and *Miranda v. Arizona*, 384 U.S. 436 (1966), teaches that the defendant may invoke the privilege simply by falling silent. Further, there is a widespread belief in the United States that an arrestee's wisest course of action is to claim the Fifth Amendment and demand to see an attorney. *Griffin* calls into question the constitutional propriety of inferring assent from a criminal defendant's silence, and the belief weakens the inference of assent from silence. In this light, it is very difficult to invoke the doctrine against an accused to generate substantive evidence of guilt. What about using the defendant's silence for the limited purpose of impeachment? The Supreme Court ventured into this thicket

to clarify the state of the law in the following case.

DOYLE v. OHIO
426 U.S. 610 (1976)

JUSTICE POWELL delivered the opinion of the Court.

The question is whether a state prosecutor may seek to impeach a defendant's exculpatory story, told for the first time at trial, by cross-examining the defendant about his failure to have told the story after receiving *Miranda* warnings at the time of his arrest. We conclude that use of the defendant's post-arrest silence in this manner violates due process.

[Bonnell, an informant, offered to assist local narcotics officers to set up drug "pushers" in return for lenient treatment in his latest legal problems. Bonnell told the officers that he had arranged a "buy" of 10 pounds of marihuana and needed $1,750 to pay for it. The police gave him $1,320. Bonnell left for the rendezvous, under surveillance by narcotics agents. After meeting petitioners Doyle and Wood, Bonnell and Wood drove in Bonnell's pickup to New Philadelphia, Ohio, while Doyle left to obtain the marihuana. The narcotics agents followed the truck. When Doyle arrived at Bonnell's truck in New Philadelphia, the two vehicles proceeded to a parking lot. Bonnell left in his truck, and Doyle and Wood departed in Doyle's car. They discovered that they had been paid $430 less than agreed on and began looking for Bonnell. They were stopped by New Philadelphia police acting on instructions from the narcotics agents. One agent, Beamer, arrested the petitioners, and gave them *Miranda* warnings. A search of the car yielded the $1,320.

Each petitioner testified at his trial and admitted practically everything except the most crucial point: who was selling marihuana to whom. According to petitioners, Bonnell framed them. The arrangement had been for Bonnell to sell Doyle 10 pounds of marihuana. Doyle had left Dover to borrow the money, but while driving by himself had decided that he wanted only one or two pounds. When Bonnell arrived with the marijuana at Doyle's car in the parking lot, Doyle explained his change of mind. Bonnell angrily threw the $1,320 into Doyle's car and took all 10 pounds of the marihuana back to his truck. According to petitioners, the ensuing chase was the petitioners' effort to catch Bonnell to find out what the $1,320 was all about. In separate trials, petitioners Doyle and Wood were convicted of selling marihuana.]

Petitioner's explanation of the events presented some difficulty for the prosecution, as it was not entirely implausible and there was little if any direct evidence to contradict it. In an effort to undercut the explanation, the prosecutor asked each petitioner why he had not told the frame up story to Agent Beamer when he arrested petitioners. In the first trial . . . of petitioner Wood, the following colloquy occurred:

Q: [By the prosecutor.] Mr. Beamer did arrive on the scene?

A: [By Wood.] Yes, he did.

Q: And I assume you told him all about what happened to you?

. . . .

A: No.

Q: You didn't tell Mr. Beamer?

. . . .

A: No.

Q: And we can't understand any reason why anyone would put money in your car and you were chasing him around town and trying to give it back?

A: I didn't understand that.

Q: You mean you didn't tell him that?

. . . .

A: Tell him what?

. . . .

Q: Mr. Wood, if that is all you had to do with this and you are innocent, when Mr. Beamer arrived on the scene why didn't you tell him?

. . . .

Q: But in any event you didn't bother to tell Mr. Beamer anything about this?

A: No, sir.

Defense counsel's timely objections to the above questions of the prosecutor were overruled. The cross-examination of petitioner Doyle at his trial contained a similar exchange, and again defense counsel's timely objections were overruled.

The State . . . argues that the discrepancy between an exculpatory story at trial and silence at time of arrest gives rise to an inference that the story was fabricated somewhere along the way, perhaps to fit within the seams of the State's case as it was developed at pretrial hearings. Noting that the prosecution usually has little else with which to counter such an exculpatory story, the State seeks only the right to cross-examine a defendant as to post-arrest silence for the limited purpose of impeachment. In support of its position the State relies upon those cases in which this Court has permitted use for impeachment purposes of post-arrest statements that were inadmissible as evidence of guilt because of an officer's failure to follow *Miranda's* dictates. *Harris v. New York*, 401 U.S. 222 (1971); *Oregon v. Hass*, 420 U.S. 714 (1975); *see also Walder v. United States*, 347 U.S. 62 (1954). Thus, although the State does not suggest petitioners' silence could be used as evidence of guilt, it contends that the need to present to the jury all information relevant to the truth of petitioners' exculpatory story fully justifies the cross-examination that is at issue.

The *Miranda* decision compels rejection of the State's position. The warnings mandated by that case, as a prophylactic means of safeguarding Fifth Amendment rights, require that a person taken into custody be advised immediately that he has the right to remain silent, that anything he says may be used against him, and that he has a right to retain or appoint counsel before submitting to interrogation.

Silence in the wake of these warnings may be nothing more than the arrestee's exercise of these *Miranda* rights. Thus, every post — arrest silence is insolubly ambiguous because of what the State is required to advise the person arrested. Moreover, while it is true that the *Miranda* warnings contain no express assurance that silence will carry no penalty, such assurance is implicit to any person who receives the warnings. In such circumstances, it would be fundamentally unfair and a deprivation of due process to allow the arrested person's silence to be used to impeach an explanation subsequently offered at trial. Mr. Justice White, concurring in the judgment in *United States v. Hale, supra,* at 182–183, put it very well:

> [W]hen a person under arrest is informed, as *Miranda* requires, that he may remain silent, that anything he says may be used against him, and that he may have an attorney if he wishes, it seems to me that it does not comport with due process to permit the prosecution during the trial to call attention to his silence at the time of arrest and to insist that because he did not speak about the facts of the case at that time, as he was told he need not do, an unfavorable inference might be drawn as to the truth of his trial testimony. . . .

We hold that the use for impeachment purposes of petitioners' silence, at the time of arrest and after receiving *Miranda* warnings, violated the Due Process Clause of the Fourteenth Amendment.[11]

NOTES AND PROBLEMS

1.   Since rendering the *Doyle* decision, the Supreme Court has revisited the issue. In *Doyle,* the defendants' silence was both post-arrest and post-warnings. In *Jenkins v. Anderson,* 447 U.S. 231, 238–40 (1980), the Court held that a prosecutor may cross-examine a defendant about pre-arrest silence for the purpose of impeachment. In *Fletcher v. Weir,* 455 U.S. 603 (1982), the Court further limited *Doyle* by announcing that a prosecutor may use post-arrest silence for impeachment if the defendant had not yet been given *Miranda* warnings.

2.   **Problem 19-6.** In *Devitt,* at trial the defendant takes the stand. During direct examination, the following occurs:

Q: What did you do after the police took you to the station?

A: I cooperated fully with the police.

Q: What do you mean by "cooperated"?

A: As best I could, I told them everything they wanted to know about where I had been and what I'd done that day.

In light of this direct testimony, would the prosecutor be able to prove that when first interrogated, Devitt claimed the Fifth Amendment? Note footnote 11 in *Doyle.*

---

[11] It goes almost without saying that the fact of post-arrest silence could be used by the prosecution to contradict a defendant who testifies to an exculpatory version of events and claims to have told the police the same version upon arrest. In that situation the fact of earlier silence would not be used to impeach the exculpatory story, but rather to challenge the defendant's testimony as to his behavior following arrest. *Cf. United States v. Fairchild,* 505 F.2d 1378, 1383 (CA5 1975).

Would the prosecutor be able to use Devitt's silence as substantive evidence of guilt or merely as impeachment?

3.   **Problem 19-7.** In *Hill*, Laroby confronts the plaintiff immediately after the collision and accuses her of being drunk. She remains silent. Is her silence automatically admissible? What would you like to know about Ms. Hill's condition at the time Laroby spoke with her? *Klever v. Elliott*, 212 Or. 490, 320 P.2d 263, 264–65 (1958) (the "plaintiff . . . indicated inability to talk about the accident because of his injury").

4.   **Problem 19-8.** Suppose that after the accident, Mr. Hill wrote a letter to the president of the manufacturer Polecat. In the letter he asserted that "you should be ashamed of yourself for marketing such a dangerous product." Neither Polecat's president nor any other officer of Polecat responded to the letter. At trial, can Ms. Hill argue that Polecat's failure to respond is an adoptive admission that its gas tank was "dangerous"? Assume alternatively that the president of the Jefferson Motor Cars dealership wrote to the president of Polecat and included a similar assertion in the letter. Jefferson Motor Cars and Polecat have dealt with each other for 15 years. In that light, would Polecat's failure to respond be an adoptive admission? *See* 2 McCORMICK, EVIDENCE § 262, at 215–17 (6th ed. 2006) (yes). While many adoptive admissions arise from failure to respond to oral accusations, some arise from a party's refusal to respond to a written accusation. *Hellenic Lines, Ltd. v. Gulf Oil Corp.*, 340 F.2d 398, 401 (2d Cir. 1965) (failure of party to respond to a letter constituted admission by silence, where circumstances reasonably called for a response).

D.   VICARIOUS ADMISSIONS

The final type of admission is the most controversial. In the case of personal and adoptive admissions, there is at least some arguable basis for inferring assent. In the case of a vicarious admission, there need be no evidence of assent or agreement. We impute vicarious admissions to the party-opponent solely on the basis of the opponent's close legal relationship with the declarant. The statement may be admissible against the opponent even when, in all probability, the opponent would never have made the same statement. The question then becomes: When is the relationship strong enough to justify burdening the opponent with the third party's statement?

1.   Civil Cases

At first, the courts virtually equated the vicarious admission standard with the agency law test for authority to serve as a spokesperson. Even if the third-party speaker was indisputably an employee of the party-opponent, the courts refused to admit the speaker's statements as the opponent's vicarious admission unless there was an affirmative showing of "authority to speak for the principal." *Rudzinski v. Warner*, 16 Wis. 2d 241, 114 N.W.2d 466 (1962). Opinions were replete with references to the RESTATEMENT OF THE LAW OF AGENCY. Under this approach, statements by Polecat's president would qualify as vicarious admissions against Polecat because the president of a company is an authorized spokesperson;

however, assertions by Worker, Roe's employee, would probably be inadmissible against Roe.

Eventually the courts came to question the facile equation between the agency and evidentiary doctrines. More and more courts came to think that the issues were distinguishable and that the evidentiary standard should be more liberal than the agency test.

Finally, at the commentators' urging, a number of courts began to repudiate the traditional view and explicitly adopt a broader standard for the vicarious admissions of agents and employees. The drafters of the Federal Rules embraced that liberalized view in Rule 801(d)(2)(C) and (D):

> (d) Statements That Are Not Hearsay. A statement that meets the following conditions is not hearsay:
>
> (2) An Opposing Party's Statement. The statement is offered against an opposing party and:
>
> (C) was made by a person whom the party authorized to make a statement on the subject;
>
> (D) was made by the party's agent or employee on a matter within the scope of that relationship and while it existed.

Subsection (C) preserves the traditional "speaking authority" route for admitting agents' statements, but (D) supplements (C) by adding a more liberal, alternative basis for imputing the statement to the employer or principal. Under (D), the declarant need not be a speaking agent (*Hill v. F.R. Tripler & Co., Inc.*, 868 F. Supp. 593, 597 (S.D.N.Y. 1994)); "authorization to speak need not be shown." *Precision Piping & Instruments, Inc. v. E.I. du Pont de Nemours & Co.*, 951 F.2d 613, 619 (4th Cir. 1991). The declarant's statement need only "concern" matters within the scope of the agency. *In re Sunset Bay Associates*, 944 F.2d 1503 (9th Cir. 1991).

NOTES AND PROBLEMS

1. Although Federal Rule 801(d)(2)(D) breaks down the equation between the evidentiary admissibility of the agent's statements against the principal and the principal's *respondeat superior* liability in tort, agency principles are still pertinent to the interpretation of the Rule. The Rule uses the expression "agent or employee," and the courts continue to look to common-law principles to determine whether the declarant is an "agent or employee." In *Boren v. Sable*, 887 F.2d 1032, 1038 (10th Cir. 1989), the court observed:

> The use of the terms "agent" or "servant" without definition evidences Congress' intent to describe the traditional master-servant relationship as understood by common law agency doctrine. Use of the term "scope of employment" in Rule 801(d)(2)(D) is additional evidence of Congress' intent that common law agency principles be used in applying Rule 801.

When a statute employs a term which has acquired a fixed meaning at common law, the courts ordinarily presume that the legislature used the term in the common law sense. Based on this reasoning, for example, the courts ordinarily refuse to treat a party's expert witnesses as agents. *Kirk v. Raymark Industries, Inc.*, 51 F.3d 1206, 1213–14 (3d Cir. 1995). For similar reasons, an outside independent contractor usually does not qualify as an agent for purposes of the rule. *United States v. Bonds*, 608 F.3d 495 (9th Cir. 2010) (Barry Bonds's personal trainer was an independent contractor, not Bonds's agent). Similarly, in the *Hill* case, the dealer, Jefferson Motor Car, would not qualify as an agent of the manufacturer, Polecat Motors. *Carlisle v. Deere & Co.*, 576 F.3d 649, 656 (7th Cir. 2009).

2. Recall *Bourjaily v. United States*, 483 U.S. 171 (1987), where the Court noted that before the adoption of the Federal Rules of Evidence, the common law "bootstrapping doctrine" was in effect. By virtue of that doctrine, a prosecutor attempting to lay the foundation for a coconspirator's hearsay declaration had to present independent evidence of such foundational facts as the existence of the conspiracy and the declarant's membership in the conspiracy; the prosecutor could not on the content of the declaration itself to lay the foundation, since doing so would amount to forbidden "bootstrapping." *Bourjaily* ruled that the doctrine did not survive the enactment of Federal Rule 104(a).

3. Notwithstanding the *Bourjaily* holding, some post-Rules civil cases asserted that "the statement to be introduced may not be relied upon to establish the alleged agency relationship." *Pappas v. Middle Earth Condominium Ass'n*, 963 F.2d 534, 538 (2d Cir. 1992). In 1997, Rule 801 (d)(2) was amended to clarify the issue:

> The contents of the statement shall be considered but are not alone sufficient to establish the declarant's authority under subdivision (C), the agency or employment relationship and the scope thereof under subdivision (D), or the existence of the conspiracy and the participation therein of the declarant and the party against whom the statement is offered under subdivision (E).

The restyled Rules contain a similar provision.

4. Problem 19-9. After the collision in *Hill*, Worker told a bystander, Ms. Karl, "I guess I just wasn't paying attention to the traffic." Ms. Hill wants to offer Worker's statement, through Ms. Karl's testimony, as a vicarious admission of Roe under Rule 801(d)(2)(D). How could she prove the fact of Worker's agency or employment? Suppose that Ms. Karl also heard Worker say, "Mr. Roe sent me to rush a package cross town, and he's going to be mad as hell when he finds out that I got into this accident on the way."

5. Problem 19-10. Suppose that Worker had recently immigrated to the United States from Mexico and that he was not yet fluent in English. He was riding with Mr. Contreras, another employee of Roe, who had been born in the United States. Rather than speaking directly to Karl, Worker spoke through Contreras, serving as an interpreter. Does the interpretation add another hearsay layer? Powell, Note, *No Comprende, No Justice: An Analysis of Applying Hearsay Exceptions to Interpreted Statements and the Impact on Iowa's Increasingly Diverse Residents, Workforce, and Justice System*, 57 DRAKE L. REV. 759 (2009) (yes). Would Rule 801(d)(2)(D) apply to that level as well? What if Mr. Contreras was another bystander, rather than a co-worker?

6. At common law, some courts adopted a strict approach to the agency rationale for vicarious admissions. 2 McCORMICK, EVIDENCE § 259, at 196–97 (6th ed. 2006). Since agency doctrines generally applied only when some third party sued the principal, these courts refused to admit an agent's internal statements to another agent or to the principal as vicarious admissions of the principal. *Id.* Did that limitation survive the adoption of Federal Rule 801(d)(2)? The Advisory Committee Note states that "[t]he rule is phrased broadly so as to encompass both" statements to outsiders and statements to insiders.

7. Perhaps the most frequent battleground for the vicarious admission doctrine today is the admissibility of statements by corporate agents in employment discrimination cases. The courts do not restrict the plaintiff to evidence of ageist, racist, or sexist statements by the plaintiff's immediate supervisor, *Maher v. City of Chicago*, 406 F. Supp. 2d 1006 (N.D. Ill. 2006), *aff'd*, 547 F.3d 817 (7th Cir. 2008), or persons with authority to make the personnel decision. *United States v. Riley*, 621 F.3d 312, 338 (3d Cir. 2010). However, they often require that the declarant have had some significant involvement, as either a participant or advisor, in the process leading to the challenged decision. *Yates v. Rexton, Inc.*, 267 F.3d 793 (8th Cir. 2001).

8. We saw earlier in this chapter that under the common law, personal admissions are admissible even if not based on the declarant's personal knowledge. Should the same rule apply to vicarious admissions by agents? Since vicarious admissions are one step removed from the party-opponent himself or herself, there is an additional concern about the probative value of the evidence. What should be the result under Federal Rule 801(d)(2)(D)? *See Brookover v. Mary Hitchcock Mem. Hosp.*, 893 F.2d 411, 415–17 (1st Cir. 1990) ("[c]ommentators and the courts differ on whether personal knowledge is a prerequisite for a vicarious admission under the Rule"). Again, the Advisory Committee Note to Rule 801(d)(2) contains a general reference to "[t]he freedom which admissions have enjoyed . . . from . . . the rule requiring firsthand knowledge." The trend is to hold that even vicarious admissions need not be based on personal knowledge. *Blackburn v. United Parcel Service, Inc.*, 179 F.3d 81, 96–97 (3d Cir. 1999); *Stagman v. Ryan*, 176 F.3d 986, 996 (7th Cir.), *cert. denied*, 528 U.S. 986 (1999).

9. At common law, the vicarious admission doctrine extended to statements by privies or predecessors in interest. 2 McCORMICK, EVIDENCE § 260 (6th ed. 2006). GEORGIA CODE ANNOTATED § 24-3-32 expressly refers to admissions by "privies in blood, . . . estate, and . . . law." For example, if a previous owner of the fee made a statement about the extent of his title to the property, the statement might be admissible against a subsequent owner. *Id.* Similarly, in many jurisdictions, if a decedent made a statement, the statement would be admissible against the decedent's personal representative or heirs in a survival or wrongful death action brought by the representative or heirs. *Id.* Thus, if Ms. Hill had died in the collision and her heirs had sued Polecat for wrongful death, her antemortem statements would be admissible against her heirs. Should such statements be admissible under Federal Rule 801(d)(2)? *Compare* Langum, *Uncodified Federal Evidence Rules Applicable to Civil Trials*, 19 WILLAMETTE L. REV. 513, 521–22 (1983) (yes), *with In re Cornfield*, 365 F. Supp. 2d 271, 277 (E.D.N.Y. 2004) (answering no but acknowledging the split of authority), *aff'd*, 156 Fed.Appx. 343 (2d Cir. 2005).

2. Criminal Cases

The criminal counterpart of the admission of agents' statements is the doctrine allowing the prosecution to use coconspirators' statements against each other. The statements may be oral or written. For example, a calendar/ledger maintained by one drug trafficker may be admitted as substantive evidence against her coconspirator. *United States v. Smith*, 893 F.2d 1573 (9th Cir. 1990). Like its civil analogue, the early common-law version of this exception looked to substantive law to define the limits of admissibility — in this instance, the vicarious responsibility of coconspirators under criminal law.

W. LaFave, Criminal Law, Ch. 12 (5th ed. 2010), sets forth the substantive law of conspiracy in a nutshell: When individuals enter into a criminal conspiracy, each of them is liable for every act, and is bound by the act and declaration of each conspirator done in furtherance of the conspiracy. That liability attaches even if the accused coconspirator was absent when the act was performed or the declaration voiced. When one conspirator commits an act to achieve the main objective of the criminal plan, the act is imputed to every other conspirator. A coconspirator escapes criminal responsibility only if the first conspirator unexpectedly goes entirely beyond the purpose to commit the crime. However, once the conspiracy comes to an end, whether by accomplishing or abandoning the criminal objective, the conspirator's vicarious liability terminates.

Evidentiary rulings on the admissibility of coconspirator's statements parallel the substantive criminal law:

- A statement qualifies under the evidentiary doctrine only if the declarant actually joined the conspiracy; if the declarant was an undercover agent who would not incur criminal responsibility, the declaration is inadmissible. *United States v. Williamson*, 450 F.2d 585 (5th Cir. 1971), *cert. denied*, 405 U.S. 1026 (1972).

- Courts generally hold that the conspiracy terminates when the conspirators either achieve or abandon their main objective. The conspiracy ordinarily ends before individual conspirators begin their personal, individual efforts to conceal the conspiracy and avoid arrest and conviction. Most courts do not infer a subsidiary conspiracy to continue to work in concert after the crime's commission and the division of the fruits of the crime. *Grunewald v. United States*, 353 U.S. 391 (1957); *Lutwak v. United States*, 344 U.S. 604 (1953); *Krulewitch v. United States*, 336 U.S. 440 (1949). To justify the admission of later statements, the prosecution must prove the formation of a *further* conspiracy to continue to act in concert.

- Just as under substantive Crimes law, the statement must be intended to further the conspiracy, though it need not have the actual effect of promoting the conspiracy. Thus, a coconspirator's statement to an undercover agent is admissible if the coconspirator mistakenly believes that the agent is a criminal negotiating for the purchase of illegal drugs. *United States v. Smith*, 441 F.2d 254 (4th Cir.), *cert. denied sub nom. Reep v. United States*, 549 U.S. 903 (2006).

Against this backdrop of the common law, consider Federal Rule of Evidence 801(d)(2)(E):

(d) Statements That Are Not Hearsay. A statement that meets the following conditions is not hearsay:

(2) An Opposing Party's Statement. The statement is offered against an opposing party and:

(E) was made by the party's coconspirator during and in furtherance of the conspiracy.

The Advisory Committee described Rule 801(d)(2)(E) as being "in the accepted [common-law] pattern."

NOTES AND PROBLEMS

1. Some reformers have urged the courts to expand the duration of the conspiracy for evidentiary purposes. Under the prevailing view, the prosecutor must establish an express agreement to extend the conspiracy into the concealment phase. *Grunewald v. United States*, 353 U.S. 391, 399–406 (1957). Critics of the prevailing view recommend implying such an agreement. Although the Georgia legislature adopted this recommendation, most jurisdictions adhere to the traditional view. *Dutton v. Evans*, 400 U.S. 74, 81 (1970). Is the duration limitation more or less defensible than the "in furtherance" requirement?

2. **Problem 19-10.** In *Devitt*, the prosecution claims that the defendant conspired with and planned the battery with a friend, Mert Bloomington. The prosecution alleges that Bloomington had worked for Paterson and that when Paterson fired him, Bloomington developed a hatred for him. At trial, the prosecutor calls Mr. Kranston as a witness. Kranston was present at several meetings between Devitt and Bloomington, and he testifies that he heard the two men discuss "getting Paterson and paying him back for what he (Paterson) had done to Bloomington." Ultimately, the prosecutor wants to elicit Kranston's testimony that Bloomington said that "Danny (Devitt) is going to nail him [Paterson] good." As soon as the prosecutor asks the question to elicit that testimony, Devitt's attorney objects and requests permission to *voir dire* Kranston and present extrinsic testimony that there was no conspiracy between Bloomington and Devitt.

Should the judge grant the defense request? Does the judge or jury decide whether there was a conspiracy, authorizing the introduction of Bloomington's statement as a vicarious admission? Reread the Supreme Court's decision in *Bourjaily* (excerpted in Chapter 5) and compare *Bourjaily* with this passage from the Assembly Committee's Comment to California Evidence Code § 403 (the California analogue to Federal Rule 104(b)): "The admission of a co-conspirator is another form of an authorized admission. Hence, the proffered evidence is admissible upon the introduction of evidence sufficient to sustain a finding of the conspiracy."

3. **Problem 19-11.** Assume the first trial in *Devitt* resulted in a hung jury and a mistrial. Before the first trial, Devitt's defense attorney anticipated that the prosecution would call Mr. Manville, who lived in the same apartment complex as

Paterson. Based on his informal conversations with Manville, the defense attorney expected Manville to testify that he had a conversation with Devitt just outside the Paterson apartment and that during that conversation Devitt had made a veiled threat toward Mr. Paterson. Devitt's attorney tries to preempt Manville's testimony by conceding, during opening statement, that Devitt made such remarks, but adds: "Ladies and gentlemen, there's a world of difference between casually making a vague threat and actually attacking that person." Manville dies unexpectedly before trial, and his testimony is never presented during the first trial. During the second trial, the prosecutor attempts to offer the defense counsel's opening statement acknowledging that Devitt made the remarks shortly before the alleged attack. Devitt has a new attorney at the second trial, and she objects that the former counsel's statement is "rank hearsay." The prosecutor argues that the prior defense counsel's statement is a vicarious admission. The prosecutor does not argue that the defense attorney was a coconspirator under (E) but contends that the attorney was an "agent" under (C) or (D). Does it make a difference that Devitt has retained new counsel for the second trial? *See United States v. McKeon*, 738 F.2d 26, 30–34 (2d Cir. 1984) (the statement was admissible against the defendant even though the defendant elected to proceed pro se at the second trial). In some respects, an attorney is unquestionably the client's agent; and on its face, Rule 801(d)(2) does not carve out any exception for attorneys. *United States v. McClellan*, 868 F.2d 210 (7th Cir. 1989); Humble, *Evidentiary Admissions of Defense Counsel in Federal Criminal Cases*, 24 AM. CRIM. L. REV. 93 (1986). However, "the routine use of attorney statements against a criminal defendant risks impairment of the privilege against self-incrimination, the right to counsel of one's choice, and the right to the effective assistance of counsel." *United States v. Valencia*, 826 F.2d 169, 172 (2d Cir. 1987) (a defense counsel's statement during bail discussions with the prosecutor did not qualify as a vicarious admission).

4. In a criminal case involving conspirators, must the prosecution rely on Rule 801(d)(2)(E), or can the prosecution invoke other theories recognized in Rule 801(d)(2)? Though Rule 801(d)(2)(D) is arguably so broad that it might never be necessary for the prosecution to resort to — and comply with — Rule 801(d)(2)(E), courts ordinarily favor statutory interpretations that give independent effect to each provision in a statute. *See Ojo v. Farmers Group, Inc.*, 565 F.3d 1175 (9th Cir. 2009).

Thus far, we have discussed the prosecution's attempts to use the various admission doctrines against the defendant. Can the defendant turn the tables on the prosecution? Suppose, for example, that, during the pretrial investigation of the case, a police officer or prosecutor makes a statement which tends to exculpate Devitt? May Devitt introduce the statement as evidence against the government on the theory that the police officer is its agent or employee? In the following case, in which the legendary trial advocacy lecturer Professor Irving Younger was the appointed defense counsel, the court addressed that question:

UNITED STATES v. SANTOS
372 F.2d 177 (2d Cir. 1967)

Waterman, Circuit Judge.

[The defendant was charged with assaulting a federal officer.]

Appellant maintains that the case should be remanded for a new trial in that it was improper and prejudicial to exclude from evidence a sworn affidavit to an officer's complaint by a narcotics agent, agent Edward R. Dower, who had witnessed the assault, in which agent Dower named another than appellant as one of the three assailants, and which sworn affidavit defendant offered at trial during the defense case as an admission against the Government. We find no merit and affirm the conviction below.

The claim of reversible error may be shortly answered by stating that inconsistent out-of-court statements or actions of a government agent said or done in the course of his employment take on quite a different probative character in a government criminal case from that which inconsistent out-of-court acts of agents acting within the scope of their employment generally take on at a trial. Though a government prosecution is an exemplification of the adversary process . . . , when the Government prosecutes, it prosecutes on behalf of all the people of the United States; therefore all persons, whether law enforcement agents, government investigators, complaining prosecuting witnesses, or the like, who testify on behalf of the prosecution, and who, because of an employment relation or other personal interest in the outcome of the prosecution, may happen to be inseparably connected with the government side of the adversary process, stand in relation to the United States and in relation to the defendant no differently from persons unconnected with the effective development of or furtherance of the success of, the prosecution.

Therefore, the inconsistent out-of-court statements of a government agent made in the course of the exercise of his authority and within the scope of that authority, which statements would be admissions binding upon an agent's principal in civil cases, are not so admissible here as "evidence of the fact."

To be sure, if the defense had adopted different trial tactics and had confronted Dower with this statement of his when cross-examining him the statement would have been admissible as evidence tending to impeach his credibility. This course the defendant elected not to adopt. The course defendant did adopt would have been successful if it had been attempted other than in a criminal prosecution. This limitation upon the use the defendant may make of a government agent's out-of-court inconsistent statement seems grossly unfair to defendants, for the prosecution may introduce against the defendant similar damaging statements by defendants' agents if made in the course of the exercise of the agent's authority and within the scope thereof and the agents' admissions have the same testimonial value as if the inconsistent statements had been made by the defendant himself.

This apparent discrimination is explained by the peculiar posture of the parties in a criminal prosecution — the only party on the government side being the Government itself whose many agents and actors are supposedly uninterested personally in the outcome of the trial and are historically unable to bind the sovereign. Apparently recognizing the seeming unfairness of this peculiar relationship Congress by enacting 18 U.S.C. § 3500 has made it a requirement that the prosecution turn over to the defense any inconsistent statements of government witnesses relating to the testimony given by those witnesses at trial so that the defense upon cross-examination can interrogate the witnesses about the inconsistent statements. But these statements are not admissible against the Government as evidentiary proof of the matter therein stated.

Judgment affirmed.

Santos still commands a following in modern cases such as the following opinion.

UNITED STATES v. YILDIZ
355 F.3d 80 (2d Cir. 2004)

PER CURIAM.

[Yildiz was convicted of conspiring to rob jewelry merchants. A substantial part of the trial evidence consisted of recorded conversations among Yildiz, his co-defendants, and a government informant. When the informant later spoke with the police, he made several statements which could be construed as exculpatory of Yildiz. However, the trial judge refused to allow the defense to introduce those statements.]

Most courts continue to follow *Santos. See, e.g., United States v. Prevatte*, 16 F.3d 767, 779 n.9 (7th Cir. 1994) . . . . [W]e write to reaffirm its holding [even] in light of legal developments that have led some courts and commentators to question its validity. *See e.g., United States v. Morgan*, 581 F.2d 933, 938, 189 U.S. App. D.C. 155 & n. 15 (D.C. Cir. 1978); 30B Michael H. Graham, *Federal Practice and Procedure: Evidence* § 7023m at 221 n. 11 (2000).

This Court has recognized that the government's attorneys can bind the government with their in-court statements, *see United States v. Salerno*, 937 F.2d 797, 810–12 (2d Cir. 1991), *rev'd on other grounds*, 505 U.S. 317, (1992), and filings, *see United States v. GAF Corp.*, 928 F.2d 1253, 1258–62 (2d Cir. 1991). These cases are consistent with Rule 801(d)(2)(B), which provides that a statement of which a party "has manifested an adoption or belief in its truth" is not hearsay, and with authority that has applied that provision against the government in criminal cases, *see United States v. Kattar*, 840 F.2d 118, 130–31 (1st Cir. 1988); Morgan, 581 F.2d at 938 & n. 15.

There is good reason, however, to distinguish sworn statements submitted to a judicial officer which the government might be said to have adopted, and those that are not submitted to a court and, consequently, not adopted, for example, statements contained in an arrest warrant, *see United States v. Warren*, 42 F.3d 647, 655-56, 310 U.S. App. D.C. 1 (D.C. Cir. 1994), and an informant's remarks. Like the Third Circuit, "we do not believe that the authors of Rule 801(d)(2)(D) intended statements by informers as a general matter to fall under the [admissions] rule, given their tenuous relationship with the police officers with whom they work."

Lippay v. Christos, 996 F.2d 1490, 1499 (3d Cir. 1993).

The 1972 Advisory Committee Notes to Rule 801(d)(2)(D) indicate that the Rule was motivated by "dissatisfaction" with the traditional rule that an agent's admission would only be admissible if made "in the scope of his employment," since "few principals employ agents for the purpose of making damaging statements." As "the Notes disclose a purpose to adhere to the common law in the application of evidentiary principles, absent express provisions to the contrary," *Tome v. United States*, 513 U.S. 150, 160–61 (1995) . . . , we hold that Rule 801(d)(2)(D) does not abrogate the common law rule articulated in *Santos*. And we hold, following *Santos*, that the out-of-court statements of a government informant are not admissible in a criminal trial pursuant to Rule 801(d)(2)(D) as admissions by the agent of a party opponent . . . Accordingly, the evidentiary ruling of the district court is affirmed.

NOTES

1.   Professor Younger continued to press his attack on the *Santos* decision after the Second Circuit's decision. Younger, *Sovereign Admissions: A Comment on United States v. Santos*, 43 N.Y.U. L. REV. 108 (1968). He passionately insisted that when a defendant "confront[s] the sovereign in court, the rules of the game [should] be the same for both." *Id.* at 108. However, as *Yildiz* suggests, both before and after the adoption of the Federal Rules, most courts have followed *Santos*. *E.g., United States v. Durrani*, 659 F. Supp. 1183, 1185–86 (D. Conn.), *aff'd*, 835 F.2d 410 (2d Cir. 1987).

2.   Do you find Judge Waterman's reasoning persuasive? When the sovereign is a party to a civil lawsuit, the courts apply the normal vicarious admission doctrine against the sovereign. *United States v. A. T. & T. Co.*, 524 F. Supp. 1331, 1333–34 (D.D.C. 1981); *Burkey v. Ellis*, 483 F. Supp. 897, 911 n.13 (N.D. Ala. 1979).

3.   Which type of statement is more likely to be reliable — a statement by a coconspirator or a statement by a government agent? Criminal conspirators are often inveterate liars. Levie, *Hearsay and Conspiracy: A Reexamination of the Co-Conspirators' Exception to the Hearsay Rule*, 52 MICH. L. REV. 1159, 1166 (1954). It may well be in the conspirator's self-interest to misrepresent the membership or aims of the conspiracy. *Id.* at 1165–66. Professor Mueller put the matter bluntly when he wrote that the coconspirator doctrine is "an embarrassment." Mueller, *The Federal Coconspirator Exception: Action, Assertion, and Hearsay*, 12 HOFSTRA L. REV. 323, 324 (1984). In contrast, the government has presumably exercised some care in hiring its employees.

4.   Consider the problem as an issue of statutory interpretation. Is the wording of Rule 801(d)(2)(D) broad enough to apply to statements by government agents? Given Rule 402, may a court continue to enforce *Santos* on the theory that if Congress had intended to overrule such a well-settled doctrine, Congress "surely" would have done so explicitly? Think back to the Supreme Court's treatment of Rule 402 in *Daubert*, 509 U.S. 579 (1993), discussed in Chapter 12. When Congress wanted to apply different rules to the prosecution and defense, it did so explicitly in the text of the Federal Rules. *E.g.*, FED. R. EVID. 804(b)(3) (prior to 2010, the corroboration requirement applied only to declarations offered by the defense).

Judge Bazelon questioned whether *Santos* is good law under the Federal Rules. *United States v. Morgan*, 581 F.2d 933, 938 n.14 (D.C. Cir. 1978). So too have the commentators. *See, e.g.*, Jonakait, *The Supreme Court, Plain Meaning, and the Changed Rules of Evidence*, 68 TEX. L. REV. 745, 774–78 (1990) ("[t]he plain-meaning standard discards the *Santos* doctrine"). There has been movement away from *Santos. E.g., United States v. Zizzo*, 120 F.3d 1338, 1351 n.4 (7th Cir.) (although this court generally "decline[s] to apply Rule 801(d)(2) to statements made by government employees in criminal cases," the court acknowledged that "a number of courts have rejected that approach when dealing with statements by government attorneys"), *cert. denied*, 522 U.S. 998 (1997); *United States v. Salerno*, 937 F.2d 797, 810–12 (2d Cir. 1991) (the government's earlier closing argument); *United States v. GAF Corp.*, 928 F.2d 1253 (2d Cir. 1991) (the government's earlier bill of particulars could be introduced against the prosecution as the admission of a party-opponent); *State v. Cardenas-Hernandez*, 579 N.W. 2d 678, 685 (Wis. 1998) ("[w]e . . . refuse to adopt a per se prohibition on the use of prior statements of prosecutors as admissions of a party-opponent"). A distinction is often made between prosecutor declarations (admissible) and declarations by police officers and their agents (inadmissible).

Chapter 20

HEARSAY: EXCEPTIONS THAT DO NOT REQUIRE PROOF OF UNAVAILABILITY

Read Federal Rule of Evidence 803, subdivisions (1–4, 6–12, 14 and 18).

A. INTRODUCTION

This chapter considers many of the exceptions listed in Federal Rule of Evidence 803, which is entitled "Exceptions to the Rule Against Hearsay — Regardless of Whether the Declarant is Available as a Witness." (The following chapter deals with exceptions that do require proof of the declarant's unavailability, which are contained in Rule 804.) The exceptions now codified in Rule 803 were recognized at common law because courts reasoned that hearsay evidence with particular features was likely to be equally or more reliable than testimony the declarant would now give from the witness stand. Hutchins & Slesinger, *Some Observations on the Law of Evidence: State of Mind in Issue*, 29 U. Colo. L. Rev. 147, 149 (1929). Thus, the key to these exceptions is an inference of the statement's reliability. That inference supplies both the circumstantial guarantees of trustworthiness (eliminating the need for cross-examination) and the element of necessity — justifying the resort to hearsay.

The Rule 803 exceptions fall into two major categories. In the first, the inference of reliability arises from circumstances strongly suggesting the declarant's sincerity. In the second, the statement takes the form of a writing and the care with which the writing was prepared creates the inference of reliability.

B. EXCEPTIONS DERIVED FROM THE COMMON LAW "RES GESTAE" THEORY

1. "Res Gestae"

Although the phrase "res gestae" does not appear in the Federal Rules of Evidence and is generally disfavored by commentators, it has a long history in the common law of evidence. Thus, you are likely to encounter the term at some point in your professional career and it is useful to have some familiarity with it. The major specific hearsay exceptions generally said to have been spawned by the res gestae theory are: excited utterances, contemporaneous statements, declarations of bodily condition, and declarations of state of mind. These four exceptions are addressed in this section.

Dean Wigmore remarked about the term res gestae that it "is inexact and indefinite in its scope. . . . The phrase 'res gestae' has long been not only entirely useless but even positively harmful." 6 J. WIGMORE, EVIDENCE § 1767, at 180, 182–83 (3d ed. 1940). Thus, having noted the traditional use of the term to refer to a group of hearsay exceptions that share a certain feature of "automaticity," this text will generally avoid using it.[1]

2. Excited or Startled Utterances

The excited or startled utterance exception is based on the intuitive rationale that when an observer makes a statement about a startling event that he or she has just witnessed, the excitement caused by the event will tend to suppress the kind of rational, purposive thought that normally accompanies lying. In colloquial terms, courts imagine that the declarant "blurts out" the utterance without thinking. In his lectures for the National Institute on Trial Advocacy, the late Professor Irving Younger pointed out that it is quite easy to recognize excited utterances: they usually begin with "My God" and end with an exclamation mark. Federal Rule of Evidence 803(2) codifies the exception:

> Rule 803. The following are not excluded by the rule against hearsay, regardless of whether the declarant is available as a witness:

> (2) **Excited Utterance.** A statement relating to a startling event or condition, made while the declarant was under the stress of excitement that it caused.

A close look at the Rule reveals two basic foundational requirements for admissibility of a hearsay statement as an excited utterance. First, the content of the statement must "relat[e] to a startling event or condition." It is not enough that the declarant was excited while speaking; the statement cannot range far from the subject of the event or condition that caused the excitement. Inherent in this foundation are the further requirements of a sufficient showing that the event actually occurred and that the declarant perceived it.

Often the evidence that the exciting event occurred comes from the hearsay statement itself. Imagine that a witness testifies that she heard the declarant shout, "Oh my God! Jerry just punched Tom in the face and knocked him out!!" The declarant's statement provides evidence that the event — Jerry punching Tom in the face — happened. One troublesome question is whether the hearsay statement may be used in this way to prove the event or whether the proponent must present independent evidence that the event occurred. Under the traditional rule, many jurisdictions had an independent evidence requirement. These courts reasoned that, without independent evidence of the event, the hearsay statement would "bootstrap" itself into evidence by providing its own foundation. Because the startling event ensures the reliability of the statement, it would be inappropriate to take the statement itself at face value as proof of the event's occurrence. Although some courts have construed the text of Rule 803(2) to codify the rule requiring

---

[1] This introductory material is based on M. LADD & R. CARLSON, CASES AND MATERIALS ON EVIDENCE 899–903 (1972).

independent proof, for example, *People v. Burton*, 433 Mich. 268, 445 N.W.2d 133 (1989), the Advisory Committee's Note to Rule 803(2) indicates that it intended the Rule to follow "the prevailing practice" dispensing with the requirement of independent evidence. This is one instance in which the available extrinsic legislative history material furnishes a relatively firm answer to a question of statutory construction. So long as a court believes that it is legitimate to consider the Advisory Committee's Note, that Note provides clear guidance.

In addition to the "relating to" requirement, the rule contains a timing requirement: the statement must have been made by the declarant while the declarant was in a state of excitement caused by that event. As noted above, such excitement is thought to guard against the testimonial infirmity of insincerity. In addition, the timing requirement tends to ensure that the statement was made in close proximity to the event, thus mitigating the testimonial infirmities of memory and perception. However, the Advisory Committee's Note makes clear that it does not favor rigid enforcement of this limitation, which is looser than the immediacy requirement that we will see when we turn to Present Sense Impressions. The following case examines the limits of both of Rule 803(2)'s foundational requirements.

UNITED STATES v. NAPIER
518 F.2d 316 (9th Cir. 1975)

SNEED, CIRCUIT JUDGE.

Defendant Napier was indicted on four counts of interstate transportation of a stolen motor vehicle in violation of 18 U.S.C. § 2312 ("Dyer Act") and one count of interstate kidnapping in violation of 18 U.S.C. § 1201 ("Lindbergh Act"). Defendant was convicted by a jury on all counts.

Counts IV and V of the indictment alleged that defendant kidnapped Mrs. Caruso in Oregon, transported her to Washington, and then drove her stolen car back to Oregon. There was very strong circumstantial evidence of defendant's involvement in the incident. Mrs. Caruso, a resident of Portland, Oregon, was found unconscious, with severe head injuries, near Vancouver, Washington. A broken rifle lay by her body. Blood and hair on the hammer of the weapon matched those of Mrs. Caruso; the barrel of the gun bore the fingerprints of the defendant. Tire tracks nearby corresponded to those of the Caruso car, which was later recovered in Oregon. Defendant's fingerprints were found on the car (including the steering wheel) and his personal papers and effects were discovered therein with Mrs. Caruso's purse.

Defendant argues that the court erred in admitting, as a "spontaneous exclamation," an out-of-court statement made by Mrs. Caruso. We find defendant's contention without merit and affirm the conviction.

Caruso was hospitalized for seven weeks following the assault, during which time she underwent two brain operations. There was testimony that she suffered brain damage which rendered her unable to comprehend the significance of an oath and therefore incapable of testifying at trial. It was also testified, although her memory was intact, that her communication with others was restricted to isolated words and simple phrases, often precipitated by situations of stress and strain. Approximately one week after Caruso returned home from the hospital, her sister, Eileen Moore, showed her a newspaper article containing a photograph of the defendant. Moore testified that Caruso looked at the photograph (but did not read the accompanying article), and her "immediate reaction was one of great distress and horror and upset," and that Caruso "pointed to it and she said very clearly, 'He killed me, he killed me.'" Moore also testified that no member of the family had attempted to discuss the incident with Caruso prior to the display of the photograph. The court admitted the statement, over defendant's objection that it was inadmissible hearsay, as a "spontaneous exclamation." We hold that the statement was properly admitted.

Although the government insists that the statement is a "verbal act" and thus not hearsay at all, we do not pass on this contention because it is our view that even if the statement is hearsay it falls within the exception for "spontaneous exclamation" or "excited utterances." Fed. R. Evid. 803(2) provides: "A statement relating to a startling event or condition made while the declarant was under the stress of excitement caused by the event or condition [is not excluded by the hearsay rule]." Appellant disputes the applicability of the "spontaneous exclamation" exception. He argues that since the statement "he killed me" refers to the assault, that event constitutes the "startling" event. Because the statement was not made under the stress of excitement caused by the assault, appellant insists that the statement is not within the exception. We reject appellant's analysis. The display of the photograph qualifies as a sufficiently "startling" event to render the statement made in response thereto admissible.

Although in most cases the "startling" events which prompt "spontaneous exclamations" are accidents, assaults, and the like, cf. McCormick, Evidence § 297 at 705 (2d ed. 1972), there is no reason to restrict the exception to those situations. Wigmore, in the classic statement of the admissibility of spontaneous exclamations, writes:

> This general principle is based on the experience that, under certain external circumstances of physical shock, a stress of nervous excitement may be produced which stills the reflective faculties and removes their control, so that the utterance which then occurs is a spontaneous and sincere response to the actual sensations and perceptions already produced by the external shock. Since this utterance is made under the immediate and uncontrolled domination of the senses, and during the brief period when considerations of self-interest could not have been brought fully to bear by reasoned reflection, the utterance may be taken as particularly trustworthy (or, at least, as lacking the usual grounds of untrustworthiness), and thus as expressing the real tenor of the speaker's belief as to the facts just observed by him; and may therefore be received as testimony to those facts. The ordinary situation presenting these conditions is an affray or a railroad accident. But the principle itself is a broad one.

6 Wigmore, Evidence § 1747, at 135 (3d ed. 1940). And McCormick writes of the nature of the event which underlies the exception: "The courts seem to look

primarily to the effect upon the declarant and, if satisfied that the event was such as to cause adequate excitement, the inquiry is ended." McCormick, Evidence § 297, at 705 (2d ed. 1972). In the instant case where Caruso, having never discussed the assault with her family, was suddenly and unexpectedly confronted with a photograph of her alleged assailant, there can be no doubt that the event was sufficiently "startling" to provide adequate safeguards against reflection and fabrication.

NOTES AND PROBLEMS

1. Does *Napier* interpret "relating to" sensibly? The court treats Mrs. Caruso's viewing of the photograph as the startling event. In the final analysis, though, what was the event Mrs. Caruso was purporting to remember?

There are now a number of cases following the *Napier* approach. Note, *Crying Wolf or an Excited Utterance? Allowing Reexcited Statements to Qualify Under the Excited Utterance Exception*, 52 CLEV. ST. L. REV. 527 (2005). By way of example, consider *Esser v. Commonwealth*, 566 S.E.2d 876 (Va. Ct. App. 2002). There, a rape victim made the alleged excited utterance two days after the attack, after her mother told her that she might take the victim again to the place where the assault occurred. The court held that the victim's fear of returning to the scene of the attack ensured the spontaneity of the statement and that the startling event need not be the crime itself, but may rather be a related occurrence.

In addition to this "trigger" or "re-excitement" theory, some courts have admitted statements involving threats on the theory that the exciting event — being threatened — continued for the period of time during which the declarant remained or felt under threat. In *United States v. Pursley*, 577 F.3d 1204 (10th Cir. 2009), the declarant was attacked in a prison holding cell; during the attack, one of the assailants warned him "not to try to get help." The court suggested that, to the extent that the declarant remained subject to this threat of future violence, there was "no lapse in time" because "it was not until [the declarant] decided to relay the inculpatory statements . . . that he experienced the immediate and direct stress of the threat of violence." *See also United States v. Ledford*, 443 F.3d 702 (10th Cir. 2005) (where police officer testified to declarant's statement that defendant had threatened to kill her if she spoke to the police, speaking to police officer could be viewed as the exciting event). Do you think that these cases stretch the foundational elements of this exception too far?

2. Part of the rationale for the timing requirement is the concern for the testimonial infirmity of memory. When the "trigger" or "continuing threat" cases cited above allow evidence of hearsay statements that concern events that might have happened days or weeks before the statements were made, this rationale begins to break down. Numerous experiments have demonstrated the alarmingly fast rate at which people forget. Gardner, *The Perception and Memory of Witnesses*, 18 CORNELL L.Q. 391, 393 (1933). In one study testing recollection of words, the typical subject forgot 90% of the information within a week. *Id.* By the time a few weeks have passed, memory decay is extensive. Stewart, *Perception, Memory, and Hearsay: A Criticism of Present Law and the Proposed Federal Rules of Evidence*, 1970 UTAH L. REV. 1, 24. As we have seen, the primary reason for

the "relating to" requirement is a concern about the quality of the declarant's memory.

3. **Problem 20-1.** In *Hill*, the plaintiff calls as a witness Mr. Bernstein. Bernstein testifies that he was at the intersection where the collision occurred. A few moments after the crash, he saw a man walking towards him. Mr. Bernstein is prepared to testify that the man said, "Did you see it? It was terrible. That guy must have been going at least 70. What an idiot!" Roe objects on the ground that the man Bernstein is quoting is unidentified. What ruling? *Powers v. Temple*, 250 S.C. 149, 156 S.E.2d 759, 765 (1967) (permitting excited utterance by unidentified declarant). There is substantial authority supporting *Powers. Boler v. State*, 240 Ga. App. 90, 522 S.E.2d 676 (1999) (admitting officer's testimony that two unidentified members of a crowd identified the defendant as the shooter); *New York, C. & St. L. R.R v. Kovatch*, 120 Ohio St. 532, 166 N.E. 682, 682–84 (1929). However, there are contrary authorities. *Lindsey v. State*, 271 Ga. 657, 522 S.E.2d 459 (1999) (statement ruled inadmissible).

4. **Problem 20-2.** In Problem 20-1, suppose that Roe had objected on the ground that there was insufficient proof that the man had personally observed the collision. Would the result be different if Bernstein had not noticed the man until five minutes after the collision? In *Cummiskey v. Chandris, S.A.*, 719 F. Supp. 1183, 1187 (S.D.N.Y. 1989), *aff'd*, 895 F.2d 107 (2d Cir. 1990), the court commented that "[i]n a case where the witness is both unidentified and unavailable, the burden [of showing personal knowledge] is greater." *Accord Shinners v. K-Mart Corp.*, 847 F. Supp. 31, 34 (D. Del. 1994) ("a heavier burden").

5. Are excited utterances by incompetent persons admissible? The mystical theory sometimes invoked by the courts is that the startling event is speaking through the person rather than the person speaking about the event. That theory can come into play when the declarant is a child or other person suffering from a mental disorder. In *State v. Burnette*, 125 Ohio App. 3d 278, 708 N.E.2d 276 (1998), the defense objected that the declarant was mentally incompetent. In upholding the introduction of the declarant's prior excited utterances, the court analogized to cases treating incompetent children's statements. The court recognized the rule that a child must be found competent at the time a statement was made before the statement can qualify under any hearsay exception, but noted that excited utterances are exempted from this general rule.

The foundational requirements explored above mainly help assure the declarant's perception and memory. The central focus of this exception, however, is the declarant's sincerity, and the indicator of sincerity is that the event observed must have been "startling" — the type of incident that could generate nervous excitement. In *Lira v. Albert Einstein Medical Center*, 384 Pa. Super. 503, 559 A.2d 550 (1989), the court considered a statement made by an attending physician during a physical examination of a patient after an operation: "Who's the butcher who [did] this?" The court held that the examination was not the type of shocking occurrence that can support admission of a statement as an excited utterance. In addition to requiring the existence of an event or condition that is objectively "startling," courts require a foundational showing that the declarant in fact was in a state of nervous excitement when he or she made the statement. Typically, courts place great emphasis on the time interval between the event and the statement. It is ideal if the declarant makes the statement "a few minutes" after the event. *Peavey v. State*, 631 S.W.2d 821 (Tex. Crim. App. 1982). However, the critical inquiry is not the duration of time between the event and the statement, but rather whether the declarant remained in a state of excitement caused by the event. This articulation of the requirement by the Court of Appeals for the Sixth Circuit is typical: "our cases do not demand a precise showing of the lapse of time between the startling event and the out-of-court statement. The exception may be based solely on 'testimony that the declarant still appeared nervous or distraught and that there was a reasonable basis for continuing [to be] emotionally upset.'" *United States v. Davis*, 577 F.3d 660, 669 (6th Cir. 2009). The Advisory Committee's Note to Rule 803(2) similarly states that "[w]ith respect to the *time element* . . . the standard of measurement is the duration of the state of excitement." Courts have admitted statements made fifteen minutes, *United States v. Golden*, 671 F.2d 369 (10th Cir. 1982), twenty minutes, *United States v. Alexander*, 331 F.3d 116, 122–24 (D.C. Cir. 2003), forty minutes, *State v. Rogers*, 585 S.W.2d 498 (Mo. Ct. App. 1979), and even seventy-five minutes after the event. *United States v. Iron Shell*, 633 F.2d 77 (8th Cir. 1980), *cert. denied*, 450 U.S. 1001 (1981). In addition to the timing, courts consider such factors as the declarant's location at the time of the statement, the declarant's intervening conduct, the declarant's condition at the time of the statement, and whether the statement was a response to a question. *United States v. Merrill*, 484 F.2d 168 (8th Cir.), *cert. denied*, 414 U.S. 1077 (1973); *Jones v. Greer*, 627 F. Supp. 1481, 1492 (C.D. Ill. 1986). The fact that a declarant resorted to curse words can also be an indication of the declarant's excited state. Slovenko, *The Impact of Profanity on Hearsay Evidence*, 1 MED. & LAW 397, 398 (1982).

Another potential factor is the age of the declarant. Many courts have been fairly liberal in admitting statements by children in sexual abuse cases under the excited utterance exception. *See, e.g., United States v. Rivera*, 43 F.3d 1291 (9th Cir. 1995) (affirming admission of statement made by a child the day after the alleged molestation where the child was described as frightened and on the verge of tears at the time of the statement); *United States v. Jennings*, 496 F.3d 344 (4th Cir. 2007), *cert. denied*, 128 S. Ct. 1300 (2008) (where alleged acts of abuse occurred during the course of a long airplane flight an hour or two before the young declarant made hearsay statement after she left the plane, court held that she was still under the stress of excitement cause by the event because she remained afraid the entire time that she was on the same flight with the defendant). Note that admission of such statements in criminal cases may raise serious questions under the Confrontation Clause of the Sixth Amendment, as discussed in Chapter 32.

PROBLEMS

1. **Problem 20-3.** In *Devitt*, Paterson is beaten so brutally that he goes into an immediate coma. Two weeks pass. Paterson is lying in a hospital bed ten miles from his house when he finally regains consciousness. At that instant, he jumps up in bed and blurts out, "Devitt — is he still here? He just attacked me. Please protect me." The prosecutor offers Nurse Holmstrom's testimony about Paterson's first words after regaining consciousness. Does the statement qualify as an excited utterance?

2. **Problem 20-4.** In *Hill*, the plaintiff calls Kathryn Manning as a witness. Ms. Manning testifies that she has a five-year-old daughter, Elise, who witnessed the collision when she was three years old. Ms. Manning will testify that she had her back turned to the intersection when she heard Elyse, in her stroller, scream, "Mommy!! The man in the truck was going so fast." It is well-settled in Morena that to be a competent witness, a person must be five years old at the time of the relevant event. Roe objects on the grounds of "the clear incompetency of the hearsay declarant." What ruling? *See* Annot., 15 A.L.R.4th 1043, 1047–54 (1982). Remember the mystical theory that the event is speaking through the person.

3. **Problem 20-5.** Suppose that the judge overrules the objection in Problem 20-4. You are Ms. Hill's attorney. The judge states, "You can proceed so long as you show that the little girl was in a state of nervous excitement at the time." You must now conduct the direct examination to lay that element of the foundation. What facts would you elicit about Elise's facial expression, tone of voice, volume of speech, pace and coherency of speech, and gestures? Be prepared to conduct this part of the direct examination in class. Notice the tightrope you need to walk as a direct examiner laying this foundation. On the one hand, the event needs to be startling enough to attract and hold the declarant's attention. On the other hand, you do not want the jury to think that the declarant was absolutely hysterical at the time of the statement.

It should be evident by now that with excited utterances, as in the case of admissions, the courts are quite liberal in finding them admissible. In some jurisdictions, these hearsay statements are admissible even though the declarant is unavailable, was unidentified, and would have been incompetent if called to testify as a witness. The courts thus place tremendous faith in the power of stress or excitement to ensure sincerity. Is that faith justified? In one commentator's view, in the past the courts have naively overestimated the length of time during which a startling event can suppress a person's ability to reflect and fabricate. Even a startled person can come to his or her senses and regain that ability in a matter of seconds. "The . . . exception, which tolerates more than a thirty minute gap between the event and the utterance, allows sufficient time for mendacity and calculation of false reports. It does not take much time to lie. . . ." Orenstein, *"My God!": A Feminist Critique of the Excited Utterance Exception to the Hearsay Rule*, 85 CAL. L. REV. 159 (1997). Moreover, even assuming that the event induces a lengthy, truthful frame of mind, witness psychologists have been critical of the excited utterance exception. The following classic article argues that the excited statement may lose more in accuracy of perception and memory than it gains in sincerity.

Hutchins & Slesinger, *Some Observations on the Law of Evidence*
28 COLUM. L. REV. 432, 437–39 (1928)

One need not be a psychologist to distrust an observation made under emotional stress; everybody accepts such statements with mental reservation. M. Gorphe cites the case of an excited witness to a horrible accident who erroneously declared that the coachman deliberately and vindictively ran down a helpless woman. Fiore tells of an emotionally upset man who testified that hundreds were killed in an accident; that he had seen their heads rolling from their bodies. In reality only one man was killed, and five others injured. Another excited gentleman took a pipe for a pistol. Besides these stories from real life, there are psychological experiments which point to the same conclusion. After a battle in a classroom, prearranged by the experimenter but a surprise to the students, each one was asked to write an account of the incident. The testimony of the most upset students was practically worthless, while those who were only slightly stimulated emotionally scored better than those left cold by the incident. Miss Hyde of Nebraska tells of an unpublished experiment, the results of which differed only in the general inaccuracy of all accounts, regardless of the amount of emotion generated.[32] The conclusion drawn from these, and other similar experiments, is that "emotion may virtually hold connected perception in abeyance so that the subject has only isolated sensations to remember instead of a logically connected unit perception."

That participants, as well as bystanders,[35] have their perceptions clouded by strong emotions will not be doubted. When a carriage containing the inevitable psychologist upset, that worthy gentleman amused himself and his companions by taking depositions while they awaited assistance. He had no known reality to check their stories against, but it was obvious that if any one was right, all the rest were wrong. That even trained observers are fallible is well brought out in an editorial in the *New York World* in which several accounts of newspaper reports of the striking of Kerensky on his recent visit to America are printed. Though the reporters were all experts, and sitting close to the platform, each one told a different story of what must have been a fairly simple event.[37]

---

[32] The amount, or presence of any emotion at all presents another interesting problem. Syz, *Observations on the Unreliability of Subjective Reports of Emotional Reactions*[,] (1920) 17 BRIT. JOUR. PSYCH. Gen. Sect. 119-26 reports the following. His subjects were hooked up to a psychogalvanometer capable of recording the electrical change which takes place in one under emotional stress. Then a list of words was given, and they were asked to report those words which caused in them an emotional feeling. Their reports and the galvanometer readings were not in accord. They reported emotion to conventional words like mother, father, etc., whereas they registered emotion with entirely different ones.

[35] It will be remembered that some courts make a distinction between the two.

[37] These are descriptions of the manner in which the young woman struck her blow:

WORLD: "Slashed him viciously across the cheek with her gloves."

NEWS: "Struck him on the left cheek with the bouquet."

AMERICAN: "Dropped her flowers and slapped him in the face with her gloves."

TIMES: "Slapped his face vigorously with her gloves three times."

HERALD TRIBUNE: "Beat him on the face and head . . . a half-dozen blows."

EVENING WORLD: Struck him across the face "several times."

MIRROR: Struck him a single time.

POST: "Vigorously and accurately slapped him." And this is what happened next:

AMERICAN: Kerensky "reeled back."

EVENING WORLD: "He stood unmoved."

NEWS: "He stepped back, maintaining a calm pose."

WORLD: He stood still, but used his arms to "wave back his friends."

The result of these observations is a dilemma. From the point of view of subjective veracity, the speed the courts demand does not necessarily guarantee truth. And from the standpoint of objective accuracy, emotion is little better. If a speedy reaction means nothing without the aid of a stopwatch, an emotional reaction means nothing without eliminating the emotion. What the emotion gains by way of overcoming the desire to lie, it loses by impairing the declarant's power of observation. On the one hand, if reflective self-interest has not had a chance to operate because of emotional stress, then the statement should be excluded because of the probable inaccuracy of observation. On the other, if little emotion is involved, clearly a very short time is sufficient to allow reflective self-interest to assume full sway. On that basis there would seem to be no reason for this hearsay exception. In fact, the emphasis should be all the other way. On psychological grounds, the rule might very well read: Hearsay is inadmissible, especially (not except) if it be a spontaneous exclamation.

NOTES

1. More modern commentators generally concur with Hutchins and Slesinger. *See* Levine & Tapp, *The Psychology of Criminal Identification: The Gap from* Wade *to* Kirby, 121 U. Pa. L. Rev. 1079 (1973). Witnesses to traumatic, startling events are particularly unreliable. *Id.* Although hearsay exceptions such as this one have "stressed the element of sincerity, . . . [i]t is believed to be the common experience of attorneys in the trial of cases, when facts are not accurately reported, that witnesses are more often found to be mistaken than committing perjury." Ladd, *The Hearsay We Admit*, 5 Okla. L. Rev. 271, 286 (1952).

Professors Levine and Tapp note, however, that it is a mistake to generalize that excitement invariably distorts perception. Levine & Tapp, *supra*, at 1098. Although great excitement tends to produce hysteria and distortion, moderate stress seems actually to improve the witness's attention without great distortion. *Id.* Indeed, the Hutchins and Slesinger excerpt above notes this phenomenon, stating that "those who were only slightly stimulated emotionally scored better than those left cold by the incident." Would it be judicially manageable for the courts to administer a hearsay exception purporting to admit only statements made under "moderate" stress?

2. The Hutchins and Slesinger article is not only the leading secondary authority on this topic, but also happens to be one of the very first authorities cited in the Advisory Committee's Note to Rule 803. Moreover, as previously stated, the Committee opted for the more conservative view restricting this hearsay exception to statements "relating to" the startling event. Some commentators have criticized several of the Rule 803 exceptions on the ground that they leave intact the common

---

HERALD TRIBUNE: He stood still, with his arms "thrown back."

JOURNAL: "He reeled."

POST: "He remained unmoved."

MIRROR: "He reeled from the blow. His supporters were stemmed by a handful of royalists. Fists flew; noses ran red; shirts and collars were torn."

law misconceptions about the relative importance of the memory and sincerity factors. Stewart, *Perception, Memory, and Hearsay: A Criticism of Present Law and the Proposed Federal Rules of Evidence*, 1970 UTAH. L. REV. 1. However, the text of Rule 803(2) and the accompanying Note suggests that "the statutory framework of Article VIII . . . directs courts to" place greater stress in the memory factor in deciding whether to admit hearsay. Imwinkelried, *The Importance of the Memory Factor in Analyzing the Reliability of Hearsay Testimony: A Lesson Slowly Learnt — and Quickly Forgotten*, 41 FLA. L. REV. 215, 229 (1989).

3. Present Sense Impressions

Like the excited utterance exception, the exception for present sense impressions is traceable to the res gestae concept. In the case of excited utterances, the idea is that event inspires spontaneity, guaranteeing sincerity. Under the present sense impression exception, contemporaneity substitutes for spontaneity. Professor Thayer argued that the courts should treat contemporaneity and spontaneity as separate, alternative methods of demonstrating reliability. Thayer, *Bedingfield's Case-Declarations as a Part of the Res Gestae*, 15 AM. L. REV. 1 (1881). In contrast, Wigmore stressed spontaneity to the virtual exclusion of contemporaneity. Following Wigmore's lead, the courts long ignored contemporaneity. The contemporaneity of the statement eliminated doubts about the quality of the hearsay declarant's memory. However, as we have seen, the conventional wisdom at common law was that the sincerity factor was far more important than the memory factor. Since there appeared to be no affirmative guarantee of the sincerity of a contemporaneous statement, the overwhelming majority of courts refused to admit such statements. Comment, *The Present Sense Impression Exception to the Hearsay Rule: Federal Rule of Evidence 803(1)*, 81 DICK. L. REV. 347, 351 (1977).

It was left to Professor Morgan to resurrect Thayer's theory. The theory first persuaded a few jurisdictions to adopt contemporaneous statements as a common law exception. *See, e.g., Houston Oxygen Co. v. Davis*, 139 Tex. 1, 161 S.W.2d 474 (1942). These cases eventually led to the Advisory Committee's decision to include the exception in Federal Rule of Evidence 803. The committee stated its decision emphatically by making the exception the very first provision in the rule:

> The following are not excluded by the hearsay rule, even though the declarant is available as a witness:
>
> (1)   Present sense impression. A statement describing or explaining an event or condition made while the declarant was perceiving the event or condition, or immediately thereafter.

Citing the Hutchins and Slesinger article, the Committee deliberately opted for what was undeniably a minority view at common law.

As in the case of the excited utterance doctrine, the foundation is designed to create an inference of reliability. First, the statement must be based on personal knowledge, which addresses the issue of the declarant's **perception.** *Bemis v. Edwards*, 45 F.3d 1369, 1373 (9th Cir. 1995). If the declarant has experienced some event or condition firsthand, Rule 803(1) permits the declarant to describe the event or condition. In contrast, the language of California Evidence Code § 1241 is much more restrictive, limiting admissible declarations to statements about the "conduct of the declarant." To be sure, the restriction strengthens the inference of accurate perception: the declarant is less likely to be mistaken about her own conduct than about the acts of other persons and objects caught up in the same event. But it is questionable whether that incremental increase in trustworthiness is worth the cost of excluding those statements that fall outside California's more limited exception.

The doctrine also contains a rigorous guarantee of the quality of the declarant's **memory.** In other words, "immediately thereafter" is a much stricter timing requirement than that under the excited utterance exception. On this timing issue, the California Evidence Code takes an even more conservative position, requiring that the declarant speak "while the declarant was engaged in such conduct." In sum, although the outer limit for excited utterances is usually a matter of hours, statements admitted as present sense impressions must ordinarily be made within a matter of minutes after the event. *E.g., Miller v. Crown Amusements, Inc.*, 821 F. Supp. 703 (S.D. Ga. 1993) (two minutes); *Hynes v. Coughlin*, 79 F.3d 285, 294 (2d Cir. 1996) ("delay of 15 to 45 minutes 'hardly qualifies as immediately'"). Calls to 911 frequently qualify when the caller phones during an event or immediately after the event occurs. *Bemis v. Edwards*, 45 F.3d 1369 (9th Cir. 1995); *Miller v. Crown Amusements, Inc.*, 821 F. Supp. 703 (S.D. Ga. 1993).

As an additional check on the declarant's perception and a guarantee of sincerity, Thayer argued that one of the conditions of admissibility should be that the witness on the stand also observed the event. Thayer, *supra*, at 83, 107 (1881). Subsequent commentators concurred. Comment, *Spontaneous Exclamations in the Absence of a Startling Event*, 46 U. Colo. L. Rev. 430, 439 (1946). At common law, most courts regarded the testifying witness's observer status as an element of the foundation. Note that Rule 803(1) makes no mention of any requirement for a corroborating witness. Do you think that the requirement survive the adoption of the Federal Rules?

PROBLEMS

1.   **Problem 20-6.** In *Hill*, three blocks before colliding with the plaintiff's car, Worker passed Mr. Grimm's car. As Worker's car passed, Grimm swerved to the right and said to his passenger, Ms. Fowler, "That jerk isn't looking where he's driving. He's goin' too fast, and he's not even all the way in his lane." At the time of his statement, Grimm was speaking in a matter-of-fact tone although he seemed a bit angry. At trial, could Ms. Fowler testify to Grimm's statement? *See Houston Oxygen Co. v. Davis*, 139 Tex. 1, 161 S.W.2d 474, 476–77 (1942). Could she do so in California under Evidence Code § 1241:

Evidence of a statement is not made inadmissible by the hearsay rule if the statement:

(a)   Is offered to explain, qualify, or make understandable conduct of the declarant; and

(b)   Was made while the declarant was engaged in such conduct.

Roe objects that Grimm's statement refers to "Worker's conduct, not his own." Suppose that at the end of his statement, Grimm added, "If I hadn't swerved, that jerk would have hit us."

2.   **Problem 20-7.** In Problem 20-6, suppose that Ms. Fowler was not in Grimm's car when Worker's car passed but instead was talking to him on his cell phone. Imagine further that Grimm recited to Ms. Fowler the license number and description of the speeding car. Does Grimm's remark qualify as a present sense impression? See *Miller v. Crown Amusements, Inc.*, 821 F. Supp. 703 (S.D. Ga. 1993) (911 call).

3.   **Problem 20-8.** Suppose that Mr. Hill also sues Roe for the damage his car sustained in the collision. At trial, attempting to prove the extent of his property damage, he testifies that he took the car to a local mechanic and stood by while the mechanic inspected the car. Immediately after the inspection, the mechanic told Mr. Hill that it would cost $3,325 to repair the damage. Roe's attorney objects that the mechanic's statement is inadmissible hearsay. What ruling? Does Rule 803(1) apply to statements of opinion? *See Makuc v. American Honda Motor Co.*, 835 F.2d 389, 392 (1st Cir. 1987). Would it make a difference if the mechanic reduced the statement to writing and handed it to Mr. Hill? *Phoenix Mut. Life Ins. Co. v. Adams*, 828 F. Supp. 379, 389 (D.S.C. 1993), *aff'd*, 30 F.3d 554 (4th Cir. 1994).

4.   Declarations of Bodily Condition

The next set of exceptions concerns statements by a declarant about his or her state of mind or body. The exceptions for statements of state of mind and body, like excited utterances and present sense impressions, also derive from the res gestae theory but differ in this important way: Whereas the latter two types of statements relate to external reality, the exceptions for declarations of bodily and mental condition concern statements that speak to an internal reality — a sensation or state of mind that the declarant experiences.

The Federal Rules of evidence group these exceptions under the following two rules:

Rule 803.

The following are not excluded by the rule against hearsay rule, regardless of whether the declarant is available as a witness:

(3) Then-existing mental, emotional, or physical condition. A statement of the declarant's then-existing state of mind (such as motive, intent, or plan), or emotional, sensory, or physical condition (such as mental feeling, pain, or bodily health), but not including a statement of memory or belief to prove the fact remembered or believed unless it relates to the validity or terms of the declarant's will.

(4) Statement Made for Medical Diagnosis or Treatment. A statement that:

(A) is made for — and is reasonably pertinent to — medical diagnosis or treatment; and

(B) describes medical history; past or present symptoms or sensations; their inception; or their general cause.

As with the other exceptions we have examined, in deciding whether to admit evidence under one of these hearsay exceptions the basic policy question is how important cross-examination of the declarant would be to allow the fact finder to assess the declarant's testimonial qualities of perception, memory, narration, and sincerity. In the case of statements of bodily condition, especially present condition, there is rarely any doubt about perception, memory, or narration. The declarant is usually in the best possible position to "perceive" whether she is experiencing pain or some other sensation. Furthermore, when the declaration relates to present bodily condition there is no serious question about the quality of memory. And the concepts of physical conditions such as pain are so elementary that there is little concern about the declarant's narrative ability.

On the other hand, there can sometimes be grave doubts about the testimonial quality of sincerity. More often than not, these exceptions are invoked in personal injury litigation and the plaintiff (the injured party) may have already begun a personal injury lawsuit — or at least foreseen that possibility — at the time she made the statement. Thus there is the potential temptation to lie. Evidence law deals with this danger by limiting the admission of these declarations to circumstances in which the risk of insincerity is thought to be lowest. To identify those circumstances, courts carefully scrutinize two related factors: (1) the purpose for which the declarant made the statement; and (2) the person to whom the declarant made the statement. This section analyzes several types of statements of mental or bodily condition — declarations of present bodily condition, statements of past bodily condition, and assertions about the cause of the bodily condition — with a view to these two factors.

a.   Declarations of Present Bodily Condition

Common sense indicates that concerns about perception, memory, and narration are relatively insubstantial when the declarant purports to describe a physical condition he or she is then experiencing. For that reason, a hearsay exception for such declarations evolved relatively early in the common law of evidence. *See Aveson v. Kinnaird*, 6 East 188, 102 Eng. Rep. 1258 (K.B. 1805); *Caspermeyer v. Florsheim Shoe Store Co.*, 313 S.W.2d 198 (Mo. Ct. App. 1958). The Federal Rules of Evidence codify the exception in Rule 803(3), as noted above.

At some point, however, the risk of insincerity can become intolerably high. Suppose that the plaintiff in the *Hill* case was examined by a physician hired solely for the purpose of testifying at trial. The purpose of this examination prompts much more serious doubts about the truthfulness of any statements that Ms. Hill may make to the doctor about her physical condition. At common law, many courts drew the line at this situation and refused to admit such statements as substantive evidence. At least until recently, this attitude was the prevailing view in the United States. However, as you can see from the language of Rule 803(4), the Federal Rules of Evidence have abandoned this restriction and the rule now permits statements made to a physician for medical diagnosis or treatment without regard to whether that physician has been hired with a possible view to litigation.

PROBLEMS

1.   **Problem 20-9.** In *Hill*, three weeks after the collision the plaintiff suffered a spontaneous miscarriage. There was so little tissue that the pathologist could not determine the age of the fetus. Ms. Hill claims that she was pregnant before the accident and that the accident caused the miscarriage. At trial, she calls Ms. Windsong, a neighbor. Ms. Windsong is prepared to testify that one week before the accident Ms. Hill told her that she "felt" pregnant. Roe objects on hearsay grounds. What ruling? *See People v. Wright*, 167 Cal. 1, 8, 138 P. 349, 352 (1914). Note that Rule 803(3) refers to "sensation, *or* physical condition" (emphasis added).

2.   **Problem 20-10.** Ms. Hill calls Dr. Nordstrom as a witness. Nordstrom is prepared to testify that during a physical examination one month after the accident Ms. Hill said she was still experiencing "excruciating pain." Before the judge allows Nordstrom to give this testimony, Roe takes Nordstrom on *voir dire* examination as follows:

Q: Doctor, isn't it true that you did not prescribe any pain-killing drugs for Ms. Hill?

A: Yes.

Q: Or any medication at all for that matter?

A: Yes.

Q: Did you order her to take physical therapy at any local hospital?

A: No.

Q: Did you require her to do physical therapy at your office?

A: No. I suggested some exercises to her when she asked, but I didn't order her.

Q: Your Honor, I renew my objection on the ground that the plaintiff consulted this witness solely for trial preparation.

Morena subscribes to the common law view that statements made to physicians consulted only for testimony fall outside the hearsay exception. What ruling under Moreno law? Under FRE 803(4)?

b.   Past Bodily Condition

Statements of the patient's past symptoms are usually styled "case history." Traditionally, most courts balked at allowing these statements as substantive proof. *Martin v. P. H. Hanes Knitting Co.*, 189 N.C. 644, 127 S.E. 688 (1925); Younger, *Statements of Past Physical Condition as an Exception to the Rule Against Hearsay*, 19 N.Y.L.F. 777 (1974). The reluctance to admit these statements is understandable. The risks of misrecollection and insincerity are higher here: the declarant is no longer speaking about a condition she is then experiencing, and the doctor or other medical professional cannot immediately verify the declarant's claimed symptoms.

In limited circumstances, however, some courts carved out a common law exception to the general rule of exclusion. One of the landmark opinions is the *Meany* case.

MEANEY v. UNITED STATES
112 F.2d 538 (2d Cir. 1940)

L. HAND, CIRCUIT JUDGE.

This is an appeal from a judgment, entered upon the verdict of a jury, dismissing a petition in an action to recover upon a policy of war risk insurance. The insured was mustered out on December 31, 1918, and the policy lapsed on January 30, 1919; he died of pulmonary tuberculosis on July 6, 1922, and the question was whether he was permanently and totally disabled when the policy lapsed. He had consulted one physician at some time, not definitely fixed in 1919, and another in December 1920, who found that he had contracted tuberculosis, and that it was already "moderately advanced." By April of 1921 the disease had so far developed that he had to go to a sanatorium, where he stayed till January 1922, only six months before his death. The only error we need consider was a ruling, made during the examination of the physician who had first examined him in December, 1920. This witness said that he had taken care of the insured both at that time and after he came back from the sanatorium; and he was allowed to testify as to what he found on his several examinations, but the judge refused to let him say what the insured had told him of the "history of the case."

The insured's declarations seem to have been offered as a narrative of his condition; so far as appears they were no part of the basis of the physician's opinion as to his condition; at least they were not offered as such. They were therefore hearsay, and moreover, they did not fall within the generally accepted exception in favor of spontaneous expressions of pain. It is quite true that this exception includes narrative statements as well as mere ejaculations, and that it has been extended to a declaration of present symptoms told by a patient to a physician. The utterances of a patient in the course of his examination, so far as they are spontaneous, may be merely ejaculatory — as when he emits a cry upon palpation — or they may be truly narrative; and it will often be impossible to distinguish rationally between the two; between an inarticulate cry, for example, and a statement such as: "That hurts." The warrant for the admission of both is the same: the lack of opportunity or motive for fabrication upon an unexpected occasion to which the declarant responds immediately, and without reflection. But most of what he tells will not ordinarily be of this kind at all; there may be, and there is in fact, good reason to receive it, but it is a very different reason. A man goes to his physician expecting to recount all that he feels, and often he has with some care searched his consciousness to be sure that he will leave out nothing. If his narrative of present symptoms is to be received as evidence of the facts, as distinguished from mere support for the physician's opinion, these parts of it can only rest upon his motive to disclose the truth because his treatment will in part depend upon what he says. That justification is not necessary in the case of his spontaneous declarations; but it is necessary for those we are now considering.

The same reasoning applies with exactly the same force to a narrative of past symptoms, and so the Supreme Court of Massachusetts, declared obiter in *Roosa v. Boston Loan Co.*, 132 Mass. 439. A patient has an equal motive to speak the truth; what he has felt in the past is as apt to be important in his treatment as what he feels at the moment. Thus, in spite of the dicta in *Northern Pacific R. E. v. Urlin*, *supra* (158 U.S. 271) and *Boston & Albany R. R. v. O'Reilly*, *supra* (158 U.S. 334) that only declarations of present symptoms are competent, several federal courts have seemed not to take the distinction between declarations of present and past symptoms, provided the patient is consulting the physician for treatment, and Professor Wigmore appears to assent. Wigmore, § 1722. It is true that this body of authority is not impressive as such, but it appears to us that if there is to be any consistency in doctrine, either declarations of all symptoms, present or past, should be competent, or only those which fall within the exception for spontaneous utterances. Nobody would choose the second, particularly as the substance of the declarations can usually be got before the jury as parts of the basis on which the physician's opinion was formed. It is indeed always possible that a patient may not really consult his physician for treatment; the consultation may be colorable. The judge has power to prevent an abuse in such cases, and here as elsewhere, when the competency of evidence depends upon a question of fact, his conclusion is final. He must decide before admitting the declarations whether the patient was consulting the physician for treatment and for that alone. Unless he is so satisfied, he must exclude them, though it is true that if he admits them, the defendant may still argue that they are untrustworthy. They will be evidence, but in estimating their truth the jury may have to decide for themselves the very issue on which the judge himself passed before he admitted them; the competency of evidence is always independent of its weight.

We hold that the insured's "history of the case" as narrated to the physician was competent and that its exclusion was error.

Judgment reversed; new trial ordered.

––––––––––

Even after *Meaney* most courts excluded statements of past bodily condition, but some courts admitted the statements when made to a physician for purposes of treatment. Like Judge Hand, these courts reasoned that when the declarant knows that his or her description of past symptoms will affect treatment, this realization is a strong motive for sincerity. The patient realizes that "otherwise, [he or she] may mislead the physician, with disastrous results" to the patient's own health. *Mackey v. Greenview Hosp.*, 587 S.W.2d 249, 254 (Ky. Ct. App. 1979). This motive largely counteracts any doubts about the declarant's sincerity. The "patient's self-interest in promoting the cure of his or her own medical ailments guarantees" the truthfulness of the declaration. *Gong v. Hirsch*, 913 F.2d 1269, 1273 (7th Cir. 1990). As with statements of present bodily condition made to physicians, as discussed above, FRE 803(4) allows statements of past bodily condition based largely on this sincerity rationale.

PROBLEMS

1. **Problem 20-11.** In *Hill*, the plaintiff rode in an ambulance to the hospital immediately after the collision. Just before the end of the ride, she had a brief conversation with the ambulance attendant, Mr. Sullivan. Sullivan asked her to "tell [him] about the accident, so that I get the info to the docs just as soon as we get to the hospital." In response, Ms. Hill told Sullivan that immediately after the collision, she experienced a sharp pain in her abdomen. An abdominal injury is one of the elements of damage she now claims at trial. When Ms. Hill attempts to elicit Sullivan's testimony about her statement, Roe cites *Meaney* as authority that to qualify as a hearsay exception, the statement "must be made directly, personally to a licensed physician." Does *Meaney* support Roe's argument? Would the argument be tenable under Federal Rule of Evidence 803(4)? In its Note to the Rule, the Advisory Committee commented that "[s]tatements to hospital attendants, ambulance drivers, or even members of the family might be included."

2. **Problem 20-12.** Would the result in Problem 20-11 be different if Sullivan had *not* said, "so that I can get the info to the docs. . . ."? Under *Meaney?* Under Federal Rule 803(4)?

3. **Problem 20-13.** After Ms. Hill arrives at the hospital and receives treatment, she hires an attorney, who immediately arranges for a physician, Dr. Stewart, to visit Ms. Hill in the hospital. The attorney tells Dr. Stewart, "I want you to examine her thoroughly with a view to testifying at trial." Ms. Hill tells Dr. Stewart about the abdominal pain she described to the ambulance attendant. At trial, Ms. Hill calls Dr. Stewart to testify about her statement. Roe cites *Meaney* for the proposition that the hearsay exception applies only if the patient consulted the physician for treatment. Consider the significance of the term "diagnosis or" in Rule 803(4). *United States v. Iron Shell*, 633 F.2d 77, 82–85 (8th Cir. 1980), *cert. denied*, 450 U.S. 1001 (1981).

c.   Statements Describing the Cause of the Declarant's Physical Condition

When a physician initially questions a patient, she usually inquires about the cause of a condition as well as the condition's existence. Determining the cause is often the key in diagnosing and prescribing treatment. However, the orthodox view is that the declarant's description of the cause is inadmissible hearsay. Even if the jurisdiction admits case history statements, courts may exclude statements about causation. *Pinter v. Parsekian*, 92 N.J. Super. 392, 223 A.2d 635 (1966); Theis, *The Doctor as Witness: Statements for Purposes of Medical Diagnosis or Treatment*, 10 Loy. U. Chi. L.J. 363, 369 (1979).

The exclusion of these statements is at least defensible. These statements pose numerous probative dangers. First, the quality of the declarant's perception is suspect. The declarant is no longer speaking about an internal reality such as pain; the reference to cause is usually an allusion to an external event such as the collision in *Hill*, and thus we have neither the spontaneity demanded by Rule 803(2) nor the contemporaneity required by Rule 803(1). If the reference is to a past event, there is also a concern about the quality of the declarant's memory. There is similarly doubt about the declarant's narrative ability. When the declarant says that the event "caused" his injuries, did he mean factual cause in the tort sense, or did the words carry the common law connotation of fault? Finally, if litigation was foreseeable, the declarant's sincerity is also suspect. For all these reasons, until recently the courts steadfastly excluded statements about causation. *Hassell v. State*, 607 S.W.2d 529 (Tex. Crim. App. 1980); *Illinois Cent. R.R. v. Sutton*, 42 Ill. 438 (1867).

However, the drafters of Federal Rule of Evidence 803(4) thought otherwise. Note the textual reference to "the inception or general character of the cause or external source." Their reasoning is similar to the reasoning supporting the extension of the hearsay exception to case history declarations: if the patient believes that the physician needs the information in order to treat him, that realization is a sufficient motive for sincerity.

NOTES AND PROBLEMS

1.   Do you agree with the Advisory Committee that the inference of sincerity outweighs the need to cross-examine the declarant about perception, memory, and narration? Remember that statements about causation raise concerns about perception and narration that are absent from case history statements. In *White v. Illinois*, 502 U.S. 346 (1992), writing for the majority, Chief Justice Rehnquist declared: "a statement made in the course of procuring medical services, where the declarant knows that a false statement may cause misdiagnosis or mistreatment, carries special guarantees of credibility that a trier of fact may not think replicated by courtroom testimony." In footnote 8 of his opinion, the Chief Justice remarked that the exception is "widely accepted among the States." *White* involved statements by a very young child to a doctor and an emergency room nurse. Many courts have invoked this exception to justify the introduction of the alleged victim's statements in child abuse prosecutions. Mosteller, *Child Sexual Abuse and Statements for the Purpose of Medical Diagnosis or Treatment*, 67 N.C. L. REV. 257 (1989). Several courts have gone so far as to admit the child's statement identifying the assailant on the theory that the assailant's identity was relevant to treatment. *United States v. George*, 960 F.2d 97, 99–100 (9th Cir. 1992) ("the exact nature and extent of" the victim's psychological injuries "often depend on the identity of the abuser"). When the alleged abuser is a member of the victim's household, the assailant's identity is arguably relevant, at least in the sense that the requisite treatment might include the child's removal from that household. In *State v. Moen*, 309 Or. 45, 786 P.2d 111 (1990), the court extended the exception to a statement by an adult victim. The defendant was charged with murder. Before her death, the victim consulted a physician for depression and despondency. The victim told the physician that she feared that the defendant would kill her. The court admitted the statement under that state's version of Rule 803(4). *See also U.S. v. Bercier*, 506 F.3d 625 (8th Cir. 2007) (in the case of an 18-year-old victim's statement to a medical professional disclosing the identity of the abuser, holding that such statements may be admissible upon the proponent's showing that "(i) the physician made clear to the victim that inquiry into the abuser's identity was essential to diagnosis and treatment, and (ii) 'the victim manifest[ed] such an understanding.'" In this case, such a showing was not made and admission of the statements was therefore error).

2. **Problem 20-14.** When Ms. Hill arrived at the emergency room, she was treated by Dr. Farnsworth. Farnsworth told her, "I can see that you have some first-degree burns on your left foot, Ms. Hill. I'm going to apply some salve immediately." Ms. Hill responded, "Please do it as fast as you can. It hurts like hell. The gas tank exploded, and there were flames everywhere." Would Ms. Hill's reference to the explosion fall within Rule 803(4)?

3. **Problem 20-15.** In addition to her statement in Problem 20-14, Ms. Hill told Dr. Farnsworth, "That idiot driver was going so fast that I never had a chance to avoid the accident. He was going way too fast." What additional difficulties does this statement present under Rule 803(4)? *United States v. Narciso*, 446 F. Supp. 252, 284–85, 288–89 (E.D. Mich. 1977).

5. Declarations of State of Mind

An utterance evidencing state of mind may not be hearsay; the utterance might be nonassertive and thus fall outside the scope of Rule 801(a). But even if it is hearsay, it may nonetheless fall within the exception admitting declarations of state of mind. Like the exception for statements of bodily condition, the "State of Mind" exception admits assertions about internal realities such as the declarant's thoughts and emotions. The case for admitting these assertions appears at least as strong as the case for allowing statements about bodily condition. When the declarant purports to describe his own present state of mind, we have few doubts about the declarant's perception, memory, or narration. And while there may be grounds to suspect the declarant's sincerity, in this setting the suspicions probably carry less weight than they do when they relate to the sincerity of a statement about bodily condition. In addition, there is a greater need to admit statements of mental condition as compared to physical conditions. A physician may be able to determine whether the patient has the physical symptoms to account for the pain the patient claims to be experiencing, but the psychiatrist has less reliable means of testing the genuineness of a claim of depression. The greater need for the evidence is generally thought to justify the risk of the declarant's insincerity.

As in the case of statements of bodily condition, the probative danger — and consequently the hearsay analysis — varies depending on the type of assertion and its use. We shall now consider the four major situations typically encountered.

a. Declarations of Present State of Mind Used to Prove State of Mind

There is virtually unanimous agreement that if the declarant's state of mind is relevant, the declarant's assertion of her then existing state of mind is admissible. The admissibility of such statements was recognized at common law, and many legislatures have sanctioned their admissibility. In the words of California Evidence Code § 1250(a)(1), an assertion of present state of mind is admissible when state of mind is "itself an issue." As noted above, Federal Rule of Evidence 803(3) sets out the federal version of the exception, which encompasses "statement[s] of the declarant's then-existing state of mind (such as motive, intent, or plan) or emotional . . . condition (such as mental feeling . . .)."

In this situation, there is little need for cross-examination at trial. The declarant is speaking about present state of mind, removing any doubt about perception or memory. Further, if the declarant is referring to a simple concept such as joy or depression, there is rarely any reason to suspect the declarant's narrative ability. Further, since the declarant is referring to present state of mind, the hearer can determine whether the declarant's nonverbal conduct matches the asserted state of mind, which provides some corroboration of the statement. If the declarant professes depression while striking a broad smile and the hearer subsequently becomes a witness, questioning the witness about the declarant's behavior will sufficiently impeach the claim of depression.

Given this reasoning, most courts admit declarations of present state of mind if the declarant's state of mind is relevant under the substantive law. For example, in *Hill*, one of the issues conditioning Roe's liability is whether Worker was acting within the scope of his employment at the time of the accident. Under the substantive law of agency, the court can consider Worker's subjective intention in determining this issue. Suppose that a few blocks before reaching the scene of the collision Mr. Worker picked up a hitchhiker, Ms. Randall. A few moments before the collision, Worker told Randall, "I've really got to move it out. See that package in the back seat? Orders from the boss — I've got to get that package 'cross town within the next hour or else." Worker makes the statement almost simultaneously with the collision, and Ms. Hill would have little difficulty persuading the trial judge to admit the statement to prove Worker's intention at the time of the accident.

NOTES AND PROBLEMS

1.   **Problem 20-16.** Suppose that Worker picked up Ms. Randall an hour before the time of the collision. He makes the statement to her that he made in the original hypothetical. Does the timing of the statement preclude its admission? How does Federal Rule of Evidence 401 figure into your analysis of this problem? See the discussion of the concept of continuity of state of mind in 2 C. McCormick, Handbook of The Law of Evidence § 274, at 270–71 (6th ed. 2006).

2.   **Problem 20-17.** An hour after the accident, Worker is speaking with Ms. Randall. He says, "I'm in such trouble. The boss is going to kill me for getting involved in that terrible accident, and he's also going to jump all over me because of the package. Remember that package on the back seat? I've still got to get that to the print shop before the close of business today, or I'll be in big time trouble with my boss." Ms. Hill calls Randall to testify to Worker's statement, but Roe objects that the statement is inadmissible "because it came after the collision." What result?

3.   In applying the concept of continuity of state of mind, what factors should you consider in addition to the time lapse? Suppose that the police questioned Worker before he had his conversation with Ms. Randall in Problem 20-17. Would it make a difference if the police officer suggested to Worker that Roe's insurance policy would cover the accident only if Worker were driving in the scope of employment? What role would Federal Rule of Evidence 403 play in the analysis? *See Colasanto v. Life Ins. Co. of North America*, 100 F.3d 203, 212–13 (1st Cir. 1996) (there was an intervening, bitter fight between the event and the letter describing the event).

b. Declarations of Present State of Mind Used to Prove Subsequent Conduct

A declaration of present state of mind can give rise to more than one inference. As we have seen, under the substantive law the relevant fact may be the declarant's state of mind at the time. If so, we can use the declaration to establish that state of mind. However, if the asserted state of mind is a plan or intention to engage in future conduct, we can also use the assertion as some evidence that the declarant later carried out the plan or intention. Under Federal Rule of Evidence 401, the asserted intention is logically relevant for that purpose: the fact that a person plans to perform an act tends to increase the likelihood that she subsequently did perform the act. Notice that Federal Rule of Evidence 803(3) expressly refers to "motive, intent, or plan" as examples of state of mind. The California Evidence Code is even more explicit: section 1250(a)(2) announces that an assertion of plan is admissible as evidence to "prove or explain [the subsequent] acts or conduct of the declarant." Whether the proponent is attempting to prove the state of mind itself or the subsequent conduct, we invoke the same hearsay exception. In both situations, the immediate inference from the declaration is the existence of the state of mind. The difference is that in the context of proving subsequent conduct, we must draw a further inference from the state of mind to the ensuing behavior of the declarant.

One of the leading cases is a famous decision by the Supreme Court.

MUTUAL LIFE INSURANCE CO. v. HILLMON
145 U.S. 285 (1892)

Justice Gray delivered the opinion of the Court.

[Action by Sallie E. Hillmon to recover on life insurance policies of her husband, John W. Hillmon. The crucial question disputed at trial was the identity of the deceased. One Walters had disappeared, and strong evidence had been introduced showing that the body alleged to have been Hillmon's was in fact the body of Walters, who allegedly had been killed by Hillmon with a view to enabling his wife to recover upon the policies. To show the probability that the body alleged to be Hillmon was Walters, letters were introduced from Walters to his sister and fiancé, which expressed the intention of leaving Wichita with Hillmon for a trip to "Colorado or parts unknown."]

There is, however, one question of evidence so important and so likely to arise upon another trial, that it is proper to express an opinion upon it.

This question is of the admissibility of the letters written by Walters on the first days of March, 1879, which were offered in evidence by the defendants, and excluded by the court. In order to determine the competency of these letters, it is important to consider the state of the case when they were offered to be read.

The matter chiefly contested at the trial was the death of John W. Hillmon, the insured; and that depended upon the question whether the body found at Crooked Creek on the night of March 18, 1879, was his body, or the body of Walters.

Much conflicting evidence had been introduced as to the identity of the body. The plaintiff had also introduced evidence that Hillmon and one Brown left Wichita in Kansas on or about March 5, 1879, and traveled together through Southern Kansas in search of a site for a cattle ranch, and that on the night of March 18 while they were in camp at Crooked Creek, Hillmon was accidentally killed, and that his body was taken thence and buried. The defendants had introduced evidence, without objection, that Walters left his home and his betrothed in Iowa in March, 1878, and was afterwards in Kansas until March, 1879; that during that time he corresponded regularly with his family and his betrothed; that the letters received from him were one received by his betrothed on March 3, and postmarked at Wichita March 2, and one received by his sister about March 4 or 5, and dated at Wichita a day or two before; and that he had not been heard from since.

The evidence that Walters was at Wichita on or before March 5, and had not been heard from since, together with the evidence to identify as his the body found at Crooked Creek on March 18, tended to show that he went from Wichita to Crooked Creek between those dates. Evidence that just before March 5 he had the intention of leaving Wichita with Hillmon would tend to corroborate the evidence already admitted, and to show that he went from Wichita to Crooked Creek with Hillmon. Letters from him to his family and his betrothed were the natural, if not the only attainable evidence of his intention.

The letters should have been admitted. A man's state of mind or feeling can only be manifested to others by countenance, attitude or gesture, or by sounds or words, spoken or written. The nature of the fact to be proved is the same, and evidence of its proper tokens is equally competent to prove it, whether expressed by aspect or conduct, by voice or pen. When the intention to be proved is important only as qualifying an act, its connection with that act must be shown, in order to warrant the admission of declarations of the intention. But whenever the intention is of itself a distinct and material fact in a chain of circumstances, it may be proved by contemporaneous oral or written declarations of the party.

The existence of a particular intention in a certain person at a certain time being a material fact to be proved, evidence that he expressed that intention at that time is as direct evidence of the fact, as his own testimony that he then had that intention would be. After his death, there can hardly be any other way of proving it; and while he is still alive, his own memory of his state of mind at a former time is no more likely to be clear and true than a bystander's recollection of what he then said, and is less trustworthy than letters written by him at the very time and under circumstances precluding a suspicion of misrepresentation.

The letters in question were competent, not as narratives of facts communicated to the writer by another, nor yet as proof that he actually went away from Wichita, but as evidence that, shortly before the time when other evidence tended to show that he went away he had the intention of going, and of going with Hillmon, which made it more probable both that he did go and that he went with Hillmon, than if there had been no proof of such intention. In view of the mass of conflicting testimony introduced upon the question whether it was the body of Walters that was found in Hillmon's camp, this evidence might properly influence the jury in determining that question.

The rule applicable to this case has been thus stated by this court: "Wherever the bodily or mental feelings of an individual are material to be proved, the usual expressions of such feelings are original and competent evidence. Those expressions are the natural reflexes of what it might be impossible to show by other testimony, this may be necessary to set the facts thus developed in their true light, and to give them their proper effect. As independent, explanatory or corroborative evidence, it is often indispensable to the due administration of justice. Such declarations are regarded as verbal acts, and are as competent as any other testimony, when relevant to the issue. Their truth or falsity is an inquiry for the jury." *Ins. Co. v. Mosley*, 75 U.S. 8 Wall 397, 404, 405.

In accordance with this rule, a bankrupt's declarations, at or before the time of leaving or staying away from home, as to his reason for going abroad, have always been held by the English courts to be competent, in an action by his assignees against a creditor, as evidence that his departure was with intent to defraud his creditors, and therefore an act of bankruptcy. *Bateman v. Bailey*, 5 TR 512.

Upon an indictment of one Hunter for the murder of one Armstrong at Camden, the Court of Errors and Appeals of New Jersey unanimously held that Armstrong's oral declarations to his son at Philadelphia, on the afternoon before the night of the murder, as well as a letter written by him at the same time and place to his wife, each stating that he was going with Hunter to Camden on business, were rightly admitted in evidence. Chief Justice Beasley said: "In the ordinary course of things, it was the usual information that a man about leaving home would communicate, for the convenience of his family, the information of his friends, or the regulation of his business. At the time it was given, such declarations could, in the nature of things, mean harm to no one, he who uttered them was bent on no expedition of mischief or wrong, and the attitude of affairs at the time entirely explodes the idea that such utterances were intended to serve any purpose but that of which they were obviously designed. If it be said that such notice of an intention of leaving home could have been given without introducing it in the name of Mr. Hunter, the obvious answer to the suggestion, I think, is that a reference to the companion who is to accompany the person leaving is as natural a part of the transaction as is any other incident or quality of it. If it is legitimate to show by a man's own declarations that he left his home to be gone a week, or for a certain destination, which seems incontestible, why may it not be proved in the same way that a designated person was to bear him company? At the time the words were uttered or written, they imported no wrong doing to any one, and the reference to the companion who was to go with him was nothing more, as matters then stood, than an indication of an additional circumstance of his going. If it was in the ordinary train of events for this man to leave word or to state where he was going, it seems to me it was equally so for him to say with whom he was going." *Hunter v. State*, 40 N.J.L. 495, 534, 536–538.

Upon principle and authority, therefore, we are of opinion that the two letters were competent evidence of the intention of Walters at the time of writing them, which was a material fact bearing upon the question in controversy; and that for the exclusion of these letters, as well as for the undue restriction of the defendants' challenges, the verdicts must be set aside, and a new trial had.

Judgment reversed, and case remanded to the Circuit Court, with directions to set aside the verdict and to order a new trial.

At first blush, *Hillmon* seems innocuous enough. We are interested in the declarant's conduct, he had earlier professed an intention to engage in the conduct, and the profession certainly passes muster under Rule 401 as logically relevant. But note the Court's statement that the letters were admissible evidence both that he did go and that he went with Hillmon. The language suggests that the insurer could use Walters' statement of intent as evidence not only of the subsequent conduct of Walters, but also that of Hillmon.

That suggestion has triggered a burning controversy. In one commentary on the *Hillmon* case, Professor Maguire condemned the suggestion:

> Even if Walters was planning to travel with Hillmon, how would we prove that Hillmon was willing to and did accept him as a companion? By Walters' hearsay declaration? Hardly, unless we drill a new and unusually deep hole in the hearsay rule. It is not customary to accept one man's extra-judicial assertions as evidence of another's mental state.

Maguire, *The Hillmon Case — Thirty-Three Years After*, 38 Harv. L. Rev. 709, 717 (1925). In his dissent in *People v. Alcalde*, 24 Cal. 2d 177, 148 P.2d 627 (1944), Justice Traynor echoed this view. Justice Traynor argued that "[a] declaration as to what one person intended to do, however, cannot safely be accepted as evidence of what another probably did." *Id.* at 189–90, 148 P.2d at 633. When one person on the stand attempts to testify directly to another person's state of mind, in the view of many judges the testimony is objectionable as improper lay speculation and lacking in personal knowledge. Fed. R. Evid. 602, 701.

Unfortunately, the adoption of the Federal Rules of Evidence has not laid this controversy to rest. As in the case of the dispute over the existence of a corroboration requirement under Rule 803(1), the root of the problem is ambiguous legislative history. In *United States v. Pheaster*, 544 F.2d 353 (9th Cir. 1976), *cert. denied sub nom. Inciso v. United States*, 429 U.S. 1099 (1977), the Ninth Circuit Court of Appeals stated that Justice Traynor's position "is definitely the minority view, stated primarily in dicta and dissent." *Id.* at 380 n.18. According to the court, most jurisdictions interpret *Hillmon* as permitting the use of the declarant's statement as proof of the third party's subsequent conduct. The court pointed out that, in its note to Rule 803(3), the Advisory Committee asserted that "[t]he rule of . . . *Hillmon* . . . is . . . left undisturbed." *Id.* at 379. The court construed the note as approving "the prevailing common law position" that *Hillmon* allows such a statement to be used to prove the third party's conduct as well as that of the declarant. *Id.* at 379–80. However, the court conceded that the report of the House Committee on the Judiciary takes a "significantly different" approach. *Id.* at 380. That report states:

> [T]he Committee intends that the Rule be construed to limit the doctrine of . . . *Hillmon* . . . so as to render statements of intent by a declarant admissible only to prove his future conduct, not the future conduct of another person. H.R. Rep. No. 93-650.

Id. at 379.

NOTES AND PROBLEMS

1. How would you resolve the seeming conflict between the Advisory Committee Note and the House Report? The House Committee is an agency of Congress. However, the Advisory Committee Notes were widely circulated with the text of the proposed rules. Jurists such as Justice Scalia and Judge Easterbrook have questioned the assumption that most legislators take the time to familiarize themselves with the contents of committee reports. Paradoxically, the Note may therefore be better evidence of congressional intent than the Report!

The House Report specifically addresses the question of the propriety of using a declarant's statement to prove a third party's subsequent conduct. Is the Advisory Committee Note as explicit? Although a number of jurisdictions allow a wide-open opportunity for a declarant not only to declare her intent but also to implicate the intention of another person, it appears that the House Report has carried the day in many state courts. For example, consider the comment to TENN. R. EVID. 803(3): "The Commission contemplates that only the declarant's conduct, *not some third party's conduct*, is provable by this hearsay exception." *See generally* Devall, Comment, *Whether Federal Rule of Evidence 803(3) Should Be Amended to Exclude Statements Offered to Prove the Subsequent Conduct of a Nondeclarant*, 78 TUL. L. REV. 911 (2004) (collecting state cases).

In the federal courts, there is a split of authority on the question. The Ninth Circuit, following *Pheaster*, has rejected the House Committee limitation on the *Hillmon* doctrine and thus allows statements of intent to do a future act together with a third party as evidence that the declarant did the act with the third party (and hence as evidence of what the third party did). In contrast, the First and Fourth Circuits have adopted the narrower reading of Rule 803(3) and do not permit inferences of third-party behavior. The Second Circuit has developed a compromise position, whereby it permits the statements so long as there is corroboration of the third party's action by independent evidence. *See U.S. v. Best*, 219 F.3d 192, 197–99 (2d Cir. 2000).

2. As a matter of policy, which view do you prefer? Was Walters' plan absolutely irrelevant to prove Hillmon's conduct and, therefore, inadmissible under Rule 401? Or when Justice Traynor remarked that Walters' declaration "cannot safely be treated as evidence" of Hillmon's conduct, was he voicing a different concern? Is the inference directly from Walters' declaration to Hillmon's conduct, or is there an implicit, intermediate inference about Hillmon's state of mind and intention? If Walters mounted the witness stand, would we allow him to opine about Hillmon's state of mind? If so, under what circumstances? Reread Federal Rule 701. In the past, the courts have focused on the hearsay issue, but perhaps the decisive doctrine is the lay opinion rule.

3. Suppose that the jurisdiction in question subscribes to Justice Traynor's view that the declarant's statement of intent is admissible only for the limited purpose of proving the declarant's own subsequent conduct. And suppose further that the declarant's statement expressed an intent to do something with another person —

for example, "I'm going to dinner tonight with Angelo." If you were the trial judge, what kind of limiting instruction would you give the jury about the testimony describing the declarant's statement? During closing argument, what could the proponent of the testimony say about the declarant's statement?

4.   Recently, law professor Marianne Wesson and biological anthropologist Dennis Van Gerven attempted to answer once and for all the question of who was killed at Crooked Creek. They were granted permission to disinter the body buried in Hillmon's grave and they obtained DNA material from living descendants of both Hillmon and Walters. Unfortunately, because of water damage there was no recoverable DNA in the grave. However, Van Gerven used an alternative technique of photo comparison and reported his opinion that the corpse indeed was that of Mr. Hillmon. *See* Dennis Van Gerven, *A Digital Photographic Solution to the Question of Who Lies Buried in Oak Hill Cemetery* (2007), available at http://thehillmoncase. com/results.html. After a lengthy historical investigation, Professor Wesson concluded that the Walters letter at issue in the *Hillmon* case was most likely a fraudulent creation of the defendant insurance companies; she argued that statements admissible under the exception created by the Supreme Court in *Hillmon* are of questionable reliability. *See* Marianne Wesson, *The Hillmon Case, the Supreme Court, and the McGuffin*, in EVIDENCE STORIES (Richard Lempert, ed. 2006).

5.   **Problem 20-18.** In *Devitt*, the prosecutor calls Mr. Sharman, who testifies that he knows the defendant, that he had a conversation with the defendant a few days before the alleged battery, and that the defendant said, "I'm working for a guy named Paterson. He's been bugging me and whining about every little slip-up I make. The next time he gives me some lip, I'm just gonna slug the jerk." The defense counsel objects that the statement is "clearly inadmissible hearsay and too vague as well." What ruling? *United States v. Curtis*, 568 F.2d 643, 645–46 (9th Cir. 1978). Does the prosecutor have to resort to the admission exemption to introduce this statement?

c.   Declarations of Present Memory to Prove Past, Remembered Events

Federal Rule of Evidence 803(3) excludes "statement[s] of memory or belief to prove the fact remembered or believed unless it relates to the validity or terms of the declarant's will." This part of the Rule codifies the prevailing common law view, which bans statements of memory to prove the remembered fact for two reasons.

First, the use of such statements as evidence of prior, remembered facts raises a grave concern about the testimonial quality of memory. Suppose that in *Hill* the police found an eyewitness, Mr. Bellows, the day after the collision. At that time Mr. Bellows stated, "I distinctly remember that the guy driving the other vehicle wasn't looking at the road. When he passed me, he seemed to be looking at something in a store window to the side." Bellows' statement is a declaration of present state of mind in the sense of present memory. However, if we use the statement as evidence of the remembered fact, the statement's evidentiary value obviously depends upon the accuracy of Bellows' memory. Absent an opportunity to cross-examine Bellows and test the quality of his memory, we cannot be assured of the statement's reliability.

The second reason for barring this use of declarations of memory is well stated in the Assembly Committee's Comment to California Evidence Code § 1250(b), setting out the same limitation as that in Rule 803(3):

> This limitation is necessary to preserve the hearsay rule. Any statement of a past event is, of course, a statement of the declarant's then existing state of mind — memory or belief — concerning the past event. If the evidence of that . . . memory . . . were admissible to show that the fact remembered or believed actually occurred, any statement narrating a past event would be, by a process of circuitous reasoning, admissible to prove that the event occurred.

These two reasons account for the general norm that statements of memory are inadmissible as proof of the recollected events and facts. However, in one situation, courts have deviated from this norm. A famous English precedent, *Sugden v. St. Leonards*, 1 Prob. Div. 154 (1876), admitted a testator's declarations made before and after a will's execution to prove the contents of the lost will. Some American jurisdictions have rejected *Sugden, see, e.g., In re Will of Bonner*, 17 N.Y.2d 9, 266 N.Y.S.2d 971, 214 N.E.2d 154 (1966), and others admit the testator's declarations only when there is independent evidence raising a presumption of the revocation of the will. *Payne v. Payne*, 229 Ga. 822, 194 S.E.2d 458 (1972). However, at common law a majority of American jurisdictions followed *Sugden* on the ground that there was a special need for the testator's declarations. It is normally difficult to prove a person's state of mind; the proponent usually resorts to this hearsay exception when the declarant, the testator or testatrix, is already deceased. The declarant's death creates an especially compelling justification for resorting to hearsay evidence. There may be doubts about the declarant's memory and sincerity, but most jurisdictions have concluded that the need for the evidence outweighs those doubts. That conclusion explains the provision in Federal Rule 803(3).

d.   Declarations of Past State of Mind

Although Rule 803(3) allows the admission of statements of present memory to prove prior events in the narrow circumstances described in the prior section, the Rule does not allow the admission of declarations of past state of mind. In *Hill*, suppose that while talking with his wife one week after the collision, Mr. Worker stated, "I feel so bad about the accident. I was rushing across town on the boss's orders to get something delivered, and I wonder if I just rushed too fast." At trial, Ms. Hill calls Mrs. Worker to testify to the first clause in her husband's second sentence. If Ms. Hill offered the testimony under Rule 803(3), the trial judge would probably sustain Mr. Roe's objection.

Why sustain the objection and exclude the evidence? The rationale for the general norm banning such statements is the same as that underlying the exclusion of most statements of present memory: the need for an opportunity to test the quality of the declarant's memory and sincerity. The declarant is not referring to a thought or emotion that he is currently entertaining. The declarant is referring to a past state of mind, and her current statement could be a product of innocent misrecollection.

Most jurisdictions follow the pattern of the Federal Rules and categorically exclude declarations of past state of mind. California is one of the few jurisdictions to allow these declarations:

§ 1251. Prior State of Mind.

Subject to Section 1252, evidence of a statement of the declarant's state of mind, emotion, or physical sensation (including a statement of intent, plan, motive, design, mental feeling, pain, or bodily health) at a time prior to the statement is not made inadmissible by the hearsay rule if

(a) The declarant is unavailable as a witness; and

(b) The evidence is offered to prove such prior state of mind or emotion, when it is itself an issue in the action and the evidence is not offered to prove any fact other than such state of mind or emotion.

§ 1252. Statement Under Circumstances Showing Lack of Trustworthiness.

Evidence of a statement is inadmissible under this article if the statement was made under circumstances such as to indicate its lack of trustworthiness.

In its commentary to §§ 1251–52, the California Law Revision Commission frankly acknowledged that the new statutes changed the prior state of the law. However, the Commission argued that when the proponent could satisfy § 1251(b), the particular need for the evidence should override doubts about the declarant's memory.

NOTE AND PROBLEMS

1. While most jurisdictions allow statements of present memory to prove past events in estate litigation, the majority exclude declarations of past state of mind. Are these positions consistent? Compare the two types of statements in terms of (a) the concern for cross-examining the declarant about perception, memory and narration, and (b) the need for the evidence. There is arguably greater need to cross-examine the declarant about perception in case of statements of present memory; the declarant is referring to an external event such as a fire that destroyed the will rather than the internal reality of an intention. Is there such a unique need in estate litigation that it is justifiable to single out that type of case? The need seems debatable, for only a handful of California cases have even discussed § 1251.

2. **Problem 20-19.** Ms. Hill offers Mrs. Worker's testimony about Worker's statement that he was "rushing across town on the boss's orders" to prove that Worker acted within the scope of his employment. Would the statement be admissible under the Federal Rules? Would it be admissible under the California Evidence Code? Would it make a difference if Worker himself died before trial?

C. EXCEPTIONS FOR WRITTEN STATEMENTS

1. Business Entries

The business entry doctrine is the most frequently employed documentary exception. The frequency of the its use reflects the significant role that businesses — sole proprietorships, partnerships, and corporations — play in American society. Business records are the repositories of a staggering amount of data, and necessity demands a convenient means of making that data accessible to the judicial system. Earlier, we saw that the courts have facilitated access by recognizing a special means of authenticating business records. The same impulse helps account for the existence of the three hearsay exceptions codified in Federal Rules of Evidence 803(6), (7), and (11):

(6) ***Records of a Regularly Conducted Activity.*** A record of an act, event, condition, opinion, or diagnosis if:

   (A) the record was made at or near the time by — or from information transmitted by — someone with knowledge;

   (B) the record was kept in the course of a regularly conducted activity of a business, organization, occupation, or calling, whether or not for profit;

   (C) making the record was a regular practice of that activity;

   (D) all these conditions are shown by the testimony of the custodian or another qualified witness, or by a certification that complies with Rule 902(11) or (12) or with a statute permitting certification; and

   (E) neither the source of information nor the method or circumstances of preparation indicate a lack of trustworthiness.

(7) ***Absence of a Record of a Regularly Conducted Activity.*** Evidence that a matter is not included in a record described in paragraph (6) if:

   (A) the evidence is admitted to prove that the matter did not occur or exist;

   (B) a record was regularly kept for a matter of that kind; and

   (C) neither the possible source of the information nor other circumstances indicate a lack of trustworthiness.

(11) ***Records of Religious Organizations Concerning Personal or Family History.*** A statement of birth, legitimacy, ancestry, marriage, divorce, death, relationship by blood or marriage, or similar facts of personal or family history, contained in a regularly kept record of a religious organization.

The Rules represent a fairly traditional version of the business records doctrine. Rule 803(6) attempts to ensure that the business entry is based on first-hand perception, expressly referring to "someone with knowledge." Personal knowledge is an element of the common law doctrine. *Lord v. Moore*, 37 Me. 208, 220 (1854).

Although the Rule is thus in accord with the majority view, a few jurisdictions have dispensed with the personal knowledge requirement. These jurisdictions follow a model act that states that "all other circumstances, including the lack of personal knowledge by the entrant or maker," affect the weight but not the admissibility of the entry.

Another guarantee of the quality of the declarant's perception is the requirement that the report must be routine. In the words of Rule 803 (6), "making the record was a regular practice" of the organization. The routine nature of the report increases the likelihood that the business's employees have developed a habit of precision in gathering the type of data reflected in the report. Before the adoption of the Federal Rules, some common law courts had begun to relax this element of the doctrine; they occasionally admitted special business reports about nonrecurring events. 5 C. Fishman, Jones on Evidence: Civil and Criminal § 33:12 (7th ed. 1998); 2 B. Witkin, California Evidence § 231 (4th ed. 2000). As with the case of the personal knowledge requirement, Congress opted for the orthodox view. Under the Rule, "[m]iscellaneous jottings" in a desk calendar are inadmissible, since there is no "demonstrable pattern of inclusion or exclusion." *United States v. Ramsey*, 785 F.2d 184, 192 (7th Cir.), *cert. denied*, 476 U.S. 1186 (1986); *Willco Kuwait Trading S.A.K. v. deSavary*, 843 F.2d 618, 628 (1st Cir. 1988) (excluding evidence of a non-routine business telex).

NOTE

How does the guarantee of personal knowledge apply to computerized business records? Even if the handwriting on an original slip of paper would have permitted the identification of the author, when a computer operator feeds the entry into the system, the entry often becomes an essentially anonymous report. Suppose that, in the *Hill* case, Polecat wanted to offer some of its computer records as evidence. How would Polecat's attorney satisfy this element of the foundation? Could Polecat's attorney use Federal Rule of Evidence 406 in laying this element of the foundation?

The common law business records doctrine attempted to ensure the declarant's memory as well as her perception. The doctrine's limitation to routine reports strengthened the inference of the quality of the witness's recollection. If the report were habitual, the declarant would presumably have acquired a habit of precisely recording the data in addition to gathering it accurately. Another indicium of memory is the mandate that the entry be prepared at or near the time of the event memorialized. At common law, the courts were fairly tolerant of time lapses and sometimes allowed the introduction of reports prepared months after the event. *Standard Oil Co. v. Moore*, 251 F.2d 188, 223 (9th Cir. 1957), *cert. denied*, 356 U.S. 975 (1958). Despite the liberality of these common law decisions, Congress was unwilling to eliminate the timing requirement. Rule 803(6) incorporates the requirement by requiring that the record have been "made at or near the time" of the event. *See Carrie Contractors, Inc. v. Blount Construction Group of Blount, Inc.*, 968 F. Supp. 662 (M.D. Ala. 1997) (delay of 17 months was fatal to the admissibility of accounting records).

Likewise, the doctrine endeavors to eliminate concerns about the declarant's narrative ability. The common law addressed this concern by restricting admissible entries to recitations of observed fact. 2 C. McCormick, Handbook of The Law of Evidence § 287 (6th ed. 2006). If the declarant used lay diction to describe a perceived event, there was little danger that the jury would misunderstand the statement. Thus, the courts readily admit business entries that are "objective observations of occurrences." Garland, *Hospital Records: Legal Requirements of Proof*, 59 Ill. B.J. 312, 313–14 (1970). However, if the declarant records an opinion, such as characterizing a mental patient's condition as "psychotic," there is a much graver risk that jurors might mistake the declarant's meaning. For that reason, when a hospital record contains a debatable diagnosis involving "judgment or discretion on complex" data, at early common law the trial judge often refused to treat the record as a business entry. Note, 56 Geo. L.J. 939, 945 (1968); Powell, *Admissibility of Hospital Records into Evidence*, 21 Md. L. Rev. 22, 43 (1961).

But here, too, courts began to relax the restrictions on the admission of business entries. *Weis v. Weis*, 147 Ohio St. 416, 72 N.E.2d 245 (1947), collects numerous authorities documenting this willingness to accept hospital record entries that were based in part on opinion:

> Types of hospital or physician's office records, which have been held admissible in evidence by the courts, are as follows: Record of examination of a patient on admission to a hospital, stating that he had no external injuries and observation that there was a deviation of the nasal septum . . . ; laboratory tests and history sheet . . . ; observation that a patient was well under the influence of alcohol . . . ; record of admission to hospital including observation, "odor of alcohol on the breath" . . . ; diagnosis of cerebral hemorrhage . . . ; report to effect patient had ulcer, chronic prostatitis and seminal vesiculitis . . . ; pathological record to show that death resulted from venereal disease . . . ; record that an insured was delirious four hours before an accident . . . ; record that patient had a fractured right clavicle . . . ; record that patient was suffering from "nephritis" . . . ; record of "moderately advanced tuberculosis" . . . ; record that patient's vomitus had odor of whiskey . . . ; record showing unruly behavior of patient and his disobedience of orders of surgeons and nurses . . . ; and record of treatment prescribed and statements made by patient concerning his symptoms . . .

NOTES AND PROBLEMS

1. What limits, if any, should there be on the admissibility of opinions in business entries? Is hearsay policy satisfied whenever we are confident that if the expert had been present in the courtroom, the expert could have voiced the opinion stated in the report? Is there a difference between a diagnosis of ulcer (mentioned in *Weis*) and a psychiatrist's evaluation of "post-traumatic stress disorder"? *Philips v. Neil*, 452 F.2d 337, 343–47 (6th Cir. 1971), *cert. denied*, 409 U.S. 884 (1972).

2. Regardless of your own policy preference, what position does Rule 803(6) take on the question of whether the business entry must be a recitation of observed fact? Do you think that the Advisory Committee intended that the courts apply the language literally?

3. Problem 20-20. In *Devitt*, the prosecutor calls Officer Dorsey as a witness. Dorsey testifies that he is the chief of the local police crime laboratory. The prosecutor hands Dorsey an exhibit, which he identifies as the report of a comparative chemical and microscopic analysis of hair strands found at the crime scene and strands taken from the defendant. The report concludes with the statement that the two sets of hair strands "are microscopically identical and indistinguishable." The prosecutor offers the report into evidence. Defense counsel objects on the ground that the entry is "insufficiently factual." What ruling? *See State v. Merritt*, 591 S.W.2d 107, 111–14 (Mo. Ct. App. 1979).

When we reach Chapter 32 on Constitutional Overrides to the Rules of Evidence (and the cases of *Crawford v. Washington*, 541 U.S. 36 (2004)), and *Melendez-Diaz v. Massachusetts*, 557 U.S. 305 (2009), you should reconsider this Problem and the next one in light of the Confrontation Clause. Beyond the hearsay issues, there are possible constitutional objections. *See* Julie Seaman, *Triangulating Testimonial Hearsay: The Constitutional Boundaries of Expert Opinion Testimony*, 96 Geo. L.J. 827 (2008).

4. Problem 20-21. In Problem 20-20, suppose that Devitt's attorney objected on the ground that there must be a specific showing of the expertise of the analyst who prepared the report. The defense attorney argues, "you can't admit the opinion until we know that if the guy had been in the courtroom, he could have given that opinion from the witness stand." *See State v. Rhone*, 555 S.W.2d 839, 841–42 (Mo. 1977).

As a final check on the reliability of business records, common law courts attempted to fashion circumstantial guarantees of the declarant's sincerity. One such guarantee is that the declarant had a business duty to gather and record the data. The accuracy of the records is a matter of paramount concern to the typical business. The declarant is usually an employee of the business and thus realizes that his continued employment, his livelihood, depends on the quality of his job performance; part of that job is collecting and recording business data. This understanding is a powerful incentive for accurate perception and memory. The following case, which is expressly mentioned in the Advisory Committee Note to Rule 803(6), is the leading authority on the requirement of a business duty.

JOHNSON v. LUTZ
253 N.Y. 124, 170 N.E. 517 (N.Y. 1930)

Hubbs, J.

This action is to recover damages for the wrongful death of the plaintiff's intestate, who was killed when his motorcycle came into collision with the defendants' truck at a street intersection. There was a sharp conflict in the testimony in regard to the circumstances under which the collision took place. A policeman's report of the accident filed by him in the station house was offered in evidence by the defendants under section 374-a of the Civil Practice Act, and was excluded. The sole ground for reversal urged by the appellants is that said report was erroneously excluded. That section reads: "Any writing or record, whether in the form of an entry in a book or otherwise, made as a memorandum or record of any act, transaction, occurrence or event, shall be admissible in evidence in proof of said act, transaction, occurrence or event, if the trial judge shall find that it was made in the regular course of any business, and that it was the regular course of such business to make such memorandum or record at the time of such act, transaction, occurrence or event, or within a reasonable time thereafter. All other circumstances of the making of such writing or record, including lack of personal knowledge by the entrant or maker, may be shown to affect its weight, but they shall not affect its admissibility. The term business shall include business, profession, occupation and calling of every kind."

Prior to the decision in the well-known case of *Vosburgh v. Thayer*, 12 Johns. 461, decided in 1815, shopbooks could not be introduced in evidence to prove an account. The decision in that case established that they were admissible where preliminary proof could be made that there were regular dealings between the parties; that the plaintiff kept honest and fair books; that some of the articles charged had been delivered; and that the plaintiff kept no clerk. At that time it may not have been a hardship to require a shopkeeper who sued to recover an account to furnish the preliminary proof required by that decision. Business was transacted in a comparatively small way, with few, if any, clerks. Since the decision in that case, it has remained the substantial basis of all decisions upon the question in this jurisdiction prior to the enactment in 1928 of section 374-a, Civil Practice Act.

Under modern conditions, the limitations upon the right to use books of account, memoranda, or records, made in the regular course of business, often resulted in a denial of justice, and usually in annoyance, expense, and waste of time and energy. A rule of evidence that was practical a century ago had become obsolete. * * *

In view of the history of section 374-a and the purpose for which it was enacted, it is apparent that it was never intended to apply to a situation like that in the case at bar. The memorandum in question was not made in the regular course of any business, profession, occupation, or calling. The policeman who made it was not present at the time of the accident. The memorandum was made from hearsay statements of third persons who happened to be present at the scene of the accident when he arrived. It does not appear whether they saw the accident and stated to him what they knew, or stated what some other persons had told them.

The purpose of the Legislature in enacting section 374-a was to permit a writing or record, made in the regular course of business, to be received in evidence, without the necessity of calling as witnesses all of the persons who had any part in making it, provided the record was made as a part of the duty of the person making it, or on information imparted by persons who were under a duty to impart such information. The amendment permits the introduction of shopbooks without the necessity of calling all clerks who may have sold different items of account. It was not intended to permit the receipt in evidence of entries based upon voluntary hearsay statements made by third parties not engaged in the business or under any duty in relation thereto. It was said, in *Mayor, etc., of New York City v. Second Ave.*

R. Co., 102 N.Y. 582, at page 581, 7 N.E. 905, 909, 55 Am. Rep. 839: "It is a proper qualification of the rule admitting such evidence that the account must have been made in the ordinary course of business, and that it should not be extended so as to admit a mere private memorandum, not made in pursuance of any duty owing by the person making it, or when made upon information derived from another who made the communication casually and voluntarily, and not under the sanction of duty or other obligation."

An important consideration leading to the amendment was the fact that in the business world credit is given to records made in the course of business by persons who are engaged in the business upon information given by others engaged in the same business as part of their duty.

"Such entries are dealt with in that way in the most important undertakings of mercantile and industrial life. They are the ultimate basis of calculation, investment, and general confidence in every business enterprise. Nor does the practical impossibility of obtaining constantly and permanently the verification of every employee affect the trust that is given to such books. It would seem that expedients which the entire commercial world recognizes as safe could be sanctioned, and not discredited, by courts of justice. When it is a mere question of whether provisional confidence can be placed in a certain class of statements, there cannot profitably and sensibly be one rule for the business world and another for the court-room. The merchant and the manufacturer must not be turned away remediless because the methods in which the entire community places a just confidence are a little difficult to reconcile with technical scruples on the part of the same persons who as attorneys have already employed and relied upon the same methods. In short, courts must here cease to be pedantic and endeavor to be practical." 3 Wigmore on Evidence (1923) § 1530, p. 278.

The Legislature has sought by the amendment to make the courts practical. It would be unfortunate not to give the amendment a construction which will enable it to cure the evil complained of and accomplish the purpose for which it was enacted. In construing it, we should not, however, permit it to be applied in a case for which it was never intended.

Judgment affirmed.

NOTE AND PROBLEMS

1. It is critical to appreciate the limited nature of the holding in *Johnson*. The court holds only that the proponent may not use the business entry exception to justify the hearsay use, under the business records exception, of bystanders' statements quoted in a police report. *Johnson* does not foreclose offering the statement for a nonhearsay purpose or invoking a different hearsay exception. *See* FED. R. EVID. 805. When hearsay — such as a bystander's statement — is contained within a document or statement that is itself hearsay, commentators use various expressions to describe the problem: double hearsay, multiple hearsay, hearsay within hearsay, or "tacking" hearsay exceptions. For each "link in the hearsay chain," the proponent must develop a nonhearsay theory or invoke an exemption or exception. *Romano v. Howarth,* 998 F.2d 101, 108 (2d Cir. 1993) ("Because the

Progress Notes contain [an] additional level of hearsay, another link in the hearsay chain is necessary to usher into evidence the officer's statements to the nurse").

2. **Problem 20-22.** Consider these variations of the *Johnson* facts:

(a) In *Hill*, a bystander told the investigating police officer that, in her opinion, Worker was driving at least 45 miles an hour. The officer recorded that statement in his report, and Ms. Hill read that statement before she filed suit. In part because of that statement, she agreed that her attorney should allege speeding in her complaint. At trial, Roe calls an accident reconstruction expert who analyzes the physical evidence at the accident scene and convincingly demonstrates that Worker was not speeding. The trial results in a defense verdict. After this trial, Roe sues Ms. Hill for the tort of malicious civil proceeding. In that suit, one issue is whether Ms. Hill had a good faith belief in the allegations she included in her complaint. At the trial of this suit, Ms. Hill attempts to testify to the contents of the police report, including the bystander's statement about Worker's speed. Does *Johnson* preclude Ms. Hill from doing so? Consider Rule 801(c) as well as Rule 803(6).

(b) Suppose that the bystander in question became a defense witness at trial. At trial, she testifies that after carefully reconstructing the accident in her mind, she believes that Worker was driving "at most 25 miles an hour." On cross-examination, Ms. Hill attempts to confront the witness with the passage in the police report. Does *Johnson* preclude Ms. Hill from doing so? Consider Rule 613 as well as Rule 803(6).

(c) Assume that the bystander is unavailable at trial but that, on its face, the police report recites enough facts to bring the bystander's statement within the excited utterance exception under Rule 803(2). During her case-in-chief, Ms. Hill produces a properly attested copy of the police report. She attempts to offer into evidence the passage quoting the bystander. Does *Johnson* bar Ms. Hill from doing so?

Johnson gives one layer of meaning to the expression, "in the regular course of business." It requires an affirmative showing that the declarant had a business motivation for gathering and recording the data. However, the *Johnson* rule does not exhaust the meaning of "in the regular course of business." The next case, which is also mentioned in the Advisory Committee Note to Rule 803(6), probes even more deeply into the significance of that language.

PALMER v. HOFFMAN
318 U.S. 109 (1943)

JUSTICE DOUGLAS delivered the opinion of the Court.

This case arose out of a grade crossing accident which occurred in Massachusetts. * * * On the question of negligence the trial court submitted three issues to the jury — failure to ring a bell, to blow a whistle, to have a light burning in the front of the train. The jury returned a verdict in favor of respondent * * * The case is here on a petition for a writ of certiorari which presents three points.

The accident occurred on the night of December 25, 1940. On December 27, 1940, the engineer of the train, who died before the trial, made a statement at a freight office of petitioners where he was interviewed by an assistant superintendent of the road and by a representative of the Massachusetts Public Utilities Commission. This statement was offered in evidence by petitioners under the Act of June 20, 1936, 28 U.S.C.A. § 695.[1] They offered to prove that the statement was signed in the regular course of business, it being the regular course of such business to make such a statement. Respondent's objection to its introduction was sustained.

We agree with the majority view below that it was properly excluded.

We may assume that if the statement was made "in the regular course" of business, it would satisfy the other provisions of the Act. But we do not think that it was made "in the regular course" of business within the meaning of the Act. The business of the petitioners is the railroad business. That business like other enterprises entails the keeping of numerous books and records essential to its conduct or useful in its efficient operation. Though such books and records were considered reliable and trustworthy for major decisions in the industrial and business world, their use in litigation was greatly circumscribed or hedged about by the hearsay rule — restrictions which greatly increased the time and cost of making the proof where those who made the records were numerous.[2] 5 Wigmore, Evidence, 3d Ed. 1940, § 1530. It was that problem which started the movement towards adoption of legislation embodying the principles of the present Act. *See* Morgan et al., The Law of Evidence, Some Proposals for its Reform (1927) c. V. And the legislative history of the Act indicates the same purpose.[3]

---

[1] "In any court of the United States and in any court established by Act of Congress, any writing or record, whether in the form of an entry in a book or otherwise, made as a memorandum or record of any act, transaction, occurrence, or event, shall be admissible as evidence of said act, transaction, occurrence, or event, if it shall appear that it was made in the regular course of any business, and that it was the regular course of such business to make such memorandum or record at the time of such act, transaction, occurrence, or event or within a reasonable time thereafter. All other circumstances of the making of such writing or record, including lack of personal knowledge by the entrant or maker, may be shown to affect its weight, but they shall not affect its admissibility. The term 'business' shall include business, profession, occupation, and calling of every kind."

[2] The problem was well stated by Judge Learned Hand in *Massachusetts Bonding & Ins. Co. v. Norwich Pharmacal Co.* (CCA 2, 1927) 18 F.2d 934, 937: "The routine of modern affairs, mercantile, financial and industrial, is conducted with so extreme a division of labor that the transactions cannot be proved at first hand without the concurrence of persons, each of whom can contribute no more than a slight part, and that part not dependent on his memory of the event. Records, and records alone, are their adequate repository, and are in practice accepted as accurate upon the faith of the routine itself, and of the self-consistency of their contents. Unless they can be used in court without the task of calling those who at all stages had a part in the transactions recorded, nobody need ever pay a debt, if only his creditor does a large enough business."

[3] Thus the report of the Senate Committee on the Judiciary incorporates the recommendation of the Attorney General who stated in support of the legislation, "The old common-law rule requires that every book entry be identified by the person making it. This is exceedingly difficult, if not impossible, in the case of an institution employing a large bookkeeping staff, particularly when the entries are made by machine. In a recent criminal case the Government was prevented from making out a prima facie case by a ruling that entries in the books of a bank, made in the regular course of business, were not admissible in evidence unless the specific bookkeeper who made the entry could identify it. Since the bank employed 18 bookkeepers, and the entries were made by bookkeeping machines, this was impossible." S. Rep. No. 1965, 74th Cong. 2d Sess., pp. 1, 2.

The engineer's statement which was held inadmissible in this case falls into quite a different category. It is not a record made for the systematic conduct of the business as a business. An accident report may affect that business in the sense that it affords information on which the management may act. It is not, however, typical of entries made systematically or as a matter of routine to record events or occurrences, to reflect transactions with others, or to provide internal controls. The conduct of a business commonly entails the payment of tort claims by the negligence of its employees. But the fact that a company makes a business out of recording its employees' versions of their accidents does not put those statements in the class of records made "in the regular course" of the business within the meaning of the Act. If it did, then any law office in the land could follow the same course, since business as defined in the Act includes the professions. We would then have a real perversion of a rule designed to facilitate admission of records which experience has shown to be quite trustworthy. Any business by installing a regular system for recording and preserving its version of accidents for which it was potentially liable could qualify those reports under the Act. The result would be that the Act would cover any system of recording events or occurrences provided it was "regular" and though it had little or nothing to do with the management or operation of the business as such. Preparation of cases for trial by virtue of being a "business" or incidental thereto would obtain the benefits of this liberalized version of the early shop book rule. The probability of trustworthiness of records because they were routine reflections of the day to day operations of a business would be forgotten as the basis of the rule. *See Conner v. Seattle*, R. & S. Ry. Co., 56 Wash. 310, 312, 313, 105 P. 634. Regularity of preparation would become the test rather than the character of the records and their earmarks of reliability (*Chesapeake & D. Canal Co. v. United States*, 250 U.S. 123, 128, 129) acquired from their source and origin and the nature of their compilation. We cannot so completely empty the words of the Act of their historic meaning. If the Act is to be extended to apply not only to a "regular course" of a business but also to any business, Congress not this Court must extend it. Such a major change which opens wide the door to avoidance of cross-examination should not be left to implication. Nor is it any answer to say that Congress has provided in the Act that the various circumstances of the making of the record should affect its weight, not its admissibility. That provision comes into play only in case the other requirements of the Act are met.

In short, it is manifest that in this case those reports are not for the systematic conduct of the enterprise as a railroad business. Unlike payrolls, accounts receivable, accounts payable, bills of lading and the like, these reports are calculated for use essentially in the court, not in the business. Their primary utility is in litigating, not in railroading.

It is, of course, not for us to take these reports out of the Act if Congress has put them in. But there is nothing in the background of the law on which this Act was built or in its legislative history which suggests for a moment that the business of preparing cases for trial should be included. In this connection it should be noted that the Act of May 6, 1910, 45 U.S.C.A. § 38, requires officers of common carriers by rail to make under oath monthly reports of railroad accidents to the Interstate Commerce Commission, setting forth the nature and causes of the accidents and the circumstances connected therewith. And the same Act (45 U.S.C.A. § 40) gives the

Commission authority to investigate and to make reports upon such accidents. It is provided, however, that "Neither the reports required by § 38 of this title nor any report of the investigation provided for in § 40 of this title nor any part thereof shall be admitted as evidence or used for any purpose in any suit or action for damages growing out of any matter mentioned in said report or investigation." 45 U.S.C.A. § 41. A similar provision, 45 U.S.C.A. § 33, bars the use in litigation of reports concerning accidents resulting from the failure of a locomotive boiler or its appurtenances. That legislation reveals an explicit congressional policy to rule out reports of accidents which certainly have as great a claim to objectivity as the statement sought to be admitted in the present case. We can hardly suppose that Congress modified or qualified by implication these long standing statutes when it permitted records made "in the regular course" of business to be introduced. Nor can we assume that Congress having expressly prohibited the use of the company's reports on its accidents impliedly altered that policy when it came to reports by its employees to their superiors. The inference is wholly the other way.

The several hundred years of history behind the Act indicate the nature of the reforms which it was designed to effect. It should of course be liberally interpreted so as to do away with the anachronistic rules which gave rise to its need and at which it was aimed. But "regular course" of business must find its meaning in the inherent nature of the business in question and in the methods systematically employed for the conduct of the business as a business . . .

NOTES AND PROBLEMS

1. **Problem 20-23.** In *Hill*, Polecat offers records of safety tests of the Polecat model that the plaintiff was driving at the time of the accident. To lay the foundation for the records, Polecat calls Mr. Granger, the head of the safety department. Granger testifies that the tests were actually conducted by Future Motors, Inc., a wholly owned subsidiary of Polecat. Future Motors' safety personnel conducted the tests, prepared the reports, and sent the reports directly to Polecat. Ms. Hill cites *Johnson* and argues that the reports are inadmissible because the declarants were not employees of Polecat. What result? *United States v. Flom*, 558 F.2d 1179, 1182–83 (5th Cir. 1977). Is the declarant's formal employment status dispositive? Do Future Motors employees have a business duty to Polecat?

Sometimes the records of Company B are incorporated or integrated into the records of Company A. There is authority that in these circumstances, an officer of Company A can lay the foundation for Company B's records as if they had originally been prepared by employees of Company A. *See* R. CARLSON, A STUDENT'S GUIDE TO ELEMENTS OF PROOF 36 (2004) (collecting authorities).

2. **Problem 20-24.** In *Hill*, the plaintiff offers a hospital record into evidence. The hospital record states, "patient complained that she was experiencing sharp pain in her right side today." Ms. Hill offers the hospital records custodian's testimony to identify the record. Polecat's attorney objects and cites *Johnson*. Is *Johnson* controlling? What is the relevance of Federal Rule of Evidence 805?

3. **Problem 20-25.** Suppose that Polecat offered a hospital record stating "patient indicated that her pain was much less severe today." Now Ms. Hill cites

Johnson to block the introduction of the record. Consider Federal Rule of Evidence 801(d)(2).

4. Problem 20-26. In *Devitt*, as in Problem 20-20, the prosecutor offers the report of the analysis of the hair strands. Now Devitt's attorney cites *Palmer* in support of the objection to the report's admission. What result? *Compare State v. Henderson*, 554 S.W.2d 117, 120 (Tenn. 1977) *with United States v. Evans*, 21 C.M.A. 579, 582, 45 C.M.R. 353, 356 (1972). Assume that Morena has not adopted the Federal Rules of Evidence.

5. The holding of *Palmer v. Hoffman* is generally understood as grounded upon the lack of trustworthiness of the records. In *Palmer*, the records were prepared in anticipation of litigation; this was the basis of the Court's holding that the records were not prepared in the regular course of business. Though accident reports are sometimes admitted under the business records exception, courts continue to scrutinize them for trustworthiness and, sometimes, to exclude them for this reason. *See, e.g., Wilkins v. Kmart Corp.*, 487 F. Supp. 2d 1216, 1222–23 (D. Kan. 2007).

2. Official Records

Closely related to the business entry doctrine is the official records exception. Like corporations, government agencies have become a major repository of data in our society. The parallel continues because, as with business records, the courts have permitted special means of authenticating official documents. To complete the parallel, the courts have fashioned a set of hearsay exceptions to facilitate the admission of official records as substantive evidence. The exceptions have been invoked to justify the admission of a wide variety of documents, including military records, weather reports, tax returns, ships' papers, and hospital reports.

The Federal Rules of Evidence include several exceptions in Rule 803, based on the official records doctrine:

(8) *Public Records.* A record or statement of a public office if:

(**A**) it sets out:

(**i**) the office's activities;

(**ii**) a matter observed while under a legal duty to report, but not including, in a criminal case, a matter observed by law-enforcement personnel; or

(**iii**) in a civil case or against the government in a criminal case, factual findings from a legally authorized investigation; and

(**B**) neither the source of information nor other circumstances indicate a lack of trustworthiness.

(9) *Public Records of Vital Statistics.* A record of a birth, death, or marriage, if reported to a public office in accordance with a legal duty.

(10) *Absence of a Public Record.* Testimony — or a certification under Rule 902 — that a diligent search failed to disclose a public record or statement if the testimony or certification is admitted to prove that:

(A) the record or statement does not exist; or

(B) a matter did not occur or exist, if a public office regularly kept a record or statement for a matter of that kind.

(12) *Certificates of Marriage, Baptism, and Similar Ceremonies.* A statement of fact contained in a certificate:

(A) made by a person who is authorized by a religious organization or by law to perform the act certified;

(B) attesting that the person performed a marriage or similar ceremony or administered a sacrament; and

(C) purporting to have been issued at the time of the act or within a reasonable time after it.

(14) *Records of Documents That Affect an Interest in Property.* The record of a document that purports to establish or affect an interest in property if:

(A) the record is admitted to prove the content of the original recorded document, along with its signing and its delivery by each person who purports to have signed it;

(B) the record is kept in a public office; and

(C) a statute authorizes recording documents of that kind in that office.

Once again, we begin our analysis of the exception by pointing to the circumstantial guarantees of the quality of perception. One common denominator with the business entry doctrine is that at common law, an official record must have been based on the declarant's firsthand knowledge. *Wetherill v. University of Chicago*, 518 F. Supp. 1387 (N.D. Ill. 1981).

The courts and legislatures have also attempted to guard against the declarant's misrecollection. For example, California Evidence Code § 1280(b) limits official records to writings "made at or near the time of the act, condition, or event" recorded. Does Federal Rule of Evidence 803(8) include any comparable language? Note the contrast in this regard between Rules 803(8) and 803(6).

To minimize the ambiguities of narration, common law courts limited official records to recitations of observed fact. Courts routinely excluded statements of medical causation or legal responsibility. Note that unlike Rule 803(6), Rule 803(8) does not contain an express reference to "opinions, or diagnoses." However, modern courts no longer categorically exclude statements of opinion or conclusion in official records. In many jurisdictions, for example, statutes require that the medical examiner or coroner state the cause and manner of death in the death certificate. 2 P. GIANNELLI & E. IMWINKELRIED, SCIENTIFIC EVIDENCE § 19-3(A), at 89 (3d ed. 1999). Although the view is not universal, many jurisdictions now admit this type of conclusory statement of cause of death as substantive evidence. *Id.*

Lastly, courts have tried to ensure the declarant's sincerity. English courts drew the inference of sincerity from the declarant's realization that the report would be subjected to public scrutiny. M. LADD & R. CARLSON, CASES AND MATERIALS ON EVIDENCE 976 (1972). In *Mercer v. Denne*, [1904] 2 Ch. D. 534, Judge Farwell stated: "The test of publicity as put by Lord Blackburn is that the public are interested in it, and entitled to go and see it, so that if there is anything wrong in it they would be entitled to protest. In that sense it becomes a statement that would be open to the public to challenge or dispute."

American authorities invoke a different theory as the basis for inferring sincerity: the declarant's official duty to gather and record the data. That duty serves as a motivation for sincerity, just as it provides the declarant with an incentive for accurate perception and memory. As Rules 803(9) and (12) imply, the duty can exist even if the declarant is a private person. For instance, under Rule 803(12), when a member of the clergy executes a marriage certificate, that person functions as a *de facto* public official. The courts have likewise been willing to treat foreign governmental documents as official records. *E.g.*, *United States v. Pintado-Isiordia*, 448 F.3d 1155 (9th Cir. 2006) (Mexican birth record); *United States v. Grady*, 544 F.2d 598, 604 (2d Cir. 1976) (records of Royal Ulster Constabulary); *United States v. Rodriguez*, 534 F.2d 7 (1st Cir. 1976) (Dominican identification card, military records, and death certificate).

The key factor in deciding whether to treat a document as an official record is the document's nature rather than the declarant's identity. The classic analysis of that problem appears in Dean Wigmore's treatise. 5 J. WIGMORE, EVIDENCE § 1636 (3d ed. 1940). Wigmore describes several basic types of official records admitted at common law. One type is a register. Registers record events of which public officials have firsthand knowledge and which typically occur on their premises. For instance, in a deed registry, a clerk records that a citizen gave the official a deed to be included in the registry. Another type is a return. As in the case of a registry, the official executing a return ordinarily has personal knowledge, but in the case of a return the record relates to an act that the official performed off the premises. An illustration would be a police officer's return on a search warrant; the officer executes the warrant away from the police station and files a return, detailing his or her acts, with the court. A third type is a certificate. In the case of a certificate, the official usually gives the record to a private citizen. When a notary public certifies a person's acknowledgment of his or her authorship of a document such as a deed, the notary is acting as a public official; rather than retaining the certificate, the notary hands the certificate to the person who appeared before him. Lastly, a report may summarize an investigation that an official conducted. As in the case of a return, a report of investigation (ROI) relates to the official's conduct away from the official's business premises. However, at least in part the report collects hearsay statements relating to events of which the official lacks personal knowledge. Since the findings in most ROIs rest in part on hearsay, at common law the courts were highly reluctant to admit such findings as substantive evidence.

Whereas Rule 803(6) essentially codifies the common law business entry exception, certain aspects of Rule 803(8) are innovative. Rule 803(8)(A)(i) is unexceptional, permitting the admission of records reflecting "the activities of the office or agency." However, Rules 803(8)(A)(ii) and (iii) deviate from the common law. Rule 803(8)(A)(i) excludes some records that were admissible at common law. The rule excludes "in a criminal case, a matter observed by law-enforcement personnel." The Court of Appeals for the Second Circuit addressed the meaning and scope of this exclusion in the following case. [ed. note that the Federal Rules of Evidence have been "restyled" since this case was decided: former Rules 803(8)(B) and (C) are now numbered as Rules 803(8)(A)(i) and (ii).]

UNITED STATES v. OATES
560 F.2d 45 (2d Cir. 1977)

[A jury convicted the defendant of possessing heroin with intent to distribute and of conspiracy to commit that substantive offense. One of the alleged coconspirators was Isaac Daniels.]

Appellant claims that the trial court committed error by admitting into evidence at trial two documentary exhibits purporting to be the official report and accompanying worksheet of the United States Customs Service chemist who analyzed the white powdery substance seized from Daniels. The documents, the crucial nature of which is beyond cavil, concluded that the powder examined was heroin. Appellant contends, first of all, that under the new Federal Rules of Evidence the documents should have been excluded as hearsay. Before discussing the merits of these contentions, which raise difficult and important issues of evidential law, it will be helpful to describe briefly the circumstances surrounding the admission of the report and the worksheet.

At trial the government had planned upon calling as one of its final witnesses a Mr. Milton Weinberg, a retired United States Customs Service chemist who allegedly had analyzed the white powder seized from Daniels. It seems that Mr. Weinberg had been present on the day the trial had been scheduled to commence but he was not able to testify then because of a delay occasioned by the unexpected length of the pretrial suppression hearing. The government claims that by the time Weinberg was rescheduled to testify he had become "unavailable" [due to a medical condition].

Before the onset of Weinberg's condition, the prosecutor had planned to call Weinberg for the purpose of eliciting from him testimony that Weinberg had analyzed the powder seized from Daniels and found it to be heroin. When Weinberg became "unavailable," the government decided to call another Customs chemist, Shirley Harrington, who, although she did not know Weinberg personally, was able to testify concerning the regular practices and procedures used by Customs Service chemists in analyzing unknown substances. Through Mrs. Harrington the government was successful in introducing Exhibits 13 and 12 which purported to be, respectively, the handwritten worksheet used by the chemist analyzing the substance seized from Daniels and the official typewritten report of the chemical analysis. When the defense voiced vigorous objection to the attempt to introduce the documents through Mrs. Harrington, the government relied upon [several] different hearsay exceptions contained in the new Federal Rules of Evidence to support its position that the documents were admissible.

[W]e believe that, on balance, appellant's emphasis on the importance of FRE 803(8) is well-founded. That the chemist's report and worksheet could not satisfy the requirements of the "public records and reports" exception seems evident merely from examining, on its face, the language of FRE 803(8). While there may be no sharp demarcation between the records covered by exception 8(B) and those referenced in exception 8(C), and there may in some cases be actual overlap, we conclude without hesitation that surely the language of item (C) is applicable to render the chemist's documents inadmissible as evidence in this case, and they might also be within the ambit of the terminology of item (B), a claim appellant argues to us persuasively.

It is manifest from the face of item (C) that "factual findings resulting from an investigation made pursuant to authority granted by law" are not shielded from the exclusionary effect of the hearsay rule by "the public records exception" if the government seeks to have those "factual findings" admitted *against* the accused in a criminal case. It seems indisputable to us that the chemist's official report and worksheet in the case at bar can be characterized as reports of "factual findings resulting from an investigation made pursuant to authority granted by law." The "factual finding" in each instance, the conclusion of the chemist that the substance analyzed was heroin, obviously is the product of an "investigation,"[19] *see, e.g., Martin v. Reynolds Metal Corp.*, 297 F.2d 49, 57 (9th Cir. 1961) (" 'investigation', when liberally construed, includes the sampling and *testing* here contemplated") (emphasis supplied), supposedly involving on the part of the chemist employment of various techniques of scientific analysis. Furthermore, in view of its reliance on the chemist's report at trial and its representation to the district court that "chemical analys[e]s of unidentified substances are indeed a regularly conducted activity of the Customs laboratory of Customs chemists," the government here is surely in no position to dispute the fact that the analyses regularly performed by United States Customs Service chemists on substances lawfully seized by Customs officers are performed pursuant to authority granted by law.

Though with less confidence, we believe that the chemist's documents might also fail to achieve status as public records under FRE 803(8)(B) because they are records of "matters observed by police officers and other law enforcement personnel." Although in characterizing the chemist's report and worksheet here it is quite accurate to designate those reports as the reports of factual findings made pursuant to an investigation, the reports in this case conceivably could also be susceptible of the characterization that they are "reports . . . setting forth . . . (B) matters observed pursuant to duty imposed by law as to which matters there was a duty to report." If this characterization is justified, the difficult question would be whether the chemists making the observations could be regarded as "other law enforcement personnel." We think this phraseology must be read broadly enough to

---

[19] That "investigation" can encompass scientific testing is clearly shown by the Advisory Committee's Notes which, while noting "the variety of situations encountered" by courts deciding the admissibility of reports of this nature, *see* Advisory Committee's Notes, Note to Paragraph (8) of Rule 803, 56 F.R.D. at 312, characterize as "evaluative reports" certificates issued pursuant to 18 U.S.C. § 4245 and findings made pursuant to 7 U.S.C. § 78.

Certificates under 18 U.S.C. § 4245 are based on psychiatric and psychological examinations while findings made pursuant to the former 7 U.S.C. § 78 could be based on testing of grain.

make its prohibitions against the use of government-generated reports in criminal cases coterminous with the analogous prohibitions contained in FRE 803(8)(C). *See United States v. Smith, supra,* 521 F.2d at 968–69, n.24. We would thus construe "other law enforcement personnel" to include, at the least, any officer or employee of a governmental agency which has law enforcement responsibilities. Applying such a standard to the case at bar, we easily conclude that full-time chemists of the United States Customs Service are "law enforcement personnel." The chemist in this case was employed by the Customs Service, a governmental agency which had clearly defined law enforcement authority in the field of illegal narcotics trafficking; the officers who actually seized the suspected contraband were employed by the Customs Service, and the unidentified substance was delivered by them to a laboratory operated by the Customs Service. The unidentified substance was then subjected to analysis by a chemist, one of whose regular functions is to test substances seized from suspected narcotics violators. Chemists at the laboratory are, without question, important participants in the prosecutorial effort. As well as analyzing substances for the express purpose of ascertaining whether the substances are contraband, and if so, participating in eventual prosecution of narcotics offenders, the chemists are also expected to be familiar with the need for establishing the whereabouts of confiscated drugs at all times from seizure until trial. Moreover, the role of the chemist typically does not terminate upon completion of the chemical analysis and submission of the resulting report but participation continues until the chemist has testified as an important prosecution witness at trial.

In short, these reports are not "made by persons and for purposes unconnected with a criminal case [but rather they are a direct] result of a test made for the specific purpose of convicting the defendant and conducted by agents of the executive branch, the very department of government which seeks defendant's conviction." *State v. Larochelle,* 112 N.H. 392, 400, 297 A.2d 223, 228 (1972) (dissenting opinion). It would therefore seem that if the chemist's report and worksheet here can be deemed to set forth "matters observed," the documents would fail to satisfy the requirements of exception FRE 803(8) for the chemist must be included within the category of "other law enforcement personnel."

The reason why such a restrictive approach was adopted can be established by referring to the Advisory Committee's Notes and by examining the way in which Congress revised the draft legislation proposed by the Advisory Committee and which the Supreme Court submitted to Congress. [A]n overriding concern of the Advisory Committee was that the rules be formulated so as to avoid impinging upon a criminal defendant's right to confront the witnesses against him . . .

> In one respect, however, the rule with respect to evaluative reports under FRE 803(8)(C) is very specific: they are admissible only in civil cases and against the government in criminal cases in view of the *almost certain collision with confrontation rights which would result from their use against an accused in a criminal case.*

Advisory Committee's Notes, Note to Paragraph (8) of Rule 803, 56 F.R.D. at 313 (emphasis supplied). This preoccupation with preserving the confrontation rights of criminal defendants was shared by a Congress which established enhanced protection for those rights by substantially amending the proposed language of FRE 803(8)(B). An amendment offered by Representative David Dennis added important qualifying language to item (B) which before the amendment deemed as "public records" under FRE 803(8) "matters observed pursuant to duty imposed by law as to which matters there was a duty to report." *See* 120 Cong. Rec. 2387 (1974). The amendment qualified the foregoing language by adding "excluding, however, in criminal cases matters observed by police officers and other law enforcement personnel." *Id.* In the debate that followed the offer of this amendment, the accused's right to confront the witnesses against him was advanced as the impetus for the proposal. . . . Representative Dennis, the sponsor of the proposal,[25] confirmed that this was the intent of the amendment by emphasizing that the amendment pertained to "criminal cases, and in a criminal case the defendant should be confronted with the accuser to give him the chance to cross examine." *Id.* Following the addition of this language excluding reports reciting matters observed by law enforcement personnel, *see* 120 Cong. Rec. 2389 (1974), the Senate added to the pending legislation a proposed FRE 804(b)(5) which would have rendered the exclusion of such reports from the scope of FRE 803(8)(B) ineffective in the event the author of the report was "unavailable" to testify. *See* S. Rep. No. 1277, 93d Cong., 2d Sess. 17 (1974). This attempt to emasculate the Dennis amendment proved to be abortive, however, for the Committee of Conference removed it from the pending legislation. *See* H.R. Rep. No. 1597, 93d Cong., 2d Sess. 12 (1974) (Joint Explanatory Statement of the Committee of Conference).

The discussion in the preceding paragraphs describes *why* Congress decided to take the approach it did with regard to the use of "evaluative" reports under FRE 803(8)(C) and reports of law enforcement personnel under FRE 803(8)(B). The *result* Congress intended was the absolute inadmissibility of records of this nature, and that this was, indeed, the result which Congress believed it had achieved by Rules 803(8)(B) and (C), could not have been articulated with any more clarity than it was by Representative William L. Hungate. As Chairman of the House Judiciary Subcommittee on Criminal Justice, Representative Hungate had been responsible for presiding over extensive hearings on the proposed Federal Rules of Evidence and must be regarded as one of the legislators most knowledgeable about the then pending legislation. . . . [H]e informed the House that the Committee of Conference had rejected the Senate's attempt to create a new hearsay exception which would have permitted admission of police reports authored by officers unavailable to testify. He explained the meaning of the remaining related provisions:

> As the rules of evidence now stand, police and law enforcement reports are not admissible against defendants in criminal cases. This is made quite clear by the provisions of rule 803(8)(B) and (C).

120 Cong. Rec. H12254 (daily ed. Dec. 18, 1974). This unequivocal language shows that it was Representative Hungate's understanding, and he was as familiar with the legislation as anyone else in Congress,[26] that the language retained in FRE

---

[25] It is, of course, well-established that the sponsor's interpretation of his proposal, when expressed prior to adoption of the legislation, is entitled to great weight. (citations omitted).

[26] It is clear that "[r]esort may be had to the statements of such an *authoritative* person," *Ideal Farms, Inc. v. Benson*, 288 F.2d 608, 616 (3d Cir. 1961) (emphasis supplied), *cert. denied*, 372 U.S. 965

803(8)(B) and (C) meant that those provisions had the *effect* of rendering absolutely inadmissible against defendants in criminal cases the "police reports" of item (B) and the "evaluative reports" of item (C).

*   *   *

[At this point, the court analyzed the substantiality of the defendant's contention that the admission of the report and worksheet violated his rights under the Confrontation Clause. The court stressed that "we do not decide whether appellant's right of confrontation was violated here." However, the court concluded that the defendant's constitutional argument raised sufficiently "serious doubts" to mandate the narrower interpretation of Rule 803(8). Concomitantly, the court ruled that the legislative history was so clear that the prosecution could not even rely on the alternative theory that the chemist's documents qualified as business entries under Rule 803(6).]

[W]e hold here, that in criminal cases reports of public agencies setting forth matters observed by police officers and other law enforcement personnel and reports of public agencies setting forth factual findings resulting from investigations made pursuant to authority granted by law cannot satisfy the standards of any hearsay exception if those reports are sought to be introduced against the accused. Inasmuch as the chemist's documents here can be characterized as governmental reports which set forth matters observed by law enforcement personnel or which set forth factual findings resulting from an authorized investigation, they were incapable of qualifying under any of the exceptions to the hearsay rule specified in FRE 803 and 804.

(1963), as Representative Hungate. What persons may be regarded as "authoritative" is equally well-established by numerous cases which have addressed this question. The sponsor of the legislation would surely be regarded as such a person. *See* note 25, *supra.* So, too, the floor managers, *see, e.g., City of New York v. Train, supra,* 494 F.2d at 1039 n.16; the members of the congressional committee which holds hearings on the proposed legislation, *See City of New York v. Train, supra,* 494 F.2d at 1039, n.16; and particularly the chairman of such a committee, *See Department of Water & Power v. Allis-Chalmers Mfg. Co., supra* at 351; and the members of the conference committee, *see, e.g., City of New York v. Train, supra,* 494 F.2d at 1039 n.16; are regarded as persons whose views, when expressed in the floor debates prior to passage of the legislation, are entitled to particular deference.

The weight to which views of any particular congressman is entitled will vary, of course, with the legislator's familiarity with, and participation in the shaping of, the legislation. It would be difficult to imagine anyone more qualified to comment on the legislation in this case than was Representative Hungate who, as member and Chairman of the House Judiciary Subcommittee on Criminal Justice, and as floor manager and as conference committee member probably had more contact with the proposed rules than any other single legislator. When such impressive credentials exist, we believe that the congressman's "statements in explaining the bill to the House, and the answers made by him to questions asked by members may be considered in construing the bill as it was subsequently enacted into law. These statements are in the nature of supplemental committee reports and are entitled to the same weight accorded to formal committee reports." *Department of Water & Power v. Allis-Chalmers Mfg. Co., supra* at 351.

NOTES

1. Even assuming that you accept the court's interpretation of Rule 803(8), as a matter of statutory construction must you read the same limitation into Rule 803(6)? Most courts have rejected the *Oates* approach. 1 P. GIANNELLI & E. IMWINKELRIED, SCIENTIFIC EVIDENCE § 6-2(A) (3d ed. 1999). Most courts exclude only arrest and lineup reports — documents describing direct adversarial confrontations which are most likely to be colored by the officer's subjective evaluation. *United States v. Enterline*, 894 F.2d 287 (8th Cir. 1990). These courts read "law enforcement personnel" more narrowly than the *Oates* court, and they generally refuse to read Rule 803(8)(C)'s exclusionary provision into Rule 803(6). *United States v. Sokolow*, 81 F.3d 397, 405 (3d Cir. 1996) ("many courts" have criticized *Oates*).

Most courts that have addressed the issue have agreed with the narrow holding of *Oates* — that a police report excluded by Rule 803(8)(B) should not be admitted through the "back-door" of Rule 803(6). *See, e.g., Air Land Forwarders, Inc. v. United States*, 172 F.3d 1338, 1344–45 (Fed. Cir. 1999). However, courts have generally rejected the broad *Oates* dicta to the effect that a Rule 803(8) exclusion should bar admissibility of the report under *any* hearsay exception. Given that much of the *Oates* reasoning rested on concerns about defendants' confrontation rights, these cases sensibly distinguish admission under exceptions that do not raise confrontation concerns. *See United States v. Picciandra*, 788 F.2d 39 (1st Cir.), *cert. denied*, 479 U.S. 847 (1986) (Rule 803(5), Recorded Recollection); *United States v. Metzger*, 778 F.2d 1195 (6th Cir. 1985) (Rule 803(10), Absence of Public Record or Entry). Based on similar reasoning, courts have admitted such records under Rule 803(6) where the author of the report testifies at trial. Indeed, the Second Circuit has itself diverged from the broad *Oates* dicta in subsequent cases. *See United States v. Yakobov*, 712 F.2d 20, 26–27 (2d Cir. 1983) (admitting evidence under Rule 803(10)).

With respect to the *Oates* court's interpretation of the term "law enforcement personnel," most courts, including the Second Circuit in subsequent cases, have read the term more narrowly so as to permit introduction of various government reports under Rule 803(8)(B). *See United States v. Rosa*, 11 F.3d 315, 331–34 (2d Cir. 1993) (autopsy report). However, the Supreme Court's recent decision in *Melendez-Diaz v. Massachusetts*, 557 U.S. 305 (2009), calls this narrow interpretation into question. Addressing the government's argument that the drug analyst's affidavit at issue in the case was a business record and/or public record and therefore was not testimonial hearsay barred by the Confrontation Clause, the Court stated:

> Documents kept in the regular course of business may ordinarily be admitted at trial despite their hearsay status. See Fed. Rule Evid. 803(6). But that is not the case if the regularly conducted business activity is the production of evidence for use at trial. Our decision in Palmer v. Hoffman, 318 U. S. 109 (1943), made that distinction clear. There we held that an accident report provided by an employee of a railroad company did not qualify as a business record because, although kept in the regular course of the railroad's operations, it was "calculated for use essentially in the court, not in the business." Id., at 114. The analysts' certificates [in this case] —

like police reports generated by law enforcement officials — do not qualify as business or public records for precisely the same reason. See Rule 803(8) (defining public records as "excluding, however, in criminal cases matters observed by police officers and other law enforcement personnel").

This passage strongly suggests that the document at issue in *Oates* — also a drug analyst's report — properly was held in that case to fall within the exclusion for "matters observed by . . . other law enforcement personnel." When we consider the Confrontation Clause in Chapter 32, we will look more closely at *Melendez-Diaz* and its holding that a government report of this sort may not be introduced against a criminal defendant absent an opportunity to cross-examine the author of the report.

2. In some respects, as an exercise in statutory interpretation, the *Oates* opinion is exemplary. The court not only marshals the extrinsic legislation history materials in detail; it also critically evaluates the deference of the materials — pausing, for example, to determine whether the source of a statement was a sponsor of the legislative and therefore entitled to greater weight. Nevertheless, some of the court's conclusions are debatable.

The court reads "an implied exception into FRE 803(6) . . . ." The proponent of a hearsay statement may ordinarily invoke the various provisions of Rules 803 and 804 as alternative theories for admissibility. For example, the proponent may argue that the statement qualifies as either a present sense impression under Rule 803(1) or a startled utterance under Rule 803(2). Does any of the legislative history cited in *Oates* manifest a clear intention to extend Rule 803(8)(B)'s exclusionary rule to Rule 803(6)? Absent a clear manifestation of that intent, is the implied exception consistent with Rule 402? However, perhaps the court does not need to this "implied exception" theory. In a sense, Rule 803(8)(A)(ii) — formerly Rule 803(8)(B) — applies *Palmer v. Hoffman* to official records: when the prosecution offers police reports against a defendant, the reports can arguably be viewed as suspect litigation reports. The Advisory Committee Note to Rule 803(6) expressly cites *Palmer* and the Supreme Court, as quoted above, cites *Palmer* in *Melendez-Diaz*.

While Rule 803(8)(A)(ii) departs from the common law by fashioning a new exclusionary provision, Rule 803(8)(A)(iii) deviates from the common law in the opposite direction by expanding the admissibility of certain types of official records. As Wigmore noted, at common law one of the most controversial issues surrounding the official records doctrine was the admissibility of statements in reports of investigation. This type of official record poses the gravest concerns about the hearsay declarant's testimonial qualities: is the declarant relating personal knowledge or second-level hearsay from a third party? When the report states conclusions and opinions, are we confident that we understand the meaning the declarant intended to convey?

If the trigger for the investigation was an event likely to lead to litigation, the declarant's sincerity may be suspect. Given those concerns, the traditional common law view was that reports of investigation did not qualify as official records. Wigmore stressed that "few officers, if any, are found vested by implication with

. . . authority" to prepare reports of investigation worthy of admission at trial. 5 J. WIGMORE, EVIDENCE § 1636 (2d ed. 1940). However, McCormick urged more liberal admission of reports. McCormick, *Can the Courts Make Wider Use of Reports of Official Investigations?*, 42 IOWA L. REV. 363, 364–68 (1957).

McCormick's article influenced the Advisory Committee, and in turn the committee persuaded the Supreme Court and Congress to include (8)(A)(iii) — formerly (8)(C) — in Rule 803. The rule provides that the official records exception now authorizes the admission "in civil actions and proceedings and against the Government in criminal cases, factual findings resulting from an investigation made pursuant to authority granted by law, unless the sources of information or other circumstances indicate lack of trustworthiness." Like the expression "law enforcement personnel" in (8)(A)(ii), the language "factual findings" in (8)(A)(iii) divided the lower courts. How broadly did Congress intend the courts to construe this new inclusionary provision? As in the case of the interpretation of (8)(A)(ii), when the courts attempted to resolve the interpretation of (8)(A)(iii), they had to struggle with "equivocal legislative history." Reid & Nettleton, *Trial by Administrative Ambush*, 16 TRIAL, Fall 1989, at 16. Ultimately, the Supreme Court provided some guidance in the following decision:

BEECH AIRCRAFT CORPORATION v. RAINEY
488 U.S. 153 (1988)

JUSTICE BRENNAN delivered the opinion of the Court.

In this case we address a longstanding conflict among the Federal Courts of Appeals over whether Federal Rule of Evidence 803(8)(C), which provides an exception to the hearsay rule for public investigatory reports containing "factual findings," extends to conclusions and opinions contained in such reports. We also consider whether, on the facts of this case, the trial court abused its discretion in refusing to admit, on cross-examination, testimony intended to provide a more complete picture of a document about which the witness had testified on direct.

This litigation stems from the crash of a Navy training aircraft at Middleton Field, Alabama, on July 13, 1982, which took the lives of both pilots on board. * * * After radio warnings from two other pilots, the plane banked sharply to the right in order to avoid the other aircraft. At that point it lost altitude rapidly, crashed, and burned.

Because of the damage to the plane and the lack of any survivors, the cause of the accident could not be determined with certainty. The two pilots' surviving spouses brought a product liability suit against petitioners Beech Aircraft Corporation, the plane's manufacturer, and Beech Aerospace Services, which serviced the plane under contract with the Navy. The plaintiffs alleged that the crash had been caused by a loss of engine power, known as "rollback," due to some defect in the aircraft's fuel control system. The defendants, on the other hand, advanced the theory of pilot error, suggesting that the plane had stalled during the abrupt avoidance maneuver.

At trial, the only seriously disputed question was whether pilot error or equipment malfunction had caused the crash. Both sides relied primarily on expert testimony. One piece of evidence presented by the defense was an investigative report prepared by Lieutenant Commander William Morgan on order of the training squadron's commanding officer and pursuant to authority granted in the Manual of the Judge Advocate General. This "JAG Report," completed during the six weeks following the accident, was organized into sections labeled "finding of fact," "opinions," and "recommendations," and was supported by some 60 attachments. The "finding of fact" included statements like the following:

> "13.   At approximately 1020, while turning crosswind without proper interval, 3E955 crashed, immediately caught fire and burned . . .

> "27.   At the time of impact, the engine of 3E955 was operating but was operating at reduced power." App. 10-12.

Among his "opinions" Lieutenant Commander Morgan stated, in paragraph five, that due to the deaths of the two pilots and the destruction of the aircraft "it is almost impossible to determine exactly what happened to Navy 3E955 from the time it left the runway on its last touch and go until it impacted the ground." He nonetheless continued with a detailed reconstruction of a possible set of events, based on pilot error, that could have caused the accident. The next two paragraphs stated a caveat and a conclusion:

> "6.   Although the above sequence of events is the most likely to have occurred, it does not change the possibility that a 'rollback' did occur.

> "7.   The most probable cause of the accident was the pilots [sic] failure to maintain proper interval." Id., at 15.

The trial judge initially determined, at a pretrial conference, that the JAG Report was sufficiently trustworthy to be admissible, but that it "would be admissible only on its factual findings and would not be admissible insofar as any opinions or conclusions are concerned." Id., at 35. The day before trial, however, the court reversed itself and ruled, over the plaintiffs' objection, that certain of the conclusions would be admitted. Id., at 40–41. Accordingly, the court admitted most of the report's "opinions," including the first sentence of paragraph five about the impossibility of determining exactly what happened, and paragraph seven, which opined about failure to maintain proper interval as "[t]he most probable cause of the accident." Id., at 97. On the other hand, the remainder of paragraph five was barred as "nothing but a possible scenario," id., at 40, and paragraph six, in which investigator Morgan refused to rule out rollback, was deleted as well.

[T]he jury returned a verdict for the petitioners. A panel of the Eleventh Circuit reversed and remanded for a new trial. . . . [holding that] the "conclusions" contained in the JAG Report should have been excluded . . .

Federal Rule of Evidence 803 provides that certain types of hearsay statements are not made excludable by the hearsay rule, whether or not the declarant is available to testify. Rule 803(8) defines the "public records and reports" which are not excludable, as follows:

> "Records, reports, statements, or data compilations, in any form, of public offices or agencies, setting forth (A) the activities of the office or agency, or (B) matters observed pursuant to duty imposed by law as to which matters

there was a duty to report, . . . or (C) in civil actions and proceedings and against the Government in criminal cases, factual findings resulting from an investigation made pursuant to authority granted by law, unless the sources of information or other circumstances indicate lack of trustworthiness."

Because the Federal Rules of Evidence are a legislative enactment, we turn to the "traditional tools of statutory construction," *INS v. Cardoza-Fonseca*, 480 U.S. 421, 446 (1987), in order to construe their provisions. We begin with the language of the Rule itself. Proponents of the narrow view have generally relied heavily on a perceived dichotomy between "fact" and "opinion" in arguing for the limited scope of the phrase "factual findings." *Smith v. Ithaca Corp.*, contrasted the term "factual findings" in Rule 803(8)(C) with the language of Rule 803(6) (records of regularly conducted activity), which expressly refers to "opinions" and "diagnoses." "Factual findings," the court opined, must be something other than opinions. 612 F.2d at 221-222. [8]

For several reasons, we do not agree. In the first place, it is not apparent that the term "factual findings" should be read to mean simply "facts" (as opposed to "opinions" or "conclusions"). A common definition of "finding of fact" is, for example, "[a] conclusion by way of reasonable inference from the evidence." Black's Law Dictionary 569 (5th ed. 1979). To say the least, the language of the Rule does not compel us to reject the interpretation that "factual findings" includes conclusions or opinions that flow from a factual investigation. Second, we note that, contrary to what is often assumed, the language of the Rule does not state that "factual findings" are admissible, but that "*reports* . . . setting forth . . . factual findings" (emphasis added) are admissible. On this reading, the language of the Rule does not create a distinction between "fact" and "opinion" contained in such reports.

Turning next to the legislative history of Rule 803(8)(C), we find no clear answer to the question of how the Rule's language should be interpreted. Indeed, in this case the legislative history may well be at the origin of the dispute. Rather than the more usual situation where a court must attempt to glean meaning from ambiguous comments of legislators who did not focus directly on the problem at hand, here the

---

[8] The court in *Smith* found it significant that different language was used in Rules 803(6) and 803(8)(C): "Since these terms are used in similar context within the same Rule, it is logical to assume that Congress intended that the terms have different and distinct meanings." 612 F.2d, at 222. The Advisory Committee notes to Rule 803(6) make clear, however, that the Committee was motivated by a particular concern in drafting the language of that Rule. While opinions were rarely found in traditional "business records," the expansion of that category to encompass documents such as medical diagnoses and test results brought with it some uncertainty in earlier versions of the Rule as to whether diagnoses and the like were admissible. "In order to make clear its adherence to the [position favoring admissibility]," the Committee stated, "the rule specifically includes both diagnoses and opinions, in addition to acts, events, and conditions, as proper subjects of admissible entries." Advisory Committee's Notes on Fed. Rule Evid. 803(6), 28 U.S.C. App., p. 723. Since that specific concern was not present in the context of Rule 803(8)(C), the absence of identical language should not be accorded much significance. See *Rainey v. Beech Aircraft Corp.*, 827 F.2d 1498-1512 (CA11 1987) (en banc) (Tjoflat, J., concurring). What is more, the Committee's report on Rule 803(8)(C) strongly suggests that that Rule has the same scope of admissibility as does Rule 803(6): "Hence the rule, *as in Exception [paragraph] (6)*, assumes admissibility in the first instance but with ample provision for escape if sufficient negative factors are present." Advisory Committee's Notes on Fed. Rule Evid. 803(8), 28 U.S.C. App., p. 725 (emphasis added).

Committees in both Houses of Congress clearly recognized and expressed their opinions on the precise question at issue. Unfortunately, however, they took diametrically opposite positions. Moreover, the two Houses made no effort to reconcile their views, either through changes in the Rule's language or through a statement in the Report of the Conference Committee.

Clearly this legislative history reveals a difference of view between the Senate and the House that affords no definitive guide to the congressional understanding. It seems clear however that the Senate understanding is more in accord with the wording of the Rule and with the comments of the Advisory Committee.[9]

The Advisory Committee's comments are notable, first, in that they contain no mention of any dichotomy between statements of "fact" and "opinions" or "conclusions." What was on the Committee's mind was simply whether what it called "evaluative reports" should be admissible. Illustrating the previous division among the courts on this subject, the Committee cited numerous cases in which the admissibility of such reports had been both sustained and denied. It also took note of various federal statutes that made certain kinds of evaluative reports admissible in evidence. What is striking about all of these examples is that these were *reports that stated conclusions. E.g., Moran v. Pittsburgh-Des Moines Steel Co.*, 183 F.2d 467-473 (CA3 1950) (report of Bureau of Mines concerning the cause of a gas tank explosion inadmissible); *Franklin v. Skelly Oil Co.*, 141 F.2d 568-572 (CA10 1944) (report of state fire marshal on the cause of a gas explosion admissible); 42 U.S.C. § 269(b) (bill of health by appropriate official admissible as prima facie evidence of vessel's sanitary history and condition). The Committee's concern was clearly whether reports of this kind should be admissible. Nowhere in its comments is there the slightest indication that it even considered the solution of admitting only "factual" statements from such reports. Rather, the Committee referred throughout to "reports," without any such differentiation regarding the statements they contained. What the Committee referred to in the Rule's language as "reports . . . setting forth . . . factual findings" is surely nothing more or less than what in its commentary it called "evaluative reports." Its solution as to their admissibility is clearly stated in the final paragraph of its report on this Rule. That solution consists of two principles: First, "the rule . . . assumes admissibility in the first instance . . . ." Second, it provides "ample provision for escape if sufficient negative factors are present."

That "provision for escape" is contained in the final clause of the Rule: evaluative reports are admissible "unless the sources of information or other circumstances indicate lack of trustworthiness." This trustworthiness inquiry — and not an arbitrary distinction between "fact" and "opinion" — was the Committee's primary safeguard against the admission of unreliable evidence, and it is important to note that it applies to all elements of the report. Thus, a trial judge has the discretion, and indeed the obligation, to exclude an entire report or portions thereof — whether narrow "factual" statements or broader "conclusions" — that she deter-

---

[9] *See* Advisory Committee's Notes on Fed. R. Evid. 803(8), 28 U.S.C. App., pp. 724-725. As Congress did not amend the Advisory Committee's draft in any way that touches on the question before us, the Committee's commentary is particularly relevant in determining the meaning of the document Congress enacted.

mines to be untrustworthy.[11] Moreover, safeguards built in to other portions of the Federal Rules, such as those dealing with relevance and prejudice, provide the court with additional means of scrutinizing and, where appropriate, excluding evaluative reports or portions of them. And of course it goes without saying that the admission of a report containing "conclusions" is subject to the ultimate safeguard — the opponent's right to present evidence tending to contradict or diminish the weight of those conclusions.

Our conclusion that neither the language of the Rule nor the intent of its framers calls for a distinction between "fact" and "opinion" is strengthened by the analytical difficulty of drawing such a line. It has frequently been remarked that the distinction between statements of fact and opinion is, at best, one of degree:

> "All statements in language are statements of opinion, *i.e.*, statements of mental processes or perceptions. So-called 'statements of fact' are only more specific statements of opinion. What the judge means to say, when he asks the witness to state the facts, is: 'The nature of this case requires that you be more specific, if you can, in your description of what you saw.'" W. King & D. Pillinger, Opinion Evidence in Illinois 4 (1942) (footnote omitted).

*   *   *

In the present case, the trial court had no difficulty in admitting as a factual finding the statement in the JAG Report that "[a]t the time of impact, the engine of 3E955 was operating but was operating at reduced power." Surely this "factual finding" could also be characterized as an opinion, which the investigator presumably arrived at on the basis of clues contained in the airplane wreckage. Rather than requiring that we draw some inevitably arbitrary line between the various shades of fact/opinion that invariably will be present in investigatory reports, we believe the Rule instructs us — as its plain language states — to admit "reports . . . setting forth . . . factual findings." The Rule's limitations and safeguards lie elsewhere: First, the requirement that reports contain factual findings bars the admission of statements not based on factual investigation. Second, the trustworthiness provision requires the court to make a determination as to whether the report, or any portion thereof, is sufficiently trustworthy to be admitted.

A broad approach to admissibility under Rule 803(8)(C), as we have outlined it,

---

[11] The Advisory Committee proposed a nonexclusive list of four factors it thought would be helpful in passing on this question: (1) the timeliness of the investigation; (2) the investigator's skill or experience; (3) whether a hearing was held; and (4) possible bias when reports are prepared with a view to possible litigation *(citing Palmer v. Hoffman*, 318 U.S. 109, 63 S. Ct. 477, 87 L. Ed. 645 (1943)). Advisory Committee's Notes on Fed. Rule Evid. 803(8), 28 U.S.C. App., p. 725; *see* Note, The Trustworthiness of Government Evaluative Reports under Federal Rule of Evidence 803(8)(C), 96 Harv. L. Rev. 492 (1982).

In a case similar in many respects to this one, the trial court applied the trustworthiness requirement to hold inadmissible a JAG Report on the causes of a Navy airplane accident; it found the report untrustworthy because it "was prepared by an inexperienced investigator in a highly complex field of investigation." *Fraley v. Rockwell Int'l Corp.*, 470 F. Supp. 1264, 1267 (S.D. Ohio 1979). In the present case, the District Court found the JAG Report to be trustworthy. App. 35. As no party has challenged that finding, we have no occasion to express an opinion on it.

is also consistent with the Federal Rules' general approach of relaxing the traditional barriers to "opinion" testimony. Rules 702-705 permit experts to testify in the form of an opinion, and without any exclusion of opinions on "ultimate issues." And Rule 701 permits even a lay witness to testify in the form of opinions or inferences drawn from her observations when testimony in that form will be helpful to the trier of fact. We see no reason to strain to reach an interpretation of Rule 803(8)(C) that is contrary to the liberal thrust of the Federal Rules.

We hold, therefore, that portions of investigatory reports otherwise admissible under Rule 803(8)(C) are not inadmissible merely because they state a conclusion or opinion. As long as the conclusion is based on a factual investigation and satisfies the Rule's trustworthiness requirement, it should be admissible along with other portions of the report.[13] As the trial judge in this case determined that certain of the JAG Report's conclusions were trustworthy, he rightly allowed them to be admitted into evidence. We therefore reverse the judgment of the Court of Appeals in respect of the Rule 803(8)(C) issue.

NOTES AND PROBLEMS

1. What questions about Rule 803(8)(C) — now 803(A)(iii) — does *Rainey* settle? What questions does the opinion leave unresolved? Does (8)(C) authorize the admission of conclusions of law set out in otherwise admissible official reports? *Hines v. Brandon Steel Decks, Inc.*, 886 F.2d 299, 302–03 (11th Cir. 1989). Read footnote 13 in the Supreme Court's opinion. How liberally should courts invoke the "trustworthiness" clause in (8)(C)? *See Anderson v. City of New York*, 657 F. Supp. 1571, 1577–90 (S.D.N.Y. 1987) (report of the Criminal Justice Subcommittee of the House Judiciary Committee); *United States v. Durrani*, 659 F. Supp. 1183 (D. Conn.) (report of the President's Special Review Board, the Tower report, on the Iran-Contra scandal), *aff'd*, 835 F.2d 410 (2d Cir. 1987). Politics can rear its ugly head in a government investigation. The opponent has the burden of coming forward with proof of facts to trigger the "trustworthiness" clause. *Johnson v. City of Pleasanton*, 982 F.2d 350, 352 (9th Cir. 1992). In effect, proof of the normal foundational elements creates a rebuttable presumption of admissibility. *Moss v. Ole South Real Estate, Inc.*, 933 F.2d 1300, 1305 (5th Cir. 1991).

2. According to Justice Brennan, what was the better evidence of legislative intent: the Advisory Committtee Note or the House Judiciary Report? Why?

3. As we have noted in the past, one of the maxims of interpretation is that, if the legislature uses different terms in different provisions of the same statutory scheme, the legislature presumptively intended different meanings. *Smith v. Ithaca Corporation*, cited in *Beech*, relied heavily on that maxim in championing the "narrow" interpretation of Rule 803(8)(C). The *Smith* court noted that unlike Rule 803(6), Rule 803(8) contained no reference to "opinions." Justice Brennan expressly rejects both that interpretation and the *Smith* court's reasoning. Why does

---

[13] We emphasize that the issue in this case is whether Rule 803(8)(C) recognizes any difference between statements of "fact" and "opinion." There is no question in this case of any distinction between "fact" and "law." We thus express no opinion on whether legal conclusions contained in an official report are admissible as "findings of fact" under Rule 803(8)(C).

Brennan attach so little weight to the maxim in *Beech*?

4. **Problem 20-27.** In *Hill*, before the accident, Polecat exchanged correspondence with the National Highway Traffic Safety Administration. The NHTSA recommended that Polecat recall the model that Ms. Hill drove. Specifically, NHTSA urged that Polecat strengthen the gas tank "because of its hazardous placement." At trial, Ms. Hill calls an NHTSA official to authenticate the letter. Polecat's attorney objects that "a mere letter can't qualify under Rule 803(8)." What ruling? *Tveraas v. Coffey*, 818 F. Supp. 75, 77–78 (D. Vt. 1993) (official letter of reprimand); *In re Multi-Piece Rims Prods. Liability Litig.*, 545 F. Supp. 149, 150–52 (W.D. Mo. 1982).

5. **Problem 20-28.** The NHTSA conducted safety tests on the Polecat model. The test inspector was Mr. Blumoff. The day after the tests, Blumoff dictated his report to his government secretary, Ms. Chernoff. During the dictation, he said, "In this inspector's opinion, the placement of the gas tank is hazardous." Ms. Chernoff was not listening closely; and when she typed the final report, she inserted the word "not" before "hazardous." Blumoff signed the report without reading it carefully. As soon as he signed it, he placed it in the NHTSA's permanent files. A year later, while browsing through the files on an unrelated case, he came across the report and noticed the error. He immediately dictated a "Corrected Final Report" and inserted it in the file. At trial, Ms. Hill calls Blumoff to offer the "Corrected Final Report." Would the report be admissible under Rule 803(8)? Under California Evidence Code § 1280(b), which requires that "the writing was made at or near the time of the act, condition, or event"? *See Apollo Fuel Oil v. United States*, 73 F. Supp. 2d 254 (E.D.N.Y.) (the inspector later changed the date on a work history sheet when he realized that it was off by one day), *aff'd*, 195 F.3d 74 (2d Cir. 1999).

6. **Problem 20-29.** In *Devitt*, the prosecutor again offers the crime laboratory report of the hair analysis. Assume that the judge accepted Devitt's argument that *Palmer* precludes admitting the report as a business entry. The prosecutor now remarks, "Well, if that's the case, Your Honor, I'll just offer it as an official record rather than a business entry. *Palmer* deals only with the business entry exception." Is there any language in Rule 803(8) that Devitt can rely on? *See* Annot., 56 A.L.R. Fed. 168, 171–72 (1982).

7. The courts generally limit the scope of Rule 803(8) to final reports approved by the government entity. Neither drafts (*Figures v. Bd. of Public Utilities*, 967 F.2d 357 (10th Cir. 1992)) nor preliminary staff reports (*Kemper Architects v. McFall, Konkel & Kimball Consulting Engineers, Inc.*, 843 P.2d 1178 (Wyo. 1992)) qualify.

Although the courts recognize that limitation on the scope of Rule 803(8)(A)(iii), they otherwise have applied the hearsay exception fairly liberally to administrative reports and investigations. *Guild v. General Motors Corp.*, 53 F. Supp. 2d 363 (W.D.N.Y. 1999); *Livingston v. Isuzu Motors, Ltd.*, 910 F. Supp.1473, 1497 (D. Mont. 1995). Yet, given Rule 803(22), most courts have balked at extending (8)(A)(iii) to judicial findings of fact. *Hairston v. Washington Metropolitan Area Transit Auth.*, 1997 U.S. Dist. LEXIS 5188 (D.D.C. Apr. 10, 1997).

8.   By this time, you should be conversant with the business entry and official record exceptions. It should be evident that the doctrines are so closely akin that it is easy to confuse them. Be prepared to list all the differences between the two hearsay exceptions.

3.   Learned Treatises

At the outset of our discussion of this hearsay exception, we must differentiate it from the preceding documentary hearsay exceptions and a credibility doctrine. The prior hearsay exceptions are distinguishable because under those exceptions, we normally admit writings reflecting specific events such as the delivery of merchandise or the service of a search warrant. In contrast, under the learned treatise exception, we typically introduce texts and articles discussing general principles in subject areas such as science, geography, and history. Thus, the content of a learned treatise differs profoundly from that of a routine business entry or official record.

To distinguish this hearsay exception from the related credibility doctrine, though, we must focus on the use of the treatise rather than its content. In an earlier chapter, we saw that on direct examination, an expert customarily states a principle or theory that serves as the major premise in the expert's syllogistic reasoning. On cross-examination in most jurisdictions, the opposing counsel may confront the expert with passages from learned treatises that contradict the principle on which the expert is relying. 2 C. McCormick, Handbook of The Law of Evidence § 321 (6th ed. 2006). Jurisdictions disagree on the extent to which learned treatises may be used to impeach the witness's testimony about the principle or theory. Some states limit the cross-examiner to texts on which the expert admits relying in forming her opinion. Other states follow the "recognition" test that the cross-examiner may resort to any text that the expert acknowledges as a standard authority in the field. Still other jurisdictions permit the cross-examiner to use any text "established as a reliable authority" by, for example, "other expert testimony or . . . judicial notice." Cal. Evid. Code § 721 (B)(3); Mich R. Evid. 707. At the extreme, some jurisdictions allow the cross-examiner to quote any contradictory passage to the witness without a preliminary identification of the text or its authoritative status. R. Habush, Cross Examination of Non-Medical Experts 20-9-10 (1981). All jurisdictions agree, however, that on this theory, the passage may not be treated as substantive evidence during summation, and the attorney may not use it as substantive proof to support any finding of fact on appeal. On request, the trial judge gives the jurors a limiting instruction stating that they are not to treat the passage as substantive evidence.

In contrast, when the learned treatise hearsay exception applies, the passage is introduced as substantive proof. Moreover, case law allows the use of learned treatises on either direct or redirect examination. *Caruolo v. John Crane, Inc.*, 226 F.3d 46, 55 (2d Cir. 2000). There is no limiting instruction, the attorney may invite the jury to accept the passage as substantive evidence, and on appeal the attorney may use the passage to support a judgment in her client's favor. Those are the procedural consequences when the attorney persuades the judge that the proffered text falls within Federal Rule of Evidence 803(18):

(18) *Statements in Learned Treatises, Periodicals, or Pamphlets.* A statement contained in a treatise, periodical, or pamphlet if:

> **(A)** the statement is called to the attention of an expert witness on cross-examination or relied on by the expert on direct examination; and
>
> **(B)** the publication is established as a reliable authority by the expert's admission or testimony, by another expert's testimony, or by judicial notice.
>
>   If admitted, the statement may be read into evidence but not received as an exhibit.

The justification for recognizing this hearsay exception is relatively straightforward. In the case of scholarly texts, there is rarely any question about the quality of the declarant's perception or memory. The declarant, the author, of the learned treatise text may be describing the results of a long-term research project. The declarant will usually have had substantial time to collect any data, record it, refine the record into a manuscript, and publish the manuscript after painstaking proofreading. Objectively, there is far less reason to question the perception or memory of the treatise author than that of a startled declarant or a bookkeeper hurriedly dashing off an invoice.

Furthermore, there is good reason to assume the declarant's sincerity. The author is not writing with a view to litigation. The *Palmer* reasoning works in reverse here; the absence of any litigation motivation supports the inference that the author wrote impartially and truthfully. Moreover, the author knows that his or her work will be subjected to close scrutiny by colleagues — and critics. The author knows that his or her professional reputation and future are at stake.

However, while the factors of perception, memory, and sincerity cut in favor of recognizing a hearsay exception for learned treatises, the testimonial quality of narration cuts in the opposite direction. 6 J. WIGMORE, EVIDENCE § 1690 (3d ed. 1940). When the author uses a technical term of art in the text, what meaning did she ascribe to the term? Did the author intend that the statement be construed literally and categorically, or would the author concede any exceptions or qualifications? At the time of trial, in the light of more recent research, would the author revise any statements in the text?

These narrative concerns are so weighty that until recently only a few jurisdictions recognized the learned treatise exception. Before the adoption of the Federal Rules, only a minority of courts, including such jurisdictions as Alabama, California, Iowa, and Wisconsin, had adopted the exception. However, with the adoption of the Federal Rules by 44 states at last count, a majority of jurisdictions now employ the learned treatise exception.

NOTES AND PROBLEMS

1. The Advisory Committee conceived of Rule 803(18) as a compromise view. In what sense is it a compromise? Note the requirement of subsection (A) of the Rule. In its Note on Rule 803(18), the Committee commented that "[t]he rule avoids the danger of misunderstanding and misapplication by limiting the use of treatises as substantive evidence to situations in which an expert is on the stand and available to explain and assist in the application of the treatise if desired." Does this compromise adequately address the narrative dangers that originally accounted for the courts' reluctance to admit treatises as substantive proof?

2. **Problem 20-30.** In *Devitt*, the prosecutor calls Dr. Norris as a witness. Dr. Norris identifies himself as a licensed psychiatrist. The prosecutor then marks a text as an exhibit. The text is entitled *The Assault Victim — A Profile* by Chang and Holguin, two practicing psychiatrists. After stating that the text is the most widely read authority on the psychiatric disorders caused by assaults, Norris reads into the record the part of the text describing post-traumatic stress disorder — the symptomatology of a person subjected to an assault. Norris then asserts that he examined Mr. Paterson and concluded that he displayed all the symptoms described by Chang and Holguin. During closing argument, the prosecutor states, "You heard the description of post-traumatic stress disorder, ladies and gentlemen. You know that Mr. Paterson matches that description perfectly." At this point, the defense objects, "Your Honor, there is no substantive proof of the nature of that syndrome. The prosecutor never offered his text into evidence." What ruling? Note the last sentence in Rule 803(18). What do "admitted" and "received" mean? How do they differ? *See Maggipinto v. Reichman*, 607 F.2d 621, 622 (3d Cir. 1979).

3. **Problem 20-31.** In *Hill*, the plaintiff attempts to introduce a Model Code of Safe Automotive Engineering, prepared by the National Highway Traffic Safety Administration. The Code contains a provision on gas tank placement, and the Polecat model involved was designed in violation of the provision. The NHTSA promulgated the Code as an advisory guide; the federal government never enacted the Code. Can Ms. Hill offer the Code under Rule 803(18)? Suppose that the Code had been promulgated by the National Association of Automotive Safety Engineers, a voluntary private organization. *See Johnson v. Ellis & Sons Iron Works, Inc.*, 604 F.2d 950, 957 (5th Cir. 1979); Annot., 58 A.L.R.3d 148, 153–55 (1974).

4. Does the treatise have to take the form of a conventional book or article? D. KAYE, D. BERNSTEIN & J. MNOOKIN, THE NEW WIGMORE: EXPERT EVIDENCE § 4.7 (2004). Does Rule 803(18) require that? In *Costantino v. Herzog*, 203 F.3d 164 (2d Cir. 2000), the court applied the exception to a videotape intended to educate physicians on the proper technique for conducting a particular medical procedure.

D.   CONCLUSION

As you studied this chapter, you undoubtedly noted the general trend toward the expansion of the exceptions recognized in Rule 803. It is useful at this juncture to pause to assess the wisdom of that trend.

The undervaluation of demeanor: Some critics have argued that the trend overlooks the importance of demeanor evidence to the trier of fact. One of the factors that originally accounted for the emergence of the hearsay doctrine was the belief that the admission of hearsay deprives the trier of fact of the opportunity to assess the declarant's demeanor while he or she is speaking. The Rule 803 exceptions arguably depreciate the importance of demeanor by admitting hearsay evidence even when there is no necessity to dispense with demeanor evidence — that is, there is no showing of the declarant's unavailability.

Some modern legal psychologists disagree with the manner in which courts routinely downplay the importance of demeanor evidence. In the Cleveland Jury Project, the researchers concluded that when witnesses disagree, jurors often decide the case by focusing on the witnesses' demeanor rather than the substance of their testimony. Austin, *Why Jurors Don't Heed the Trial*, NAT'L L.J., Aug. 12, 1985, at 18. Communications experts commonly assert that when one person speaks to another, nonverbal conduct accounts for more than 50% of the information communicated. J. KESTLER, QUESTIONING TECHNIQUES AND TACTICS § 2.49 (1982). If the speaker's statement is laden with emotion, more than 90% of the message may be communicated nonverbally. K. TAYLOR, R. BUCHANAN & D. STRAWN, COMMUNICATION STRATEGIES FOR TRIAL ATTORNEYS 49 (1984). Further, when the listener perceives a conflict between the speaker's statement and the accompanying nonverbal cues, the listener usually opts to disbelieve the statement. J. KESTLER, *supra*, at § 3.34; Peskin, *Non-Verbal Communication in the Courtroom*, 3 TRIAL DIPL. J. 8 (Winter 1980). In light of these findings, should the courts be so ready to admit hearsay and dispense with demeanor?

The counterpoint to this criticism, though, is that although laypersons might attach significant weight to demeanor in evaluating a witness's credibility, there is mounting evidence that demeanor is a poor indicator of the witness's subjective truthfulness, much less the objective trustworthiness of the witness's testimony. Wellborn, *Demeanor*, 76 CORNELL L. REV. 1075 (1991). As Professor Wellborn has written:

> If ordinary people in fact possess the capacity to detect falsehood or error on the part of others by observing their nonverbal behavior, then it should be possible . . . to demonstrate such a capacity under controlled conditions. Over the past twenty-five years, a large number of experiments involving thousands of subjects have searched for this capacity. With remarkable consistency, the experiments have shown that it simply does not exist.

Id. at 1104. Other commentators concur. Blumenthal, *A Wipe of the Hands, a Lick of the Lips: The Validity of Demeanor Evidence in Assessing Witness Credibility*, 72 NEB. L. REV. 1157 (1993); Seaman, *Black Boxes*, 58 EMORY L. J. 427 (2008).

The overvaluation of sincerity: A second criticism has been leveled against the current state of law on the Rule 803 exceptions — a criticism that seemingly has more merit than the first. By now, it should be obvious that in deciding whether to admit a type of hearsay, the common law attached great, often decisive, significance to an inference of the declarant's sincerity. If the declarant's nervous excitement or business duty strongly suggested that her subjective motivation was truthful, the courts were inclined to characterize the statement as sufficiently reliable to be admitted.

The early common law stress on sincerity is understandable, given its virtual obsession with the prevention of perjury. The preamble to the original English Statute of Frauds referred to the "fraudulent practices which are commonly endeavored to be upheld by perjury and subornation." 6 HOLDSWORTH, HISTORY OF

ENGLISH LAW 379–97 (1924). One of the reasons for the emergence of the authentication requirement (the courts' refusal to follow the practice of "every-day affairs of business and social life" of taking documents at face value) was that the courts believed that the requirement would be "a necessary check on the perpetration of fraud." 2 C. McCORMICK, EVIDENCE § 219 (6th ed. 2006).

It is to be expected that courts so intent on preventing perjury would be readily impressed by an inference of subjective sincerity. However, the question is whether the courts have been overly impressed — whether their focus on sincerity has led them to neglect serious doubts about the declarant's perception, memory, or narration. E. MORGAN, SOME PROBLEMS OF PROOF UNDER THE ANGLO-AMERICAN SYSTEM OF LITIGATION 139–40 (1956). The inference of sincerity may be an adequate substitute for the oath; but when there are substantial questions about the declarant's other testimonial qualities, it is doubtful whether it is wise to waive the opportunity for cross-examination. *Id.* at 164–66.

Trial attorneys' experience and witness psychologists' research suggest the need for a rethinking of the stress on sincerity. Although most hearsay exceptions "stress the element of sincerity . . . , [i]t is believed to be the common experience of attorneys in the trial of cases, when facts are not accurately reported, that witnesses are more often found to be mistaken than committing perjury." Ladd, *The Hearsay We Admit*, 5 OKLA. L. REV. 271, 286 (1952). The traditional exceptions sanction the admission of many types of hearsay that witness psychology tells us are likely to be inaccurate. Stewart, *Perception, Memory, and Hearsay: A Criticism of Present Law and the Proposed Federal Rules of Evidence*, 1970 UTAH L. REV. 1, 9–10, 28. The excited utterance doctrine is particularly suspect. Psychologists have charged that excited utterances are "[t]he most unreliable type of evidence admitted under hearsay exceptions." *Id.* at 28.

NOTE

As a matter of policy, is it time for a wholesale revision of the hearsay exceptions discussed in this chapter? If so, what form should the revision take: (a) the abolition of exceptions such as excited utterance? (b) The revision of the exceptions to require more extensive foundations? or (c) a general directive to the trial judges administering the hearsay rule to make a more searching inquiry into the declarant's perception, memory, and narration?

Chapter 21

HEARSAY: EXCEPTIONS THAT REQUIRE PROOF OF UNAVAILABILITY

Read Federal Rules of Evidence 803(5) and 804. Reread Federal Rule of Evidence 612.

A. INTRODUCTION

Thus far we have considered hearsay exceptions contained in Rule 803. For statements offered under Rule 803 exception, the availability of the declarant is not relevant to the admissibility of the hearsay statement because — at least in theory — statements satisfying those exceptions are of equal or even greater value than the potential trial testimony by the declarant on the same point. For example, the declarant's present sense impression utterance at the time of the event is arguably better evidence than a present recollection of an event that likely occurred many months prior to the trial. (Note that the exception for recorded recollections, contained in Rule 803(5), is a special case and is included in this chapter because it requires a special kind of unavailability.)

In contrast, each of the exceptions contained in Rule 804 requires a showing that the declarant is unavailable before the hearsay statements may be admitted. These hearsay statements are clearly of a "second-best" nature: we would rather have the live testimony of the witness, but if that is impossible due to unavailability, then under certain circumstances we will accept the hearsay statement instead. Thus, the first order of business when considering the Rule 804 exceptions is to understand the five possible grounds of unavailability set out in Rule 804(a).

B. PROOF OF THE DECLARANT'S UNAVAILABILITY

Because the hearsay exceptions discussed in this chapter emerged one by one pursuant to common law development, the courts developed individualized standards for judging unavailability under each of the various exceptions. In the case of dying declarations, for example, the traditional view recognized the declarant's death as the only acceptable showing of unavailability. For other exceptions, though, a showing of lack of memory or physical infirmity was sufficient to invoke the exception. While in principle it might be justifiable to have a different unavailability standard for each hearsay exception, in practice using a different unavailability standard for each exception was unwieldy and confusing.

To eliminate that confusion, most jurisdictions have adopted a uniform unavailability standard for all exceptions requiring proof of unavailability. Federal Rule of

Evidence 804(a) is in line with that trend:

Rule 804 (a) Criteria for Being Unavailable. A declarant is considered to be unavailable as a witness if the declarant:

(1)   is exempted from testifying about the subject matter of the declarant's statement because the court rules that a privilege applies;

(2)   refuses to testify about the subject matter despite a court order to do so;

(3)   testifies to not remembering the subject matter;

(4)   cannot be present or testify at the trial or hearing because of death or a then-existing infirmity, physical illness, or mental illness; or

(5)   is absent from the trial or hearing and the statement's proponent has not been able, by process or other reasonable means, to procure:

    (A)   the declarant's attendance, in the case of a hearsay exceptopn under Rule 804(b)(1) or (5); or

    (B)   the declarant's attendance or testimony, in the case of a hearsay exception under Rule 804(b)(2), (3), or (4).

But this subdivision (a) does not apply if the statement's proponent procured or wrongfully caused the declarant's unavailability as a witness in order to prevent the declarant from attending or testifying.

Rule 804(a) states a rather liberal definition of unavailability. For example, the risks attendant to a late pregnancy can render a female witness unavailable. *United States v. McGuire*, 307 F.3d 1192, 1205 (9th Cir. 2002). Subsection (2) treats a witness's "refus[al] to testify" as a species of unavailability, which was contrary to the common-law view in some jurisdictions. Some critics argue that characterizing refusal as unavailability gives the witness's proponent an incentive to encourage the witness to refuse; the proponent gets the benefit of the favorable hearsay, and the opponent cannot effectively cross-examine the witness on the stand. Does the last sentence of Rule 804(a) adequately protect the opponent against that danger?

Subsection (3) treats a witness's lack of memory as adequate unavailability. Like subsection (2), this provision departs from the common law in a number of states. Some commentators have argued that recognizing forgetfulness as a criterion of unavailability encourages perjured claims of loss of memory; they also worry that the trial judge will be unable to make a reliable determination whether a witness's forgetfulness is genuine. Courts sometimes find that a claimed lack of memory is feigned and that it therefore does not satisfy the requirements of a hearsay exception.

Subsection 804(b)(6) was added in 1997. It authorizes the receipt of a hearsay statement when the opposing party "wrongfully caused — or acquiesced in wrongfully causing — the declarant's unavailability as a witness, and did so intending that result." The accompanying Advisory Committee Note specifies that "[t]he usual Rule 104(a) preponderance of the evidence standard has been adopted." In other words, the preliminary factual question whether the defendant wrongfully caused the declarant's unavailability is one that the judge must decide by a preponderance of the evidence standard. Where the declarant is unavailable because she was murdered, and where the defendant is on trial for that crime, the rule creates the prospect that a court might admit incriminating hearsay statements of the victim upon finding it more likely than not that the defendant is guilty of killing her. This "bootstrapping" of such statements raises constitutional as well as evidentiary issues and will be further addressed in Chapter 32.

Another difficult question raised by Rule 804(b)(6) is whether the defendant must personally have intimidated the hearsay declarant in order to trigger forfeiture under the rule. After surveying the case law, one commentator has concluded that there is little authority for extending the rule to fact situations in which "a defendant . . . used a proxy to intimidate the witness." Flanagan, *Forfeiture by Wrongdoing and Those Who Acquiesce in Witness Intimidation: A Reach Exceeding Its Grasp and Other Problems with Federal Rule of Evidence 804(b)(6)*, 51 Drake L. Rev. 459, 543–44 (2003). However, some courts have held that one conspirator's waiver-by-misconduct may be imputed to another conspirator when the misconduct occurs within the scope and furtherance of the conspiracy. *United States v. Thompson*, 286 F.3d 950 (7th Cir. 2002), *cert. denied*, 537 U.S. 1134 (2003).

Finally, courts have struggled to define the requisite state of mind for a defendant who commits the misconduct leading to the declarant's unavailability at trial. While some have argued that Rule 804(b)(6), by its text, is limited to cases where the violence against the declarant was specifically aimed at preventing the declarant from testifying, others have suggested that the principle should be understood to reach all situations where the defendant is responsible for the witness's absence.

In *Giles v. California*, 554 U.S. 353 (2008), decided in 2008, the Supreme Court settled this question under the forfeiture doctrine of the Confrontation Clause and suggested that the same standard applies under the hearsay rule (*see* infra, Chapter 32). The Court reversed a homicide conviction, holding that forfeiture of a Confrontation Clause claim to introduction of hearsay requires proof of a specific intent to prevent the witness's testimony; simple knowledge that unavailability would result from the act is insufficient.

PROBLEMS

1.   **Problem 21-1.** Morena allows depositions in criminal cases. Morena also permits the introduction of the deposition transcript as substantive evidence at trial if the deponent is then unavailable. Before trial in *Devitt*, the prosecution deposes Mr. Prentiss. At the deposition, Prentiss claims that he and Devitt planned the attack on Paterson. At the time of trial, Prentiss is incarcerated in a state prison in Missouri. The prosecutor argues that Prentiss's imprisonment automatically makes him unavailable. Both Morena and Missouri have adopted the Uniform Act to Secure the Attendance of Witnesses from Without a State in Criminal Proceedings. Devitt's attorney argues that the admission of Prentiss's deposition would "violate both Rule 804 and the Constitution." What ruling? *See Barber v. Page*, 390 U.S. 719, 722–25 (1968) (a violation).

2. **Problem 21-2.** Suppose that at the time of trial Prentiss had moved to Australia. Prentiss is still an American citizen, but he has become a permanent resident of Australia. Is this sufficient proof of unavailability? *See Mancusi v. Stubbs*, 408 U.S. 204, 209–13 (1972) (The witness became unavailable when he took up permanent residence in Sweden). The *Mancusi* court relied on 28 U.S.C. § 1783(a). When *Mancusi* arose, the statute read: "A court of the United States may subpoena, for appearance before it, a citizen or resident of the United States who . . . is beyond the jurisdiction of the United States and whose testimony in a criminal proceeding is desired by the Attorney General." (1958 ed.). Section 1783 now provides that "[a] court of the United States may order the issuance of a subpoena requiring the appearance as a witness before it, or before a person or body designated by it, of a national or resident of the United States who is in a foreign country." Unlike the earlier version of the statute, the amendment authorizes federal process to compel an American citizen to return for a state trial. Would the amendment of § 1783 affect the result in *Mancusi* and this problem?

3. **Problem 21-3.** Assume that *Mancusi* is still good law. The prosecutor does not have any testimony that Prentiss has taken up residence in Australia. However, the prosecutor calls Ms. Ferguson, a friend of Prentiss. Ferguson testifies that a month before trial, Prentiss told her that he was "moving to Australia in two weeks at the latest." Without more, is Ferguson's testimony sufficient proof of Prentiss's unavailability? *See United States v. Arthur*, 22 C.M.R. 482, 484 (A.C.M.R. 1956) (no).

C.   EXCEPTIONS REQUIRING PROOF OF UNAVAILABILITY

1.   Former or Prior Testimony

If a party is involved in multiple hearings, several legal doctrines might come into play. Under civil procedure law, decisions rendered in the first proceeding may have issue or claim preclusive effects in the second case. Alternatively, under Federal Rule of Evidence 803(22), the judgment in the prior case may be admissible as evidence in the second case to prove the truth of the elements of the prior crime.

Under the hearsay exception contained in Rule 804(b)(1), testimony given in trial #1 may be admissible as evidence in trial #2:

Rule 804(b) The Exceptions. The following are not excluded by the rule against hearsay if the declarant is unavailable as a witness:

(1)   Former Testimony. Testimony that:

   (A)   was given as a witness at a trial, hearing, or lawful deposition, whether given during the current proceeding or a different one; and

   (B)   is now offered against a party who had — or, in a civil case, whose predecessor in interest had — an opportunity and similar motive to develop it by direct, cross-, or redirect examination.

As we saw in Chapter 19 with the common law evolution of the vicarious admission doctrine, the early law of former testimony was dominated by related civil procedure rules. More recently, courts have been freeing the former testimony doctrine from the grip of those rules and relaxing the admissibility of prior testimony. As in the case of vicarious admissions, the focus has shifted to the reliability of the evidence rather than reliance on rigid doctrines of privity and agency. The guarantees of reliability in the case of former testimony are compelling: The foundation includes proof of the declarant's unavailability at the present hearing, the presentation of the testimony at an earlier hearing, and a showing that the opponent had a fair chance to develop the testimony at the prior hearing. While the first element creates the necessity for resorting to the prior testimony, the other elements supply the indicia of reliability.

The first reliability guarantee is that ***the witness gave the prior testimony at a fair adversary hearing.*** The testimony must have been given under oath; and if the hearing was a critical stage in a criminal prosecution, the state must have afforded the defendant a right to counsel. *Pointer v. Texas*, 380 U.S. 400 (1965) (the testimony was given at preliminary hearing at which the accused was denied counsel). However, the most important procedural safeguard is the one most central to hearsay policy — the opportunity to examine the witness at the prior proceeding. It is well-settled that if the party had no opportunity to cross-examine, the evidence cannot be admitted under the former testimony exception. *Edgerley v. Appleyard*, 110 Me. 337, 86 A. 244 (1913). In *California v. Green*, 399 U.S. 149 (1970), the Supreme Court sustained the admission of a witness's preliminary hearing testimony and stressed that the previous opportunity for cross-examination at the preliminary hearing served to satisfy the mandates of both the hearsay rule and the Confrontation Clause. So long as that opportunity is afforded, even a deposition conducted under foreign law can qualify; the deposition can be admitted even if the foreign deposition procedure differs radically from American procedure. *United States v. Kelly*, 892 F.2d 255 (3d Cir. 1989) (Belgian deposition), *cert. denied*, 497 U.S. 1006 (1990); *United States v. Casamento*, 887 F.2d 1141, 1174 (2d Cir. 1989) (Swiss depositions), *cert. denied*, 493 U.S. 1081 (1990);*United States v. Salim*, 664 F. Supp. 682 (E.D.N.Y. 1987), *aff'd*, 855 F.2d 944 (2d Cir. 1988) (under French law, the attorneys' only participation was the ability to submit written interrogatories, and all questions were asked by the judge).

PROBLEMS

(1) Problem 21-4. In *Devitt*, one witness, Ms. Farrell, testified before the grand jury that returned the indictment against the defendant. Farrell testified that she saw Devitt leave Paterson's apartment at the time of the alleged battery and that at the time Devitt appeared to be upset and in a rush. Farrell died before trial. Can the prosecutor introduce Farrell's grand jury testimony at the trial under the former testimony exception? *Young v. United States*, 406 F.2d 960, 962 n. 2 (D.C.Cir. 1968)(no).

(2) Problem 21-5. In *Hill*, the state of Morena brought an administrative action against Worker to suspend his license. At the license revocation hearing, Ms. Pepperidge testified that in her opinion Worker was driving at least fifteen miles an hour in excess of the speed limit. Pepperidge dies before trial. Can Ms. Hill introduce Pepperidge's testimony under Rule 804(b)(1)? Does it matter that the hearing was "administrative" rather than "judicial"? Would Ms. Hill have to name Worker as a defendant before invoking Rule 804(b)(1)?

At common law, the second traditional guarantee of reliability was *"identity" of parties*, which required that the parties to suit #2 be the same as the parties to suit #1 or be in a relationship of strict privity. However, as Wigmore noted, the limits of privity are not necessarily the extent of reliability; it was very questionable whether this rule, imported from the arena of civil procedure, made sense in the context of a hearsay exception.

The logic of Wigmore's position eventually prevailed, and courts adopted the position that the cross-examination requirement is satisfied when the party against whom the prior testimony is now offered was a party to the earlier trial. So long as that party had an opportunity to cross-examine or otherwise develop the testimony of the witness in trial #1, there is a sufficient guarantee of reliability for the witness's prior testimony to be admissible at trial #2. Indeed, the original version of Rule 804(b)(1) explicitly referred to "the party against whom the testimony is now offered."

Some commentators argued that the exception for former testimony should be even broader and that such evidence should be admissible even where the opposing party was not a party to the prior action, if the party it was offered against in trial #1 was similarly situated — that is, possessed a similar interest and motive to develop the testimony. If that party had the necessary interest and motive, it would have cross-examined and probed the prior testimony to ensure that it was trustworthy. Hence, there would be a safeguard of reliability even if the party against whom the testimony is now offered was not a party (or in technical privity with a party) in trial #1. Although the Federal Rules did not go this far, the California legislature accepted this reasoning for civil cases in Evidence Code § 1292(a):

Evidence of former testimony is not made inadmissible by the hearsay rule if:

(1)   The declarant is unavailable as a witness;

(2)   The former testimony is offered in a civil action; and

(3)   The issue is such that the party to the action or proceeding in which the former testimony was given had the right and opportunity to cross-examine the declarant with an interest and motive similar to that which the party against whom the testimony is offered has at the hearing.

In analyzing the admissibility of hearsay under the former testimony exception it is usually best to focus initially on hearing #2. At hearing #2, who is the party against whom the evidence is being offered? Then look at hearing #1 and ask: Was this party: (a) a party to hearing #1, (b) in privity with a party to hearing #1, or (c) under the California statute, similarly situated to a party to hearing #1?

NOTES AND PROBLEMS

1. **Problem 21-6.** Before the *Hill* case came to trial, Roe sued Worker for indemnification for the property damage to Roe's truck. At the trial, Roe called Ms. Pepperidge as a witness. She testified that she believed that Worker was speeding. Pepperidge died before the trial in *Hill.* In *Hill,* the plaintiff offers the transcript of Pepperidge's testimony against Roe. Does the evidence qualify under the former testimony exception? Did Roe have an opportunity to "cross-examine" Pepperidge in the prior trial? *See* FED. R. EVID. 804(b)(1).

2. **Problem 21-7.** Before the trial in *Hill,* Ms. Oppenheimer brought a similar lawsuit against Polecat to trial. At that trial, Oppenheimer called Professor Vincent as an expert witness on safety design. He testified that in his opinion the placement of the gas tank was hazardous. Professor Vincent dies before the trial in *Hill.* May Ms. Hill offer evidence of Vincent's testimony against Polecat in the present trial?

3. Several courts applying Rule 804(b)(1) have found the phrase "predecessor in interest" troublesome. *E.g., New England Life Ins. Co. v. Anderson,* 888 F.2d 646, 651–52 (10th Cir. 1989) (distinguishing between "realistic . . ." and "formalistic" interpretations of "predecessor in interest"). Three possible interpretations have emerged:

- Some courts construe the expression in the narrow property sense of privity;

- Others go to the opposite extreme and find a predecessor in interest whenever there is similarity of motive between the earlier litigant and the party in the instant suit. *Supermarket of Marlinton v. Meadow Gold Dairies,* 875 F. Supp. 340, 344–45 (W.D. Va. 1994).

- Still others have embraced a compromise position and insist on a unique relationship between the two parties that ensures similarity of interest and motive.

The current Reporter for the Federal Rules of Evidence Advisory Committee, Professor Daniel Capra, touches on this issue in ADVISORY COMMITTEE NOTES TO THE FEDERAL RULES OF EVIDENCE THAT MAY REQUIRE CLARIFICATION (Fed. Jud. Center 1998). On the one hand, he points out that given the way the expression "predecessor in interest" is ordinarily used, the statute appears to require proof of "some kind of [technical] privity relationship." *Id.* at 20–21. On the other hand, he observes that the Advisory Committee Note uses broader language. Further, as he reads the cases, the courts "have generally opted . . . for the Advisory Committee approach" and permitted the Note to "supersede" the statutory text. *Id.* at 21–22. *New Jersey Turnpike Authority v. PPG Industries,* 197 F.3d 96, 110 n.21 (3d Cir. 1999) bears out Professor Capra's observation. *See also Cordance Corp. v. Amazon.com, Inc.,* 639 F. Supp. 2d 406, 431 (D. Del. 2009) ("[p]rivity is not required").

Look again at Rule 804(b)(1). By its terms, in addition to requiring that the party to the prior hearing was "a predecessor in interest," the rule imposes a separate requirement that the party had a "similar motive to develop the testimony." Does that express requirement strengthen or weaken the argument for an expansive construction of "predecessor in interest"? When a legislature uses different terms — "interest" as opposed to "motive" — courts normally presume that the legislature meant different things. The legislative history is of little help. 2 McCormick, Evidence § 303, at 351–52 (6th ed. 2006) ("the House Subcommittee that drafted this [language] intended it to require a 'formal relationship' between the parties. [But h]ow much weight to give such obscure indications of legislative intent is . . . unclear, particularly since even the Senate Judiciary Committee did not appear to understand the significance of the modification").

The last guarantee of reliability takes the form of a requirement that there be *identity of issues between the two hearings*. Although courts usually refer to "issues," it is more precise to think about the issue in the singular — a comparison between the fact that the testimony was offered to prove in trial one and the fact that it is now offered to establish. The requirement of similarity of issues is embodied in Rule 804(b)(1)'s requirement that the party against whom the evidence is now offered have had a "similar motive" to develop the testimony at the prior trial or hearing.

The modern understanding of the requirements for identity of parties and issues is that both requirements are merely means to an end — ensuring that at the prior hearing, the testimony was probed with roughly the same vigor that it would have been challenged with in the current trial. In a civil case, that necessitates inquiring whether the stakes in the prior hearing were roughly equivalent to the stakes in the current trial. If Ms. Oppenheimer's prior suit against Polecat had been a claim for only $2,000 in property damage to her car, we cannot be confident that Professor Vincent's testimony was tested as rigorously as it would be in *Hill* with hundreds of thousands of dollars in issue. The motive and incentive to cross-examine would be much greater in *Hill*. As the Assembly Committee's Comment to California Evidence Code § 1291 states, "[t]he determination of similarity of interest and motive in cross-examination should be based on practical considerations and not merely on the similarity of the party's position in the two cases. For example, testimony contained in a deposition that was taken, but not offered in evidence at the trial, in a different action should be excluded if the judge determines that the deposition was taken for discovery purposes and that the party did not subject the witness to a thorough cross-examination because he sought to avoid a premature revelation of the weakness in the testimony of the witness or in the adverse party's case."

NOTE

It is generally understood that criminal defense counsel use preliminary hearings for discovery. Unlike Perry Mason — who won all his cases at the preliminary hearing — most defense counsel do not present a full case at the hearing; rather, they sit back and discover the case the police have amassed against their client. Given that common practice, is there sufficient identity of issues between the preliminary hearing and the trial? *Compare California v. Green*, 399 U.S. 149, 166 (1970) ("although . . . the preliminary hearing is ordinarily a less searching exploration into the merits of a case than a trial, . . . 'there may be some justification for holding that the opportunity for cross-examination of a witness at a preliminary hearing satisfies the demands of the confrontation clause'") *with*

Ohio v. Roberts, 448 U.S. 56, 61–62, 69–72 (1980) (strongly hinting that the mere opportunity for cross-examination satisfies the Confrontation Clause). *See Trigones v. Bissonette*, 296 F.3d 1, 11–13 (1st Cir. 2002) (the defendant had the same motive to cross-examine at a suppression hearing that he would have had at trial).

Just as the defense's motivation might change from the preliminary hearing to the trial, the prosecution's motivation can change from the grand jury to the trial. In *United States v. Salerno*, 937 F.2d 797 (2d Cir. 1991), the defendants, alleged Cosa Nostra members, were charged with rigging bids on construction projects. The indictment alleged that the defendants did so by allocating contracts among a "Club" of six concrete companies. Two witnesses, DeMatteis and Bruno, testified before a grand jury but invoked their privilege against self-incrimination at trial. The witnesses owned a construction company. In their grand jury testimony, these two witnesses stated that neither they nor their company participated in the Club. At trial, the defense offered this grand jury testimony and the government objected that there was insufficient similarity of issues between the two proceedings. The trial judge excluded the evidence, but the Second Circuit reversed. The circuit court noted that although the witnesses were unavailable to testify at trial, as a practical matter the prosecution could — if it chose — make the witnesses available by granting them immunity. The court therefore held that "since these witnesses were available to the government at trial through a grant of immunity, the government's motive in examining the witnesses at the grand jury was irrelevant." The government appealed, and the Supreme Court handed down the following decision:

UNITED STATES v. SALERNO
505 U.S. 317 (1992)

JUSTICE THOMAS delivered the opinion of the Court.

The District Court refused to admit the grand jury testimony. It observed that Rule 804(b)(1) permits admission of former testimony against a party at trial only when that party had a "similar motive to develop the testimony by direct, cross, or redirect examination." The District Court held that the United States did not have this motive, stating that the "motive of a prosecutor in questioning a witness before the grand jury in the investigatory stages of a case is far different from the motive of a prosecutor in conducting the trial." A jury subsequently convicted the respondents . . . . The . . . Court of Appeals for the Second Circuit reversed, holding that the District Court . . . erred in excluding [the] grand jury testimony. Although the Court of Appeals recognized that "the government may have had no motive . . . to impeach Bruno or DeMatteis" before the grand jury, it concluded that "the government's motive in examining the witnesses . . . was irrelevant." The Court . . . decided that, in order to maintain "adversarial fairness," Rule 804(b)(1)'s similar motive element should "evaporat[e]" when the government obtains immunized testimony in a grand jury proceeding from a witness who refuses to testify at trial. We . . . reverse . . . .

Rule 804(b)(1) . . . establishes an exception to the hearsay rule for former testimony. This exception provides: "The following are not excluded by the hearsay rule if the declarant is unavailable as a witness: Former Testimony. Testimony given as a witness at another hearing . . . if the party against whom the testimony is now offered . . . had an opportunity and similar motive to develop the testimony by direct, cross, or redirect examination."

Nothing in the language of Rule 804(b)(1) suggests that a court may admit former testimony absent satisfaction of each of the Rule's elements. The United States thus asserts that, unless it had a "similar motive," . . . the District Court properly excluded DeMatteis and Bruno's testimony as hearsay. The respondents . . . urge us not to read Rule 804(b)(1) in a "slavishly literal fashion." They contend that "adversarial fairness" prevents the United States from relying on the similar motive requirement in this case. We agree with the United States.

When Congress enacted the prohibition against admission of hearsay in Rule 802, it placed 24 exceptions in Rule 803 and 5 additional exceptions in Rule 804. Congress thus presumably made a careful judgment as to what hearsay may come into evidence and what may not. To respect its determination, we must enforce the words it enacted. The respondents . . . have no right to introduce DeMatteis and Bruno's grand jury testimony under Rule 804(b)(1) without showing a "similar motive."

The respondents . . . assert that adversarial fairness requires us to infer that Rule 804(b)(1) contains implicit limitations. They observe, for example, that the Advisory Committee Note to Rule 804 makes clear that the former testimony exception applies only to statements made under oath or affirmation, even though the Rules does not state this restriction explicitly. The respondents maintain that we likewise may hold that Rule 804(b) does not require a showing of similar motive in all instances.

The respondents' example does not persuade us . . . . If the Rules applies only to sworn statements, it does so not because adversarial fairness implies a limitation, but simply because the word "testimony" refers only to statements made under oath or affirmation. *See* BLACK'S LAW DICTIONARY 1476 (6th ed. 1990). We see no way to interpret the text of Rule 804(b)(1) to mean that defendants sometimes do not have to show "similar motive."

The question remains whether the United States had a "similar motive" in this case. The United States asserts that the District Court specifically found that it did not and that we should not review its factual determinations. It also argues that a prosecutor generally will not have the same motive to develop testimony in grand jury proceedings as he does at trial. A prosecutor, it explains, must maintain secrecy during the investigatory stages of the criminal process and therefore may not desire to confront grand jury witnesses with contradictory evidence. It further states that a prosecutor may not know, prior to indictment, which issues will have importance at trial and accordingly may fail to develop grand jury testimony effectively.

The respondents . . . characterize the District Court's ruling as one of law, rather than fact, because the District Court essentially ruled that a prosecutor's motives at trial always differ from his motives in grand jury proceedings. The respondents contend further that the grand jury transcripts in this case show that the United States thoroughly attempted to impeach DeMatteis and Bruno.

The Court of Appeals . . . erroneously concluded that the respondents did not have to demonstrate a similar motive in this case to make use of Rule 804(b)(1). It therefore declined to consider fully the arguments now presented by the parties about whether the United States had such a motive. Rather than address this issue here in the first instance, we think it prudent to remand the case for further consideration.

NOTES

1. When potential defense witnesses possessing exculpatory information refuse to testify on the grounds of self-incrimination, defendants have sometimes argued that their constitutional Due Process rights require that the prosecution grant the witness immunity in order to make the exculpatory testimony available. For the most part, the courts have rejected this argument. *United States v. Khan*, 728 F.2d 676 (5th Cir. 1984). Given the failure of the constitutional argument, defendants have turned to non-constitutional, evidentiary arguments such as the former testimony rationale advanced in *Salerno*.

2. The starting point of Justice Thomas' opinion is predictable — the text of the statute. The defense urged the Court not to adopt a "slavishly literal" reading of Rule 804(b)(1). The defense's proposed statutory interpretation was rather novel. In effect, the defense conceded that Rule 804(b)(1) controlled, but the defense contended that it did not have to comply with one of the requirements set out on the face of Rule 804(b)(1). Did the defense articulate a convincing justification for singling out the motive requirement and obviating the need to satisfy it?

3. What "extrinsic" source did Justice Thomas consult to determine the meaning of the word "testimony" in Rule 804(b)(1)? According to some commentators, reliance on dictionaries can be treacherous. Cunningham et al., *Plain Meaning and Hard Cases*, 103 YALE L.J. 1561, 1615 (1994). "[T]here are a wide variety of dictionaries from which to choose, and all of them usually provide several entries for each word. The selection of a particular dictionary and a particular definition is not obvious and must be defended on some other grounds of suitability." Note, *Looking It Up: Dictionaries and Statutory Interpretation*, 107 HARV. L. REV. 1437, 1445 (1994).

4. Assume that the motive requirement is applicable. On the facts, who has the better of the argument over whether the prosecution had a similar motive before the grand jury? In dissent in *Salerno*, Justice Stevens argued that the requirement was satisfied. On remand, a panel of the Second Circuit agreed, 974 F.2d 231 (2d Cir. 1992), but the Second Circuit then reheard the case *en banc*, vacated the panel decision, and held that the government did not have a sufficiently similar motive. *United States v. DiNapoli*, 8 F.3d 909, 915 (2d Cir. 1993). However, the result in *Salerno* does not mean that the government's motive at trial can never be sufficiently similar to its motive at the grand jury stage. *E.g., United States v. McFall*, 558 F.3d 951 (9th Cir. 2009) (the government had the same motive and opportunity to question the witness when it brought him before the grand jury).

5. Several courts have found that the government had a different motive at a pretrial plea hearing than it had at a later trial. *United States v. Preciado*, 336 F.3d 739, 746 (8th Cir. 2003) ("[t]he government's motive at Preciado's change of plea hearing was to ensure that the plea was knowing, voluntary, and intelligent and that there was an adequate factual basis to accept it — it had no need or motive to develop testimony about Sanchez"), *cert. denied*, 540 U.S. 1134 (2004); *United States v. Jackson*, 335 F.3d 170, 178 (2d Cir. 2003) (a co-conspirator's statements at his plea allocution were not admissible against the government; "the Government does not have the same motive to examine the defendant at a plea hearing as it does at other proceedings"); *Commonwealth v. Colon*, 846 A.2d 747 (Pa. Super. Ct. 2004) (the Commonwealth's motive at a co-defendant's aborted guilty plea proceeding). *See also S.E.C. v. Jasper*, 678 F.3d 1116, 1128 (9th Cir. 2012)("'during the investigatory stage of the proceedings, as opposed to the accusatory stage, . . . the trial . . . , the motive is different'").

2. Declarations Against Interest

In the case of former testimony, the circumstantial guarantee of trustworthiness is the prior opportunity to test the declarant's perception, memory, narration, and sincerity by cross-examination. There is a different basis for inferring reliability in the case of declarations against interest. Here the inference arises from the fact that it is against the person's rational self-interest to have made the statement: we assume that people are self-interested and do not say things that are against their interest unless those things are actually true. The further requirement of firsthand knowledge contributes to the inference of the statement's reliability.

Rule 804(b)(3) provides:

> (b) The Exceptions. The following are not excluded by the rule against hearsay if the declarant is unavailable as a witness:

> (3) Statement Against Interest. A statement that:

> (A) a reasonable person in the declarant's position would have made only if the person believed it to be true because, when made, it was so contrary to the declarant's proprietary or pecuniary interest or had so great a tendency to invalidate the declarant's claim against someone else or to expose the declarant to civil or criminal liability; and

> (B) is supported by corroborating circumstances that clearly indicate its trustworthiness, if it is offered in a criminal case as one that tends to expose the declarant to criminal liability.

Again, the key circumstantial guarantee of sincerity is the declarant's realization that the statement is contrary to his or her interests and therefore the realization must exist when the declarant makes the statement. This timing requirement is an important distinction between statements of party-opponents ("admissions") admissible under Rule 801(d)(2) and declarations against interest. While it is true that an Rule 801(d)(2) admission is presumably against the party's interest *at the trial* (since it must be offered against the party to fall under the rule) it need not have been against the declarant's interest at the time it was made. In contrast, the reliability rationale for declarations against interest rests on an inference of sincerity, and inferring sincerity requires a finding that the statement was against the declarant's interest at the time it was said.

Under the common-law understanding of the exception, the test for whether a statement was against the declarant's interest was, in principle, a subjective one — the crucial issue was whether the declarant actually believed the statement to be against her interest. Morgan, *Declarations Against Interest*, 5 VAND. L. REV. 451, 477 (1952). Of course, the state of mind of the hypothetical reasonable person is relevant; if a reasonable person would have thought that the statement was disserving, that is some evidence that the actual declarant entertained that thought. The reasonable person's hypothetical belief is circumstantial evidence of the declarant's actual belief. Does Rule 804(b)(3) treat the reasonable person's state of mind as circumstantial evidence? The federal courts seem to interpret the rule literally. They have declared that the test is "objective" *(United States v. Turner*, 475 F. Supp. 194 (E.D. Mich. 1978)), based on the perception of a reasonable person in the declarant's position rather than the declarant herself. *United States v. Satterfield*, 572 F.2d 687 (9th Cir.), *cert. denied*, 439 U.S. 840 (1978).

A difficult issue that has arisen with respect to statements against interest is how to treat statements that are generally against interest but, arguably, partially self-serving or neutral. The classic example is a confession of a cooperating coconspirator in a criminal case. While criminal confessions are obviously against the declarant's interest, to the extent that they shift blame or attempt to curry favor with the government they can also be self-serving. Should such statements qualify under the hearsay exception? That question was addressed by the Supreme Court in the following case:

WILLIAMSON v. UNITED STATES
512 U.S. 594 (1994)

JUSTICE O'CONNOR delivered the opinion of the Court, except as to Part II–C.

In this case we clarify the scope of the hearsay exception for statements against penal interest. Fed. Rule Evid. 804(b)(3).

[A sheriff stopped a rental car driven by Harris. When a search of the car revealed cocaine, Harris was arrested. After his arrest, Harris was questioned by DEAAgent Walton. Harris said that the cocaine belonged to Williamson and that it was to be delivered that night to a particular dumpster.

When Walton took steps to arrange a controlled delivery of the cocaine to the dumpster, Harris said, "I can't let you do that. That's not true, I can't let you go up there for no reason." Harris then told Walton that he had lied about the plans and that in truth he was driving the cocaine to Atlanta for Williamson. He said that Williamson had been traveling in front of him in anothercar and that, after Harris' car was stopped by police, Williamson turned around, drove past, and must have seen Harris' car trunk open. Harris said that since Williamson had apparently seen the police searching the car, it would now be impossible to make a controlled delivery.

Harris refused to testify at Williamson's trial, even though the prosecution gave him use immunity. The District Court ruled that, under Rule 804(b)(3), Agent Walton could relate what Harris had said to him. The court reasoned that "defendant Harris' statements clearly implicated himself, and therefore, are against his penal interest. Second, defendant Harris, the declarant, is unavailable. And third . . . there are sufficient corroborating circumstances in this case to ensure the trustworthiness of his testimony." Williamson was convicted and the Court of Appeals for the Eleventh Circuit affirmed.]

The hearsay rule, Fed. Rule Evid. 802, is premised on the theory that out-of-court statements are subject to particular hazards. The declarant might be lying; he might have misperceived the events which he relates; he might have faulty memory; his words might be misunderstood or taken out of context by the listener. And the ways in which these dangers are minimized for in-court statements — the oath, the witness' awareness of the gravity of the proceedings, the jury's ability to observe the witness' demeanor, and, most importantly, the right of the opponent to cross-examine — are generally absent for things said out of court.

Nonetheless, the Federal Rules of Evidence . . . recognize that some kinds of out-of-court statements are less subject to these hearsay dangers, and therefore except them from the general rule that hearsay is inadmissible. One such category covers statements that are against the declarant's interest. . . . Fed. Rule Evid. 804(b)(3).

To decide whether Harris' confession is made admissible under Rule 804(b)(3), we must first decide what the Rule means by "statement," which Federal Rule of Evidence 801(a)(1) defines as "an oral or written assertion." One possible meaning, "a report or narrative," WEBSTER'S THIRD NEW INTERNATIONAL DICTIONARY 2229, defn. 2(a) (1961), connotes an extended declaration. Under this reading, Harris' entire confession — even if it contains both self-inculpatory and non-self-inculpatory parts — would be admissible so long as in the aggregate the confession sufficiently inculpates him. Another meaning of "statement," "a single declaration or remark," *ibid.*, defn. 2(b), would make Rule 804(b)(3) cover only those declarations or remarks within the confession that are individually self-inculpatory.

Although the text of the Rule does not directly resolve the matter, the principle behind the Rule, so far as it is discernible from the text, points clearly to the narrower reading. Rule 804(b)(3) is founded on the commonsense notion that reasonable people, even reasonable people who are not especially honest, tend not to make self-inculpatory statements unless they believe them to be true. This notion simply does not extend to the broader definition of "statement." The fact that a person is making a broadly self-inculpatory confession does not make more credible the confession's non-self-inculpatory parts. One of the most effective ways to lie is to mix falsehood with truth, especially truth that seems particularly persuasive because of its self-inculpatory nature.

[T]he most faithful reading of Rule 804(b)(3) is that it does not allow admission of non-self-inculpatory statements, even if they are made within a broader narrative that is generally self-inculpatory. The district court may not just assume for purposes of Rule 804(b)(3) that a statement is self-inculpatory because it is part of a fuller confession, and this is especially true when the statement implicates someone else. "[T]he arrest statements of a codefendant have traditionally been viewed with special suspicion. Due to his strong motivation to implicate the defendant and to exonerate himself, a codefendant's statements about what the defendant said or did are less credible than ordinary hearsay evidence." *Lee v. Illinois*, 476 U.S. 530, 541 (1986).

In this case, . . . we cannot conclude that all that Harris said was properly admitted. Some of Harris' confession would clearly have been admissible under Rule 804(b)(3); for instance, when he said he knew there was cocaine in the suitcase, he essentially forfeited his only possible defense to a charge of cocaine possession, lack of knowledge. But other parts of his confession, especially the parts that implicated Williamson, did little to subject Harris himself to criminal liability. A reasonable person in Harris' position might even think that implicating someone else would decrease his practical exposure to criminal liability, at least so far as sentencing goes. Small fish in a big conspiracy often getshorter sentences than people who are running the whole show . . . , especially if the small fish are willing to help the authorities catch the big ones. . . .

Nothing in this record shows that the District Court . . . inquired whether each of the statements in Harris' confession was truly self-inculpatory. [T]his can be a fact-intensive inquiry, which would require careful examination of all the circumstances surrounding the criminal activity; we therefore remand to the Court of Appeals to conduct this inquiry in the first instance.

JUSTICE SCALIA, concurring.

I quite agree with the Court that a reading of the term "statement" to connote an extended declaration (and which would allow both self-inculpatory and non-self-inculpatory parts of a declaration to be admitted so long as the declaration in the aggregate was sufficiently inculpatory) is unsupportable.

[A] declarant's statement is not magically transformed from a statement against penal interest into one that is inadmissible merely because the declarant names another person. . . . For example, if a lieutenant in an organized crime operation described the inner workings of an extortion and protection racket, naming some of the other actors and thereby inculpating himself . . . , some of those remarks could be admitted as statements against penal interest. Of course, naming another person, if done . . . in a context where the declarant is minimizing culpability or criminal exposure, can bear on whether the statement meets the Rule 804(b)(3) standard. The relevant inquiry, however — and one that is not furthered by clouding the waters with manufactured categories such as "collateral neutral" and "collateral self-serving" . . . — must always be whether the particular remark at issue (and not the extended narrative) meets the standard set forth in the rule.

JUSTICE GINSBURG, with whom JUSTICE BLACKMUN, JUSTICE STEVENS, and JUSTICE SOUTER join, concurring in part and concurring in the judgment.

[These justices would have ruled that "Harris' statements . . . do not fit, even in part, within" Rule 804(b)(3). Harris had been "caught red-handed with 19 kilos of cocaine." The self-inculpatory parts of his statements "provided only marginal or cumulative evidence of his guilt." Overall, the circumstances "project an image of a person acting not against his penal interest, but striving mightily to shift personal responsibility to someone else." In that light, "none of Harris' hearsay statements were admissible under Rule804(b)(3)."]

JUSTICE KENNEDY, with whom THE CHIEF JUSTICE and JUSTICE THOMAS join, concurring in the judgment.

There has been a long-running debate among commentators over the admissibility of collateral statements. Dean Wigmore took the strongest position in favor of admissibility, arguing that "the statement may be accepted, not merely as to the specific fact against interest, but also as to every fact contained in the same statement." 5 J. WIGMORE, EVIDENCE § 1465 (3d ed. 1940). According to Wigmore, because "the statement is made under circumstances fairly indicating the declarant's sincerity and accuracy," the entire statement should be admitted. Dean McCormick's approach regarding collateral statements was more guarded. He argued for the admissibility of collateral statements of a neutral character; and for the exclusion of collateral statements of a self-serving character. For example, in the statement "John and I robbed the bank," the words "John and" are neutral (save for the possibility of conspiracy charges). On the other hand, the statement, "John, not I, shot the bank teller" is to some extent self-serving and therefore might be inadmissible. *See* C. McCORMICK, LAW OF EVIDENCE § 256 (1954). Professor Jefferson took the narrowest approach, arguing that the reliability of a statement against interest stems only from the disserving fact stated and so should be confined "to the proof of the fact which is against interest." Jefferson, *Declarations Against Interest: An Exception to the Hearsay Rule*, 58 HARV. L. REV. 1 (1944). Under the Jefferson approach, neither collateral neutral nor collateral self-serving statements would be admissible.

The text of Rule [804(b)(3)] does not tell us whether collateral statements are admissible. . . . Because the text of Rule 804(b)(3) expresses no position regarding the admissibility of collateral statements, we must determine whether there are other authoritative guides on the question. In my view, three sources demonstrate that Rule 804(b)(3) allows the admission of some collateral statements: the Advisory Committee Note, the common law . . . , and the general presumption that Congress did not enact statutes that have almost no effect.

First, the Advisory Committee Note establishes that some collateral statements are admissible. In fact, it refers in specific terms to the issue we here confront: "[o]rdinarily the third-party confession is thought of in terms of exculpating the accused, but this is by no means always or necessarily the case; it may include statements implicating him, and under the general theory of declarations against interest they would be admissible as related statements." This language seems a forthright statement that collateral statements are admissible under Rule 804(b)(3). When as here the text of a Rule of Evidence does not answer a question . . . , and . . . the Advisory Committee Note does answer the question, . . . we should pay attention to the Advisory Committee Note. We have referred often to those Notes in interpreting the Rules of Evidence, and I see no reason to jettison that well-established practice here. *See Huddleston v. United States*, 485 U.S. 681

(1988); *United States v. Owens*, 484 U.S. 554 (1988); *Bourjaily v. United States*, 483 U.S. 171 (1987); *United States v. Abel*, 469 U.S. 45 (1984).

Second, even if the Advisory Committee Note were silent about collateral statements, I would not adopt a rule excluding all statements collateral or related to the specific words against penal interest. Absent contrary indications, we can presume that Congress intended the principles and terms used in the Federal Rules of Evidence to be applied as they were at common law. *See Daubert v. Merrell Dow Pharmaceuticals, Inc.*, 509 U.S. 579 (1993); *Green v. Bock Laundry Machine Co.*, 490 U.S. 504 (1989). . . . Application of that interpretive principle indicates that collateral statements should be admissible. "From the very beginning of this exception, it has been held that a declaration against interest is admissible, not only to prove the disserving fact but also to prove other facts contained in collateral statements connected with the disserving statement." Jefferson, 58 HARV. L. REV. at 57. . . . I would not assume that Congress gave the common law rule a silent burial in Rule 804(b)(3).

There is yet a third reason weighing against the Court's interpretation. . . . [W]e should assume that Congress intended the penal interest exception for inculpatory statements to have some meaningful effect. That counsels against adopting a rule excluding collateral statements. "[T]he exclusion of collateral statements would cause the exclusion of almost all inculpatory statements." Comment, 66 CALIF. L. REV. at 1207. To be sure, under the approach adopted by the court, there are some situations where the Rule would still apply. For example, if the declarant said that he stole certain goods, the statement could be admitted in a prosecution of the accused for receipt of stolen goods in order to show that the goods were stolen. But . . . it is likely to be the rare case where the precise self-inculpatory words of the declarant, without more, also inculpate the defendant. I would not presume that Congress intended the penal interest exception . . . to have so little effect with respect to statements that inculpate the accused.

In sum, I would adhere to the following approach with respect to statements against penal interest that inculpate the accused. A court first should determine whether the declarant made a statement that contained a fact against penal interest. If so, the court should admit all statements related to the precise statement against penal interest, subject to two limits. Consistent with the Advisory Committee Note, the court should exclude a collateral statement that is so self-serving as to render it unreliable (if, for example, it shifts blame to someone else for a crime the defendant could have committed). In addition, in cases where the statement was made under circumstances where it is likely that the declarant had a significant motivation to obtain favorable treatment, as when the government made an explicit offer of leniency in exchange for the declarant's admission of guilt, the entire statement should be inadmissible.

NOTES

1. What was the very first source Justice O'Connor considered when she attempted to ascertain the meaning of "statement" in Rule 804(b)(3)? Remember Justice Thomas's analysis of the word "testimony" in Rule 804(b)(1) in *Salerno* and the commentators' criticism of heavy reliance on dictionaries.

2.   Under the definition of "statement" in Rule 801(a), what is the unit of analysis — the individual assertion or the larger declaration or writing including the assertion? *United States v. Canan*, 48 F.3d 954 (6th Cir. 1995), *cert. denied*, 516 U.S. 1050 (1996), reads *Williamson* as requiring "sentence by sentence" analysis. According to *United States v. Sims*, 879 F. Supp. 828, 832, 835 (N.D. Ill. 1995), *Williamson* mandates that the trial judge engage in "a segmented, not aggregate, analysis" to determine whether "each part of a proffered statement is . . . against . . . interest." Would it be more precise to say that the analysis must proceed assertion by assertion? Like Rule 801(a), the text of Rule 804(b)(3) purports to refer to a "statement" in the singular.

3.   Some commentators claim that the key issue in modern "legisprudence" is not *whether* to consult extrinsic legislative materials but rather *how much* such materials — such as the Advisory Committee Notes to the rules of evidence — should "count" in a court's interpretive decision. W. Eskridge & P. Frickey, Cases and Materials on Legislation: Statutes and the Creation of Public Policy 698 (1988). Does the disagreement between Justices O'Connor and Kennedy bear out that claim? Some view *Williamson* as a turning point away from a strict textualist approach by the Court. Taslitz, Daubert's *Guide to the Federal Rules of Evidence: A Not-So-Plain-Meaning Jurisprudence*, 32 Harv. J. On Legis. 3, 71–73 (1995). Think back to the *Tome* case (discussed in Chapter 18), which also relied heavily on the Advisory Committee Notes.

4.   The opinions in *Williamson* make reference to these categories of statements: self-inculpatory, disserving, non-self-inculpatory, self-serving, and neutral. How would you characterize the following hypothetical statements by Harris:

(a) "Williamson and I arranged the drug delivery." At the time of the statement Harris was on probation, one of the probation conditions was that he not associated with convicted felons, and Williamson was a convicted felon. Is Harris's reference to Williamson disserving to Harris's interest? Admitting involvement in the drug buy exposes Harris to the risk of prosecution for the drug offense. What else does the reference to Williamson expose Harris to?

(b) "Williamson and I arranged the drug delivery." Before Harris made the statement, he had been arrested. The police made it clear to Harris that they knew Williamson was a "big fish" in the drug ring and that Harris would receive more lenient treatment if he helped them build a case against Williamson.

(c) "Williamson and I arranged the drug delivery." However, as far as Harris can tell at the time he makes the statement, it is a matter of indifference to the police whether he names Williamson rather than C, D, or anybody else.

5.   Although *Williamson* involved a declaration against penal interest proffered in a criminal case, courts have extended the ruling to other contexts. *Silverstein v. Chase*, 260 F.3d 142 (2d Cir. 2001) (pecuniary interest), *aff'd*, 61 Fed.Appx. 743 (2d Cir. 2003); *Federated Mut. Ins. Co. v. Williams Trull Co.*, 838 F.Supp.2d 370, 408-11 (M.D.N.C. 2011)(civil case);*In re September 11 Litigation*, 621 F. Supp. 2d 131 (S.D.N.Y. 2009) (civil case). Are these extensions justified?

6.   While *Williamson* is based on the Court's construction of the Federal Rules of Evidence, in *Lilly v. Virginia*, 527 U.S. 116 (1999), the Court considered

Confrontation Clause limitations on the admission of statements that might qualify as declarations against interest under state law. The *Williamson* and *Lilly* decisions are kindred, since they both evince skepticism about custodial confessions. However, *Lilly* does not mandate as a matter of constitutional law that the state courts follow *Williamson*. Thus, "state courts need not follow the federal courts' parcel-by-parcel approach to interpreting their own versions of the statement-against-interest exception to the hearsay rule." *Bailey v. Pitcher*, 86 Fed.Appx. 110 (6th Cir. 2004).

Another controversy surrounding the declaration against interest exception centers on the **type of interest** to which the statement must be contrary. Logically, it would seem that there should be no limitation on the type of interest that is disserved. The only questions should be the magnitude of the interest and the degree to which the statement is contrary to the interest. Whatever the type, the declarant's realization that the statement is directly contrary to a weighty interest supplies an inference of reliability. Notwithstanding this logic, the common law sharply differentiated among various types of interest. The early common law narrowly recognized only pecuniary and proprietary interest. If Mr. Hill admitted that he owed Jefferson Motor Car Co. $100 on a late installment payment on the car, that statement would be admissible. Similarly, if he confessed that he did not have full title to the car and that Jefferson retained a security interest, that statement would be sufficiently disserving. The American cases strained to broaden the categories of pecuniary and proprietary interest to include statements that exposed the declarant to civil liability. *E.g., Weber v. Chicago, R.I. & P. Ry.*, 175 Iowa 358, 151 N.W. 852 (1915). However, in an 1844 British decision the House of Lords drew the line at pecuniary and proprietary interest and refused to recognize penal interest. The acceptance of penal interest in the United States has come grudgingly.

In *People v. Spriggs*, 60 Cal. 2d 868, 36 Cal. Rptr. 841, 389 P.2d 377 (1964), Justice Roger Traynor presented a persuasive argument that the doctrine should extend to penal interest. In time, Justice Traynor's argument won over the Supreme Court. Even before the adoption of the Federal Rules of Evidence, the Court had accepted the view that a statement against penal interest can be trustworthy precisely because of its disserving character. *United States v. Matlock*, 415 U.S. 164 (1974); *Chambers v. Mississippi*, 410 U.S. 284 (1973); *United States v. Harris*, 403 U.S. 573 (1971). Rule 804(b)(3) specifically mentions statements "subject[ing] the declarant to . . . criminal liability". While most jurisdictions now accept statements against penal interest under the exception, there are still occasional judicial opinions declaring that penal interest does not qualify. *E.g., State v. Turner*, 623 S.W.2d 4 (Mo. 1981), *cert. denied*, 456 U.S. 931 (1982); *State v. Hill*, 614 S.W.2d 744, 752 (Mo. Ct. App. 1981) ("[I]t has consistently been held that declarations against penal interest are not admissible").

Statements against social interest more broadly, however, are not covered by the exception in most jurisdictions. Congress decided against including social interest in Rule 804(b)(3). However, eleven states have adopted a version of Rule 804(b)(3) recognizing social interest. Note, *Sin, Suffering, and "Social Interest": Exception for Statements Subjecting the Hearsay Declarant to "Hatred, Ridicule, or Disgrace,"* 4 REV. LITIG. 367 (1985). Under California Evidence Code § 1230, a statement is admissible if the declarant realized that the statement would make "him an object of hatred, ridicule, or social disgrace in the community." In these jurisdictions, the courts often treat statements on the following topics as declarations against social interest: sexual impropriety, illegitimacy, criminal activity, suicide, insanity, or professional business incompetence, malpractice, or misconduct. Is Congress's decision defensible on the ground that it is more difficult to determine whether a statement will make a person "an object of . . . social disgrace" than to decide whether the statement would subject him to prosecution?

NOTES AND PROBLEMS

1. **Problem 21-8.** In *Devitt*, the defense counsel calls Mr. Napier as a witness. Napier is prepared to testify that he knows a Mr. Johnson and that Johnson confided in him that he had attacked Paterson. Johnson died a month before trial. The prosecutor objects on hearsay grounds. The defense counsel responds that the statement qualifies as a declaration against interest. What result? *See Harris v. State*, 387 A.2d 1152, 1155–56 (Md. Ct. Spec. App. 1978) (the third party's confession should be "received . . . unless it is clearly collusive, frivolous, or otherwise obviously untrustworthy"). Suppose that Johnson had said that he "alone had attacked Paterson." *Commonwealth v. Colon*, 461 Pa. 577, 584, 337 A.2d 554, 558 (1975) (if a part of a statement implicates the declarant and a distinct part exonerates the defendant, the portion exonerating the defendant is not against the declarant's interest), *cert. denied*, 423 U.S. 1056 (1976).

2. Note the last sentence in Rule 804(b)(3), which requires corroboration of statements against penal interest offered in criminal cases. The rationale for this requirement is that unless corroboration is required, it would be too easy for a defendant to obtain perjured testimony about third-party confessions. Courts differ, however, over what exactly must be corroborated. The credibility of the in-court witness's report that the hearsay declarant made the statement? *United States v. Lubell*, 301 F. Supp. 2d 88, 91 (D. Mass. 2004). The general credibility of the hearsay declarant? The trustworthiness of the specific statement allegedly made by the hearsay declarant? *United States v. Lumpkin*, 192 F.3d 280 (2d Cir. 1999).

3. The original version of Rule 804(b)(3) did not impose the same requirement on prosecution evidence. Tague, *Perils of the Rulemaking Process: The Development, Application, and Unconstitutionality of Rule 804(b)(3)'s Penal Interest Exception*, 69 Geo. L.J. 851, 978–1011 (1981) argued that the statute was therefore unconstitutional. To moot the constitutional issue, several courts read a corroboration requirement for prosecution evidence into the statute. *American Automative Accessories, Inc. v. Fishman*, 175 F.3d 534, 541 (7th Cir. 1999) ("[w]e believe it best to . . . utilize a unitary standard for applying Rule 804(b)(3) to statements offered both to exculpate and to inculpate a third party"); *United States v. Candoli*, 870 F.2d 496, 509 (9th Cir. 1989) (citing Second, Third, Fifth, and Eighth Circuit cases imposing a corroboration requirement). As a matter of statutory interpretation, it was strained to read in the requirement. Some commentators contended that the courts had in effect rewritten the statute and stretched the constitutional avoidance maxim too far. In 2010, the statute was amended to extend the corroboration requirement to prosecution evidence.

3. Dying Declarations

One of the more mystical hearsay exceptions is the dying declaration doctrine. This doctrine allows the admission of dramatic evidence of deathbed statements on the assumption that the declarant would not want to meet her maker with a lie on her lips. At common law, this exception required proof of the following foundational facts: (1) At the time of the statement, the declarant had "a settled hopeless expectation of immediately impending death." The declarant had to believe that death was both certain and imminent. (2) The declarant had personal knowledge of the facts recited in the statement. (3) The declaration had to relate to "the circumstances directly leading up to the declarant's death." (4) The accusatory pleading had to charge the accused with the declarant's murder. (5) At the time of trial, the declarant had to be dead. Death was the only acceptable showing of the declarant's unavailability.

The first requirement is obviously defensible. Throughout the history of this exception, the courts have stressed the declarant's evident sincerity as the basis for inferring reliability. The inference arises from the declarant's belief that imminent death is certain. At one time, the courts were exceedingly strict in demanding proof of the declarant's belief in certain and imminent death. Nowadays, they will accept numerous types of circumstantial evidence of that belief, including the condition or severity of the wound, the administration of last rites to the declarant, and the declarant's own statements.

The second and third requirements are based on the rationale of guarding against the hearsay dangers of misperception and misrecollection. Like the "relating to" restriction in Rule 803(2) governing excited utterances, the third limitation evidences concern about the quality of the declarant's memory. When the declarant refers to preceding events such as earlier arguments with the alleged killer, there is a much greater risk of misrecollection.

In contrast, some of the other requirements enforced at common law made little or no sense. For instance, at early common law, the courts limited the doctrine to statements by deceased declarants, named as the victim in homicide prosecutions. The courts reasoned that the most compelling need was for the declarations of homicide victims. If the declarant recovered, or the declarant was not the named victim, or the case was not a homicide prosecution, the courts barred the evidence. These restrictions were subjected to pointed criticism. 5 J. Wigmore, Evidence § 1433 (3d ed. 1940). Under the Federal Rules of Evidence, it is no longer necessary that the declarant be dead at the time of trial. The only requirements are that the declarant meet the general unavailability test announced in Rule 804(a) and that the declarant make the statement "while believing the declarant's death to be imminent." Fed. R. Evid. 804(b)(2), Advisory Committee Note.

The exception's limitation to declarants named as victims in the pleading was also assailed. The limitation led to seemingly absurd results: If the defendant killed two persons by the same blow but the indictment named only one as the victim, the other victim's statements were excluded. *Westberry v. State*, 175 Ga. 115, 164 S.E. 905 (1932). McCormick concurred with Wigmore's remark, "Could one's imagination devise a more senseless rule of exclusion . . . ?" 2 C. McCormick,

EVIDENCE § 311 (6th ed. 2006) (*citing* 5 J. WIGMORE, EVIDENCE § 1433 (3d ed. 1940)). The Advisory Committee also agreed and did not include the restriction in Rule 804(b)(3).

Finally the exception's limitation to homicide prosecutions came under attack. Even before the adoption of the Federal Rules, several state legislatures had made inroads on this aspect of the orthodox rule. After much debate, Congress adopted a compromise position in Rule 804(b)(2):

> (b) The Exceptions. The following are not excluded by the rule against hearsay if the declarant is unavailable as a witness:

> (2) Statement Under the Belief of Imminent Death. In a prosecution for homicide or in a civil case, a statement that the declarant, while believing the declarant's death to be imminent, made about its cause or circumstances.

NOTES AND PROBLEMS

1. **Problem 21-9.** In *Devitt*, suppose that Paterson died after the attack and that Devitt is charged with murder. The prosecutor calls Patrolman Winslow as a witness. Winslow is prepared to testify that just before Paterson died at the scene he said, "That bastard Devitt did this to me. I'll get him for this. I'll pay him back. He never would have." The defense counsel objects that the statement does not fall within Rule 804(b)(2). What ruling?

2. **Problem 21-10.** Paterson told Winslow, "That bastard Devitt did this to me. He did it on purpose." The defense objects that the second sentence is irrelevant and incompetent hearsay because "it is too highly conclusory and opinionated." *See Pippin v. Commonwealth*, 117 Va. 919, 86 S.E. 152, 154–55 (1915) ("[t]he opinion rule has no application to dying declarations").

3. **Problem 21-11.** Paterson told Winslow, "That bastard Devitt did this to me. He said before that if I pushed him too far, something bad would happen. He lived up to his word." Does this testimony relate to the "cause and circumstances" of Paterson's death?

4. Although dying declarations have long been admissible, there has always been a strain of skepticism about them. Several jurisdictions require that the judge give the jury a cautionary instruction about dying declarations. Some jurisdictions demand that the judge tell the jury that a dying declaration is entitled to less weight than other evidence in the case. Others require that both the judge and jury pass on the admissibility of the declaration. Quick, *Some Reflections on Dying Declarations*, at 6 HOW. L.J. 109, 128 (1960).

Is this skepticism about dying declarations warranted? Perhaps the skepticism reflects a growing realization of the common law's overemphasis on the sincerity factor. Or is the fear that the evidence is so dramatic that the jury will attach too much weight to it?

5. Be prepared to list in class the differences between the excited utterance and dying declaration doctrines.

4.   Past Recollection Recorded

In the last section, we considered the hearsay exception that traditionally requiring the most extreme showing of necessity — the declarant's death. The next exception, for recorded recollections, is at the other extreme. Although the exception requires some showing of necessity, it accepts a very minimal showing: the witness's present inability to remember. In part because there is such a lax standard of unavailability for this exception, it is codified in Rule 803 rather than Rule 804.

a.   Contrasted with Present Recollection Refreshed

Before considering the past recollection recorded exception in detail, we should distinguish the exception from a related doctrine with which it is often confused — present recollection refreshed (or revived). By virtue of the latter doctrine, if the witness on the stand temporarily forgets a fact, the attorney may present the witness with an object such as a prior writing to revive the witness's memory. The object serves only to jog the memory of the witness; the actual evidence is the oral testimony from the witness's refreshed recollection. The doctrine thus rests on the psychological phenomenon of association. The witness associates the memory of a fact with a certain writing or object, and permitting the witness to inspect the writing or object will hopefully help the witness retrieve the associated memory. *See, e.g., Aponte-Rivera v. DHL Solutions (USA), Inc.*, 650 F.3d 803 (1st Cir. 2011).

Like past recollection recorded, the present recollection refreshed doctrine requires a showing of necessity before the attorney may resort to the document. "Most jurisdictions require a foundation that the witness cannot now recall all the facts about an event, or that the witness' memory is exhausted." Tanford, *An Introduction to Trial Law*, 51 Mo. L. Rev. 623, 667 (1986). Once the witness asserts a lack of memory, the attorney ordinarily inquires: "Is there anything — any writing, for example — that might help you remember?" The witness then identifies the document. The attorney marks the document as an exhibit for identification and presents it to the witness. The witness reads the document silently to himself. The attorney next asks: "Having read plaintiff's exhibit number three for identification, can you now recall the license number?" If the witness answers yes, the witness proceeds to testify unaided by the exhibit. Since the real evidence is the witness's testimony, the exhibit is not formally admitted into evidence; it remains only an exhibit for identification. *United States v. Faulkner*, 538 F.2d 724 (6th Cir.), *cert. denied*, 429 U.S. 1023 (1976).

This procedure raises several questions. To begin with, what types of documents may the witness use to refresh his memory? When we consider past recollection recorded, we shall see a number of restrictions on the documents usable under that theory. Some jurisdictions apply the same restrictions to writings employed to refresh recollection. 1 McCormick, Evidence § 9 (6th ed. 2006). However, "the wiser practice" and prevailing view is that "any memorandum . . . without restriction . . . as to authorship, guaranty of correctness, or time of making" can be used. *Id.* at 19. For example, there is substantial case authority that the witness may use documents prepared by third parties.

Consider the doctrine from the perspective of the opposing counsel. May the opponent inspect the document that the witness uses to refresh his memory? Courts concur on the proposition that the opponent has a right to inspect any document that the witness consults while on the witness stand. The more difficult question is whether the opponent has a right to inspect documents that the witness uses before trial. This question has divided the courts into three schools of thought.

The traditional view was that these documents are nondiscoverable. *Goldman v. United States*, 316 U.S. 129, 132 (1942); Annot., 82 A.L.R.2d 473 (1962). It is a common practice among trial attorneys to prepare their witnesses by reviewing the witnesses' statements with the witnesses before trial. The courts regarded this as a legitimate practice, and they feared that recognizing the discoverability of writings used before trial would create a disincentive for adequate pretrial preparation of the witnesses; the attorneys would fear that they were rendering the document discoverable by showing it to the witness during the pretrial conference.

Other jurisdictions repudiated the traditional view and declared that the opponent has a right to discover documents reviewed prior to trial. They asserted that the distinction between documents used at the trial and those reviewed pretrial is "artificial." *Commonwealth v. Marsh*, 354 Mass. 713, 242 N.E.2d 545 (1968). In their minds, a document used before trial is the "functional equivalent" of one used on the witness stand. *Ballew v. State*, 640 S.W.2d 237, 244 (Tex. Crim. App. 1982).

The trend in the case law and statutes is toward a third view, according the trial judge discretion to order the production of documents used before trial. Federal Rule of Evidence 612 is illustrative. Rule 612(a)(2) states that the opponent may examine a document used "before testifying, if the court decides that justice requires the party to have those options." The early cases in this line of authority were criminal decisions, but the trend soon spread to civil cases as well. On its face, Rule 612 applies to both types of proceedings. The boldest cases not only hold that the document is generally discoverable, but also announce that, by using the document before trial to refresh the witness's recollection, the party waives any privilege that would otherwise attach to the document. Belcour, *Use It and Lose It — Privileged Documents, Preparing Witnesses, and Rule 612 of the Federal Rules of Evidence*, 31 FED. B. NEWS & J. 171, 172 (1984). The more "cautious" cases hold that Rule 612 comes into play only when the record shows both that the witness consulted the document and that the witness did so for the specific purpose of refreshing memory to testify. *United States v. Sheffield*, 55 F.3d 341 (8th Cir. 1995); Applegate, *Preparing for Rule 612*, 19 LITIGATION, Spr. 1993, at 17, 20.

NOTES

1.   Why require a showing of necessity before permitting the witness to resort to a document to refresh her memory? Some have argued that liberally permitting witnesses to consult documents would probably improve the accuracy of courtroom testimony. Suppose that the witness prepared the notes with a view to using them while she was on the witness stand. Assume further that the attorney helped the witness prepare the notes. *See NLRB v. Federal Dairy Co.*, 297 F.2d 487, 489 (1st Cir. 1962) ("it [is] necessary to forbid the use of . . . artificial written aids capable of misuse so as to put into the witness' mouth a story which is . . . fictitious . . . ").

2. Are documents the only objects that the witness should be permitted to use to revive her memory? What if the witness stated that seeing a photograph or listening to a recording might refresh her memory? *Baker v. State*, 35 Md. App. 593, 371 A.2d 699 (1977), contains the following colorful passage:

> It may be a line from Kipling or the dolorous strain of "The Tennessee Waltz"; a whiff of hickory smoke; the running of the fingers across a swatch of corduroy; the sweet carbonation of a chocolate soda; the sight of a faded snapshot in a long-neglected album. All that is required is that it may trigger the Proustian moment. It may be anything that produces the desired testimonial prelude, "It all comes back to me now."

b. Past Recollection Recorded

Unlike present recollection refreshed, past recollection recorded is a full-fledged hearsay exception. Under the traditional view, an exhibit representing past recollection recorded is formally admitted because the writing is the actual evidence. What showing of reliability and necessity must the proponent make to justify the admission of the exhibit as past recollection recorded? Federal Rule of Evidence 803(5) addresses that question:

> The following are not excluded by the rule against hearsay, regardless of whether the declarant is available as a witness:

> (5) Recorded recollection. A record that: (A) is on a matter the witness once knew about but now cannot recall well enough to testify fully and accurately; (B) was made or adopted by the witness when the matter was fresh in the witness's memory; and (C) accurately reflects the witness's knowledge. If admitted, the record may be read into evidence but may be received as an exhibit only if offered by an adverse party.

At common law and under the Federal Rules, the foundation for past recollection recorded entails proof of both the writing's reliability and the necessity for resorting to it. The foundational requirements relate to three distinct points in time: the time of the recorded event, the time of the preparation of the record, and the time of trial.

The Time of the Event

The initial requirement concerns the time of the event which is recorded. As one mark of reliability, the writing must be based on personal knowledge of the fact or event recorded. When Rule 803(5) refers to "knowledge," the term means firsthand or personal knowledge in the Rule 602 sense.

The Time of the Preparation of the Record

The next two requirements relate to the time of the preparation of the record. One requirement speaks to the question of *who* prepares the record. The doctrine demands that the firsthand observer participate in preparing the writing. It is ideal if the observer herself prepared the writing. In *Devitt*, suppose that another tenant saw a car race away from Paterson's apartment and had the sense to note the car's license number, but she cannot remember the number at trial. Every jurisdiction would treat the note as past recollection recorded if the tenant herself wrote the note. Likewise, every jurisdiction will accept the note if the observer dictated the information to a third-party writer and then personally checked the note for accuracy. Imagine, for example, that one tenant, the wife, is standing by the window and sees the car race away. She immediately relays the license number to her husband sitting at the kitchen table. He records the number on a note pad, and his wife immediately walks over, picks up the note pad, and ensures that her husband correctly recorded the number.

It is more troublesome if the observer neglects to verify the writing at the time of the event. Suppose that the wife did not bother to walk across the room to check the number her husband recorded on the note pad. At common law, the courts dubbed this problem a "cooperative report." These records were admitted only if both witnesses testified at trial: the wife testified that she observed the car and relayed the license number to her husband, and the husband testified that he accurately recorded the number his wife gave him.

NOTES

1. Note the language of Rule 803(5): "made or adopted by the witness when the matter was fresh in the witness's memory." Is that language broad enough to include cooperative reports? Many courts continue to accept such cooperative records, as they did at common law. *E.g., Boehmer v. LeBoeuf,* 650 A.2d 1336 (Me. 1994). The Advisory Committee Note reads: "Multiple person involvement in the process of observing and recording, as in *Rathbun v. Brancatella,* 93 N.J.L. 222, 107 A. 279, 280 (1919), is entirely consistent with the exception." Is the statutory language at least ambiguous enough to permit resort to this legislative history material? Does a court have to find an ambiguity on the face of the statute before it may legitimately resort to extrinsic legislative history materials such as the Advisory Committee's Note? In his article on the interpretation of the Federal Rules (excerpted in Chapter 2), Professor Cleary states that sometimes, when there is a "collision . . . between legislative history and the seemingly unmistakable meaning of [the text] of a Rule," the *text* must yield. Would Judge Easterbrook agree? This may be another instance in which a court's construction of the statute turns on the court's philosophy of statutory interpretation.

2. Must courts stretch the language of Rule 803(5) to continue employing the common-law cooperative reports doctrine? Consider Rule 803(1), the exception for present sense impressions. Could the proponent argue that Rule 803(1) applies when, after observing the car race away, the wife turns and immediately tells the license number to her husband? Given Rule 803(1), would both the wife and the husband need to testify at trial to permit the introduction of the note recording the license number? *Cf. Cargill, Inc. v. Boag Cold Storage Warehouse, Inc.,* 71 F.3d 545, 554–55 (6th Cir. 1995) (no).

The exception for recorded recollections requires assurances of accurate memory as well as indications of firsthand knowledge; thus, a further requirement relates to *when* the record is prepared. The proponent must demonstrate that the declarant prepared or adopted the document while shestill had a good memory of the event. The strict common law requirement was that the writer had to draft the document at or near the time of the event. *Gigliotti v. United Illuminating Co.*, 151 Conn. 114, 193 A.2d 718 (1963). The modern common-law view is more liberal: courts often tolerate delays of as long as a few days in preparing the writing. Their tolerance is in accord with the state of modern witness psychology research. The data indicate that the psychological curve of memory declines rapidly after one or two days. E. LOFTUS, J. DOYLE & J. DYSART, EYEWITNESS TESTIMONY § 3.2 (4th ed. 2007); Stewart, *Perception, Memory, and Hearsay: A Criticism of Present Law and the Proposed Federal Rules of Evidence*, 1970 UTAH L. REV. 1. However, when the time lapse is longer — for example, approaching a week — the memory decay becomes extensive. *Id.* at 16; Gardner, *The Perception and Memory of Witnesses*, 18 CORNELL L.Q. 391, 393 (1933) (in a study of word recollection, the typical subject forgot 90% of the information in a week). Rule 803(5) refers directly to the quality of the declarant's memory rather than the time lapse, requiring only that the memory be "fresh" at the time that the record is made.

PROBLEM

Problem 21-12. In *Devitt*, the tenant, Mrs. Murchison, saw the license plate number of Devitt's car as he drove away from Paterson's apartment. Mrs. Murchison prides herself on her memory and felt no need to write the number down. However, there were delays in bringing Devitt to trial; after ten months had elapsed, Mrs. Murchison became concerned that she might forget. At that point, she sat down and wrote the license number on a note pad. She is prepared to testify that when she wrote on the pad she still "distinctly recalled" the license number she had seen. Can her notation qualify under Rule 803(5)? *See United States v. Patterson*, 678 F.2d 774, 778–80 (9th Cir.) (yes), *cert. denied*, 459 U.S. 911 (1982).

The Time of Trial

The past recollection recorded exception demands still another guarantee of the quality of memory: at the time of trial, the witness must vouch that the document was accurate when prepared. In the words of Rule 803(5), the document must be shown to have been "made or adopted by the witness when the matter was fresh in the witness's memory and [to] accurately reflect the witness's knowledge." It is certainly sufficient if the witness testifies that she recalls recording the data and recognizing the recorded data as correct. The proponent may also use habit evidence to lay this element of the foundation. If the writer had been a police officer entering the license number in his notebook, the officer could vouch that he is aware of the importance of this sort of entry and habitually double-checks such entries in his notebook. Some jurisdictions have even permitted a witness to vouch for himself: they admit the document where the witness says that he recognizes his handwriting and is positive that he would not have recorded the information if it had not been true. *Walker v. Larson*, 284 Minn. 99, 169 N.W.2d 737 (1969).

Finally, at the time of trial, the proponent must also establish a degree of necessity for introducing the writing. At early common law, the witness virtually had to say that he had drawn a complete blank; even after reviewing the writing on the witness stand, he could not remember any of the recorded data. *Bennefield v. State*, 281 Ala. 283, 202 So. 2d 55 (1967). However, in some cases, it was clearly absurd to require that the witness lack any current memory. If the writing listed several hundred items, it was altogether plausible that an honest witness would remember some items but forget others. The next step in liberalizing the standard was to adoption the test codified in Rule 803(5): Even after reviewing the document, the witness "cannot recall well enough to testify fully and accurately."

NOTES

1.   How does the unavailability standard for recorded recollections differ from the unavailability for the other exceptions covered in this chapter? Does it make sense to require a stronger showing of unavailability in the case of former testimony that has already been subjected to cross-examination? Do the witness's physical presence and availability for cross-examination justify a more relaxed standard of unavailability in the case of past recollections recorded?

2.   Sometimes the trial judge must draw a line between past recollection recorded and present recollection refreshed. If the witness testifies that even after viewing the document, he or she cannot remember, the foundation is laid for past recollection recorded. In contrast, if the witness testifies that after viewing the document, he or she can remember, the foundation is appropriate for present recollection refreshed. Suppose that the witness purports to remember, but her demeanor leads the judge to believe that the witness is lying? Does the judge have to accept the witness's statement at face value? *Fendi Adele v. Burlington Coat Factory Warehouse*, 689 F. Supp. 2d 585, 593–94 (S.D.N.Y. 2010) ("The district court has broad discretion.").

3.   The traditional view was that once the proponent had lain a complete foundation of reliability and necessity, the writing itself was admitted as substantive evidence. *Fisher v. Swartz*, 333 Mass. 265, 130 N.E.2d 575, 579 (1955). Does Rule 803(5) codify the traditional view? Like Rule 803(18) on learned treatises, Rule 803(5) uses the expressions "admitted" and "received." In *Maggipinto v. Reichman*, 607 F.2d 621, 622 (3d Cir. 1979), construing Rule 803(18), the court interpreted "admitted" as meaning formally introduced into evidence and "received" as referring to physical receipt of the exhibit by the trier of fact. When a legislature repeats the same words in different sections of the same statutory scheme, the courts ordinarily presume that the legislature intended the words to bear the same meaning in both sections. *Barnson v. United States*, 816 F.2d 549, 554 (10th Cir.), *cert. denied*, 484 U.S. 896 (1987). Under the Rule, how would the mechanics of handling a past recollection recorded differ from those for a document used to revive recollection?

4.   Rule 803(5) accords "an adverse party" the right to offer the document into evidence. Why might the adverse party want to offer the document?

5.   Depositions Otherwise Admissible Under Federal Rule of Civil Procedure 32(a)

Federal Rule of Civil Procedure 32(a) contains provisions authorizing the use of pretrial depositions at later trials in the same civil proceeding. Under Rule 32(a)(3)(B), a party may introduce the deposition so long as "the witness is at a greater distance than 100 miles from the place of trial or hearing . . . ." That showing of unavailability does not satisfy Rule 804(a). However, some courts have held that "Federal Rule of Civil Procedure 32(a) 'creates of its own force an exception to the hearsay rule' with respect to deposition testimony." *Orr v. Bank of America*, 285 F.3d 764 (9th Cir. 2002). These courts reason that the provision creates an "independent" (*id.*) "freestanding exception to the hearsay rule." *Ueland v. United States*, 291 F.3d 993 (7th Cir. 2002). If Rule 804 makes no mention of such a hearsay exception, how can these courts justify recognizing the exception? Note the reference to "other rules" in the text of Federal Rule of Evidence 802.

D. CONCLUSION

A comparison between Rules 803 and 804 suggests a tension in hearsay jurisprudence. To invoke most of the 803 exceptions, the proponent does not have to make any showing of necessity. At most, these exceptions assume a relative necessity: the hearsay evidence is likely to be more reliable than testimony now given on the witness stand. However, to trigger the 804 exceptions, the proponent must prove some species of unavailability: death, presence beyond the territorial reach of compulsory process, or lack of present memory. At least where the proponent can establish the declarant's unavailability, there is a genuine need for dispensing with otherwise valuable demeanor evidence and instead allowing hearsay.

Common sense suggests an inverse relationship between the factors of reliability and necessity; the greater the necessity, the less demanding we should be regarding proof of reliability. If that were the case, since the 804 exceptions require proof of necessity, we would ordinarily assume that they rest on a weaker inference of reliability than the exceptions in 803. Do you think that is an accurate description of the rules?

If the law of hearsay is inconsistent in this respect, what should we do to harmonize it? Would the solution be to liberalize Rule 804 by dispensing with proof of unavailability? In *People v. Spriggs*, 60 Cal. 2d 868, 875–76, 36 Cal. Rptr. 841, 845-46, 389 P.2d 377, 381–82 (1964), the California court struck that requirement from the foundation for declarations against interest. (The California legislature later adopted the state evidence code, and the code reinstated the unavailability requirement.) Or would it be better to tighten up Rule 803 to require much greater reliability?

Chapter 22

THE FUTURE OF THE RULE AGAINST HEARSAY: RESIDUAL EXCEPTION

Read Federal Rules of Evidence 803–04, 807.

A. INTRODUCTION

In our review of hearsay, we have highlighted the most important exclusions and exceptions. However, there are certain hearsay exceptions that we have glossed over or ignored entirely. For example, Rule 803(20) allows the admission of community reputation about "boundaries of land in the community or customs that affect the land" as well as "general historical events important to that community." Furthermore, when a matter of "general history or boundaries . . . could be proved by evidence of reputation," Rule 803(23) authorizes the use of a prior judgment to prove the matter. A whole host of exceptions — Rules 803(13), 803(19), 803(23), and 804(b)(4) — feature in estate litigation to help litigants prove family relationships. Moreover, because of the special reliability of judgments, Rule 803(22) broadly permits the introduction of certain prior criminal judgments in civil cases to "prove any fact essential to the judgment."

Rather than attempt to cover all of the exceptions, including rarely encountered ones, we focus in this chapter on the future of the rule against hearsay. The contours of the rule have changed over the past few decades and we likely can expect still more change in the future. One of the most thoughtful statements by the drafters of the Federal Rules appears in the Note to Rule 803(24), one of the predecessors to current Rule 807:

> The preceding . . . exceptions . . . are designed to take full advantage of the accumulated wisdom and experience of the past in dealing with hearsay. It would, however, be presumptuous to assume that all possible desirable exceptions to the hearsay rule have been catalogued and to pass the hearsay rule to oncoming generations as a closed system. [R]oom is left for growth and development of the law of evidence in the hearsay area. . . .

Based on that reasoning, the Advisory Committee added residual hearsay exceptions at the end of Rules 803 and 804 — these were consolidated and moved to Rule 807 in later amendments to the rules. To invoke the residual exception, the proponent must show both that the statement is reliable and that there is an element of necessity. The residual exception is particularly important because it creates a window into the common-law process.

Rule 807 provides:

(a) In General. Under the following circumstances, a hearsay statement is not excluded by the rule against hearsay even if the statement is not specifically covered by a hearsay exception in Rule 803 or 804:

    (1) the statement has equivalent circumstantial guarantees of trustworthiness;

    (2) it is offered as evidence of a material fact;

    (3) it is more probative on the point for which it is offered than any other evidence that the proponent can obtain through reasonable efforts; and

    (4) admitting it will best serve the purposes of these rules and the interests of justice.

(b) Notice. The statement is admissible only if, before the trial or hearing, the proponent gives an adverse party reasonable notice of the intent to offer the statement and its particulars, including the declarant's name and address, so that the party has a fair opportunity to meet it.

The future of the hearsay doctrine will be shaped in part by the statutory construction of the residual exception. As we shall see, the courts are badly divided over the proper interpretation of this exception. The future of the doctrine is also likely to be impacted by empirical research. For example, one of the most heated hearsay debates is whether there should be a special exception for statements by alleged victims in child abuse prosecutions. The outcome of that debate will likely depend in part on the ultimate findings of ongoing psychological investigations into the trustworthiness of such statements.

B. FUTURE LEGISLATIVE CHANGES

1. Abolition of the Hearsay Exclusion

Although the hearsay doctrine is a creature of the common law, most of the major recent changes have been effected by legislation. What legislative changes could occur in the near future?

The most drastic possibility would be the abolition of the hearsay rule altogether. In the last century, the English Parliament has taken major steps toward legislating the hearsay rule out of existence, particularly in civil cases.[1] The English Civil Evidence Acts of 1995 and 1968, and their predecessor the Evidence Act of 1938, dramatically relaxed the barriers to admitting hearsay evidence. LAW ON CIVIL HEARSAY, HERBERT SMITH BRIEFING 5–6 (Mar. 1996); St. 1968, c. 64, Civil Evidence; St. 1938, c. 28, Evidence. Birch, *The Evidence Provisions*, 1989 CRIM. L.

---

[1] In the Criminal Justice Act of 2003, Parliament significantly relaxed the hearsay rule in criminal cases, but the question has arisen as to whether that relaxation passes muster under the European convention for the Protection of Human Rights and Fundamental Freedoms. Mulcahy, Unfair Consequences: How the Reforms to the Rule Against Hearsay in the Criminal Justice Act 2003 Violate a Defendant's Right to Fair Trial Under the European Convention on Human Rights, 28 B.C. INT'L & COMP. L. REV. 405 (2005).

REV.15. England's relaxation of the hearsay rule "seem[s] obviously to have been inspired by the virtual disappearance in that country of jury trial in civil cases." 2 McCORMICK, EVIDENCE § 327, at 424 (6th ed. 2006). "[J]uries in Britain today decide only 1 percent of the civil trials and 5 percent of the criminal trials." Kimel, *Does the Jury System Need Repair?*, LEGAL TIMES, Jan. 30, 1995, at 58. In the United States, the debate over proposals to abolish the hearsay rule is also tied to the future of the jury system. As we saw in Chapter 1, Thayer claimed that the exclusionary rules, including the hearsay rule, are "the child of the jury" — the product of our fears that lay jurors would not be skeptical enough of hearsay testimony. J. THAYER, PRELIMINARY TREATISE ON EVIDENCE 47 (1898). In the words of a leading modern commentator, our continued adherence to the hearsay rule reflects a fear of the "danger of jury overvaluation of hearsay. . . ." Park, *A Subject Matter Approach to Hearsay Reform*, 86 MICH. L. REV. 51, 122 (1987).

Concerns about the limited competence of lay jurors are undeniably alive today. Former Chief Justice Warren Burger advocated the study of alternatives to the current jury system. *Alternatives to Complex Jury Cases?*, CAL. LAW., Apr. 1982, at 35. Speaking before the Conference of Chief Justices, Justice Burger declared that "when the framers of the Constitution were engaged in the practice of law in the colonies, they were not dealing with the kinds of complex cases that are the daily fare of the courts in the second half of the 20th century." Sylvester, *Jury's Still Out on Jury Trials*, NAT'L L.J., Mar. 1, 1982, at 1. The concern about jurors' competence has been compounded by the belief that jury trials aggravate the problem of crowded dockets. At an annual meeting of the American Bar Association, Justice Stevens stated that court time is a "scarce resource" in the United States. Corboy, *The Right to Trial by Jury*, TRIAL, May 1980, at 17. The Justice added that given the backlog of cases, the right to jury trial is "a luxury that perhaps we may not be able to afford to the extent we have over the years." *Id.*

Yet, there is a large, growing body of research data indicating that the doubts about jurors' competence to critically evaluate hearsay evidence are overstated. Kovera, Park & Penrod, *Jurors' Perceptions of Eyewitness and Hearsay Evidence*, 76 MINN. L. REV. 703, 722 (1992) ("this study's results suggest that in general, jurors are skeptical of the quality and usefulness of hearsay testimony. More specifically, jurors in this study were able to differentiate among accurate and inaccurate hearsay witnesses"); Landsman & Rakos, *Research Essay: A Preliminary Empirical Enquiry Concerning the Prohibition of Hearsay Evidence in American Courts*, 15 LAW & PSYCHOL. REV. 65, 66 (1991) ("preliminary empirical data . . . suggest the incompetence [thesis] is open to doubt"); Miene, Park & Borgida, *Juror Decision Making and the Evaluation of Hearsay Evidence*, 76 MINN. L. REV. 683, 699 (1992) ("the data from this study suggest that hearsay as a form of testimony is not overvalued by jurors. . . . [S]ubjects in this study did not give much weight to hearsay evidence. . . .").

Despite some notorious jury verdict debacles, it is fair to say that there is still widespread support for the present jury system — especially among federal and state trial judges. Guinther, *The Jury in America, in* THE AMERICAN CIVIL JURY 44, 53 (1987) ("In one national survey, nearly 90% of the responding judges expressed faith in the jury system"). And, of course, the right to a jury trial is protected by the Constitution in the Sixth and Seventh Amendments as well as Article III. In

2004, the A.B.A. launched its American Jury Project to reinvigorate the institution of the jury. That project was part of a widespread reform movement that has led, for example, to increased juror questioning of witnesses in some jurisdictions. For its part, the United States Supreme Court has recently reinvigorated the role of the jury. In a line of cases including such decisions as *United States v. Booker*, 543 U.S. 220 (2005), the Court has held that the jury — not the judge — must decide the existence of sentence enhancements which can have the effect of exposing the defendant to a period of imprisonment exceeding the statutory maximum authorized for the charged offense. Given such support, the jury system in America is likely to survive relatively intact for the foreseeable future. Hence, rather than focus on complete abolition of the hearsay rule, it is probably more realistic to look at other proposed reforms.

2. Recognition of New Hearsay Exceptions

The least controversial step toward reforming the hearsay rule would be to recognize new specific hearsay exceptions.[2] One exception in particular warrants discussion.

Child Hearsay Statements

The nationwide campaign against child abuse has wrought numerous changes in American evidence law. Raeder, *Navigating Between Scylla and Charybdis: Ohio's Efforts to Protect Children Without Eviscerating the Rights of Criminal Defendants — Evidentiary Considerations and the Rebirth of Confrontation Clause Analysis in Child Abuse Cases*, 25 U. Tol. L. Rev. 43 (1993–94). The campaign has led to relaxed competency standards for prospective child witnesses, special procedures such as the use of videotaping or closed-circuit television to make the experience of testifying less traumatic for children, and novel types of expert testimony including child sexual abuse accommodation syndrome (CSAAS).

In addition, the campaign has created pressure on state legislatures and courts to facilitate the more liberal admission of hearsay statements by young victims of alleged sexual abuse. In some cases, the courts have liberally applied existing hearsay exceptions to achieve that result. In *White v. Illinois*, 502 U.S. 346 (1992), for example, the child's statements were admitted under the excited utterance exception and the exception covering statements made for medical purposes. In *Idaho v. Wright*, 497 U.S. 805 (1990), the prosecution attempted to invoke the residual exception.

Several jurisdictions have taken the next step and recognized a new specific hearsay exception for statements made by alleged child victims. In some jurisdictions, courts fashioned this new exception as a matter of case law. *E.g.*, *State v. Boston*, 46 Ohio St. 3d 108, 545 N.E.2d 1220 (1989). Special statutes are in effect in roughly half the states. Mosteller, *Remaking Confrontation Clause and Hearsay Doctrine Under the Challenge of Child Sexual Abuse Prosecutions*, 1993 U. Ill. L. Rev. 691, 697. These statutes vary in detail, but typically they admit

---

[2] This section is based in part on M. Ladd & R. Carlson, Cases and Materials on Evidence 1023-28 (1972).

statements of children below a certain age (*e.g.*, under 10) who have been the victims of specified crimes, usually sexual abuse. The Pennsylvania statute is illustrative. Section 5985.1(a)(1) of title 42 provides:

> An out-of-court statement made by a child victim or witness, who at the time the statement was made was 12 years of age or younger, describing indecent contact, sexual intercourse or deviate sexual intercourse performed with or on the child by another, not otherwise admissible by statute or rule of evidence, is admissible in evidence in any criminal proceeding if . . . [t]he court finds . . . that the time, content and circumstances of the statement provide sufficient indicia of reliability.

In addition to mandating some showing of the statement's reliability, the statutes typically speak to the subject of the child's availability as a witness. Most statutes "require that the child either testify or be found unavailable." Mosteller, *supra*, at 699. The Pennsylvania statute fits the mold; section 5985.1(b)(2) conditions the admission of the statement on a showing that "[t]he child either (i) testifies at the proceeding; or (ii) is unavailable as a witness and there is corroborative evidence of the act."

Some jurisdictions have expanded the unavailability standard in child abuse cases to authorize admission at trial of pretrial videotaping of the child victim's testimony in lieu of live testimony if the prosecution can show that the experience of live testimony in the defendant's presence would traumatize the child. *E.g., Miller v. State*, 517 N.E.2d 64 (Ind. 1987); Graham, *The Confrontation Clause, the Hearsay Rule, and Child Sexual Abuse Prosecutions: The State of the Relationship*, 72 MINN. L. REV. 523, 558–62 (1988).

The Criminal Rules Advisory Committee thought that a clarifying amendment regarding availability would be useful in federal practice. That Committee proposed adding the following language to end of 804(a)(4): "or there is substantial likelihood that the testifying would result in serious physical, psychological, or emotional trauma to a declarant of tender years." However, as of 2012, that proposal has yet to be approved.

As the preceding paragraphs indicate, the general trend has been toward a growing recognition and expansion of special exceptions for children's statements in criminal cases. However, as we will see in Chapter 32, the Supreme Court's 2004 Confrontation Clause decision in *Crawford v. Washington* has sharply curtailed this trend. *Crawford* held that if a hearsay declaration is "testimonial," the statement cannot be admitted unless the defendant had a prior opportunity to question the declarant and the declarant is unavailable at trial. Although the Court is still in the process of defining the term "testimonial hearsay," to the extent that a child's hearsay statement is found to be testimonial, it cannot be admitted in a criminal case consistent with the Confrontation Clause unless the defendant has the opportunity to cross-examine the declarant.

NOTES

1. In *Maryland v. Craig*, 497 U.S. 836 (1990), the Court announced that a trial judge may deny a defendant face-to-face confrontation with a child accuser and allow an alternative means of testimony (such as via closed-circuit television or behind a screen) only when the judge makes a case-specific finding that "the child witness would be traumatized, not by the courtroom generally, but by the presence of the defendant." In deciding whether there is an adequate showing of unavailability under the special statutory hearsay exceptions for child statements, many courts analogize to *Craig*. Does the state of the psychological research permit the trial judge to make the sort of case-specific finding contemplated by *Craig*? For a skeptical analysis, *see* Crump, *Child Victim Testimony, Psychological Trauma, and the Confrontation Clause: What Can the Scientific Literature Tell Us?*, 8 ST. JOHN'S J. LEGAL COMMENT. 83, 95–96 (1992) ("it is scientifically unsound to imagine that a judge, psychotherapist, or anyone else can predict the long-term effects, into adulthood, of vigorously cross-examining an abused child").

2. Although the results of recent research seem to reflect favorably on the general trustworthiness of child witnesses, there is ongoing debate over the particular factors that courts should consider in deciding whether a particular child hearsay statement is sufficiently reliable to be admissible. Honts, *Assessing Children's Credibility: Scientific and Legal Issues in 1994*, 70 N.D. L. REV. 879 (1994) (discussing the use of the Statement Validity Assessment technique); Cacciola, Comment, *The Admissibility of Expert Testimony in Intrafamily Child Sexual Abuse Cases*, 34 UCLA L. REV. 175 (1986). In numerous cases, courts have asserted that the child's consistent repetition of the statement and the lack of leading questions are indicia of trustworthiness. Lord, Note, *Determining Reliability Factors in Child Hearsay Statements: Wright and Its Progeny Confront the Psychological Research*, 79 IOWA L. REV. 1149, 1166, 1177 (1994). However, critics characterize those assertions as "unsupported by empirical findings." *Id.* at 1177. *See also* Montoya, *Lessons from Akiki and Michaels on Shielding Child Witnesses*, 1 PSYCHOL. PUB. POL'Y & L. 340 (1995).

3. Creating Broad Exceptions to the Hearsay Rule

The Model Code

Some critics of the present hearsay rule have not been content to urge new, narrow exceptions. Rather, they favor wholesale exceptions that would markedly increase the admissibility of hearsay. The critics are especially fond of Model Code of Evidence Rule 503:

> Evidence of a hearsay declaration is admissible if the judge finds that the declarant:
>
> (a)   is unavailable as a witness, or
>
> (b)   is present and subject to cross-examination.

The brevity and simplicity of the statute should not mislead you. If adopted, the statute would revolutionize hearsay law. Moreover, it could pose major constitutional problems if invoked against a criminal defendant. We shall return to this question in Chapter 32, which is devoted to the constitutional overrides to the rules of evidence. For now, suffice it to say that any broad exception to the hearsay rule raises serious constitutional questions if it is to be applied against a criminal defendant.

The Common Law

Dean Wigmore long ago synthetized the common law of hearsay by observing that most hearsay exceptions were grounded in both reliability and necessity. During the 1950s, New Hampshire courts explicitly recognized a residual hearsay exception based on these two factors. In cases such as *Gagnon v. Pronovost*, 97 N.H. 500, 92 A.2d 904 (1952), and *Perry v. Parker*, 101 N.H. 295, 141 A.2d 883 (1958), courts admitted reliable, necessary hearsay that did not fall within any recognized exception. They thus converted the common denominators of the existing exceptions into criteria for admitting hearsay that did not fall within any existing exception.

The most famous case adopting this approach is the Fifth Circuit's decision in *Dallas County v. Commercial Union Assurance Co.*, 286 F.2d 388 (5th Cir. 1961). In that case, the county sued its insurer when the county courthouse collapsed. The county claimed that lightning had struck the courthouse. The policy's coverage included lightning as a risk. The county offered evidence that the debris included charred timbers. However, the insurer denied liability, claiming that the collapse was due to the building's structural weakness. To explain away the charred timbers, the insurer attempted to introduce a copy of the June 9, 1901, SELMA MORNING TIMES, which carried an article referring to a fire during the construction of the courthouse. The judge admitted the newspaper, and the county appealed. Judge Wisdom began the opinion by famously noting that there is no legal "canon against the exercise of common sense in deciding the admissibility of hearsay evidence." *Id.* at 397. The judge stressed that the newspaper reporter had no motive to lie and that the community was so small that any lie would have been immediately unmasked. *Id.* In the judge's mind, it was sufficient justification for the admission of the newspaper article that the article was "necessary and trustworthy." *Id.* at 398. Thus, even before the adoption of the Federal Rules, Judge Weinstein could remark that "the current clear tendency" at federal common law was to admit "necessary and trustworthy hearsay." *United States v. Barbati*, 284 F. Supp. 409, 412 (E.D.N.Y. 1968).

Federal Rule of Evidence 807

In the process leading to adoption of the Federal Rules of Evidence, there was extensive Congressional discussion about the wisdom of conferring discretion on trial judges to admit hearsay that did not fall within a specific exception. The idea of a residual hearsay exception engendered vigorous debate. The Senate Judiciary Committee cautioned against granting trial judges "broad license" or "unbridled discretion," stating that "an overly broad residual hearsay exception could emasculate the hearsay rule and the recognized exceptions or vitiate the rationale behind codification of the rules." S. Rep. No. 1277, 93rd Cong. 2d Sess. 6 (1974).

The enactment of the residual hearsay exceptions in the Federal Rules (now Rule 807) did not end the debate. In the 1970s, there was a sharp split of authority. In *United States v. Mathis*, 559 F.2d 294, 299 (5th Cir. 1977), the court asserted that "tight reins must be held" over the residual exception. During this period, many courts followed the "near miss" theory: If a statement seemed to be covered by a specific hearsay exception but nearly missed satisfying that exception's requirements, the statement could not be admitted under a residual exception. *United States v. Popenas*, 780 F.2d 545 (6th Cir. 1985). In contrast, *United States v. American Cyanamid Co.*, 427 F. Supp. 859 (S.D.N.Y. 1977), rejected the narrow construction of the residual exceptions. The court stressed that on its face, the language of the residual exceptions in the Rules is not limited to exceptional cases or evidence with extraordinary probative value.

The 1980s witnessed a marked trend toward a more expansive construction of the residual exceptions. This trend was particularly noticeable in cases admitting grand jury testimony under the exceptions. Similarly several jurisdictions began to rely on the residual exceptions as the basis for admitting hearsay statements by child sex-abuse victims. *State v. Dollinger*, 20 Conn. App. 530, 568 A.2d 1058 (1990).

This generally liberal trend persisted into the 1990s. At the outset of the decade, the First Circuit handed down one of the most liberal applications of the residual exception in *United States v. Zannino*, 895 F.2d 1 (1st Cir.), *cert. denied*, 494 U.S. 1082 (1990). In *Zannino*, a witness had testified at a codefendant's trial. The prosecution realized that the testimony could not be admitted against the defendant under the former testimony exception. However, the prosecutor offered the evidence on the alternative theory that the testimony satisfied the residual exception and the court sustained its admission on that theory. At the earlier trial, the codefendant's counsel had vigorously cross-examined the witness, and the testimony consequently "bore . . . staunch hallmarks of reliability. . . ." *Id.* at 7. In the mid 1990s, one commentator catalogued 14 different types of hearsay statements that courts had admitted under the residual exceptions, including accomplices' grand jury testimony, statements by sexually abused children, newspaper articles, diary entries, affidavits, bystander's accounts, and telexes from government agencies. The author concluded that as of the mid-1990s, there was a discernible trend to "expand . . ." the residual exceptions. Cole, *The Federal Hearsay Rule and Its Exceptions*, 19 Litigation, Sum. 1993, at 17, 23. *See also National Western Life v. Merrill, Lynch, Pierce*, 213 F. Supp. 2d 331 (S.D.N.Y. 2002) (notes taken by attorneys of interviews of a corporate investor's officer), *vacated*, 2004 U.S. App. LEXIS 317 (2d Cir. 2004); *Rotec Industries, Inc. v. Mitsubishi Corp.*, 181 F. Supp. 2d 1173, 1178–79 (D. Or. 2002) (a Chinese official's letter to the commercial attached of the United States Embassy in Beijing), *aff'd*, 348 F.3d 1116 (9th Cir. 2003), *cert. denied*, 541 U.S. 1063 (2004); *Burt Rigid Box Inc. v. Travelers Property Cas.*, 126 F. Supp. 2d 596, 620–22 (W.D.N.Y. 2001) (information in a subsidiary's annual financial statements sent to the parent corporation), *aff'd in part, rev'd in part*, 302 F.3d 83 (2d Cir. 2002).

In contrast, more recently the general tendency has been to apply the residual exception quite cautiously. This trend has manifested itself in several ways. To begin with, courts discussing the exception frequently hark back to the 1970s cases and generalize that the exception should be invoked only rarely and in exceptional circumstances. *Bohler-Uddeholm America, Inc. v. Ellwood Group*, 247 F.3d 79 (3d Cir. 2001), *cert. denied*, 534 U.S. 1162 (2002); *Steinberg v. Obstetrics-Gynecological*, 260 F. Supp. 2d 492, 495–96 (D. Conn. 2003). In the words of one court, the exception "is extremely narrow and require[s] testimony to be very important and very reliable." *Hall v. C.I.A.*, 538 F. Supp. 2d 64, 70 (D.D.C. 2008). The courts sometimes stress that the trial judge must exercise rigor in evaluating the trustworthiness of the proffered testimony. *Coyle v. Kristjan Palusalu Maritime Co., Ltd.*, 83 F. Supp. 2d 535, 545 (E.D. Pa. 2000), *aff'd*, 254 F.3d 1077 (3d Cir. 2001). In product liability cases, courts have balked at admitting videotaped statements made by claimants who died before trial. *Brown v. Philip Morris Inc.*, 228 F. Supp. 2d 506 (D.N.J. 2002) (suit against cigarette manufacturers); *Sternhagen v. Dow Co.*, 108 F. Supp. 2d 1113 (D. Mont. 1999) (suit against herbicide manufacturer).

Perhaps most significantly, the Supreme Court's 2004 decision in *Crawford v. Washington* will restrict the use of the residual exception in criminal cases. After *Crawford*, the trial judge must inquire whether, on the particular facts of the specific case, the police or prosecutors were involved in the production of "testimonial" hearsay by a declarant who should have realized that her statement could be used for prosecutorial purposes. Professor Raeder has pointed out that before *Crawford* the courts often invoked the residual exception to justify admitting grand jury testimony and statements by allegedly abused children. Raeder, *Finding the Proper Balance in Hearsay Policy: The Uniform Rules Attempt to Stem the Hearsay Tide in Criminal Cases Without Prohibiting All Nontraditional Hearsay*, 54 OKLA L. REV. 631 (2001). *Crawford* forecloses the use of the exception to allow the introduction of grand jury testimony unless the declarant testifies at the trial and is subject to cross-examination by the defendant because even a target defendant has no opportunity to question witnesses before the grand jury. Likewise, the involvement of law enforcement in questioning a child who is the alleged victim of abuse would likely render the child's statement "testimonial" under *Crawford*. Nored & Lange, Crawford v. Washington: *An Examination of the Impact on Child Abuse Prosecutions*, 47 CRIM. L. BULL. 66 (Jan.–Feb. 2011); Carter & Lyons, *The Potential Impact of* Crawford v. Washington *on Child Abuse, Elderly Abuse and Domestic Violence Litigation*, 28 THE CHAMPION 21 (Sep./Oct. 2004). Several courts have applied *Crawford* to statements by child victims. *People v. Sisavath*, 118 Cal. App. 4th 1396, 13 Cal. Rptr. 3d 753, 756–58 (2004); *People v. Espinoza*, 2004 Cal. App. Unpub. LEXIS 6573 (July 13, 2004) (unpublished); *People v. Vigil*, 104 P.3d 258 (Colo. Ct. App. 2004); *State v. Courtney*, 682 N.W.2d 185, 194–97 (Minn. Ct. App. 2004). Relying on *Crawford*, another court has invalidated a statutory hearsay exception for alleged victims of elder abuse. *People v. Pirwani*, 119 Cal. App. 4th 770, 14 Cal. Rptr.3d 673 (2004).

The current inclination to apply the residual exception conservatively will make it all the more important that the proponent attempt to justify the introduction of the testimony under one of the specific hearsay exceptions codified in Rules 803 and 804.

NOTES AND PROBLEMS

1. Consider the problem of interpreting the residual exception as one of statutory construction. Does the statutory language lend itself to the narrow interpretation given it in the 1970s by the *Mathis* case? Is the language ambiguous enough to allow a court to resort to extrinsic legislative materials such as the Senate Report? The problem of the legislative history of the residual exception is a case study in the danger of taking isolated statements in a statute's legislative history at face value. There are passages in the congressional hearings that both sides of the dispute can seize upon. When legislative history materials "lend great comfort to both sides," the legislative history materials are "of no real assistance in interpreting the statute." *American Chicle Co. v. United States*, 41 F. Supp. 537, 543 (Ct. Cl. 1941), *aff'd*, 316 U.S. 450 (1942). Has Congress in reality delegated the policy choice to the courts? (Chapter 24 notes that in Federal Rule 501, Congress expressly tasked the courts to continue the evolution of privilege doctrine by common-law process.)

2. On its face, the residual exception neither requires a showing of extraordinary probative value nor is limited in its scope to unusual situations. However, there is a plausible statutory construction argument for the "near miss" theory. The rules as originally drafted referred to "[a] statement not specifically covered by any of the foregoing exceptions." In *United States v. Dent*, 984 F.2d 1453, 1465–66 (7th Cir.), *cert. denied*, 510 U.S. 858 (1993), the court reasoned that the jurisdictions liberally reading the residual exceptions "treat Rule 804(b)(5) as if it began: 'A statement not specifically admissible under any of the foregoing exceptions . . . .' Rule 804(b)(5) reads more naturally if we understand that evidence of a kind specifically addressed ('covered') by one of the four other subsections must satisfy the conditions laid down for its admission." Since Rule 807 retains the same language, the *Dent* court's argument is still viable.

3. **Problem 22-1.** In *Hill*, the plaintiff offers a notebook that one of the Polecat test drivers kept as a personal record at home. The test driver was an independent contractor rather than a Polecat employee. There was no company policy requiring her to keep the record, but she wanted a daily diary of her professional work. One entry in the diary indicates that one of the designers of the Polecat model Ms. Hill was driving told her to be especially careful in collisions in the test because, "God knows what will happen if you crack the rear end near that damn gas tank." Assume that the trial judge rules that the notebook does not qualify under Rule 803(6). *See Gagnon v. Pronovost*, 97 N.H. 500, 92 A.2d 904, 905–06 (1952) ("It has an aura of being truthful and of some help . . ."). As you analyze the problem, consider the fundamental probative dangers — perception, memory, narration, and sincerity.

4. **Problem 22-2.** In *Devitt*, the prosecutor calls Mr. Carmody as a witness. Carmody testifies that he owns a small hardware store near Paterson's apartment. Carmody says that he was closing his shop to go home when he heard someone scream, "I've been attacked," and the sound of a car racing away. At that instant, Carmody saw two people standing just outside his closed glass entrance door. One was a woman whom the witness recognized as a customer, though he cannot remember her name. The other was a young man looking off in the direction of the car speeding away. Although Carmody could not hear the young man, he saw the

man's lips move. The lady turned to Carmody and told him that the young man had "gotten the car's license plate number." She immediately told Carmody the number. The number is Devitt's license plate. Neither the woman nor the young man is available at trial. Devitt objects to Carmody's testimony as inadmissible hearsay. Should the court admit it under the residual exception? *United States v. Medico*, 557 F.2d 309, 314–16 (2d Cir.) (in the trial court, Judge Weinstein ruled the evidence admissible), *cert. denied*, 434 U.S. 986 (1977).

Chapter 23

OPINION EVIDENCE: LAY AND EXPERT

Read Federal Rules of Evidence 701 through 706.

A. THE TRADITIONAL NORM EXCLUDING LAY OPINION TESTIMONY

1. The Rationale for Exclusion

In the typical case, the fact-finding process can operate in the following fashion. Because of the requirement of personal knowledge, the witness bases all of his or her testimony on facts and events personally observed. Further, because of the opinion prohibition, the witness limits the testimony to recitation of observed facts. Finally, the trier of fact decides which inferences and conclusions to draw from the facts testified to. In the usual case, the witness is capable of verbalizing the observed facts and the lay jurors are competent to draw the necessary inferences. In the typical situation, therefore, the model works well.

However, in some situations, the model breaks down. Those situations highlight the reasons for *admitting* lay opinion testimony. The following case sheds some light on those reasons.

GOVERNMENT OF THE VIRGIN ISLANDS v. KNIGHT
989 F.2d 619 (3d Cir. 1993)

Cowen, Circuit Judge.

[Henry Knight repeatedly struck Andreas Miller in the head with a pistol. The gun eventually discharged and killed Miller. At Knight's trial for second degree murder, there was evidence that Miller had stolen property from Knight, and that Knight was confronting Miller about this when the fatal encounter occurred. Defense counsel proffered eyewitness testimony that Knight never threatened to shoot Miller or pointed the gun at him. The district court permitted this testimony, but precluded the eyewitness, as well as an investigating police officer, from testifying to their opinions that the firing of the gun was accidental.]

Federal Rule of Evidence 701 states:

If the witness is not testifying as an expert, the witness' testimony in the form of opinions or inferences is limited to those opinions or inferences which are (a) rationally based on the perception of the witness and (b) helpful to a clear understanding of the witness' testimony or the determination of a fact in issue.

The requirement that a lay opinion be rationally based on the witness' perception requires that the witness have firsthand knowledge of the factual predicates that form the basis for the opinion. Fed. R. Evid. 701(a) Advisory Committee's Note. The district court properly excluded the investigating police officer's opinion because he did not observe the assault. In contrast, the eyewitness obviously had first-hand knowledge of the facts from which his opinion was formed.

Having met the firsthand knowledge requirement of Rule 701(a), the eyewitness' opinion was admissible if it would help the jury to resolve a disputed fact. The "modern trend favors admissibility of opinion testimony." *Leo*, 941 F.2d at 193 (quoting *Teen-Ed Inc. v. Kimball Int'l, Inc.*, 620 F.2d 399, 403 (3d Cir. 1980)). The relaxation of the standards governing the admissibility of opinion testimony relies on cross-examination to reveal any weaknesses in the witness' conclusions. Fed. R. Evid 701(b) advisory committee's note. If circumstances can be presented with greater clarity by stating an opinion, then that opinion is helpful to the trier of fact. *See United States v. Skeet*, 665 F.2d 983, 985 (9th Cir.1982). Allowing witnesses to state their opinions instead of describing all of their observations has the further benefit of leaving witnesses free to speak in ordinary language. *See Stone v. United States*, 385 F.2d 713, 716 (10th Cir. 1967), *cert. denied*, 391 U.S. 966, 88 S. Ct. 2038, 20 L. Ed. 2d 880 (1968).

In this case, an eyewitness' testimony that Knight fired the gun accidentally would be helpful to the jury. The eyewitness described the circumstances that led to his opinion. It is difficult, however, to articulate all of the factors that lead one to conclude a person did not intend to fire a gun. Therefore, the witness' opinion that the gunshot was accidental would have permitted him to relate the facts with greater clarity, and hence would have aided the jury. Based on an assessment of the witness' credibility, the jury then could attach an appropriate weight to this lay opinion.

Although the district court should not have excluded this opinion, the exclusion of the opinion was harmless error as it did not prejudice Knight.

NOTES

1. Why does the *Knight* court approve the admission of the opinion testimony of the eyewitness? Notice that there are two distinct justifications, clarity as well as the difficulty of articulating all the factors that lead to a conclusion. Shakespeare seems to have had the latter rationale in mind when he wrote of our "poor, poor power of speech." Other courts have used slightly different formulations. For example, in *Baltimore & O. R.R. v. Schultz*, 43 Ohio St. 270, 282, 1 N.E. 324, 332 (1885), the court stated that lay opinions are admissible "where it is not practicable to place before the jury all the primary facts upon which they are founded. . . ." *Id.* at 332.

2.   At common law, a lay witness's inability to articulate the underlying sensory data was held to satisfy the requirement of necessity for resorting to the witness's opinion. Rule 701 liberalized the admissibility of lay opinion testimony by eliminating this requirement of necessity. The Advisory Committee Note to Rule 701(b) states that "[w]itnesses often find difficulty in expressing themselves in language which is not that of an opinion or conclusion." Note also that Rule 701(b) uses the word "helpful" rather than "necessary."

3.   The objection can sometimes be advanced that lay opinion is not needed to guide the jury. *United States v. Garcia-Ortiz*, 528 F.3d 74, 80–81 (1st Cir. 2008) (police testimony that photograph of another individual resembled defendant was improper opinion testimony). A similar objection may be raised as to expert opinion testimony. *See, e.g., Bly v. State*, 283 Ga. 453, 660 S.E.2d 713 (2008) (where average person can draw conclusion from facts, no expert opinions are needed to guide the jury).

2.   The Acceptable Types of Lay Opinion Testimony

Focus on the language of Rule 701:

> If the witness is not testifying as an expert the form of an opinion is limited to one that is:
>
> (a) rationally based on the witness's perception;
>
> (b) helpful to clearly understanding the witness's testimony or to determining a fact in issue; and
>
> (c) not based on scientific, technical or other specialized knowledge within the scope of Rule 702.

The language would lead the reader to believe that admissible lay opinion testimony comes in some unified format. In fact, there are at least two distinct types of lay opinion testimony, and there is a fundamental difference between the two types. In both types of lay opinion, there is an element of necessity for resorting to opinionated testimony; the witness is likely to have difficulty verbalizing the underlying data. However, the foundational requirements for the two types of lay opinion differ. The foundational requirements are designed to ensure that both types of lay opinion are reliable as well as necessary.

These foundational requirements are particularly important because the empirical studies indicate that lay opinion is error prone. Previously, we mentioned studies documenting the unreliability of lay opinions about handwriting identification and lay opinions identifying voices. More recently, the accuracy of eyewitness identification testimony has become controversial. *See* Noah Clements, *Flipping a Coin: A Solution for the Inherent Unreliability of Eyewitness Identification Testimony*, 40 IND. L. REV. 271, 271 (arguing that eyewitness testimony is inherently unreliable).

a. Collective Fact, Composite Fact or Shorthand Rendition Lay Opinions

Under this first doctrine, a lay witness may express an opinion on such subjects as whether a person was drunk, *Bunting v. State*, 854 N.E.2d 921 (Ind. Ct. App. 2006) (admitting police opinion testimony that defendant was intoxicated); or as in *Knight*, whether a killing was accidental or intentional (*Ex parte White*, 160 S.W.3d 46 (Tex. Crim. App. 2004) (finding admissible eyewitness opinion testimony that the defendant had intentionally run over the victims with his truck). The courts usually refer to this doctrine as the collective fact, composite fact, or shorthand rendition doctrine.

Delaware Rule of Evidence 701 states the principle in an interesting format: "If a witness is not testifying as an expert, his testimony about what he perceived may be in the form of inference and opinion, when: . . . The witness cannot readily, and with equal accuracy and adequacy, communicate what he has perceived to the trier of fact without testifying in terms of inferences or opinions. . . ." The doctrine permits lay persons to opine on such varied subjects as relative darkness, speed, sound, size, age, weight, and distance. *See also Gust v. Jones*, 162 F.3d 587 (10th Cir. 1998) (permitting lay testimony on the speed of vehicles involved in a collision). In keeping with the requirement of a basis in personal observation, lay opinion based upon the observations of others will not be allowed. *United States v. Freeman*, 498 F.3d 893, 904 (9th Cir. 2007) (finding that lay testimony interpreting a conversation was improper when based on speculation). In contrast, expert witnesses are routinely permitted to advance opinions based upon findings, conclusions or reports supplied by other persons.

PROBLEM

23-1. In *Hill*, an eyewitness seeks to testify that worker was driving the truck "real fast." There is an objection by Roe that "the witness must testify in the form of estimated m.p.h., not simply 'fast' or 'real fast.' " What result?

To trigger the collective fact doctrine, the proponent must lay a foundation proving two elements:

The witness's opinion is based on personally observed facts. As we previously noted, Federal Rule of Evidence 701(a) requires that the inference be "rationally based on the perception of the witness. . . ." Proof of perception should precede the question eliciting the opinion. *State v. Palmer*, 606 S.W.2d 207 (Mo. Ct. App. 1980) (police observation that defendant's eyes were glassy and bloodshot, as well as the way the defendant recited the alphabet and performed the finger-to-nose test supported the lay opinion that the defendant was drunk). This requirement is as much a product of Rule 602 as it is of Rule 701.

By adding the adverb "rationally," the drafters suggest that the judge must not merely inquire whether the opinion has some underlying factual basis; rather, the judge must also assess the sufficiency or adequacy of the basis. This suggestion parallels the law governing expert opinion testimony that we shall study in the next part of the chapter. There, too, the judge must not only examine the quality of the bases of the expert's opinion-that is, inquire whether each basis is proper; but the judge must also assess the quantity of the bases and determine that cumulatively, they are sufficient to support a rational opinion on the subject.

A number of courts have vigorously enforced this foundation requirement. For example, in *Gross v. Burggraf Constr. Co.*, 53 F.3d 1531, 1544 (10th Cir. 1995), the defendant was charged with sexual harassment. The plaintiff, a female truck driver, complained about the attitude of Anderson, supervisor of the construction project where plaintiff worked. Plaintiff offered a witness's alleged statement that "Anderson had a problem with women who were not between the ages of 19 and 25 and who weighed more than 115 pounds." The court rejected the conclusion: "[The witness'] opinion regarding Anderson's idiosyncratic impression about female beauty was inadmissible under Rule 701(a) of the Federal Rules of Evidence because it was not based on his personal knowledge of any statement Anderson may have made about his preferences concerning a woman's appearance."

Similarly, in *Alexis v. McDonald's Restaurants of Massachusetts*, 67 F.3d 341 (1st Cir. 1995), the court demanded an evidentiary foundation for an inference of racial animus. In *Alexis*, an African-American restaurant customer was arrested by a police officer for allegedly causing a disturbance at a fast food restaurant. At issue was the testimony of an eyewitness to the events who opined that "had Alexis been 'a rich white woman' she would not have been treated in the same manner." *Id.* at 347. In Alexis' civil rights action against the restaurant and the police officer, exclusion of the lay opinion was approved on appeal because of the lack of foundation for an inference of racial animus. As noted by the Seventh Circuit, Rule 701 does not authorize the admission of "flights of fancy, speculations, hunches, intuitions, or rumors. . . ." *Visser v. Packer Engineering Associates, Inc.*, 924 F.2d 655, 659 (7th Cir. 1991) (excluding for lack of foundation co-workers' affidavits that plaintiff was fired because of her age).

Other courts have required an identifiable basis supported by personal observation of the facts which form the foundation for a lay person's opinion. A lay witness was barred from "reconstructing" the dynamics of a vehicle accident through his opinions in *Muehlhauser v. Erickson*, 621 N.W.2d 24 (Minn. Ct. App. 2000). A minivan was propelled into the path of a truck carrying a load of metal pipes. The collision dislodged the pipes, and one of them struck a van passenger in the head and killed her. The lay witness surmised that the van came straight up over the top of the truck and that when the van landed it tore the pipe rack off the truck. The van then flipped upside-down and landed with pipe underneath the van. The trial court would not allow the witness to speculate and instead confined the witness to a description of the height of the truck and the height of the van which came over the truck.

PROBLEMS

1. Problem 23-2. In *Devitt*, you are the defense counsel ultimately desiring to elicit the witness's testimony that Devitt was drunk. What foundation must you lay?

- The witness's bare assertion that he "saw" Devitt?

- The witness's testimony that he saw Devitt in a bar?

- Testimony that he saw Devitt consume four drinks?

- Testimony that Devitt's speech was slurred and his eyes hazy?

- Testimony that he has seen drunks on previous occasions?

How extensive a foundation does the collective fact doctrine require?

2. **Problem 23-3.** In the last problem, after laying a foundation for an opinion regarding intoxication, the defense asks the witness: "In your opinion, was Devitt impaired by alcohol?" The prosecutor objects. Then, in addition to urging her objection, the prosecutor requests permission to take the witness on *voir dire* before the judge rules finally on her objection. She states, "Your Honor, I think a short *voir dire* will show exactly how scanty the basis for any opinion is here." The defense opposes any prosecution *voir dire*. Should the judge permit the *voir dire*?

3. **Problem 23-4.** In *Devitt*, a witness, Mr. Kilgore, saw Devitt burst through the door leaving the apartment building. He got a good look at the man. In addition, Kilgore had seen Devitt on a prior occasion. Kilgore had talked to Devitt in Paterson's apartment building. This was a few months prior to the alleged assault, during one of the times Devitt was there to do some repair work on another apartment. The prosecutor shows Kilgore a March 15 videotape from the hallway security camera in the building hallway as Devitt is moving away from Paterson's apartment. The images in the tape are somewhat blurry and grainy, but visible. Kilgore is asked by the prosecutor:

Q: Do you recognize the man on the video?

A: Yes.

Q: Will you tell us who he is?

There was a defense objection. Devitt is sitting in the courtroom in full view of the jury while the lawyers argue the issue. Kilgore was prepared to say the man on the videotape was Devitt. What ruling?

4. There is debate in the cases over the admissibility of lay opinion on the question of whether a defendant is the person depicted in a videotape. Not admissible, says *Carter v. State*, 598 S.E.2d 76 (Ga. Ct. App. 2004). The Georgia court said that it was not convinced that jurors are helped by such testimony. It observed that when jurors can take the same elements and factors that would guide a witness' opinion and make an equally intelligent judgment of their own, that is what they should do. The court did not believe that familiarity with a defendant would enable a witness to decide better than an average juror whether or not the defendant is the person in a videotape.

On the other hand, at least two other courts came to a different conclusion. The defendant in *United States v. Pierce*, 136 F.3d 770 (11th Cir. 1998), appealed the trial court's admission of a lay witness's identification of him from a surveillance photograph. The Eleventh Circuit held this was not error because the witness's familiarity with the defendant made his identification testimony more helpful than merely allowing the jury to identify the defendant from the photograph.

In accord with the latter decision is *State v. Finan*, 843 A.2d 630 (Conn. App. Ct. 2004). The Connecticut court said that the testimony of individuals who knew the defendant for a number of years and in a variety of circumstances offered the jury a perspective it could not have acquired in its limited exposure to the defendant during the trial. This was especially true in this case, the court said, because the depiction of the defendant in the videotape was not particularly clear and his appearance was brief. The majority of jurisdictions which have addressed the issue have affirmed the admission of lay testimony under Rule 701. The court noted that in federal courts, such lay opinions are admissible so long as there is some basis to conclude that the witness is more likely than a third person to identify the defendant from the videotape.

Which line of reasoning, that embraced in *Carter* or the competing view, do you prefer?

5. **Problem 23-5.** In the *Hill* case, the witness is Ms. Hill herself. After testifying about the accident, she begins describing her damages. May she testify about her current medical condition? How detailed may she be? May she testify in terms of her "diagnosis"? What may she say about her treatment? Compare *Rogers v. State of Ala. Dept. of Mental Health*, 825 F. Supp. 986 (M.D. Ala. 1993) (patient's testimony about status of her mental health allowed under Rule 701) with *In re Mosley*, 494 F.3d 1320 (11th Cir. 2007) (debtor's testimony about how his medical condition affected his ability to obtain work admissible because it was not medical prognosis).

———

The opinion is the type of inference that lay persons commonly and reasonably draw. As we shall see, there are some inferences that only an expert can draw; the expert's knowledge or skill enables the expert to draw conclusions beyond the capacity of laypersons. Thus, this element of the foundation is the dividing line between lay and expert opinion testimony. If expert knowledge or skill is necessary to draw a particular inference, lay persons cannot commonly draw the inference; and, hence, lay opinion on that subject would be inadmissible. The dividing line has become increasingly blurred because the courts are now quite receptive to lay opinion testimony. *See Teen-Ed, Inc. v. Kimball Intern, Inc.*, 620 F.2d 399, 403 n.4 (3d Cir. 1980) (holding that although accountant might have been qualifiable as an expert, his lay opinion testimony about lost profits was nevertheless admissible because it was based on his personal observation of the plaintiff's balance sheet). However, trial courts must continue to exercise some care. Improvident admission of lay opinion can lead to reversible error. *See Hester v. BIC Corp.*, 225 F.3d 178 (2d Cir. 2000) (holding that co-worker's testimony that supervisor's treatment of plaintiff was race-based was improper opinion testimony).

The following problems test the limits of the liberality of admitting lay opinion testimony.

PROBLEMS

1. **Problem 23-6.** In our torts case, an eyewitness to the accident saw the plaintiff's car being operated by Ms. Hill just before the collision and is ready to testify "she was driving recklessly." The defense lawyer will also ask this witness: "Did she seem to be driving in disregard of human life?" Will you admit these opinions? *United States v. Sheffey*, 57 F.3d 1419 (6th Cir. 1995) (lay witnesses permitted to answer such questions because they do not embrace "specialized legal terms"), *cert. denied*, 116 S. Ct. 749 (1996). In contrast, courts usually prevent witnesses (lay or expert) from opining that an actor's conduct was "negligent" or "legally negligent."

2. **Problem 23-7.** In the same case, Silverstein, who lived near the accident scene and observed the accident, was prepared to testify that "any car that would behave that way has to be just plain unsafe." Would you admit that opinion? *See Randolph v. Collectramatic, Inc.*, 590 F.2d 844, 847–48 (10th Cir. 1979) (excluding plaintiff's opinion testimony that pressure cooker was defectively designed).

3. **Problem 23-8.** In the *Devitt* prosecution, defendant wanted to testify that as far as he could tell, Paterson "seemed to have trouble on his mind" after he finished his beer. In the past, many judges routinely excluded such opinions on the ground that the question calls for improper "speculation" or "conjecture" about another person's state of mind. Some courts continue to bar such opinions under Rule 701. *United States v. Guzzino*, 810 F.2d 687, 699 n.15 (7th Cir.) (collecting cases excluding proffered lay opinions about another person's intention, meaning, or reason), *cert. denied*, 481 U.S. 1030 (1987). However, under Rule 701, many courts have been surprisingly liberal in admitting lay opinions about the state of mind of third persons. *United States v. Hoffner*, 777 F.2d 1423, 1425 (10th Cir. 1985) ("[C]ourts have been liberal in admitting witnesses' testimony as to another's state of mind. . . ."); *John Hancock Mut. Life Ins. Co. v. Dutton*, 585 F.2d 1289, 1294 (5th Cir. 1978) (testimony of decedent's daughter that she did not believe that the decedent's wife would ever shoot him); *United States v. McClintic*, 570 F.2d 685 (8th Cir. 1978) (third party was aware of a fact); *United States v. Smith*, 550 F.2d 277, 281 (5th Cir.), *cert. denied*, 434 U.S. 841 (1977) (third party "knew and understood" certain requirements). How would you rule as trial judge?

Consider a case in which the trial court allowed a rape complainant to testify that the defendants "knew that I was trying to get away." Sometimes such testimony is excluded as speculation; on the other hand, it may be deemed to be admissible as a firsthand impression. The latter approach was followed in *State v. Ayala*, 178 Ariz. 385, 873 P.2d 1307 (Ct. App. 1994). In similar fashion in a business litigation context, see *Winant v. Bostic*, 5 F.3d 767 (4th Cir. 1993) (witness concluded that land developers never intended to do what they had promised).

4. **Problem 23-9.** No witness, lay or expert, is allowed to state directly that another witness who testified earlier in the case lied when he gave his testimony. *United States v. Akitoye*, 923 F.2d 221 (1st Cir. 1991). How far removed from this is it when a witness opines that a criminal defendant "feigned grief" over his wife's death? In *United States v. Meling*, 47 F.3d 1546 (9th Cir.), *cert. denied*, 116 S. Ct. 130 (1995), a paramedic was allowed to give his impression that the defendant was feigning grief when the paramedic was treating defendant's wife. One potential

distinction is that the witness is not characterizing the accused's demeanor and truthfulness *at trial*.

Just as a witness cannot tell the trial jury that a witness who previously testified was lying, affirmations that another witness gave honest testimony are barred. "Vouching testimony" came in the form of opinion testimony by lay witnesses that a rape complainant was sincere when she told them about the crime in *Maurer v. Minnesota*, 32 F.3d 1286 (8th Cir. 1994). Admission of the vouching testimony was held to have denied the defendant due process of law.

b. Skilled Lay Observer Testimony

There is a second type of opinion that lay persons are often permitted to express on the witness stand. The courts sometimes use the label, "skilled lay observer" testimony. The courts admit this type of opinion on such subjects as the identification of a defendant as the person in a surveillance photograph (*United States v. Borrelli*, 621 F.2d 1092 (10th Cir.), *cert. denied*, 449 U.S. 956 (1980)); sanity (*Spillman v. Estate of Spillman*, 587 S.W.2d 170 (Tex. Civ. App. 1979)); *Estate of Clegg v. Wiebe*, 87 Cal. App. 3d 594, 151 Cal. Rptr. 158 (1978), the identification of handwriting style, or the recognition of a voice.

In one key respect, collective fact opinion and skilled lay observer opinion are alike. The reliability model breaks down here as it does in the case of collective fact opinion testimony. Remember that if the witness wants to give skilled lay observer testimony identifying Devitt's handwriting style on a letter containing a relevant admission, under Evidence Rule 901(b)(2) the witness must have "familiarity" with Devitt's handwriting. Just as it is practically impossible for a lay witness to verbalize all the primary sensory data leading to the conclusion that a color was red, it seems virtually impossible for a lay witness to describe the bases for the familiarity in complete detail. The witness may have observed the purported author's handwriting style on hundreds of prior occasions. It would be ridiculous to expect the witness to articulate every prior observation, and it hardly seems worth the effort so long as the witness has some substantial basis for familiarity.

If we make the threshold policy decision to admit skilled lay observer opinions, two questions then naturally arise. The first is how do we distinguish between collective fact and skilled lay observer opinions. If a lay witness is going to express a collective fact opinion on a subject such as color or speed, the foundation need not include the witness's explicit testimony that on prior occasions, he or she has seen red objects or observed passing automobiles. We assume that most normal persons have had such observations; given that assumption, in most cases, requiring proof of prior observation would be a waste of time.

NOTES AND PROBLEMS

1. Contrast the practice for collective fact opinion with the practice for skilled lay observer testimony. If a lay person is going to express an opinion on a subject such as handwriting style or sanity, the opinion must be preceded by testimony about the witness's familiarity with the person whose handwriting or sanity is in issue. *See Avery v. State*, 609 S.W.2d 52, 53 (Ark. 1980) (excluding lay opinion testimony on defendant's mental state to establish insanity defense). Do you think that it is sound to treat the two types of lay opinion differently in this respect? Is this an argument for deleting the foundational requirement for skilled lay observer opinion — or for at least occasionally adding that requirement for collective fact opinion?

2. **Problem 23-10.** In the *Devitt* case, Ms. Mussio, a prosecution witness, is prepared to testify that shortly after the alleged assault on Paterson, she saw Devitt and observed "bloodstains" on his shirt. Would you classify that opinion as collective fact or skilled lay observer? What foundation would you lay before eliciting the final opinion? *See State v. Boucher*, 376 A.2d 478, 480–81 (Me. 1977) (finding testimony that "the matter appeared to be blood" was admissible as a short-hand way of describing the witness's perception).

3. **Problem 23-11.** In the last problem, assume that the judge rules that "you need a foundation, counselor." What foundation would be adequate?

- Ms. Mussio's statement "I am familiar with blood"?

- Her testimony that "I've seen blood before"?

- Her statement "I've seen blood on tens of occasions"?

- Her testimony that she served as a Red Cross aide in a combat zone in Vietnam in 1972?

- Her testimony that she presently works as a technician in a medical clinic?

How does Rule 701's language, "rationally based on the perception of the witness," apply to skilled lay observer testimony?

The second question that should occur to you is how do we distinguish between skilled lay observer and expert opinions. Sometimes, the law permits us to use both types of opinion on the same subject. For example, a friend of Devitt's could give skilled lay observer testimony on the subject of whether Devitt appeared insane or irrational shortly after the alleged attack but we would also permit a psychiatrist who had evaluated Devitt to testify on the subject of Devitt's sanity.

NOTES

1. A number of cases allow lay witnesses to state that an accused person "seemed irrational" on the day of a crime. Other related opinions have been allowed as well. *United States v. Rea*, 958 F.2d 1206, 1215 (2d Cir. 1992) ("there is no theoretical prohibition against allowing lay witnesses to give their opinions as to the mental states of others. Accordingly, these Rules do not, in principle, bar a lay witness from testifying as to whether a defendant in a criminal prosecution had the requisite knowledge").

2. In one respect, lay opinion testimony may be more liberally admissible than expert opinion. Federal Rule of Evidence 704(b) prohibits an expert in a criminal case from testifying "as to whether the defendant did or did not have the mental state or condition constituting an element of the crime charged or of a defense

thereto. Such ultimate issues are matters for the trier of fact alone." Some courts have held that this prohibition is inapplicable to lay opinion testimony and that consequently, otherwise admissible lay opinions may directly address those questions. *United States v. Rea, supra,* at 1215. The *Rea* court conceded that "the last sentence [of 704(b)], if read literally, could be understood to bar even opinions of lay witnesses on the ultimate issue of the state of mind of a defendant in a criminal case. . . ." However, the court argued that "there would have been no need to include the word 'expert' in the first sentence" if 704 (b) applied to lay opinion testimony.

c.   Other "Lay" Opinion Testimony

At common law, the courts often allowed owners to testify about the value of their personal or real property. Some courts extended the practice and permitted people to testify about the value of their services, as in *General Aggregate Corp. v. Labrayere,* 666 S.W.2d 901 (Mo. Ct. App. 1984). In these cases, the courts admitted these lay opinions liberally. *See Bower v. Processor and Chem. Serv.,* 672 S.W.2d 30 (Tex. Ct. App. 1984) (holding that the witness could testify about the value of his own property even though he would not be permitted to express a similar opinion about the value of other persons' property in the same area).

NOTE

The general rule is that an owner may testify as to the value of his or her own land. *Hidden Oaks Ltd. v. City of Austin,* 138 F.3d 1036 (5th Cir. 1998). Similarly, the owner or officer of a business may testify to the projected profits of the business; a corporate employee may give an opinion about the value of corporate property, and a business owner may testify to the damages done to his business as the result of another's action. *E.g., Craig v. Outdoor Advertising v. Viacom Outdoor, Inc.,* 528 F.3d 1001 (8th Cir. 2008); *Downeast Ventures, LTD v. Washington County,* 450 F. Supp. 2d 106 (D. Me. 2006). However, the owner of the business may not speculate. *United States Salt, Inc. v. Broken Arrow, Inc.,* 563 F.3d 687 (8th Cir. 2009).

3. Summary and Preview

To better understand these rules and contrast them with the next section on expert opinion, it may be helpful to visualize the rules in this fashion:

Lay Opinion Testimony

The lay witness can verbalize all the primary data underlying the inference	The lay witness cannot verbalize all the underlying data; but he or she can draw a reliable inference from the data	Only an expert can draw a reliable inference from the data
(Therefore, lay opinion testimony is excluded as unnecessary)	(Therefore, lay opinion testimony is admitted as necessary and trustworthy)	(Therefore, lay opinion testimony is excluded as untrustworthy)

At common law, the preference for factual testimony by lay witnesses yields when the lay opinion is both necessary and reliable. On the one hand, when the lay witness can readily verbalize the underlying factual data, the courts exclude the witness' opinion as unnecessary. On the other hand, when the subject is so arcane that only an expert can draw a trustworthy inference, the courts exclude lay opinions as unreliable. In the parlance of Rule 701, to be admissible, a lay opinion must be both "helpful" and reliable in the sense that it is "rationally based on the perception of the witness."

B. EXPERT OPINION TESTIMONY

1. Introduction

As noted in Chapter 12, expert opinion testimony has become one of the most important types of evidence. In criminal cases, lay jurors have come to expect expert proof of guilt in such forms as fingerprints. In the words of one prosecutor, expert testimony has become "the backbone of every circumstantial evidence case." Clark, *Scientific Evidence, in* THE PROSECUTOR'S DESKBOOK 542 (1971). In major civil cases, expert testimony has become virtually indispensable, especially on the issues of causation and damages.

The presence of experts has become so commonplace that commentators have suggested that the American judicial hearing is becoming trial by expert. *See* Pizzi, *Expert Testimony in the US*, 145 NEW L.J. 82 (Jan. 27, 1995). In 1974, the Jury Verdict Reporter for Cook County, Illinois, listed only 188 regularly testifying experts. Blum, *Experts: How Good Are They?*, NAT'L L.J., Aug. 24, 1989, at 1. "Today, there are more than 3,100 — a 1,540% increase." *Id.* In the late 1980's, the Cook County state courts averaged one expert per trial. *Id.*

In some areas, the trend is even more pronounced.

Modern juries expect to see scientific and expert evidence. Observers have noted the "CSI effect" in cases where prosecutors failed to produce DNA or other forensic proof, and jurors acquitted the defendant. Because of the enhanced expectation that every crime scene will yield substantial scientific evidence, jurors may vote against a party if the party fails to use the technologies which the jurors see on TV. *See* R Carlson, *Navigating the Nuances of Modern Expert Witness Law: How to Teach About Experts*, 50 St. L.U.L.J. 1115 (2006).

As we have seen, the common law's preference is that lay witnesses restrict their testimony to recitations of observed fact; the common law assumes that jurors are competent to draw their own inferences from the underlying sensory data. In the preceding materials, we saw one deviation from this norm: the common law accepts lay opinion testimony when the lay witness cannot verbalize the underlying data. Expert witness testimony involves another deviation from the norm of personal observation.

-----

2.   Laying the Foundation for an Expert Opinion

a.   The Educating Witness

First, the proponent must get the witness to explain the underlying scientific theory, the empirical basis for the theory, and the methodology used to implement the theory. The proponent calls this expert to elicit the opinions that the theory is valid and that the methodology (including instrumentation) involved is reliable.

In some cases, live testimony on the theory and instrument will be unnecessary. When we studied judicial notice in Chapter 2, we saw that if a scientific theory qualifies as "a readily verifiable certainty," the judge can judicially notice the theory's validity. On occasion the judge may dispense with the need for proof of the reliability of an instrument. Courts routinely judicially notice the validity of the theories such as those underlying DNA typing and the reliability of instruments such as the stationary radar speedmeter. However, when judicial notice is unavailable under Federal Rule of Evidence 201, the proponent should elicit live testimony from the teaching witness about his or her qualifications, the theory's validity, and lastly the instrument's reliability

b.   The Reporting Witness

After the teaching witness leaves the stand, the proponent calls the reporting witness. This witness is frequently the laboratory technician who personally conducted the test. The witness will describe both the test and the test result. In the process of describing the test, this witness will venture the opinions that proper test procedures were used and that any equipment used was in good working order.

1)   The Qualifications to Conduct the Test

The qualifications required of the person who conducts a test may differ in kind from those required of the first, teaching witness. Suppose that in *Devitt*, when the defendant is arrested, the police administer a breathalyzer test to him. They want to determine if he is intoxicated. The police may be qualified to conduct the test, but they are not necessarily qualified to explain the theory underlying the instrument or evaluate the significance of the test result. The tasks of maintaining and operating the equipment are essentially mechanical, and the technician can develop the skill to perform those tasks on the job. The extent of the requisite training can vary greatly; it obviously requires more sophistication to operate a nuclear reactor than to use a breathalyzer. However, in both instances, in qualifying the witness, the emphasis will be on proof of mechanical skills rather than academic knowledge, as in the case of the teaching witness. In the words of Rule 702, the reporting witness can qualify as an expert by virtue of "skill" gained through "experience [and] training."

2)   Proof That the Reporter Received the Object to be Tested

To establish the logical relevance of the reporter's testimony, the proponent must show that the reporter tested the same object that was found at the crime or accident scene. This showing ordinarily necessitates proof of a chain of custody satisfying Federal Rule of Evidence 104(b); the proponent traces the chain from the time the object was originally found to the reporter's initial receipt of the object. Having identified the object to be tested, the proponent turns to the equipment used to conduct the test. Chapter 10 discussed the chain of custody concept in detail.

3)   Proof That Any Instrument Involved Was In Proper Working Order

In most jurisdictions, the proponent must affirmatively show that at the time of the test, any equipment used was in good, working order. There are often several methods of proving the equipment's operational condition. For example, in the case of the radar speedmeter, there are three satisfactory methods. First, the officers could testify to a road test; the officer ran a chase car through the speedmeter's operational zone, and the officers checked the speedmeter readout against the chase car's speedometer. Second, the officer may use a tuning fork to determine whether the speedmeter is correctly registering frequencies. Finally, the mechanic from the police motorpool could testify that she ran an internal electronic function test on the speedmeter shortly before the speedmeter was used to clock the defendant. One or a combination of these methods would suffice to lay this element of the foundation.

Problem 12-12. Assume that Morena allocates the burden of proving the instrument's reliability to the proponent. In our torts case, the attending physician had an electroencephalogram conducted to determine whether Ms. Hill sustained any brain damage in her accident. To prove that the EEG was in working order, the plaintiff calls Mr. Furniss, a hospital employee. Furniss testifies that he and another employee, Graves, are responsible for the maintenance of the EEG equipment at the hospital; they work as a team, Furniss checking four functions of the equipment and Graves testing another four; they checked the EEG before the test of the plaintiff; and on that date, the EEG seemed to be in working order. As defense counsel, what objection might you raise to Furniss' testimony. Consider both Fed. R. Evid. 801 and Rule 104(a). Focus on the last sentence of Rule 104(a). *See State v. Cardone*, 146 N.J. Super. 23, 368 A.2d 952, 954–55 (1976) (finding calibration and accuracy certificate of radar machine calibrated with a tuning fork admissible). As you may recall, in the *Bourjaily* case excerpted in Chapter 5, the Supreme Court had occasion to construe the last sentence in Rule 104(a).

4)   Proof That the Proper Test Procedures Were Used

This topic has produced a split of authority among the courts. Some courts "have indicated that [this] question goes to the weight of the evidence, not the admissibility. . . ." *People v. Castro*, 144 Misc. 2d 956, 545 N.Y.S.2d 985, 987 (Sup. Ct. 1989) (excluding DNA identification testimony for failure to use proper methodology in testing while noting that some courts thought this issue went to weight rather than admissibility).

At common law most jurisdictions required foundational proof that the witness used the proper test procedures on the occasion in question. Some jurisdictions have recently reaffirmed the common law view. *See People v. Venegas*, 18 Cal. 4th 47, 74 Cal. Rptr. 2d 262, 954 P.2d 525 (1998) (while finding that there was general acceptance of the ceiling principle in DNA technology, it was error to admit the DNA evidence because the FBI failed to use correct procedures in its statistical calculations). The majority view is attractive; many of the proficiency studies of forensic laboratories point to improper test procedure as a common cause of erroneous test outcomes. Flawed test procedure is often the Achilles heel of expert testimony. The December 1, 2000 amendment to Federal Rule of Evidence 702 codified the majority view, adding a requirement that the proponent demonstrate that "the witness has applied the principles and methods reliably to the facts of the case."

There is a strong policy case for the majority view. *See* Imwinkelried, *The Debate in the DNA Cases Over the Foundation For the Admission of Scientific Evidence: The Importance of Human Error as a Cause of Forensic Misanalysis*, 69 WASH. U. L.Q. 19 (1991). The teaching witness often relies on "controlled" experimentation to validate the underlying theory and technique. The experiments are "controlled" in the sense that the researcher controls certain variables: If the test is conducted under these controlled conditions, this is the expected outcome. That research does not furnish support for the validity of the second witness's testimony unless, in conducting the test, he or she duplicated the conditions that obtained during the validating research.

Even the courts subscribing to the majority view, though, usually accept rather conclusory testimony from the witness: "I followed the standing operating procedure in running the test." If the proponent wants to go into a bit more detail, the proponent can proceed in this fashion. The proponent initially spends a minute or two having the witness describe the various steps in the customary procedure for conducting the test. Then the proponent asks, "And on the occasion in question, what procedures did you use in conducting the test?" When the witness responds that he or she followed the customary procedure they previously described, the foundation is complete. If you were the trial judge, would you deem that testimony sufficient?

5)   Statement of the Test Result

At the end of his or her testimony, the reporting witness describes the test result. This element of the foundation is an ideal opportunity for using physical evidence. For example, the proponent may use a photographic enlargement of a developed fingerprint or a polygram chart. Remember that validating the scientific evidence is itself a logical relevance problem. A second logical relevance issue, the authentication of the photograph, arises if the proponent attempts to use a photographic enlargement or enhancement of the fingerprint. In effect, it is an authentication problem within an authentication problem. Previously, we noted the peculiar issues that arise when a technician uses digital enhancement technology to manipulate an image supposedly to improve its clarity.

c.   The Interpreting or Evaluating Witness

The third, interpreting witness explains the significance of the test results. In some cases, the proponent will not need a third witness. For instance, sometimes the test result is self-explanatory; some breathalyzers register "Pass" or "Fail" rather than yielding a numerical blood alcohol concentration reading. Moreover, in part as a result of the national campaign against drunk drivers, 41 states have enacted laws making it a crime to drive on the highways with a certain level of blood alcohol — so-called *per se* laws. Under these laws, proof of the blood alcohol level is sufficient to establish the crime. Or there may be a statutory presumption that obviates the necessity for a third witness. Thus, even in a driving under the influence prosecution in most jurisdictions, when a breathalyzer yields a numerical test result, the prosecutor does not need to call a toxicologist or physician to testify that a 0.08 BAC (blood alcohol concentration) level indicates intoxication; there will be a statutory presumption to that effect. *See* Tenth Annual Criminal Advocacy Institute (Practising Law Institute 1978) (collecting the state statutes). Finally, in many cases, the reporting witness will also have the qualifications to interpret the test result. The two sets of qualifications do not necessarily equate, but the reporting witness will often qualify to both conduct and evaluate the test. For example, in the case of polygraphy, the same person administers the test and evaluates the polygram chart.

However, when the proponent's evidence does not fall within one of the above situations, the proponent may need a third witness to complete the foundation. This witness will express an opinion, interpreting the test result and explaining its significance to the jurors.

1)   The Qualifications to Interpret the Test Result

As we have seen, the teaching witness needs relatively heavy academic credentials. In contrast, the reporter's qualifications are usually experiential, normally on-the-job training. The ideal evaluating witness is a hybrid with both academic and experiential qualifications. The jury tends to attach more weight to the witness's testimony if, for example, the expert testifying in a products liability case has not only advanced degrees in the field but also practical experience in the industry. The forensic pathologist is perhaps the preeminent example of this third type of witness. In addition to completing four or five years of graduate training, forensic pathologists have "observed or participated in 400-500 autopsies." 2 P. GIANNELLI & E. IMWINKELRIED, SCIENTIFIC EVIDENCE § 19-2, at 78 (3d ed. 1999). The pathologist's background combines an impressive academic background with extensive practical experience.

2)   Explaining the Significance of the Test Result

The basic function of the interpreting witness is to evaluate the significance of the test results described by the reporting witness. The interpreting witness will base his or her opinion on those results. We shall study the bases for expert opinion later when we discuss Federal Rule of Evidence 703 in Chapter 23. Briefly stated, in most jurisdictions, the expert may base an opinion on: (a) facts the expert has personally observed; (b) facts that are the type of data customarily considered by practitioners of the specialty; and (c) hypothetically assumed facts.

It is, of course, ideal if the interpreter was present when the reporter conducted the test. In that situation, the interpreter may testify to the test result from personal knowledge. However, even when the interpreter lacks firsthand knowledge, many jurisdictions now permit the interpreter to base an opinion on the test result so long as that is a widespread practice within the interpreter's scientific discipline. Lastly, if all else fails, the proponent may include the test result in a hypothetical question and invite the interpreter to base an opinion on the assumed facts in the hypothesis. The next question to arise is what standard the interpreter employs to evaluate the test result.

3)   The Interpretive Standard Used to Evaluate the Test Result

The interpreter must explain why the tests "fit" the issues that must be resolved in the case. Then the interpreter must actually apply the results of the tests to the question at issue. If the test result is not self-explanatory, the witness must serve as an interpreter for the trier of fact. Because Federal Rule of Evidence 704 permits experts to testify in the form of an ultimate opinion (except opinions about whether "the defendant did or did not have a mental state or condition that constitutes an element of the crime charged or of a defense"), experts are given wide latitude in the way in which they do this. Although Evidence law does not formally require that the expert articulate the interpretive standards used to evaluate the test results, a competent proponent almost always asks the expert to do so in order to make the opinion understandable. For example, in fingerprint identification testimony, an expert may use a particular standard called ACE-V —

for analysis, comparison, and evaluation — to assert that the expert's test results, according to these standards, show that the defendant's fingerprints match those of the crime scene. *See U.S. v. Pena*, 586 F.3d 105 (1st Cir. 2009) (holding that expert fingerprint testimony identifying a latent print from the crime scene as defendant's, based on ACE-V methodology was admissible). The subjectivity of these standards is often highly controversial.

3. The Statement of the Expert's Qualifications

As we discussed in Chapter 12, a proper foundation must be laid for expert opinion. Permitting an expert witness to testify in areas deemed to be beyond his or her expertise can be dangerous for the trial judge. *State v. Villanueva*, 49 P.3d 481 (Kan. 2003) (erroneous admission of testimony of unlicensed social worker that alleged victim's behavior was consistent with that of rape trauma victims was not harmless; expert did not have professional qualifications to render medical diagnosis, in the view of the court). In addition, the following decision handed down in 2004 by the Michigan Supreme Court also makes the point.

GILBERT v. DAIMLERCHRYSLER CORPORATION
685 N.W.2d 391 (Mich. 2004)

YOUNG, J.

In this appeal, defendant seeks reversal or remittitur of the largest recorded compensatory award for a single-plaintiff sexual harassment suit in the history of the United States. The $21 million verdict awarded, according to plaintiff, barely compensates her for the lasting effects of the sexual harassment she endured as an employee of defendant, DaimlerChrysler, by whom she is still employed and earning almost $100,000 a year. She contended during her trial that defendant's failure to deal adequately with sexual harassment in her plant led to a permanent change in her "brain chemistry" and a relapse into substance abuse and depression, and that these conditions will soon lead to her untimely and excruciating death.

The foundation for this theory of recovery was laid by the expert opinion testimony of a social worker who had a longstanding relationship with plaintiff's counsel. This witness not only lacked any training, education, or experience in medicine, but also testified falsely about his credentials. Nevertheless, plaintiff asked the jury to treat this witness' testimony as a "prognosis," and to compensate plaintiff for the loss of her health and, eventually, her life. Plaintiff's counsel evoked images of physical abuse and torture, compared his client to survivors of the Holocaust, and argued that defendant Daimler Chrysler thought of itself as "God Almighty," exempt from the legal norms that govern others. Thus, in defendant's view, the verdict was the product of inflammatory rhetoric, unscientific "expert" testimony, fraud on the court, and attorney misconduct.

* * *

It is undisputed that plaintiff, Linda Gilbert, has long waged a losing battle with substance abuse. Her personal struggles were thoroughly documented in medical records that plaintiff introduced at trial in order to establish damages. According to those records, Ms. Gilbert began drinking at fourteen and began using cocaine at twenty years of age. Most of her adult life has since been marked by excessive drinking. At one point during her employment with defendant, she reported to her substance abuse counselors that she was consuming a pint to one-fifth gallon of alcohol a day. Her cocaine use also continued during her employment with defendant, as documented by records from St. John Hospital and Sacred Heart Rehabilitation Center.

Ms. Gilbert sought professional assistance on a number of occasions and has been treated on both an inpatient and outpatient basis for substance abuse. On the basis of the testimony at trial, however, it appears that none of these treatments has been entirely successful. Indeed, the foundation of plaintiff's claim for $140 million in damages was the assertion that plaintiff's substance abuse would continue until it resulted in her death.

Plaintiff's work life contrasts markedly with her personal difficulties. In the mid-eighties, plaintiff began an apprenticeship to train for a career as a millwright. By 1990, plaintiff had become a journeyman millwright and was hired two years later by the Chrysler Corporation. Plaintiff was the first female millwright to work at Chrysler's Jefferson North Assembly Plant in Detroit. To our knowledge, plaintiff continues to work for defendant and, according to her attorney, earns "nearly $100,000 per year" with overtime pay.

Plaintiff initiated the present sexual harassment action against defendant on March 25, 1994, complaining that a hostile work environment existed in defendant's Jefferson North plant. At that time, plaintiff had reported two specific instances of harassment through defendant's formal discrimination reporting procedure. The first incident took place on May 22, 1993, a little over a year after plaintiff began working for defendant. Plaintiff reported that she found a lewd cartoon taped to her toolbox. It depicted a woman in a bar engaged in an "armwresting" match with a man's penis. Plaintiff's name was written above the woman in the cartoon, and the name of a coworker was written on the man whose penis was being wrestled.

After receiving plaintiff's oral report of this cartoon, plaintiff's supervisor and area coordinator apologized to plaintiff, stated that defendant "did not condone such action" and that they would address the problem by speaking with employees in the area and distributing copies of defendant's written policy against sexual harassment. Defendant's internal memo notes that an employee in Chrysler's human resources department and several other employees spoke with the workers in plaintiff's and distributed the company's sexual harassment guidelines following plaintiff's report.

[The employee reported other incidents, which the company handled in a somewhat similar fashion. A social worker was called to testify about the impact of these incidents upon the plaintiff.]

It is well-established that the proponent of evidence "bears the burden of establishing relevance and admissibility." At the time this case was tried, the proponent of expert opinion evidence bore the burden of establishing admissibility according to the *Davis-Frye* "general acceptance" standard. MRE 702 has since been amended explicitly to incorporate *Daubert's* standards of reliability. But this modification of MRE 702 changes only the factors that a court may consider in determining whether expert opinion evidence is admissible. It has not altered the court's fundamental duty of ensuring that *all* expert opinion testimony — regardless of whether the testimony is based on "novel" science — is reliable.

Thus, properly understood, the court's gatekeeper role is the same under *Davis-Frye* and *Daubert*. Regardless of which test the court applies, the court may admit evidence only once it ensures, pursuant to MRE 702, that expert testimony meets that rule's standard of reliability. In other words, both tests require courts to exclude junk science; *Daubert* simply allows courts to consider more than just "general acceptance" in determining whether expert testimony must be excluded.

[The trial court received in evidence a number of the plaintiff's hospital records, and the social worker was asked to interpret those records. He was questioned on direct examination.]

Q: Will [plaintiff] be able to work in light of what you know about her condition as recently as yesterday? Will she continue to be physically able to work?

A: No. *Her medical complications at this point have progressed to the point where she is going to be physically unable to work fairly soon.*

Q: Do you have any idea what was the cause of her problems as they exist in this lady as late as yesterday?

A: Alcoholism, major depression precipitated by work stresses, and sexual harassment. That is the bottom line.

. . . .

Where the subject of the proffered testimony is far beyond the scope of an individual's expertise — for example, where a party offers an expert in economics to testify about biochemistry — that testimony is *inadmissible* under MRE 702. In such cases, it would be inaccurate to say that the expert's lack of expertise or experience merely relates to the weight of hr testimony. An expert who lacks "knowledge" in the field at issue cannot "assist the trier of fact."

Here, according to plaintiff's counsel, Mr. Hnat gave plaintiff a "prognosis" on the basis of his interpretation of records from medical and treatment facilities. The medical "prognosis" of a social worker who has no training in medicine and lacks any demonstrated ability to interpret medical records meaningfully is of little assistance to the trier of fact.

[The verdict for the plaintiff was reversed by the Michigan Supreme Court, and the case remanded to the Wayne Circuit Court for a new trial.]

NOTES AND PROBLEMS

1.   Problem 23-15. Devitt raises an insanity defense. He calls Dr. Miguel, a general practitioner physician. By happenstance, the physician saw Devitt a few days before the alleged offense, and Dr. Miguel is prepared to testify that in her opinion, Devitt was "mentally disturbed." The witness testifies that she had some formal psychiatric training during medical school. On *voir dire* by the prosecutor, she admits:

Q: Isn't it true that psychiatry is a recognized specialty within the medical profession?

A: Yes.

Q: And you are not a specialist in that field. Are you?

A: No.

Q: Moreover, you can be certified as a specialist in that field by a special board. Isn't that true?

A: Yes.

Q: Isn't it true that you are not board certified in the field of psychiatry?

A: Yes.

Q: Isn't it also a fact that as a general proposition, the opinion of a board certified psychiatrist would be more expert than the opinion of a general practitioner on a psychiatric issue?

A: I guess so, as a general proposition.

Would you sustain the prosecutor's objection to the witness's proposed testimony? *See Alvarado v. Weinberger,* 511 F.2d 1046, 1048–49 (1st Cir. 1975).

2.   State statutes sometimes provide that when a witness proposes to testify on a medical question, the witness must be a currently licensed physician in the jurisdiction. Several jurisdictions impose that requirement for witnesses who propose to testify to the standard of care in medical malpractice actions. *Dawsey v. Olin Corp.,* 782 F.2d 1254, 1262 (5th Cir. 1986) (discussing the Louisiana statute). However, licensure in the forum is usually unnecessary to qualify as an expert witness. *Mulholland v. DEC Int'l Corp.,* 432 Mich. 395, 405 n.4, 443. W.2d 340, 345 n.4 (1989) ("Michigan has no statute prohibiting unlicensed professionals from testifying as experts. States which prohibit such testimony continue to constitute a small minority of the jurisdictions in this country").

3.   Lawyers who wish to challenge the qualifications of an expert sometimes do so immediately upon the completion of the expert's background information. The voir dire examination by opposing counsel probes the expert's qualifications, seeking to exclude the expert by showing he is unqualified. *Dimambro Northend Associates v. Williams,* 169 Ga. App. 219, 312 S.E.2d 386, 389–90 (1983) (opposing party must be afforded the opportunity, if he so requests it, to cross-examine the witness on the question of his qualifications *before* the discretionary determination of admissibility is made by the trial court). Often this request for an out-of-order cross examination regarding credentials comes right after the expert is tendered by the proponent of the witness.

4.   The Bases of Expert Testimony

One way to look at the presentation of expert testimony to the jury is as a syllogistic exercise. The proponent can present the expert's testimony as major premise, minor premise, and conclusion. The major premise is usually the principle or theory that the expert proposes to use to evaluate the data in the case. For example, in our torts case, after qualifying a witness as a safety expert in the automobile industry, Ms. Hill's attorney could have the witness describe the safety standards recognized within the industry. *See* Maslow, *Products Liability Comes of Age*, JURIS. DR., Feb. 1975, at 23–25. In some cases, the expert derives the general principle from practical experience. For example, a veteran D.E.A. agent may testify about the general operational procedures of narcotics dealers. *See United States v. Mang Sun Wong*, 884 F.2d 1537, 1543 (2d Cir. 1989), *cert. denied*, 493 U.S. 1082 (1990) (permitting DEA agent to testify that the money found on defendant was part of a drug transaction, in a pre-*Daubert* case). In other cases, the expert will rely on a principle or theory derived by scientific experimentation.

In addition to the relevance /reliability concerns of Federal Rule of Evidence 702, the application of Rules 703 and 705 are sometimes the subject of dispute. As noted in Chapter 12, expert testimony may, but need not, be based on personal observation. A fingerprint expert may, for example, rely on the visual comparison of ridge patterns observed in the latent print taken from the crime scene with those of prints taken from the defendant. In forming her opinion, she may also rely on information that she has been made aware of in the case, such as trial testimony and exhibits, or as presented in lawyers' hypothetical questions. Two major caveats, however: First, the underlying facts or data must be of the kind reasonably relied on by experts in forming an opinion; second, if the expert relies on inadmissible facts or data to reach an opinion (hearsay, for example), those underlying facts and data are inadmissible (absent judicial balancing). As the court explained in *Presley v. Commercial Moving and Rigging, Inc.*, 25 A.3d 873, 893 (D.C. Cir. 2011), in excluding an accident report, "while experts may rely on hearsay to form their opinions, their testimony is not a vehicle by which evidence that is otherwise inadmissible may be introduced."

Rule 703. Bases of an Expert's Opinion Testimony An expert may base an opinion on facts or data in the case that the expert has been made aware of or personally observed. If experts in the particular field would reasonably rely on those kinds of facts or data in forming an opinion on the subject, they need not be admissible for the opinion to be admitted. But if the facts or data would otherwise be inadmissible, the proponent of the opinion may disclose them to the jury only if their probative value in helping the jury evaluate the opinion substantially outweighs their prejudicial effect. Rule 703 makes it clear that experts may rely on other scientists' studies and reports, as long as they are the kind of information that experts in the field generally rely upon. This can cause something of a conundrum for the courts because these third party studies are most likely hearsay, and therefore would be inadmissible under the common law. No problem, says Rule 703, just don't admit these third party studies into evidence. If the third party studies are crucial to understanding the expert's opinion, the judge can perform a balancing test to determine if their probative value substantially outweighs their prejudicial effect. *See i4i Ltd. Partnership v. Microsoft Corp.*, 670 F. Supp. 2d 568 (E.D. Tex. 2009) (noting that Rule 703 provides an independent basis for admitting evidence that is otherwise inadmissible). But what happens if the opposing party wishes to attack the basis of the expert opinion in cross-examination? Rule 705 addresses this issue:

> **Rule 705. Disclosing the Facts or Data Underlying an Expert's Opinion**
> Unless the court orders otherwise, an expert may state an opinion — and give the reasons for it — without first testifying to the underlying facts or data. But the expert may be required to disclose those facts or data on cross-examination.

The interplay between Federal Rules of Evidence 702, 703 and 705 is examined in the following case

PINEDA v. FORD MOTOR CO.
520 F.3d 237 (3rd Cir. 2008)
(most footnotes omitted, eds.)

IRENAS, Senior District Judge.: Appellant Jose Pineda is an automobile technician who was injured when the rear liftgate glass of a 2002 Ford Explorer shattered. He filed a products liability action against Appellee Ford Motor Company in the United States District Court for the Eastern District of Pennsylvania and retained an expert to support his claims. After extensive discovery and a *Daubert* hearing,[1] the District Court ruled that Pineda's proffered expert witness was not qualified to testify and that his methodology was not reliable. The District Court then granted Ford's motion to exclude the testimony of Pineda's expert and its motion for summary judgment. For the reasons set forth below, we will reverse both decisions and remand for further proceedings.

I

Pineda was employed as an automobile technician by Murphy Lincoln-Mercury in West Chester, Pennsylvania. On July 18, 2002, he worked to replace several components of the rear liftgate on a 2002 Ford Explorer. Pineda initially examined the Explorer on July 2, when the owner brought the vehicle to the dealership for repair because the rear liftgate would not close properly. Pineda determined that one of the hinges that connected the liftgate glass to the body of the Explorer was damaged. He also knew that, in April of 2001, Ford issued a Special Service Instruction for repair of the liftgate brackets on 2002 Explorers built between February 5 and March 30, 2001. The brackets connected the lift cylinders, which supported the rear liftgate in the open position, to each side of the liftgate glass.

---

[1] A Daubert hearing refers to a pretrial hearing where a court determines whether a proffered expert witness's testimony is both relevant and reliable, and thus admissible as evidence, pursuant to Federal Rule of Evidence 702 and Daubert v. Merrell Dow Pharms., Inc., 509 U.S. 579, 113 S.Ct. 2786, 125 L.Ed.2d 469 (1993).

Pineda told the owner of the vehicle to refrain from using the rear liftgate until it could be repaired. He then ordered replacement lift cylinders, liftgate brackets, and liftgate hinges, all of which were available for installation on July 18.

That morning, Pineda replaced the lift cylinders and liftgate brackets without incident. Later in the afternoon, he began to replace the liftgate hinges. During his deposition, Pineda described what happened next:

> It was right after lunch, somewhere around 1:00, when I finished to install the hinge on the left side and moved to the right side. I got the book because [there] was no information related to the torque specs on the hinge, so I got the book, torqued the hinge [on the glass side] to the specs of the book, then put the nut on the body side. When I finished torquing the nut on the body side, I hear a click and felt like the glass was exploding. I closed my eyes and I felt something hit my leg. . . . . I stepped back with my eyes closed, two steps. I was in so much pain on my leg that I have to open my eyes, and I saw my calf wide open.

Pineda filed a complaint against Ford on July 16, 2004, in the Eastern District of Pennsylvania. The complaint alleged that the liftgate glass and hinges on the 2002 Ford Explorer were defective in design and that Ford failed to adequately warn of the dangerous condition.

In order to satisfy his burden of proof on the products liability claims, Pineda retained Craig D. Clauser, P.E., as an expert. Clauser produced a report on September 30, 2005. It concluded that the liftgate glass shattered because its "design was defective in that it was only marginally able to resist fracture in its intended service and the pertinent manual and bulletins lacked adequate instructions and warnings." Clauser's report noted that "[n]o improper action by Mr. Pineda caused this incident to occur."

Ford deposed Clauser on March 31, 2006. He stated at the deposition that his design defect opinion was based on his comparison of warranty claims for 2002 and 2003 model year Ford Explorers. Specifically, his analysis of performance reviews based on the warranty claims led him to conclude that 2002 models had a design defect related to the liftgate glass and hinges. His opinion was also based on third-party opinions he found on the internet . . .

As to his failure to warn opinion, Clauser testified that the 2002 Explorer's service manual did not provide specific, step-by-step instructions for replacing the liftgate brackets and hinges and reconnecting them to the liftgate glass. He further testified that the service manual failed to warn that the need for following such instructions was a safety issue. Clauser admitted that, in reaching his conclusions, he did not perform any objective testing of his own, e.g., stress analysis or other experiments on the liftgate glass of the vehicle at issue or on 2002 Explorers generally.

After the deposition, Ford filed motions to exclude Clauser's testimony and for summary judgment. Alternatively, it moved for a pretrial *Daubert* hearing. The bases for these motions were that Clauser was unqualified to provide expert testimony and that, even if he were qualified, Clauser's testimony was unreliable under Federal Rule of Evidence 702 and *Daubert*. The District Court granted the motion for a *Daubert* hearing, which was held on September 28, 2006. Prior to the hearing, on July 11, 2006, Clauser provided a supplemental report, in which his opinions from the first report remained unchanged. Nonetheless, at the start of the hearing, Pineda voluntarily withdrew his design defect claim and proceeded only on his failure to warn claim.

Clauser was the only witness to testify at the *Daubert* hearing. Pineda's counsel first asked Clauser to discuss his credentials as a professional engineer with experience in materials analysis and systems failure analysis. Clauser admitted that he was not a warnings expert, except to the extent that "a warning and instructions" are "solution[s] to an engineering problem." He also testified about Ford's 2004 Safety Recall Instruction (the "SRI"), which described the procedure for replacing the liftgate brackets and hinges on the 2002 Ford Explorer. Clauser stated that the SRI, unlike the 2002 service manual used by Pineda, provided adequate warnings and proper, detailed instructions for the replacement of the liftgate brackets and hinges.

By Opinion and Order dated November 15, 2006, the District Court granted Ford's motion to exclude Clauser's testimony in its entirety because: (1) Clauser admitted that he was not qualified as a warnings expert; (2) when discussing alternative warnings, Clauser could not compare the 2002 service manual to the SRI pursuant to Federal Rule of Evidence 407; and (3) Clauser's testimony was not based on an accepted methodology, i.e., his testimony was unreliable. The District Court held Ford's motion for summary judgment in abeyance pending Pineda's response to the issue of whether he could withstand summary judgment without expert testimony.

Pineda did not file the requested response by the District Court's imposed deadline of November 29, 2006. He sought an extension of time until December 13, which the District Court granted, but Pineda failed to meet that deadline as well. On December 19, the District Court granted Ford's motion for summary judgment and incorporated its November 15 *243 decision by reference. Pineda filed a timely notice of appeal on January 18, 2007. His appeal does not challenge the District Court's conclusion that "in the absence of expert testimony, a jury could not render a just and proper decision" on his failure to warn claim. Thus, the only issue before us is whether the District Court erred in its decision to exclude Clauser's proffered expert testimony.[9]

II.

. . .

We apply an abuse-of-discretion standard when reviewing a District Court's decision to admit or exclude expert testimony. *See Kumho Tire Co. v. Carmichael*, 526 U.S. 137, 152, 119 S.Ct. 1167, 143 L.Ed.2d 238 (1999); *see also In re TMI Litig.*,

---

[9] Because we find that the District Court erred in excluding Clauser's testimony, the District Court's grant of summary judgment in favor of Ford was necessarily erroneous since that decision was based entirely on the absence of expert testimony on behalf of Pineda.

193 F.3d 613, 666 (3d Cir.1999). "An abuse of discretion arises when the District Court's decision rests upon a clearly erroneous finding of fact, an errant conclusion of law or an improper application of law to fact." *TMI*, 193 F.3d at 666 (internal quotation marks omitted). We will not interfere with the district court's decision "unless there is a definite and firm conviction that the court below committed a clear error of judgment in the conclusion it reached upon a weighing of the relevant factors." *Id.* (internal quotation marks omitted). To the extent that the District Court's decision involved a legal interpretation of the Federal Rules of Evidence, our review is plenary. *See id.*

III.

Under the Federal Rules of Evidence, a trial judge acts as a "gatekeeper" to ensure that "any and all expert testimony or evidence is not only relevant, but also reliable." *Kannankeril v. Terminix Int'l, Inc.*, 128 F.3d 802, 806 (3d Cir.1997) (citing *Daubert v. Merrell Dow Pharms., Inc.*, 509 U.S. 579, 589, 113 S.Ct. 2786, 125 L.Ed.2d 469 (1993)). The Rules of Evidence embody a strong preference for admitting any evidence that may assist the trier of fact. *Id.*; *see also* Fed.R.Evid. 401 (defining "relevant evidence," all of which is generally admissible, to mean "evidence having *any* tendency to make the existence of *any* fact that is of consequence to the determination of the action more probable or less probable than it would be without the evidence" (emphases added)). "Rule 702, which governs the admissibility of expert testimony, has a liberal policy of admissibility." *Kannankeril*, 128 F.3d at 806.

Rule 702 has three major requirements: (1) the proffered witness must be an expert, i.e., must be qualified; (2) the expert must testify about matters requiring scientific, technical or specialized knowledge; and (3) the expert's testimony must assist the trier of fact. *Id.* (citing *In re Paoli R.R. Yard PCB Litig.*, 35 F.3d 717, 741–42 (3d Cir.1994)). We have interpreted the second requirement to mean that " 'an expert's testimony is admissible so long as the process or technique the expert used in formulating the opinion is reliable.' " *Id.* (quoting *Paoli*, 35 F.3d at 742).

The District Court found that Clauser failed to meet the first requirement of Rule 702 because he was not qualified as an expert on warnings. It also found that Clauser did not satisfy the second requirement because his methodology was not reliable. When the District Court considered whether Clauser's methodology was reliable, it ruled that he could not compare the 2002 service manual to the SRI pursuant to Federal Rule of Evidence 407.

We will first address the District Court's finding that Clauser was not qualified as an expert. Then we will discuss the District Court's legal interpretation of the Federal Rules of Evidence. Finally, we will address the District Court's finding that Clauser's methodology was not reliable.

. . . . [The court first addresses the expert's qualifications, and finds that it was abuse of discretion to exclude the witness, " that Clauser should have been qualified as an expert even though he may not have been the "best qualified" expert or did not have the "specialization" that the District Court deemed necessary."]

B. Federal Rules of Evidence 407 and 703

At the *Daubert* hearing, Clauser addressed the issue of alternative instructions and warnings for the safe replacement of the rear liftgate brackets and hinges on 2002 Ford Explorers. Without opining on the precise language, he asserted that the SRI issued by Ford in 2004 was an appropriate alternative to the 2002 service manual language. In its November 15 Opinion and Order, the District Court summarily ruled that Federal Rule of Evidence 407 **[subsequent remedial measures, eds.]** precluded such a comparison. . . .

Pineda argues that he only sought to admit the SRI as an example of effective language for an alternative instruction and warning, and not to prove Ford's "culpable conduct" or the "need for a warning or instruction." According to Pineda, any concern of unfair prejudice can be addressed by either a limiting instruction from the District Court or by admitting the language of the SRI without attributing it to Ford. Ford counters that a plain reading of Rule 407 supports the District Court's ruling. We hold that the Court erred because it focused exclusively on Rule 407 and failed to consider Rule 703, which governs the bases of opinion testimony by experts. . . .

The District Court and the parties conflate the separate issues of whether the SRI itself can be admitted into evidence and whether Clauser's opinion can be admitted if it is based on a consideration of the SRI. Rule 703 is clear that the SRI does not need to be admissible evidence in order for Clauser's opinion that the 2002 service manual lacked adequate instructions and warnings to be admitted. The Rule's only requirement is that the data be "of a type reasonably relied upon by experts in the particular field in forming opinions or inferences upon the subject." We find that it is reasonable for an engineer to rely upon a warning and alternative safety instruction subsequently issued by a manufacturer in forming an opinion that an earlier service manual fails to provide adequate instructions and warnings to automobile technicians. Thus, despite Rule 407's general exclusion of subsequent remedial measure evidence, we hold that Rule 703 permits Clauser to base his opinion on a consideration of the SRI.

Rule 703, as amended on April 17, 2000, permits otherwise inadmissible evidence to be disclosed to the jury if the trial court determines that the probative value in assisting the jury *substantially* outweighs the prejudicial effect. However, the Rule's balancing test clearly establishes a presumption against disclosure to the jury of otherwise inadmissible evidence. *See* Fed.R.Evid. 703 advisory committee's notes (2000 Amendments). While we express no opinion as to whether the SRI should be admitted into evidence, the advisory committee's notes implicitly endorse the possible solution proposed by Pineda with regard to a limiting instruction: "If the otherwise inadmissible information is admitted under this balancing test, the trial judge must give a limiting instruction upon request, informing the jury that the underlying information must not be used for substantive purposes." *Id.* However, Rule 703's presumption against the disclosure of otherwise inadmissible evidence is only applicable when the evidence is offered by the proponent of the expert. *Id.* If Ford elects to cross-examine Clauser on the bases of his opinion, which would include the SRI, it would become part of the record for the jury to consider. *See* Fed.R.Evid. 705 ("The expert may in any event be required to disclose the underlying facts or data [supporting his opinion] on cross-examination."); *see also Stecyk v. Bell Helicopter Textron, Inc.*, 295 F.3d 408, 414 (3d Cir.2002) ("Rule 705, together with Rule 703, places the burden of exploring the facts and assumptions underlying the testimony of an expert witness on opposing counsel during cross-examination.").

C. Reliability

As we recognized earlier, pursuant to the second requirement of Rule 702, "an expert's testimony is admissible so long as the process or technique the expert used in formulating the opinion is reliable." *Paoli*, 35 F.3d at 742 (citing *Daubert*, 509 U.S. at 589, 113 S.Ct. 2786). While a litigant has to make more than a prima facie showing that his expert's methodology is reliable, we have cautioned that "[t]he evidentiary requirement of reliability is lower than the merits standard of correctness." *Id.* at 744; *see also TMI*, 193 F.3d at 665 (stating that "the standard for determining reliability is not that high, even given the evidentiary gauntlet facing the proponent of expert testimony under Rule 702" (internal quotation marks and citation omitted)); *Kannankeril*, 128 F.3d at 806 ("Admissibility decisions focus on the expert's methods and reasoning; credibility decisions arise after admissibility has been determined.").

A trial court should consider several factors in evaluating whether a particular methodology is reliable. These factors, enunciated in *Daubert* and this Court's decision in *United States v. Downing*, 753 F.2d 1224 (3d Cir.1985), may include: (1) whether a method consists of a testable hypothesis; (2) whether the method has been subject to peer review; (3) the known or potential rate of error; (4) the existence and maintenance of standards controlling the technique's operation; (5) whether the method is generally accepted; (6) the relationship of the technique to methods which have been established to be reliable; (7) the qualifications of the expert witness testifying based on the methodology; and (8) the non-judicial uses to which the method has been put. *Paoli*, 35 F.3d at 742 n. 8.

The factors drawn from *Daubert* and *Downing*, however, "are neither exhaustive nor applicable in every case." *Kannankeril*, 128 F.3d at 806–07; *see also Kumho Tire*, 526 U.S. at 151, 119 S.Ct. 1167 (noting that *Daubert* itself "made clear that its list of factors was meant to be helpful, not definitive"); *Milanowicz v. The Raymond Corp.*, 148 F.Supp.2d 525, 536 (D.N.J.2001) (reconfiguring *Daubert* for application to "technical" or "other specialized" subjects such as engineering and identifying several factors for trial courts to consider in evaluating reliability, including relevant literature, evidence of industry practice, and product design and accident history). "The inquiry envisioned by Rule 702 is . . . a flexible one." *Daubert*, 509 U.S. at 594, 113 S.Ct. 2786.

Here, the District Court focused its analysis extensively on "indicia of reliability specific to warnings and instructions." The Court determined that Clauser's opinion that the 2002 service manual failed to provide adequate instructions and warnings was based on nothing more than his "generalized experience." In particular, it criticized Clauser for declining to offer proposed alternative language for a warning, for failing to test the effectiveness of a possible alternative warning, and for failing to compare the language of the 2002 service manual with the language provided by other automobile manufacturers. The District Court also held that Clauser could not adequately testify as to whether the service manual's lack of instructions actually caused Pineda's injury because Clauser did not test the 2002 Ford Explorer at issue or any other 2002 Explorers.

The District Court's inquiry of the reliability of Clauser's methodology did not demonstrate the appropriate level of flexibility required by Rule 702 and our past precedent. First, the District Court focused too narrowly on Clauser's failure either to offer proposed alternative language for a warning or to test the effectiveness of alternative warnings. Pineda proffered Clauser as an engineering expert who understood the stresses and forces that might cause glass to fail. Clauser's specialized, rather than generalized, experience in this area allowed him to recognize that exerting a force on one area of the rear liftgate glass before exerting a force on another area of the glass could lead to its shattering. Clauser did not have to develop or test alternative warnings to render an opinion that the 2002 service manual did not provide adequate, step-by-step instructions to account for the different stresses that might be exerted when an automobile technician replaces the rear liftgate brackets and hinges, or that the lack of instructions was a safety issue for the technician.

In addition, as we discussed above, Rule 703 permits Clauser to base his opinion on a comparison of the 2002 service manual language with the language of the SRI, regardless of whether Rule 407 might render the SRI inadmissible in evidence. As a result, Clauser did not have to compare the language of the 2002 service manual with the language provided by other manufacturers in order to render a reliable opinion that Ford's service manual failed to provide adequate instructions or warnings.

Finally, the District Court erred in holding that Clauser failed to establish a causal link between the alleged defect in the service manual language and Pineda's injury. It relied on cases that found such a connection lacking in situations where cause was far more attenuated. For example, one case excluded an expert's testimony because the expert could not address any defect in the design of a computer keyboard or any causal association between the keyboard and plaintiffs' wrist injuries. *See Allen v. IBM*, No. 94-264-LON, 1997 U.S. Dist. LEXIS 8016 (D.Del. May 19, 1997). The issue in *Allen* was not whether a lack of an instruction or warning caused injuries, but rather whether the product itself caused injuries. Here, there can be no doubt that the shattered liftgate glass caused Pineda's injuries. Clauser has opined that the instructions and warnings in the 2002 service manual were inadequate and that an automobile technician with thorough repair instructions and an adequate safety warning would not have been injured as a result of the rear liftgate glass shattering. *See Pavlik*, 135 F.3d at 886 (noting the general presumption that an individual will read and heed any warnings attached to a product). Any dispute between the parties about the strength of the evidence in this case should be resolved by the jury. . . .

NOTES AND PROBLEMS

1.   Suppose that the expert is premising her testimony on a scientific principle. In addition to describing the theory and its experimental verification, to what else should the witness testify? Think back to our previous study of the validation of scientific evidence. Do *Frye* and *Daubert* apply here?

2.   Problem 23-16.   In the last problem, Devitt wants to elicit Dr. Miguel's testimony that even though she is only a general practitioner, the psychiatric theory she applied in Devitt's case is widely accepted by specialists. Dr. Miguel is prepared to refer to four articles and two texts (all written by board-certified psychiatrists) that subscribe to the same theory. When she attempts to do so, the prosecutor objects on hearsay grounds. As trial judge, would you sustain the objection? Consider Federal Rules of Evidence 703 and 803(18). *Compare Chorzelewski v. Druker*, 546 So. 2d 1118 (Fla. Dist. Ct. App. 1989) (on direct examination, an expert could not read from a medical treatise to "bolster his own opinion testimony") *with* Imwinkelried, *The "Bases" of Expert Testimony: The Syllogistic Structure of Scientific Testimony*, 67 N.C. L. Rev. 1, 9 (1988) ("Would we require a modern accident reconstruction expert to replicate Newton's seventeenth century experiments to derive the laws of motion? Suppose that a physicist is testifying about the safety of a nuclear power plant. If the physicist contemplates relying on the words of Fermi or Oppenheimer, would we require that the physicist duplicate their research?"). Should the hearsay rule apply when the witness attempts to refer to another researcher's work to establish the validity of the theory the witness contemplates relying on?

3.   Previously, we attempted to visualize the restrictions on lay opinion testimony. We can similarly depict the limitations on the expert's major premise:

Expert Opinion Testimony

Even a layperson could draw a reliable inference	Only an expert can draw a reliable inference	Even an expert cannot draw a reliable inference
(Therefore, expert testimony is excluded as unnecessary under the introductory clause in Rule 702)	(Therefore, expert testimony is admitted as necessary and trustworthy)	(Therefore, expert testimony is excluded as untrustworthy under *Frye* or *Daubert*)

As in the case of lay opinion testimony, the preferential rule excluding opinions yields when the proponent can demonstrate that the opinion is necessary as well as reliable. Although the common law required that expert opinions be strictly necessary, Rule 702 now provides that the expert need only be helpful and "assist the trier of fact." The split of authority over *Daubert* and *Frye* relates to the second component of the required showing by the proponent. Jurisdictions following *Frye* demand that the expert vouch that her theory is generally accepted, while *Daubert* jurisdictions require that the expert establish that the theory has been experimentally verified.

Frequently, this determination turns on the reliability of the expert's methods of reasoning. Where the proponent demonstrates that the expert used a reliable methodology, the expert opinion is likely to be admitted. *E.g., Pineda v. Ford Motor Co.*, 520 F.3d 237 (3d Cir. 2008).

5.   The Factual Bases or Data to which the Expert Will Apply the Theory

An important part of structuring a foundation for expert testimony is setting out the factual data which form the bases of the opinion. For example, after stating the diagnostic criteria for a particular mental illness (her major premise), an expert might describe the case history of the patient in question. Unless an appropriate foundation is laid for the expert's opinion, it may be excluded. *Concord Boat Corp. v. Brunswick Corp.*, 207 F.3d 1039 (8th Cir. 2000) (expert opinion should not have been admitted because it did not incorporate all of the needed underlying data; because of deficiencies in foundation, the expert's conclusions were deemed to be "mere speculation"). By and large, however, court are deferential toward the expert in determining the basis for her opinion. The rule also broadly permits the expert to base her opinion on the work product of other professionals. *See Ohio Environmental Development v. Envirotest Systems*, 478 F. Supp. 2d 963 (N.D. Ohio 2007) (holding that an appraiser could rely on the architect's repair estimates when giving a damages opinion).

There are three permissible bases or sources for data the expert factors into her conclusions: her own personal observation, the trial attorney's hypothesis, or a third party's hearsay report:

Facts the expert personally observed. Even at early common law, there was universal agreement that an expert could properly base an opinion on factual data he or she had personally observed. The example that comes most readily to mind is the physician describing the nature and extent of personal injuries the physician has personally examined and diagnosed. Personal observation is obviously a trustworthy source of factual data to support an opinion, and the acceptance of this basis is consistent with the common law reliability model. Revisit Federal Rule of Evidence 703. The Rule's language, "those [facts] perceived by . . . him," continues the common law view.

Facts the proponent asks the expert to assume hypothetically. The following is a familiar courtroom litany:

Q: Doctor, please assume the following facts: One, in the accident, the plaintiff sustained a cut four inches in length and one-quarter inch in depth on the right front part of his head. Two, the plaintiff bled profusely from the cut. Three, immediately after the accident, the plaintiff began experiencing sharp, painful headaches in the right front of his head.

A: Yes.

Q: On the basis of those facts, do you have an opinion about the nature of the plaintiff's illness?

A: Yes.

Q: Doctor, what is that opinion?

This litany is the hypothetical question technique.

The initial question that should occur to you is whether we should permit hypothetical questions at all. Bear in mind the policy considerations which dictate such usage. If we restrict expert opinions to conclusions based on personally observed facts, we would thereby restrict the parties' access to experts. If the expert is too busy to personally study the facts before trial or if the party could not afford that expense, requiring personal knowledge would effectively keep that expert off the witness stand. Thus, it can be argued that restricting the bases of experts' opinions to observed facts is neither desirable nor necessary. The expert can contribute to the fact-finding process even when he or she has not personally observed the underlying data before trial. So long as the proponent presents admissible, independent evidence of the data, the hypothetical question techniques seem useful.

On the other hand, the technique's critics have indicted the technique because of the practical problems related to the use of hypothetical questions. To begin with, the proponent can virtually deliver a closing argument under the guise of asking a question. Wellman cites the following example:

> To illustrate the lengths to which the hypothetical question has gone, I may mention a contested will case recently tried in New York, in which a hypothetical question was propounded to three experts on each side. The two questions together consisted of about 36,000 words, that is, about 36 columns of newspaper print, and occupied more than four hours in the reading.

F. Wellman, The Art of Cross-Examination 109 (4th ed. 1936).

Consider the effect of such a lengthy hypothesis on the jurors. It is unrealistic to assume that the jurors can properly evaluate the weight of an opinion resting on such a gargantuan hypothesis. Worse still, some jurisdictions permit the proponent to ask an expert witness who has been sitting in the courtroom during the prior testimony to assume the truth of "the prior testimony" or the testimony of a particular witness. That form of hypothetical question increases the danger of jury confusion. The danger is especially acute if the number of witnesses who have already testified is large or if there were some discrepancies between the testimony of the prior witnesses. The Advisory Committee attempted, in drafting Rule 705, to remedy the weaknesses of the hypothetical question. The Committee explained:

> The hypothetical question has been the target of a great deal of criticism as encouraging partisan bias, affording an opportunity to sum up in the middle of the case, and as complex and time consuming. While the rule allows counsel to make disclosure of the underlying facts or data as a preliminary to the giving of an expert opinion, if he chooses, the instances in which he

is required to do so are reduced. This is true whether the expert bases his opinion on data furnished him at secondhand or observed by him at firsthand.

Illustrating a hypothetical used to elicit expert opinion about methods of operation of street drug operatives, see *State v. Nesbitt*, 888 A.2d 472 (N.J. 2006).

NOTE

A technique which is related to use of the hypothetical question is that of allowing the expert to remain in the courtroom to hear other witnesses. Thereafter, she may give her opinion based on their testimony. For example, highly qualified Dr. X is consulted by the plaintiff in an injury case and remains in the courtroom during testimony of the plaintiff and the plaintiff's attending physician. Based on what she hears, Dr. X testifies that the injuries are permanent. Note that this tactic requires creative use of Federal Evidence Rule 615(3).

Hearsay reports of third parties. Before the adoption of Federal Evidence Rule 703, experts were often limited to facts the experts have personally observed and facts to which other witnesses testify from personal knowledge and that the expert is asked to assume hypothetically. At common law, the expert could not base an opinion, even in part, on hearsay reports from third parties if the report was not within a hearsay exception and hence independently admissible. With the adoption of Rule 703, however, if the practitioners within a specialty customarily consider a particular type of hearsay data in forming their opinions, that very practice furnishes an argument for relaxing the traditional view. The Advisory Committee explained:

> [T]he rule is designed . . . to bring the judicial practice into line with the practice of the experts themselves when not in court. Thus a physician in his own practice bases his diagnosis on information from numerous sources and of considerable variety, including statements by patients and relatives, reports and opinions from nurses, technicians, and other doctors, hospital records, and x-rays. The physician makes life-and-death decisions in reliance upon them. His validation, expertly performed and subject to cross-examination, ought to suffice for judicial purposes.

To what extent should evidence law defer to the practice within the expert's own specialty?

NOTES AND PROBLEM

1. As previously stated, one underlying policy question is the extent to which the courts should defer to experts' selection of information to be included in the data supporting her opinion. Assume *arguendo* that the question arises in a *Frye* jurisdiction. *Frye* rests on a judgment that the courts should defer to experts' judgment on the validity of scientific theories; the courts should admit testimony based on a theory only if the theory has gained the status of general acceptance.

Does that judgment dictate the conclusion that the courts should also defer to the experts' judgment as to the proper type of case-specific information to rely on?

> There is much less reason to defer to the scientist's choice of the information functioning as her minor premise. An expert's willingness to rely on a report about the facts in the instant case is no guarantee of the report's trustworthiness. As an expert in medicine, a physician is in a better position than the judge or jury to determine that the presence of symptoms A, B, and C is the distinctive symptomatology for disease D. That determination is an exercise in scientific analysis. Suppose, however, that symptom A is nausea, and the patient tells the physician that she experienced nausea the day before visiting the doctor's office. The patient is the plaintiff in a personal injury action, and the question is whether plaintiff truthfully described her symptoms. Does the physician's medical degree make the physician a better judge of character than the judge or jury? A physician's medical school coursework does not include any specialized training in determining credibility. The determination of the content of expert's minor premise is predominantly an exercise in factual analysis rather than true scientific analysis. To make that determination, the expert temporarily "step[s] into the shoes of the factfinder" at trial. We do not assign that final determination to experts because the determination amounts to "factfinding, not the application of expertise." Empowering experts to finally decide the facts constituting the minor premise would "usurp . . . and derogate . . . the function of the factfinder."

Imwinkelried, *supra*, at 67 N.C. L. REV. 1, 10–11.

2. What is the relationship between Rules 702 and 703? The Advisory Committee Note to revised Rule 703 sought to clarify the issue:

> There has been some confusion over the relationship between Rules 702 and 703. The amendment makes clear that the sufficiency of the basis of an expert's testimony is to be decided under Rule 702. Rule 702 sets forth the overarching requirement of reliability, and an analysis of the sufficiency of the expert's basis cannot be divorced from the ultimate reliability of the expert's opinion. In contrast, the "reasonable reliance" requirement of Rule 703 is a relatively narrow inquiry. When an expert relies on inadmissible information, Rule 703 requires the trial court to determine whether that information is of a type reasonably relied on by other experts in the field. If so, the expert can rely on the information in reaching an opinion. However, the question whether the expert is relying on a *sufficient* basis of information — whether admissible information or not — is governed by the requirements of Rule 702.

3. We turn now from the question of evidentiary policy to the problem of statutory construction. Does the use of "reasonably" in Rule 703 give the trial judge the power to second guess the customary practice of the specialty? *Compare In re Japanese Elec. Prods. Antitrust Litig.*, 723 F.2d 238, 275–79 (3d Cir. 1983) *with In re "Agent Orange" Prod. Liab. Litig.*, 611 F. Supp. 1223, 1243–45 (E.D.N.Y. 1985) (*citing* Carlson, *Collision Course in Expert Testimony: Limitations on Affirmative Introduction of Underlying Data*, 36 U. FLA. L. REV. 234 (1984)). *See also* Carlson,

Policing the Bases of Modern Expert Testimony, 39 VAND. L. REV. 577 (1986); *In re Paoli R.R. Yard PCB Litigation*, 35 F.3d 717, 748 (3d Cir. 1994), *cert. denied*, 115 S. Ct. 1253 (1995) (empowering the trial judge to rule that the specialty's customary practice is unreasonable).

4.   Problem 23-17. In our torts case, Dr. Knopf is prepared to testify about the extent of Ms. Hill's injuries. He has personally examined her, but before trial the doctor told you frankly that his diagnosis rests in significant part on the records of the hospital where Ms. Hill was first treated and a report from Dr. Mason, the consulting burn expert. The records and reports themselves are inadmissible for some reason such as the hearsay doctrine. Under Rule 703, what foundation must the plaintiff lay if the plaintiff nevertheless wants the doctor to base an opinion on the reports? *People v. Ward*, 61 Ill. 2d 559, 338 N.E.2d 171, 176–77 (1975). Be prepared to conduct a short direct examination of Dr. Knopf in class to lay this foundation.

5.   Assume that in the last problem, the plaintiff laid a proper foundation to permit the use of the reports for the limited purpose of establishing the bases of the expert's opinion. Should the written records be formally admitted into evidence and shown to the jurors? Some trial judges apparently construe Rule 703 as permitting both the formal admission of the reports and their submission to the jury. *See* Carlson, *Collision Course in Expert Testimony: Limitations on Affirmative Introduction of Underlying Data*, 36 U. FLA. L. REV. 234, 235, 242–43 (1984). Is that interpretation sound? What light does the wording of Rules 612 and 803(18) shed on the proper construction of Rule 703? Citing Professor Carlson, the Minnesota drafting committee revised that state's version of Rule 703 to add this provision:

> (b) Underlying expert data must be independently admissible in order to be received upon direct examination; provided that when good cause is shown in civil cases and the underlying data is particularly trustworthy, the court may admit the data under this rule for the limited purpose of showing the basis for the expert's opinion.

However, at least one commentator feels strongly that the jury must learn the full basis for the expert's opinion. Rice, *Inadmissible Evidence as a Basis for Expert Opinion Testimony: A Response to Professor Carlson*, 40 VAND. L. REV. 583 (1987). The competing positions are analyzed in D. Caudill & L. LaRue, NO MAGIC WAND: THE IDEALIZATION OF SCIENCE IN LAW, 32–33 (2006), and Mahoney, *Houses Built on Sand: Police Expert Testimony in California Gang Prosecutions*, 3 HASTINGS CONST. L.Q. 385, 397 (debate over whether expert witnesses should be able to introduce hearsay evidence into the trial record is really part of a larger question: how active should the trial court be in policing expert testimony?).

6.   The debate continues. *See* Epps, *Clarifying the Meaning of Federal Rule of Evidence 703*, 36 B.C. L. REV. 53 (1994); Allen & Miller, *The Common Law Theory of Experts: Deference or Education?*, 87 Nw. U. L. REV. 1131 (1993). A modern study underlines the advisability of enactments like the Minnesota rule set forth in the prior section. *See* Schuller, *Expert Evidence and Hearsay: The Influence of "Secondhand" Information on Jurors' Decisions*, 19 LAW & HUM. BEHAV. 345 (1995). Participants in an experiment were exposed to unsubstantiated and secondhand information conveyed by means of an expert relating her background investigations to the jury. Mock juror simulations indicated that expert background hearsay was used to reach verdict decisions, despite judicial instructions to ignore the substantive facts asserted in the hearsay statements. The results underline the danger in allowing experts to freely relate otherwise inadmissible hearsay.

7. A December 1, 2000 amendment to Rule 703 "provides a presumption against disclosure to the jury of otherwise inadmissible information used as the basis of an expert's opinion or inference, where that information is offered by the proponent of the expert." Advisory Committee Note to Rule 703. The revised rule provides that if facts or data are otherwise inadmissible, they "shall not be disclosed to the jury by the proponent of the opinion or inference unless . . . their probative value . . . substantially outweighs their prejudicial effect." This dimension to Rule 703 is discussed in Carlson, *Is Revised Expert Witness Rule 703 a Critical Modernization for the New Century?*, 52 FLA. L. REV. 715 (2000).

8. Following the December 1, 2000, amendment to Rule 703, a number of courts have denied admission to an expert's underlying data. *Turner v. Burlington N. R.R. Co.*, 338 F.3d 1058 (9th Cir. 2003) is a good example. Applying the presumption against disclosure supplied under federal law when the information is offered by the proponent of the expert, the court rejected a lab report. At issue was the cause of a fire. Instead of the railroad's negligence, the railroad sought to prove the fire was the result of arson. Samples of debris piles from the railroad's property were sent to Armstrong Forensic Laboratory in Arlington, Texas for analysis. The lab apparently claimed that gasoline was detected. Nobody from the lab came to the *Turner* trial. However, the lab's report was going to be used by a local fire investigator to conclude that an arsonist started the fire. The court rejected the testimony. "The lab report was otherwise inadmissible hearsay evidence in the absence of foundation testimony by the laboratory that conducted the testing. The prejudice that would result from admission of this evidence was substantial, whereas its probative value was minimal. Because the probative value of this otherwise inadmissible evidence does not outweigh its prejudicial effect, our inquiry is ended under Fed. R. Evid. 703."

9. Sometimes a similar result is reached without the benefit of the 2000 federal amendment. Iowa Evidence Rule 703 did not contain the extra language of the federal rule when the Iowa Supreme Court decided *Gacke v. Pork Extra, L.L.C.*, 684 N.W.2d 168 (Iowa 2004). Hearsay declarants affirmed in writing an odor problem emanating from nearby hog confinement facilities. Plaintiff collected these responses, and medical experts testified to medical and breathing problems based upon them. The trial court allowed the testimony and the written hearsay into evidence. This created a problem. Although the Iowa rule generally allowed such information to be received in evidence to show the basis for an expert's opinion, the wholesale entry into the record of so much raw hearsay was too much for the court. Judgment for the plaintiffs was reversed.

10. Ethics questions sometimes accompany the foregoing legal considerations Professor Daniel Blinka poses this scenario:

Direct examination of an expert witness. The expert witness has relied on written and oral reports by non-testifying experts, as is her custom; however, they do not fall within any apparent hearsay exception. Proponent nonetheless wants the jury to hear this information and asks the witness to describe it. Proponent is convinced that opposing counsel will not object either because he fails to grasp the hearsay issue or doesn't want to accentuate the evidence by objecting. The witness describes the hearsay reports without objection and proponent later uses this material in closing argument. Was proponent's conduct proper?

D. Blinka, *Ethics, Evidence and the Modern Adversarial Trial*, 19 GEO. J.L. ETHICS 1, 4 (2006).

11.   The wisdom of the Advisory Committee in enacting the December 1, 2000 amendment becomes apparent when we look at states laboring without the guidance of such an amendment. For example, Maryland adopted Rule 703 in 1994. While Maryland Rule 5-703(a) tracks the first part of the federal rule, Maryland Rule 703(b) was new and invited introduction of otherwise inadmissible evidence when that data is relied upon by an expert. Maryland did not adopt the 2000 federal amendment. In 2008, a Maryland case raised the issue of when a jury could receive otherwise inadmissible evidence under Maryland Rule 5-703. Although parts of an environmental testing report contained some allegedly irrelevant and prejudicial data, an unredacted version was admitted into evidence. The proponent of the report argued that since a trial expert had relied on the document, the jury could see it in its entirety. The Court of Special Appeals agreed, stating that "even data that might not otherwise be admissible, may . . . be properly admitted if it is relied upon by an expert." *Brown v. Daniel Realty Co.*, 180 Md. App. 102, 118, 949 A.2d 6 (2008). In civil cases, this interpretation opens the process to abuse, as described above. In criminal trials, such an approach might raise *Crawford* violations.

6.   The Statement of the Ultimate Opinion

This topic presents two main issues. First, some jurisdictions still insist that the expert vouch for the ultimate opinion to a "reasonable scientific (or medical) certainty." Although the meaning of "reasonable certainty" is open to interpretation, an opinion lacking this formulation may be inadmissible as a matter of law.

Do you see any justification for imposing that limitation? At first, the limitations may seem arbitrary, but there is a connection between this limitation and the *Frye* rule. As we have seen, in part *Frye* rests on the fear that the lay jurors will assume that virtually all scientific testimony is infallible. If we work from that premise, it makes sense to limit expert testimony to opinions that merit the weight we think the jurors will accord the opinions. If jurors are likely to give scientific evidence certain or conclusive weight, it is arguable that only scientific opinions of that degree of certitude should be admitted. On the other hand, if we abandon the traditional rule and permit experts to express probabilities and even possibilities, that shift would seem to diminish the danger that the jury will attach undue weight to the evidence. Forcing the expert to characterize every courtroom opinion as a certainty may heighten the very danger on which *Frye* rests. The trend is toward abandoning the traditional view and permitting the expert to specify a lesser degree of certitude with which he or she feels comfortable. *See Jahn v. Equine Servs.*, PSC, 233 F.3d 382 (6th Cir. 2000) (suit against veterinary hospital and surgeons followed death of a horse; testimony by plaintiff's experts about the "most likely" cause of the horse's death was proper, and expert testimony need not eliminate all other possible causes of an injury).

Are defense experts required to testify with the same degree of medical or scientific certainty as experts for plaintiffs — *e.g.*, "reasonable probability"? Some courts fear that requiring defense experts to do so impermissibly shifts the burden of proof on causation from plaintiff to defendant. Defense experts may testify in terms of alternative "possible" causes, *see, e.g., Haas v. Zaccaria*, 659 So. 2d 1130 (Fla. Dist. Ct. App. 1995) (defendant doctor not precluded from offering possible alternative explanation to negligence in medical malpractice action). *See also* Strachan, *Possible Defense Responses to Plaintiff's Experts*, 17 Utah B.J. 12 (Aug/Sept 2004).

While Rule 704(a) permits experts to opine on an ultimate issue of fact, while Rule 704(b) creates an exception in criminal cases, where "an expert witness must not state an opinion about whether the defendant did or did not have a mental state or condition that constitutes an element of the crime charged or of a defense" reserving those issues for the trier of fact. Federal Rule of Evidence 704(b)

Subsection (b) was added in 1984 as part of the Comprehensive Crime Control Act, primarily in reaction to several high-profile insanity defense cases, including Hinckley's attempted assassination of President Reagan. The subsection purports to resurrect the ultimate fact prohibition in a specific context. The legislative history indicates that in enacting the subsection, Congress intended to "eliminate the confusing spectacle of competing expert witnesses testifying to directly contradictory conclusions as to the ultimate legal issue to be found by the trier of fact." S. Rep. No. 225, 98th Cong., 1st. Sess. 230 (1983). The rationale for subsection (b) is that "insanity involves a legal (moral), not a medical issue, and therefore, no matter how the test for insanity is phrased, a psychiatrist or psychologist is no more qualified than any other person to give an opinion whether a particular defendant's mental condition satisfies the legal test for insanity." P. Giannelli & E. Imwinkelried, Scientific Evidence § 9-3(B), at 286 (1986).

Sometimes defense evidence needs to be looked at very carefully. Does it violate Rule 704, or not? While at first blush it may seem to abridge Rule 704, upon closer examination a different conclusion sometimes evolves. The next case illustrates.

UNITED STATES v. FINLEY
301 F.3d 1000 (9th Cir. 2002)

Bright, J.

[Finley owned a law bookstore and ran a bar review course for students of non-accredited law schools. Finley began looking for investors to assist him in opening a chain of approximately twenty bookstores across the United States. Finley apparently could not obtain traditional bank financing because of a dispute he had with the IRS over a large tax claim. His efforts to get financing resulted in three counts of bank fraud, and Finley was convicted of two of them. His conviction was reversed when the Court of Appeals determined that the trial court erred in striking the testimony of Finley's psychological expert, Dr. Wicks].

*   *   *

Expert testimony that compels the jury to conclude that the defendant did or did not possess the requisite *mens rea* does not "assist the trier of fact" under Rule 702 because such testimony encroaches on the jury's vital and exclusive function to make credibility determinations. Specifically, Rule 704(b) "limits the expert's testimony by prohibiting him from testifying as to whether the defendant had the mental state or condition that constitutes an element of the crime charged." [*United States v.] Morales*, 108 F.3d at 1035. The "rationale for precluding ultimate opinion testimony applies . . . "to any ultimate mental state of the defendant that is relevant to the legal conclusion sought to be proven.' " *United States v Campos*, 217 F.3d 707, 711 (9th Cir. 2000) (quoting S. Rep. 98-225 at 231). However, Rule 704(b) allows expert testimony on a defendant's mental state so long as the expert does not draw the ultimate inference or conclusion for the jury. *Morales*, 108 F.3d at 1037–38. It is, therefore, essential that we distinguish between expert opinions that "necessarily compel" a conclusion about the defendant's *mens rea* and those that do not.

In *Morales*, we concluded that the district court erred in barring expert testimony under Rule 704(b) because the expert's testimony did not compel the conclusion that Morales lacked the *mens rea* of the crime. Morales, charged with willfully making false bookkeeping entries, wanted an accounting expert to testify that her "understanding of accounting principles" was "weak." *Id.* at 1037. We stated:

> Even if the jury believed [the] expert testimony that Morales had a weak grasp of bookkeeping knowledge (and there was evidence to the contrary), the jury would still have had to draw its own inference from that predicate testimony to answer the ultimate factual question — whether Morales willfully made false entries. Morales could have had a weak grasp of bookkeeping principles and still knowingly made false entries. *Id.* at 1037.

In *Morales*, we also cited with approval *United States v. Rahm*, in which we reversed the district court's exclusion of a defense expert who was going to testify that Rahm had poor visual perception and consistently overlooked important visual details. *Morales*, 108 F.3d at 1038. In *Rahm*, we drew a distinction between the ultimate issue — whether Rahm knew the bills were counterfeit — and the proffered testimony of the defendant's poor vision, from which the jury could, but was not compelled, to infer that she did not know the bills were counterfeit. *Id.* (citing *Rahm*, 993 F.2d at 1411–12).

On the other hand, we have applied Rule 704(b) to prohibit certain testimony that does compel a conclusion about *mens rea*. In *Campos*, we upheld a district court's exclusion of a polygraph expert from testifying that the defendant was truthful when she stated she did not know she was transporting marijuana. 217 F.3d at 711. We determined that the testimony compelled the conclusion that the defendant did not possess the requisite knowledge to commit the crime because polygraph test results offer an implicit opinion about whether the accused is being deceptive about the very matters at issue in the trial. *Id.* at 712.

Dr. Wicks' expert diagnosis that Finley has an atypical belief system falls into the

Morales/Rahm line of reasoning and can be distinguished from *Campos*. The jury could have accepted the atypical belief diagnosis and still concluded that Finley knowingly defrauded the banks. If credited, Dr. Wicks' testimony established only that Finley's beliefs were rigid and he would distort or disregard information that ran counter to those beliefs. Dr. Wicks did not, and would not be allowed to, testify about Finley's specific beliefs with regard to the financial instruments. The jury was free to conclude that Finley knew the notes were fraudulent, despite the rigidity of his belief system. Just as in *Morales* and *Rahm*, the defense was entitled to present evidence so that the jury could infer from the expert's testimony that the defendant lacked the necessary intent to defraud, but such a conclusion was not necessarily compelled by the diagnosis. A psychological diagnosis, unlike a lie detector test, does not automatically entail an opinion on the truth of a patient's statements. Furthermore, the psychological diagnosis can be limited such that it in no way touches upon the specific issues of fact to be resolved by the jury.

We also observe that a jury is free to reject Dr. Wicks' testimony. A jury might decide that Finley was untruthful with Dr. Wicks, as the government so strenuously argues in its brief to this court. *See Vallejo*, 237 F.3d at 1020 ("allowing the expert testimony would not displace the role of the jury because, after hearing the expert testimony, the jury was free to decide that the reason for the discrepancy was Vallejo's lack of credibility — not his communications disorder").

NOTES

1. How broad is the prohibition in Rule 704(b)? To be sure, the Rule prohibits at least "opinions incorporating the statutory language of the insanity standard." Note, *Resurrection of the Ultimate Issue Rule: Federal Rule of Evidence 704(b) and the Insanity Defense*, 72 CORNELL L. REV. 620, 639 (1987). However, it remains to be seen whether the courts will extend the prohibition to opinions that "go to the very brink," that is, opinions so closely related to the ultimate issue that they indirectly communicate to the jury the expert's opinion on the ultimate issue. *Id.* Suppose that Devitt raised an insanity defense. Would Rule 704(b) prohibit an expert from testifying that, at the time of the assault, Devitt believed that he was merely dreaming? Or assume that the expert was willing to testify that Devitt did not understand that he was actually beating Paterson. Could the expert testify that Devitt did not understand the nature of the act? *Id.* at 638. In *United States v. Masat*, 896 F.2d 88, 93 (5th Cir. 1990), the court indicated that Rule 704(b) applies to "only a direct statement on the issue of intent." Testimony that the accused did not possess the requisite mens rea was excluded in *United States v. Campos*, 217 F.3d 707 (9th Cir. 2000). The *Campos* case is discussed in the *Finley* decision, *supra*.

2. After Rule 704(a), what remains of the ultimate fact rule? While there is support for the view that an expert may voice limited opinions on mixed questions of law and fact where such opinions form part of the vocabulary in the expert's field, there are boundaries. Consider this excerpt from the Advisory Committee Note on Rule 704:

The abolition of the ultimate issue rule does not lower the bars so as to admit all opinions. Under Rules 701 and 702, opinions must be helpful to the trier of fact, and Rule 403 provides for exclusion of evidence which wastes time. These provisions afford ample assurances against the admission of opinions which would merely tell the jury what result to reach, somewhat in the manner of the oath-helpers of an earlier day. They also stand ready to exclude opinions phrased in terms of inadequately explored legal criteria. Thus the question, "Did T have capacity to make a will?" would be excluded, while the question, "Did T have sufficient mental capacity to know the nature and extent of his property and the natural objects of his bounty and to formulate a rational scheme of distribution?" would be allowed. McCormick § 12.

3.   Does the expression, "ultimate issue," in 704(a) allow opinions only upon the "ultimate factual issue"? Does a dichotomy emerge whereby Rule 704(a) authorizes, for the most part, ultimate opinions of fact but continues to bar admission of opinions on mixed questions of law and fact? *Compare Carol Barnhart Inc. v. Economy Cover Corp.*, 773 F.2d 411 (2d Cir. 1985) *with Bammerlin v. Navistar Int'l Transportation Corp.*, 30 F.3d 898, 900–01 (7th Cir. 1994). Judge Easterbrook's view in the latter case on the law speaks volumes:

> [Plaintiff] wants Professor Lloyd Weinreb to testify as an expert witness about the copyright process in general, and the copyrightability of mannequin heads in particular . . . [It] objects to what it sees as undue restrictions on Professor Weinreb's testimony. . . . Professor Weinreb is a distinguished scholar, but he will not be allowed to testify in this case.
>
> Whether mannequin heads in general, or these mannequin heads in particular, are copyrightable is a question of law, which the court will decide (perhaps in response to dispositive motions soon to be filed). A jury has nothing to do with this subject. . . . If the court determines that mannequin heads are copyrightable subject matter, the jury will be so instructed. Similarly, the court will provide the jury with any necessary general information about the operation of the copyright system. There is no need for expert testimony on this subject; in a trial there is only one legal expert — the judge. *Pivot Point International, Inc. v. Charlene Products, Inc.*, 932 F. Supp. 220, 225 (N.D. Ill. 1996).

7.   The Future of Expert Opinion Testimony

The net effect of the adoption of Article VII of the Federal Rules of Evidence is to liberalize the admission of expert opinion testimony. In sum, we are likely to encounter "the battle of the experts" in the courtroom more frequently in the future. The basic policy question is whether that battle belongs in the courtroom. To some degree, we continue to adhere to the view that expert testimony is admissible only if the subject matter is beyond the comprehension or ken of the jurors. But if that is true, are the jurors capable of evaluating the proper weight to assign to the evidence and resolving a dispute between two experts?

One of the recurring criticisms of expert opinion testimony is that each side finds a partisan expert and presents the expert most willing to slant his or her testimony in favor of the party calling — and paying — the expert. Many commentators suggested that this problem could be remedied by a more liberal use of the courts' power to appoint impartial experts. The drafters of the Federal Rules attempted to implement that suggestion in Rule 706. The Rule provides that the court may appoint expert witnesses agreed upon by the parties or of its own selection. Witnesses so appointed must advise the parties of their findings and be available to be deposed by any party. They may be called to testify by the court or any party and shall be subject to cross-examination by any party, including the proponent of such witnesses.

Courts have been hesitant to use their power to appoint experts; consequently Rule 706 is underused. This is in contrast to most of the countries in Europe where the judge makes the final selection of the experts to be called as witnesses. "The experts [in civil-law jurisdictions] are formally appointed as the court's own witnesses and compensated for their services with public funds. . . . The pattern is radically different in most common-law jurisdictions like the United States and the United Kingdom." Imwinkelried, *The Court Appointment of Expert Witnesses in the United States: A Failed Experiment*, 8 MED. & LAW 601 (1989).

NOTE

Should American judges be eager or reluctant to appoint experts under Rule 706? In countries where expert testimony has been largely privatized like the United States, the attorneys representing private parties play the major role in selecting experts. Is this preferable to the approach in most civil law countries? While considerations such as ensuring a witness's scientific objectivity may be aided by the European practice, does it introduce a larger measure of judicial bias into the dispute? *See* Diamond, *The Fallacy of the Impartial Expert*, 3 ARCHIVES OF CRIM. PSYCHODYNAMICS 221 (1959). Which approach is more in keeping with an adversary model of adjudication? On the partisan battles between experts in modern trials, see J. Mnookin, *Idealizing Science and Demonizing Experts: An Intellectual History of Expert Evidence*, 52 VILL. L. REV. 763 (2007).

Chapter 24

THE BEST EVIDENCE RULE: THE ADMISSIBILITY OF COPIES, SUMMARIES, ETC.

Read Federal Rules of Evidence 1001 through 1007

A. INTRODUCTION

As Chapter 18 noted, the hearsay, opinion, and best evidence rules are all designed to implement a reliability model that prefers live testimony to hearsay, statements of fact to opinions, and the production of writings to testimony about their contents. The best evidence doctrine implements the last element of that model. *United States ex rel. El-Amin v. George Washington Univ.*, 522 F. Supp. 2d 135, 145 (D.D.C. 2007).

The best evidence rule assumes that one type of evidence — the original document — has superior trustworthiness. The rule enforces that assumption by demanding that the proponent either produce or account for the original document when the document's terms are in issue. However, courts realize that sometimes, through no fault of the proponent's, the original will be unavailable at trial. In this situation, the common law relents and accepts "secondary evidence" of the contents of the document.

As you might have noticed, this approach parallels hearsay analysis. As we saw in Chapters 20–22 most hearsay exceptions are based on a combined showing of the reliability of the out-of-court statement and some necessity to resort to the hearsay. Similarly, the best evidence rule works to ensure that the secondary evidence is both necessary and reliable by defining both the acceptable excuses for nonproduction of the original and the admissible secondary evidence. In short, the best evidence rule operates as a preferential doctrine rather than as a categorical exclusionary rule.

The doctrine is codified in Rule 1002: Requirement of Original.

> An original writing, recording, or photograph is required in order to prove its content unless these rules or a federal statute provides otherwise.

The federal approach can be restated as follows: When the terms of a document are in issue, the proponent must either: (a) produce an original or duplicate, *or* (b) both establish an excuse for the nonproduction of the document and offer a satisfactory type of secondary evidence.

To understand the doctrine, we must analyze five questions: (1) What is a "document" for purposes of the best evidence rule?, (2) When are the terms of a document "in issue"?, (3) How should we define an "original" or "duplicate"?, (4)

What are adequate excuses for the nonproduction of the original?, (5) And, finally, what are the acceptable types of secondary evidence?

As we trace the evolution of the answers to those questions from the common law to the Federal Rules of Evidence, you will notice the gradual but steady, liberalization of the admissibility of secondary evidence of a document's contents. The conservative, common-law best evidence rule "has its roots in a time before word processors, copier machines, typewriters or even carbon paper." McElhaney, *The Best Evidence*, 75 A.B.A. J. 72 (Jan. 1989). To a large extent, scientific advances have driven the liberalization of this rule.

B. WHAT IS A "DOCUMENT" FOR PURPOSES OF THE BEST EVIDENCE RULE?

The modern doctrine traces its origins to a statement by Chief Justice Holt in *Ford v. Hopkins*, 1 Salk 283, 91 Eng. Rep. 250 (K.B. 1700): "the best proof that the nature of the thing will afford is only required." Although Holt's language is broad enough to apply to non-documentary evidence, in the 19th century Professor Thayer's writings persuaded most courts that the rule should be confined to documents.

Taking their cue from Thayer, many commentators have noted that the label "best evidence rule" is a misnomer. The phrase suggests that there is a general requirement that the proponent must generally produce the most trustworthy evidence possible. Such a broad requirement exists, if at all, only in the principle that an opposing party generally may comment on the proponent's failure to produce more reliable evidence presumably within the proponent's possession. However, there is no general rule excluding evidence simply because more trustworthy evidence may be available.

The rationale for the rule's limitation to documents was grounded in the historical dangers of copying mistakes and fraud, particularly given the law's "special regard" for the importance of the written word. As you know, words are very carefully chosen in legal documents and statutes; what may seem like a minor word change can have enormous legal consequences. Under substantive contract law, for example, it can make a huge difference whether a clause reads "unless" rather than "until." When a case turns on the precise wording of an agreement or deed, it is vital to minimize the risk of mistransmission or misdescription of the document's contents. Thus, early common law placed great importance on originals.

The primacy of this rationale helps explain the liberalization of the rule over time, since science has generated better and better mechanical means of reproduction "which virtually eliminate the possibility of unintentional mistransmission." 2 McCormick, Evidence § 233, at 89 (6th ed. 2006). The other policy concern — prevention of fraud — originally stemmed from suspicion that a litigant who failed to produce an original might be trying to hide something or deceive the court. In the era before pretrial discovery, it could be difficult to detect fraudulent copies or fabricated secondary evidence. The advent of modern discovery has lessened — but not entirely eliminated — the latter concern.

These twin policy concerns have been influential in shaping the meaning of "document" and of "duplicate" under the best evidence rule. There are four types of evidence most commonly considered documents under the rule.

1.   Conventional Writings

The most obvious candidate for inclusion within the rule's scope is a conventional writing. Federal Rule of Evidence 1001(a) offers a broad definition of the term "writing." In our torts case, if Ms. Hill's attorney wanted to introduce the written contract of purchase, the best evidence rule would unquestionably apply. In the *Devitt* case, if the prosecutor offered a laboratory report to establish the presence of bloodstains on Paterson's shirt, again the rule would come into play. Or suppose that, with the help of a police artist, Paterson prepared an Identikit drawing of the assailant's face. The prosecutor might want to introduce the drawing to show a striking similarity between the features in the drawing and Devitt's facial features. The drawing would be a writing, triggering the rule. *Seiler v. Lucasfilm, Ltd.*, 808 F.2d 1316 (9th Cir. 1986), *cert. denied*, 484 U.S. 826 (1987).

NOTE

In *United States v. Bennett*, 363 F.3d 947, 954 (9th Cir.), *cert. denied*, 543 U.S. 950 (2004), the court ruled that the definition of writing in Rule 1001(a) is broad enough to include a GPS (Global Positioning System) display. The court noted that "the government [did] not offer any record evidence that it would have been impossible or even difficult to download or print out the data on [the] GPS. . . . We therefore hold that [the] GPS-based testimony was inadmissible under the best evidence rule." Do you read the rule to *require* the creation of a writing? Was the display on the GPS screen a "writing"?

2.   Tape Recordings

The traditional common-law definition of "document" emerged before tape recordings or audiotapes even existed. When tape recordings developed, the question naturally arose whether the best evidence rule should extend to audiotapes, and courts ultimately held that it should. Suppose that in the *Devitt* case, the police had a tape recording of a threatening call the attacker made anonymously to Paterson the week before the incident. The prosecutor wants to have a police officer testify about the tape recording. The best evidence rule would require the prosecutor to produce the audiotape recording itself. *See People v. Kirk*, 43 Cal. App. 3d 921, 117 Cal. Rptr. 345 (1974). The same result obtains under Federal Evidence Rule 1001(a).

3.   Photographs

Another technological innovation that affected the scope of the best evidence rule was the development of the photographic process. Assume that in the *Devitt* case, shortly after his arrest the police searched Devitt's apartment. During the search, the officers found several photographs of Paterson's apartment and the vicinity — suggesting that Devitt had been "casing" the apartment for some time. The prosecutor wants one of the searching officers to testify to this discovery. At common law, many courts balked at extending the best evidence rule to photographs. It is true that a photograph is not a conventional writing, but many of the same policy considerations are pertinent. The Federal Rules of Evidence include photographs within the scope of the rule. *See* Rule 1001(c).

4.   Inscribed Chattels

Suppose that in *Devitt*, Mr. Paterson testifies that the assailant brandished a knife and the police find a knife on Devitt's person at the time of arrest. Without producing the knife, the prosecutor could elicit the arresting officer's testimony about the knife. *Redman v. State*, 580 S.W.2d 945 (Ark. 1979). Or in our torts case, Ms. Hill might have a testing laboratory subject the metal from which the gas tank is made to a thin layer chromatography (TLC) test to determine its chemical composition. The test is run on plates; the length and color of the streaks on the plate indicate the chemical composition of the unknown metal. It is well-settled that the chemist may testify to describe the test result without producing the TLC plates. *United States v. Gavic*, 520 F.2d 1346 (8th Cir. 1975).

Although we begin with the assumption that a chattel — a thing — is not a document for purposes of the best evidence rule, there may be circumstances in which a chattel should functionally be treated as a document. In the *Devitt* hypothetical above, suppose Paterson said that when the assailant brandished the knife, he saw the inscription "Buck Knives" on the blade. The police officer might attempt to testify that Devitt's knife bore that inscription without producing the knife in the courtroom. In this situation, some jurisdictions refuse to apply the best evidence rule even though the testimony technically describes the contents of "a writing." Others invoke the rule whenever the focus shifts to an inscription on a chattel. These jurisdictions reason that the concern for detail that inspires the best evidence rule applies equally to an inscription on a chattel as to the writing in a conventional document. These courts argue that limiting the rule's scope to documents in the orthodox sense is arbitrary. Still others, probably the majority at common law, give the trial judge discretion to decide whether to treat the chattel as a document for purposes of the best evidence rule.

NOTES AND PROBLEM

1.   In exercising its discretion in the case of an inscribed chattel, what factors should the court consider? What is the significance of the length of the inscription? Suppose that the knife could easily be brought into the courtroom. How does that factor cut? Should it affect the ruling if the issue of Devitt's identification as the assailant were a close one?

2.   In almost all jurisdictions, inscribed chattels represent the outer limit of the definition of "document." For that reason, courts have refused to hold, for example, that in drug prosecutions the government must produce the drugs themselves; the drugs are not inscribed in any sense. However, suppose the defense argued that the drugs are such vital evidence in these prosecutions that the best evidence rule should be extended? What policy arguments might the defense make? *See G.E.G. v.*

State, 417 So. 2d 975, 977–78 (Fla. 1982) (a rule of nonproduction could "thwart the [defense's] ability to make certain objections, particularly objections to chain of custody").

3. **Problem 24-1.** Suppose that in the *Devitt* hypothetical, the Morena legislature has adopted Federal Evidence Rules 1001–08. As trial judge, how would you rule on defense counsel's objection to the testimony about the inscription on the knife blade? Be prepared to point to the statutory language that you think is dispositive. Under Rule 1001(a), does the judge have discretion whether to treat the inscription as a writing, or is the application of the definition to inscriptions mandatory? *Compare United States v. Yamin*, 868 F.2d 130, 134 (5th Cir.) (the judge has discretion whether to treat the Rolex inscription on allegedly counterfeit watches as a writing), *cert. denied*, 492 U.S. 924 (1989), *with* 2 B. JEFFERSON, CALIFORNIA EVIDENCE BENCHBOOK § 31.12, at 647 (3d ed. 1997) (arguing that under a very similar California statute, the application is mandatory).

C. WHEN ARE THE DOCUMENT'S TERMS "IN ISSUE"?

Even if the object in question is a "document," the best evidence rule does not come into play unless the document's terms are in issue. In the words of Federal Rule of Evidence 1002, the rule applies only when the proponent is attempting "[t]o prove []the content" of a writing, recording, or photograph. The proponent can freely elicit testimony about the existence, physical characteristics, or execution of a writing without triggering the best evidence rule. *O'Brien v. Ed Donnelly Enterprises, Inc.*, 575 F.3d 567, 598 (6th Cir. 2009) ("to prove something besides the 'content' " of the writing). However, when the document's terms or contents are in issue, the concern for accuracy underlying the best evidence rule mandates its application. Courts customarily find that a document's terms are in issue in two situations.

1. When the Material Facts of Consequence Automatically Place the Document's Terms in Issue

In our torts case, suppose that the complaint specifically alleges that Ms. Hill's husband purchased a Polecat automobile from Jefferson Motor Car Company by a written contract. That allegation places the contract's contents squarely within the range of issues in the case. (Indeed, in most jurisdictions, a copy of the writing is attached to the complaint as an exhibit, and the complaint will purport to incorporate the terms of the writing by reference.) Given that allegation, Ms. Hill may not testify orally to the contents of the written contract between her husband and Jefferson Motor Car without excusing the nonproduction of the contract itself.

Distinguish the above situation from the deceptively similar situation in which both non-documentary and documentary evidence of the same fact exist. If an eyewitness observed the fact or event without relying upon a document that also memorializes that fact or event, then the fact or event exists "independently" of the document and oral testimony about the fact or event is not subject to the best evidence rule. For example, to recover on her claim, Ms. Hill must prove that her husband fulfilled his obligations under the contract with Jefferson Motor Car

Company. May she testify that she paid his monthly installments, without producing the written receipts Jefferson gave him? The best evidence rule is not triggered merely because the witness is testifying to facts that also happen to be conveniently "contained in a writing." *Moschale v. Mock*, 591 S.W.2d 415, 419 (Mo. Ct. App. 1979). The rule does not "prohibit a witness from testifying to a fact simply because the fact can be supported by written documentation." *McKeown v. Woods Hole*, 9 F. Supp. 2d 32, 40 (D. Mass. 1998). The law does not "require[] the plaintiff to prove her case by documentary rather than testimonial evidence." *Negron v. Caleb Brett U.S.A., Inc.*, 212 F.3d 666, 673 (1st Cir. 2000).

PROBLEMS

1. **Problem 24-2.** Suppose that in *Devitt*, it became relevant to show that Paterson reported the battery to the police shortly after the alleged incident. During cross-examination of Paterson, the defense implied that there was no attack; the defense counsel suggested that Paterson did not report the incident promptly. To rehabilitate Paterson's credibility, the prosecutor would like a police officer to testify that shortly after the alleged battery, Paterson phoned and reported that he had just been attacked. A few minutes after receiving the telephone call, the officer recorded the report in a police log. Could the officer testify to the report without bringing the log into the courtroom? Or suppose that the police department routinely tape-records all incoming calls. Could the officer testify to the report without producing the audiotape? *United States v. Fagan*, 821 F.2d 1002, 1009 n.1 (5th Cir. 1987) ("The prosecution was not trying to show the contents of the tape, but rather the contents of the conversation . . . ."), *cert. denied*, 484 U.S. 1005 (1988).

2. **Problem 24-3.** In *Hill*, it so happened that Mr. Michelson was standing at the intersection where Ms. Hill's and Mr. Worker's cars collided. He was using his video camera to film his wife standing in front of the old courthouse near the intersection. While he was taking the video of his wife, he happened to see the collision occur and got it on video. At trial, Ms. Hill calls Michelson as a witness. Polecats' attorney objects that Michelson may not testify without first accounting for the film. As trial judge, would you sustain the objection?

2. When the Proffered Testimony Contains an Express or Implied Reference to the Contents of a Document

Sometimes, even when the material facts of consequence do not require the proponent to resort to documentary proof, the proponent does so. For example, the proponent can prove the fact of a marriage ceremony without producing the marriage certificate. The marriage ceremony occurs independently of the certificate, and an eyewitness can observe the entire ceremony without ever seeing the certificate. Indeed, typically the certificate does not even exist at the time of the ceremony; the official presiding at the ceremony usually signs the certificate after the ceremony. However, at the time of trial, the proponent may be unable to locate an eyewitness to the marriage ceremony. The unavailability of eyewitnesses might force the proponent to resort to the certificate, and in that situation the proponent would have to comply with the best evidence rule.

NOTES AND PROBLEMS

1. **Problem 24-4.** As we have seen, to make out a prima facie case, Ms. Hill must prove not only that her husband formed a contract to purchase the Polecat automobile but also that he fulfilled all of his conditions under the contract, including the down payment of the purchase price. When he made the down payment, a Jefferson employee gave him a receipt. Ms. Hill witnessed the delivery of the receipt. As trial judge, would you permit Ms. Hill to testify, "And I've got a receipt to prove it," to corroborate her testimony?

2. **Problem 24-5.** In *Devitt*, the officer who originally received the complaint of the battery testifies. On direct examination, he purports to recall Paterson's report. However, on cross-examination, the officer admits that he has received so many reports of batteries and other crimes in his years of service as an officer that he cannot presently recall that particular telephone call. He admits that he is relying on his entry in the log book. At that point, what should the defense attorney do? Assuming that the log book is not in the courtroom, how should the trial judge rule?

3. What if an expert relies on the contents of a writing as part of the basis for his or her opinion under Rule 703? Does that use of the writing trigger the best evidence rule? *Guzman v. Memorial Hermann Hosp. System*, 637 F. Supp. 2d 464, 476 (S.D. Tex. 2009) ("Nor does the rule apply 'when an expert testifies based in part on having reviewed writings . . . because Rule 703 allows an expert to express opinions based on matters not put into evidence' ").

4. In *United States v. Smith*, 566 F.3d 410 (4th Cir. 2009), the prosecution sought to prove that the firearms in question were manufactured outside of North Carolina. The prosecution called an A.T.F. agent who testified on the basis of certain written reference material. The defense challenged the testimony as a violation of Rule 1002. In rejecting the challenge, the Fourth Circuit explained:

> In this case, the government never sought to prove the content of any writing or recording relating to the firearms or their places of manufacture. It sought only to prove the fact that the firearms were manufactured in States other than North Carolina . . . . The place of the firearms' manufacture was a fact existing independently of the content of any . . . writing.

The independent existence argument can defeat the contention that the material facts automatically place the document's terms in issue, but does it also surmount the contention that the proffered testimony refers to or is based on the writing's contents? However, consider Note 3, *supra*.

D.   THE DEFINITIONS OF "ORIGINAL" AND "DUPLICATE"

As we have seen, if a document's terms are in issue, the best evidence rule applies. In such a case, the preference under both the common law and the Federal Rules is that the proponent introduce **primary evidence**, which under the best evidence rule refers to either the original document or a "duplicate original" (sometimes called a counterpart). Originals and duplicates are equally admissible;

if the proponent can persuade the trial judge that the evidence qualifies as either an original or duplicate, the evidence is admissible — and there is no necessity to account for or produce any other document. Thus, it is critical to understand the definitions of "original" and "duplicate."

1.   The Definition of "Original"

The common law recognized only a single "original" writing, which in most cases was the document produced first in point of time. The legal definition of the original is that it is the document that has legal significance under the substantive law.

To illustrate the point, consider this hypothetical. Suppose that in our torts case, Mr. Hill and Jefferson Motor Car entered into the contract for the purchase of the automobile by correspondence. Mr. Hill types an offer to buy the car on his computer, prints out the offer, makes a photocopy, and mails the photocopy to the Jefferson Motor Car Company. The typed document was prepared first in point of time. However, that document is not the "original." To identify the original, we must resort to the substantive law of contracts. Under contract law, a document does not become legally effective as an offer until the offeree receives the document. The upshot is that the document created second is actually the "original" under the best evidence rule.

Federal Rule of Evidence 1001(d) defines 'original' as follows: "An original of a writing or recording means the writing or recording itself or any counterpart intended to have the same effect by the person who executed or issued it. For electronically stored information, 'original' means any printout — or other output readable by sight — if it accurately reflects the information. An 'original' of a photograph includes the negative or a print from it."

NOTE

Does this rule codify the traditional, common-law definition of "original"? If not, how does the rule differ from the common law? Is the definition broader or narrower? To what extent do the scientific advances in reproduction technology help to explain the changes? Under this definition, will there necessarily be only one "original" writing? Are multiple "originals" possible under Rule 1001(d)?

2.   The Definition of "Duplicate" or "Counterpart"

At common law, to qualify a document as a "duplicate original" — admissible without accounting for the absence of any other "original" — the proponent had to demonstrate that:

(a)   The document was an exact copy of the original;

(b)   The parties made the copy at the same time as the original;

(c)   The parties intended the copy to have the same legal effect as the original; and

(d)   The parties executed the copy with roughly the same formalities as the original.

Until recently, all subsequently prepared copies were treated as secondary evidence. The rationale for this strict requirement was that a "Bob Cratchit fingers numbed by cold in the counting house and fraught with anxiety over the health of Tiny Tim, might distractedly misplace a decimal point, invert a pair of digits or drop a line. Yet a Xerox machine, by way of contrast, does not worry about Tiny Tim and does not, therefore, misplace decimal points, invert digits, drop lines, or suffer any of the mental lapses that flesh is heir to." *Equitable Life Assur. Soc'y v. Starr*, 241 Neb. 609, 489 N.W.2d 857, 863 (1992). Understandably, as modern technology spawned superior methods for document reproduction, the common law's strict requirements became less important as a means of assuring the copy's accuracy. The crucial issue became *how* the document was prepared — not *when* it was prepared.

The drafters of the Federal Rules of Evidence focused on that issue. Federal Rule 1001(e) defines "duplicate" as follows:

A "duplicate" means a counterpart produced by a mechanical, photographic, chemical, electronic, or other equivalent process or technique that accurately reproduces the original.

A "duplicate" under the Federal Rules is quite different than the common-law "duplicate original" — there is no requirement that the parties *intended* the duplicate to be the functional equivalent of an original. The Rule 1001(e) also dispenses with the timing requirement. In common parlance, a duplicate under the Rule is simply a copy.

NOTES AND PROBLEMS

1.   Note one peculiarity of the Federal Rules. At common law, a duplicate was admissible exactly as if it were an original; the proponent needn't account for the original or for any other duplicates. Is that true under the Federal Rules? Carefully read Rule 1003:

A duplicate is admissible to the same extent as an original unless a genuine question is raised about the original's authenticity or the circumstances make it unfair to admit the duplicate.

Does Rule 1003 reflect the continuing vitality of the secondary rationale for the original document rule, namely, fraud prevention?

Consider also the accompanying Advisory Committee Note to Rule 1003:

Therefore, if no genuine issue exists as to authenticity and no other reason exists for requiring the original, a duplicate is admissible under the rule. This position finds support in the decisions, *Myrick v. United States*, 332 F.2d 279 (5th Cir. 1964), no error in admitting photostatic copies of checks instead of original microfilm in absence of suggestion to trial judge that photostats were incorrect; *Johns v. United States*, 323 F.2d 421 (5th Cir. 1963), not error to admit concededly accurate tape recording made from original wire recording; *Sauget v. Johnston*, 315 F.2d 816 (9th Cir. 1963), not error to admit copy of agreement when opponent had original and did not on appeal claim any discrepancy. Other reasons for requiring the original may be present when only a part of the original is reproduced and the remainder is needed for cross-examination or may disclose matters qualifying the part offered or otherwise useful to the opposing party. *United States v. Alexander*, 326 F.2d 736 (4th Cir. 1964).

The above quotation from the Note attempts to illustrate the exceptions in Rule 1003. What must the opposing attorney do to invoke Rule 1003's provision about "a genuine question"? Is it sufficient to assert that there is a question about the authenticity of the original, or must the opponent have available, admissible evidence calling the original's authenticity into question? *United States v. Leight*, 818 F.2d 1297, 1305 (7th Cir.)(no; 'only speculation'), *cert. denied*, 484 U.S. 958 (1987). In *Carroll v. Leboeuf, Lamb, Greene & Macrae, LLP*, 614 F. Supp. 2d 481 (S.D.N.Y. 2009), the court found that the testimony raised a general question as to the authenticity of the original letters. The promoter testified that he did not write the letters and that the signatures on the letters were not his.

However, *Carroll* may be an outlier. One commentator contends that since the enactment of Rule 1003, duplicates have been admitted more often than originals in the reported decisions. Miller, *Even Better Than the Real Thing: How Courts Have Been Anything But Liberal in Finding Genuine Questions Raised as to the Authenticity of Originals Under Rule 1003*, 68 MD. L. REV. 160 (2008). The author states that courts "almost never" find a genuine question and argues that judges should be more liberal in finding such questions. The report of the House Committee on the Judiciary indicates that Congress expected that courts would be "liberal in deciding" that a genuine question existed. The author concludes that courts ought to find a genuine question when there are "inconsistencies within and between witnesses' testimony or between the testimony and the duplicate itself" or when there is "expert evidence questioning the authenticity of [the] originals."

2. **Problem 24-6.** Assume that in *Hill*, rather than finalizing the contract by correspondence, Mr. Hill visited Jefferson Motor Car's showroom to sign the contract of purchase. Jefferson's representative handed Mr. Hill a carbon manifold: an original form on top, a sheet of carbon paper, and an exact copy on the bottom. When Mr. Hill and Jefferson's sales manager signed the original form on top, the signatures were impressed through the carbon paper and onto the copy on the bottom. Would the carbon copy qualify as a duplicate? Under the common law? Under Rule 1001(4)?

3. **Problem 24-7.** In *Hill*, when Mr. Hill and Jefferson's sales manager signed the contract, they both signed one document; there was no carbon copy in existence at the time of signature. However, before Mr. Hill left, Jefferson's sales manager made a photocopy of the signed document and handed the copy to Mr. Hill. Under the Federal Rules, would the copy qualify as either an original or a duplicate?

4. **Problem 24-8.** Assume that in Problem 24-6, the copy qualifies as at least a duplicate. At trial, Jefferson's attorney offers the copy in evidence. The copy shows marks crossing out several of the warranty provisions of the contract. Mr. Hill testifies that the copy is "just plain wrong — there were no marks striking out the

warranty provisions when I signed it." Would the copy be automatically admissible in the face of that testimony? What else would Jefferson have to prove? Suppose that Mr. Hill's testified instead that he "cannot recall" marks striking out the warranty provisions.

5.   **Problem 24-9.** Suppose that Ms. Hill is attempting to prove that her husband fulfilled all of the conditions under his contract with Jefferson. Unfortunately, he cannot actually remember making the monthly installment payments. However, he has the cancelled checks he wrote to make the payments. Rather than bring the checks to trial, he photographs them. Are the photographs admissible? *United States v. Patten*, 826 F.2d 198 (2d Cir.) (yes), *cert. denied*, 484 U.S. 968 (1987); *Arizona Dept. of Law. Civil Rights Div. v. Asarco*, 844 F.Supp.2d 957, 979 (D.Ariz. 2011)(yes).

E.   ADEQUATE EXCUSE FOR NONPRODUCTION OF THE ORIGINAL

The best evidence rule is a preferential doctrine rather than an absolute exclusionary rule. The preference is for an original or exact duplicate, but after an appropriate showing, secondary evidence is permitted instead. As those great existential philosophers, the Rolling Stones, remind us, "You can't always get what you want." However, in most jurisdictions at common law, before a judge would allow the introduction of secondary evidence, the proponent had to persuade the trial judge that there was some necessity for resorting to secondary evidence: the proponent had to establish an adequate excuse for nonproduction of the original and *all* duplicate originals.

The Federal Rules' stance on excuses for nonproduction is a bit ambivalent. In one respect, the Rules liberalize admissibility standards. Under Rule 1004, the proponent must establish excuses only for the nonproduction of "originals" — there is no duty to excuse the nonproduction of duplicates. However, in other respects the Federal Rules merely codify the received orthodoxy. Rule 1004 catalogues most of the recognized common law excuses:

The original is not required, and other evidence of the contents of a writing, recording, or photograph is admissible if —

(a)   all the originals are lost or destroyed, and not by the proponent acting in bad faith;

(b)   an original cannot be obtained by any available judicial process;

(c)   the party against whom the original would be offered had control of the original; was at that time put on notice, by pleadings or otherwise, that the original would be a subject of proof at the trial or hearing; and fails to produce it at the trial or hearing; or

(d)   the writing, record, or photograph is not closely related to a controlling issue.

While in large part Rule 1004 is a straightforward codification of the common-law excuses, there are some differences worth noting. At common law, if the excuse was that the original had been lost, the proponent had to have made a recent, diligent search for the original. Some jurisdictions even laid down a hard and fast rule that the proponent must have personally contacted the last known custodian. What is the federal standard? *Bianchi v. Florists Mut. Ins. Co.*, 660 F. Supp. 2d 434 (E.D.N.Y. 2009) (a diligent but unsuccessful search).

Similarly, most jurisdictions concur that there is an adequate excuse when the original is beyond the territorial reach of compulsory process. Some states limit the doctrine to their own compulsory process. Thus, a Pennsylvania proponent must show only that the original is beyond the reach of Pennsylvania's compulsory process. Even if it is clear that the original is in Nevada, the proponent need not investigate the possibility that Nevada courts would give some extraterritorial effect to Pennsylvania process. Is that true under the Federal Rule? Furthermore, in some jurisdictions even when the document is in the possession of a third party beyond the reach of compulsory process, the proponent must either attempt to contact that person to induce that person to voluntarily send the document to the site of trial or show that any contact would be futile because, for example, of the person's hostility to the proponent. Does the Federal Rule incorporate that requirement? Consider the pertinent Advisory Committee Note:

> When the original is in the possession of a third person, inability to procure it from him by resort to process or other judicial procedure is a sufficient explanation of nonproduction. Judicial procedure includes subpoena duces tecum as an incident to the taking of a deposition in another jurisdiction. No further showing is required.

Rule 1004(c) reflects a frequently used excuse. The opponent in possession of the original can be put "on notice" in a variety of ways. If the complaint specifically refers to the written contract, that will obviously put the defendant on notice that the original will be needed at trial. What other means can the proponent use to give the opponent notice? Compulsory process, such as a motion to produce, certainly suffices. Even an informal notice or demand can put the opponent on notice that "the contents (of the original) will be a subject of proof at the hearing."

With respect to Rule 1004(d), some jurisdictions define "collateral" in a technical sense. As we saw earlier in Chapter 16, a fact is collateral (and therefore cannot be proven by extrinsic evidence) if its only logical relevance is to a witness's credibility. Using that technical definition, these courts permit the use of copies of prior written inconsistent statements. Rule 1004(d) rejects that technical definition. The drafters reasoned that the concern for detail is an acute consideration only when the document plays a central role in the case. If the document's role is less central, we can relax the best evidence rule.

Rule 1005 codifies another, frequently used excuse for nonproduction relative to Public Records:

> The proponent may use a copy to prove the content of an official record — or of a document that was recorded or filed in a public office as authorized by law — if these conditions are met: the record or document is otherwise admissible; and the copy is certified as correct in accordance with Rule 902(4) or is testified to be correct by a witness who has compared it with the

original. If no such copy can be obtained by reasonable diligence, then the proponent may use other evidence to prove the content.

At first glance, Rule 1005 does not even appear to deal with the question of excuses for nonproduction. However, by affirmatively authorizing the admission of a certified copy, Rule 1005 impliedly dispenses with the production of the original. Here, too, the Federal Rules differ slightly from the common law. At early common law, some jurisdictions restricted this excuse to documents, the removal of which from official custody was forbidden by statute or regulation. Rule 1005 is broader. Many jurisdictions still restrict the excuse to official records, that is, documents created by government agencies and remaining in official custody; these jurisdictions do not extend the doctrine to private documents that have found their way into official custody. What position does Rule 1005 take on this issue?

Rule 1006 also incorporates an often invoked excuse for nonproduction:

Rule 1006. Summaries to Prove Content

> The proponent may use a summary, chart, or calculation to prove the content of voluminous writings, recordings, or photographs that cannot be conveniently examined in court. The proponent must make the originals or duplicates available for examination or copying, or both, by other parties at a reasonable time and place. And the court may order the proponent to produce them in court.

More and more attorneys appreciate the need to shorten and streamline their presentations in complex cases, and to that end they increasingly turn to Rule 1006 summaries. By its terms, Rule 1006 does not require that the underlying records actually be introduced into evidence. Fishman, *Summary Evidence*, 25 Litig. 38 (Spring 1999) surveys the Rule 1006 case law and exposes a number of "mythical" limitations such as the supposed requirements that the witness herself must prepare the chart, the underlying documents must be admitted in evidence, the underlying documents must be produced in court, the number of documents must be so large that it would be impossible for the jury to review them, the jury itself must perform any calculation, and the summary chart must reflect all the data. However, trial judges do review the wording of rule 1006 charts to ensure that they do not contain "argumentative" "editorializing" of the facts. *Henry v. City of Tallahassee*, 216 F. Supp. 2d 1299, 1309 n.14 (N.D. Fla. 2002).

PROBLEM AND NOTE

1. **Problem 24-10.** Suppose that before marketing the model Mr. Hill purchased, Polecat Motors ran extensive safety tests. The results of the tests are compiled in a 5,000-page report. During discovery, Ms. Hill obtained the report and submitted the report for analysis by her safety expert, Dr. D'Antoni. At trial, the doctor wants to testify to express his opinion of the model's safety. May the doctor present an oral summary of the report or prepare a written "chart, summary, or calculation"? What is the meaning of the expression "conveniently examined in court" in Rule 1006? *United States v. Stephens*, 779 F.2d 232, 238–39 (5th Cir. 1985) (abuse of discretion standard of review).

2. Distinguish Rule 1006 summaries from charts used for illustrative purposes. The use of such charts is governed by Rule 611(a), not Rule 1006. Unlike Rule 1006 charts, pedagogical aids are not substantive evidence and cannot be sent to the jury during deliberations. *United States v. Ogba*, 526 F.3d 214, 225 (5th Cir.), *cert. denied*, 555 U.S. 897 (2008). However, such charts can be used for purposes other than summarizing documents; they can, for instance, be used to summarize testimony. *United States v. Ollison*, 555 F.3d 152 (5th Cir. 2009). Further, pedagogic devices are allowed to "reflect . . . , through captions or other organizational devices of description, the inferences and conclusions drawn from the underlying evidence." *United States v. Milkiewicz*, 470 F.3d 390 (1st Cir. 2006). It is quite common for counsel to employ such charts during closing argument.

Lastly, Rule 1007 supplies one final excuse for nonproduction.

Testimony or Statement of a Party to Prove Content

> The proponent may prove the content of a writing, recording, or photograph by the testimony, deposition, or written statement of the party against whom the evidence is offered. The proponent need not account for the original.

Some common-law jurisdictions do not recognize any admission excuse, while others treat any alleged admission as an adequate excuse. The latter courts have been known to apply the excuse even when the alleged admission was oral and the opponent flatly denied making the admission. In this situation, there is a risk that the opponent in fact never made the admission. Rule 1007 thus represents a compromise between these opposite extreme positions taken at common law.

QUESTIONS AND NOTES

1. In what sense is Rule 1007 a compromise between these two views?

2. Rule 1007 is only a partial excuse. In the case of most excuses for nonproduction, once the excuse is proven, any type of secondary evidence is admissible. However, in the case of Rules 1005–1007, even after the excuse is established, only certain, specified types of secondary evidence are admissible.

Before we close on this topic, consider one last issue of statutory construction. In common-law jurisdictions, trial judges can always be creative and recognize a new excuse for nonproduction. Does the trial judge retain that power under the Federal Rules? Or is the list of excuses in Rules 1004–1007 exhaustive? Do Rules 1004–1007 answer that question, or must we look elsewhere in the Rules? Contrast the wording of Rule 1002 with that of Rules 404(b) ("such as") and 901(b) ("examples"). Does Article X leave any window to the common law? Consider Rule 1004(d). Substantively, Article X is a relatively conservative statutory scheme which, for the most part, merely tinkers with the common-law excuses for nonproduction. Rule 1004(d) is arguably the only real safety valve in Article X.

F. IF THERE IS AN ADEQUATE EXCUSE FOR NONPRODUCTION, WHAT TYPES OF SECONDARY EVIDENCE ARE ADMISSIBLE?

If the proponent demonstrates an adequate excuse for nonproduction of the original, secondary evidence becomes admissible, subject to certain limitations. These limitations ensure that the secondary evidence admitted is reliable as well as necessary.

1. The Types of Secondary Evidence

There are two general categories of secondary evidence that might be introduced as proof of a document's contents. First, a witness could testify that he or she once read the document and can presently recall its contents. The cases liberally permit such testimony so long as the witness satisfies the personal knowledge requirement of Rule 602.

The other type of secondary evidence is a written copy that does not qualify as a "duplicate." The courts ordinarily insist that the copy be complete and verbatim. In some jurisdictions, the judge may admit an abstract of an official record. As with all non-testimonial evidence, the requisite foundation includes authentication under Article IX.

2. The Degrees of Secondary Evidence

By now you ought to be wondering: Given the rationale of the best evidence rule, should we not also prefer the written copy over the oral recollection testimony when we consider admissibility of secondary evidence? And if that is the case, ought we not require the proponent to excuse the nonproduction of any written copies before resorting to oral recollection testimony? Logic suggests that the hierarchy should be primary evidence, secondary copies, and finally oral recollection testimony. That was the majority view in the United States at common law — the so-called "American rule." Indeed, some jurisdictions such as Georgia codified the majority view. GA. CODE ANN. § 24-5-5.

The American rule is undeniably consistent with the policy underlying the best evidence rule. But some courts have gone even further: they prefer a firsthand copy (a copy made from an original or duplicate) over a secondhand copy (a copy made from a copy). Those courts take the logic of the best evidence rule far indeed.

Sensing the need to draw a line to identify the point of diminishing returns, even at common law a minority of courts rejected the proposition that there are degrees of secondary evidence, adopting the so-called "English view." Under this view, except for a preference for a certified copy of official records there are no degrees of secondary evidence; the proponent can introduce oral recollection testimony without any necessity for accounting for written copies.

NOTES AND PROBLEMS

1. Which view do the Federal Rules adopt? Consider the following excerpts from the Advisory Committee Notes to Rules 1004–05:

(Rule 1004)

The rule recognizes no "degrees" of secondary evidence. While strict logic might call for extending the principle of preference beyond simply preferring the original, the formulation of a hierarchy of preferences and a procedure for making it effective is believed to involve unwarranted complexities. Most, if not all, that would be accomplished by an extended scheme of preferences will, in any event, be achieved through the normal motivation of a party to present the most convincing evidence possible and the arguments and procedures available to his opponent if he does not.

(Rule 1005)

Public records call for somewhat different treatment. Removing them from their usual place of keeping would be attended by serious inconvenience to the public and to the custodian. As a consequence judicial decisions and statutes commonly hold that no explanation need be given for failure to produce the original of a public record. McCormick § 204; 4 Wigmore §§ 1215-1228. This blanket dispensation from producing or accounting for the original would open the door to the introduction of every kind of secondary evidence of contents of public records were it not for the preference given certified or compared copies. Recognition of degrees of secondary evidence in this situation is an appropriate *quid* pro quo for not applying the requirement of producing the original.

2. As we have seen, a best evidence objection can raise several preliminary issues: whether something is a document for purposes of the rule, whether its terms are in issue, etc. Which issues does the judge finally decide, and which issues are reserved for the jury? Reread Federal Rules of Evidence 104(a) and (b) and then consider Rule 1008.

Rule 1008. Functions of Court and Jury.

Ordinarily, the court determines whether the proponent has fulfilled the factual conditions for admitting other evidence of the content of a writing, recording, or photograph under Rule 1004 or 1005. But in a jury trial, the jury determines — in accordance with Rule 104(b) — any issue about whether:

(a) an asserted writing, recording, or photograph ever existed;

(b) another one produced at the trial or hearing is the original; or

(c) other evidence of content accurately reflects the content.

G. CONCLUSION

A proponent encountering a best evidence objection can respond by arguing that:

- The testimony does involve a writing, recording, or photograph; or

- The document's terms are not in issue; or

- The evidence qualifies as an "original"; or

- The evidence qualifies as a "duplicate"; or

- There is an adequate excuse for the non-production of the original, and the proffered evidence qualifies as an admissible type of secondary evidence.

As one 2007 opinion noted, "[b]ecause of [the] numerous avenues of escape from the mechanical application of the requirement of the original, a party is rarely precluded from producing significant relevant evidence because of the best evidence rule." *United States ex rel. El-Amin v. George Washington Univ.*, 522 F. Supp. 2d 135, 145–46 (D.D.C. 2007).

Part 4

ADMISSIBILITY RULES BASED ON SOCIAL POLICY

Chapter 25

PRIVILEGE: A GENERAL ANALYTICAL APPROACH

Read Federal Rules of Evidence 501 and 502.

A. INTRODUCTION

Thus far, we have looked at admissibility doctrines premised on the supposed unreliability of certain types of evidence. In the case of privileged information, in contrast, the concern is not unreliability but extrinsic social policy. The evidentiary privileges often exclude trustworthy — sometimes even crucial — evidence. When privileged information is excluded, it is done not to promote the intrinsic truth finding function of the trial but rather to to promote some extrinsic social policy such as the protection of a socially important relationship. Precisely because privileges affect important relationships outside the courtroom, privilege doctrine arguably has greater social significance than any other area of evidence law.

We must be frank, though, about the effect of applying privileges. At least if we consider only the microcosm — the particular case in which the privilege is invoked — the enforcement of a privilege can exact a high cost by suppressing the truth and obstructing the factual inquiry. Given that cost, many courts are hostile to privileges. They are reluctant to recognize new privileges, *In re Sealed Case*, 148 F.3d 1073 (D.C. Cir. 1998) (declining to recognize a privilege between the President and his Secret Service agents), and, whenever possible, will interpret existing privileges narrowly. *Miller v. Transamerican Press, Inc.*, 621 F.2d 721, 725 (5th Cir. 1980). In *Herbert v. Lando*, 441 U.S. 153 (1979), the Supreme Court voiced the prevailing sentiment of most American courts: "Evidentiary privileges in litigation are not favored. . . ."

Proponents of the privileges counter that the true cost of recognizing privileges is minimal. They typically rely on Dean Wigmore's instrumental or utilitarian rationale for evidentiary privileges. Wigmore assumed that people would be very concerned about later, compelled disclosure of their sensitive communications. Indeed, he posited that absent the assurance of confidentiality furnished by an evidentiary privilege, they ordinarily would not consult with or disclose confidential information to such service providers as lawyers and psychiatrists. If that assumption is correct, it would follow that there is no cost to recognizing a privilege. As one court stated the argument, the enforcement of privileges "results in little evidentiary detriment [because] the evidence lost would simply never come into being if the privilege did not exist." *Folb v. Motion Picture Indus. Pension & Health Plans*, 16 F. Supp. 2d 1164, 1178 (C.D. Cal. 1998). However, as our review of privilege law progresses, we shall see that the existing empirical research calls into question that basic assumption.

Although there is substantial judicial hostility to the recognition of new privileges and serious doubt about the validity of the traditional instrumental justification, there are a surprisingly large number of privileges, especially statutory, in the various jurisdictions. For example, 50 states recognize privileges for communications with doctors, social workers, rape crisis counselors, banks, and accountants. Over time, the number of privileges has gradually increased. To a greater extent than any other area of Evidence law, privilege doctrine has resisted the general trend in evidence law toward liberalization and greater admissibility. In the final analysis, since privileges are viewed as a means of protecting privacy, a large part of the explanation is probably American society's growing concern about privacy. A. ETZIONI, THE LIMITS OF PRIVACY (1999).

The history of the privilege provisions of the Federal Rules is a case in point. When the Advisory Committee drafted the Federal Rules, it included 13 detailed privilege provisions in Article V. However, Congress ultimately balked and instead enacted a single rule — Rule 501 — which stated:

Except as otherwise required by the Constitution of the United States or provided by Act of Congress or in the rules prescribed by the Supreme Court pursuant to statutory authority, the privilege of a witness, person, government, State, or political subdivision thereof shall be governed by the principles of the common law as they may be interpreted by the courts of the United States in the light of reason and experience. However, in civil actions and proceedings, with respect to an element of a claim or defense as to which State law supplies the rule of decision, the privilege of a witness, person, government, State, or political subdivision thereof shall be determined in accordance with State law.

The tortured genesis of Rule 501 is the great paradox in the history of the Federal Rules of Evidence. Congress intervened to block the Supreme Court's adoption of the draft as court rules primarily because Congress received so many complaints about the privilege provisions in draft Article V. According to Representative Hungate who chaired the House hearings on the draft rules, "50% of the complaints . . . relate[d] to the [article] on privileges." PROPOSED RULES OF EVIDENCE: HEARINGS BEFORE THE SPECIAL SUBCOMM. ON REFORM OF FED. CRIM. LAWS, HOUSE COMM. JUD., 93d Cong., 1st Sess. 555, 557 (Feb. 7, 8, 22, 28 and Mar. 9, 15, 1973). However, Congress came to realize that if it attempted to legislate on such issues as the attorney-client or medical privilege, there was a tremendous risk of offending powerful special interest groups. The House committee developed the basic outline of current Rule 501 as a compromise. Representative Hungate warned his colleagues in Congress that if they "open[ed] this issue up," they would discover that it was "very difficult" to decide which groups deserved the protection of a privilege and that "the social workers and the piano tuners" all would "want a privilege." Id. Rather than opening this Pandora's box, Congress punted and, in Rule 501, authorized the federal courts to continue to develop privilege doctrine by common-law methodology.

Rule 501 is the most explicit window into the common law in the Federal Rules of Evidence. It empowers the courts to continue to evolve privilege doctrine by decisional process. Nonetheless, issues of statutory construction still arise. For example, what inferences should courts draw from Congress's refusal to enact the specific privilege rules originally proposed by the Advisory Committee? One of the murkiest problems in statutory interpretation is the significance of legislative inaction such as a legislature's refusal to enact a proposed bill. W. ESKRIDGE & P. FRICKEY, CASES AND MATERIALS ON LEGISLATION: STATUTES AND THE CREATION OF PUBLIC POLICY 772–74 (1988). As we shall see, several of the privilege rules proposed by the Advisory Committee would have effected innovative changes in privilege law. Notwithstanding Congress' refusal to enact those rules, are the courts free to embrace those changes under Rule 501?

The Supreme Court has attached great significance to the draft provisions on privilege. In *United States v. Gillock*, 445 U.S. 360 (1980), the Court cited the draft provisions in support of its decision not to recognize a privilege for state legislators, noting that the draft provisions did not contain any such privilege. In *Jaffee v. Redmond*, 518 U.S. 1 (1996), the Court cited the draft provisions in support of its decision to recognize a psychotherapist privilege. Draft Fed. R. Evid. 504 provided for such a privilege. In *Tennenbaum v. Deloitte & Touche*, 77 F.3d 337, 340 (9th Cir. 1996), the Ninth Circuit described the draft rules as "a convenient comprehensive guide to the federal law of privilege as it now stands." Indeed, by 2012 every privilege proposed in the draft of Article V had been recognized by either the Supreme Court or a lower federal court. Moreover, the federal courts have generally rejected pleas that they recognize privileges not included in the draft rule. *Id.*

B.   THE RATIONALES FOR PRIVILEGE PROTECTION

In discussions of evidentiary privilege, two alternative rationales emerge: The instrumental or utilitarian rationale generally associated with Wigmore; and the "humanistic" rationale, which focuses on privacy, autonomy, and freedom from governmental intrusion into certain special relationships. In the United States, the instrumental rationale seems to have won the day in the courts, though as we have noted above the jury is still out on whether it is empirically supportable. But the humanistic rationale continues to have an influence in the scholarly literature, state legislatures, and very likely as an undercurrent even in the courts that explicitly invoke instrumental reasoning.

The reference in the text of Rule 501 to "reason" is certainly broad enough to permit federal courts to rely on a humanistic rationale in shaping privilege doctrine. While it is true that during the Congressional hearings on the draft Federal Rules many witnesses appealed to instrumental arguments, there were also pointed criticisms of the instrumental rationale. In addition, several members of Congress and witnesses explicitly invoked humanistic arguments. For example, Representative Holtzman discussed privacy considerations as an alternative basis for formulating privilege doctrine. Professor Charles Black submitted a letter assailing the original draft of Article V as a "diminishment of human privacy." There was never any suggestion — either by members of Congress present at the hearings or witnesses — that humanistic policies should be rejected out of hand.

However, for decades the dominant view has been the utilitarian approach. In both *Jaffee v. Redmond*, 518 U.S. 1 (1996) and *Swidler & Berlin v. United States*, 524 U.S. 399 (1998), although the lower courts had relied in part on humanistic reasoning, the Supreme Court relied exclusively on instrumental rationales that view privilege as a means to the end of promoting the free and candid flow of information within certain valued social relationships. As you read the materials in this section, consider whether a humanistic rationale might ground some of the privileges and might support creation of others, such as one for the child-parent relationship. As Joseph Raz pointed out in THE MORALITY OF FREEDOM (1986), although we often view government as the enemy of liberty, government can sometimes promote freedom. Evidentiary privileges, fashioned by government, can help create private enclaves for a citizen to consult confidants such as spiritual advisors, attorneys, and physicians to enhance the quality of the citizen's life preference choices.

C. THE CRITERIA FOR DETERMINING WHETHER TO RECOGNIZE A PRIVILEGE

Given his instrumental conception of privileges, Wigmore famously prescribed the following four conditions as necessary for recognizing a communications privilege:

1. The communications must originate in a *confidence* that they will not be disclosed;

2. This element of *confidentiality must be essential* to the full and satisfactory maintenance of the relation between the parties;

3. The *relation* must be one which in the opinion of the community ought to be sedulously *fostered*; and

4. The *injury* that would inure to the relation by the disclosure of the communications must be *greater than the benefit* thereby gained for the correct disposal of litigation.

8 J. WIGMORE, EVIDENCE § 2285 (McNaughton rev. 1961).

NOTES

1.   Focus on the second of Wigmore's four criteria. If privileges protect only communications which would not occur but for the existence of a privilege, there is no net cost to the legal system to recognize privileges. As Professor Leslie has written, "In a perfect [Wigmorean] world, . . . the privilege would shield no evidence. . . . Eliminate the privilege, and the communication disappears." Leslie, *The Costs of Confidentiality and the Purpose of Privilege*, 2000 WIS. L. REV. 31. Wigmore assumed that the typical potential lay client or patient was so concerned about later compelled judicial disclosure of his or her confidential communications that but for the assurance of confidentiality furnished by a privilege, the layperson would not consult or confide. That assumption explains why Wigmore insisted that communications privileges be absolute in the sense that they cannot be defeated

later by a showing of compelling need for the privileged information. On Wigmore's assumption, at the very time that he or she is deciding whether to confide, the layperson must be able to predict with confidence whether the court will later protect the communication. If, at a later point in time, a judge could override the privilege on the basis of an ad hoc showing of need, the layperson could not make that prediction.

2. This empirical assumption has proven to be highly debatable. Part B of Chapter 26 discusses two studies on the attorney-client privilege that do not bear out the generalization that but for the privilege, the average client would not consult or confer. Wydick, *The Attorney-Client Privilege: Does It Really Have Life Everlasting?*, 87 KY. L.J. 1165, 1170–75 (1999). Similar results have emerged from studies of the psychotherapist privilege. Article, *The Rivalry Between Truth and Privilege: The Weakness of the Supreme Court's Instrumental Reasoning in* Jaffee v. Redmond, *518 U.S. 1 (1996)*, 49 HASTINGS L.J. 969, 980–82 (1998). The existing research, though limited, suggests that only a minority of persons would be chilled from communicating with their lawyers or therapists if the privileges did not protect those communications (though written communications would be more circumspect). The psychological literature on self-disclosure is also at odds with the empirical assumptions underlying the instrumental rationale. Article, *A Psychological Critique of the Assumptions Underlying the Law of Evidentiary Privileges: Insights from the Literature on Self-Disclosure*, 38 LOY. L.A. L. REV. 707 (2004). That literature paints a much more complex picture of self-disclosure than the simplistic model posited by the instrumental theory.

3. What are the implications of these studies for privilege law? Do the studies undermine Wigmore's instrumental theory? At the very least do they call into question the assumption that privileges need to be absolute? Do the findings make a humanistic theory more attractive?

D. AN ANALYTICAL OUTLINE

With respect to the confidential communications privileges, there are certain common questions that arise regardless of which particular privilege is at issue. Thus, we can set out a general framework for privilege issues that will guide our analysis as we turn to look more closely at specific privileges such as the attorney-client privilege, the spousal privileges, or the doctor-patient privilege. Before we can resolve a claim of privilege, we need to answer the following questions:

1.   To what types of proceedings does the privilege apply?

2.   Who holds the privilege?

3.   What is the nature of the privilege?

4.   What type of information is privileged?

5.   Has the privilege been waived?

6.   Does any exception apply?

7.   Is the privilege absolute or qualified?

1. To What Types of Proceedings Does the Privilege Apply?

As noted above, most modern rely primarily on the instrumental rationale in interpreting evidentiary privileges, reasoning that a privilege encourages full and free communication between persons standing in the privileged relationships.

Given that rationale, it follows that the, privileges apply in a wide variety of legal proceedings: criminal cases such as the *Devitt* prosecution, civil actions such as the *Hill* case, and even administrative proceedings. If the harm to the relationship would result from disclosure of the confidential communication, then the privilege must be expansively applied to all stages of any proceeding. California Evidence Code § 901 is typical. It defines "proceeding" as:

> any action, hearing, investigation, inquest, or inquiry (whether conducted by a court, administrative agency, hearing officer, administrator, legislative body, or any other person authorized by law) in which, pursuant to law, testimony can be compelled to be given.

Currently, the only major dispute is whether the privileges apply as a matter of right to legislative hearings. Occasionally, congressional committees have asserted their prerogative to disregard claims of evidentiary privilege. Note, *The Attorney-Client Privilege in Congressional Investigations*, 88 COLUMB. L. REV. 145, 146 (1988).

While most privileges apply in all types of proceedings, the statutes creating privileges sometimes specifically provide that the privilege is inapplicable to certain types of proceedings. For instance, in most jurisdictions, the statutory physician-patient privilege does not apply to criminal cases or workers' compensation actions. Under California Evidence Code § 986, the spousal privilege is inapplicable to juvenile court proceedings. These restrictions are founded on the judgment that those types of proceedings trigger special, countervailing policies that override the policy supporting the privilege. These restrictions can also be viewed as special exceptions to the scope of these privileges. It would be dishonest to contend that disclosure in such proceedings does not tend to chill the freedom of communication between the parties, but the legislatures in these cases have determined that there are relevant policies that outweigh any chill.

2. Who is the Holder of the Privilege?

Suppose that in the *Devitt* case, the prosecutor calls Paterson's doctor as a witness and that Morena recognizes a physician-patient privilege in criminal cases. The doctor describes the results of his examination of Paterson immediately after the battery, and the prosecutor next asks the doctor to relate what Paterson told him about the battery. Devitt may be able to object successfully on hearsay grounds. However, Devitt cannot properly object on the ground of Paterson's doctor-patient privilege. He cannot assert the privilege because he is not the holder. This represents a crucial distinction between objection based on privilege and other types of objections.

The holder is not necessarily even a party to the action. Although Paterson is not a formal party to the prosecution, he could appear and invoke the physician-patient privilege to prevent his doctor from disclosing his confidential communications. A person claiming a privilege can intervene in a proceeding specially for the purpose of asserting a privilege.

a. The Original Holder

In the case of the professional privileges such as the one protecting attorney-client communications, the holder is the person seeking professional services — the client. As a general matter, the holder of the privilege is normally whoever is the intended beneficiary of the privacy protection the privilege confers.

The penitent-clergy privilege, which is protected by statute in many states and enjoys some support in federal case law, is unique in terms of which party to the relationship holds the privilege. For most of the professional privileges, the layperson seeking services is the only holder. However, many of the jurisdictions recognizing the clergy-penitent privilege allow the clergyperson to assert the privilege even if it has been waived by the penitent. For example, California Evidence Code § 1033 grants a privilege to the penitent, but § 1034 confers a separate privilege on the clergyperson. If Devitt confesses to a priest in California and then publicly acknowledges guilt, the priest nevertheless can refuse to disclose the confession. The Virginia Code is to the same effect. *Seidman v. Fishburne-Hudgins Educ. Found., Inc.*, 724 F.2d 413, 415–16 (4th Cir. 1984) (construing Va. Code § 8.01-400).

NOTES

1.   As we have seen, in the case of most privileges, the policy is protecting the confidentiality that the layperson reposes in the professional and thereby encouraging free communication. In the case of the clergy-penitent privilege, does another policy come into play? Can you construct an argument that the policy has constitutional stature? Suppose that out of religious scruple the priest refuses to divulge the content of a confession. If the priest has no privilege to refuse, the tribunal could imprison him for contempt until he discloses the communication.

2.   An entity such as a corporation obviously cannot hold the penitent or spousal privilege. However, with respect to the professional privileges such as attorney-client and accountant-client, the almost universal assumption is that entities can hold such privileges. The Supreme Court adopted that view in both *CFTC v. Weintraub*, 471 U.S. 343 (1985) and *Upjohn Co. v. United States*, 449 U.S. 383 (1981). Of course, the privileges have to be adapted to the reality that the holder is an artificial, legal construct. Thus, there are differences in the courts' application of those privileges to entities as opposed to natural persons. We will look more closely at this issue when we consider the attorney-client privilege in Chapter 26.

b. Successor Holders

Suppose that Ms. Hill's attorney discovered that another person had been killed in a strikingly similar accident involving one of the defendant's cars, manufactured on the very same day as the car which injured Ms. Hill. The plaintiff's attorney believes that evidence of the third party's accident might be admissible against

Polecat Motors in the *Hill* trial on an issue such as causation. Ms. Hill serves a subpoena *duces tecum* on the decedent's physician to obtain a copy of the records of the injury and subsequent treatment. The decedent's surviving son moves to quash the subpoena on the ground of the Morena physician-patient privilege. This motion poses the question whether the privilege survives the original holder's death.

The jurisdictions are badly divided on this issue. In some, privileges terminate when the original holder dies. In others, a privilege lasts until the formal discharge of the decedent's personal representative, that is, the administrator or executor. *In re John Doe Grand Jury Investigation*, 408 Mass. 480, 562 N.E.2d 69 (1990). In still others, the privilege lasts indefinitely and passes like intestate property — a type of property exempt from the Rule against Perpetuities. *United States v. King*, 536 F. Supp. 253, 263 n.17 (C.D. Cal. 1982). *Swidler & Berlin v. United States*, 524 U.S. 399 (1998) is in accord with respect to the federal attorney-client privilege, as we shall see in the following chapter.

c.   Agents of the Privilege Holder

In the case of most professions bound by confidentiality, the profession's own code of ethics requires the professional to claim the privilege in the holder's absence. For example, an attorney has an ethical duty to assert the privilege on behalf of a client.

However, the rules of professional ethics are not coextensive with evidentiary rules. Some jurisdictions have bridged the gap and, in certain circumstances, make the lawyer's ethical duty also a legal obligation. For example, the California Evidence Code not only gives the lawyer authority to make a legally effective privilege claim in the holder's absence, section 955 *requires* the lawyer to assert the privilege on the client's behalf:

> The lawyer who received or made a communication subject to the privilege under this article shall claim the privilege whenever he is present when the communication is sought to be disclosed and is authorized to claim the privilege under subdivision (c) of Section 954.

3.   What is the Nature of a Privilege?

We ordinarily refer to a particular "privilege" in the singular. In truth, the term really subsumes at least three distinct rights.

a.   The Right Personally to Refuse to Disclose the Privileged Information

When we use the expression "privilege," we ordinarily mean the holder's right personally to refuse to disclose certain information. For example, assume that the prosecutor was cross-examining Devitt, and the following occurred:

Q: Mr. Devitt, isn't it a fact that you admitted to your attorney that you committed this battery?

A: I refuse to answer the question. I'm claiming my attorney-client privilege.

If the trial judge sustains the privilege claim, Devitt cannot be held in contempt for refusing to answer. Federal Rule of Civil Procedure 26(b) restricts the scope of permissible discovery to "any matter, *not privileged*, which is relevant to the subject matter involved in the pending action . . . ." (emphasis added).

b.   The Right to Prevent a Third Party Disclosing the Privileged Communication

A holder such as a client not only has a right personally to refuse to disclose privileged information; the holder can also prevent the other party to the communication, such as the attorney, from disclosing it. If the attorney-client privilege precludes the prosecutor from forcing Devitt to disclose an attorney-client communication, the privilege also bars the prosecutor from eliciting the information from the attorney over Devitt's privilege claim.

Other types of third parties have proven a bit more troublesome. The traditional view was that that at least inadvertent eavesdroppers and interceptors were not bound by the privilege. If a third party accidentally overheard Devitt's consultation with his attorney, most courts permitted the eavesdropper to testify to the communication. Courts following the traditional view granted the holder protection only when the intended recipient (here, the attorney) "connived with" the third party. For example, if the attorney secretly hated Devitt and told a third party exactly where and when to station himself with a parabolic microphone to overhear the conversation, even under the strict traditional rule Devitt would be allowed to prevent the third party from disclosing the overheard communication.

The recent trend in both the case law and the statutes has been to show more sensitivity to the interest in privacy of communications and to silence a third party who intentionally overheard or intercepted an otherwise confidential communication. For that matter, a significant number of jurisdictions silence all third parties, even inadvertent eavesdroppers.

PROBLEM

Problem 25-1. Suppose that Devitt's attorney breached his ethical duty of confidentiality by informing the police that Devitt had told him (the attorney) that he (Devitt) had confessed the battery to his brother. The police follow up on the investigative lead and confront Devitt's brother. Devitt's brother reluctantly agrees to testify against his brother. At trial, can Devitt object to his brother's testimony on the ground that the testimony is derived from a breach of Devitt's attorney-client privilege? Most courts answer that question in the negative. *State v. Sandini*, 395 So. 2d 1178, 1180–81 (Fla. Dist. Ct. App. 1981); *United States v. Seiber*, 12 U.S.C.M.A. 520, 31 C.M.R. 106, 107–10 (1961).

Under the Fourth Amendment exclusionary rule, courts exclude derivative evidence ("the fruit of the poisonous tree"). *Wong Sun v. United States*, 371 U.S. 471, 484–93 (1963). Yet less than a handful of courts have expressed a willingness to exclude evidence derived from a violation of a non-constitutional privilege. Comment, *Evidentiary Privileges and the Exclusion of Derivative Evidence: Commentary and Analysis*, 26 SAN. DIEGO L. REV. 625 (1989). All of the federal circuit courts of appeals now refuse to apply the fruit of the poisonous tree doctrine to "nonconstitutional" privileges, including the attorney-client privilege. *See* United States v. Warshak, 631 F.3d 266 (6th Cir. 2010); Mosteller, *Admissibility of Fruits of Breached Evidentiary Privileges: The Importance of Adversarial Fairness, Party Culpability, and Fear of Immunity*, 81 WASH. U. L.Q. 961, 962–63, 1010–16 (2003) (generally supporting the majority view).

c. The Right to Prevent Trial Comment on the Invocation of the Privilege

In the Fifth Amendment context, it is well-settled that neither the judge nor the prosecutor can comment on a defendant's invocation of the privilege. In pronouncing that rule, the Supreme Court reasoned that it would be inconsistent to grant the Fifth Amendment privilege and yet make its assertion at trial "costly." *Griffin v. California*, 380 U.S. 609 (1965). However, there is no such constitutional prohibition in civil cases.

Roughly half the jurisdictions in the United States apply the same "no comment" rule to all privileges: Neither the judge nor the opposing party may invite the jury to draw an adverse inference from the invocation of the privilege at trial. In jurisdictions that do permit comment, it may create a substantial deterrent to invoking the privilege. For example, if Polecat Motors invoked the attorney-client privilege to protect a memorandum the corporate president sent the corporate counsel, these jurisdictions would permit Ms. Hill's attorney not only to elicit that fact during cross-examination of the president, but also to argue the point during summation:

> Remember, ladies and gentlemen, that the defendant's president admitted that they refused to show us that memo about the accident. Why? I think we all know the answer. They're hiding something from us; they're afraid to let us see what's in that memo. For all we know, that memo could say, 'There's no question; we're at fault in this accident.'

Furthermore, some jurisdictions would even permit the trial judge to instruct the jury on permissible adverse inferences. Note that proposed Federal Rule of Evidence 513 would have forbidden such cross-examination, argument, and jury instructions. Which view do you prefer?

4. What Type of Information is Privileged?

In order to be protected by a privilege, there must be (a) a communication that is (b) confidential, which occurs (c) between properly related parties and (d) is incident to the relationship. The concept thus encompasses four requirements — lacking any one will defeat the privilege in a particular case.

a. A "Communication"

The policy underlying the creation of privileges is to promote communication between persons standing in certain relations. Given that policy, along with the general assumption that the search for truth should be obstructed only to the extent necessary, privileges protect only information in the nature of *communication.* In most cases, courts construe "communication" according to the ordinary usage of the term.

NOTES AND PROBLEM

1. **Problem 25-2.** Decide whether the following items should qualify as "communications" for purposes of privilege law. Why or why not?

(a)   An oral statement Devitt made to his attorney during the initial interview.

(b)   The fact that Devitt nodded when the attorney asked, "Did you actually do it?"

(c)   The fact that Devitt said nothing and glanced down when the attorney asked, "Did you actually do it?"

(d)   A letter Devitt wrote his attorney about the case.

(e)   A copy of a threatening letter Devitt had previously sent Paterson and decided to send to the attorney to help the attorney prepare for trial. Can you distinguish this letter from the previous letter? In terms of the policy underlying the privilege, is it significant that the second letter did not come into existence as an attorney-client communication? If Devitt retained the second letter, could he refuse to comply with compulsory process demanding the production of the letter? *See Fisher v. United States,* 425 U.S. 391, 403–04 (1976) (no).

(f)   Suppose that Devitt verbally told his attorney where he hid the clothes he wore during the battery. Could the prosecutor force the attorney to disclose the whereabouts of the evidence?

2.   When the privilege relates to a professional relationship, the question arises as to whether the privilege is a two-way street. Does the privilege attach to the attorney's communications to the client as well as the client's communications to the attorney? There is virtual unanimity that to some extent the professional's communications are also cloaked. *Families for Freedom v. U.S. Customs and Border,* 797 F. Supp. 2d 375, 387 (S.D.N.Y. 2011). There is some dispute, though, over the extent of the protection. 1 E. IMWINKELRIED, THE NEW WIGMORE: EVIDENTIARY PRIVILEGES § 6.6.4 (2d ed. 2010).

•   The most conservative view is the classical position that the privilege applies to the professional's statements only when they tend to reveal the content of communications from the client or patient.

•   The intermediate view is that the privilege attaches to the professional's communications that are "based upon" the client's or patient's communications, as when a client's question prompts a communication from the attorney.

•   The broadest position is the view that the privilege applies to any communication by the professional incident to the protected relationship. Which view do you prefer? Why?

We shall see in Chapter 26 that certain privileges, notably the spousal and medical privileges, sometimes incorporate a more expansive definition of "communication."

b. Confidentiality

It is not enough that the information qualifies as a communication; to be protected, the communication must have been confidential. It is true that it would maximally promote freedom of communication to protect all communications. But not all types of communication need the protection of a privilege. If the holder did not manifest an intent to maintain secrecy at the time of communication, the court will not confer confidentiality later in the courtroom. Ordinarily, a showing of confidentiality requires proof of two things.

First, at the time of communication, the parties must have had physical privacy. Assume that Devitt spoke to his attorney in the presence of a third party — and that Devitt realized that the third party was present. That realization usually negates confidentiality. Note the distinction between this rule and the traditional eavesdropper rule: Under the traditional view, if an eavesdropper overheard a communication without Devitt's knowledge, the eavesdropper could testify but the attorney would still be bound by the privilege. However, if Devitt knew that the third party was present, the privilege would never attach and no one would be bound.

Second, in addition to showing physical privacy, the party claiming the privilege must show that, at the time of communication, there was an intent to maintain secrecy. *United States v. Bump*, 605 F.2d 548 (10th Cir. 1979).

NOTES AND PROBLEMS

1. **Problem 25-3.** Both courts and legislatures have recognized numerous exceptions to the norm that the third party's presence negates confidentiality. Suppose Devitt were deaf or not fluent in English, and the attorney hired an interpreter. Should the interpreter's presence preclude the privilege from attaching? *Duckett v. Touhey*, 36 Md. App. 238, 373 A.2d 323 (1977).

2. Can you think of any other situations in which a third party's presence is realistically necessary for effective communication? In the context of professional privileges such as the attorney-client privilege, courts generally permit the presence of "secretaries, file clerks, telephone operators, messengers, clerks not yet admitted to the bar, and aides of other sorts." *von Bulow v. von Bulow*, 811 F.2d 136, 146 (2d Cir.), *cert. denied*, 481 U.S. 1015 (1987). California has taken the most liberal position on this issue. Under Cal. Evid. Code § 952, the third party's presence does not negate confidentiality so long as the third party was "present to further the interest of the client in the consultation." Does that provision go too far? Should we draw the line at the fact situation at which there is some degree of necessity for the third party's presence?

3. We have already noted some of the parallels between privilege doctrine and the Fourth Amendment exclusionary rule. Under Justice Harlan's celebrated

concurrence in *Katz v. United States*, 389 U.S. 347 (1967), a person invoking the exclusionary rule must show that he or she had a reasonable expectation of privacy. Under privilege law, similarly, the claimant must establish that he or she had an expectation of confidentiality; in many jurisdictions, it must be "reasonable." Given the similar language, it is easy to confuse the two concepts, and that confusion can sometimes result in mischief. Mosteller & Broun, *The Danger to Confidential Communications in the Mismatch Between the Fourth Amendment's "Reasonable Expectation of Privacy" and the Confidentiality of Evidentiary Privileges*, 32 CAMPBELL L. REV. 147 (2010). Thus, it is important to clearly define the confidentiality expectation required by privilege law.

4. **Problem 25-4.** Does the intent of both parties to the conversation govern the intent to maintain secrecy? Whose intent is critical? *See Apex Mun. Fund v. N-Group Securities*, 841 F. Supp. 1423, 1426–27 (S.D. Tex. 1993) (the client's intent is controlling). Suppose that at the initial attorney-client interview in our torts case, Ms. Hill's attorney told her that he needed some information for "the complaint I'll put on file with the court." How would that statement affect your confidentiality analysis? If you were the attorney, how would you have phrased the statement? *See In re Grand Jury Proceedings*, 727 F.2d 1352, 1356–58 (4th Cir. 1984) (preparation of a securities prospectus); *In re Grand Jury Investigation*, 842 F.2d 1223 (11th Cir. 1987) (preparation of a tax return); *United States v. Bohonnon*, 628 F. Supp. 1026 (D. Conn.) (preparation of a tax return), *aff'd*, 795 F.2d 79 (2d Cir. 1985). Has Ms. Hill in effect delegated to her attorney the choice of the information to include in the complaint? Has Ms. Hill agreed to disclose "only so much of the information . . . as the attorney concludes should be . . ." included in the complaint? *Schenet v. Anderson*, 678 F. Supp. 1280, 1283 (E.D. Mich. 1988).

c. Between "Properly Related Parties"

We have already noted that politics can influence a legislature's decision as to whether to create a particular privilege. Some critics have suggested that the existence of many professional privileges represents successful lobbying by a special interest group rather than a principled legislative judgment that a particular social relation warrants privilege protection. Remember Representative Hungate's fear that even the "piano tuners" would lobby for a privilege.

As you review the subject of privilege, ask yourself these questions: Are these relationships sufficiently important to warrant this extraordinary legal protection? Can we justify protecting these relationships while denying protection to relationships such as student-teacher and parent-child in most jurisdictions? Initially, you should analyze these questions under the dominant instrumental theory, thinking back to Wigmore's classic criteria set out at the beginning of this chapter. Alternatively, you might ask yourself whether a humanistic theory would justify conferring a privilege on various types of relationships. In THE MORALITY OF FREEDOM (1986), Joseph Raz argues that government should play a positive role in promoting freedom. By conferring privileges on certain relationships and thereby creating a private enclave for consultation with different kinds of professional or spiritual advisors, government can assist citizens in making intelligent, considered life choices.

d. "Incident to the Relationship"

It is not enough that the client consult an attorney. The cases tell us that the privilege comes into play only when the client is consulting the attorney *qua* attorney — in the person's capacity *as a lawyer*. The requirement that the communication be "incident to the relationship" is another way of saying that the purpose of the client's communication must relate to obtaining legal advice. Some authorities go even further and hold that the privilege attaches only if the client consults the attorney "primarily" to obtain legal advice. *Resolution Trust Corp. v. Diamond*, 773 F. Supp. 597 (S.D.N.Y. 1991).

This issue often arises in the context of a company's consultation with corporate counsel, who may act in both a business advisory roll as well as a legal advisory roll. Does it make sense to limit the privilege to communications incident to the legal advisory relationship only? Perhaps the limitation is best supported by the theory that we are attempting to balance the courts' truth-seeking function against protection of only certain special advisory relationships. The protected relationship weighs more heavily in the balance when the communication is *directly* related. Moreover, following the utilitarian rationale, if the communication were not directly germane to securing legal advice, the holder likely would have made the statement even absent the privilege. If, in our torts case, we conclude that Polecat Motors' president was consulting the corporate counsel in her capacity as business advisor, we can assume that the president would have made the statement even without an attorney-client privilege. *See Hercules, Inc. v. Exxon Corp.*, 434 F. Supp. 136 (D. Del. 1977).

NOTES

Once we have decided to impose the incidence requirement, we face the task of defining when a communication is incident to the particular relationship. When would a communication be "incident" to the attorney-client relation? The physician-patient relation? The penitent-clergy relation? The following California Evidence Code provisions contain language phrasing the incidence requirement for the various privileges protected under California law:

§ 951 (attorney-client) ("for the purpose of retaining the lawyer or securing legal service or advice from him in his professional capacity");

§ 991 (general medical)" for the purpose of securing a diagnosis or preventive, palliative, or curative treatment of his physical or mental or emotional condition");

§ 1011 (psychotherapy) ("for the purpose of securing a diagnosis or preventive, palliative, or curative treatment of his mental or emotional condition or who submits to an examination of his mental or emotional condition for the purpose of scientific research on mental or emotional problems"); and

§ 1032 (penitential communication) ("a communication made . . . to a clergyman who, in the course of the discipline or practice of his church, denomination, or organization, is authorized or accustomed to hear such communications and, under the discipline or tenets of his church, denomination, or organization, has a duty to keep such communications secret").

Consider the wording of § 1032. Should the privilege be confined to required confessional statements? In the Catholic faith, a penitent must confess to a priest, who must be male. Suppose that Devitt were Catholic and had a good friend, Sister Teresa, a nun whom he frequently conferred with as a spiritual consultant. After his encounter with Paterson, Devitt experiences a deep sense of guilt and goes to talk to Sister Teresa. Should the privilege be rejected simply because she is a nun rather than a priest? *See Eckmann v. Board of Educ.*, 106 F.R.D. 70, 72–73 (E.D. Mo. 1985) (recognizing the privilege under similar circumstances).

5.   Has There Been a Waiver of the Privilege?

Under Federal Rule of Evidence 104(a), the person claiming a privilege has the burden of proving the above four elements of communication, confidentiality, properly related parties, and incidence. If that person persuades the judge that the right type of holder is claiming the right type of privilege for the right type of information in an appropriate proceeding, there is a prima facie case for sustaining the privilege claim. However, the opponent can still defeat the privilege by showing either a waiver or a special exception. The proposed Federal Rules of Evidence contained the following waiver provisions:

Rule 511. Waiver of Privilege by Voluntary Disclosure

A person upon whom these rules confer a privilege against disclosure of the confidential matter or communication waives the privilege if he or his predecessor while holder of the privilege voluntarily discloses or consents to disclosure of any significant part of the matter or communication. This rule does not apply if the disclosure is itself a privileged communication.

Rule 512. Privileged Matter Disclosed Under Compulsion or Without Opportunity to Claim Privilege

Evidence of a statement or other disclosure of privileged matter is not admissible against the holder of the privilege if the disclosure was (a) compelled erroneously or (b) made without opportunity to claim the privilege.

Where the opponent claims a waiver of the privilege, a court must address two related issues: (a) whether the privilege has been waived, and (b) if so, the extent of the waiver.

a.   Whether There Has Been a Waiver

The holder may either assert or waive the privilege. Since courts are generally hostile to claims of privilege, they are generally eager to find waivers.

Automatic Waiver By Plaintiff

As noted in *Zenith Radio Corp. v. United States*, 588 F. Supp. 1443 (U.S. Ct. Int'l Trade 1984), some courts are so hostile to privileges that they have "adopted the automatic waiver rule . . . on the theory that when a party seeks judicial relief, he waives whatever privilege he has." *Id.* at 1445. *In re County of Erie*, 546 F.3d 222 (2d Cir. 2008) is sharply critical of the automatic waiver doctrine, and the vast majority of courts reject this rule. It seems Draconian and arbitrary for a person to forfeit a privilege simply because he or she happens to be the plaintiff in a legal action. After all, under modern civil procedure, including the availability of declaratory actions, a person's normal role as plaintiff or defendant can be reversed.

"At Issue" Waivers

Even if the mere act of filing suit does not effect a waiver, the specific allegations in the litigant's pleadings may result in a waiver. Many courts find a waiver when three criteria are met: (1) assertion of the privilege was a result of some affirmative act, such as filing suit, by the asserting party; (2) through this affirmative act, the asserting party put the protected information at issue by making it relevant to the case; and (3) application of the privilege would have denied the opposing party access to information vital to his defense. *Hearn v. Rhay*, 68 F.R.D. 574 (E.D. Wash. 1975). This is the so-called "at issue" or "in issue" doctrine: Filing suit waives a privilege if the allegations in the pleading place the contents of a privileged communication in issue. For example, in a jurisdiction requiring the plaintiff in a fraud action to establish the reasonableness of his or her reliance on the defendant's misrepresentation, the plaintiff might aver that he or she consulted an attorney about the representation. *Clark v. Kellogg Co.*, 205 F.3d 1079 (8th Cir. 2000). Similarly, in his or her answer, a copyright infringement defendant could allege that they acted in good faith rather than willfully because they consulted an attorney about the possibility of infringement. Under such circumstances, the party will have waived the privilege as to those attorney-client communications.

Waiver by Disclosure

Most courts find a waiver when the holder voluntarily discloses a substantial part of the privileged information. Proposed Rule 512 essentially restated the common law in requiring that, to effect a waiver, a disclosure must be voluntary.

The issue of voluntariness arises frequently during pretrial discovery: One party seeks document production, the other party inadvertently produces privileged material, and the question arises as to whether the inadvertent production effected a waiver. Prior to 2008, there was a three-way split of authority on this question: Some courts treated inadvertent disclosure as an automatic waiver; others refused to do so; still others examined the surrounding circumstances such as whether the disclosing party had taken reasonable steps to prevent unintended disclosures. The trend was toward the last view, under which courts considered such factors as the number of documents involved and the period of time which the party had to review the documents. The number of documents may have been so large and the period of time so short that it is understandable that the party's review did not identify all the privileged documents.

To resolve the split of authority, in 2008 Congress approved new Federal Rule of Evidence 502. Rule 502(b) announces a general rule that inadvertent disclosure in a federal judicial or administrative proceeding does not effect a waiver. In addition, several other provisions in the new Rule specify fact situations in which there is no waiver. For instance, Rule 502(d) states that there is no waiver if the prior disclosure was connected to litigation pending in federal court and the federal court entered an order that the disclosure in question would not waive the privilege. Federal court discovery orders sometimes include "quick peek" and "claw back" provisions. In a "quick peek" situation, the party with custody of the information produces the documents to enable the other party to peek and determine which materials it would like to copy. The former party then conducts a privilege review of only those materials. In a "claw back" situation, the producing party can request the return of documents until the status of the documents is resolved by the court.

NOTE AND PROBLEMS

1. Professor Richard Marcus has argued persuasively that it is a mistake to analyze the waiver issue solely in terms of the holder's subjective intent. Marcus, *The Perils of Privilege: Waiver and the Litigator*, 84 MICH. L. REV. 1605 (1986). He emphasizes that the primary objection to privileges is that they obstruct the search for truth. In that light, he contends that "the focus should be on unfairness flowing from . . . selective use of privileged materials to garble the truth. . . . [T]he opponent [should have] access to related material to set the record straight." *Id.* at 1607. His position has gained numerous judicial adherents. *In re Southern and Eastern Dist. Asbestos Litig.*, 730 F. Supp. 582 (S.D.N.Y. 1990) (a party may not use privilege doctrine to "distort" the search for truth); *McLaughlin v. Lunde Truck Sales, Inc.*, 714 F. Supp. 916, 918 (N.D. Ill. 1989) (privileges "may not be manipulated to the advantage of the party asserting the privilege").

2.   Problem 25-5. Would you find a waiver in the following variations of our torts case? (Assume that Morena recognizes a physician-patient privilege in such cases.)

(a)   Polecat Motors calls Ms. Hill's physician. On direct examination, the defense attorney asks, "Isn't it true that three days after the accident, the plaintiff told you that she was feeling 'fairly well'?" Ms. Hill's attorney fails to object.

(b)   Ms. Hill takes the witness stand. On direct examination, she refers to the treatment she received and adds that "I had several conversations with Dr. Tyler."

(c)   Assume that you found a waiver in the last variation. Should the result be the same if Ms. Hill instead made the reference during cross-examination? In some jurisdictions, the holder's responses during cross-examination do not effect a waiver. Is that view sound?

(d)   Assume that you did *not* find a waiver in (b). Would your answer be the same if Ms. Hill said, "I had several conversations about the accident with Dr. Tyler"? If she said, "I had several conversations about the accident with Dr. Tyler, and I told him how Worker's car injured me"? How specific must the reference be before there is a waiver? Should the answer depend upon whether the privilege at stake is the attorney-client or physician-patient privilege? As we shall see, the definition of "communication" is often much broader under the physician-patient privilege. Do you see a connection between the breadth of the concept of "communication" and the ease with which a court can find a waiver? The breadth of the definition of "communication" can be a two-edged sword; it can both make it easier to find both a communication and to find a waiver.

(e)   Ms. Hill tells her husband what she told her doctor. (Note that a waiver can occur outside the courtroom.)

(f)   At the first trial of her lawsuit, Ms. Hill recovers a huge verdict. The verdict is so highly publicized that a publisher approaches Ms. Hill's attorney and asks him to write a book about the trial, and he does so. In one passage, he refers to a privileged conversation with Ms. Hill. The attorney gives Ms. Hill a copy of the manuscript to review before he mails it to the publisher. She browses through the manuscript and vaguely notices that the manuscript refers to her conversation with the attorney. She makes no objection to the release of the book. Has Ms. Hill waived the attorney-client privilege? See *In re von Bulow*, 828 F.2d 94, 100 (2d Cir. 1987) (discussing Professor Alan Dershowitz' book, REVERSAL OF FORTUNE — INSIDE THE VON BULOW CASE (1986)).

(g)   During preparation for the trial of Ms. Hill's lawsuit, her attorney shares one of her letters to him with a paralegal in the firm in order to obtain suggestions for conducting her direct examination. Does the attorney's disclosure effect a waiver? What if the disclosure occurs outside the law firm? Suppose that to prepare for her direct examination related to the personal injuries resulting from the accident, the attorney shares the letter with a physician. According to California Evidence Code § 952, a disclosure does not result in waiver if it "is reasonably necessary for . . . the accomplishment of the purpose for which the lawyer is consulted." These are sometimes referred to as protected, "facilitative" communications.

In which of these problems, if any, would it make a difference whether the court employed the traditional analysis, based on the holder's subjective intent, or the fairness analysis favored by Professor Marcus?

b.   The Extent of the Waiver

Even if there has been a waiver, the privilege is not necessarily lost in its entirety. In most cases finding a waiver, courts rationalize the result on the theory that the holder has consented to surrendering the protection of the privilege. If we begin with that theory as the premise, there is a strong argument that the holder can exercise some control over the scope of the waiver. If waiver doctrine is grounded in voluntary consent, shouldn't the holder be able to influence — if not determine — the extent to which he or she loses the protection of the privilege?

NOTE AND PROBLEMS

1.   Think back to the discussion of Professor Marcus' view in the preceding subsection. Is that view relevant here as well? If there has been a waiver, one could argue that the fairness concept should also determine the extent of that waiver. Imagine that a party has disclosed one document. The opponent argues that the waiver should extend to another document that has not been disclosed. The two

documents might be so integrally related that presenting the jury with only the first document would be a misleading half-truth. New Rule 502(a) reflects this reasoning. Under that provision, a waiver effected by disclosure of certain information extends to other, as yet undisclosed information only if three conditions concur:

- The previous waiver was "intentional";

- The "disclosed and undisclosed communications or information concern the same subject matter . . . ."; and

- The disclosed and undisclosed information "ought in fairness to be considered together."

2.   Problem 25-6.

(a)   Mr. Grant, a plaintiff in another case, sues the *Hill* defendants based on a similar accident involving the same model as the car involved in *Hill.* Ms. Hill and Mr. Grant hire the same attorney. The court concludes that by failing to claim the privilege during pretrial discovery, Grant has waived the attorney-client privilege. Can Ms. Hill still claim it?

(b)   Prior to trial, Ms. Hill consults two doctors, Dr. Tyler and Dr. Gibson. At trial, Ms. Hill calls Dr. Tyler as a witness to testify about the extent and permanency of her injuries. Can she still claim a privilege for her communications with Dr. Gibson? *Helman v. Murray's Steaks, Inc.*, 728 F. Supp. 1099, 1103 (D. Del. 1990) ("privilege is waived as to the same subject matter"). Should it make a difference whether the plaintiff consulted the doctors individually or jointly?

(c)   After Ms. Hill sues Polecat Motors, she sues Turner Company, the parts supplier that furnished the gas tank on her car. Ms. Hill had called Dr. Tyler as a witness in the first suit. Can the plaintiff assert the physician-patient privilege for Dr. Tyler's testimony in the second suit?

(d)   A year after the Polecat lawsuit, Ms. Hill sues a cosmetic company for scalp injuries she sustained when she used a shampoo it manufactured. Dr. Tyler treated her for the scalp injuries. If the plaintiff had waived the physician-patient privilege by calling Dr. Tyler as a witness in the first suit, can she still assert the privilege as against the cosmetic company? Does the waiver at the first trial extend to the second trial?

(e)   Before the trial in Ms. Hill's lawsuit against Polecat Motors, Dr. Tyler submitted two reports to Ms. Hill's attorney dealing with Ms. Hill's injuries that allegedly resulted from the collision. During her case-in-chief, Ms. Hill introduces the first report. Does her introduction of that report waive her privilege for the second report? Suppose that the first report dealt with Ms. Hill's burn injuries but the second report related to bone fractures caused by the accident. Would it make a difference that the second report addressed the cause and the extent of the bone fractures? *See Helman, supra*, at 1103–04 (a different "subject").

(f)   Before Ms. Hill filed suit against Polecat Motors, a federal consumer agency conducted an investigation into practices in the automotive industry.

During the investigation, the agency made it clear to Polecat that unless it cooperated, the agency might initiate an administrative action against Polecat. Polecat decided to cooperate and voluntarily turned over a document covered by the attorney-client privilege. When it delivered the document to the federal authorities, Polecat attached a letter "reserving any privileges in any subsequent litigation with third parties." Ms. Hill's attorney learns about the investigation and argues that Polecat waived its privilege by handing over the document to the federal agency. What result? Although one federal circuit has recognized the concept of "selective" waiver, it is a distinct minority view. *See Diversified Industries, Inc. v. Meredith*, 572 F.2d 596, 611 (8th Cir. 1977). Most courts do not allow the holder to use the privilege as both a sword and a shield. *See 2 RICE, ATTORNEY-CLIENT PRIVILEGE IN THE UNITED STATES § 9:28 (2d ed. 1999). Can you articulate arguments for and against allowing selective waiver in such cases?

As originally proposed, Rule 502(c) addressed the issue of selective waiver. The original draft read:

Selective waiver. In a federal or state proceeding, a disclosure of a communication or information covered by the attorney-client privilege or work product protection — when made to a federal public office or agency in the exercise of its regulatory, investigative, or enforcement authority — does not operate as a waiver of the privilege or protection in favor of non-governmental persons or entities. The effect of disclosure to a state or local government agency, with respect to non-governmental persons or entities, is governed by applicable state law.

In the end, the drafters deleted the authorization for selective wavier from new Rule 502, and the Advisory Committee's Note to the final version of Rule 502 specifically states that the Rule does not attempt to resolve the question.

6. Is There a Pertinent Special Exception to the asserted Privilege?

As we have seen, privileges are based on extrinsic social policies. Of course, those policies can collide with other social policies. Such collisions have led courts and legislatures to carve out exceptions to the scope of the various privileges. While these exceptions are far too numerous to detail here, there are several recurring themes that run through the exceptions.

One theme is an allowance for *the interpretative intent of the holder.* Interpretative intent is a concept borrowed from a branch of philosophy: It is the intent a person probably would have had if the person had foreseen a problem that materialized later. For example, under the "testamentary" exception, after the client's death an attorney is permitted to disclose the client's otherwise privileged statements about dispositive instruments the attorney drafted for the client. The assumption is that if the decedent had foreseen the dispute that arose after his or her death, he or she would have wanted full disclosure to ensure that the court effectuated his or her actual intent.

A second theme is that of *fairness*. When we consider the legal and medical privileges, we shall see that there is a "crime or tort" exception. There is no privilege if the services of the professional were sought or obtained in order to commit a crime, fraud or tort. When the client has such an intent, communications are not protected because the consultation amounts to an attempt to abuse the privilege for socially undesirable ends.

Finally, in Wigmore's view, any exceptions to a privilege should be clearly articulated ex ante. Although Wigmore acknowledged that in some exceptional cases privileges should yield, he insisted that any exceptions be announced beforehand and phrased in crystal clear terms. Under the instrumental rationale, it is essential that *at the time they are deciding whether to communicate and reveal sensitive information*, the parties must be able to predict with relative confidence whether a privilege will attach and protect their communication. That ability would be undermined if the privileges were subject to exceptions that are either vague or announced after the fact.

7. Is the Privilege Absolute or Qualified

In a similar vein, in order for privileges to facilitate and encourage open communication, they must not be subject to ad hoc balancing or qualifications after the fact. Some privileges, such as attorney-client, are thus considered "true" or "absolute" privileges: They are absolute in the technical sense that they cannot be surmounted by a showing of necessity in a particular case. If the party claiming the privilege establishes the requisite foundation, the opposing party cannot defeat the privilege claim by showing a compelling, case-specific need for the privileged information. In the case of such "absolute" privileges, normally the only way to defeat the privilege is by proving waiver or a special exception.

However, not all privileges are "absolute." Some privileges such as the medical privilege in several states are "qualified." Even if the privilege attaches, the party seeking discovery can obtain the privileged information by demonstrating an overriding need for the information. Qualified privileges allow the court the discretion to weigh the importance of confidentiality against countervailing social policies. For example, although 32 states have enacted statutes granting reporters a privilege to withhold the identity of confidential sources of information, in most states the privilege will yield when the source of information possesses information vital to the disposition of criminal charges. The privilege rests on a legitimate extrinsic policy, but in this circumstance that policy collides with another, weightier extrinsic policy — the criminal defendant's right to a fair trial.

Moreover, as we shall see in Chapter 32, even purportedly absolute privileges may be rendered qualified by constitutional concerns. In extreme cases when a criminal defendant has shown a truly compelling need for privileged information, courts have overridden virtually every type of privilege, including attorney-client, spousal, medical, and psychotherapist. E. IMWINKELRIED & N. GARLAND, EXCULPATORY EVIDENCE: THE ACCUSED'S CONSTITUTIONAL RIGHT TO INTRODUCE

FAVORABLE EVIDENCE Ch. 10 (3d ed. 2004). Several cases have recognized that civil litigants have a similar procedural due process right that sometimes overrides evidentiary privileges. *Id.* at Ch. 2A.

Finally, there is some tendency, particularly among lower courts, to treat privileges, especially new ones, as qualified. However, in its two most recent privilege decisions, *Swidler v. Berlin v. United States*, 524 U.S. 399 (1998) (attorney-client) and *Jaffee v. Redmond*, 518 U.S. 1 (1996) (psychotherapist-patient), the Supreme Court has ruled that those privileges were absolute. In both cases, the Court did so even though lower courts had treated the privileges as qualified. Furthermore, in each case the Court expressly endorsed Dean Wigmore's instrumental theory. However, the available empirical studies do not validate that theory's underlying assumption that but for the existence of a privilege, the typical client or patient would not consult or confide. The lower courts seem to be more responsive to the findings of the empirical studies than the Supreme Court.

Chapter 26

PRIVILEGE: SPECIALIZED ASPECTS

Read Federal Rule of Evidence 501 and 502.

In the last chapter, we referred to several of the communications privileges as examples and illustrations of the general themes of privilege doctrine. This chapter offers a more in-depth consideration of several of the most important privileges: attorney-client; spousal (and other family relations); medical and psychotherapist-patient; and government secrets. Although most of the evidentiary doctrines discussed in this chapter are classic communications privileges, some such as the doctrine protecting military secrets are topical privileges.

A. THE ATTORNEY-CLIENT PRIVILEGE

Overview

The attorney-client privilege is the most ancient and probably the most important of the privileges. Proposed Article V of the Federal Rules of Evidence included Rule 503, which provided:

Lawyer-Client Privilege

(a) Definitions. As used in this rule:

   (1) A "client" is a person, public officer, or corporation, association, or other organization or entity, either public or private, who is rendered professional legal services by a lawyer, or who consults a lawyer with a view to obtaining professional legal services from him.

   (2) A "lawyer" is a person authorized, or reasonably believed by the client to be authorized, to practice law in any state or nation.

   (3) A "representative of the lawyer" is one employed to assist the lawyer in the rendition of professional legal services.

   (4) A communication is "confidential" if not intended to be disclosed to third persons other than those to whom disclosure is in furtherance of the rendition of professional legal services to the client or those reasonably necessary for the transmission of the communication.

(b) General rule of privilege. A client has a privilege to refuse to disclose and to prevent any other person from disclosing confidential communications made for the purpose of facilitating the rendition of professional legal services to the client, (1) between himself or his representative and his lawyer or his lawyer's representative, or (2) between his lawyer and the lawyer's representative, or (3) by him or his lawyer to a lawyer representing another in a matter of common interest, or (4) between representatives of the client or between the client and a representative of the client, or (5) between lawyers representing the client.

(c) Who may claim the privilege. The privilege may be claimed by the client, his guardian or conservator, the personal representative of a deceased client, or the successor, trustee, or similar representative of a corporation, association, or other organization, whether or not in existence. The person who was the lawyer at the time of the communication may claim the privilege but only on behalf of the client. His authority to do so is presumed in the absence of evidence to the contrary.

(d) Exceptions. There is no privilege under this rule:

(1) *Furtherance of crime or fraud.* If the services of the lawyer were sought or obtained to enable or aid anyone to commit or plan to commit what the client knew or reasonably should have known to be a crime or fraud; or

(2) *Claimants through same deceased client.* As to a communication relevant to an issue between parties who claim through the same deceased client, regardless of whether the claims are by testate or intestate succession or by *inter vivos* transaction; or

(3) *Breach of duty by lawyer or client.* As to a communication relevant to an issue of breach of duty by the lawyer to his client or by the client to his lawyer; or

(4) *Document attested by lawyer.* As to a communication relevant to an issue concerning an attested document to which the lawyer is an attesting witness: or

(5) *Joint clients.* As to a communication relevant to a matter of common interest between two or more clients if the communication was made by any of them to a lawyer retained or consulted in common, when offered in an action between any of the clients.

1. The Wisdom of Recognizing the Privilege

Since the time of Jeremy Bentham, critics of privileges have underscored their cost: the suppression of relevant, often highly reliable, evidence. What benefits allegedly offset this cost and justify recognizing a privilege? As we have seen, Wigmore's instrumental argument is that, without the assurance of the privilege, the average client would be reluctant to disclose sensitive information to his or her attorney. For many years, this argument was based on intuition; now, however, there is some relevant empirical data:

Zacharias *Rethinking Confidentiality*
74 Iowa L. Rev. 351 (1989)

The Yale Study on Attorney-Client Privilege

In 1962, the *Yale Law Journal* conducted a study of the importance and effect of attorney-client privilege rules. Its primary mission was to compare the privilege accorded the bar to that granted other professions. The *Journal* distributed questionnaires and accumulated responses from 108 laypersons, 125 lawyers, and between 12 and 51 members of several other professions, including psychology, psychiatry, social work, marriage counseling, and accounting.[119]

The survey revealed widespread misinformation concerning privileges, particularly the attorney-client privilege. Interestingly, "[l]awyers, significantly more than laymen, believe the privilege encourages free disclosure to them." Seventy-one of 108 laypersons surveyed understood that, as a general matter, attorneys would not disclose confidential matter. But a significant percentage of the laypersons thought that lawyers, if questioned in court, would have an obligation to reveal confidences.

Several aspects of the survey are telling. First, the figures on lay perceptions of attorneys suggest that, while a preference for nondisclosure rules exists, a substantial majority of laypersons would continue to use lawyers even if secrecy were limited. Indeed, many of the subjects believed that the privilege rules should be confined. Second, the comparative figures suggest that laypersons do not perceive any dramatic contrast in the way different professionals will protect their communications. What makes these results particularly significant is that most of the nonlegal professions are *not* governed by the same highly protective privilege that is applicable to the legal profession. That the professions continue to thrive despite the "theoretical" lay hesitation to disclose absent confidentiality suggests that either consumer ignorance or a simple need for professional services is what really controls the marketplace.[134]

The Tompkins County Study on Confidentiality

In connection with this Article, I conducted a survey of attorneys and laypersons in Tompkins County, New York. . . . Neither subject pool was large or diverse enough to represent the country as a whole. Although the sixty-three responding lawyers probably make up a majority of active Tompkins County practitioners, the community in which they practice is rural and university oriented. . . . One might therefore surmise that the surveyed laypersons were more legally sophisticated

---

[119] Note, *Functional Overlap Between the Lawyer and Other Professionals: Its Implications for the Privileged Communications Doctrine*, 71 Yale L.J. 1226, 1227 (1962). There are several reasons to caution against too much reliance on the Yale study. First, the number of subjects was limited. Second, subjects were not chosen with sufficient randomness to assure the significance of the results. *See id.* at 1227 n.6. Third, the study was conducted by a legal periodical, without statistical rigor. Still, the study contains the only available empirical data. The results provide valuable food for thought.

[134] See Moore, *Limits to Attorney-Client Confidentiality: A "Philosophically Informed" and Comparative Approach to Legal and Medical Ethics*, 36 Case W. Res. L. Rev. 177, 196–211 (1985) (comparing confidentiality in medical and legal professions).

than typical individual clients, but not so educated as business clients one would find in commercial urban litigation.

Several responses support the proposition that some form of confidentiality rule serves confidentiality's basic rationales. Approximately half of the lay respondents predicted that they would withhold information from attorneys if no firm obligation of confidentiality existed. A substantial number of the surveyed clients claimed to have relied upon confidentiality; nearly 30% stated that they gave information to their attorneys that "they would not have given without a guarantee of confidentiality."

. . .

As in the Yale study, a comparison of lawyers with other professionals proved enlightening on the subject of the significance of secrecy rules to clients. [A] large majority of clients responded that lawyers are no more obligated to preserve confidences than doctors, psychologists, and psychiatrists; a healthy minority believed the same held true for accountants and social workers. A similar pattern appeared when clients were asked whether "attorneys in fact guard client confidences more carefully than" the other professionals.

Even more interesting were client responses to the question, "Assuming you needed the assistance of each of the following professionals, would you be more likely to give information to attorneys than to [blank]?" On the whole, the clients accepted that lawyers have a higher legal obligation to preserve confidences than accountants and social workers. Yet only half of the clients were more likely to give information to attorneys. Few were prepared to trust lawyers over priests, doctors, psychologists, or psychiatrists.

Confidentiality's effect in inducing client communication. Most lawyers surveyed believed that they would get the same information from clients even if they never informed the clients about confidentiality. A higher percentage, 85.9%, believed they would get enough information to represent clients competently.[173] The answers at least suggest that strict rules are not essential to maintaining an adversary system.

The client survey further supports this conclusion. . . . The survey asked whether the subjects would withhold information from their attorney "if [the] attorney told you that he/she could not guarantee confidentiality but that, except in unusual cases, he/she would keep information secret." A majority of laypersons answered that they would withhold information. But when the same respondents were asked whether they would still withhold information if the lawyer "promised confidentiality except for specific types of information which he/she described in advance," only 15.1% said they would withhold. That is not significantly different from the 11.3% of the surveyed clients who admitted to withholding information from their attorneys under current confidentiality rules. These results suggest that

---

[173] T.C. Table L1, at 5. Similarly, lawyers do not seem to share the code drafters' concern with client lies or withholding of information. Few of the lawyers surveyed believed their clients lied in more than a quarter of their cases. T.C. Table L1, at 10 (23.4%). When, however, lawyers thought their clients lied or withheld information, only 19.3% of the lawyers believed the failure to disclose significantly affected more than 25% of the cases. T.C. Table L1, at 10.

the general sense of trust in attorneys as professionals — rather than particularly strict confidentiality rules — is what fosters client candor.

NOTES AND QUESTIONS

1. In the 1980s, Professor Vincent Alexander released the results of another study. Alexander, *The Corporate Attorney-Client Privilege: A Study of the Participants*, 63 St. John's L. Rev. 191 (1989). He interviewed corporate executives, in-house counsel, and other corporate attorneys — a total of 182 interviews. Three out of four high-ranking executives stated that the existence of the privilege encouraged candor. Yet the executives' responses indicated that in their interactions with counsel they relied more heavily on their trust in the individual attorney than on any assumption about evidence law. *Id.* at 248. More specifically, Professor Alexander found that curtailment of the privilege would have little effect on the frequency of consultation, that oral consultations would generally be as candid as they had been in the past, but that some communication would be more guarded. *Id.* at 248, 264, 269–70, 370–71, 374.

2. Does this empirical data warrant reform of the attorney-client privilege? If so, in what respect? Should the privilege be converted into a more qualified protection like that applied to attorney work product?

2. The Scope of the Privilege

a. The Identity of the Client

Suppose that after the battery and before any arrest, Devitt contacts an attorney. Devitt describes the crime to the attorney and hires the attorney to defend him against any charge that might be filed against him. The attorney decides to check on Paterson's status. He learns that Paterson is in the hospital and visits the hospital, identifying himself to the floor nurse. The nurse reports to the police that an attorney stopped by. The police then contact the attorney and demand that he divulge his client's identity. When he refuses, the police persuade the district attorney to initiate a grand jury investigation. The attorney is subpoenaed before the grand jury, which demands that he identify his client. At this point, can he assert the attorney-client privilege to refuse to divulge Devitt's identity?

Although it is a well-established general rule that the client's identity is *not* within the privilege, *Frank v. Tomlinson*, 351 F.2d 384 (5th Cir. 1965), *cert. denied*, 382 U.S. 1028 (1966). On infrequent occasions, though, some courts have held that a client's identity is protected. *See, e.g., Matter of Kozlov*, 398 A.2d 882 (N.J. 1979). A leading case, *United States v. Hodge & Zweig*, 548 F.2d 1347 (9th Cir. 1977), announced this test:

> As a general rule, . . . the identity of an attorney's clients and the nature of his fee arrangements with his clients are not confidential communications protected by the attorney-client privilege. The general rule, however, is qualified by an important exception: A client's identity and the nature of that client's fee arrangements may be privileged where the person invoking

the privilege can show that a strong probability exists that disclosure of such information would implicate that client in the very criminal activity for which legal advice was sought.

Id. at 1353. This doctrine is sometimes referred to as the "legal advice" exception to the general rule. Note the verb "implicate" in the last sentence quoted from *Hodge & Zweig.* Rather than resting exclusively on the attorney-client privilege, this exception is based on the interplay between that privilege and the Fifth Amendment privilege against self-incrimination.

Although the "legal advice" exception has some judicial support, other courts have adopted the "last link" exception. *Baird v. Koerner,* 279 F.2d 623 (9th Cir. 1960), declared:

The name of the client will be considered privileged matter where the circumstances of the case are such that the name of the client is material only for the purpose of showing an acknowledgment of guilt on the part of such client of the very offenses on account of which the attorney was employed.

Id. at 633. Following *Baird,* some courts apply the privilege when the revelation of the client's identity would furnish "the last link in an existing chain of incriminating evidence likely to lead to the client's indictment." Przypyszny, *supra,* at 356. Like the "legal advice" exception, this doctrine has a hybrid rationale, resting on Fifth Amendment concerns as well as the attorney-client privilege.

However, there is a third doctrine based squarely on the privilege — the "confidential communication" exception. *Id.* at 359. In *United States v. Liebman,* 742 F.2d 807 (3d Cir. 1984), the Internal Revenue Service asked a law firm to identify all clients that the firm had erroneously advised that certain fees in connection with a particular real estate transaction were deductible. The court held that, in these limited circumstances, the clients' identities were privileged; by revealing the clients' identities, the firm would implicitly simultaneously disclose the substance of the communication between the firm and the client. In cases such as *Liebman,* the courts expand the protection of the privilege to cloak the client's identity as a means to the end of protecting the privileged communications themselves. The trend in the case law has been toward this doctrine.

b. Confidentiality — Clients with Shared Interests

Suppose that Devitt was being tried with a codefendant and that they contemplated a joint defense. Courts have generally extended the privilege to so-called "allied party exchanges" of information. The court thus would probably apply the privilege to cloak exchanges of information between counsel for Devitt and his co-defendant. Or assume that, in the *Hill* case, Ms. Hill's attorney decided to share information with the attorney representing another plaintiff pressing a similar product liability claim against Polecat. Again, the court would likely apply the privilege to protect the information exchanged. Under this "common interest" doctrine, the privilege protects the exchanged information so long as the parties' *legal* interests are "substantially identical." *In re Regents of the University of California,* 101 F.3d 1386 (Fed. Cir. 1996). In essence, there is a broader circle of confidence. Litigation need not be pending at the time of the exchange, and the parties can be in the position of potential co-plaintiffs or co-defendants in a civil case or co-defendants in a criminal proceeding.

NOTES

1. The rationale advanced in favor of the common interest doctrine is that by facilitating the pooling of information by litigants, this extension of the privilege promotes the efficient operation of the litigation system. Do you agree?

2. What does "common interest" mean? Suppose that an employee agrees to cooperate in a corporation's internal investigation conducted because of the threat of a suit that might be filed against both employee and employer. Is that enough to establish a common interest? *In re Grand Jury Subpoena: Under Seal*, 415 F.3d 333, 341 (4th Cir. 2005) (no — "some form of joint strategy is necessary").

3. Many courts limit the scope of the common interest extension to communications made in the presence of an attorney. *In re Teleglobe Communications Corp.*, 493 F.3d 345 (3d Cir. 2007). They refuse to apply the extension to communications directly between the clients. After all, the privilege protects only attorney-client communications. But what if one client is relaying a message from his or her attorney to the other client about coordinating their legal strategies?

c. Attorney-Client Communications in the Corporate Context

The threshold question is whether, like a natural person, a corporate entity can qualify as a client. Given the size of many corporations, the extension of the privilege to corporations has a greater potential for obstructing the search for truth than the application of the privilege to individual natural persons. A tremendous volume of data could be secreted in the millions of corporate file cabinets. However, a corporate entity has the same legitimate need for legal counsel as do individuals. Consequently, a consensus exists that to some extent an entity such as a corporation may hold the attorney-client privilege.

Communications with corporate employees. Suppose that soon after Ms. Hill files her complaint, the in-house counsel for Polecat Motors begins a factual investigation to prepare for trial. The counsel wants to persuade the jury that the defendant corporation is intensely concerned about quality control of safety features. Consequently, the attorney interviews both executive officers, such as the president and also lower-level employees such as assembly line workers. He compiles the interviews into a single report, retains one copy of the report, and sends the only other copy to the outside firm defending the litigation. Subsequently, in response to an interrogatory, the defendant discloses the existence of the report and Ms. Hill's attorney then moves for production of the report. Can the defendant successfully resist production of the entire report or any part of it on the ground of the attorney-client privilege?

Beyond the question whether the privilege should apply to organizations or other entities, there is the much more complex question of scope of protection afforded to such entities. Given the size of many corporations, the extension of the privilege to corporations has a greater potential for obstructing the search for truth than the application of the privilege to individual natural persons. In the following case, the Supreme Court struggled with a split of authority over that question.

UPJOHN CO. v. UNITED STATES
449 U.S. 383 (1981)

JUSTICE REHNQUIST delivered the opinion of the Court.

We granted certiorari in this case to address important questions concerning the scope of the attorney-client privilege in the corporate context. [H]owever, we . . . decide concrete cases and not abstract propositions of law. We decline to lay down a broad rule . . . to govern all conceivable future questions in this area . . . . We . . . do, however, conclude that the attorney-client privilege protects the communications involved in this case from compelled disclosure.

[Upjohn sells pharmaceuticals abroad. Accountants auditing one of its foreign subsidiaries discovered that the subsidiary had paid foreign government officials to secure government business and they informed Upjohn's General Counsel., who consulted the Board Chairman. They decided that Upjohn should conduct an internal investigation of the "questionable payments." Upjohn's attorneys sent a letter and questionnaire to all foreign general and area managers. Responses were sent directly to the General Counsel. Upjohn's attorneys also interviewed the recipients of the questionnaire and some 33 other Upjohn officers or employees.

Later, Upjohn submitted a report disclosing certain questionable payments to the Internal Revenue Service, which initiated its own investigation. Upjohn provided a list of all the interviewees and questionnaire respondents. The I.R.S. issued a summons demanding production of all questionnaires, responses, and interview notes. Upjohn asserted the attorney-client privilege.]

The Court of Appeals . . . considered the application of the privilege in the corporate context to present a "different problem," since the client was an inanimate entity and "only the senior management, guiding and integrating the several operations, . . . can be said to possess an identity analogous to the corporation as a whole." 600 F.2d at 1226. The first case to articulate the so-called "control group test" adopted by the court below, *City of Philadelphia v. Westinghouse Electric Corp.*, 210 F. Supp. 483, 485 (E.D. Pa.), petition for mandamus and prohibition denied, 312 F.2d 742 (CA3 1962), cert. denied, 372 U.S. 943 (1963), reflected a similar conceptual approach:

> Keeping in mind that the question is, Is it the corporation which is seeking the lawyer's advice when the asserted privileged communication is made?, the most satisfactory solution . . . is that if the employee making the communication, of whatever rank he may be, is in a position to control or even to take a substantial part in a decision about any action which the corporation may take upon the advice of the attorney, . . . then, in effect, *he is (or personifies) the corporation* when he makes his disclosure to the lawyer and the privilege would apply.

Such a view . . . overlooks the fact that the privilege exists to protect not only the giving of professional advice to those who can act on it but also the giving of information to the lawyer to enable him to give sound and informed advice. The first step in the resolution of any legal problem is ascertaining the factual background and sifting through the facts with an eye to the legally relevant. *See* ABA Code of Professional Responsibility, Ethical Consideration 4-1:

> A lawyer should be fully informed of all the facts of the matter he is handling in order for his client to obtain the full advantage of our legal system. It is for the lawyer in the exercise of his independent professional judgment to separate the relevant and important from the irrelevant and unimportant. The observance of the ethical obligation of a lawyer to hold inviolate the confidences and secrets of his client not only facilitates the full development of facts essential to proper representation of the client but also encourages laymen to seek early legal assistance.

> In the case of the individual client, the provider of information and the person who acts on the lawyer's advice are one and the same. In the corporate context, however, it will frequently be employees beyond the control group as defined by the court below — "officers and agents . . . responsible for directing [the company's] actions in response to legal advice" — who will possess the information needed by the corporation's lawyers. Middle-level — and indeed lower-level — employees can, by actions within the scope of their employment, embroil the corporation in serious legal difficulties, and it is only natural that these employees would have the relevant information needed by corporate counsel if he is adequately to advise the client with respect to such actual or potential difficulties . . . .

The communications at issue were made by Upjohn employees to counsel for Upjohn acting as such, at the direction of corporate superiors in order to secure legal advice from counsel. As the magistrate found, "Mr. Thomas consulted with the Chairman of the Board and outside counsel and thereafter conducted a factual investigation to determine the nature and extent of the questionable payments *and to be in a position to give legal advice to the company with respect to the payments*." Information, not available from upper-echelon management, was needed to supply a basis for legal advice concerning compliance with securities and tax laws, foreign laws, currency regulations, duties to shareholders, and potential litigation in each of these areas. The communications concerned matters within the scope of the employees' corporate duties, and the employees themselves were sufficiently aware that they were being questioned in order that the corporation could obtain legal advice. The questionnaire identified Thomas as "the company's General Counsel" and referred . . . to the possible illegality of payments such as the ones on which information was sought. A statement of policy accompanying the questionnaire clearly indicated the legal implications of the investigation. It began "Upjohn will comply with all laws and regulations," and stated that commissions or payments "will not be used as a subterfuge for bribes or illegal payments" and that all payments must be "proper and legal." Any future agreements with foreign distributors or agents were to be approved "by a company attorney" and any questions concerning the policy were to be referred "to the company's General

Counsel." Pursuant to explicit instructions from the Chairman of the Board, the communications were considered "highly confidential" when made, and have been kept confidential by the company. Consistent with the underlying purposes of the attorney-client privilege, these communications must be protected against compelled disclosure.

The Court of Appeals declined to extend the attorney-client privilege beyond the limits of the control group test for fear that doing so would entail severe burdens on discovery and create a broad "zone of silence" over corporate affairs. Application of the attorney-client privilege to communications such as those involved here, however, puts the adversary in no worse position than if the communications had never taken place. The privilege only protects disclosure of communications; it does not protect disclosure of the underlying facts by those who communicated with the attorney:

> The protection of the privilege extends only to *communications* and not to facts. A fact is one thing and a communication concerning that fact is an entirely different thing. The client cannot be compelled to answer the question "What did you say or write to the attorney?" but may not refuse to disclose any relevant fact within his knowledge merely he incorporated a statement of such fact into his communication to his attorney. *City of Philadelphia v. Westinghouse Electric Corp.*, 205 F. Supp. 830, 831 (E.D. Pa. 1962).

Here the Government was free to question the employees who communicated with Thomas and outside counsel. Upjohn has provided the IRS with a list of such employees . . . . While it would probably be more convenient for the Government to secure the results of petitioner's internal investigation by simply subpoenaing the questionnaires and notes taken by petitioner's attorneys, such considerations of convenience do not overcome the policies served by the attorney-client privilege. As Justice Jackson noted in his concurring opinion in *Hickman v. Taylor*, 329 U.S., at 516: "Discovery was hardly intended to enable a learned profession to perform its functions . . . on wits borrowed from the adversary."

[W]e decide only the case before us, and do not undertake to draft a set of rules which should govern challenges to investigatory subpoenas. Any such approach would violate the spirit of F.R.E. 501. While such a "case-by-case" basis may to some slight extent undermine desirable certainty in the boundaries of the attorney-client privilege, it obeys the spirit of the Rules. At the same time we conclude that the narrow "control group test" sanctioned by the Court of Appeals in this case cannot, consistent with "the principles of the common law as . . . interpreted . . . in light of reason and experience," F.R.E. 501, govern the development of the law in this area.

Accordingly, the judgment of the Court of Appeals is reversed, and the case remanded for further proceedings.

CHIEF JUSTICE BURGER, concurring in part and concurring in the judgment.

I agree fully with the Court's rejection of the so-called "control group" test, its reasons for doing so, and its ultimate holding that the communications at issue are privileged. As the Court states, however, "if the purpose of the attorney-client privilege is to be served, the attorney and the client must be able to predict with some degree of certainty whether particular discussions will be protected." For this very reason, . . . we should articulate a standard that will govern similar cases and afford guidance to corporations, counsel advising them, and federal courts.

[T]o say we should not reach all facets of the privilege does not mean that we should neglect our duty to provide guidance in a case that squarely presents the question in a traditional adversary context. Indeed, because Federal Rule of Evidence 501 provides that the law of privileges "shall be governed by the principles of the common law as they may be interpreted by the courts of the United States in light of reason and experience," this Court has a special duty to clarify aspects of the law of privileges properly before us. Simply asserting that this failure "may to some slight extent undermine desirable certainty" neither minimizes the consequences of continuing uncertainty and confusion nor harmonizes the inherent dissonance of acknowledging that uncertainty while declining to clarify it.

NOTES

1.   Do you agree with the *Upjohn* Court? Are the communications of the lower echelon employees (outside the control group) as likely to be affected by the existence *vel non* of a privilege as the communications of control group members? Is it not safe to assume that lower echelon employees will normally report data to their superiors out of a general sense of business duty — rather than because of any motivation to obtain legal advice? If the operational level employees refuse to cooperate, they can be fired.

2.   Unlike a natural person, an entity cannot represent itself in court. Thus, whenever there is a realistic possibility of litigation, the entity must turn to counsel. Further, the turnover rate in the American workforce is quite high. "According to a BNA survey, one in seven permanent employees switched jobs in 1999 . . . ." Semmes, *Rising Employee Turnover Rate Puts Spotlight on Agreements to Protect Trade Secrets*, 69 U.S.L.W. (BNA) 2211 (Oct. 17, 2000). Hence, an entity would take a huge legal risk if it did not order its employees to disclose relevant information to counsel immediately. If a corporation has such strong practical incentives to order its employees to reduce information in their possession to written form, is the further protection of a privilege necessary?

3.   Should the scope of the corporate privilege be limited to persons who are formal employees of the entity? Many corporations have downsized and outsourced functions to persons who are technically independent contractors. Suppose, for example, that a company outsourced accounting. The "outside" accountants are frequently now the repositories of the type of information typically maintained by "inside" employees in the past. If the company becomes involved in litigation involving accounting data, the company's counsel will have to obtain the information from the "outside" accountants. These independent contractors are arguably the functional equivalent of employees. Beardslee, *The Corporate Attorney-Client Privilege: Third-Rate Doctrine for Third-Party Consultants*, 62 SMU L.Rev. 727, 748, 774–77 (2009).

d. *The Involvement of an Intermediary*

Normally the client and attorney communicate directly, but sometimes such direct communication is not possible. Suppose, for instance, that Devitt was not fluent in English. Common sense would move the attorney to have an interpreter present during the interview of Devitt. In this situation, it makes sense that the interpreter's presence should not negate the privilege, and indeed that is the prevailing doctrine. Now suppose that Devitt were charged with a tax offense and he therefore brings to the attorney-client interview not only his voluminous records but also an accountant to help him interpret the records for the attorney. Under these circumstances, there is authority that the accountant's presence similarly does not negate the privilege. *See United States v. Kovel*, 296 F.2d 918 (2d Cir. 1961); *In re Consolidated Litig. Concerning Int'l Harvester's Disposition of Wis. Steel*, 666 F. Supp. 1148, 1157 (N.D. Ill. 1987). The extension of the attorney-client privilege to communications with experts in some circumstances now appears to be the majority view. *Miller v. District Court*, 737 P.2d 834 (Colo. 1987); *Haynes v. State*, 103 Nev. 309, 739 P.2d 497 (1987).

In these fact situations, the information being interpreted emanates from the client, but the client lacks the expertise to effectively interpret the information for the attorney. The expert's intervention is necessary for effective communication between attorney and client. Under such circumstances, some courts have extended the privilege to: (a) the client's disclosures to the expert (*People v. Goldbach*, 27 Cal. App. 3d 563, 103 Cal. Rptr. 800 (1972); *contra Granviel v. Estelle*, 655 F.2d 673 (5th Cir. 1981)); (b) the knowledge the expert acquires and the opinion the expert forms (*San Francisco v. Superior Court*, 37 Cal. 2d 227, 231 P.2d 26 (1951)); and (c) any written report the expert submits to the attorney. *Jones v. Superior Court*, 58 Cal. 2d 56, 22 Cal. Rptr. 879, 372 P.2d 919 (1962).

Clearly, the privilege should extend to (a). As Chapter 25 noted, many courts protect these revelations as "facilitative" communications. But are (b) and (c) distinguishable? It might be argued that those extensions of the privilege in effect convert the doctrine into a much broader doctrine rendering the expert incompetent as a witness against the side which originally hired the expert. Do those extensions permit — or, worse still, encourage — the attorney to safely "shop around" among experts until the attorney finds an expert who will testify to the opinion the attorney wants? If they are not privileged, should (b) and (c) nonetheless be covered by a qualified work product protection?

PROBLEMS

1. **Problem 26-1.** In *Devitt*, the defense decides to raise an insanity defense. To prepare for trial, the defense attorney sends Devitt to a psychiatrist for an evaluation. Will the attorney-client privilege attach? *State v. Pratt*, 284 Md. 516, 398 A.2d 421, 423–24 (1979) (yes); *but see State v. Carter*, 641 S.W.2d 54, 57 (Mo. 1982).

2. **Problem 26-2.** In *Hill*, the attorney for Polecat Motors hires a safety engineer and sends the engineer to the site of the accident to identify any features of the section of road that might have caused the accident. Will the privilege attach to the report the expert prepares on that subject? *See Grand Lake Drive-In v. Superior Court*, 179 Cal. App. 2d 122, 125–28, 3 Cal. Rptr. 621, 624–27 (1960) (no).

3. Special Exceptions to the Attorney-Client Privilege

The California statutes list most of the recognized exceptions to this privilege:

§ 956. Lawyer Obtained to Aid in Planning, Committing Crime.

There is no privilege under this article if the services of the lawyers were sought or obtained to enable or aid anyone to commit or plan to commit a crime or a fraud.

§ 957. Communication Between Parties Claiming Under Deceased Client.

There is no privilege under this article as to a communication relevant to an issue between parties all of whom claim through a deceased client, regardless of whether the claims are by testate or intestate succession or by inter vivos transaction.

§ 958. Communications of Issue of Breach of Duty — Lawyer-Client. There is no privilege under this article as to a communication relevant to an issue of breach, by the lawyer or by the client, of a duty arising out of the lawyer-client relationship.

§ 959. Communication of Intention or Competence of Client Executing Attested Document.

There is no privilege under this article as to a communication relevant to an issue concerning the intention or competence of a client executing an attested document of which the lawyer is an attesting witness, or concerning the execution.

§ 960. Communication of Intention of Deceased Client with Respect to Writing Affecting Property Interest.

There is no privilege under this article as to a communication relevant to an issue concerning the intention of a client, now deceased, with respect to a deed of conveyance, will, or other writing, executed by the client, purporting to affect an interest in property.

§ 961. Validity of Writing by Deceased Client Affecting Interest in Property.

There is no privilege under this article as to a communication relevant to an issue concerning the validity of a deed of conveyance, will, or other writing, executed by a client, now deceased, purporting to affect an interest in property.

§ 962. Communication Made Where Two or More Clients Retain Same Lawyer *in Matter of Common Interest.*

Where two or more clients have retained or consulted a lawyer upon a matter of common interest, none of them, nor one successor in interest of any of them, may claim a privilege under this article as to a communication made in the course of that relationship when such communication is offered in a civil proceeding between one of such clients (or his successor in interest) and another of such clients (or his successor in interest).

California Evidence Code § 956 codifies the crime-fraud exception. Although there is no corresponding statute or Rule in federal practice, the federal courts recognized the exception as a matter of common law well before the adoption of the Federal Rules. In the following case, the Supreme Court confronted two questions: (1) whether the exception survived the passage of the Federal Rules; and (2) if so, whether and under what circumstances the trial judge may order the party claiming the privilege to submit the allegedly privileged material to the judge for *in camera* examination. Think back to the discussion of preliminary fact-finding procedures under Rule 104 in Chapter 5. Remember that the last sentence of Rule 104(a) reads: "In making its determination [the court] is not bound by the rules of evidence except those with respect to privileges."

The catalyst for this case was a high-profile Internal Revenue Service investigation of the Church of Scientology and its founder, L. Ron Hubbard. In an earlier California state case, the church had sued a former member, Gerald Armstrong, who had allegedly stolen church documents. The parties to the state case filed several documents under seal, including some tapes about the church's activities. The IRS served a summons on Zolin, the court clerk, to produce the tapes. In support of its petition to enforce the summons, the IRS submitted partial transcripts of the tapes to the federal district court, claiming that it lawfully obtained the transcripts from a confidential source. When the church opposed the summons on the ground that the tapes were privileged attorney-client communications, the IRS countered that the tapes were subject to the crime-fraud exception.

UNITED STATES v. ZOLIN
491 U.S. 554 (1989)

JUSTICE BLACKMUN delivered the opinion of the Court.

The attorney-client privilege is not without its costs. "[S]ince the privilege has the effect of withholding relevant information from the factfinder, it applies only where necessary to achieve its purpose." *Fisher*, 425 U.S., at 403. The attorney-client privilege must necessarily protect the confidences of wrongdoers, but the reason for that protection — the centrality of open client and attorney communication to the proper functioning of our adversary system of justice — "ceas[es] to operate at a certain point, namely, where the desired advice refers *not to prior wrongdoing*, but to *future wrongdoing*." 8 Wigmore, § 2298, p. 573. . . . It is the purpose of the crime-fraud exception to the attorney-client privilege to assure that the "seal of secrecy" . . . between lawyer and client does not extend to communications "made for the purpose of getting advice for the commission of a fraud" or crime. *O'Rourke v. Darbishire*, [1920] A.C. 581, 604.

The District Court and the Court of Appeals found that the tapes at issue in this case recorded attorney-client communications. [That] finding [is] not at issue here. [T]he remaining obstacle to respondents' successful assertion of the privilege is the IRS' contention that the recorded attorney-client communications were made in furtherance of a future crime or fraud.

[W]e need not decide the quantum of proof necessary ultimately to establish the applicability of the crime-fraud exception. *Cf. Clark*, 289 U.S., at 15. Rather, we are concerned here with the *type* of evidence that may be used to make that ultimate showing. Within that general area of inquiry, the initial question in this case is whether a district court, at the request of the party opposing the privilege, may review the allegedly privileged communications *in camera* to determine whether the crime-fraud exception applies. If such *in camera* review is permitted, the second question . . . is whether some threshold evidentiary showing is needed before the district court may undertake the requested review. Finally, if a threshold showing is required, we must consider the type of evidence the opposing party may use to meet it: *i.e.*, in this case, whether the partial transcripts the IRS possessed may be used for that purpose.

At first blush, two provisions of the Federal Rules of Evidence would appear . . . relevant. Rule 104(a) provides: "Preliminary questions concerning the qualification of a person to be a witness, *the existence of a privilege*, or the admissibility of evidence shall be determined by the court. . . . In making its determination it is not bound by rules of evidence *except those with respect to privileges.*" Rule 1101(c) provides: "The rule with respect to privileges applies at all stages of all actions, cases, and proceedings." Taken together, these Rules might be read to establish that in a summons-enforcement proceeding, attorney-client communications cannot be considered by the district court in making its crime-fraud ruling: to do otherwise, under this view, would be to make the crime-fraud determination without due regard to the existence of the privilege.

Even those scholars who support this reading of Rule 104(a) acknowledge that it leads to an absurd result:

"Because the judge must honor claims of privilege made during his preliminary fact determinations, many exceptions to the rules of privilege will become 'dead letters,' since the preliminary facts that give rise to these exceptions can never be proved. For example, an exception to the attorney-client privilege provides that there is no privilege if the communication was made to enable anyone to commit a crime or fraud. There is virtually no way in which the exception can ever be proved, save by compelling disclosure of the contents of the communication; Rule 104(a) provides that this cannot be done." 21 C. Wright & K. Graham, Federal Practice & Procedure: Evidence § 5055, p. 276 (1977).

We find this Draconian interpretation of Rule 104(a) inconsistent with the Rule's plain language. The Rule does not provide by its terms that all materials as to which a "clai[m] of privilege" is made must be excluded from consideration. In that critical respect, the language of Rule 104(a) is markedly different from the comparable California evidence rule, which provides that "the presiding officer may not require disclosure of information *claimed to be privileged* under this division in order to rule on the claim of privilege." Cal. Evidence Code § 915(a).[10] There is no reason to read

---

[10] A good example of the effect of the California rule is provided by the record in this case. While the disputed matters were being briefed in Federal District Court, the state Superior Court held a hearing on a motion by Government attorneys seeking access to materials in the Armstrong case for ongoing litigation in Washington, D.C. The transcript of the hearing was made part of the record before the District Court in this case. Regarding the tapes, the Government argued to the Superior Court that the attorney-client conversations on the tapes reflect the planning or commission of a crime or fraud.

Rule 104(a) as if its text were identical to that of the California rule.

In fashioning a standard for determining when *in camera* review is appropriate, we begin with the observation that "*in camera* inspection . . . is a smaller intrusion upon the confidentiality of the attorney-client relationship than is public disclosure." *Fried, Too High a Price for Truth: The Exception to the Attorney-Client Privilege for Contemplated Crimes and Frauds*, 64 N.C.L.Rev. 443, 467 (1986). We therefore conclude that a lesser evidentiary showing is needed to trigger *in camera* review than is required ultimately to overcome the privilege. *Ibid.* The threshold we set . . . need not be a stringent one.

[T]he following standard strikes the correct balance. Before engaging in *in camera* review to determine the applicability of the crime-fraud exception, "the judge should require a showing of a factual basis adequate to support a good faith belief by a reasonable person," *Caldwell v. District Court*, 644 P. 2d 26, 33 (Colo. 1982), that *in camera* review of the materials may reveal evidence to establish the claim that the crime-fraud exception applies. . . .

The question remains as to what kind of evidence a district court may consider in determining whether it has the discretion to undertake an *in camera* review of an allegedly privileged communication at the behest of the party opposing the privilege. Here the issue is whether the partial transcripts may be used by the IRS in support of its request for *in camera* review of the tapes. The answer to that question . . . must be found in Rule 104(a), which establishes that materials that have been determined to be privileged may not be considered in making the preliminary determination of the existence of a privilege. Neither the District Court nor the Court of Appeals made factual findings as to the privileged nature of the partial transcripts, so we cannot determine on this record whether Rule 104(a) would bar their consideration. Assuming for the moment, however, that no rule of privilege bars the IRS' use of the partial transcripts, we fail to see what purpose would be served by excluding the transcripts from the District Court's consideration. . . . Permitting district courts to consider this type of evidence would aid them substantially in rapidly and reliably determining whether *in camera* review is appropriate. . . . [T]he party opposing the privilege may use any nonprivileged evidence in support of its request for *in camera* review, even if its evidence is not "independent" of the contested communications. . . .

We . . . hold . . . that before a district court may engage in *in camera* review at the request of the party opposing the privilege, that party must present evidence sufficient to support a reasonable belief that *in camera* review may yield evidence that establishes the exception's applicability. [Further], . . . the threshold showing to obtain *in camera* review may be met by using any relevant evidence, lawfully obtained, that has not been adjudicated to be privileged. . . .

Transcripts of Hearing of February 11, 1985, p. 52. That claim was supported by several declarations and other extrinsic evidence. The Government noted, however, that "the tape recordings themselves would . . . be the best evidence of exactly what was going on." *Id.*, at 53. The intervenors stressed that, as a *matter of California* law, "you can't show the tapes are not privileged by the contents." *Id.*, 58; *see also Id.*, at 68. The Superior Court acknowledged the premise that "you can't look at the conversation itself to make [the crime-fraud] determination," *Id.*, at 74, and concluded that the extrinsic evidence was not sufficient to make out a prima facie case that the crime-fraud exception applies. *Id.*, at 75–76.

NOTES

1.   On remand in *Zolin*, the court found that the crime-fraud exception applied to the tapes in question. 905 F.2d 1344 (9th Cir. 1990), *cert. denied*, 499 U.S. 920 (1991).

2.   Based on *Zolin*, what procedural steps must a litigant follow if he or she wants to invoke the crime-fraud exception as a basis for discovering otherwise privileged information? *Zolin* seems to contemplate a two-step procedure, a preliminary judicial examination of the allegedly privileged records and a final ruling by the judge. What guidance does *Zolin* provide as to each step? In particular, does the Court settle the issue of the measure of the final burden of proof on the question of the applicability of the crime-fraud exception?

3.   Prior to the adoption of the Federal Rules, federal judges had asserted common-law power to require *in camera* examinations. The *Zolin* Court concludes that that practice is still good law under Rule 104(a). Is the Court's reasoning persuasive? Justice Blackmun asserts that a contrary interpretation of Rule 104(a) would "lead . . . to an absurd result." It is an ancient maxim of statutory interpretation that, whenever possible, the court should reject a construction which would lead to an absurd result. *Crooks v. Harrelson*, 282 U.S. 55, 60 (1930); *In re Jones*, 591 F.3d 308 (4th Cir. 2010). However, the maxim is a dangerous one; a judge may attempt to conceal a debatable policy judgment by mongering the label "absurd." Has Justice Blackmun in effect said that California Evidence Code § 915 is "absurd"? Do you think that the Court would be willing to invalidate § 915 as a violation of due process? In 2009, the California Supreme Court affirmed that § 915 bars *in camera* examination. *Costco Wholesale Corp. v. Superior Court*, 219 P.3d 736 (Cal. 2009).

4.   Consider the situation in which a client tells her lawyer that she plans to commit fraud, robbery, or assault. Must or may the lawyer disclose the client's plan to the authorities? Many jurisdictions permit the lawyer to do so, but the answer can depend upon whether the jurisdiction follows the Model Code of Professional Responsibility, Model Rules of Professional Conduct, or special state law. *See generally* Zacharias, *Federalizing Legal Ethics*, 73 TEX. L. REV. 335 (1994).

The crime-fraud exception is not the only recognized exception to the attorney-client privilege. Many jurisdictions also recognize the so-called self-defense exception.

PROBLEM

1.   **Problem 26-3.** If Devitt subsequently accuses his attorney of ineffective representation or if Ms. Hill later sues her attorney for malpractice, should the attorney be permitted to use otherwise privileged communications to respond? Suppose that the ethics committee of the State Bar leveled that charge. Should the result be the same? What result under California Evidence Code § 958?

4.   The Duration of the Privilege

SWIDLER & BERLIN v. UNITED STATES
524 U.S. 399 (1998)

CHIEF JUSTICE REHNQUIST delivered the opinion of the Court.

This dispute arises out of an investigation . . . by the Office of the Independent Counsel into whether various individuals made false statements, obstructed justice, or committed other crimes during investigations of the 1993 dismissal of employees from the White House Travel Office. [Foster was Deputy White House Counsel during the Clinton Administration when the firings occurred. Foster met petitioner Hamilton, an attorney at petitioner Swidler & Berlin, to seek legal advice about the firings. During a meeting, Hamilton took handwritten notes. One of the first entries in the notes is the word "Privileged." Nine days later, Foster committed suicide.

A federal grand jury issued subpoenas to Hamilton and the firm for Hamilton's notes. Petitioners moved to quash, arguing that the notes were protected by the attorney client privilege. After examining the notes in camera, the District Court concluded they were protected from disclosure and denied enforcement of the subpoenas.

The Court of Appeals reversed. It reasoned that the risk of posthumous revelation, when confined to the criminal context, has little to no chilling effect on client communication, but that the costs of protecting communications after death are high. The court ruled that the privilege is not absolute in such circumstances, and that a balancing test should apply.]

The Independent Counsel argues that the attorney-client privilege should not prevent disclosure of confidential communications where the client has died and the information is relevant to a criminal proceeding. There is some authority for this position. One state appellate court, *Cohen v. Jenkintown Cab. Co.*, 238 Pa.Super. 456, 357 A.2d 689 (1976), [has] . . . held the privilege may be subject to posthumous exceptions in certain circumstances. *Cohen*, a civil case, . . . recognized that the privilege generally survives death, but concluded that it could make an exception where the interest of justice was compelling and the interest of the client in preserving the confidence was insignificant. *Id.*, 462–464, 357 A.2d, at 692–693.

But other than [those few] decisions, cases addressing the existence of the privilege after death — most involving the testamentary exception — uniformly presume the privilege survives even if they do not so hold. See, *e.g.*, *Mayberry v. Indiana*, 670 N.E.2d 1262 (Ind.1996); *Morris v. Cain*, 39 La. Ann. 712, 1 So. 797 (1887); *People v. Podzelewski*, 611 N.Y.S.2d 22, 203 A.D.2d 594 (1994). Several State Supreme Court decisions expressly hold that the attorney-client privilege extends beyond the death of the client, even in the criminal context. See *In re John Doe Grand Jury Investigation*, 408 Mass. 480, 481–483, 562 N.E.2d 69, 70 (1990); *State v. Doster*, 276 S.C. 647, 650–651, 284 S.E.2d 218, 219 (1981); *State v. Macumber*, 112 Ariz. 569, 571, 544 P.2d 1084, 1086 (1976). . . .

. . . [V]arious commentators have criticized this rule, urging that the privilege should be abrogated after the client's death where extreme injustice would result, as long as disclosure would not seriously undermine the privilege by deterring client communication. See, *e.g.*, C. Mueller & L. Kirkpatrick, 2 Federal Evidence § 199, at 380–381 (2d ed. 1994). . . . But even these critics . . . recognize that established law supports the continuation of the privilege and that a contrary rule would be a modification of the common law . . . .

Despite the scholarly criticism, . . . there are weighty reasons that counsel in favor of posthumous application. Knowing that communications will remain confidential even after death encourages the client to communicate fully and frankly with counsel. While the fear of disclosure, and the consequent withholding of information from counsel, may be reduced if disclosure is limited to posthumous disclosure in a criminal context, it seems unreasonable to assume that it vanishes altogether. Clients may be concerned about reputation, civil liability, or possible harm to friends or family. Posthumous disclosure of such communications may be as feared as disclosure during the client's lifetime.

The Independent Counsel . . . suggests that his proposed exception would have minimal impact if confined to criminal cases, or . . . if it is limited to information of substantial importance to a particular criminal case. However, there is no case authority for the proposition that the privilege applies differently in criminal and civil cases . . . . In any event, a client may not know at the time he discloses information to his attorney whether it will later be relevant to a civil or a criminal matter, let alone whether it will be of substantial importance. Balancing ex post the importance of the information against client interests, even limited to criminal cases, introduces substantial uncertainty into the privilege's application. For just that reason, we have rejected use of a balancing test in defining the contours of the privilege. See *Upjohn*, 449 U.S., at 393; *Jaffe, supra*, at 17–18.

In a similar vein, the Independent Counsel argues that existing exceptions to the privilege, such as the crime-fraud exception and the testamentary exception, make the impact of one more exception marginal. However, these exceptions do not demonstrate that the impact of a posthumous exception would be insignificant, and there is little empirical evidence on this point.[4] A "no harm in one more exception" rationale could contribute to the general erosion of the privilege. . . .

Finally, the Independent Counsel, relying on cases such as *United States v. Nixon*, 418 U.S. 683, 710 (1974), and *Branzburg v. Hayes*, 408 U.S. 665 (1972), urges that privileges be strictly construed because they are inconsistent with the

---

[4] Empirical evidence on the privilege is limited. Three studies do not reach firm conclusions on whether limiting the privilege would discourage full and frank communication. Alexander, The Corporate Attorney Client Privilege: A Study of the Participants, 63 St. John's L. Rev. 191 (1989); Zacharias, Rethinking Confidentiality, 74 Iowa L. Rev. 352 (1989); Comment, Functional Overlap Between the Lawyer and Other Professionals: Its Implications for the Privileged Communications Doctrine, 71 Yale L.J. 1226 (1962). These articles note that clients are often uninformed or mistaken about the privilege, but suggest that a substantial number of clients and attorneys think the privilege encourages candor. Two of the articles conclude that a substantial number of clients and attorneys think the privilege enhances open communication, Alexander, *supra*, at 244–246, 261, and that the absence of a privilege would be detrimental to such communication, Comment, 71 Yale L.J., *supra*, at 1236. The third article suggests instead that while the privilege is perceived as important to open communication, limited exceptions to the privilege might not discourage such communication, Zacharias, *supra*, at 382, 386.

paramount judicial goal of truth seeking. But both *Nixon* and *Branzburg* dealt with the creation of privileges not recognized by the common law, whereas here we deal with one of the oldest recognized privileges in the law. And we are asked not simply to "construe" the privilege, but to narrow it, contrary to the weight of the existing body of caselaw.

Reversed.

JUSTICE O'CONNOR, with whom JUSTICE SCALIA and JUSTICE THOMAS join, dissenting.

[A] criminal defendant's right to exculpatory evidence or a compelling law enforcement need for information may, where the testimony is not available from other sources, override a client's posthumous interest in confidentiality.

[A] deceased client may retain a personal, reputational, and economic interest in confidentiality. But, after death, the potential that disclosure will harm the client's interest has been greatly diminished, and the risk that the client will be held criminally liable has abated altogether. Thus, . . . terminating the privilege upon the client's death "could not to any substantial degree lessen the encouragement for free disclosure which is [its] purpose." 1 J. Strong, McCormick on Evidence § 94, p. 350 (4th ed. 1992). This diminished risk is coupled with a heightened urgency for discovery of a deceased client's communications in the criminal context. The privilege does not "protect disclosure of the underlying facts by those who communicated with the attorney," *Upjohn*, [449 U.S. at 395 . . . , and were the client living, prosecutors could grant immunity and compel the relevant testimony. After a client's death, however, if the privilege precludes an attorney from testifying in the client's stead, a complete "loss of crucial information" will often result, see 24 C. Wright & K. Graham, Federal Practice and Procedure § 5498, p. 484 (1986).

[T]he costs of recognizing an absolute posthumous privilege can be inordinately high. Extreme injustice may occur, for example, where a criminal defendant seeks disclosure of a deceased client's confession to the offense. See *State v. Macumber*, 112 Ariz. 569, 571, 544 P.2d 1084, 1086 (1976). [T]he paramount value that our criminal justice system places on protecting an innocent defendant should outweigh a deceased client's interest in preserving confidences.

Moreover, . . . there is authority . . . that a deceased client's communications may be revealed, even in circumstances outside of the testamentary context. California's Evidence Code, for example, provides that the attorney-client privilege continues only until the deceased client's estate is finally distributed . . . Cal. Evid. Code Ann. § 954 . . . . [A] state appellate court has admitted an attorney's testimony concerning a deceased client's communications after "balanc[ing] the necessity for revealing the substance of the [attorney-client conversation] against the unlikelihood of any cognizable injury to the rights, interests, estate or memory of [the client]." *Cohen*, 357 A.2d, at 693. The American Law Institute . . . has . . . recommended withholding the privilege when the communication "bears on a litigated issue of pivotal significance" and has suggested that courts "balance the interest in confidentiality against any exceptional need for the communication."

Restatement (Third) of the Law Governing Lawyers § 127, at 431, Comment d; see also 2 C. Mueller & L. Kirkpatrick, Federal Evidence, § 199, p.380 (2d ed. 1994) ("[I]f a deceased client has confessed to criminal acts that are later charged to another, surely the latter's need for evidence sometimes outweighs the interest in preserving the confidences").

Where the exoneration of an innocent criminal defendant or a compelling law enforcement interest is at stake, the harm of precluding critical evidence that is unavailable by any other means outweighs the potential disincentive to forthright communication. [T]he cost of silence warrants a narrow exception to the rule that the attorney-client privilege survives the death of the client. . . .

NOTES AND QUESTIONS

1. There are several parallels between *Swidler & Berlin* and *Jaffe v. Redmond*, 518 U.S. 1 (1996), *infra*, the case announcing the existence of a federal psychotherapist privilege. As in *Jaffe*, although the lower court cited both instrumental and humanistic rationales for the privilege, the Supreme Court chose to rely exclusively on instrumental reasoning.

2. A further parallel is that, as in *Jaffe*, the lead opinion in *Swidler & Berlin* appeals in a footnote to empirical research to justify its decision. The Court's decision to rely on the instrumental theory helps explain why the Court felt obliged to point to empirical evidence supporting the behavioral assumption that clients would not consult attorneys or make necessary revelations but for the existence of a privilege. However, as we saw in Section A.1 *supra*, on close scrutiny the studies cited in *Jaffe* did not bear out the generalization that in the typical case the patient would either not consult a therapist or divulge essential information but for the assurance of confidentiality furnished by an evidentiary privilege. Other commentators have reached the same conclusion about the attorney-client studies in *Swidler & Berlin*. Wydick, *The Attorney-Client Privilege: Does It Really Have Life Everlasting?*, 87 Ky. L.J. 1165, 1173–74 (1999).

3. The Court pointed out that the weight of authority favored the view that the privilege both survived and remained absolute in character even after the client's death. In the Court's view, the Independent Counsel was proposing a novel exception to the scope of an existing privilege. As we pointed out in Chapter 25, as a general proposition, the Supreme Court and the lower federal courts have recognized every privilege that was set out in draft article V and refused to recognize the privileges omitted from the draft. Here, we see the Court similarly refusing to recognize an exception that was not set out in the draft rules.

B. THE SPOUSAL PRIVILEGES AND OTHER CONFIDENTIAL FAMILY COMMUNICATIONS

In Chapter 7, we considered the question of spousal *incompetency* — now abolished everywhere. In this section, we first turn to the doctrine of spousal *disqualification*, the power to disqualify a person and effectively render him or her incompetent as a witness. In some jurisdictions, this power enables the party spouse to prevent the witness spouse from testifying against her; in other jurisdictions, it entitles the witness spouse to refuse to testify against the party spouse; in still other jurisdictions, both spouses enjoy the power. In addition, in virtually all jurisdictions there is a related, but fundamentally different, *privilege* protecting confidential communications between spouses. Thus, there are two distinct spousal privileges: a testimonial privilege and a confidential communications privilege.

1. The Disqualification Power

Although both the testimonial and communications privileges promote the general policy of protecting the marital relationship, there are significant procedural differences. Unlike the testimonial privilege, the communications privilege does not keep the witness entirely off the stand; rather, it merely prevents the witness spouse from answering questions calling for the substance of confidential conversations with the other spouse. The communications privilege differs in another respect; the testimonial privilege can be invoked only during the marriage, but the communications privilege survives the marriage's termination and can be asserted later. *Pereira v. United States*, 347 U.S. 1, 6 (1954).

The proposed Article V of the Federal Rules of Evidence contained a marked departure from the common law: they would have retained the testimonial disqualification but abolished the communications privilege.

Draft Rule 505 — Husband-Wife Privilege

(a) General rule of privilege. An accused in a criminal proceeding has a privilege to prevent his spouse from testifying against him.

(b) Who may claim the privilege. The privilege may be claimed by the accused or by the spouse on his behalf. The authority of the spouse to do so is presumed in the absence of evidence to the contrary.

(c) Exceptions. There is no privilege under this rule (1) in proceedings in which one spouse is charged with a crime against the person or property of the other or of a child of either, or with a crime against the person or property of a third person committed in the course of committing a crime against the other, or (2) as to matters occurring prior to the marriage, or (3) in proceedings in which a spouse is charged with importing an alien for prostitution or other immoral purpose in violation of 8 U.S.C. § 1328, with transporting a female in interstate commerce for immoral purposes or other offense in violation of 18 U.S.C. §§ 2421–2424, or with violation of other similar statutes.

The Advisory Committee Note to proposed Rule 505 declared:

> While some 10 jurisdictions recognize a privilege not to testify against one's spouse in a criminal case, and a much smaller number do so in civil cases, the great majority recognize no privilege on the part of the testifying spouse and this is the position taken by the rule. . . .
>
> The rule recognizes no privilege [for spousal communications]. . . . The traditional justifications for privileges . . . have been the prevention of

marital dissension and the repugnancy of requiring a person to condemn or be condemned by his spouse. These considerations bear no relevancy to marital communications. Nor can it be assumed that marital conduct will be affected by a privilege . . . of whose existence the parties in all likelihood are unaware. The other communication privileges, by way of contrast, have as one party a professional person who can be expected to inform the other of the existence of the privilege.

However, as we have seen, the Committee failed to persuade Congress. As a matter of case law, the Supreme Court has adopted a spousal testimonial privilege that differs from proposed Rule 505 and many state court versions of the privilege.

TRAMMEL v. UNITED STATES
445 U.S. 40 (1980)

CHIEF JUSTICE BURGER delivered the opinion of the Court.

We granted certiorari to consider whether an accused may invoke the privilege against adverse spousal testimony so as to exclude the voluntary testimony of his wife. This calls for a re-examination of *Hawkins v. United States*, 358 U.S. 74 (1958).

[Trammel was indicted for conspiring to import heroin into the United States. The indictment named several unindicted co-conspirators, including his wife. According to the indictment, Mrs. Trammel traveled to Thailand where she purchased drugs. During a customs search on her return, the drugs were discovered, and she was arrested. After discussions with Drug Enforcement Administration agents, she agreed to cooperate with the Government. Prior to trial, Trammel attemted to prevent her from testifying against him by asserting a spousal testimonial privilege. The District Court ruled that although Mrs. Trammel could not disclose any confidential communications with her husband, she was otherwise a competent prosecution witness. At trial, her testimony constituted virtually the entire case against Trammel. He was found guilty.]

In the Court of Appeals petitioner's only claim of error was that the admission of the adverse testimony of his wife . . . contravened this Court's teaching in *Hawkins v. United States* . . . . The Court of Appeals rejected this contention. It concluded that *Hawkins* did not prohibit "the voluntary testimony of a spouse who appears as an unindicted co-conspirator under grant of immunity from the Government in return for her testimony."

The privilege claimed by petitioner has ancient roots. Despite its medieval origins, this rule of spousal disqualification remained intact in most common-law jurisdictions well into the 19th century. It was applied by this Court in *Stein v. Bowman*, 13 Pet. 209, 220–23 (1839) and again in *Jin Fuey Moy v. United States*, 254 U.S. 189, 195 (1920). It was not until 1933, in *Funk v. United States*, 290 U.S. 371, that this Court abolished the testimonial disqualification in the federal courts to permit the spouse of a defendant to testify in the defendant's behalf. *Funk*, however, left undisturbed the rule that either prevent the other from giving adverse testimony. *Id.*, at 373. The rule thus evolved into one of privilege rather than one of absolute disqualification. *See* J. Maguire, Evidence, Common Sense and Common Law 78-92 (1947).

The modern justification for this privilege against adverse spousal testimony is its perceived role in fostering the harmony and sanctity of the marriage relationship. Notwithstanding this benign purpose, the rule was sharply criticized. Professor Wigmore termed it "the merest anachronism in legal theory and an indefensible obstruction to truth in practice." 8 Wigmore § 2228, at 221. In its place, Wigmore suggested a privilege protecting only private marital communications, modeled on the privilege between attorney and client. *See* 8 Wigmore § 2332 *et seq.*

In *Hawkins v. United States*, 358 U.S. 74 (1958), this Court considered the continued vitality of the privilege against adverse spousal testimony in the federal courts. There the District Court had permitted petitioner's wife, over his objection, to testify against him. With one questioning concurring opinion, the Court held the wife's testimony inadmissible; it took note of the critical comments that the common-law rule had engendered but chose not to abandon it. Also rejected was the Government's suggestion that the Court modify the privilege by vesting it in the witness spouse, with freedom to testify or not independent of the defendant's control. The Court viewed this proposed modification as antithetical to the widespread belief, evidenced in the rules then in effect in a majority of the States and in England, "that the law should not force or encourage testimony which might alienate husband and wife, or further inflame existing domestic differences."

Since 1958, when *Hawkins* was decided, support for the privilege against adverse spousal testimony has been corroded further. Thirty-one jurisdictions then allowed an accused a privilege to prevent adverse spousal testimony. The number has now declined to 24 . . . . The trend in state law toward divesting the accused of the privilege to bar adverse spousal testimony[10] has special relevance because the law of marriage and domestic relations are concerns traditionally reserved to the states.

[T]he *Hawkins* privilege is not needed to protect information privately disclosed between husband and wife in the confidence of the marital relationship . . . . Those confidences are privileged under the independent rule protecting confidential marital communications. *Blau v. United States*, 340 U.S. 332 (1951). The *Hawkins* privilege is invoked, not to exclude private marital communications, but rather to exclude evidence of criminal acts and of communications made in the presence of third persons.

No other testimonial privilege sweeps so broadly. The privileges between priest and penitent, attorney and client, and physician and patient limit protection to private communications. The *Hawkins* rule stands in marked contrast to these three privileges. Its protection is not limited to confidential communications; rather it permits an accused to exclude all adverse spousal testimony. As Jeremy Bentham

---

[10] In 1965, California took the privilege from the defendant-spouse and vested it in the witness-spouse, accepting a study commission recommendation that the "latter [was] more likely than the former to determine whether or not to claim the privilege on the basis of the probable effect on the marital relationship." *See* Cal. Evid. Code Ann. §§ 970-973 (West 1966 and Supp. 1979) and 1 California Law Revision Commission, Recommendation and Study relating to the Marital "For and Against" Testimonial Privilege, at F-5 (1956).

observed, such a privilege goes far beyond making "every man's house his castle," and permits a person to convert his house into "a den of thieves." 5 Rationale of Judicial Evidence 340 (1827).

The ancient foundations for so sweeping a privilege have long since disappeared. Nowhere in the common law world . . . is a woman regarded as chattel or demeaned by denial of a separate legal identity. The contemporary justification for affording an accused such a privilege is also unpersuasive. When one spouse is willing to testify against the other in a criminal proceeding — whatever the motivation — their relationship is almost certainly in disrepair; there is probably little in the way of marital harmony for the privilege to preserve. In these circumstances, a rule of evidence that permits an accused to prevent adverse spousal testimony seems far more likely to frustrate justice than to foster family peace.[12] Indeed, there is reason to believe that vesting the privilege in the accused could actually undermine the marital relationship. For example, in a case such as this, the Government is unlikely to offer a wife immunity and lenient treatment if it knows that her husband can prevent her from giving adverse testimony. If the Government is dissuaded from making such an offer, the privilege can have the untoward effect of permitting one spouse to escape justice at the expense of the other. It hardly seems conducive to the preservation of the marital relation to place a wife in jeopardy solely by virtue of her husband's control over her testimony.

"Reason and experience" no longer justify so sweeping a rule as that found in *Hawkins*. [T]he existing rule should be modified so that the witness spouse alone has a privilege to refuse to testify adversely; the witness may be neither compelled to testify nor foreclosed from testifying. This modification — vesting the privilege in the witness spouse — furthers the important public interest in marital harmony without unduly burdening legitimate law enforcement needs.

NOTES

1.   Both *Trammel* and the case it overruled, *Hawkins*, made certain sociological assumptions about the general state of the institution of marriage in the United States. Those assumptions "were hardly indisputable." 2 McCormick, Evidence § 328, at 386 (4th ed. 1992). Are the *Trammel* Court's assumptions justifiable? Or is *Trammel* simply another illustration of the courts' unfortunate tendency to confuse *a priori* conjecture with empirical fact? How does the Court know that those assumptions are true? Before indulging in those assumptions, should the Court demand empirical verification of the assumptions?

2.   Do you agree with the Court's reasoning in *Trammel*? One respected authority, Professor Lempert, does not. Lempert, *A Right to Every Woman's Evidence*, 66 Iowa L. Rev. 725 (1981). Professor Lempert points out that the government can pressure a wife into "consenting" to testify against her husband and that while the *Hawkins* case was pending before the Court, the Court

---

[12] It is argued that abolishing the privilege will permit the Government to come between husband and wife, pitting one against the other. That, too, misses the mark. Neither *Hawkins*, nor any other privilege, prevents the Government from enlisting one spouse to give information concerning the other or to aid in the other's apprehension. It is only the spouse's testimony in the courtroom that is prohibited.

discovered that "Hawkins' wife had been imprisoned as a material witness and released only after giving a three thousand dollar bond conditioned upon her appearance in court as a witness for the United States." *Id.* at 733. *Hawkins* illustrates how the prosecution can obtain "apparently voluntary testimony" from an unwilling spouse. *Id.*

Would Professor Lempert's argument still have merit if, in applying *Trammel*, the courts allowed the defendant to challenge the voluntariness of his spouse's consent to testifying?

3. In the full opinion, the *Trammel* Court cites both current Federal Rule 501 and draft Rule 505. Remember that Congress balked at enacting Rule 505. Nevertheless, the Court treated the issue of the continued existence of the disqualification as an Article V problem. Suppose alternatively that the Court had decided that Rule 601 governed. If the Court had given Rule 601 a plain meaning reading, could the Court have justified recognizing any disqualification? What are the legitimate uses of the unenacted provisions of Article V and the accompanying Advisory Committee Notes: as an indication of what Congress considered a "privilege" problem governed by Article V; as an indication of what the evidentiary norms should be in the privilege area; or as a mere description of what the prevailing privileges rules are — or at least were when the Notes were written? *Article V. Privileges, in* EMERGING PROBLEMS UNDER THE FEDERAL RULES OF EVIDENCE 85, 111–13 (3d ed. 1998).

4. Courts have divided over whether there should be a "joint participants" exception — that is, whenever both spouses conspired or participated in committing the charged crime — to the disqualification power. Assume, for example, that Devitt's wife helped him plan the crime and that Morena follows the *Trammel* decision. At trial, Mrs. Devitt asserts her right under *Trammel* to refuse to testify against her husband. Should she be compelled to testify over Devitt's objection? (Assume there is no self-incrimination problem; ordinarily, the witness will be given immunity or some sort of "deal.") To date, the majority of federal circuits that have considered such an exception have adopted it. *See, e.g., United States v. Keck*, 773 F.2d 759, 766 (7th Cir. 1985). However, the Second and Third Circuits have rejected the exception. *In re Koecher*, 755 F.2d 1022 (2d Cir.), *cert. granted*, 474 U.S. 815 (1985), *vacated as moot*, 475 U.S. 133 (1986); *Appeal of Malfitano*, 633 F.2d 276, 279 (3d Cir. 1980).

2. The Spousal Communications Privilege

Trammel recognizes a privilege that, in some cases, keeps the witness spouse altogether off the witness stand. Another evidentiary doctrine provides a second layer of protection for the spousal relationship: the privilege for confidential spousal communications. This privilege comes into play after the witness takes the stand, when the question would require the witness spouse to disclose a protected communication.

a.   The Types of Information Protected by the Spousal Communications Privilege

1)   The Definition of "Confidential Communication"

In the last chapter we examined the conventional definition of the word "communication." In the case of most privileges, "communication" has the ordinary lay usage of information conveyed orally or in writing from one person to another. The issue is whether that definition obtains here. To answer that question, consider this excerpt from a seminal Supreme Court decision on the spousal communications privilege:

BLAU v. UNITED STATES
340 U.S. 332 (1951)

JUSTICE BLACK delivered the opinion of the Court.

Petitioner was summoned to appear before a federal district grand jury. He . . . refused to reveal the whereabouts of his wife, who was wanted by the grand jury as a witness in connection with the same investigation. As to this refusal to testify, petitioner asserted his privilege against disclosing confidential communications between husband and wife. The district judge overruled [the-claim[] of privilege and sentenced petitioner to . . . prison for contempt of court. The Court of Appeals for the Tenth Circuit affirmed.

[We must] . . . consider[] the validity of the sentence insofar as it rests on the failure of petitioner to disclose the whereabouts of his wife. In *Wolfle v. United States*, 291 U.S. 7, this Court recognized that a confidential communication between husband and wife was privileged. It is not disputed in the present case that petitioner obtained his knowledge as to where his wife was by communication from her. Nevertheless, the Government insists that he should be denied the benefit of the privilege because he failed to prove that the information was privately conveyed. This contention ignores the rule that marital communications are presumptively confidential. *Wolfle v. United States, supra*, at 14; Wigmore, Evidence, § 2336. The Government made no effort to overcome the presumption. In this case, moreover, the communication to petitioner was of the kind likely to be confidential. Petitioner's wife, according to the district judge, knew that she and a number of others were "wanted" as witnesses by the grand jury but she "hid out, apparently so that the process . . . could not be served upon her." Several of the witnesses who appeared were put in jail for contempt of court. Under such circumstances, it seems highly probable that Mrs. Blau secretly told her husband where she could be found. Petitioner's refusal to betray his wife's trust therefore was both understandable and lawful. We have no doubt that he was entitled to claim his privilege.

QUESTIONS

1. Justice Black speculates that "it seems highly probable that Mrs. Blau secretly told her husband where she could be found." Under the federal statutory scheme, the trial judge should assess that probability under Rule 104(a). Justice Black's statement raises two issues. The first is procedural: Who has the burden of proving the basis of Blau's knowledge of his wife's whereabouts? Since the person invoking the privilege knows the basis of his or her knowledge, that party usually assumes the burden. But note the presumption Justice Black mentions. Many lower courts have construed Justice Black's statement as creating a presumption that "communications between spouses are . . . confidential." *Proctor & Gamble Co. v. Bankers Trust Co.*, 909 F. Supp. 525, 527 (S.D. Ohio 1995).

2. The second issue is substantive: As a matter of policy, should information standing alone be protected? Certainly, it would have been objectionable if the questioner had asked what his wife told Blau about her whereabouts. On its face, that question calls for the revelation of spousal communications. But the questioner was not quite so blatant in *Blau*. Would we reach the same result if Blau's knowledge of his wife's whereabouts rested only partially on her communication? Suppose that after speaking with her, Blau had visited her. Should that fact change the result in *Blau?*

3. *Blau* raises the question of when the normal definition of "communication" should be expanded to include information. Some courts have taken another step in expanding the definition of communication for purpose of the spousal privilege. The following article discusses the expansion.

Comment, *The Husband-Wife Privileges of Testimonial Non-Disclosure*
56 Nw. U. L. Rev. 208, 220–22 (1961)

There is a wide variance in the decisions purporting to define communication, though they may be categorized in one of five areas, *viz.*, (1) verbal exchanges whether oral or written, (2) acts performed with manifest intent to convey information, (3) acts performed with intent to convey information, the intent being implied from the propinquity of the marital relation, (4) acts performed with knowledge that they might convey information, but apparently lacking in intent to so convey, and (5) any act or effect observed by the actor's spouse accidentally, but consequent upon the marital relation.

Most of the cases adhere to the first definition, though an increasing number of courts seem prone to privilege acts which are manifestly intended to impart information, such as displaying stolen goods to one's wife.

The third category may be illustrated by the husband who develops a mental problem or disease. Though he may seek to conceal it, the very closeness of a normal marital relation will cause its revelation; and in the event that his wife's knowledge may constitute prejudicial testimony at a later date, the courts should look to the circumstances inducing his attempted concealment, and imply intent to communicate by virtue of propinquity, thus preserving the privilege where it would be manifestly against the policy of inducing and protecting marital confidence to deny it, and likewise offensive to society. The lack of overt intent to convey information results from false pride or shame, and should not prevent the application of the privilege to the knowledge acquired by the partner spouse. Some courts have been willing to extend the privilege to the knowledge acquired by the partner spouse. Some courts have been willing to extend the privilege to this third category and the opinions seem well reasoned.

Though some courts have extended the privilege in the fourth category, they seem to torture the policy by disallowing disclosure of actions performed without express or implied intent to convey information, simply because such actions are fortuitously observed by the actor's spouse. No privilege should be allowed ostensibly to protect and foster communication when, in fact, the communicator had no intent to impart knowledge. Like considerations apply also to the fifth category, which is illustrated by the situation wherein a husband places papers in his desk knowing and relying on his knowledge that his wife is not wont to look into his desk, but she chances to see them.

NOTES AND PROBLEMS

1.   **Problem 26-4.** Assume Devitt was married at the time of the battery. That evening, Mrs. Devitt hears a noise in the backyard. She walks into the backyard to find Devitt digging a hole to bury property he had stolen from Paterson's apartment. Could she testify over the defense objection that she would be testifying to a spousal communication from Devitt?

2.   **Problem 26-5.** Later Devitt divorces his wife. May Devitt's former wife testify about Devitt's action over a defense objection that she is revealing a spousal communication?

3.   Is there something about the nature of the marital relationship that necessitates broadening the concept of communication? The Advisory Committee's Note to proposed Rule 505 states: "[T]he relationships for which those [professional] privileges arise are essentially and almost exclusively verbal in nature, quite unlike marriage." The Note opposed recognizing a privilege; but once the policy decision is made to recognize a privilege, the large nonverbal component of the spousal relationship arguably cuts in favor of a broad privilege.

2)   The Requirement that the Communication Occur Between Properly Related Parties

At first glance, the application of this requirement to the spousal privilege seems to be a simple matter: We apply the privilege only if the parties were "married" at the time of the communication. However, the issue is not that clear-cut.

The initial question is whether we should limit the evidentiary privilege to persons who are formally married. In the past four decades, we have witnessed a revolution in society's attitude toward the cohabitation of unmarried persons. We now extend many of the legal protections formerly reserved for married persons to cohabiting persons. If we begin to treat cohabitation as the functional legal equivalent of marriage in some respects, why not in this respect as well? Suppose that Devitt were cohabiting with the woman in the last hypothetical rather than being married to her. If they had been cohabiting for a substantial period of time and had bought personal and real property together, why deny them the protection of the evidentiary privilege? The received orthodoxy is that they are not entitled to any privilege. What problems or issues do you see in extending the privilege to cohabiting parties?

Additionally, even when the marriage is technically valid, the marriage may be a "sham." In *Lutwak v. United States*, 344 U.S. 604 (1953), the defendants had been convicted of conspiring to defraud the United States by obtaining illegal entry under the War Brides Act. Writing for the majority, Justice Minton specifically stated that "[w]e do not believe that the validity of the marriages is material." (*id.* at 611).

NOTES AND PROBLEM

1. Even assuming that a particular marriage was valid at the time of the ceremony, it may no longer be viable at the time of the communication. Should that affect the application of the spousal privilege? The traditional view is that even here we must uphold the privilege. However, some courts have been willing to rethink the assumptions underlying a mechanical application of the privilege. *People v. D'Amato*, 105 Misc. 2d 1048, 430 N.Y.S.2d 521, 522–24 (Sup. Ct. 1980).

2. **Problem 26-6.** The stated justification for the spousal privilege is protecting the marital relationship. If Devitt's marriage had been in shambles, would it make any sense to apply the privilege at the cost of suppressing the truth? Remember the Supreme Court's reasoning in *Trammel v. United States*, 445 U.S. 40 (1980). Does the answer depend on whether the deterioration occurred by the time of (a) the communication or (b) the trial? Even if Devitt's marriage had been in shambles, would a refusal to apply the privilege chill the candor between other spouses? For that matter, can courts frame judicially manageable standards to determine when a marriage is in such disarray that it no longer merits the protection of the privilege? Even if courts are generally unwilling to inquire whether a marriage has deteriorated, should they recognize a privilege when the spouses are permanently separated? *United States v. Byrd*, 750 F.2d 585, 591–94 (7th Cir. 1984).

3. What about same-sex relations? While most jurisdictions deny a privilege to heterosexual couples who cohabit, those couples have chosen not to avail themselves of the opportunity to marry that the law affords them. Comment, *The Husband-Wife Evidentiary Privileges: Is Marriage Really Necessary?*, Teri S. O'Brien, 1977 ARIZ. ST. L.J. 411. At present, there are only a few jurisdictions in which same-sex couples may marry. *Varnum v. Brien*, 763 N.W.2d 862 (Iowa 2009). Thus, the case for a privilege for same-sex couples seems stronger, since in most states they currently do not have that choice.

3)   The Requirement that the Communication Be Incident to the Relationship

Even a confidential communication between properly related persons is unprotected unless it occurs incident to the relationship. In the case of the professional privileges, it is usually rather easy for the courts to administer that requirement.

It is more difficult to apply such a requirement to spousal communications. The marital relationship is so broad, encompassing such a wide range of human activities, that it is difficult to find a subject that spouses would not discuss with each other in the normal course of their marital relation. As a practical matter, the spousal privilege is the hardest privilege to defeat on the theory that the communication was not incident to the relationship.

While it is difficult to do so, it is not impossible. The party resisting the privilege claim typically attempts to prove that there was another relationship between the spouses and that the communication occurred incident to that relationship.

PROBLEMS

1.   **Problem 26-7.** Suppose that in our torts case, Ms. Hill and her husband were partners in a landscaping and gardening business. It was a small business, and both Ms. Hill and her husband did a good deal of manual labor involved in the landscaping and gardening. Approximately one month before trial, Ms. Hill and her husband had a long, detailed discussion of the extent of her physical injuries. Polecat Motors' attorney believes that during the discussion, Ms. Hill told her husband that her injuries are not as severe as she claims in her complaint. At trial, Polecat Motors' attorney calls Ms. Hill's husband as an adverse witness. The following occurs:

Q: And both of you do some of the manual work in this business?

A: Yes.

Q: So your wife's physical condition is of interest to you as her business partner. Isn't that correct?

A: Right.

Q: How much money you make as her partner depends in part on how much landscaping she is capable of doing?

A: Yes.

Q: Isn't it true that during that conversation you admitted you had with your wife, she told you that she expected to be back at work and "right as rain" within three months?

D: Your Honor, I object to that question on the ground that it calls for privileged information.

P: Your Honor, it's clear that Ms. Hill gave the witness this information because he is her business partner. This wasn't a husband-wife communication.

As trial judge, how would you rule on the objection? Must Polecat Motors' attorney convince you that the statement related only to the business partnership, or is it enough that you conclude that Ms. Hill would have made the statement to the witness even if they had not been married?

2. **Problem 26-8.** Suppose that Devitt's wife hated Paterson and had helped Devitt plan an assault on the complainant. Mrs. Devitt would then be chargeable as a coconspirator. Should her status as a coconspirator defeat the privilege? *See United States v. Picciandra*, 788 F.2d 39, 43 (1st Cir. 1986) (yes); *People v. Watkins*, 89 Misc. 2d 870, 393 N.Y.S.2d 283, 285–86 (1977), *aff'd*, 63 A.D.2d 1033, 406 N.Y.S.2d 343, *cert. denied*, 439 U.S. 984 (1978) (yes). The case for overriding the privilege seems especially strong when the other relationship between the spouses is one of criminal agency.

b. Special Exceptions to the Spousal Privilege

Compared to the other privileges, the spousal privilege is subject to relatively few exceptions. Though the number of exceptions is small, the exceptions represent important inroads on the privilege's scope. In some cases, the exceptions are common to most privileges. For example, California Evidence Code § 984 provides:

There is no privilege under this article in

(a) A proceeding brought by or on behalf of one spouse against the other spouse.

(b) A proceeding between a surviving spouse and a person who claims through the deceased spouse, regardless of whether such claim is by testate or intestate succession or by inter vivos transaction.

Section 981 reads:

There is no privilege under this article if the communication was made, in whole or in part, to enable or aid anyone to commit or plan to commit a crime or a fraud.

We have already seen that most privileges yield when the purpose of the communication was "to enable or aid anyone to commit or plan to commit a crime or a fraud." It is important, though, to understand the limited scope of this exception. Would it come into play if Devitt disclosed the battery to his wife the day after the battery? Suppose that the day before the battery, he suggested to his wife that he was planning on committing the battery. What facts must you add before the exception comes into play?

Other exceptions are unique to the spousal privilege. Most jurisdictions recognize an injured spouse exception to both the privilege and the disqualification. California Evidence Code § 985 codifies the exception in this fashion:

There is no privilege under this article in a criminal proceeding in which one spouse is charged with:

(a)   A crime committed at any time against the person or property of the other spouse or of a child of either.

(b)   A crime committed at any time against the person or property of a third person committed in the course of committing a crime against the person or property of the other spouse.

(c)   Bigamy.

(d)   A crime defined by Section 270 [child neglect] or 270a [non-support of wife] of the Penal Code.

There is an element of inconsistency and unfairness when the defendant commits "offenses against the marital relation" while simultaneously invoking the spousal privilege and attempting to "hide the truth behind" the same marital relation.

Finally, consider California Evidence Code § 987:

> There is no privilege under this article in a criminal proceeding in which the communication is offered in evidence by a defendant who is one of the spouses between whom the communication was made.

In the case of most of the other exceptions, the rationale is a variation of the theme that society has countervailing interests that override the interests of the holder of the privilege. In this case, the focus is different; the party seeking disclosure is the defendant spouse. Like California, as a matter of common law or statutory evidence law many jurisdictions permit the defendant to override the privilege; and a few have gone to the length of granting the defendant a constitutional right to do so. However, not all jurisdictions agree that the correct balance favors disclosure. How should the balance be struck?

PROBLEM

Problem 26-9. Suppose that Devitt's attack on Paterson was part of a rampage that afternoon, which began with a violent attack on his wife an hour before his attack on Paterson. Devitt and his wife had quarreled violently, and the quarrel triggered both attacks. Could the prosecutor call Devitt's wife as a witness to the quarrel and Devitt's battery on her to prove the motive for the subsequent battery? *See People v. Love*, 339 N.W.2d 493, 496–97 (Mich. Ct. App. 1983) ("a crime committed against a third person as part of the same criminal transaction as a crime committed against a spouse 'grows out of a personal wrong or injury' done to the spouse . . .").

What if Paterson and Devitt's wife were acquaintances and Mrs. Devitt had referred to Paterson during the quarrel immediately before Devitt's attack on his wife. Do these facts change the result?

3.   A Parent-Child Privilege?

Once we accept the proposition that the spousal relation warrants the protection of an evidentiary privilege, the question naturally arises whether we should grant similar protection to other close family relationships such as parent and child or siblings. The analogy is at least superficially appealing. Even if we should not allow a child to disqualify a parent as a potential witness against the child, the analogy suggests that we ought to give the child or the parent the more limited protection of an evidentiary privilege for confidential communications. Given the high divorce rate in the United States, a person's parent-child relationship can be much longer lasting than a spousal relationship. As we shall see later in this chapter, in *Jaffee v. Redmond*, 518 U.S. 1 (1996), Justice Scalia asked in dissent: "Would your mental health be more significantly impaired by preventing from seeing a psychotherapist, or preventing from getting advice from your mom?"

Many academic commentators favor recognizing a parent-child privilege. *See, e.g.*, Comment, 16 SAN DIEGO L. REV. 811 (1979); Comment, 47 FORDHAM L. REV. 771 (1979); Comment, 1978 BYU L. REV. 1002. Other legal traditions recognize a parent-child privilege. Note, *Parent-Child Loyalty and Testimonial Privilege*, 100 HARV. L. REV. 910, 912 (1987). "[T]he prevailing view in the civil law countries of Western Europe is that no person will be forced to divulge confidences between him or herself and another family member." Watts, *The Parent-Child Privilege: Hardly a New or Revolutionary Concept*, 28 WM. & MARY L. REV. 583, 593 (1987). The American Bar Association's Criminal Justice Section has proposed a model statute generally providing that "[n]either a parent nor the parent's child may be compelled to answer a question concerning confidential communications [between them]." *Id.* at 619–31.

Three states (Idaho, Massachusetts, and Minnesota) have enacted statutes recognizing some form of testimonial or communications privilege. Watts, *Do We Need a Parent-Child Privilege? Yes*, 2 CRIM. JUST. 11, 34 (Summer 1987). In *In re Agosto*, 553 F. Supp. 1298 (D. Nev. 1983), analogizing to *Trammel*, Chief Judge Clairborne recognized a child's right to refuse to testify adversely to a parent:

> Applying this rationale to the case at bar, it is reasonable to hold that Charles Agosto may claim the parent-child privilege not only for confidential communications which transpired between his father and himself, but he may likewise claim the privilege for protection against being compelled to be a witness and testify adversely against his father in any criminal proceeding.

Id. at 1325.

However, the vast majority of courts have refused to recognize such a privilege. With the exception of New York and one federal district court, most jurisdictions recognize neither a testimonial nor a communications privilege for the parent-child relationship. *In re Doe*, 842 F.2d 244 (10th Cir.), *cert. denied*, 488 U.S. 894 (1988); *In re Santarelli*, 740 F.2d 816, 816–17 (11th Cir. 1984), *United States v. Ismail*, 756 F.2d 1253, 1258 (6th Cir. 1985).

Is the parent-child relationship sufficiently analogous to the spousal relation to justify a disqualification power or a more limited communications privilege? *People v. Doe*, 61 A.D. 2d 426, 403 N.Y.S.2d 375 (1978), accepted the analogy. However, some commentators argue that the analogy to the spousal relation is specious. Is a young child likely to be sufficiently aware of a disqualification or privilege to be influenced by its existence? Does a child need the encouragement of a privilege to consult his or her parents?

C. MEDICAL PRIVILEGE: PHYSICIAN, PSYCHOTHERAPIST, ETC.

1. Overview

The American Medical Association imposed a confidentiality duty on its members in its first code of ethics in 1847. The AMA still prescribes that duty:

> A physician may not reveal the confidence entrusted to him in the course of medical attendance, or the deficiencies he may observe in the character of patients, unless he is required to do so by law or unless it becomes necessary in order to protect the welfare of the individual or of the community.

AMERICAN MEDICAL ASSOCIATION, PRINCIPLES OF MEDICAL ETHICS § 9.

Although the medical privileges did not exist at common law, they were among the first to be codified. The first statute was enacted in New York in 1928, and statutes creating some form of medical privilege now exist in at least 42 states. The very existence of these statutes demonstrates the courts' reluctance to recognize a medical privilege as a matter of decisional law. Courts routinely declare that there is no common-law medical privilege. *Whalen v. Roe*, 429 U.S. 589, 602 n.28 (1977); *Patterson v. Caterpillar, Inc.*, 70 F.3d 503, 506–07 (7th Cir. 1995); *Perkins v. United States*, 877 F. Supp. 330, 332 (E.D. Tex. 1995). Even Congress' enactment of the Health Insurance Portability and Accountability Act has not changed the state of the common law, and there is no general federal medical privilege.

What do you think accounts for that reluctance? Is the medical relationship somehow less important than the legal relationship? Is there less need for a medical privilege? Given the stakes in medical care — the preservation of life and the prevention of pain — will the absence of a privilege deter the patient from making full disclosure to the physician? In its 1996 decision in *Jaffee v. Redmond*, 518 U.S. 1 (1996), which recognized a psychotherapist-patient privilege, the Court made clear that it thinks that there is a much weaker case for recognizing a general medical privilege. Justice Stevens noted that:

> [t]reatment by a physician for physical ailments can often proceed successfully on the basis of a physical examination, objective information supplied by the patient, and the results of diagnostic tests. Effective psychotherapy, by contrast, depends upon an atmosphere of confidence and trust in which the patient is willing to make a frank and complete disclosure of facts, emotions, memories, and fears.

Id. at 10. Yet, public opinion polls consistently show that the public attaches a great deal of importance to the privacy of medical information. A. ETZIONI, THE LIMITS OF PRIVACY 148, 158 (1999). In 2004, then Senator Clinton introduced a bill to amend the Federal Rules of Evidence to incorporate a general medical privilege, but the bill never became law.

When it drafted the Federal Rules of Evidence, the Advisory Committee decided to omit a general physician-patient privilege, opting instead for only a psychotherapist-patient privilege. In the Note accompanying proposed Rule 504 on the psychotherapist-patient privilege, the Committee asserted that the courts and legislatures have recognized so many exceptions to the physician-patient privilege that "little if any basis for the privilege" remains. Even the advocates of medical privileges ordinarily concede than the case for a psychotherapist privilege is stronger than the case for a general physician-patient privilege.

NOTES AND PROBLEMS

1. **Problem 26-10.** Suppose that in the *Devitt* case, the defendant consulted a physician the day after the alleged battery. If Devitt told the physician: "I've got some bruises on my chest where a guy punched me," that statement would fall within the orthodox definition of "communication" and be protected by many state versions of the doctor-patient privilege. However, assume that rather than making that statement, Devitt took off his shirt, displayed the bruises and scratches to the physician, and winced painfully when touched. Could the physician testify to his or her observation of the injuries over Devitt's objection? Most statutes codifying the privilege contain broad definitions of "communication." California Evidence Code § 992 is illustrative: "information, including information transmitted by an examination of the patient, transmitted between a patient and his physician."

2. **Problem 26-11.** Suppose that the physician orders a blood test of Devitt and the technician informs the physician that Devitt's blood type is A. Can Devitt preclude the physician from revealing that fact?

3. ***Treatment vs. forensic purposes.*** Chapter 20 discussed the hearsay exception for statements made for medical purposes. In most jurisdictions that exception is limited to statements the patient makes with a view to treatment or diagnosis. The medical privilege is similarly limited. In *Devitt*, assume that as part of pretrial preparation, defense counsel sends Devitt to a serologist for a blood grouping test. The medical privilege would not attach, since the purpose is legal rather than medical. However, what if defense counsel sends Devitt to a psychotherapist and Devitt discloses his inner-most thoughts?

4. **Problem 26-12.** To prepare for trial, Ms. Hill's attorney sends her to Dr. Legomsky for a physical evaluation. Prior to this evaluation, Ms. Hill had never consulted Dr. Legomsky. As she walks into Legomsky's examination room, Ms. Hill tells the doctor, "my attorney sent me. I'm here for that exam to get ready for trial." Legomsky says, "Fine. I'll get all the facts and send the report straight to your lawyer." Dr. Legomsky spends an hour examining Ms. Hill. Just before she leaves, Legomsky says, "you know, it wouldn't be a bad idea if you started using a salve on those real bad burns on your ankles. In addition, twice-a-day baths with oil might help restore some of that skin tissue." Legomsky sends his report to Ms. Hill's attorney. Is the report protected by the physician-patient privilege? What if, as Ms. Hill walks into the examination room, she tells Dr. Legomsky, "I'm here for that exam to get ready for trial. In addition, Doc, the burnt skin around my ankles has been very sensitive lately; it hurts all the time. I'd really appreciate it if you could advise me." Protected?

5. Many jurisdictions recognize a special exception to the medical privilege in child abuse cases. These states have enacted statutes requiring physicians to report

suspected child abuse to the authorities and eliminating any privilege precluding the physician from testifying about the child's injuries at a subsequent prosecution. *E.g.*, Minn. Stat. § 626.556 (the Minnesota Maltreatment of Minors Reporting Act).

2.   Specialized Aspects: The Psychotherapist Privilege

At first, there was no separate psychotherapist-patient privilege. The only available protections were the traditional state physician-patient privileges. Thus, if the psychotherapist was a licensed physician practicing psychiatry, the communications would be protected in a state that recognized a general doctor-patient privilege; otherwise, there was no protection. Non-M.D. psychotherapists argued that confidentiality is even more essential to their profession than it is to the practice of generalized medicine. They have been persuasive. In its commentary on the California statutory privilege, the Report of the California Senate Committee on the Judiciary explained:

> A broad privilege should apply to both psychiatrists and certified psychologists. Psychoanalysis and psychotherapy are dependent upon the fullest revelation of the most intimate and embarrassing details of the patient's life. Research on mental or emotional problems requires similar disclosure. Unless a patient or research subject is assured that such information can and will be held in utmost confidence, he will be reluctant to make the full disclosure upon which diagnosis and treatment or complete and accurate research depends.

> The Law Revision Commission has received several reliable reports that persons in need of treatment sometimes refuse such treatment from psychiatrists because the confidentiality of their communications cannot be assured under existing law. Many of these persons are seriously disturbed and constitute threats to other persons in the community. Accordingly, this article establishes a new privilege that grants to patients of psychiatrists a privilege much broader in scope than the ordinary physician-patient privilege. Although it is recognized that the granting of the privilege may operate in particular cases to withhold relevant information, the interests of society will be better served if psychiatrists are able to assure patients that their confidences will be protected.

The same Federal Rules Advisory Committee that rejected a general physician-patient privilege was willing to codify a psychotherapist-patient privilege. The committee alluded to the psychotherapist's "special need to maintain confidentiality." Given that special need, the Committee proposed Rule 504:

Psychotherapist-Patient Privilege

(a) Definitions.

(1)   A "patient" is a person who consults or is examined or interviewed by a psychotherapist.

(2)   A "psychotherapist" is (A) a person authorized to practice medicine in any state or nation, or reasonably believed by the patient so to be, while engaged in the diagnosis or treatment of

a mental or emotional condition, including drug addiction, or (B) a person licensed or certified as a psychologist under the laws of any state or nation, while similarly engaged.

(3)   A communication is "confidential" if not intended to be disclosed to third persons other than those present to further the interest of the patient in the consultation, examination, or interview, or persons reasonably necessary for the transmission of the communication, or persons who are participating in the diagnosis and treatment under the direction of the psychotherapist, including members of the patient's family.

(b) General rule of privilege. A patient has a privilege to refuse to disclose and to prevent any other person from disclosing confidential communications, made for the purposes of diagnosis or treatment of his mental or emotional condition, including drug addiction, among himself, his psychotherapist, or persons who are participating in the diagnosis or treatment under the direction of the psychotherapist, including members of the patient's family.

. . .

Although Congress decided against enacting the Rule, the Supreme Court later recognized a psychotherapist privilege:

JAFFEE v. REDMOND
518 U.S. 1 (1996)

JUSTICE STEVENS delivered the opinion of the Court.

After a traumatic incident in which she shot and killed a man, a police officer received extensive counseling from a licensed clinical social worker. The question we address is whether statements the officer made to her therapist during the counseling sessions are protected from compelled disclosure in a federal civil action brought by the family of the deceased. [T]he question is whether it is appropriate for federal courts to recognize a "psychotherapist privilege" under Rule 501 of the Federal Rules of Evidence.

Like the spousal and attorney-client privileges, the psychotherapist-patient privilege is "rooted in the imperative need for confidence and trust." *Trammel*, 445 U.S. at 51. Treatment by a physician for physical ailments can often proceed successfully on the basis of a physical examination, objective information supplied by the patient, and the results of diagnostic tests. Effective psychotherapy, by contrast, depends upon an atmosphere of confidence and trust in which the patient is willing to make a frank and complete disclosure of facts, emotions, memories, and fears. Because of the sensitive nature of the problems for which individuals consult psychotherapists, disclosure of confidential communications made during counseling sessions may cause embarrassment or disgrace. For this reason, the mere possibility of disclosure may impede development of the confidential relationship necessary for successful treatment . . . .

The psychotherapist privilege serves the public interest by facilitating the provision of appropriate treatment for individuals suffering the effects of a mental or emotional problem. The mental health of our citizenry, no less than its physical health, is a public good of transcendent importance.[10] In contrast to the significant public and private interests supporting recognition of the privilege, the likely evidentiary benefit that would result from the denial of the privilege is modest. If the privilege were rejected, confidential conversations between psychotherapists and their patients would surely be chilled, particularly when it is obvious that the circumstances that give rise to the need for treatment will probably result in litigation. Without a privilege, much of the desirable evidence to which litigants such as petitioner seek access — for example, admissions against interest by a party — is unlikely to come into being. This unspoken "evidence" will therefore serve no greater truth-seeking function than if it had been spoken and privileged.

That it is appropriate for the federal courts to recognize a psychotherapist privilege under Rule 501 is confirmed by the fact that all 50 States and the District of Columbia have enacted into law some form of psychotherapist privilege. We have previously observed that the policy decisions of the States bear on the question whether federal courts should recognize a new privilege or amend the coverage of an existing one . . . . Because state legislatures are fully aware of the need to protect the integrity of the fact finding functions of their courts, the existence of a consensus among the States indicates that "reason and experience" support recognition of the privilege. In addition, given the importance of the patient's understanding that her communications with her therapist will not be publicly disclosed, any State's promise of confidentiality would have little value if the patient were aware that the privilege would not be honored in a federal court.

[W]e hold that confidential communications between a licensed psychotherapist and her patients in the course of diagnosis or treatment are protected from compelled disclosure under Rule 501 of the Federal Rules of Evidence.

All agree that a psychotherapist privilege covers confidential communications made to licensed psychiatrists and psychologists. [T]he federal privilege should also extend to confidential communications made to licensed social workers in the course of psychotherapy. . . . Today, social workers provide a significant amount of mental health treatment. . . . Their clients often include the poor and those of modest means who could not afford the assistance of a psychiatrist or psychologist, . . . but whose counseling sessions serve the same public goals. [T]he vast majority of States explicitly extend a testimonial privilege to licensed social workers. . . .

---

[10] This case amply demonstrates the importance of allowing individuals to receive confidential counseling. Police officers engaged in the dangerous and difficult tasks associated with protecting the safety of our communities not only confront the risk of physical harm but also face stressful circumstances that may give rise to anxiety, depression, fear, or anger. The entire community may suffer if police officers are not able to receive effective counseling and treatment after traumatic incidents, either because trained officers leave the profession prematurely or because those in need of treatment remain on the job.

JUSTICE SCALIA, with whom THE CHIEF JUSTICE joins . . . , dissenting.

The Court has discussed . . . the benefit that will be purchased by creation of the evidentiary privilege in this case: the encouragement of psychoanalytic counseling. It has not mentioned the purchase price: occasional injustice. That is the cost of every rule which excludes reliable and probative evidence . . . .

[E]ffective psychotherapy undoubtedly is beneficial to individuals with mental problems, and surely serves some larger social interest in maintaining a mentally stable society. But merely mentioning these values does not answer the critical question: are they of such importance, and is the contribution of psychotherapy to them so distinctive, and is the application of normal evidentiary rules so destructive to psychotherapy, as to justify making our federal courts occasional instruments of injustice? On that central question the Court's analysis [is un]convincing . . . .

When is it . . . that the psychotherapist came to play such an indispensable role in the maintenance of the citizenry's mental health? For most of history, men and women have worked out their difficulties by talking to, inter alios, parents, siblings, best friends and bartenders — none of whom was awarded a privilege against testifying in court. Ask the average citizen: Would your mental health be more significantly impaired by preventing you from seeing a psychotherapist, or by preventing you from getting advice from your mom? I have little doubt what the answer would be. Yet there is no mother-child privilege . . . .

The Court's failure to put forward a convincing justification of its own could perhaps be excused if it were relying upon the unanimous conclusion of state courts in the reasoned development of their common law. It cannot do that, since no State has such a privilege apart from legislation. What it relies upon, instead, is "the fact that all 50 States and the District of Columbia have [1] enacted into law [2] some form of psychotherapist privilege." Let us consider both the verb and its object: The fact [1] that all 50 States have enacted this privilege argues not for, but against, our adopting the privilege judicially. At best it suggests that the matter has been found not to lend itself to judicial treatment . . . . At worst it suggests that the privilege commends itself only to decision making bodies in which reason is tempered . . . by political pressure from organized interest groups (such as psychologists and social workers), and decision making bodies that are not overwhelmingly concerned (as courts of law . . . should be) with justice . . . .

NOTES

1.   Recall that Chapter 25 quoted Representative Hungate's remark, at the beginning of the Senate Committee deliberations on the draft of the Federal Rules, to the effect that if Congress was foolish enough to open the Pandora's box of Article V every special interest group, including "social workers and piano tuners," would want a privilege. It is an irony of the *Jaffee* decision that, in part at least, his remark turned out to be more prophetic than facetious.

2.   The lower court decision in *Jaffee* had cited both instrumental and humanistic justifications in support of a psychotherapist privilege. *Jaffee v. Redmond*, 51 F.3d 1346 (7th Cir. 1995). Did the Supreme Court rely at all on humanistic

reasoning?

3.   What light does *Jaffee* shed on the meaning of "experience" in Rule 501? Justice Scalia seems inclined to limit the term to judicial experience. In contrast, the majority appears to construe the term more expansively to include either legal or social experience. The title and text of Rule 201 indicate that the drafters knew how to use the limiting adjective "judicial" when they intended to do so. If either more expansive interpretation of "experience" (legal or social) is appropriate, did the majority reach the right result? After all, all 50 states and D.C. concurred. That fact alone distinguishes *Jaffee* from all the prior cases in which the Court has balked at recognizing a new privilege or in the situation where the states are split over the wisdom of fashioning a particular privilege.

4.   In a footnote, the *Jaffee* Court pointed to a number of "authorities" which supposedly substantiated the generalization that in the typical case, a patient would either not consult a mental health expert or not make necessary disclosures without the assurance of confidentiality furnished by an evidentiary privilege. That characterization of the cited studies has been challenged. *See* Imwinkelried, *The Rivalry Between Truth and Privilege: The Weakness of the Supreme Court's Instrumental Reasoning in* Jaffe v. Redmond, 518 U.S. 1, 49 Hastings L.J. 969 (1998). In some cases, the studies turn out to be surveys of mental health experts rather than actual and prospective patients. In other cases, the surveys indicate that the patients are far more concerned about unsupervised, out-of-court disclosure to employers than judicially supervised disclosure. A close examination of the empirical studies arguably indicates that the *Jaffee* Court understated the evidentiary costs of the privilege.

5.   Once a separate psychotherapist-patient privilege is recognized, the problem becomes one of relating the specific contours of the privilege to that of the general medical privilege, if any, recognized in the jurisdiction. Often the psychotherapist privilege is broader. Many jurisdictions do not recognize the physician-patient privilege in criminal cases. Thus, if Devitt attempted to prevent his treating physician from testifying to bruises the physician observed on Devitt's chest, the trial judge would routinely overrule the objection. In contrast, suppose that after the battery, Devitt began experiencing guilt and suicidal tendencies. He consulted a psychotherapist rather than a physician. During the consultation, Devitt described what he believed to be the cause of his mental problems: his revulsion at the realization that he attacked Paterson. The trial judge would not permit the psychotherapist to testify to Devitt's admissions.

6.   Another way in which the privileges can differ relates to the type of "professional" the patient consults. California Evidence Code § 990 defines "physician" as "a person authorized, or reasonably believed by the patient to be authorized, to practice medicine in any state or nation." Section 990 defines "psychotherapist" to include the foregoing but also:

(b)   A [state] licensed psychologist

(c)   A [state] licensed clinical social worker when he is engaged in applied psychotherapy of a nonmedical nature

(d)   A person who is serving as a school psychologist and holds a credential authorizing such service issued by the state

(e)   A [state] licensed marriage, family and child counselor

7.   *Jaffee* not only left unanswered questions about the types of confidants covered by the new privilege; it also raised issues about exceptions to the privilege. At the end of the lead opinion, Justice Stevens stated that future litigation would be necessary to define the "full contours" of the privilege. 518 U.S. at 18. In an accompanying footnote, the Justice asserted:

> Although it would be premature to speculate about most future develop-
> ments in the federal psychotherapist privilege, we do not doubt that there
> are situations in which the privilege must give way, for example, if a serious
> threat of harm to the patient or to others can be averted only by means of
> a disclosure by the therapist. *Id.* at 18 n. 19.

The lower federal courts have subsequently divided over the question of the existence of a so-called dangerous-patient exception.

UNITED STATES v. CHASE
340 F.3d 978 (9th Cir. 2003) (en banc), *cert. denied*, 540 U.S. 1220 (2004)

GRABER, CIRCUIT JUDGE:

[Chase was treated by a Kaiser Permanente psychiatrist Kay Dieter. During a counseling session, Chase showed Dieter his day planner, which referred to several persons, including two FBI agents who had investigated complaints lodged by Chase. He confided to Dieter that he had thought about injuring or killing these people. Dieter became concerned that Chase might act on his threats, and she warned him that if he told her specifics about whom he planned to kill, she would . . . disclose the threats to the intended victims. Dieter discussed the threats with Kaiser Permanente legal counsel, who advised her to contact the police in Chase's home town. After she did so, the FBI contacted her and she disclosed Chase's threats to the FBI. . . .

Chase and Dieter met again and he reiterated his frustration with the legal system, including the FBI, and said that if a lien against his house was not dropped, "he would get his guns . . . and have himself some justice." Chase told Dieter that he had gathered more information about the people he intended to kill and that he had located most of them. Dieter spoke again with the FBI, which then arrested Chase. Chase claimed that his "threats" were merely "hypothetical."]

. . . The district court held that Dr. Dieter's testimony was admissible. The court reasoned that the federal psychotherapist-patient privilege did not apply because Dr. Dieter properly had determined that Defendant's threats were serious when uttered, that harm was imminent, and that disclosure to authorities was the only means of averting the threatened harm . . . .

[T]he jury convicted Defendant [of threatening the FBI agents]. Defendant . . . appealed his conviction, arguing that admission of Dr. Dieter's testimony violated the psychotherapist-patient privilege . . . . A . . . panel of this court affirmed the district court's evidentiary rulings and affirmed the conviction. . . . We then agreed to rehear this case en banc. . . .

A. *Defendant's communication to Dr. Dieter was confidential under state law and privileged under both state and federal law.*

At the outset, we differentiate two distinct concepts: confidentiality and testimonial privilege. By "confidentiality," we refer to the broad blanket of privacy that state laws place over the psychotherapist-patient relationship. By "privilege," we mean the specific right of a patient to prevent the psychotherapist from testifying in court.

All 50 states and the District of Columbia have enacted laws protecting psychotherapist-patient confidentiality. *See* 3 Jack B. Weinstein & Margaret E. Berger, Weinstein's Federal Evidence ¶ 504.03[4][b], at p. 504-11 & n. 12 (2d ed.1997). . . . These laws commonly perform two functions: They establish a testimonial privilege, and they also create a more general blanket of confidentiality to cover the relationship in all contexts. A psychiatrist who is subject to such a law may not testify in court as to therapeutic conversations with her patient; neither may she gossip about them with her grocer. Oregon, where Defendant received treatment . . . , is no exception. Confidentiality is protected by statute. *See, e.g.*, Or. Rev. Stat. § 677.190(5) . . . . A concomitant state-court testimonial privilege is provided in Oregon Evidence Code § 504(2).

Defendant's statements were made in the course and scope of treatment. Accordingly, Defendant's communications to Dr. Dieter were confidential under state law. . . . Defendant's disclosures to his psychiatrist also were subject to a testimonial privilege in federal court, unless some exception applies. *Jaffe v. Redmond*, 51 F.3d 1346, 1355 (7th Cir.1995), *aff'd*, 518 U.S. 1 (1996). Despite its . . . endorsement [of the privilege], the Court in *Jaffe* declined to delineate the "full contours" of the psychotherapist privilege. *Id.* at 18. In a footnote . . . , the Court noted:

> Although it would be premature to speculate about most future developments in the federal psychotherapist privilege, we do not doubt that there are situations in which the privilege must give way, for example, if a serious threat of harm to the patient or to others can be averted only by means of a disclosure by the therapist.

Id. at 18 n. 19. We read that footnote as endorsing . . . a duty to disclose threats to the intended victim and to the authorities, the issue to which we turn next.

B. *Dr. Dieter properly disclosed the threats to the authorities.*

Most states have a dangerous-patient exception to their psychotherapist-patient confidentiality laws. *United States v. Hayes*, 227 F.3d 578, 583 (6th Cir. 2000). Some of these exceptions allow, and some require, a psychotherapist to disclose threats made by a patient during therapeutic sessions if the psychotherapist determines that the patient poses a risk of serious harm to self or others. This exception is often referred to as the *Tarasoff* duty, . . . after the California case that first introduced it. *See Tarasoff v. Regents of Univ. of Cal.*, 17 Cal.3d 425, 131 Cal.Rptr. 14, 551 P.2d 334, 340 (1976). . . .

Oregon recognizes this exception to the rule of confidentiality. Or.Rev.Stat. § 179.505(12). In the circumstances of this case, . . . Dr. Dieter properly disclosed the threats that Defendant had related regarding several specific individuals. The more difficult question under Rule 501 is . . . whether we should recognize a dangerous-patient exception to the federal *testimonial privilege* arising out of, or coextensive with, the dangerous-patient exceptions to states' rules of *confidentiality*.

C. *We decline to recognize a dangerous-patient exception to the federal testimonial privilege.*

We are faced with an even split between the two circuits that have considered the question under Rule 501. [While the Tenth Circuit recognized an exception to the privilege in *United States v. Glass*, 133 F.3d 1356, 1360 (10th Cir.1998), the Sixth Circuit reached a contrary conclusion. *Hayes*, 227 F.3d at 585–86.] We agree with the Sixth Circuit for . . . four reasons. . . .

1. *The States' Experiences*

The *Tarasoff* duty . . . lifts the blanket of *confidentiality* covering psychotherapist-patient communications under state law. Ordinarily, however, the *Tarasoff* duty does not abrogate the *testimonial privilege* in state courts. *Id.* at 585. Generally, the psychotherapist may (or must) warn the authorities or the intended victims of a dangerous patient, but still may not testify to confidential communications in state-court proceedings.[3] Of the states in the Ninth Circuit, only California has an *evidentiary* dangerous-patient exception. *See id.* Almost all the states . . . recognize the distinction between confidentiality (which is affected by the *Tarasoff* duty) and testimonial privilege (which is not). In Oregon, . . . the distinction has been explained this way by the state's supreme court:

> The public interest to be served by notifying the police, in most cases, could be achieved by divulging only that information needed to show why a clear and immediate danger is believed to exist. It would . . . never justify a full disclosure in open court, long after any possible danger has passed.

2. *Differing Purposes of State Confidentiality Laws and the Federal Testimonial Privilege*

The Sixth Circuit . . . saw only a marginal connection . . . between a psychotherapist's action in notifying a third party . . . of a patient's threat to kill or injure him and a court's refusal to permit the therapist to testify about such threat . . . in

---

[3] Many states carve out separate testimonial exceptions, which permit psychotherapists to testify at commitment hearings and other identified proceedings. *See, e.g.*, Cal. Evid.Code § 1004 ("There is no privilege under this article in a proceeding to commit the patient or otherwise place him or his property, or both, under the control of another because of his alleged mental or physical condition.").

a later prosecution of the patient for making it. State law requirements that psychotherapists take action to prevent serious and credible threats from being carried out serve a far more immediate function than the proposed "dangerous patient" exception. [T]he threat articulated by a defendant [who makes a threat in the course of therapy] is rather unlikely to be carried out once court proceedings have begun against him. *Id.* at 583–84.

[O]rdinarily testimony at a later criminal trial focuses on establishing a past act. There is not necessarily a connection between the goals of protection and proof. If a patient was dangerous at the time of the *Tarasoff* disclosure, but by the time of trial the patient is stable and harmless, the protection rationale that animates the exception to the states' confidentiality laws no longer applies.

3. *The 1972 Proposed Rule*

In 1972 the Chief Justice of the United States . . . submitted nine proposed testimonial privileges to Congress. One of these privileges, embodied in Proposed Rule 504, was a psychotherapist-patient privilege. The Proposed Rule establishing that privilege also created three exceptions. Conspicuously absent from the list was a dangerous-patient exception. [T]he "omission was deliberate. The exceptions allowed were patterned after those in [a] then-existing Connecticut statute." *Harris*, 74 Wash. L.Rev. at 37. The Proposed Rules cited an article by two authors of the Connecticut statute. *See* 56 F.R.D. at 243–44 (*citing* Abraham S. Goldstein & Jay Katz, *Psychiatrist-Patient Privilege: The GAP Proposal and the Connecticut Statute*, 36 Conn. B.J. 175, 182 (1962)). Professors Goldstein and Katz wrote:

> [O]ur committee deliberately chose not to write a "future crime" exception into the bill. Its members were persuaded that, as a class, patients willing to express to psychiatrists their intention to commit crime are . . .[5] making a plea for help. The very making of these pleas affords the psychiatrist his unique opportunity to work with patients in an attempt to resolve their problems. Such resolutions would be impeded if patients were unable to speak freely for fear of possible disclosure at a later date in a legal proceeding.

Goldstein & Katz, 36 Conn. B.J. at 188.

[B]ecause "the Supreme Court has officially recognized the psychotherapist-patient privilege, and cited favorably to [Proposed Rule 504] as initially proposed, the contents of the [Proposed Rule] have considerable force and should be consulted when the psychotherapist-patient privilege is invoked." 3 Weinstein's Federal Evidence ¶ 504.02, at 504–7.

---

[5] In this case, Dr. Dieter did not inform Defendant that she might testify against him in court, although she did warn him that she would disclose his threats for the purpose of protecting intended victims. We need not decide whether the result would be different if a psychotherapist informed a patient ahead of time that she would testify in court; arguably, the patient in that circumstance would be agreeing that the subsequent communication was not confidential.

4. *Public Policy*

The justification for the dangerous-patient exception to states' confidentiality rules is . . . the health and safety of the potential victim of the patient. The potential victim's well-being is as important as that of the patient. The difficult question is how to balance the patient's need for candor, in service of therapy, against the potential victim's need for protection. . . .

[T]he initial disclosure to the target or to the authorities can be damaging to the psychotherapist-patient relationship. But we think that a patient will retain significantly greater residual trust when the therapist can disclose only for protective, rather than punitive, purposes. As the Sixth Circuit expressed it:

> While early advice to the patient that, in the event of the disclosure of a serious threat of harm to an identifiable victim, the therapist will have a duty to protect the intended victim, may have a marginal effect on a patient's candor in therapy sessions, an additional warning that the patient's statements may be used against him in a subsequent criminal prosecution would certainly chill and very likely terminate open dialogue.

On balance, . . . the gain from refusing to recognize a dangerous-patient exception to the psychotherapist-patient testimonial privilege in federal criminal trials outweighs the gain from recognizing the exception.

Dr. Dieter testified about some of her conversations with Defendant during therapeutic sessions. Because . . . there is no dangerous-patient exception to the federal privilege that otherwise applies, . . . , the admission of Dr. Dieter's testimony about Defendant's communications to her was erroneous. [However, the court concluded that the admission of Dr. Dieter's testimony was harmless error.]

AFFIRMED.

KLEINFELD, CIRCUIT JUDGE, with whom CIRCUIT JUDGES T.G. NELSON and CLIFTON join, concurring in the result:

. . . I dissent from the majority's view that the psychotherapist-patient privilege applies even to a patient's imminent, seriously intended, and properly disclosed threat to commit murder.

Sometimes a warning may suffice to protect the victim, sometimes not. FBI agents, the prospective victims in this case, carry guns and know how to use them, so perhaps they . . . could protect themselves if they know who to look out for. But most people cannot. What, exactly, is one to do if a psychotherapist calls up and says "I have a deranged patient who plans to kill you, and he's serious"? Call the police? They do not provide bodyguard services. Seek state civil commitment proceedings . . . ? How shall the threatened individual assemble the money for lawyers and experts and persuade the involved bureaucracies and individuals to act fast enough to prevent realization of the threat? The fastest way to get someone locked up who threatens to kill a federal official . . . may well be a federal criminal proceeding in which the psychotherapist testifies about what the patient says.

Beyond these practical concerns, there is . . . the concern with having the truth vindicated and justice done. . . . [T]his is a case where the threat was understood by the psychiatrist to be so serious as to require disclosure, and she had disclosed what her patient told her. The confidentiality of the therapeutic relationship had already been breached, and the patient knew it. [T]he social interest in assuring that the judge and jury know the whole truth greatly exceeds the value of preserving any remaining shreds of the confidential therapeutic relationship. The jury ought . . . to know the truth about what Chase said. The cat being already out of the bag, trial is no occasion for stuffing it back in.

NOTES

1.　Do you agree with the majority's policy analysis? What is the policy rationale for the dangerous patient exception? Would it serve that policy to apply the exception in fact situations such as *Chase?*

2.　Do you agree with the majority's statutory construction argument? Like *Trammel* and *Jaffee*, the court turns to the enacted draft of Article V of the Federal Rules. In *Trammel*, the Court looked to the unenacted provisions for the limited purpose of deciding whether Congress had considered the spousal disqualification an Article V problem rather than an Article VI issue. In *Jaffee*, the Court relied on the unenacted provisions as support for its general threshold decision to recognize a psychotherapist privilege. How does the *Chase* court's use of the unenacted provisions compare with that of the treatment of those provisions in *Trammel* and *Jaffee*. Is it just as legitimate to rely on specific, fine details in an unenacted bill as a basis for inferring legislative intent?

D.　GOVERNMENT SECRETS

1.　Overview

Most of the privileges we have considered so far are communications privileges. They shield confidential communications about facts, but not the facts themselves. Thus, at a deposition, a client who has been involved in a traffic accident could refuse to answer questions about her communications about the accident with her attorney, but she could not refuse to answer otherwise proper questions about the accident itself. However, some privileges are topical in nature and directly protect facts. For example, the original draft of Article V would have recognized topical privileges for trade secrets and for a person's vote.

There are also a large number of topical privileges for various sorts of government information in various jurisdictions. One court has fashioned a privilege for complaints made to a state ombudsman office. *Shabazz v. Scurr*, 662 F. Supp. 90 (S.D. Iowa 1987). Another court has recognized a privilege for confidential communications between a judge and his or her law clerks. *In re Certain Complaints Under Investigation by an Investigating Comm. of Judicial Council of Eleventh Circuit*, 783 F.2d 1488, 1518–20 (11th Cir. 1986). The courts have derived other evidentiary privileges for governmental actors from such constitutional provisions as the speech and debate clause. *United States v. Gillock*, 445 U.S. 360 (1980); *Gravel v. United States*, 408 U.S. 606, *reh'g denied*, 409 U.S.

902 (1972). In a survey course such as this, we can highlight only the government privileges encountered most frequently in practice.

2. Military and State Secrets

Federal case law has created an absolute privilege for important government secrets. The seminal case is *Totten v. United States*, 92 U.S. (2 Otto) 105 (1875). There the Supreme Court barred a lawsuit based on an employment contract that President Lincoln had allegedly authorized for a Civil War spy's services. The Court declared that permitting the lawsuit to proceed "would inevitably lead to the disclosure of matters which the law itself regards as "confidential." In *Totten*, the allegations on the face of the complaint made it clear that the very subject matter of the case qualified as a state secret. In the following case, the Court was convinced that the processes of pretrial discovery and trial proof would similarly imperil the protection of military secrets.

UNITED STATES v. REYNOLDS
345 U.S. 1 (1953)

CHIEF JUSTICE VINSON delivered the opinion of the Court.

[Three civilians were killed in the crash of a B-29 military aircraft. The purpose of the flight was to test secret electronic equipment. The decedents' widows sued the United States under the Federak Tort Claims Act. During pretrial discovery, the plaintiffs moved for production of the Air Force's accident investigation report and the statements of the surviving crew members. The Secretary of the Air Force filed a formal "Claim of Privilege" objecting to production of the documents "for the reason that the aircraft in question, together with the personnel on board, were engaged in a highly secret mission of the Air Force." An affidavit of the Air Force Judge Advocate General added that the material could not be furnished "without seriously hampering national security . . . and the development of highly technical and secret military equipment." The Government instead offered to produce the surviving crew members for questioning. These witnesses would be allowed to refresh their memories from their Air Force statements and to testify about any unclassified matter.

The District Court ordered the Government to produce the documents in order that the court might determine whether they contained privileged matter. When the Government refused, the court ordered that the facts on the issue of negligence would be taken as established in plaintiffs' favor. The Court of Appeals affirmed.]

Judicial experience with the privilege which protects military and state secrets has been limited in this country. English experience has been more extensive, but still relatively slight compared with other evidentiary privileges. Nevertheless, the principles which control the application of the privilege emerge quite clearly from the available precedents. The privilege belongs to the Government and must be asserted by it; it can neither be claimed nor waived by a private party. It is not to be lightly invoked. There must be a formal claim of privilege, lodged by the head of the department which has control over the matter, after actual personal consideration by that officer. The court itself must determine whether the circumstances are appropriate for the claim of privilege, and yet do so without forcing a disclosure of the very thing the privilege is designed to protect. The latter requirement is the only one which presents real difficulty. As to it, we find it helpful to draw upon judicial experience in dealing with an analogous privilege, the privilege against self-incrimination.

The privilege against self-incrimination presented the courts with a similar sort of problem. Too much judicial inquiry into the claim of privilege would force disclosure of the thing the privilege was meant to protect, while a complete abandonment of judicial control would lead to intolerable abuses. Indeed, in the earlier stages of judicial experience with the problem, both extremes were advocated, some saying that the bare assertion by the witness must be taken as conclusive, and others saying that the witness should be required to reveal the matter behind his claim of privilege to the judge for verification. Neither extreme prevailed, and a sound formula of compromise was developed. [I]n substance it is agreed that the court must be satisfied from all the evidence and circumstances and "from the implications of the question, in the setting in which it is asked, that a responsive answer to the question or an explanation of why it cannot be answered might be dangerous because injurious disclosure could result." *Hoffman v. United States*, 341 U.S. 479, 486–487 (1951). If the court is so satisfied, the claim of the privilege will be accepted without requiring further disclosure.

[S]ome like formula of compromise must be applied here. Judicial control over the evidence in a case cannot be abdicated to the caprice of executive officers. Yet we will not go so far as to say that the court may automatically require a complete disclosure to the judge before the claim of privilege will be accepted in any case. It may be possible to satisfy the court, from all the circumstances of the case, that there is a reasonable danger that compulsion of the evidence will expose military matters which, in the interest of national security, should not be divulged. When this is the case, the occasion for the privilege is appropriate, and the court should not jeopardize the security which the privilege is meant to protect by insisting upon an examination of the evidence, even by the judge alone, in chambers.

[T]his is a time of vigorous preparation for national defense. Experience in [World War II] has made it common knowledge that air power is one of the most potent weapons in our scheme of defense, and that newly developing electronic devices have greatly enhanced the effective use of air power. [T]hese electronic devices must be kept secret if their full military advantage is to be exploited in the national interests. On the record before the trial court it appeared that this accident occurred to a military plane which had gone aloft to test secret electronic equipment. Certainly there was a reasonable danger that the accident investigation report would contain references to the secret electronic equipment which was the primary concern of the mission.

In each case, the showing of necessity which is made will determine how far the court should probe in satisfying itself that the occasion for invoking the privilege is appropriate. Where there is a strong showing of necessity, the claim of privilege should not be lightly accepted, but even the most compelling necessity cannot overcome the claim of privilege if the court is ultimately satisfied that military secrets are at stake. *A fortiori*, where necessity is dubious, a formal claim of privilege, made under the circumstances of this case, will have to prevail. Here, necessity was greatly minimized by an available alternative, which might have given respondents the evidence to make out their case without forcing a showdown on the claim of privilege. By their failure to pursue that alternative, respondents have posed the privilege question for decision with the formal claim of privilege set against a dubious showing of necessity.

There is nothing to suggest that the electronic equipment, in this case, had any causal connection with the accident. Therefore, it should be possible for respondents to adduce the essential facts as to causation without resort to material touching upon military secrets. Respondents were given a reasonable opportunity to do just that when petitioner formally offered to make the surviving crew members available for examination. We think that offer should have been accepted.

NOTES AND QUESTIONS

1. Given the absolute nature of the privilege, it is important to develop a manageable definition of military and state secrets. The statutes recognizing the privilege often attempt to define its scope in terms of the effect of disclosing the information: "exceptionally grave damage to the Nation" or "detrimental to the national security." Zagel, *The State Secrets Privilege*, 50 MINN. L. REV. 875, 881 (1966). The Advisory Committee proposed a rule, Federal Rule of Evidence 509, on government secrets, including state secrets. The proposed rule would have defined a state secret as "a governmental secret relating to the national defense or the international relations of the United States." *See* PROPOSED FED. R. EVID. 509.

2. In 2003, the heirs to the plaintiffs in *Reynolds* filed a petition for a writ of error coram nobis with the Supreme Court. Coyle, *New Light on an Old Defense of "Secrets,"* NAT'L L.J., Mar. 10, 2003, at A1. The Air Force had declassified the accident report on the crash. According to the heirs' attorney, "[t]he accident report . . . contained nothing remotely like a military secret." The attorney claimed that in *Reynolds*, the government had perpetrated a fraud on the Court. The government asked the Court to dismiss the writ. "The government . . . contend[ed] that there was no fraud: 'The Secretary [of the Air Force] was legitimately concerned that information about the confidential equipment and mission of this aircraft might be disclosed if the report and witness statements were released.'" "On June 23, [2003], the Supreme Court issued a one-sentence order denying the motion. This order did not expressly state whether the court's ruling was based on procedural or substantive grounds. . . ." Churchill & Goldenberg, *Who Will Guard the Guardians? Revisiting the State Secrets Privilege of* United States v. Reynolds, 72 U.S.L.W. (BNA) 2227, 2231 (Oct. 28, 2003). Some commentators have suggested that the subsequent revelations in *Reynolds* "should prompt the Court to rethink the degree of deference given to government privilege claims." *Id.* at 2231–32.

3. Since the 9/11 terrorist attacks, there have been claims that the Executive branch has asserted the privilege at an unprecedented rate. According to SECRECY REPORT CARDS 2007, "[s]ince 2001, the state secrets privilege had been invoked 39 times, an average of six times per year in 6.5 years, which is more than double the average in the previous 24 years." *But see* Coyle, *Balancing the Force of State*

Secrets, Nat'l L.J., Mar. 24, 2008, at 21 (research by Professor Robert Cheney "has rebutted claims that the Bush Administration has used the state secrets privilege more broadly than prior administrations"). In any event, these concerns have led to proposals to alter the privilege. For example, some suggest that trial judges should always examine the allegedly secret material *in camera*. Glasionov, Note, *In Furtherance of Transparency and Litigants' Rights: Reforming the State Secrets Privilege*, 77 Geo. Wash. L. Rev. 458 (2009).

4. Is there a fundamental difference between the fact situations in *Totten* and *Reynolds*? In *Totten* situations where the pleadings' allegations implicate state secrets, should the trial judge be more willing to dismiss the case before trial? *Mohamed v. Jeppesen Dataplan, Inc.*, 614 F.3d 1070 (9th Cir. 2010) (en banc) (dismissing the claims of alleged victims of the government's "extraordinary rendition" program; rejecting the contention that the trial judge cannot dismiss pretrial in *Reynolds* situations); Bernstein, Comment, *Over Before it Even Began:* Mohamed v. Jeppesen Dataplan *and the Use of the State Secrets Privilege in Extraordinary Rendition Cases*, 34 Fordham Int'l L.J. 1400 (2011).

5. The consequences of the successful assertion of the privilege depend on the procedural context. When the sovereign asserting the privilege is not a party to the litigation, the assertion merely renders the evidence unavailable to the litigants. *Farnsworth Cannon, Inc. v. Grimes*, 635 F.2d 268, 270–73 (4th Cir. 1980). If the litigant needed the evidence to sustain its initial burden of production, the litigant will suffer a nonsuit. However, suppose that the sovereign is a party to the lawsuit, as when the federal government asserts the privilege in a federal prosecution. In that situation, the assertion may lead to the dismissal of charges. In Judge Hand's words, "The government must choose; either it must leave the transactions in the obscurity from which a trial will draw them, or it must expose them fully." *United States v. Andolschek*, 142 F.2d 503, 506 (2d Cir. 1944). The government can avoid a dismissal if it can prepare a summary of the evidence (omitting the privileged material) which will enable the defendant to fairly litigate the merits. The Classified Information Procedure Act, 18 U.S.C. App. IV §§ *et seq.*, prescribes procedures for preparing such summaries.

3. Confidential Government Information

Besides the *Reynolds* privilege, the government has an array of other protections for its confidential information. One, frequently encountered in criminal work, is the qualified privilege for an informant's identity: there may be secrecy for the identity of persons who furnish information regarding violations of law to enforcement agents such as police and prosecutor. That privilege helps ensure the flow of useful information *to* government. However, the discovering party typically can defeat the privilege by showing substantial need for disclosure of the information. *See Roviaro v. United States*, 353 U.S. 53 (1957); Proposed Fed. R. Evid. 510.

Other major areas of qualified governmental privileges are the executive privilege, agency deliberative privileges, and law enforcement investigative information privileges. *See, e.g., United States v. Nixon*, 418 U.S. 683 (1974). The federal courts often invoke the predecisional or deliberative process privilege. *See*

Falcone v. Internal Revenue Serv., 479 F. Supp. 985 (E.D. Mich. 1979). This privilege helps ensure the flow of opinions, recommendations, and analysis *within* government. The purpose of this privilege is to encourage candor in government decision-making. The rationale is that if government decision-makers are assured confidentiality, their internal discussions will be franker and the end product — the final government decision — will be better. To be protected, a document must be *both* predecisional *and* deliberative; the document must be generated as part of a government decision-making process, and the contents of the document must reflect the "give-and-take" of opinions in that process. *Dow, Lohnes & Albertson v. Presidential Comm'n on Broadcasting to Cuba*, 624 F. Supp. 572 (D.D.C. 1984). The document "must bear on the formulation or exercise of policy-oriented judgment." *Ethyl Corp. v. U.S.E.P.A.*, 25 F.3d 1241, 1248 (4th Cir. 1994).

There are several limitations on this privilege. First, it generally does not protect raw, factual data the government gathers during decision-making. Weaver & Jones, *The Deliberative Process Privilege*, 54 Mo. L. Rev. 279, 297 (1989). Next, the privilege does not protect a final opinion adopted by the agency. *Falcone v. Internal Revenue Serv, supra.* Finally, the privilege can be overcome by a showing of compelling need. *United States v. Farley*, 11 F.3d 1385, 1389 (7th Cir. 1993). In deciding whether to uphold the privilege, courts consider: (1) the relevance of the information sought, (2) the availability of alternative evidence, (3) the seriousness of the litigation, (4) the role of the government in the litigation (in particular whether there is an allegation of government misconduct), and (5) the possibility of future timidity by government employees who will realize that their secrets are violable. *In re Franklin Nat'l Bank Securities Litig.*, 478 F. Supp. 577 (E.D.N.Y. 1979).

E. THE FUTURE OF PRIVILEGE

Since World War II, the basic trend in American evidence law has been to liberalize the standards of admissibility — a gradual triumph of logical relevance over both legal irrelevance and competence restrictions. Stein, *The Foundation of Evidence Law*, 8 Canad. J.L. & Juris. 279 (1996). The common-law courts began the trend, and the Federal Rules of Evidence accelerated it. However, the major privileges — spousal, attorney-client, physician-patient, and the like — have proved remarkably resistant to that trend.

At first blush, the two most recent Supreme Court privilege decisions seem to suggest that the Court has adopted a more receptive attitude toward claims of novel privileges. However, it would be a mistake to read too much into either *Jaffee v. Redmond*, 518 U.S. 1 (1996) or *Swidler & Berlin v. United States*, 524 U.S. 399 (1998). In both cases, the Court approvingly cited precedents that emphasized the Court's reluctance to fashion new privileges or expand old privileges. In *Jaffee*, the case for recognizing the psychotherapist privilege was exceptionally strong. Not only had the draft Federal Rules included the privilege, but as the Court noted at several points in its opinion all 50 states had opted to recognize the privilege. In *Swidler*, the Court was not extending the attorney-client privilege; rather, it was rejecting the Independent Counsel's attempt to contract the common-law scope of the doctrine. In short, a litigant urging a court to recognize a new privilege still faces an uphill battle.

More broadly, what are the prospects for the evolution of privilege doctrine?

Privileges are largely designed to affect behavior outside the courtroom; in the final analysis, many of the controversies over privilege doctrine are reducible to questions of whether a particular privilege protection will have the presumed effects. Further social science research can help resolve these questions. To what extent would the lack of a privilege deter mental patients from either seeking assistance or disclosing sensitive information to treating experts? Will forced testimony by children against their parents or parents against their children inflict psychological harm on the children? Would the quality of legal representation suffer without the very strong (and even posthumous) protection afforded client communications? These questions cannot be answered by abstract reasoning. They can be resolved only by additional experimentation and investigation.

Suppose that the further research were to validate Wigmore's assumption that absent the assurance of confidentiality furnished by a privilege, the typical layperson would not consult with or confide in mental health professionals. That research would have two effects. First, it would strengthen the case for classifying privileges as absolute. If laypersons are in fact acutely concerned about later compelled judicial disclosure, at the time of communication they must be able to predict with relative confidence whether their disclosures will be protected. A qualified privilege — one that can be defeated by a subsequent showing of need for the information — would make it quite difficult for them to make that prediction.

Second, such research would support statutory codification of privileges. Although Congress refused to enact the specific privilege statutes proposed by the Advisory Committee, most of the states which have enacted a version of the Federal Rules have adopted specific privilege statutes. To use a Biblical metaphor, "[t]he stone which the builders rejected has become the cornerstone." Psalms 118:22. In fact, most of those statutes have gone to the extreme of closing the window to the common law which Federal Rule 501 opened; their statutory schemes "foreclose . . . common law development and restrict . . . privileges to those specifically provided for by constitution, statute or court rule." 1 G. JOSEPH & S. SALTZBURG, EVIDENCE IN AMERICA: THE FEDERAL RULES IN THE STATES § 23.2 (1987). Assuming the validity of Dean Wigmore's theory, it would make eminently good sense to legislate privilege doctrine. Statutes often provide clearer rules that make it easier for laypersons to forecast whether a privilege would attach to their revelations.

Alternatively, what if further research continues to show that some privileges do not have the pronounced effect on laypersons' out-of-court conduct that Wigmore hypothesized. Perhaps courts would come to rely more heavily on a humanistic rationale and less on instrumental theories. It might also become more difficult to defend the conventional wisdom that communications privileges must be "absolute" in character. Significantly, in both *Jaffee v. Redmond* and *Swidler & Berlin v. United States*, the lower courts not only relied on humanistic reasoning but also treated the privileges in question as qualified. Such findings would also weaken the case for codification of privilege doctrine. In a regime of qualified privileges, courts need flexible standards to make *ad hoc* determinations whether the demonstrated need for the privileged information outweighs the policies favoring protection in the particular case. It might well be preferable to rely on common-law methodology to give courts that flexibility.

In sum, thinking about the future of privilege law highlights the two overarching themes of this text — the importance of legisprudence, and the crucial role of empirical investigation into the underlying behavioral assumptions of evidence law.

Chapter 27

COMPROMISE

Read Rules of Evidence 408–10.

A. INTRODUCTION

It would be difficult to overestimate the importance of settlement and settlement negotiations in the dispute resolution process. Roughly 97% of all civil claims that come into attorneys' offices are settled before trial. Kelner, *Settlement Techniques — Part One*, TRIAL, Feb. 1980, at 46. Many civil claims are settled before a lawsuit is even filed. Of the claims that are filed, over 90% are settled before trial. Plea bargaining plays an equally vital role in criminal proceedings. Approximately 96% of the arrestees who are booked plead guilty, and in most instances the plea is negotiated. Beall, *Negotiating the Disposition of Criminal Charges*, TRIAL, Oct. 1980, at 46; *Gannett Co. v. De Pasquale*, 443 U.S. 368, 389 (1979) (Burger, C. J., concurring). If anything, the current trend is toward settling an even higher percentage of cases. *DOJ Reports Huge Decline in Tort Cases Resolved Through U.S. District Court Trial*, 74 U.S.L.W. 2104 (Aug. 23, 2005); Post, *79% Decline: Federal Tort Trials Continue a Downward Spiral*, NAT'L L.J., Aug. 22, 2005, at 7. In 1962, 11.5% of all federal cases were disposed of by trial. In the early 21st century, that percentage has plummeted to 1.8%. Refo, *The Vanishing Trial*, 30 LITIG. 1, 2 (Winter 2004) (summarizing the findings of an A.B.A. Litigation Section research project entitled "The Vanishing Trial").

Thus, only a tiny — and declining — percentage of cases are tried, yet even this small percentage strains our judicial system. REPORT OF THE FEDERAL COURTS STUDY COMMITTEE 4–10 (1990). In many major metropolitan areas, litigants can expect to wait one to three years from the time their case is filed before it is tried; in some very crowded dockets it is not unheard of to wait five years for a civil trial date. In the words of one commentator, "[e]xisting court calendar backlogs and prosecutors' and public defenders' case-loads make the social costs of an even larger number of trials unacceptable, especially in view of the longer delays in civil dockets that would also inevitably result." Welch, *Settling Criminal Cases*, 6 LITIG., Winter 1980, at 32. More and more jurisdictions are experimenting with alternative dispute resolution (ADR) techniques, such as arbitration and mediation, to ease crowded dockets and expedite the processing of cases.

It is therefore understandable that courts and legislatures not only depend on out-of-court settlements, they also actively seek to encourage them. One method of facilitating settlement is to recognize exclusionary rules for statements the parties make in the process of bargaining. For example, some 35 states have enacted "Apology Laws," providing that if a physician apologizes to a patient for a medical mishap, the apology cannot be used as evidence in a subsequent malpractice action. Pearlmutter, *Physcian Apologies and General Admissions of Fault: Amending the Federal Rules of Evidence*, 72 OHIO ST. L.J. 687, 689 (2011). These legislatures and courts reason that such exclusionary rules encourage candid exchange during bargaining. More informed parties presumably can better evaluate their cases and reach agreement. In short, the rationale for such exclusionary rules is to "encourage nonlitigious solutions to disputes." *Reichenbach v. Smith*, 528 F.2d 1072 (5th Cir. 1976).

Some critics question whether these exclusionary rules are needed. After all, there are already powerful factors pressuring the parties to settle — case-loads, economics, and the desirability of avoiding exposure to higher damages awards and sentences. Given these pressures, it seems doubtful that an exclusionary rule will have an appreciable impact on the parties' willingness to negotiate. As in the case of privileges, it is questionable whether the typical layperson is aware of (and, therefore, affected by) evidentiary doctrines protecting statements made during settlement negotiations. Critics therefore argue that it is fanciful to assume that these exclusionary rules have an significant effect on settlement negotiations, and that courts and legislators have overestimated the impact of these rules on the parties' negotiating behavior outside of court.

Proponents of such exclusionary rules counter that, in most negotiations, the parties are represented by attorneys who are likely to know the rules and to be concerned about subsequent evidentiary use of their clients' statements. In any event, most courts and many legislatures have steadfastly adhered to the exclusionary rules. Unfortunately, there has been little empirical research into the question of the impact of these rules on parties' behavior during negotiation.

In addition to extrinsic policy justifications, these rules also rest in part on the sorts of institutional concerns that underlie FRE 403. As we saw in Chapter 13, one of the classic 403 probative dangers is the risk that the jury will overvalue an item of evidence. Especially if he or she has never been involved in litigation, a lay juror might not appreciate the extreme practical pressure on even a litigant with a meritorious claim to settle rather than going to trial. A juror might mistakenly think that a litigant's willingness to talk about settlement is a strong indication of the weakness of the party's position in the litigation. Given the dual rationales for this type of exclusionary rule, some commentators have dubbed them "quasi-privileges." 23 C. WRIGHT & K GRAHAM, FEDERAL PRACTICE AND PROCEDURE: EVIDENCE § 5423, at 698, § 5424, at 703 (1980).

B.   SETTLEMENT OFFERS, STATEMENTS DURING NEGOTIATIONS, AND SURROUNDING CONDUCT IN CIVIL CASES

1.   The General Exclusionary Rule

With some changes that we shall highlight later, Federal Evidence Rule 408 codifies the traditional common-law rule:

Rule 408. Compromise Offers and Negotiations and Offers to Compromise.

(a)   Prohibited uses. — Evidence of the following is not admissible — on behalf of any party — either to prove or disprove the validity or amount of a disputed claim or to impeach by a prior inconsistent statement or a contradiction:

(1)   Furnishing, promising, or offering — or accepting, promising to accept, or offer to accept — a valuable consideration in compromising or attempting to compromise the claim; and

(2)   Conduct or a statement made during compromise negotiations about the claim, except when offered in a criminal case and when the negotiations related to a claim by a public office in the exercise of regulatory, investigative, or enforcement authority.

(b)   Exceptions. — The court may admit evidence for another purpose, such as proving a witness's bias or prejudice, negating a contention of undue delay, or proving an effort to obstruct a criminal investigation or prosecution.

Under this Rule, certain persons have a right to prevent the introduction of certain types of statements made during negotiation over certain types of claims for specified purposes. The Rule raises several sub-issues: (1) Who has the right to object and invoke the rule?, (2) What types of claims and evidence are covered?, (3) What constitutes "compromise negotiation"?, (4) What alternative uses of the evidence are permissible?

a.   Who May Invoke the Rule?

As we have seen, the exclusionary rule codified in FRE 408 rests in part on the extrinsic social policy of encouraging settlement of civil claims. Given that rationale for the rule, its protection arguably should apply only to participants in the settlement negotiations and not to third parties. Does Rule 408 impose that limitation?

Chapter 25 pointed out that a person who holds a privilege is capable of waiving the privilege. Thus, a related question is whether the party who made the statement during compromise negotiations should be able to waive Rule 408 and introduce evidence of the statement. The Advisory Committee Note accompanying the 2006 amendment to Rule 408 addresses this point:

The amendment makes clear that Rule 408 excludes compromise evidence even when a party seeks to admit its own settlement offer or statements made in settlement negotiations. If a party were to reveal its own statement or offer, this could itself reveal the fact that the adversary entered into settlement negotiations. The protections of Rule 408 cannot be waived unilaterally because the rule, by definition, protects both parties from having the fact of negotiation disclosed to the jury. *See generally Pierce v. F.R.Tripler & Co.*, 955 F.2d 820, 828 (2d Cir. 1992) (settlement offers are excluded under Rule 408 even if it is the offeror who seeks to admit them.).

b.   What Types of Claims Are Covered?

Assuming that the party objecting under FRE 408 has standing to invoke the rule, does the rule apply even if the negotiations were with someone other than the current opponent? Courts are divided on the question. *See, e.g., Portugues-Santana v. Rekomdiv Intern.*, 657 F.3d 56, 63 (1st Cir. 2011) ; *Lyondell Chemical Co. v. Occidental Chemical Corp.*, 608 F.3d 284, 295–300 (5th Cir. 2010) (noting the split of authority); Narechania & Kirklin, *An Unsettling Development: The Use of Settlement-Related Evidence for Damages Determinations in Patent Litigation*, J. Law, Tech. & Pol'y 1, 11-14 (2012). There are at least three possible answers:

- The Rule applies only when the negotiations occurred between the same parties and relate to the specific claim which is the subject-matter of the current suit.

- The Rule applies if the negotiations occurred between the same parties and relate to the same general transaction underlying the current suit.

- When the negotiations relate to the same general transaction, Rule 408 applies even if the negotiations were with a third party.

Which view is most consistent with the language of Rule 408? Which makes the most sense as a matter of policy?

c.   Which Discussions Qualify as "Compromise Negotiations"?

The next question that arises is whether the parties engaged in "compromise negotiations" for purposes of the Rule. Rule 408 repeatedly uses the expression, "compromise," and also requires that the claim in question be "disputed." *Molinos Valle del Cibao, C. Por A. v. Lama*, 633 F.3d 1330, 1354 (11th Cir. 2011). The policy underlying Rule 408 certainly warrants extending its protection to negotiations in which the parties attempt to resolve a bona fide dispute over liability or the amount of damages. *Master-Halco, Inc. v. Scillia, Dowling & Natarelli*, 739 F. Supp. 2d 125, 129 (D. Conn. 2010). Those are the types of disputes that would otherwise require judicial resolution. By applying Rule 408 to statements made during such negotiations, we will hopefully encourage the pretrial settlement of those disputes and ease the burden on the courts. The issue is whether the rule applies to other types of disputes.

NOTES AND PROBLEM

1. **Problem 27-1.** Polecat Motors learns that Ms. Hill is desperate for cash. The plaintiff's medical bills are mounting, and she is in imminent danger of losing her house because of delinquent mortgage payments. Sensing the possibility of a "cheap" settlement, Polecat's agent approaches Ms. Hill and says, "We'll admit that your claim is valid. We're even willing to concede that the amount of your claim is fair; we've checked out the damages you claim and everything seems to be on the up and up. But face facts: You need cash right now. We're prepared to pay you $15,000 cash right now to settle this claim." The plaintiff rejects the settlement offer, and the case goes to trial. Can Ms. Hill introduce the statements of Polecat's agent? *See* Michaels, *Rule 408: A Litigation Mine Field*, 19 Litig., Fall 1992, at 36 ("The statement by a debtor, 'Of course I owe you the money, but unless you are willing to settle for less you will have to sue me for it' is, according to Weinstein, admissible. [T]here is no policy reason to exclude evidence when a debtor merely tries to induce a creditor to settle an admittedly due amount for a lesser sum".)

2. By its terms, Rule 408 is limited to claims disputed as to either "validity or amount." The courts have divided over the interpretation of that expression. *See* Michaels, *supra*, at 35 ("The Federal Circuit has held . . . that an acknowledged 'probability' of an eventual court battle is not sufficient . . . if the claim has not yet been contested. [T]he Tenth Circuit reached a similar result; [i]t held that 'threatened litigation' is a clear point for invoking Rule 408 protection. Statements made before threatened litigation are . . . not within the purview of the Rule."). In *Affiliated Manufacturers, Inc. v. Aluminum Co. of America*, 56 F.3d 521 (3d Cir. 1995), the court ruled that a clear difference of opinion between the parties is sufficient to bring 408 into play even though the disagreement had not yet crystallized to the stage of threatened litigation. However, *Kraemer v. Franklin and Marshall College*, 909 F. Supp. 267, 268 (E.D. Pa. 1995), holds that while litigation " 'need not have commenced for Rule 408 to apply,' there must be some dispute which the parties are attempting to resolve through discussion." In that case, the court found that "[a]lthough there is a difference of view between the parties as to the validity of Plaintiff's claim, no compromise negotiations or offers to settle occurred."

d. Which Statements Are Covered?

The next question that arises is what types of statements are protected. That question has long been disputed. Though there is broad agreement that offers and acceptances of offers themselves are covered by the rule, there is considerable disagreement about other statements and conduct that occur during the negotiations.

Waltz & Huston, *The Rules of Evidence in Settlement*
5 Litig., Fall 1978, at 11

Courts at common law consistently ruled that offers to settle a disputed claim by compromise were inadmissible when offered at a later trial to substantiate the plaintiff's claim. Inconsistency set in, however, when courts considered the admis-

sibility of subsidiary or collateral conversations occurring during settlement talks.
. . .

Prior to Rule 408's advent, all federal and most state courts excluded offers of compromise as irrelevant to the substantive issues; such offers, they said, implied merely a desire for peace, not a concession of a wrong done. The result was different when an offer of compromise was extended before any dispute had hardened. *E.g., Perzinski v. Chevron Chemical Company*, 503 F.2d 654 (7th Cir. 834 COMPRO- MISE CH. 27 1974). If the driver of a vehicle that struck and injured a pedestrian dropped by the victim's hospital room on the day after the accident to offer payment of his medical bills, his words would rise to haunt him at a subsequent trial since they preceded any negotiations to dispose of an actual dispute.

Once a dispute arose, the only true offer of compromise was "an offer to pay an amount conditioned on the denial of liability." . . . If unqualified, independent fact statements surrounded the offer, they would not be shielded at a later trial if the parties' settlement efforts broke down. *E.g., Brown v. Hyslop*, 153 Neb. 669, 45 N.W.2d 743 (1951). . . . [I]t often was difficult to separate the collateral evidence, which was admissible, from the offer of compromise itself, which was inadmissible.

A few courts excluded compromise offers on a contract theory. *E.g., White v. Old Dominion S.S. Co.*, 102 N.Y. 550, 6 N.E. 289 (1886). Anything said or done during compromise negotiations was later admissible unless it had been accompanied by an express or presumed "without prejudice" reservation. The offer itself was presumed to have been made without prejudice to future denials of liability but the collateral conversation was not. If an offer of compromise was not accepted, the courts reasoned, there was no contract between the parties and the defendant's offer was stripped of its evidentiary impact, but the force of unqualified fact admissions lingered on.

If the contract theory was excessively conceptualistic, the relevance theory was excessively unrealistic. The offer of $500.00 in a disputed lawsuit with a million dollar prayer is either a nuisance offer aimed at avoiding costly combat or a bad case of whistling in the dark. An offer of $500,000 in the same suit is a definite straw in the wind. . . . [S]o substantial an offer of compromise reflected a sense of pessimism by defendant on the liability issue. Pessimism of that magnitude was surely probative.

Faced with two flawed theories, some courts faced up to realities and frankly excluded offers of compromise because to do otherwise would inhibit free discourse during bargaining and frustrate the public policy favoring the extrajudicial dispo- sition of disputes. This policy-based version of the exclusionary rule sounded very much like a privilege.

. . . [A] crucial flaw in both the relevance and the contract theories at common law was that they required courts to draw a distinction between the actual offer and the words or conduct surrounding it. One test, Dean Wigmore's, emphasized the form of the proffered statement. 4 J. WIGMORE, EVIDENCE IN TRIALS AT COMMON LAW § 1061 at 41 (Chadbourne Rev.1972). Wigmore thought the speaker's intention was the key and the form of his statement was the best indicator of that intent. If the offeror did not intend his fact statement to be an assertion of his actual belief about the facts, he would phrase it hypothetically or conditionally. ("Fred, we don't believe it for a minute but just for the sake of argument let's assume that we've got a defective product here. What would you say to $150,000?") Conversely, if the offeror intended his comment as an assertion of belief — that is, as an admission — he would probably speak in explicit, unconditional terms, or so Dean Wigmore thought. ("Let's face it, Fred, we put out a defective gear box on this motorbike and we know we're going to have to pay for it.") Under Wigmore's test, only unconditional collateral assertions were admissible if settlement negotiations aborted. Thus counsel's first remark to Fred would not be admissible later; the second comment, an unqualified admission, would be.

A second test tried to focus on the relationship of the proffered collateral evidence and the offer of compromise or the subject matter of the discussions. *See, e.g., M'Neil v. Holbrook*, 37 U.S. 84 (1838). The closer, the more intimately intertwined the relationship, the more likely it was that the collateral evidence would be held inadmissible at trial. The most commonly encountered litmus was whether the proffered words had been "in furtherance" of compromise.

It has been said that Wigmore's test victimized the unsophisticated, who might fail to tack endless conditions and disclaimers onto their settlement offers. The relationship or "in furtherance" test was so unpredictable it left everyone vulnerable. These difficulties made the privilege theory look good: since collateral fact assertions could be as hurtful as proof of an outright offer when introduced later, the policy-based privilege theory excluded the collateral evidence along with the offer. The workability of this approach helps to explain the form given to Federal Rule of Evidence 408 by the U.S. Supreme Court's Advisory Committee, and ultimately, by the Congress.

The Advisory Committee was dissatisfied with the common law rule that excluded offers of compromise on a theory of irrelevance. It preferred to base the rule on the public policy favoring the compromise and settlement of meritorious disputes; in other words, it opted for the privilege approach. Advisory Committee Note to Court, Rule 408, 56 F.R.D. 183, 227–228 (1972). Consistent with its privilege approach, the Advisory Committee fashioned a rule that made collateral evidence, as well as offers of compromise, inadmissible to prove liability for, or the amount of, a disputed claim.

NOTES AND PROBLEMS

1. **Problem 27-2.** You represent Polecat Motors in the *Hill* case. You have completed most of your pretrial discovery, and you are ready to make a serious settlement offer to Ms. Hill. On the one hand, you want to go into enough detail about the facts of the case to enable Ms. Hill's attorney to appreciate your case evaluation. On the other hand, you want to be certain that none of your factual statements will come back to haunt you at trial. How would you word a settlement letter to ensure that you will be able to invoke Rule 408 if Ms. Hill's attorney attempts to offer the letter against you at trial? *See Layne Christensen v. Bro-Tech Corp.*, 836 F.Supp.2d 1203, 1229 (D.Kan. 2011)('In this letter, Purolite began by stating its desire to settle outstanding payments at issue between the parties . . . .');*Civic Center Drive Apts. Ltd. v. SW Bell Video*, 295 F. Supp. 2d 1091, 1099 n.3

(N.D. Cal. 2003) ("For Settlement Purposes Only").

2. **Problem 27-3.** Shortly after the accident, Ms. Hill's attorney spoke with Mr. Flesher, the head of Polecat Motors' Claims Department. A week before the meeting, Ms. Hill's attorney had sent a demand letter to Flesher. The demand was for $350,000. During their meeting, Flesher made a counteroffer for $50,000. Flesher told Ms. Hill's attorney that Ms. Hill had "a pretty good case." Flesher also stated that "our preliminary investigation uncovered no evidence that your client was guilty of any contrib." At common law, would Flesher's last statement be admissible against Polecat Motors? Under Rule 408?

3. A number of decisions have extended the scope of Rule 408 to exclude evidence of consent decrees entered in administrative or judicial proceedings. *Price v. Trans Union, L.L.C.*, 839 F.Supp.2d 785 (E.D.Pa. 2012); *New Jersey Turnpike Authority v. PPG Industries*, 16 F. Supp. 2d 460 (D.N.J. 1998) (civil consent decree with a state environmental agency), *aff'd*, 197 F.3d 96 (3d Cir. 1999); *Option Resource Group v. Chambers Development Company, Inc.*, 967 F. Supp. 846 (W.D. Pa. 1996) (consent judgment in civil proceeding and compromise settlement in Securities and Exchange Commission proceeding). Is the statutory text of Rule 408 broad enough to support that extension?

e.   What are the Permissible Uses of Covered Statements?

Remember the characterization of this rule as a "quasi-privilege." In the case of a true privilege, ordinarily the judge must exclude the evidence regardless of the proponent's intended use of the evidence. As we have seen, Wigmore's instrumental theory of privilege dictates that true privileges be absolute in that sense. Either the evidence is privileged or it is not; and if it is, the proponent's theory of logical relevance for proffering the evidence is immaterial. In this respect, Rule 408 differs markedly from a true privilege.

The structure of FRE 408 is similar to that of the uncharged misconduct doctrine, FRE 404(b). Rule 408(b) makes it clear that the evidence is not excluded so long as the proponent can articulate a theory of logical relevance other than the forbidden purposes specified in Rule 408(a). *See Sterling Sav. Bank v. Citadel Development Co.*, 656 F. Supp. 2d 1248, 1255 (D. Or. 2009) ("The list of example uses in 408(b) is illustrative, not exhaustive"); Michaels, *Rule 408: A Litigation Mine Field*, 19 LITIG., Fall 1992, at 37 ("Settlement evidence has been admitted for the following purposes: to show notice; to rebut a contention of failure to mitigate damages; to show that the incident in question was not the result of accident or mistake; to show a course of reckless and outrageous conduct; to explain the absence of settling defendants who were previously in court; to assist the jury in understanding why certain individuals were not litigants; and to show the intent to commit fraud").

NOTES AND PROBLEM

1. **Problem 27-4.** Ms. Hill settles with Roe before trial, and Roe agrees to testify for Ms. Hill at trial. The settlement between Hill and Roe is a so-called "Mary Carter" agreement. Ms. Hill not only releases her claim against Roe; Ms.

Hill also promises to pay or credit Roe a portion of any future recovery obtained against Polecat Motors. *Clayton v. Volkswagenwerk A.G.*, 606 S.W.2d 15, 17 (Tex. Civ. App. 1980). A "Mary Carter" agreement gives the settling defendant a direct financial interest in the plaintiff's recovery. *Lubbock Mfg. Co. v. Perez*, 591 S.W.2d 907, 919 (Tex. Civ. App. 1979). May Polecat use evidence of the settlement to impeach any trial testimony by Roe that seems to aid Hill? *Houston v. Sam P. Wallace & Co.*, 585 S.W.2d 669, 673–74 (Tex. 1979).

Rule 408(b) is often applied in cases arising from traffic accidents. Suppose that the defendant's truck injured both the driver and the guest in a passenger car. Before trial, the defendant settles with the guest. At trial, the guest appears as a defense witness and testifies that the plaintiff was inattentive and, hence, guilty of contributory negligence. Under 408(a), the plaintiff may not prove the witness's settlement with the defendant to show the defendant's fault directly or to prove the defendant's consciousness of fault. However, under 408(b), there is a perfectly sound alternative theory of logical relevance: bias. If the proponent relies on that theory, the judge would give the jury a limiting instruction permitting the jurors to treat the evidence as proof of bias but forbidding them from inferring fault from the settlement. The proponent would have to observe a similar limitation during his or her closing argument.

2. Another theory of independent relevance is the use of evidence of compromise negotiations to rebut a contract defendant's claim that the plaintiff failed to mitigate damages. For example, if a defendant contractor walked off a construction project, in a subsequent suit by the landowner the contractor might allege that the landowner failed to mitigate damages by unreasonably delaying hiring a new contractor. The landowner can respond by explaining that there were pending compromise negotiations and that she delayed hiring a new contractor because she thought the defendant might "come to his senses," return to work, and finish the construction project. *But see Stockman v. Oakcrest Dental Center*, 480 F.3d 791 (6th Cir. 2007) ("under both federal and Michigan law, a defendant may raise the defense that the plaintiff failed to mitigate this damages by seeking and accepting employment. The goal of mitigation is the prevention of unnecessary economic loss, and therefore mitigation [evidence] necessarily goes to the amount of the claim" and is consequently inadmissible under Rule 408).

3. If the statement amounts to an independent violation of law and the proponent offers the statement to prove that violation, the exclusionary rule is inapplicable. *Carney v. American University*, 151 F.3d 1090 (D.C. Cir. 1998). In one court's words, "Rule 408 is . . . inapplicable when the claim is based upon some wrong that was committed in the course of settlement negotiations; e.g. libel, assault, breach of contract, unfair labor practices, and the like. . . ." *Uforma/Shelby Business Forms, Inc. v. National Labor Relations Board*, 111 F.3d 1284 (6th Cir. 1997).

4. At this point, if you are familiar with alternative dispute resolution (ADR), you may wonder why Rule 408 seems to be confined to situations in which the parties are formally litigating their dispute or contemplating litigation. The simple answer is that Rule 408 was enacted before the recent growth in interest in non-judicial dispute resolution. Although most federal courts are contra, a few have recognized a general settlement privilege under Rule 501. *Goodyear Tire & Rubber v. Chiles Power Supply*, 332 F.3d 976 (6th Cir. 2003). There has been much more activity at the state level. All 50 states have either statutes or court rules conferring some protection on the confidentiality of ADR proceedings, especially mediation. Kentra, *Hear No Evil, See No Evil, Speak No Evil: The Intolerable Conflict for Attorney-Mediators Between the Duty to Maintain Confidentiality and the Duty to Report Fellow Attorney Misconduct*, 1997 BYU L. REV. 715, 733, 757–76 (1997).

Many of these statutes and court rules purport to create true privileges. However, the wording of the state statutes and rules varies widely. Some resemble true privileges in that, unlike a party faced with a Rule 408 objection, the proponent cannot defeat this objection by identifying an alternative theory of logical relevance. These statutes purport to prohibit any use of the evidence. For example, North Carolina Statute Section 50-13 states that "all verbal or written communications from either or both parties to the mediator or between the parties in the presence of the mediator made in a proceeding pursuant to this section are absolutely privileged and inadmissible in court." Other statutes and court rules resemble the conditional work product immunity in that the proponent can surmount the objection by establishing a compelling, case-specific need for the information. Comment, Christopher DeMayo, *The Mediation Privilege and Its Limits*, 5 HARV. NEGOTIATION. L. REV. 383 (2000). In short, when one of these statutes or court rules comes into play, it can present significant interpretive issues.

5.   Rule 408(a) was amended in 2006 to prohibit the use of compromise evidence "to impeach through a prior inconsistent statement or contradiction." Prior to the amendment, the courts were divided over the question. The Advisory Committee Note accompanying the amendment asserts that "[s]uch broad impeachment would tend to swallow the exclusionary rule. . . ."

6.   A 2006 amendment to Rule 408 also carved out an exception permitting the use of compromise statements "when offered in a criminal case and the negotiations related to a claim by a public office or agency in the exercise of regulatory, investigative, or enforcement authority." The accompanying Advisory Committee Note explains the amendment's intended purpose:

> Where an individual makes a statement in the presence of government agents, its subsequent admission in a criminal case should not be unexpected. The individual can seek to protect against subsequent disclosure through negotiation and agreement with the civil regulator or an attorney for the government. . . .
>
> In contrast, statements made during compromise negotiations of other disputed claims are not admissible in subsequent criminal litigation, when offered to prove liability for, invalidity of, or amount of those claims. When private parties enter into compromise negotiations they cannot protect against the subsequent use of statements in criminal cases by way of private ordering. The inability to guarantee protection against subsequent use could lead to parties refusing to admit fault, even if by doing so they could favorably settle the private matter. Such a chill on settlement negotiations would be contrary to the policy of Rule 408.

The amendment creates an acute danger for a party involved in parallel civil and criminal actions. Thompson, *To Speak or Not to Speak? Navigating the Treacherous Waters of Parallel Investigations Following the Amendment to Federal Rule of Evidence 408* , 76 U. Cin. L. Rev. 939, 949–50 (2008) ("[t]he [Advisory Committee] Notes state that where a defendant seeks to protect statements made during compromise negotiations with the government, the defendant should seek . . . an agreement with the government agency that would prohibit subsequent disclosure").

2. Payments by the Potential Defendant to the Potential Plaintiff of Medical Expenses

Rule 409 provides: "Evidence of furnishing, promising to pay, or offering to pay medical, hospital, or similar expenses resulting from an injury is not admissible to prove liability for the injury." The scope of this rule is broader and more absolute than Rule 408 in that it excludes the evidence for all purposes. Yet it is narrower than Rule 408 because it excludes only the offer or promise to pay or the actual payment itself and not surrounding statements. The differences between Rules 408 and 409 would certainly be indefensible if, like Rule 408, Rule 409 rested solely on the same policy of encouraging compromise negotiations. However, another policy comes into play when we shift from statement to payments. In *Ferguson v. Graddy*, 565 S.W.2d 600 (Ark. 1978), the Arkansas Supreme Court discussed Arkansas Evidence Rule 409, modeled after the federal rule. The court asserted that Rule 409 designed to encourage Good Samaritans: "It is in the best interest of society and in keeping with the mores of the community that humanitarian and benevolent instincts not be hobbled by the hazard that assistance to an injured person be taken as an admission of liability."

QUESTIONS

1.   Compare Rules 408 and 409. Rule 408 explicitly limits its scope to statements incident to negotiation over "a disputed claim." Does Rule 409 contain a similar limitation?

2.   The proponent can defeat a Rule 408 objection by articulating a theory of independent logical relevance. Can the proponent overcome a Rule 409 objection by the same tactic? Is the text of Rule 409, "to prove liability for the injury," more or less restrictive than the language of Rule 408?

C. STATEMENTS MADE DURING CRIMINAL PLEA BARGAINING

1. Offers and Statements

a. Plea Bargaining

Plea bargaining can raise a number of evidentiary issues. For example, if a defendant's guilty or *nolo* plea in one case is later offered as evidence in another case, it may give rise to a hearsay objection posing the issue whether the statement qualifies as the admission of a party opponent as discussed in Chapter 19. Here, however, we consider evidence other than and falling short of the final, accepted plea: offers to plead or accept a plea, statements related to the offer, and withdrawn pleas.

As with Rule 408, there has been virtually no empirical investigation of the impact of the criminal exclusionary rule on plea bargaining behavior, though there have been numerous studies on the potential impact of the abolition of plea bargaining altogether. *E.g.*, M. RUBINSTEIN, S. CLARKE & T. WHITE, ALASKA BANS PLEA BARGAINING (1980); Callan, *An Experience in Justice Without Plea Negotiation*, 13 LAW & SOC'Y REV. 327 (1979). However, our concern here is with a radically different question: Given that we currently have a plea bargaining system, should there also be an exclusionary rule for plea offers, related statements, and withdrawn pleas? As with civil settlement negotiations, there are numerous practical incentives for defendants to engage in plea bargaining. Furthermore, as on the civil side, the number of criminal trials is declining; and the percentage of cases disposed of via plea bargaining is enormous. In 1962, there were over 5,000 criminal trials in federal court. Refo, *The Vanishing Trial*, 30 LITIG. 1, 2 (Winter 2004). In 2002, although the number of cases filed had doubled, there were fewer than 4,000 criminal trials. *Id.*

Like civil settlement negotiations, plea bargaining is recognized as a legitimate part of our litigation process and the rules are crafted in order to encourage, or at least not to discourage, negotiations. In the words of one California court:

> Exclusion of admissions made in the course of plea negotiations is . . . important to the proper functioning of the criminal justice system. In deciding whether a settlement in a criminal case is in the public interest, a district attorney must be influenced by his assessment of the defendant's culpability. Indeed, one of the advantages of plea bargaining is that it allows a fine adjustment of the criminal charge to the facts of the particular offense. (*See People v. West*, 3 Cal. 3d 595, 605, 91 Cal. Rptr. 385, 477 P.2d 409.) Accordingly, if we wish to encourage negotiated pleas, defendant's actual guilt should not be a forbidden topic of discussion. That exclusion of admissions will promote this form of candor and thus facilitate settlements seems beyond dispute. Failure to exclude such admissions would not only hamper efforts to reach an agreement but also, by discouraging plain speaking, would perpetuate the deviousness in the plea negotiation procedure so much condemned by our Supreme Court.

People v. Tanner, 45 Cal. App. 3d 345, 119 Cal. Rptr. 407 (1975). In *United States v. Verdoorn*, 528 F.2d 103, 107 (8th Cir. 1976), the Eighth Circuit echoed these sentiments: "[I]t is essential that plea negotiations remain confidential to the parties if they are unsuccessful. Meaningful dialogue between the parties would, as a practical matter, be impossible if either party has to assume the risk that plea offers would be admissible in evidence."

That belief led to the enactment of Federal Rule of Evidence 410:

Rule 410. Inadmissibility of Pleas, Plea Discussions, and Related Statements.

   (a)   Prohibited Uses. In a civil or criminal case, evidence of the following is not admissible against the defendant who made the plea or participated in the plea discussions:

      (1)   a plea of guilty that was later withdrawn;

      (2)   a plea of nolo contendere;

      (3)   any statement made during a proceeding on either of those pleas under Federal Rule of Criminal Procedure 11 or a comparable state procedure; or

      (4)   any statement during plea discussions with an attorney for the prosecuting authority if the discussions did not result in a guilty plea or they resulted in a later-withdrawn guilty plea.

   (b)   Exceptions. The court may admit a statement described in Rule 410(a)(3) or (4):

      (1)   In any proceeding in which another statement made during the same plea or plea discussions has been introduced, if in fairness the statements ought to be considered together; or

      (2)   In a criminal proceeding for perjury or false statement, if the defendant made the statement under oath, on the record, and with counsel present.

For all practical purposes, Rule 410 is identical to Federal Rule of Criminal Procedure 11(e)(6).

Just as Rule 408 does not cover all communications between potential plaintiffs and potential defendants, Rule 410 does not apply to all discussions between the defendant and law enforcement authorities. In deciding whether particular statements or pleas are excluded, we must ask (1) whether the discussions amounted to "plea bargaining;" (2) whether they were said to the appropriate type of government official; and (3) whether they fall under any exception in the rule.

As we have just seen, Rule 408 applies only if the statements were made during "compromise" negotiations. For Rule 410, the question is whether the statements were made during "plea bargaining." The definition of "plea bargaining" is tied to the concept of one party seeking a *quid pro quo* from another party. *United States v. Geders*, 566 F.2d 1227 (5th Cir. 1978), *cert. denied*, 441 U.S. 922 (1979). When a defendant negotiates over a plea, the points of dispute typically are (1) the precise charge the defendant will plead to, and (2) the sentence concessions the defendant can obtain. Courts understand "sentence concessions" broadly; they may include such features as immunity, forfeiture, and civil penalties. *United States v. Boltz*, 663 F. Supp. 956 (D. Alaska 1987). Furthermore, the exclusionary rule applies both to statements made after the beginning of discussions over sentence concessions and to "statements made in an effort to initiate plea bargaining. . . ." *United States v. Bridges*, 46 F. Supp. 2d 462, 465 (E.D. Va. 1999).

NOTES AND PROBLEMS

1. **The defendant's state of mind:** Focus first on the defendant's side of the bargaining table. In 1979, Rule 410 was amended to restrict its protection of surrounding statements to those made during plea discussions "with an attorney for the prosecuting authority." Prior to that amendment, it often was difficult for courts to determine whether inculpatory statements by a defendant had been made during "plea negotiations." For example, a defendant might seek to exclude statements made to a police officer or investigator, claiming that he believed he was engaged in plea negotiations. The leading case on the question was, *U.S. v. Robertson*, 582 F.2d 1356 (5th Cir. 1978), which articulated the following two-tiered analysis:

> To determine whether a discussion should be characterized as a plea negotiation and as inadmissible, the trial court should carefully consider the totality of the circumstances . . . . [T]he accused's assertions concerning his state of mind are critical in determining whether a discussion should be characterized a plea negotiation. However, under a totality of the circumstances approach, an accused's subsequent account of his prior subjective mental impressions cannot be considered the sole determinative factor. Otherwise, every confession would be vulnerable to such subsequent challenge. The trial court must apply a two-tiered analysis and determine, first, whether the accused exhibited an actual subjective expectation to negotiate a plea at the time of the discussion, and, second, whether the accused's expectation was reasonable given the totality of the objective circumstances (citations omitted).

2. It is questionable whether *Robertson* remains good law under the current version of Rule 410. The Fifth Circuit formulated its two-tiered analysis in 1978 under the original version of Rule 410, which did not specify that plea discussions had to be conducted with "an attorney from the prosecuting authority." Though most courts assume that the two-tiered approach is still valid, *e.g., United States v. Kearns*, 109 F. Supp. 2d 1309, 1315 (D. Kan. 2000); *United States v. Leon Guerrero*, 847 F.2d 1363, 1367 (9th Cir. 1988), others no longer enforce the requirement that the defendant's beliefs have been objectively reasonable. *State v. Fox*, 760 P.2d 670, 674–75 (Haw. 1988). These courts point out that Rule 410 now purports to apply broadly to any "statement made during plea discussions."

3. **The type of government agent:** Now focus on the government agents on the other side of the bargaining table. The amended version of Rule 410 severely restricts the scope of excludable statements and withdrawn pleas to those made to a prosecuting attorney. Is this a trap for the unwary defendant? Suppose a detective implies that she is willing to help the defendant in exchange for inculpatory statements. Should those statements be excluded at a later trial if the defendant in

fact (and reasonably) believed that the discussions amounted to a plea negotiation? Consider the fairness issues raised as you work through the problems below.

4.   Problem 27-5. While in jail, Devitt tells the jailer that he would like to speak with the detectives assigned to the case. When the detectives come to Devitt's cell, he tells them that he wants "to cop a plea and strike a deal." The detectives assure him that they will bring his cooperation to the prosecutor's attention. At that point, Devitt makes an admission that complies with all the pertinent criminal procedure rules. Does Rule 410 bar the statement's admission under the former version of Rule 410? *See United States v. Posey*, 611 F.2d 1389, 1390–91 (5th Cir. 1980) (no). Under the current version?

5.   Problem 27-6. Now assume instead that the police initiate the discussion with Devitt. Under Morena law, they lack actual authority to grant or offer Devitt any concessions. However, they do not make that clear to Devitt; rather, they suggest to him that they are so "tight with the DA" that they "can probably deliver" if Devitt has "the right sort of story to tell." Devitt does not formally offer to plead guilty during this meeting; but in response to the police officers' urgings, he makes several damaging admissions. Would the former version of Rule 410 have barred the introduction of these admissions? *United States v. Geders*, 566 F.2d 1227, 1229–32 (5th Cir. 1978), *cert. denied*, 441 U.S. 922 (1979) (the court favored "a liberal interpretation of when plea bargaining commences"); *United States v. Herman*, 544 F.2d 791, 795–99 (5th Cir. 1977) ("the inappropriateness of giving the rule an inhospitable reading"). What about the current version? *See United States v. Perez-Franco*, 873 F.2d 455, 461 (1st Cir. 1989) ("This rule has been consistently interpreted by the courts to protect only those statements made by a defendant to the prosecuting attorney himself"); *United States v. Glaspie*, 993 F. Supp. 448, 461 (W.D. La. 1998) (the rule does not apply to "confession bargaining" with the police), *aff'd*, 184 F.3d 819 (5th Cir. 1999). *But see United States v. Millard*, 139 F.3d 1200, 1205 n.4 (8th Cir.) ("Agent Hein represented to the Millards that he was working directly with Assistant United States Attorney Lester Paff. Furthermore, during the course of these conversations, Hein telephoned Paff and discussed with Paff what deal they could offer the Millards."), *cert. denied*, 525 U.S. 949 (1998); *State v. Smallwood*, 594 N.W.2d 144 (Minn. 1999) (the police acted as agents of the prosecutor in bringing the offer to the prosecutor's attention and relaying information back to the defendant).

6.   Suppose that the defendant made the statement during plea bargaining with local or state authorities. Does Rule 410 forbid the receipt of the statement in a federal case? Or assume that the defendant made the statement bargaining with foreign authorities? Does Rule 410 reach that far? *United States v. Orlandez-Gamboa*, 320 F.3d 328 (2d Cir. 2003) (Colombia).

As the above materials indicate, Rule 410 reaches fairly far in protecting the defendant. However, the defendant still faces some dangerous pitfalls. Rule 410 clearly excludes withdrawn pleas, pleas of *nolo contendere*, and statements made during federal Rule 11 proceedings or comparable state proceedings. In addition, Rule 410 by its terms, protects "any statement made during plea discussions with an attorney for the prosecuting authority." As we have seen, in the civil context the traditional rule was that surrounding statements of fact were protected only if they were expressly made hypothetical, for example, "arguendo" or "without prejudice." But from early on, the same standard was not applied to criminal plea bargaining. This may reflect an assumption that the average arrestee engaged in plea bargaining lacks the sophistication of the typical businessperson attempting to compromise a civil claim. In *People v. Tanner*, for example, the California Supreme court extended protection to accompanying statements of fact, although on its face the California statute refers only to offers. Rule 410, of course, expressly applies to "statements."

Another pitfall relates to the timing of the defendant's statement. The question sometimes arises whether a particular statement — even if made (as required by the current version of the rule) to the prosecuting attorney — was made "during" plea discussions. Several courts have held that statements made by a defendant after the plea agreement has been entered into are not covered by the rule because they were not made during plea discussions. *See, e.g., U.S. v. Marks*, 209 F.3d 577 (6th Cir. 2000); *U.S. v. Lloyd*, 43 F.3d 1183 (8th Cir. 1994). *But see* Graham, *Plea Bargaining Pursuant to Fed. R. Evid. 410: "Criminal Defendant Beware!!!!*, 44 CRIM. L. BULL. 960, 977–79 (Nov.–Dec. 2008) ("[a]s a matter of textual interpretation, the Fed. R. Evid. 410(3) proviso of 'made in the course of plea discussions' is plainly broad enough to encompass and, as a matter of fairness, should be interpreted to encompass subsequently made cooperation statements when a plea of guilty for any reason is not eventually entered and not withdrawn").

b. Exceptions to the Exclusionary Rule

The three rules discussed in this chapter cover the spectrum from completely protective to relatively loose. Rule 409, governing evidence of payment of medical expenses by a potential defendant, is an absolute ban on the introduction of the evidence. In contrast, Rule 408 permits introduction of compromise offers and statements so long as the proponent can develop some theory of independent logical relevance. Rule 410 differs from both of these rules: It does not create an absolute ban, but the Rule recognizes only a very limited number of specified exceptions. (Reread the last sentence of Rule 410(b).)

NOTES AND PROBLEM

1. **Problem 27-7.** Imagine that Devitt makes a statement during plea bargaining, the bargain "falls through," and at the subsequent trial Devitt gives testimony that contradicts his plea bargaining statement. Would Rule 410 permit the prosecutor to use the plea bargaining statement as a prior inconsistent statement to impeach Devitt's testimony? Though at one time the Rule expressly allowed the prosecution to use plea bargaining statements to impeach the suspect's subsequent testimony, Congress later amended the Rule to delete the general exception for impeachment. *United States v. Martinez*, 536 F.2d 1107, 1108 (5th Cir.), *cert. denied*, 429 U.S. 985 (1976).

2. On the impeachment issue, which version of Rule 410 is preferable as a matter of policy? The prosecutor will undoubtedly analogize to *Harris v. New York*, 401 U.S. 222, 223–25 (1971), which allows the impeachment use of statements

obtained in violation of *Miranda.* The Supreme Court has read this impeachment exception very expansively. *See United States v. Havens,* 446 U.S. 620, 624–28 (1980). How strong is the analogy between plea bargaining statements and the situation in *Harris? State v. Vargas,* 618 P.2d 229, 230–31 (Ariz. 1980) ("This analogy . . . is without basis"). Is the policy underlying Rule 410 strong enough to override the law's abhorrence for perjury? *People v. Benniefield,* 88 Ill. App. 3d 150, 410 N.E.2d 455, 458 (1980) (yes).

3. Suppose that the defense attempts to offer a statement made by the *prosecutor* during plea bargaining. Disregarding any potential hearsay objection, may the prosecution invoke Rule 410 to exclude the statement? *See United States v. Verdoorn,* 528 F.2d 103, 107 (8th Cir. 1976) (prosecution may invoke the rule). Does *Verdoorn* reach the correct result as a matter of statutory construction? Consider this sentence in the last paragraph of the Criminal Advisory Committee's Note on the last version of Rule 410 prior to the 2011 restyling: "[N]o disapproval is intended of such decisions as *United States v. Verdoorn.*" Does this legislative history justify a court in allowing the government to use Rule 410 against the defense?

4. Consider whether the government can instead invoke Rule 408 in these circumstances. Prior to the 2006 amendment to Rule 408, the circuits were split on the question whether Rule 408 applied in criminal cases. *Compare United States v. Bailey,* 327 F.3d 1131, 1146 (10th Cir. 2003) (Rule 408 applies in criminal cases); *United States v. Arias,* 431 F.3d 1327 (11th Cir. 2005) ("we join the Fifth and Tenth Circuits in holding that Rule 408 applies to both civil and criminal proceedings") *with United States v. Prewitt,* 34 F.3d 436 (7th Cir. 1994). Following the amendment, and in particular 408(a)(2), what is the correct application of Rule 408 in a later criminal case?

2. Withdrawn Pleas

Rule 410 provides that withdrawn pleas cannot be used as evidence against the defendant at his later trial To be sure, the exclusion of even withdrawn pleas furthers the policy of encouraging plea bargaining. However, in the leading precedent, *Kercheval v. United States,* 274 U.S. 220, 224 (1927), Justice Butler added another justification for the norm of inadmissibility:

> [O]n timely application, the court will vacate a plea of guilty shown to have been unfairly obtained or given through ignorance, fear or inadvertence. Such an application does not involve any question of guilt or innocence. *Commonwealth v. Crapo,* 212 Mass. 209. The court in exercise of its discretion will permit one accused to substitute a plea of not guilty and have a trial if for any reason the granting of the privilege seems fair and just. *Swang v. State,* 2 Coldw.(Tenn.) 212.

The Supreme Court reasoned that the effect of the trial court's order permitting the withdrawal was to adjudge that the plea of guilty should not have been entered. Its subsequent use as evidence against petitioner was in direct conflict with that determination. When the plea was annulled, it ceased to be evidence.

While *Kercheval* is a well-respected precedent, its rationale has come under some criticism:

> The *Kercheval* rationale is based upon the mistaken assumption that pleas of guilt are permitted to be withdrawn only when the court has some reason to believe the plea was unfairly obtained and is therefore unreliable. This is not the case. Federal trial judges will often permit a plea of guilt to be withdrawn at any time up to sentence if the attorney for the defendant wishes it withdrawn . . . . He has a constitutional right to be proved guilty beyond a reasonable doubt and courts are reluctant to hold a defendant to a waiver of this fundamental right.

> Since Rule 11(e)(6) of the Rules of Criminal Procedure which supersedes Rule 410 excludes evidence of any withdrawn plea in any proceeding regardless of knowledge and willingness of the pleader, the line of cases permitting withdrawn pleas to be used if withdrawal was not approved by the court is overruled. The *Kercheval* rationale is no longer adequate.

> A franker rationale for exclusion is that permitting use of the withdrawn plea would make the granting of a trial meaningless. Cases which permitted the withdrawn plea to be admitted into evidence were based upon the assumption that proper instructions to the jury would insure that it would use the plea merely as evidence of conduct inconsistent with the defendant's claim of innocence. Courts have increasingly doubted the efficacy of such cautionary instructions.

2 J. Weinstein & M. Berger, Weinstein's Evidence ¶ 410[03] 410-36 to 410-37 (1986). The same criticisms are reiterated in 2 Weinstein's Federal Evidence ¶ 410.02[2] (rev. 2012).

NOTE

Which justification do you find more persuasive? If the second rationale proposed by Weinstein and Berger is sounder, does the exclusion of withdrawn pleas rest on extrinsic policy or intrinsic relevancy considerations?

3. Waiver

In *United States v. Mezzanatto*, 513 U.S. 196 (1995), the Supreme Court held that a suspect may waive the protection of Rule 410. Increasingly, prosecutors now demand that the suspect execute a written waiver as a precondition to entering into plea bargaining discussions. Depending on the wording of the proffer agreement, it might allow the prosecution to use the statements for impeachment of the defendant if he testifies at trial; some agreements go further and permit the prosecution to offer the statements as substantive proof during its case-in-chief. *United States v. Krilich*, 159 F.3d 1020, 1024–25 (7th Cir. 1998), *cert. denied*, 528 U.S. 810 (1999); *United States v. Burch*, 156 F.3d 1315 (D.C. Cir. 1998), *cert. denied*, 526 U.S. 1011 (1999). Depending on the language of the waiver, it might even be permissible for the prosecution to use the statement to impeach any defense evidence, not only the defendant's personal testimony. *United States v. Velez*, 354

F.3d 190, 198–99 (2d Cir. 2004) (while the *Mezzanatto* Court dealt with a narrow waiver provision, its reasoning goes farther). For an excellent discussion of *Mezzanatto* and the issues it raises, see Christopher Slobogin, *The Story of Rule 410 and United States v. Mezzanatto: Using Plea Statements at Trial, in* Evidence Stories 103 (2006).

Of course, even if the wording of the agreement is broad, the suspect might later be able to establish that the waiver was unknowing and therefore ineffective. *E.g., United States v. Young,* 73 F. Supp. 2d 1014 (N.D. Iowa 1999) (defendant was not advised of the nature or existence of a right to have the statements excluded). Should the voluntariness test under Rule 410 be the same as the standard under the Fifth Amendment? If not, should the standard be more relaxed or more rigorous?

Chapter 28

REMEDIAL MEASURES

Read Federal Rule of Evidence 407.

A. INTRODUCTION

Modern American society is extremely safety-conscious. Accordingly, our courts are committed to promoting the social policy of encouraging remedial or safety measures. That policy is reflected in one of the most controversial evidentiary rules, the so-called "subsequent remedial measures" doctrine. The doctrine excludes certain evidence of remedial measures that the defendant implements after an accident.

Federal Rule of Evidence 407 codifies this exclusionary rule:

Rule 407. When measures are taken that would have made an earlier injury or harm less likely to occur, evidence of the subsequent measures is not admissible to prove:

- negligence;

- culpable conduct;

- a defect in a product or its design; or

- a need for a warning or instruction.

But the court may admit this evidence for another purpose, such as impeachment or — if disputed — proving ownership, control, or the feasibility of precautionary measures.

Courts and commentators differ somewhat over the policy justification for this rule. Some argue that such evidence should be excluded on the theory that it is irrelevant. At the very least, it can be argued that there is a risk that lay jurors will attach too much weight to evidence that a defendant took remedial measures after an accident involving the plaintiff. Others take the position that such evidence should be excluded as a matter of social policy, since subsequent repairs, alterations, or precautions ought to be encouraged in order to prevent future accidents. If these improvements could be introduced as evidence of the prior negligence of the person who made the repairs, it would deter repair of the place or thing that caused the injury.

Thus, like Rule 408 (governing evidence of compromise statements), Rule 407 appears to have a dual rationale. D. LEONARD, THE NEW WIGMORE: SELECTED RULES OF LIMITED ADMISSIBILITY section 2.3 (rev.ed. 2002).

And like Rule 408, Rule 407 could be thought of as a "quasi-privilege." Consequently, like Rule 408, Rule 407 poses a standing issue: Should a litigant be able to object based on Rule 407 only if he or she was the one who actually made the subsequent repair? Does the language of Rule 407 prescribe that limitation? If the focus is on the logical relevance rationale for this doctrine, it should not make any difference whether the person is a litigant or a non-party. However, if the focus is the policy rationale, it makes sense to limit the exclusionary rule to changes effected by a party to the litigation. Under that rationale, when that person is not joined as a litigant, the litigants lack standing to invoke the exclusionary rule. Eight federal circuits take this view. *Millenium Partners, L.P. v. Colmar Storage, LLC*, 494 F.3d 1293, 1303 (11thCir. 2007).

B. THE CURRENT STATUS OF THE EXCLUSIONARY RULE

1. The Exclusionary Rule

Our analysis must begin with a discussion of two definitional questions. What is the meaning of "subsequent" in the statute, and what is a "remedial measure" for purposes of Rule 407?

"Subsequent"

First, what does **subsequent** mean in this context? "Subsequent" could mean "after the accident." The doctrine should certainly apply when the defendant makes the repairs after the accident in which the plaintiff is injured. The accident may heighten the defendant's fear that a repair will come back to haunt him or her as evidence in later litigation with the plaintiff.

However, that meaning does not exhaust the definitional possibilities. A second possible meaning is "after the sale of the product to the plaintiff." In *Shatz v. TEC Technical Adhesives*, 415 A.2d 1188 (N.J. Super. Ct. App. Div. 1980), the plaintiff had some workers install a slate floor in his house. The workers were using TEC 21F cement manufactured by the defendant. The defendant's container warned only against using the cement near flame. The workers utilized the cement near electrical wires. A wire fell onto the floor, igniting vapors from the cement and starting a fire that destroyed the plaintiff's house. At trial, the plaintiff proffered evidence that sometime before the fire, the defendant added a warning to the container label to use its cement with cross-ventilation to prevent a vapor build-up. The defendant objected that the evidence amounted to proof of a subsequent remedial measure. The court refused to exclude the evidence, reasoning that it was unrealistic to think that a manufacturer would forego safety improvements to avoid adverse inferences in cases arising from accidents that had not yet occurred.

NOTES

1.   Prior to 1997, courts were divided over definition of "subsequent" under the original wording of Rule 407 omitting the language "after an injury or harm allegedly caused by an event." A number of courts extended Rule 407 to safety improvements implemented after the date of the sale but before the accident. *Petree v. Victor Fluid Power, Inc.*, 831 F.2d 1191 (3d Cir. 1987). The extension also enjoyed scholarly support. Note, Roger W. Frazier, *Excluding Subsequent Design Modifications in Product Liability Litigation: The Propriety of a Post-Sale Versus a Post-Accident Exclusion*, 29 ARIZ. L. REV. 621 (1987).

2.   In 1997, Rule 407 was amended to add the phrase: "after an injury or harm allegedly caused by an event." The Advisory Committee Note states that the amendment was "added to clarify that the rule applies only to changes made after the occurrence that produced the damages giving rise to the action. Evidence of measures taken by the defendant prior to the 'event' causing 'injury or harm' does not fall within the exclusionary scope of Rule 407 even if they occurred after the manufacture or design of the product." Applying the amendment, *Thakore v. Universal Machine Co. of Pottstown, Inc.*, 670 F. Supp. 2d 705, 731–32 (N.D. Ill. 2009) admitted evidence of pre-accident remediation. The amendment has resolved the 407 issue in federal practice. Although the amendment settles the question in federal court, some states with evidence codes modeled after the Federal Rules have not adopted the amendment. Thus, the question remains a lively one in those jurisdictions.

3.   Which view is sounder as a matter of policy? Is it fanciful to think that a manufacturer would be concerned about the admissibility of the design modification? Given the high incidence of product liability suits, a manufacturer well might consider the admissibility of the evidence even before any accidents have occurred. Which manufacturer is more responsible — the one that makes changes only after accidents or the one which implements changes even before accidents? Under *Shatz*, which manufacturer enjoys the protection of Rule 407?

4.   Does amended Rule 407 apply if the defendant made the decision to change the design before the accident but implemented the redesign after the accident? *Martin v. Norfolk Southern Railway Co.*, 271 S.W.3d 76 (Tenn. 2008) (noting the split of authority).

"Remedial Measure"

Whereas the trend has been to narrow the meaning of "subsequent," the courts have tended to construe **remedial measure** broadly. In *Vander Missen v. Kellogg-Citizens Nat'l Bank*, 481 F. Supp. 742 (E.D. Wis. 1979), the plaintiff alleged that the defendant bank unlawfully denied her credit because of her husband's unfavorable credit rating. On a motion to compel an answer to an interrogatory, the plaintiff argued that she was entitled to discover whether the bank had taken any steps to ensure that future credit applicants would not be discriminated against on the basis of sex. The court sustained the defendant's Rule 407 objection. In *Ford v. Schmidt*, 577 F.2d 408 (7th Cir.), *cert. denied*, 439 U.S. 870 (1978), inmates challenged a prison policy forbidding possession of negotiable items within the prison. To show the prison officials' realization that their policy was invalid, the inmates offered evidence that after the incident triggering the suit, the officials adopted a new policy allowing the possession of some negotiable items. Again, the court cited Rule 407 as the basis for excluding the evidence.

Similarly, many courts routinely exclude evidence that after an alleged tort, the defendant employer fired the employees who were personally involved in the incident, *Nolan v. Memphis City Schools*, 589 F.3d 257, 273–74 (6th Cir. 2009), or required them to undergo remedial training. *Alfieri v. Carmelite Nursing Home Inc.*, 29 Misc. 3d 509 (N.Y. Civ. Ct. 2010). *See also Rosa v. Taser Intern., Inc.*, 684 F.3d 941 (9th Cir. 2012)(a warning on a stun gun); *Ekco Group, Inc. v. Travelers Indem. Co. of Ill.*, 273 F.3d 409, 415–16 (1st Cir. 2001) (change in the standard form language of an insurance policy); *Mahaney ex rel. Estate of Kyle v. Novartis Pharma.*, 835 F.Supp.2d 299, 314 (W.D.Ky. 2011)(labeling changes); *World Boxing Council v. Cosell*, 715 F. Supp. 1259, 1267 (S.D.N.Y. 1989) ("Courts have applied the broad language of this rule 'to exclude evidence of . . . installation of safety devices, changes in company rules, and discharge of employees.' ").

NOTES AND PROBLEMS

1.   Although courts and commentators sometimes dub this the "subsequent repair" doctrine, that label is inaccurate. Rule 407 does not use the word "repair." The operative language is "remedial measure." How would you define that expression? Would "precautionary" or "preventative" measure be more precise? Revisit the introductory clause in Rule 407. Does that clause suggest a working definition? A repair can involve a mere replacement, in the sense of merely returning something to its previous, undamaged condition. Suppose, for example, that the tires to Worker's truck were damaged in the accident, and Roe had them replaced with the identical product. Is that the type of remedial measure to which Rule 407 applies? Would that repair even be relevant in the suit between Roe and Ms. Hill? The definition should arguably capture two elements: The nature of the measure was such both that (1) its earlier implementation would have reduced the probability of the accident occurring and (2)its implementation would logically support an inference of antecedent fault.

2.   Consider the definitional issue in light of the facts of *Patrick v. South Cent. Bell Tel. Co.*, 641 F.2d 1192, 1195–97 (6th Cir. 1980). The plaintiff's decedent was electrocuted in an industrial accident. His repair truck came into contact with a tree-damaged power line. Before the accident, the defendant had strung the line 30 feet above the ground. Immediately after the accident, the defendant restored the cable to its original 30 feet. Later the defendant elevated the cable another 10 feet. Does Rule 407 exclude proof of the defendant's initial conduct in restoring of the cable to 30 foot height? What about the later height increase?

3.   To invoke Rule 407, does the defendant have to establish that the sole or primary motivation for the change was "safety concerns"? *Chlopek v. Federal Ins. Co.*, 499 F.3d 692 (7th Cir. 2007) answers that question in the negative. Do you think that is the right answer as a matter of statutory interpretation? As a matter of policy?

4.   **Problem 28-1.** A related issue, the admissibility of a defendant's recall letters and campaigns, raises intriguing questions about the relationship between the relevance doctrine and the extrinsic policy considerations underlying Rule 407.

Suppose that Polecat Motors sent out a recall letter mentioning the position of the gas tank as a defect and proposing a bumper modification to increase the protection of the gas tank. Could Ms. Hill's attorney offer a copy of the recall letter at trial? At first blush, Rule 407 would seem to govern this problem and bar the admission of the recall evidence. *Gauche v. Ford Motor Co.*, 226 So. d 198, 210–11 (La. Ct. App. 1969).

But consider whether the deterrence rationale applies in this situation. The National Traffic and Motor Vehicle Safety Act of 1966, 15 U.S.C. § 1411, requires automobile manufacturers to issue recall letters when they discover defects. Given that legislation, will the admissibility of the recall letter discourage Polecat from issuing the letter? *See Barry v. Manglass*, 55 A.D.2d 1, 389 N.Y.S.2d 870, 874–77 (1976) (no). Maine Evidence Rule 407(b) explicitly permits proof of recall letters. *See O'Dell v. Hercules, Inc.*, 904 F.2d 1194, 1204 (8th Cir. 1990) ("An exception to Rule 407 is recognized for evidence of remedial action mandated by superior governmental authority . . ."). On the other hand, while the legislation may undercut the Rule 407 objection, the legislation arguably gives rise to a different possible objection based on hearsay and the admissions doctrine (*see* Chapter 19). *Vockie v. General Motors Corp., Chevrolet Div.*, 66 F.R.D. 57, 60–62 (E.D. Pa.), *aff'd without op.*, 523 F.2d 1052 (3d Cir. 1975) (an admission must be voluntary).

5.   **Problem 28-2.** Suppose that in Problem 28-1, there was no statute or regulation compelling the recall; Polecat issued the recall letter voluntarily as a safety measure, and the judge decides to apply Rule 407 to the letter itself. *Hughes v. Boston Scientific Corp.*, 669 F. Supp. 2d 701 (S.D. Miss. 2009) (evidence of a voluntary recall is inadmissible). Before deciding to issue the recall letter, Polecat conducted a study of the crash-worthiness of the design of the gas tank. Polecat initiated the study with a view to deciding whether to issue a recall letter. Does Rule 407 bar the admission of the study? *Compare Martel v. Mass. Bay Transp. Auth.*, 403 Mass. 1, 525 N.E.2d 662 (1988) (yes because the study was a prerequisite to the safety measure) *with Rocky Mountain Helicopters v. Bell Helicopters*, 805 F.2d 907, 918 (10th Cir. 1986) ("It would strain" the language of Rule 407 "to extend its shield" that far). The question is whether the Rule applies not only to "theactual remedial measures" but also to "the initial steps toward ascertaining whether any remedial measures are called for." *In re Aircrash in Bali, Indonesia*, 871 F.2d 812, 816 n.2 (9th Cir.), *cert. denied sub nom. Pan American World Airways v. Causey*, 493 U.S. 917 (1989); *Prentiss & Carlisle Co. v. Koehring-Waterous Div. of Timberjack, Inc.*, 972 F.2d 6, 10 (1st Cir. 1992) (after an accident, the defendant conducted an internal investigation of the incident; while Rule 407 required redacting the parts of the report of investigation discussing possible remedial measures, the "analysis" section of the report was admissible).

6.   At one time, these questions were not as critical as they are today. During the 1970s and 1980s there was a strong trend toward recognizing a separate "self-critical analysis" privilege. Bacon, Note, *The Privilege of Self-Critical Analysis: Encouraging Recognition of the Misunderstood Privilege*, 8 Kan. J. L. & Pub.

POL'Y 221, 225 (1999). For example, if a corporation conducted an internal investigation into its compliance with environmental laws, the conditional self-critical analysis privilege might attach to the report documenting the investigation. Thus, even if Rule 407 did not cloak a study, this privilege might. However, in 1990, the Supreme Court handed down its decision in *University of Pennsylvania v. Equal Employment Opportunity Commission*, 493 U.S. 182 (1990). In that decision, the Court rejected a self-critical privilege for university tenure reviews. Since the rendition of that decision, most federal courts have rejected claims of the self-critical privilege. Pollard, *Unconscious Bias and Self-Critical Analysis: The Case for a Qualified Evidentiary Equal Employment Opportunity Privilege*, 74 WASH. L. REV. 913, 989, 993 (1999).

2. The "Exceptions" to the Exclusionary Rule

The contours of the subsequent remedial measures doctrine are strikingly similar to the structure of the uncharged misconduct doctrine, discussed in Chapter 14. We noted the two formulations of that doctrine — the exclusionary and inclusionary views — and that the exclusionary view has gradually given way to the inclusionary approach.

Traditional commentators often suggest that there is a general exclusionary rule regarding subsequent remedial measures, with a finite list of recognized exceptions. That suggestion is inconsistent with the language of Rule 407. Courts have admitted evidence of subsequent repairs or corrective measures to establish: notice of a prior defect; the cause of an accident; the condition at the time of an accident; control of the premises in question; the duty of the defendant to repair; the feasibility of avoiding the accident; and rebuttal or impeachment. One commentator has argued that the rule is no longer one of general exclusion, but rather a positive rule of admissibility subject only to the exception where the evidence is used as an admission of negligence. Comment, *Ault v. International Harvester Co. — Death Knell to the Exclusionary Rule Against Subsequent Remedial Conduct in Strict Products Liability*, 13 SAN DIEGO L. REV. 208 (1975).

When the judge finds that an "exception" applies, the judge overrules the Rule 407 objection and admits the evidence. However, the evidence still cannot be used for the purpose of inferring negligence or fault. Consequently, Federal Evidence Rule 105 applies and the defendant is entitled to a limiting instruction. Rule 105 reads: "If the court admits evidence that is inadmissible . . . for a purpose — but not . . . for another purpose — the court, on timely request, must restrict the evidence to its proper scope and instruct the jury accordingly." The limiting instruction will restrict what the proponent of the evidence may say about the testimony during closing argument.

NOTES AND PROBLEMS

1.   **Problem 28-3.** In our torts case, Ms. Hill has sued Roe on a *respondeat superior* theory. In his answer, Roe denies that Worker was acting in the course and scope of his employment. Would it be permissible for Ms. Hill's attorney to prove at trial that after the accident, one of Roe's tow trucks picked up Worker's damaged

car and brought it back to the Roe motor-pool for repairs? Is there any language in Rule 407 that controls this situation? *See Lee v. E I Dupont De Nemours & Co.*, 249 F.3d 362, 365–66 (5th Cir. 2001) ("de facto control"). Is this problem distinguishable from a variation of the case in which Roe denies owning the truck that Worker was driving at the time of the accident?

2.   **Problem 28-4.** Seven months after Mr. Hill bought the Polecat — six months after the accident but before trial — Polecat Motors' safety engineers redesigned the rear of the Polecat model Ms. Hill was driving at the time of the accident. The new design positioned the gas tank farther toward the front of the car and strengthened the bumper to give the gas tank additional protection. At trial, Ms. Hill calls Mr. Foster, the head of Polecat Motors' Production Design Division, as an adverse witness. Ms. Hill's attorney attempts to elicit Foster's admission that the rear of that model of Polecat was redesigned after the accident. The following occurs at sidebar:

O: Your Honor, I must object to that question. It patently calls for evidence in violation of Rule 407.

Q: Your Honor, I'm not offering this to prove fault in general. I have a much more specific purpose in mind.

J: Namely?

Q: I'm offering this to prove that it would have been feasible for Polecat to have designed a safer car. This is a products liability case, and I think I'm entitled to show that, Your Honor.

What ruling?

3.   **Problem 28-5.** Would the result in the last problem be the same if the defendant had presented expert testimony about the "state of the art"? Assume that during the defense case-in-chief, Polecat had called Ms. Judd, a safety engineer, who had testified that "when it rolled off the assembly line, that model not only had the safest gas tank on any model car, domestic or foreign; its gas tank incorporated every protective feature we safety engineers were familiar with at the time." *See Johnson v. State of Arizona*, 233 P.3d 1133 (Ariz. 2010) ("exaggerated claims that the condition was the safest possible . . . ."); *Blythe v. Sears, Roebuck & Co.*, 586 So. 2d 861 (Ala. 1991) (the safety expert testifies either in superlatives or in a false, misleading manner). Note "if disputed" in the second sentence in Rule 407. Why did the drafters add that language? *Stecyk v. Bell Helicopter Textron, Inc.*, 295 F.3d 408, 415 (3d Cir. 2002) ("While the text of Rule 407 permits admission of subsequent remedial measures for impeachment, we have cautioned against permitting the exception to 'swallow' the rule"); *Complaint of Consolidation Coal Co.*, 123 F.3d 126, 136 (3d Cir. 1997) ("a court must interpret the impeachment exception to Rule 407 circumspectly because 'any evidence of subsequent remedial measures might be thought to contradict and so in a sense impeach [a party's] testimony . . . .' Accordingly, the evidence offered for impeachment must contradict the witness's testimony directly"), *cert. denied*, 523 U.S. 1054 (1998).

4.   What degree of dispute is necessary to satisfy the "if disputed" requirement in Rule 407? How sharp must the dispute be? In *Grenada Steel Indus. v. Alabama Oxygen Co.*, 695 F.2d 883, 888–89 (5th Cir. 1983), the court rejected the plaintiff's

contention that feasibility is inherently in issue in any design defect case. In the same spirit, *Werner v. Upjohn Co.*, 628 F.2d 848, 855 (4th Cir. 1980), *cert. denied*, 449 U.S. 1080 (1981), brushed aside a plaintiff's contention that the defendant must formally admit feasibility to remove the issue from controversy. *Cf. Tuer v. McDonald*, 347 Md. 507, 701 A.2d 1101 (1997) (discussing a more expansive view as to when feasibility is sufficiently controverted). As a judge, where would you draw the line?

5. In the typical case, the plaintiff offers testimony about the subsequent repair made by the defendant. However, in some cases, the defense is the proponent of the testimony. For instance, in a case in which the plaintiff seeks punitive damages, the defense might proffer the testimony in order to show its good faith. Does Rule 407 bar this use of the evidence? *Swinton v. Potomac Corporation*, 270 F.3d 794, 814–15 (9th Cir. 2001) (no), *cert. denied*, 535 U.S. 1018 (2002). Alternatively, is this testimony objectionable as good character evidence? Is there a noncharacter theory of logical relevance?

C. THE CURRENT CONTROVERSY OVER THE SCOPE OF THE EXCLUSIONARY RULE

The subsequent remedial measures doctrine crystallized long before strict products liability became a common basis for imposing tort damages. Thus, it initially was not necessary to answer the question whether evidence of subsequent remedial measures was inadmissible in products liability cases to the same extent that it was excluded in negligence actions. However, as products liability became a more popular basis for tort liability, it was inevitable that courts would have to address the question. When they did, they at first made the easy assumption that the doctrine was equally applicable to this type of case. That assumption, however, quickly came under attack. Just as the California Supreme Court's tort decisions were instrumental in expanding strict products liability, that court vigorously attacked the assumption that the exclusion applied in such cases. The following decision construes the expression "culpable conduct" in California Evidence Code § 1151 and explains the controversy over application of the exclusionary rule to strict liability cases.

AULT v. INTERNATIONAL HARVESTER CO.
13 Cal. 3d 113, 117 Cal. Rptr. 812, 528 P.2d 1148 (1974)

Mosk, Justice.

[Plaintiff was injured in an accident involving a "Scout" vehicle manufactured by defendant. He alleged that the accident was caused by a design defect in the vehicle; he argued that he was entitled to recovery under theories of strict liability and negligence.]

The gear box of the Scout involved in the accident was manufactured of aluminum 380, a material which plaintiff asserts was defective for that purpose. At the trial evidence established that after the accident defendant changed from aluminum 380 to malleable iron in the production of the gear box. A jury returned a verdict of $700,000 in plaintiff's favor. On the appeal defendant maintains that the trial court erred in . . . admi[tting] into evidence of the change to malleable iron in the manufacture of the gear box, contending that the receipt of this evidence violates the prohibition contained in section 1151 of the Evidence Code.[1]

Defendant asserts that the admission of the evidence it changed from aluminum 380 to malleable iron after the accident violated the proscription of section 1151. In our view, however, the language and the legislative history of section 1151 demonstrate that the section is designed for cases involving negligence or culpable conduct on the part of the defendant, rather than to those circumstances in which a manufacturer is alleged to be strictly liable for placing a defective product on the market. Furthermore, we are not persuaded that the rationale which impelled the Legislature to adopt the rule set forth in the section for cases involving negligence is applicable to suits founded upon strict liability, and we therefore decline to judicially extend the application of the section to litigation founded upon that theory.

Section 1151 by its own terms excludes evidence of subsequent remedial or precautionary measures only when such evidence is offered to prove negligence or culpable conduct. In an action based upon strict liability against a manufacturer, negligence or culpability is not a necessary ingredient. The plaintiff may recover if he establishes that the product was defective, and he need not show that the defendants breached a duty of due care. (*Greenman v. Yuba Power Products, Inc.* (1963) 59 Cal. 2d 57, 62–63.)[2]

Defendant maintains that the phrase "culpable conduct" in section 1151 is sufficiently broad to encompass strict liability. It concedes that the term "culpable" implies blameworthiness, and that a manufacturer in a strict liability action may not be blameworthy in a legal sense. However, asserts defendant, a manufacturer who has placed a defective product on the market is blameworthy in a moral sense, and is therefore guilty of "culpable conduct" within the meaning of section 1151. We are unpersuaded by this tenuous construction. It is difficult to escape a contrary conclusion: if the Legislature had intended to encompass cases involving strict liability within the ambit of section 1151, it would have used an expression less related to and consistent with affirmative fault than "culpable conduct" — a term which, under defendant's theory, would embrace a moral rather than a legal duty.[3]

---

[1] Section 1151 provides, "When, after the occurrence of an event, remedial or precautionary measures are taken, which, if taken previously, would have tended to make the event less likely to occur, evidence of such subsequent measures is inadmissible to prove negligence or culpable conduct in connection with the event." All statutory references will be to the Evidence Code, unless otherwise noted.

[2] The clear theoretical distinction between these two bases of recovery impelled this court in a recent decision to hold that contrary to the Restatement (Rest. 2d Torts, § 402a), a plaintiff is not required, in order to prevail on the theory of strict liability, to show that a product is unreasonably dangerous to the use, and that it is sufficient if he demonstrates that it contained a defect which caused him injury. Cronin v. J. B. E. Olson Corp. (1972) 8 Cal. 3d 121, 135.

[3] Another argument of defendant is that unless "culpable conduct" is interpreted to include strict liability, the phrase has no meaning in section 1151 because it would then be synonymous with "negligence." However, there are types of faulty conduct other than negligence which are encompassed within "culpable conduct," such as wanton and reckless misconduct. Donnelly v. Southern Pac. Co. (1941) 18 Cal. 2d 863, 869; Rest.2d Torts, § 500.

[C]ourts and legislatures . . . retained the exclusionary rule in negligence cases as a matter of "public policy," reasoning that the exclusion of such evidence may be necessary to avoid deterring individuals from making improvements or repairs after an accident has occurred. Section 1151 rests explicitly on this "public policy" rationale. In explaining the purpose of the section, the draftsmen's comment states: "The admission of evidence of subsequent repair *to prove negligence* would substantially discourage persons from making repairs after the occurrence of an accident." (Law Revision Com. comment to Evid. Code § 1151.)

While the provisions of section 1151 may fulfill this anti-deterrent function in the typical negligence action, the provision plays no comparable role in the products liability field. Historically, the common law rule codified in section 1151 was developed with reference to the usual negligence action, in which a pedestrian fell into a hole in a sidewalk (*see, e.g., City of Miami Beach v. Wolfe* (Fla. 1955) 83 So. 2d 774) or a plaintiff was injured on unstable stairs (*see, e.g., Hadges v. New York Rapid Transit Corporation* (1940), 18 N.Y.S.2d 304); in such circumstances, it may be realistic to assume that a landowner or potential defendant might be deterred from making repairs if such repairs could be used against him in determining liability for the initial accident.

When the context is transformed from a typical negligence setting to the modern products liability field, however, the "public policy" assumptions justifying this evidentiary rule are no longer valid. The contemporary corporate mass producer of goods, the normal products liability defendant, manufactures tens of thousands of units of goods; it is manifestly unrealistic to suggest that such a producer will forego making improvements in its product, and risk innumerable additional lawsuits and the attendant adverse effect upon its public image, simply because evidence of adoption of such improvement may be admitted in an action founded on strict liability for recovery on an injury that preceded the improvement. In the products liability area, the exclusionary rule of section 1151 does not affect the primary conduct of the mass producer of goods, but serves merely as a shield against potential liability. In short, the purpose of section 1151 is not applicable to a strict liability case and hence its exclusionary rule should not be gratuitously extended to that field.

This view has been advanced by others. It has been pointed out that not only is the policy of encouraging repairs and improvements of doubtful validity in an action for strict liability since it is in the economic self-interest of a manufacturer to improve and repair defective products, but that the application of the rule would be contrary to the public policy of encouraging the distributor of mass-produced goods to market safer products. (Note, *Products Liability and Evidence of Subsequent Repairs*, 1972 Duke L.J. 837, 845–852.)[4]

---

[4] In a cogent analysis of the policy considerations underlying the admission of evidence of post-occurrence changes in a products liability context, the author states, "The assumption that the admission of evidence of subsequent repairs discourages defendants from making required repairs may be erroneous. Manufacturers and distributors of mass-produced products may not be so callous to the safety of the consumer as the general exclusionary rule presumes. Furthermore, to the extent that admission of such evidence results in recovery by injured plaintiffs, it can be argued that evidence of subsequent repairs *encourages* future remedial action. A distributor of mass-produced goods may have

The judgment is affirmed.

WRIGHT, C. J., and McCOMB, TOBRINER, SULLIVAN AND BURKE, JJ., concur. CLARK, JUSTICE (dissenting).

Lack of probative value is the basis for the exclusionary rule according to Professor Wigmore, although . . . some courts have also relied on public policy to avoid discouraging persons from making repairs following an accident. 2 Wigmore on Evidence (3d ed. 1940) pp. 151-159. There is even less probative value when evidence of subsequent change is offered to prove an admission in product liability cases. Change in a product is frequently made for reasons unrelated to the remedial nature of the change. Among the motivations for change are the desires to decrease production cost or to increase efficiency or salability. The most striking illustration of lack of probative value is supplied by the automobile industry. Each year hundreds of changes are made in a new model. It is absurd to suggest that each change reflects an admission the modification was made to remedy a defect.

Notwithstanding the lack of probative value, juries . . . may conclude the change reflects an admission of negligence or defect and . . . give great and decisive weight to the perceived admission. The danger of such misuse of evidence is at least as great in product liability cases as in negligence cases.

* * *

As the majority opinion and dissent in *Ault* indicate, there is a longstanding division of authority over the proper scope of the subsequent remedial measures doctrine. Annot., 50 A.L.R. Fed. 935 (1980). Several jurisdictions, including New York and South Dakota, followed *Ault* as a matter of decisional law. *Caprara v. Chrysler Corp.*, 52 N.Y.2d 114, 436 N.Y.S.2d 251, 417 N.E.2d 545 (N.Y. Ct. App. 1981); *Shaffer v. Honeywell, Inc.*, 249 N.W.2d 251 (S.D. 1976). The official comment to Colorado's version of Rule 407 declares that the exclusionary rule does not apply to strict liability design defect cases. A number of jurisdictions, including Maine, Oklahoma, and Wyoming, have amended their version of the rule to expressly allow the admission of subsequent repair evidence in strict products liability cases.

---

thousands of goods on the market. If his products are defective, the distributor would probably face greater total liability by allowing such defective products to remain on the market or by continuing to put more defective products on the market than he would by being adjudged liable in one particular case where evidence of subsequent repairs was introduced. Also, concern on the part of the distributors for consumer protection is promoted by consumer organizations, federal agencies, and mass media exposure of product defects. To some extent, the economic self-interest of product distributors requires that they repair and improve defective products to avoid adverse publicity which might result from future litigation. Since a prior jury finding of product defectiveness is admissible in a subsequent suit when the product causing the second injury is substantially similar to the first, distributors of defective products are under pressure to repair or alter their products to insulate themselves from a finding of defectiveness which may be used against them in subsequent litigation.

In conclusion, excluding evidence of subsequent repairs to encourage future remedial action may preclude recovery under theories of products liability which are themselves designed to ensure safety in marketed products. Relevant evidence should not be excluded from a products liability case by an obsolete evidentiary rule when modern legal theories, accompanied by economic and political pressures, will achieve the desired policy goals." (*Id.* at pp. 848-850.)

However, most jurisdictions found Justice Mosk's reasoning unpersuasive. They adamantly continue to apply the exclusionary doctrine in products liability actions. In *Gauthier v. AMF, Inc.*, 788 F.2d 634, 637 (9th Cir. 1986), the court stated that "[t]he overwhelming trend in the federal courts has been to exclude evidence of subsequent remedial measures in products liability cases." *Accord, Prentiss & Carlisle Co. v. Koehring-Waterous Div. of Timberjack, Inc.*, 972 F.2d 6, 10 (1st Cir. 1992) ("Like the majority of circuits, this court has held that Rule 407 applies to strict product liability actions").

In 1997, Federal Rule 407 was amended to extend the exclusionary rule to proffers of subsequent repair evidence to prove "a defect in a product, a defect in a product's design, or a need for a warning or instruction." The accompanying Advisory Committee Note acknowledges the prior split of authority. However, the Note states that the amendment is intended to codify the "view of a majority of the circuits that have interpreted Rule 407 to apply to product liability actions." Only the Tenth Circuit appears to refuse to extend Rule 407 to such actions. Stephenson, *Alone and Out of Excuses: The Tenth Circuit's Refusal to Apply Federal Rule of Evidence 407 to Product Liability Actions*, 36 N.M.L.REV. 391 (2006).

NOTES

1. Does Justice Mosk cite any empirical support for his assertion that the threat of tort exposure will counteract the repair disincentive created by limiting the subsequent remedial measures doctrine? Some courts seem to think that Justice Mosk's assertion is a self-evident proposition. *Shaffer v. Honeywell, Inc.*, 249 N.W.2d 251, 257, n.7 (S.D. 1976) ("In an age of mass production it is not reasonable to assume that manufacturers would forego improvements in a product and subject themselves to mass liability for a defect just because evidence of an improvement is admissible in a pre-improvement liability case. The pure economics of the situation dictate otherwise."). Justice Mosk relies heavily on the DUKE LAW JOURNAL Note — rather than an article from an economics journal. In turn, the cited pages of the Duke Note rely on cases and law review articles — rather than empirical economic research. The justice describes the Note's analysis as "cogent." The analysis may be plausible. But has it been validated and proven? One of the lessons from the judicial experience with scientific testimony is that it can be a huge mistake to treat the plausible as the proven.

2. The key juncture is the point in time at which the manufacturer has to decide whether to make the subsequent repair. At that point, is there not at least a possibility that any subsequent plaintiff will sue on a negligence theory as well as strict products liability? Consider the complaint in *Hill*. If so, do the mass manufacturers that Justice Mosk is describing also need the protection of Rule 407?

3. Does Justice Mosk's position go too far or not far enough? The drafters of the Maine Rules of Evidence pursued what they thought to be the internal logic of the *Ault* decision in enacting Maine Rule 407(a):

(a) Subsequent Remedial Measures. When, after an event, measures are taken which, if taken previously, would have made the event less likely to occur, evidence of the subsequent measures is admissible.

The Note accompanying the Maine rule declares: "The public policy behind the rule against admissibility was that it would deter repairs. This rationale is unpersuasive today." The Maine drafters saw the real issue posed by *Ault*: Is it time to abolish the subsequent remedial measures doctrine even in negligence cases involving mass producer defendants? In your opinion, has the time arrived to deliver the coup de grace to this exclusionary rule?

Chapter 29

LIABILITY INSURANCE

Read Federal Rule of Evidence 411.

A. THE RULE PRECLUDING ANY MENTION OF LIABILITY INSURANCE

Suppose in our torts case, Ms. Hill learns during discovery that Polecat Motors carries a public liability policy with a limit of $25,000,000 per incident. The existence of the liability policy is logically relevant to a material fact of consequence, since the existence of the policy arguably makes it more likely that the defendant would be careless. The defendant's agents might think that any judgment against their employer will come "out of the insurer's pocket" rather than out of the corporate funds used to pay their wages. The inference is admittedly weak, since it depends on an assumption that Polecat's employees or agents were aware of the insurance. Moreover, there is an equally plausible contrary inference: we normally assume that persons who go the trouble to obtain insurance are more — not less — careful.

While the evidence of liability insurance thus may have some logical relevance, it also carries a danger of unfair prejudice. If the jury hears the evidence of the defendant's liability insurance, the jury may be tempted to decide the case on an improper basis. The jurors may find for the plaintiff — not because they believe that the defendant was careless but rather because they feel that the insurer is better able to absorb the loss. The fear that the jury may succumb to this temptation underlies the common law exclusionary rule barring mention of the defendant's insurance. Federal Rule of Evidence 411 codifies the rule:

Rule 411. Liability Insurance.

Evidence that a person was or was not insured against liability is not admissible to prove whether the person acted negligently or otherwise wrongfully. But the court may admit this evidence for another purpose, such as proving a witness's bias or prejudice or proving agency, ownership, or control.

There has been little research to validate the fear underlying this exclusionary rule. The following article reports some of the extant research on the subject.

Kalven *The Jury, The Law, and The Personal Injury Damage Award*
19 Oʜɪᴏ Sᴛ. L. J. 1 58, 170–72 (1958)

[T]he points I should like to underscore here are three. First that liability insurance, at least in auto cases and for the business enterprise defendant, is now so frequent that its impact on the jury is probably reduced. Second that it may have a somewhat different relevance for jury thinking on damages than for their thinking about liability. There is the arresting suggestion in some of our data that the effect of insurance may be not so much to inflate damages as it is to persuade the jury that the full loss be placed on the defendant. That is, doubts as to insurance are likely to cause the jury to award less than what it regards as the adequate award, out of regard to the burden it places on the defendant. And finally there is the underlying premise which an occasional juror puts into words. Insurance and ability to pay are relevant only in the case of real doubt. There is no simple jury rule that the insured defendant cannot win. Rather it is that where there is doubt and consequently the risk of injustice and error in deciding the case either way, it is better to risk error against the insurance fund than against the injured plaintiff. The result therefore is a subtle shift of the burden of proof, particularly on damage issues, to the insurance fund.

This last observation invites a strong note of caution as to what has been said in this section. I have been reporting primarily on what the jury talks about when confronted with the various damage issues. For several reasons such data although relevant must not be taken too literally as prediction of jury decision. On many points we have at most suggestive anecdotes, not systematic data. Again what has been reported is almost always the reactions of some individual jurors, not the consensus of the jury as a whole and it is the jury as a whole that makes the decision. The give and take of the deliberation *process* and the requirement of a group decision operates to limit greatly extreme tendencies to do equity as one or two jurors may see it. The jury is likely to be more conventional and in accord with the law than is the individual juror. Jury discussion is highly fluid, arguments are frequently rationalizations or rhetoric or face saving gestures making possible changes in position and there may be a wide gulf between the way the jury talks and how it finally decides.

NOTES

1. Consider the note of caution Professor Kalven sounds at the end of the excerpt. Throughout this text, we have cited empirical "jury" studies as a basis for critiquing evidentiary doctrine. Some commentators are highly skeptical of the value of these studies. What problems may arise when the researchers use mock jurors — persons who know that their decision will not in fact deprive an accused of his liberty or a civil defendant of her money? What problems may be present even when the researchers interview actual jurors? Do these problems raise concerns about the internal or external validity of the studies?

2. For purposes of argument, accept ProfessorKalven's tentative findings. How should this research data affect: (a) the scope of the exclusionary rule; and (b) the

courts' attitude toward the enforcement of the rule? Many courts previously enforced this rule with remarkable vigor. Annot., 40 A.L.R. Fed. 541 (1978). The rule's violation led to many a sustained objection and a reversed judgment. In the past, trial judges often enforced the rule by declaring a mistrial where there was any mention at all of the defendant's insurance. *Id.* However, as the following case illustrates, more recently judges have beenless willing to grant the drastic relief of a mistrial declaration.

EDE v. ATRIUM SOUTH OB-GYN, INC.
71 Ohio St.3d 124, 642 N.E.2d 365 (1994)

[As administrator of his wife's estate, Charles Ede filed a medical malpractice action against Dr. Dakoske and the corporation of which he was the president, Atrium South OB-GYN, Inc. Dakoske performed surgery on Mrs. Ede. She died four days later. Appellant alleged that Dakoske's negligent post-operative care caused her death.]

The focus of this appeal is whether the trial court properly precluded appellant from eliciting testimony at trial regarding the commonality of insurance interests between Dakoske and other physicians testifying as [defense] experts. . . . Before trial, Dakoske's counsel . . . filed a motion *in limine*, seeking to exclude from the trial any mention . . . that Dakoske and other testifying physicians are insured by Physicians' Mutual Insurance Company ("PIE"). Appellant argued that since PIE is a mutual insurance company, each insured's policy is evidence of some fractional part ownership in PIE. Appellant argued that PIE-insured medical experts have a built-in bias — fewer successful malpractice claims means lower premiums charged for malpractice insurance.

. . . During . . . argument on the motion, the trial judge asked Dakoske's counsel whether PIE's insurance rates were related to whether an insured agreed to testify on behalf of another insured. Dakoske'scounsel . . . stated that they were not. The trial judge did not, however, seek to determine whether insurance rates for a particular classification of doctor might be affected by the outcome of a particular case.

At trial, Dr. Martin Schneider . . . testified on behalf of Dakoske. Appellant's cross-examination included questioning regarding Schneider's possible bias. Appellant established that Dakoske's counsel, Jacobson, Maynard, Tuschman&Kalur, previously had defended Schneider in his own malpractice case, and that Schneider had also testified as an expert in cases defended by the same firm.

Appellant's counsel then sought to establish that Schneider and Dakoskewere insured by the same malpractice insurer, PIE, and asked Schneider the following question:

> "Have you ever entered into any contractual relationship with any Ohio corporation for which the law firm of Jacobson, Maynard, Tuschman&Kalur provided legal services?"

Dakoske's counsel objected, which objection the trial judge sustained . . . . Appellant's counsel again argued that Schneider had a potential bias and financial interest in the outcome of the case due to the terms of his insurance contract with

PIE, and that the matter of insurance may be brought up pursuant to Evid. R. 411 if used to show bias. The trial judge responded:

> "[W]e had inquiry before and I was told and it was represented that the premium rates for each of those physicians are determined according to their classification and practice and that they would not be affected by whether or not a physician, ah, determined to testify on behalf of the insurance company or didn't."

The trial judge thus precluded appellant from embarking on any questioning relevant to insurance. A jury returned a verdict in favor of Dakoske and Atrium South . . . . The appellate court affirmed, finding that the trialcourt's exclusion of the insurance evidence did not amount to an abuse of discretion. The appellate court did make clear, however, that admission of the evidence, coupled with a limiting instruction, would likewise not have amounted to an abuse of discretion. The appellate court noted that "[d]epending upon the directness and scope of the potential pecuniary impact of an adverse award upon the expert witness, admission of this type of evidence upon cross-examination, coupled with the limiting instruction as to its permitted use, would seem to be the preferred choice."

The trial court in this case pointed to Evid. R. 403 in determining that the issue of the commonality of interests between Drs. Dakoske and Schneider could not be demonstrated through evidence of a common insurance carrier. The trial court ruled that the danger of prejudice outweighed the probative value of such testimony. We find that determination to be unreasonable, and therefore reversible error, for two reasons.

First, the trial court did not appreciate the probative value of establishing that Dakoske and Schneider were both insured by PIE. The trial court focused its inquiry on only one thing — whether a doctor's premiums could be raised by PIE if the doctor refused to testify on behalf of another PIE-insured doctor. Thus, the trial court sought to determine whether PIE coerced Schneider's testimony, but did not seem to consider Schneider's personal bias resulting from his insurance relationship. Satisfied by Dakoske's attorney's assurance that Schneider was not being coerced by PIE, the trial court failed to consider other possible biases created by Schneider's relationship with PIE. The trial court was not responsive to appellant's argument that as a fractional part-owner of PIE, Schneider's own premiums might fluctuate due to the result of the case. Such testimony would have been probative of bias.

Second, the trial court erred by grossly overestimating to what extent testimony that Dakoske was insured would prejudice the jury. The second sentence of Evid. R. 411 exists for a reason — it recognizes that testimony regarding insurance is not always prejudicial. However, too often courts have a Pavlovian response to insurance testimony — immediately assuming prejudice. It is naive to believe that today's jurors, bombarded for years with information about health care insurance, do not already assume in a malpractice case that the defendant doctor is covered by insurance. The legal charade protecting juries from information they already know keeps hidden from them relevant information that could assist them in making their determinations. Our Rules of Evidence are designed with truth and fairness in mind; they do not require that courts should be blind to reality. . . .

Given the sophistication of our juries, the first sentence of Evid. R. 411 ("[e]vidence that a person was or was not insured against liability is not admissible upon the issue [of] whether he acted negligently or otherwise wrongfully") does not merit the enhanced importance it has been given. Instead of juries knowing the truth about the existence and extent of coverage, they are forced to make assumptions which may have more prejudicial effect than the truth.

Thus, the second sentence of Evid. R. 411, which allows courts to operate in a world free from truth-stifling legal fictions, ought to be embraced. In such instances as the case at hand, truth should win out over a naively inspired fear of prejudice.

Therefore, we hold that in a medical malpractice action, evidence of a commonality of insurance interests between a defendant and an expert witness is sufficiently probative of the expert's bias as to clearly outweigh any potential prejudice evidence of insurance might cause. Thus, in the present case, the trial court acted unreasonably in excluding evidence regarding the commonality of insurance interests of Drs. Dakoske and Schneider. The judgment of the court of appeals is reversed and the cause is remanded to the trial court for a new trial.

NOTES

1. At the end of the last chapter, we considered the question whether it is time to scrap the exclusionary rule for subsequent remedial measures. Likewise, here perhaps it is time to substitute an instruction to the jury in place of the old exclusionary rule set out in Rule 411. Many jurors simply assume that a defendant has insurance; we fear that this assumption will influence the jurors' evaluation of the evidence of liability. In cases in which the defendant lacks insurance, why not deal with the problem in an honest, straightforward fashion and tell the jury that the defendant lacks insurance? Or why not tell them in every case that whether the defendant carries insurance is irrelevant? To use Professor Kalven's words, why "leave . . . the jury in the dark"?

2. Diamond, Casper, & Ostergren, three psychology researchers, have challenged the practice of "blindfolding the jury." *Blindfolding the Jury*, 52 LAW & CONTEMP. PROBS. 247 (1989). They argue:

> Jurors hold expectations that influence their perceptions and judgments. Not all of those expectations are accurate, and when the inaccuracies go uncorrected at trial because of blindfolding, such false expectations may influence jury verdicts. For example, jurors may generally expect defendants to carry insurance that will cover the total cost of a damage award, but the general rule is that the jury cannot be told whether or to what extent the parties are insured against liability. Faced with an injured plaintiff, the jury will presumably be overgenerous if it thinks that an insurance company will pay.

Id. at 252. The authors attack "the . . . fiction that the jury operates on a blank slate, influenced only by what it hears and sees in court, and uninfluenced by . . . expectations." *Id.* at 251.

3. To an extent, this exclusionary rule can be justified on the basis of the same type of extrinsic social policy rationale that underlies Rules 407 and 409: We do not want to create a disincentive for persons to act responsibly. Based on this rationale, should only the insured have the right to raise a Rule 411 objection? Does the statutory text prescribe that limitation?

B. THE "EXCEPTIONS" TO THE RULE

Reread the last sentence of Federal Rule of Evidence 411. The structure of the Rule is similar to that of the uncharged misconduct doctrine codified in Rule 404(b). As in that rule, there is one purpose for which the evidence may not be offered: in the words of Rule 411, "to prove whether the person acted negligently or otherwise wrongfully." To defeat an objection based on the exclusionary rule, the proponent need not cram the evidence intoa pigeonhole exception. The proponent need only articulate a theory of independent logical relevance: "the court may admit this evidence for another purpose, such as." There are several well-accepted theories of independent logical relevance. The following problems illustrate some of those theories.

NOTES AND PROBLEMS

1. In the typical case, the plaintiff attempts to introduce evidence that the defendant carried insurance and the defense objects. Suppose, though, that the defense wishes to introduce the evidence. Does Rule 411 apply? Does the defense need to find an applicable exception? Consider in this regard Rules 404 and 405: Is the defense offering the evidence to show that the defendant is a careful person? Is this forbidden good character evidence?

2. Problem 29-1. In our torts case, after the accident, Polecat Motors' president told Ms. Hill, "Don't worry. We carry over $25,000,000 in liability insurance." In offering this statement in evidence, what inference does the plaintiff want the jury to draw? Does the judge have to construe this statement as an admission of liability by the defendant? *Brainard v. Cotner*, 59 Cal. App. 3d 790, 795–96, 130 Cal. Rptr. 915, 918 (1976) (the statement "was not necessarily an admission of fault by the defendant; therefore it was not an abuse of discretion to exclude it"). Assume that the judge interprets the statement in that fashion. Should the admission drag the mention of insurance into evidence with it? *See Keown v. Monks*, 491 So. 2d 914, 915–16 (Ala. 1986) ("I've got insurance and I'm just real sorry.").

3. Problem 29-2. Would the result be different if the statement read: "Don't worry. We're at fault, but we're good for it. We carry over $25,000,000 in liability insurance." Is the difference purely linguistic?

4. Problem 29-3. Ms. Hill has added Roe, Mr. Worker's employer, as a defendant. In his answer, Roe denies that Worker was one of his agents. Would it be permissible for Ms. Hill to prove that at the time of the accident, Roe's liability insurance policy included Worker on Schedule B, the list of employees whose acts were covered by the policy? *See Cherry v. Stockton*, 75 N.M. 488, 406 P.2d 358, 360 (1965) ("a circumstance to be considered in determining whether the workman is an employee . . . .").

5.   Problem 29-4. In his answer, Roe denies owning the truck involved in the accident. Could Ms. Hill prove that Schedule C, the list of covered instrumentalities, mentioned the car? *See Dobbins v. Crain Bros.*, 432 F. Supp. 1060, 1069–70 (W.D. Pa. 1976) ("some evidence of . . . ownership and control . . . ."), *modified*, 567 F.2d 559 (3d Cir. 1977). Does the language of Rule 411 support your conclusion?

6.   Problem 29-5. During its case-in-chief, Polecat Motors calls Dr. Vaughn, who testifies that in his opinion Ms. Hill's injuries are not permanent in character and that the prognosis is a complete recovery. Vaughn is being paid by the defendant's liability insurer, Allstate. In the past three years, Allstate has hired Vaughn to give similar testimony in 10 other cases. What is the logical relevance of the evidence of defendant's liability insurance? Does this theory qualify as a theory of independent relevance? *Charter v. Chleborad*, 551 F.2d 246, 248 (8th Cir.), *cert. denied*, 434 U.S. 856 (1977) (yes). Again, is there any textual support for your conclusion in Rule 411? *See Oliveira v. Jacobson*, 846 A.2d 822 (R.I. 2004) (at a medical malpractice trial, a defense witness held a paid position with a medical malpractice insurance company, but not the one which insured the defendant doctor; "The trial justice properly concluded that Dr. Lerner's professional working relationship with a medical malpractice insurance company and the fact that he failed to disclose that information in his curriculum vitae or in response to a direct question was an impeachable omission not excluded by the provisions of Rule 411. The fact that Dr. Lerner was a paid advocate or representative of an insurance company and was paid substantial compensation was relevant and probative of his potential for bias").

7.   Note the contrast between Rules 411 and 407, dealing with evidence of subsequent remedial measures. Rule 407 expressly requires that the fact the evidence is offered to prove be "disputed." Rule 411 omits that language. Can the judge nevertheless exclude insurance evidence under Rule 403 if the evidence is offered to prove an issue that is only technically in dispute? 23 C. WRIGHT & K GRAHAM, FEDERAL PRACTICE AND PROCEDURE: EVIDENCE § 5365, at 455 (1980). Assume that, in a fact situation like Problem 29-3 or 29-4, the issue which Ms. Hill offered the evidence to prove was undisputed. For example, Roe's attorney might offer to stipulate that Worker was one of Roe's employees or that Roe owned the truck involved in the accident. May the judge exclude the evidence under Rule 403?

Should the court read the requirement for a bona fide dispute into Rule 411 on the theory that the drafters' omission was inadvertent? One commentator has characterized the omission as an "oversight" by the drafters. Schmertz, *Relevance and Its Policy Counterweights: A Brief Excursion Through Article IV of the Proposed Federal Rules of Evidence*, 33 FED. B.J. 1, 20 (1974). Some students of legislation believe that "scrivener's errors" are relatively common. Eskridge, *The New Textualism*, 37 UCLA L. REV. 621, 687 (1990). Courts occasionally assert the power to effectively insert words into a statute to correct legislative drafting "scriveners mistakes." *Amalgamated Transit. Local 1309 v. Laidlaw Transit*, 448 F.3d 1092, 1097 (9th Cir. 2006); *Tax Analysts v. I.R.S.*, 214 F.3d 179, 182 n.1 (D.C. Cir. 2000). However, the courts do not "lightly" exercise that power. *People v. Guzman*, 35 Cal.4th 577, 25 Cal. Rptr. 3d 761, 767, 107 P.3d 860 (2005). That power must be exercised cautiously due to separation of power considerations. W.

ESKRIDGE & P. FRICKEY, CASES AND MATERIALS ON LEGISLATION: STATUTES AND THE CREATION OF PUBLIC POLICY 633 (1988). In some states, including Michigan and Texas, the drafters added an adjective, either "controverted" or "disputed," to Rule 411 to moot this issue of statutory interpretation. 23 C. WRIGHT & K. GRAHAM, FEDERAL PRACTICE AND PROCEDURE: EVIDENCE § 5365 (1980).

The Kalven article excerpted above mentions a closely related issue that can arise earlier during the *voir dire* examination of the prospective jurors. If the defendant has an insurer, one of the insurer's stockholders or employees may be a venireperson. The venireperson may even be challengeable for cause on that very ground. During *voir dire*, many jurisdictions permit counsel to ask prospective jurors whether there are any "policyholders, stockholders, present employees, past employees, or claims adjusters" of an insurance company among them. *George v. Howard Constr. Co.*, 604 S.W.2d 685 (Mo. Ct. App. 1980). *But see Parento v. Palumbo*, 677 F.2d 3, 4–5 (1st Cir. 1982) (noting the split of authority).

NOTE

Although this inquiry is logically relevant to a ground for challenge, the inquiry also serves as a transparent device for suggesting the presence of insurance to the jury. If, as judge, you permitted the attorney to question prospective jurors regarding the "insurance question," how far would you allow the attorney to go? In particular, would you permit the attorney to mention the specific insurer involved in the case? In addition, if you allowed inquiry, what type of instruction would you give the jury? Does our toleration of this *voir dire* practice suggest that the time is ripe to abandon the exclusionary rule?

Part 5

SUFFICIENCY OF THE EVIDENCE

Chapter 30

THE INITIAL BURDEN OF GOING FORWARD

Read Federal Rules of Evidence 301 and 302.

A. INTRODUCTION

In Parts 3 and 4 of this text we examined questions relating to the admissibility of various types of evidence. In this Part, we shift our focus to a different issue: the cumulative sufficiency of all the evidence to prove a particular element of the case. Even if the plaintiff or prosecutor wins the battle over the admission of any particular item of evidence, she may lose the war. The judge may conclude that the cumulative probative value of all the admitted items of evidence is insufficient to establish a fact the plaintiff or prosecutor must prove and, on that ground, direct a defense verdict.

There are several ways to establish a fact during a trial. As we saw in Chapter 2, some facts are so well known or easily verifiable that they are subject to judicial notice under Federal Rule 201. The parties may also establish a fact by stipulation. In most instances, however, neither of these shortcuts is available and one of the parties will bear the burden of introduce enough evidence to persuade the judge and jury that the fact exists.

In evaluating the sufficiency of the evidence to prove a disputed fact, there are two distinct steps. First, the judge must assess the legal sufficiency of the evidence by determining whether it has sufficient probative value to permit a rational trier of fact to conclude that the fact exists. In other words, the judge inquires whether the proponent has sustained its initial burden of going forward (sometimes called **the burden of production**). If the proponent satisfies this burden, the proponent has made out a submissible case and will reach the jury. However, if the proponent fails to meet the burden of production, the judge takes the issue away from the jury and announces that the opponent has prevailed on the issue "as a matter of law."

Even if the proponent sustains the initial burden of production, the proponent has still another hurdle: persuading the trier of fact (the jury or, in a bench trial, the judge). This second burden is typically referred to as the **burden of persuasion**; together, the burdens of production and persuasion make up the overall **burden of proof.** In ruling on the first step, however, the judge decides only whether a rational trier of fact could decide that the fact exists. For example, in *Devitt* the prosecutor must persuade the judge that Paterson's identification of Devitt as the assailant is definite enough to permit a rational juror to find that Devitt committed the battery. Only after the judge has made that initial finding does the trier of fact assess the factual sufficiency of the evidence. The trier of fact evaluates the evidence to decide whether the fact exists: the prosecutor now faces the heavier burden of convincing the jury, beyond a reasonable doubt (the burden in a criminal case), that Devitt in fact attacked Paterson.

There is one further complication to this scheme: the concept of presumptions. **A presumption** is a statutory or decisional rule that operates to allow a party to meet a burden of production and/or persuasion. A presumption provides that proof of a certain designated fact will have a predetermined effect in establishing the existence of another fact. Presumptions can be highly useful. One common presumption is that if a letter is properly stamped, addressed, and mailed, the addressee received the letter. *See Baldwin County Welcome Ctr. V. Brown*, 466 U.S. 147, 148 n.1 (1984) (presuming receipt within three days). There is a related presumption that the letter was mailed on the date shown. *See Celestine v. Cold Crest Care Center*, 495 F. Supp. 2d 428 (S.D.N.Y. 2007) (in a disability suit, court notes a rebuttable presumption that government mailed notice on date shown).

At the outset, you may be struck by the fact that the number of rules governing the admissibility of evidence in our system dwarfs the number governing the sufficiency of evidence. In contrast, civil law systems traditionally had quite detailed rules for determining the sufficiency of the evidence — for example, two witnesses or a witness's testimony corroborated by documentary evidence might be required to establish a proposition.

In Anglo-American evidence law, on the other hand, "[t]here are few formal rules governing questions of" the sufficiency of evidence. Twining, *The Rationalist Tradition of Evidence Scholarship*, in WELL AND TRULY TRIED 211, 221 (E. Campbell & L. Waller, eds. 1982). Rather than fashioning "artificial legal rules," our system relies primarily on "the natural processes of the mind" to determine the legal sufficiency of evidence. J. WIGMORE, 1 THE SCIENCE OF JUDICIAL PROOF 5 (3d ed. 1937). Occasionally, common law jurisdictions recognize numerical rules. For instance, Pennsylvania follows a "two witness" rule in contract reformation cases. *See Giant Eagle, Inc. v. Federal Ins. Co.*, 92 F.3d 205, 212 (3d Cir. 1996), and the federal and many state constitutions commonly impose corroboration requirements in prosecutions for the most serious offenses against the state. For example, § 3 of Article III of the national constitution provides that "[n]o person shall be convicted of Treason unless on the Testimony of two Witensses to the same overt Act. . . ." As a general proposition, though, the testimony of a single witness is sufficient to support any finding of fact. CAL. EVID. CODE § 411; GA. CODE ANNOT. § 24-4-8.

B.   THE INITIAL BURDEN OF GOING FORWARD: AN OVERVIEW

The burden of production may be thought of as a duty owed by one of the parties to the trial judge. The duty is the obligation to convince the judge that the proponent's evidence is strong enough to allow a rational trier of fact to return a verdict in the proponent's favor. There are various ways that this burden has been articulated: The proponent's evidence must be sufficient to make out a "submissible" case; a case strong enough to submit to a rational jury; the issue must be "trial-worthy." *Colantuoni v. Alfred Calcagni & Sons, Inc.*, 44 F.3d 1 (1st Cir. 1994).

In deciding whether the evidence would support a logical inference by a rational jury, "[t]he key . . . is the reasonable probability that the conclusion flows from the evidentiary datum because of past experience in human affairs." *Levendos v. Stern Entertainment Co.*, 909 F.2d 747, 753 (3d Cir. 1990) (*quoting* R. ALDISERT, LOGIC FOR LAWYERS: A GUIDE TO CLEAR LEGAL THINKING 29 (1989)).

Suppose, for example, that at the close of Ms. Hill's case-in-chief, Polecat Motors' attorney believes that Ms. Hill has not presented sufficient evidence of negligent manufacture or an unreasonably dangerous defect. Polecat's attorney should move for a nonsuit or judgment as a matter of law. If the judge agrees that Ms. Hill has presented insufficient proof of negligence or defect, the judge would grant the motion and proclaim a defense victory. For purposes of ruling on this motion, the judge assumes the truth of all Ms. Hill's evidence. To grant the motion and declare a defense victory, the judge must conclude that even if the jury chose to believe all of Ms. Hill's evidence, the evidence of negligence or a defect is insufficient to support a rational plaintiff's verdict. To shield Polecat Motors from an irrational verdict, the judge thus takes the case from the jury and enters a judgment for the defense. The term for this type of ruling varies from jurisdiction to jurisdiction: nonsuit, directed verdict, judgment as a matter of law, finding of not guilty, or judgment of acquittal. FED. R. CIV. P. 50 (motion for "judgment as a matter of law"); FED. R. CRIM. P. 29 ("motion for judgment of acquittal"). The common denominator is the judge's decision to preclude the possibility of an irrational verdict by taking the case from the jury and announcing the result "as a matter of law."

There remains the question of which party has the initial burden of production for a particular fact. Thus far in this discussion, we have assumed that the plaintiff or prosecutor has the burden of production on any given issue, but this is not necessarily the case. We shall consider the allocation of the ultimate burden of persuasion in detail in the next chapter. At this point, you should begin with the rule of thumb that the party with the ultimate burden of persuasion will also have the initial burden of production. In *Hill*, the plaintiff has both the initial and ultimate burdens on the factual issues of negligent manufacture and the existence of an unreasonably dangerous design defect. However, it would be wasteful and unduly burdensome to assign to plaintiff the initial burden to anticipate and negate all conceivable affirmative defenses. *See Barton Group, Inc. v. NCR Corp.*, 796 F. Supp. 2d 473, 498 (S.D.N.Y. 2011) (noting that a contractual party pleading breach by the suing party is asserting an affirmative defense, and has the burden of proving it). In most jurisdictions, for example, if Roe wants to raise the issue of Ms. Hill's contributory negligence, Roe must assume the initial and ultimate burdens on the issue.

1. The General Mechanics of the Burden

The following excerpt lays out a framework for analyzing burdens of production, including presumptions and their potential effect in shifting burdens of production or persuasion. Pay close attention to the various types of presumptions and to the (rather confusing) array of terms that are used to describe different types of presumptions.

2 E. IMWINKELRIED, P. GIANNELLI, F. GILLIGAN & F. LEDERER, COURTROOM CRIMINAL EVIDENCE §§ 2904–12
(5th ed. 2011)

Attempting to Sustain the Burden Many evidence students have complained that this area of law is abstract to the point of being metaphysical. At the outset, diagramming the steps the proponent and opponent progress through is helpful. The following is a discussion of the most important steps depicted on the diagram.

The Proponent Fails to Sustain the Burden. In the first step, the proponent's evidence is insufficient to sustain the burden. The older view is that a mere scintilla of evidence is sufficient to sustain the burden. More recently, the prevailing view is that the evidence must have sufficient probative value to permit the jurors to rationally infer that the disputed fact exists.

. . . [By virtue of *Jackson v. Virginia*, 443 U.S. 307 (1979), a] stricter standard applies in criminal cases. This view is that the test in criminal cases is whether the evidence is so weak that the jurors must have a remaining lingering reasonable doubt; even if there is a permissive inference of the fact's existence, the evidence is insufficient if it would necessarily leave rational jurors with a lingering doubt about the defendant's guilt.

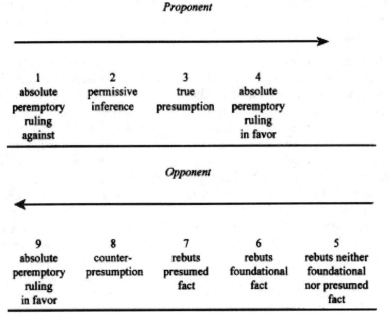

Suppose that the defendant attempts to raise the defense of insanity. The judge allocates the defendant the initial burden of going forward on that issue. Suppose further that the defendant's only evidence of insanity is the testimony of a lay witness to the crime. That witness gives conclusory testimony that several hours before the crime, the defendant was acting "a bit peculiar." At the instructions conference, the defense attorney requests an instruction on insanity. The judge will undoubtedly deny the request, for logically, the evidence lacks sufficient probative value to support an inference of insanity. Thus to control the rationality of the jury's findings, the judge will withdraw the issue from the jury. This ruling can be restated symbolically. The proponent, the defense, has presented credible evidence of fact A, the defendant's slightly peculiar behavior before the offense. The ultimate material fact in dispute is E, the defendant's sanity. In effect, the judge has ruled that *even if the jurors believe the evidence of A, they may not infer E.* A is the foundational or basic fact. E is the presumed fact. In this case, the foundational or basic fact does not have sufficient probative worth to permit an inference that E exists.

What is the procedural consequence if the proponent reaches only this step? As a matter of law, the judge will make an absolute peremptory ruling against the proponent. If the prosecution has the burden on an issue and prosecution reaches only step #1, the judge will grant a motion for directed verdict, judgment of acquittal, or finding of not guilty. When the defense has the burden on a defense and reaches only step #1, the judge will not instruct the jury on the defense. The proponent suffers an absolute defeat on the issue.

The Proponent Barely Sustains the Burden. In the second step, the proponent barely sustains the burden of going forward. The proponent ordinarily reaches this step by presenting sufficient evidence to support a rational jury finding of the existence of the fact in dispute. Under *Jackson v. Virginia*, when the prosecution has the burden, the evidence must be sufficient to permit a hypothetical juror to infer guilt beyond a reasonable doubt. The judge assesses the probative value of the proponent's evidence and concludes that the value is sufficient to sustain the burden. Alternatively, for policy reasons the legislature can declare that if the proponent proves specified foundational facts, the jury may infer the fact in dispute. [T]he creation of an inference by legislative fiat poses serious constitutional questions in criminal cases.

Returning to the original hypothetical, suppose that the defense attorney now presents more extensive lay testimony. The lay witness states that he or she has known the defendant intimately for several years; at the time of the offense, the defendant was absolutely incoherent, lacked muscular control, and had a dazed appearance; and in the witness' opinion, the defendant was insane. Once again, the defense attorney requests an instruction on insanity. Now the judge will probably grant the request. The proponent defense has presented evidence of fact B, detailed testimony about bizarre behavior on the part of the defendant whom the witness knew well. The judge rules that *if the jurors believe the evidence of B, they may infer E.*

At this stage, the proponent has created a permissive inference or presumption of fact. The procedural consequence is that the judge will submit the issue to the jury. If the proponent reaches only step #2, neither party will be subject to a peremptory ruling by the judge.

The Proponent Creates a True Presumption. In the third step, the proponent goes beyond barely sustaining the burden, presenting sufficient evidence to create a true presumption or mandatory inference. In the second step, the proponent creates a mere permissive inference; the jury may infer the existence of the fact in dispute from the foundational evidence. The third step is qualitatively different. There is such a necessary or highly probable connection between the foundational fact and the fact in dispute that the inference is mandatory; if the jurors believe the foundational evidence, they must infer the existence of the fact in dispute. The California statutes clearly draw the distinction. California Evidence Code § 600(b) defines an inference as "a deduction of fact that may logically and reasonably be drawn from another fact or group of facts." In contrast, Evidence Code § 600 (a) declares that a presumption is "an assumption of fact that the law requires to be made from another or group of facts." Ordinarily the proponent must rely upon the evidence's sheer probative value to carry the proponent to the third step. Of course, as in the second step, a legislature may create a presumption by fiat, declaring that if the jury finds that specified foundational facts exist, they must infer the fact in dispute. Here again, in criminal cases, such legislative declarations pose constitutional issues.

Revisiting the hypothetical, suppose that the defense attorney presents a properly authenticated copy of a judgment showing that shortly before the alleged offense, a court of competent jurisdiction adjudged the defendant permanently insane. If the defendant suffered from a relatively permanent mental disorder such a short time before the offense, he or she was probably insane at the time of the alleged *actus reus*. The foundational evidence is so powerful that it creates a mandatory inference or true presumption of insanity. The foundational evidence, fact C, gives rise to a mandatory inference of the existence of the fact in dispute. The judge would rule that *if the jurors believe the evidence of C, they must infer E.*

The proponent has now created a mandatory inference or presumption of law or prima facie case. A true presumption has one and sometimes two procedural consequences. The first is that if the presumption does not disappear from the case, it will entitle the proponent to a conditional peremptory ruling which takes the form of a favorable instruction to the jury. Because the presumption does not entitle the proponent to an absolute peremptory ruling, the judge will not instruct the jury that E, the fact in dispute, exists. Rather, the ruling is conditional, and the condition is the jury's belief of the foundational evidence. Thus the judge instructs the jury that they must infer E if they believe the evidence of C. The conditional ruling is peremptory because the judge has withdrawn from the jury the issue of the connection between C and E, telling the jury that a necessary connection exists between the two facts. However, the jury must nevertheless decide whether to believe the evidence of C.

In some jurisdictions, a second procedural consequence flowing from the creation of a presumption is a shift of the ultimate burden of proof. This consequence could conceivably operate against a criminal defendant. In a homicide case, the prosecution must prove the death of the alleged victim. Some jurisdictions recognize a burden-shifting presumption that a person is dead if he or she has not been heard from in seven years. In a bigamy case, the prosecution must establish the validity of the first marriage. Several jurisdictions recognize a burden-shifting presumption that a ceremonial marriage is valid. Some statutes creating burden-shifting presumptions expressly provide that the presumption may not operate against a criminal defendant.

The Proponent Obtains an Absolute Peremptory Ruling. In the first step, the judge makes an absolute peremptory ruling against the proponent; the judge withdraws the issue from the jury and announces the proponent's loss. In the fourth step, the judge makes an absolute peremptory ruling in the proponent's favor; the judge withdraws the issue from the jury and announces the proponent's victory. In this situation the proponent presents such overwhelming evidence and the opponent presents such meager evidence that the jury's finding against the proponent would be irrational.

Understandably, a proponent rarely reaches the fourth step. The fifth and fourteenth amendments preclude absolute peremptory rulings against the defendant on essential elements of the charged offense. However, occasionally, some defendants have won absolute peremptory ruling. In the original hypothetical, suppose that the defense presented extensive expert psychiatric testimony of schizophrenia, and the prosecution did not present even lay rebuttal testimony. Under these circumstances, some defendants have won absolute peremptory rulings which dismiss the charges against them. There is also authority that if the defendant presents uncontradicted evidence of entrapment, the defendant is entitled to dismissal. Such cases share several common elements. First, the proponent presents extensive, credible evidence of the foundational facts. Second, the opponent presents no or very meager rebuttal evidence. Third, the opponent usually has the ultimate burden of proof on the issue. In the insanity cases, although the defense has the initial burden of going forward on the insanity issue, in most jurisdictions the prosecution has the ultimate burden of proof. If all three elements are present, an absolute peremptory ruling in the proponent's favor is appropriate.

Here the foundational evidence is D. The judge rules that *(1) the jury must believe the evidence of D and (2) the jury must infer E from D.* In the third step, the judge makes only the second ruling — the conditional peremptory ruling that a necessary connection exists between C and E. However, the judge does not direct the jury to believe the evidence of C. In the fourth step, the judge concludes that the jury's disbelieving the evidence of D would be irrational. Therefore, the judge removes the condition and makes an absolute ruling. For example, if several reputable psychiatrists testify that the defendant was suffering from a psychosis and the prosecution presents no rebuttal, the defense is entitled to an absolute peremptory ruling. The ruling for the defense takes the form of a directed verdict, judgment of acquittal, or finding of not guilty.

Attempting to Rebut the Evidence

Assume that the proponent reaches either step #2 or #3. If the proponent reaches step #2, the proponent has barely sustained the burden; if the proponent reaches step #3, the proponent creates a true presumption. In both cases, the proponent has satisfied the burden of going forward. However, so long as the proponent does not reach step #4, the opponent escapes an absolute peremptory ruling. Moreover, the opponent usually has the opportunity to present rebuttal evidence to demonstrate that the presumed fact does not exist, for most presumptions are rebuttable. Although the proponent gains the benefit of a permissive or mandatory inference that E exists, the opponent may introduce evidence that E does not exist.[22]

The Opponent Does Not Present Sufficient Evidence to Rebut Either the Foundational or the Presumed Fact. In the fifth step, the opponent fails to present sufficient evidence to rebut either the foundational fact or the presumed fact. The form of the instruction the jury hears depends upon whether the proponent attained the second or the third step. If the proponent reached the second step, the instruction is that *if the jurors believe the evidence of B, they may infer E*. If the proponent attained the third step, the instruction is that *if the jurors believe the evidence of C, they must infer E*.

The Opponent Presents Sufficient Evidence to Rebut the Foundational Fact. In the sixth step, the opponent still fails to present sufficient evidence to rebut the ultimate fact in dispute, E. However, the opponent does succeed in presenting sufficient evidence to rebut the foundational fact. With one exception, the jury instructions are the same as they are in the fifth step. This exception is that judge must call the jury's attention to the fact that the parties have presented conflicting evidence on the foundational fact. There is now a disputed question of fact over whether the foundational fact exists. The judge instructs that *the jurors must resolve the conflict in the evidence over whether the foundational fact, B or C, exists*. The judge then delivers the instructions previously outlined.

The Opponent Presents Sufficient Evidence to Rebut the Presumed Fact. In the seventh step, the opponent mounts a sufficient rebuttal against E itself, the ultimate fact in dispute. Two questions arise. The first is the standard for determining when the opponent has presented sufficient rebuttal evidence. The second is the procedural effect of the opponent's presentation of sufficient rebuttal evidence.

The Sufficiency of the Rebuttal Evidence. The courts have unfortunately articulated numerous conflicting standards for testing the sufficiency of the opponent's rebuttal evidence, including "substantial evidence to the contrary, any contradictory evidence, some evidence to the contrary, competent evidence, evi-

---

[22] There are conclusive or irrebuttable presumptions. Such presumptions are in this form: If the jurors believe the evidence of C, they must infer E. That statement is elliptical; to state the matter more starkly, if the jurors believe the evidence of C, they must infer E even if the opponent has credible evidence that E does not exist. The truth of the matter is that a conclusive presumption is a substantive rule of law rather than an evidentiary rule. 9 WIGMORE, EVIDENCE § 2492 (3d ed. 1940).

The legal consequence flows from the foundational facts, and the existence or non-existence of the presumed fact is immaterial.

Consider this statutory presumption for criminal nonsupport actions. A child born while a husband and wife are cohabiting is conclusively presumed to be the husband's natural offspring. In a nonsupport action, the defendant husband could attack the foundational facts. The husband could introduce evidence that the woman was not his lawful wife or that they were not cohabiting when the child was born. However, the husband could not attack the presumed fact, the child's legitimacy. The husband could not introduce another man's admission that he considered himself the father. In reality, the child's legitimacy is immaterial in the nonsupport action. By enacting the statutory evidentiary presumption, the legislature has effectively promulgated a substantive rule of law that a husband has a legal duty to support a child born of his wife while they are cohabiting. *Brian C. v. Ginger K.*, 77 Cal. App. 4th 1198, 92 Cal. Rptr. 2d 294, 298 (2000) ("While nominally a rule of evidence, there is no doubt that the conclusive presumption is a substantive rule of law . . .").

dence of equal weight, evidence legally sufficient to overcome the presumption, and testimony that outweighs the presumption." Nevertheless, the wealth of verbal formulae is reducible to five primary standards: the Model Code standard of "any evidence contrary thereto, regardless of whether it is credible or substantial"; substantial evidence to the contrary; evidence sufficient, standing alone, to support a finding that the material fact in dispute does not exist; evidence sufficient to leave the issue in equipoise; and finally, evidence which makes the fact's non-existence more likely than its existence.

The Effect of the Presentation of Sufficient Rebuttal Evidence. Suppose that under the prevailing standard in the jurisdiction, the judge decides that the opponent has presented sufficient rebuttal evidence. What is the procedural consequence? There are two schools of thought on this question.

The first is the majority view, the "bursting bubble" theory, advocated by Thayer, Wigmore, and the drafters of the Model Code. Their view is that the presumption disappears or self-destructs as soon as the opponent presents sufficient rebuttal evidence. If the opponent presents such evidence, the judge will not mention a mandatory inference or even the word presumption in the final jury charge. This school theorizes that presumptions are merely procedural devices for allocating the burden of going forward during the trial. If the judge has decided that the case should be submitted to the jury, the presumption has already spent its force and fulfilled its function.

Only the presumption has disappeared; the proponent is no longer at step #3. Usually a permissive inference remains, for the evidence of the foundational facts is still in the record, and that evidence ordinarily has sufficient probative value to keep the proponent at step #2, thus preventing an absolute peremptory ruling against the proponent. Conceivably, when the presumption disappears, the proponent could revert back to step #1. This possibility arises because, as previously stated, a legislature may create a presumption by fiat. If the foundational facts specified in the statute do not have sufficient probative value to support a permissive inference of the existence of the ultimate fact, E, the presentation of sufficient rebuttal evidence is fatal to the proponent's case. The immediate effect is the disappearance of the presumption; the proponent is no longer at step #3. More importantly, because the foundational facts do not support a permissive inference of E, the proponent reverts to step #1 and suffers an unfavorable absolute peremptory ruling.

The second school of thought asserts that the presumption remains in the case even after opponent presents sufficient rebuttal evidence. The adherents of this view include Morgan, McCormick, Bohlen, and the drafters of the Uniform Rules. This view has significant procedural consequences. First, even after the opponent reaches step #7, the proponent remains at step #3. Hence, it is impossible for the proponent to revert to step #1 and suffer an unfavorable absolute peremptory ruling. Second, regardless of the rebuttal evidence, the proponent obtains a favorable jury instruction. However, even the courts subscribing to the second school of thought disagree over the instruction's wording.

Some courts prefer merely to inform the jury that the presumption exists and do not even attempt to explain the presumption's operation to the jury. Other courts inform the jury of the presumption's existence and then describe the presumption itself as evidence. Still other courts use the term, presumption, but describe the presumption as a permissive inference. The final group of courts urge that the presumption not only remains in the case but also shifts the ultimate burden of proof to the opponent. They instruct the jury *if the jurors believe the evidence of C, they must infer E unless the opponent proves by a certain measure of proof that E does not exist* — for example, by a preponderance of the evidence. Morgan and McCormick would apply this view to all true presumptions.

NOTES AND PROBLEMS

1.   Note the similarity in mode of analysis between Rule 104(b) admissibility determinations and sufficiency decisions under the initial burden of going forward. Under 104(b), the judge accepts the foundational testimony at face value to determine whether the proffered item of evidence is admissible and may be presented to the jury. Under the initial burden, the judge accepts the testimony on the historical merits at face value and decides whether the proponent's case may be submitted to the jury. The judge cannot "play thirteenth juror." *United States v. Genova*, 333 F.3d 750, 757 (7th Cir. 2003). The only notable exception is the "physical facts rule." *Harris v. General Motors Corp.*, 201 F.3d 800, 802 (6th Cir. 2000). The judge may reject testimony that is "impossible under the laws of nature." *United States v. Okoronkwo*, 46 F.3d 426, 430 (5th Cir.) ("defies physical laws"), *cert. denied*, 516 U.S. 833 (1995); *United States v. Bermea*, 30 F.3d 1539, 1552 (5th Cir. 1994) ("incredible as a matter of law"), *cert. denied sub nom. Rodriguez v. United States*, 513 U.S. 1156 (1995); *United States v. Blas*, 947 F.2d 1320 (7th Cir. 1991), *cert. denied*, 502 U.S. 1118 (1992); *United States v. Boyd*, 792 F. Supp. 1083 (N.D. Ill. 1992) (immutable laws of nature).

2.   Although the mailed letter presumption applies to regular mail, it is particularly strong in the case of certified mail. However, in the case of certified mail, the presumption does not arise unless the sender receives the requested return receipt. Recently, courts have extended the presumption to apply to the use of telegrams and email. *Am. Boat Co. v. Unknown Sunken Barge*, 418 F.3d 910, 913–14 (8th Cir. 2005), *aff'd*, 567 F.3d 348 (8th Cir. 2009), and even private courier service. *Murray v. TXU Corp.*, 279 F. Supp. 2d 799 (N.D. Tex. 2003).

3.   **Problem 30-1.** In *Hill*, the Morena legislature enacts a statute creating a presumption that when an injury results from an automobile accident, the manufacturer's negligence in manufacturing the auto was one of the causes of the accident. At trial, Ms. Hill requests the judge to give the jury an instruction based on the statutory presumption. Polecat Motors' attorney opposes the request and assails the statute's constitutionality. *See also B & G Const. v. Director, Workers' Comp'n Programs*, 662 F.3d 233, 254 (3d Cir. 2011) ("A plurality of the Supreme Court has rejected the theory that a legislature's use of an irrebuttable presumption automatically violates the Due Process Clause"); *Delong v. Department of Health and Human Services*, 264 F.3d 1334, 1341 (Fed. Cir. 2001) (civil "statutes creating conclusive presumptions are judged under the same due process standards as other statutes"); *Brian C. v. Ginger K.*, 77 Cal. App. 4th 1198, 92 Cal. Rptr. 2d 294, 298 (2000) ("While nominally a rule of evidence, there is no doubt that the conclusive

presumption [of paternity under Cal. Fam. Code § 7540] is a substantive rule of law.
. . .").

(a) Do the underlying facts, the accident and resulting injury, support a permissive inference of negligence on the manufacturer's part?

(b) If not, what argument should Ms. Hill make to support the statute? Assume that as a matter of substantive due process, it would be constitutional for the Morena legislature to impose strict liability on automobile manufacturers for deaths resulting from the use of their products.

See *Ferry v. Ramsey*, 277 U.S. 88, 94–95 (1928).

3. **Problem 30-2.** In Morena, the plaintiff in a negligence action has the ultimate burden of proving freedom from contributory negligence to recover. However, the Morena legislature has enacted a statutory "presumption" that persons injured in automobile accidents exercised due care in attempting to avoid the accident. During their defense case-in-chief, Polecat Motors attempts to rebut the charge of design defect and Roe attempts to disprove the allegation of negligent operation; but neither presents affirmative evidence of Ms. Hill's negligence. At the close of all the evidence, Ms. Hill requests an instruction based on the presumption. As trial judge, would you give an instruction? If so, how would you word it? Should the instruction include the word "must"? Should the instruction include the word "presume" or "presumption"?

4. Is the presumption of innocence a true presumption? Does the defendant have to prove any foundational facts to avail himself or herself of the "presumption"? See *Carr v. State*, 192 Miss. 152, 156, 4 So. 2d 887, 888 (1941). Would it be more accurate to refer to the doctrine as an "assumption"?

5. **Problem 30-3.** During her cross-examination, Ms. Hill gives the following testimony:

Q: Were you watching the road at the time of the collision?

A: No.

Q: Isn't it true that you were searching through your purse for a cigarette lighter?

A: Maybe.

Q: Yes or no, Ms. Hill.

A: Yes.

Q: And you were doing that for five or six seconds before the collision. Weren't you?

A: Yes.

Q: With your eyes off the road?

A: Yes.

At the close of the plaintiff's case-in-chief, Roe's attorney moves for a directed verdict on the ground of contributory negligence. What ruling? See *Fidelity & Guar. Ins. Underwriters, Inc. v. Mendoza*, 588 S.W.2d 612, 615–16 (Tex. Civ. App. 1979);

Note, *Directing a Verdict in Favor of the Party with the Burden of Proof*, 16 WAKE FOREST L. REV. 607, 612 (1980).

6. **Problem 30-4.** Suppose that rather than giving the testimony in Problem 30-3, Ms. Hill had admitted that she was driving "about 10 — 12 miles over the speed limit." Should the trial judge direct a defense verdict on the basis of that testimony? Is the testimony in this variation of the hypothetical distinguishable from that in Problem 30-3? *See Smith v. Secrist*, 590 S.W.2d 386, 389–90 (Mo. Ct. App. 1979).

7. **Problem 30-5.** Revisit Problem 30-2. During his defense case-in-chief, Mr. Roe calls Mr. Taylor as a witness. Taylor states that he observed Ms. Hill "for about five or six seconds before impact, and she didn't seem to be watching the road at all." As in Problem 30-2, Ms. Hill requests an instruction based on the statute. In a jurisdiction following the Morgan-McCormick view, how would you phrase the instruction?

8. Which view is sounder? The proponents of the Morgan-McCormick view point out that lay jurors are unaccustomed to working with the formal rules of logic and circumstantial evidence. In his classic article on the subject, Dean McCormick asserted that lay "[p]ersons unaccustomed to weighing evidence . . . are notoriously suspicious of circumstantial inferences." McCormick, *What Shall the Trial Judge Tell the Jury About Presumptions?*, 13 WASH. L. REV. 185, 188 (1938). The commentators argue that the presumption instruction gives the jury needed guidance in evaluating the circumstantial evidence. Does that argument really lead to the conclusion that the judge should instruct on a presumption? Could the judge give the jury sufficient guidance by informing them that a certain configuration of circumstantial evidence would sustain a permissive inference? Is there any need to resort to the words "must" or "presume"?

9. Which view does Federal Rule of Evidence 301 adopt? *See Texas Dept. of Community Affairs v. Burdine*, 450 U.S. 248, 254–55 (1981); *Usery v. Turner Elkhorn Mining Co.*, 428 U.S. 1, 27 (1976); *St. Mary's Honor Center v. Hicks*, 509 U.S. 502, 510 (1993) ("The presumption, having fulfilled its role of forcing the defendant to come forward with some response, simply drops out of the picture"). When the Supreme Court submitted proposed Article III of the Federal Rules of Congress, that article suffered a fate similar to proposed Article V on privileges. The Court's proposal included draft Rule 3-03(b), reading that "[a] presumption imposes on the party against whom it is directed the burden of proving that the nonexistence of the presumed fact is more probable than its existence." Congress refused to enact the proposed rule. Instead, Congress adopted the current Rule 301. The Conference Report states that, under Rule 301, "[i]f the adverse party . . . offer[s] evidence contradicting the presumed fact, the court cannot instruct the jury that it may presume the existence of the presumed fact from proof of the basic fact." Thus, unless there is a contrary statute, the federal courts generally apply the "bursting bubble" theory. *Cappuccio v. Prime Capital Funding LLC*, 649 F.3d 180, 189–90 (3d Cir. 2011). The single notable exception to this general rule is maritime law. There, even without the benefit of a statute, the courts sometimes recognize presumptions shifting the ultimate burden of proof. Admiralty law tends to "stand . . . apart from other areas of federal law." *Hood v. Knappton Corp., Inc.*, 986 F.2d 329 (9th Cir.

1993); *Kelly v. Armstrong*, 141 F.3d 799, 802 (8th Cir. 1998) ("th[e] inference or presumption of negligence [on an admiralty law issue] . . . is not governed by Rule 301 . . . [but] is determined as a matter or substantive law . . .").

10.   Note the eighth step on the diagram, the opponent's creation of a counter presumption. The step can arise in a case in which conflicting presumptions could conceivably apply. Suppose, for example, that there is a contest over a decedent's estate. Ms. Hill died in the collision, and two men — Arthur and Gilbert — both claim to be her surviving husband and heir-at-law. Gilbert has evidence that he married the decedent in 1973. Morena has a presumption that, once created, a condition or status such as marriage continues. However, Arthur has evidence of a ceremonial marriage with the decedent in 1978. Morena also has a presumption of the validity of ceremonial marriages. *See* CAL. EVID. CODE § 663; *Daimlerchrysler Corp. Healthcare Benefits Plan v. Durden*, 448 F.3d 918 (6th Cir. 2006). This problem has divided the courts into four different schools of thought.

One school of thought is the double bursting bubble — the presumptions negate each other, and both presumptions disappear from the case. The judge calls the jurors' attention to the evidence on both sides of the issue, allocates the ultimate burden of proof, and tells the jury nothing more.

Another view is that the judge should identify the "weightier" presumption and instruct on that presumption. *See Rader v. Thrasher*, 57 Cal. 2d 244, 252, 18 Cal. Rptr. 736, 740-41, 368 P.2d 360, 364–65 (1962). In weighing the presumption, the judge considers such factors as the probative value of the foundational facts and the magnitude of any social policy that the presumption implements.

A third position — Wigmore's view — denies that there are "conflicting" presumptions. Wigmore argued that there are successive presumptions rather than conflicting presumptions. The first presumption arises when Gilbert presents his evidence of the 1973 marriage, but that bubble bursts as soon as Arthur proves the 1978 marriage. The only remaining presumption is the presumption of the validity of the 1978 ceremonial marriage. *See Montpelier v. Calais*, 114 Vt. 5, 39 A.2d 350, 356 (1944).

The fourth approach is to tailor a third presumption for the case to resolve the conflict between the first two presumptions. For instance, the court might mediate the conflict in our hypothetical by fashioning a presumption that the first marriage terminated by divorce. *See Hewitt v. Firestone Tire & Rubber Co.*, 490 F. Supp. 1358, 1362 (E.D. Va. 1980); *Vargas v. Superior Ct.*, 9 Cal. App. 3d 470, 473, 88 Cal. Rptr. 281, 283 (1970).

2.   The Sufficiency of "Naked" Statistical Evidence to Satisfy the Burden

In Chapter 12, we saw that there is a heated controversy over the admissibility of statistical evidence. On that issue, the trend appears to be toward the more liberal admission of this type of evidence. The admissibility question, though, is by no means the end of the controversy over statistical evidence. Suppose that the plaintiff or prosecutor does not present any individualized or particularistic evidence about the parties in the case but presents only statistical evidence to prove a particular fact on which she has the burden of production. Is a case consisting of naked statistical evidence sufficient to go to the jury? The following case represents the traditional answer to that question.

SMITH v. RAPID TRANSIT, INC.
58 N.E.2d 754 (Mass. 1945)

SPALDING, JUSTICE.

The decisive question in this case is whether there was evidence for the jury that the plaintiff was injured by a bus of the defendant that was operated by one of its employees in the course of his employment. If there was, the defendant concedes that the evidence warranted the submission to the jury of the question of the operator's negligence in the management of the bus. The case is here on the plaintiff's exception to the direction of a verdict for the defendant.

These facts could have been found: While the plaintiff at about 1:00 A.M. on February 6, 1941, was driving an automobile on Main Street, Winthrop, in an easterly direction toward Winthrop Highlands, she observed a bus coming toward her which she described as a "great big, long, wide affair." The bus, which was proceeding at about forty miles an hour, "forced her to turn to the right," and her automobile collided with a "parked car." The plaintiff was coming from Dorchester. The department of public utilities had issued a certificate of public convenience or necessity to the defendant for three routes in Winthrop, one of which included Main Street,[1] and this was in effect in February, 1941.

"There was another bus line in operation in Winthrop at that time but not on Main Street." According to the defendant's time-table, buses were scheduled to leave Winthrop Highlands for Maverick Square via Main Street at 12:10 A.M., 12:45 A.M., 1:15 A.M., and 2:15 A.M. The running time for this trip at that time of night was thirty minutes. The direction of a verdict for the defendant was right. The ownership of the bus was a matter of conjecture. While the defendant had the sole franchise for operating a bus line on Main Street, Winthrop, this did not preclude private or chartered buses from using this street; the bus in question could very well have been one operated by someone other than the defendant. It was said in *Sargent v. Massachusetts Accident Co.*, 307 Mass. 246, at page 250, 29 N.E.2d 825, at page 827, that it is "not enough that mathematically the chances somewhat favor a proposition to be proved; for example, the fact that colored automobiles made in the current year outnumber black ones would not warrant a finding that an undescribed automobile of the current year is colored and not black, nor would the fact that only a minority of men die of cancer warrant a finding that a particular man did not die of cancer." The most that can be said of the evidence in the instant case is that perhaps the mathematical chances somewhat favor the proposition that a bus of the defendant caused the accident. This was not enough. A "proposition is proved by a preponderance of the evidence if it is made to appear more likely or probable in the sense that actual belief in its truth, derived from the evidence, exists in the mind or minds of the tribunal notwithstanding any doubts that may still linger

---

[1] The defendant in its brief concedes that this route included the place where the accident occurred.

there." *Sargent v. Massachusetts Accident Co.*, 307 Mass. 246, at page 250, 29 N.E.2d 825 at page 827.

In cases where it has been held that a vehicle was sufficiently identified so as to warrant a finding that it was owned by the defendant, the evidence was considerably stronger than that in the case at bar. *See*, for example, *Kelly v. Railway Express Agency, Inc.*, 315 Mass. 301, 52 N.E.2d 411; *Gallagher v. R. E. Cunniff, Inc.*, 314 Mass. 7, 8, 9, 49 N.E.2d 448; *Breen v. Dedham Water Co.*, 241 Mass. 217, 135 N. E. 130; *Heywood v. Ogasapian*, 224 Mass. 203, 112 N.E. 619; *Hopwood v. Pokrass*, 219 Mass. 263, 106 N.E. 997.

The evidence in the instant case is no stronger for the plaintiff than that in *Atlas v. Silsbury-Gamble Motors Co.*, 278 Mass. 279, 180 N.E. 127, or in *Cochrane v. Great Atlantic & Pacific Tea Co.*, 281 Mass. 386, 183 N.E. 757, where it was held that a finding that the vehicle in question was owned by the defendant was not warranted.

Exceptions overruled.

NOTES

1. The orthodox view has been that if a party relied on naked statistical evidence, as a matter of law the party's case was legally insufficient; "the evidence would never reach the jury." Nesson, *The Evidence or the Event? On Judicial Proof and the Acceptability of Verdicts*, 98 HARV. L. REV. 1357, 1380 (1985). Professor Nesson cites *Smith* as authority for that proposition. However, other commentators argue that "the support for the proposition that courts are reluctant to let cases be decided on 'statistical evidence' is greatly exaggerated in the literature." Allen, *A Reconceptualization of Civil Trials*, 66 B.U. L. REV. 401, 429 n.67 (1986). Today there are signs that the courts are more inclined to uphold the sufficiency of cases consisting of statistical evidence. *See Kaminsky v. Hertz Corp.*, 94 Mich. App. 356, 288 N.W.2d 426, 427 (1979).

2. Professor Allen disputes the characterization of *Smith* as a case involving naked statistical evidence. The plaintiff "did not rely on any such evidence. She merely asserted that she was forced off the road by a bus and in addition proved that Rapid Transit, Inc., was the only bus line operating regularly on the road where the accident occurred." Allen, *supra.* In *Smith*, did the plaintiff establish that more than 50% of the buses on that road belonged to the defendant?

3. Why not uphold a case based on statistical evidence? If statistical evidence generates a 51% probability of all the relevant events and the normal test for the sufficiency of the evidence is whether a rational juror could find a 51% probability, why take the case away from the jury? To use Dean Wigmore's expression, if "the natural processes of the mind" would lead a juror to conclude that the test has been satisfied, why create an "artificial legal rule" that the evidence is insufficient? In the final analysis, like the traditional support for the *Frye* test, the reluctance of some courts to uphold cases based on statistical evidence may bespeak the courts' fear that the jurors will overvalue the scientific testimony. However, several empirical studies indicate that, rather than being overwhelmed by statistical evidence, jurors tend to underutilize statistical evidence during their deliberations. *See* Kaye & Koehler, *Can Jurors Understand Probabilistic Evidence?*, 154 J. ROYAL STAT. SOC.

75, 79–80 (1991) ("[t]he clearest and most consistent finding"); Thompson & Shumann, *Interpretation of Statistical Evidence in Criminal Trials: The Prosecutor's Fallacy and the Defense Attorney's Fallacy*, 11 Law & Hum. Behav. 167, 183 (1987) ("[F]inal judgments of guilt . . . tended to be significantly lower than a Bayesian analysis suggests they should have been"); Faigman & Baglioni, *Bayes' Theorem in the Trial Process: Instructing Jurors on the Value of Statistical Evidence*, 12 Law & Hum. Behav. 1, 13–16 (1988). There is a natural distrust of the unfamiliar, and that distrust may be operative here.

4. Students of the application of probability theory to jury trials have developed several hypotheticals supposedly illustrating the dangers of upholding cases resting on naked statistical evidence.

One is the hypothetical of the blue bus, based on *Smith*. *See* Kaye, *The Laws of Probability and the Law of the Land*, 47 U. Chi. L. Rev. 34, 40 (1979). The evidence establishes that the plaintiff was negligently run over by a blue bus and that the defendant operates four-fifths of all the blue buses in town. *See* Kaye, *Paradoxes, Gedanken Experiments and The Burden of Proof: A Response to Dr. Cohen's Reply*, 1981 Ariz. St. L.J. 635, 636–37.

Another is the hypothetical of the gatecrasher. L. Cohen, The Probable and the Provable 49-120 (1977); Cohen, *Subjective Probability and the Paradox of the Gatecrasher*, 1981 Ariz. St. L.J. 627. The management of a rodeo sold 499 tickets. When they take attendance, they discover that there are 1,000 people in the seats — and a hole in the fence. There are 499 legal entrants, and 501 trespassers. They pick one attendee at random and sue him for the cost of admission. Of course, there is a better than 50% probability that he is a trespasser.

Are the two hypotheticals distinguishable? The argument against recovery in the gatecrasher hypothetical is a species of argument *reductio ad absurdum*; the management could present the same case against all 1,000 attendees and could possibly recover then even from the 499 legal entrants. Does permitting recovery in the blue bus hypothetical lead to the same absurd consequences?

It is not only arguable that the blue bus hypothetical is distinguishable. Professor Kaye has advanced a further argument for resolving the supposed paradox of the blue bus hypothetical: When more particularized evidence is readily available, a rational juror would find naked statistical evidence insufficient. Should jurors consider not only the evidence the parties have furnished but also data that conspicuously has been not supplied? Should jurors consider the completeness of the evidence? It may be helpful to remember that the various burdens of proof express "degree[s] of the jury's belief." 2 C. McCormick, Handbook of the Law of Evidence § 339, at 483 (6th ed. 2006).

Professor Shaviro goes further. *Statistical-Probability Evidence and the Appearance of Justice*, 103 Harv. L. Rev. 530 (1989). He notes that all testimony implicitly involves uncertainty. *Id.* at 536. Eyewitness identification testimony is unquestionably prone to error, and "the exact error rate" has not been quantified. Yet the courts routinely sustain criminal guilty verdicts on the basis of such testimony. He concedes that statistical evidence is more overtly uncer tain and probabilistic. *Id.* at 546. Although in the past courts have been squeamish about relying on statistical evidence, Professor Shaviro argues that the admission of such testimony can improve the accuracy of fact-finding and thereby strengthen society's commitment to minimize injustice. *Id.* at 548.

5. In section B.1 of this chapter, we saw that given *Jackson v. Virginia*, 443 U.S. 307, 318 (1979), there is a higher standard for the burden of going forward in criminal cases. The prosecution evidence must not only create a permissive inference of the existence of every element of the charged crime; the evidence must be capable of banishing every reasonable doubt from the mind of the hypothetical juror. Since the test is more rigorous in criminal trials, it would be consistent to hold that a naked statistical evidence case is sufficient in civil practice but not in a prosecution. Does Professor Kaye's argument in the blue bus hypothetical show that there is less than a 50% probability or that at least the hypothetical juror should have a lingering, reasonable doubt about the defendant's liability?

6. In sum, there are at least four positions a court can take on this controversy: A case consisting of naked statistical evidence is sufficient; the case is sufficient unless, as in the gatecrasher hypothetical, upholding the sufficiency of the evidence leads to absurd consequences; the case is legally insufficient; and the case is legally insufficient in a criminal trial. Which view do you prefer? Why?

C. THE BURDEN OF PRODUCTION IN CRIMINAL CASES

Distinctive problems arise when we attempt to analyze the operation of the burden of production in criminal cases. The burden's primary function is to regulate the rationality of jury findings. However, in criminal cases, the solicitude for the defendant's liberty interest is so strong that we tolerate some irrational jury behavior in the defendant's favor. For example, because of the use of a general verdict and the secrecy of jury deliberations, the jury has the power to nullify the substantive law by acquitting an obviously guilty defendant; the Supreme Court has recognized the power. *See Sparf & Hanson v. United States*, 156 U.S. 51 (1895). To protect defendants from oppressive laws, the courts have acknowledged "the undisputed power of the jury to acquit, even if its verdict is contrary to the law . . . and the evidence." *United States v. Moylan*, 417 F.2d 1002, 1006 (4th Cir. 1969), *cert. denied*, 397 U.S. 910 (1970) (holding that the reasonable doubt standard has constitutional stature, so that juveniles are entitled to proof beyond a reasonable doubt of all elements of the crime charged). Moreover, due process mandates that the judge instruct the jury that they cannot convict the defendant unless they are convinced of the existence of all the crime's elements beyond a reasonable doubt. *See In re Winship*, 397 U.S. 358 (1970). Though this standard of proof may lead to erroneous acquittals of guilty persons, we tolerate those errors as the cost of society's decision to minimize the risk of the wrongful conviction of the innocent.

It is understandable, then, that the initial burden must be modified to adapt to criminal cases. To some extent, this need is reflected in the interpretation of statutes purporting to create "presumptions." As previously stated, the term "presumption" is often used in a vague, imprecise manner. In the technical, common law sense, a presumption is a mandatory inference. When a statute uses a term which has acquired a technical meaning at common law, courts ordinarily assume that the legislature intended the term in its common law sense. However, when a "presumption" is designed to operate against a criminal defendant, there is a countervailing interpretive consideration: the rule of lenity. *See Busic v. United States*, 446 U.S. 398, 406 (1980). When a criminal statute is ambiguous, the rule operates in the accused's favor and counsels the court to strictly construe the statute. *See United States v. Gray*, 633 F. Supp. 1311 (D. Mont. 1986), *aff'd*, 809 F.2d 579 (9th Cir.), *vacated on other grounds*, 484 U.S. 807 (1987). Hence, despite the fact that a statute uses the term "presumption," a court might interpret the statute as recognizing only a permissive inference in a criminal case.

As the preceding paragraph indicates, constitutional considerations indirectly influence the construction of statutes relating to presumption law. However, those considerations do not merely affect statutory interpretation; in several respects, they can also directly restrict the operative effect of the presumptions.

1.   Reaching Step #2 — Barely Sustaining the Burden

To begin with, the Constitution demands that the initial burden be applied in a modified fashion in criminal cases. One constitutional modification affects the standard for determining whether the proponent, the prosecutor, has sustained the burden. Until 1979, many jurisdictions applied the same standard in civil and criminal cases; whether the standard was a scintilla of evidence or substantial evidence, the same test governed both types of cases. However, in *Jackson v. Virginia*, 443 U.S. 307 (1979), the Supreme Court shattered the equation. In *Jackson*, Justice Stewart drew heavily on *Winship*. Although on its face *Winship* deals with only the measure of the ultimate burden of proof, Justice Stewart treated *Winship* as evidence of the preeminent value attached to the liberty interest — a value that warrants toughening the initial burden as well as the ultimate burden in criminal cases. On that reasoning, Justice Stewart announced that due process requires a directed verdict when the judge concludes "that upon the record evidence adduced at trial, no rational trier of fact could have found proof of guilt beyond a reasonable doubt." *Id.* at 324. The justice thus incorporated the expression, "beyond a reasonable doubt," into the test for sustaining the initial burden. *Id.* at 316.

NOTES AND PROBLEMS

1.   Problem 30-6. In *Devitt*, the attacker covered his face with a handkerchief. Paterson had a clear view of only the assailant's eyes and the bridge of his nose. At trial, Paterson admits that he had a "very limited" view of the attacker's face but nevertheless expresses "complete confidence that that man (pointing to Devitt) is the attacker." At the close of the prosecution case-in-chief, the defense attorney moves for a directed verdict. The defense attorney asserts that "although there might be barely a permissive inference of my client's identity as the assailant, that's not enough under *Jackson*, Your Honor. In a case as flimsy as this, any reasonable juror would necessarily have a lingering doubt about my client's innocence." What ruling? *See United States v. Sears*, 332 F.2d 199, 200–01 (7th Cir. 1964) (antedating *Jackson v. Virginia*).

2. Problem 30-7. Before trial, Paterson picked out Devitt's picture in a photograph spread at the police station. However, at trial, he could not identify Devitt; he testified, "It sorta looks like him, but I just can't be sure. I don't wanta guess." The trial judge admitted Paterson's pretrial identification of Devitt and treated it as substantive evidence of Devitt's identity as the assailant under Rule 801(d)(1)(C). At the close of the prosecution case-in-chief, the defense attorney again moves for a directed verdict. What ruling? Is Paterson's out-of-court statement entitled to as much weight as in-court testimony? *See People v. Valenzuela,* 175 Cal. App. 3d 381, 222 Cal. Rptr. 405, 410–11 (1985). Would it make a difference if the pretrial identification has been a corporeal lineup rather than a photographic spread? *See* Annot., 29 A.L.R.4th 104, 130–33 (1984).

3. Problem 30-8. Vary the facts in Problem 30-7. At a preliminary hearing, Paterson identifies Devitt as the attacker. However, at trial he is uncertain of the identification. On the witness stand, he states that Devitt "sorta looks like the guy. However, I've got to be honest with you, and I can't truthfully say that that's even probably the guy who attacked me. If I'm forced to say, I don't think it's him." At that point, the trial judge permits the prosecution to introduce Paterson's preliminary hearing identification as substantive evidence under Federal Rule 801(d)(1)(A). The prosecution rests without presenting further evidence of Devitt's identity as the attacker. The defense moves for a directed verdict. What ruling? *See People v. Gould,* 54 Cal. 2d 621, 631, 7 Cal. Rptr. 273, 278, 354 P.2d 865, 870 (1960) (en banc); Goldman, *Guilt by Intuition: The Insufficiency of Prior Inconsistent Statements to Convict,* 65 N.C. L. REV. 1, 40 (1986).

4. The British courts have taken a different approach to the problem of the sufficiency of eyewitness identification testimony; they have been more impressed by the scientific evidence of the unreliability of eyewitness testimony. The Court of Appeal, Criminal Division, has announced corroboration requirements. Theresby, *A Turnaround in the Use of Identification Evidence,* 62 A.B.A. J. 1343–44 (1976). The trial judge assesses the quality of the eyewitness testimony by considering such factors as the lighting conditions and the length of the opportunity for observation. If the caliber of the testimony is high, the judge submits the case to the jury with a cautionary instruction. "But if the quality was poor, as for instance if it depended solely on a fleeting glance, then the judge should withdraw the case from the jury and direct an acquittal, unless there was other evidence to support the correctness of the identification." *Id.*

2. Reaching Step #3 — Creating a True Presumption

The next modification is a constitutionally mandatory test for determining the validity of presumptions in criminal cases. The Court first addressed the issue in *Tot v. United States,* 319 U.S. 463 (1943). In *Tot,* the Court invalidated a statutory presumption that a firearm found in an ex-convict's possession had been received in interstate commerce. The Court rejected the "greater includes the lesser" theory applicable in civil cases. The Court declared that in a criminal case, "a statutory presumption cannot be sustained if there be no rational connection between the fact proved and the ultimate fact presumed, if the inference of the one from proof of the other is arbitrary because of lack of connection between the two in common experience." *Id.* at 467.

The *Tot* Court did not define "rational connection." Did the term mean logical relevance or sufficiency? Was it enough that the foundational fact was relevant to the presumed fact under Federal Rule of Evidence 401, or did the foundational fact have to have at least sufficient probative value to support an inference that the presumed fact exists? The Court embraced the second interpretation in 1969 in *Leary v. United States*, 395 U.S. 6 (1969). Speaking for the Court, Justice Harlan stated that "a criminal statutory presumption must be regarded as 'irrational' or 'arbitrary' and hence unconstitutional, unless it can at least be said with substantial assurance that the presumed fact is more likely than not to flow from the proved fact on which it is made to depend." *Id.* at 36.

However, even *Leary* did not satisfy the most ardent advocates of extending *Winship*'s protection to criminal defendants. For example, in *Turner v. United States*, 396 U.S. 398 (1970), the defense invited the Court to adopt "the more exacting reasonable doubt standard normally applicable in criminal cases." *Id.* at 416. Do the foundational facts have to have enough probative value to establish the presumed fact beyond a reasonable doubt? The Court declined the invitation in *Turner;* and three years later in *Barnes v. United States*, 412 U.S. 837, 843 (1973), the Court confessed that "the teaching" of its prior precedents was "not altogether clear." The Court did not bring needed clarity to this area of law until 1979. In that year, in *Ulster County Ct. v. Allen*, 442 U.S. 140 (1979), the Court passed on New York's statutory presumption that a firearm's presence in an automobile is evidence of its illegal possession by all the occupants. In the course of upholding the presumption, Justice Stevens wrote:

> Inferences and presumptions are a staple of our adversarial system of fact finding. It is often necessary for the trier of fact to determine the existence of an element of the crime — that is, an "ultimate" or "elemental" fact — from the existence of one or more "evidentiary" or "basic" facts. *E.g., Barnes v. United States*, 412 U.S. 837, 843–844; *Tot v. United States*, 319 U.S. 463, 467. The value of these evidentiary devices, and their validity under the Due Process Clause, vary from case to case, however, depending on the strength of the connection between the particular basic and elemental facts involved and on the degree to which the device curtails the factfinder's freedom to assess the evidence independently. Nonetheless, in criminal cases, the ultimate test of any device's constitutional validity in a given case remains constant: the device must not undermine the factfinder's responsibility at trial, based on evidence adduced by the State, to find the ultimate facts beyond a reasonable doubt. *See In re Winship*, 397 U.S. 358, 364.
>
> The most common evidentiary device is the entirely permissive inference or presumption, which allows — but does not require — the trier of fact to infer the elemental fact from proof by the prosecutor of the basic one and that places no burden of any kind on the defendant. *See, e.g., Barnes v. United States, supra*, at 840 n.3. In that situation the basic fact may constitute prima facie evidence of the elemental fact. *See, e.g., Turner v. United States*, 396 U.S. 398, 402 n.2. When reviewing this type of device, the

Court has required the party challenging it to demonstrate its invalidity as applied to him. *E.g., Barnes v. United States, supra*, at 845; *Turner v. United States, supra*, at 419–424. Because this permissive presumption leaves the trier of fact free to credit or reject the inference and does not shift the burden of proof, it affects the application of the "beyond a reasonable doubt" standard only if, under the facts of the case, there is no rational way the trier could make the connection permitted by the inference. For only in that situation is there any risk that an explanation of the permissible inference to a jury, or its use by a jury, has caused the presumptively rational factfinder to make an erroneous factual determination.

A mandatory presumption is a far more troublesome evidentiary device. For it may affect not only the strength of the "no reasonable doubt" burden but also the placement of that burden; it tells the trier that he or they must find the elemental fact upon proof of the basic fact, at least unless the defendant has come forward with some evidence to rebut the presumed connection between the two facts. *E.g., Turner v. United States, supra*, at 401–402, and n.1; *Leary v. United States*, 395 U.S. 6, 30; *United States v. Romano*, 382 U.S. 136, 137, and n.4, 138, 143; *Tot v. United States, supra*, at 469.[16] In this situation, the Court has generally examined the presump-

---

[16] This class of more or less mandatory presumptions can be subdivided into two parts: presumptions that merely shift the burden of production to the defendant, following the satisfaction of which the ultimate burden of persuasion returns to the prosecution; and presumptions that entirely shift the burden of proof to the defendant. The mandatory presumptions examined by our cases have almost uniformly fit into the former subclass, in that they never totally removed the ultimate burden of proof beyond a reasonable doubt from the prosecution. *E.g., Tot v. United States, supra*, at 469. To the extent that a presumption imposes an extremely low burden of production — *e.g.*, being satisfied by "any" evidence — it may well be that its impact is no greater than that of a permissive inference and it may be proper to analyze it as such. *See generally Mullaney v. Wilbur, supra*, 421 U.S., at 703 n.31.

In deciding what type of inference or presumption is involved in a case, the jury instructions will generally be controlling, although their interpretation may require recourse to the statute involved and the cases decided under it. *Turner v. United States, supra*, provides a useful illustration of the different types of presumptions. It analyzes the constitutionality of two different presumption statutes (one mandatory and one permissive) as they apply to the basic fact of possession of both heroin and cocaine, and the presumed facts of importation and distribution of narcotic drugs. The jury was charged essentially in the terms of the two statutes.

The importance of focusing attention on the precise presentation of the presumption to the jury and the scope of that presumption is illustrated by a comparison of *United States v. Gainey*, 380 U.S. 63 with *United States v. Romano*, 382 U.S. 136 (1965). Both cases involved statutory presumptions based on proof that the defendant was present at the site of an illegal still. In *Gainey* the Court sustained a conviction "for carrying on" the business of the distillery in violation of 26 U.S.C. § 5601(a)(4), whereas in *Romano*, the Court set aside a conviction for being in "possession, custody, and control" of such a distillery in violation of § 5601(a)(1). The difference in outcome was attributable to two important differences between the cases. Because the statute involved in *Gainey* was a sweeping prohibition of almost any activity associated with the still, whereas the *Romano* statute involved only one narrow aspect of the total undertaking, there was a much higher probability that mere presence could support an inference of guilt in the former case than in the latter.

Of perhaps greater importance, however, was the difference between the trial judge's instructions to the jury in the two cases. In *Gainey* the judge had explained that the presumption was permissive; it did not require the jury to convict the defendant even if it was convinced that he was present at the site. On the contrary, the instructions made it clear that presence was only "a circumstance to be considered

tion on its face to determine the extent to which the basic and elemental facts coincide. *E.g., Turner v. United States, supra,* at 408–418; *United States v. Romano, supra,* at 140–41; *Tot v. United States, supra,* at 468. To the extent that the trier of fact is forced to abide by the presumption, and may not reject it based on an independent evaluation of the particular facts presented by the State, the analysis of the presumption's constitutional validity is logically divorced from those facts and based on the presumption's accuracy in the run of cases.[17] It is for this reason that the Court has held it irrelevant in analyzing a mandatory presumption, but not in analyzing a purely permissive one, that there is ample evidence in the record other than the presumption to support a conviction. *E.g., Turner v. United States, supra,* at 407; *Leary v. United States, supra,* at 31–32; United States v. Romano, *supra,* at 138–139.

Without determining whether the presumption in this case was mandatory, the Court of Appeals analyzed it on its face as if it were. In fact, it was not, as the New York Court of Appeals had earlier pointed out.

The trial judge's instructions make it clear that the presumption was merely a part of the prosecution's case, that it gave rise to a permissive inference available only in certain circumstances, rather than a mandatory

---

along with all the other circumstances in the case." As we emphasized, the "jury was thus specifically told that the statutory [presumption] was not conclusive." Gainey, 380 U.S., at 69–70. In *Romano* the trial judge told the jury that the defendant's presence at the still "shall be deemed sufficient evidence to authorize conviction." Romano, 382 U.S., at 182. Although there was other evidence of guilt, that instruction authorized conviction even if the jury disbelieved all of the testimony except the proof of presence at the site. This Court's holding that the statutory presumption could not support the *Romano* conviction was thus dependent, in part, on the specific instructions given by the trial judge. Under those instructions it was necessary to decide whether, regardless of the specific circumstances of the particular case, the statutory presumption adequately supported the guilty verdict.

[17] In addition to the discussion of *Romano* in n. 16, *supra*, this point is illustrated by *Leary v. United States, supra.* In that case, Dr. Timothy Leary, a professor at Harvard University was stopped by customs inspectors in Laredo, Texas as he was returning from the Mexican side of the international border. Marihuana seeds and a silver snuff box filled with semi refined marihuana and three partially smoked marihuana cigarettes were discovered in his car. He was convicted of having knowingly transported marihuana which he knew had been illegally imported into this country in violation of 21 U.S.C. § 176a. That statute includes a mandatory presumption: "possession shall be deemed sufficient evidence to authorize conviction [for importation] unless the defendant explains his possession to the satisfaction of the jury." Leary admitted possession of the marihuana and claimed that he had carried it from New York to Mexico and then back.

Justice Harlan for the Court noted that under one theory of the case, the jury could have found direct proof of all of the necessary elements of the offense without recourse to the presumption. But he deemed that insufficient reason to affirm the conviction because under another theory the jury might have found knowledge of importation on the basis of either direct evidence or the presumption, and there was accordingly no certainty that the jury had not relied on the presumption. 395 U.S., at 31–32. The Court therefore found it necessary to test the presumption against the Due Process Clause. Its analysis was facial. Despite the fact that the defendant was well educated and had recently traveled to a country that is a major exporter of marihuana to this country, the Court found the presumption of knowledge of importation from possession irrational. It did so not because Dr. Leary was unlikely to know the source of the marihuana but instead because "a majority of possessors" were unlikely to have such knowledge. *Id.* at 53. Because the jury had been instructed to rely on the presumption even if it did not believe the Government's direct evidence of knowledge of importation (unless, of course, the defendant met his burden of "satisfying" the jury to the contrary), the Court reversed the conviction.

conclusion of possession, and that it could be ignored by the jury even if there was no affirmative proof offered by defendants in rebuttal. The judge explained that possession could be actual or constructive, but that constructive possession could not exist without the intent and ability to exercise control or dominion over the weapons. He also carefully instructed the jury that there is a mandatory presumption of innocence in favor of the defendants that controls unless it, as the exclusive trier of fact, is satisfied beyond a reasonable doubt that the defendant possessed the handguns in the manner described by the judge. In short, the instructions plainly directed the jury to consider all the circumstances tending to support or contradict the inference that all four occupants of the car had possession of the two loaded handguns and to decide the matter for itself without regard to how much evidence the defendants introduced. Our cases considering the validity of permissive statutory presumptions such as the one involved here have rested on an evaluation of the presumption as applied to the record before the Court. None suggests that a court should pass on the constitutionality of this kind of statute "on its face." It was error for the Court of Appeals to make such a determination in this case.

NOTE

Under *Ulster County, supra*, the substantive test for and the mode of analyzing the constitutionality of mandatory inferences (step #3) differ from those for permissive inferences (step #2). Be prepared to state the test and mode of analysis for each type of inference. *See People v. McCall*, 128 Cal. Rptr. 2d 917, 924 (Cal. Ct. App. 2002) ("A mandatory presumption may be constitutional if it is accurate beyond a reasonable doubt"), *superseded*, 132 Cal. Rptr. 2d 713, 66 P.3d 718 (Cal. 2003).

3. Reaching Step #4 — Obtaining an Absolute Peremptory Ruling

Still another modification peculiar to criminal cases is that the prosecutor cannot reach step four and obtain a peremptory ruling. *See People v. Mayberry*, 15 Cal. 3d 143, 125 Cal. Rptr. 745, 542 P.2d 1337 (1975) (reversing rape and kidnapping convictions). The judge may not direct a verdict of guilty, in whole or in part. *See United States v. Bosch*, 505 F.2d 78 (5th Cir. 1974) (a "trial judge is prohibited from entering a judgment of conviction or directing the jury to come forward with such verdict"). The judge may not do so even if the prosecution's evidence is overwhelming (*People v. Mayberry, supra*) or seemingly conclusive. *See Connecticut v. Johnson*, 460 U.S. 73, 83 (1983) (plurality opinion finding error in district court's failure to instruct the jury on the elements of conspiracy with intent to distribute; and its direction that a negative answer to the issue of immunity would mandate a finding of guilty).

4. Limitations on the Effect of Presumptions — The Operation of Truly Mandatory Presumptions

The previous subsections discuss the question of whether the prosecution can or has reached three of the various steps in sustaining the ultimate burden of proof: Has the prosecution established a permissive inference and attained step #2? Has the prosecution created a mandatory inference and achieved step #3? And, finally, has the prosecution reached Step #4, an absolute ruling? In contrast, this subsection assumes that the prosecution has otherwise reached step #3. The question that now arises is the permissible effect of a presumption at step #3.

NOTE AND PROBLEM

1. **Problem 30-9.** In *Devitt*, Paterson tells the prosecutor that although he had not seen Devitt in the week before the attack, during that week he, Paterson, had mailed Devitt a letter, firing him and stating that Devitt had done such shoddy carpentry work that he would not pay him anything for the work Devitt had already done. The prosecution contends that the contents of the letter gave Devitt a motive to attack Paterson. Morena normally presumes the addressee's receipt of a properly addressed, stamped, and mailed letter. 2 McCormick, Evidence § 343, at 502 (6th ed. 2006). At trial, Paterson testifies that he properly addressed, stamped, and mailed the letter to Devitt. Devitt does not take the stand. The prosecutor requests that the judge instruct the jury that "if you believe Mr. Paterson's testimony, you must conclude that Devitt received his letter." Devitt's attorney objects that "the instruction would violate *Ulster County*." What result? Does *Ulster County* apply to this instruction? Is the presumed fact ultimate or evidentiary? Should that make a difference? *United States v. Waldemer*, 50 F.3d 1379, 1386 (7th Cir. 1995) ("A mandatory presumption occurs where an instruction requires the jury to presume the existence of an ultimate fact, that is an element of the offense charged"); *In re Ivey*, 85 Cal. App. 4th 793, 102 Cal. Rptr. 2d 447, 455 (2000) ("The use of a mandatory presumption in a criminal case is unconstitutional whether the presumption is conclusive or rebuttable. However, a mandatory inference may be reconfigured as a permissive inference for use in a criminal case"); Hug, *Presumptions and Inferences in Criminal Law*, 56 Mil. L. Rev. 81, 91, 105 (1972).

2. Although some courts which preclude the operation of mandatory inferences against an accused rely on *Ulster County* as authority, other courts premise their ruling on *Sandstrom* discussed in the next subsection. Revisit this question after you have read *Sandstrom*.

5. Limitations on the Effect of Presumptions — Conclusive Presumptions and Presumptions that Shift the Ultimate Burden of Proof to the Defense

Winship (discussed in subsection C, *supra*) has also necessitated modifications relating the effect of presumptions in another respect, namely, the stage in which the opponent attempts to overcome a presumption. May a conclusive presumption operate against a defendant? May a presumption shift the ultimate burden to the defendant? The Court reached those questions in the following case, in which the trial judge gave a homicide jury the instruction that "the law presumes that a person intends the ordinary consequences of his voluntary acts." As of 1979, the instruction was a traditional one. Indeed, the first sentence of California Evidence Code § 665 reads: "A person is presumed to intend the ordinary consequences of his voluntary Act."

SANDSTROM v. MONTANA
442 U.S. 510 (1979)

JUSTICE BRENNAN delivered the opinion of the Court.

The threshold inquiry in ascertaining the constitutional analysis applicable to this kind of jury instruction is to determine the nature of the presumption it describes. *See Ulster County Court v. Allen*, [442 U.S. 140,] 99 S. Ct. 2213 (1979). That determination requires careful attention to the words actually spoken to the jury, *see id.*, at n. 16, for whether a defendant has been accorded his constitutional rights depends upon the way in which a reasonable juror could have interpreted the instruction.

Respondent argues, first, that the instruction merely described a permissive inference — that is, it allowed but did not require the jury to draw conclusions about defendant's intent from his actions — and that such inferences are constitutional. These arguments need not detain us long, for even respondent admits that "it's possible" that the jury believed they were required to apply the presumption. Sandstrom's jurors were told that "the law presumes that a person intends the ordinary consequences of his voluntary acts." They were not told that they had a choice, or that they might infer that conclusion; they were told only that the law presumed it. It is clear that a reasonable juror could easily have viewed such an instruction as mandatory. *See generally* Montana Rules of Evidence 301(a).[4]

In the alternative, respondent urges that even if viewed as a mandatory presumption rather than as a permissive inference, the presumption did not conclusively establish intent but rather could be rebutted. On this view, the instruction required the jury, if satisfied as to the facts which trigger the presumption, to find intent unless the defendant offered evidence to the contrary. Moreover, according to the State, all the defendant had to do to rebut the presumption was produce "some" contrary evidence; he did not have to "prove" that he lacked the required mental state. Thus, "[a]t most, it placed a burden of production on the petitioner," but "did not shift to petitioner the burden of persuasion with respect to any element of the offense. . . ." Brief for Respondent 3. Again, respondent contends that presumptions with this limited effect pass constitutional muster.

We need not review respondent's constitutional argument on this point either, however, for we reject this characterization of the presumption as well. Respondent

---

[4] "Rule 301 (a) Presumption defined. A presumption is an assumption of fact that the law requires to be made from another fact or group of facts found or otherwise established in the action or proceeding."

concedes there is a "risk" that the jury, once having found petitioner's act voluntary, would interpret the instruction as automatically directing a finding of intent. Tr. of Oral Arg. 29. Moreover, the State also concedes that numerous courts "have differed as to the effect of the presumption when given as a jury instruction without further explanation as to its use by the jury," and that some have found it to shift more than the burden of production, and even to have conclusive effect. Brief for Respondent 17. Nonetheless, the State contends that the only authoritative reading of the effect of the presumption resides in the Supreme Court of Montana. And the State argues that by holding that "[d]efendant's sole burden under instruction No. 5 was to produce some evidence that he did not intend the ordinary consequences of his voluntary acts, not to disprove that he acted 'purposely' or 'knowingly,' " 580 P.2d, at 109, the Montana Supreme Court decisively established that the presumption at most affected only the burden of going forward with evidence of intent — that is, the burden of production.

The Supreme Court of Montana is, of course, the final authority on the legal weight to be given a presumption under Montana law, but it is not the final authority on the interpretation which a jury could have given the instruction. If Montana intended its presumption to have only the effect described by its Supreme Court, then we are convinced that a reasonable juror could well have been misled by the instruction given, and could have believed that the presumption was not limited to requiring the defendant to satisfy only a burden of production. Petitioner's jury was told that "the law presumes that a person intends the ordinary consequences of his voluntary acts." They were not told that the presumption could be rebutted, as the Montana Supreme Court held, by the defendant's simple presentation of "some" evidence; nor even that it could be rebutted at all. Given the common definition of "presume" as "to suppose to be true without proof," Webster's New Collegiate Dictionary 911 (1974), and given the lack of qualifying instructions as to the legal effect of the presumption, we cannot discount the possibility that the jury may have interpreted the instruction in either of two more stringent ways.

First, a reasonable jury could well have interpreted the presumption as "conclusive," that is, not technically as a presumption at all, but rather, as an irrebuttable direction by the court to find intent once convinced of the facts triggering the presumption. Alternatively, the jury may have interpreted the instruction as a direction to find intent upon proof of the defendant's voluntary actions (and their "ordinary" consequences), unless the defendant proved the contrary by some quantum of proof which may well have been considerably greater than "some" evidence — thus effectively shifting the burden of persuasion on the element of intent. Numerous federal and state courts have warned that instructions of the type given here can be interpreted in just these ways. *See generally United States v. Wharton*, 433 F.2d 451, 139 U.S. App. D.C. 293 (1970); *State v. Roberts*, 88 Wash. 337, 341–42, 562 P.2d 1259, 1261–1262 (1977). And although the Montana Supreme Court held to the contrary in this case, Montana's own Rules of Evidence expressly state that the presumption at issue here may be overcome only "by a preponderance of evidence contrary to the presumption." Montana Rules of Evidence 301 (b)(2). Such a requirement shifts not only the burden of production, but also the ultimate burden of persuasion on the issue of intent.

We do not reject the possibility that some jurors may have interpreted the challenged instruction as permissive, or, if mandatory, as requiring only that the defendant come forward with "some" evidence in rebuttal. However, the fact that a reasonable juror could have given the presumption conclusive or persuasion shifting effect means that we cannot discount the possibility that Sandstrom's jurors actually did proceed upon one or the other of these latter interpretations. And that means that unless these kinds of presumptions are constitutional, the instruction cannot be adjudged valid. *Ulster County Court v. Allen*, 99 S. Ct. 2213 n. 17. It is the line of cases urged by petitioner, and exemplified by *In re Winship*, 397 U.S. 358 (1970), that provides the appropriate mode of constitutional analysis for these kinds of presumptions.

We consider first the validity of a conclusive presumption. This Court has considered such a presumption on at least two prior occasions. In *Morissette v. United States*, 342 U.S. 246 (1952), the defendant was charged with willful and knowing theft of government property. Although his attorney argued that for his client to be found guilty, "the taking must have been with felonious intent," the trial judge ruled that "[t]hat is presumed by his own act." *Id.*, at 249. After first concluding that intent was in fact an element of the crime charged, and after declaring that "[w]here intent of the accused is an ingredient of the crime charged, its existence is a . . . jury issue," *Morissette* held:

> It follows that the trial court may not withdraw or prejudge the issue by instruction that the law raises a presumption of intent from an act. It often is tempting to cast in terms of a "presumption" a conclusion which a court thinks probable from given facts. . . . [But] [we] think presumptive intent has no place in this case. A conclusive presumption which testimony could not overthrow would effectively eliminate intent as an ingredient of the offense. A presumption which would permit but not require the jury to assume intent from an isolated fact would prejudge a conclusion which the jury should reach of its own volition. A presumption which would permit the jury to make an assumption which all the evidence considered together does not logically establish would give to a proven fact an artificial and fictional effect. In either case, this presumption would conflict with the overriding presumption of innocence with which the law endows the accused and which extends to every element of the crime. 342 U.S., at 274–275.

Just last Term, in *United States v. United States Gypsum*, 438 U.S. 422 (1978), we reaffirmed the holding of *Morissette*. In that case defendants, who were charged with criminal violations of the Sherman Act, challenged the following jury instruction:

> The law presumes that a person intends the necessary and natural consequences of his acts. Therefore, if the effect of the exchanges of pricing information was to raise, fix, maintain, and stabilize prices, then the parties to them are presumed, as a matter of law, to have intended that result. 438 U.S., at 430.

After again determining that the offense included the element of intent, we held

[A] defendant's state of mind or intent is an element of a criminal antitrust offense which . . . cannot be taken from the trier of fact through reliance on a legal presumption of wrongful intent from proof of effect on prices. "Although an effect on prices may well support an inference that the defendant had knowledge of the probability of such a consequence at the time he acted, the jury must remain free to consider additional evidence before accepting or rejecting the inference . . . [U]ltimately, the decision on the issue of intent must be left to the trier of fact alone. The instruction given invaded this fact finding function. *Id.*, at 435, 446.

As in *Morissette* and *United States Gypsum*, a conclusive presumption in this case would "conflict with the overriding presumption of innocence with which the law endows the accused and which extends to every element of the crime," and would "invade [the] fact finding function" which in a criminal case the law assigns solely to the jury. The instruction announced to David Sandstrom's jury may well have had exactly these consequences. Upon finding proof of one element of the crime (causing death), and of facts insufficient to establish the second (the voluntariness and "ordinary consequences" of defendant's action), Sandstrom's jurors could reasonably have concluded that they were directed to find against defendant on the element of intent. The State was thus not forced to prove "beyond a reasonable doubt . . . every fact necessary to constitute the crime . . . charged," 397 U.S., at 364, and defendant was deprived of his constitutional rights as explicated in *Winship*.

A presumption which, although not conclusive, had the effect of shifting the burden of persuasion to the defendant, would have suffered from similar infirmities. If Sandstrom's jury interpreted the presumption in that manner, it could have concluded that upon proof by the State of the slaying, and of additional facts not themselves establishing the element of intent, the burden was shifted to the defendant to prove that he lacked the requisite mental state. Such a presumption was found constitutionally deficient in *Mullaney v. Wilbur*, 421 U.S. 684 (1975). In *Mullaney* the charge was murder, which under Maine law required proof not only of intent but of malice. The trial court charged the jury that "malice aforethought is an essential and indispensable element of the crime of murder." *Id.*, at 686. However, it also instructed that if the prosecution established that the homicide was both intentional and unlawful, malice aforethought was to be implied unless the defendant proved by a fair preponderance of the evidence that he acted in the heat of passion on sudden provocation. *Mullaney v. Wilbur*, 421 U.S., at 686. As we recounted just two Terms ago in *Patterson v. New York*, "[t]his Court . . . unanimously agreed with the Court of Appeals that Wilbur's due process rights had been invaded by the presumption casting upon him the burden of proving by a preponderance of the evidence that he had acted in the heat of passion upon sudden provocation." 432 U.S., at 214. And *Patterson* reaffirmed that "a State must prove every ingredient of an offense beyond a reasonable doubt, and . . . may not shift the burden of proof to the defendant" by means of such a presumption.

Because David Sandstrom's jury may have interpreted the judge's instruction as constituting either a burden-shifting presumption like that in *Mullaney*, or a conclusive presumption like those in *Morissette* and *United States Gypsum*, and because either interpretation would have deprived defendant of his right to the due process of law, we hold the instruction given in this case unconstitutional.

NOTES

1. Revisit Problem 30-9 in the previous subsection. Does *Sandstrom* make it clearer that it is unconstitutional to permit a truly mandatory presumption of the existence of an element of the charged crime to operate against an accused? In 1985, the Supreme Court revisited this topic in *Francis v. Franklin*, 471 U.S. 307 (1985). In large part, *Francis* reaffirmed *Sandstrom*. Several courts have interpreted *Francis* as announcing a categorical rule that a mandatory inference may not operate against a criminal defendant on an ultimate fact in issue. For example, in *Coleman v. Butler*, 816 F.2d 1046, 1048 (5th Cir. 1987), the court stated that "[a] mandatory presumption, one that instructs a criminal jury that it must infer a presumed fact if the state proves the predicate facts or fact, is unconstitutional." *Potts v. Kemp*, 814 F.2d 1512 (11th Cir. 1987), reaches the same conclusion.

2. In light of *Sandstrom*, you should be able to answer the questions posed at the beginning of this subsection. May the state erect a conclusive presumption of the existence of an element of the charged crime? May a presumption shift the ultimate burden of proof to the defense?

3. Prior to 1989, the lower courts' broad reading of *Sandstrom* and *Francis* was debatable. In both cases, the defense presented a case-in-chief and attempted to rebut the presumed fact. In terms of the diagram found in section B.1. of this chapter, the defense was at step #7. At that step, under the second school of thought, the presumption remains in the case but shifts the burden of proof. The proponents of the second school would want the trial judge to instruct the jury: "If you believe the prosecution's evidence of C (the foundational fact), you must infer E (the presumed fact) unless the defense convinces you of non E." Of course, the "unless" clause is the language shifting the burden of proof to the defense.

In *Francis*, the majority commented that "[w]e are not required to decide in this case whether a mandatory presumption that shifts only a burden of production to the defendant is consistent with the Due Process Clause, and we express no opinion on that question." *Francis, supra*, at 314 n.3. Suppose that, in *Francis*, the defense had not presented any evidence rebutting the presumed fact. Or suppose that the defense did not present any case-in-chief. The final step of the record would then be step #3 on the diagram. At that step, under the common law conception of a presumption, the judge would direct the jury: "If you believe the prosecution's evidence of C, you must infer E." Since there is no defense rebuttal evidence, there would be no need for the judge to add the "unless" clause at the end of the instruction. Thus, strictly speaking, there is no necessity to even reach the question of shifting the ultimate burden of proof. Would this instruction violate *Francis*?

In 1989, the Court decided *Carella v. California*, 491 U.S. 263 (1989). In that case, unlike *Sandstrom* and *Francis*, the defendant did not attempt to rebut the presumed fact. The trial judge directed the jury that, if they believed the prosecution evidence of the foundational facts, the fact in issue "shall be presumed." Since the defense had not offered any rebuttal evidence, there was no need for the trial judge to add an "unless" clause at the end of the instruction. Nevertheless, the Court held that the instruction ran afoul of *Francis*. *Carella* strengthens the case for the lower courts' expansive interpretation of *Sandstrom* and *Francis*.

Chapter 31

THE ULTIMATE BURDEN OF PERSUASION

Read Federal Rules of Evidence 301 and 302.

A. INTRODUCTION

In the preceding chapter, we examined the initial burden of producing evidence in support of each issue of fact. Now we encounter the second aspect, the ultimate burden of persuading the trier of fact that a given fact in issue is proved by the applicable standard of proof (preponderance of the evidence, clear and convincing evidence, or beyond a reasonable doubt). The burden is sometimes referred to as the "risk of nonpersuasion" because it allocates the loss to the party who fails to persuade the trier of fact that the evidence meets the requisite standard. In the words of the Supreme Court, the burden embodies "the notion that if the evidence is evenly balanced, the party that bears the burden of persuasion must lose." *Director, Office of Workers' Compensation Programs, Dep't of Labor v. Greenwich Collieries*, 512 U.S. 267 (1994) (discussing preponderance standard). The concept of a risk of nonpersuasion is critical in decision-making both within and outside the judicial system. *See* R. GASKINS, BURDENS OF PROOF IN MODERN DISCOURSE (1993). If we need to reach closure on a question on which knowledge is incomplete and truth uncertain, the allocation of that risk often determines the outcome.

The burden of persuasion differs from the burden of production in several respects. First, whereas the burden of production is analogous to a duty owed by the party to the judge, the burden of persuasion is akin to a duty owed to the trier of fact. (The term "trier of fact" includes the judge sitting as a trier of fact in a bench trial.) Once the parties have satisfied their respective burdens of going forward on various facts, the remaining fact issues are for the jury.

Second, whether a party has satisfied the burden of persuasion on a given issue is a question of fact. The status of the burden of going forward is an issue of law for the judge (although it often requires the judge to evaluate the factual evidence). In passing on the legal sufficiency of the evidence, the judge accepts the evidence at face value without evaluating the witnesses' credibility; in this respect, the judge's ruling on the sufficiency of the evidence is similar to the judge's ruling on the admissibility of evidence under Federal Rule of Evidence 104(b). The judge must draw every permissive inference favoring the fact the proponent is attempting to establish. In contrast, the jury may choose to disbelieve a witness; and the jury may select what it believes to be the most realistic of the competing permissive inferences from the evidence.

Third, the penalty for failing to sustain the burden of persuasion is an adverse finding by the jury. The penalty for failing to satisfy the burden of going forward is a peremptory ruling by the judge, except that in a criminal case, the judge cannot direct a verdict against the defendant.

Finally, the burden of persuasion is allocated by a rule of law; once allocated, it rarely shifts from one party to the other. The exception is the unusual case of Morgan-McCormick presumptions, addressed in the last chapter, which shift the ultimate burden of proof. In contrast, the burden of production on an issue may shift back and forth during the trial, as first one party and then the other introduces evidence relevant to that issue.

B. THE ALLOCATION OF THE BURDEN OF PERSUASION

1. The Common Law

The common law (and occasionally a statute) allocates the burden of proof (production and persuasion) for each issue of fact to one of the parties. Usually (but not invariably) this is the party who must plead the existence of the fact. Allocation of these burdens is a question of procedural or substantive law, not of evidence. The following excerpt describes the primary criteria for allocating the burden of proof.

F. JAMES, G. HAZARD & J. LEUBSDORF, CIVIL PROCEDURE § 7.16
(5th ed. 2001)

There is no a priori test for allocating the burden of persuasion or the burden of producing evidence. The party who must establish the affirmative proposition is sometimes said to have the burden of proof on the issue. But any proposition can be stated either affirmatively or negatively. Breach of promise, for example, may be termed nonfulfillment; negligence can be described as the failure to exercise due care; a declaration of nonliability is in substance the same as an affirmative defense. Similarly, the burden of proof is sometimes said to rest on the party to whose case the fact in question is essential, and so it is. But this simply restates the question: To which party's case is the fact essential?

Every jurisdiction has rules of allocation governing most types of claims. As new legal rights are established by decisional law or statute, corresponding decisions have to be made on allocation of the burden of proof. The burden of proof does not follow the burden of pleading in all cases. Many jurisdictions, for example, require plaintiffs to plead non-payment of an obligation sued on but do not require them to prove it. In federal courts defendant must plead contributory negligence as an affirmative defense to an action for injuries negligently caused, but federal courts in diversity cases will follow a local rule that puts the burden of proof on plaintiffs. The burden of pleading is itself allocated on pragmatic considerations of fairness, convenience, and policy rather than on any general principle of pleading. Since the burden of proof is allocated on very much the same basis, an inquiry to determine the pleading rule (absent clear authority) would simply parallel the inquiry needed to determine the burden of proof rule in the first instance.

Access to proof. The burden of proof traditionally is placed on the party having the readier access to knowledge about the fact in question. This consideration, however, has never been controlling. Plaintiff usually has the burden to prove what the defendant's conduct was in negligence and breach of contract. Even more starkly, a plaintiff who has been defrauded has the burden of proving the falsity of the representations and, under classic fraud doctrine, the fact that the falsity was known to defendant but not to plaintiff. If access to facts were a determining factor in allocating the burden of proof, it would be bizarre to require plaintiff to prove in court facts about which he or she was deceived in the underlying transaction. The alleged wrongdoer's greater access to evidence as a factor in procedural justice is thus offset by another such factor — the sense that a charge of serious wrongdoing should be proven by the person making it.

Access to evidence is a much diminished basis for allocating burden of proof in modern liberal discovery. Whatever testimony is available from an opposing party ordinarily can be elicited through deposition before trial and be at hand for use in evidence. Also, in this era of reporting and recordkeeping, large amounts of relevant evidence are compiled in documents accessible by subpoena duces tecum and, in the case of public records, freedom of information laws. From this perspective, the critical element in allocation is not the burden of coming forward with evidence but the burden of persuasion in the face of evidence of ambiguous significance.

Substantive policy. Finally, substantive considerations are influential in allocation of burden of proof. For real or supposed reasons of policy the law sometimes disfavors certain types of claims and defenses. Burden of proof is often used as a handicap against the disfavored contention. Thus, the defendant in libel and slander formerly was required to prove the truth of the objectionable words to escape liability. The evolved interpretation of the First Amendment, however, requires plaintiff to prove the falsity of a statement in news media about a subject of public interest.

Another substantively influenced rule of allocation is associated with the concept of res ipsa loquitur in tort litigation. This concept responds to the injuries suffered by people whose safety is dependent on conditions under the control of others. Res ipsa loquitur, in at least one of its formulations, holds that under certain circumstances plaintiff can satisfy the burden of coming forward with evidence to prove negligence without directly proving a specific negligent act. The conditions specify that (1) the injury-inflicting instrument be in defendant's exclusive control in circumstances in which injury does not ordinarily occur without negligence, and (2) the evidence shows no fault on the part of the injured person. This is enough to submit the case to the jury. For somewhat similar reasons, courts have sometimes thrown the burden on each of several tort-feasors to disprove responsibility for a plaintiff's injuries.

NOTES

1. The excerpt above mentions several factors that courts consider in allocating the burden of proof. In your opinion, which factor is the most important? Which factor is the least important? Why? The courts treat the following doctrines as affirmative defenses on which the defense has the burden: the statute of limitations (*F.T.C. v. National Business Consultants, Inc.*, 376 F.3d 317, 320 (5th Cir. 2004), cert. denied, 544 U.S. 904 (2005)), release (*Auslander v. Helfand*, 988 F. Supp. 576 (D. Md. 1997)), and fair use in copyright infringement cases (*Lyons Partnership v. Giannoulas*, 14 F. Supp. 2d 947 (N.D. Tex. 1998), aff'd, 179 F.3d 384 (5th Cir. 1999)). Would the professors agree that all these doctrines be treated in that fashion? If not, why not?

2. If a statute creates a cause of action or crime, courts look for manifestations of legislative intent on the allocation of the burden. *See United States v. Moore*, 613 F.2d 1029, 1044 (D.C. Cir. 1979). In making the determination, many courts rely heavily on matters of form. If the statute describes the cause of action or crime and, in a separate clause or sentence, refers to grounds for avoiding responsibility, the courts tend to treat the reference as an affirmative defense and allocate the burden to the defendant. In many cases, however, the legislature may not have considered the procedural issue of allocating the burden; rather, its primary concern may have been simply announcing a new crime or substantive civil rule. How ambiguous must the statute be before a court should consider itself free to make its own allocation of the burden by independently evaluating the factors listed by James, Hazard, and Leubsdorf?

2. Constitutional Limitations on the Allocation of the Ultimate Burden

As we noted in the last chapter, a legislature is not free to allocate the burden of persuasion in criminal cases as it wishes. The first in a line of decisions on this topic, *In re Winship*, 397 U.S. 358 (1970), held that in a criminal case, due process requires the government to prove beyond a reasonable doubt every fact necessary to constitute the crime charged. This requirement is deceptively simple. What elements are "necessary" to the crime charged?

In *Mullaney v. Wilbur*, 421 U.S. 684 (1975), the defendant was convicted of murder in a Maine state court. Maine's statute defined murder as the unlawful killing of a human being "with malice aforethought, either express or implied." Manslaughter was a killing "in the heat of passion, on sudden provocation, without express or implied malice aforethought." Under Maine law, "malice aforethought" was defined as the absence of "heat of passion on sudden provocation." The Maine courts assigned the defendant the burden of proving by a preponderance of the evidence that he had killed in the "heat of passion, on sudden provocation." "Heat of passion" was an affirmative defense by which an accused could reduce murder to manslaughter.

In a unanimous decision, the United States Supreme Court held that the Maine rule unconstitutionally placed this burden on the defendant. The Court reasoned that the absence of "heat of passion on sudden provocation" (*i.e.*, malice aforethought under Maine law) was a necessary element of the crime, and under *Winship* the burden of proof of such an element must rest and remain on the government.

While this may seem reasonably clear on its face, the *Winship/Mullaney* rule introduced a new complexity into sufficiency-of-proof issues in criminal cases. Does *Mullaney* apply only if the fact in question negates an element of the definition of the crime? Or does *Mullaney* mean that whenever defendant raises an issue that would lessen the degree of the offense, the government must disprove the existence of that element? In some cases, courts have had little difficulty deciding the proper allocation. They routinely assign the government the burden on alibi, for example, while requiring the defendant to assume the burden on entrapment. *See United States v. Blassingame*, 197 F.3d 271 (7th Cir. 1999) (distinguishing between alibi and entrapment).

Other allocation decisions, such as the burden on complex *mens rea* elements in homicide cases, have proved more troublesome. The Supreme Court revisited the issue in the following case.

PATTERSON v. NEW YORK
432 U.S. 197 (1977)

JUSTICE WHITE delivered the opinion of the Court.

The question here is the constitutionality under the Fourteenth Amendment's Due Process Clause of burdening the defendant in a New York State murder trial with proving the affirmative defense of extreme emotional disturbance as defined by New York Law.

After a brief and unstable marriage, the appellant, Gordon Patterson, Jr., became estranged from his wife, Roberta. Roberta resumed an association with John Northrup, a neighbor to whom she had been engaged prior to her marriage to appellant. On December 27, 1970, Patterson borrowed a rifle from an acquaintance and went to the residence of his father-in-law. There, he observed his wife through a window in a state of semiundress in the presence of John Northrup. He entered the house and killed Northrup by shooting him twice in the head.

Patterson was charged with second-degree murder. In New York there are two elements of this crime: (1) "intent to cause the death of another person"; and (2) "caus[ing] the death of such person or of a third person." NY Penal Law § 125.25. Malice aforethought is not an element of the crime. In addition, the State permits a person accused of murder to raise an affirmative defense that he "acted under the influence of extreme emotional disturbance for which there was a reasonable explanation or excuse."[2]

---

[2] Section 125.25 provides in relevant part: "A person is guilty of murder in the second degree when:
   1.   With intent to cause the death of another person, he causes the death of such person or of a third person; except that in any prosecution under this subdivision, it is an affirmative defense that: (a) The defendant acted under the influence of extreme emotional disturbance for which there was a reasonable explanation or excuse, the reasonableness of which is to be determined

New York also recognizes the crime of manslaughter. A person is guilty of manslaughter if he intentionally kills another person "under circumstances which do not constitute murder because he acts under the influence of extreme emotional disturbance."[3] Appellant confessed before trial to killing Northrup, but at trial he raised the defense of extreme emotional disturbance.

The jury was instructed as to the elements of the crime of murder. Focusing on the element of intent, the trial court charged:

> Before you can convict this defendant or anyone of murder, you must believe and decide that the People have established beyond a reasonable doubt that he intended, in firing the gun, to kill either the victim himself or some other human being. . . .

> Always remember that you must not expect or require the defendant to prove to your satisfaction that his acts were done without the intent to kill. Whatever proof he may have attempted, however far he may have gone in an effort to convince you of his innocence or guiltlessness, he is not obligated to prove anything. It is always the People's burden to prove his guilt, and to prove that he intended to kill in this instance beyond a reasonable doubt.

The jury was further instructed, consistently with New York law, that the defendant had the burden of proving his affirmative defense by a preponderance of the evidence. The jury was told that if it found beyond a reasonable doubt that appellant had intentionally killed Northrup but that appellant had demonstrated by a preponderance of the evidence that he had acted under the influence of extreme emotional disturbance, it had to find appellant guilty of manslaughter instead of murder.

The jury found appellant guilty of murder. Judgment was entered on the verdict, and the Appellate Division affirmed. While appeal to the New York Court of Appeals was pending, this Court decided *Mullaney v. Wilbur*, 421 U.S. 684 (1975), in which the Court declared Maine's murder statute unconstitutional.

In the Court of Appeals appellant urged that New York's murder statute is functionally equivalent to the one struck down in *Mullaney* and that therefore his conviction should be reversed.

The Court of Appeals rejected appellant's argument. The Court distinguished

---

from the viewpoint of a person in the defendant's situation under the circumstances as the defendant believed them to be. Nothing contained in this paragraph shall constitute a defense to a prosecution for, or preclude a conviction of, manslaughter in the first degree or any other crime.

[3] Section 125.20(2). NY Penal Law § 125.20(2) provides: "A person is guilty of manslaughter in the first degree when:

2. With intent to cause the death of another person, he causes the death of such person or of a third person under circumstances which do not constitute murder because he acts under the influence of extreme emotional disturbance, as defined in paragraph (a) of subdivision one of section 125.25. The fact that homicide was committed under the influence of extreme emotional disturbance constitutes a mitigating circumstance reducing murder to manslaughter in the first degree and need not be proved in any prosecution initiated under this subdivision.

Mullaney on the ground that the New York statute involved no shifting of the burden to the defendant to disprove any fact essential to the offense charged, since the New York affirmative defense of extreme emotional disturbance bears no direct relationship to any element of murder. This appeal ensued. We affirm.

In determining whether New York's allocation to the defendant of proving the mitigating circumstances of severe emotional disturbance is consistent with due process, it is relevant to note that this defense is a considerably expanded version of the common-law defense of heat of passion on sudden provocation and that at common law the burden of proving the latter, as well as other affirmative defenses — indeed, "all . . . circumstances of justification, excuse or alleviation" — rested on the defendant. 4 W. Blackstone, Commentaries *201. This was the rule when the Fifth Amendment was adopted, and it was the American rule when the Fourteenth Amendment was ratified. *Commonwealth v. York*, 50 Mass. 93 (1845).

In 1895 the common-law view was abandoned with respect to the insanity defense in federal prosecutions. *Davis v. United States*, 160 U.S. 469 (1895). This ruling had wide impact on the practice in the federal courts with respect to the burden of proving various affirmative defenses, and the prosecution in a majority of jurisdictions in this country sooner or later came to shoulder the burden of proving the sanity of the accused and of disproving the facts constituting other affirmative defenses, including provocation. *Davis* was not a constitutional ruling, however, as *Leland v. Oregon*, 343 U.S. 790 (1952) made clear.

At issue in *Leland v. Oregon* was the constitutionality under the Due Process Clause of the Oregon Rule that the defense of insanity must be proved by the defendant beyond a reasonable doubt. Noting that *Davis* "obviously establish[ed] no constitutional doctrine," 343 U.S., at 797, the Court refused to strike down the Oregon scheme, saying that the burden of proving all elements of the crime beyond a reasonable doubt, including the elements of premeditation and deliberation, was placed on the State under Oregon procedures and remained there throughout the trial. To convict, the jury was required to find each element of the crime beyond reasonable doubt, based on all the evidence, including the evidence going to the issue of insanity. Only then was the jury "to consider separately the issue of legal sanity per se. . . ." *Id.*, at 795. This practice did not offend the Due Process Clause even though among the 20 States then placing the burden of proving his insanity on the defendant, Oregon was alone in requiring him to convince the jury beyond a reasonable doubt.

In 1970, the Court declared that the Due Process Clause "protects the accused against conviction except upon proof beyond a reasonable doubt of every fact necessary to constitute the crime with which he is charged." *In re Winship*, 397 U.S. 358, 364 (1970). Five years later, in *Mullaney v. Wilbur*, 421 U.S. 684 (1975), the Court further announced that under the Maine law of homicide, the burden could not constitutionally be placed on the defendant of proving by a preponderance of the evidence that the killing had occurred in the heat of passion on sudden provocation. The Chief Justice and Mr. Justice Rehnquist, concurring, expressed their understanding that the *Mullaney* decision did not call into question the ruling in *Leland v. Oregon* with respect to the proof of insanity.

Subsequently, the Court confirmed that it remained constitutional to burden the defendant with proving his insanity defense when it dismissed, as not raising a substantial federal question, a case in which the appellant specifically challenged the continuing validity of *Leland v. Oregon*. This occurred in *Rivera v. Delaware*, 429 U.S. 877 (1976), an appeal from a Delaware conviction which, in reliance on *Leland*, had been affirmed by the Delaware Supreme Court over the claim that the Delaware statute was unconstitutional because it burdened the defendant with proving his affirmative defense of insanity by a preponderance of the evidence. The claim in this Court was that *Leland* had been overruled by *Winship* and *Mullaney*. We dismissed the appeal as not presenting a substantial federal question.

We cannot conclude that Patterson's conviction under the New York law deprived him of due process of law. The crime of murder is defined by the statute, which represents a recent revision of the state criminal code, as causing the death of another person with intent to do so. The death, the intent to kill, and causation are the facts that the State is required to prove beyond a reasonable doubt if a person is to be convicted of murder. No further facts are either presumed or inferred in order to constitute the crime. The statute does provide an affirmative defense — that the defendant acted under the influence of extreme emotional disturbance for which there was a reasonable explanation — which, if proved by a preponderance of the evidence, would reduce the crime to manslaughter, an offense defined in a separate section of the statute. It is plain enough that if the intentional killing is shown, the State intends to deal with the defendant as a murderer unless he demonstrates the mitigating circumstances.

Here, the jury was instructed in accordance with the statute, and the guilty verdict confirms that the State successfully carried its burden of proving the facts of the crime beyond a reasonable doubt. Nothing in the evidence, including any evidence that might have been offered with respect to Patterson's mental state at the time of the crime, raised a reasonable doubt about his guilt as a murderer; and clearly the evidence failed to convince the jury that Patterson's affirmative defense had been made out. It seems to us that the State satisfied the mandate of *Winship* that it prove beyond a reasonable doubt "every fact necessary to constitute the crime with which [Patterson was] charged." 397 U.S. at 364.

In convicting Patterson under its murder statute, New York did no more than *Leland* and *Rivera* permitted it to do without violating the Due Process Clause. Under those cases, once the facts constituting a crime are established beyond a reasonable doubt, based on all the evidence including the evidence of the defendant's mental state, the State may refuse to sustain the affirmative defense of insanity unless demonstrated by a preponderance of the evidence.

The New York law on extreme emotional disturbance follows this pattern. This affirmative defense, which the Court of Appeals described as permitting "the defendant to show that his actions were caused by a mental infirmity not arising to the level of insanity, and that he is less culpable for having committed them," does not serve to negative any facts of the crime which the State is to prove in order to convict of murder. It constitutes a separate issue on which the defendant is required to carry the burden of persuasion; and unless we are to overturn *Leland* and *Rivera*, New York has not violated the Due Process Clause, and Patterson's conviction must be sustained.

We are unwilling to reconsider *Leland* and *Rivera*. But even if we were to hold that a State must prove sanity to convict once that fact is put in issue, it would not necessarily follow that a State must prove beyond a reasonable doubt every fact, the existence or nonexistence of which it is willing to recognize as an exculpatory or mitigating circumstance affecting the degree of culpability or the severity of the punishment. Here, in revising its criminal code, New York provided the affirmative defense of extreme emotional disturbance, a substantially expanded version of the older heat-of-passion concept; but it was willing to do so only if the facts making out the defense were established by the defendant with sufficient certainty. The State was itself unwilling to undertake to establish the absence of those facts beyond a reasonable doubt, perhaps fearing that proof would be too difficult and that too many persons deserving treatment as murderers would escape that punishment if the evidence need merely raise a reasonable doubt about the defendant's emotional state. It has been said that the new criminal code of New York contains some 25 affirmative defenses which exculpate or mitigate but which must be established by the defendant to be operative. The Due Process Clause, as we see it, does not put New York to the choice of abandoning those defenses or undertaking to disprove their existence in order to convict of a crime which otherwise is within its constitutional powers to sanction by substantial punishment.

We decline to adopt as a constitutional imperative, operative countrywide, that a State must disprove beyond a reasonable doubt every fact constituting any and all affirmative defenses related to the culpability of an accused. Traditionally, due process has required that only the most basic procedural safeguards be observed; more subtle balancing of society's interests against those of the accused have been left to the legislative branch. We therefore will not disturb the balance struck in previous cases holding that the Due Process Clause requires the prosecution to prove beyond a reasonable doubt all of the elements included in the definition of the offense of which the defendant is charged. Proof of the nonexistence of all affirmative defenses has never been constitutionally required; and we perceive no reason to fashion such a rule in this case and apply it to the statutory defense at issue here.

This view may seem to permit state legislatures to reallocate burdens of proof by labeling as affirmative defenses at least some elements of the crimes now defined in their statutes. But there are obviously constitutional limits beyond which the States may not go in this regard. "[I]t is not within the province of a legislature to declare an individual guilty or presumptively guilty of a crime." *McFarland v. American Sugar Rfg. Co.*, 241 U.S. 79, 86 (1916). The legislature cannot "validly command that the finding of an indictment, or mere proof of the identity of the accused, should create a presumption of the existence of all the facts essential to guilt." *Tot v. United States*, 319 U.S. 463, 469 (1943).

It is urged that *Mullaney v. Wilbur* necessarily invalidates Patterson's conviction. In *Mullaney* the charge was murder, which the Maine statute defined as the unlawful killing of a human being "with malice aforethought, either express or implied." The trial court instructed the jury that the words "malice aforethought" were most important because "malice aforethought is an essential and indispensable element of the crime of murder." Malice, as the statute indicated and as the court instructed, could be implied and was to be implied from "any deliberate, cruel act committed by one person against another suddenly . . . or without a considerable provocation," in which event an intentional killing was murder unless by a preponderance of the evidence it was shown that the act was committed "in the heat of passion, on sudden provocation." The instructions emphasized that " 'malice aforethought and heat of passion on sudden provocation are two inconsistent things'; thus, by proving the latter the defendant would negate the former." 421 U.S., at 686–687.

Mullaney surely held that a State must prove every ingredient of an offense beyond a reasonable doubt, and that it may not shift the burden of proof to the defendant by presuming that ingredient upon proof of the other elements of the offense. This is true even though the State's practice, as in Maine, had been traditionally to the contrary. Such shifting of the burden of persuasion with respect to a fact which the State deems so important that it must be either proved or presumed is impermissible under the Due Process Clause.

It was unnecessary to go further in *Mullaney*. The Maine Supreme Judicial Court made it clear that malice aforethought, which was mentioned in the statutory definition of the crime, was not equivalent to premeditation and that the presumption of malice traditionally arising in intentional homicide cases carried no factual meaning insofar as premeditation was concerned. Even so, a killing became murder in Maine when it resulted from a deliberate, cruel act committed by one person against another, "suddenly without any, or without a considerable provocation." *State v. Lafferty, supra* at 665. Premeditation was not within the definition of murder; but malice, in the sense of the absence of provocation, was part of the definition of that crime. Yet malice, *i.e.*, lack of provocation, was presumed and could be rebutted by the defendant only by proving by a preponderance of the evidence that he acted with heat of passion upon sudden provocation. In *Mullaney* we held that however traditional this mode of proceeding might have been, it is contrary to the Due Process Clause as construed in *Winship*.

As we have explained, nothing was presumed or implied against Patterson; and his conviction is not invalid under any of our prior cases. The judgment of the New York Court of Appeals is affirmed.

NOTES AND PROBLEMS

1. The dissenters in *Patterson* charged that the distinctions the majority drew between *Patterson* and *Mullaney* were "indefensibly formalistic." Do you agree? Is the majority elevating form over substance?

2. The majority opinion accords the legislature great latitude in defining crimes and allocating burdens, but the majority is quick to add that "there are obviously constitutional limits beyond which the States may not go." What limits does the majority identify? *See* Allen, *Structuring Jury Decision Making in Criminal Cases: A Unified Constitutional Approach to Evidentiary Devices*, 94 HARV. L. REV. 321, 342–48 (1980).

3. The majority argues that the Court should not "put New York to the choice of abandoning those defenses or undertaking to disprove their existence in order to convict of a crime which otherwise is within its constitutional powers to sanction." Would a broad interpretation of *Mullaney* put New York to that choice? If so, which option is New York likely to choose? Would a broad reading of *Mullaney* be counterproductive?

4. One of the most important progeny of *Patterson* is *Martin v. Ohio*, 480 U.S. 228 (1987). In *Martin*, the Court sustained the constitutionality of state legislation, allocating the defendant the burden of proof on self-defense. The Ohio statutes defined murder as "purposely causing the death of another with prior calculation or design." *Id.* at 233. The prosecution had the burden of proof on the elements of the crime. The Court acknowledged that the evidence the defendant offered on self-defense might also be logically relevant to the question of whether the defendant "purposely killed with prior calculation and design." *Id.* "[E]vidence [relevant] to prove [self-defense] will often tend to negate [the elements of aggravated murder]." *Id.* at 234. However, the Court concluded that "when read as a whole," the trial judge's instruction permitted the jury to consider the self-defense evidence on the question of whether there was a reasonable doubt as to any element of the crime. The judge merely charged the jury that, when they turned to the separate issue of self-defense, the defense had the burden of proof by a preponderance of the evidence.

In 1996, in *Montana v. Egelhoff*, 518 U.S. 37 (1996), a majority of the Court indicated that they read *Patterson* and *Martin* as permitting the legislature to go quite far in redefining the *mens rea* elements of offenses. In *Egelhoff*, the question was the constitutionality of a Montana statute providing that in determining whether the defendant had purposely or knowingly caused a death, the jury could not consider any evidence of the defendant's voluntary intoxication. Justices Scalia, Kennedy, and Thomas filed the lead, plurality opinion, joined by the Chief Justice. Justice Ginsburg concurred in the judgment. While the plurality Justices indicated that they were willing to uphold the statute as either an evidentiary rule or a substantive redefinition of *mens rea*, Justice Ginsburg characterized the statue as "a redefinition of the mental-state element of the offense." She wrote that "when a State's power to define criminal conduct is challenged under the Due Process Clause, we inquire only whether the law offends some principle of justice so rooted in the traditions and conscience of our people as to be ranked as fundamental." She emphasized the portion of the plurality opinion noting the English tradition that voluntary intoxication may not serve as an excuse in a criminal case. She also noted that "a significant minority of the States" adhere to the English position even "today." She concluded that "comprehended as a measure redefining mens rea," the statute "encounters no constitutional shoal."

5.   Problem 31-1. Suppose that Paterson's daughter had interrupted the burglary in the *Devitt* case and that before fleeing, the perpetrator raped her. Just before the incident, the Morena legislature passed and the governor signed the following Penal Code provision:

(a)   Rape is the carnal knowledge of a woman by a man not her husband without her actual consent.

(b)   Sexual assault [a lesser offense] is the carnal knowledge of a woman by a man not her husband without her actual consent, but with her apparent consent. "Apparent consent" is words or conduct or both that create in another the genuine but unreasonable belief that consent was given.

(c)   Apparent consent is an affirmative defense that must be raised by the defendant and proved by him by a preponderance of the evidence.

Is this statute constitutional? In *State v. Camara*, 113 Wash. 2d 631, 781 P.2d 483 (1989), the court upheld state legislation providing that, in a rape case, the victim's consent is an affirmative defense. The court conceded that, in the past, it had inquired "whether . . . an element of the defense 'negates' an element of the crime charged." *Id.* at 781 P.2d at 487. However, the court then added:

> In light of [*Martin v. Ohio*], we have substantial doubt about the correctness of the "negates" analysis and thus decline to apply it in this case. In *Martin* . . . , [a]cknowledging an overlap between self-defense and the elements of purpose and prior calculation and design, the Court nevertheless held that the State's burden to prove the elements of the crime was unrelieved.

Id. The court ruled that "while there is a conceptual overlap between the consent defense and the rape crime's element of forcible compulsion, we cannot hold that for that reason alone the burden of proof on consent must rest with the State." *Id.* In the passage in *Martin* which the *Camara* court alluded to, the Supreme Court stated that "the elements of aggravated murder and self-defense overlap in the sense that evidence to prove the latter will often tend to negate the former." 480 U.S. at 234. Does *Camara* properly interpret *Martin*? There was an evidentiary overlap in *Martin*; there were items of evidence which were logically relevant both to the question of purposeful killing and the issue of self defense. Was there also a "conceptual overlap" in *Martin*, as there was in *Camara*? Does *Martin* govern apply in fact situations such as *Camara* where there is a conceptual overlap as well as an evidentiary one?

6.   **Problem 31-2.** In the original *Devitt* battery prosecution, Devitt is charged with a specific intent assault, assault with intent to inflict grievous bodily injury. His friend, James Woodley, is prepared to testify that Devitt was "roaring drunk" an hour before the alleged assault. Morena recognizes voluntary intoxication as a defense to specific intent crimes. May Morena assign Devitt the burden of proof on the issue of intoxication? *See United States ex rel. Goddard v. Vaughn*, 614 F.2d 929, 936 (3d Cir. 1980).

7.   **Problem 31-3.** Assume that in *Devitt*, Woodley was a codefendant. The prosecution theory is that while they were drinking together, Devitt and Woodley entered into a conspiracy to attack Paterson. Woodley intends to defend on the theory that although he initially "went along" with Devitt, Woodley withdrew from the conspiracy. May Morena require Woodley to assume the burden of proving withdrawal? *See United States v. Read*, 658 F.2d 1225, 1232–36 (7th Cir. 1981).

8.   **Problem 31-4.** Devitt is charged with battery, a general intent crime under Morena law. He concedes that he physically touched Paterson, but he claims that the touching was accidental. He testifies that after they argued, he was attempting

to leave; and he was passing Paterson in the hallway of the apartment when he tripped on one of his tools and fell into Paterson. May Morena assign Devitt the burden on the issue of accident? *See Fornash v. Marshall*, 686 F.2d 1179, 1183 (6th Cir. 1982).

9.   The Supreme Court's most recent decision in this line of authority is *Dixon v. United States*, 548 U.S. 1 (2006). There the question presented was whether it violates due process to allocate the defendant the burden of proof on the question of duress. The Court answered that question in the negative.

C.   THE MEASURE OF THE BURDEN OF PERSUASION

1.   The Common Law

Different standards for meeting the burden of persuasion have been devised for different types of cases and issues. The standards reflect the different levels of confidence which society thinks that the trier of fact should have before making various legal decisions. *Conservatorship of Wendland*, 93 Cal. Rptr. 2d 550, 571 (Cal. Ct. App.), *superseded*, 97 Cal. Rptr. 2d 511, 2 P.3d 1065 (2000). The following explanation is taken from M. Ladd & R. Carlson, Cases and Materials on Evidence 1189-90 (1972):

The standards are designed to control the mental processes of the jury through fixing a measure of the persuasive force required for fulfilling the burden of proof. The tests generally fit into three categories: proof by a preponderance of evidence, proof by clear and convincing evidence, and proof beyond a reasonable doubt.

In principle, the court's choice of a measure for the burden should reflect the stakes in the case; the more important the stakes, the higher the burden should be. Saltzburg, *Standards of Proof and Preliminary Questions of Fact*, 27 Stan. L. Rev. 271, 278-80, 304 (1975). The court should weigh the risk of error before selecting a measure. *Motor & Equipment Mfrs. Ass'n v. E.P.A.*, 627 F.2d 1095, 1122 (D.C. Cir. 1979). However, the reader should also realize that to some extent, the particular measure of the burden on an issue depends on the vagaries of historical accident. "The forms of action we have buried, but they still rule us from their graves." F. Maitland, The Forms of Action at Common Law 2 (1936 ed.). At the risk of oversimplification, the civil law courts generally used the standard of preponderance of the evidence, the equity courts employed the extraordinary measure of clear and convincing proof, and the criminal courts developed the test of proof beyond a reasonable doubt. Consider each of the three standards.

Preponderance of the evidence. In most civil cases, the test requires that there must be a preponderance of evidence in favor of the party who has the burden of proof. *See, e.g., Grogan v. Garner*, 498 U.S. 279, 286 (1991); *Valley Housing LP v. City of Derby*, 802 F. Supp. 2d 359 (D. Conn. 2011). Preponderance and greater weight of evidence are synonymous terms. *See Almerfedi v. Obama*, 654 F.3d 1 (D.C. Cir. 2011) (the trier of fact must make a comparative judgment about the evidence presented by the two sides). The trier of fact must believe that the existence of a fact is more probable than its nonexistence. The court's instruction usually includes a cautionary statement that the greater weight or preponderance of evidence does not necessarily mean the greater quantity of evidence or the larger number of witnesses but is the greater weight of proof. Some courts have struggled over the meaning of preliminary words in the instruction such as informing the jury that they must be "satisfied" by a preponderance of evidence. Most courts refuse to quantify the standard by, for example, informing the jury that the standard represents a "fifty-one per cent/forty-nine percent" rule. *See Ortiz v. Principi*, 274 F.3d 1361, 1365 (Fed. Cir. 2001). Some take the view that satisfaction would require more proof than a preponderance, and others feel that a jury might be satisfied with less than a preponderance. The cases tend to overemphasize the niceties of expression. Such linguistic nuances probably have little or no effect upon the thinking process of the average juror.

In *Livanovitch v. Livanovitch*, 99 Vt. 327, 131 A. 799 (1926), the court emphasized how easily the proponent can establish a preponderance of the evidence:

> The slightest preponderance of the evidence in his favor entitle[s] the plaintiff to a verdict. All that is required in a civil case of one who has the burden of proof is that he establish his claim by a preponderance of the evidence. When the equilibrium of proof is destroyed, and the beam inclines toward him who has the burden, however slightly, he has satisfied the requirement of the law, and is entitled to the verdict. "A bare preponderance is sufficient, though the scales drop but a feather's weight."

As CALIFORNIA JURY INSTRUCTIONS — CIVIL CACI 200 (2005) illustrates, the judge can convey this concept to the jury without using the classical expression, "preponderance":

> When I tell you that a party must prove something, I mean that the party must persuade you, by the evidence presented in court, that what he or she is trying to prove is more likely to be true than not true. This is sometimes referred to as the "burden of proof." After weighing all of the evidence, if you cannot decide whether a party has satisfied the burden of proof, you must conclude that the party did not prove the fact. In criminal trials, the prosecution must prove facts showing that the defendant is guilty beyond a reasonable doubt. But in civil trials, such as this one, the party who is required to prove a fact need only prove that the fact is more likely to be true than not true.

California is one of the 11 jurisdictions that have adopted "plain English" instructions in the past decade. *See* Maclean, *Calif. Puts It in Plain English*, NAT'L L.J., Aug. 22, 2005 at 4.

NOTE AND PROBLEM

1. Do not assume that the preponderance standard applies only in civil cases. Not only do equity courts often use the standard, criminal courts sometimes employ the preponderance measure. In many jurisdictions, preponderance is the measure on the issue of the defendant's competency to stand trial. *See United States v. Digilio*, 538 F.2d 972, 988 (3d Cir. 1976). Further, a number of states use preponderance as the test for the sufficiency of the evidence of criminal venue and

jurisdiction. *See* Annot., 67 A.L.R.3d 988 (1975). What common denominator do these issues — competency, venue, and jurisdiction — share?

2. Problem 31-5. In *Devitt*, the prosecution attempts to prove that the defendant mailed Mr. Paterson a threatening letter a week before the alleged attack. An acquaintance of the defendant, Mr. McManis, is prepared to identify the letter's handwriting style as Devitt's. However, the defense has a questioned document examiner, Ms. Mussio, who will give contrary testimony. Does the letter's authenticity fall under Federal Rule of Evidence 104(a) or 104(b)? Who finally decides the letter's authenticity — the judge or jury? What standard of proof applies to the question of the letter's genuineness?

Clear and convincing evidence. This standard of proof lies somewhere between a preponderance of evidence and proof beyond reasonable doubt. *See U.S. v. Francis*, 686 F.3d 265, 274 (4th Cir. 2012) ("Clear and convincing evidence produces in the mind of a fact finder a firm belief or conviction, without hesitancy, about the truth of the allegations"). The standard is often applied "in civil suits where 'particularly important individual interests' are at stake, under circumstances where the interests are substantially more important than the 'mere loss of money,' or where there are accusations of 'quasi-criminal wrongdoing.' " *Forshey v. Gober*, 226 F.3d 1299, 1305 (Fed. Cir. 2000), *withdrawn*, 239 F.3d 1224 (Fed. Cir. 2001). *See, also, Shales v. T. Manning Concrete, Inc.*, 847 F.Supp.2d 1102 (N.D. Ill. 2012) (clear and convincing evidence is the standard for civil contempt). The common expression is "clear and convincing evidence." Other similar expressions are used such as "clear, precise, and indubitable," "clear conviction with-out hesitation," and "clear, satisfactory, and convincing." This higher standard of proof is required in "a limited range" actions in which it is thought that the status quo should not be changed by a mere preponderance of evidence. *In re Marriage of Haines*, 33 Cal. App. 4th 277, 294 n.9, 39 Cal. Rtpr. 2d 673, 684 (1995). *See also In re Diaz*, 647 F.3d 1073 (11th Cir. 2011) (civil contempt); *Cooley v. Lincoln Elec. Co.*, 776 F. Supp. 2d 511 (N.D. Ohio 2011) (punitive damages); *Mattco Forge, Inc. v. Arthur Young & Co.*, 52 Cal. App. 4th 820 n.4, 60 Cal. Rptr. 2d 780, 800–01 n.4 (1997) (listing 11 different types of actions in which California courts require clear and convincing evidence). Illustrative are actions to reform a written contract because of mutual mistake, to show civil contempt, to establish the existence and content of a lost will or deed, to prove that a deed of land was in fact a mortgage, to impeach a notary's certificate of acknowledgment, to establish the malice required to recover punitive damages, to prove a ground for disbarment of an attorney, to establish the facts triggering promissory estoppel, to show the invalidity of a patent, and to prove fraud.

> This standard was applied in equity and in law where the claimant either sought extraordinary relief or based his claim on disfavored grounds, or where he sought relief which would have serious social consequences or harsh effects on an individual beyond the mere award of money damages.

See Comment, 24 EMORY L.J. 105, 114 (1975). In 2011, in a patent infringement case, the Supreme Court ruled that a defendant challenging the validity of a patent must establish that defense by clear and convincing evidence. *See Microsoft Corp. v. i4i Ltd. Partnership*, 131 S. Ct. 2238 (2011).

As in the case of the preponderance standard, do not think that the standard is confined to civil actions. To begin with, the Supreme Court has mandated the standard in eyewitness identification cases. In *United States v. Wade*, 388 U.S. 218 (1967), the Court recognized a limited Sixth Amendment right to counsel at lineups. The Court added that when the pretrial lineup violates the defendant's right to counsel, the eyewitness' in-court identification is admissible only if the government "establish[es] by clear and convincing evidence that the in-court identifications were based upon observations of the suspect other than the lineup identification." *Id.* at 240. In the Fourth Amendment context, if the prosecution relies on the defendant's consent as the basis for a warrantless search, some jurisdictions require the prosecutor to prove consent by clear and positive evidence. *See also Latif v. Obama*, 677 F.3d 1175 (D.C. Cir. 2012) (clear evidence is necessary to rebut the presumption of regularity that supports the official acts of public officers).

NOTES

1.   Who decides the issues of consent and the propriety of an in-court identification — the judge or jury? Does that help explain why the courts apply a more rigorous standard of proof? Remember that the standard originated in equity suits. Is there usually a jury in equity suits?

2.   The clear and convincing proof standard now applies in several types of cases tried by juries. 2 C. McCormick, Handbook of the Law of Evidence § 340 (6th ed. 2006). As trial judge, how would you explain the concept of clear and convincing proof to lay jurors? The concept refers to the quality of the evidence rather than any particular quantum of proof. *See Nguyen v. IBP, Inc.*, 905 F. Supp. 1471, 1481 n.2 (D. Kan. 1995) (the court added that "[t]he evidence is clear 'if it is certain, unambiguous, and plain to the understanding. It is convincing if it is reasonable and persuasive enough to cause the trier of facts to believe it' "); *Modern Air Conditioning, Inc. v. Cinderella Homes, Inc.*, 226 Kan. 70, 78, 596 P.2d 816 (1979) ("the witness to a fact must be found to be credible; the facts to which the witness testifies must be distinctly remembered; the details in connection with the transaction must be narrated exactly and in order, . . . and the witness must be lacking in confusion as to the facts at issue"). Some courts merely tell the jury that the truth of the contention must be "highly probable." *See Freeland v. Financial Recovery Services, Inc.*, 790 F. Supp. 2d 991 (D. Minn. 2011); McBaine, *Burden of Proof: Degrees of Belief*, 32 Cal. L. Rev. 242, 246, 253–54 (1944). According to that suggestion, the pattern instruction in California directs the jury that " 'clear and convincing' evidence means evidence of such a convincing force that it demonstrates . . . a high probability of the truth of the fact for which it is offered as proof." Book of Approved Jury Instructions § 2.62 (2005).

It has been observed that this standard "takes into account the subjective belief of the factfinder as to the validity of the proposition . . . rather than simply weighing [the] evidence. . . ." Comment, 24 Emory L.J. 105, 114 (1975). The Nebraska Supreme Court has described this quantum of evidence as "that amount . . . which produces in the trier of fact a firm belief or conviction." *Haines v. Mensen*, 233 Neb. 543, 446 N.W.2d 716, 719 (1989). The following year, the United States Supreme Court elaborated on the concept as evidence which "produces in the mind of the trier of fact a firm belief or conviction as to the truth of the allegations sought to be established, evidence so clear, direct, and weighty and convincing as to enable the fact finder to come to a clear conviction, without hesitancy, of the truth of the precise facts." *Cruzan v. Director, Missouri Dept. of Health*, 497 U.S. 261, 285 n.11 (1990).

Proof beyond a reasonable doubt. In *Commonwealth v. Webster*, 59 Mass. 295, 320 (1850), Chief Justice Shaw coined the classic definition of a reasonable doubt:

> It is that state of the case, which after the entire comparison and consideration of all the evidence, leaves the minds of the jurors in that condition that they cannot say they feel an abiding conviction, to a moral certainty, of the truth of the charge.

Many states' pattern jury instructions incorporate this precise language, and some jurisdictions have gone to the length of codifying the definition. CAL. PENAL CODE § 1096.

Most trial judges treat Shaw's definition as if it were irreducible; they refuse to amplify on the definition. Their refusal is understandable; in many states, the trial judge risks reversal by the appellate court whenever he or she attempts to explain the concept further.

However, some judges believe that the jury needs additional guidance. In some jurisdictions, the judge may add that the doubt is the kind of doubt that would make a reasonable person hesitate to act. *See United States v. Dunmore*, 446 F.2d 1214, 1222 (8th Cir. 971), *cert. denied*, 404 U.S. 1041 (1972). The judge should negatively stress hesitancy to act rather than affirmative willingness to act. The judge can err by telling the jury that proof beyond a reasonable doubt is evidence "of such a convincing character that you would be willing to rely upon it unhesitatingly in the most important of your own affairs." *United States v. Williams*, 505 F.2d 947, 948 n.1 (8th Cir. 1974). Even in jurisdictions allowing the judge to refer to the jury's willingness to act in important affairs, the judge risks reversal if the judge takes the next step and gives the jury examples of important affairs. In *Commonwealth v. Ferreira*, 364 N.E.2d 1264 (Mass. 1977), the judge listed several "important decisions" in the jury charge: whether to get married or stay single, to buy a house or continue renting, to leave school, to get a job, or to move to another community. The appellate court reversed, expressing the fear that some of the trial judge's examples understated and trivialized the standard in the jury's mind. *See also People v. Johnson*, 115 Cal. App. 4th 1169, 1171–72, 9 Cal. Rptr. 2d 781, 783–84 (2004) (the trial judge erred by analogizing reasonable doubt to the thought processes of people planning vacations or scheduling flights; the explanation had the effect of lowering the prosecution's burden of proof).

As previously stated, this measure does not apply to every issue in a criminal case. Thus, it does not govern the proof of either venue or jurisdiction. In the past, the conventional wisdom was that the standard applied only to the essential elements of the charged crime or offense. Given that assumption, the courts did not extend the standard to factual issues during sentencing. However, in 2000 the Supreme Court undermined that assumption. In that year, the Court handed down its decision in *Apprendi v. New Jersey*, 530 U.S. 466 (2000). The Court announced that other than the fact of a prior conviction, any fact that increases the penalty for a crime beyond the prescribed statutory maximum must be submitted to the jury and proved beyond a reasonable doubt. In 2004 in *Blakely v. Washington*, 542 U.S. 296 (2004), the Court clarified its holding in *Apprendi*. The *Blakely* Court defined "the prescribed statutory maximum." The Court explained:

> [T]he 'statutory maximum' for *Apprendi* purposes is the maximum sentence a judge may impose solely on the basis of the facts reflected in the jury verdict or admitted by the defendant. In other words, the relevant 'statutory maximum' is not the maximum sentence a judge may impose after finding additional facts, but the maximum he may impose without any additional findings. When a judge inflicts punishment that the jury's verdict alone does not allow, the jury has not found all the facts 'which the law makes essential to the punishment,' . . . [so that] the judge exceeds his proper authority.

Post *Apprendi*, the proof beyond a reasonable doubt standard extends to many sentencing factors as well as the essential elements of the charged crime. *United States v. Booker*, 125 S. Ct. 738 (2005) (invalidating the mandatory aspect of the Sentencing Guidelines).

NOTES

1. It was once common practice to give the jury a specially refined definition of proof beyond a reasonable doubt when the prosecution relied on circumstantial evidence. Thus, in *State v. DeRaad*, 164 N.W.2d 108, 110 (Iowa 1969), the court directed the trial judge to instruct the jury that:

> [W]here circumstantial evidence alone is relied on . . . , the . . . circumstances must be entirely consistent with defendant's guilt and wholly inconsistent with any rational hypothesis of defendant's innocence. . . .

However, *Holland v. United States*, 348 U.S. 121, 139–40 (1954), is a watershed in the history of that instruction. *Holland* asserted that the instruction probably succeeds only in confusing the jurors. Since the *Holland* decision, all the federal circuits have abandoned the hypothesis of innocence phraseology. *See United States v. Bell*, 678 F.2d 547, 549 n.3 (5th Cir. 1982). The instruction has also fallen into disrepute in most states.

2. Is the analogy to a chain of circumstances leading to a conviction of guilt open to the argument that a chain is no stronger than its weakest link and that the weak link is sufficient to create a reasonable doubt? Is a better analogy to a cable made up of many strands that together give the evidential force to establish guilt beyond reasonable doubt, although each strand alone would be insufficient and the separate strands might vary considerably in their strength? *See* M. LADD & R. CARLSON, CASES AND MATERIALS ON EVIDENCE 1214 (1972).

3. There has been very little empirical research into the jury's understanding of the various measures of the burden. One of the few studies to explore that question was the London School of Economics Jury Project. Cornish & Sealy, *Juries and the*

Rules of Evidence, 1973 CRIM. L. REV. 208, *cited in Addington, infra.* In the study, the subjects heard several variations of an instruction on the measure. Some were told that they had to be convinced of guilt "beyond reasonable doubt," others were instructed that they had to be "sure and certain" of guilt, and still others were directed that they had to "feel satisfied that it is more likely than not that the accused is guilty." *Id.* at 213–14. In a hypothetical theft case, under the three instructions, the percentage of convictions increased from 31% to 35% to 46%. The results in two other hypothetical cases, though, were more mixed; while the subjects receiving the last instruction convicted more frequently than the subjects receiving the first instruction, the lowest conviction rate was under the "sure and certain" instruction. *Id.* at 216–17. The researchers acknowledged that they had conducted a limited study. *Id.* at 221. However, they added that the results of the study indicated that "jurors are not influenced" by instructions on the measure of the burden to the extent that is commonly assumed. *Id.* at 219.

4. In the vast majority of cases, the proof beyond a reasonable doubt standard is applied in prosecutions rather than civil actions. However, in rare cases, the standard comes into play in civil cases. By way of example, when a litigant seeks rescission of a contract on the ground of unilateral mistake, Mississippi law requires proof of the mistake beyond a reasonable doubt. *Crosby-Mississippi Resources, Ltd. v. Prosper Energy Corp.*, 974 F.2d 612 (5th Cir. 1992). Similarly, by statute, Colorado requires that certain elements of a claim for punitive damages be proven beyond a reasonable doubt. *Karnes v. SCI Colorado Funeral Services, Inc.*, 162 F.3d 1077, 1082 (10th Cir. 1998) (discussing Colo. Rev. Stat. § 13-25-127).

2. Constitutional Requirements

ADDINGTON v. TEXAS
441 U.S. 418 (1979)

CHIEF JUSTICE BURGER delivered the opinion of the Court.

The question in this case is what standard of proof is required by the Fourteenth Amendment to the Constitution in a civil proceeding brought under state law to commit an individual involuntarily for an indefinite period to a state mental hospital.

On seven occasions between 1969 and 1975, appellant was committed temporarily to various Texas state mental hospitals and was committed for indefinite periods to Austin State Hospital on three different occasions. On December 18, 1975, when appellant was arrested on a misdemeanor charge of "assault by threat" against his mother, the county and state mental health authorities therefore were well aware of his history of mental and emotional difficulties.

Appellant's mother filed a petition for his indefinite commitment in accordance with Texas law. The county psychiatric examiner interviewed appellant while in custody and after the interview issued a Certificate of Medical Examination for Mental Illness. In the certificate, the examiner stated his opinion that appellant was "mentally ill and require[d] hospitalization in a mental hospital."

Appellant retained counsel and a trial was held before a jury to determine in accord with the statute:

   (1)   whether the proposed patient is mentally ill, and if so

   (2)   whether he requires hospitalization in a mental hospital for his own welfare and protection or the protection of others, and if so

   (3)   whether he is mentally incompetent.

Art. 5547-51 (Vernon 1958). The trial on these issues extended over six days.

The State offered evidence that appellant suffered from serious delusions, that he often had threatened to injure both of his parents and others, that he had been involved in several assaultive episodes while hospitalized and that he had caused substantial property damage both at his own apartment and at his parents' home. From these undisputed facts, two psychiatrists, who qualified as experts, expressed opinions that appellant suffered from psychotic schizophrenia and that he had paranoid tendencies. They also expressed medical opinions that appellant was probably dangerous both to himself and to others. They explained that appellant required hospitalization in a closed area to treat his condition because in the past he had refused to attend outpatient treatment programs and had escaped several times from mental hospitals.

Appellant did not contest the factual assertions made by the State's witnesses; indeed, he conceded that he suffered from a mental illness. What appellant attempted to show was that there was no substantial basis for concluding that he was probably dangerous to himself or others.

The trial judge submitted the case to the jury with the instructions in the form of two questions:

   1.   Based on clear, unequivocal and convincing evidence, is Frank O'Neal Addington mentally ill?

   2.   Based on clear, unequivocal and convincing evidence, does Frank O'Neal Addington require hospitalization in a mental hospital for his own welfare and protection or the protection of others?

Appellant objected to these instructions on several grounds, including the trial court's refusal to employ the "beyond a reasonable doubt" standard of proof.

The jury found that appellant was mentally ill and that he required hospitalization for his own or others' welfare. The trial court then entered an order committing appellant as a patient to Austin State Hospital for an indefinite period.

Appellant appealed that order to the Texas Court of Civil Appeals, arguing, among other things, that the standards for commitment violated his substantive due process rights and that any standard of proof for commitment less than that required for criminal convictions, i.e., beyond a reasonable doubt, violated his procedural due process rights. The Court of Civil Appeals agreed with appellant on the standard of proof issue and reversed the judgment of the trial court. Because of its treatment of the standard of proof, that court did not consider any of the other issues raised in the appeal.

On appeal, the Texas Supreme Court reversed the Court of Civil Appeals' decision. In so holding, the supreme court relied primarily upon its previous decision in *State v. Turner*, 556 S.W.2d 563 (1977), *cert. denied*, 435 U.S. 929 (1978).

In *Turner*, the Texas Supreme Court held that a "preponderance of the evidence" standard of proof in a civil commitment proceeding satisfied due process. The court declined to adopt the criminal law standard of "beyond a reasonable doubt" primarily because it questioned whether the State could prove by that exacting standard that a particular person would or would not be dangerous in the future. It also distinguished a civil commitment from a criminal conviction by noting that under Texas law the mentally ill patient has the right to treatment, periodic review of his condition, and immediate release when no longer deemed to be a danger to himself or others. Finally, the *Turner* court rejected the "clear and convincing" evidence standard because under Texas rules of procedure juries could be instructed only under a beyond-a-reasonable-doubt or a preponderance standard of proof.

Reaffirming *Turner*, the Texas Supreme Court in this case concluded that the trial court's instruction to the jury, although not in conformity with the legal requirements, had benefited appellant, and hence the error was harmless. Accordingly, the court reinstated the judgment of the trial court.

We noted probable jurisdiction. After oral argument it became clear that no challenge to the constitutionality of any Texas statute was presented. Under 28 U.S.C. § 1257(2) no appeal is authorized; accordingly, construing the papers filed as a petition for a writ of certiorari, we now grant the petition.

The function of a standard of proof, as that concept is embodied in the Due Process Clause and in the realm of fact finding, is to "instruct the factfinder concerning the degree of confidence our society thinks he should have in the correctness of factual conclusions for a particular type of adjudication." *In re Winship*, 397 U.S. 358, 370 (1970). The standard serves to allocate the risk of error between the litigants and to indicate the relative importance attached to the ultimate decision.

Generally speaking, the evolution of this area of the law has produced across a continuum three standards or levels of proof for different types of cases. At one end of the spectrum is the typical civil case involving a monetary dispute between private parties. Since society has a minimal concern with the outcome of such private suits, plaintiff's burden of proof is a mere preponderance of the evidence. The litigants thus share the risk of error in roughly equal fashion.

In a criminal case, on the other hand, the interests of the defendant are of such magnitude that historically and without any explicit constitutional requirement they have been protected by standards of proof designed to exclude as nearly as possible the likelihood of an erroneous judgment. In the administration of criminal justice, our society imposes almost the entire risk of error upon itself. This is accomplished by requiring under the Due Process Clause that the state prove the guilt of an accused beyond a reasonable doubt. *In re Winship, supra.*

The intermediate standard, which usually employs some combination of the words "clear," "cogent," "unequivocal," and "convincing," is less commonly used, but nonetheless "is no stranger to the civil law," *Woodby v. INS*, 385 U.S. 276, 285 (1966). One typical use of the standard is in civil cases involving allegations of fraud or some other quasi-criminal wrongdoing by the defendant. The interests at stake in those cases are deemed to be more substantial than mere loss of money and some jurisdictions accordingly reduce the risk to the defendant of having his reputation tarnished erroneously by increasing the plaintiff's burden of proof. Similarly, this Court has used the "clear, unequivocal and convincing" standard of proof to protect particularly important individual interests in various civil cases. *See, e.g., Woodby v. INS, supra*, at 285 (deportation); *Chaunt v. United States*, 364 U.S. 350, 353 (1960) (denaturalization); *Schneiderman v. United States*, 320 U.S. 118, 125, 159 (1943) (denaturalization).

Candor suggests that, to a degree, efforts to analyze what lay jurors understand concerning the differences among these three tests or the nuances of a judge's instructions on the law may well be largely an academic exercise; there are no directly relevant empirical studies. Indeed, the ultimate truth as to how the standards of proof affect decision making may well be unknowable, given that fact finding is a process shared by countless thousands of individuals throughout the country. We probably can assume no more than that the difference between a preponderance of the evidence and proof beyond a reasonable doubt probably is better understood than either of them in relation to the intermediate standard of clear and convincing evidence. Nonetheless, even if the particular standard-of-proof catch words do not always make a great difference in a particular case, adopting a "standard of proof is more than an empty semantic exercise." *Tippett v. Maryland*, 436 F.2d 1153, 1166 (CA4 1971), *cert. dismissed sub nom. Murel v. Baltimore City Criminal Court*, 407 U.S. 355 (1972). In cases involving individual rights, whether criminal or civil, "[t]he standard of proof [at a minimum] reflects the value society places on individual liberty." 436 F.2d, at 1166.

In considering what standard should govern in a civil commitment proceeding, we must assess both the extent of the individual's interest in not being involuntarily confined indefinitely and the state's interest in committing the emotionally disturbed under a particular standard of proof.

This Court repeatedly has recognized that civil commitment for any purpose constitutes a significant deprivation of liberty that requires due process protection. *See, e.g., Jackson v. Indiana*, 406 U.S. 715 (1972). Moreover, it is indisputable that involuntary commitment to a mental hospital after a finding of probable dangerousness to self or others can engender adverse social consequences to the individual. Whether we label this phenomena "stigma" or choose to call it something else is less important than that we recognize that it can occur and that it can have a very significant impact on the individual.

The state has a legitimate interest under its parens patriae powers in providing care to its citizens who are unable because of emotional disorders to care for themselves; the state also has authority under its police power to protect the community from the dangerous tendencies of some who are mentally ill. Under the Texas Mental Health Code, however, the State has no interest in confining individuals involuntarily if they are not mentally ill or if they do not pose some danger to themselves or others. Since the preponderance standard creates the risk of increasing the number of individuals erroneously committed, it is at least unclear to what extent, if any, the state's interests are furthered by using a preponderance standard in such commitment proceedings.

The expanding concern of society with problems of mental disorders is reflected in the fact that in recent years many states have enacted statutes designed to protect the rights of the mentally ill. However, only one state by statute permits involuntary commitment by a mere preponderance of the evidence, Miss. Code. Ann. § 41-21-75, and Texas is the only state where a court has concluded that the preponderance of the evidence standard satisfies due process. We attribute this not to any lack of concern in those states, but rather to a belief that the varying standards tend to produce comparable results. As we noted earlier, however, standards of proof are important for their symbolic meaning as well as for their practical effect.

At one time or another every person exhibits some abnormal behavior which might be perceived by some as symptomatic of a mental or emotional disorder, but which is in fact within a range of conduct that is generally acceptable. Obviously, such behavior is no basis for compelled treatment and surely none for confinement. However, there is the possible risk that a factfinder might decide to commit an individual based solely on a few isolated instances of unusual conduct. Loss of liberty calls for a showing that the individual suffers from something more serious than is demonstrated by idiosyncratic behavior. Increasing the burden of proof is one way to impress the factfinder with the importance of the decision and thereby perhaps to reduce the chances that inappropriate commitments will be ordered.

The individual should not be asked to share equally with society the risk of error when the possible injury to the individual is significantly greater than any possible harm to the state. We conclude that the individual's interest in the outcome of a civil commitment proceeding is of such weight and gravity that due process requires the state to justify confinement by proof more substantial than a mere preponderance of the evidence.

Appellant urges the Court to hold that due process requires use of the criminal law's standard of proof — "beyond a reasonable doubt." He argues that the rationale of the *Winship* holding that the criminal law standard of proof was required in a delinquency proceeding applies with equal force to a civil commitment proceeding.

*   *   *

There are significant reasons why different standards of proof are called for in civil commitment proceedings as opposed to criminal prosecutions. In a civil commitment state power is not exercised in a punitive sense. . . .[4]

In addition, the "beyond a reasonable doubt" standard historically has been reserved for criminal cases. This unique standard of proof, not prescribed or defined

---

[4] The State of Texas confines only for the purpose of providing care designed to treat the individual. As the Texas Supreme Court said in *State v. Turner*, 556 S.W.2d 563, 566 (1977): "The involuntary mental patient is entitled to treatment, to periodic and recurrent review of his mental condition, and to release at such time as he no longer presents a danger to himself or others."

in the Constitution, is regarded as a critical part of the "moral force of the criminal law," *In re Winship*, 397 U.S., at 364, and we should hesitate to apply it too broadly or casually in noncriminal cases.

The heavy standard applied in criminal cases manifests our concern that the risk of error to the individual must be minimized even at the risk that some who are guilty might go free. *Patterson v. New York*, 432 U.S. 197, 208 (1977). The full force of that idea does not apply to a civil commitment. It may be true that an erroneous commitment is sometimes as undesirable as an erroneous conviction, 5 J. Wigmore, Evidence § 1400 (Chadbourn rev. 1974). However, even though an erroneous confinement should be avoided in the first instance, the layers of professional review and observation of the patient's condition, and the concern of family and friends generally will provide continuous opportunities for an erroneous commitment to be corrected. Moreover, it is not true that the release of a genuinely mentally ill person is no worse for the individual than the failure to convict the guilty. One who is suffering from a debilitating mental illness and in need of treatment is neither wholly at liberty nor free of stigma. *See* Chodoff, *The Case for Involuntary Hospitalization of the Mentally Ill*, 133 Am. J. Psychiatry 496, 498 (1976); Schwartz, Myers, & Astrachan, *Psychiatric Labeling and the Rehabilitation of the Mental Patient*, 31 Arch. Gen. Psychiatry 329, 334 (1974). It cannot be said, therefore, that it is much better for a mentally ill person to "go free" than for a mentally normal person to be committed.

Finally, the initial inquiry in a civil commitment proceeding is very different from the central issue in either a delinquency proceeding or a criminal prosecution. In the latter cases the basic issue is a straightforward factual question — did the accused commit the act alleged? There may be factual issues to resolve in a commitment proceeding, but the factual aspects represent only the beginning of the inquiry. Whether the individual is mentally ill and dangerous to either himself or others and is in need of confined therapy turns on the meaning of the facts which must be interpreted by expert psychiatrists and psychologists. Given the lack of certainty and the fallibility of psychiatric diagnosis, there is a serious question as to whether a state could ever prove beyond a reasonable doubt that an individual is both mentally ill and likely to be dangerous. Note, *Civil Commitment of the Mentally Ill: Theories and Procedures*, 79 Harv. L. Rev. 1288, 1291 (1966); Note, *Due Process and the Development of "Criminal" Safeguards in Civil Commitment Adjudications*, 42 Fordham L. Rev. 611, 624 (1974).

The subtleties and nuances of psychiatric diagnosis render certainties virtually beyond reach in most situations. The reasonable-doubt standard of criminal law functions in its realm because there the standard is addressed to specific, knowable facts. Psychiatric diagnosis, in contrast, is to a large extent based on medical "impressions" drawn from subjective analysis and filtered through the experience of the diagnostician. This process often makes it very difficult for the expert physician to offer definite conclusions about any particular patient. Within the medical discipline, the traditional standard for "fact finding" is a "reasonable medical certainty." If a trained psychiatrist has difficulty with the categorical "beyond a reasonable doubt" standard, the untrained lay juror — or indeed even a trained judge — who is required to rely upon expert opinion could be forced by the criminal law standard of proof to reject commitment for many patients desperately in need of institutionalized psychiatric care. *See ibid.* Such "freedom" for a mentally ill person would be purchased at a high price.

*   *   *

Having concluded that the preponderance standard falls short of meeting the demands of due process and that the reasonable doubt standard is not required we turn to a middle level of burden of proof that strikes a fair balance between the rights of the individual and the legitimate concerns of the state. We note that 20 states, most by statute, employ the standard of "clear and convincing" evidence; three states use "clear, cogent, and convincing" evidence; and two states require "clear, unequivocal and convincing" evidence.

In *Woodby v. INS*, 385 U.S. 276 (1966), dealing with deportation, and *Schneiderman v. United States*, 320 U.S. at 125, 159, dealing with denaturalization, the Court held that "clear, unequivocal, and convincing" evidence was the appropriate standard of proof. The term "unequivocal," taken by itself, means proof that admits of no doubt, a burden approximating, if not exceeding, that used in criminal cases. The issues in *Schneiderman* and *Woodby* were basically factual and therefore susceptible of objective proof and the consequences to the individual were unusually drastic — loss of citizenship and expulsion from the United States.

We have concluded that the reasonable doubt standard is inappropriate in civil commitment proceedings because, given the uncertainties of psychiatric diagnosis, it may impose a burden the state cannot meet and thereby erect an unreasonable barrier to needed medical treatment. Similarly, we conclude that use of the term "unequivocal" is not constitutionally required, although the states are free to use that standard. To meet due process demands, the standard has to inform the factfinder that the proof must be greater than the preponderance of the evidence standard applicable to other categories of civil cases.

We noted earlier that the trial court employed the standard of "clear, unequivocal and convincing" evidence in appellant's commitment hearing before a jury. That instruction was constitutionally adequate. However, determination of the precise burden equal to or greater than the "clear and convincing" standard which we hold is required to meet due process guarantees is a matter of state law which we leave to the Texas Supreme Court. Accordingly, we remand the case for further proceedings not inconsistent with this opinion.

Vacated and remanded.

NOTES AND PROBLEMS

1. In *Santosky v. Kramer*, 455 U.S. 745, 768–69 (1982), the Court extended *Addington* to proceedings to terminate natural parents' rights in their children. The Court declared that the child and the natural parents share a "vital interest in preventing erroneous termination of their relationship." *Id.* at 760. However, in *Rivera v. Minnich*, 483 U.S. 574 (1987), the Court refused to extend *Santosky* to paternity litigation between private parties. The Court distinguished *Santosky* on

several grounds, including the private character of the litigants. The Court noted that, in all the cases in which it has held that an enhanced standard of proof is constitutionally required, "the contestants" have been "the State and an individual." *Id.* at 581. In each case, it was "appropriate for society to impose upon itself a disproportionate share of the risk of error" because "the State has superior resources," and the private individual faced "especially severe consequences." *Id.* However, in paternity litigation between private parties, the competing interests are in relative "equipoise." *Id.* Analogously, some courts have held that in proceedings to terminate a parent's custody of a child on the ground that continued custody would be detrimental to the child, due process requires that the finding of detriment be supported by clear and convincing evidence. *In re Z.K.*, 133 Cal. Rptr. 3d 597, 609 (Cal. Ct. App. 2011).

2.   Like *Mullaney*, *Addington* relies on *Winship*. Should *Mullaney*, like *Addington*, now extend to civil cases? Even if you would not apply *Mullaney* in the typical civil action, would you apply it in a termination proceeding as in *Santosky*? Suppose that the government assigned the natural parents the burden of proving that they had not neglected the child.

3.   Over the years, the Supreme Court has designated several interests as "fundamental": voting, free speech, and travel. *See* Case Comment, 26 U. FLA. L. REV. 155, 156 (1973). Does *Santosky* augur the application of *Addington* to all proceedings in which a fundamental interest is at stake?

4.   In many jurisdictions, the prosecution's burden at pretrial motion hearings is a mere preponderance. *See, e.g., United States v. Tucker*, 495 F. Supp. 607, 613 (E.D.N.Y. 1980). The Supreme Court itself has sanctioned that burden. *See Lego v. Twomey*, 404 U.S. 477, 488 (1972). However, in light of *Addington*, is that minimal burden suspect?

5.   In *Addington*, the appellant argued that the clear and convincing evidence standard was too low. A decade later in *Cruzan v. Director, Missouri Dept. of Health*, 497 U.S. 261 (1990), the co-guardians of a petitioner presented the converse argument that the standard was too high. In *Cruzan*, the petitioner, Nancy Cruzan, had been rendered incompetent by virtue of injuries sustained in an automobile accident. Her parents were her co-guardians, and they became convinced that she had virtually no chance of recovering her cognitive faculties. They then sought a court order directing the withdrawal of the petitioner's artificial life support equipment. The Missouri Supreme Court denied relief for the stated reason that there was no clear and convincing evidence of the petitioner's desire to have life-sustaining treatment withdrawn. Writing for the majority, Chief Justice Rehnquist stated that Missouri's choice of an enhanced standard was defensible, since "the interests at stake . . . are more substantial, both on an individual and societal level, than those involved in the run-of-the-mine civil dispute." The Chief Justice stated:

> In *Santosky*, one of the factors which led the Court to require proof by clear and convincing evidence in a proceeding to terminate parental rights was that a decision in such a case was final and irrevocable. The same must surely be said of the decision to discontinue hydration and nutrition of a patient such as Nancy Cruzan, which all agree will result in her death.

6. *Cooper v. Oklahoma*, 517 U.S. 348 (1996), was the next case in the *Addington* line of authority. Cooper attacked the constitutionality of a state law requiring him to prove his alleged incompetence to stand trial by clear and convincing evidence. The Supreme Court invalidated the law. Oklahoma had invoked *Addington* in its attempt to persuade the Court to uphold the law. Writing for a unanimous Court, Justice Stevens distinguished *Addington*:

> Our decision today is in complete agreement with the basis for our ruling in *Addington*. Both cases concern the proper protection of fundamental rights in circumstances in which the State proposes to take drastic action against an individual. The requirement that the grounds for civil commitment be shown by clear and convincing evidence protects the individual's fundamental interest in liberty. The prohibition against requiring the criminal defendant to demonstrate incompetence by clear and convincing evidence safeguards the fundamental right not to stand trial while incompetent.

7.   Problem 31-6. In *Devitt*, the defendant is convicted. In addition to alleging the battery, the initial indictment charged that Devitt is a "special dangerous violent offender." Under Morena law, once convicted, the defendant faces an enhanced punishment if the prosecution can prove other violent misconduct. During sentencing, the prosecutor intends to offer evidence of three other assaults by Devitt. The defense attorney learns of the prosecutor's intention and objects, citing *Winship*. The defense attorney asserts that "just like the charged battery, these assaults have to be proven beyond a reasonable doubt." You are the judge. What ruling? *Compare Specht v. Patterson*, 386 U.S. 605, 609–11 (1967) *with United States v. Inendino*, 604 F.2d 458, 463 (7th Cir. 1979).

8.   Problem 31-7. In *Devitt*, the defendant is acquitted. However, the prosecutor immediately files a new proceeding to have Devitt involuntarily committed as a mentally disordered violent offender (MDVO). The Morena statutes refer to this type of proceeding as "a civil action." The statutes authorize involuntary commitment when on the basis of past violent misconduct, the judge finds that the subject is "predisposed" to commit future violent crimes. During the proceeding, the prosecutor intends to offer the evidence of the battery and three assaults mentioned in Problem 31-6. At a pretrial hearing, the defense attorney argues that the past acts relied on as the basis for the prediction of future violent misconduct must be proved beyond a reasonable doubt. What ruling? *See People v. Burnick*, 14 Cal. 3d 306, 313–26, 121 Cal. Rptr. 488, 492-500, 535 P.2d 352, 356–64 (1975).

Part 6

CONSTITUTIONAL OVERRIDES TO THE RULES OF EVIDENCE

Chapter 32

CONSTITUTIONAL OVERRIDES: CONFRONTATION, COMPULSORY PROCESS, AND DUE PROCESS

A. INTRODUCTION

To understand the Supreme Court's jurisprudence on constitutional overrides to the rules of evidence — particularly the Sixth Amendment Confrontation Clause — it is helpful to know a bit of history. The events surrounding the evolution of the right to confrontation make it one of the most fascinating chapters of legal history. *See* Pollitt, *The Right of Confrontation: Its History and Modern Dress*, 8 J. Pub. L. 381 (1959).

One of the major historical incidents that shaped the American Constitution was the trial of Sir Walter Raleigh in 1603. Catherine Drinker Bowen, in her majestic work, The Lion and the throne (Little, Brown and Co. 1956) provides an indelible historical vignette.

THE TRIAL OF SIR WALTER RALEIGH
State Trials, Vol. 2 (1603)
(Cobbett's Complete Collection, Howell ed. 1809, pp. 1–46)

[The following excerpt is from Waltz & Park, Evidence, (Foundation Press 8th ed. 1995) pp. 82-83:] The general rule excluding hearsay statements did not become firmly fixed in England until the latter part of the 17th Century. Thus Sir Walter Raleigh had his problems with hearsay earlier in that century.

(Raleigh was tried for a conspiracy of treason to dethrone Elizabeth and to put Arabella Stuart in her place, by the aid of Spanish money and intrigue. Sir Edward Coke, attorney-general, conducted the prosecution. The principal evidence against him was the assertion of Lord Cobham, a supposed fellow-conspirator, who had betrayed Raleigh in a sworn statement made before trial. Cobham himself was in prison, and was not produced on the trial.) . . .

Raleigh. "But it is strange to see how you press me still with my Lord Cobham, and yet will not produce him; it is not for gaining of time or prolonging my life that I urge this; he is in the house hard by, and may soon be brought hither; let him be produced, and if he will yet accuse me or avow this confession of his, it shall convict me and ease you of further proof."

Lord Cecil. "Sir Walter Raleigh presseth often that my Lord Cobham should be brought face to face; if he ask a thing of grace and favour, they must come from him only who can give them; but if he ask a matter of law, then, in order that we, who sit here as commissioners, may be satisfied, I desire to hear the opinions of my Lords, the judges, whether it may be done by law."

The Judges all answered, "that in respect it might be a mean to cover many with treasons, and might be prejudicial to the King, therefore, by the law, it was not sufferable."

Popham, C.J. "There must not such a gap be opened for the destruction of the King as would be if we should grant this; you plead hard for yourself, but the laws plead as hard for the King. Where no circumstances do concur to make a matter probable, then an accuser may be heard; but so many circumstances agreeing and confirming the accusation in this case, the accuser is not to be produced; for, having first confessed against himself voluntarily, and so charged another person, if we shall now hear him again in person, he may, for favour or fear, retract what formerly he hath said, and the jury may, by that mean, be inveigled." . . .

Raleigh. — "I never had intelligence with Cobham since I came to the Tower."

Lord Cecil. — "Sir Walter Raleigh, if my Lord Cobham will now affirm, that you were acquainted with his dealings with Count Aremberg, that you knew of the letter he received, that you were the chief instigator of him, will you then be concluded by it?"

Raleigh. — "Let my Lord Cobham speak before God and the King, and deny God and the King if he speak not truly, and will then say that ever I knew of Arabella's matter, or the money out of Spain, or the Surprising Treason, I will put myself upon it."

Lord Henry Howard. — "But what if my Lord Cobham affirm anything equivalent to this; what then?"

Raleigh. — "My Lord, I put myself upon it."

Attorney-General. — "I shall now produce a witness viva voce:"

He then produced one *Dyer*, a pilot, who, being sworn, said, "Being at Lisbon, there came to me a Portuguese gentleman, who asked me how the King of England did, and whether he was crowned? I answered him, that I hoped our noble king was well, and crowned by this; but the time was not come when I came from the coast of Spain. 'Nay,' said he 'your king shall never be crowned, for Don Cobham and Don Raleigh will cut his throat before he come to be crowned.' And this, in time, was found to be spoken in mid July."

Raleigh. — "This is the saying of some wild Jesuit or beggarly priest; but what proof is it against me?"

Attorney-General. — "It must perforce arise out of some preceding intelligence, and shews that your treason had wings." . . .

Thus on the single evidence of Cobham, never confronted with Raleigh, who retracted his confession, and then (according to the advocates of the Crown) recalled his retraction, did an English jury, to the amazement and horror of the bystanders, and the perpetual disgrace of the English name, find the most illustrious of their fellow subjects guilty of high treason.

RALEIGH'S SENTENCING

[Excerpt from Bowen, *supra*, at 216–17:] Raleigh was led to the bar. Chief Justice Popham stood up, bareheaded. In his hand he held the black cap that signified a death sentence. "Sir Walter Raleigh," he said, "I am sorry to see this fallen upon you this day. You have always been taken for a wise man. And I cannot but marvel to see that a man of your wit, as this day you have approved it, could be entangled with so many treasons. I grieve to find that a man of your quality would have sold yourself for a spy to the enemy of your country for 1500 pounds a year. This covetousness is like a canker, that eats the iron place where it lives . . . ."

There was more; to Raleigh it must have been well nigh unendurable. "O God!" he had written to his wife from the Tower, "I cannot live to think how I am derided, the scorns I shall receive, the cruel words of lawyers, the infamous taunts and despites, to be made a wonder and a spectacle! O death, destroy the memory of these and lay me up in dark forgetfulness!"

Of all these cruel taunts, Popham's solemn pronouncement was the worst. Coke had raved but Raleigh could answer him. Now, for Raleigh, denial and affirmation were forever blocked. What the Chief Justice said, the world (or so thought Raleigh) would take as truth. "It now comes to my mind," Popham continued, "why you may not have your accuser brought face to face: for such a one is easily brought to retract when he seeth there is no hope of his own life. . . . It now only remaineth to pronounce the judgment, which I would to God you had not to receive this day of me. I never saw the like trial, and I hope I shall never see the like again."

Raising both hands with the deliberation of an aged man, Popham set the black cap on his head. "Sir Walter Raleigh," he said, "since you have been found guilty of these horrible treasons, the judgment of this court is, That you shall be had from hence to the place whence you came, there to remain until the day of execution. And from thence you shall be drawn upon a hurdle through the open streets to the place of execution, there to be hanged and cut down alive, and your body shall be opened, your heart and bowels plucked out, and your privy members cut off and thrown into the fire before your eyes. Then your head to be stricken off from your body, and your body shall be divided into four quarters, to be disposed of at the King's pleasure.

"And God have mercy upon your soul."

POSTSCRIPT

Raleigh was condemned in 1603. The death sentence was commuted to imprisonment in the Tower. After 13 years in the Tower, Raleigh was freed (but not pardoned) by James I to embark on a 2-year voyage to Guiana in search of gold. Raleigh was eventually executed in 1621; his last words were to become legend. As Sir Walter knelt by the block, the headsman bade him face east as he lay down. "What matter how the head lie," said Raleigh, "so the heart be right?" *Id.* at 414, 416.

B. NEGATIVE OVERRIDES: EXCLUDING OTHERWISE ADMISSIBLE EVIDENCE

In our legal system there is a hierarchy: the Constitution overrides statutory and common law evidentiary rules. Such an override can work either negatively or affirmatively. Negatively, the Constitution may preclude the introduction of evidence that would otherwise be admissible; affirmatively, the Constitution may operate to require admission of evidence that would otherwise be inadmissible.

We begin with Supreme Court opinions interpreting the Confrontation Clause of the Sixth Amendment — where Raleigh's ghost looms largest. The Confrontation Clause provides: "In all criminal prosecutions, the accused shall enjoy the right . . . to be confronted with the witnesses against him."

In 1965, in *Pointer v. Texas*, 380 U.S. 400 (1965), the Court made the Confrontation Clause binding upon the states by holding that the right to Confrontation was "incorporated" into the Due Process Clause of the Fourteenth Amendment. Since then, the Court has struggled with the intersection between the Confrontation Clause and the rule against hearsay. If a hearsay declarant is always a "witness against" the defendant, then the Constitution would always be implicated by introduction of hearsay by the prosecution in a criminal trial. On the other hand, if the Clause were read to refer only to in-court witnesses, then there would be no overlap between the Constitution and the hearsay rule. The Court has never adhered to either of these extreme views, but it has been inconsistent as to precisely when the Constitution is violated by introduction of hearsay statements by a declarant who has not been subject to cross-examination.

In *California v. Green*, 399 U.S. 149 (1970), the Court sustained the admission of the preliminary hearing testimony of a witness who claimed at trial that he could not remember his prior testimony. Under the applicable California Evidence Rule, the statement was admissible both substantively and for impeachment purposes as a prior inconsistent statement. The California Supreme Court construed the Confrontation Clause to require exclusion of the prior testimony because it was not adequately amenable to cross-examination by the defendant. The United States Supreme Court disagreed, holding that the declarant's presence at trial obviated any Confrontation Clause problem because he was subject at trial to cross-examination about the prior testimony (although belated and perhaps impaired by the claimed memory loss).

But what if the declarant is not present at trial? In *Ohio v. Roberts*, 448 U.S. 56 (1980), the Court fashioned a new, two-part standard: if the declarant is unavailable, the out-of-court statement must either (1) fall within a "firmly rooted" hearsay exception or (2) have particularized guarantees of trustworthiness such that adversarial testing would be expected to add little, if anything, to the statement's reliability. *Id.* at 65–6. *Roberts* involved former testimony — an exception that has always required unavailability and that carries high degree of comfort about trustworthiness. Since the former testimony doctrine is a traditional exception, the Court held that it was firmly rooted and that the evidence passed muster under the *Roberts* test.

Over the course of the following two-and-a-half decades, the Court decided a number of Confrontation Clause cases and held that several of the traditional hearsay exceptions were "firmly rooted" and, therefore, that admission of such statements against a criminal defendant did not violate the Confrontation Clause. The difficulty arose with statements admitted pursuant to non-traditional or evolving exceptions, particularly the residual exception in Rule 807 or state equivalents. Evidence admitted under such exceptions had to satisfy the second prong of the *Roberts* test. In *Idaho v. Wright*, 497 U.S. 805 (1990), the trial court admitted the hearsay statements of a child to a doctor under the state's residual hearsay exception, which was identical to the federal rule. The Supreme Court held that the Confrontation Clause had been violated, noting that the residual exception is not "firmly rooted," and that the hearsay did not demonstrate particularized guarantees of trustworthiness.

Roberts and its progeny represent the high point of a flexible, liberal approach to application of the Sixth Amendment Confrontation Clause that put courts in the central position of determining the reliability, for constitutional purposes, of hearsay introduced against a criminal defendant. With respect to most of the traditional hearsay exceptions, *Roberts* essentially constitutionalized the hearsay doctrine by holding that admissible hearsay was likewise admissible under the Confrontation Clause. Though there are some advantages to this approach — especially for the prosecution — one difficulty lay in the obvious tension with the original historical meaning and purpose of the Sixth Amendment. The *Roberts* rule was subject to much criticism. In the years leading up to the *Crawford* decision, excerpted below, the United States as amicus had argued that the Court should adopt a much stricter view of the reach of the Confrontation Clause, limiting its application to certain types of hearsay that more closely resembled the scenarios about which the Confrontation Clause was historically concerned. The Court rejected these arguments in two Confrontation cases prior to *Crawford*, but ultimately adopted a version of this approach:

CRAWFORD v. WASHINGTON
541 U.S. 36 (2004)

Justice Scalia delivered the opinion of the Court.

Petitioner Michael Crawford stabbed a man who allegedly tried to rape his wife, Sylvia. At his trial, the State played for the jury Sylvia's tape-recorded statement to the police describing the stabbing, even though he had no opportunity for cross-examination. The Washington Supreme Court upheld petitioner's conviction after determining that Sylvia's statement was reliable. The question presented is whether this procedure complied with the Sixth Amendment's guarantee that, "[i]n all criminal prosecutions, the accused shall enjoy the right . . . to be confronted with the witnesses against him."

On August 5, 1999, Kenneth Lee was stabbed at his apartment. Police arrested petitioner later that night. After giving petitioner and his wife *Miranda* warnings, detectives interrogated each of them twice. Petitioner eventually confessed that he and Sylvia had gone in search of Lee because he was upset over an earlier incident in which Lee had tried to rape her. The two had found Lee at his apartment, and a fight ensued in which Lee was stabbed in the torso and petitioner's hand was cut.

Petitioner gave the following account of the fight:

Q: Okay. Did you ever see anything in [Lee's] hands?

A: I think so, but I'm not positive.

Q: Okay, when you think so, what do you mean by that?

A: I could a swore I seen him goin' for somethin' before, right before everything happened. He was like reachin', fiddlin' around down here and stuff . . . and I just . . . I don't know, I think, this is just a possibility, but I think, I think that he pulled somethin' out and I grabbed for it and that's how I got cut . . . but I'm not positive. I, I, my mind goes blank when things like this happen. I mean, I just, I remember things wrong, I remember things that just doesn't, don't make sense to me later." (punctuation added).

Sylvia generally corroborated petitioner's story about the events leading up to the fight, but her account of the fight itself was arguably different — particularly with respect to whether Lee had drawn a weapon before petitioner assaulted him:

Q: Did Kenny do anything to fight back from this assault?

A: (pausing) I know he reached into his pocket . . . or somethin' . . . I don't know what.

Q: After he was stabbed?

A: He saw Michael coming up. He lifted his hand . . . his chest open, he might [have] went to go strike his hand out or something and then (inaudible).

Q: Okay, you, you gotta speak up.

A: Okay, he lifted his hand over his head maybe to strike Michael's hand down or something and then he put his hands in his . . . put his right hand in his right pocket . . . took a step back . . . Michael proceeded to stab him . . . then his hands were like . . . how do you explain this . . . open arms . . . with his hands open and he fell down . . . and we ran (describing subject holding hands open, palms toward assailant).

Q: Okay, when he's standing there with his open hands, you're talking about Kenny, correct?

A: Yeah, after, after the fact, yes.

Q: Did you see anything in his hands at that point?

A: (pausing) um um (no)." (punctuation added).

The State charged petitioner with assault and attempted murder. At trial, he claimed self-defense. Sylvia did not testify because of the state marital privilege, which generally bars a spouse from testifying without the other spouse's consent. *See* Wash. Rev. Code § 5.60.060(1) (1994). In Washington, this privilege does not extend to a spouse's out-of-court statements admissible under a hearsay exception, see *State v. Burden*, 120 Wash.2d 371, 377, 841 P.2d 758, 761 (1992), so the State sought to introduce Sylvia's tape-recorded statements to the police as evidence that the stabbing was not in self-defense. Noting that Sylvia had admitted she led petitioner to Lee's apartment and thus had facilitated the assault, the State invoked the hearsay exception for statements against penal interest, Wash. Rule Evid. 804(b)(3) (2003).

Petitioner countered that, state law notwithstanding, admitting the evidence would violate his federal constitutional right to be "confronted with the witnesses against him." According to our description of that right in *Ohio v. Roberts*, 448 U.S. 56 (1980), it does not bar admission of an unavailable witness's statement against a criminal defendant if the statement bears "adequate 'indicia of reliability.' " *Id.*, at 66. To meet that test, evidence must either fall within a "firmly rooted hearsay exception" or bear "particularized guarantees of trustworthiness." *Ibid.* The trial court here admitted the statement on the latter ground, offering several reasons why it was trustworthy: Sylvia was not shifting blame but rather corroborating her husband's story that he acted in self-defense or "justified reprisal"; she had direct knowledge as an eyewitness; she was describing recent events; and she was being questioned by a "neutral" law enforcement officer. The prosecution played the tape for the jury and relied on it in closing, arguing that it was "damning evidence" that "completely refutes [petitioner's] claim of self-defense." The jury convicted petitioner of assault.

The Washington Court of Appeals reversed. It applied a nine-factor test to determine whether Sylvia's statement bore particularized guarantees of trustworthiness, and noted several reasons why it did not: The statement contradicted one she had previously given; it was made in response to specific questions; and at one point she admitted she had shut her eyes during the stabbing. The court considered and rejected the State's argument that Sylvia's statement was reliable because it coincided with petitioner's to such a degree that the two "interlocked." The court determined that, although the two statements agreed about the events leading up to the stabbing, they differed on the issue crucial to petitioner's self-defense claim: "[Petitioner's] version asserts that Lee may have had something in his hand when he stabbed him; but Sylvia's version has Lee grabbing for something only after he has been stabbed."

The Washington Supreme Court reinstated the conviction, unanimously concluding that, although Sylvia's statement did not fall under a firmly rooted hearsay exception, it bore guarantees of trustworthiness: "[W]hen a codefendant's confession is virtually identical [to, *i.e.*, interlocks with,] that of a defendant, it may be deemed reliable." 147 Wash.2d 424, 437, 54 P.3d 656, 663 (2002) (quoting *State v. Rice*, 120 Wash.2d 549, 570, 844 P.2d 416, 427 (1993)). ***

We granted certiorari to determine whether the State's use of Sylvia's statement violated the Confrontation Clause.

* * * [Part II — historical background is omitted — eds.] * * *

[Part III A]

This history supports two inferences about the meaning of the Sixth Amendment.

First, the principal evil at which the Confrontation Clause was directed was the civil-law mode of criminal procedure, and particularly its use of *ex parte* examinations as evidence against the accused. It was these practices that the Crown deployed in notorious treason cases like Raleigh's; that the Marian statutes invited; that English law's assertion of a right to confrontation was meant to prohibit; and that the founding-era rhetoric decried. The Sixth Amendment must be interpreted with this focus in mind.

Accordingly, we once again reject the view that the Confrontation Clause applies of its own force only to in-court testimony, and that its application to out-of-court statements introduced at trial depends upon "the law of Evidence for the time being." 3 Wigmore § 1397, at 101; accord, *Dutton v. Evans*, 400 U.S. 74, 94 (1970) (Harlan, J., concurring in result). Leaving the regulation of out-of-court statements to the law of evidence would render the Confrontation Clause powerless to prevent even the most flagrant inquisitorial practices. Raleigh was, after all, perfectly free to confront those who read Cobham's confession in court.

This focus also suggests that not all hearsay implicates the Sixth Amendment's core concerns. An off-hand, overheard remark might be unreliable evidence and thus a good candidate for exclusion under hearsay rules, but it bears little resemblance to the civil-law abuses the Confrontation Clause targeted. On the other hand, *ex parte* examinations might sometimes be admissible under modern hearsay rules, but the Framers certainly would not have condoned them.

The text of the Confrontation Clause reflects this focus. It applies to "witnesses" against the accused — in other words, those who "bear testimony." 1 N. Webster, An American Dictionary of the English Language (1828). "Testimony," in turn, is typically "[a] solemn declaration or affirmation made for the purpose of establishing or proving some fact." *Ibid.* An accuser who makes a formal statement to government officers bears testimony in a sense that a person who makes a casual remark to an acquaintance does not. The constitutional text, like the history underlying the common-law right of confrontation, thus reflects an especially acute concern with a specific type of out-of-court statement.

Various formulations of this core class of "testimonial" statements exist: "*ex parte* in-court testimony or its functional equivalent — that is, material such as affidavits, custodial examinations, prior testimony that the defendant was unable to cross-examine, or similar pretrial statements that declarants would reasonably expect to be used prosecutorially," Brief for Petitioner 23; "extrajudicial statements . . . contained in formalized testimonial materials, such as affidavits, depositions, prior testimony, or confessions," *White v. Illinois*, 502 U.S. 346, 365 (1992) (THOMAS, J., joined by SCALIA, J., concurring in part and concurring in judgment); "statements that were made under circumstances which would lead an objective witness reasonably to believe that the statement would be available for use at a later trial," Brief for National Association of Criminal Defense Lawyers et al. as *Amici Curiae*

3. These formulations all share a common nucleus and then define the Clause's coverage at various levels of abstraction around it. Regardless of the precise articulation, some statements qualify under any definition — for example, *ex parte* testimony at a preliminary hearing. ***

In sum, even if the Sixth Amendment is not solely concerned with testimonial hearsay, that is its primary object, and interrogations by law enforcement officers fall squarely within that class.[4]

B

The historical record also supports a second proposition: that the Framers would not have allowed admission of testimonial statements of a witness who did not appear at trial unless he was unavailable to testify, and the defendant had had a prior opportunity for cross-examination. The text of the Sixth Amendment does not suggest any open-ended exceptions from the confrontation requirement to be developed by the courts. Rather, the "right *** to be confronted with the witnesses against him," is most naturally read as a reference to the right of confrontation at common law, admitting only those exceptions established at the time of the founding. *See Mattox v. United States*, 156 U.S. 237, 243 (1895);. *** As the English authorities above reveal, the common law in 1791 conditioned admissibility of an absent witness's examination on unavailability and a prior opportunity to cross-examine. The Sixth Amendment therefore incorporates those limitations. The numerous early state decisions applying the same test confirm that these principles were received as part of the common law in this country.

We do not read the historical sources to say that a prior opportunity to cross-examine was merely a sufficient, rather than a necessary, condition for admissibility of testimonial statements. They suggest that this requirement was dispositive, and not merely one of several ways to establish reliability. This is not to deny, as THE CHIEF JUSTICE notes, that "[t]here were always exceptions to the general rule of exclusion" of hearsay evidence. *Post*, at 5. Several had become well established by 1791. *See* 3 Wigmore § 1397, at 101;. *** But there is scant evidence that exceptions were invoked to admit testimonial statements against the accused in a criminal case.[6] Most of the hearsay exceptions covered statements that by their

---

[4] We use the term "interrogation" in its colloquial, rather than any technical legal, sense. *Cf. Rhode Island v. Innis*, 446 U.S. 291, 300–301 (1980). Just as various definitions of "testimonial" exist, one can imagine various definitions of "interrogation," and we need not select among them in this case. Sylvia's recorded statement, knowingly given in response to structured police questioning, qualifies under any conceivable definition.

[6] The one deviation we have found involves dying declarations. The existence of that exception as a general rule of criminal hearsay law cannot be disputed. *See, e.g., Mattox v. United States*, 156 U.S. 237, 243–244 (1895); *King v. Reason*, 16 How. St. Tr. 1, 24–38 (K.B.1722); 1 D. Jardine, Criminal Trials 435 (1832); Cooley, Constitutional Limitations, at *318; 1 G. Gilbert, Evidence 211 (C. Lofft ed. 1791); see also F. Heller, The Sixth Amendment 105 (1951) (asserting that this was the only recognized criminal hearsay exception at common law). Although many dying declarations may not be testimonial, there is authority for admitting even those that clearly are. *See Woodcock, supra*, at 501–504, 168 Eng. Rep., at 353–354; *Reason, supra*, at 24-38; Peake, Evidence, at 64; *cf. Radbourne, supra*, at 460–462, 168 Eng. Rep., at 332–333. We need not decide in this case whether the Sixth Amendment incorporates an exception for testimonial dying declarations. If this exception must be accepted on historical grounds, it is *sui generis*.

nature were not testimonial — for example, business records or statements in furtherance of a conspiracy. We do not infer from these that the Framers thought exceptions would apply even to prior testimony. Cf. *Lilly v. Virginia*, 527 U.S. 116, 134 (1999) (plurality opinion) ("[A]ccomplices' confessions that inculpate a criminal defendant are not within a firmly rooted exception to the hearsay rule").[7]

IV

Our case law has been largely consistent with these two principles. Our leading early decision, for example, involved a deceased witness's prior trial testimony. *Mattox v. United States*, 156 U.S. 237 (1895). In allowing the statement to be admitted, we relied on the fact that the defendant had had, at the first trial, an adequate opportunity to confront the witness: "The substance of the constitutional protection is preserved to the prisoner in the advantage he has once had of seeing the witness face to face, and of subjecting him to the ordeal of a cross-examination. This, the law says, he shall under no circumstances be deprived of. . . ." *Id.*, at 244.

Our later cases conform to *Mattox's* holding that prior trial or preliminary hearing testimony is admissible only if the defendant had an adequate opportunity to cross-examine. *See Mancusi v. Stubbs*, 408 U.S. 204, 213–216 (1972); *California v. Green*, 399 U.S. 149, 165–168 (1970); *Pointer v. Texas*, 380 U.S., at 406–408; cf. *Kirby v. United States*, 174 U.S. 47, 55–61 (1899). Even where the defendant had such an opportunity, we excluded the testimony where the government had not established unavailability of the witness. *See Barber v. Page*, 390 U.S. 719, 722–725 (1968); ***. We similarly excluded accomplice confessions where the defendant had no opportunity to cross-examine. *See Roberts v. Russell*, 392 U.S. 293, 294–295 (1968) (*per curiam*); *Bruton v. United States*, 391 U.S. 123, 126–128 (1968); *Douglas v. Alabama*, 380 U.S. 415, 418-420 (1965). In contrast, we considered reliability factors beyond prior opportunity for cross-examination when the hearsay statement at issue was not testimonial. *See Dutton v. Evans*, 400 U.S., at 87–89 (plurality opinion).

Even our recent cases, in their outcomes, hew closely to the traditional line. *Ohio v. Roberts*, 448 U.S., at 67–70 admitted testimony from a preliminary hearing at which the defendant had examined the witness. *Lilly v. Virginia*, *supra*, excluded testimonial statements that the defendant had had no opportunity to test by cross-examination. And *Bourjaily v. United States*, 483 U.S. 171, 181–184 (1987), admitted statements made unwittingly to an FBI informant after applying a more general test that did not make prior cross-examination an indispensable require-ment.[8]

---

[7] We cannot agree with THE CHIEF JUSTICE that the fact "[t]hat a statement might be testimonial does nothing to undermine the wisdom of one of these [hearsay] exceptions." *Post*, at 6. Involvement of government officers in the production of testimony with an eye toward trial presents unique potential for prosecutorial abuse — a fact borne out time and again throughout a history with which the Framers were keenly familiar. This consideration does not evaporate when testimony happens to fall within some broad, modern hearsay exception, even if that exception might be justifiable in other circumstances.

[8] One case arguably in tension with the rule requiring a prior opportunity for cross-examination when the proffered statement is testimonial is *White v. Illinois*, 502 U.S. 346 (1992), which involved, *inter alia*, statements of a child victim to an investigating police officer admitted as spontaneous declarations. *Id.*,

* * *

Our cases have thus remained faithful to the Framers' understanding: Testimonial statements of witnesses absent from trial have been admitted only where the declarant is unavailable, and only where the defendant has had a prior opportunity to cross-examine.[9]

V

Although the results of our decisions have generally been faithful to the original meaning of the Confrontation Clause, the same cannot be said of our rationales. *Roberts* conditions the admissibility of all hearsay evidence on whether it falls under a "firmly rooted hearsay exception" or bears "particularized guarantees of trustworthiness." 448 U.S., at 66. This test departs from the historical principles identified above in two respects. First, it is too broad: It applies the same mode of analysis whether or not the hearsay consists of *ex parte* testimony. This often results in close constitutional scrutiny in cases that are far removed from the core concerns of the Clause. At the same time, however, the test is too narrow: It admits statements that do consist of *ex parte* testimony upon a mere finding of reliability. This malleable standard often fails to protect against paradigmatic confrontation violations.

Members of this Court and academics have suggested that we revise our doctrine to reflect more accurately the original understanding of the Clause. *See, e.g., Lilly,* 527 U.S., at 140–143 (Breyer, J., concurring); *White,* 502 U.S., at 366 (Thomas, J., joined by Scalia, J., concurring in part and concurring in judgment); A. Amar, The Constitution and Criminal Procedure 125-131 (1997); Friedman, Confrontation: The Search for Basic Principles, 86 Geo. L.J. 1011 (1998). They offer two proposals: First, that we apply the Confrontation Clause only to testimonial statements, leaving the remainder to regulation by hearsay law — thus eliminating the overbreadth referred to above. Second, that we impose an absolute bar to statements that are testimonial, absent a prior opportunity to cross-examine — thus eliminating the excessive narrowness referred to above.

---

at 349–55. It is questionable whether testimonial statements would ever have been admissible on that ground in 1791; to the extent the hearsay exception for spontaneous declarations existed at all, it required that the statements be made "immediat[ely] upon the hurt received, and before [the declarant] had time to devise or contrive any thing for her own advantage." *Thompson v. Trevanion,* Skin. 402, 90 Eng. Rep. 179 (K.B.1694). In any case, the only question presented in *White* was whether the Confrontation Clause imposed an unavailability requirement on the types of hearsay at issue. *See* 502 U.S., at 348–349. The holding did not address the question whether certain of the statements, because they were testimonial, had to be excluded even if the witness was unavailable. We "[took] as a given . . . that the testimony properly falls within the relevant hearsay exceptions." *Id.*, at 351, n. 4.

[9] *** Finally, we reiterate that, when the declarant appears for cross-examination at trial, the Confrontation Clause places no constraints at all on the use of his prior testimonial statements. *See California v. Green,* 399 U.S. 149, 162 (1970). It is therefore irrelevant that the reliability of some out-of-court statements " 'cannot be replicated, even if the declarant testifies to the same matters in court.' " *Post*, at 6 (quoting *United States v. Inadi,* 475 U.S. 387, 395 (1986)). The Clause does not bar admission of a statement so long as the declarant is present at trial to defend or explain it. (The Clause also does not bar the use of testimonial statements for purposes other than establishing the truth of the matter asserted. *See Tennessee v. Street,* 471 U.S. 409, 414 (1985).)

In *White*, we considered the first proposal and rejected it. 502 U.S., at 352–353. Although our analysis in this case casts doubt on that holding, we need not definitively resolve whether it survives our decision today, because Sylvia Crawford's statement is testimonial under any definition. This case does, however, squarely implicate the second proposal.

A

Where testimonial statements are involved, we do not think the Framers meant to leave the Sixth Amendment's protection to the vagaries of the rules of evidence, much less to amorphous notions of "reliability." Certainly none of the authorities discussed above acknowledges any general reliability exception to the common-law rule. Admitting statements deemed reliable by a judge is fundamentally at odds with the right of confrontation. To be sure, the Clause's ultimate goal is to ensure reliability of evidence, but it is a procedural rather than a substantive guarantee. It commands, not that evidence be reliable, but that reliability be assessed in a particular manner: by testing in the crucible of cross-examination. The Clause thus reflects a judgment, not only about the desirability of reliable evidence (a point on which there could be little dissent), but about how reliability can best be determined *** .

The *Roberts* test allows a jury to hear evidence, untested by the adversary process, based on a mere judicial determination of reliability. It thus replaces the constitutionally prescribed method of assessing reliability with a wholly foreign one. In this respect, it is very different from exceptions to the Confrontation Clause that make no claim to be a surrogate means of assessing reliability. For example, the rule of forfeiture by wrongdoing (which we accept) extinguishes confrontation claims on essentially equitable grounds; it does not purport to be an alternative means of determining reliability. *See Reynolds v. United States*, 98 U.S. 145, 158–159 (1879).

The Raleigh trial itself involved the very sorts of reliability determinations that *Roberts* authorizes. In the face of Raleigh's repeated demands for confrontation, the prosecution responded with many of the arguments a court applying *Roberts* might invoke today: that Cobham's statements were self-inculpatory, that they were not made in the heat of passion, and that they were not "extracted from [him] upon any hopes or promise of Pardon,". *** It is not plausible that the Framers' only objection to the trial was that Raleigh's judges did not properly weigh these factors before sentencing him to death. Rather, the problem was that the judges refused to allow Raleigh to confront Cobham in court, where he could cross-examine him and try to expose his accusation as a lie.

Dispensing with confrontation because testimony is obviously reliable is akin to dispensing with jury trial because a defendant is obviously guilty. This is not what the Sixth Amendment prescribes.

B

The legacy of *Roberts* in other courts vindicates the Framers' wisdom in rejecting a general reliability exception. The framework is so unpredictable that it fails to provide meaningful protection from even core confrontation violations.

Reliability is an amorphous, if not entirely subjective, concept. There are countless factors bearing on whether a statement is reliable; the nine-factor balancing test applied by the Court of Appeals below is representative. *See, e.g., People v. Farrell*, 34 P.3d 401, 406–407 (Colo. 2001) (eight-factor test). Whether a statement is deemed reliable depends heavily on which factors the judge considers and how much weight he accords each of them. Some courts wind up attaching the same significance to opposite facts. ****

The unpardonable vice of the *Roberts* test, however, is not its unpredictability, but its demonstrated capacity to admit core testimonial statements that the Confrontation Clause plainly meant to exclude. Despite the plurality's speculation in *Lilly*, 527 U.S., at 137 that it was "highly unlikely" that accomplice confessions implicating the accused could survive *Roberts*, courts continue routinely to admit them ***.

To add insult to injury, some of the courts that admit untested testimonial statements find reliability in the very factors that *make* the statements testimonial. As noted earlier, one court relied on the fact that the witness's statement was made to police while in custody on pending charges — the theory being that this made the statement more clearly against penal interest and thus more reliable. *Nowlin, supra*, at 335–338, 579 S.E.2d, at 371–372. Other courts routinely rely on the fact that a prior statement is given under oath in judicial proceedings. *E.g., Gallego, supra*, at 168 (plea allocution); *Papajohn, supra*, at 1120 (grand jury testimony). That inculpating statements are given in a testimonial setting is not an antidote to the confrontation problem, but rather the trigger that makes the Clause's demands most urgent. It is not enough to point out that most of the usual safeguards of the adversary process attend the statement, when the single safeguard missing is the one the Confrontation Clause demands.

C

Roberts' failings were on full display in the proceedings below. Sylvia Crawford made her statement while in police custody, herself a potential suspect in the case. Indeed, she had been told that whether she would be released "depend[ed] on how the investigation continues." In response to often leading questions from police detectives, she implicated her husband in Lee's stabbing and at least arguably undermined his self-defense claim. Despite all this, the trial court admitted her statement, listing several reasons why it was reliable. In its opinion reversing, the Court of Appeals listed several *other* reasons why the statement was *not* reliable. Finally, the State Supreme Court relied exclusively on the interlocking character of the statement and disregarded every other factor the lower courts had considered. The case is thus a self-contained demonstration of *Roberts'* unpredictable and inconsistent application.

Each of the courts also made assumptions that cross-examination might well have undermined. The trial court, for example, stated that Sylvia Crawford's statement was reliable because she was an eyewitness with direct knowledge of the events. But Sylvia at one point told the police that she had "shut [her] eyes and . . .

didn't really watch" part of the fight, and that she was "in shock." The trial court also buttressed its reliability finding by claiming that Sylvia was "being questioned by law enforcement, and, thus, the [questioner] is . . . neutral to her and not someone who would be inclined to advance her interests and shade her version of the truth unfavorably toward the defendant." The Framers would be astounded to learn that *ex parte* testimony could be admitted against a criminal defendant because it was elicited by "neutral" government officers. But even if the court's assessment of the officer's motives was accurate, it says nothing about Sylvia's perception of her situation. Only cross-examination could reveal that.

The State Supreme Court gave dispositive weight to the interlocking nature of the two statements — that they were both ambiguous as to when and whether Lee had a weapon. The court's claim that the two statements were *equally* ambiguous is hard to accept. Petitioner's statement is ambiguous only in the sense that he had lingering doubts about his recollection: "A. I coulda swore I seen him goin' for somethin' before, right before everything happened . . . [B]ut I'm not positive." Sylvia's statement, on the other hand, is truly inscrutable, since the key timing detail was simply assumed in the leading question she was asked: "Q. Did Kenny do anything to fight back from this assault?" Moreover, Sylvia specifically said Lee had nothing in his hands after he was stabbed, while petitioner was not asked about that.

The prosecutor obviously did not share the court's view that Sylvia's statement was ambiguous — he called it "damning evidence" that "completely refutes [petitioner's] claim of self-defense." We have no way of knowing whether the jury agreed with the prosecutor or the court. Far from obviating the need for cross-examination, the "interlocking" ambiguity of the two statements made it all the more imperative that they be tested to tease out the truth.

We readily concede that we could resolve this case by simply reweighing the "reliability factors" under *Roberts* and finding that Sylvia Crawford's statement falls short. But we view this as one of those rare cases in which the result below is so improbable that it reveals a fundamental failure on our part to interpret the Constitution in a way that secures its intended constraint on judicial discretion. Moreover, to reverse the Washington Supreme Court's decision after conducting our own reliability analysis would perpetuate, not avoid, what the Sixth Amendment condemns. The Constitution prescribes a procedure for determining the reliability of testimony in criminal trials, and we, no less than the state courts, lack authority to replace it with one of our own devising.

We have no doubt that the courts below were acting in utmost good faith when they found reliability. The Framers, however, would not have been content to indulge this assumption. They knew that judges, like other government officers, could not always be trusted to safeguard the rights of the people; the likes of the dread Lord Jeffreys were not yet too distant a memory. They were loath to leave too much discretion in judicial hands. Cf. U.S. Const., Amdt. 6 (criminal jury trial); Amdt. 7 (civil jury trial); *Ring v. Arizona*, 536 U.S. 584, 611–612 (2002) (SCALIA, J., concurring). By replacing categorical constitutional guarantees with open-ended balancing tests, we do violence to their design. Vague standards are manipulable, and, while that might be a small concern in run-of-the-mill assault prosecutions like this one, the Framers had an eye toward politically charged cases like Raleigh's — great state trials where the impartiality of even those at the highest levels of the judiciary might not be so clear. It is difficult to imagine *Roberts'* providing any meaningful protection in those circumstances.

*   *   *

Where nontestimonial hearsay is at issue, it is wholly consistent with the Framers' design to afford the States flexibility in their development of hearsay law — as does *Roberts*, and as would an approach that exempted such statements from Confrontation Clause scrutiny altogether. Where testimonial evidence is at issue, however, the Sixth Amendment demands what the common law required: unavailability and a prior opportunity for cross-examination. We leave for another day any effort to spell out a comprehensive definition of "testimonial."[10] Whatever else the term covers, it applies at a minimum to prior testimony at a preliminary hearing, before a grand jury, or at a former trial; and to police interrogations. These are the modern practices with closest kinship to the abuses at which the Confrontation Clause was directed.

In this case, the State admitted Sylvia's testimonial statement against petitioner, despite the fact that he had no opportunity to cross-examine her. That alone is sufficient to make out a violation of the Sixth Amendment. *Roberts* notwithstanding, we decline to mine the record in search of indicia of reliability. Where testimonial statements are at issue, the only indicium of reliability sufficient to satisfy constitutional demands is the one the Constitution actually prescribes: confrontation.

The judgment of the Washington Supreme Court is reversed, and the case is remanded for further proceedings not inconsistent with this opinion.

It is so ordered.

CHIEF JUSTICE REHNQUIST, with whom JUSTICE O'CONNOR joins, concurring in the judgment.

I dissent from the Court's decision to overrule *Ohio v. Roberts*, 448 U.S. 56 (1980). I believe that the Court's adoption of a new interpretation of the Confrontation Clause is not backed by sufficiently persuasive reasoning to overrule long-established precedent. Its decision casts a mantle of uncertainty over future criminal trials in both federal and state courts, and is by no means necessary to decide the present case.

The Court's distinction between testimonial and nontestimonial statements, contrary to its claim, is no better rooted in history than our current doctrine. ***

I therefore see no reason why the distinction the Court draws is preferable to our precedent. Starting with Chief Justice Marshall's interpretation as a Circuit Justice in 1807, 16 years after the ratification of the Sixth Amendment, *United States v.*

---

[10] We acknowledge THE CHIEF JUSTICE's objection [that our refusal to articulate a comprehensive definition in this case will cause interim uncertainty. But it can hardly be any worse than the status quo.] The difference is that the *Roberts* test is *inherently*, and therefore *permanently*, unpredictable.

Burr, 25 F. Cas. 187, 193 (No. 14,694) (CC Va. 1807), continuing with our cases in the late 19th century, *Mattox v. United States*, 156 U.S. 237, 243–244 (1895); *Kirby v. United States*, 174 U.S. 47, 54–57 (1899), and through today, *e.g.*, *White v. Illinois*, 502 U.S. 346, 352–353 (1992), we have never drawn a distinction between testimonial and nontestimonial statements. And for that matter, neither has any other court of which I am aware. I see little value in trading our precedent for an imprecise approximation at this late date.

* * *

In choosing the path it does, the Court of course overrules *Ohio v. Roberts*, 448 U.S. 56 (1980), a case decided nearly a quarter of a century ago. Stare decisis is not an inexorable command in the area of constitutional law, see *Payne v. Tennessee*, 501 U.S. 808, 828 (1991), but by and large, it "is the preferred course because it promotes the evenhanded, predictable, and consistent development of legal principles, fosters reliance on judicial decisions, and contributes to the actual and perceived integrity of the judicial process," *id.*, at 827. And in making this appraisal, doubt that the new rule is indeed the "right" one should surely be weighed in the balance. Though there are no vested interests involved, unresolved questions for the future of everyday criminal trials throughout the country surely counsel the same sort of caution. The Court grandly declares that "[w]e leave for another day any effort to spell out a comprehensive definition of 'testimonial.'" But the thousands of federal prosecutors and the tens of thousands of state prosecutors need answers as to what beyond the specific kinds of "testimony" the Court lists, see *ibid.*, is covered by the new rule. They need them now, not months or years from now. Rules of criminal evidence are applied every day in courts throughout the country, and parties should not be left in the dark in this manner.

To its credit, the Court's analysis of "testimony" excludes at least some hearsay exceptions, such as business records and official records. To hold otherwise would require numerous additional witnesses without any apparent gain in the truth-seeking process.

But these are palliatives to what I believe is a mistaken change of course. It is a change of course not in the least necessary to reverse the judgment of the Supreme Court of Washington in this case. The result the Court reaches follows inexorably from *Roberts* and its progeny without any need for overruling that line of cases. In *Idaho v. Wright*, 497 U.S. 805, 820–824 (1990), we held that an out-of-court statement was not admissible simply because the truthfulness of that statement was corroborated by other evidence at trial. As the Court notes, the Supreme Court of Washington gave decisive weight to the "interlocking nature of the two statements." No re-weighing of the "reliability factors," which is hypothesized by the Court is required to reverse the judgment here. A citation to *Idaho v. Wright, supra*, would suffice. For the reasons stated, I believe that this would be a far preferable course for the Court to take here.

NOTES AND PROBLEMS

1. Problem 32-1. In *Devitt*, the prosecutor calls Paterson as a witness, but Paterson refuses to answer questions in any meaningful way. His responses are "I don't know," "I can't remember," and "I won't answer that." The prosecutor argues that since Paterson is physically present in the courtroom, his prior out-of-court statements to police are admissible, citing footnote 9 of Justice Scalia's *Crawford* opinion.

Since *California v. Green*, 399 U.S. 149 (1970), there has been controversy over whether the presence of the declarant at trial, without more, satisfies the Confrontation Clause. Professor Mosteller argued that *Green* should be limited to situations in which the witness/declarant is actually responsive (*i.e.*, cases in which the opponent has a meaningful opportunity to cross-examine the declarant at trial). Mosteller, *Remaking Confrontation Clause and Hearsay Doctrine Under the Challenge of Child Sexual Abuse Prosecutions*, 1993 U. ILL. L. REV. 691, 729. Does the dictum in footnote 9 assume more than bare physical presence of the declarant at trial? In *U.S. v. Owens*, 484 U.S. 554 (1988), the Supreme Court held that a victim who had suffered severe brain damage in the attack at issue in the defendant's trial was "available" for cross-examination about his prior identification despite his having no recollection of making the statement nor of identifying the defendant. The Court held that the Confrontation Clause was not violated by the admission of the prior statements.

2. The testimonial/non-testimonial distinction is a linchpin of the majority opinion. In Part III.A, Justice Scalia states that the constitutional requirements apply to "a specific type of out-of-court statement." Near the end of the opinion, the Court acknowledges the Chief Justice's criticism that the majority decides to "leave for another day any effort to spell out a comprehensive definition of 'testimonial.'" However, the majority opinion does offer some guidance. For example, the Court refers to "[v]arious formulations of this core class of 'testimonial' statements," including "statements that declarants would reasonably expect to be used prosecutorially" and "statements that were made under circumstances which would lead an objective witness reasonably to believe that the statement would be available for use at a later trial." Given this general guidance, consider whether the following are testimonial under *Crawford*:

- A deposition

- Grand jury testimony

- Preliminary hearing testimony

- An affidavit

- A custodial statement given to the police, proffered as a declaration against penal interest

- A business record

- An official record

- A statement falling within the co-conspirator exemption to the hearsay rule

- An excited utterance

- "An offhand . . . remark to an acquaintance" falling within the present sense impression hearsay exception

- A dying declaration

3. Notice the Court's reference, in footnote 6, to dying declarations. In applying the testimonial/non-testimonial distinction, should the focus be on the categorical hearsay exception cited by the proponent, or on the specific circumstances surrounding the proffered statement?

4. It seems reasonably certain that the term "testimonial" encompasses prior courtroom-type testimony. Justice Scalia's opinion gives several examples, including prior trials, preliminary hearings, depositions, grand jury hearings, and plea allocutions. Further, the concept clearly extends to formalized out-of-court statements, since the majority opinion cites an affidavit as an example of a testimonial statement.

Beyond these easier cases, however, *Crawford* leaves the definition of "testimonial" very murky. One question that *Crawford* left unanswered concerns the test for whether a statement is testimonial: Is the standard subjective or objective; and should the standard be applied from the perspective of the declarant, the listener, or some combination? When Justice Scalia uses phrases such as "declarants would reasonably expect" and "lead an objective witness reasonably to believe," the focus appears to be on the objective intent of the declarant, though other aspects of the decision suggest a focus on the role of the government in eliciting the statement.

In *Davis v. Washington*, 547 U.S. 813 (2006), the Court revisited and clarified the definition and test for "testimonial hearsay" somewhat. Once again, Justice Scalia authored the majority opinion. With respect to statements made during questioning by law enforcement, which was at issue both in *Davis* and in the companion case *Hammon v. Indiana*, the Court stated:

> Statements are nontestimonial when made in the course of police interrogation under circumstances objectively indicating that the primary purpose of the interrogation is to enable police assistance to meet an ongoing emergency. They are testimonial when the circumstances objectively indicate that there is no such ongoing emergency, and that the primary purpose of the interrogation is to establish or prove past events potentially relevant to later criminal prosecution.

Davis, 547 U.S. at 822.

The Court's most recent pronouncement on this question came in *Michigan v. Bryant*, with a majority opinion authored by Justice Sotomayor. 131 S. Ct. 1143 (2011). *Bryant* involved statements made by a shooting victim to police under circumstances in which the victim had driven himself from the scene of the shooting to a nearby gas station. When police officers arrived at the gas station, the victim "appeared to be in great pain, and spoke with difficulty." In response to police questioning, the victim implicated defendant Bryant in the shooting. After being taken to a hospital, the victim died within a few hours.

Addressing the definition of "testimonial hearsay," the Court made clear that the relevant question is the "primary purpose" of the statement. First, the Court stated that "th[is] inquiry is objective:"

> The circumstances in which an encounter occurs — e.g., at or near the scene of the crime versus at a police station, during an ongoing emergency or afterwards — are clearly matters of objective fact. The statements and actions of the parties must also be objectively evaluated. That is, the relevant inquiry is not the subjective or actual purpose of the individuals involved in a particular encounter, but rather the purpose that reasonable participants would have had, as ascertained from the individuals' statements and actions and the circumstances in which the encounter occurred.

Next, the Court made clear that the focus of the inquiry is not limited to either the declarant or the questioner: "In addition to the circumstances in which an encounter occurs, the statement and actions of both the declarant and interrogators provide objective evidence of the primary purpose of the interrogation. . . . Davis requires a combined inquiry that accounts for both the declarant and the interrogator."

Finally, the Court engaged in a multifactorial, contextual analysis to conclude that the declarant's statements in *Bryant* were non-testimonial:

> When he made the statements, Covington was lying in a gas station parking lot bleeding from a mortal gunshot wound to his abdomen. His answers to the police officers' questions were punctuated with questions about when emergency medical services would arrive . . . He was obviously in considerable pain and had difficulty breathing and talking . . . From this description of his condition and report of his statements, we cannot say that a person in Covington's situation would have had a 'primary purpose' 'to establish or prove past events potentially relevant to later criminal prosecution.'
>
> For their part, the police responded to a call that a man had been shot. As discussed above, they did not know why, where, or when the shooting had occurred. Nor did they know the location of the shooter or anything else about the circumstances in which the crime occurred. The questions they asked — 'what had happened, who had shot him, and where the shooting occurred,' . . . — were the exact type of questions necessary to allow the police to 'assess the situation, the threat to their own safety, and possible danger to the potential victim; and to the public . . . including to allow them to ascertain 'whether they would be encountering a violent felon.' . . . in other words, they solicited the information necessary to enable them 'to meet an ongoing emergency . . . .
>
> Finally, we consider the informality of the situation and the interrogation. This situation is more similar, though not identical, to the informal, harried 911 call in Davis than to the structured, station-house interview in Crawford. . . . the situation was fluid and somewhat confused: the officers arrived at different times . . . they did not conduct a structured interrogation. . . . The informality suggests that the interrogators' primary

purpose was simply to address what they perceived to be an ongoing emergency, and the circumstances lacked any formality that would have alerted Covington to or focused him on the possible future prosecutorial use of his statements.

Because the circumstances of the encounter as well as the statements and actions of Covington and the police objectively indicate that the 'primary purpose of the interrogation' was 'to enable police assistance to meet an ongoing emergency,' Covington's identification and description of the shooter and the location of the shooting were not testimonial hearsay. The Confrontation Clause did not bar their admission at Bryant's trial.

Bryant, slip op. (internal citations omitted).

In a scathing dissent, Justice Scalia accused the Court of reviving the *Roberts* reliability standard in the guise of its contextual approach: "We tried that approach to the Confrontation Clause for nearly 25 years before *Crawford rejected* it as an unworkable standard unmoored from the text and the historical roots of the Confrontation Clause." According to Justice Scalia's dissent, among the many problems with the Court's approach in *Bryant*, the opinion showed signs of collapsing the constitutional and hearsay analyses.

Also dissenting, Justice Ginsburg pointed out that the Court had yet to clarify whether dying declarations were a sui generis exception to the *Crawford* doctrine.

5. Where testimonial hearsay is at issue, the rule set down in *Crawford* strictly requires exclusion absent an opportunity to cross-examine by the defendant. As we have seen, based on its historical analysis the Court left open the possibility of a dying declaration exception to this otherwise uncompromising rule. In another part of the opinion, the Court mentioned one other possible exception: that a defendant might waive or forfeit his confrontation right by procuring the unavailability of the witness whose testimonial hearsay is offered against him.

In the wake of *Crawford*, prosecutors and advocates for domestic and child victims expressed concern that the new rule would make successful prosecution of these cases much more difficult because of the reluctance — and sometimes inability — of many of these victims to testify against their abusers. Given these circumstances, and seizing upon *Crawford*'s forfeiture suggestion, several commentators argued that the exception should apply to allow testimonial statements by victims to be admitted against defendants in such cases. They argued that the particular dynamics of an ongoing abusive relationship serve to make many victims unavailable sufficient to satisfy the constitutional and evidentiary forfeiture rules (for a discussion of the forfeiture by wrongdoing exception to the rule against hearsay, see Chapter 21). According to this argument, where the abuser actually kills the victim and is prosecuted for homicide, the victim's testimonial hearsay statements should be admissible if the court finds that the defendant caused the witness's unavailability by killing her. In response, others argued that such a rule would intrude upon the defendant's right to a jury trial by permitting the trial judge's determination of guilt to bootstrap the testimonial hearsay of the victim into evidence.

In *Giles v. California*, the Supreme Court resolved this debate over the proper contours of the constitutional forfeiture rule. The Court held that it is not sufficient that the judge find that the defendant's wrongful act caused the witness's unavailability. Rather, the judge must find that the defendant's *purpose* was to cause the witness to be unavailable to testify. On the other hand, language in the opinion suggested that a history of abuse could be relevant to this inquiry:

> The domestic-violence context is, however, relevant for a separate reason. Acts of domestic violence often are intended to dissuade a victim from resorting to outside help, and include conduct designed to prevent testimony to police officers or cooperation in criminal prosecutions. Where such an abusive relationship culminates in murder, the evidence may support a finding that the crime expressed the intent to isolate the victim and to stop her from reporting abuse to the authorities or cooperating with a criminal prosecution — rendering her prior statements admissible under the forfeiture doctrine. Earlier abuse, or threats of abuse, intended to dissuade the victim from resorting to outside help would be highly relevant to this inquiry, as would evidence of ongoing criminal proceedings at which the victim would have been expected to testify. 554 U.S. 353 (2008).

6. Problem 32-2. As the criminal case file for the *Devitt* prosecution indicates, after the alleged beating Mr. Paterson went to Matilda Larson's apartment. When he arrived at her door, Mrs. Larson observed that Paterson was a bit incoherent and bleeding. She immediately called 911. When she explained what had happened, the dispatcher asked to speak directly to Mr. Paterson. Mrs. Larson handed Paterson the phone. As soon as Paterson was on the line, the dispatcher asked, "What help do you need? Tell me what happened." After stating that he needed an ambulance, Paterson added that he had just been attacked by Devitt. Is Paterson's statement testimonial?

In *Davis v. Washington, supra*, one of the statements was the product of a 911 call. In characterizing the statement as non-testimonial, Justice Scalia emphasized that the declarant was making a call for help and that the dispatcher's questions were intended to gather information about a current, ongoing emergency. Would it make a difference in Problem 32-2 if the dispatcher identified himself as a police officer to Mrs. Larson and, when she handed the phone to Paterson, she said, "The police officer wants to speak to you"? Consider the discussion in *Bryant* in your response to this problem.

7. Problem 32-3. Assume that at the outset of the telephone conversation in Problem 32-2, Paterson's statements would not be deemed testimonial. However, suppose that the conversation continues for five minutes. During that time, Paterson becomes more composed, and at that point the dispatcher begins asking specific questions about Devitt's conduct. At that point, would Paterson's responses be testimonial? In *Davis*, the Court stated:

> This is not to say that a conversation which begins as an interrogation to determine the need for emergency assistance cannot . . . "evolve into testimonial statements . . . ." In this case, for example, after the operator gained the information needed to address the exigency of the moment, the emergency appears to have ended. . . . The operator then told McCottry to

be quiet, and proceeded to pose a battery of questions. It could readily be maintained that, from that point on, McCottry's statements were testimonial.

Assume further that at some point in the conversation with Paterson, the dispatcher informs him that he, the officer, is tape recording the call. Would Paterson's statements now be considered testimonial? In *Hammon*, which involved a domestic violence police "show up," Justice Scalia characterized some of the statements as testimonial in part because the police had the alleged victim execute a battery affidavit.

8. **Problem 32-4.** Assume that in Problems 32-2 and 32-3, none of the statements was ruled testimonial. After the 911 call, the police respond to the scene. Which, if any, of the following statements is testimonial?

(a) Police question Paterson at the scene, and he makes oral statements in response to their questions.

(b) Next, they take him to the emergency room. Paterson makes further oral statements to the police while he is being treated at the ER. What if Paterson responds to a question by a nurse after police request that the nurse ask the question?

(c) After he is treated, they transport him to the police station and take a written statement from him.

9. After *Crawford*, lower courts as well as commentators were divided on the proper treatment on non-testimonial hearsay under the Confrontation Clause. Some argued that the *Roberts* reliability test continued to apply to non-testimonial hearsay, while others argued that such hearsay did not raise any constitutional question.

Davis v. Washington offered additional ammunition to those who suggested that non-testimonial hearsay is entirely exempt from scrutiny under the Confrontation Clause. At the outset of his opinion, Justice Scalia stated that the question posed was whether the proffered statements were testimonial "and thus subject to the requirements of the Sixth Amendment's Confrontation Clause." In his separate opinion in *Davis*, Justice Thomas described testimonial statements as "the evidence targeted by the Confrontation Clause."

Michigan v. Bryant seems to settle the question once and for all. The Court stated that where the primary purpose of a statement is "not to create a record for trial" that statement "is not within the scope of the [Confrontation] Clause" and "the admissibility of [such] a statement is the concern of state and federal rules of evidence, not the Confrontation Clause."

10. **The issue of forensic reports.** At one point in *Crawford*, the Court generalizes that business records are not testimonial. Is the test whether the record is made for a purpose associated with ordinary business activities or for a purpose of prosecution? Suppose that the business record in question is the report of a forensic analysis conducted by the police crime laboratory — should such a report be considered testimonial for purposes of the Confrontation Clause?

In *Melendez-Diaz v. Massachusetts*, 557 U.S. 305 (2009), the United States Supreme Court addressed this question and held that the introduction at trial of affidavits reporting the results of a forensic drug analysis, absent testimony by the analysts who prepared the reports, violated the defendant's Confrontation rights. In an opinion once again authored by Justice Scalia, the Court stated:

> There is little doubt that the documents at issue in this case fall within the "core class of testimonial statements" thus described [in *Crawford*]. Our description of that category mentions affidavits twice . . . . The documents at issue here, while denominated by Massachusetts law "certificates," are quite plainly affidavits: "declaration[s] of facts written down and sworn to by the declarant before an officer authorized to administer oaths." Black's Law Dictionary 62 (8th ed. 2004). They are incontrovertibly a " 'solemn declaration or affirmation made for the purpose of establishing or proving some fact.' " . . . The fact in question is that the substance found in the possession of Melendez-Diaz and his codefendants was, as the prosecution claimed, cocaine — the precise testimony the analysts would be expected to provide if called at trial. The "certificates" are functionally identical to live, in-court testimony, doing "precisely what a witness does on direct examination." Davis v. Washington, 547 U. S. 813, 830 (2006) (emphasis deleted).

> Here, moreover, not only were the affidavits " 'made under circumstances which would lead an objective witness reasonably to believe that the statement would be available for use at a later trial,' " Crawford, supra, at 52, but under Massachusetts law the sole purpose of the affidavits was to provide "prima facie evidence of the composition, quality, and the net weight" of the analyzed substance, Mass. Gen. Laws, ch. 111, § 13. We can safely assume that the analysts were aware of the affidavits' evidentiary purpose . . . .

> In short, under our decision in Crawford the analysts' affidavits were testimonial statements, and the analysts were "witnesses" for purposes of the Sixth Amendment. Absent a showing that the analysts were unavailable to testify at trial and that petitioner had a prior opportunity to cross-examine them, petitioner was entitled to " 'be confronted with' " the analysts at trial. Crawford, supra, at 54.

The Court's 5-4 decision in *Melendez-Diaz* generated much discussion and controversy. The dissent predicted that the Court's ruling "threatens to disrupt if not end many prosecutions where guilt is clear but a newly found formalism now holds sway." In an unusual move, the Supreme Court granted review in *Briscoe v. Virginia*, a case that presented essentially the same question that was decided in *Melendez-Diaz*. The Court's action led to speculation that the Court, with new Justice Sotomayor having replaced Justice Souter (a member of the *Melendez-Diaz* majority), might overrule the case just one term after it had been decided. However, after a spirited oral argument in January 2010, the Court handed down a one-paragraph per curiam order that left *Melendez-Diaz* intact.

Indeed, the holding and reasoning of *Melendez-Diaz* were extended in the Court's recent opinion in *Bullcoming v. New Mexico*, 564 U.S. ___, 131 S. Ct. 2705 (2011). Following *Melendez-Diaz*, some courts had held that so-called "surrogate experts" could stand in for the analyst who actually prepared a forensic report so long as the surrogate was familiar with the testing procedures of the lab. In *Bullcoming*, the prosecution had introduced a forensic lab report that certified that the defendant's blood alcohol level was high enough to qualify him for a conviction of aggravated DUI. Rather than call the analyst who had actually performed the test on Bullcoming's blood sample, the state called a different analyst — who had neither participated in nor observed the specific analysis of the defendant's sample — to validate the lab report. The Court held that this use of a "surrogate analyst" violated the defendant's Confrontation right. In a 5-4 decision, the Court forcefully reaffirmed the rule laid out in *Crawford*:

> As a rule, if an out-of-court statement is testimonial in nature, it may not be introduced against the accused at trial unless the witness who made the statement is unavailable and the accused has had a prior opportunity to confront that witness. Because the new Mexico Supreme Court permitted the testimonial statement of one witness, i.e. Caylor [the analyst who performed the analysis], to enter into evidence through the in-court testimony of a second person, i.e. Razatos [the analyst who testified in his place], we reverse . . . .

131 S. Ct. at 2713. The Court dismissed concerns, expressed by Justice Kennedy in dissent (and joined by Chief Justice Roberts and Justices Alito and Breyer), that its holding would unduly burden state prosecutorial resources. "The constitutional requirement, we reiterate, 'may not [be] disregard[ed] . . . at our convenience . . . .'" *Id.* at 16 (alterations in original).

Justice Sotomayor, concurring in part, wrote separately to "highlight some of the factual circumstances that this case does *not* present," among which were:

> Second, this is not a case in which the person testifying is a supervisor, reviewer, or someone else with a personal, albeit limited, connection to the scientific test at issue. Razatos conceded on cross-examination that he played no role in producing the BAC report and did not observe any portion of Curtis Caylor's conduct of the testing. App. 58. The court below also recognized Razatos' total lack of connection to the test at issue. 226 P. 3d, at 6. It would be a different case if, for example, a supervisor who observed an analyst conducting a test testified about the results or a report about such results. We need not address what degree of involvement is sufficient because here Razatos had no involvement whatsoever in the relevant test and report.

> Third, this is not a case in which an expert witness was asked for his independent opinion about underlying testimonial reports that were not themselves admitted into evidence. See Fed. Rule Evid. 703 (explaining that facts or data of a type upon which experts in the field would reasonably rely in forming an opinion need not be admissible in order for the expert's opinion based on the facts and data to be admitted). As the Court notes, ante, at 12, the State does not assert that Razatos offered an independent, expert opinion about Bullcoming's blood alcohol concentration. Rather, the State explains, "[a]side from reading a report that was introduced as an exhibit, Mr. Razatos offered no opinion about Petitioner's blood alcohol

content . . . ." Brief for Respondent 58, n. 15 (citation omitted). Here the State offered the BAC report, including Caylor's testimonial statements, into evidence. We would face a different question if asked to determine the constitutionality of allowing an expert witness to discuss others' testimonial statements if the testimonial statements were not themselves admitted as evidence.

Finally, this is not a case in which the State introduced only machine-generated results, such as a printout from a gas chromatograph. The State here introduced Caylor's statements, which included his transcription of a blood alcohol concentration, apparently copied from a gas chromatograph printout, along with other statements about the procedures used in handling the blood sample. See ante, at 10; App. 62 ("I certify that I followed the procedures set out on the reverse of this report, and the statements in this block are correct"). Thus, we do not decide whether, as the New Mexico Supreme Court suggests, 226 P. 3d, at 10, a State could introduce (assuming an adequate chain of custody foundation) raw data generated by a machine in conjunction with the testimony of an expert witness. See Reply Brief for Petitioner 16, n. 5.

This case does not present, and thus the Court's opinion does not address, any of these factual scenarios.

131 S. Ct. 2722–23 (Sotomayor, J., concurring in part).

The most recent case to consider this issue was decided in June 2012. In *Williams v. Illinois*, 132 S. Ct. 2221 (2021), an expert witness testified about the results of a DNA test conducted by other analysts in a lab to which the government had sent the crime samples. The forensic report itself was not introduced into evidence; the witness testified that the profile in the lab's report matched the defendant's DNA profile, which was on file because of a prior arrest. The expert relied on the report in forming her opinion, pursuant to Rule 703. The Supreme Court held that this testimony did not violate the Confrontation Clause. In a plurality opinion, Justice Alito wrote that such "non-hearsay" use of the report was permissible, and in the alternative that the report was not testimonial because it was created before the defendant was even a suspect in the case. This latest case represents a significant limitation to the robust Confrontation right announced in *Crawford. See* Seaman, *Triangulating Testimonial Hearsay: The Constitutional Boundaries of Expert Opinion Testimony*, 96 Geo. L. J. 827 (2008) (arguing that using Rule 703 to avoid the Confrontation Clause should not be permitted).

11. In *Whorton v. Bockting*, 549 U.S. 406 (2007), Justice Alito, writing for a unanimous court, declined to make *Crawford* retroactive. In addition, the Court has held that Confrontation Clause violations are subject to harmless error analysis.

C. AFFIRMATIVE OVERRIDES: ADMITTING OTHERWISE INADMISSIBLE EVIDENCE

Thus far in this chapter we have considered negative constitutional overrides — precluding the admission of otherwise admissible evidence. Now we turn to overrides with the opposite effect — requiring the admission of otherwise inadmissible evidence.

1. Criminal Cases

WASHINGTON v. TEXAS
388 U.S. 14 (1967)

Mr. Chief Justice Warren delivered the opinion of the Court.

We granted certiorari in this case to determine whether the right of a defendant in a criminal case under the Sixth Amendment[1] to have compulsory process for obtaining witnesses in his favor is applicable to the States through the Fourteenth Amendment, and whether that right was violated by a state procedural statute providing that persons charged as principals, accomplices, or accessories in the same crime cannot be introduced as witnesses for each other.

Petitioner, Jackie Washington, was convicted in Dallas County, Texas, of murder with malice and was sentenced by a jury to 50 years in prison. The prosecution's evidence showed that petitioner, an 18-year-old youth, had dated a girl named Jean Carter until her mother had forbidden her to see him. The girl thereafter began dating another boy, the deceased. Evidently motivated by jealousy, petitioner with several other boys began driving around the City of Dallas on the night of August 29, 1964, looking for a gun. The search eventually led to one Charles Fuller, who joined the group with his shotgun. After obtaining some shells from another source, the group of boys proceeded to Jean Carter's home, where Jean, her family and the deceased were having supper. Some of the boys threw bricks at the house and then ran back to the car, leaving petitioner and Fuller alone in front of the house with the shotgun. At the sound of the bricks the deceased and Jean Carter's mother rushed out on the porch to investigate. The shotgun was fired by either petitioner or Fuller, and the deceased was fatally wounded. Shortly afterward petitioner and Fuller came running back to the car where the other boys waited, with Fuller carrying the shotgun.

Petitioner testified in his own behalf. He claimed that Fuller, who was intoxicated, had taken the gun from him, and that he had unsuccessfully tried to persuade Fuller to leave before the shooting. Fuller had insisted that he was going to shoot someone, and petitioner had run back to the automobile. He saw the girl's mother come out of the door as he began running, and he subsequently heard the shot. At the time, he had thought that Fuller had shot the woman. In support of his version of the facts, petitioner offered the testimony of Fuller. The record indicates that

---

[1] "In all criminal prosecutions, the accused shall enjoy the right . . . to have compulsory process for obtaining witnesses in his favor. . . ."

Fuller would have testified that petitioner pulled at him and tried to persuade him to leave, and that petitioner ran before Fuller fired the fatal shot.

It is undisputed that Fuller's testimony would have been relevant and material, and that it was vital to the defense. Fuller was the only person other than petitioner who knew exactly who had fired the shotgun and whether petitioner had at the last minute attempted to prevent the shooting. Fuller, however, had been previously convicted of the same murder and sentenced to 50 years in prison, and he was confined in the Dallas County jail. Two Texas statutes provided at the time of the trial in this case that persons charged or convicted as coparticipants in the same crime could not testify for one another, although there was no bar to their testifying for the State. On the basis of these statutes the trial judge sustained the State's objection and refused to allow Fuller to testify. Petitioner's conviction followed, and it was upheld on appeal by the Texas Court of Criminal Appeals. We granted certiorari. We reverse.

[The majority then ruled that the due process clause of the Fourteenth Amendment incorporates the compulsory process guarantee of the Sixth Amendment and renders the guarantee enforceable against the states.]

Since the right to compulsory process is applicable in this state proceeding, the question remains whether it was violated in the circumstances of this case. The testimony of Charles Fuller was denied to the defense not because the State refused to compel his attendance, but because a state statute made his testimony inadmissible whether he was present in the courtroom or not. We are thus called upon to decide whether the Sixth Amendment guarantees a defendant the right under any circumstances to put his witnesses on the stand, as well as the right to compel their attendance in court. The resolution of this question requires some discussion of the common-law context in which the Sixth Amendment was adopted.

Joseph Story, in his famous Commentaries on the Constitution of the United States, observed that the right to compulsory process was included in the Bill of Rights in reaction to the notorious common-law rule that in cases of treason or felony the accused was not allowed to introduce witnesses in his defense at all. Although the absolute prohibition of witnesses for the defense had been abolished in England by statute before 1787, the Framers of the Constitution felt it necessary specifically to provide that defendants in criminal cases should be provided the means of obtaining witnesses so that their own evidence, as well as the prosecution's, might be evaluated by the jury.

Despite the abolition of the rule generally disqualifying defense witnesses, the common law retained a number of restrictions on witnesses who were physically and mentally capable of testifying. To the extent that they were applicable, they had the same effect of suppressing the truth that the general proscription had had. Defendants and codefendants were among the large class of witnesses disqualified from testifying on the ground of interest. A party to a civil or criminal case was not allowed to testify on his own behalf for fear that he might be tempted to lie. Although originally the disqualification of a codefendant appears to have been based only on his status as a party to the action, and in some jurisdictions co-indictees were allowed to testify for or against each other if granted separate trials, other jurisdictions came to the view that accomplices or co-indictees were incompetent to testify at least in favor of each other even at separate trials, and in spite of statutes making a defendant competent to testify in his own behalf. It was thought that if two persons charged with the same crime were allowed to testify on behalf of each other, "each would try to swear the other out of the charge." This rule, as well as the other disqualifications for interest, rested on the unstated premises that the right to present witnesses was subordinate to the court's interest in preventing perjury, and that erroneous decisions were best avoided by preventing the jury from hearing any testimony that might be perjured, even if it were the only testimony available on a crucial issue.

The federal courts followed the common-law restrictions for a time, despite the Sixth Amendment. In *United States v. Reid*, 12 How. 361 (1852), the question was whether one of two defendants jointly indicted for murder on the high seas could call the other as a witness. Although this Court expressly recognized that the Sixth Amendment was designed to abolish some of the harsh rules of the common law, particularly including the refusal to allow the defendant in a serious criminal case to present witnesses in his defense, it held that the rules of evidence in the federal courts were those in force in the various States at the time of the passage of the Judiciary Act of 1789, including the disqualification of defendants indicted together. The holding in *United States v. Reid* was not satisfactory to later generations, however, and in 1918 this Court expressly overruled it, refusing to be bound by "the dead hand of the common law rule of 1789," and taking note of "the conviction of our time that the truth is more likely to be arrived at by hearing the testimony of all persons of competent understanding who may seem to have knowledge of the facts involved in a case, leaving the credit and weight of such testimony to be determined by the jury or by the court. . . ." *Rosen v. United States*, 245 U.S. 467, 471.

Although *Rosen v. United States* rested on nonconstitutional grounds, we believe that its reasoning was required by the Sixth Amendment. In light of the common-law history, and in view of the recognition in the *Reid* case that the Sixth Amendment was designed in part to make the testimony of a defendant's witnesses admissible on his behalf in court, it could hardly be argued that a State would not violate the clause if it made all defense testimony inadmissible as a matter of procedural law. It is difficult to see how the Constitution is any less violated by arbitrary rules that prevent whole categories of defense witnesses from testifying on the basis of *a priori* categories that presume them unworthy of belief.

The rule disqualifying an alleged accomplice from testifying on behalf of the defendant cannot even be defended on the ground that it rationally sets apart a group of persons who are particularly likely to commit perjury. The absurdity of the rule is amply demonstrated by the exceptions that have been made to it. For example, the accused accomplice may be called by the prosecution to testify against the defendant. Common sense would suggest that he often has a greater interest in lying in favor of the prosecution rather than against it, especially if he is still awaiting his own trial or sentencing. To think that criminals will lie to save their fellows but not to obtain favors from the prosecution for themselves is indeed to clothe the criminal class with more nobility than one might expect to find in the public at large. Moreover, under the Texas statutes the accused accomplice is no longer disqualified if he is acquitted at his own trial. Presumably, he would then be free to testify on behalf of his comrade, secure in the knowledge that he could incriminate himself as freely as he liked in his testimony, since he could not again be prosecuted for the same offense. The Texas law leaves him free to testify when he has a great incentive to perjury, and bars his testimony in situations where he has a lesser motive to lie.

We hold that the petitioner in this case was denied his right to have compulsory process for obtaining witnesses in his favor because the State arbitrarily denied him the right to put on the stand a witness who was physically and mentally capable of testifying to events that he had personally observed, and whose testimony would have been relevant and material to the defense.[21] The Framers of the Constitution did not intend to commit the futile act of giving to a defendant the right to secure the attendance of witnesses whose testimony he had no right to use. The judgment of conviction must be reversed.

NOTES

1. To justify his conclusion, Chief Justice Warren resorts to *reductio ad absurdum* reasoning: The Chief Justice argues that it would obviously be unconstitutional if "a State . . . made all defense testimony inadmissible as a matter of procedural law." The Chief Justice states that it is equally clear that "the Constitution is . . . violated by arbitrary rules that prevent whole categories of defense witnesses from testifying on the basis of *a priori* categories that presume them unworthy of belief." Assume that such evidentiary rules would be patently unconstitutional. Did the Court have to imply a right to present evidence from the Sixth Amendment compulsory process clause to find a doctrinal basis for holding those rules unconstitutional? What other doctrinal basis could the Court have invoked to invalidate a truly "arbitrary" rule? Is arbitrariness the sole concern?

2. What is the significance of footnote 21? Does *Washington* apply only to sweeping incompetency rules which have the effect of altogether barring testimony by a witness? The Illinois Supreme Court construed footnote 21 in that fashion. *People v. Scott*, 52 Ill. 2d 432, 288 N.E.2d 478 (1972). In the *Scott* court's view, the right announced in *Washington* required only that the state put the defense witness on the stand; the right did not regulate the validity of the state evidentiary rules governing the content of the witness's testimony. As the next opinion demonstrates, the Supreme Court ultimately reached a contrary conclusion in the following landmark case:

---

[21] Nothing in this opinion should be construed as disapproving testimonial privileges, such as the privilege against self-incrimination or the lawyer-client or husband-wife privileges, which are based on entirely different considerations from those underlying the common-law disqualifications for interest. Nor do we deal in this case with nonarbitrary state rules that disqualify as witnesses persons who, because of mental infirmity or infancy, are incapable of observing events or testifying about them.

CHAMBERS v. MISSISSIPPI
410 U.S. 284 (1973)

Mr. Justice Powell delivered the opinion of the Court.

Petitioner, Leon Chambers, was tried by a jury in a Mississippi trial court and convicted of murdering a policeman. *** Subsequently, the petition for certiorari was granted, to consider whether petitioner's trial was conducted in accord with principles of due process under the Fourteenth Amendment. We conclude that it was not.

The events that led to petitioner's prosecution for murder occurred in the small town of Woodville in southern Mississippi. On Saturday evening, June 14, 1969, two Woodville policemen, James Forman and Aaron "Sonny" Liberty, entered a local bar and pool hall to execute a warrant for the arrest of a youth named C. C. Jackson. Jackson resisted and a hostile crowd of some 50 or 60 persons gathered. The officers' first attempt to handcuff Jackson was frustrated when 20 or 25 men in the crowd intervened and wrestled him free. Forman then radioed for assistance and Liberty removed his riot gun, a 12-gauge sawed-off shotgun, from the car. Three deputy sheriffs arrived shortly thereafter and the officers again attempted to make their arrest. Once more, the officers were attacked by the onlookers and during the commotion five or six pistol shots were fired. Forman was looking in a different direction when the shooting began, but immediately saw that Liberty had been shot several times in the back. Before Liberty died, he turned around and fired both barrels of his riot gun into an alley in the area from which the shots appeared to have come. The first shot was wild and high and scattered the crowd standing at the face of the alley. Liberty appeared, however, to take more deliberate aim before the second shot and hit one of the men in the crowd in the back of the head and neck as he ran down the alley. That man was Leon Chambers.

Officer Forman could not see from his vantage point who shot Liberty or whether Liberty's shots hit anyone. One of the deputy sheriffs testified at trial that he was standing several feet from Liberty and that he saw Chambers shoot him. Another deputy sheriff stated that, although he could not see whether Chambers had a gun in his hand, he did see Chambers "break his arm down" shortly before the shots were fired. The officers who saw Chambers fall testified that they thought he was dead but they made no effort at that time either to examine him or to search for the murder weapon. Instead, they attended to Liberty, who was placed in the police car and taken to a hospital where he was declared dead on arrival. A subsequent autopsy showed that he had been hit with four bullets from a .22-caliber revolver.

Shortly after the shooting, three of Chambers' friends discovered that he was not yet dead. James Williams, Berkley Turner, and Gable McDonald loaded him into a car and transported him to the same hospital. Later that night, when the county sheriff discovered that Chambers was still alive, a guard was placed outside his room. Chambers was subsequently charged with Liberty's murder. He pleaded not guilty and has asserted his innocence throughout.

The story of Leon Chambers is intertwined with the story of another man, Gable McDonald. McDonald, a lifelong resident of Woodville, was in the crowd on the evening of Liberty's death. Sometime shortly after that day, he left his wife in Woodville and moved to Louisiana and found a job at a sugar mill. In November of that same year, he returned to Woodville when his wife informed him that an acquaintance of his, known as Reverend Stokes, wanted to see him. Stokes owned a gas station in Natchez, Mississippi, several miles north of Woodville, and upon his return McDonald went to see him. After talking to Stokes, McDonald agreed to make a statement to Chambers' attorneys, who maintained offices in Natchez. Two days later, he appeared at the attorneys' offices and gave a sworn confession that he shot Officer Liberty. He also stated that he had already told a friend of his, James Williams, that he shot Liberty. He said that he used his own pistol, a nine-shot .22-caliber revolver, which he had discarded shortly after the shooting. In response to questions from Chambers' attorneys, McDonald affirmed that his confession was voluntary and that no one had compelled him to come to them. Once the confession had been transcribed, signed, and witnessed, McDonald was turned over to the local police authorities and was placed in jail.

One month later, at a preliminary hearing, McDonald repudiated his prior sworn confession. He testified that Stokes had persuaded him to confess that he shot Liberty. He claimed that Stokes had promised that he would not go to jail and that he would share in the proceeds of a lawsuit that Chambers would bring against the town of Woodville. On examination by his own attorney and on cross-examination by the State, McDonald swore that he had not been at the scene when Liberty was shot but had been down the street drinking beer in a café with a friend, Berkley Turner. When he and Turner heard the shooting, he testified, they walked up the street and found Chambers lying in the alley. He, Turner, and Williams took Chambers to the hospital. McDonald further testified at the preliminary hearing that he did not know what had happened, that there was no discussion about the shooting either going to or coming back from the hospital, and that it was not until the next day that he learned that Chambers had been felled by a blast from Liberty's riot gun. In addition, McDonald stated that while he once owned a .22-caliber pistol he had lost it many months before the shooting and did not own or possess a weapon at that time. The local justice of the peace accepted McDonald's repudiation and released him from custody. The local authorities undertook no further investigation of his possible involvement.

Chambers' case came on for trial in October of the next year. At trial, he endeavored to develop two grounds of defense. He first attempted to show that he did not shoot Liberty. Only one officer testified that he actually saw Chambers fire the shots. Although three officers saw Liberty shoot Chambers and testified that they assumed he was shooting his attacker, none of them examined Chambers to see whether he was still alive or whether he possessed a gun. Indeed, no weapon was ever recovered from the scene and there was no proof that Chambers had ever owned a .22-caliber pistol. One witness testified that he was standing in the street near where Liberty was shot, that he was looking at Chambers when the shooting began, and that he was sure that Chambers did not fire the shots.

Petitioner's second defense was that Gable McDonald had shot Officer Liberty. He was only partially successful, however, in his efforts to bring before the jury the testimony supporting this defense. Sam Hardin, a lifelong friend of McDonald's, testified that he saw McDonald shoot Liberty. A second witness, one of Liberty's cousins, testified that he saw McDonald immediately after the shooting with a pistol in his hand. In addition to the testimony of these two witnesses, Chambers endeavored to show the jury that McDonald had repeatedly confessed to the crime. Chambers attempted to prove that McDonald had admitted responsibility for the murder on four separate occasions, once when he gave the sworn statement to Chambers' counsel and three other times prior to that occasion in private conversations with friends.

In large measure, he was thwarted in his attempt to present this portion of his defense by the strict application of certain Mississippi rules of evidence. Chambers asserts in this Court, as he did unsuccessfully in his motion for new trial and on appeal to the State Supreme Court, that the application of these evidentiary rules rendered his trial fundamentally unfair and deprived him of due process of law. It is necessary, therefore, to examine carefully the rulings made during the trial.

Chambers filed a pretrial motion requesting the court to order McDonald to appear. Chambers also sought a ruling at that time that, if the State itself chose not to call McDonald, he be allowed to call him as an adverse witness. Attached to the motion were copies of McDonald's sworn confession and of the transcript of his preliminary hearing at which he repudiated that confession. The trial court granted the motion requiring McDonald to appear but reserved ruling on the adverse-witness motion. At trial, after the State failed to put McDonald on the stand, Chambers called McDonald, laid a predicate for the introduction of his sworn out-of-court confession, had it admitted into evidence, and read it to the jury. The State, upon cross-examination, elicited from McDonald the fact that he had repudiated his prior confession. McDonald further testified, as he had at the preliminary hearing, that he did not shoot Liberty, and that he confessed to the crime only on the promise of Reverend Stokes that he would not go to jail and would share in a sizable tort recovery from the town. He also told his own story of his actions on the evening of the shooting, including his visit to the café down the street, his absence from the scene during the critical period, and his subsequent trip to the hospital with Chambers.

At the conclusion of the State's cross-examination, Chambers renewed his motion to examine McDonald as an adverse witness. The trial court denied the motion, stating: "He may be hostile, but he is not adverse in the sense of the word, so your request will be overruled." On appeal, the State Supreme Court upheld the trial court's ruling, finding that "McDonald's testimony was not adverse to appellant" because "[n]owhere did he point the finger at Chambers." 252 So. 2d, at 220.

Defeated in his attempt to challenge directly McDonald's renunciation of his prior confession, Chambers sought to introduce the testimony of the three witnesses to whom McDonald had admitted that he shot the officer. The first of these, Sam Hardin, would have testified that, on the night of the shooting, he spent the late evening hours with McDonald at a friend's house after their return from the hospital and that, while driving McDonald home later that night, McDonald stated that he shot Liberty. The State objected to the admission of this testimony on the ground that it was hearsay. The trial court sustained the objection.

Berkley Turner, the friend with whom McDonald said he was drinking beer when the shooting occurred, was then called to testify. In the jury's presence, and without objection, he testified that he had not been in the café that Saturday and had not had any beers with McDonald. The jury was then excused. In the absence of the jury, Turner recounted his conversations with McDonald while they were riding with James Williams to take Chambers to the hospital. When asked whether McDonald said anything regarding the shooting of Liberty, Turner testified that McDonald told him that he "shot him." Turner further stated that one week later, when he met McDonald at a friend's house, McDonald reminded him of their prior conversation and urged Turner not to "mess him up." Petitioner argued to the court that, especially where there was other proof in the case that was corroborative of these out-of-court statements, Turner's testimony as to McDonald's self-incriminating remarks should have been admitted as an exception to the hearsay rule. Again, the trial court sustained the State's objection.

The third witness, Albert Carter, was McDonald's neighbor. They had been friends for about 25 years. Although Carter had not been in Woodville on the evening of the shooting, he stated that he learned about it the next morning from McDonald. That same day, he and McDonald walked out to a well near McDonald's house and there McDonald told him that he was the one who shot Officer Liberty. Carter testified that McDonald also told him that he had disposed of the .22-caliber revolver later that night. He further testified that several weeks after the shooting, he accompanied McDonald to Natchez where McDonald purchased another .22 pistol to replace the one he had discarded.[5] The jury was not allowed to hear Carter's testimony. Chambers urged that these statements were admissible, the State objected, and the court sustained the objection. On appeal, the State Supreme Court approved the lower court's exclusion of these witnesses' testimony on hearsay grounds. 252 So. 2d, at 220.

In sum, then, this was Chambers' predicament. As a consequence of the combination of Mississippi's "party witness" or "voucher" rule and its hearsay rule, he was unable either to cross-examine McDonald or to present witnesses in his own behalf who would have discredited McDonald's repudiation and demonstrated his complicity. Chambers had, however, chipped away at the fringes of McDonald's story by introducing admissible testimony from other sources indicating that he had not been seen in the café where he said he was when the shooting started, that he had not been having beer with Turner, and that he possessed a .22 pistol at the time of the crime. But all that remained from McDonald's own testimony was a single written confession countered by an arguably acceptable renunciation. Chambers' defense was far less persuasive than it might have been had he been given an opportunity to subject McDonald's statements to cross-examination or had the other confessions been admitted.

The right of an accused in a criminal trial to due process is, in essence, the right to a fair opportunity to defend against the State's accusations. The rights to confront and cross-examine witnesses and to call witnesses in one's own behalf have long been recognized as essential to due process. Mr. Justice Black, writing for the

---

[5] A gun dealer from Natchez testified that McDonald had made two purchases. The witness' business records indicated that McDonald purchased a nine-shot .22-caliber revolver about a year prior to the murder. He purchased a different style .22 three weeks after Liberty's death.

Court in *In re Oliver*, 333 U.S. 257, 273 (1948), identified these rights as among the minimum essentials of a fair trial:

> A person's right to reasonable notice of a charge against him, and an opportunity to be heard in his defense — a right to his day in court — are basic in our system of jurisprudence; and these rights include, as a minimum, a right to examine the witnesses against him, to offer testimony, and to be represented by counsel.

See also Jenkins v. McKeithen, 395 U.S. 411, 428–29 (1969). Both of these elements of a fair trial are implicated in the present case.

Chambers was denied an opportunity to subject McDonald's damning repudiation and alibi to cross-examination. He was not allowed to test the witness' recollection, to probe into the details of his alibi, or to "sift" his conscience so that the jury might judge for itself whether McDonald's testimony was worthy of belief. *Mattox v. United States*, 156 U.S. 237, 242–243 (1895). The right of cross-examination is more than a desirable rule of trial procedure. It is implicit in the constitutional right of confrontation, and helps assure the "accuracy of the truth-determining process." *Dutton v. Evans*, 400 U.S. 74, 89 (1970). It is, indeed, "an essential and fundamental requirement for the kind of fair trial which is this country's constitutional goal." *Pointer v. Texas*, 380 U.S. 400, 405 (1965). [I]ts denial or significant diminution calls into question the ultimate " 'integrity of the fact-finding process' " and requires that the competing interest be closely examined. *Berger v. California*, 393 U.S. 314, 315 (1969).

In this case, petitioner's request to cross-examine McDonald was denied on the basis of a Mississippi common-law rule that a party may not impeach his own witness. ***

Whatever validity the "voucher" rule may have once enjoyed, and apart from whatever usefulness it retains today in the civil trial process, it bears little present relationship to the realities of the criminal process. It might have been logical for the early common law to require a party to vouch for the credibility of witnesses he brought before the jury to affirm his veracity. Having selected them especially for that purpose, the party might reasonably be expected to stand firmly behind their testimony. But in modern criminal trials, defendants are rarely able to select their witnesses: they must take them where they find them. Moreover, as applied in this case, the "voucher" rule's impact was doubly harmful to Chambers' efforts to develop his defense. Not only was he precluded from cross-examining McDonald, but, he was also restricted in the scope of his direct examination by the rule's corollary requirement that the party calling the witness is bound by anything he might say. He was, therefore, effectively prevented from exploring the circumstances of McDonald's three prior oral confessions and from challenging the renunciation of the written confession.

    ***

The argument that McDonald's testimony was not "adverse" to, or "against," Chambers is not convincing. The State's proof at trial excluded the theory that more than one person participated in the shooting of Liberty. To the extent that McDonald's sworn confession tended to incriminate him, it tended also to exculpate

Chambers. And, in the circumstances of this case, McDonald's retraction inculpated Chambers to the same extent that it exculpated McDonald. It can hardly be disputed that McDonald's testimony was in fact seriously adverse to Chambers. The availability of the right to confront and to cross-examine those who give damaging testimony against the accused has never been held to depend on whether the witness was initially put on the stand by the accused or by the State. We reject the notion that a right of such substance in the criminal process may be governed by that technicality or by any narrow and unrealistic definition of the word "against." The "voucher" rule, as applied in this case, plainly interfered with Chambers' right to defend against the State's charges.

We need not decide, however, whether this error alone would occasion reversal since Chambers' claimed denial of due process rests on the ultimate impact of that error when viewed in conjunction with the trial court's refusal to permit him to call other witnesses. The trial court refused to allow him to introduce the testimony of Hardin, Turner, and Carter. Each would have testified to the statements purportedly made by McDonald, on three separate occasions shortly after the crime, naming himself as the murderer. The State Supreme Court approved the exclusion of this evidence on the ground that it was hearsay.

The hearsay rule, which has long been recognized and respected by virtually every State, is based on experience and grounded in the notion that untrustworthy evidence should not be presented to the triers of fact. A number of exceptions have developed over the years to allow admission of hearsay statements made under circumstances that tend to assure reliability and thereby compensate for the absence of the oath and opportunity for cross-examination. Among the most prevalent of these exceptions is the one applicable to declarations against interest — an exception founded on the assumption that a person is unlikely to fabricate a statement against his own interest at the time it is made. Mississippi recognizes this exception but applies it only to declarations against pecuniary interest. It recognizes no such exception for declarations, like McDonald's in this case, that are against the penal interest of the declarant. *Brown v. State*, 99 Miss. 719, 55 So. 961 (1911).

This materialistic limitation on the declaration-against-interest hearsay exception appears to be accepted by most States in their criminal trial processes, although a number of States have discarded it. Declarations against penal interest have also been excluded in federal courts under the authority of *Donnelly v. United States*, 228 U.S. 243, 272–273 (1913), although exclusion would not be required under the newly proposed Federal Rules of Evidence. ***

The hearsay statements involved in this case were originally made and subsequently offered at trial under circumstances that provided considerable assurance of their reliability. First, each of McDonald's confessions was made spontaneously to a close acquaintance shortly after the murder had occurred. Second, each one was corroborated by some other evidence in the case — McDonald's sworn confession, the testimony of an eyewitness to the shooting, the testimony that McDonald was seen with a gun immediately after the shooting, and proof of his prior ownership of a .22-caliber revolver and subsequent purchase of a new weapon. The sheer number of independent confessions provided additional corroboration for each. Third, whatever may be the parameters of the penal-interest rationale, each confession here was in a very real sense self-incriminatory and unquestionably against interest. *See United States v. Harris*, 403 U.S. 573, 584 (1971); *Dutton v. Evans*, 400 U.S., at 89. McDonald stood to benefit nothing by disclosing his role in the shooting to any of his three friends and he must have been aware of the possibility that disclosure would lead to criminal prosecution. Indeed, after telling Turner of his involvement, he subsequently urged Turner not to "mess him up." Finally, if there was any question about the truthfulness of the extrajudicial statements, McDonald was present in the courtroom and was under oath. He could have been cross-examined by the State, and his demeanor and responses weighed by the jury. *See California v. Green*, 399 U.S. 149 (1970). The availability of McDonald significantly distinguishes this case from the prior Mississippi precedent, *Brown v. State, supra*, and from the *Donnelly*-type situation, since in both cases the declarant was unavailable at the time of trial.

Few rights are more fundamental than that of an accused to present witnesses in his own defense. *E.g., Washington v. Texas*, 388 U.S. 14, 19 (1967). In the exercise of this right, the accused, as is required of the State, must comply with established rules of procedure and evidence designed to assure both fairness and reliability in the ascertainment of guilt and innocence. Although perhaps no rule of evidence has been more respected or more frequently applied in jury trials than that applicable to the exclusion of hearsay, exceptions tailored to allow the introduction of evidence which in fact is likely to be trustworthy have long existed. The testimony rejected by the trial court here bore persuasive assurances of trustworthiness and thus was well within the basic rationale of the exception for declarations against interest. That testimony also was critical to Chambers' defense. In these circumstances, where constitutional rights directly affecting the ascertainment of guilt are implicated, the hearsay rule may not be applied mechanistically to defeat the ends of justice.

We conclude that the exclusion of this critical evidence, coupled with the State's refusal to permit Chambers to cross-examine McDonald, denied him a trial in accord with traditional and fundamental standards of due process. In reaching this judgment, we establish no new principles of constitutional law. Nor does our holding signal any diminution in the respect traditionally accorded to the States in the establishment and implementation of their own criminal trial rules and procedures. Rather, we hold quite simply that under the facts and circumstances of this case the rulings of the trial court deprived Chambers of a fair trial.

The judgment is reversed and the case is remanded to the Supreme Court of Mississippi for further proceedings not inconsistent with this opinion.

NOTES

1. *Chambers* establishes that the accused can invoke the constitutional right of Due Process to surmount essentially procedural rules, such as the restriction on the leading form of questions, as well as substantive evidentiary rules, such as hearsay. Westen, *Confrontation and Compulsory Process: A Unified Theory of Evidence for Criminal Cases*, 91 Harv. L. Rev. 567, 609, 612–13 (1978).

2. Commentators typically focus on the Court's holding that McDonald's declaration against his penal interest was so reliable that its exclusion constituted constitutional error. Did the Court also modify the unavailability standard for declarations against penal interest? Was McDonald unavailable within the meaning of that expression in Federal Rule of Evidence 804(a)? *State v. Barts*, 321 N.C. 170, 362 S.E.2d 235 (1987).

3. In *Chambers*, the Court found two constitutional errors which cumulatively denied the defendant a fair trial. Suppose that there had been only one error. Without more, does the exclusion of demonstrably reliable, exculpatory hearsay violate the defendant's constitutional right to present evidence? The Court implicitly answered that question in *Green v. Georgia*, 442 U.S. 95 (1979). In *Green*, the only error was the exclusion of the hearsay. Despite that difference, the *Green* court treated *Chambers* as dispositive. *Foster v. State*, 297 Md. 191, 464 A.2d 986 (1983), *cert. denied*, 464 U.S. 1073 (1984), characterizes *Green* as clarifying the scope of *Chambers*.

4. Like *Washington*, *Chambers* left significant questions about its scope unanswered. In *Chambers*, the Court had overridden the hearsay rule, an exclusionary doctrine based on doubts about the reliability of uncross-examined testimony. It makes sense to say that that type of exclusionary rule must yield to a strong showing of the trustworthiness of defense evidence. However, as we have seen, there are other types of exclusionary rules. Would they also be subject to constitutional attack? The next case addresses this issue.

DAVIS v. ALASKA
415 U.S. 308 (1974)

MR. CHIEF JUSTICE BURGER delivered the opinion of the Court.

We granted certiorari in this case to consider whether the Confrontation Clause requires that a defendant in a criminal case be allowed to impeach the credibility of a prosecution witness by cross-examination directed at possible bias deriving from the witness' probationary status as a juvenile delinquent when such an impeachment would conflict with a State's asserted interest in preserving the confidentiality of juvenile adjudications of delinquency.

When the Polar Bar in Anchorage closed in the early morning hours of February 16, 1970, well over a thousand dollars in cash and checks was in the bar's Mosler safe. About midday, February 16, it was discovered that the bar had been broken into and the safe, about two feet square and weighing several hundred pounds, had been removed from the premises.

Later that afternoon the Alaska State Troopers received word that a safe had been discovered about 26 miles outside Anchorage near the home of Jess Straight and his family. The safe, which was subsequently determined to be the one stolen from the Polar Bar, had been pried open and the contents removed. Richard Green, Jess Straight's stepson, told investigating troopers on the scene that at about noon on February 16 he had seen and spoken with two Negro men standing alongside a late-model metallic blue Chevrolet sedan near where the safe was later discovered.

The next day Anchorage police investigators brought him to the police station where Green was given six photographs of adult Negro males. After examining the photographs for 30 seconds to a minute, Green identified the photograph of petitioner as that of one of the men he had encountered the day before and described to the police. Petitioner was arrested the next day, February 18. On February 19, Green picked petitioner out of a lineup of seven Negro males.

At trial, evidence was introduced to the effect that paint chips found in the trunk of petitioner's rented blue Chevrolet could have originated from the surface of the stolen safe. Further, the trunk of the car contained particles which were identified as safe insulation characteristic of that found in Mosler safes. The insulation found in the trunk matched that of the stolen safe.

Richard Green was a crucial witness for the prosecution. He testified at trial that while on an errand for his mother he confronted two men standing beside a late-model metallic blue Chevrolet, parked on a road near his family's house. The man standing at the rear of the car spoke to Green asking if Green lived nearby and if his father was home. Green offered the men help, but his offer was rejected. On his return from the errand Green again passed the two men and he saw the man with whom he had had the conversation standing at the rear of the car with "something like a crowbar" in his hands. Green identified petitioner at the trial as the man with the "crowbar." The safe was discovered later that afternoon at the point, according to Green, where the Chevrolet had been parked.

Before testimony was taken at the trial of petitioner, the prosecutor moved for a protective order to prevent any reference to Green's juvenile record by the defense in the course of cross-examination. At the time of the trial and at the time of the events Green testified to, Green was on probation by order of a juvenile court after having been adjudicated a delinquent for burglarizing two cabins. Green was 16 years of age at the time of the Polar Bar burglary, but had turned 17 prior to trial.

In opposing the protective order, petitioner's counsel made it clear that he would not introduce Green's juvenile adjudication as a general impeachment of Green's character as a truthful person but, rather, to show specifically that at the same time Green was assisting the police in identifying petitioner he was on probation for burglary. From this petitioner would seek to show — or at least argue — that Green acted out of fear or concern of possible jeopardy to his probation. Not only might Green have made a hasty and faulty identification of petitioner to shift suspicion away from himself as one who robbed the Polar Bar, but Green might have been subject to undue pressure from the police and made his identifications under fear of possible probation revocation. Green's record would be revealed only as necessary to probe Green for bias and prejudice and not generally to call Green's good character into question.

The trial court granted the motion for a protective order, relying on Alaska Rule of Children's Procedure 23,[1] and Alaska Stat. § 47.10.080 (g) (1971).[2]

---

[1] Rule 23 provides: "No adjudication, order, or disposition of a juvenile case shall be admissible in a court not acting in the exercise of juvenile jurisdiction except for use in a presentencing procedure in a criminal case where the superior court, in its discretion, determines that such use is appropriate."

[2] Section 47.10.080 (g) provides in pertinent part: "The commitment and placement of a child and

Although prevented from revealing that Green had been on probation for the juvenile delinquency adjudication for burglary at the same time that he originally identified petitioner, counsel for petitioner did his best to expose Green's state of mind at the time Green discovered that a stolen safe had been discovered near his home. Green denied that he was upset or uncomfortable about the discovery of the safe. He claimed not to have been worried about any suspicions the police might have been expected to harbor against him, though Green did admit that it crossed his mind that the police might have thought he had something to do with the crime.

Defense counsel cross-examined Green in part as follows:

Q:　　　　　Were you upset at all by the fact that this safe was found on your property?

A:　　　　　No, sir.

Q:　　　　　Did you feel that they might in some way suspect you of this?

A:　　　　　No.

Q:　　　　　Did you feel uncomfortable about this though?

A:　　　　　No, not really.

Q:　　　　　The fact that a safe was found on your property?

A:　　　　　No.

Q:　　　　　Did you suspect for a moment that the police might somehow think that you were involved in this?

A:　　　　　I thought they might ask a few questions is all.

Q:　　　　　Did that thought ever enter your mind that you — that the police might think that you were somehow connected with this?

A:　　　　　No, it didn't really bother me, no.

Q:　　　　　Well, but. . . .

A:　　　　　I mean, you know, it didn't — it didn't come into my mind as worrying me, you know.

Q:　　　　　That really wasn't — wasn't my question, Mr. Green. Did you think that — not whether it worried you so much or not, but did you feel that there was a possibility that the police might somehow think that you had something to do with this, that they might have that in their mind, not that you. . . .

A:　　　　　That came across my mind, yes, sir.

Q:　　　　　That did cross your mind?

A:　　　　　Yes.

Q:　　　　　So as I understand it you went down to the — you drove in with the police in — in their car from mile 25, Glenn Highway down to the city police station?

---

evidence given in the court are not admissible as evidence against the minor in a subsequent case or proceedings in any other court . . . ."

A: Yes, sir.

Q: And then went into the investigators' room with Investigator Gray and Investigator Weaver?

A: Yeah.

Q: And they started asking you questions about — about the incident, is that correct?

A: Yeah.

Q: Had you ever been questioned like that before by any law enforcement officers?

A: No.

MR. RIPLEY: I'm going to object to this, Your Honor, it's a carry-on-with rehash of the same thing. He's attempting to raise in the jury's mind. . . .

THE COURT: I'll sustain the objection."

Since defense counsel was prohibited from making inquiry as to the witness' being on probation under a juvenile court adjudication, Green's protestations of unconcern over possible police suspicion that he might have had a part in the Polar Bar burglary and his categorical denial of ever having been the subject of any similar law-enforcement interrogation went unchallenged. The tension between the right of confrontation and the State's policy of protecting the witness with a juvenile record is particularly evident in the final answer given by the witness. Since it is probable that Green underwent some questioning by police when he was arrested for the burglaries on which his juvenile adjudication of delinquency rested, the answer can be regarded as highly suspect at the very least. The witness was in effect asserting, under protection of the trial court's ruling, a right to give a questionably truthful answer to a cross-examiner pursuing a relevant line of inquiry; it is doubtful whether the bold "No" answer would have been given by Green absent a belief that he was shielded from traditional cross-examination. It would be difficult to conceive of a situation more clearly illustrating the need for cross-examination. The remainder of the cross-examination was devoted to an attempt to prove that Green was making his identification at trial on the basis of what he remembered from his earlier identifications at the photographic display and lineup, and not on the basis of his February 16 confrontation with the two men on the road.

The Alaska Supreme Court affirmed petitioner's conviction, concluding that it did not have to resolve the potential conflict in this case between a defendant's right to a meaningful confrontation with adverse witnesses and the State's interest in protecting the anonymity of a juvenile offender since "our reading of the trial transcript convinces us that counsel for the defendant was able adequately to question the youth in considerable detail concerning the possibility of bias or motive." 499 P. 2d 1025, 1036 (1972). Although the court admitted that Green's denials of any sense of anxiety or apprehension upon the safe's being found close to his home were possibly self-serving, "the suggestion was nonetheless brought to the attention of the jury, and that body was afforded the opportunity to observe the demeanor of the youth and pass on his credibility." *Ibid.* The court concluded that, in light of the indirect references permitted, there was no error.

Since we granted certiorari limited to the question of whether petitioner was denied his right under the Confrontation Clause to adequately cross-examine Green, 410 U.S. 925 (1973), the essential question turns on the correctness of the Alaska court's evaluation of the "adequacy" of the scope of cross-examination permitted. We disagree with that court's interpretation of the Confrontation Clause and we reverse.

The Sixth Amendment to the Constitution guarantees the right of an accused in a criminal prosecution "to be confronted with the witnesses against him." This right is secured for defendants in state as well as federal criminal proceedings under *Pointer v. Texas*, 380 U.S. 400 (1965). Confrontation means more than being allowed to confront the witness physically. "Our cases construing the [confrontation] clause hold that a primary interest secured by it is the right of cross-examination." *Douglas v. Alabama*, 380 U.S. 415, 418 (1965). Professor Wigmore stated:

> The main and essential purpose of confrontation is *to secure for the opponent the opportunity of cross-examination.* The opponent demands confrontation, not for the idle purpose of gazing upon the witness, or of being gazed upon by him, but for the purpose of cross-examination, which cannot be had except by the direct and personal putting of questions and obtaining immediate answers. 5 J. Wigmore, Evidence § 1395, p. 123 (3d ed. 1940). (Emphasis in original.)

Cross-examination is the principal means by which the believability of a witness and the truth of his testimony are tested. Subject always to the broad discretion of a trial judge to preclude repetitive and unduly harassing interrogation, the cross-examiner is not only permitted to delve into the witness' story to test the witness' perceptions and memory, but the cross-examiner has traditionally been allowed to impeach, *i.e.*, discredit, the witness. One way of discrediting the witness is to introduce evidence of a prior criminal conviction of that witness. By so doing the cross-examiner intends to afford the jury a basis to infer that the witness' character is such that he would be less likely than the average trustworthy citizen to be truthful in his testimony. The introduction of evidence of a prior crime is thus a general attack on the credibility of the witness. A more particular attack on the witness' credibility is effected by means of cross-examination directed toward revealing possible biases, prejudices, or ulterior motives of the witness as they may relate directly to issues or personalities in the case at hand. The partiality of a witness is subject to exploration at trial, and is "always relevant as discrediting the witness and affecting the weight of his testimony." 3A J. Wigmore, Evidence § 940, p. 775 (Chadbourn rev. 1970). We have recognized that the exposure of a witness' motivation in testifying is a proper and important function of the constitutionally protected right of cross-examination. *Greene v. McElroy*, 360 U.S. 474, 496 (1959).

In the instant case, defense counsel sought to show the existence of possible bias and prejudice of Green, causing him to make a faulty initial identification of petitioner, which in turn could have affected his later in-court identification of petitioner.

We cannot speculate as to whether the jury, as sole judge of the credibility of a witness, would have accepted this line of reasoning had counsel been permitted to fully present it. But we do conclude that the jurors were entitled to have the benefit of the defense theory before them so that they could make an informed judgment as to the weight to place on Green's testimony which provided "a crucial link in the proof . . . of petitioner's act." *Douglas v. Alabama*, 380 U.S., at 419. The accuracy and truthfulness of Green's testimony were key elements in the State's case against petitioner. The claim of bias which the defense sought to develop was admissible to afford a basis for an inference of undue pressure because of Green's vulnerable status as a probationer, as well as of Green's possible concern that he might be a suspect in the investigation.

We cannot accept the Alaska Supreme Court's conclusion that the cross-examination that was permitted defense counsel was adequate to develop the issue of bias properly to the jury. While counsel was permitted to ask Green *whether* he was biased, counsel was unable to make a record from which to argue *why* Green might have been biased or otherwise lacked that degree of impartiality expected of a witness at trial. On the basis of the limited cross-examination that was permitted, the jury might well have thought that defense counsel was engaged in a speculative and baseless line of attack on the credibility of an apparently blameless witness or, as the prosecutor's objection put it, a "rehash" of prior cross-examination. On these facts it seems clear to us that to make any such inquiry effective, defense counsel should have been permitted to expose to the jury the facts from which jurors, as the sole triers of fact and credibility, could appropriately draw inferences relating to the reliability of the witness. Petitioner was thus denied the right of effective cross-examination which " 'would be constitutional error of the first magnitude and no amount of showing of want of prejudice would cure it.' *Brookhart v. Janis*, 384 U.S. 1, 3." *Smith v. Illinois*, 390 U.S. 129, 131 (1968).

The claim is made that the State has an important interest in protecting the anonymity of juvenile offenders and that this interest outweighs any competing interest this petitioner might have in cross-examining Green about his being on probation. The State argues that exposure of a juvenile's record of delinquency would likely cause impairment of rehabilitative goals of the juvenile correctional procedures. This exposure, it is argued, might encourage the juvenile offender to commit further acts of delinquency, or cause the juvenile offender to lose employment opportunities or otherwise suffer unnecessarily for his youthful transgression.

We do not and need not challenge the State's interest as a matter of its own policy in the administration of criminal justice to seek to preserve the anonymity of a juvenile offender. *Cf. In re Gault*, 387 U.S. 1, 25 (1967). Here, however, petitioner sought to introduce evidence of Green's probation for the purpose of suggesting that Green was biased and, therefore, that his testimony was either not to be believed in his identification of petitioner or at least very carefully considered in that light. Serious damage to the strength of the State's case would have been a real possibility had petitioner been allowed to pursue this line of inquiry. In this setting we conclude that the right of confrontation is paramount to the State's policy of protecting a juvenile offender. Whatever temporary embarrassment might result to Green or his family by disclosure of his juvenile record — if the prosecution insisted on using him to make its case — is outweighed by petitioner's right to probe into the influence of possible bias in the testimony of a crucial identification witness.

In *Alford v. United States*, 282 U.S. 687 (1931), we upheld the right of defense counsel to impeach a witness by showing that because of the witness' incarceration in federal prison at the time of trial, the witness' testimony was biased as "given under promise or expectation of immunity, or under the coercive effect of his detention by officers of the United States." 282 U.S., at 693. In response to the argument that the witness had a right to be protected from exposure of his criminal record, the Court stated:

> [N]o obligation is imposed on the court, such as that suggested below, to protect a witness from being discredited on cross-examination, short of an attempted invasion of his constitutional protection from self incrimination, properly invoked. There is a duty to protect him from questions which go beyond the bounds of proper cross-examination merely to harass, annoy or humiliate him. *Id.*, at 694.

As in *Alford*, we conclude that the State's desire that Green fulfill his public duty to testify free from embarrassment and with his reputation unblemished must fall before the right of petitioner to seek out the truth in the process of defending himself.

The State's policy interest in protecting the confidentiality of a juvenile offender's record cannot require yielding of so vital a constitutional right as the effective cross-examination for bias of an adverse witness. The State could have protected Green from exposure of his juvenile adjudication in these circumstances by refraining from using him to make out its case; the State cannot, consistent with the right of confrontation, require the petitioner to bear the full burden of vindicating the State's interest in the secrecy of juvenile criminal records. The judgment affirming petitioner's convictions of burglary and grand larceny is reversed and the case is remanded for further proceedings not inconsistent with this opinion.

NOTES AND PROBLEMS

1. How strong a showing of the reliability of its evidence must the defense make to trigger the constitutional right? The *Chambers* court stressed that the excluded hearsay statements had "considerable assurance of their reliability" — their spontaneity, the corroboration, their disserving character, and their "sheer number." If *Chambers* is the appropriate benchmark, it may be difficult for an accused to successfully invoke the constitutional right.

However, in the parts of his opinion describing the reliability of the defense evidence, Justice Powell analogized to the reliability of prosecution hearsay which the Court had previously held to pass muster under the Confrontation Clause. That symmetry has an attractive even-handedness: Under the Compulsory Process Clause, the defense should have the right to introduce hearsay as reliable as the hearsay that the prosecution may introduce under the Confrontation Clause.

Moreover, the Court seemingly lowered the threshold showing of reliability in *Rock v. Arkansas*, 483 U.S. 44 (1987). In that case, the defendant was charged with shooting her husband. Before trial, she had difficulty remembering the precise details of the shooting. She underwent hypnosis by a neuropsychologist to revive her memory. Only after hypnosis did she remember that her gun was defective and had accidentally misfired. The prosecutor filed a pretrial motion to bar the defendant's testimony about the events recalled only after hypnosis. The state court adopted the rule that hypnotically enhanced testimony is *per se* inadmissible. On appeal to the Supreme Court, the majority held that the exclusion violated the accused's right under *Washington.* In so holding, the majority acknowledged that "the current medical . . . view" of the reliability of enhanced testimony "is unsettled." *Id.* at 59. *But cf. United States v. Scheffer,* 523 U.S. 303 (1998) (polygraph evidence) and note 6 below.

2. For their part, some lower courts have aggressively enforced the accused's right to present evidence. In some jurisdictions, the courts have relied on the right in according the defense a right to introduce otherwise inadmissible polygraph evidence. 1 P. GIANNELLI & E. IMWINKELRIED, SCIENTIFIC EVIDENCE § 8-3(D) (3d ed. 1999). Many courts have invoked the right to override evidentiary privileges blocking the admission of defense evidence. Note, *Defendant v. Witness: Measuring Confrontation and Compulsory Process Rights Against Statutory Communications Privileges,* 30 STAN. L. REV. 935, 990 (1978); *Doe v. Diamond,* 964 F.2d 1325 (2d Cir. 1992) (psychotherapist-patient privilege); *People v. Boyette,* 201 Cal. App. 3d 1527, 247 Cal. Rptr. 795 (1988) (psychotherapist-patient privilege); *People v. Adamski,* 198 Mich. App. 133, 497 N.W.2d 546 (1993) (psychologist-patient privilege); *State v. Juarez,* 570 A.2d 1118 (R.I. 1990) (attorney-client privilege).

3. **Problem 32-6.** Devitt informs his defense attorney that before Paterson filed battery charges against him, he found him engaged in sexual intercourse with a minor. Devitt had threatened to inform the authorities and have Paterson prosecuted for statutory rape. He tells his defense attorney that he suspects Paterson filed a false battery charge against him "to beat me to the punch." The state rape shield law would otherwise bar cross-examining Paterson about the incident with the minor. The defense cites *Davis* and argues that application of the statute would deny Devitt his constitutional right to present evidence. What ruling? *See State v. Jalo,* 27 Or. App. 845, 557 P.2d 1359 (1976).

4. When the defense invokes this constitutional right, it might be able to use empirical evidence to support its argument. For instance, the defense may marshal empirical evidence to diminish the magnitude of the countervailing government interest. Suppose that the exclusionary rule in question is an evidentiary privilege. Those doctrines rest on the assumption that laypersons such as clients and patients would be unwilling to communicate with professional counselors without the protection of a privilege; yet, as we saw in Chapter 26, the few empirical investigations to date call the validity of the assumption into question.

5. **Problem 32-7.** Devitt is charged with a specific intent offense, assault with intent to cause serious bodily injury. The defense contemplates offering psychiatric testimony to negate the intent. State law declares that mental health expert testimony is admissible to establish a full-fledged insanity defense but not to disprove specific intent. The defense argues that it violates *Washington* and *Chambers* for the state law to flatly declare expert testimony irrelevant to negate specific intent. What ruling? *See Hughes v. Matthews,* 576 F.2d 1250, 1255–56 (7th Cir. 1978); *People v. Bobo,* 229 Cal. App. 3d 1417, 1442, 3 Cal. Rptr. 2d 747 (1990) ("if a crime requires a particular mental state, the Legislature *cannot* deny a defendant

the opportunity to prove that he did not entertain that state") (emphasis in original). *See Clark v. Arizona*, 548 U.S. 735 (2006); *Montana v. Egelhoff*, 518 U.S. 37 (1996).

6. In *Washington, Chambers, and Davis*, the defense succeeded in persuading the Supreme Court to override a statutory or common law exclusionary rule of evidence. Yet, a similar defense argument failed in *United States v. Scheffer*, 523 U.S. 303 (1998). In that case, the question was the constitutionality of Military Rule of Evidence 707, a blanket prohibition on the admission of polygraph evidence in courts-martial. Justice Thomas authored the lead opinion. *Scheffer* does not purport to overrule any of the prior precedents in the *Washington* line of cases. However, Justice Thomas's opinion reads those precedents narrowly as standing for the limited proposition that statutory and common law evidentiary rules violate the accused's constitutional right only when they are "arbitrary" or "disproportionate to the purposes they are designed to serve." *Id.* at 308. *Scheffer* may be a "harbinger" that in the future, the Court will be more reluctant to invalidate evidentiary rules. Nagareda, *Reconceiving the Right to Present Witnesses*, 97 MICH. L. REV. 1063, 1098 (1999). As Professor Nagareda has observed,

> Of the five Justices who voted to strike down the per se ban on hypnotically-enhanced testimony in *Rock [v. Arkansas]*, only one — Justice Stevens — remains on the current Court, and he was the lone dissenter in *Scheffer*. By contrast, three of the four dissenters in *Rock* — Chief Justice Rehnquist and Justices O'Connor and Scalia — subsequently voted to uphold the per se rule in *Scheffer*.

Id. at 1098.

On the other hand, it may be a mistake to read too much into *Scheffer*. Justice Thomas's opinion is susceptible to a limited reading. It could be argued that the lead opinion treats polygraph as *sui generis*. In his opinion, the justice distinguished polygraph testimony from "the analysis of fingerprints, ballistics, or DNA." 523 U.S. at 313. Thus, the opinion can be interpreted as stopping short of placing all expert testimony beyond the reach of the accused's Sixth Amendment right. While Justice Thomas wrote the lead opinion, Justice Kennedy filed a concurrence, and Justice Stevens filed a dissent. The dissent would have rejected Rule 707 in part because it was an absolute, per se ban on polygraph evidence. 523 U.S. at 321. More importantly, Justice Kennedy's concurrence asserts that "some later case might present a more compelling case for introduction of testimony than this one does." *Id.* at 318. Hence, although Justice Kennedy voted to uphold Rule 707 as applied in the instant case, he was unwilling to sustain it as an absolute ban. Three justices joined in his concurrence. The upshot is that between the concurrence and the dissent, five justices refused to completely foreclose an as-applied attack on Rule 707's constitutionality.

7. The most recent decision in this line of authority is *Holmes v. South Carolina*, 547 U.S. 319 (2006). In his very first opinion as a Justice of the Supreme Court, Justice Alito wrote for a unanimous Court to strike down a state restriction . . . The Court struck down a state restriction on defense evidence that a third party was guilty of the crime that the defendant was charged with. The defendant claimed that the real killer was Jimmy McCaw White. Like Gable McDonald in *Chambers*, White had admitted to the crime. However, the prosecution had forensic evidence, including DNA analysis and a palm print, connecting the defendant to the crime. The defense countered with expert testimony that the DNA samples had been contaminated and that the palm print had been planted. The South Carolina courts held that given the forensic evidence, the defense evidence of White's guilt was insufficient to raise a reasonable doubt as to Holmes's guilt. Justice Alito wrote:

> Just because the prosecution's evidence, if credited, would provide strong support for a guilty verdict, it does not follow that evidence of third-party guilt has only a weak logical connection to the central issues in the case. [W]here the credibility of the government's witnesses or the reliability of its evidence is not conceded, the strength of the prosecution's case cannot be assessed without making the sort of factual findings that have traditionally been reserved for the trier of fact. . . .

8.   Does a convicted defendant have a due process right to access DNA evidence that he claims would prove his "actual innocence"? In *District Attorney's Office for the Third Judicial District v. Osborne*, 557 U.S. 52 (2009), the Supreme Court answered the question in the negative, holding that neither procedural nor substantive due process required the state to permit Osborne to test DNA evidence at his own expense. Furthermore, the Court noted that it has yet to decide the question whether a convicted defendant has a "federal constitutional right to be released upon proof of 'actual innocence' " where he can show no constitutional defect in his trial.

2.   Civil Cases

Washington, Chambers, and *Davis* all are criminal cases. The premises for those decisions are constitutional guarantees peculiar to criminal cases, namely, the Sixth Amendment compulsory process and confrontation provisions. It has, however, been argued that under Fifth Amendment procedural due process, *civil* litigants should be accorded a similar constitutional right to introduce demonstrably reliable, critical evidence. Imwinkelried, *The Case for Recognizing a New Constitutional Entitlement: The Right to Present Favorable Evidence in Civil Cases*, 1990 UTAH L. REV. 1. The courts are beginning to recognize such a right.

In *Adams v. St. Francis Regional Medical Center*, 264 Kan. 144, 955 P.2d 1169 (1998), the Kansas Supreme Court held that certain statutory health care privileges, invoked by the providers to shield an investigative review by the state board of nursing and peer review/disciplinary records of the hospital, unconstitutionally abridged the malpractice plaintiff's right to due process:

> In the present case the legislature granted a peer review privilege to health care providers to maintain staff competency by encouraging frank and open discussions and thus improving the quality of medical care in Kansas. We must weigh that privilege against the plaintiffs' right to due process and the judicial need for the fair administration of justice. There can be no question that in granting the privilege, the legislature did not intend to restrict or eliminate a plaintiff's right to bring a medical malpractice action against a health care provider. To allow the hospital here to insulate from discovery

the facts and information which go to the heart of the plaintiffs' claim would deny plaintiffs that right. . . .

In the present case, we conclude that although the interest in creating a statutory peer review privilege is strong, it is outweighed by the fundamental right of the plaintiffs to have access to all the relevant facts. The district court's protective order and order granting other discovery relief denied plaintiffs that access and thus violated plaintiff's right to due process and a fair determination of their malpractice action against the defendants.

NOTES

1. Assume *arguendo* that the courts extend the right to present reliable, critical evidence to civil cases. Is that extension likely to have as much impact as the existence of the parallel right on the criminal side? Consider the difference in the ultimate burden of proof between civil and criminal cases. In a criminal prosecution, to gain an acquittal, an accused need only raise a reasonable doubt about an element of the charged offense. Can a civil defendant gain a defense verdict as easily? Even if other courts decide to follow the lead of the *Adams* decision, the recognition of the constitutional override in the civil arena might have a less dramatic effect.

2. In *Baptist Memorial Hospital-Union County v. Johnson*, 754 So. 2d 1165 (Miss. 2000), the Mississippi Supreme Court reached a result in accord with the outcome in *Adams*. In *Baptist Memorial*, the plaintiff mother gave birth to her child at the defendant hospital. A nurse in the defendant's employ misdelivered the child to another woman to be nursed. The latter woman breast-fed the child. When the plaintiff and her husband later discovered the mix-up, they sued the hospital for negligence. In order to determine whether the breast-feeding endangered their child's health, they sought discovery of the other woman's identity and medical records. On the one hand, the court ruled that the medical privilege applied to the woman's identity and that the hospital could assert the privilege on behalf of the unidentified woman. On the other hand, the court concluded that the plaintiffs had such a "compelling" need for the information that their constitutional rights surmounted the medical privilege.

D. CONCLUSION

Washington, Chambers, and *Davis* all reach the same conclusion: The Constitution sometimes mandates the introduction of otherwise inadmissible defense evidence. However, while *Washington* and *Chambers* rely on an implication from the Compulsory Process Clause, *Chambers* also relies heavily on due process, and *Davis* premises the decision on the Confrontation Clause. The advent of this constitutional jurisprudence has had a two-fold impact on codified evidentiary rules.

One impact is indirect: The existence of the right may give the proponent of evidence at least a colorable argument that a narrow construction of a rule of evidence would be unconstitutional and, thus, enable the proponent to argue for a more expansive interpretation, admitting his or her evidence. In *Commonwealth v.*

Joyce, for example, the accused was charged with rape and sought to introduce evidence of the victim's alleged prior sexual activity. 382 Mass. 222 (1981). In that case, the accused was charged with rape. The accused sought to introduce evidence of the victim's alleged prior sexual activity. The prosecutor objected on the ground that the state rape shield statute barred the evidence. The defense had argued that, as construed by the prosecutor, the statute abridged the accused's constitutional right to present evidence. The court found the defense argument persuasive. The court emphasized that, in that jurisdiction, it was well-settled that "a 'statute must be construed, if fairly possible so as to avoid not only the conclusion that it is unconstitutional but also grave doubts upon that score.' " *Id.* at 185 n.5.

The other impact is direct: If the court concludes that the proponent's interest in introducing the evidence outweighs the public interest underlying the exclusionary rule, the court holds that that application of the statute in a specific case violates the Constitution. Suppose, for instance, that in the *Devitt* case, a trial judge rules that, although it is technically inadmissible under the statutory hearsay rules in the jurisdiction, certain defense hearsay is so demonstrably reliable that the Constitution mandates its admission. The immediate effect is the creation of a differential standard: the normal statutory standard which the prosecution must satisfy and the relaxed standard for the criminal defendant under *Chambers*.

Crawford and *Davis v. Alaska* illustrate, respectively, the negative and affirmative strictures that the Confrontation Clause imposes upon the operation of hearsay doctrine. Together, they are likely to engender the kind of differential standard mentioned above: a heightened standard for "testimonial" hearsay sought to be admitted against the accused and a reduced standard when the same type of evidence is offered by the accused.

Is the existence of a differential standard inconsistent with the philosophy of the adversary system? Or does it preserve a fair state-individual balance? As a matter of practical politics, is its existence likely to motivate prosecutors to argue for a liberalization of evidentiary standards?

Appendix

THE FEDERAL RULES OF EVIDENCE

DECEMBER 1, 2011

ARTICLE I
GENERAL PROVISIONS

Rule 101. Scope; Definitions

(a) Scope. These rules apply to proceedings in United States courts. The specific courts and proceedings to which the rules apply, along with exceptions, are set out in Rule 1101.

(b) Definitions. In these rules:

(1) "civil case" means a civil action or proceeding;

(2) "criminal case" includes a criminal proceeding;

(3) "public office" includes a public agency;

(4) "record" includes a memorandum, report, or data compilation;

(5) a "rule prescribed by the Supreme Court" means a rule adopted by the Supreme Court under statutory authority; and

(6) a reference to any kind of written material or any other medium includes electronically stored information.

Rule 102. Purpose

These rules should be construed so as to administer every proceeding fairly, eliminate unjustifiable expense and delay, and promote the development of evidence law, to the end of ascertaining the truth and securing a just determination.

Rule 103. Rulings on Evidence

(a) Preserving a claim of error. A party may claim error in a ruling to admit or exclude evidence only if the error affects a substantial right of the party and:

(1) if the ruling admits evidence, a party, on the record:

(A) timely objects or moves to strike; and

(B) states the specific ground, unless it was apparent from the context; or

(2) if the ruling excludes evidence, a party informs the court of its substance by an offer of proof, unless the substance was apparent from the context.

(b)   Not needing to renew an objection or offer of proof. Once the court rules definitively on the record — either before or at trial — a party need not renew an objection or offer of proof to preserve a claim of error for appeal.

(c)   Court's statement about the ruling; directing an offer of proof. The court may make any statement about the character or form of the evidence, the objection made, and the ruling. The court may direct that an offer of proof be made in question-and-answer form.

(d)   Preventing the jury from hearing inadmissible evidence. To the extent practicable, the court must conduct a jury trial so that inadmissible evidence is not suggested to the jury by any means.

(e)   Taking notice of plain error. A court may take notice of a plain error affecting a substantial right, even if the claim of error was not properly preserved.

Rule 104.   Preliminary Questions

(a)   In general. The court must decide any preliminary question about whether a witness is qualified, a privilege exists, or evidence is admissible. In so deciding, the court is not bound by evidence rules, except those on privilege.

(b)   Relevance that depends on a fact. When the relevance of evidence depends on whether a fact exists, proof must be introduced sufficient to support a finding that the fact does exist. The court may admit the proposed evidence on the condition that the proof be introduced later.

(c)   Conducting a hearing so that the jury cannot hear it. The court must conduct any hearing on a preliminary question so that the jury cannot hear it if:

(1) the hearing involves the admissibility of a confession;

(2) a defendant in a criminal case is a witness and so requests; or

(3) justice so requires.

(d)   Cross-examining a defendant in a criminal case. By testifying on a preliminary question, a defendant in a criminal case does not become subject to cross-examination on other issues in the case.

(e)   Evidence relevant to weight and credibility. This rule does not limit a party's right to introduce before the jury evidence that is relevant to the weight or credibility of other evidence.

Rule 105.   Limiting Evidence That Is Not Admissible Against Other Parties or for Other Purposes

If the court admits evidence that is admissible against a party or for a purpose — but not against another party or for another purpose — the court, on timely request, must restrict the evidence to its proper scope and instruct the jury accordingly.

Rule 106.   Remainder of or Related Writings or Recorded Statements

If a party introduces all or part of a writing or recorded statement, an adverse party may require the introduction, at that time, of any other part — or any other writing or recorded statement — that in fairness ought to be considered at the same time.

ARTICLE II
JUDICIAL NOTICE

Rule 201.   Judicial Notice of Adjudicative Facts

(a)   Scope. This rule governs judicial notice of an adjudicative fact only, not a legislative fact.

(b)   Kinds of facts that may be judicially noticed. The court may judicially notice a fact that is not subject to reasonable dispute because it:

    (1) is generally known within the trial court's territorial jurisdiction; or

    (2) can be accurately and readily determined from sources whose accuracy cannot reasonably be questioned.

(c)   Taking notice. The court:

    (1) may take judicial notice on its own; or

    (2) must take judicial notice if a party requests it and the court is supplied with the necessary information.

(d)   Timing. The court may take judicial notice at any stage of the proceeding.

(e)   Opportunity to be heard. On timely request, a party is entitled to be heard on the propriety of taking judicial notice and the nature of the fact to be noticed. If the court takes judicial notice before notifying a party, the party, on request, is still entitled to be heard.

(f)   Instructing the jury. In a civil case, the court must instruct the jury to accept the noticed fact as conclusive. In a criminal case, the court must instruct the jury that it may or may not accept the noticed fact as conclusive.

ARTICLE III
PRESUMPTIONS IN CIVIL CASES

Rule 301.   Presumptions in Civil Cases Generally

In a civil case, unless a federal statute or these rules provide otherwise, the party against whom a presumption is directed has the burden of producing evidence to rebut the presumption. But this rule does not shift the burden of persuasion, which remains on the party who had it originally.

Rule 302.   Applying State Law to Presumptions in Civil Cases

In a civil case, state law governs the effect of a presumption regarding a claim or defense for which state law supplies the rule of decision.

ARTICLE IV
RELEVANCE AND ITS LIMITS

Rule 401. Test for Relevant Evidence

Evidence is relevant if: (a) it has any tendency to make a fact more or less probable than it would be without the evidence; and (b) the fact is of consequence in determining the action.

Rule 402. General Admissibility of Relevant Evidence

Relevant evidence is admissible unless any of the following provides otherwise:

- the United States Constitution;

- a federal statute;

- these rules; or

- other rules prescribed by the Supreme Court.

Irrelevant evidence is not admissible.

Rule 403. Excluding Relevant Evidence for Prejudice, Confusion, Waste of Time, or Other Reasons

The court may exclude relevant evidence if its probative value is substantially outweighed by a danger of one or more of the following: unfair prejudice, confusing the issues, misleading the jury, undue delay, wasting time, or needlessly presenting cumulative evidence.

Rule 404. Character Evidence; Crimes or Other Acts

(a) Character evidence.

(1) Prohibited Uses.

Evidence of a person's character or character trait is not admissible to prove that on a particular occasion the person acted in accordance with the character or trait.

(2) Exceptions for a Defendant or Victim in a Criminal Case.

The following exceptions apply in a criminal case:

(A) a defendant may offer evidence of the defendant's pertinent trait, and if the evidence is admitted, the prosecutor may offer evidence to rebut it;

(B) subject to the limitations in Rule 412, a defendant may offer evidence of an alleged victim's pertinent trait, and if the evidence is admitted, the prosecutor may:

(i) offer evidence to rebut it; and

(ii) offer evidence of the defendant's same trait; and

(C) in a homicide case, the prosecutor may offer evidence of the alleged victim's trait of peacefulness to rebut evidence that the victim was the first aggressor.

(3)　Exceptions for a Witness.

Evidence of a witness's character may be admitted under Rules 607, 608, and 609.

(b)　Crimes, wrongs, or other acts.

(1)　Prohibited Uses.

Evidence of a crime, wrong, or other act is not admissible to prove a person's character in order to show that on a particular occasion the person acted in accordance with the character.

(2)　Permitted Uses; Notice in a Criminal Case.

This evidence may be admissible for another purpose, such as proving motive, opportunity, intent, preparation, plan, knowledge, identity, absence of mistake, or lack of accident. On request by a defendant in a criminal case, the prosecutor must:

(A) provide reasonable notice of the general nature of any such evidence that the prosecutor intends to offer at trial; and

(B) do so before trial — or during trial if the court, for good cause, excuses lack of pretrial notice.

Rule 405.　Methods of Proving Character

(a)　By reputation or opinion. When evidence of a person's character or character trait is admissible, it may be proved by testimony about the person's reputation or by testimony in the form of an opinion. On cross-examination of the character witness, the court may allow an inquiry into relevant specific instances of the person's conduct.

(b)　By specific instances of conduct. When a person's character or character trait is an essential element of a charge, claim, or defense, the character or trait may also be proved by relevant specific instances of the person's conduct.

Rule 406.　Habit; Routine Practice

Evidence of a person's habit or an organization's routine practice may be admitted to prove that on a particular occasion the person or organization acted in accordance with the habit or routine practice. The court may admit this evidence regardless of whether it is corroborated or whether there was an eyewitness.

Rule 407.　Subsequent Remedial Measures

When measures are taken that would have made an earlier injury or harm less likely to occur, evidence of the subsequent measures is not admissible to prove:

- negligence;
- culpable conduct;
- a defect in a product or its design; or
- a need for a warning or instruction.

But the court may admit this evidence for another purpose, such as impeachment or — if disputed — proving ownership, control, or the feasibility of precautionary measures.

Rule 408. Compromise Offers and Negotiations

(a) Prohibited uses. Evidence of the following is not admissible — on behalf of any party — either to prove or disprove the validity or amount of a disputed claim or to impeach by a prior inconsistent statement or a contradiction:

(1) furnishing, promising, or offering — or accepting, promising to accept, or offering to accept — a valuable consideration in compromising or attempting to compromise the claim; and

(2) conduct or a statement made during compromise negotiations about the claim — except when offered in a criminal case and when the negotiations related to a claim by a public office in the exercise of its regulatory, investigative, or enforcement authority.

(b) Exceptions. The court may admit this evidence for another purpose, such as proving a witness's bias or prejudice, negating a contention of undue delay, or proving an effort to obstruct a criminal investigation or prosecution.

Rule 409. Offers to Pay Medical and Similar Expenses

Evidence of furnishing, promising to pay, or offering to pay medical, hospital, or similar expenses resulting from an injury is not admissible to prove liability for the injury.

Rule 410. Pleas, Plea Discussions, and Related Statements

(a) Prohibited uses. In a civil or criminal case, evidence of the following is not admissible against the defendant who made the plea or participated in the plea discussions:

(1) a guilty plea that was later withdrawn;

(2) a nolo contendere plea;

(3) a statement made during a proceeding on either of those pleas under Federal Rule of Criminal Procedure 11 or a comparable state procedure; or

(4) a statement made during plea discussions with an attorney for the prosecuting authority if the discussions did not result in a guilty plea or they resulted in a later-withdrawn guilty plea.

(b) Exceptions. The court may admit a statement described in Rule 410(a)(3) or (4):

(1) in any proceeding in which another statement made during the same plea or plea discussions has been introduced, if in fairness the statements ought to be considered together; or

(2) in a criminal proceeding for perjury or false statement, if the defendant made the statement under oath, on the record, and with counsel present.

Rule 411.   Liability Insurance

Evidence that a person was or was not insured against liability is not admissible to prove whether the person acted negligently or otherwise wrongfully. But the court may admit this evidence for another purpose, such as proving a witness's bias or prejudice or proving agency, ownership, or control.

Rule 412.   Sex-Offense Cases: The Victim's Sexual Behavior or Pre-disposition

(a)   Prohibited uses. The following evidence is not admissible in a civil or criminal proceeding involving alleged sexual misconduct:

    (1) evidence offered to prove that a victim engaged in other sexual behavior; or

    (2) evidence offered to prove a victim's sexual predisposition.

(b)   Exceptions.

    (1)   Criminal Cases.

The court may admit the following evidence in a criminal case:

    (A) evidence of specific instances of a victim's sexual behavior, if offered to prove that someone other than the defendant was the source of semen, injury, or other physical evidence;

    (B) evidence of specific instances of a victim's sexual behavior with respect to the person accused of the sexual misconduct, if offered by the defendant to prove consent or if offered by the prosecutor; and

    (C) evidence whose exclusion would violate the defendant's constitutional rights.

    (2)   Civil Cases.

In a civil case, the court may admit evidence offered to prove a victim's sexual behavior or sexual pre-disposition if its probative value substantially outweighs the danger of harm to any victim and of unfair prejudice to any party. The court may admit evidence of a victim's reputation only if the victim has placed it in controversy.

(c)   Procedure to determine admissibility.

    (1)   Motion.

If a party intends to offer evidence under Rule 412(b), the party must:

    (A) file a motion that specifically describes the evidence and states the purpose for which it is to be offered;

    (B) do so at least 14 days before trial unless the court, for good cause, sets a different time;

    (C) serve the motion on all parties; and

    (D) notify the victim or, when appropriate, the victim's guardian or representative.

    (2)   Hearing.

Before admitting evidence under this rule, the court must conduct an in camera hearing and give the victim and parties a right to attend and be heard. Unless the court orders otherwise, the motion, related materials, and the record of the hearing must be and remain sealed.

(d) Definition of "victim." In this rule, "victim" includes an alleged victim.

Rule 413. Similar Crimes in Sexual-Assault Cases

(a) Permitted uses. In a criminal case in which a defendant is accused of a sexual assault, the court may admit evidence that the defendant committed any other sexual assault. The evidence may be considered on any matter to which it is relevant.

(b) Disclosure to the defendant. If the prosecutor intends to offer this evidence, the prosecutor must disclose it to the defendant, including witnesses' statements or a summary of the expected testimony. The prosecutor must do so at least 15 days before trial or at a later time that the court allows for good cause.

(c) Effect on other rules. This rule does not limit the admission or consideration of evidence under any other rule.

(d) Definition of "sexual assault." In this rule and Rule 415, "sexual assault" means a crime under federal law or under state law (as "state" is defined in 18 U.S.C. § 513) involving:

(1) any conduct prohibited by 18 U.S.C. chapter 109A;

(2) contact, without consent, between any part of the defendant's body — or an object — and another person's genitals or anus;

(3) contact, without consent, between the defendant's genitals or anus and any part of another person's body;

(4) deriving sexual pleasure or gratification from inflicting death, bodily injury, or physical pain on another person; or

(5) an attempt or conspiracy to engage in conduct described in subparagraphs (1)–(4).

Rule 414. Similar Crimes in Child-Molestation Cases

(a) Permitted uses. In a criminal case in which a defendant is accused of child molestation, the court may admit evidence that the defendant committed any other child molestation. The evidence may be considered on any matter to which it is relevant.

(b) Disclosure to the defendant. If the prosecutor intends to offer this evidence, the prosecutor must disclose it to the defendant, including witnesses' statements or a summary of the expected testimony. The prosecutor must do so at least 15 days before trial or at a later time that the court allows for good cause.

(c) Effect on other rules. This rule does not limit the admission or consideration of evidence under any other rule.

(d) Definition of "child" and "child molestation." In this rule and Rule 415:

(1) "child" means a person below the age of 14; and

(2) "child molestation" means a crime under federal law or under state law (as "state" is defined in 18 U.S.C. § 513) involving:

    (A) any conduct prohibited by 18 U.S.C. chapter 109A and committed with a child;

    (B) any conduct prohibited by 18 U.S.C. chapter 110;

    (C) contact between any part of the defendant's body — or an object — and a child's genitals or anus;

    (D) contact between the defendant's genitals or anus and any part of a child's body;

    (E) deriving sexual pleasure or gratification from inflicting death, bodily injury, or physical pain on a child; or

    (F) an attempt or conspiracy to engage in conduct described in subparagraphs (A)–(E).

Rule 415.　Similar Acts in Civil Cases Involving Sexual Assault or Child Molestation

(a)　Permitted uses. In a civil case involving a claim for relief based on a party's alleged sexual assault or child molestation, the court may admit evidence that the party committed any other sexual assault or child molestation. The evidence may be considered as provided in Rules 413 and 414.

(b)　Disclosure to the opponent. If a party intends to offer this evidence, the party must disclose it to the party against whom it will be offered, including witnesses' statements or a summary of the expected testimony. The party must do so at least 15 days before trial or at a later time that the court allows for good cause.

(c)　Effect on other rules. This rule does not limit the admission or consideration of evidence under any other rule.

ARTICLE V
PRIVILEGES

Rule 501.　Privilege in General

The common law — as interpreted by United States courts in the light of reason and experience — governs a claim of privilege unless any of the following provides otherwise:

- the United States Constitution;

- a federal statute; or

- rules prescribed by the Supreme Court.

But in a civil case, state law governs privilege regarding a claim or defense for which state law supplies the rule of decision.

Rule 502. Attorney-Client Privilege and Work Product; Limitations on Waiver

The following provisions apply, in the circumstances set out, to disclosure of a communication or information covered by the attorney-client privilege or work-product protection.

(a) Disclosure made in a federal proceeding or to a federal office or agency; scope of a waiver. When the disclosure is made in a federal proceeding or to a federal office or agency and waives the attorney-client privilege or work-product protection, the waiver extends to an undisclosed communication or information in a federal or state proceeding only if:

(1) the waiver is intentional;

(2) the disclosed and undisclosed communications or information concern the same subject matter; and

(3) they ought in fairness to be considered together.

(b) Inadvertent disclosure. When made in a federal proceeding or to a federal office or agency, the disclosure does not operate as a waiver in a federal or state proceeding if:

(1) the disclosure is inadvertent;

(2) the holder of the privilege or protection took reasonable steps to prevent disclosure; and

(3) the holder promptly took reasonable steps to rectify the error, including (if applicable) following Federal Rule of Civil Procedure 26(b)(5)(B).

(c) Disclosure made in a state proceeding. When the disclosure is made in a state proceeding and is not the subject of a state-court order concerning waiver, the disclosure does not operate as a waiver in a federal proceeding if the disclosure:

(1) would not be a waiver under this rule if it had been made in a federal proceeding; or

(2) is not a waiver under the law of the state where the disclosure occurred.

(d) Controlling effect of a court order. A federal court may order that the privilege or protection is not waived by disclosure connected with the litigation pending before the court — in which event the disclosure is also not a waiver in any other federal or state proceeding.

(e) Controlling effect of a party agreement. An agreement on the effect of disclosure in a federal proceeding is binding only on the parties to the agreement, unless it is incorporated into a court order.

(f) Controlling effect of this rule. Notwithstanding Rules 101 and 1101, this rule applies to state proceedings and to federal court-annexed and federal court-mandated arbitration proceedings, in the circumstances set out in the rule. And notwithstanding Rule 501, this rule applies even if state law provides the rule of decision.

(g) Definitions. In this rule:

(1) "attorney-client privilege" means the protection that applicable law provides for confidential attorney-client communications; and

(2) "work-product protection" means the protection that applicable law provides for tangible material (or its intangible equivalent) prepared in anticipation of litigation or for trial.

ARTICLE VI
WITNESSES

Rule 601.   Competency to Testify in General

Every person is competent to be a witness unless these rules provide otherwise. But in a civil case, state law governs the witness's competency regarding a claim or defense for which state law supplies the rule of decision.

Rule 602.   Need for Personal Knowledge

A witness may testify to a matter only if evidence is introduced sufficient to support a finding that the witness has personal knowledge of the matter. Evidence to prove personal knowledge may consist of the witness's own testimony. This rule does not apply to a witness's expert testimony under Rule 703.

Rule 603.   Oath or Affirmation to Testify Truthfully

Before testifying, a witness must give an oath or affirmation to testify truthfully. It must be in a form designed to impress that duty on the witness's conscience.

Rule 604.   Interpreter

An interpreter must be qualified and must give an oath or affirmation to make a true translation.

Rule 605.   Judge's Competency as a Witness

The presiding judge may not testify as a witness at the trial. A party need not object to preserve the issue.

Rule 606.   Juror's Competency as a Witness

(a)   At the trial. A juror may not testify as a witness before the other jurors at the trial. If a juror is called to testify, the court must give a party an opportunity to object outside the jury's presence.

(b)   During an inquiry into the validity of a verdict or indictment.

(1)   Prohibited Testimony or Other Evidence.

During an inquiry into the validity of a verdict or indictment, a juror may not testify about any statement made or incident that occurred during the jury's deliberations; the effect of anything on that juror's or another juror's vote; or any juror's mental processes concerning the verdict or indictment. The court may not receive a juror's affidavit or evidence of a juror's statement on these matters.

(2)   Exceptions.

A juror may testify about whether:

(A) extraneous prejudicial information was improperly brought to the jury's attention;

(B) an outside influence was improperly brought to bear on any juror; or

(C) a mistake was made in entering the verdict on the verdict form.

Rule 607. Who May Impeach a Witness

Any party, including the party that called the witness, may attack the witness's credibility.

Rule 608. A Witness's Character for Truthfulness or Untruthfulness

(a)   Reputation or opinion evidence. A witness's credibility may be attacked or supported by testimony about the witness's reputation for having a character for truthfulness or untruthfulness, or by testimony in the form of an opinion about that character. But evidence of truthful character is admissible only after the witness's character for truthfulness has been attacked.

(b)   Specific instances of conduct. Except for a criminal conviction under Rule 609, extrinsic evidence is not admissible to prove specific instances of a witness's conduct in order to attack or support the witness's character for truthfulness. But the court may, on cross-examination, allow them to be inquired into if they are probative of the character for truthfulness or untruthfulness of:

(1) the witness; or

(2) another witness whose character the witness being cross-examined has testified about.

By testifying on another matter, a witness does not waive any privilege against self-incrimination for testimony that relates only to the witness's character for truthfulness.

Rule 609. Impeachment by Evidence of a Criminal Conviction

(a)   In general. The following rules apply to attacking a witness's character for truthfulness by evidence of a criminal conviction:

(1) for a crime that, in the convicting jurisdiction, was punishable by death or by imprisonment for more than one year, the evidence:

(A) must be admitted, subject to Rule 403, in a civil case or in a criminal case in which the witness is not a defendant; and

(B) must be admitted in a criminal case in which the witness is a defendant, if the probative value of the evidence outweighs its prejudicial effect to that defendant; and

(2) for any crime regardless of the punishment, the evidence must be admitted if the court can readily determine that establishing the elements of the crime required proving — or the witness's admitting — a dishonest act or false statement.

(b)   Limit on using the evidence after 10 years. This subdivision (b) applies if more than 10 years have passed since the witness's conviction or release from confinement for it, whichever is later. Evidence of the conviction is admissible only if:

   (1) its probative value, supported by specific facts and circumstances, substantially outweighs its prejudicial effect; and

   (2) the proponent gives an adverse party reasonable written notice of the intent to use it so that the party has a fair opportunity to contest its use.

(c)   Effect of a pardon, annulment, or certificate of rehabilitation. Evidence of a conviction is not admissible if:

   (1) the conviction has been the subject of a pardon, annulment, certificate of rehabilitation, or other equivalent procedure based on a finding that the person has been rehabilitated, and the person has not been convicted of a later crime punishable by death or by imprisonment for more than one year; or

   (2) the conviction has been the subject of a pardon, annulment, or other equivalent procedure based on a finding of innocence.

(d)   Juvenile adjudications. Evidence of a juvenile adjudication is admissible under this rule only if:

   (1) it is offered in a criminal case;

   (2) the adjudication was of a witness other than the defendant;

   (3) an adult's conviction for that offense would be admissible to attack the adult's credibility; and

   (4) admitting the evidence is necessary to fairly determine guilt or innocence.

(e)   Pendency of an appeal. A conviction that satisfies this rule is admissible even if an appeal is pending. Evidence of the pendency is also admissible.

Rule 610.   Religious Beliefs or Opinions

Evidence of a witness's religious beliefs or opinions is not admissible to attack or support the witness's credibility.

Rule 611.   Mode and Order of Examining Witnesses and Presenting Evidence

(a)   Control by the court; purposes. The court should exercise reasonable control over the mode and order of examining witnesses and presenting evidence so as to:

   (1) make those procedures effective for determining the truth;

   (2) avoid wasting time; and

   (3) protect witnesses from harassment or undue embarrassment.

(b)   Scope of cross-examination. Cross-examination should not go beyond the subject matter of the direct examination and matters affecting the witness's credibility. The court may allow inquiry into additional matters as if on direct examination.

(c) Leading questions. Leading questions should not be used on direct examination except as necessary to develop the witness's testimony. Ordinarily, the court should allow leading questions:

(1) on cross-examination; and

(2) when a party calls a hostile witness, an adverse party, or a witness identified with an adverse party.

Rule 612. Writing Used to Refresh a Witness's Memory

(a) Scope. This rule gives an adverse party certain options when a witness uses a writing to refresh memory:

(1) while testifying; or

(2) before testifying, if the court decides that justice requires the party to have those options.

(b) Adverse party's options; deleting unrelated matter. Unless 18 U.S.C. § 3500 provides otherwise in a criminal case, an adverse party is entitled to have the writing produced at the hearing, to inspect it, to cross-examine the witness about it, and to introduce in evidence any portion that relates to the witness's testimony. If the producing party claims that the writing includes unrelated matter, the court must examine the writing in camera, delete any unrelated portion, and order that the rest be delivered to the adverse party. Any portion deleted over objection must be preserved for the record.

(c) Failure to produce or deliver the writing. If a writing is not produced or is not delivered as ordered, the court may issue any appropriate order. But if the prosecution does not comply in a criminal case, the court must strike the witness's testimony or — if justice so requires — declare a mistrial.

Rule 613. Witness's Prior Statement

(a) Showing or disclosing the statement during examination. When examining a witness about the witness's prior statement, a party need not show it or disclose its contents to the witness. But the party must, on request, show it or disclose its contents to an adverse party's attorney.

(b) Extrinsic evidence of a prior inconsistent statement. Extrinsic evidence of a witness's prior inconsistent statement is admissible only if the witness is given an opportunity to explain or deny the statement and an adverse party is given an opportunity to examine the witness about it, or if justice so requires. This subdivision (b) does not apply to an opposing party's statement under Rule 801(d)(2).

Rule 614. Court's Calling or Examining a Witness

(a) Calling. The court may call a witness on its own or at a party's request. Each party is entitled to cross-examine the witness.

(b) Examining. The court may examine a witness regardless of who calls the witness.

(c)   Objections. A party may object to the court's calling or examining a witness either at that time or at the next opportunity when the jury is not present.

Rule 615.   Excluding Witnesses

At a party's request, the court must order witnesses excluded so that they cannot hear other witnesses' testimony. Or the court may do so on its own. But this rule does not authorize excluding:

(a) a party who is a natural person;

(b) an officer or employee of a party that is not a natural person, after being designated as the party's representative by its attorney;

(c) a person whose presence a party shows to be essential to presenting the party's claim or defense; or

(d) a person authorized by statute to be present.

ARTICLE VII
OPINIONS AND EXPERT TESTIMONY

Rule 701.   Opinion Testimony by Lay Witnesses

If a witness is not testifying as an expert, testimony in the form of an opinion is limited to one that is:

(a) rationally based on the witness's perception;

(b) helpful to clearly understanding the witness's testimony or to determining a fact in issue; and

(c) not based on scientific, technical, or other specialized knowledge within the scope of Rule 702.

Rule 702.   Testimony by Expert Witnesses

A witness who is qualified as an expert by knowledge, skill, experience, training, or education may testify in the form of an opinion or otherwise if:

(a) the expert's scientific, technical, or other specialized knowledge will help the trier of fact to understand the evidence or to determine a fact in issue;

(b) the testimony is based on sufficient facts or data;

(c) the testimony is the product of reliable principles and methods; and

(d) the expert has reliably applied the principles and methods to the facts of the case.

Rule 703.   Bases of an Expert's Opinion Testimony

An expert may base an opinion on facts or data in the case that the expert has been made aware of or personally observed. If experts in the particular field would reasonably rely on those kinds of facts or data in forming an opinion on the subject, they need not be admissible for the opinion to be admitted. But if the facts or data would otherwise be inadmissible, the proponent of the opinion may disclose them to the jury only if their probative value in helping the jury evaluate the opinion substantially outweighs their prejudicial effect.

Rule 704. Opinion on an Ultimate Issue

(a) In general — not automatically objectionable. An opinion is not objectionable just because it embraces an ultimate issue.

(b) Exception. In a criminal case, an expert witness must not state an opinion about whether the defendant did or did not have a mental state or condition that constitutes an element of the crime charged or of a defense. Those matters are for the trier of fact alone.

Rule 705. Disclosing the Facts or Data Underlying an Expert's Opinion

Unless the court orders otherwise, an expert may state an opinion — and give the reasons for it — without first testifying to the underlying facts or data. But the expert may be required to disclose those facts or data on cross-examination.

Rule 706. Court-Appointed Expert Witnesses

(a) Appointment process. On a party's motion or on its own, the court may order the parties to show cause why expert witnesses should not be appointed and may ask the parties to submit nominations. The court may appoint any expert that the parties agree on and any of its own choosing. But the court may only appoint someone who consents to act.

(b) Expert's role. The court must inform the expert of the expert's duties. The court may do so in writing and have a copy filed with the clerk or may do so orally at a conference in which the parties have an opportunity to participate. The expert:

(1) must advise the parties of any findings the expert makes;

(2) may be deposed by any party;

(3) may be called to testify by the court or any party; and

(4) may be cross-examined by any party, including the party that called the expert.

(c) Compensation. The expert is entitled to a reasonable compensation, as set by the court. The compensation is payable as follows:

(1) in a criminal case or in a civil case involving just compensation under the Fifth Amendment, from any funds that are provided by law; and

(2) in any other civil case, by the parties in the proportion and at the time that the court directs — and the compensation is then charged like other costs.

(d) Disclosing the appointment to the jury. The court may authorize disclosure to the jury that the court appointed the expert.

(e) Parties' choice of their own experts. This rule does not limit a party in calling its own experts.

ARTICLE VIII
HEARSAY

Rule 801.   Definitions That Apply to This Article; Exclusions from Hearsay

(a)   Statement. "Statement" means a person's oral assertion, written assertion, or nonverbal conduct, if the person intended it as an assertion.

(b)   Declarant. "Declarant" means the person who made the statement.

(c)   Hearsay. "Hearsay" means a statement that: (1) the declarant does not make while testifying at the current trial or hearing; and (2) a party offers in evidence to prove the truth of the matter asserted in the statement.

(d)   Statements that are not hearsay. A statement that meets the following conditions is not hearsay: (1) A Declarant-Witness's Prior Statement. The declarant testifies and is subject to cross-examination about a prior statement, and the statement:

   (A) is inconsistent with the declarant's testimony and was given under penalty of perjury at a trial, hearing, or other proceeding or in a deposition;

   (B) is consistent with the declarant's testimony and is offered to rebut an express or implied charge that the declarant recently fabricated it or acted from a recent improper influence or motive in so testifying; or

   (C) identifies a person as someone the declarant perceived earlier.

   (2)   An Opposing Party's Statement.
The statement is offered against an opposing party and:

   (A) was made by the party in an individual or representative capacity;

   (B) is one the party manifested that it adopted or believed to be true;

   (C) was made by a person whom the party authorized to make a statement on the subject;

   (D) was made by the party's agent or employee on a matter within the scope of that relationship and while it existed; or

   (E) was made by the party's coconspirator during and in furtherance of the conspiracy.

The statement must be considered but does not by itself establish the declarant's authority under (C); the existence or scope of the relationship under (D); or the existence of the conspiracy or participation in it under (E).

Rule 802.   The Rule Against Hearsay

Hearsay is not admissible unless any of the following provides otherwise:

   • a federal statute;

   • these rules; or

• other rules prescribed by the Supreme Court.

Rule 803. Exceptions to the Rule Against Hearsay — Regardless of Whether the Declarant Is Available as a Witness

The following are not excluded by the rule against hearsay, regardless of whether the declarant is available as a witness:

(1) Present Sense Impression.

A statement describing or explaining an event or condition, made while or immediately after the declarant perceived it.

(2) Excited Utterance.

A statement relating to a startling event or condition, made while the declarant was under the stress of excitement that it caused.

(3) Then-Existing Mental, Emotional, or Physical Condition.

A statement of the declarant's then-existing state of mind (such as motive, intent, or plan) or emotional, sensory, or physical condition (such as mental feeling, pain, or bodily health), but not including a statement of memory or belief to prove the fact remembered or believed unless it relates to the validity or terms of the declarant's will.

(4) Statement Made for Medical Diagnosis or Treatment.

A statement that:

(A) is made for — and is reasonably pertinent to — medical diagnosis or treatment; and

(B) describes medical history; past or present symptoms or sensations; their inception; or their general cause.

(5) Recorded Recollection.

A record that:

(A) is on a matter the witness once knew about but now cannot recall well enough to testify fully and accurately;

(B) was made or adopted by the witness when the matter was fresh in the witness's memory; and

(C) accurately reflects the witness's knowledge. If admitted, the record may be read into evidence but may be received as an exhibit only if offered by an adverse party.

(6) Records of a Regularly Conducted Activity.

A record of an act, event, condition, opinion, or diagnosis if:

(A) the record was made at or near the time by — or from information transmitted by — someone with knowledge;

(B) the record was kept in the course of a regularly conducted activity of a business, organization, occupation, or calling, whether or not for profit;

(C) making the record was a regular practice of that activity;

(D) all these conditions are shown by the testimony of the custodian or another qualified witness, or by a certification that complies with Rule 902(11) or (12) or with a statute permitting certification; and

(E) neither the source of information nor the method or circumstances of preparation indicate a lack of trust-worthiness.

(7)   Absence of a Record of a Regularly Conducted Activity.

Evidence that a matter is not included in a record described in paragraph (6) if:

(A) the evidence is admitted to prove that the matter did not occur or exist;

(B) a record was regularly kept for a matter of that kind; and

(C) neither the possible source of the information nor other circumstances indicate a lack of trustworthiness.

(8)   Public Records.

A record or statement of a public office if:

(A) it sets out:

(i) the office's activities;

(ii) a matter observed while under a legal duty to report, but not including, in a criminal case, a matter observed by law-enforcement personnel; or

(iii) in a civil case or against the government in a criminal case, factual findings from a legally authorized investigation; and

(B) neither the source of information nor other circumstances indicate a lack of trustworthiness.

(9)   Public Records of Vital Statistics.

A record of a birth, death, or marriage, if reported to a public office in accordance with a legal duty.

(10)   Absence of a Public Record.

Testimony — or a certification under Rule 902 — that a diligent search failed to disclose a public record or statement if the testimony or certification is admitted to prove that:

(A) the record or statement does not exist; or

(B) a matter did not occur or exist, if a public office regularly kept a record or statement for a matter of that kind.

(11)   Records of Religious Organizations Concerning Personal or Family History.

A statement of birth, legitimacy, ancestry, marriage, divorce, death, relationship by blood or marriage, or similar facts of personal or family history, contained in a regularly kept record of a religious organization.

(12)   Certificates of Marriage, Baptism, and Similar Ceremonies.

A statement of fact contained in a certificate:

(A) made by a person who is authorized by a religious organization or by law to perform the act certified;

(B) attesting that the person performed a marriage or similar ceremony or administered a sacrament; and

(C) purporting to have been issued at the time of the act or within a reasonable time after it.

(13) Family Records.

A statement of fact about personal or family history contained in a family record, such as a Bible, genealogy, chart, engraving on a ring, inscription on a portrait, or engraving on an urn or burial marker.

(14) Records of Documents That Affect an Interest in Property.

The record of a document that purports to establish or affect an interest in property if:

(A) the record is admitted to prove the content of the original recorded document, along with its signing and its delivery by each person who purports to have signed it;

(B) the record is kept in a public office; and

(C) a statute authorizes recording documents of that kind in that office.

(15) Statements in Documents That Affect an Interest in Property.

A statement contained in a document that purports to establish or affect an interest in property if the matter stated was relevant to the document's purpose — unless later dealings with the property are inconsistent with the truth of the statement or the purport of the document.

(16) Statements in Ancient Documents.

A statement in a document that is at least 20 years old and whose authenticity is established.

(17) Market Reports and Similar Commercial Publications.

Market quotations, lists, directories, or other compilations that are generally relied on by the public or by persons in particular occupations.

(18) Statements in Learned Treatises, Periodicals, or Pamphlets.

A statement contained in a treatise, periodical, or pamphlet if:

(A) the statement is called to the attention of an expert witness on cross-examination or relied on by the expert on direct examination; and

(B) the publication is established as a reliable authority by the expert's admission or testimony, by another expert's testimony, or by judicial notice.

If admitted, the statement may be read into evidence but not received as an exhibit.

(19) Reputation Concerning Personal or Family History.

A reputation among a person's family by blood, adoption, or marriage — or among a person's associates or in the community — concerning the person's birth, adoption, legitimacy, ancestry, marriage, divorce, death, relationship by blood, adoption, or marriage, or similar facts of personal or family history.

(20) Reputation Concerning Boundaries or General History.

A reputation in a community — arising before the controversy — concerning boundaries of land in the community or customs that affect the land, or concerning general historical events important to that community, state, or nation.

(21) Reputation Concerning Character.

A reputation among a person's associates or in the community concerning the person's character.

(22) Judgment of a Previous Conviction.

Evidence of a final judgment of conviction if:

(A) the judgment was entered after a trial or guilty plea, but not a nolo contendere plea;

(B) the conviction was for a crime punishable by death or by imprisonment for more than a year;

(C) the evidence is admitted to prove any fact essential to the judgment; and

(D) when offered by the prosecutor in a criminal case for a purpose other than impeachment, the judgment was against the defendant.

The pendency of an appeal may be shown but does not affect admissibility.

(23) Judgments Involving Personal, Family, or General History, or a Boundary.

A judgment that is admitted to prove a matter of personal, family, or general history, or boundaries, if the matter:

(A) was essential to the judgment; and

(B) could be proved by evidence of reputation.

(24) [Other Exceptions.]

[Transferred to Rule 807.]

Rule 804. Exceptions to the Rule Against Hearsay — When the Declarant Is Unavailable as a Witness

(a) Criteria for being unavailable. A declarant is considered to be unavailable as a witness if the declarant:

(1) is exempted from testifying about the subject matter of the declarant's statement because the court rules that a privilege applies;

(2) refuses to testify about the subject matter despite a court order to do so;

(3) testifies to not remembering the subject matter;

(4) cannot be present or testify at the trial or hearing because of death or a then-existing infirmity, physical illness, or mental illness; or

(5) is absent from the trial or hearing and the statement's proponent has not

been able, by process or other reasonable means, to procure:

(A) the declarant's attendance, in the case of a hearsay exception under Rule 804(b)(1) or (6); or

(B) the declarant's attendance or testimony, in the case of a hearsay exception under Rule 804(b)(2), (3), or (4).

But this subdivision (a) does not apply if the statement's proponent procured or wrongfully caused the declarant's unavailability as a witness in order to prevent the declarant from attending or testifying.

(b)   The exceptions. The following are not excluded by the rule against hearsay if the declarant is unavailable as a witness:

(1)   Former Testimony.

Testimony that:

(A) was given as a witness at a trial, hearing, or lawful deposition, whether given during the current proceeding or a different one; and

(B) is now offered against a party who had — or, in a civil case, whose predecessor in interest had — an opportunity and similar motive to develop it by direct, cross-, or redirect examination.

(2)   Statement Under the Belief of Imminent Death.

In a prosecution for homicide or in a civil case, a statement that the declarant, while believing the declarant's death to be imminent, made about its cause or circumstances.

(3)   Statement Against Interest.

A statement that:

(A) a reasonable person in the declarant's position would have made only if the person believed it to be true because, when made, it was so contrary to the declarant's proprietary or pecuniary interest or had so great a tendency to invalidate the declarant's claim against someone else or to expose the declarant to civil or criminal liability; and

(B) is supported by corroborating circumstances that clearly indicate its trustworthiness, if it is offered in a criminal case as one that tends to expose the declarant to criminal liability.

(4)   Statement of Personal or Family History.

A statement about:

(A) the declarant's own birth, adoption, legitimacy, ancestry, marriage, divorce, relationship by blood, adoption, or marriage, or similar facts of personal or family history, even though the declarant had no way of acquiring personal knowledge about that fact; or

(B) another person concerning any of these facts, as well as death, if the declarant was related to the person by blood, adoption, or marriage or was so intimately associated with the person's family that the declarant's information is likely to be accurate.

(5)   [Other Exceptions.]

[Transferred to Rule 807.]

(6)   Statement Offered Against a Party That Wrongfully Caused the Declarant's Unavailability.

A statement offered against a party that wrongfully caused — or acquiesced in wrongfully causing — the declarant's unavailability as a witness, and did so intending that result.

Rule 805.   Hearsay Within Hearsay

Hearsay within hearsay is not excluded by the rule against hearsay if each part of the combined statements conforms with an exception to the rule.

Rule 806.   Attacking and Supporting the Declarant's Credibility

When a hearsay statement — or a statement described in Rule 801(d)(2)(C), (D), or (E) — has been admitted in evidence, the declarant's credibility may be attacked, and then supported, by any evidence that would be admissible for those purposes if the declarant had testified as a witness. The court may admit evidence of the declarant's inconsistent statement or conduct, regardless of when it occurred or whether the declarant had an opportunity to explain or deny it. If the party against whom the statement was admitted calls the declarant as a witness, the party may examine the declarant on the statement as if on cross-examination.

Rule 807.   Residual Exception

(a)   In general. Under the following circumstances, a hearsay statement is not excluded by the rule against hearsay even if the statement is not specifically covered by a hearsay exception in Rule 803 or 804:

(1) the statement has equivalent circumstantial guarantees of trustworthiness;

(2) it is offered as evidence of a material fact;

(3) it is more probative on the point for which it is offered than any other evidence that the proponent can obtain through reasonable efforts; and

(4) admitting it will best serve the purposes of these rules and the interests of justice.

(b)   Notice. The statement is admissible only if, before the trial or hearing, the proponent gives an adverse party reasonable notice of the intent to offer the statement and its particulars, including the declarant's name and address, so that the party has a fair opportunity to meet it.

ARTICLE IX
AUTHENTICATION AND IDENTIFICATION

Rule 901. Authenticating or Identifying Evidence

(a) In general. To satisfy the requirement of authenticating or identifying an item of evidence, the proponent must produce evidence sufficient to support a finding that the item is what the proponent claims it is.

(b) Examples. The following are examples only — not a complete list — of evidence that satisfies the requirement:

(1) Testimony of a Witness with Knowledge.
Testimony that an item is what it is claimed to be.

(2) Nonexpert Opinion About Handwriting.
A nonexpert's opinion that handwriting is genuine, based on a familiarity with it that was not acquired for the current litigation.

(3) Comparison by an Expert Witness or the Trier of Fact.
A comparison with an authenticated specimen by an expert witness or the trier of fact.

(4) Distinctive Characteristics and the Like.
The appearance, contents, substance, internal patterns, or other distinctive characteristics of the item, taken together with all the circumstances.

(5) Opinion About a Voice.
An opinion identifying a person's voice — whether heard firsthand or through mechanical or electronic transmission or recording — based on hearing the voice at any time under circumstances that connect it with the alleged speaker.

(6) Evidence About a Telephone Conversation.
For a telephone conversation, evidence that a call was made to the number assigned at the time to:

(A) a particular person, if circumstances, including self-identification, show that the person answering was the one called; or

(B) a particular business, if the call was made to a business and the call related to business reasonably transacted over the telephone.

(7) Evidence About Public Records.
Evidence that:

(A) a document was recorded or filed in a public office as authorized by law; or

(B) a purported public record or statement is from the office where items of this kind are kept.

(8) Evidence About Ancient Documents or Data Compilations.

For a document or data compilation, evidence that it:

> (A) is in a condition that creates no suspicion about its authenticity;

> (B) was in a place where, if authentic, it would likely be; and

> (C) is at least 20 years old when offered.

(9)   Evidence About a Process or System.

Evidence describing a process or system and showing that it produces an accurate result.

(10)   Methods Provided by a Statute or Rule.

Any method of authentication or identification allowed by a federal statute or a rule prescribed by the Supreme Court.

Rule 902.   Evidence That Is Self-Authenticating

The following items of evidence are self-authenticating; they require no extrinsic evidence of authenticity in order to be admitted:

(1)   Domestic Public Documents That Are Sealed and Signed.

A document that bears:

> (A) a seal purporting to be that of the United States; any state, district, commonwealth, territory, or insular possession of the United States; the former Panama Canal Zone; the Trust Territory of the Pacific Islands; a political subdivision of any of these entities; or a department, agency, or officer of any entity named above; and

> (B) a signature purporting to be an execution or attestation.

(2)   Domestic Public Documents That Are Not Sealed but Are Signed and Certified.

A document that bears no seal if:

> (A) it bears the signature of an officer or employee of an entity named in Rule 902(1)(A); and

> (B) another public officer who has a seal and official duties within that same entity certifies under seal — or its equivalent — that the signer has the official capacity and that the signature is genuine.

(3) **Foreign Public Documents.** A document that purports to be signed or attested by a person who is authorized by a foreign country's law to do so. The document must be accompanied by a final certification that certifies the genuineness of the signature and official position of the signer or attester — or of any foreign official whose certificate of genuineness relates to the signature or attestation or is in a chain of certificates of genuineness relating to the signature or attestation. The certification may be made by a secretary of a United States embassy or legation; by a consul general, vice consul, or consular agent of the United States; or by a diplomatic or consular official of the foreign country assigned or accredited to the United States. If all parties have been given a reasonable opportunity to investigate the document's authenticity and accuracy, the court may, for good cause, either:

(A) order that it be treated as presumptively authentic without final certification; or

(B) allow it to be evidenced by an attested summary with or without final certification.

(4)   Certified Copies of Public Records.

A copy of an official record — or a copy of a document that was recorded or filed in a public office as authorized by law — if the copy is certified as correct by:

(A) the custodian or another person authorized to make the certification; or

(B) a certificate that complies with Rule 902(1), (2), or (3), a federal statute, or a rule prescribed by the Supreme Court.

(5)   Official Publications.

A book, pamphlet, or other publication purporting to be issued by a public authority.

(6)   Newspapers and Periodicals.

Printed material purporting to be a newspaper or periodical.

(7)   Trade Inscriptions and the Like.

An inscription, sign, tag, or label purporting to have been affixed in the course of business and indicating origin, ownership, or control.

(8)   Acknowledged Documents.

A document accompanied by a certificate of acknowledgment that is lawfully executed by a notary public or another officer who is authorized to take acknowledgments.

(9)   Commercial Paper and Related Documents.

Commercial paper, a signature on it, and related documents, to the extent allowed by general commercial law.

(10)   Presumptions Under a Federal Statute.

A signature, document, or anything else that a federal statute declares to be presumptively or prima facie genuine or authentic.

(11)   Certified Domestic Records of a Regularly Conducted Activity.

The original or a copy of a domestic record that meets the requirements of Rule 803(6)(A)–(C), as shown by a certification of the custodian or another qualified person that complies with a federal statute or a rule prescribed by the Supreme Court. Before the trial or hearing, the proponent must give an adverse party reasonable written notice of the intent to offer the record — and must make the record and certification available for inspection — so that the party has a fair opportunity to challenge them.

(12)   Certified Foreign Records of a Regularly Conducted Activity.

In a civil case, the original or a copy of a foreign record that meets the requirements of Rule 902(11), modified as follows: the certification, rather than complying with a federal statute or Supreme Court rule, must be signed in a manner that, if falsely made, would subject the maker to a criminal penalty in the country where the certification is signed. The proponent must also meet the notice requirements of Rule 902(11).

Rule 903. Subscribing Witness's Testimony

A subscribing witness's testimony is necessary to authenticate a writing only if required by the law of the jurisdiction that governs its validity.

ARTICLE X
CONTENTS OF WRITINGS, RECORDINGS, AND PHOTOGRAPHS

Rule 1001. Definitions That Apply to This Article

In this article:

(a) A "writing" consists of letters, words, numbers, or their equivalent set down in any form.

(b) A "recording" consists of letters, words, numbers, or their equivalent recorded in any manner.

(c) A "photograph" means a photographic image or its equivalent stored in any form.

(d) An "original" of a writing or recording means the writing or recording itself or any counterpart intended to have the same effect by the person who executed or issued it. For electronically stored information, "original" means any printout — or other output readable by sight — if it accurately reflects the information. An "original" of a photograph includes the negative or a print from it.

(e) A "duplicate" means a counterpart produced by a mechanical, photographic, chemical, electronic, or other equivalent process or technique that accurately reproduces the original.

Rule 1002. Requirement of the Original

An original writing, recording, or photograph is required in order to prove its content unless these rules or a federal statute provides otherwise.

Rule 1003. Admissibility of Duplicates

A duplicate is admissible to the same extent as the original unless a genuine question is raised about the original's authenticity or the circumstances make it unfair to admit the duplicate.

Rule 1004. Admissibility of Other Evidence of Content

An original is not required and other evidence of the content of a writing, recording, or photograph is admissible if:

(a) all the originals are lost or destroyed, and not by the proponent acting in bad faith;

(b) an original cannot be obtained by any available judicial process;

(c) the party against whom the original would be offered had control of the original; was at that time put on notice, by pleadings or otherwise, that the original would be a subject of proof at the trial or hearing; and fails to produce it at the trial or hearing; or

(d) the writing, recording, or photograph is not closely related to a controlling issue.

Rule 1005. Copies of Public Records to Prove Content

The proponent may use a copy to prove the content of an official record — or of a document that was recorded or filed in a public office as authorized by law — if these conditions are met: the record or document is otherwise admissible; and the copy is certified as correct in accordance with Rule 902(4) or is testified to be correct by a witness who has compared it with the original. If no such copy can be obtained by reasonable diligence, then the proponent may use other evidence to prove the content.

Rule 1006. Summaries to Prove Content

The proponent may use a summary, chart, or calculation to prove the content of voluminous writings, recordings, or photographs that cannot be conveniently examined in court. The proponent must make the originals or duplicates available for examination or copying, or both, by other parties at a reasonable time and place. And the court may order the proponent to produce them in court.

Rule 1007. Testimony or Statement of a Party to Prove Content

The proponent may prove the content of a writing, recording, or photograph by the testimony, deposition, or written statement of the party against whom the evidence is offered. The proponent need not account for the original.

Rule 1008. Functions of the Court and Jury

Ordinarily, the court determines whether the proponent has fulfilled the factual conditions for admitting other evidence of the content of a writing, recording, or photograph under Rule 1004 or 1005. But in a jury trial, the jury determines — in accordance with Rule 104(b) — any issue about whether:

(a) an asserted writing, recording, or photograph ever existed;

(b) another one produced at the trial or hearing is the original; or

(c) other evidence of content accurately reflects the content.

ARTICLE XI
MISCELLANEOUS RULES

Rule 1101. Applicability of the Rules

(a) To courts and judges. These rules apply to proceedings before:

- United States district courts;

- United States bankruptcy and magistrate judges;

- United States courts of appeals;

- the United States Court of Federal Claims; and

- the district courts of Guam, the Virgin Islands, and the Northern Mariana Islands.

(b)　To cases and proceedings. These rules apply in:

- civil cases and proceedings, including bankruptcy, admiralty, and maritime cases;

- criminal cases and proceedings; and

- contempt proceedings, except those in which the court may act summarily.

(c)　Rules on privilege. The rules on privilege apply to all stages of a case or proceeding.

(d)　Exceptions. These rules — except for those on privilege — do not apply to the following:

(1) the court's determination, under Rule 104(a), on a preliminary question of fact governing admissibility;

(2) grand-jury proceedings; and

(3) miscellaneous proceedings such as:

- extradition or rendition;

- issuing an arrest warrant, criminal summons, or search warrant;

- a preliminary examination in a criminal case;

- sentencing;

- granting or revoking probation or supervised release; and

- considering whether to release on bail or otherwise.

(e)　Other statutes and rules. A federal statute or a rule prescribed by the Supreme Court may provide for admitting or excluding evidence independently from these rules.

Rule 1102.　Amendments

These rules may be amended as provided in 28 U.S.C. § 2072.

Rule 1103.　Title

These rules may be cited as the Federal Rules of Evidence.

TABLE OF CASES

[References are to pages]

[References are to pages]

[References are to pages]

[References are to pages]

D

[References are to pages]

[References are to pages]

[References are to pages]

I

J

[References are to pages]

[References are to pages]

[References are to pages]

[References are to pages]

[References are to pages]

[References are to pages]

[References are to pages]

[References are to pages]

INDEX

[References are to sections.]

A

ABSOLUTE PRIVILEGE
Generally . . . 25[D][7]

ADMISSIBILITY
Generally . . . 6[A]
Competency of witnesses (See COMPETENCY OF WITNESSES)
Foundational facts, proof of . . . 5[D]
Hearsay rule (See HEARSAY RULE)
Judge's discretion to exclude otherwise admissible conviction . . . 16[E][2][b]
Judges role in (See JUDGES, subhead: Admissibility of evidence, role in)
Logical relevance (See LOGICAL RELEVANCE)
Other acts evidence
    Generally . . . 14[C][2][b]
    Prejudicial character of evidence
        . . . 14[C][2][b][2]
    Prosecution's need for evidence
        . . . 14[C][2][b][1]
Petit jurors, role of (See PETIT JURORS, ROLE OF)
Preliminary facts conditioning admissibility of evidence
    Petit jurors, role of . . . 5[C][3]
    Trial judge, role of . . . 5[B][2]
Prior consistent statements, of . . . 17[C][1]
Scientific evidence, validation of (See SCIENTIFIC EVIDENCE, VALIDATION OF, subhead: Admissibility standards)

ADMISSIONS
Adoptive admissions (See HEARSAY RULE, subhead: Adoptive admissions)
Attorney, role of (See ATTORNEYS, subhead: Admission and exclusion of evidence, role in)
Personal admissions . . . 19[B]
Vicarious admissions (See HEARSAY RULE, subhead: Vicarious admissions)

ADOPTIVE ADMISSIONS (See HEARSAY RULE, subhead: Adoptive admissions)

ADVERSARY SYSTEM
Generally . . . 1[B]

ATTORNEY-CLIENT PRIVILEGE
Generally . . . 26[A]
Clients
    Identity of . . . 26[A][2][a]
    Shared interests, with . . . 26[A][2][b]
Communications in corporate context
    . . . 26[A][2][c]
Confidentiality . . . 26[A][2][b]
Corporate context, communications in
    . . . 26[A][2][c]
Duration of . . . 26[A][4]
Exceptions to, special . . . 26[A][3]

ATTORNEY-CLIENT PRIVILEGE—Cont.
Identity of client . . . 26[A][2][a]
Intermediary, involvement of . . . 26[A][2][d]
Recognition of . . . 26[A][1]
Special exceptions to . . . 26[A][3]

ATTORNEYS
Admission and exclusion of evidence, role in
    Pretrial motions to . . . 5[A][1]
    Trial
        Objections to evidence at . . . 5[A][3]
        Offering evidence at . . . 5[A][2]
Competent witness, as . . . 7[E][2][c]

AUTHENTICATION
Physical evidence (See PHYSICAL EVIDENCE, subhead: Identification of)
Underlying logical relevance . . . 8[D][2][b]
Writings (See WRITINGS, subhead: Authentication of)

B

BARGAINING (See COMPROMISES)

BEST EVIDENCE RULE
Generally . . . 24[A]; 24[G]
Conventional writings . . . 24[B][1]
Counterpart, defined . . . 24[D][2]
Document for purposes of
    Generally . . . 24[B]
    Conventional writings . . . 24[B][1]
    Inscribed chattels . . . 24[B][4]
    Photographs . . . 24[B][3]
    Tape recordings . . . 24[B][2]
Duplicate, defined . . . 24[D][2]
Inscribed chattels . . . 24[B][4]
Original
    Generally . . . 24[D]
    Defined . . . 24[D][1]
    Nonproduction of, excuses for
        Generally . . . 24[E]; 24[F]
        Secondary evidence (See subhead: Secondary evidence offered upon excuses for nonproduction of original)
    Secondary evidence offered upon excuses for nonproduction of (See subhead: Secondary evidence offered upon excuses for nonproduction of original)
Photographs . . . 24[B][3]
Secondary evidence offered upon excuses for nonproduction of original
    Generally . . . 24[F]
    Degrees . . . 24[F][2]
    Types . . . 24[F][1]
Tape recordings . . . 24[B][2]
Terms in issue, document 's
    Generally . . . 24[C]

I-1

[References are to sections.]

[References are to sections.]

[References are to sections.]

IMPEACHMENT EVIDENCE—Cont.
Cross-examination to prove bias—Cont.
    Probative value and prejudice, balancing
       . . . 16[C][3][a][2]
    Relevance of bias impeachment
       . . . 16[C][3][a][1]
Opinion testimony, reputation and (See subhead:
    Reputation and opinion testimony)
Prior inconsistent statements and acts
    Generally . . . 16[B][1]
    Cross-examination about . . . 16[B][1][a]
    Extrinsic evidence of . . . 16[B][1][b]
Reputation and opinion testimony
    Generally . . . 16[D][3][a]
    Cross-examination . . . 16[D][3][a][2]
    Direct examination . . . 16[D][3][a][1]
Specific contradiction . . . 16[B][2]
Untruthfulness, character trait of witness of (See
    subhead: Character trait of witness of untruthful-
    ness)
Who can be impeached . . . 15[D][2]
Witness of untruthfulness, character trait of (See
    subhead: Character trait of witness of untruthful-
    ness)

INSCRIBED CHATTELS
Best evidence rule . . . 24[B][4]

INSTRUCTIONS
Jury, to . . . 3[B][10]

INSURANCE, LIABILITY
Exceptions to rule . . . 29[B]
Mention of, preclusion of . . . 29[A]

INTERPRETING WITNESSES (See EXPERT
    OPINION TESTIMONY, subhead: Witness test
    result, interpretation or evaluation of)

J

JUDGES
Admissibility of evidence, role in
    Generally . . . 5[B]
    Preliminary facts conditioning . . . 5[B][2]
    Questions of law . . . 5[B][1]
Competent witness, as . . . 7[E][2][a]
Discretion to exclude otherwise admissible convic-
    tion . . . 16[E][2][b]
Instruction or charge to jury . . . 3[B][10]
Jury, instruction or charge to . . . 3[B][10]
Witnesses
    Called by . . . 3[B][8]
    Questions posed to . . . 4[A][3]

JUDICIAL NOTICE (See EVIDENCE LAW, sub-
    head: Judicial notice)

JURORS
Competent witness, as . . . 7[E][2][b]
Lay jurors, use of . . . 1[C]
Petit jurors, role of (See PETIT JURORS, ROLE
    OF)
Questions by . . . 4[A][4]

JURY TRIAL
Generally . . . 3[A]
Case-in-chief
    Defense . . . 3[B][5]
    Plaintiff's . . . 3[B][3]
    Prosecutor's . . . 3[B][3]
Closing argument . . . 3[B][9]
Defense
    Case-in-chief . . . 3[B][5]
    Directed verdict, motion for . . . 3[B][4]
    Nonsuit, motion for . . . 3[B][4]
    Surrebuttal . . . 3[B][7]
Judge's instruction or charge to jury . . . 3[B][10]
Opening statements . . . 3[B][2]
Organization of trial as a whole
    Case-in-chief (See subhead: Case-in-chief)
    Closing argument . . . 3[B][9]
    Defense (See subhead: Defense)
    Judge's instruction or charge to jury
       . . . 3[B][10]
    Opening statements . . . 3[B][2]
    Plaintiff
       Case-in-chief . . . 3[B][3]
       Rebuttal . . . 3[B][6]
    Prosecutor
       Case-in-chief . . . 3[B][3]
       Rebuttal . . . 3[B][6]
    Selection, jury . . . 3[B][1]
    Summation . . . 3[B][9]
    Voir dire . . . 3[B][1]
    Witnesses called by trial judge . . . 3[B][8]
Plaintiff
    Case-in-chief . . . 3[B][3]
    Rebuttal . . . 3[B][6]
Prosecutor
    Case-in-chief . . . 3[B][3]
    Rebuttal . . . 3[B][6]
Selection, jury . . . 3[B][1]
Summation . . . 3[B][9]
Trial judge, witnesses called by . . . 3[B][8]
Voir dire . . . 3[B][1]
Witnesses called by trial judge . . . 3[B][8]

L

LAY OBSERVER TESTIMONY
Generally . . . 11[A][3]

LAY OPINION TESTIMONY
Generally . . . 23[A][3]
Acceptable types
    Collective fact, composite fact or shorthand
       rendition . . . 23[A][2][a]
    Other lay opinion testimony . . . 23[A][2][c]
    Skilled lay observer testimony
       . . . 23[A][2][b]
Rationale for exclusion . . . 23[A][1]

LIABILITY INSURANCE
Exceptions to rule . . . 29[B]
Mention of, preclusion of . . . 29[A]

LOGICAL RELEVANCE
Generally . . . 8[A]; 8[B][1]; 8[E]

[References are to sections.]

[References are to sections.]

[References are to sections.]

[References are to sections.]